Sociology:

A Down-to-Earth Approach

Second Edition

▼

James M. Henslin
Southern Illinois University
Edwardsville

Allyn and Bacon
Boston London Toronto Sydney Tokyo Singapore

11-98

Executive Editor: Karen Hanson
Vice President, Publisher: Susan Badger
Editorial Assistant: Sarah L. Dunbar
Developmental Editor: Hannah Rubenstein
Cover Administrator: Linda Knowles
Composition and Prepress Buyer: Linda Cox
Manufacturing Buyer: Megan Cochran
Marketing Manager: Joyce Nilsen
Signing Representative: Ward Moore
Photo Researcher: Susan Duane
Fine Art Researcher: Laurie Frankenthaler
Editorial-Production Service: The Book Company
Text Designer: Wendy Calmenson for The Book Company
Page Composition: MediaLink Associates, Inc.

Chapter 1: *Crowd IV*, 1993 by Diana Ong/Superstock

Chapter 2: *Spring Arrival*, 1994 by Dan V. Lomahaftewa. Collagraph, 42" x 30". Courtesy of El Cerro Graphics.

Chapter 3: *Men Exist for the Sake of One Another. Teach Them or Bear With Them*, 1958 by Jacob Lawrence. National Museum of American Art, Washington DC/Art Resource, NY. Courtesy of the artist and Francine Seders Gallery, Seattle, WA.

Chapter 4: *Builders (Green and Red Ball)*, 1979 by Jacob Lawrence. Gouache on paper, 30" x 22". New Jersey State Museum Collection, Trenton, NJ. Purchase, FA1987.28. Courtesy of the artist and Francine Seders Gallery, Seattle, WA.

Chapter 5: *Two Realities*, 1992 by Wendy Seller. Oil on canvas, 36" H x 28" W. © 1992 Wendy Seller. In the collection of Dr. and Mrs. Newton Scherl.

Chapter 6: *Can Fire in the Park*, 1946 by Beauford Delaney. Oil on canvas, 24" x 30". Copyright National Museum of American Art. Washington, DC, USA/Art Resource, NY.

Chapter 7: *Sign of the Watchmaker: Enseigne de l'Horloger*. Contemporary Folk Art, West Africa. From the Girard Foundation Collection in the Museum of International Folk Art, a unit of the Museum of New Mexico.

Chapter 8: *Untitled*, 1989 by Ilona Anderson. Acrylic on Canvas.

Chapter 9: *Haitians Waiting at Guantanamo Bay*, 1994 by Pacita Abad. Oil on canvas, stitched with buttons, beads, collaged with painted fabric and padded with cotton, 96" x 70". Photo by Paul Tanedo.

Chapter 10: *Social Climbers*, 1993 by Randy Stevens. Mixed media pastel. © 1993 Randy Stevens. Courtesy of Newbury Fine Arts.

Chapter 11: *Dissension*, 1993 by Wendy Seller. Oil on canvas, 34" H x 30" W. © 1993 Wendy Seller. In the collection of Robert and Elayne Simandl.

Chapter 12: *Korean Shopkeepers*, 1993 by Pacita Abad. Acrylic and oil on canvas, stitched with plastic buttons, yarn, fabric and padded canvas, 97" x 58". Photo by Paul Tanedo.

Chapter 13: *Sisters, Too*, 1992 by Deidre Scherer. Fabric and thread, 23" x 18". © 1992 Deidre Scherer. Photo by Jeff Baird.

Chapter 14: "City Building" from *America Today*, 1930 by Thomas Hart Benton. Distemper and egg tempera with oil glaze on gessoed linen, 92 x 117 inches. Collection, The Equitable Life Assurance Society of the United States

Chapter 15: *L.A. Liberty*, 1993 by Pacita Abad. Acrylic on canvas, stitched with cotton yarn, plastic buttons, broken glass, gold thread, fabric and padded canvas, 97" x 58". Photo by Paul Tanedo.

Chapter 16: *Sandia/Watermelon*, 1986 by Carmen Lomas Garza. Gouache painting, 20" x 28". © 1986 Carmen Lomas Garza. Photo by Wolfgang Dietze. Collection of Dudley D. Brooks & Tomas Ybarra-Frausto, Seattle, WA.

Chapter 17: *Tribute to the American Working People*, 1986 by Honore Desmond Sharrer. Detail of 5 part painting. Copyright National Museum of American Art, Washington, DC, USA/Art Resource, NY.

Chapter 18: *Oracion*, 1989 by Orlando Agudelo-Botero. Multi-media on papier d'Arches, 29" x 41".

Chapter 19: "Drs. Neftali Rodriquez and Antonio Diaz Lombardo," detail from mural *The History of Medicine in Mexico: The People's Demand for Better Health*, 1953 by Diego Rivera. Hospital de la Raza, Mexico City, Mexico. Schalkwijk/Art Resource, NY.

Chapter 20: *Subway* (detail) from *Ruckus Manhattan*, 1976 by Red Grooms. Mixed media, 9' x 18'7" x 37'2". Courtesy, Marlborough Gallery, NY.

Chapter 21: *Parade in Moscow*, 1956 by Diego Rivera. Oil on canvas, 135.2 x 108.3 cm. Collection Banco National de Mexico, Mexico City.

Chapter 22: *Between Flights*, 1993 by Lisa Houck. Watercolor, 6" x 9". © 1993 Lisa Houck.

Photo credits appear on page xvi, which is a continuation of this copyright page.

ISBN: 0-205-16158-8

Printed in the United States of America

10 9 8 7 6 5 4 3   99 98 97 96 95

BRIEF CONTENTS

CONTENTS

Part One The Sociological Perspective

Part Three Social Inequality

Part Five Social Change

BOXES

▼ Thinking Critically About Social Controversy

PREFACE

If you like to watch people and try to figure out why they do what they do, you will like sociology. Sociology pries open the doors of society, so you can see what goes on behind them.

In this book, you will especially see how social class sets us on different paths in life, how in one direction they lead to better health, more education, higher income, even better marriages—and in the other to more illness and disease, dropping out of school, low income, and higher chances of having your marriage fail. Those paths even affect your chances of making it to your first birthday, as well as of getting in trouble with the police—and of reading this book in the first place.

When I took my first course in sociology, I was "hooked." Seeing how marvelously my life had been affected by these larger group influences opened my eyes to a new world, one that has been fascinating to explore. I hope that this will be your experience also.

From how people become homeless to how they become presidents, from why women are treated as second-class citizens around the world to why people commit suicide—all are part of sociology. This breadth, in fact, is what makes sociology so intriguing. We can place the sociological lens on broad features of society, such as social class, gender, and race, and then immediately turn our focus on the small-scale level. If we look at two people interacting—whether quarreling or kissing—we see how these broad features of society are being played out in their lives.

We aren't born with instincts. We don't come into this world with preconceived notions of what life should be like. At birth, we have no ideas of race, gender, age, social class, of how people "ought" to be. Yet we all learn such things as part of growing up in our society. Uncovering the "hows" and the "whys" of this process is also part of sociology's fascination.

One of sociology's many pleasures is that as we study life in groups (which can be taken as a definition of sociology), whether those groups be in some far off part of the world (if there still are far-off places) or in some nearby corner of our own society, we constantly gain insights into our own selves. As we see how their customs affect them, effects of our own society on ourselves become more visible.

You can look forward to reading this book, then, for it can lead you to a new way of looking at the social world—and in the process, help you to better understand both society and yourself.

I have done my best to communicate the fascination of sociology in a down-to-earth manner. If there are sections of this text that you especially enjoy, or that you wish to comment on for whatever reason, don't hesitate to write me. I enjoy communicating with students.

ACKNOWLEDGMENTS

The gratifying response to the first edition indicates that my efforts at making sociology down to earth have succeeded. The years that have gone into writing this text are a culmination of the many more years that preceded its writing, from graduate school to what now have become decades in the classroom. But no text comes solely from its author. Although I am responsible for the final words on the printed page, I have depended heavily on feedback from instructors who used the first edition. I especially want to thank:

Sandra L. Albrecht *The University of Kansas*
Kenneth Ambrose *Marshall University*
Alberto Arroyo *Baldwin-Wallace College*
Karren Baird-Olsen *Kansas State University*
Linda Barbera-Stein *The University of Illinois*
John K. Cochran *The University of Oklahoma*
Russell L. Curtis *University of Houston*
John Darling *University of Pittsburgh-Johnstown*
Ray Darville *Stephen F. Austin State University*
Nanette J. Davis *Portland State University*
Lynda Dodgen *North Harris Community College*
Helen R. Ebaugh *University of Houston*
Obi N. Ebbe *State University of New York-Brockport*
David O. Friedrichs *University of Scranton*
Norman Goodman *State Univeristy of New York-Stony Brook*
Donald W. Hastings *The University of Tennessee—Knoxville*
Michael Hoover *Missouri Western State College*
Charles E. Hurst *The College of Wooster*
Mark Kassop *Bergen Community College*
Alice Abel Kemp *University of New Orleans*
Dianna Kendall *Austin Community College*
Gary Kiger *Utah State University*
Abraham Levine *El Camino Community College*
Ron Matson *Wichita State University*
Armaund L. Mauss *Washington State University*
Evelyn Mercer *Southwest Baptist University*
Robert Meyer *Arkansas State University*
W. Lawrence Neuman *University of Wisconsin—Whitewater*
Charles Norman *Indiana State University*
Laura O'Toole *University of Delaware*

Phil Piket *Joliet Junior College*
Adrian Rapp *North Harris Community College*
Howard Robboy *Trenton State College*
Walt Shirley *Sinclair Community College*
Marc Silver *Hofstra University*
Roberto E. Socas *Essex County College*
Susan Sprecher *Illinois State University*
Randolph G. Ston *Oakland Community College*
Kathleen A. Tiemann *University of North Dakota*
Larry Weiss *University of Alaska*
Douglas White *Henry Ford Community College*
Stephen R. Wilson *Temple University*
Stuart Wright *Lamar University*

I also am indebted to the capable staff of Allyn and Bacon. I wish to specifically acknowledge the contributions of Karen Hanson and Susan Badger, who saw the promise of the early manuscript and have seen it through its many trials. The influence of Hannah Rubenstein, the development editor, on this book has been extraordinary. Her sharp mind, creativity, insightful questioning, ability to see the connection of the part to the whole, and acute perception of the relevance of social events have left an idelible mark on the final product. George Calmenson of The Book Company and Wendy LaChance of By Design also deserve special mention for their capable handling of both the routine and the urgent. Without such capable professional support, this book would not exist.

James M. Henslin
Department of Sociology
Southern Illinois University
Edwardsville, IL 62026

JAMES M. HENSLIN, who was born in Minnesota, graduated from high school and junior college in California and from college in Indiana. He earned his Master's and doctorate in sociology at Washington University in St. Louis, Missouri. His primary interests in sociology are the sociology of everyday life, deviance, social psychology, and the homeless. Among his more than a dozen books is Down to Earth Sociology (Free Press), now in its eighth edition, a book of readings that reflects these sociological interests. He has also published widely in sociology journals, including *Social Problems* and *American Journal of Sociology*.

While a graduate student, James Henslin taught at the University of Missouri at St. Louis. After completing his doctorate, he joined the faculty at Southern Illinois University, Edwardsville, where he is Professor of Sociology. He requests the introductory course, teaching it several times each year. He says, "I've always found the introductory course enjoyable to teach. I love to see students' faces light up when they first glimpse the sociological perspective and begin to see how society has become an essential part of how they view the world."

Henslin enjoys spending time with his family, reading, and fishing. His two favorite activities are writing and traveling. He especially enjoys living in other cultures, for this brings him face to face with behaviors that he cannot take for granted, experiences that "make sociological principles come alive."

Sociology:

A Down-to-Earth Approach

Diana Ong, Crowd IV, 1993

CHAPTER

1

The Sociological Perspective

*E*VEN FROM THE DIM GLOW *of the faded red-and-white exit sign, its light barely reaching the upper bunk, I could see that the sheet was filthy. Resigned to another night of fitful sleep, I reluctantly crawled into bed—tucking my clothes firmly around my body, like a protective cocoon.*

The next morning, I joined the long line of disheveled men leaning against the chain-link fence. Their faces were as downcast as their clothes were dirty. Not a glimmer of hope among them.

No one spoke as the line slowly inched forward. When my turn came, I was handed a styrofoam cup of coffee, some utensils, and a bowl of semiliquid that I couldn't identify. It didn't look like any food I had seen before. Nor did it taste like anything I had ever eaten.

My stomach fought the foul taste, every spoonful a battle. But I was determined. "I will experience what they experience," I kept telling myself. My stomach reluctantly gave in and accepted its morning nourishment.

The room was eerily silent. Hundreds of men were eating, but each was sunk deeply into his own private hell, his head aswim with disappointment, remorse, bitterness.

As I stared at the styrofoam cup holding my solitary postbreakfast pleasure, I noticed what looked like teeth marks. I shrugged off the thought, telling myself that my long weeks as a sociological observer of the homeless were finally getting to me. "That must be some sort of crease from handling," I concluded.

I joined the silent ranks of men turning in their bowls and cups. When I saw the man behind the counter swishing out styrofoam cups in a washtub of water, I began to feel sick at my stomach. I knew then that the jagged marks on my cup really had come from a previous mouth.

How much longer did this research have to last? I felt a deep longing to return to my family—to a welcome world of clean sheets, healthy food, and "normal" conversations.

The Sociological Perspective

Why were these men so silent? Why did they receive such despicable treatment? What was I doing in that homeless shelter? (After all, I hold a respectable, secure professional position, and I have a home and family.)

Sociology offers a perspective, a view of the world. The **sociological perspective** (or imagination) opens a window onto unfamiliar worlds, and offers a fresh look at familiar worlds. In this text you will find yourself in the midst of Nazis in Germany, chimpanzees in Africa, and warriors in South America. But you will also find yourself looking at your own world in a different light. As you look at other worlds, or your own, the sociological perspective casts a light that enables you to gain a new vision of social life. In fact, this is what many find appealing about sociology.

The sociological perspective has been a motivating force in my own life. Ever since I took my first introductory course in sociology, I have been enchanted by the perspective that sociology offers. I have thoroughly enjoyed both observing other groups and questioning my own assumptions about life. I sincerely hope that the same happens to you.

Seeing the Broader Social Context

The sociological perspective stresses the broader context of life in society. To find out why people do what they do, sociologists look at **social location,** where people are located in history and in a particular society. Sociologists focus on such characteristics of people

sociological perspective: an approach to understanding human behavior by placing it within its broader social context

social location: people's group memberships because of their location in history and society

4

as their jobs, income, education, gender, and race. At the center of the sociological perspective is the question of how people are influenced by **society**—a group of people who share a culture and a territory. Take, for example, how growing up identified with a group called females or a group called males affects people's ideas of what they should attain in life.

Sociologist C. Wright Mills (1959b) said that the sociological perspective enables us to grasp the connection between history and biography. Because of its history, a society has certain broad characteristics—such as its commonly accepted ideas of the proper roles of men and women. By biography, Mills meant the individual's specific experiences in society. This intersection of history and biography results in people having particular values, goals, aspirations, and even self-concept. In short, in the sociological view people don't do what they do because of some sort of inherited internal mechanism, such as instincts. Rather, external influences—people's experiences—become internalized, become part of an individual's thinking and motivations.

An example will make this point obvious. If we were to take a newborn baby away from its U.S. parents today and place that infant with a Yanomamo Indian tribe in the jungles of South America, you know that when that child begins to speak, his or her sounds will not be in English. You also know that the child will not think like an American. He or she will not grow up wanting credit cards, for example, or designer jeans, a new car, and the latest video game. Equally, the child will unquestioningly take his or her place in Yanomamo society—perhaps as a food gatherer, a hunter, or a warrior—and will not even know about the world left behind at birth. And, whether male or female, that child will grow up, not debating whether to have one, two, or three children, but assuming that it is natural to want many children.

People around the globe take their particular world for granted. Something inside us Americans tells us that hamburgers are delicious, small families attractive, and designer clothing desirable. Yet something inside some of the Sinai Desert Arab tribes used to tell them that warm, fresh camel's blood makes a fine drink and that everyone should have a large family and wear flowing robes (Murray 1935; McCabe and Ellis 1990). And that something certainly isn't an instinct. As sociologist Peter Berger (1963) phrased it, that "something" is "society within us."

Although obvious, this point frequently eludes us. We often think and talk about people's behavior as though it is caused by their sex, their race, or some other factor transmitted by their genes. The sociological perspective helps us to escape from this cramped personal view by exposing the broader social context that underlies human behavior. It helps us to see the links between what people do and the social settings that shape their behavior.

Examining the broad social context in which people live is essential to the sociological perspective, for this context shapes our beliefs and sets the guidelines for what we do. From this photo, you can see how distinctive those guidelines are for the Yanomamo Indians of Brazil. How have these Yanomamo youths been influenced by their group? How has your behavior been influenced by your groups?

society: a term used by sociologists to refer to a group of people who share a culture and a territory

Sociology and the Other Sciences

Just as humans today have an intense desire to unravel the mysteries around them, people in ancient times also attempted to understand their world. Their explanations, however, were not based only on observations, but were mixed with magic and superstition as well.

To satisfy their basic curiosities about the world around them, humans gradually developed **science,** systematic methods used to study the social and natural worlds, as well as the knowledge obtained by those methods. **Sociology,** the scientific study of society and human behavior, is one of the sciences that modern civilization has developed.

A useful way of comparing these sciences—and of gaining a better understanding of sociology's place—is to first divide them into the natural and the social sciences.

The Natural Sciences

The **natural sciences** are the intellectual and academic disciplines designed to comprehend, explain, and predict the events in our natural environment. The natural sciences are divided into specialized fields of research according to subject matter, such as biology, geology, chemistry, and physics. These are further subdivided into even more highly specialized areas, with a further narrowing of content. Biology is divided into botany and zoology, geology into mineralogy and geomorphology, chemistry into its inorganic and organic branches, and physics into biophysics and quantum mechanics. Each area of investigation examines a particular "slice" of nature (Henslin 1993).

The Social Sciences

People have not limited themselves to investigating nature. In the pursuit of a more adequate understanding of life, people have also developed fields of science that focus on the social world. These, the **social sciences,** examine human relationships. Just as the natural sciences attempt to objectively understand the world of nature, the social sciences attempt to objectively understand the social world. Just as the world of nature contains ordered (or lawful) relationships that are not obvious but must be discovered through controlled observation, so the ordered relationships of the human or social world are not obvious, and must be revealed by means of controlled and repeated observations.

Like the natural sciences, the social sciences are divided into specialized fields based on their subject matter. These divisions are anthropology, economics, political science, psychology, and sociology. And the social sciences, too, are subdivided into further specialized fields. Thus, anthropology is divided into cultural and physical anthropology; economics has macro (large-scale) and micro (small-scale) specialties; political science has theoretical and applied branches; psychology may be clinical or experimental; and sociology has its quantitative and qualitative branches. Since our focus is sociology, let us contrast sociology with each of the other social sciences.

Political Science   *Political science* focuses on politics and government. Political scientists study how people govern themselves: the various forms of government, their structures, and their relationships to other institutions of society. Political scientists are especially interested in how people attain ruling positions in their society, how they then maintain those positions, and the consequences of their activities for those who are governed. In studying a system of government with a constitutional electorate, such as that of the United States, political scientists also focus on voting behavior.

Economics   *Economics* also concentrates on a single social institution. Economists study the production and distribution of the material goods and services of a society.

science: the application of systematic methods to obtain knowledge and the knowledge obtained by those methods

sociology: the scientific study of society and human behavior

natural sciences: the intellectual and academic disciplines designed to comprehend, explain, and predict events in our natural environment

social sciences: the intellectual and academic disciplines designed to understand the social world objectively by means of controlled and repeated observations

They want to know what goods are being produced at what rate and at what cost, and how those goods are distributed. They are also interested in the choices that determine production and consumption, for example, the factors that lead a society to produce a certain item instead of another.

Anthropology   *Anthropology*, in which the primary focus has been preliterate or tribal peoples, is the sister discipline of sociology. The chief concern of anthropologists is to understand *culture*, a people's total way of life. Culture includes (1) the group's artifacts such as its tools, art, and weapons; (2) the group's structure, that is, the hierarchy and other patterns that determine its members' relationships to one another; (3) a group's ideas and values, especially how its belief system affects people's lives; and (4) the group's forms of communication, especially language. The anthropologists' traditional focus on tribal groups is now giving way to the study of groups in industrialized settings.

Psychology   The focus of *psychology* is on processes that occur *within* the individual, within the "skin-bound organism." Psychologists are primarily concerned with mental processes: intelligence, emotions, perception, and memory. Some concentrate on attitudes and values; others focus on personality, mental aberration (psychopathology, or mental illness), and how individuals cope with the problems they face.

Sociology   *Sociology* has many similarities to the other social sciences. Like political scientists, sociologists study how people govern one another, especially the impact of various forms of government on people's lives. Like economists, sociologists are concerned with what happens to the goods and services of a society—but sociologists place their focus on the social consequences of production and distribution. Like anthropologists, sociologists study culture; they have a particular interest in the social consequences of material goods, group structure, and belief systems, as well as in how people communicate with one another. Like psychologists, sociologists are also concerned with how people adjust to the difficulties of life.

Given these overall similarities, then, what distinguishes sociology from the other social sciences? Unlike political scientists and economists, sociologists do not concentrate on a single social institution. Unlike anthropologists, sociologists focus primarily on industrialized societies. And unlike psychologists, sociologists stress factors *external* to the individual to determine what influences people. In succeeding chapters, these distinctions will become clearer. The Down-to-Earth Sociology box on page 8 revisits an old fable about how members of different disciplines perceive the same subject matter.

The Goals of Science

The first goal of each science is to *explain* why something happens. The second goal is to make **generalizations,** that is, to go beyond the individual case and make statements that apply to a broader group or situation. For example, a sociologist wants to explain not only why Mary went to college or became an armed robber but also why people with her characteristics are more likely than others to go to college or to become armed robbers. To achieve generalizations, sociologists and other scientists look for **patterns,** recurring characteristics or events. The third scientific goal is to *predict*, to specify what will happen in the future in the light of current knowledge.

To attain these goals, scientists must rely not on magic, superstition, or common beliefs but on conclusions based on systematic studies. They need to examine evidence with an open mind, in such a way that it can be checked by others. Secrecy, prejudice, and other biases, with their inherent closures, go against the grain of science.

Sociologists and other scientists also move beyond **common sense,** those ideas that prevail in a society that "everyone knows" are true. Just because "everyone" knows something is true does not make it so. "Everyone" can be mistaken, today just as easily as

generalization: a statement that goes beyond the individual case and is applied to a broader group or situation

patterns: recurring characteristics or events

common sense: those things that "everyone knows" are true

▼▲▼▲▼▲▼▲▼▲▼▲▼▲▼▲▼▲▼▲▼▲▼▲▼▲▼▲▼▲▼▲▼▲▼▲

Down-To-Earth Sociology

An Updated Version of the Old Elephant Story

IT IS SAID THAT in the recent past five wise men and women, all blindfolded, were led to an elephant and asked to explain what they "saw." The first, a psychologist, feeling the top of the head, said, "This is the only thing that counts. All feeling and thinking takes place inside here. To understand this beast, we need study only this."

The second, an anthropologist, tenderly touching the trunk and the tusks, said, "This is really primitive. I feel very comfortable here. Concentrate on these."

The third, a political scientist, feeling the gigantic ears, said, "This is the power center. What goes in here controls the entire beast. Concentrate your studies here."

The fourth, an economist, feeling the mouth, said, "This is what counts. What goes in here is distributed throughout the body. Concentrate your studies on this."

Then came the sociologist (of course!), who, after feeling the entire body, said, "You can't understand the beast by concentrating on only one part. Each is but part of the whole. The head, the trunk and tusks, the ears, the mouth—all are important. But so are the parts of the beast that you haven't even mentioned. We must remove our blindfolds so we can see the larger picture. We have to see how everything works together to form the entire animal."

Pausing for emphasis, the sociologist added, "And we also need to understand how this creature interacts with similar creatures. How does their life in groups influence their behaviors?"

I wish I could conclude this fable by saying that the psychologist, the anthropologist, the political scientist, and the economist, dazzled upon hearing the wisdom of the sociologist, amidst gasps of wonderment threw away their blindfolds and, joining together, began to examine the larger picture. But, alas and alack! Upon hearing this sage advice, each stubbornly bound their blindfolds even tighter to concentrate all the more on the single part. And if you listened very, very carefully you could even hear them saying, "The top of the head is mine—stay away from it." "Don't touch the tusks." "Take your hand off the ears." "Stay away from the mouth—that's my area."

---

when common sense dictated that the world was flat or that no human could ever walk on the moon. As sociologists examine people's assumptions about the world, their findings may contradict commonsense notions about social life. The Down-to-Earth Sociology box on page 9 provides a number of examples.

Sometimes the explorations of sociologists take them into nooks and crannies that people would prefer remain unexplored. For example, a sociologist might study how people make decisions to commit a crime or to cheat on their spouses. Because sociologists want above all to understand social life, they cannot cease their studies because people feel uncomfortable. With all realms of human life considered legitimate avenues of exploration by sociologists, their findings sometimes challenge even cherished ideas.

As they examine how groups operate, sociologists often confront prejudice and attempts to keep things secret. It seems that every organization, every group, nourishes a pet image that it presents to the public. Sociologists are interested in knowing what is really going on behind the scenes, however, so they peer beneath the surface to get past that sugarcoated image of suppressed facts (Berger 1963). This approach sometimes brings sociologists into conflict with people who feel threatened by that information—which is all part of the adventure, and risk, of being a sociologist.

The Development of Sociology

Just how did sociology begin? Has it always been around? Or is it relatively new?

In some ways it is difficult to answer these questions. By the time Jesus Christ was born, the Greeks and Romans had already developed intricate systems of philosophy about human behavior. Even preliterate peoples made observations about their tribal lives and were likely aware, for example, which classes of people were more privileged and powerful. They also analyzed *why* life was as it was, but in doing so they often depended on magic and superstition, such as explanations based on the positions of the stars.

Simple assertions of truth—or observations mixed with magic or superstition or the stars—are not adequate. *All science requires the development of theories that can be proved or disproved by systematic research.*

This standard simplifies the question of the origin of sociology. Measured by this standard sociology is clearly a recent discipline. It emerged about the middle of the nineteenth century when European social observers began to use scientific methods to test their ideas. Three factors combined to lead to the development of sociology.

The first was social upheaval in Europe. By the middle of the nineteenth century, Europe found itself in the midst of the Industrial Revolution. This change from agriculture to factory production brought violent changes to people's lives. Masses of people were forced off the land. They moved to the cities in search of work where they were met with anonymity, crowding, filth, and poverty. Their ties to the land, to the generations that had lived there before them, and to their way of life were abruptly broken. The city greeted them with horrible working conditions: low pay; long, exhausting hours; dangerous work; bad ventilation; and much noise. To survive, families had to permit their children to work in these same conditions, some of them even chained to factory machines to make certain they did not run away.

With the successes of the American and French revolutions, in which the idea that individuals possess inalienable rights caught fire, the political systems in Western countries slowly began to give way to more democratic forms. As the traditional order was challenged, religion lost much of its force as the unfailing source of answers to life's perplexing questions. Each fundamental social change further undermined traditional explanations of human existence.

When tradition reigns supreme, it provides a ready answer: "We do this because it has always been done this way." Such societies offer minimal encouragement for original

---

Down-To-Earth Sociology

Enjoying a Sociology Quiz—Sociological Findings Versus Common Sense

SOME FINDINGS OF SOCIOLOGY support commonsense understandings of social life, while others contradict them. Can you tell the difference? If you want to enjoy this quiz fully, before turning the page to check your answers complete *all* the questions.

1. True/False The earnings of U.S. women have just about caught up with those of U.S. men.

2. True/False When faced with natural disasters such as floods and earthquakes, people panic and social organization disintegrates.

3. True/False Revolutions are more likely to occur when conditions are consistently bad than when they are improving.

4. True/False Most people on welfare are lazy and looking for a handout. They could work if they wanted to.

5. True/False Most U.S. Roman Catholics oppose birth control.

6. True/False Compared with men, women touch each other more while they are conversing.

7. True/False Compared with women, men maintain more eye contact while they are conversing.

8. True/False Because of the rapid rise in the divorce rate in the United States, U.S. children are much more likely to live in single-parent households now than they were a century ago.

9. True/False The more available alcohol is (as measured by the number of places to purchase alcohol per one hundred people), the more alcohol-related injuries and fatalities occur on U.S. highways.

10. True/False Couples who live together before marriage usually report higher satisfaction with their marriages than couples who do not live together before marriage.

▼▲▼▲▼▲▼▲▼▲▼▲▼▲▼▲▼▲▼▲▼▲▼▲▼▲▼▲▼▲▼▲▼

Down-To-Earth Sociology

Sociological Findings Versus Common Sense—Answers to the Sociology Quiz

1. False. Over the years, the income gap has narrowed, but only slightly. On average, full-time working women earn only about 65 percent of what full-time working men earn; this low figure is actually an improvement, for in the 1970s women's incomes averaged about 60 percent of men's.

2. False. Following such disasters, people develop *greater* cohesion, cooperation, and social organization to deal with the catastrophe.

3. False. Just the opposite is true. When conditions are consistently bad people are more likely to be resigned to their fate, while rapid improvement causes their aspirations to outrace their circumstances, which can increase frustrations and foment revolution.

4. False. Most people on welfare are children, the old, the sick, the mentally and physically handicapped, or young mothers with few skills. Less than 2 percent meet the common stereotype of an able-bodied male—and many of these are actively looking for jobs.

5. False. About 80 percent of U.S. Roman Catholics favor birth control.

6. False. It is men who touch each other more during conversations (Henley et al. 1985; Whyte 1989).

7. False. Female speakers maintain considerably more eye contact (Henley and Hamilton 1985).

8. False. Strange as it may sound, the proportion of children who live with one parent is roughly the same today as it was one hundred years ago. A century back, many parents died at an early age, leaving only one parent to rear the children. With today's advances in public health and medicine, few people die young. Although death as a source of one-parent families is now lower, our much higher divorce rate has made up the difference.

9. False. In California, researchers compared the number of alcohol outlets per population with the alcohol-related highway injuries and fatalities. They found that counties in which alcohol is more readily available do not have more alcohol-related injuries and fatalities (Kohfeld and Leip 1991).

10. False. The opposite is true. The reasons are unknown, but researchers suggest that many couples who marry after cohabiting are less committed to marriage in the first place—and a key to marital success is firm commitment to one another (Larson 1988).

---

thinking. Since the answers are already provided, there is little impetus to search for explanations. Sweeping change, however, does the opposite: by upsetting the existing order, it encourages questioning and demands answers.

The second factor that encouraged the development of sociology was the development of imperialism. The Europeans had been successful in conquering many parts of the world. Their new colonial empires, stretching from Asia through Africa to North America, exposed them to radically different cultures. Startled by these contrasting ways of life, they began to ask why cultures differed.

The third impetus for the development of sociology was the success of the natural sciences. Just at the time when the Industrial Revolution and imperialism moved people to question fundamental aspects of their social worlds, **the scientific method**—objective, systematic observations to test theories—used in chemistry and physics had begun to transform the world. Given these successes, it seemed logical to apply this method to the questions now being raised about the social world.

Auguste Comte

the scientific method: the use of objective systematic observations to test theories

positivism: the application of the scientific approach to the social world

This idea of applying the scientific method to the social world, known as **positivism,** was apparently first proposed by Auguste Comte (1798–1857). With the French Revolution still fresh in his mind, Comte left the small, conservative town in which he had grown up and moved to Paris. The changes he himself experienced, combined with those France underwent in the revolution, led Comte to become interested in the twin problems of social order and social change (which he called "social statics" and "social

This eighteenth-century painting by Giraudon depicts the taking of the Bastille. The French Revolution of 1789 overthrew not only the aristocracy but upset the entire social order. With change so extensive, and the past no longer a sure guide to the present, Auguste Comte (1798–1857) began to analyze how societies change, thus ushering in the science of sociology.

dynamics"). What holds society together? he wondered. Why is there social order instead of anarchy or chaos? And once society becomes set on a particular course, what causes it to change? Why doesn't it always continue in the direction it began?

As he pondered these questions, Comte concluded that the right way to answer them was to apply the scientific method to social life. Just as it had revealed the law of gravity, so, too, it would uncover the laws that underlie society. This new science, based on positivism, not only would discover social principles but it would also apply them to social reform. Comte called this new science *sociology*—"the study of society" (from the Greek *logos*, "study of," and the Latin *socius*, companion, "being with others").

Comte had some ideas that today's sociologists find humorous. For example, as Comte saw matters, there were only six sciences—mathematics, physics, chemistry, biology, astronomy, and sociology—with sociology far superior to the others (Bogardus 1929). To Comte, applying the scientific method to social life apparently referred to "armchair philosophy"—drawing conclusions from informal observations of social life. He did not do what today's sociologists would call research, and his conclusions have been abandoned.

Nevertheless, Comte's insistence that we cannot be dogmatic about social life, but that we must observe and classify human activities in order to uncover society's fundamental laws, is well taken. Because he developed this idea and coined the term *sociology*, Comte is often credited with being the founder of sociology.

Auguste Comte (1798-1857), who is identified as the founder of sociology, began to analyze the bases of the social order. Although he stressed that the scientific method should be applied to the study of society, he did not apply it himself.

Herbert Spencer

Herbert Spencer (1820–1903), who grew up in England, is sometimes called the second founder of sociology. He, too, believed that society operates according to fixed laws. Spencer became convinced that societies evolve from lower ("barbarian") to higher ("civilized") forms. As generations pass, he said, the most capable and intelligent ("the fittest") members of a society survive, while the less capable die out. Thus, over time, societies steadily improve.

Spencer called this principle "the survival of the fittest." Although Spencer coined this phrase, it is usually attributed to his contemporary, Charles Darwin, who proposed that living organisms evolve over time as they survive the conditions of their environment. Because of their similarities, Spencer's views of the evolution of societies became known as *social Darwinism*.

Unlike Comte, Spencer did not think sociology should guide social reform. In fact, he was convinced that no one should intervene in the evolution of society. The fittest members didn't need any help. They would always survive on their own and produce a more advanced society unless misguided do-gooders got in the way and helped the less fit survive. Consequently, Spencer's ideas—that charity and helping the poor were wrong, whether carried out by individuals or by the government—appalled many. Not surprisingly, wealthy industrialists, who saw themselves as "the fittest" (superior), found Spencer's ideas attractive. And not coincidentally, his views also helped them avoid feelings of guilt for living like royalty while people around them starved.

Like Comte, Spencer was more of a social philosopher than a sociologist. Also like Comte, Spencer did not conduct scientific studies, but simply developed ideas about society. Eventually, after gaining a wide following in England and the United States, Spencer's ideas about social Darwinism were discredited.

Karl Marx

Karl Marx (1818–1883), a third individual who influenced sociology, also left his mark on world history. Marx's influence has been so great that even that staunch advocate of capitalism, the *Wall Street Journal*, has called him one of the three greatest modern thinkers (the other two being Sigmund Freud and Albert Einstein).

Like Comte, Marx thought that people should take active steps to change society. Marx, who came to England after being exiled from his native Germany for proposing revolution, believed that the key to human history was **class conflict.** He said that the *bourgeoisie* (the controlling class of *capitalists*, those who own the means to produce wealth—capital, land, factories, and machines) are locked in inevitable conflict with the *proletariat* (the exploited class, the mass of workers who do not own the means of production). This bitter struggle can end only when members of the working class unite in revolution and throw off their chains of bondage. The result will be a classless society, one free of exploitation in which all individuals will work according to their abilities and receive according to their needs (Marx and Engels 1848/1967).

Marxism is not the same as communism. Although Marx stood firmly behind revolution as the only way for the proletariat to gain control of society, he did not develop the political system called *communism*, which was a later application of his ideas (and rapidly changing ones at that). Indeed, Marx himself felt disgusted when he heard debates about his insights into social life. After listening to some of the positions attributed to him, he even declared, "I am not a Marxist" (Dobriner 1969:222).

Unlike Comte and Spencer, Marx did not think of himself as a sociologist. He spent years studying in the library of the British Museum in London, where he wrote widely on history, philosophy, and, of course, economics and political science. Because of his insights into the relationship between the social classes, especially the class struggle between the "haves" and the "have-nots," many sociologists today claim Marx as a significant early sociologist. He also introduced one of the major perspectives in sociology, conflict theory, which is discussed on pages 25–26.

Harriet Martineau

At this time in history, it was difficult for women to obtain an education as the men who ran society felt that formal education for females was unnecessary and dangerous: unnecessary as they did not need it to run a household, and dangerous for it might make them

Karl Marx (1818–1883) believed that the roots of human misery lay in the exploitation of the proletariat, or propertyless working classes, by the capitalist class, which owned the means of production. Social change, in the form of the overthrow of the capitalists by the proletariat, was inevitable from Marx's perspective. Although Marx did not consider himself a sociologist, his ideas have profoundly influenced many in the discipline, particularly conflict theorists.

Interested in social reform, Harriet Martineau, (1802–1876) turned to sociology, where she discovered the writings of Comte. An active advocate for the abolition of slavery, she traveled widely and wrote extensively.

class conflict: Marx's term for the struggle between the proletariat and the bourgeoisie

discontent with their subservient role to men. A handful of women from wealthy families, however, managed to get an education. One of these was Harriet Martineau (1802–1876), a native of England, who studied social life in both the United States and Great Britain. In 1837, she published *Society in America*, in which she reported on this new nation's family customs, race relations, gender relations, politics, and religion. She also helped to popularize Comte's ideas by translating them into English.

Emile Durkheim

Emile Durkheim (1858–1917), who was born and reared in eastern France, was educated in both Germany and France. Durkheim received the first academic appointment in sociology in a French university, teaching first at the University of Bordeaux in 1887, and moving to the more prestigious Sorbonne in 1906 (Coser 1977).

Durkheim insisted on rigorous research. In a study still quoted today, he compared the suicide rates of several European countries. He (1897/1966) found that each country's suicide rate was different and that it remained remarkably stable year after year. He also found that different groups within a country had different suicide rates. For example, Protestants, the wealthy, males, and the unmarried killed themselves at a higher rate than did Catholics, Jews, the poor, females, and the married. From this, Durkheim drew the highly insightful conclusion that suicide is not simply a matter of individuals here and there deciding to take their lives for personal reasons. Rather, *social factors underlie suicide*, and this is what keeps those rates fairly constant year after year.

Durkheim identified **social integration,** the degree to which people are tied to their social group, as a key social factor in suicide. He found that people with weak social ties were more likely to commit suicide. This factor explained the higher suicide rate of Protestants, males, the wealthy, and the unmarried. Protestantism, Durkheim argued, encourages greater freedom of thought and action; males are more independent than females; wealthy people have greater choices in life; and the unmarried are less socially integrated than those bound by the ties and responsibilities of marriage. In other words, because their social integration is weaker, people in these groups have fewer social ties that keep them from committing suicide.

Although strong social bonds help to protect people from suicide, Durkheim noted that in some instances strong bonds can encourage suicide. To illustrate this type of suicide, which he termed *altruistic suicide*, Durkheim used the example of grieving people who kill themselves following the death of a dearly loved spouse. Their own feelings are so integrated with those of their spouse that they prefer death rather than life without the one who gave meaning to life. Another example of altruistic suicide is the Japanese kamikaze pilots in World War II, whose missions were to ram their bomb-laden planes into enemy ships.

Almost one hundred years later, Durkheim's work is still quoted because of its scientific rigor and excellent theoretical interpretations. Durkheim's research was so thorough that its principles still apply to contemporary life: People who are less socially integrated continue to have a higher rate of suicide. Those same categories of people that Durkheim identified— Protestants, males, the wealthy, and the unmarried—are still more likely to kill themselves than are others.

Durkheim was concerned about the tendency of modern society to produce what he called anomie, and thereby suicide. By **anomie,** Durkheim referred to a breaking down of the controlling influences of society, which leaves people without the moral guidance that societies usually offer. People become detached from society, they lack social support, and their desires are no longer regulated by clear norms (Coser 1977). Durkheim's analysis of suicide provides a good example of the sociological perspective we reviewed earlier—the idea that human behavior (even suicide) cannot be understood simply in individualistic terms, that it must be understood within its larger social context.

The French sociologist Emile Durkheim (1858-1917) contributed many important concepts to sociology. His systematic study comparing suicide rates among several countries revealed an underlying social factor: People were more likely to commit suicide if their ties to others in their communities were weak. Durkheim's identification of the key role of social integration on social life remains central to sociology today.

social integration: the degree to which people feel a part of social groups

anomie: Durkheim's term for a condition of society in which people become detached, cut loose from the norms that usually guide their behavior

Emile Durkheim used the term anomie *to refer to lack of a sense of intimate belonging. Durkheim believed that modern societies produce feelings of isolation especially as a result of the division of labor. In contrast, members of traditional societies, who till the soil and work alongside family and neighbors, experience a high degree of social integration—the opposite of anomie.*

Max Weber (1864–1920) was another early sociologist who left a profound impression on sociology. He used cross-cultural and historical materials in order to determine how extensively culture affects people's orientations to life and to trace the causes of social change.

Like Comte, Durkheim (1893/1933) also proposed that sociologists actively intervene in society. To overcome anomie, he suggested that new social groups be created. Standing somewhere between the state and the family, those groups would help meet the need for a sense of belonging that the impersonality of industrial society was eroding.

Max Weber

Max Weber (1864–1920) (Mahx VÁY-ber), a German sociologist and a contemporary of Durkheim's, also held professorships in the new academic discipline of sociology. He was a renowned scholar who, like Marx, wrote in several academic fields. He agreed with much of what Marx wrote, but he strongly disagreed that economics is the central force in social change. That role, he said, belongs to religion. Weber (1904/1958) theorized that the belief system provided by Roman Catholicism encouraged Roman Catholics to hold onto traditional ways of life, while the belief system of Protestantism encouraged its members to embrace change. To test his theory, Weber compared the economic development of several countries with the dominance of Protestantism or Catholicism within those countries. His conclusion—that Protestantism, specifically Calvinism, encouraged people to work hard, to save money, and to invest it, and thus was the central factor in the rise of capitalism in those countries—was controversial when he developed it and is still debated by scholars today (Dickson and McLachlan 1989). Weber's analysis of the significance of religion in economic development is discussed in more detail on pages 164–166.

▼▲   ## The Role of Values in Social Research

value free: the view that a sociologist's personal values or biases should not influence social research

values: ideas about what is good or worthwhile in life; attitudes about the way the world ought to be

objectivity: total neutrality

Weber also raised another issue that remains controversial among sociologists when he declared that sociology should be **value free.** By this, he meant that a sociologist's **values,** personal beliefs about what is good or worthwhile in life and the way the world ought to be, should not affect his or her social research. Weber wanted **objectivity,** total neutrality, to be the hallmark of sociological research. If values influence research, he said, sociological findings will be biased.

Objectivity as an ideal is not a matter of debate in sociology. On the one hand, all sociologists agree that objectivity is a proper goal, in the sense that sociologists should not distort data to make them fit preconceived ideas or personal values, and that research

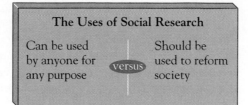

Figure 1.1

The Debate over Values.

reports must accurately reflect actual, not desired findings. On the other hand, it is equally clear that no sociologist can escape values entirely. Like everyone else, sociologists are members of a particular society at a given point in history and are therefore infused with values of all sorts, and these inevitably play a role in their research. For example, values are part of the reason that one sociologist chooses to do research on the Mafia, while another turns a sociological eye on kindergarten students. To overcome the distortions that values can cause, sociologists stress **replication,** that is, the repetition of a study by other researchers to see how the results compare. If values have unwittingly influenced research findings, replication by other sociologists should uncover this problem and correct it.

In spite of the consensus, however, the proper role of values in sociology is still hotly debated (Seubert 1991). The problem especially concerns ideas about the proper purposes and uses of sociological research. Regarding the *purpose* of sociology, some sociologists take the position that sociology's proper role is to advance understanding. Sociologists should gather data on any aspect of social life in which they are interested and then use the best theory available to interpret their findings. Others are convinced that it is the responsibility of sociologists to explore harmful social arrangements of society—to investigate what causes poverty, crime, war, and other forms of human exploitation.

Regarding the *uses* of sociology, those who say that understanding is sociology's proper goal take the position that the knowledge gained by social research belongs to the scientific community and to the world. Accordingly, it can be used by anyone for any purpose. In contrast, those who say that sociology should explore harmful social arrangements take the position that sociological knowledge should be used to reform society. They say that sociologists should use their studies to alleviate human suffering and make society a better place to live. (See Figure 1.1.)

Although the debate about the proper role of values in social research is infinitely more complicated than the argument presented here—few sociologists take such one-sided views—the preceding sketch does identify its major issues. Perhaps sociologist John Galliher (1991) best expresses the majority position:

> Some argue that social scientists, unlike politicians and religious leaders, should merely attempt to describe and explain the events of the world but should never make value judgments based on those observations. Yet a value-free and nonjudgmental social science has no place in a world that has experienced the Holocaust, in a world having had slavery, in a world with the ever-present threat of rape and other sexual assault, in a world with frequent, unpunished crimes in high places, including the production of products known by their manufacturers to cause death and injury as has been true of asbestos products and continues to be true of the cigarette industry, and in a world dying from environmental pollution by these same large multinational corporations.

Verstehen **and Social Facts**

Weber **and** Verstehen

Weber also stressed that one cannot understand human behavior simply by looking at statistics. Those cold numbers may represent people's activities, he said, but they must be interpreted. To do so, he said that we should use **Verstehen** (a German word meaning

replication: repeating a study in order to check the findings of a previous study

Verstehen: a German word used by Weber that is perhaps best understood as "to have insight into someone's situation"

"to understand"). Perhaps the best translation of this term is "to grasp by insight." By emphasizing *Verstehen*, Weber meant that the best interpreter of human action is someone who "has been there," someone who can understand the feelings and motivations of the people they are studying. In short, we must pay attention to what are called **subjective meanings,** the ways in which people interpret their own behavior. We can't understand what people do, Weber insisted, unless we look at how people themselves view and explain their own behavior.

To better understand this term, let's return to the homeless in the opening vignette. Why were the men so silent? Why were they so unlike the noisy, sometimes boisterous college students in their dorms and cafeterias?

Verstehen can help explain this. When I interviewed men in the shelters (and in other settings, homeless women), they talked about their despair. As someone who knows—at least on some level—what the human emotion of despair is, you are immediately able to apply it to their situation. You know that people in despair feel a sense of hopelessness. The future looks bleak, hardly worth plodding toward. Consequently, what is there worth talking about anyway? Who wants to hear another hard-luck story?

By applying *Verstehen*—your own understanding of what it means to be human and to face various situations in life—you gain an understanding of people's behavior, in this case the silence, the lack of communication, among the homeless.

Durkheim and Social Facts

In contrast to Weber's use of *Verstehen*, or subjective meanings, Durkheim stressed what he called **social facts.** By this term, he meant the patterns of behavior that characterize a social group. (Note however that Weber did not disagree about the significance of social facts, for they are the basis of his conclusions about Protestantism and capitalism.) Examples of social facts in the United States include June being the most popular month for weddings, suicide being higher among people 65 and over, and more births occurring on Tuesdays than any other day of the week.

Durkheim said that we must use social facts to interpret social facts. In other words, each pattern reflects some underlying condition of society. People all over the country don't just coincidentally decide to do similar things, whether getting married or committing suicide. If that were the case, in some years middle-aged people would be the most likely to kill themselves, in other years, young people, and so on. Patterns that hold true year after year, however, indicate that as thousands and even millions of people make their individual decisions, they are responding to conditions in their society. It is the job of the sociologist, then, to uncover social facts and then to explain them through other social facts. In the following section, we shall see how these particular social facts are explained by the school year, conditions of the aged, and the social organization of medicine, respectively.

How Social Facts and *Verstehen* Fit Together

Social facts and *Verstehen* go hand in hand. As a member of U.S. society, you know how June weddings are related to the end of the school year and how this month, now locked in tradition, common sentiment, and advertising, carries its own momentum. As for suicide among the elderly (see chapter 13), you probably already have a sense of the greater despair that many Americans of this age feel.

But do you know why more Americans are born on Tuesday than any other day of the week? One would expect Tuesday to be no more common than any other day, and that is how it used to be. But no longer. To understand this change, we need a combination of social facts and *Verstehen*. Four social facts are relevant: First, technological developments have made the hospital a dominating force in the U.S. medical system. Second, current technology has made delivery by cesarean section safer. Third, as discussed in chapter 19, males took over the delivery of babies. Fourth, profit is a top goal of medicine in the United States. As

subjective meanings: the meanings that people give their own behavior

social facts: Durkheim's term for the patterns of behavior that characterize a social group

a result, an operation that used to be reserved for emergencies has become so routine that one-fourth of all U.S. babies are now delivered in this manner (*Statistical Abstract* 1992:86), the highest rate of such births in the world (Wolff et al. 1992). To these social facts, then, we add *Verstehen*. In this instance, it is understanding the preferences of mothers-to-be to give birth in a hospital, and their perceived lack of alternatives. Consequently, physicians schedule large numbers of deliveries for their own convenience, with most finding that Tuesdays fit their week best.

Sociology in North America

Transplanted to U.S. soil in the late nineteenth century, sociology first took root at the University of Chicago and at Atlanta University, then an all-black school. From there, academic specialties in sociology spread throughout U.S. higher education. The growth was gradual, however. Although the first departments of sociology in North America opened in 1889 at the University of Kansas and in 1892 at the University of Chicago, it was not until 1922 that McGill University gave Canada its first department of sociology. Harvard University did not open its department of sociology until 1930, and the University of California at Berkeley did not follow until the 1950s.

At first, sociology in the United States was dominated by the department at the University of Chicago, founded by Albion Small (1854–1926), who also founded the *American Journal of Sociology* and was its editor from 1895 to 1925. Members of this first sociology department whose ideas continue to influence today's sociologists include Robert E. Park (1864–1944), Ernest Burgess (1886–1966), and George Herbert Mead (1863–1931), who developed the symbolic interactionist perspective examined below.

In the late 1800s, the dominant sentiment was that a woman's place was in the home. Women who became sociologists during this period were not welcome as professors, and many turned to doing practical work with the poor. The outstanding example is Jane Addams (1860–1935), the founder of Hull-House in Chicago in 1889. She came from a privileged background and attended The Women's Medical College of Philadelphia, dropping out due to illness. On one of her many trips to Europe, she was impressed with work being done on behalf of London's poor. From then on, she tirelessly worked for social justice, concentrating on housing, education, and the working conditions of the poor, especially immigrants. Hull-House, located in the midst of Chicago's slums, was open to people who needed refuge—to the sick, the aged, the poor. Sociologists from nearby University of Chicago were frequent visitors at Hull-House. With her piercing insights into the social classes, the adjustment of peasant immigrants to industrializing cities, and the exploitation of workers, Addams constantly strived to bridge the gap between the powerful and the powerless. Her efforts at social reform were so outstanding, and so effective, that in 1931 she was a co-winner of the Nobel Peace Prize (Addams 1910/1981).

W. E. B. Du Bois (1868–1963), an African American who completed his education at the University of Berlin, created a sociological laboratory at Atlanta University in 1897. His lifetime research interest was relations between whites and African Americans in the United States, and he published a book on this subject every year between 1896 and 1914. At first, Du Bois was content simply to collect and interpret objective data. Later, frustrated at the continuing exploitation of blacks, Du Bois turned to social action and helped found the National Association for the Advancement of Colored People (NAACP). Continuing to battle racism both as a sociologist and as a journalist, he embraced revolutionary Marxism. Dismayed that so little improvement had been made in race relations, when he was 93 he moved to Ghana, where he is buried (Stark 1989).

Like Du Bois, and following the advice of Comte, many of the early North American sociologists combined the role of sociologist with that of social reformer. They saw society, or parts of it, as corrupt and in need of serious reform. During the 1920s and 1930s,

Jane Addams, 1860–1935, a recipient of the Nobel Peace Prize, tirelessly worked on behalf of poor immigrants. With Ellen G. Starr, she founded Hull House, a center to help immigrants in Chicago. She was also a leader in women's rights (women suffrage) and in the peace movement.

W(illiam) E(dward) B(urghardt) Du Bois (1868–1963) spent his lifetime studying relations between African Americans and whites. Like many early North American sociologists, Du Bois combined the role of academic sociologist with that of social reformer. He was also the editor of Crisis, an influential journal of the time.

Park and Burgess not only studied prostitution, crime, drug addiction, and juvenile delinquency, but they also offered suggestions for how to alleviate these social problems.

During the 1940s, the sociology departments at Harvard, Michigan, Wisconsin, and Columbia universities challenged the preeminent position of the University of Chicago. At the same time, the academic emphasis shifted from social reform to social theory. Talcott Parsons (1902–1979), for example, developed abstract models of society that exerted great influence on sociology. These models of how the parts of society harmoniously work together did nothing to stimulate social activism.

Robert K. Merton (b. 1910) stressed the need for sociologists to develop **middle-range theories,** explanations that tie together many research findings but avoid sweeping generalizations that attempt to account for everything. Such theories, he claimed, are preferable because they can be tested. Grand theories, in contrast, while attractive because they seem to account for so much of social life, are of little value because they cannot be tested. Merton (1968) developed a middle-range theory of crime and deviant behavior (discussed on pages 204–205) that explains how U.S. society's emphasis on attaining material wealth encourages crime.

C. Wright Mills (1916–1962) deplored the theoretical abstractions of this period, which he said were accompanied by empty research methods. Mills (1956) urged sociologists to get back to social reform, seeing imminent danger to freedom in the coalescing of interests of the power elite—the wealthy, the politicians, and the military. After his death, the turbulence in U.S. society in the 1960s and 1970s, fueled by the Vietnam War, also disturbed U.S. sociology. As interest in social activism revived, Mills's ideas became popular among a new generation of sociologists.

The Present   Since the 1970s, U.S. sociology has not been dominated by any one theoretical orientation or by any single concern. Three theoretical frameworks are most commonly used, as we shall see later, and social activism remains an option for sociologists. Some sociologists are content to study various aspects of social life, interpret their findings, and publish these findings in sociology journals. Others direct their research and publications toward social change and actively participate in community affairs to help bring about their vision of a more just society.

During the past two decades, the activities of sociologists have broadened. Once just about the only occupation open to a graduate in sociology was teaching. Although most sociologists still enter teaching, the government has now become their second-largest source of employment. Many other sociologists work for private firms in management and planning positions. Still others work in criminology and demography, in social work, and as counselors. Sociologists put their training to use in such diverse efforts as tracking the spread of AIDS and helping teenage prostitutes escape from pimps. This book later looks more closely at some of these applications of sociology.

At this point, however, let's concentrate on a better understanding of sociological theory.

Theoretical Perspectives in Sociology

middle-range theories: explanations of human behavior that go beyond a particular observation or research but avoid sweeping generalizations that attempt to account for everything

theory: a general statement about how some parts of the world fit together and how they work; an explanation of how two or more facts are related to one another

Facts never interpret themselves. They always must be interpreted by being placed into a framework. That conceptual framework is called a theory. A **theory** is a general statement about how some parts of the world fit together and how they work. It is an explanation of how two or more facts are related to one another. By providing a framework in which to fit observations, each theory interprets reality in a distinct way.

Three major theories have emerged within the discipline of sociology: symbolic interactionism, functional analysis, and conflict theory. Let us first look at the main elements of these theories and then apply each theory to the question of why the divorce rate in the United States is so high that only about a *third* of people who marry today can expect their marriage to last (Bumpass 1990).

	Table 1.1			
Major Theoretical Perspectives in Sociology				
Perspective	*Usual Level of Analysis*	*Focus of Analysis*	*Key Terms*	*Applying the Perspectives to the Divorce Rate of the United States*
Symbolic Interactionism	Microsociological—examines small-scale patterns of social interaction	Face-to-face interaction; how people use symbols to create social life	Symbols Interaction Meanings Definitions	Industrialization and urbanization change marital roles and lead to a redefinition of the nature of love, marriage, children, and divorce
Functional Analysis (*also called Functionalism and Structural Functionalism*)	Macrosociological—examines large-scale patterns of society	Relationships among the parts of society; how these parts are *functional* (have beneficial consequences) or *dysfunctional* (have negative consequences)	Structure Functions (manifest and latent) Dysfunction Equilibrium	As social change erodes the traditional functions of the family, family ties are weakened and the divorce rate increases
Conflict Theory	Macrosociological—examines large-scale patterns of society	The struggle for scarce resources by groups in a society; how dominant elites use power to control the less powerful	Inequality Power Conflict Competition Exploitation	When men control economic life, the divorce rate is low because women find few alternatives to a bad marriage; the rising divorce rate reflects a shift in the balance of power between men and women

Symbolic Interactionism

We can trace the origins of **symbolic interactionism** to the Scottish moral philosophers of the eighteenth century, who noted that people evaluate their own conduct by comparing themselves with others (Stryker 1990). In the United States, a long line of thinkers added to this analysis, including the pioneering psychologist William James (1842–1910) and the educator John Dewey (1859–1952), who analyzed how people use symbols to encapsulate their experiences. This theoretical perspective was brought into sociology by sociologists Charles Horton Cooley (1864–1929), William I. Thomas (1863–1947), and George Herbert Mead (1863–1931). Cooley's and Mead's analyses of how symbols lie at the basis of the self-concept are discussed on pages 65–67.

Symbolic interactionists view symbols—things to which we attach meaning—as the basis of social life. First, without symbols our social relations would be limited to the animal level, for we would have no mechanism for perceiving others in terms of relationships (aunts and uncles, employers and teachers, and so on). Strange as it may seem, only because we have symbols can we have aunts and uncles, for it is these symbols that define for us what such relationships entail. Second, without symbols we could not coordinate our actions with others; we would be unable to make plans for a future date, time, and place. Unable to specify times, materials, sizes, or goals, we could not build bridges and highways. Without symbols, there would be no books, movies, or musical instruments. We would have no schools or hospitals, no government, no religion. In short, as symbolic interactionists point out, symbols make social life possible. Third, even the self is a symbol, for it consists of the ideas that we have about who we are.

symbolic interactionism: a theoretical perspective in which society is viewed as composed of symbols that people use to establish meaning, develop their views of the world, and communicate with one another

George Herbert Mead (1863–1931) is one of the founders of symbolic interactionism, a major theoretical perspective in sociology. He taught at the University of Chicago, where his lectures were very popular. Though he wrote very little, after his death his students compiled his lectures into an influential book, Mind, Self, and Society.

And it is a changing symbol, for as we interact with others, we constantly adjust our views of the self based on how we interpret the reactions of others.

Symbolic interactionists analyze how our behaviors depend on how we define ourselves and others. For example, if you think of someone as an aunt or uncle, you behave in certain ways, but if you think of that person as a boyfriend or girlfriend, you behave quite differently. It is as though everyday life is a stage on which we perform, switching roles to suit our changing audiences. This topic is examined in detail on pages 107–110. For now, keep in mind that symbolic interactionists primarily examine face-to-face interaction, looking at how people work out their relationships and make sense out of life and their place in it.

Applying Symbolic Interactionism   To better understand symbolic interactionism, let us see how changing symbols (meanings) help to explain the high U.S. divorce rate (Henslin 1992).

1 *Emotional satisfaction.* In the earlier part of this century, symbolic interactionists observed that the basis for family solidarity was changing. As early as 1933, sociologist William Ogburn noted that personality was becoming more important in mate selection. Then in 1945, sociologists Ernest Burgess and Harvey Locke found that family solidarity was coming to depend more and more on mutual affection, understanding, and compatibility. What these sociologists had observed was a fundamental shift in U.S. marriage: Husbands and wives were coming to expect—and demand—greater emotional satisfaction from one another.

As this trend intensified, intimacy became the core of marriage. At the same time, as society grew more complex and impersonal, Americans came to see marriage as a solution to the tensions that society produced (Lasch 1977). This new form, "companionate marriage," contributed to divorce, for it encouraged people to expect that their spouse would satisfy "each and every need." Consequently, sociologists say, marriage became an "overloaded institution."

2 *The love symbol.* Our symbol of love also helps to "overload" marriage. Unrealistic expectations that "true love" will be a constant source of emotional satisfaction set people up for crushed hopes, for when dissatisfactions enter marriage, as they inevitably do, spouses tend to blame one another for what they see as the other's failure. Their engulfment in the symbol of love at the time of marriage blinds them to the basic unreality of their expectations.

3 *The meaning of children.* Ideas about childhood have undergone a deep historical shift with far-reaching consequences for the contemporary U.S. family (Henslin 1992a). In medieval European society children were seen as miniature adults, and there was no sharp separation between the worlds of adults and children (Ariès 1962). Boys were apprenticed at about age 7, while girls at the same age learned the homemaking duties associated with the wifely role. In the United States, just three generations ago children "became adults" when they graduated from eighth grade and took employment. The contrast is amazing: From miniature adults, children have been culturally fashioned into impressionable, vulnerable, and innocent beings.

4 *The meaning of parenthood.* These changed notions of childhood have had a corresponding impact on our ideas of good parenting. Today's parents are expected not only to provide unending amounts of affection, love, and tender care but also to take responsibility for ensuring that their children "reach their potential." Today's child rearing lasts longer and is more demanding, pushing the family into even greater "emotional overload" (Lasch 1977).

5 *Marital roles.* In earlier generations, newlyweds knew what they could legitimately expect from each other, for the responsibilities and privileges of husbands and wives were clearly defined. In contrast, today's much vaguer guidelines leave couples to work out more aspects of their respective roles on their own. Many find it difficult to figure out how to divide up responsibilities for work, home, and children.

6 *Perception of alternatives.* While the above changes in marriage expectations were taking place, another significant social change was under way: More and more women began taking jobs outside the home. As they earned paychecks of their own, many wives began for the first time to see alternatives to remaining in unhappy marriages. Symbolic interactionists consider the perception of an alternative an essential first step to making divorce possible.

7 *The meaning of divorce.* As these various factors coalesced—greater expectations of emotional satisfaction and changed marital and parental roles, accompanied by a new perception of alternatives to an unhappy marriage—divorce steadily increased. (Figure 1.2 shows the increase in divorce in the United States, from practically zero in 1890 to the current 1.2 million divorces a year. The plateau for both marriage and divorce since 1980 is probably due to increased cohabitation.)

As divorce became more common, its meaning changed. Once a symbol of almost everything negative   failure, irresponsibility, even immorality—divorce became infused with new meanings—personal change, opportunity, even liberation. This symbolic change from failure to self-fulfillment reduced the stigma of divorce, setting the stage for divorce on an even larger scale.

8 *Changes in the law.* The law, itself a powerful symbol, began to reflect these changed ideas about divorce—and to encourage divorce. Where previously divorce was granted only when the most rigorous criteria, such as adultery, were met, legislators now made "incompatibility" legitimate grounds for divorce. Eventually, states pioneered "no-fault" divorce, in which couples could dissolve their marriage without accusations of wrongdoing. Some even provide do-it-yourself divorce kits.

▼ **In Sum** Symbolic interactionists explain an increasing divorce rate in terms of the changing symbols (or meanings) associated with both marriage and divorce. Changes in people's ideas—about divorce, marital satisfaction, love, the nature of children and parenting, and the roles of husband and wife—have put extreme pressure on today's married couples. No single change is *the* cause, but taken together, these changes provide a strong "push" toward divorce.

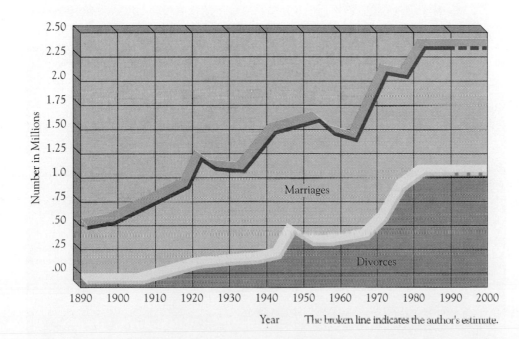

Figure 1.2

American Marriage, American Divorce

(*Source:* For 1950–1990, *Statistical Abstract 1992:* Table 80; early editions for earlier years.)

Are these changes good or bad? Central to symbolic interactionism is the position that to make a value judgment about change (or anything else) requires a value framework from which to view the change. Symbolic interactionism provides no such value framework. In short, symbolic interactionists, like other sociologists, can analyze social change, but they cannot pass judgment on that change.

Functional Analysis

Functional analysis, also known as *functionalism* and *structural functionalism,* is rooted in the origins of sociology (Turner 1978). Auguste Comte and Herbert Spencer used an organic analogy to analyze society, viewing it as a kind of living organism. Just as a biological organism has interrelated tissues and organs that function together, they wrote, so does society. Like an organism, if society is to function smoothly, its various parts must work together in harmony.

Emile Durkheim also saw society as composed of many parts, each with its own function. When all the parts of society fulfill their functions, society is in a "normal" state. If they do not fulfill their functions, society is in an "abnormal" or "pathological" state. To understand society, then, functionalists say that we need to look at both *structure*—how the parts of a society fit together to make the whole—and *function*—how each part contributes to society.

Although Robert K. Merton dismissed the organic analogy, he continued the essence of functionalism—the image of society as a whole composed of interrelated parts. Merton used the term *functions* to refer to the beneficial consequences of people's actions that help to maintain the equilibrium of a social system. In contrast, *dysfunctions* are consequences that undermine a system's equilibrium.

Functions can be either manifest or latent. Merton called an action intended to help a system's equilibrium a *manifest function.* For example, suppose the tuition at your college is doubled. The intention, or manifest function, of such a sharp increase may be to raise faculty salaries and thus recruit better faculty. Merton pointed out that people's

functional analysis: a theoretical framework in which society is viewed as composed of various parts, each with a function that, when fulfilled, contributes to society's equilibrium; also known as functionalism and structural functionalism

Sociologists who use the functionalist perspective stress that the traditional functions of the family have been undermined by industrialization and urbanization, leading to dysfunctions, or a weakening of family ties. One traditional function of the family that has been largely replaced by strangers is taking care of the dead. Wakes in the home, once common in the United States, are becoming rare—although still evident in certain parts of the country, as in this scene of an open casket in the living room of a family in Kentucky.

actions can also have *latent functions*, unintended consequences that help a system adapt. Let us suppose that the tuition increase worked, that the quality of the faculty improved so greatly that your college gained a national reputation overnight. As a result, it was flooded with new applicants and was able to expand both its programs and its campus. The expansion contributed to the stability of your college, but it was unintended. Therefore, it is a *latent* function of the tuition increase.

Sometimes human actions have the opposite effect, of course, and hurt the system. Because such consequences are usually unintended, Merton called them *latent dysfunctions*. Let's assume that doubling the tuition backfired, that half the student body couldn't afford the increase and dropped out. With this loss of income, the college had to reduce salaries. They managed to get through one year this way, but then folded. Because these results were not intended and actually harmed the social system (in this case, the college), they represent a latent dysfunction of the tuition increase.

In Sum From the perspective of functional analysis, then, the group is a functioning whole, with each part related to the whole. Whenever we examine a smaller part, we need to look for its functions and dysfunctions to see how it is related to the larger unit. This basic approach can be applied to any social group, whether an entire society, a college, or even a group as small as a family.

Applying Functional Analysis Now let's apply functional analysis to the U.S. divorce rate. Functionalists stress that industrialization and urbanization undermined the traditional functions of the family, namely economic production, the socialization of children, care of the sick and elderly, recreation, sexual control of family members, and reproduction. Let us see how each of these basic functions has changed.

1 *Economic production.* Prior to industrialization, the family constituted an economic team. Most families found the availability of food uncertain, and family members had to cooperate in producing what they needed to survive. When industrialization moved production from home to factory, it disrupted this family team and weakened the bonds that tied family members together. Especially significant was the transfer of the husband/father to the factory, for this move separated him from the family's daily routine. In addition, the wife/mother and children now contributed less to the family's economic survival.

2 *Socialization of children.* As these sweeping economic changes occurred, the government, growing larger and more powerful, usurped many family functions. To name just one example, local schools took the responsibility of educating children away from the family. In so doing, they assumed much of the responsibility for socializing children. To make certain that families went along with this change, states passed laws requiring that children attend school and threatened parents with jail if they did not send their children.

3 *Care of the sick and elderly.* As the central government expanded and its agencies multiplied, care of the aged changed from a family concern to a government obligation. With new laws governing medical schools and hospitals, institutionalized medicine grew more powerful, and medical care gradually shifted from the family to outside medical specialists.

4 *Recreation.* As more disposable income became available to Americans, business enterprises sprang up to compete for that income. This cost the family much of its recreational function, for much entertainment and "fun" changed from home-based, family-centered activities to attendance at paid events.

5 *Sexual control of members.* Even the control of sexuality was not left untouched by the vast social changes that swept the country. Traditionally, only sexual relations within marriage were considered legitimate. Although this sexual control was always more ideal than real, for even among the Puritans matrimony never did enjoy a monopoly over sexual relations (Smith and Hindus 1975), it is now considerably weaker than it used to be. The "sexual revolution" of the past few decades has opened many alternatives to marital sex.

Figure 1.3

Percentage of Births to Unmarried Mothers by Country

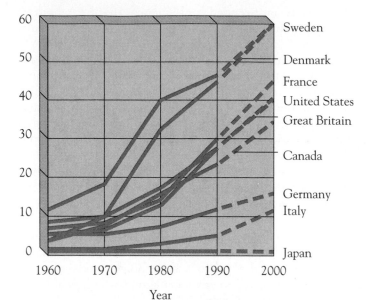

Year

Source: *Statistical Abstract 1992: 1365.* Dotted lines are the author's projections.

6 *Reproduction.* On the surface, the only family function that seems to have been left untouched is reproduction. Yet even this vital and seemingly inviolable function has not gone unchallenged. A prime example is the greater number of single women who are having children. Figure 1.3 shows that in the United States unmarried women now account for more than one-quarter of all births—and that the same trend is common throughout the industrialized world. (Japan is the only exception.) Even schools and private agencies have taken over some of the family's control over reproduction. A married woman, for example, can get an abortion without informing her husband, and some high schools distribute condoms.

A Glimpse of the Past   To see how sharply family functions have changed, it may be useful to take a glimpse of family life in the 1800s.

> When Phil became sick, he was nursed by Ann, his wife. She cooked for him, fed him, changed the bed linen, bathed him, read to him from the Bible, and gave him his medicine. (She did this in addition to doing the housework and taking care of their six children.) Phil was also surrounded by the children, who shouldered some of his chores while their father was sick.
>
> When Phil died, the male neighbors and relatives made the casket while Ann, her mother, and female friends washed and dressed the body. Phil was then "laid out" in the front parlor (the formal living room), where friends, neighbors, and relatives viewed him, paying their last respects. From there friends moved his body to the church for the final message, and then to the grave they had dug.

As you can see from this event, the functions of the family were diverse, covering many aspects of life and death that are now handled by outside agencies. Not only did the care of the sick take place almost exclusively within the family, but death was also a family affair—from preparing the body to burying it. Today we assume that such functions *properly* belong to specialized agencies, and few of us can even imagine preparing the body of a close relative for burial. Such an act may even seem grotesque, almost barbarous, for our current customs also guide our feelings, another fascinating aspect of social life, but one, regrettably, that I do not have time to pursue. (On pages 70–71, I return to the topic of emotions.)

conflict theory: a theoretical framework in which society is viewed as composed of groups competing for scarce resources

▼   **In Sum**   The family has lost many of its traditional functions, while others are presently under assault. From a functionalist perspective, these changes have weakened the family unit. The fewer functions that family members have in common, the fewer their "ties that bind." This erosion of family functions has made the family more fragile and an increase in divorce inevitable. Thus, functionalists attribute the high divorce rate in the United States to a weakening or loss of family functions, which previously had held a husband and wife together in spite of the problems they experienced.

Conflict Theory

Conflict theory provides a third perspective on social life. Karl Marx, the founder of conflict theory, witnessed the Industrial Revolution that transformed Europe. He saw that peasants who had left the land to seek work in urbanizing areas had to work at wages that barely provided enough to eat. (The average worker died at age 30, the wealthy at age 50 [Edgerton 1992:87]). Shocked by the suffering and exploitation he witnessed, Marx began to analyze society and history. As he did so, he developed **conflict theory,** concluding that the key to all human history is class struggle. In each society, some small group controls the means of production and exploits those who do not. In industrialized societies the struggle is between the **bourgeoisie,** the small group of capitalists who own the means to produce wealth, and the **proletariat,** the mass of workers exploited by the bourgeoisie. The capitalists also control politics, so that when workers rebel the capitalists are able to call on the power of the state to control them (Angell 1965).

When Marx made his observations, capitalism was in its infancy and workers were at the mercy of their employers. Workers had none of what we take for granted today—the right to strike, minimum wages, eight-hour days, coffee breaks, five-day work weeks, paid vacations and holidays, medical benefits, sick leave, unemployment compensation, Social Security. His analysis reminds us that these benefits came not from generous hearts, but from workers who forced concessions from their employers.

Some current conflict sociologists use conflict theory in a much broader sense. Ralf Dahrendorf (b. 1929) sees conflict as inherent in all relations that have authority. He points out that **authority,** or power that people consider legitimate, runs through all layers of society—whether small groups, a community, or the entire society. People in positions of authority try to enforce conformity, which in turn creates resentment and resistance. The result is a constant struggle throughout society to determine who has authority over what (Turner 1978).

Another sociologist, Lewis Coser (b. 1913), pointed out that conflict is especially likely to develop among people who are in close relationships. Such people are connected by a network of responsibilities, power, and rewards and to change something can easily upset arrangements that they have so carefully worked out. Consequently, we can think even of close relationships as a balancing act—of maintaining and reworking a particular distribution of responsibilities, power, and rewards.

▼   **In Sum** Unlike the functionalists who view society as a harmonious whole, with its parts working together, conflict theorists see society as composed of groups fiercely competing for scarce resources. Although alliances or cooperation may prevail on the surface, beneath that surface is a struggle for power. Marx focused on struggles between the bourgeoisie and proletariat, but today's conflict theorists have expanded this perspective to include smaller groups and even basic relationships.

Applying Conflict Theory   If we apply conflict theory's emphasis on competition and exploitation to divorce, a sharply contrasting picture emerges. Conflict theorists look at men's and women's relationships in terms of basic inequalities—men dominate and exploit, while women are dominated and exploited. They also point out that marriage reflects the basic male–female relationship of society and is one of the means by which men maintain their domination and exploitation of women.

The Historical Record.   Conflict theorists stress that women have traditionally been regarded as property and passed by one male, the father, to another, the husband (Dobash and Dobash 1981). Just as the law allowed fathers to discipline daughters, so it allowed husbands to disci-

bourgeoisie: Karl Marx's term for capitalists, those who own the means to produce wealth

proletariat Marx's term for the exploited class, the mass of workers who do not own the means of production

authority: power that people consider legitimate

pline their wives—and that included beating them. In society after society, women have been assigned the role of taking care of the personal needs of men—their fathers, husbands, and brothers—and the home has been the place in which they were relegated to lifetime servitude. Because marriage still reflects these millennia-old patterns of female subordination, it remains the basic arena for the ongoing struggle between the sexes. Changing relationships of power and inequality, then, are the keys to understanding the current divorce rate.

Different Experiences of Marriage.   Because of their unequal statuses, say conflict theorists, men and women have experienced marriage quite differently (Bernard 1992). If a woman's main goal in life is to be a wife and mother, the search for security guides her mate selection. Women with this goal are more anxious than males about dating, mate selection, and the outcome of marriage. In contrast, males who find their basic security in the workplace are less concerned about the marital relationship. The consequence has been an unequal balance of power in marriage, with wives more dependent on its outcome and investing more in the relationship.

The Struggle for Power.   The relationship between men and women is undergoing fundamental change. Because today's females increasingly participate in social worlds beyond the home, they refuse to bear burdens previously accepted as inevitable and are much more likely to dissolve a marriage that has become intolerable. At the center of marriage today, then, is a struggle for power (Bernard 1992). Recent increases in the number of women who work outside the home and in women's organizations advocating changes in male–female relationships have upset traditional imbalances of rights and obligations. Conflict in marriage is primarily due to husbands' resentment of their decreasing power and wives' resentment of their husbands' reluctance to share marital power.

▼   **In Sum**   Conflict theorists see marriage as reflecting a society's basic inequalities between males and females. Higher divorce rates result from changed male–female power relationships, especially as wives attempt to resolve basic inequalities and husbands resist those efforts. From the conflict perspective, then, the increase in divorce is not a sign that marriage has weakened but, rather, a sign that women are finally making headway in their historical struggle with men.

Levels of Analysis: Macro and Micro

A major difference between the theoretical orientations described above is their level of analysis. The functionalist and conflict perspectives focus on **macro-level analysis;** that is, they examine large-scale patterns of society. In contrast, the symbolic interactionist perspective tends to focus more on **micro-level analysis,** on **social interaction,** or what people do when they are in one another's presence. (See Table 1.1, p. 19)

Let's return to the example of homelessness to make this distinction between micro and macro levels clearer. In studying the homeless, symbolic interactionists would focus on what they say and what they do. They would analyze what homeless people do when they are in shelters and on the streets, focusing especially on their communications, both their talk and their **nonverbal interaction** (how they communicate by gestures, silence, use of space, and so on). The observations that I made earlier about the despair and silence of the homeless, for example, would be areas of interest to symbolic interactionists.

This micro level, however, would not interest functionalists and conflict theorists. They would focus instead on the macro level. Functionalists would examine how changes in the parts of society are related to homelessness. They might look at how changing relationships in the family (smaller, more divorce) and economic conditions (higher rents, inflation, fewer unskilled jobs, loss of jobs overseas) cause homelessness among people who are unable to find jobs and do not have a family to fall back on. For their part, conflict theorists would stress the struggle between social classes, especially how the policies of the wealthy push certain groups into unemployment and homelessness. That, they would point out, accounts for the disproportionate number of African Americans who are homeless. Chapter 4 focuses on the distinctions between macro and micro levels of analysis.

macro-level analysis: an examination of large-scale patterns of society

micro-level analysis: an examination of small-scale patterns of society

social interaction: what people do when they are in one another's presence

nonverbal interaction: communication without words through gestures, space, silence, and so on

Putting the Theoretical Perspectives Together

Which theoretical perspective should we use to study human behavior? Which level of analysis is the correct one? As you have seen, these theoretical perspectives provide different and often sharply contrasting pictures of our world. No theory or level of analysis encompasses all of reality. Rather, by focusing on different features of social life, each provides a distinctive interpretation. Consequently, it is necessary to use all three theoretical lenses to analyze human behavior. By putting the contributions of each perspective and level of analysis together, we gain a more comprehensive picture of social life.

As you can see, the sociological perspective leads to an entirely different understanding of divorce than the commonsense understanding of "They were simply incompatible." To take this larger view of human events, which is the sociological perspective, gives us a different way of viewing social life. This will become even more apparent in the following chapters as we explore topics as broad as sexism and as highly focused as a kindergarten classroom.

▼▲▼▲▼▲▼▲▼▲▼▲▼▲▼▲▼▲▼▲▼▲▼▲▼▲▼▲▼▲▼

Down-To-Earth Sociology

Sociologists at Work: What Applied Sociologists Do

APPLIED SOCIOLOGISTS WORK IN a wide variety of settings—from counseling children to improving work relationships. To give you an idea of that variety, let's look over the shoulders of four sociologists.

Leslie Green, who does marketing research at Vanderveer Group in Philadelphia, Pennsylvania, earned her bachelor's degree in sociology at Shippensburg University. To develop marketing strategies so doctors will choose to prescribe a particular drug, her company has physicians meet in groups to discuss prescription drugs. Green sets up the meetings, locates moderators for the discussion groups, and arranges payments to the physicians who participate in the research. "My training in sociology," she says, "helps me in 'people skills.' It helps me to understand the needs of different groups, and to interact with them."

Stanley Capela, whose master's degree is from Fordham University, works as an applied sociologist at HeartShare Human Services in New York. He evaluates how children's programs—such as housing, AIDS, care in group homes, and preschool programs for developmentally disabled children—actually work, compared with what they are supposed to do. He spots problems and suggests solutions. One of his projects was to find out why adoption was taking so long, why there was a backlog of unadopted children although there was a list of eager adoptive parents. He identified the problem as an inefficient information system; that is, the paperwork got bogged down as it was routed through the system. The solution was to improve the flow of paperwork.

Laurie Banks, who received her master's degree in sociology from Fordham University, works for the New York City Health Department, where she analyzes vital statistics. By examining data on death certificates, she identified high-and low-cancer areas in the city. She found that a Polish neighborhood had high rates of stomach cancer. Follow-up interviews by the Centers for Disease Control traced the cause to eating large amounts of sausage. In another case, she compared birth certificates and school records and found that problems at birth—low birth weight, lack of prenatal care, and birth complications—were linked to low reading skills and behavior problems in school.

Ross Cappell, whose doctorate is from Temple University, runs his own research company, Social Research Corporation, in Philadelphia. His work, too, is filled with variety—from surveying the customers of a credit card company in order to help the company understand its market to analyzing the impact of fare increases in public transportation. In one case, Cappell was asked to evaluate the services that unemployed workers received when a steel mill closed down. He found that the services and training were not particularly helpful. Too many workers were retrained in a single field, such as air conditioner repair, and the local market was flooded with more specialists than it could use. When Cappell testified before Congress, he stressed how the training given to displaced workers must match the needs of the local labor market.

From just this small sample, you can catch a glimpse of the amazing variety of work that applied sociologists do. You can see that some applied sociologists work for corporations, some for government and private agencies, and others operate their own firms. You can also see that a doctorate is not necessary to work as an applied sociologist. For another example of an applied sociologist at work, see the Down-to-Earth Sociology box on page 132.

Applied and Clinical Sociology

Sociologists Paul Lazarsfeld and Jeffrey Reitz (1989) divide sociology into three phases. First, as we have already seen, when sociology began it was indistinguishable from attempts to reform society. The primary concern of early sociologists was to make the world a better place. The point of analyzing social conditions was to use the information to improve social life. Albion Small, one of the first presidents of the American Sociological Society (1912–1913), said that the primary reason for the existence of sociology was its "practical application to the improvement of social life." Sociologists, he said, should use science to gain knowledge and then use that knowledge to "realize visions" (Fritz 1989). This first phase of sociology lasted until the 1920s.

During the second phase, it became the goal of sociologists to establish sociology as a respected field of knowledge. To this end, sociologists sought to develop **pure** or **basic sociology,** that is, research and theory aimed at making discoveries about life in human groups, but not at making changes in those groups. This goal was soon achieved, and within a generation sociology was incorporated into almost every college and university curriculum in the United States. World War II marked the end of this phase.

During the third and current phase, there has been an attempt to merge sociological knowledge and practical work. Dissatisfied with "knowledge for the sake of knowledge," many sociologists use their sociological skills to bring about social change, to make a difference in social life. The final results of this phase are not yet known, but the emphasis on applying sociology has gained much momentum in just the past few years.

Efforts to blend sociological knowledge and practical results are known as **applied sociology.** This term refers to the use of sociology to solve problems. Applied sociologists work in a variety of settings, recommending practical changes that can be implemented. A business firm may hire a sociologist to solve a problem in the workplace; sociologists may do research for government commissions or agencies investigating social problems such as pornography, crime, violence, or environmental pollution. The Down-to-Earth Sociology box on p. 27 features sociologists who do applied sociology.

Some applied sociologists not only make recommendations for change based on their findings but they themselves become directly involved in solving problems. This type of applied sociology is called **clinical sociology.** Clinical sociologists who work in industrial settings may try to change work conditions to reduce job turnover. Others work with drug addicts and ex-convicts, while still others are family counselors who try to change basic relationships between a husband and wife or between children and their parents. Figure 1.4 contrasts basic and applied sociology.

pure or basic sociology: sociological research whose only purpose is to make discoveries about life in human groups, not to make changes in those groups

applied sociology: the use of sociology to solve problems—from the micro level of family relationships to the macro level of crime and pollution

clinical sociology: the direct involvement of sociologists in bringing about social change

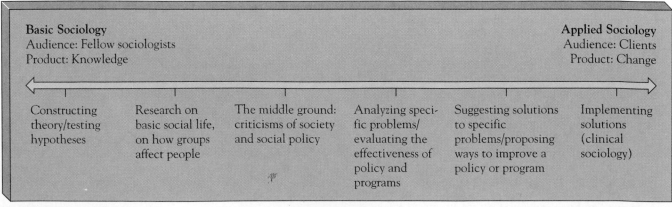

Basic Sociology
Audience: Fellow sociologists
Product: Knowledge

Applied Sociology
Audience: Clients
Product: Change

| Constructing theory/testing hypotheses | Research on basic social life, on how groups affect people | The middle ground: criticisms of society and social policy | Analyzing specific problems/ evaluating the effectiveness of policy and programs | Suggesting solutions to specific problems/proposing ways to improve a policy or program | Implementing solutions (clinical sociology) |

Source: Based on De Martini 1982.

Figure 1.4

Comparing Basic and Applied Sociology

▼▲

Perspectives

CULTURAL DIVERSITY AROUND THE WORLD

Sociology in a World in Turmoil

THE SOCIOLOGICAL PERSPECTIVE EMPHASIZED in this text does not come "naturally," and in some cases it is even vigorously resisted. People often have good reason to keep their minds closed. If they can keep social arrangements unexamined, their "old way" of doing things is not threatened. In contrast, by explaining how the various parts of society work together, sociology opens the possibility of liberating change.

This point was driven home by Mikhail Gorbachev, the former head of the former Soviet Union. When he declared *perestroika*, the "reconstruction" of his nation, Gorbachev committed himself to developing a new structure for Soviet society. This required an objective, "outside" view of the structure that existed at the time. Consequently, one of Mikhail Gorbachev's first initiatives in higher education was to authorize graduate students to come to the United States. To study what? Engineering? Chemistry? Computer science? Physics? English? None of these. It was to study *sociology*.

This graduate exchange between the former Soviet Union and the United States was worked out between the American Sociological Association and its Soviet counterpart. Soviet students were placed in fifteen sociology programs around the United States. In addition, what was then the Soviet Union began to set up sociology departments in its own universities.

At this radical juncture in history, the world is poised between opportunity and potential disaster. Economic markets and technology are being globalized (see Chapter 14). So is democracy. As traditional social orders are swept away, sociology has the potential to provide an understanding of these events—of the opportunities that the world's societies face, as well as the land mines that can destroy those opportunities.

Sociology often makes people uncomfortable, however, for as sociologists analyze the interconnections between the parts of a society, they also expose its underbelly. Ruling parties become upset when sociologists show how a society's interconnections produce its social problems. For example, sociologists point out how social injustices are built into U.S. society. They stress how as a result of social arrangements some groups are deprived of opportunity, income, and education, thus increasing their chances of being malnourished, getting sick, dying young, getting divorced, having their children become juvenile delinquents or getting involved in drugs, and their adults committing street crimes. Such analysis challenges people's comfortable assumptions about why "those people" do what "they" do—and about their own place in society.

Closed societies feel especially threatened by sociology. For example, after the Tiananmen Square massacre, China moved away from sociology, for its leaders did not want to be confronted with social analysis. They wanted no one to question their social arrangements. Chinese students of sociology in the United States and elsewhere became suspect on returning home.

In contrast, societies that want to understand themselves tend to welcome sociology, for sociological analysis of relations at work, school, and home, relations between ethnic groups, discrimination against women, the effects of social class, provides useful knowledge.

In short, sociologists bring a society's interconnections into the open, where they can be examined. From this process arises the possibility of productive social change, which is the promise of sociology in a world in turmoil.

Sources: Based on Boden et al. 1990 and the author's interviews with Chinese graduate students studying sociology in the United States.

The Future Sociology is now swinging full circle. From an initial concern with improving society, sociologists switched their focus to developing abstract knowledge. Currently sociologists are again seeking ways to apply their findings. These efforts have gained momentum in recent years, and the future is likely to see much more applied sociology (see the Perspectives box above). Many departments of sociology now offer courses in applied sociology, and some offer specialties, and even internships, in applied sociology at both the graduate and undergraduate levels.

These changes are taking sociology closer to its starting point. They provide renewed contact with the discipline's roots, promising to invigorate sociology as they challenge us to grasp a vision of what society can become—and what sociology's role can be in that process of change.

Summary and Review

The Sociological Perspective

What is the sociological perspective?

The **sociological perspective** stresses that people's social experiences—the groups to which they belong and their particular experiences within these groups—underlie their behavior. C. Wright Mills referred to this as the intersection of biography (the individual) and history (social factors acting on the individual). Pp. 4–5.

Sociology and the Other Sciences

What is science, and where does sociology fit in?

Science is the application of systematic methods to obtain knowledge and the knowledge obtained by those methods. The sciences are divided into the **natural sciences**, which seek to comprehend, explain, and predict events in the natural environment; and the **social sciences**, which seek to understand the social world objectively by means of controlled and repeated observations. **Sociology** is the scientific study of society and human behavior. Pp. 6–8.

The Development of Sociology

When did sociology first appear as a separate discipline, and what factors contributed to its emergence?

Sociology emerged as a separate discipline in the mid-1800s in western Europe, during the onset of the Industrial Revolution. Industrialization brought social changes so sweeping they affected all aspects of human existence—where people lived, the nature of their work, and interpersonal relationships. Early sociologists who focused on these social changes include Auguste Comte, Herbert Spencer, Karl Marx, Harriet Martineau, Emile Durkheim, and Max Weber. Pp. 8–14.

The Role of Values in Social Research

Should the purpose of social research be only to advance human understanding or also to reform society?

All sociologists concur that social research should be **value free**: the researcher's personal beliefs should be set aside in order to permit objective findings. But sociologists do not agree on the uses and purposes of social research. Some believe its purpose should be only to advance understanding of human

behavior; others, that its goal should be to reform harmful social arrangements. Pp. 14–15.

Verstehen and Social Facts

How do sociologists use *Verstehen* and social facts to investigate human behavior?

According to Weber, to understand why people act as they do, sociologists must try to put themselves in their shoes. He used the German term **Verstehen,** "to grasp by insight," to describe this essentially subjective approach. Although not denying the importance of *Verstehen*, Emile Durkheim emphasized the importance of uncovering "social facts" that influence human actions. **Social facts** are objective social conditions that influence how people behave. Contemporary sociology uses both approaches to understand human behavior. Pp. 15–17.

Sociology in North America

How recently were academic departments of sociology established in the United States?

The earliest departments of sociology were established around the turn of the nineteenth century at the universities of Kansas, Chicago, and Atlanta, respectively. During the 1940s sociology was dominated by the University of Chicago. Today, no single university or theoretical perspective dominates. Pp. 17–18.

Theoretical Perspectives in Sociology

What is a theory?

A **theory** is a general statement about how sets of facts are related to one another. A theory provides a conceptual framework within which facts are interpreted. P. 18.

What are the major theoretical perspectives?

Sociologists make use of three primary theoretical frameworks to interpret social life. **Symbolic interactionism** examines how people use symbols to develop and share their views of the world. Symbolic interactionists usually focus at the micro level—on small-scale patterns of human interaction. **Functional analysis,** in contrast, focuses on the macro level—on large-scale patterns of society. Functional theorists stress that a social system is made up of various parts. When working properly, each part contributes to the stability of the whole, fulfilling a function that contributes to a system's equilibrium. **Conflict theory** also focuses on large-scale patterns of society. Conflict theorists stress that society is composed of competing groups struggling for scarce resources.

Because no single theory encompasses all of reality, at different times sociologists may use any or all of the three theoretical lenses. With each perspective focusing on certain features of social life and each providing its own interpretation, their combined insights yield a more comprehensive picture of social life. Pp. 19–27.

Applied and Clinical Sociology

What is the difference between pure and applied sociology?

Pure sociology is sociological research whose only purpose is to make discoveries. In contrast, **applied sociology** is the use of sociology to solve problems. Pp. 28–29.

Where can I read more on this topic?

Suggested readings for this chapter are listed on page 637.

Dan V. Lomahaftewa, Spring Arrival, 1994

Culture

I HAD NEVER FELT HEAT LIKE this before. *If this was northern Africa, I wondered what it must be like closer to the equator. The sweat poured off me as the temperature soared past 110 degrees Fahrenheit.*

As we were herded into the building—without air conditioning—hundreds of people lunged toward the counter at the rear of the building. With body crushed against body, we waited as the uniformed officials behind the windows leisurely examined each passport. It was at times like this that I wondered what I was doing in Africa.

When I had arrived in Morocco, I found the sights that greeted me exotic—not far removed from my memories of Casablanca, Raiders of the Lost Ark, and other movies that over the years had become part of my collective memory. The men, women, and even the children did wear those white robes that reached down to their feet. What was especially striking was the fact that the women were almost totally covered. In spite of the heat, every woman wore not only a full-length gown, but also a head covering that reached down over the forehead and a veil that covered her face from the nose down. All you could make out were their eyes—and every eye the same shade of brown.

And how short everyone was! The Arab women looked to be on average 5 feet, and the men only about three or four inches more. As the only blue-eyed, blonde 6-foot-plus person around, wearing jeans and a pullover shirt, in a world of white-robed short people, I stood out like a sore thumb. Everyone stared. No matter where I went, they stared. Wherever I looked, I found brown eyes watching intensely. Even staring back at those many dark brown eyes had no effect. It was so different from home, where, if you caught someone staring at you, the person would immediately look embarrassed and glance away.

And lines? The concept apparently didn't even exist. Buying a ticket for a bus or train meant pushing and shoving toward the ticket man (always a man—no women were visible in any public position), who just took the money from whichever outstretched hand he decided on.

And germs? That notion didn't seem to exist here either. Flies swarmed over the food in the restaurants and the unwrapped loaves of bread in the stores. Shopkeepers would considerately shoo off the flies before handing me a loaf. They also had home delivery of bread. I still remember a bread vendor delivering an unwrapped loaf to a woman standing on a second-floor balcony. She first threw her money to the bread vendor, and he then threw the unwrapped bread up to her. Only, his throw was off. The bread bounced off the wrought-iron balcony railing and landed in the street filled with people, wandering dogs, and the ever-present burros. The vendor simply picked up the loaf and threw it again. This certainly wasn't his day, for again he missed. But the man made it on his third attempt. And the woman smiled, satisfied, as she turned back into her apartment, apparently to prepare the noon meal for her hungry family.

As I stood in the oppressive heat of the Moroccan–Algerian border, the crowd had once again become unruly. Another fight had broken out. And once again, the little man in uniform appeared, shouting and knocking people aside as he forced his way to the little wooden box nailed onto the floor. Climbing onto this makeshift platform, he would shout at the crowd, his arms flailing about him. The people would become silent. But just as soon as the man would leave, the shoving and shouting would begin again as the people clamored to get their passports stamped.

The situation had become unbearable. Pressed body to body, the man behind me had decided that this was a good time to take a nap. Determining that I made a good support, he placed his arm against my back and leaned his head against his arm. Sweat streamed from my back at the point that his arm and head touched me.

Finally, I realized that I had to abandon U.S. customs. I pushed my way forward, forcing my frame into every space I could make. At the counter, I shouted in English. The official looked up at the sound of this strange tongue, and, thrusting my long arms over the heads of three persons, I shoved my passport into his hand.

Citizens of industrialized nations take it for granted that if they can afford it (an important qualification) the supply of food is plentiful. In the former Soviet Union, however, this cultural assumption does not exist. Shortages have long been a fact of life, both under communism and since its demise. At this state in Russia's transformation to capitalism, more goods are available, but rampant inflation has continued to make them elusive to the average consumer.

What Is Culture? ▲▼

What is culture? The concept is sometimes easier to grasp by description than by definition. For example, suppose you meet a young woman who has just arrived in the United States from India. That her culture is different from yours is immediately evident. You first see it in her clothing, jewelry, makeup, and hairstyle. Next you hear it in her language. It then becomes apparent by her gestures. Later, you will hear her express unfamiliar beliefs about the world and opinions about what is valuable in life. All these characteristics are indicative of **culture,** the language, beliefs, values, norms, behaviors, and even material objects that are passed from one generation to the next.

In northern Africa, I was surrounded by a culture quite alien to my own. It was evident in everything I saw and heard. The **material culture**—such things as jewelry, art, buildings, weapons, machines, and even eating utensils, hairstyles, and clothing—provided a sharp contrast to what I was used to seeing. There is nothing inherently "natural" about material culture. That is, it is no more natural (or unnatural) to wear gowns on the street than it is to wear jeans.

I also found myself immersed in a contrasting **nonmaterial culture,** that is, a group's ways of thinking (its beliefs, values, and other assumptions about the world) and doing (its common patterns of behavior, including language, gestures, and other forms of interaction). North African assumptions about crowding to buy a ticket and staring in public are examples of nonmaterial culture. So are U.S. assumptions about not doing either of these things. Like material culture, neither custom is "right." People simply become comfortable with the customs they learn during childhood, and—as in the case of my visit to northern Africa—uncomfortable when their basic assumptions about life are challenged.

Culture and Taken-for-Granted Orientations to Life

To develop a sociological imagination, it is essential to understand how culture affects people's lives. While meeting someone from a different culture may make us aware of culture's pervasive influence, attaining the same level of awareness regarding our own culture is quite another matter. *Our* speech, *our* gestures, *our* beliefs, and *our* customs are usually taken for granted. We assume that they are "normal" or "natural," and we

culture: the language, beliefs, values, norms, behaviors, and even material objects that are passed from one generation to the next

material culture: the material objects that distinguish a group of people, such as their art, buildings, weapons, utensils, machines, hairstyles, clothing, and jewelry

nonmaterial culture: a group's ways of thinking (including its beliefs, values, and other assumptions about the world) and doing (its common patterns of behavior, including language and other forms of interaction) almost always follow them without question. As anthropologist Ralph Linton (1936) said, "The last thing a fish would ever notice would be water." So it is with people: except in unusual circumstances, the effects of our own culture generally remain imperceptible to us.

Yet culture's significance is profound; it touches almost every aspect of who and what we are. We came into this life without a language, without values and morality, with no ideas about religion, war, money, love, use of space, and so on. We possessed none of these fundamental orientations that we take for granted and that are so essential in determining the type of people we are. Yet at this point in our lives we all have them. Sociologists call this culture *within* us. These learned and shared ways of believing and of doing (another definition of culture) penetrate our beings at an early age and quickly become part of our taken-for-granted assumptions concerning normal behavior. *Culture becomes the lens through which we perceive and evaluate what is going on around us*. Seldom do we question these assumptions, for, like water to a fish, the framework from which we view life remains largely beyond our ordinary perception.

The rare instances in which these assumptions are challenged, however, can be upsetting. Although as a sociologist I should be able to look at my own culture "from the outside," my trip to Africa quickly revealed how fully I had internalized my own culture. My upbringing in Western industrialized society had given me strong assumptions about aspects of social life that had become deeply rooted in my being—staring, hygiene, and the use of space. But in this part of Africa these assumptions were useless for helping me get through daily life. No longer could I count on people to stare only surreptitiously, to take precautions against invisible microbes, or to stand in an orderly way one behind the other on the basis of time of arrival to obtain a service.

As you can tell from the opening vignette, I personally found these different assumptions upsetting, for they violated my basic expectations of "the way people *ought* to be"—although I did not even know I held these expectations until they were so abruptly challenged. When my nonmaterial culture failed me—when it no longer enabled me to make sense out of the world—I experienced a disorientation known as **culture shock.** In the case of buying tickets, the fact that I was several inches taller than most Moroccans and thus able to outreach almost everyone helped me to adjust partially to their different ways of doing things. But I never did get used to the idea that pushing ahead of others was "right," and I always felt guilty when I used my size to receive preferential treatment.

An important consequence of culture within us is **ethnocentrism,** a tendency to use our own group's ways of doing things as the yardstick for judging others. All of us learn that the ways of our own group are good, right, proper, and even superior to other ways of life. As sociologist William Sumner (1906), who developed this concept, said, "One's own group is the center of everything, and all others are scaled and rated with reference to it." Ethnocentrism has both positive and negative consequences. On the positive side, it creates in-group loyalties. On the negative side, ethnocentrism can lead to harmful discrimination against people whose ways differ from ours.

The effects of culture on our lives fascinate sociologists. By examining more explicitly just how profoundly culture affects everything we are, this chapter will serve as a basis from which you can start to analyze your previously unquestioned assumptions of reality and thus help you gain a different perspective on social life and your role in it.

▼   **In Sum**   To avoid losing track of the ideas under discussion, let's pause for a moment to summarize, and in some instances clarify, the principles we have covered.

1   There is nothing "natural" about material culture. Arabs wear gowns on the street and feel that it is natural to do so; Americans do the same with jeans.

2   There is nothing "natural" about nonmaterial culture; it is just as arbitrary to stand in line as it is to push and shove.

culture shock: the disorientation that people experience when they come in contact with a fundamentally different culture and can no longer depend on their taken-for-granted assumptions about life

ethnocentrism: the use of one's own culture as a yardstick for judging the ways of other individuals or societies, generally leading to a negative evaluation of their values, norms, and behaviors

3 Culture penetrates deep into the recesses of our spirits, becoming a taken-for-granted aspect of our lives.

4 Culture provides the lens through which we see the world and obtain our perception of reality.

5 Culture provides implicit instructions that tell us what we ought to do in various situations. It provides a fundamental basis for our decision making.

6 Culture also provides a "moral imperative"; that is, by internalizing a culture, people learn ideas of right and wrong. (I, for example, deeply believed that it was unacceptable to push and shove to get ahead of others.)

7 Coming into contact with a radically different culture challenges our basic assumptions of life. (I experienced culture shock when I discovered that my deeply ingrained cultural ideas about the use of space and hygiene no longer applied.)

8 Although the particulars of culture differ from one group of people to another, culture itself is universal. That is, all people have culture. There are no exceptions. A society cannot exist without developing shared, learned ways of dealing with the demands of life.

9 All people are ethnocentric, which has both functional and dysfunctional consequences.

Practicing Cultural Relativism

Rather than using one's own culture as a standard to judge another culture, to practice **cultural relativism** is to try to understand a culture on its own terms. It is to look at how the various elements of a culture fit together, without judging those elements as superior or inferior to one's own way of life. The Down-to-Earth Sociology box on page 39 illustrates this point.

Cultural relativism presents a challenge to ordinary thinking, for we tend to use our own culture to judge another. For example, Americans may have strong feelings against raising bulls for the sole purpose of stabbing them to death in front of crowds shouting "Olé!" According to cultural relativism, however, bullfighting must be viewed strictly within the context of the culture in which it takes place—*its* history, *its* folklore, *its* ideas of bravery, and *its* ideas of sex roles.

As an American, you may still regard bullfighting as wrong, of course, since your culture, which lies deep within you, has no history of bullfighting. Americans possess culturally specific ideas about cruelty to animals, ideas that have evolved slowly and match other cultural elements. Consequently, practices that once were common in some areas—cock fighting, dog fighting, bear–dog fighting, and so on—have been gradually weeded out (Bryant 1993).

None of us can be entirely successful at practicing cultural relativism; we simply cannot help viewing a contrasting way of life through the lens that our own culture provides. Cultural relativism, however, is an attempt to mute that lens and thereby appreciate other ways of life rather than simply asserting, "Our way is right."

Although cultural relativism is a worthwhile goal and helps us to avoid cultural smugness, this view has come under attack. Anthropologist Robert Edgerton, in a provocative book, *Sick Societies* (1992), points out that some cultures endanger their people's health, happiness, or survival. He suggests that we develop a scale to evaluate cultures on their "quality of life," much as we do for U.S. cities. He also asks why we should consider cultures that practice female genital mutilation, gang rape, wife beating, or that sell daughters into prostitution as morally equivalent to those that do not. Cultural values that result in exploitation, he says, are inferior to those that enhance people's lives.

Edgerton's sharp questions and incisive examples bring us to a point that will come up repeatedly in this text—disagreements that arise among scholars as they confront changing views of reality. It is such questioning of assumptions that keeps sociology interesting.

cultural relativism: understanding a people from the framework of its own culture

Components of Culture

The Symbolic Basis of Culture

Sociologists sometimes refer to nonmaterial culture as **symbolic culture** because a central component is the symbols that people use to communicate. A **symbol** is something to which people attach meaning and which they then use to communicate. Symbols are the basis of culture. They include gestures, language, values, norms, sanctions, folkways, and mores. Let's look at each of these components of symbolic culture.

Gestures

Gestures, the use of one's body to communicate with others, are useful shorthand ways to give messages without using words. While people in every culture of the world use gestures, their meaning may change completely from one culture to another. North Americans, for example, communicate a succinct message by raising the middle finger in a short, upward stabbing motion. I wish to stress "North Americans," for that gesture does not convey the same message in South America or most other parts of the world.

I was once surprised to find that this particular gesture was not universal, having internalized it to such an extent that I thought everyone knew what it meant. When I was comparing gestures in Mexico, however, this gesture drew a blank look from friends. After I explained its intended meaning, they laughed and showed me their rudest gesture—placing the hand under the armpit. To me, they simply looked as if they were imitating a monkey, but to them the gesture meant "Your mother is a whore," absolutely the worst possible insult in that culture.

Gestures thus not only facilitate communication but, since they differ around the world, can also lead to misunderstandings, embarrassment, or worse. Once in Mexico, for example, I raised my hand to a certain height to indicate how tall a child was. My hosts began to laugh. It turned out that Mexicans have a more complicated system of hand gestures to indicate height: one for people, a second for animals, and a third for plants. (See Figure 2.1.) What had amused them was that I had ignorantly used the plant gesture to indicate the child's height.

To get along in another culture, then, it is important to learn the gestures of that culture. If you don't, you will not only fail to achieve the simplicity of communication that gestures allow but you will also miss much of what is happening, run the risk of appearing foolish, and possibly offend people. In many cultures, for example, you would provoke deep offense if you were to offer food or a gift with your left hand, because the left hand is reserved for dirty tasks, such as wiping after going to the bathroom. Left-handed Americans visiting Arabs please note!

symbolic culture: another term for nonmaterial culture

symbol: something to which people attach meanings and then use to communicate with others

gestures: the ways in which people use their bodies to communicate with one another

indicates animal height   indicates plant height   indicates human height

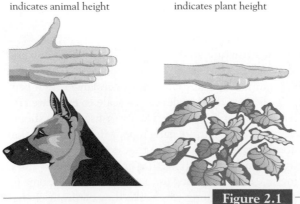

Figure 2.1

Gestures to Indicate Height, Southern Mexico

▼▲▼▲▼▲▼▲▼▲▼▲▼▲▼▲▼▲▼▲▼▲▼▲▼▲▼▲▼

Down-To-Earth Sociology

Communicating Across Cultural Boundaries

WHEN VIEWED FROM AFAR, cultural differences among human groups may be only a matter of interest. But when there is **culture contact,** that is, when people come into contact with people from different cultures, those differences can lead to problems in communication.

It is not only travelers who face this problem. Increasingly, business has become international, making cultural differences a practical problem for businesspeople. And at times, even highly knowledgeable and experienced firms don't quite manage to break through those cultural barriers. General Motors, for example, was very successful in marketing its automobile, the Nova, in the United States. When they decided to export that success south of the border, they were perplexed when the car sold very, very slowly. Finally, someone let them in on the secret: In Spanish, "*No va*" is an entire sentence that means, "It does not go."

Not all results are negative, of course, and businesspeople are also able to capitalize on cultural differences. For example, Japanese women are greatly embarrassed by the sounds they make in public toilets. To drown out the offensive sounds, they flush the toilet an average of 2.7 times a visit (Lori 1988). This wastes water, however, and that creates its own problems. Some enterprising American saw money-making possibilities in this and developed a battery-powered device that is mounted next to the toilet. When the woman activates the device, it emits a 25-second flush-ing sound. Although a toilet-sound duplicator may seem useless for our culture, the Japanese government and private companies are buying about three thousand of these devices a month.

Let's suppose that you were publishing a magazine about sports heroes in Japan. It wouldn't surprise you to know that your readers expect you to chronicle their idol's height and hobbies. But they also expect to read about their hero's blood type, for it is viewed as a sort of zodiac birth sign (Ono 1993). If you ran a golf course, you would have to understand why Japanese golfers are alarmed if they are so unlucky as to shoot a hole-in-one: it obligates them to buy expensive gifts for their fellow players, to throw a drinking party, and to plant a commemorative tree near the tee to mark their "joy." Of course, to ward off such a catastrophe, for $100 golfers can buy $5,000 hole-in-one insurance before a game (Hardy 1993a).

Japanese trying to get along in U.S. culture, of course, also face cultural hurdles, but at least they have a plain-talking phrase book to learn from, called *New York English* (Hardy 1993b). There they will learn how "real" Americans talk, memorizing such phrases as "suck face" and "chill out." But what about the subtle differences, such as when *not* to say the phrase (which this book teaches) "Get outta my face, you lying bag of scum!"? (Probably at this point the Japanese value of martial arts comes in handy.)

▲▼▲▼▲▼▲▼▲▼▲▼▲▼▲▼▲▼▲▼▲▼▲▼▲▼▲▼▲

Now suppose for a moment that you are visiting southern Italy. After eating one of the best meals in your life you are so pleased that when you catch the waiter's eye, you smile broadly and use the standard American "A-OK" gesture of putting your thumb and forefinger together and making a large "O." The waiter looks horrified, and you are struck speechless when the manager asks you to leave. What have you done? Nothing on purpose, of course, but in that culture that gesture refers to a part of the human body that is not mentioned in polite company (Ekman et al. 1984).

Is it really true that there are no universal gestures? There is some disagreement on this point. Some anthropologists claim that no gestures are universal. They point out that even nodding the head up and down to indicate "yes" is not universal, since in some parts of the world, such as areas of Turkey, nodding the head up and down means "no" (Ekman et al. 1984). Ethologists, researchers who study biological bases of behavior, however, claim that expressions of anger, pouting, fear, and sadness are built into our biology and are universal (Eibl-Eibesfeldt 1970:404). They point out that even infants who are born blind and deaf, who have had no chance to learn these gestures, express themselves in the same way.

Although this matter is not yet settled, we can note that gestures tend to vary remarkably around the world. It is also significant that gestures can create emotions. Some gestures are so associated with emotional messages that the gesture itself summons up an emotion. For example, my introduction to Mexican gestures took place at a dinner table. It was evident that my husband-and-wife hosts were trying to hide their embarrassment at actually using this obscene gesture at their dinner table. And I felt the same

culture contact: encounter between people from different cultures, or contact with some parts of a different culture

way—not about *their* gesture, of course, which meant absolutely nothing to me—but about the one I was teaching them.

Language

The primary way in which people communicate with one another is through **language**—a system of symbols that can be put together in an infinite number of ways for the purpose of communicating abstract thought. Each word is actually a symbol, a sound to which we have attached a particular meaning so that we can then use it to communicate with one another. Language itself is universal in the sense that all human groups have language, but there is nothing universal about the meanings given to particular sounds. Thus, like gestures, in different cultures the same sound may mean something entirely different—or may have no meaning at all.

The significance of language for human life is difficult to overstate, as will become apparent from the following discussion of the primary ways that language allows culture to exist.

Language Allows Human Experience to Be Cumulative   By means of language one generation is able to pass significant experiences on to the next and allow that next generation to build on experiences it may not itself undergo. This building process enables humans to modify their behavior in the light of what previous generations have learned. Hence the central sociological significance of language: *Language allows culture to develop by freeing people to move beyond their immediate experiences.*

Without language, human culture would be little more advanced than that of the lower primates. People would be limited to communicating by some system of grunts and gestures, which would greatly shorten the temporal dimension of human life and limit communication to a small time zone surrounding the immediate present: events now taking place, those which have just taken place, or those which will immediately take place—a sort of "slightly extended present." You can grunt and gesture, for example, that you want a drink of water, but in the absence of language how could you share ideas concerning past or future events? There would be little or no way to communicate to others what event you had in mind, much less the greater complexities that humans communicate—ideas and feelings about events.

Language Provides a Social or Shared Past   Even without language an individual would still have memories of experiences and events. Those memories, however, would be extremely limited, for people associate experiences with words and then use words to recall the experience. Such memories as would exist in the absence of language would also be highly individualized, for they could be but rarely and incompletely communicated to others, much less discussed and agreed on. With language, however, events can be codified, that is, attached to words and then recalled so they can be discussed in the present.

Language Provides a Social or Shared Future   Language also extends our time horizons forward. When people talk about past events, they share meanings that allow them to decide how they will or should act in similar circumstances in the future. Because language enables people to agree with one another concerning times, dates, and places, it also allows them to plan activities with one another.

Think about it for a moment. Without language how could people ever plan future events? How could they possibly communicate goals, purposes, times, and plans? Whatever planning could exist would have to be limited to extremely rudimentary communications, perhaps to an agreement to meet at a certain place when the sun is in a certain position. But think of the difficulty, perhaps impossibility, of conveying just a slight change in this simple arrangement, such as "I can't make it tomorrow."

language: a system of symbols that can be combined in an infinite number of ways and can represent not only objects but also abstract thought

Language Allows Shared Perspectives or Understandings Our ability to speak, then, allows us a social past and future; these two vital aspects of our humanity represent a watershed that distinguishes us from animals. But speech does much more than this. When humans talk with one another, they are exchanging ideas about events, that is, exchanging perspectives. Their words are the embodiment of their experiences, distilled and codified into a readily exchangeable form, mutually intelligible for people who have learned that language. Talking about events allows people to arrive at the shared understandings that form the essence of social life.

Language Allows Complex, Shared, Goal-Directed Behavior Common understandings further enable people to establish a *purpose* for getting together. Let us suppose that you want to go on a picnic. You use speech not only to plan the picnic but also to decide on reasons for the picnic—which may be anything from "because it's a nice day and it shouldn't be wasted studying" to "because it's my birthday." Language permits you to blend individual activities into an integrated sequence. In other words, through discussion you decide where you will go; who will drive; who will bring the hamburgers, the potato chips, the soda; where you will meet; and so on. Only because of language can you participate in such a common yet complex event.

Language and Perception: The Sapir-Whorf Hypothesis In the 1930s, two anthropologists, Edward Sapir and Benjamin Whorf, became intrigued when they noted that the Hopi Indians of the southwestern United States had no words to distinguish between the past, the present, and the future. English, in contrast, as well as German, French, Spanish, and so on, distinguish carefully just when something takes place. From this observation, Sapir and Whorf concluded that the common sense idea that words are merely labels that people attach to things was wrong. They developed the hypothesis that thinking and perception are not only expressed through language but actually shaped by language. Because language has embedded in it a way of looking at the world, learning a language involves learning not only words but also a particular way of thinking and perceiving (Sapir 1949; Whorf 1961; Landes 1983; Garrison 1990).

The implications of the **Sapir-Whorf hypothesis,** which alerts us to how extensively language affects us, are far-reaching. *The Sapir-Whorf hypothesis reverses common sense:* It indicates that rather than objects and events forcing themselves onto our consciousness, it is our very language that determines our consciousness, and hence our perception, of objects and events. Eskimos, for example, have many words for snow. As Eskimo children learn their language, they learn distinctions between types of snowfalls that are imperceptible to non-Eskimo speakers. Others might learn to see heavy and light snowfalls, wet and dry snowfalls, and so on; but not having words for "fine powdery," "thicker powdery," and "more granual" snowfalls actually prevents them from perceiving snow in the same way as Eskimos do.

Although Sapir's and Whorf's observation that the Hopi do not have tenses was incorrect (Edgerton 1992:27), we still need to take their conclusion seriously, for the classifications that we humans develop as we try to make sense of our worlds do direct our perception. Sociologist Eviatar Zerubavel (1991) gives a good example. Hebrew, his native language, does not differentiate between jam and jelly. Only when Zerubavel learned English could he "see" this difference, which is "obvious" to native English speakers. Similarly, if you learn to classify students as "dweebs," "dorks," "nerds," "brains," and so on, you will perceive a student who asks several questions during class or remains after class to talk about a lecture in an entirely different way from someone who does not know these classifications.

▼ **In Sum** The significance of language is that it takes us beyond the world of apes and allows culture to develop. Language frees us from the present by providing a past and a future, giving us the capacity to share understandings about the past and to develop common perceptions about the future, as well as to establish underlying

Sapir-Whorf hypothesis: Edward Sapir and Benjamin Whorf's hypothesis that language itself creates a particular way of thinking and perceiving

purposes for our current activities. Consequently, as in the case of the picnic, each individual is able to perform a small part of a larger activity, aware that others are carrying out related parts. In this way a series of separated, isolated activities become united into a larger whole.

Language also allows us to expand our connections far beyond our immediate, face-to-face groups, so that our *individual* biological and social needs are met by extended networks of people. This development in turn leads to far-flung connections with our fellow humans, facilitating, for example, the cooperative actions ultimately responsible for our worldwide networks of production and distribution. Although language by no means *guarantees* cooperation among people, language is an *essential* precondition of collaboration. Without language, extended cooperative human endeavors simply could not exist (Malinowski 1945; Hertzler 1965; Blumer 1966).

Learning a language means not just learning words but also acquiring the perceptions embedded in that language. In other words, language both reflects and shapes cultural experiences. Precisely because language is such a primary shaper of experience and culture, difficulties arise among people who live among each other but do not share a language as illustrated in the Perspectives box on page 43.

In short, our entire way of life is based on language, although, like most aspects of culture, its *linguistic base* is usually invisible to us.

Values, Norms, and Sanctions

To learn a culture is to learn people's **values,** their ideas of what is desirable in life. When we uncover people's values, we learn a great deal about them, for values are the standards by which people define good and bad, beautiful and ugly. Values underlie their preferences, guide their choices, and indicate what they hold worthwhile in life.

Every group develops both values and expectations concerning the right way to reflect them. Sociologists use the term **norms** to describe those expectations, or rules of behavior, that develop out of a group's values. They use the term **sanctions** to refer to positive or negative reactions to the ways in which people follow norms. **Positive sanction** refers to an expression of approval given for following a norm, while **negative sanction** denotes disapproval for breaking a norm. Positive sanctions can be material, such as a money reward, a prize, or a trophy, but in everyday life they usually consist of hugs, smiles, a clap on the back, soothing words, or even handshakes. Negative sanctions can also be material—a fine is one example—but they, too, are more likely to consist of gestures, such as frowns, stares, harsh words, or raised fists. Being awarded a raise at work is a positive sanction, indicating that the norms clustering around work values have been followed, while being fired is a negative sanction, indicating the opposite. The North American finger gesture discussed earlier is, of course, a negative sanction.

Folkways and Mores

Norms that are not strictly enforced are called **folkways.** We expect people to comply with folkways, but we are likely to shrug our shoulders and not make a big deal about it if they don't. If someone insists on passing you on the left side of the sidewalk, for example, you are unlikely to take corrective action—although if the sidewalk is crowded and you must move out of the way, you might give the person a dirty look.

Other norms, however, are taken much more seriously. We think of them as essential to our core values, and we insist on conformity. These are called **mores** (MORE-rays). A person who steals, rapes, and kills has violated some of society's most important mores. As sociologist Ian Robertson (1987:62) put it,

> A man who walks down a street wearing nothing on the upper half of his body is violating a folkway; a man who walks down the street wearing nothing on the lower half of his body is violating one of our most important mores, the requirement that people cover their genitals and buttocks in public.

values: the standards by which people define what is desirable or undesirable, good or bad, beautiful or ugly

norms: the expectations, or rules of behavior, that develop out of values

sanction: an expression of approval or disapproval given to people for upholding or violating norms

positive sanction: a reward given for following norms, ranging from a smile to a prize

negative sanction: an expression of disapproval for breaking a norm, ranging from a mild, informal reaction such as a frown to a formal prison sentence

folkways: norms that are not strictly enforced

mores: (MORE-rays) norms that are strictly enforced because they are thought essential to core values

▼▲▼

Perspectives

CULTURAL DIVERSITY IN U.S. SOCIETY

Miami—Language and a Changing City

IN THE YEARS SINCE Castro seized power in Cuba, the city of Miami has been transformed from a quiet southern city to a Latin-American mecca. Few things better capture Miami today than its ethnic divisions, especially its long-simmering fight over language: English versus Spanish. The 1990 census found that half of the city's 358,548 residents have trouble speaking English—possibly the highest proportion in any large U.S. city. This reflects the recent influx of Hispanic and Creole-speaking Haitian immigrants.

As this chapter stresses, language is a primary means by which people learn—and communicate—their social worlds. Consequently, language differences in Miami reflect not just cultural diversity but people who live in separate worlds. Although the ethnic stew makes Miami culturally one of the richest cities in the United States, the language gap sometimes creates anger and misunderstanding. The aggravation of Anglos—tinged with hostility—is seen in the bumper stickers reading, "Will the Last American Out Please Bring the Flag?"

But Hispanics, now a majority in Miami, are equally frustrated. Many feel Anglos should be able to speak at least some Spanish. Nicaraguan immigrant Pedro Falco, for example, is studying English and wonders why more people won't try to learn his language. "Miami is the capital of Latin America," he says. "The population speaks Spanish."

In the past ten years, Miami's population grew only 3.4 percent, but its Spanish-speaking population grew 15 percent, making the city 62 percent Hispanic. Throughout the United States, 83 percent of residents speak English at home, but only 25 percent of Miami residents do so.

Language and cultural flare-ups sometimes make headlines in the city. The Hispanic-American community was outraged when an employee at the Coral Gables Board of Realtors lost her job for speaking Spanish at the office. And protesters swarmed a Publix supermarket after a cashier was fired for chatting with a friend in Spanish.

What's happening in Miami, says University of Chicago sociologist Douglas Massey, is what happened in cities such as Chicago at the beginning of the century. Then, as now, the rate of immigration exceeded the speed with which new residents learned English, creating a pile-up effect in the proportion of non-English speakers. Becoming comfortable with English is a slow process, he points out, whereas immigration is fast.

Massey expects the city's proportion of non-English speakers to rise with continuing immigration. But he says that this "doesn't mean in the long run that Miami is going to end up being a Spanish-speaking city." Instead, Massey believes, bilingualism will prevail. "Miami is the first truly bilingual city," he says. "The people who get ahead are not monolingual English speakers or monolingual Spanish speakers. They're people who speak both languages."

Source: Copyright 1992, *USA Today*. Reprinted by permission.

It should also be noted that what are folkways to one group in society may constitute mores to another. Although a male walking down the street with the upper half of his body uncovered is deviating from a folkway, a female doing the same thing is violating accepted mores. In addition, the folkways and mores of a subculture (the topic of the next section) may be the opposite of the general culture. For example, to walk down the sidewalk in a nudist camp with the entire body uncovered would not violate the mores of that subculture—but, rather, conform to *their* folkways.

A **taboo** refers to a norm so strongly ingrained even the thought of its violation is greeted with revulsion. Eating human flesh and having sex with one's parents are examples of such behaviors (Benales 1973; Read 1974; Henslin 1995b).

Subcultures and Countercultures

All groups, no matter what their size, have their own values, norms, and sanctions. Most groups are microcosms of the larger society to which they belong and thus reflect its values. Obvious examples are the Future Farmers of America and the Chamber of Commerce. In

> **taboo:** a norm so strong that it brings revulsion if violated

contrast, the values and related behaviors of some groups are so distinct that they set its members off from the general culture. Sociologists use the term **subculture** to refer to such groups. Each subculture, *a world within the larger world* of the dominant culture, has a distinctive way of looking at life (Gordon 1947; Komarovsky and Sargent 1949). U.S. society contains thousands of subcultures, some as broad as the way of life we associate with teenagers, others as narrow as those represented by skateboarders and body builders (Klein 1994). Ethnic groups also often form subcultures. They pride themselves on how they differ from the dominant culture and may place special value on their language, distinctive foods, religious practices, or other customs.

Occupations are a rich source of subcultures, and many of them develop a special language marking out their distinctive experiences. Thus cabdrivers (Davis 1959; Henslin 1967, 1993a), artists (McCall 1980), pool hustlers (Polsky 1967), police (Pepinsky 1980), prostitutes (Davis 1971), thieves (Sutherland 1937), and construction workers (Haas 1972) form subcultures. So do sociologists (Tiryakian 1971; Prus 1980), who, as you are learning, also have developed a unique language for carving up the world.

Unlike a subculture, in which a group carves out its own identity but remains compatible with the dominant culture, the values of some groups set their members in opposition to the dominant culture. Sociologists use the term **counterculture** to describe such groups. Heavy metal adherents who glorify satanism, hatred, cruelty, rebellion, sexism, violence, and death, are an example of a counterculture. Note that motorcycle enthusiasts—who emphasize personal freedom and speed, while maintaining the accepted cultural value of success—are members of a subculture. In contrast, the members of an outlaw motorcycle gang—who also stress freedom and speed, but add the values of dirtiness and despising women and work—form part of a counterculture (Watson 1988). Countercultures do not have to be negative. The Mormons, for example, were originally a counterculture when its members challenged the culture's core value of monogamy in the 1800s.

Often, members of the broader culture feel threatened by a counterculture, and they sometimes move against it in the attempt to affirm their own values. The Mormons, for example, were driven out of several states before they finally settled in Utah, what was then a wilderness. Even there the federal government would not let them practice polygyny (one man having more than one wife) and Utah's statehood was made conditional on its acceptance of monogamy (Anderson 1942, 1966).

subculture: the values and related behaviors of a group that distinguish its members from the larger culture; a world within a world

counterculture: a group whose values place its members in opposition to the values of the broader culture

The norms and values of counterculture groups are at odds with the dominant culture. Shown here are members of a Cambodian gang in Long Beach, California. This youth gang, like its counterparts across the United States, provides its members with a sense of belonging, but at the same time its clashing norms and values isolate them from the dominant culture.

Values in U.S. Society

As you well know, the United States is a **pluralistic society,** made up of many different groups. The United States has numerous religious, racial, and ethnic groups, as well as countless interest groups centering on such divergent activities as collecting dolls and hunting animals. This state of affairs makes the job of specifying U.S. values difficult. Nonetheless, sociologists have tried to identify the underlying core values that are shared by the many groups that make up U.S. society. Sociologist Robin Williams (1965) identified the following:

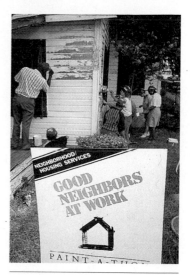

Humanitarianism is one of the core values that sociologists have identified in U.S. culture. Thousands of U.S. organizations, centered around this value, are dedicated to helping others.

1 *Achievement and success.* Americans place a high value on personal achievement, especially outdoing others. This value includes getting ahead at work and school, and the goal of attaining wealth, power, and prestige.

2 *Individualism.* Americans have traditionally prized success through individual efforts and initiative. They cherish the ideal that an individual can rise from the bottom to the very top of society. If someone does not "make it" or fails to "get ahead" to the degree that others expect, Americans generally find fault with that individual, rather than with the social system for placing roadblocks in his or her path. They tend to judge the person as having failed either through lack of ability or lack of effort.

3 *Activity and work.* Americans expect people to work hard and to be busily engaged in some activity even when not at work. Work is an end in itself, and, as Williams says, "It is no accident that the business so characteristic of the culture can also be spelled 'busyness.' "

4 *Efficiency and practicality.* Americans award high marks for getting things done efficiently. Even in everyday life, Americans consider it important to do things as fast or as well as possible, and constantly seek changes to increase efficiency.

5 *Science and technology.* Americans have a passion for applied science, for using science to control nature—to tame rivers and harness winds—and to develop new technology, from carburetors to electronic pinsetters.

6 *Progress.* Americans expect continued, rapid technological change. They believe that they should constantly build "more and better" gadgets and attain an ever-increasing national product. They also anticipate that change helps them move toward some vague goal called "progress."

7 *Material comfort.* Americans expect a high level of material comfort. This comfort includes not only nutrition, medical care, and housing, but also late-model cars and recreational playthings—from boats to computer games.

8 *Humanitarianism.* Americans emphasize helpfulness, personal kindness, aid in mass disasters, and organized philanthropy.

9 *Freedom.* This core value pervades U.S. life. It underscored the American Revolution, and Americans today bristle at the suggestion of any limitation on personal freedom. The Perspectives box (page 47) highlights some startling research on this core value and Native Americans.

10 *Democracy.* By this term, Americans refer to majority rule, to the right of everyone to express an opinion, and to representative government.

11 *Equality.* It is impossible to understand Americans without being aware of the central role that the value of equality plays in their lives. Equality of opportunity, an important concept in the ideal culture discussed later, has significantly influenced U.S. history and continues to mark relations between the groups that make up U.S. society.

12 *Racism and group superiority.* Although it sharply contradicts freedom, democracy, and equality, Americans value some groups more than others and have done so throughout their history. The institution of slavery in earlier U.S. society is the most notorious example. We shall examine consequences of sexism and racism in Chapters 11 and 12.

pluralistic society: a society made up of many different groups

In an earlier publication (Henslin 1975), I updated Williams's analysis by adding the following three values.

13 *Education.* Americans are expected to go as far in school as their abilities and finances allow. Over the years, the definition of an "adequate" education has changed sharply, and today the expectation of a college education is held as an appropriate goal for most Americans. Some even view people who have an opportunity for higher education and who do not take it as doing something "wrong," not merely making a bad choice, but somehow involved in an immoral act.

14 *Religiosity.* There is a feeling that "every true American ought to be religious." This does not mean that everyone is expected to join a church or synagogue, but that everyone ought to acknowledge a belief in a Supreme Being and follow some set of matching precepts. This value is so pervasive that Americans stamp "In God We Trust" on their money and declare in their national pledge of allegiance that they are "one nation under God." We shall examine this value in Chapter 18.

15 *Romantic love and monogamy.* Americans feel that the only proper basis for marriage is romantic love. Songs, literature, mass media, and "folk beliefs" all stress this value, and sometimes include the theme that "love conquers all." Similarly, the idea that the only proper form of marriage is that of one man to one woman overwhelmingly predominates in U.S. society. In some respects this value has changed somewhat; Americans now tolerate more than one spouse—but still only one at a time, a marital practice some call "serial monogamy."

Value Clusters

As you can see, values are not independent units; some cluster together to form a larger whole. In the **value cluster** surrounding success, for example, we find hard work, education, efficiency, material comfort, and individualism all bound up together. Americans are expected to go far in school, to work hard afterward, to be efficient, and then to attain a high level of material comfort, which, in turn, demonstrates success. Success is attributed to the individual's own efforts, the lack of success to his or her own faults.

Value Contradictions and Social Change

Not all values fall into neat, integrated packages. Some, indeed, contradict one another. The **value contradiction** noted earlier—group superiority—contradicts freedom, democracy, and equality. There simply cannot be full expressions of freedom, democracy, equality, racism, and sexism at the same time. Something has to give. One way in which Americans sidestepped this contradiction in the past was to say that the values of freedom, democracy, and equality apply only to certain groups. The contradiction was bound to surface over time, however, and so it did. Americans have responded by continuing to stress the values of freedom, equality, and democracy, extending these values to more groups and reducing emphasis on group superiority.

As society changes, then, some values are challenged and undergo modification. Although the Civil War put an end to slavery, this did not mean the end of some of the values that belonged to its cluster. Values that support racial superiority have only gradually been modified. Values of male supremacy in U.S. society have also changed, but slowly, as they have been challenged by contradictory values of equality. *It is precisely at the point of value contradictions that one can see a major force for social change in a society.*

Emerging Values

A value cluster of three interrelated core values—leisure, physical fitness, and self-fulfillment—appears to be emerging in the United States. A fourth emerging core value—concern for the environment—can also be identified.

value clusters: a series of interrelated values that together form a larger whole

value contradictions: values that contradict one another; to follow the one means to come into conflict with the other

▼▲

Perspectives

CULTURAL DIVERSITY IN U.S. SOCIETY

Why Do Native Americans Like Westerns?

U.S. AUDIENCES (AND EVEN German, French, and Japanese) devour westerns. In the United States, it is easy to see why Anglos like this genre, for it is they who seemingly defy odds and emerge victorious. It is they who are portrayed as heroically taming a savage wilderness, who fend themselves from cruel, barbaric Indians intent on their destruction. But why would Indians like westerns?

Sociologist JoEllen Shively, a Chippewa who grew up on Indian reservations in Montana and North Dakota, found that westerns are so popular that Native Americans bring bags of paperbacks into taverns to trade with one another. They even call one another "cowboy."

Intrigued, Shively decided to investigate the matter by showing a western movie to adult Native Americans and Anglos in a reservation town. Shively (1991, 1992) previewed over seventy westerns and then chose a John Wayne movie, *The Searchers*, because it focuses not only on conflict between Indians and cowboys but also shows the cowboys defeating the Indians. The Native Americans and Anglos were matched on education, age, income, and percentage of unemployment. After the movie, she had the viewers fill out questionnaires and interviewed them.

Shively found something surprising: *all* Native Americans and Anglos identified with the cowboys; *none* identified with the Indians.

The ways in which Anglos and Native Americans identified with the cowboys, however, were quite different, for each projected a different fantasy onto the story. While An-

glos saw the movie as an accurate portrayal of the Old West and a justification of their own status in the social system, Native Americans saw it as embodying a free, natural way of life. In fact, Native Americans said that they were the "real cowboys." They said, "Westerns relate to the way I wish I could live"; "He's not tied down to an eight-to-five job, day after day"; "He's his own man." Shively adds,

What appears to make Westerns meaningful to Indians is the fantasy of being free and independent like the cowboy. . . . Indians . . . find a fantasy in the cowboy story in which the important parts of their ways of life triumph and are morally good, validating their own cultural group in the context of a dramatically satisfying story. (1992)

To express their real identity—a combination of marginality on the one hand, with a set of values which are about the land, autonomy, and being free—they (use) a cultural vehicle (that is) written for Anglos about Anglos, but it is one in which Indians invest a distinctive set of meanings that speak to their own experience, which they can read in a manner that affirms a way of life they value, or a fantasy they hold to. (1991)

In other words, values, not ethnicity, are the central issue. If a Native American film industry were to portray Native Americans with the same values as the Anglo movie industry projects onto cowboys, then Native Americans would identify with their own group. Thus, says Shively, Native American viewers make cowboys "honorary Indians," for the cowboys express their values of bravery, autonomy, and toughness.

16 *Leisure.* The emergence of leisure as a value is reflected in the rapid growth of a huge recreation industry—from computer games, boats, and motor homes, to sports arenas, vacation homes, and a gigantic travel and vacation industry (Caplow 1991; Hamilton 1991). For an interesting cross-cultural comparison of leisure, see the Perspectives box on page 49.

17 *Physical fitness.* Physical fitness is not a new U.S. value, but the increased emphasis on it is moving it into the core. This trend can be seen in the "natural" foods craze; brew bars; obsessive concerns about weight and diet; the many joggers, runners, cyclists, and backpackers; and, of course, the mushrooming of health clubs and physical fitness centers.

18 *Self-fulfillment.* This value is reflected in the "human potential" movement, a preoccupation with becoming "all one can be," "self-help," "relating," and "personal development."

This emerging value cluster is a logical response to new needs and interests resulting from fundamental changes in U.S. society. Americans used to be largely preoccupied with forging a nation and fighting for economic survival. They now

Concern for the environment is an emerging value in many nations. Change in values does not come easily, however, and people who hold this new value come up against business, politics, and other interests that feel they can exploit of nature can continue indefinitely. Environmental concern is likely to become a core American value.

have come to a point in their economic development where millions of people are freed from long hours of work, and millions more are able to retire from work when they can still expect decades of life ahead of them. This value cluster centers around enabling them to enjoy those years of retirement, or to maintaining their health and vigor during their younger years while they look forward to a life of leisure.

19 *Concern for the environment.* During most of U.S. history, the environment was seen as a challenge—a wilderness to be settled, forests to be chopped down, rivers and lakes to be fished, and animals to be hunted. The lack of concern for the environment that characterized earlier Americans is illustrated by the near extinction of the bison and the extinction in 1914 of the passenger pigeon, a bird previously so numerous that its annual migration would darken the skies for days. Today, Americans have developed a genuine, and (we can hope) long-term, concern for the environment, as illustrated by pressures that citizen groups have put on Congress to improve the quality of the country's air and water, a federal list of endangered species that merit special protection, and the requirement that construction projects file environmental impact statements. This emergent value of environmental concern is also related to the current stage of U.S. economic development, a point that becomes clearer when we note that people act on environmental concerns only after basic needs are met. At this point in their development, for example, Third World nations, have a much more difficult time "affording" this value.

Reactions to Changes in Core Values

Core values do not change without meeting strong resistance from traditionalists who hold them dear. Consequently, many people are upset at the changes swirling around them, seeing their way of life challenged and their future growing insecure. A major criticism of the emerging value cluster just identified is that it encourages individualism at the cost of social responsibility. Because self-indulgent people neglect the needs of others, this value cluster will break down community, and, ultimately, undermine the family, religion, and the economy (Etzioni 1982; Bellah et al. 1985). The new concern for the environment is also under attack, but for quite different reasons. Among the traditionalists who are threatened by this emergent value are hunters, contractors, and developers who feel that their rights are being trampled on by extremists.

Values as Blinders

Values and their supporting beliefs paint a unique picture of reality, as well as forming a view of what life *ought* to be like. Because Americans value individualism so highly, for example, they tend to see people as free to pursue whatever legitimate goals they desire. This value blinds them to the many social circumstances that impede people's efforts. The dire consequences of family poverty, parents' low education, and dead-end jobs tend to drop from sight. Instead, Americans cling to the notion that anyone can make it—with the right amount of effort. And to prove it, dangled before their eyes are success stories of individuals who have succeeded in spite of huge handicaps.

"Ideal" Versus "Real" Culture

Many of the norms that surround cultural values are only partially followed. Differences always exist between what a group holds out as its cultural ideal and what its members actually do. Consequently, sociologists use the term **ideal culture** to refer to the ideal values and norms of a people, to the goals they hold out. The idea of success, for example, is part of ideal culture. Americans glorify academic progress, hard work, and the display of material goods as signs of individual achievement. What people actually do, however, usually falls short of the cultural ideal. Compared with their capacities, for

ideal culture: the ideal values and norms of a people, the goals held out for them

▼▲▼▲▼▲▼▲▼▲▼▲▼▲▼▲▼▲▼▲▼▲▼▲▼▲▼▲▼▲▼▲▼

Perspectives

CULTURAL DIVERSITY AROUND THE WORLD

The Government Says, "You Will Have Fun."

JAPAN HAS LONG BEEN guided by a powerful work ethic. Its internationally envied steamroller of economic expansion made 12-hour workdays, accompanied by long commutes, typical. The country's guiding maxim has been "Real workers don't take vacations." If the company needs it, workers will toil until midnight several nights in a row. Many workers take only two days off in an entire year. The company takes care of them, and they take care of the company.

Although this ethic of unflinching devotion to duty is in no danger of dying out anytime soon, tiny cracks have begun to appear. Facing severe criticism abroad for its trade surplus and for its obsession with production, and now engulfed in a nearly worldwide economic downturn, the nation's leaders have declared that Japan will become a *seikatsu taikoku,* or "lifestyle superpower." The government has vowed to enact new laws that will allow workers to leave the office early enough to spend evenings at concerts or even to chat with their families. Accordingly, in Japanese style, companies have set up "leisure creation committees." One company has begun to fine its employees for every vacation day they don't take. Another now insists that at least one day a week all employees must leave at 5:10 P.M. and must submit written explanations if they stay late. Even public schools have begun to let their students out on Saturdays— once a month, that is.

The Japanese have so revered the work ethic that they have a hard time grasping the concept of leisure. Some wonder why the company no longer needs them as much. Forty percent of workers across the nation say they wouldn't know what to do with a month off. An enterprising author has written a book called *Master of the Weekend* to try to fill this gap, suggesting such radical steps as having parties at home, or making friends with neighbors. The National Recreation Association of Japan even offers a year-long course on how to enjoy life, awarding a diploma certifying that each graduate is a bona fide "leisure life promoter." The course at least helps to fill time for a year, avoiding the dread of actually facing leisure time itself.

Source: Based on Ono and Schlesinger 1992.

example, most people don't go as far as they could in school or work as hard as they can. Sociologists call the norms and values that people actually follow **real culture.**

Cultural Universals

With the amazing variety of human cultures around the world, are there any **cultural universals**—values, norms, or other cultural traits that are found everywhere?

Anthropologist George Murdock (1945) sought to answer this question. After combing through data gathered by anthropologists on hundreds of groups around the world, he drew up a list of customs concerning courtship, cooking, marriage, funerals, games, laws, music, myths, incest taboos, and even toilet training. He found that although such activities are present in all cultures, *the specific customs differ from one group to another.* There is no universal form of the family, no universal way of disposing of the dead. Similarly, specific games, rules, songs, stories, and methods of toilet training differ from one culture to another.

Anthropologists have even found that incest is defined differently from group to group. For example, the Mundugumors of New Guinea extend the incest taboo so far that seven of every eight women are ineligible marriage partners (Mead 1950). Other groups go in the opposite direction and allow some men to marry their own daughters (La Barre 1954). In certain circumstances, some groups even require that brothers and sisters marry one another (Beals and Hoijer 1965). The Burundi of Africa even insisted that, to remove a certain curse, a son have sexual relations with his mother (Albert

real culture: the norms and values that people actually follow

cultural universal: a value, norm, or other cultural trait that is found in every group

Cultural universals are those values, norms, rites, customs, or other cultural traits that are found in all societies. Although there are universal human activities, there is no universal way of doing the activity. Marriage is such an example. Although marriage is found in all human groups, the form varies widely around the world.

1963). Such sexual relations were allowed only for special people (royalty) or in a special situation (such as that of a lion hunter before a dangerous hunt), however, and no society permits generalized incest for its members.

In short, although there are universal human activities (speech, music, storytelling, marrying, disposing of the dead, preparing food, and so on), there is no universally accepted way of doing any of them. Humans have no biological imperative that results in one particular form of behavior throughout the world. As indicated in the following Thinking Critically section, a few sociologists do take the position that genes significantly influence human behavior, although almost all sociologists reject this view.

▼▲▼▲▼▲▼▲▼▲▼▲▼▲▼▲▼▲▼▲▼▲▼▲▼▲▼▲▼▲

Thinking Critically About Social Controversy

Are We Prisoners of Our Genes? Sociobiology

▼   A CONTROVERSIAL VIEW OF human behavior called **sociobiology** provides a sharp contrast to the perspective presented in this chapter. Instead of looking at human behavior as shaped by culture, sociobiologists stress natural selection as responsible for humans' particular biological characteristics, which, in turn, shape human behavior.

According to Charles Darwin (1859), natural selection is based on four principles. First, reproduction occurs within a natural environment. Second, the genes of a species, the basic units of life that contain the individual's traits, are passed on to offspring. These genes have a degree of random variability; that is, different characteristics are distributed among the members of a species. Third, because the members of a species possess different characteristics, some members have a better chance of surviving in the natural environment than do others—and of passing their particular genetic traits to the next generation. Fourth, over thousands of generations, those genetic traits that aid survival in the natural environment tend to become common in a species, while those that do not tend to disappear.

Natural selection is used to explain not only the physical characteristics of plants and animals, but also their behavior, for over countless generations instincts emerged. Edward O. Wilson (1975), an insect specialist, claims that the principles of natural selection that led to human physical characteristics also cause human behavior. Human behavior, he said, is no different from the behavior of cats, dogs, rats, bees, or mosquitoes—it has been bred into *Homo sapiens* through evolutionary principles.

Wilson deliberately set out to create a storm of protest, and he succeeded. He claims that religion, competition and cooperation, slavery and genocide, war and peace, envy and altruism—all can be explained through sociobiology. He provocatively adds that because human behavior can be explained in terms of genetic programming, the new discipline of sociobiology will eventually absorb sociology—as well as anthropology and psychology.

Obviously, most sociologists find Wilson's position unacceptable. Not only is it a direct attack on their discipline, but it also bypasses the essence of what sociologists focus on: humans designing their own cultures, their own unique ways of life. Sociologists do not deny that biology underlies human behavior, at least not in the sense that it takes a highly developed brain to develop human culture, that there would be no speech if humans had no tongue or larnyx, that abstract thought could not exist if we did not have a highly developed cerebral cortex.

But sociologists find the claim that human behavior is due to genetic programming to be quite another matter (Howe et al. 1992). Pigs act alike because they don't have a cerebral cortex, and instincts control their behavior. So it is for spiders, elephants, and so on. But humans are far from being driven simply by instincts. Humans possess a self and have abstract thought. They discuss principles that underlie what they do. They decide on rational courses of action. They develop purposes and goals. They consider, reflect, and make choices.

This controversy has turned into much more than simply an academic debate among scientists. Homosexuals have found its outcome to be of high personal interest. If homosexuality is due to a choice of lifestyle, then those who consider that lifestyle immoral will use this as a basis to exclude homosexuals from full social participation. If, however, homosexuality is not a choice, but is due to genetic traits, then that reason for social exclusion is removed. Over the

sociobiology: a framework of thought that views human behavior as the result of natural selection and considers biological characteristics to be the fundamental cause of human behavior

years, biological researchers have suggested a genetic basis for both heterosexuality and homosexuality (Bailey 1993; Burr 1993; Pillard and Weinrich 1993). So far, follow-up studies with
different samples have failed to confirm the initial research (Denney and Quadagno 1992).
Final answers are far from in, and the controversy continues strong.

In short, sociobiologists and sociologists stand on opposite sides, the one looking at human
behavior as determined by instincts, the other as determined by social learning, by experiences in the human group. Sociologists point out that if humans were prisoners of their genes,
we would not have developed such a variety of fascinating ways of life around the world—we
would live in a monoculture of some sort.

For Your Consideration

Why do sociologists discredit the sociobiologists' claim that all human behavior can be traced
to genetic programming? Are you aware of any research that poses a valid challenge to the sociological premise that humans have no biological imperative that results in a particular form
of behavior that is common around the world? ▲

Animals and Culture

Let us digress for a moment to follow a fascinating and related issue: Do animals have
culture? And, do animals have language?

Do Animals Have Culture?

According to our definition of culture as a learned way of life that is passed on to others, it would seem that animals could not have culture. They certainly could not if animal behavior is entirely under the control of *instincts,* inherited patterns of behavior
common to all normal members of a species. Instinctual behaviors, such as the distinctive nest building of a Baltimore oriole, are not learned. By definition, then, they do
not constitute culture.

*Instead of assuming the answer,
scientists have increasingly studied
animals to observe the extent to
which their behavior is learned, and
not simply transmitted genetically.*

The basic sociological question is this: Are there any behaviors that animals teach each other across generations—even though those behaviors may appear to be due to instincts? The answer to this question was revealed in a rather surprising way. Eight-year-old Jane Goodall decided that when she grew up she would go to Africa and live with wild animals. Not many adults are able to live out their childhood fantasies, but in 1957, when she was a 22-year-old secretary in London, a schoolfriend invited her to visit her parents' farm in Kenya, Africa. Later, in Nairobi, she met Louis Leakey, a world-renowned anthropologist and paleontologist. When Leakey learned of Goodall's interest in animals, he hired her as a secretary.

Leakey had been working just across the border where he was collecting fossils in an area called the Olduvai Gorge. He invited her to go on a dig with him there, and on that trip he asked her if she would like to study some chimpanzees living on the shores of a lake. Leakey explained that because the remains of early humans were often found on lakeshores it was possible that "an understanding of chimpanzee behavior today might shed light on the behavior of our stone age ancestors" (Van Lawick-Goodall 1971).

Bear in mind that Goodall had no college degree, much less a doctorate, nor did she have any training in fieldwork. Secretarial training was not exactly preparation for studying wild animals. Also, the "lake site" was in the remote jungle eight hundred miles from Nairobi—and working there would require her to live in isolation for years. Yet Goodall eagerly accepted the famous anthropologist's invitation. An obstacle to their plans arose, however, for when Tanzanian officials learned that a young woman was planning to live in a jungle by herself, they refused to grant a permit for the work. Only when Goodall's mother agreed to live with her did they issue the permit. Before Goodall (1971) left, she spent three weeks on an uninhabited island in Lake Victoria, which, she says, taught her "a good deal about such things as note taking in the field, the sort of clothes to wear, the movements a wild monkey will tolerate in a human observer and those it will not."

Afterward, she went on to her destination. At first, things didn't go well. While her mother remained in the camp on the shores of Lake Tanganyika, Goodall would spend her days unsuccessfully searching for chimpanzees. She was seldom even able to catch a glimpse of the wary chimps, who made sure they kept their distance from this strange intruder. You can imagine the frustration Goodall felt each evening, telling her mother that another day's effort had yielded nothing.

Goodall persisted, however, and about six months later the situation changed abruptly. That day began like all the preceding ones, just another big disappointment. When Goodall spotted some chimpanzees through her binoculars, she tried to sneak up on them. All she found were empty branches of a fruit tree.

> The same old feeling of depression clawed at me. Once again the chimpanzees had seen me and silently fled. Then all at once my heart missed several beats.
>
> Less than twenty yards away from me two male chimpanzees were sitting on the ground staring at me intently. Scarcely breathing, I waited for the sudden panic-stricken flight that normally followed a surprise encounter between myself and the chimpanzees at close quarters. But nothing of the sort happened. The two large chimps simply continued to gaze at me. Very slowly I sat down, and after a few more moments, the two calmly began to groom one another.
>
> As I watched, still scarcely believing it was true, I saw two more chimpanzee heads peering at me over the grass from the other side of a small forest glade: a female and a youngster. They bobbed down as I turned my head toward them, but soon reappeared, one after the other, in the lower branches of a tree about forty yards away. There they sat, almost motionless, watching me. (1971)

About ten minutes later, as the sun was going down, the two chimps stopped their grooming. One stood and carefully looked Goodall over. Then the two turned and slowly walked away.

Goodall was naturally elated by this unexpected event. It was almost as if the chimps had given her an invitation to get to know them. Goodall practically ran down the mountainside to tell her mother about this exciting breakthrough. The exultation she felt at that moment made the depression and despair of the past months seem as nothing. After this overture, the chimpanzees gradually let Goodall get close to them. Eventually she made friends with the band, and over the next ten years she practically lived with them. Slowly she learned to understand how they communicated, and eventually she was able to participate in their gestures, hoots, and facial expressions. She continued her research for the next thirty years, living in a house made of "concrete blocks with a thin, corrugated tin roof and thatch, no running water, and windows covered in mesh to keep the baboons out" (Walters 1990).

The exotic nature of this fieldwork apart, what did Goodall actually learn that might help us decide whether animals have culture? Goodall noticed that, amazingly, the chimps made and used **tools;** they actually modified objects and used them for specific purposes. Until Goodall made this observation, it was assumed that only humans used tools. The tool itself was very simple, but tool it was. The chimps would first pick a blade of grass, then strip off its leaves and lick one end. Next they would poke the sticky end into a nest of termites. After waiting a bit, they would pull it out covered with termites, then savor the taste as they licked off the stick.

Encouraged by Goodall's discovery, scientists began trying to determine the extent of **animal culture**—learned, shared behavior among animals. They separated infant animals from their parents and others of their species to determine which behaviors remained constant. The surprise, of course, was not the behaviors that animals raised in isolation continued to have in common with their species. These were to be expected. And, indeed, squirrels raised in isolation still bury nuts, and spiders still spin distinctive webs. The surprise was the behaviors that did *not* continue. For example, although many birds raised in soundproof chambers will sing the songs unique to their species, a bullfinch raised with canaries will sing like a canary (Eibl-Eibesfeldt 1970).

One of the more interesting findings was that even the mating behavior of some animals is learned. Mating certainly appears as instinctual as cats bathing themselves, but it is not, and zookeepers have been disappointed that many of their captives did not reproduce. Gorillas, for example, are notorious for not mating in captivity. The keepers constantly had to replenish their supply of these animals from the wild. When there was a seemingly endless supply of wild animals, and numerous hunters made their living by capturing them alive, the situation was a minor nuisance. With increasing numbers of endangered species, however, coupled with growing international restrictions on capturing and importing animals, it has become a major problem. In one of the more humorous footnotes to scientific endeavors to understand the extent of animal culture, zookeepers in Sacramento, California, noted that young gorillas seemed to want to mate, but didn't seem to know how (Stark 1989). To solve the problem, they showed them a movie—of two adult gorillas mating. The lesson turned out to be a success.

Goodall's research and subsequent experiments answer our question: on a rudimentary level animal culture exists. Although the principle has been established, however, we do not yet know the particulars. What animals? What specific behaviors are learned? The initial answers, enticing though they may be, only point to further provocative questions.

Do Animals Have Language?

A related question that has intrigued scientists and nonscientists alike is whether animals have language. Do those barks and meows your pets make constitute language?

Social scientists think of language as more complex than mere sounds. They view language as symbols that can be infinitely strung together to communicate abstract thought. Animal sounds, however, appear to be much like infant cries. Although a baby will cry when in pain, the cry of distress that brings a parent running is not language. The cry is merely a biological response to pain, similar to reflexes.

Social scientists, then, seem to be in agreement that animals do not have language. For the most part, that is true. Animals do not even have the vocal apparatus necessary

tool: an object that is modified for a specific purpose

animal culture: learned, shared behavior among animals

Jane Goodall's research demonstrated that animals have a primitive culture; that is, they teach one another behavior that is transmitted across generations. Such culture is very limited, however, because, unlike humans, animals do not have language.

to utter the complex sounds that make up language. But not all animals are incapable of learning language.

In a remarkable series of experiments, researchers have tried to teach chimpanzees to talk. In the earliest of these efforts, a husband-and-wife team at Indiana University tried to "humanize" a baby chimp, Gua. For nine months, the Kelloggs (1933) raised Gua together with their own infant son, Donald. Gua and Donald grew very close, and they would hold hands and hug one another. They would also imitate one another: like Donald, Gua began to push a baby buggy, but, to the parents' surprise, Donald began to make the chimp "barking" sound for food, to carry objects in his mouth, and even to scrape the wall with his teeth (1933:144–145). At the end of the experiment 18-month-old Donald could respond appropriately to 68 words and phrases, while 16-month-old Gua could respond to 58. Gua did not learn to speak, and Donald's speech development was retarded—which may be why the Kelloggs ended their experiment.

Is the absence of chimpanzee speech due to the lack of intelligence (the inability to learn speech), or to the inability to make the sounds of speech? Noticing that chimps in the wild use many more hand signals than vocal signals, Allen and Beatrice Gardner (1969), psychologists at the University of Nevada, decided to teach chimps a gestural language instead of a verbal one (Fleming 1974). Their first pupil was Washoe, a female chimpanzee who was born in the wild. In 1966, when Washoe was 1 year old, her language training began. Washoe was like a human baby. She slept a lot, had just begun to crawl, and her daily routine centered on diapers and bottles. The Gardners tried to teach Washoe American Sign Language, a system of communication in which hand gestures correspond to individual words. They never spoke in her presence, and they played a lot of games that promoted interaction between Washoe and themselves.

The Gardners were greatly encouraged when Washoe began to learn some of the signs, and they were elated when she began to generalize, to apply a sign learned in one situation to other situations. For example, they taught her the sign for "open" using three particular doors in the house trailer she lived in. Washoe transferred that sign to all doors, drawers, containers, the refrigerator, and even the water faucet.

Within a year, Washoe had become inventive and was putting signs together in the equivalent of simple sentences. She even made up combinations, such as joining the sign for "give me" with "tickle" to indicate that she wanted to be tickled. At the end of four years, Washoe could use 160 signs.

The Gardners then transferred Washoe to the care of Roger Fouts, a graduate student who was moving to the University of Oklahoma to continue his studies in animal communication. When Washoe arrived, she did something that showed both the extent of her ability to understand language and her creativity with language. Until then Washoe had been raised apart from other monkeys and had only once before seen one of her own kind. Now, as she joined other monkeys, she was taught the sign for "monkey." She used this sign correctly. But in referring to a particular monkey who had threatened her when she arrived, she would add the sign for "dirty." Previously, she had used "dirty" only for feces or for something that had become filthy, but now she would call him only "dirty monkey."

Washoe did just what my son would do at that age: When he didn't like a particular food, he would say, "It tastes like poop!"—a phrase we definitely had not taught him. Later, like a spoiled child, Washoe would use this sign for teachers who refused to grant her wishes.

Another intriguing experiment is taking place at Northwestern University. Irene Pepperberg has taught Alex, an African Gray parrot, to name eighty objects, such as wool, walnut, and shower; to identify the color of objects; and to tell how many objects there are in groups up to six. Unconvinced, skeptics reply that the only thing that distinguishes Alex from pigeons taught to peck buttons for food is that his responses sound like English (Stipp 1990).

To answer the question of whether or not animals have the capacity for language, we must wait for more evidence. That evidence is now being collected. What we currently have, however, are data with intriguing implications.

Cultural Diffusion and Cultural Leveling

For most of human history, cultures had little contact with one another. Communication was limited and travel slow. Consequently, in their relative isolation groups of people developed highly distinctive ways of life in response to the particular situations they faced. The characteristics they developed that distinguished one culture from another tended to change little over time.

One group, the Tasmanians who lived on an inaccessible island off the coast of Australia, for at least thousands of years had no contact with any other culture. They were so isolated that they did not even know how to make clothing or fire (Edgerton 1992). Except in such rare instances, however, there is always *some* contact with other groups. During these contacts, groups learn from one another, adapting some part of the other's way of life. In this process, called **cultural diffusion,** groups are most open to a change in their material culture. They are usually eager, for example, to adopt superior weapons, tools, and implements. In remote jungles in South America one can find metal cooking pots, steel axes, and even bits of clothing spun in mills in South Carolina. Although the direction of cultural diffusion today is primarily from the West to other parts of the world, cultural diffusion is not a one-way street, as bagels, woks, and hammocks in the United States show.

When it comes to their nonmaterial culture, however, groups are less open to change. Nevertheless, as cultures come in contact with one another, such changes also occur. An example is the parliament of India, modeled after that of Great Britain, its former colonial ruler.

With today's technology in travel and communications, cultural diffusion is occurring rapidly around the globe. Air travel has made it possible to journey halfway across the globe in a matter of hours. In the not-so-distant past, a trip from the United States to Africa was so unusual that only a few hardy people made it. Now hundreds of thousands make the trip each year. Communication has been similarly transformed. Until a

cultural diffusion: the spread of cultural characteristics from one group to another

century ago, communication was limited to face-to-face speech and to visual signals such as smoke, light reflected from mirrors, sending the written word from hand to hand, and so on. People in distant parts of the United States did not hear about the end of the Civil War until weeks and months after it was over. Today's electronic systems of communication transmit messages across the globe in a matter of seconds, and we can find out almost instantaneously what is happening on the other side of the world.

In fact, we are being united by travel and communication to such an extent that there almost is no "other side of the world" anymore. One result of this communications revolution and our current remarkable rate of cultural diffusion is **cultural leveling,** a process in which cultures become similar to one another as expanding industrialization brings not only technology but also Western culture to the rest of the world. Japan, for example, is no longer a purely Eastern culture. It has adapted not only Western economic production but also Western forms of dress and music. These changes, superimposed on Japanese culture, have turned Japan into a blend of Western and Eastern cultures.

Cultural leveling, occurring rapidly around the world, is apparent to any traveler. The Golden Arches of McDonald's welcome today's visitors to Tokyo, Paris, London, Madrid, and even Moscow and Hong Kong. In the Indian Himalayan town of Dharmsala, a Buddhist monk and two Indian boys, sitting on benches in a shack with a dirt floor waiting for a videotaped U.S. movie to begin, watch a Levis commercial on MTV (Brauchli 1993). In a remote part of China, a peasant farmer living in a mud hut with pigs running freely from room to room tunes into "The Rich and the Famous"—thanks to a satellite dish perched atop his wood-planked roof ("Of Channel Jockeys and Tyrants," 1993). In Taiwan a million homes tune in to their favorite program, "Hill Street Blues." In South Korea, a U.S. album, "Bodyguard" by Whitney Houston, sold 800,000 copies. A New Delhi tailor works late to meet the eager demand for his copies of U.S. clothing shown on TV. "Thanks to MTV," says an Indian girl in Calcutta, "I can wear a miniskirt to a disco" (Brauchli 1993).

Although the bridging of geography and culture by electronic signals does not in itself mark the end of traditional cultures, it inevitably will result in some degree of cultural leveling, some blander, less distinctive way of life—U.S. culture with French, Japanese, and Bulgarian accents, so to speak. Although the "cultural accent" remains, something is lost forever.

cultural leveling: the process by which cultures become similar to one another, and especially by which Western industrial culture is imported and diffused into developing nations

In today's swiftly changing world, with its rapid communications and transportation, cultural diffusion is occurring at an unprecedented rate. The direction of change is almost exclusively from the industrialized to the nonindustrialized nations. At times, as with the event depicted here, the results are incongruous.

Summary and Review

What Is Culture?

All human groups possess **culture**—language, beliefs, values, norms, and material objects passed from one generation to the next. **Material culture** consists of objects (art, buildings, clothing, tools). **Nonmaterial** (or **symbolic) culture** is a group's ways of thinking and patterns of behavior. **Ideal culture** is a group's ideal values and norms, and their goals. **Real culture** is people's actual behavior, often falls short of their cultural ideals. Pp. 35–37.

What are cultural relativism and ethnocentrism?

People are naturally **ethnocentric;** that is, they use their own culture as a yardstick for judging the ways of others. In contrast, those who embrace **cultural relativism** try to understand other cultures on those cultures' own terms. P. 37.

Components of Culture

What are the components of nonmaterial culture?

The central component is **symbols,** anything to which people attach meaning and use to communicate with others. Universally, the symbols of nonmaterial culture are **gestures, language, values, norms, sanctions, folkways,** and **mores.** Pp. 38–43.

Why is language so significant to culture?

Language allows human experience to be goal directed, cooperative, and cumulative. It also lets humans move beyond the present and share past, future, and other common perspectives. According to the **Sapir-Whorf hypothesis,** language even shapes our thoughts and perceptions. Pp. 40–42.

How do values, norms, folkways, mores, and sanctions reflect culture?

All groups have **values,** standards by which they define what is desirable or undesirable, and **norms,** rules or expectations about behavior. Groups use **positive sanctions** to show approval of those who follow their norms, and **negative sanctions** to show disapproval of those who do not. Norms that are not strictly enforced are called **folkways,** while **mores** are norms to which groups demand conformity because they reflect core values. Pp. 42–43.

Subcultures and Countercultures

How do subcultures and countercultures differ?

A **subculture** is a group whose values and related behaviors distinguish its members from the general culture in any way. A **counterculture** holds values that at least in some ways stand in opposition to those of the dominant culture. Pp. 43–44.

Values in U.S. Society

What are the dominant U.S. values?

Although the United States is a **pluralistic society,** made up of many groups, each with its own set of values, certain values dominate; chiefly achievement and success, individualism, activity and work, efficiency and practicality, science and technology, progress, material comfort, equality, freedom, democracy, humanitarianism, racism and group superiority, education, religiosity, romantic love and monogamy. Some values cluster together (**value clusters**) to form a larger whole. **Value contradictions** (such as equality and racism) indicate areas of social tension, which are likely points of social change. Changes in a society's fundamental values are opposed by people who hold strongly to traditional values. Leisure, physical fitness, self-fulfillment, and concern for the environment are emerging core values. Pp. 45–49.

Cultural Universals

Do cultural universals exist?

Cultural universals are values, norms, or other cultural traits that are found in all cultures. Although all human groups have customs concerning cooking, funerals, weddings, and so on, because the specific forms these customs take vary from one culture to another there are no cultural universals. Pp. 49–50.

Animals and Culture

Do animals have culture?

To the extent that some animals teach their young certain behaviors, animals also have a rudimentary culture. No animals have language in the sociological sense of the term, although some experiments indicate that some animals may have a limited capacity to learn language. Pp. 50–55.

Cultural Diffusion and Cultural Leveling

What are the world's main cultural trends?

With today's technological advances in travel and communications, **cultural diffusion** is occurring rapidly. This leads to **cultural leveling,** whereby many groups are adopting Western culture in place of their own customs. Much of the richness of the world's diverse cultures is being lost in the process. Pp. 55–56.

Where can I read more on this topic?

Suggested readings for this chapter are listed on page 637.

Jacob Lawrence, Men Exist for the Sake of One Another. Teach Them or Bear With Them, 1958.

Socialization

THE OLD MAN WAS HORRIFIED when he found out. Life never had been good since his daughter had lost her hearing when she was just two years old. She couldn't even talk—just fluttered her hands around trying to tell him things. Over the years, he had gotten used to that. But now . . . he shuddered at the thought of her being pregnant. No one would be willing to marry her; he knew that. And the neighbors, their tongues would never stop wagging. Everywhere he went, he could hear people talking behind his back.

If only his wife were still alive, maybe she could come up with something. What should he do? He couldn't just kick his daughter out into the street.

After the baby was born, the old man tried to shake his feelings, but they wouldn't let loose. Isabelle was a pretty name, but every time he looked at the baby he felt sick to his stomach.

He hated doing it, but there was no way out. His daughter and her baby would have to live in the attic.

Unfortunately, this is a true story. Isabelle was discovered in Ohio in 1938 when she was about 6 1/2 years old, living in a dark room with her deaf-mute mother. Isabelle couldn't talk, but she did use gestures to communicate with her mother. An inadequate diet and lack of sunshine had given Isabelle a disease called rickets. Her legs

> *were so bowed that as she stood erect the soles of her shoes came nearly flat together, and she got about with a skittering gait. Her behavior toward strangers, especially men, was almost that of a wild animal, manifesting much fear and hostility. In lieu of speech she made only a strange croaking sound. (Davis 1988:77)*

When the newspapers reported this case, sociologist Kingsley Davis decided to find out what happened to Isabelle after her discovery. We'll come back to that later, but first let's use the case of Isabelle to give us some insight into what human nature is.

What Is Human Nature?

For centuries, people have been intrigued with the question of what is human about human nature. How much of people's characteristics comes from "nature" (heredity) and how much from "nurture" (the **social environment,** contact with others)? Scientists have made many attempts to unravel this matter (see the Down-to-Earth Sociology box on the next page). One way to answer this question would be to examine people who have been raised without human contact. Although ethics forbid us to conduct such an experiment, some insight into human nature may be gleaned from feral, isolated, and institutionalized children.

Feral Children

Over the centuries, the discovery of **feral** (wild) **children** has been reported from time to time. Supposedly, these children were abandoned or lost by their parents at a very early age and then raised by animals. In one instance, a feral child, known as the wild boy of Aveyron, was studied by the scientists of his day (Itard 1962). This boy, who was found in the forests of France in 1798, walked on all fours, and pounced on small animals, devouring them uncooked. He could not speak, and he gave no indication of feeling the cold. Other reports of feral children have claimed that on discovery, these children acted like wild animals: They could not speak; they bit, scratched, growled, and walked on all fours; they ate grass, tore ravenously at meat, drank by lapping water; and showed an insensitivity to pain and cold (Malson 1972).

social environment: the entire human environment, including direct contact with others

feral children: children assumed to have been raised by animals, in the wilderness isolated from other humans

Most social scientists today dismiss the significance of feral children, taking the position that children cannot be raised by animals and that children found in the woods were reared by their parents as infants but abandoned, probably because they were retarded. But what if this were not the case? Could it be that by nature, if untouched by society, we would all be like feral children?

Isolated Children

Cases like Isabelle's surface from time to time. Because they are well documented, what can they tell us about human nature? We can first conclude that humans have no natural language, for Isabelle, and others like her, are unable to speak.

But maybe Isabelle was not normal. Perhaps Isabelle was retarded, as most scientists claim feral children are, and could not go through the normal stages of development that depend on biology, not society. As noted, Kingsley Davis followed up on this case. After Isabelle was discovered, she scored practically zero on an intelligence test. Apparently, she was severely retarded.

▼▼▼▼▼▼▼▼▼▼▼▼▼▼▼▼▼▼▼▼▼▼▼

Down-To-Earth Sociology

Heredity or Environment? The Case of Oskar and Jack, Identical Twins

IDENTICAL TWINS SHARE EXACT genetic heredity. One fertilized egg divides to produce two embryos. If heredity is the cause of personality (or of people's attitudes, temperament, and basic skills), then identical twins should be identical not only in their looks but also in these characteristics.

The fascinating case of Jack and Oskar helps us unravel this mystery. From their experience, we can see the far-reaching effects of the environment—how social experiences override biology.

Jack Yufe and Oskar Stohr are identical twins born in 1932 to a Jewish father and a Catholic mother. They were separated as babies after their parents divorced. Oskar was reared in Czechoslovakia by his mother's mother, who was a strict Catholic. When Oskar was a toddler, Hitler annexed this area of Czechoslovakia, and Oskar learned to love Hitler and to hate Jews. He became involved with the Hitler Youth (a sort of Boy Scout organization designed to instill the "virtues" of patriotism, loyalty, obedience—and hatred).

Jack's upbringing provides an almost total contrast. Reared in Trinidad by his father, he learned loyalty to Jews and hatred of Hitler and the Nazis. After the war, Jack emigrated to Israel, where, at the age of 17, he joined a kibbutz. Later, Jack served in the Israeli army.

In 1954, the two brothers met. It was a short meeting, and Jack had been warned not to tell Oskar that they were Jews. Twenty-five years later, in 1979, when they were 47 years old, social scientists at the University of Minnesota brought them together again. These researchers figured that since Jack and Oskar had the same genes, whatever differences they showed would have to be due to the environment—to their different social experiences.

Not only were Oskar's and Jack's attitudes toward the war, Hitler, and Jews different, so, too, were their other basic orientations to life. In their politics, Oskar is quite conservative, while Jack is more liberal. Oskar turned out to be domineering in his attitude toward women, while Jack is more accepting of feminism. Oskar enjoys leisure, while Jack is a workaholic. And, as you can predict, Jack is very proud of being a Jew. Oskar, however, won't even mention it.

That would seem to settle the matter. But there is another side to the findings. The researchers also found that Oskar and Jack both like sweet liqueur and spicy foods, excelled at sports as children but had difficulty with math, and have the same rate of speech. Each even flushes the toilet both before and after using it.

Heredity or environment? How much influence does *each* have? The question is not yet settled, but at this point it seems fair to conclude that the *limits* of certain physical and mental abilities are established by heredity (such as ability at sports and mathematics), while such basic orientations to life as attitudes are the result of the environment. We can put it this way: For some parts of life, the blueprint is drawn by heredity; but even here the environment can redraw those lines. For other parts, the individual is a blank slate, and it is entirely up to the environment to determine what is written on that slate.

Sources: Based on Begley 1979, Chen 1979.

At least that is what people first thought. But when Isabelle was given intensive language training, a surprising thing happened. She progressed through the learning stages that are characteristic of the first six years of life in the proper order and in rapid succession. In only two months, Isabelle was able to speak in short sentences. In about a year, she could write a few words, do simple addition, and retell stories after hearing them. Seven months later, she had a vocabulary of almost two thousand words. It took only two years for Isabelle to reach the intellectual level normal for her age. She then went on to school, where she was "bright, cheerful, energetic . . . and participated in all school activities as normally as other children" (Davis 1988:78).

As discussed in the last chapter, language is the key to human behavior. Without language, people have no mechanism for developing thought. Unlike animals, humans have no instincts that take the place of language. If an individual lacks language, he or she lives in an isolated world, a world of internal silence, without shared ideas, without connections to others.

Without language, there can be no culture—no shared way of life—and culture is the key to what people become. Each of us possesses a biological heritage, but this heritage does not determine specific behaviors, attitudes, or values. It is our culture that superimposes the specifics of what we become on to our biological heritage.

Institutionalized Children

But what besides language is required if a child is to develop into what we consider a healthy, balanced, intelligent human being? The key is stimulating interaction.

Two or three generations ago, when we had a much higher death rate, orphanages dotted the United States. Children raised in orphanages tended to be smaller than other children, to have difficulty establishing close bonds with others, and to have lower IQs—if they survived, that is, for their death rates were much higher than average (Spitz 1945). These orphanages were not Dickensian institutions where ragged children were beaten and denied food. The children were kept clean and given simple but nutritious food. Nevertheless, the contrast with today's standards is remarkable. Here is an account of a good orphanage in Iowa during the 1930s.

> Until about six months, they were cared for in the infant nursery. The babies were kept in standard hospital cribs that often had protective sheeting on the sides, thus effectively limiting visual stimulation; no toys or other objects were hung in the infants' line of vision. Human interactions were limited to busy nurses who, with the speed born of practice and necessity, changed diapers or bedding, bathed and medicated the infants, and fed them efficiently with propped bottles. (Skeels 1966)

Although everyone knew that the cause of mental retardation was biological ("They're just born that way"), two psychologists who consulted in this Iowa orphanage, H. M. Skeels and H. B. Dye (1939), began to suspect that the absence of stimulating social interaction was the basic problem, not some biological incapacity on the part of the children. To test their controversial idea, they placed thirteen infants whose mental retardation was so obvious that no one wanted to adopt them, in Glenwood State School, an institution for the mentally retarded. Each infant, then about 19 months old, was assigned to a separate ward of women ranging in mental age from 5 to 12 and in chronological age from 18 to 50. The women were pleased with this arrangement. They not only did a good job taking care of the infants' basic physical needs—diapering, feeding, and so on—but they also loved to play with the children, to cuddle them, and to shower them with attention. They even competed to see which ward would have "its baby" walking or talking first. One woman would become

> particularly attached to him (or her) and figuratively "adopted" him (or her). As a consequence, an intense one-to-one adult–child relationship developed, which was supplemented by the less intense but frequent interactions with the

Human interaction—especially that which expresses love, affection, acceptance, and self-worth—is essential to the development of valued human traits. These children, either abandoned by their parents or left orphans, have been classified as mentally ill and are warehoused in an orphanage in Romania. Like the Rhesus monkeys in the Harlows' experiment, their chances of becoming "normal" adults are very slim.

other adults in the environment. Each child had some one person with whom he (or she) was identified and who was particularly interested in him (or her) and his (or her) achievements. (Skeels 1966)

The researchers left a control group of twelve infants, also retarded but higher in intelligence, at the orphanage, where they received the usual care. Two and a half years later, Skeels and Dye tested all the children's intelligence. Their findings were startling: Those assigned to the retarded women had gained an average of twenty-eight IQ points while those who remained in the orphanage had lost thirty points.

What happened after these children were grown? Did these initial differences matter? Twenty-one years later, Skeels and Dye did a follow-up study. Those in the control group that had remained in the orphanage averaged less than third grade in education. Four still lived in state institutions, while the others held low-level jobs. Only two had married. In contrast, the average level of education for the thirteen individuals in the experimental group was twelve grades (about normal for that period). Five had completed one or more years of college. One had not only earned a B.A. but had gone on to graduate school. Eleven had married. All thirteen were self-supporting and had higher-status jobs or were homemakers (Skeels 1966). The attention that the retarded "mothers" had lavished on "their" babies had achieved startling benefits.

Apparently, then, characteristics that we take for granted as being basic "human" traits—such as high intelligence, cooperative behavior, and friendliness—result from early close relations with other humans. The pathetic story of Genie underscores the point that intelligence and the ability to establish close bonds with others in later life are dependent on early interactions.

In 1970, California authorities found Genie, a 13 1/2-year-old girl who had been kept locked in a small room since she was 20 months old. Apparently her father (70 years old when Genie was discovered) hated children, and had probably caused the death of two of Genie's siblings. Her 50-year-old mother was partially blind and frightened of her husband. Genie could not speak, did not know how to chew, was unable to stand upright, and could not straighten her hands and legs. On intelligence tests, she scored at the level of a 1-year-old. After intensive training, Genie learned to walk and use simple sentences (although they were garbled). Her language remained primitive, and at the age of 21, Genie went to live in a home for adults who cannot live alone (Pines 1981).

Like humans, monkeys also need interaction to thrive. Those raised under conditions of total isolation are unable to interact satisfactorily with others. In this photograph, we see one of the monkeys described in the text. Purposely frightened by the experimenter, the monkey has taken refuge in the soft terrycloth draped over an artificial "mother."

A final lesson can be gained by looking at animals that have been deprived of normal interaction.

Deprived Animals

In the last chapter, we saw that because animals lack language they cannot have a social or shared past or future. We also saw that some animal behavior that we assume is instinctual is actually learned. Let's take another look at animals, this time those that have been deprived of normal learning.

In a series of experiments with rhesus monkeys, psychologists Harry and Margaret Harlow demonstrated the importance of early learning. The Harlows (1962) raised baby monkeys in isolation. They gave each monkey two artificial mothers, shown in the photograph. One "mother" was only a wire frame with a wooden head, but it did have a nipple from which the baby could nurse. The frame of the other "mother," which had no bottle, was covered with soft terrycloth. For their food, the baby monkeys nursed at the wire frame. But when the Harlows (1965) frightened the babies with a large mechanical bear or dog, the babies did not run to the wire frame "mother"; instead, they would cling pathetically to their terrycloth "mother." The Harlows drew the significant conclusion that infant–mother bonding is due not to feeding but rather to what they termed "intimate physical contact." To most of us, this phrase means cuddling.

It is also significant that the monkeys raised in isolation were never able to adjust to monkey life. The experimenters placed them with other monkeys when they were grown. But because they didn't know how to enter into "monkey interaction"—to play and to engage in pretend fights—they were rejected by the other monkeys. Neither did they know how to engage in sexual intercourse, in spite of futile attempts to do so. The experimenters designed a special device, which allowed some females to become pregnant. After giving birth, however, these monkeys were "ineffective, inadequate, and brutal mothers . . . [who] . . . struck their babies, kicked them, or crushed the babies against the cage floor."

In another experiment, the Harlows (1965) divided baby monkeys into three groups. In the first group, each monkey was raised in total isolation, seeing no living being other than itself. In the second, each baby was allowed to be only with its mother. In the third, the baby monkeys were raised only with other baby monkeys. After these monkeys were grown, they, too, were placed with adult monkeys. And again the Harlows observed what happened. The monkeys that had been raised in total isolation were the most abnormal. They would cower in the corner, avoid contact with others, and would not defend themselves. Those raised with just the mother were not much better adjusted. Those raised only with other baby monkeys, however, made a fairly good adjustment. As infants, they had obtained comfort and security by clinging to one another, and while they were growing up they had played together. From this experiment the Harlows concluded that interaction with peers is essential to normal development.

In one of their many other experiments, the Harlows isolated baby monkeys for different lengths of time. They found that monkeys isolated for short periods (about three months) were able to overcome the effects of their isolation, whereas those isolated for six months or more were unable to adjust to normal monkey life. In other words, the longer the isolation, the more difficult it is to overcome its effects. There also may be a critical learning stage that, if missed, may be impossible to overcome. That may have been the case with Genie.

Because humans are not monkeys, we must always be careful about extrapolating from animal studies to human behavior. The Harlow experiments, however, strongly corroborate what we know about the effects on children of being raised in isolation.

In Sum: Society Makes Us Human

Apparently, warm, intimate interaction is essential to vital aspects of human development: biological, mental, emotional, moral, and social growth. Or, as psychologist Urie Bronfenbrenner (1992) says, to develop properly, "Kids need people who are crazy about them." Usually, loving, concerned parents provide this kind of interaction for their children.

Somewhat more radically, we can claim that babies do not "naturally" develop into human adults. Although their bodies certainly get bigger, if raised in isolation they become little more than big animals. Without the concepts of language, they can't experience or even grasp relations between people (the "connections" we call brother, sister, parent, friend, teacher, and so on). They aren't "friendly" in the accepted sense of the term, nor do they cooperate with others. They do not think in terms of a past and a future. Indeed, they do not appear to think at all in any meaningful way.

In short, to develop into adults with the characteristics that we take for granted as "human," children need to be surrounded by people who care for them. Only then can they develop into social adults within the limits set by their biology, for it is through human contact that people learn to be members of the human community. This interaction is what sociologists have in mind when they say, "Society makes us human."

The Social Development of the Self, Mind, and Emotions

Let's now turn our attention to **socialization,** the process by which we learn the ways of society (or of particular groups). As you will see, this process is so fundamental to our identity that it even shapes the way we think and feel.

Cooley and the Looking-Glass Self

Back in the 1800s, Charles Horton Cooley (1864–1929), a symbolic interactionist who taught at the University of Michigan, wondered how human infants develop a **self**—the ability to see themselves "from the outside." Cooley saw the self as our interpretation of how others see us, the ability to contemplate our existence, to project ourselves into the past, into the future, and into various situations in life. Cooley concluded that this unique aspect of "humanness" is *socially created;* that is, our sense of self develops from interaction with others. He coined the term **looking-glass self** (1902) to describe the process by which a sense of self develops, which he summarized in the following couplet:

> Each to each a looking-glass
> Reflects the other that doth pass.

The looking-glass self contains three elements:

1 *We imagine how we appear to those around us.* For example, we may think that others see us as tall and slim or short and fat.

2 *We interpret others' reactions.* We come to conclusions about how others evaluate us. Do they like us being tall and slim? Do they dislike us for being short and fat?

3 *We develop a self-concept.* Based on our interpretations of the reactions of others, we develop feelings and ideas about ourselves. A favorable reflection in this "social mirror" leads to a positive self-concept, a negative reflection to a negative self-concept.

Note that the development of the self does *not* depend on accurate evaluations. Even if we grossly misinterpret how others think about us, those misjudgments become part of our self-concept. It is also important to note that *the development of the self is an*

socialization: the process by which people learn the characteristics of their group—the attitudes, values and actions thought appropriate for them

self: the concept, unique to humans, of being able to see ourselves "from the outside"; to gain a picture of how others see us

looking-glass self: a term coined by Charles Horton Cooley to refer to the process by which our self develops through internalizing others' reactions to us

ongoing, lifelong process. Although the self-concept begins in childhood, it continues to develop throughout life. The three steps of the looking-glass self are an everyday part of our lives, and our ongoing monitoring of how other people react to us continually modifies the self. This process applies to all stages of life, even to old age. Significantly, then, the self is never a finished product but is always in process.

Mead and Role Taking

Another symbolic interactionist, George Herbert Mead (1863–1931), who taught at the University of Chicago, was also interested in how the self develops. He agreed with Cooley that the self develops during social interaction. Mead added that play is critical to the development of a self. In play, children learn to **take the role of the other,** that is, to put themselves in someone else's shoes—to understand how someone else feels and thinks and to anticipate how that person will act.

Young children attain this ability only gradually (Mead 1934; Coser 1977). In a simple experiment, psychologist J. Flavel (1968) asked 14-year-olds and 8-year-olds to explain a board game to some children who were blindfolded and to others who were not. The 8-year-olds gave the same instructions to everyone, while the 14-year-olds gave more detailed instructions to those who were blindfolded. The younger children could not yet take the role of the other, while the older children could.

As they develop this ability, at first children are able to take only the role of **significant others,** individuals who significantly influence their lives, such as parents or siblings. By assuming their roles during play, such as dressing up in their parents' clothing, children cultivate the ability to put themselves in the place of significant others.

As the self gradually develops, children internalize the expectations of larger numbers of people. The ability to take on roles eventually extends to being able to take the role of an abstract entity, "the group as a whole." To this, our perception of how people in general think of us, Mead gave the term **generalized other.**

When parents socialize their children, their goal is to teach them to fit into the human group—first into the family, then the peer group, and later school and work. To take the role of significant others and the generalized other is essential to this goal, because it gives children the ability to modify their behavior by anticipating the reactions of others—something Genie never learned.

Mead identified three stages in role taking:

1   *Imitation*. Children under 3 can only mimic others. They do not yet have a sense of self separate from others, and they can only imitate people's gestures and words. (This stage is actually not role taking, but it prepares the child for it.)

2   *Play*. During the second stage, from the age of about 3 to 5 or 6, children pretend to take the roles of specific people. They might pretend that they are a firefighter, a wrestler, the Lone Ranger, Supergirl, Batman, and so on. They also like costumes at this stage and enjoy dressing up in their parents' clothing, or tying a towel around their necks to "become" Superman or Wonder Woman.

3   *Games*. The third stage, that of organized play, or team games, begins roughly with the early school years. The significance for the self is that to play these games the individual must be able to take multiple roles. One of Mead's favorite examples was that of a baseball game, in which each player must be able to take the role of all the other players. To play baseball, then, the child must know not only his or her own role but must also be able to anticipate who will do what when the ball is hit or thrown.

Mead also distinguished between the "I" and the "me" in the development of the self. The "*I*" is *the self as subject,* the active, spontaneous, creative part of the self. In contrast, the "*me*" is *the self as object,* made up of attitudes internalized from our interactions with others. Mead chose pronouns to indicate these two aspects of the self because in our language "I" is the active agent, as in "I shoved him," while "me" is the

taking the role of the other: putting oneself in someone else's shoes; understanding how someone else feels and thinks and thus anticipating how that person will act

significant other: an individual who significantly influences someone else's life

generalized other: the norms, values, attitudes, and expectations of people "in general"; the child's ability to take the role of the generalized other is a significant step in the development of a self

object of action, as in "He shoved me." Mead stressed that the individual is not only a "me"—like a computerized robot passively absorbing the responses of others. Rather, the "I" actively makes sense of those responses. By this, Mead meant that people (their "I") react to their social environments—evaluating the reactions of others and organizing them into a unified whole. Mead added that the "I" even monitors the "me," fine-tuning our actions to help us better match what others expect of us.

Mead also drew a conclusion that some find startling—that *not only the self but also the human mind is a social product*. Mead stressed that we cannot think without symbols. But where do these symbols come from? Only from society, which gives us our symbols by giving us language. If society did not provide the symbols, we would not be able to think, and thus would not possess what we call the mind. Mind, then, like language, is a product of society.

Piaget and the Development of Thinking

To the informal observations and theorizing of Cooley and Mead, Swiss psychologist Jean Piaget (1896–1980) added rigorous observation and testing of children to learn how the thinking process developed (Piaget 1950, 1954; Phillips 1969). Piaget's research was prompted by his observation that when young children take intelligence tests, they give *consistently* wrong answers, while older children are able to give the expected answer. Piaget concluded that younger children use some sort of incorrect rule in arriving at their answers. If so, this would mean that children go through a process of development as they acquire reasoning skills.

To test this idea, Piaget began to study what he called cognitive development—hat is, how the minds of children mature. Piaget discovered that children pass through four stages: (1) sensorimotor, (2) preoperational, (3) concrete operational, and (4) formal operational. (If you equate the term **operational** with reasoning skills or abstract thought, Piaget's findings will be easier to understand.)

At each stage, children develop new rules of reasoning, thinking skills that allow them to go on to the next stage. As will be apparent, a considerable range of mental abilities exists within each stage, and the reasoning skills that characterize the beginning or middle of a stage are quite different from those evident at the end of a stage. Also keep in mind that the pace at which children move through these stages varies.

1 *The sensorimotor stage* (from birth to about age 2)

During this first stage, understanding is limited to direct contact with the environment. It is based on sucking, touching, listening, seeing. Infants do not think in any sense that we understand. During the first part of this stage they, do not even know that their bodies are separate from the environment. Indeed, they have yet to discover that they have toes. Neither can infants recognize cause and effect. That is, they do not know that their actions cause something to happen.

During the earlier parts of this stage, what is "out of sight" is literally "out of mind." Infants are not aware that objects have a permanent existence. (Piaget called this **object permanence.**) If you show an infant a piece of candy, he or she will reach for it. But if you then place the candy under a napkin in full sight of the infant, he or she will make no attempt to reach for it. As far as the infant is concerned, if it cannot be seen, it does not exist. At about ten months of age, however, infants discover object permanence: hide the candy, and they will reach for it.

2 *The preoperational stage* (from about age 2 to age 7)

During this stage, children *develop the ability to use symbols*. They do not yet understand common concepts, however, such as numbers, size, speed, weight, volume, or causation. Although they can count, they do not really understand what numbers mean. For example, if you spread out six flowers and six pennies, a child can count to six and will say that the flowers and pennies are equal in number. But if you then

According to sociologist Herbert Mead, the self develops through three stages of role taking—imitation, play, and games. The 3 year-olds in this day care center, mimicking adults they have seen talking on the telephone, are in the imitation stage.

operational: Piaget's term for abstract reasoning skills

object permanence: Piaget's term for children's ability to realize that objects continue to exist even when they are not visible

place the pennies in a single pile, the child will say there are more flowers than pennies. Pile the flowers together and spread the pennies out, and the child will say there are more pennies than flowers (Phillips 1969).

Children at this stage do not yet have the ability to take the role of the other. Piaget asked preoperational children to describe a clay mountain range and found that they could do so. But when he asked them to describe how the mountain range looked from where another child was sitting, they could not do so. They could only repeat what they saw from their view.

3 *The concrete operational stage* (from the age of about 7 to 12)

During this stage, children's reasoning abilities are much more developed. Their reasoning, however, remains *concrete*. That is, they can understand numbers, causation, and speed, and they are able to take the role of the other and to participate in team games, but without concrete examples they are unable to talk about such concepts as truth, honesty, or justice. They can explain why Jane's answer was a lie, but they cannot describe what truth itself is.

4 *The formal operational stage* (after the age of about 12)

During this stage, children are capable of abstract thinking. They can talk about concepts, come to conclusions based on general principles, and use rules to solve abstract problems. During this stage, they are likely to become young philosophers (Kagan 1984). For example, a child at the concrete operational stage might have said, "That is wrong!" in response to a televised depiction of U.S. slavery. Now, however, he or she is more likely to ask, "If our country was founded on equality, how could people have owned slaves?"

As emphasized in Chapter 2, the content of culture varies from group to group. These differences in content are extremely significant in human thinking. Although children around the world apparently go through these stages in the same order, the *content* of their reasoning differs markedly. For example, Americans learn to think of the abstract concepts of democracy and freedom in one way; the Chinese will use those same concepts in quite a different way, while in the jungles of South America the Yanomamo will never learn such ideas.

Researchers have concluded that not everyone reaches the fourth level of cognitive development (Kohlberg and Gilligan 1971). Apparently some adults get stuck in the concreteness of the third stage and are unable to reason abstractly. Two factors may be responsible. First, *biology* may set limits on an individual's capacity for cognitive development; that is, by nature some people may be more intelligent than others. Second, *social experiences* develop the capacity of some people for abstract thought, while limiting that development in others. For example, since the college experience is built around the fourth stage, college students increase their mental ability to manipulate principles and concepts (abstract reasoning).

Along with the development of the mind and the self comes the development of emotions. Let us look at how theorists explain this development.

Freud and the Development of Personality

In Vienna at the turn of the century, Sigmund Freud (1856–1939), a physician, founded psychoanalysis, a technique for treating emotional problems through long-term, intensive exploration of the subconscious mind. We shall look at that part of his thought that applies to the development of personality.

Freud believed that personality consists of three elements. Each child is born with the first, an **id,** Freud's term for inborn drives for self-gratification. The id of the newborn is evident in cries of hunger or pain. The pleasure-seeking id operates throughout life, demanding the immediate fulfillment of basic needs: attention, safety, food, sex, aggression, and so on.

id: Freud's term for the individual's inborn basic drives

But the id's drive for immediate and complete satisfaction runs directly against the needs of other people. As the child comes up against norms and other constraints (usually represented by parents), he or she must adapt to survive. To help adapt to these constraints that block his or her desires, a second component of the personality emerges, which Freud called the **ego.** The ego is the balancing force between the id and the demands of society that suppress it. The ego also serves to balance the id and the **superego,** the third component of the personality, more commonly called the conscience.

The superego represents *culture within us*, the norms and values that we have internalized from our social groups. As the *moral* component of the personality, the superego gives us feelings of guilt or shame when we break social rules, or pride and self-satisfaction when we follow them.

According to Freud, when the id gets out of hand, we follow our desires for pleasure and break society's norms. When the superego gets out of hand, we become overly rigid in following those norms, finding ourselves bound in a straitjacket of rules that inhibit our lives. The ego, the balancing force, tries to prevent either the superego or the id from dominating. In the emotionally healthy individual, the ego succeeds in balancing these conflicting demands of the id and the superego. In the maladjusted individual, however, the ego cannot control the inherent conflict between the id and the superego, and the result is internal confusion and problem behaviors.

Sociological Evaluation What sociologists appreciate about Freud is his emphasis on socialization—that the social group into which we are born transmits norms and values that restrain our biological drives. Sociologists, however, object to the view that inborn and unconscious motivations are the primary reasons for human behavior, for this view denies the central tenet of sociology: that social factors such as social class, religion, and education shape people's behaviors (Epstein 1988; Bush and Simmons 1990). Feminist sociologists have been especially critical of Freud. Although what we just summarized applies to both females and males, Freud viewed what is "male" as "normal," filtered feminine experiences through the model of male dominance, and even analyzed females as inferior, castrated males (Gilligan 1982; Chodorow 1990).

The Sequential Development of Emotions

Researchers have found that the development of human emotions parallels the growth in reasoning skills discovered by Piaget. Emotions, too, develop in an orderly sequence (Kagan 1984). Humans are born with what we might call "emotional reflexes." During the first three to four months, an infant will show surprise, joy, distress, and excitement—all without learning. Surprisingly, fear is not one of these emotional reflexes.

Between the ages of 4 and 10 months, fear appears, as does anger. During the second year, many other emotions appear, including sadness (at the loss of a familiar object), anxiety (at not being able to do what was asked), and affection or tenderness. In line with Cooley's and Mead's theories, a child of this age shows no indication of perceiving others as having separate identities. The child also does not exhibit a sense of self; for example, he or she will look behind a mirror to find the person who must be there.

By the age of 4, children show guilt and shame. This indicates that a sense of self is developing, for these emotions require an awareness of being judged by others. By the age of 5 children also display pride, humility, envy, and jealousy—emotions that indicate greater "self-awareness." By age 6 or 7, having developed the ability to take the role of the other, children express emotions that indicate a judgment of the self in comparison with qualities that others possess. That is, they exhibit feelings about their own relative abilities, attractiveness, honesty, bravery, dominance, and popularity.

By puberty children can express the entire range of emotions, including those that require abstract thought. For example, do you feel sorry for the Moravians? Who are the Moravians? you might ask. That is precisely the point. One must first be capable of identifying the group, and then be capable of sympathizing with their problems—and that requires abstract thought.

ego: Freud's term for a balancing force between the id and the demands of society

superego: Freud's term for the conscience, the internalized norms and values of our social groups

Although males are socialized to express less emotion than are females, such socialization apparently goes quite contrary to their nature. In certain settings, as shown here, however, males are allowed to be openly emotional, even demonstrative, with one another.

Socialization into Emotions

As we have seen, socialization provides the particulars that go into human reasoning. Emotions, too, are not simply the results of biology. They also depend on socialization (Hochschild 1975; Pollak and Thoits 1989; Johnson 1992; Wouters 1992).

This conclusion may sound strange. Don't all people get angry? Doesn't everyone cry? Don't we all feel guilt, shame, sadness, remorse, happiness, fear? What has socialization to do with emotions?

Let's start with the obvious. Certainly people around the world all feel these particular emotions, but the way in which they express them varies from one social group to another. This variation becomes evident when we compare cultures. Let's consider, for example, the case of very close male friends reunited after a separation of several months. Americans in this situation might shake hands vigorously or even give each other a little clap on the back. Japanese might bow, while Arabs will kiss. A good part of childhood socialization centers on learning to express emotions correctly, for each culture has "norms of emotion" that demand conformity (Clark 1991).

The expression of emotions is not only dependent on culture but also on one's social location, in this case, gender, for in the preceding example U.S. women are more likely to hug than to merely shake hands. Similarly, college professors probably show their pleasure at having done well, such as having given a good lecture, with a simple smile. In contrast, football players show their pleasure at having done well, such as having made a touchdown, by jumping up and down, throwing the ball to the ground, shouting, lifting one another into the air, clapping one another on the shoulders, or patting one another's rear. But there is something much deeper going on here, more than just the display of emotion. Because their socialization differs, these individuals actually experience different emotions. The college professor *feels* satisfaction or pride at a job well done. In contrast, the football player *feels* an intense triumph that borders on pure ecstasy.

As you know, our emotions are also influenced by people around us. For example, we are likely to feel sad (or happy) when around sad (or happy) people. But there is a deeper level in which people influence our emotions. They give cues regarding how to *label*

Socialization plays a key role both in the kinds of emotions we feel and in how we express these emotions. Thus each culture has its own "norms of emotions" that determine the nature and expression of feelings. These Moslem priests protect themselves from the rain as they pray in the central cemetery at Sarajevo.

our internal states. This labeling, in turn, influences what we actually feel. In an interesting, although ethically questionable, experiment, psychologists Stanley Schachter and Jerome Singer (1962) injected three groups of volunteers with epinephrine, a synthetic adrenalin, which causes the heart to pound and the hands to tremble. The first group, who did not know what the drug would do, were put together with people who acted euphoric—bounding around, happily wadding paper into balls, and hooking shots into the wastebasket. These subjects reported feelings of euphoria and also began to show their happiness. The second group, who also were ignorant of the drug's effects, were put with people who acted angry. They reported that they experienced anger. Members of the third group were told what the drug would do. Some were placed with people who acted angry, others with people who acted euphoric. These subjects reported neither anger nor euphoria, only physical reactions.

Finally, in some cultures people learn to experience emotions quite unlike ours. For example, the Ifaluk, who live on the Western Caroline Islands of Micronesia, use the word *fago* to refer to feelings provoked by seeing someone suffer or in need of help, something close to what we refer to as sympathy or compassion. But they also use this term to describe their feelings when they are around someone who has high status, someone who is highly admired or respected (Kagan 1984). To us, these are two distinct emotions, and they require distinct terms.

In short, as we are socialized into a culture, we learn not only how to express our emotions, but also what emotions to feel. Because feelings are a significant influence on behavior, to understand emotions is to broaden our understanding of human behavior in general. Let's look at how even our anticipation of emotions influences what we do.

The Self and Emotions as Social Constraints on Behavior

Most socialization is intended to turn us into conforming members of society. The self and emotions are essential to this process, for both serve as social constraints on our behavior. Although we like to think we are "free," consider for a moment just some of the factors that influence how we act: the expectations of friends, parents, and teachers; classroom norms; college rules; and federal and state laws. For example, if for some reason, such as a moment of intense frustration or a devilish desire to shock people, you wanted to tear off your clothes and run naked down the street, what would stop you?

The answer is your socialization—*society within you*. Your experiences in society have resulted in a self that thinks along certain lines and feels particular emotions. This keeps you in line. Thoughts such as "What would happen if I got caught?" "Would I be sent to jail?" "Would I be kicked out of school?" represent a sense of self, an awareness of the self in relationship to others. Your social mirror is also likely to reflect another important element of socialization, the desire to avoid feelings of shame and embarrassment, and you might wonder, "What would my friends (family, teachers, acquaintances) think if they found out?" "How would I *feel* if they were to find out?" In fact, socialization into emotions is so effective that you might experience embarrassment just thinking about running nude in public! By socializing us into emotions, then, society sets up effective controls over our behavior.

Socialization into Gender

Society also channels our behavior through **gender socialization.** By expecting different behaviors from people *because* they are male or female, the social group nudges boys and girls in separate directions from an early age, laying down a foundation of contrasting orientations to life that carry over from childhood into adulthood. As a result of intensive and extensive socialization into gender, most men and women act, think, and feel according to the lines laid down by their culture as appropriate for their sex.

gender socialization: the ways in which society sets children onto different courses in life *because* they are male or female

Peer groups are second only to the family in terms of their role as agents of socialization. During adolescence, with fitting in a primary concern, peer groups become the single most important socializing force. The peer group's values compete with, and often outweigh, those of the family.

How do people learn "gender appropriate" orientations to life? How do societies convince their men and women that certain activities are "masculine," others "feminine," and on that basis proper for them or not? Of the many areas of our society that convey gender messages, we shall look at just two: the family and the mass media.

Gender, the Family, and Sex-Linked Behaviors

We spend much of the time that follows birth learning what our assigned **gender role** requires. Our parents are the first significant others who teach us our part in this symbolic division of the world. Sometimes they do so self-consciously, perhaps by bringing into play pink and blue, colors that have no meaning in themselves but have social associations with gender. But our parents' own gender orientations are so firmly established that they also teach us gender roles without being aware of what they are doing.

In what has become a classic study, psychologists Susan Goldberg and Michael Lewis (1969) asked mothers to bring their 6-month-old infants into their laboratory, supposedly to observe the infants' development. Secretly, however, the researchers also observed the mothers. They found that the mothers kept their female children closer to them and that they touched and spoke more to their daughters. By the time the children were 13 months old, the girls stayed closer to their mothers during play, and they returned to them sooner and more often than did boys of the same age. When Goldberg and Lewis set up a barrier to separate the mothers, who were holding toys, from their children, the girls cried and motioned for help more than the boys, who attempted to circumvent the barrier more actively. Goldberg and Lewis concluded that in our society mothers unconsciously reward female children for being passive and dependent and male children for being active and independent.

Teaching males to be more active and express greater independence continues during childhood. Preschool boys are allowed to roam farther from home than their preschool sisters, and they are subtly encouraged to participate in more rough-and-tumble play—even to get dirtier and to be more defiant (Henslin 1993b). This process that begins in the family is completed as the child is exposed to other aspects of society (Thorne 1990). Teachers, for example, expect male and female students to be different. They nurture the "natural" differences they find, with the result that boys and girls develop different aspirations in life.

Gender Images in the Mass Media

The mass media reinforce society's expectations of gender in many ways, through children's books, television, music, and newspapers.

gender role: the behaviors and attitudes considered appropriate because one is a female or a male

Children's Books In 1972, a research team led by sociologist Lenore Weitzman examined the children's books that had won the American Library Association's prestigious Caldecott Medal for the best illustrations. Winning books are ordered by almost all children's libraries in the United States. Because women in the United States represent about 51 percent of the population, it would be reasonable to expect about half the characters in the illustrations to be female. The researchers, however, found females virtually invisible. Almost all told stories about male adventures and featured boys, men, and even male animals. (For every female animal, ninety-five male animals were depicted!) Girls were portrayed as passive and doll-like, boys as active and adventuresome. Most of the girls were depicted as trying to please their brothers and fathers, while the boys, in contrast, engaged in tasks requiring independence and self-confidence.

Following this study, feminists began a campaign to change this situation. They compiled lists of books they felt presented more positive images of females, and they even formed publishing companies to produce nonsexist books (Williams et al. 1987). Their goal was to have "Dick . . . speak of his feelings of tenderness without embarrassment and Jane . . . reveal her career ambitions without shame or guilt." The results? By the 1980s females had become more visible, but the illustrations still showed twice as many males as females (Dougherty and Engel 1987; Heintz 1987). Traditional stereotypes also continued to dominate these books. Girls were more likely to be shown indoors and as dependent, submissive, and passive, while boys were more likely to be portrayed outdoors in independent, competitive activities. Researchers (Williams et al. 1987) came to the following conclusion:

> . . . females appear to have begun to move outside the home, but not into the labor market. . . . Not only does Jane express no career goals, but there is no adult female model to provide any ambition. One woman in the entire 1980s collection of twenty-four books has an occupation outside the home, and she works as a waitress at the Blue Tile Diner. How can we expect Dick to express tender emotions without shame when only two adult males in this collection of books have anything resembling tender emotions and one of them is a mouse?

Television Television also reinforces stereotypes of the sexes. Children's shows overwhelmingly feature more males than females. In cartoons, males outnumber females by four or five to one (Morgan 1982, 1987). Adult television picks up this message of male dominance. On prime-time television, male characters outnumber female characters by two to one, with the male characters more likely to be portrayed in higher-status positions (Vande Berg and Streckfuss 1992). Although there are some exceptions—Murphy Brown is depicted as stronger than her weak, sniveling boss—females are more likely to be portrayed as passive and indecisive. Men are much more likely to dominate women than the other way around. In commercials, women's voices are rarely used as the voice-over. The significance is not lost on viewers, for the more television people watch, the more they tend to have restrictive ideas about women's role in society (Signorielli 1989, 1990).

Music Music also helps to form our images of the sexes. Many songs directed toward teenagers give boys the message that they should dominate male–female relationships, and girls that they should be sexy, dependent, and submissive. In music videos, males are more likely to be portrayed as aggressive and domineering, females as affectionate, dependent, and nurturing (Seidman 1992). On MTV, three-quarters of music videos show only male performers (Vincent et al. 1987). Of those that do show females, 10 percent portray violence against women and 74 percent either "put women down" or "keep them in their place." Perhaps the most damning finding, however, is that females are generally irrelevant, presented simply as background ornaments for male action.

Newspapers   Researchers have found that newspapers perpetuate similar images. A study of 5,500 stories in eight newspapers showed that men are main characters *eleven* times more often than women. Whether in front-page stories, editorials, the business section, or the sports pages, men are more likely to be featured. When a story does feature a woman, it has smaller headlines and is shorter (Davis 1982). For every photo of a woman, about two photos of men are run (Luebke 1989).

   In Sum   All of us are born into a society in which "male" and "female" are significant symbols. Sorted into separate groups from childhood, girls and boys come to have sharply different ideas of themselves and of one another, beginning within the family and later reinforced by other social institutions. Each of us learns the meanings our society associates with the sexes. These symbols become integrated into our view of the world, forming a picture that forces an interpretation of the world in terms of gender.

Thus do gender messages shape our world of ideas. Mostly beneath our level of awareness, these messages mold the ways in which we see females and males. The net result is that gender serves as a primary basis for **social inequality,** giving privileges and obligations to one group of people while denying them to another.

Agents of Socialization

People and groups that influence the development of our self-concept, emotions, attitudes, and behavior are called **agents of socialization.** Of the many agents of socialization that prepare us to take our place in society, we shall examine the family, religion, school, peers, sports, mass media, and workplace.

The Family

Around the world, the first group to have a major impact on humans is the family. Unlike some animals, we cannot survive by ourselves, and as babies we are utterly dependent on our family. Our experiences in the family are so intense that they have a lifelong impact on us. They lay down our basic sense of self, establishing our initial motivations, values, and beliefs (Gecas 1990). The family gives us ideas about who we are and what we deserve out of life. It is in the family that we begin to think of ourselves as strong or weak, smart or dumb, good-looking or ugly—or somewhere in between. And as already noted, here we begin the lifelong process of defining ourselves as female or male.

To study this process, sociologists have observed parents and young children in public settings, where their act of observing does not interfere with the natural interaction. Researchers using this unobtrusive technique have consistently noted what they call the "stroller effect" (Mitchell et al. 1992). Fathers are more likely to push the stroller when the child is in it, the mother when the stroller is empty. In addition, the father is more likely to carry the child. From these observations, the researchers conclude that parents send their children subtle messages about expected differences between men and women. Indeed, probably most of the ways by which parents teach their children gender roles is not by specific instruction, but by such nonverbal cues.

The Family and Social Class   To see how far-reaching, yet subtle, social class is, let us compare how working-class and middle-class parents rear their children. Sociologist Melvin Kohn (1959, 1963, 1976, 1977, 1983; Kohn et al. 1986) found that the main concern of working-class parents is their children's outward conformity. They want their children to be obedient, neat, and clean, to follow the rules, and to stay out of trouble. They are likely to use physical punishment to make their children obey. In contrast, mid-

social inequality: a state in which privileges and obligations are given to some but denied to others

agents of socialization: people or groups that affect our self-concept, attitudes, or other orientations toward life

Schools are one of the primary agents of socialization. One of their chief functions is to sort young people into the adult roles thought appropriate for them, as well as to teach them them the attitudes that match those roles. What sorts of attitudes and adult roles do you think these "Redskinettes" are being socialized into? Is this a manifest or a latent function? Is it a dysfunction?

dle-class parents focus on developing their children's curiosity, self-expression, and self-control. They show greater concern about the motivations for their children's behavior and are less likely to use physical punishment than to reason with their children or to withdraw privileges and affection.

Kohn was not satisfied with simply documenting these differences. Just *why* should working-class and middle-class parents rear their children so differently? From his sociological imagination, Kohn knew that life experiences of some sort held the key. Kohn found this key in the world of work. Blue-collar workers are usually supervised very closely. Their bosses expect them to do exactly as they are told. Since blue-collar parents expect their children's lives to be similar to their own, they draw on these experiences as they rear their children. Consequently, they stress obedience and conformity. Middle-class parents, in contrast, especially those in management and the professions, experience a much freer workplace. They have greater independence, are encouraged to be imaginative, and advance by taking the initiative. Expecting their children to work at similar jobs, they, in turn, socialize them into these qualities—which they assume will be essential to their well-being.

What still puzzled Kohn was that the class differences in child rearing were only tendencies. Not all working-class or middle-class parents treat their children alike; instead, some working-class parents act more like middle-class parents, and vice versa. As Kohn probed this puzzle, the pieces fell into place. He found that the parents' specific type of job was even more important than their social class. Many middle-class office workers, for example, have little freedom and are closely supervised. Kohn found that such workers follow the working-class pattern of child rearing, for they stress outward conformity. In contrast, some blue-collar workers, such as those who do home repairs, have a good deal of freedom. These workers follow the middle-class model in rearing their children (Pearlin and Kohn 1966; Kohn and Schooler 1969).

Religion

Religion plays a significant role in the socialization of most Americans. It especially influences morality, becoming a key component in people's ideas of right and wrong. Religion is

Families are a primary agent of socialization. Social class and occupation of parents are key determinants in the initial values and orientations that children learn.

so important to Americans that 65 percent are official members of a local congregation, while during a typical week 40 percent of Americans attend a religious service (*Statistical Abstract* 1992:75). Religion is significant even for persons reared in nonreligious homes, for religious ideas pervade U.S. society, providing basic ideas of morality that become significant for us all.

The influence of religion extends to other areas of our lives as well. For example, participation in religious services teaches us not only beliefs about the hereafter but also ideas about the dress, speech, and manners appropriate for formal occasions. Religion is so significant that we shall treat this social institution in a separate chapter.

The School

As discussed in Chapter 1, functionalists analyze how the parts of a social system fit together. They stress that each part has manifest and latent functions. The **manifest function,** or intended purpose, of formal education is not difficult to identify. Schooling is intended to transmit the skills and values thought appropriate for earning a living and for being a "good citizen." Accordingly, our schools teach reading, writing, arithmetic, and so on. Teachers also stress such values as managing money and voting.

Our schools also have several **latent functions,** unintended consequences that help the social system. First, by placing children under the direct control of teachers—people who are not their friends, neighbors, or relatives—schooling broadens their social horizons. It exposes them to new attitudes, values, and ways of looking at the world. Second, as children move beyond a world in which they may have been the almost exclusive focus of doting parents, they learn to be part of a large group of people of similar age. Third, children learn universality—that the same rules and the same sanctions apply to everyone, regardless of who their parents are or how special they may be at home. Fourth, children gradually come to realize that their behavior is recorded in permanent, official records that will have important and lasting consequences. Such latent functions help prepare the child to take a role in the world beyond the family.

The Perspectives box on page 78 explores the socialization of a Mexican-American writer who as a schoolchild learned to become an American. Only as an adult did he painfully realize that as a consequence of his school socialization, he thereby lost many of the values and ways of looking at the world unique to his Hispanic heritage.

Sociologists have also identified a *hidden curriculum* in our schools. By this, they refer to values that are not explicitly taught but form an inherent part of a school's activities. The wording of math problems and stories intended to teach English grammar, for example, brings lessons in patriotism, democracy, justice, and honesty—all characteristics the community deems desirable for its students to become "good citizens" and to take their place in the work force.

manifest function: the intended consequences of people's actions designed to help some part of a social system

latent functions: the unintended consequences of people's actions that help to keep a social system in equilibrium

In addition to their manifest functions of teaching knowledge and skills, schools also have such latent functions as initiating us into the acceptable attitudes, values, and roles of the larger culture. Thus wealthy children who attend private schools not only learn knowledge and skills, but also how to assume a superior place in the economic system. What did you learn in your school about your proper adult roles? About your place in the economic system? How does this compare with what these children are learning?

As conflict theorists point out, the hidden curriculum means that our schools in effect teach young people the prevailing "correct" attitude toward the economic system (Marger 1987). In other words, when schools teach young people to think that our economic system is basically just, it simultaneously teaches them to think that social problems such as poverty and homelessness have nothing to do with economic power, oppression, and exploitation.

Peer Groups

As a child's experiences with agents of socialization broaden, the influence of the family lessens. Entry into school marks only one of many steps in this transfer of allegiance. One of the most significant aspects of education is that it exposes children to peer groups. A **peer group** is a group of individuals roughly the same age who are linked by common interests. Examples of peer groups, which exert such profound influence on children, are friends, clubs, gangs, and "the kids in the neighborhood."

For five years, while playing the roles of parent, friend, coach, and student teacher, sociologists Patricia Adler, Steven Kless, and Peter Adler (1992) observed children at two public elementary schools in Colorado. They found that the peer group provides an enclave in which boys and girls resist the efforts of parents and schools to socialize them their way, and in which they separate themselves by sex and develop their own worlds with unique norms and values. The norms that make boys popular are athletic ability, coolness, and toughness. For girls, they are family background, physical appearance (clothing and ability to use makeup), and interest in more mature social concerns (such as the ability to attract popular boys). Interestingly, in the child's subculture, academic achievement works in opposite directions: for boys, to do well academically hurts popularity, while getting good grades increases a girl's standing among her peers.

As you well know from personal experience, peer groups are compelling. It is almost impossible to go against a peer group, whose cardinal rule seems to be "conformity or rejection." Three basic reasons underlie the immense power of peer groups. First, they are based on common interests, which represent issues critical for the individual at the moment. Second, they provide guidelines for vital aspects of life. A group of teenagers, for example, may seem to be "simply" shooting baskets or shopping, but they are always doing much more than that. They also are trying their best to give the right impression, reacting to how others express the self, and in all likelihood also talking about the opposite sex. As they engage in these "side activities"—which may be the most significant part of what they are doing—they form norms that they enforce on one another. Third, peer groups are voluntary. As such, they hold the threat of expulsion: Anyone who doesn't do what the others want becomes an "outsider," a "nonmember," an "outcast." For preteens and teens just learning their way around in the world, it is not surprising that the peer group is king.

For example, it is almost exclusively the peer group that sets the standards. If your peers listen to rap, heavy metal, rock and roll, country, folk, gospel, classical, or any other kind of music, it is almost inevitable that you also prefer that kind of music. It is the same for clothing styles and dating standards. Peer influences also extend to behaviors that violate social norms. If your peers are college bound and upwardly striving, that is most likely what you will be; but if they use drugs, cheat, and steal, you are likely to do so, too.

Sports

Sports are also a powerful socializing agent. Everyone recognizes that sports teach values, and, in fact, "teaching youngsters to be team players" is often given as the justification for financing organized sports. How effective sports are in socializing boys is the topic of the Down-to-Earth Sociology box on page 80.

The Mass Media

The **mass media,** forms of communication directed to large audiences, also socialize us. Radio and television, newspapers and magazines do not merely entertain us; as already noted concerning gender socialization, they also shape our attitudes, values, and other basic orientations to life.

peer group: a group of individuals roughly the same age linked by common interests

Perspectives

CULTURAL DIVERSITY IN U.S. SOCIETY

Caught Between Two Worlds

JUST AS AN INDIVIDUAL is socialized into becoming a member of a culture, so a person can lose a culture through socialization. If you are exposesd to a new culture as an adult, as older immigrants are, you can selectively adopt aspects of the new culture without entirely relinquishing your native culture. The first remains dominant, the second an enriching addition. If the immersion occurs as a child, however, the second culture may vie for dominance with your native heritage. This, in turn, can lead to inner turmoil. To cut ties with your first culture—one way of handling the conflict—can create a sense of loss that is recognized only later in life.

Richard Rodriguez, a literature professor and essayist, was born in the 1950s to working-class Mexican immigrants. Wanting their son to be successful in the adopted land, his parents named him Richard instead of Ricardo. While his Spanish-English hybrid name indicated the parents' aspirations for their son, it was also a portent of the conflict Richard would experience.

Like other children of Mexican immigrants, Richard's first language was Spanish—a rich mother tongue that provided his orientation to the world. Until the age of 5 when he began school, he knew but fifty words in English. He described what happened when he began school.

The change came gradually but early. When I was beginning grade school, I noted to myself the fact that the classroom environment was so different in its styles and assumptions from my own family environment that survival would essentially entail a choice between both worlds. When I became a student, I was literally "remade"; neither I nor my teachers considered anything I had known before as relevant. I had to forget most of what my culture had provided, because to remember it was a disadvantage. The past and its cultural values became detachable, like a piece of clothing grown heavy on a warm day and finally put away.

Like millions of immigrants before him, whose parents spoke German, Polish, Italian, and so on, English and education eroded family and class ties. But for Rodriguez, they also ate away at his racial and ethnic ties. For him, language and education were not simply devices that eased the transition to the dominant culture. Instead, they transformed Richard into a *pocho*, "a Mexican with gringo aspirations." They slashed at the roots that had given him life.

Facing such inner turmoil, some withdraw from the new culture—one clue to the high dropout rate of Hispanic Americans from educational institutions. Others cut ties with their family and cultural roots and wholeheartedly adopt the new culture. Rodriguez took the second course. He performed well in his new language—so well, in fact, that he went to Stanford University and then became a graduate student in English at the University of California at Berkeley. He was even awarded a prestigious Fulbright fellowship to study English Renaissance literature at the British Museum.

But the past wouldn't let him alone. Prospective employers were impressed with his knowledge of Renaissance literature. Yet at job interviews, they would ask if he would teach the Mexican novel in translation and be an adviser to Hispanic-American students. Rodriguez was haunted by the image of his grandmother, the culture he had left behind, the language to which he was now a stranger.

Richard Rodriguez represents millions of immigrants—not just those of Hispanic origin but millions from other cultures, too—who want to be a part of the United States without betraying their past. They fear that to integrate into U.S. culture is to lose their roots. They are caught between two cultures, each beckoning, each offering rich rewards.

Sources: Based on Richard Rodriguez 1975, 1982, 1990, 1991.

Television has become the dominant medium, and children in the United States spend more time in front of a television (15,000 hours) than they do in school (11,000 hours). Because it is so cheap, and children will sit transfixed for hours before its dancing images, many parents even use this medium as an electronic babysitter—although the values presented on it may sharply conflict with their own.

Since most U.S. children are exposed to so much television, it is not surprising that some social analysts have become concerned about the *content* of what children see. As Joshua Meyrowitz (1984) points out, to use television as an electronic babysitter

is equivalent to a broad social decision to allow young children to be present at wars and funerals, courtships and seductions, criminal plots and cocktail parties . . . television exposes children to many topics and behaviors that adults have spent several centuries trying to keep hidden from them.

Violence on television has become a special concern. Researchers have found that by the age of 18 the average U.S. adolescent has watched about 18,000 people being strangled, smothered, stabbed, shot, poisoned, blown up, drowned, run over, beaten to death, or otherwise ingeniously done in (Messner 1986) and another 160,000 rapes, armed robberies, and assaults (Comstock and Strasburger 1990).

The big question, of course, is What effects does televised violence have on its viewers? Researchers have probed this question for decades, but with highly mixed results. Then, in the 1980s, researchers found a unique opportunity to help determine the answer. Two nearby Canadian towns were similar in size, race, and social class, but one had television (called "MultiTel"), and the other did not (called "NoTel"). The researchers tested the children and found that NoTel's children were less aggressive, both physically and verbally. Two years after NoTel began to receive television, the researchers again measured the children. NoTel's children had become just as aggressive as the children in MultiTel (Williams 1986).

Researchers at the University of Michigan have concluded that the effects of television violence don't stop with childhood (Comstock and Strasburger 1990). In a longitudinal study (the same people are studied over time), they measured the television viewing and aggression of all the 8-year-olds in a county in upstate New York. The children who watched more television were also the more violent. When the children turned 19, the researchers again measured their antisocial behavior. They were surprised to find the same results. At age 30, they measured their levels of aggression once more. This time they were stunned to find results as strong as those that show cigarettes cause lung cancer. The adults who had watched the most television at the age of 8 had more arrests for drunk driving and more arrests for violent crime. They even had more aggressive children.

If these findings are supported by further research, we still must deal with the question of *how* televised violence can have such effects. Some researchers suggest that scripts are the answer. One researcher put it this way:

> In a new social situation, how do you know how to behave? You search for scripts to follow. Where is a likely place for those scripts to come from? From what you've observed others doing in life, films, TV. So, as a child, you see (violence on television). . . . Even years later, the right kind of scene can trigger that script and suggest a way to behave that follows it. . . . Moreover, we find that watching TV violence affects the viewer's beliefs and attitudes about how people are going to behave. (Institute for Social Research 1994)

The Workplace

Another major agent of socialization that comes into play somewhat later in life is the workplace. Here we rub shoulders with a group of people who become influential in forming our values and orientations. Those initial jobs that we take—part-time work after school and in college—are much more than a way to earn a few dollars. They are like school itself. From them, we learn not only a set of skills but also matching attitudes and values. And just as peer groups play a significant role at school, here, too, we form friendships that teach us a perspective on the world as well as on work.

To become committed to a field of work is the end result of a long process of socialization. Sociologist Wilbert Moore (1968) found that career socialization involves four phases. First comes *career choice*, the selection of some field of work and preparation for it. Second is **anticipatory socialization,** the process of learning to play a role before entering it, a sort of mental rehearsal for some future activity. As a person identifies with a role, he or she becomes aware of some of its expectations and rewards, which supposedly makes it easier to move into the new role (Bush and Simmons 1990). Anticipatory socialization may involve reading novels about people who work in one's chosen career, talking to them, or taking a summer internship. The third phase is *conditioning and commitment*. This refers to the act of going to work, finding that many dull or unpleasant tasks are associated with the work, and yet committing to that occupation. The fourth is *continuing commitment*, sticking with the work in spite of difficulties or alternatives that may arise.

An interesting aspect of work as a socializing agent is that the more you participate in a line of work, the more the work becomes a part of your self-concept. Eventually you come to think of yourself so much in terms of the job that if someone asks you to describe yourself, you are likely to include the job in your initial self-description by saying, "I am a teacher, accountant, nurse" or whatever.

anticipatory socialization: because one anticipates a future role, one learns parts of it now

Down-To-Earth Sociology

Of Boys and Sports

IN SOME SPORTS THE "male values" of competition and rough physical contact, akin to violence, are exalted, and those who play these sports learn to be "real men." Although not playing themselves, even boys and men who intensely follow sports are openly affirming male cultural values and displaying their own masculinity.

Sociologist Michael Messner (1990) interviewed former male professional athletes and other men for whom sports provided a central identity during and after high school. He found that boys who become active in organized sports are encouraged to do so by men and other boys. For many, it is the father, older brother, or uncle who encourages a boy to develop his athletic abilities, or who serves as a role model for the boy's later success. A former professional football player, whose two older brothers had gained wide reputations for sports, said,

My brothers were role models. I wanted to prove—especially to my brothers—that I had heart, you know, that I was a man. . . . And . . . as I got older, I got better and I began to look around me and see, well hey! I'm competitive with these guys, even though I'm younger, you know?

Success at sports, then, brings recognition from others—and to the self—that one has achieved manly characteristics. This same football player also said,

And then of course all the compliments come—and I began to notice a change, even in my parents—especially in my father—he was proud of that, and that was very important to me. He was extremely important . . . he showed me more affection, now that I think of it.

In other words, success at sports brought recognition, not only from a community of peers, but as Messner found, especially from an often emotionally distant father, who warmed up at his son's success.

Although significant to many boys' self-concepts, intense sports competition can also bring high cost. Messner recounts a haunting scene during his visit to a summer basketball camp headed by a professional basketball coach:

The youngest boys, about eight years old (who could barely reach the basket with their shots) played a brief scrimmage. Afterwards, the coaches lined them up in a row in front of the older boys who were sitting in the grandstands. One by one, the coach would stand behind each boy, put his hand on the boy's head (much in the manner of a priestly benediction), and the older boys in the stands would applaud and cheer, louder or softer, depending on how well or poorly the young boy was judged to have performed. The two or three boys who were clearly the exceptional players looked confident that they would receive the praise they were due. Most of the boys, though, had expressions ranging from puzzlement to thinly disguised terror on their faces as they awaited the judgments of the older boys.*

Messner also noted that the *meaning* of sports success differs by social class. As is well known, many poor people see sports as a way out of poverty. Even though the parents of a poor boy may stress education over sports, his experiences in school and community are likely to *narrow* his perceptions and opportunities. In contrast, although middle-class boys also see sports achievement as highly desirable, it is only one of many options open to their success in life. Consequently, middle-class boys are more easily able to discard sports and to invest energy and self-identity in a future career.

Thinking about the analysis Although there is little controversy about Messner's findings, some of his conclusions are controversial. A common theme, he says, is for boys to use sports as an attempt to overcome insecurity and loneliness, a way to "connect" with other people, especially with fathers. He asserts that "the rule-bound, competitive, hierarchical world of sports offers boys an attractive means of establishing an emotionally distant (and thus 'safe') connection with others." In order to be accepted in the competitive sports world, the boys must become "winners." Thus, they tend to develop a "conditional self-worth," which leads them to construct instrumental (useful, goal-directed, not emotional) relationships with themselves and others. This, in turn, makes it difficult for them to develop intimate relationships, for they try to relate instrumentally to females who are taught to construct identities on meaningful relationships, not competitive success.

Resocialization

What does a woman who has just become a nun have in common with a man who has just divorced? The answer is that they both are undergoing the process of **resocialization**; that is, they are learning new norms, values, attitudes, and behaviors. In its most common form, resocialization occurs each time we learn something contrary to our previous experiences. A new boss who insists on a different way of doing things is resocializing you. Such resocialization is mild, however, ordinarily but a slight modification of procedures already learned.

resocialization: the process of learning new norms, values, attitudes, and behaviors

Resocialization is often a gentle process as we are usually gradually exposed to different ways of thinking and doing. Sometimes, however, it can be sudden and brutal, as with these recruits in basic training. What new values, behaviors, and ways of looking at the world do you think they are learning?

Resocialization can be intense, however. People who join Alcoholics Anonymous (AA), for example, expose themselves to a barrage of testimony about the destructive effects of excessive drinking. Some students also find the process of leaving high school and entering college to be an intense period of resocialization—especially during those initially scary, floundering days before becoming comfortable and fitting in. Even more so are psychotherapy or joining a cult, for they expose people to ideas that conflict with their previous ways of looking at the world. If these ideas "take," not only does the individual's behavior change, but he or she has also learned a fundamentally different way of looking at life.

The Case of Total Institutions

Relatively few of us experience the powerful mechanism Erving Goffman (1961) called the **total institution.** He coined this term to refer to a place in which people are cut off from the rest of society and where they come under almost total control of the officials who run the place. Boot camp, prisons, concentration camps, convents, some religious cults, and some boarding schools, such as West Point, are total institutions.

A person entering a total institution is greeted with a **degradation ceremony** (Garfinkel 1956), an attempt to remake the self by stripping away the individual's current identity and stamping a new one in its place. This may involve fingerprinting, photographing, shaving the head, and banning the person's **personal identity kit** (items such as jewelry, hairstyles, clothing, and other body decorations used to express individuality). Newcomers may be ordered to strip, examined (often in humiliating, semipublic settings), and then given a uniform to designate their new status. (For prisoners, the public reading of the verdict and being led away in handcuffs by armed police also form part of the degradation ceremony.)

Total institutions are extremely effective in stripping away people's personal freedom. They are isolated from the public (the walls, bars, or other barriers not only keep the inmates in but also keep outsiders from interfering). They suppress preexisting statuses (inmates learn that their previous roles such as spouse, parent, worker, or student mean nothing, and that the only thing that counts is their current role). Total institutions suppress the norms of "the outside world," replacing them with their own rules and values, and interpretation of life. They also closely supervise the entire lives of the residents—eating, sleeping, showering, recreation are all standardized. Finally, they control information, helping the institution to shape the inmates' ideas and "picture" of the world. This includes control of rewards and punishment. (Under conditions of deprivation, simple rewards for compliance such as sleep, a television program, a letter from home, a little extra food, or even a cigarette, act as powerful incentives in controlling behavior.) The institution correspondingly holds the power to punish rule breaking—often severely, such as by solitary confinement, or "not seeing" what other inmates do when they want to get even for something.

total institution: a place in which people are cut off from the rest of society and are almost totally controlled by the officials who run the place

degradation ceremony: a term coined by Harold Garfinkel to describe an attempt to remake the self by stripping away an individual's self-identity and stamping a new identity in its place

personal identity kit: items people use to decorate their bodies

No one leaves a total institution unscathed, for the experience leaves an indelible mark on the individual's self that colors the way he or she sees the world. Many people who have gone through boot camp talk about it as one of the most significant experiences of their lives, and as the passing years dim its harshness, may even remember it with fondness. Boot camp is brutal, but swift. Prison, in contrast, is brutal and prolonged, and few former prisoners recall that experience with fondness. Neither recruit nor prisoner, however, has difficulty in pinpointing how the institution affected the self.

Socialization Through the Life Course

Some compare our lives to an empty canvas on which a series of portraits are painted, others to the seasons of the year. Each analogy depicts an image of personal change as we touch, and are touched by, events in which we are immersed. That series of major events, the stages of our lives from birth to death, is called the **life course** (Elder 1975).

The sociological significance of the life course is that *when* you live makes a huge difference for the type of person you become. In addition, social location—such as those of social class, ethnicity, and gender—separates people into different worlds of experience. Consequently, the typical life courses of males and females, the rich and poor, and so on, differ markedly. The "experts" do not agree on a standard division of the life course and have proposed slightly different stages (Levinson 1978; Helson 1984; Baum 1990; Schlossberg 1990). Consequently, the following sketch, a composite of the life courses described by social analysts, provides only a general outline. Each individual's life course may be diverted from "typical" events outlined here due to poor health or late education; different ages at marriage (or not marrying); having children early, late, or not at all; or other "out of sequence" or atypical experiences. See the Down–to–Earth Sociology box on page 85.

The First Stage: Childhood

Like the other developmental points in our lives, childhood (from birth to about age 12) is more than a biological stage. As discussed in the previous chapter, the culture in which we are raised shapes our fundamental orientations to life. Each of us lives in a particular society at some specific point in history, and that social context lays a framework over our biology. Although a child's *biological* characteristics (such as youth and dependency) are universal, the *social* experiences of the child (what others expect of the child) are not. In short, what a child "is" differs from one society to another.

To understand this point better, let's take a look at childhood in the past, so that you can see how different your childhood would have been if you had grown up then. When historian Philippe Ariès (1965) examined European paintings from the Middle Ages, such as the one on this page, he noticed that children were always dressed up in adult clothing. If children were not stiffly posed for a family portrait, they were depicted as engaging in adult activities. Ariès concluded that at that time and in that place childhood was not regarded as a special time of life. Rather, the Europeans considered children miniature adults. Ariès also pointed out that boys were apprenticed at very early ages. At the age of 7, for example, a boy might leave home for good to learn to be a jeweler or a stonecutter. A girl, in contrast, stayed home until she married, but by the age of 7 she had to do her daily share of household tasks.

Childhood also used to be harsh. Another historian, Lloyd DeMause (1975), documented the nightmare of childhood in ages past. To beat children used to be *the norm*. Parents who did not beat their children were considered neglectful of their social duty to keep them off the road to hell. Even teachers were expected to beat their students, and one nineteenth-century German schoolteacher methodically recorded every beating he administered. His record shows 124,000 lashes with a whip, 911,527 hits with a stick, 136,715 slaps with his hand, and 1,115,800 cuffs across the ears. Beating children

In contemporary Western societies such as the United States, children are viewed as innocent and in need of protection from adult demands such as work and self-support. Historically and cross-culturally, however, ideas of childhood vary. For instance, as illustrated by this painting of Sir Walter Raleigh and son (artist unknown), in fifteenth-century Europe children were viewed as miniature adults who assumed adult roles at the earliest opportunity.

life course: the sequence of events that we experience as we journey from birth to death

was so general that even future kings didn't escape brutal punishment. Louis XIII, for example, "was whipped every morning, starting at the age of two, simply for being 'obstinate.'" He was even whipped on the day of his coronation at the age of 9 (McCoy 1985:392).

To keep children in line, parents and teachers also felt it their moral duty to use psychological terror. They would lock children in dark closets for an entire day and frighten them with tales of death and hellfire. It was also common to terrify children into submission by forcing them to witness gruesome events.

> A common moral lesson involved taking children to visit the gibbet [an upraised post on which executed bodies were left hanging from chains], where they were forced to inspect rotting corpses hanging there as an example of what happens to bad children when they grow up. Whole classes were taken out of school to witness hangings, and parents would often whip their children afterwards to make them remember what they had seen. (DeMause 1975)

Obviously, times have changed. To treat a child this way now would horrify the neighbors and land the parents in jail. Young children today are not even allowed to work for wages except in special, highly controlled situations, much less can they be beaten. The current view is that children are tender and "innocent." Parents are expected to guide their physical, emotional, intellectual, and social development while providing them with care, comfort, and protection. Now that is quite a change.

The Second Stage: Adolescence

In earlier centuries, societies did not mark out adolescence (ages 13–17) as a distinct time of life. People simply moved from childhood into young adulthood, with no stopover in between. The Industrial Revolution brought such an abundance of material surpluses, however, that for the first time millions of teenagers were able to remain outside the labor force. At the same time, the demand for education grew. The convergence of these two forces in industrialized societies created a gap between childhood and adulthood. In the early part of this century, the term *adolescence* was coined to indicate this new stage in life (Hall 1904), one that has become renowned for inner turmoil.

Preliterate societies hold initiation rites to ground the self-identity and mark the passage of children into adulthood (Gilmore 1990), but adolescents in the industrialized world must "find" themselves on their own. As they attempt to carve out an identity distinct from both the "younger" world being left behind and the "older" world still out of range, adolescents develop their own standards of clothing, hairstyles, language, and music (McAlexander and Schouten 1989). Although these outward patterns are readily visible, we usually fail to realize that adolescence is a social creation: It is contemporary society, not biological age, that makes these years a period of turmoil.

The Third Stage: Young Adulthood

If society invented adolescence as a special period in life, can it also invent other periods? Historian Kenneth Keniston suggested it could. He noted that industrialized societies seem to be adding a period of prolonged youth to the life course, in which postadolescents (ages 18–29) continue to postpone adult responsibilities and are "neither psychological adolescents nor sociological adults" (Keniston 1960:3). From the end of high school through extended education, including vocational schools, college, and even graduate school, many young adults remain free from adult responsibilities, such as a full-time job, marriage, and home ownership.

Somewhere during this period of extended preparation before "settling down," early adults gradually ease into adult responsibilities. They finish school, take a full-time job, engage in courtship rituals, get married—and go into debt. The self is considerably more stable during the latter part of this period than it was during adolescence.

The Fourth Stage: The Middle Years

The Early Middle Years   During the next period, the early middle years (ages 30–49), most people are much surer of themselves and of their goals in life than before. As with any point in the life course, however, the self can receive severe jolts—in this case from such circumstances as divorce or being fired (Dannefer 1984). It may take years for the self to stabilize after such ruptures.

Because of recent social change, the early middle years pose a special challenge for U.S. women, who increasingly have been given the message, especially by the media, that they can "have it all." They can be superworkers, superwives, and super-moms—all at the same time. During this stage, many women face a reality of too many conflicting pressures, of too many demands to be satisfied, and find that something has to give. Attempts to resolve this dilemma are often compounded by another hard reality—that during gender socialization their husbands learned that child care and housework are not "masculine." In short, adjustments continue in this and all phases of life.

The Later Middle Years   A major characteristic of this period (ages 50–65) is that people attempt to evaluate the past and to come to terms with what lies ahead. They compare what they have accomplished with how far they had hoped to get. Many do not like the gap they see between where they now are and where they had planned to be. Looking at the years ahead, most people conclude that they are not likely to get much farther, that their job or career is likely to consist of "more of the same." During this time of life, many people find themselves caring not only for their own children but also their aging parents. Because of this often crushing set of twin burdens, people in the later middle years are sometimes referred to as the "sandwich generation."

Health and mortality also begin to loom large as individuals feel physical changes in their own bodies and especially if they watch their parents become frail, ill, and die. The consequence is a fundamental reorientation in thinking—*from time since birth to time left to live* (Neugarten 1976). This combination of concerns centering on attainment and mortality is commonly termed the "mid-life crisis." This crisis, if it occurs, is also likely to take place during the later middle years.

Life during this stage, however, is far from filled only with such concerns. Many people find this to be the most comfortable period of their entire lives in which they enjoy job security and a higher standard of living than ever before, a bigger house (perhaps paid for), newer cars, and more exotic vacations. The children are grown, the self is firmly planted, and fewer upheavals are likely to occur.

As they anticipate the next stage of life, most people do not like what they see.

The Fifth Stage: The Older Years

In industrialized societies, this stage begins around the mid-60s. This, too, is recent. People in preindustrial societies had a much shorter life span, and they considered old age to begin in the 40s. They also apparently gave the elderly high respect. Since adult roles changed very little from one generation to the next, the elderly were thought to possess knowledge valuable to the young. The elderly might also hold almost all the wealth and power, which wouldn't exactly hurt their status either.

Our situation today stands in marked contrast to the past. Industrialization brought with it a delay in the onset of old age, and for those in good health being over 65 is often experienced more as an extension of the middle years than being old. This is so particularly for older people who continue to work or to be active in other rewarding social activities (Neugarten 1977). They do not see themselves as old. For people in poor health, however, it is a different story. Beside health and meaningful social activities, some social analysts also see the seventy-fifth and eighty-fifth birthdays as significant markers in perceiving one's own entry into old age (Neugarten 1974). Although frequency of sex declines during this period, most men and women in their 60s and 70s are sexually active (Denney and Quadagno 1992).

During this stage in life, most people "wind down" (Cumming 1976). They retire from work and reduce their involvement in community affairs. Winding down brings the opportunity to participate in activities that replace previous involvements (Keith 1982). For some who can afford it, this means taking trips they only dreamed about when they were younger. For many, it means becoming actively involved in the socialization of their grandchildren or even great-grandchildren.

During this stage of life people also grapple with the idea of their own death. Because we have a self and can reason abstractly, we can contemplate death. Initially death is something vaguely "out there," but as people see their friends die and their own bodies no longer functioning as before, death becomes less abstract. Increasingly, people feel that "time is closing in" on them, and many feel a burning desire to "be remembered," to leave a legacy of some kind, even if it is only a small inheritance to their children.

Down-To-Earth Sociology

Social Change and Your Life Course

DOES THE LIFE COURSE model outlined here adequately picture your past and future? Although this sketch picks up broad features of people's common experiences, and it does pass the sociological test—accounting for how deeply people's lives are grounded in the unique events of their particular society—due to social change your own experiences may differ considerably.

Only a few years ago, for example, an apparently unending economic expansion provocatively beckoned with a cornucopia of opportunities. Abruptly, during the adolescence of today's college students, that picture changed when we entered a worldwide economic downturn and many opportunities closed up. College graduates, who just a few years ago would have been snapped up by recruiters, now dejectedly take jobs in fast food restaurants. Consequently, what this generation experiences at various stages in the life course may differ sharply from the experiences of earlier generations.

So it is with the "big" events of history: political stability or instability, an era of racial-ethnic harmony or of tension and violence, as well as an entire series of "befores" and "afters"—before and after automobiles, television, the Cold War, international satellite transmissions, computers, and so on. Similarly, AIDS will have its own impact on the life course. No longer can college students take for granted that the worst health hazard of sexual experiences is something that can be cured with penicillin. We don't yet know the effects on this generation of the chilling possibility of death in exchange for sexual promiscuity, but its touch on the life course will leave marks not felt by previous generations.

As is apparent, then, the life course is much more than biology (Rossi 1974). As sociologist Glen Elder (1975) put it, "Birth, puberty, and death are biological facts in the life course, but their meanings in society are social facts or constructions." And as sociologist C. Wright Mills (1959) would say, because college recruiters are beating down the door of your school, or failing to do so, you are more inclined to marry, to buy a house, and to start a family—or to postpone these life course events, perhaps indefinitely. A major change in the life course may even now be glimpsed: due to changes in the economy, what was unthinkable in the past may become routine in the present, that of young adults inclined to remain in the security of their parents' home.

Are We Prisoners of Socialization?

From our discussion of socialization, you might conclude that sociologists think of people as little robots: The socialization goes in, and the behavior comes out. People cannot help what they do, think, or feel, for everything is simply a result of their exposure to socializing agents.

Sociologists do *not* think of people in this way. Although socialization is powerful, and profoundly affects us all, we have a self. Laid down in childhood and continually modified by later experience, the self is dynamic. It is not a sponge that passively absorbs influences from the environment but a vigorous, essential part of our being that allows us to act upon our environment (Wrong 1961; Meltzer et al. 1975; Couch 1989).

Indeed, it is precisely because individuals are not little robots that their behavior is so hard to predict. The countless reactions of the many people important to us merge in each person—as discussed earlier, even twins do not receive identical reactions from others. As the self develops, we internalize or "put together" these innumerable reactions, producing a unique whole that we call the individual. And, each unique individual uses his or her own mind to reason and to make choices in life.

In this way, each of us is actively involved in the social construction of the self. For example, although our experiences in the family lay down the basic elements of our personality, including fundamental orientations to life, we are not doomed to keep those orientations if we do not like them. We can purposely expose ourselves to groups and ideas that we prefer. Those experiences, in turn, will have their own effects on our self. In short, in spite of the powerful influences we experience, within the limitations of the framework laid down by society we can change even the self. And that self—along with the options available within society—is the key to our behavior.

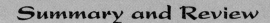

Summary and Review

What Is Human Nature?

How much of our human characteristics come from "nature" (heredity) and how much from "nurture" (the social environment)?

Observations of feral, isolated, and institutionalized children help answer this question, as do experiments with monkeys that have been isolated during infancy. All these studies indicate that language and intimate social interaction—functions of "nurture"—are essential to the development of what we consider to be human characteristics. Pp. 60–65.

The Social Development of Self, Mind, and Emotions

How do we acquire a self?

Humans are born with the *capacity* to develop a **self**, but the self must be socially constructed; that is, its contents depend on social interaction. According to Charles Horton Cooley's concept of the **looking-glass self**, our self develops as we internalize others' reactions to us. George Herbert Mead identified the ability to **take the role of the other** as essential to the development of the self. Mead concluded that even the mind is a social product. Pp. 65–67.

According to Piaget, how do children's thinking processes develop?

Jean Piaget identified four stages that children go through as they develop the ability to reason: (1) *sensorimotor*, in which understanding is limited to sensory stimuli such as touching, seeing, and listening; (2) *preoperational*, the ability to use symbols; (3) *concrete operational*, in which reasoning ability is more complex but not yet capable of complex abstractions; and (4) *formal operational*, abstract thinking. Researchers have also found that emotions develop in an orderly sequence. Pp. 67–68.

How do sociologists evaluate Freud's psychoanalytic theory of personality development?

Freud viewed personality development as the result of self-centered inborn desires, the **id**, clashing with social constraints. The **ego** develops to balance the id as well as the **superego**, the conscience. In contrast, sociologists do not examine inborn and unconscious motivations, but, rather, how social factors—social class, gender, religion, education, and so forth—underlie personality development. Pp. 68–69.

How does socialization influence emotions?

Socialization influences not only *how* we express our emotions, but also *what* emotions we feel. Socialization into emotions is a major means by which society produces conformity. Pp. 69–71.

Socialization into Gender

How does gender socialization affect our sense of self?

Gender socialization—sorting males and females into different roles—is a primary means of controlling human behavior. Children learn **gender roles** beginning in infancy. A society's ideals of sex-linked behaviors are reinforced by its social institutions. Pp. 71–74.

Agents of Socialization

What are the main agents of socialization?

The main agents of socialization are family, religion, school, peer groups, the mass media, sports, and the workplace. Each has its particular influences in socializing us into becoming full-fledged members of society. Pp. 74–80.

Resocialization

What is resocialization?

Resocialization is the process of learning new norms, values, attitudes, and behaviors. Intense resocialization occurs in **total institutions**. Most resocialization is voluntary, but some, as with prisoners, is involuntary. Pp. 80–82.

Socialization Through the Life Course

Does socialization end when we enter adulthood?

Socialization occurs throughout the life course. In industrialized societies, the **life course** can be divided into childhood, adolescence, young adulthood, the early middle years, the later middle years, and old age. Typical patterns include obtaining education, becoming independent from parents, building a career, finding a mate, rearing children, and confronting aging. Life course patterns vary by social location such as gender, ethnicity, and social class, as well as by individual experiences such as health and age at marriage. Social change also modifies the life course. Pp. 82–85.

Are We Prisoners of Socialization?

Although socialization is powerful, we are not merely the sum of our socialization experiences. Just as socialization influences human behavior, so humans act on their environment and influence it. P. 86.

Where can I read more on this topic?

Suggested readings for this chapter are listed on page 638.

Jacob Lawrence, Builders (Green and Red Ball), 1979

Social Structure and Social Interaction

M Y CURIOSITY HAD GOTTEN THE *better of me. When the sociology convention finished, I climbed aboard the first city bus that came along. I didn't know where the bus was going, and I didn't even know where I was going to spend the night.*

"Maybe I overdid it this time," I thought as the bus began winding down streets I had never seen before. Actually, since this was my first visit to Washington, D.C., I hadn't seen any of the streets before. I had no direction, no plans, not even a map. I carried no billfold, just a driver's license shoved into my jeans for emergency identification and a $10 bill tucked into my socks. My goal was simple: If I see something interesting, I'll get off and check it out.

"Nothing but the usual things," I mused, as we passed row after row of apartment buildings and stores. I could see myself riding buses the entire night. Then something caught my eye. Nothing spectacular—just groups of people clustered around a large circular area where several streets intersected.

I climbed off the bus and made my way to what turned out to be Dupont Circle. I took a seat on a sidewalk bench and began to observe. As the scene came into focus, I noted several street corner men drinking and joking with one another. One of the men broke from his companions and sat down next to me. As we talked, I mostly listened.

As night fell, the men said that they wanted to get another bottle of wine. I contributed. They counted their money and asked if I wanted to go with them.

Although I felt a churning inside—emotions combining hesitation and fear—I heard a confident "Sure!" coming out of my mouth. As we left the circle, the three men began to cut through an alley. "Oh, no," I thought. "That's not what I had in mind."

I had but a split second to make a decision. I found myself continuing to walk with the men, but holding back half a step so that none of the three was behind me. As we walked, they passed around the remnants of their bottle. When my turn came, I didn't know what to do. I shuddered to think about the diseases lurking within that bottle. I made another decision. In the semidarkness I faked it, letting only my thumb and forefinger touch my lips and nothing enter my mouth.

When we returned to Dupont Circle, the men finished their new bottle of Thunderbird. I couldn't fake it in the light, so I passed, pointing at my stomach to indicate that I was having problems.

Suddenly one of the men jumped up, smashed the emptied bottle against the sidewalk, and thrust the jagged neck in a menacing gesture. He stared straight ahead at another bench, where he had spotted someone with whom he had some sort of unfinished business. As the other men told him to cool it, I moved slightly to one side of the group—ready to flee, just in case.

Levels of Sociological Analysis

Macrosociology and Microsociology

On this sociological adventure, I almost got myself in over my head. Fortunately, it turned out all right. The man's "enemy" didn't look our way, the broken bottle was set down next to the bench "just in case he needed it," and until dawn I was introduced to a life that up to then I had only read about.

Sociologists Elliot Liebow (1967) and Elijah Anderson (1978) have written fascinating accounts about men like these. Although street corner men may appear to be disorganized, simply coming and going as they please and doing whatever feels good at the moment, these sociologists have analyzed how, like us, these men are also influenced by the norms and beliefs of our society. This will become more apparent as we examine the two levels of analysis that sociologists use.

The first, **macrosociology,** places the focus on broad features of society. Sociologists who use this approach analyze such things as social class and how groups are related to one another. If macrosociologists were to analyze street corner men, for example, they would stress that these men are located at the bottom of the U.S. social class system. Their low status means that many opportunities are closed to them: the men have few skills, little education, hardly anything to offer an employer. As "able-bodied" men, however, they are not eligible for welfare. This means that they must hustle to survive. As a consequence, they spend their lives on the streets.

Conflict theory and functionalism, both of which focus on the broader picture, are examples of this macrosociological approach. In these theories, the goal is to examine the large-scale social forces that influence how groups are organized and positioned within a social system.

The second approach sociologists use is **microsociology.** Here the emphasis is placed on **social interaction,** what people do when they come together. Sociologists who use this approach are likely to focus on the men's survival strategies ("hustles"); their rules for dividing up money, wine, or whatever other resources they have; their relationships with girlfriends, family, and friends; where they spend their time and what they do there; their language; their pecking order; and so on. With its focus on face-to-face interaction, symbolic interactionism is an example of microsociology.

A form of symbolic interactionism that is sometimes used to analyze individual behavior is **exchange theory.** This perspective, developed by sociologist George Homans (1958, 1961), looks at human behavior in terms of rewards and costs. Exchange theorists assume that the basic motivation in human behavior is seeking pleasure and avoiding pain. Thus, people do what they do to gain the maximum rewards (such as money, approval, and recognition) and to minimize costs (such as punishment, withdrawal of approval, loss of money).

With their different emphases, macrosociology and microsociology yield distinctive perspectives, and both are needed to gain a more complete understanding of social life. We cannot adequately understand street corner men, for example, without using macrosociology. It is essential that we place the men within the broad context of how groups in U.S. society are related to one another—for, as with ourselves, the social class of these men helps to shape their attitudes and behavior. Nor can we adequately understand these men without microsociology, for their everyday situations also form a significant part of their lives.

To better grasp these two contrasting approaches in sociology, and their relative contributions to our understanding of social life, let's take a look at each. As we do so, you may find yourself feeling more comfortable with one approach than the other. That is what happens with sociologists. For reasons of personal background and professional training, sociologists find themselves more comfortable with one approach and tend to use it in their research. Both approaches, however, are necessary for a full understanding of life in society.

macrosociology: analysis of social life focusing on broad features of social structure, such as social class and the relationships of groups to one another; an approach usually used by functionalist and conflict theorists

microsociology: analysis of social life focusing on social interaction; an approach usually used by symbolic interactionists

social interaction: what people do when they are in the presence of one another

exchange theory: a theory of behavior that assumes human actions are motivated by a desire to maximize rewards and minimize costs

The Macrosociological Perspective: Social Structure

Why do street people act as they do? Why do most of us avoid them? Why, perhaps, are most of us at least somewhat intimidated by them?

To better understand human behavior, we need to see how social structure *establishes limits on our behavior.* **Social structure** is the framework of society that was already laid out before you were born; it is the patterns of a society, such as the relationships between men and women or students and teachers that characterize a particular society.

Because the term *social structure* may seem vague, consider first how you personally experience social structure in your own life. As I write this, I do not know if you are African American, white, Latino, Native American, Asian American. I do not know

social structure: the relationship of people and groups to one another; the characteristics of groups—all of which give direction to and set limits on behavior

your religion. I do not know if you are young or old, tall or short, male or female. I do not know if you were reared on a farm, in the suburbs, or in the inner city. I do not know if you went to a public high school or an exclusive prep school. But I do know that you are in college. And that, alone, tells me a great deal about you.

From that one piece of information, I can assume that the social structure of your college is now shaping what you do. For example, let us suppose that today you felt euphoric over some great news. I can be fairly certain (not absolutely, mind you, but relatively certain) that when you entered the classroom, social structure overrode your mood. That is, instead of shouting at the top of your lungs and joyously throwing this book into the air, you entered the classroom fairly subdued and took your seat.

The same social structure influences your instructor, even if, on the one hand, he or she is facing a divorce or has a child dying of cancer, or, on the other, has just been awarded a promotion or a million-dollar grant. The instructor may feel like either retreating into seclusion or celebrating wildly, but it is most likely that he or she will conduct class. In short, personal feelings and desires tend to be overridden by social structure.

Just as social structure influences you and your instructor, so it also establishes limits for street people. They, too, find themselves in a specific social location in the U.S. social structure—although it is quite different than your's or your instructor's. Consequently, they are affected differently—and nothing about their social location leads them to take notes or to lecture. Their behaviors are as logical an outcome of where they find themselves in the social structure as are your own. It is just as "natural" in their position in the social structure to drink wine all night as it is for you to stay up studying all night for a crucial examination. It is just as "natural" for you to nod and say, "Excuse me," when you enter a crowded classroom late and have to claim a desk on which someone has already placed books or a coat as it is for them to break off the head of a wine bottle and glare at an enemy.

In short, people learn certain behaviors and attitudes because of their location in the social structure (whether privileged, deprived, or in between), and they act accordingly. This is equally true of street people. *The difference is not in biology (race, sex, or any other supposed genetic influences on behavior), but in people's location in the social structure.* Switch places with street people and watch your behaviors and attitudes change!

To better understand social structure, read the Down-to-Earth Sociology box on page 93. Because social structure so critically affects who we are and what we are like, let us look in turn at each of its major components: culture, social class, social status, roles, groups, and institutions.

Culture

In Chapter 2, we looked in detail at how culture affects us. At this point, let's simply review the main impact of culture, the largest envelope that surrounds us. Sociologists use the term *culture* to refer to a group's language, beliefs, values, behaviors, and even gestures. Culture also includes the material objects used by a group. In short, culture is our social inheritance, what we learn from the people around us. Culture is the broadest framework that determines what kind of people we become. If we are reared in Eskimo, Japanese, Russian, or American culture, we will grow up to be like most Eskimos, Japanese, Russians, or Americans. On the outside, we will look and act like them; and on the inside, we will think and feel like them.

Social Class

social class: a large number of people with similar amounts of income and education who work at jobs that are roughly comparable in prestige

To understand people, we must examine the particular social locations that they hold in life. Especially significant is **social class**, which is based on income, education, and occupational prestige. Large numbers of people who have similar amounts of income and education and who work at jobs that are roughly comparable in prestige make up a **social class.** It is hard to overemphasize this aspect of social structure, for our social class

Down-To-Earth Sociology

College Football as Social Structure

TO GAIN A BETTER idea of what social structure is, think of college football (cf. Dobriner 1969). You know the various positions on the team: center, guards, tackles, ends, quarterback, and running backs. Each is a *status*; that is, each is a recognized social position. For each of these statuses, there is a *role*; that is, each of these positions has particular expectations attached to it. The center is expected to snap the ball, the quarterback to pass it, the guards to block, the tackles to tackle or block, the ends to receive passes, and so on. Those role expectations guide each player's actions; that is, the players try to do what their particular role requires. Since not everyone plays the role in precisely the same way, different *role performances* result. Each quarterback, for example, has a particular "style" of play.

Let's suppose that football is your favorite sport and you never miss a home game at your college. Let's also suppose that you graduate and move across the country. Five years later you return to your campus for a nostalgic visit. The climax of your visit is the biggest football game of the season. When you get to the game, you might be surprised to see a different coach, but you are not surprised that each of the playing positions is occupied by people you don't know.

All the players you knew have graduated, and their places have been filled by others.

This scenario mirrors *social structure*, which is the framework around which a group exists. In this football example, that framework consists of the coaching staff and the eleven playing positions. The game does not depend on any particular individual, but rather on the positions that the individuals occupy. When someone leaves a position, the game can go on because someone else takes over the position and plays the role. The game will continue even though not a single individual remains the same from one period of time to the next. Notre Dame's football team endures today even though Knute Rockne, the gipper, and his teammates are long dead.

Even though you may not play football, you nevertheless live your life within a clearly established social structure. Society determines the statuses, roles, and so on, that its members will play—and when you were born, these essential components of social structure were already in place. You take your particular positions in life, others do the same, and society goes about its business. Although the specifics change with time, the game—whether of life or of football—goes on.

heavily influences not only our behaviors but even our ideas and attitudes. We have this in common, then, with the street people described in the opening vignette—both they and we are influenced by our location in the social class structure. Theirs may be a considerably less privileged position, but it is no less influential to their experience. Social class is so significant that we shall spend an entire chapter (Chapter 10) examining social classes in the United States.

Sociologists use two levels of analysis to study social life—macrosociology and microsociology. When studying street corner men, or the homeless or other social phenomena, sociologists who use the macrosociological approach study how broad forces, such as the economy and the system of social class operating in a society, contribute to existing conditions. Sociologists who use the microsociological approach to study social life analyze how people interact in everyday situations.

Each of us occupies several statuses. Among the statuses of Princess Diana are wife, mother, and Princess of Wales. Because she married into the Royal Family, her status as Princess of Wales is an achieved rather than an ascribed status. If she and Prince Charles divorce, she will lose this ascribed status and add others, among them those of divorcee, former Princess, and former wife. The woman touching Princess Diana's feet is a member of the Untouchable caste in India. Her caste status is ascribed, or involuntary.

status: the position that someone occupies in society or a social group

status set: all the statuses or positions that an individual occupies

ascribed statuses: positions an individual either inherits at birth or receives involuntarily later in life

achieved statuses: positions that are earned, accomplished, or involve at least some effort or activity on the individual's part

status symbols: items used to identify a status

Social Status

When you hear the word *status*, you are likely to think of prestige. These two words are welded together in common thinking. Sociologists, however, use **status** in a different way: to refer to the position that an individual occupies. That position may have a great deal of prestige, as in the case of a judge or an astronaut, or it may carry very little prestige, as in the case of a gas station attendant or a hamburger flipper at a fast-food restaurant. The status may also be looked down on, as in the case of a street corner man, an ex-convict, or a bag lady.

All of us occupy several positions at the same time. You may be simultaneously a son or daughter, a worker, a date, and a student. Sociologists use the term **status set** to refer to all the statuses or positions that you occupy. Obviously your status set changes as your particular statuses change; for example, if you graduate from college and take a full-time job, get married, buy a home, have children, and so on, your status set changes to include the positions of worker, spouse, homeowner, and parent.

The significance of statuses is that, like other aspects of social structure, they are part of our basic framework of living in society. The example given earlier of students and teachers doing what others expect of them in spite of their temporary moods is an illustration of how statuses affect our actions—and those of the people around us. Our statuses—whether daughter or son, worker or date—serve as guides for our behavior.

Ascribed Statuses and Achieved Statuses   The first type, **ascribed statuses,** are involuntary. You do not ask for them, nor can you choose them. Some you inherit at birth such as your race, sex, and the social class of your parents, as well as your statuses as female or male, daughter or son, niece or nephew, and granddaughter or grandson. Others are given to you later in life. These are related to the life course discussed in Chapter 3, the ages that give us such labels as teenager, young adult, middle aged, and so on.

The second type, **achieved statuses,** are voluntary. These you earn or accomplish. As a result of your efforts you become a student, a friend, a spouse, a rabbi, minister, priest, or nun. Or, for lack of effort (or efforts that others fail to appreciate), you become a school dropout, a former friend, an ex-spouse, or a defrocked rabbi, priest, or nun. In other words, achieved statuses can be either positive or negative; both college president and bank robber represent achieved statuses.

The significance of social statuses for understanding human behavior is that each status provides guidelines for how people are to act and feel. Like other aspects of social structure, they set limits on what people can and cannot do. Because social statuses are an essential part of the social structure, they are found within all human groups.

Status Symbols   People who are very pleased with their particular social status may want others to recognize that they occupy that status. To gain this recognition, they use **status symbols,** signs that identify a status. For example, people wear wedding rings to announce their marital status; uniforms, guns, and badges to proclaim that they are police officers (and to not so subtly let you know that their status gives them authority over you); and "backward" collars to declare that they are Lutheran ministers or Roman Catholic or Episcopalian priests.

Some social statuses are negative, and so, therefore, are their status symbols. The scarlet letter in Nathaniel Hawthorne's book by the same title is one example. Another is the CONVICTED DUI bumper sticker that some U.S. counties require convicted drunk drivers to display if they wish to avoid a jail sentence.

All of us use status symbols to announce our statuses to others and to help smooth our interactions in everyday life. You might consider your own status symbols. For example, how does your clothing announce your statuses of sex, age, and college student?

Master statuses overshadow our other statuses. Shown here is Stephen Hawking, who is severely disabled by Lou Gehrig's disease. For many, his master status is that of a disabled person. Because Hawking is one of the greatest physicists who has ever lived, his astounding accomplishments have given him another status, that of world-class physicist in the ranking of Einstein. Thus, Hawking occupies two master statuses simultaneously, the one ascribed and the other achieved.

Master Statuses   A **master status** is one that cuts across the other statuses that you hold. Some master statuses are ascribed. An example is your sex. Whatever you do, people perceive you as a male or as a female. If you are working your way through college by flipping burgers, people see you not only as a burger flipper and a student but as a *male* or *female* burger flipper and a *male* or *female* college student. Other master statuses are race and age.

Some master statuses are achieved. If you become very, very wealthy (and it does not matter if your wealth comes from an invention or the lottery—it is still *achieved* as far as sociologists are concerned), your wealth is likely to become a master status. No matter what else, people are likely to say, "She is a very rich burger flipper." (Or more likely, "She's very rich, and she used to flip burgers!")

Similarly, individuals who become disabled or disfigured find, to their dismay, that their condition becomes a master status. For example, a person whose face is extremely scarred, will be viewed through this unwelcome master status no matter what the individual's occupation or accomplishments. Persons confined to wheelchairs can attest to how "disabled" becomes a master status, how it overrides all their other statuses and determines others' perceptions of everything they do.

Although our statuses usually fit together fairly well, sometimes a contradiction or mismatch between statuses occurs; this is known as **status inconsistency.** A 14-year-old college student is an example of status inconsistency. So is a 40-year-old married woman on a date with a 19-year-old college sophomore.

From these examples you can understand an essential aspect of social statuses: Like other components of social structure, they come with a set of built-in *norms* (that is, expectations) that provide guidelines for behavior. When statuses mesh well, as they usually do, we know what to expect of people. Status inconsistency, however, upsets our expectations. In the preceding examples, how are you supposed to act? Are you supposed to treat the 14-year-old as you would a teenager or as you would your college classmate? The married woman as the mother of your friend or as a classmate's date?

Roles

All the world's a stage
And all the men and women merely players.
They have their exits and their entrances;
And one man in his time plays many parts . . .
  William Shakespeare, *As You Like It*, Act II, Scene 7

master status: a status that cuts across the other statuses that an individual occupies

status inconsistency: a contradiction or mismatch between statuses

Like Shakespeare, sociologists, too, see roles as essential to social life. When you were born, **roles**—the behaviors, obligations, and privileges attached to a status—were already set up for you. Society was waiting with outstretched arms to teach you how it expected you to act as a boy or a girl. And whether you were born poor, rich, or somewhere in between, certain behaviors, obligations, and privileges were attached to your statuses.

The difference between role and status is that you *occupy* a status, but you *play* a role (Linton 1936). For example, being a son or daughter is your status, but your right to receive food and shelter from your parents—as well as their expectations that you show respect to them—is your role.

Our roles are a sort of fence that helps keep us doing what society wants us to do. That fence leaves us a certain amount of freedom, but for most of us that freedom doesn't go very far. Suppose a female decides that she is not going to wear dresses—or a male that he will not wear suits and ties—regardless of what anyone says. In most situations they probably won't. When a formal occasion comes along, however, such as a family wedding or a funeral, they are likely to cave in to norms that they find overwhelming. Almost all of us stay within the fences that mark out what is "appropriate" for our roles. Most of us are little troubled by such constraints, for our socialization is so thorough that we usually *want* to do what our roles indicate is appropriate.

The sociological significance of roles is that they are an essential component of culture. They lay out what is expected of people, and as individuals throughout society perform their roles, those roles mesh together to form this thing called society. As Shakespeare put it, people's roles provide "their exits and their entrances" on the stage of life. In short, roles are remarkably effective at keeping people in line—telling them when they should "enter" and when they should "exit," as well as what to do in between.

The section on social interaction will examine roles in more detail. For now, let us turn to groups, another major component of social structure.

Groups

A **group** consists of people who regularly and consciously interact with one another. Ordinarily, the members of a group share similar values, norms, and expectations. Just as our actions are influenced by our social class, statuses, and roles, so, too, the groups to which we belong represent powerful forces in our lives. In fact, *to belong to a group is to yield to others the right to make certain decisions about our behavior.* If we belong to a group, we assume an obligation to act according to the expectations of other members of that group.

Although this principle holds true for all groups, some groups wield influence only over small segments of our behavior. If you belong to a stamp club, for example, the group's influence probably extends to your attendance at meetings and display of knowledge about

role: the behaviors, obligations, and privileges attached to a status

group: people who regularly and consciously interact with one another

Social groups to which we choose to belong are called voluntary memberships. How many voluntary memberships do you have? To count, they need not be formal organizations, for informal groups, such as a group of friends, are also voluntary memberships.

stamps. Other groups, however, control many aspects of our behavior. The family is an example. When parents say to their 15-year-old daughter, "As long as you are living under my roof, you had better be home by midnight," they show their expectation that their children, as members of the family, will conform to their ideas about many aspects of life, in this instance their views on curfew. They are saying that so long as the daughter wants to remain a member of the household her behavior must conform to their expectations.

To belong to any group is to relinquish to others at least *some* control over our lives. Those social groups that provide little option to belong are called **involuntary memberships** (or involuntary associations). These include our family and the sexual, ethnic, and racial groups into which we are born. Groups to which we choose to belong are called **voluntary memberships** (or voluntary associations). These include the scouts, professional associations, church groups, clubs, and work groups. If we want to remain members in good standing, we must conform to what people in those groups expect of us. Both voluntary and involuntary memberships are vital in affecting who we are, for our participation in them shapes our ideas and orientations to life.

Social Institutions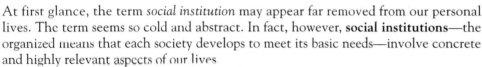

At first glance, the term *social institution* may appear far removed from our personal lives. The term seems so cold and abstract. In fact, however, **social institutions**—the organized means that each society develops to meet its basic needs—involve concrete and highly relevant aspects of our lives.

Sociologists have identified nine social institutions common to all societies. These include the family and religious, legal, political, economic, educational, medical, scientific, and military institutions. In industrialized societies, these are highly developed separate institutions, while in preliterate societies they are less developed and more informal. In industrialized societies, for example, the social institution of education is highly structured, while in preliterate societies education may consist of informally learning expected roles. Figure 4.1 on the next page summarizes the basic social institutions. Note that each institution has its own set of roles, values, and norms. Part IV of this text focuses on social institutions. For now, let's look at an emerging social institution.

The Mass Media: An Emerging Social Institution   Although not all sociologists agree, the **mass media** can be considered an emerging social institution, as shown on Figure 4.1. Although there is considerable disagreement concerning the media's exact influences, few parts of our lives remain untouched by them. Far beyond serving simply as sources of information, the media also influence our attitudes toward social issues, other people, and even our self-concept. Because the media are such significant shapers of public opinion, all totalitarian governments attempt to maintain tight control over them.

The mass media are a relatively recent historical development, owing their origins to the invention of the printing press in the 1400s. This invention had immediate and profound consequences on virtually all other social institutions. The printing of the Bible altered religion, for instance, while the publication of political broadsides and newspapers dramatically altered politics. From these beginnings, a series of inventions— from radio and movies to television and, more recently, the microchip—have made the media an increasingly powerful force.

Indeed, one of the most significant questions we can ask about this new social institution is, Who controls it? That control, which in totalitarian countries is obvious, is much less visible in democratic nations. From a functionalist perspective, we might conclude that the media in a democratic nation represent the varied interests of the many groups that make up that nation. Conflict theorists, however, would see a different scenario: the mass media—at least a country's most influential newspapers and television stations—represent the interests of the political elite, the wealthy and powerful who use the media to mold public opinion.

involuntary memberships: (or involuntary associations) groups in which people are assigned membership rather than choosing to join

voluntary memberships: (or voluntary associations) groups that people choose to join

social institutions: the organized, usual, or standard ways by which society meets its basic needs

Social Institution	Basic Needs	Some Groups or Organizations	Some Values	Some Roles	Some Norms
Family	Regulate reproduction, socialize and protect children	Relatives, kinship groups	Sexual fidelity, providing for your family, keeping a clean house, respect for parents	Daughter, son, father, mother, brother, sister, aunt, uncle, grandparent	Have only as many children as you can afford; be faithful to your spouse
Religion	Concerns about life after death, the meaning of suffering and loss; desire to connect with the Creator	Congregation, synagogue, denomination, charitable association	Reading and adhering to holy texts such as the Bible, Koran, and the Torah; honoring God	Priest, minister, rabbi, worshipper, teacher, disciple, missionary, prophet, convert	Attend worship services, contribute money, follow the teachings
Law	Maintain social order	Police, courts, prisons	Trial by one's peers, innocence until proven guilty	Police officer, lawyer, judge, defendant, prison guard	Give true testimony, follow the rules of evidence
Politics	Establish a hierarchy of power and authority	Political parties, congresses, parliaments, monarchies	Majority rule, the right to vote as a sacred trust	President, senator, lobbyist, spin doctor, candidate	One vote per person, voting as privilege and right
Economics	Produce and distribute goods and services	Credit unions, banks, credit bureaus, buying clubs	Making money, paying bills on time, producing efficiently	Worker, boss, buyer, seller, creditor, debtor, advertiser	Maximize profits, "the customer is always right," work hard
Education	Transmit knowledge and skills across the generations	School, college, student senate, sports team, PTA	Academic honesty, good grades, being "cool"	Teacher, student, dean, principal, football player, cheerleader	Do homework, prepare lectures, don't snitch on classmates
Science	Master the environment	Local, state, regional, national, and international associations	Unbiased research, open dissemination of research findings	Scientist, researcher, technician, administrator	Follow scientific method, fully disclose research findings
Medicine	Heal the sick and injured, care for the dying	AMA, hospitals, pharmacies, insurance companies	Hippocratic oath, staying in good health, following doctor's orders	Doctor, nurse, patient, pharmacist, medical insurer	Don't exploit patients, give best medical care available
Military	Protection from enemies, support of national interests	Army, navy, air force, marines, coast guard, national guard	To die for one's country is an honor, obedience unto death	Soldier, recruit, enlisted person, officer, prisoner, spy	Be ready to go to war, obey superior officers, don't question orders
Mass Media (An emerging institution?)	Disseminate information, mold public opinion, report events	Television networks, radio stations, publishers	Timeliness, accuracy, large audiences, freedom of the press	Journalist, newscaster, author, editor, publisher	Be accurate, fair, timely, and profitable

Figure 4-1

Social Institutions in Industrialized Societies

Since the mass media are so influential, the answer to this question of control is of more than passing interest, and further sociological research on it can contribute to our better understanding of contemporary society.

Comparing Functionalist and Conflict Perspectives

To understand social institutions is to realize how profoundly social structure affects our lives. Much of their influence lies beyond our ordinary awareness. For example, because of our economic institution, we consider it normal to work 8 hours a day for five days every week. There is nothing natural about this pattern, however. Its regularity is only an arbitrary arrangement for dividing work and leisure. Yet this one aspect of a single social institution has far-reaching effects on how we structure our free time and activities, how we deal with our family and friends, how we meet our personal needs and nonwork obligations, and even how we view our own place in society as a whole.

Each of the other social institutions has similarly far-reaching effects on our lives. By weaving the fabric of society, they establish the context in which we live, shaping almost everything that is of concern to us. Social institutions are so significant that if our institutions were different, we, too, would be different people. We certainly could not remain the same, for social institutions influence our ideas and attitudes and other orientations to the social world, and even to life itself.

Let us compare the functionalist and conflict perspectives on this vital aspect of social life.

The Functionalist Perspective   Functionalists stress that social institutions exist because they perform vital functions for society. No society, they point out, is without social institutions. A group may be too small to have people specializing in education or the military, but it will have its own established ways of teaching skills and ideas to the young, and it will have some mechanism of self-defense. Every society must meet its basic needs (or **functional requisites**) to survive; and according to functionalists, that is the purpose of social institutions.

What are those basic needs? Functionalists have identified five functional requisites that each society must fulfill if it is to survive (Aberle et al. 1950; Mack and Bradford 1979).

1 *Replacing members.* If a society does not replace its members, it cannot continue to exist. Because reproduction is so fundamental to a society's existence, and there is such a vital need to protect infants and children, all groups have developed some version of the family. The family also functions to control people's sex drive and to maintain orderly reproduction. The family also gives the newcomer to society a sense of belonging by providing a "lineage," an account of how he or she is related to others.

2 *Socializing new members.* People who are born into a human group must also be taught what it means to be a full-fledged member. To accomplish this, each human group establishes elaborate devices to ensure that its newcomers learn the group's basic expectations. As the primary "bearer of culture," the family is essential to this process, but other social institutions, such as religion and education, aid in meeting this functional requisite.

3 *Producing and distributing goods and services.* Every human group must obtain and distribute basic resources, from food and clothing to shelter and education. Consequently, every society establishes an *economic* institution, a means of producing such resources along with routine ways to distribute them.

4 *Preserving order.* Societies face two threats of disorder: one internal, the potential of chaos, and the other external, the possibility of being conquered. To defend themselves against external conquest, they develop some means of defense, some form of

functional requisites: the major tasks that a society must fulfill if it is to survive

the military. To protect themselves from internal threat, they develop some system of policing themselves, ranging from formal organizations of armed groups to informal systems of gossip.

5   *Providing a sense of purpose.* For people to cooperate with one another and willingly give up self-centered, short-term gains in favor of working with and for others, they need a sense of purpose. They need to be convinced that it is worth sacrificing for the common good. Human groups develop various ways of establishing such belief systems, but a primary one is religion, which attempts to answer questions about ultimate meaning. All of a society's institutions are actually involved in meeting this functional requisite, for the family provides one part of an interrelated set of answers about the sense of purpose, the school another, and so on.

The Conflict Perspective   Although conflict theorists agree that social institutions were originally designed to meet basic survival needs, they do not see social institutions as working harmoniously for the common good. On the contrary, conflict theorists stress that a society's institutions are controlled by an elite that manipulates them in order to maintain its own privileged position of wealth and power (Domhoff 1983, 1990, 1991; Useem 1988).

As evidence of their position, conflict theorists point out that a fairly small group of people has garnered the lion's share of the nation's wealth. Members of this elite sit on the boards of major corporations and of the country's most prestigious universities. They make strategic campaign contributions to control the nation's lawmakers, and it is they who make the major decisions in this society: to go to war or to refrain from war, to raise or to lower taxes, to raise or to lower interest rates, to pass laws that favor or impede moving capital, technology, and jobs out of the country.

Feminist sociologists (both female and male) have used conflict theory to gain a better understanding of how social institutions affect gender relations. Their basic insight is that gender, too, is an element of social structure, not simply a characteristic of individuals (Hess 1990). In other words, throughout the world social institutions separate males and females into separate groups that have unequal access to their society's resources.

Functional theorists have identified five key functional requisites for the survival of a society. One, providing a sense of purpose, is often met through religion. To most people, snake handling, as in this church service in Jolo, West Virginia, is nonsensical. From a functional perspective, however, it makes a great deal of sense. Can you identify its sociological meaning?

Watching the nightly news or reading the daily headlines can make one wonder if society is falling (or flying) apart. To ask what holds society together is to ask a basic sociological question. As indicated in the text, one indication of a Gesellschaft *society is the use of formal means of social control.*

▼ **In Sum**   Conflict theorists regard our social institutions as having a single primary purpose—to preserve the social order—which they interpret as preserving the wealthy and powerful in their privileged positions. Functionalists, in contrast, view social institutions as working together to meet universal human needs.

Changes in Social Structure

This enveloping system that we call social structure, which so powerfully affects our lives, is not static. Our culture changes as it responds to new technology, to innovative ideas from home and abroad, and to evolving values. Culture contact, so extensive in this era of "globalization," brings us into significant contact with the customs of other people, exerting profound changes in our basic orientations to life. Nor do social classes remain immune to the winds of change, for growth and contraction in the economy move people in and out of positions of relative privilege, while shifting relationships between racial and ethnic groups also bring with them changes in relative power and prestige. Similarly, groups that did not exist, such as the IRS, come into being, and afterward wield extraordinary power over our lives.

What Holds Society Together?

As is discussed in depth in Chapter 6, sociologists define *society* as a people who share a culture and a territory. If a society contains many different groups and undergoes extensive social change, how does it manage to stay together? Many sociologists have grappled with this question. Let us examine two main answers their efforts have yielded.

Mechanical and Organic Solidarity   Sociologist Emile Durkheim (1893, 1933) found the key to **social cohesion**—the degree to which members of a society feel united by shared values and other social bonds—in what he called **mechanical solidarity.** By this term Durkheim meant that people develop a collective consciousness when they perform the same or similar tasks. Think of an agricultural society, in which everyone is involved in planting, cultivating, and harvesting. Members of this group have so much

social cohesion: the degree to which members of a group or a society feel united by shared values and other social bonds

mechanical solidarity: a shared consciousness that people experience as a result of performing the same or similar tasks

in common that it is possible for them to know what most others feel like. This shared consciousness, or sense of a similar identity and fate, unites them into a common whole.

As societies increase in size, however, their **division of labor** (how they divide up tasks) becomes more specialized. Instead of almost everyone doing the same jobs, some become jewelers, while others become artists, authors, shopkeepers, soldiers, and so on. Rather than splitting society apart, however, the division of labor makes people depend on one another—for the activities of each contribute to the welfare of the whole. Durkheim called this new form of solidarity based on interdependence **organic solidarity.** To see why he used this term, think about how you depend on your teacher to guide you through this introductory course in sociology, just as your teacher depends on you and other students to keep his or her job. The two of you are like organs in the same body. Although each of you performs different tasks, your dependence on one another creates a form of unity.

Due to the change from mechanical to organic solidarity, people no longer cooperate with one another because they *feel* alike (mechanical solidarity), but because they *depend* on one another's activities for their own survival (organic solidarity). In the past, societies tolerated little diversity in thinking and attitudes, for their unity depended on similar thinking. With this change to organic solidarity, modern societies can tolerate many differences among people and still manage to work as a whole. Note that both past and present societies are based on social solidarity but that the types of solidarity are remarkably different in each case.

Gemeinschaft and Gesellschaft   Ferdinand Tönnies (1887/1988) also saw a new type of society emerging. Tönnies used the term *Gemeinschaft* (Guh-MINE-shoft), "intimate community," to describe the traditional type of society in which life is intimate, a community in which everyone knows everyone else and people share a sense of togetherness. In such a society people toe the line because they are acutely sensitive to the opinions of others and know that if they deviate, others will gossip and damage their reputation. Although their lives are sharply controlled by the opinions of others, they draw comfort from being part of an intimate group.

Tönnies saw that industrialization was tearing at this intimate fabric of village life. He noted that this new society was made up increasingly of strangers and impersonal, short-term relationships. In it, personal ties, family connections, and lifelong friendships were growing less important. Instead, individual accomplishments and self-interests were

division of labor: the splitting of a group's or a society's tasks into specialties

organic solidarity: solidarity based on the interdependence brought about by the division of labor

Gemeinschaft: a type of society in which life is intimate; a community in which everyone knows everyone else and people share a sense of togetherness

Modern societies, in which people live and work among strangers, are largely Gesellschaft in nature. Many would argue that even though the United States and France are both highly industrialized nations, the United States is more thoroughly Gesellschaft than France. In France many people continue to live in small rural villages, where they gather to socialize in neighborhood cafes. Such cafes represent a perpetuation of Gemeinschaft society.

being emphasized. Tönnies called this new type of society **Gesellschaft** (Guh-ZELL-shoft), "impersonal association." As much as anyone might hate it, in *Gemeinschaft* society informal mechanisms such as gossip had been effective in controlling people. In this new world of *Gesellschaft*, however, gossip was of little use, and to keep people in line society had to depend on more *formal* agencies, such as the police and courts.

▽   **In Sum**   Both Durkheim and Tönnies documented a fundamental change in the social structure. What they regretfully noted was the passing of a major form of social life, one unlikely ever to be seen again. Note that whether the terms used are *Gemeinschaft* and *Gesellschaft* or *mechanical solidarity* and *organic solidarity*, they indicate that social structure sets limits on what we do, feel, and think. In short, social structure is at the basis of what kind of people we become. The Perspectives box on page 104 describes one of the few remaining *Gemeinschaft* societies in the United States.

The Microsociological Perspective: Social Interaction in Everyday Life

While the macrosociological approach stresses the broad features of society, the microsociological approach has a narrower focus, placing its emphasis on *face-to-face social interaction*, or what people do when they are in the presence of one another.

Symbolic Interaction

For symbolic interactionists, the most significant part of life in society is social interaction. Symbolic interactionists are especially interested in the symbols that people use to define their worlds. They want to know how people look at things and how that, in turn, affects their behavior.

Stereotypes in Everyday Life   You are familiar with how first impressions "set the tone" for interaction. When you first meet someone, you cannot help but notice certain highly visible and distinctive features, such as the person's sex, race, age, and physical appearance. Despite your best intentions, your first impressions are shaped by the assumptions you make about such characteristics (Snyder 1991). You probably also know that these assumptions affect not only your ideas about the person, but also how you act toward that person.

Mark Snyder, a psychologist, wondered if **stereotypes**—the assumptions we make of what people are like—might be self-fulfilling. He noted that our reactions to people are shaped by our stereotypes, and he began to wonder if those reactions might actually produce behaviors that match the stereotype. He came up with an ingenious way to test this idea. He (1991) gave a number of college men a Polaroid snapshot of a woman, supposedly taken just moments before, and told them that they would be introduced to her after they talked with her on the telephone. Actually, the photograph, which showed either a physically attractive or unattractive woman, had been prepared before the experiment began. The one given to the subject had been chosen at random.

Stereotypes of physical attractiveness came into play even before the men spoke to the women they were going to meet. As Snyder gave each man the photograph, he asked him what he thought the woman would be like. The men who had been given the photograph of an attractive woman said they expected to meet a poised, humorous, outgoing woman. The men who had been given a photo of an unattractive woman described the person they were going to meet as awkward, serious, and unsociable.

These stereotypes then influenced the men's behavior. As each man talked on the telephone to the woman he was expecting to meet, the stereotype affected his style of getting acquainted. Men who had seen the photograph of an attractive woman were

Gesellschaft: a type of society dominated by impersonal relationships, individual accomplishments, and self-interest

stereotype: assumptions of what people are like, based on previous associations with them or with people who have similar characteristics, or based on information, whether true or false

▼▲▼▲▼▲▼▲▼▲▼▲▼▲▼▲▼▲▼▲▼▲▼▲▼▲▼▲▼▲▼▲▼

Perspectives

CULTURAL DIVERSITY IN U.S. SOCIETY

The Amish—Gemeinschaft Community in a Gesellschaft Society

U.S. SOCIETY EXHIBITS ALL the characteristics Ferdinand Tönnies identified as those of a *Gesellschaft* society. Impersonal associations pervade everyday life. Local, state, and federal governments regulate many activities. Impersonal corporations hire people not based on long-term, meaningful relationships, but on their value to the bottom line. Similarly, when it comes to firing workers, the bottom line takes precedence over personal relationships. And, perhaps even more significantly, millions of Americans do not even know their neighbors.

Within the United States, a handful of small communities exhibit characteristics that depart from those of the larger society. One such example is the Old Order Amish, followers of a sect that broke away from the Swiss-German Mennonite church in the late 1600s, settling in Pennsylvania around 1727. Today, more than 130,000 Old Order Amish live in the United States. The largest concentration, about 14,000, reside in Lancaster County, Pennsylvania. The Amish can also be found in about twenty other states and in Ontario, Canada, but 75 percent live in just three states: Pennsylvania, Ohio, and Indiana. The Amish, who believe that birth control is wrong, have doubled in size in just the past two decades.

To the nearly five million tourists that pass through Lancaster County each year, the quiet pastures and almost identical white farmhouses, simple barns, horse- or mule-drawn carts, and clothes flapping on lines to dry convey a sense of peace and wholeness reminiscent of another era. Although just sixty-five miles from Philadelphia, "Amish country" is a world away.

The Amish faith rests on separation from the world, taking Christ's Sermon on the Mount literally, and obedience to the church's teachings and leaders. This rejection of worldly concerns, Donald Kraybill writes in *The Riddle of Amish Culture*, "provides the foundation of such Amish values as humility, faithfulness, thrift, tradition, communal goals, joy of work, a slow-paced life, and trust in divine providence."

The village life that Tönnies identified as fostering *Gemeinschaft* communities—and which he correctly predicted was fast being lost to industrialization—is very much alive among the Amish. The Amish make their decisions in weekly meetings, where, by consensus, they follow a set of rules, or *Ordnung,* to guide their behavior. Religion and the discipline that it calls for are the glue that holds these communities together. Brotherly love and the welfare of the community are paramount values. Most Amish farm plots of one hundred acres or less, keeping their farms small so that horses can be used instead of tractors and neighbors can pitch in with the chores. In these ways, intimacy—a sense of community—is maintained.

The Amish are bound by many other communal ties, including language (a dialect of German known as Pennsylvania Dutch), a distinctive style of plain dress that has remained unchanged for almost three hundred years, and church-sponsored schools. Nearly all Amish marry, and divorce is forbidden. The family is a vital ingredient in Amish life; all major events take place in the home, including weddings and worship services, even births and funerals. Most Amish children attend church schools only until the age of 13. To go to school beyond the eighth grade would expose them to "worldly concerns" and give them information considered of no value to farm life. The Amish pay local, state, and federal taxes, but they pool their resources to fund their own welfare system, and therefore do not pay Social Security taxes. They won the right to be left out of the Social Security system only after drawn-out court battles. They believe that all violence is bad, even in personal self-defense, and register as conscientious objectors during times of war.

The Amish cannot resist all change, of course. Instead, they attempt to adapt to social change in ways that will cause the least harm to their core values. Because of the high cost of land due to urbanization, about 30 percent of married Amish men work at jobs other than farming, most in farm-related businesses, cottage industries, and woodworking trades. They go to great lengths to avoid leaving the home. The Amish believe that when the husband works away from the home, all aspects of life, from the marital relationship to the care of the children, seem to change—certainly an excellent sociological insight. They also believe that if a man receives a paycheck he will think that his work is of more value than his wife's. For the Amish, intimate, or *Gemeinschaft,* society is absolutely essential to their way of life.

Sources: Hostetler 1980; Kraybill 1989; Bender 1990; Jones 1990; Raymond 1990; Ruth 1990; Ziegenhals 1991; Kephart and Zellner 1994.

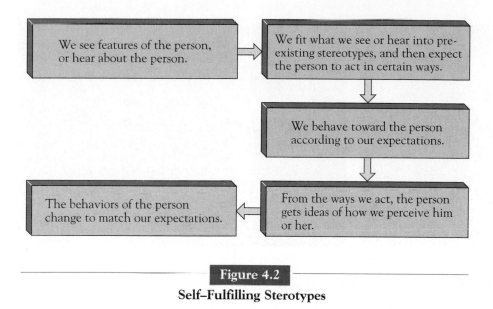

| We see features of the person, or hear about the person. | We fit what we see or hear into pre-existing stereotypes, and then expect the person to act in certain ways. |

| We behave toward the person according to our expectations. |

| The behaviors of the person change to match our expectations. | From the ways we act, the person gets ideas of how we perceive him or her. |

Figure 4.2

Self–Fulfilling Sterotypes

warm, friendly, humorous, and highly animated. Those who had seen the photograph of an unattractive woman were cold, reserved, and humorless.

These differences, in turn, affected the women's behavior. Those who (unknown to them) were believed to be attractive responded to the men in a warm, friendly, and sociable manner, while those who were perceived as physically unattractive became cool, reserved, and humorless. In short, *stereotypes tend to bring out the very kinds of behavior that fit the stereotype.*

A number of experiments have been conducted to see how stereotypes of gender, race, ability, and intelligence influence people (Snyder 1991). In one, a welding instructor in a vocational training center was told that five men in his training program had an unusually high aptitude for welding. Although the five had actually been chosen at random and knew nothing about the experiment, the effects were dramatic. These men were absent less often than other trainees, learned the basics of welding in about half the usual time, and scored ten points higher than the other men on their final welding test. The difference was noted even by the other trainees, who singled these five out as their preferred co-workers. The men were no different in their initial abilities, but the instructor's behavior brought about a change in their performance.

In sum, people's stereotypes influence their expectations and behaviors which, in turn, tend to *produce behaviors that conform to the stereotypes.* (This principle is illustrated in Figure 4.2.)

Personal Space Symbolic interactionists also study how people use personal space. Each of us surrounds ourself with a "personal bubble" that we go to great lengths to protect. We open the bubble to intimates—to close friends, children, parents, and so on—but are careful to keep most people out of this space. In the hall, we might walk with books clasped in front of us (a strategy often chosen by females); we carefully line up at the drinking fountain, making certain there is space between us so we don't touch the person in front of us, and we aren't touched by the person behind us.

At times we extend our personal space. In the library, for example, you may place your coat on the chair next to you—claiming that space for yourself even though you are not using it. If you want to really extend your space, you might even spread books in front of the other chairs, keeping the whole table to yourself by giving the impression that others have just stepped away.

Among the many aspects of social life that sociologists with a microsociological focus study is personal space. What do you see in common in the above two photos?

Anthropologist Edward Hall (1959, 1966) studied the use of personal space in several cultures. He found that the amount of space people prefer varies from one culture to another. South Americans, for example, like to be closer when they speak to others than do people reared in the United States. Hall (1959) recounts a conversation with a man from South America who had attended one of his lectures.

> He came to the front of the class at the end of the lecture to talk over a number of points made in the preceding hour. . . . We started out facing each other and as he talked I became dimly aware that he was standing a little too close and that I was beginning to back up. Fortunately I was able to suppress my first impulse and remain stationary because there was nothing to communicate aggression in his behavior except the conversational distance. . . .
>
> By experimenting I was able to observe that as I moved away slightly, there was an associated shift in the pattern of interaction. He had more trouble expressing himself. If I shifted to where I felt comfortable (about twenty-one inches), he looked somewhat puzzled and hurt, almost as though he were saying, "Why is he acting that way? Here I am doing everything I can to talk to him in a friendly manner and he suddenly withdraws. Have I done anything wrong? Said something I shouldn't?" Having ascertained that distance had a direct effect on his conversation, I stood my ground, letting him set the distance.

As you can see, in spite of his training and extensive knowledge of other cultures, Hall still felt uncomfortable in this conversation. He first interpreted the invasion of his personal space as possible aggression, for people get close (and jut out their chins and chests) when they are hostile. But when he realized that was not the case, Hall resisted his impulse to move.

After Hall (1969) analyzed situations like this, he observed that North Americans use four different "distance zones."

1 *Intimate distance.* This is the zone that the South American unwittingly invaded. It extends to about 18 inches from our bodies. We reserve this space for lovemaking and wrestling, comforting, and protecting.

2 *Personal distance.* This zone extends from 18 inches to 4 feet. We reserve it for friends and acquaintances and ordinary conversations. This is the zone in which Hall would have preferred speaking with the South American.

3 *Social distance.* This zone, extending out from us about 4 to 12 feet, marks impersonal or formal relationships. We use this zone for such things as job interviews.

4 *Public distance.* This zone, extending beyond 12 feet, marks an even more formal relationship. It is used to separate dignitaries and public speakers from the general public.

Touching Do you get uncomfortable if a stranger touches you? Many of us do. Just as
we observe unwritten rules about speaking distance, so from our culture we learn rules
about touching—and only the "cultural boor" dares to break them. Researchers who
observed couples in coffee shops around the world concluded that the United States is
a "low-touch" culture (Thayer 1988). In Gainesville, Florida, couples averaged only
two touches an hour, while in Paris they touched 110 times an hour. The touching
record, however, was made in San Juan, Puerto Rico, where couples touched 180 times
an hour. The lowest-touch city, however, was not Gainesville, but London, where couples averaged zero touches per hour.

Not only does frequency of touching differ across cultures, but so does the meaning
of touching within a culture. In general, higher-status individuals do more touching.
Thus you are much more likely to see teachers touch students and bosses touch secretaries than the other way around. Apparently it is considered unseemly for lower-status
individuals to put their hands on superiors. An interesting experiment with surgery patients illustrates how touching can have different meanings. When the nurse came in
to tell patients about their coming surgery and after-care, she touched the patients twice,
once briefly on the arm when she introduced herself, and then for a full minute on the
arm during the instruction period. When she left, she shook the patient's hand.

Men and women reacted very differently. Touching lowered the blood pressure and
anxiety of females, both before the surgery and for more than an hour afterward. The
touching upset the men, however. Their blood pressure and anxiety rose. Apparently
men in the United States find it harder to acknowledge dependency and fear than
women do. For men, then, instead of a comfort, a well-intentioned touch may be a
threatening reminder of their vulnerability (Thayer 1988).

Let us now turn to dramaturgy, a special area of symbolic interactionism.

*Cultural rules of touching, including
kissing, vary widely around the
world. This scene of two world
leaders kissing after a successful
summit will not occur among North
American leaders—whether they are
male or female. At most, they might
hug, but much more likely is a formal handshake, with a possible
brief, light touch on the other's back.*

Dramaturgy: The Presentation of Self in Everyday Life

> It was their big day, two years in the making. Jennifer Mackey wore a white
> wedding gown adorned with an 11-foot train and 24,000 seed pearls that she
> and her mother had sewn onto the dress. Next to her at the altar in Lexington,
> Kentucky, stood her intended, Jeffrey Degler, in black tie. They said their vows,
> then turned to gaze for a moment at the four hundred guests.
>
> That's when groomsman Daniel Mackey collapsed. As the shocked organist strug-
> gled to play Mendelssohn's "Wedding March," Mr. Mackey's unconscious body was
> dragged away, his feet striking—loudly—every step of the altar stairs.
>
> "I couldn't believe he would die at my wedding," the bride said. (Hughes 1990)

Sociologist Erving Goffman (1922–1982) added a new twist to symbolic interactionism
when he developed **dramaturgy** (or dramaturgical analysis). By this term he meant
that social life was like a drama or the stage: Birth ushers us onto the stage of everyday
life, and our socialization really consists of learning to perform on that stage.

Everyday life, he said, involves playing our assigned roles. We have **front stages** on
which to perform them, as did Jennifer and Jeffrey. (By the way, Daniel Mackey didn't really die—he had just passed out from the excitement of it all.) But we don't have to
look at weddings to find front stages. Everyday life is filled with them. Where your
teacher lectures is a front stage. And if you make an announcement at the dinner table,
you are using a front stage. In fact, you spend most of your time on front stages, for a front
stage is wherever you deliver your lines. We also have **back stages,** places where we can
retreat and let our hair down. When you close the bathroom or bedroom door for privacy, for example, you are entering a back stage.

dramaturgy: an approach, pioneered by Erving Goffman, analyzing social life in terms of
drama or the stage, also called
dramaturgical analysis

front stage: where performances are given

back stage: where people rest
from their performances, discuss their presentations, and
plan future performances

The same setting can serve as both a back and a front stage. For example, when you get into your car by yourself and look over your hair in the mirror or check your makeup, you are using the car as a back stage. But when you wave at friends or give that familiar gesture to someone who has just cut in front of you in traffic, you are using your car as a front stage.

Everyday life brings with it many roles. The same person may be a student, a teenager, a shopper, a worker, a date, as well as a daughter or a son. While a role lays down the basic outline for a performance, it also allows a great deal of freedom. The particular emphasis or interpretation that an individual gives a role, the person's "style," is known as **role performance.** Take your role as son or daughter as an example. You may play the role of ideal daughter or son, being very respectful, coming home at the hours your parents set, and so forth. Or that description may not even come close to your particular role performance.

Ordinarily our roles are sufficiently separated that conflict between them is minimized. Occasionally, however, what is expected of us in one role is incompatible with what is expected of us in another role. This problem, known as **role conflict,** makes us very uncomfortable, as illustrated in Figure 4.3, in which family, friendship, student, and work roles come clashing together. Usually, however, we manage to avoid role conflict by segregating our roles, which in some instances may require an intense juggling act.

Sometimes the *same* role presents inherent conflict, a problem known as **role strain.** Suppose that you are exceptionally prepared for a particular class assignment. Although the instructor asks an unusually difficult question, you find yourself knowing the answer when no one else does. If you want to raise your hand, yet don't want to make your fellow students look bad, you will experience role strain. As illustrated in Figure 4.3, the difference between role conflict and role strain is that role conflict is conflict *between* roles, while role strain is conflict *within* a role.

A fascinating characteristic of roles is that *we tend to become the roles we play.* That is, roles become incorporated into the self-concept, especially those for which we prepare long and hard and which become part of our everyday lives. When sociologist Helen Ebaugh (1988) interviewed people who had left marriages, police work, and military,

role performance: the ways in which someone performs a role within the limits that the role provides; showing a particular "style" or "personality"

role conflict: conflicts that someone feels *between* roles because the expectations attached to one role are incompatible with the expectations of another role

role strain: conflicts that someone feels *within* a role

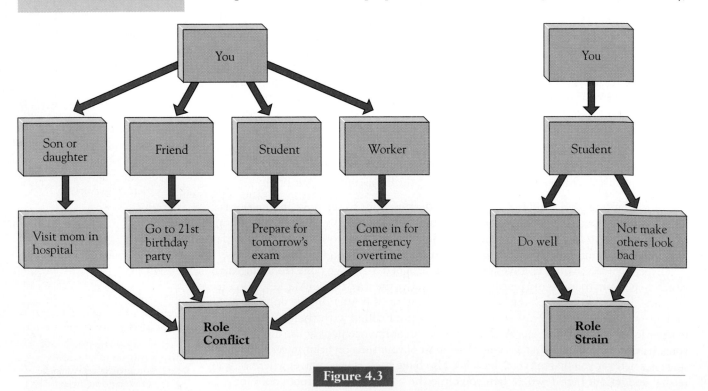

Figure 4.3

Role Strain and Role Conflict

medicine, and religious vocations, she found that these roles had become so intertwined with the subjects' self-concepts that leaving them threatened their very identity. The common question over which they struggled was "Who am I, now that I am not a nun (or physician, wife, colonel, etc.)?" Even years after leaving these roles, in their dreams many continued to perform them.

How these roles, having become such a part of the person, linger on after the individual has left them is illustrated by one of my own respondents, who said,

> After I left the (Protestant) ministry, I felt like a fish out of water. *Wearing that turned-back collar had become a part of me.* It was especially strange on Sunday mornings when I'd listen to someone else give the sermon. I knew that I should be up there preaching. I felt as though I had left God.

At the center of our performances in everyday life is the self and how we want others to think of us. We use our roles to communicate to others ideas that we want them to form about us. Goffman calls these efforts to manage the impressions that others receive of us **impression management.**

To communicate information about the self, we use three types of **sign-vehicles:** the social setting, our appearance, and our manner. The **social setting** is the place where the action unfolds. This is where the curtain goes up on your personal performances, where you find yourself on stage playing parts and delivering lines. A social setting might be an office, dorm, living room, church, gym, or bar. It is wherever you interact with others. Your social setting includes *scenery,* the furnishings you use to communicate messages, such as desks, blackboards, scoreboards, couches, and so on.

The second sign-vehicle is **appearance,** or how we look when we play our roles. Appearance includes *props,* which are like scenery, but they decorate the person rather than the setting. The teacher has books, lecture notes, and chalk, while the football player wears a special costume called a uniform. Although few of us carry around a football, we all use makeup, hairstyles, and clothing to communicate messages about ourselves. Props and other aspects of appearance serve as a sort of grease for everyday life: By letting us know what to expect from others, they tell us how we should react. Think of the messages that props communicate. Some people use clothing to say that they are college students, others that they are old; some that they are clergy, others that they are prostitutes. Similarly, people use different brands of cigarettes, liquor, and automobiles to convey messages of the self.

The third sign-vehicle is **manner,** the attitudes we demonstrate as we play our roles. We use manner to communicate information about our feelings and moods. By communicating anger or indifference, sincerity or good humor, for example, we indicate to others what they can expect of us as we play our roles. To try to make certain that the social setting is correct, that our manner is what people expect, and that our appearance is right is a goal of all role players. This becomes especially apparent, however, when we look at teenagers who are just beginning to date. For some reason, they are likely to take several showers a day, to stand before a mirror for hours combing and recombing their hair, and to change and rechange their clothing. In spite of our best efforts to manage the impressions that others receive of us, however, we sometimes fail. One of my favorite television scenes is of the character Molly Dodd trying to impress a date. She went to the "powder room," a backstage fix-up place reserved for women, where she did the usual things. Satisfied that she looked good, she made a grand entrance, with exaggerated movements and an expectant smile on her face—all the while trailing a long piece of toilet paper from her shoe. The scene is humorous because it highlights the fact that an incongruity of elements creates *embarrassment,* which in dramaturgical terms is a feeling that results when a performance fails.

To show ourselves as adept role players brings positive recognition from others, something that we all covet. To accomplish this, said Goffman, we often use **teamwork,** whereby two or more people work together to make certain that a performance goes off as planned. When a performance doesn't come off quite right, however, it may require **face-saving behavior.** We may, for example, ignore someone's flaws in performance,

impression management: the term used by Erving Goffman to describe people's efforts to control the impressions that others receive of them

sign-vehicles: the term used by Goffman to refer to how people use social setting, appearance, and manner to communicate information about the self

social setting: the place where the action of everyday life unfolds

appearance: how an individual looks when playing a role

manner: the attitudes that people show as they play their roles

teamwork: the collaboration of two or more persons interested in the success of a performance to manage impressions jointly

face-saving behavior: techniques used to salvage a performance that is going sour which Goffman defines as *tact*. Suppose your teacher is about to make an important point. Suppose also that her lecturing has been outstanding and the class is hanging on every word. Just as she pauses for emphasis, her stomach lets out a loud growl. She might then use a face-saving technique by remarking, "I was so busy preparing for class that I didn't get breakfast this morning." It is more likely, however, that both class and teacher will simply ignore the sound, both giving the impression that no one heard a thing—a face-saving technique called *studied nonobservance*. This allows the teacher to make the point, or as Goffman would say, it allows the performance to go on.

Before closing this section, we should note that impression management is not limited to individuals. Families, corporations, colleges, sports teams, in fact probably all groups, try to manage impressions. So do nations. An interesting example occurred when the International Olympic Committee was looking for a nation to host the Olympic 2000 games. Because hosting these games is so prestigious, the committee had a long list of candidates from which to choose. To impress the committee, China tried to put on a different face, to show that it was no longer repressive. With fanfare, China released a political prisoner six months before he had finished serving his fifteen-year sentence (Brauchli 1993). Unfortunately, this was impression management only, not a fundamental change, and after China lost its bid for the games, repression of political dissenters resumed in earnest.

Ethnomethodology: Uncovering Background Assumptions

As discussed in Chapter 1, symbolic interactionists stress that the events of life do not come with built-in meanings. Rather, we give meaning to things by classifying them. When we place objects and events into the classifications provided by our culture, we are doing more than naming things—we are interpreting our world.

Ethnomethodologists study how people make sense of life. They try to uncover people's basic assumptions as they interpret their everyday worlds. To better understand **ethnomethodology,** consider the word's three basic components. "Ethno" means folk or people; "method" means how people do something; "ology" means "the study of." Putting them together, then, *ethno/method/ology* means "the study of how people do things." Specifically, ethnomethodology is the study of how people use commonsense understandings to make sense out of their lives.

Let us suppose that you go to a doctor and she says that she doesn't feel like "doing doctoring" today. She then hands you the name of another physician, stares at your hair for a minute and takes out a pair of scissors and tries to give you a haircut. This would violate basic assumptions about what doctors are supposed to do. At the very least, you expect your doctor to listen to your medical problems and prescribe medicines. We all expect that of doctors. Haircuts, however, are simply not part of our expectations.

These assumptions about the way life is and the way things ought to work (what ethnomethodologists call **background assumptions**) lie at the root of social life. Exactly how these background assumptions work is what ethnomethodologists try to discover. They are so deeply embedded in our consciousness that we are seldom aware of them, for almost everyone fulfills them unquestioningly. Thus, your doctor does not offer you a haircut, even if he or she is good at cutting hair and you need one!

The founder of ethnomethodology, sociologist Harold Garfinkel, conducted some interesting exercises to uncover our background assumptions. Garfinkel (1967) asked his students to act as though they did not understand the basic rules of social life. Some tried to bargain with supermarket clerks; others would inch closer to people and stare directly at them. They were met with surprise, bewilderment, even anger. One of the more interesting exercises that Garfinkel's students conducted was to act as though they were boarders in their own homes. When they returned from class they addressed their parents as "Mr." and "Mrs.," asked permission to use the bathroom, sat stiffly, were extremely courteous, and spoke only when spoken to. The other family members were stupefied (Garfinkel 1967):

background assumptions: deeply embedded common understandings, or basic rules, concerning our view of the world and of how people ought to act

They vigorously sought to make the strange actions intelligible and to restore the situation to normal appearances. Reports (by the students) were filled with accounts of astonishment, bewilderment, shock, anxiety, embarrassment, and anger, and with charges by various family members that the student was mean, inconsiderate, selfish, nasty, or impolite. Family members demanded explanations: What's the matter? What's gotten into you? . . . Are you sick? . . . Are you out of your mind or are you just stupid?

In another exercise Garfinkel asked students to take words and phrases literally. This is what happened when one student asked his girlfriend what she meant when she said that she had a flat tire:

> What do you mean, "What do you mean?"? A flat tire is a flat tire. That is what I meant. Nothing special. What a crazy question!

Another conversation went like this.

> *Acquaintance:* How are you?
>
> *Student:* How am I in regard to what? My health, my finances, my schoolwork, my peace of mind, my . . . ?
>
> *Acquaintance* (red in the face): Look! I was just trying to be polite. Frankly, I don't give a damn how you are.

Students who are given the assignment to break background assumptions can be highly creative. The young children of one of my students were surprised one morning when they came down for breakfast to find a sheet spread across the living room floor. On it were dishes, silverware, burning candles—and ice cream. They, too, wondered what was going on—but they dug eagerly into the ice cream before their mother could change her mind.

▽ **In Sum** Ethnomethodologists explore background assumptions, our taken-for-granted ideas about the world, which underlie our behavior and are violated only with risk. These basic rules of social life are an essential part of the social structure. Deeply embedded in our minds, they give us basic directions for living everyday life. Although we are seldom aware of how extensively our background assumptions guide us through our daily lives, they are constantly present.

The Social Construction of Reality

Usually we assume that reality is something "out there," that it hits us in the face. *It* is something that independently exists, and we must deal with it. Symbolic interactionists, however, point out that we define our own reality and then live within those definitions. Our definitions are so important that what we define as real is, for us, real. As sociologist W. I. Thomas said, in what has become known as the **Thomas theorem,** "If people define situations as real, they are real in their consequences."

The process by which we take the various elements available in our society and put them together to form a view of reality is called **the social construction of reality.** Consider the following incident:

> On a visit to Morocco, in Northern Africa, I decided to buy a watermelon. When I indicated to the street vendor that the knife he was going to use to cut the watermelon was dirty (encrusted with filth would be more apt), he was very obliging. He immediately bent down and began to wash the knife in a puddle on the street. I shuddered as I looked at the passing burros, freely defecating and urinating as they went. Quickly, I indicated by gesture that I preferred my melon uncut after all.

For that vendor, germs did not exist. For me, they did. And each of us acted according to our definition of the situation. In other words, our perception and behavior result not from the fact that germs are real but *because we grew up in a society that teaches they are real.* It is not the reality of microbes that impresses itself upon us, but society that impresses the reality of microbes on us. Microbes, of course, *objectively* exist, and whether or not germs are part of our thought world makes no difference to whether we are infected by them. Our behavior, however, does not depend on the *objective* existence of something but, rather, on our *subjective interpretation*, on our definition of reality.

Thomas theorem: basically, that people live in socially constructed worlds; that is, people jointly build their own realities; summarized in William I. Thomas's statement "If people define situations as real, they are real in their consequences."

the social construction of reality: what people define as real because of their background assumptions and life experiences

We are so immersed in our own society's definitions that we are seldom aware of them. The definitions that we learn from our culture, and that we help to construct, underlie not only what we do but also what we perceive, feel, and think. Let me provide an example common to our society, although one that is difficult for males to identify with.

A gynecological nurse, Mae Biggs, and I did research on pelvic examinations. Reviewing about 14,000 cases, we looked at how the medical profession constructs social reality in order to define the examination of the vagina as nonsexual (Henslin and Biggs 1993). This desexualization is accomplished by painstakingly controlling the sign-vehicles—the setting, appearance, and manner.

The pelvic examination unfolds much as a stage play does. I will use "he" to refer to the physician because only male physicians participated in this study. Perhaps the results would be different with female gynecologists.

Scene 1 (The Patient as Person) In this scene, the doctor maintains eye contact with his patient, calls her by name, and discusses her problems in a professional manner. If he decides that a vaginal examination is necessary, he tells a nurse, "Pelvic in room 1." By this statement, he is announcing that a major change will occur in the next scene.

Scene 2 (From Person to Pelvic) This scene is the depersonalizing stage. In line with the doctor's announcement, the patient begins the transition from a "person" to a "pelvic." The doctor leaves the room, and a female nurse enters to help the patient make the transition. The nurse prepares the "props" for the coming examination and answers any questions the woman might have.

What occurs at this point is essential for the social construction of reality, for *the doctor's absence at this point removes even the suggestion of sexuality*. The act of undressing in front of him could suggest either a striptease or intimacy, thus undermining the reality in the process so carefully being defined, that of nonsexuality.

The patient also wants to remove any hint of sexuality in the coming interaction, and during this scene she may express concern about what to do with her panties, perhaps muttering to the nurse, "I don't want him to see these." Most women solve the problem by either slipping their panties under their clothes or placing them in their purse.

Scene 3 (The Person as Pelvic) This scene opens with the doctor entering the room. Before him is a woman lying on a table, her feet in stirrups, her knees tightly together, and her body covered by a drape sheet. The doctor seats himself on a low stool before the woman, tells her, "Let your knees fall apart" (rather than the sexually loaded "Spread your legs"), and begins the examination.

The drape sheet is critical in this process of desexualization, for it *dissociates the pelvic area from the person:* Bending forward and with the drape sheet above his head, the physician can see only the vagina, not the patient's face. Thus dissociated from the individual, the vagina is dramaturgically transformed into an object of analysis. If the doctor examines the patient's breasts, he also dissociates them from her person by examining them one at a time, with a towel covering the unexamined breast. Like the vagina, each breast becomes an isolated unit dissociated from the person.

In this critical scene, the patient cooperates in being an object, becoming for all practical purposes a pelvis to be examined. She withdraws eye contact, from the doctor for certain but usually from the nurse as well, is likely to stare at the wall or at the ceiling, and avoids initiating conversation.

Scene 4 (From Pelvic to Person) In this scene the patient becomes "repersonalized." The doctor has left the examining room; the patient dresses and takes care of any problems with her hair and makeup. Her re-emergence as person is indicated by such statements as, "My dress isn't too wrinkled, is it?", indicating a need for reassurance from the nurse that the metamorphosis from "pelvic" back to "person" has been completed satisfactorily.

Scene 5 (The Patient as Person) In this scene, the patient is once again treated as a person rather than an object. The doctor makes eye contact with her and addresses her by name. She, too, makes eye contact with the doctor, and the usual middle-class interaction patterns are followed. She has been fully restored.

To an outsider to our culture, the custom of single and married women going to a male stranger for a vaginal examination might seem strange. But not to us. We assume that such behavior is normal, and females in our society are encouraged to participate in this process *because they have been taught that such examinations are nonsexual in nature*. That definition of reality is a social process, accomplished by teamwork, and brought about by such techniques as those just outlined.

In Sum It is not just pelvic examinations, germs, and craps that make up our definitions of reality. Rather, *all of our reality is socially constructed.* As sociologists Peter Berger and Thomas Luckmann (1967) point out, the members of a society agree on definitions of what is going on and then cooperate to maintain those definitions. Symbolic interactionists stress that this is actually what society consists of—our definitions and our interactions based on them.

The Need for Both Macrosociology and Microsociology

As noted earlier in this chapter, to understand social life adequately, we need both microsociology and macrosociology. Each makes a vital contribution to our understanding of human behavior, and our understanding would be vastly incomplete without one or the other.

To illustrate this point, consider the research on two groups of high school boys conducted by sociologist William Chambliss (1993). Both groups attended Hanibal High School. One group was composed of eight promising young students, boys who came from "good" families and were perceived by the community as "going somewhere." Chambliss calls this group the "Saints." The other group consisted of six lower-class boys who were seen as going down a dead-end road. Chambliss calls this group the "Roughnecks."

Both groups were seriously delinquent. Both skipped school, drank a lot, and committed criminal acts, especially fighting and vandalism. The Saints were actually the more delinquent. They were truant much more often, and they committed more acts of vandalism. Yet it was the Saints who had the good reputation, while the Roughnecks were seen by teachers, the police, and the general community as no good and heading for trouble.

These reputations followed the boys throughout life. Seven of the eight Saints went on to graduate from college. Three studied for advanced degrees: one finished law school and became active in state politics, one finished medical school and set up a practice near Hanibal, and one went on to earn a Ph.D. The four other college graduates entered managerial or executive training with large firms. After his parents divorced, one Saint failed to graduate from high school on time and had to repeat his senior year. Although this boy tried to go to college by attending night school, he never finished. He was unemployed the last time Chambliss saw him.

In contrast, only four of the Roughnecks even finished high school. Two of these boys did exceptionally well in sports and received athletic scholarships to college. They both graduated from college and became high school coaches. Of the two others who graduated from high school, one became a small-time gambler and the other disappeared "up north" where he was last reported to be driving a truck. Of the two who did not complete high school, each was last heard of serving time in state penitentiaries for separate murders.

To understand what happened to the Saints and the Roughnecks, we need to grasp *both* social structure and social interaction. That is, we need both macrosociology and microsociology. Using macrosociology, we can place these boys within the larger framework of the U.S. social class system. This context reveals how opportunities open or close to people depending on their membership in the middle or lower social class, and how different goals are instilled in youngsters as they grow up in these vastly different groups. We can then use microsociology to follow their everyday lives. We can see how the Saints used their "good" reputations to skip classes repeatedly and how their access to automobiles allowed them to transfer their troublemaking to different communities and thus prevent damage to their local reputations. In contrast, lacking access to automobiles, the Roughnecks were highly visible. Their lawbreaking activities, limited to a small area, readily came to the attention of the community. Microsociology also reveals how their respective reputations opened doors of opportunity to the first group of boys while closing them to the other.

Thus we need both kinds of sociology, and both will be stressed in the following chapters.

Summary and Review

Levels of Sociological Analysis

What are the two levels of analysis that sociologists use?

Sociologists use macro- and microsociological levels of analysis. In **macrosociology,** the focus is placed on large-scale features of social life, while in **microsociology,** the focus is on **social interaction.** Functionalists and conflict theorists tend to use a macrosociological approach, while symbolic interactionists are more likely to use a microsociological approach. Pp. 90–91.

The Macrosociological Perspective: Social Structure

How does social structure influence our behavior?

The term **social structure** refers to a society's framework, the patterns that characterize a people. These patterns form an envelope around us, establishing limits on our behavior. Social structure consists of culture, social class, social statuses, roles, groups, and social institutions; together these serve as foundations for how we view the world.

Our location in the social structure underlies our perceptions, attitudes, and behaviors. Culture lays the broadest framework, while **social class** divides people according to income, education, and occupational prestige. Each of us receives **ascribed statuses** at birth; later we add various **achieved statuses.** Our behaviors and orientations are further influenced by the **roles** we play, the groups to which we belong, and our experiences with the institutions of our society. These components of society work together to help maintain social order. Pp. 91–97.

Social Institutions

What are social institutions?

Social institutions are the organized and standard means that a society develops to meet its basic needs. Sociologists have identified nine social institutions—the family, religion, law, politics, economics, education, medicine, science, and the military—summarized in Figure 4.1. From the functionalist perspective, social institutions meet universal group needs, or **functional requisites.** From the conflict perspective, the elite use social institutions to maintain its privileged position. Pp. 97–101.

When societies are transformed by social change, how do they manage to hold together?

In agricultural societies, said Emile Durkheim, people are united by **mechanical solidarity** (similar views and feelings). With industrialization comes **organic solidarity** (people depend on one another to do their jobs). Ferdinand Tönnies pointed out that the informal means of control of *Gemeinschaft* (small, intimate) societies are replaced by formal mechanisms in *Gesellschaft* (larger, more impersonal) societies. Pp. 101–103.

The Microsociological Perspective: Social Interaction in Everyday Life

What is the focus of symbolic interactionism?

In contrast to functionalists and conflict theorists, who as macrosociologists focus on the "big picture," symbolic interactionists tend to be microsociologists who focus on face-to-face social interaction. Symbolic interactionists analyze how people use symbols to define their worlds, which, in turn, affects their behavior. P. 103.

How do stereotypes affect interaction?

Stereotypes are assumptions of what people are like. When we first meet people, we classify them according to our perceptions of their visible characteristics and our ideas about those characteristics. These assumptions guide our behavior toward them, which, in turn, influences them to behave in ways that reinforce our stereotypes. Pp. 103–105.

Do all human groups share a similar sense of personal space?

In examining how people use physical space, symbolic interactionists stress that each of us is surrounded by a "personal bubble" that we carefully protect. People from different cultures have "personal bubbles" of varying sizes, so the answer to the question is no. Americans typically use four different "distance zones": intimate, personal, social, and public distance. Pp. 105–107.

What is dramaturgy?

Erving Goffman developed **dramaturgy** (or dramaturgical analysis), which analyzes everyday life in terms of the stage. At the core of this analysis are the impressions we attempt to make on others. For that, we use the **sign-vehicles** of setting, appearance, and manner. Our performances often call for **teamwork** and **face-saving behavior.** Pp. 107–110.

What is the social construction of reality?

Ethnomethodology is the study of how people make sense of everyday life. Ethnomethodologists try to uncover our **background assumptions,** which form the basic core of our reality.

The phrase **the social construction of reality** refers to how our actions depend on how we define our worlds. Pp. 110–113.

The Need for Both Macrosociology and Microsociology

Why are both levels of analysis important?

Because each in its own way adds to our knowledge of human experience, both **microsociology** (a focus on social interaction) and **macrosociology** (a focus on social structure) are necessary for us to understand social life. P. 113–114.

Where can I read more on this topic?

Suggested readings for this chapter are listed on page 638.

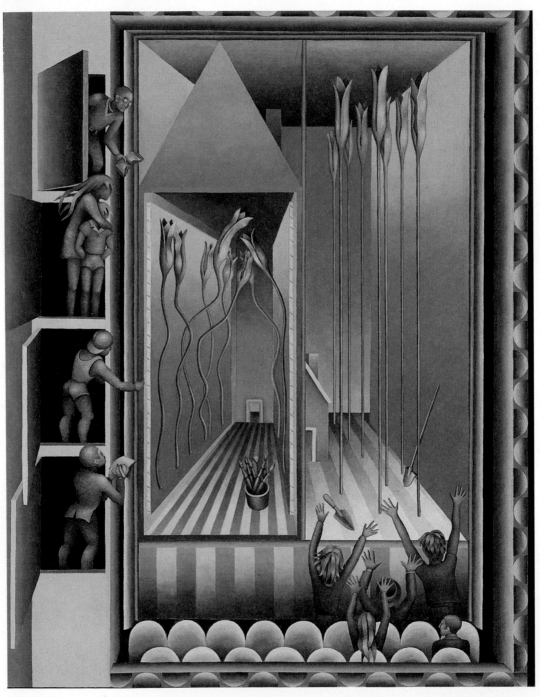

Wendy Seller, Two Realities, 1992

How Sociologists Do Research

R ENÉE HAD NEVER FELT FEAR *before, at least not like this. It had begun as a vague feeling that something wasn't quite right. Then she had felt it creep up her spine, slowly tightening as it clawed its way upward. Now it was like a fist pounding inside her skull.*

Renée never went anywhere with strangers. Hadn't her parents hammered that into her head since she was a child? And yet here she was at 19, in a car with a man she didn't know. He had seemed nice enough at first. And it wasn't as though he was some stranger on the side of the road or anything.

Renée had met George at Patricia's party, attracted by the dark eyes that seemed to light up his entire face when he smiled. When he asked her to dance, Renée felt flattered. He was a little older, a little more sure of himself than most of the guys she knew. Renée liked that; it seemed a sign of maturity. As the evening wore on and he continued to be attentive to her, it seemed natural to accept his offer to take her home.

But then they passed the turn to her dorm. When Renée told him he had missed it, he mumbled a reply about "getting something." It was then, as he continued driving, heading off into the country, that the clawing feeling at the back of her neck had begun.

His eyes, now cold, almost pierced the darkness as he looked at her. "It's time to pay, babe," he said, as he grabbed at her blouse.

Renée won't talk about that night. She doesn't want to remember anything that happened after that.

What Is a Valid Sociological Topic?

Sociologists research just about every area of human behavior. On the macro level, they study such broad matters as war (Cuzzort 1989), voting patterns (Piven and Cloward 1988), race relations (Wilson 1987), and city growth (Logan and Molotch 1987). On the micro level, they study such individualistic matters as waiting in public places (Schwartz 1991), meat packers at work (Thompson 1993), interactions between people on street corners (Whyte 1991), and even how people decorate their homes for Christmas (Caplow 1991). What happened to Renée in our opening vignette—is that, too, a valid topic for sociologists to research? If so, how should we research this topic?

As discussed in Chapter 1, sociologists study social interaction. Although rape consists of someone forcing himself on someone else, it meets the definition of people doing things with one another (in this case, *to* someone). As discussed in Chapter 1 also, no human behavior is ineligible for sociological research—whether that behavior is routine or unusual, respectable or reprehensible, free or forced. The question of *how* to do research, however, is a little more complicated, and needs to be examined in greater detail.

Common Sense and the Need for Sociological Research

First, why do we need sociological research? Why can't we simply depend on common sense, on "what everyone knows." As noted in Chapter 1 (pages 7–8), commonsense ideas may or may not be true. Common sense, for example, tells us that the rape was a significant event in Renée's life. And common sense also tells us that rape has ongoing effects, that it can trigger fears and anxieties, and that it can make women distrust men.

Although these particular ideas are accurate, we still need social research to test them, because not all commonsense ideas are true. After all, common sense tells some people that women's revealing clothing is one reason that men rape. To others, common sense indicates that men who rape are sexually deprived. Research, however, does not support either of these ideas. Studies show that men who rape don't care what a woman wears. (Most rapists don't even care who the woman is; she is simply an object to satisfy their lust and drive for power.) And some rapists are sexually deprived, while others are not—the same as men who do not rape. Many rapists have a wife or girlfriend with whom they have an ongoing sexual relationship.

If neither provocative clothing nor sexual deprivation is the underlying cause of rape, then what is? Although we may want to know why men rape, we might also want to know what the victims' reactions are. Or we may want to know something entirely different about rape. That, of course, brings us to the need for sociological research.

Regardless of the particular question that we want to answer, the point is that we want to move beyond guesswork and common sense. We want to *know* what really is going on. And for accurate answers, we need sociological research. Let us look, then, at how sociologists do their research.

A Research Model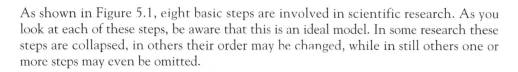

As shown in Figure 5.1, eight basic steps are involved in scientific research. As you look at each of these steps, be aware that this is an ideal model. In some research these steps are collapsed, in others their order may be changed, while in still others one or more steps may even be omitted.

1. Selecting a Topic

The first step is to select a topic. What do you want to know more about? Many sociologists simply follow their curiosity, their drive to know. They become interested in a particular topic, and they pursue it, as I did in studying the homeless. Some sociologists choose a topic because funding is available to study it, others because a particular social problem such as rape has become a pressing issue, and the sociologist wants to gather data that will help people better understand it—and perhaps to solve it.

For sociologists, any human behavior is a valid research topic. With Durkheim's classic research published in 1897, suicide was one of the first behaviors studied by sociologists. Shown here is a man leaping to his death from an overpass in Manhattan, as the police officers who tried to "talk him down" look on.

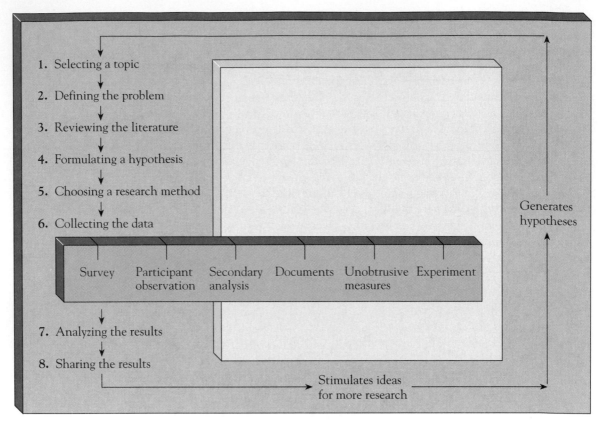

1. Selecting a topic
2. Defining the problem
3. Reviewing the literature
4. Formulating a hypothesis
5. Choosing a research method
6. Collecting the data

| Survey | Participant observation | Secondary analysis | Documents | Unobtrusive measures | Experiment |

7. Analyzing the results
8. Sharing the results

Generates hypotheses

Stimulates ideas for more research

(*Source:* Modification of Fig. 2–2 of Schaefer 1989)

Figure 5-1

The Research Model

2. Defining the Problem

The second step is to define the problem, to specify exactly what you want to learn about the topic. My interest in the homeless grew until I wanted to learn about homelessness across the nation. Ordinarily, sociologists' interests are much more focused than this. They develop a researchable question that focuses on a specific area or problem. For example, they may want to compare the work experiences, the relative isolation, or the attitudes of homeless women and men. Or they may want to know why men rape, or what can be done to reduce rape.

3. Reviewing the Literature

The third step is to review the literature to see if the question has already been answered. Nobody wants to reinvent the wheel. In addition, a review of what has been written on the topic can stimulate ideas, further refining the problem to be investigated.

4. Formulating a Hypothesis

The fourth step is to formulate a **hypothesis,** a statement of what you expect to find according to predictions from a theory. A hypothesis predicts a relationship between or among **variables,** factors that change, or vary, from one person or situation to another. For example, the statement, "Men who are more socially isolated are more likely to rape than are men who are more socially integrated" is a hypothesis. Hypotheses need **operational definitions**—that is, precise ways to measure their variables. In this example, we would need operational definitions for three variables: social isolation, social integration, and rape.

hypothesis: a statement of the expected relationship between variables according to predictions from a theory

variable: a factor or concept thought to be significant for human behavior, which varies from one case to another

operational definitions: the way in which a variable in a hypothesis is measured

Another unusual topic of sociological research is human behavior following natural disasters, such as that of Hurricane Andrew, which devastated parts of southern Florida. Sociological findings on natural disasters are reported in Chapter 21.

5. Choosing a Research Method

The means by which sociologists collect data are called **research methods.** Sociologists use six basic research methods, outlined in the next section. They select the method that will best answer the particular questions they want to solve.

6. Collecting the Data

The next step is to gather the data. Sociologists take great care to assure both the validity and reliability of their data. **Validity** is the extent to which operational definitions measure what they are intended to measure. In our example, we would need to be certain that we were really measuring social isolation, social integration, and rape and not something else.

Validity is a persistent problem for researchers. For example, just how should we measure social isolation and integration? Can we simply find out how frequently an individual interacts with others? Don't we also have to measure how much the individual identifies or feels a part of other people, a much more difficult matter? Even an operational definition for rape is not as simple to determine as it may seem. For example, in the United States the law recognizes various degrees of sexual assault, and some acts of forced sex are classified as rape in some states but not in others. In other words, we must be extremely careful that we know precisely what we are measuring.

Reliability is the extent to which studies yield consistent results. Inadequate operational definitions and sampling (covered later) will undermine reliability. For example, if our measure of rape is adequate and other researchers apply it to the same group of people we studied, they would include the individuals whom we included and exclude those whom we excluded. Clear measures, however, are just the first step toward reliability. Even though our operational definitions are clear and other researchers can follow them, we won't know that our study is reliable until other research produces similar results.

research method (or research design): one of six procedures sociologists use to collect data: surveys, participant observation, secondary analysis, documents, unobtrusive measures, and experiments

validity: the extent to which an operational definition measures what was intended

reliability: the extent to which data produce consistent results

Table 5.1

How to Read a Table

Rapists' Accounts of Alcohol and Drug Use Prior to Their Crime

These are the results of interviews with men imprisoned for rape in seven maximum- or medium-security prisons in Virginia. *Admitters* are men who define their acts as rape, *deniers* those who do not define their acts as rape.

Use of Alcohol and Drugs	Admitters n = 39	Deniers n = 25
Neither the rapist nor the victim used alcohol or drugs.	23%	16%
The rapist used alcohol or drugs.	77%	72%
The rapist was affected by the alcohol or drugs.	69%	40%
The victim used alcohol or drugs.	26%	72%
The victim was affected by the alcohol or drugs.	15%	56%
Both the rapist and the victim used and were affected by alcohol or drugs.	15%	16%

Source: Modification of Table 2 in Scully and Marolla 1984.

A table is a concise way of presenting information. Because sociological findings are often presented in tabular form, it is important to understand how to read a table. Tables contain six elements: title, headnote, headings, columns, rows, and source. When you understand how these elements work together, you know how to read a table.

1. The *title* states the topic of a table. It is located at the top of the table. What is the title of this table? Please determine your answer before looking at the correct answer below.

2. The *headnote* is not always included in a table. When it is, it is located just below the title. Its purpose is to give more detailed information about how the data were collected or how data are presented in the table. What are the first seven words of the headnote of this table?

3. The *headings* of a table tell what kind of information is contained in the table. There are three headings in this table. What are they? In the second heading, what does *n* = 39 mean?

4. The *columns* in a table present vertically arranged information. What is the fourth number in the second column and the second number in the third column?

5. The *rows* in a table present information arranged horizontally. In the sixth row, who is listed as using and being affected by alcohol and drugs?

6. The *source* of a table, usually listed at the bottom, provides information on where the data shown in the table originated. Often, as in this instance, the information is specific enough for you to consult the original source. What is the source for this table?

Some tables are much more complicated than this one, but all follow the same basic pattern. To apply these concepts to a table with more information, see pages 332 and 333.

Answers

1. Rapists' Accounts of Alcohol and Drug Use Prior to Their Crime.
2. These are the results of interviews with.
3. Use of Alcohol and Drugs, Admitters, Deniers. The *n* is an abbreviation for number, and *n* = 39 means that 39 men were admitters.
4. 26%, 72%.
5. Both the rapist and the victim.
6. A 1984 article by Scully and Marolla (listed in the References section of this text).

7. Analyzing the Results

content analysis: the examination of a source, such as a magazine article, a television program, or even a diary, to identify its themes

After the data are gathered, it is time to analyze them. Sociologists have specific techniques for doing this, each of which requires special training. They range from statistical tests (of which there are many, each with its own rules for application) to **content analysis,** which involves examining the content of something in order to identify its themes—in this case perhaps television programs about rape, or even diaries kept by women who have been raped.

If a hypothesis has been part of the research—and not all social research makes use of hypotheses—it is during this step that it is tested.

The computer has become an especially powerful tool for analyzing sociological data. It has four main values for sociologists. First, the computer will take huge amounts of quantitative information and reduce them to basic patterns. Second, it takes much of the drudgery out of analyzing data. What used to take tedious hours, and even days or weeks, of mathematical analyses of data can now be performed in an instant. Third, researchers can easily try various statistical tests to see which prove the most valuable for the data they have. Fourth, by freeing researchers from the time-consuming tasks of number crunching, the computer allows them to think more about what the numbers mean. Consequently, the use of this tool to analyze data is part of sociological training. The basic program that sociologists, even many undergraduates, learn is the Statistical Package for the Social Sciences (SPSS).

8. Sharing the Results

Now it is time to wrap up the research, or, if it is a broad project, at least some part of it. In this step the researchers write a report to share their findings with the scientific community. The report includes a review of the preceding steps to help others judge the research results. It also shows how the findings are related to the literature, the published results of other research on the topic. When research is published, usually in a scientific journal or a book, it then "belongs" to the scientific community. Table 5.1 is an example of published research. These findings are available for **replication;** that is, others can repeat the study to test the results. In this way, scientific knowledge builds slowly as finding is added to finding.

Let us look in greater detail at the fifth step and examine the research methods that sociologists use.

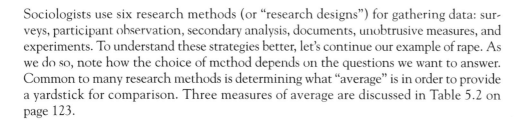

Six Research Methods

Sociologists use six research methods (or "research designs") for gathering data: surveys, participant observation, secondary analysis, documents, unobtrusive measures, and experiments. To understand these strategies better, let's continue our example of rape. As we do so, note how the choice of method depends on the questions we want to answer. Common to many research methods is determining what "average" is in order to provide a yardstick for comparison. Three measures of average are discussed in Table 5.2 on page 123.

Surveys

Let us suppose that your goal is to know how many females are raped each year. An appropriate method for this purpose would be the **survey,** in which people are asked a series of questions. Before using this method, however, you must deal with practical matters that face all researchers—selecting a sample, asking neutral questions, using questionnaires or interviews, and establishing rapport. Let us look at each of these practical problems.

Selecting a Sample   Ideally, you may want to learn about all the females in the world. Obviously, however, your resources will not permit such a study, and you must narrow your **population,** the target group that you will study.

Let us assume that your resources allow you only to investigate rape on your college campus. Let us also suppose that your college enrollment is large, making it impractical to survey all female students. Now you must select a **sample,** individuals from among your target population. How you choose a sample is critical, for the choice will affect the results of your study. For example, to survey only first-year females—or only se-

> **replication:** repeating a study in order to test its findings
>
> **survey:** the collection of data by having people answer a series of questions
>
> **population:** the target group to be studied
>
> **sample:** the individuals intended to represent the population to be studied

---

Table 5.2

Three Ways to Measure "Average"

The Mean

The term *average* seems clear enough. As you learned in grade school, to find the average you add a group of numbers and then divide the total by the number of cases that were added. For example, assume that the following numbers represent men convicted of rape who are incarcerated in seven different prisons

321
229
57
289
136
57
1,795

The total is 2,884. Divided by 7 (the number of cases), the average is 412. Sociologists call this form of average the *mean*.

The mean can be deceptive because it is strongly influenced by extreme scores, either low or high. Note that six of the seven cases are less than the mean.

Two other ways to compute averages are the median and the mode.

The Median

To compute the second average, the *median,* first arrange the cases in order—either from the highest to the lowest or the lowest to the highest. In this example, that arrangement will produce the following distribution:

57
57
136
229
289
321
1,795

Then look for the middle case, the one that falls halfway between the top and the bottom. That figure is 229, for three numbers are lower and three numbers higher. When there is an even number of cases, the median is the halfway mark between the two middle cases.

The Mode

The third measure of average, the *mode* is simply the cases that occur the most often. In this instance the mode is 57, which is way off the mark. Because the mode is often deceptive, and only by chance comes close to either of the other two averages, sociologists seldom use it. In addition, it is obvious that not every distribution of cases has a mode. And if two or more different numbers appear with the same frequency, you can have more than one mode.

---

niors, or only those enrolled in introductory sociology courses, or only those in advanced physics classes—will produce unrepresentative results in each case.

To be able to generalize your findings to the entire campus, you must select a sample that is representative of the campus (called a "representative sample"). What kind of sample will allow you to do this?

The best is a **random sample.** This does *not* mean that you stand on some campus corner and ask questions of whomever happens to walk by. *In a random sample, everyone in the population has the same chance of being included in the study.* In this case, since the population is every female enrolled in your college, all such females—whether first-year or graduate students—must have the same chance of being included in the sample. Equally, such factors as a woman's major, her age, marital status, grade-point average, or whether she is a day or evening or full- or part-time student must not affect her chance of becoming part of your study.

How can you get a random sample? First you need a list of all the female students enrolled in your college. You then would assign a number to each name on the list and, using a table of random numbers, determine which students become part of your sample. (Random numbers are available on tables in statistics books, or they can be generated by a computer.)

Because a random sample represents the population—in this case female students at your college—you can generalize your findings to all the female students on your campus, whether they were included in the sample or not.

Social scientists have developed a variation of this sampling technique that you might want to consider. Suppose you want to compare the experiences of freshmen and

random sample: a sample in which everyone in the target population has the same chance of being included in the study

▼ ◣ ▼ ◣ ▼ ◣ ▼ ◣ ▼ ◣ ▼ ◣ ▼ ◣ ▼ ◣ ▼ ◣ ▼ ◣ ▼ ◣ ▼ ◣ ▼ ◣ ▼

Down-To-Earth Sociology

Loading the Dice: How Not to Do Research

THE METHODS OF SCIENCE lend themselves to distortion, misrepresentation, and downright fraud. Consider the following information. Surveys show that

- Americans overwhelmingly prefer Toyotas to Chryslers.
- Americans overwhelmingly prefer Chryslers to Toyotas.

- Americans think that cloth diapers are better for the environment than disposable diapers.
- Americans think that disposable diapers are better for the environment than cloth diapers.

Obviously such opposites cannot both be true. Both sets of findings are misrepresentations, although each does come from surveys conducted by so-called independent researchers. These researchers, however, are biased, not independent and objective.

It turns out that some consumer researchers load the dice. Hired by firms that have a vested interest in the outcome of the research, they deliver the results their clients are looking for. There are six basic ways of loading the dice.

1. *Choose a biased sample.* For example, if you wanted to know if Americans prefer Chryslers or Toyotas, and you chose unemployed union workers who trace their job loss to Japanese imports as your sample, the answer is fairly predictable.

2. *Ask biased questions.* Even if researchers choose an unbiased sample, they can phrase their questions in such a way that most people see only one logical choice. The diaper survey just cited is a case in point. When the disposable diaper industry paid for the survey, the researchers used an excellent sample, but they worded the question this way: "It is estimated that disposable diapers account for less than 2 percent of the trash in today's landfills. In contrast, beverage containers, third-class mail and yard waste are estimated to account for about 21 percent. Given this, in your opinion, would it be fair to ban disposable diapers?"

    Is it surprising, then, that 84 percent of the respondents said that disposable diapers are better for the environment than cloth diapers? Similarly, when the cloth diaper industry funded its survey, the wording of their questions loaded the dice in their favor.

Consider the following finding, which is every bit as factual as those just cited.

- An overwhelming 91 percent of Americans want laws to limit contributions to political candidates.

Now, it is almost impossible to get 91 percent of Americans to agree on anything, much less some political issue, but researchers for Ross Perot did so by wording the question this way: "Should laws be passed to eliminate all possibilities of special interests giving huge sums of money to candidates?" This question is obviously designed to channel people's thinking toward a predetermined answer—quite contrary to the standards of scientific research.

3. *List biased choices.* Another way to load the dice is to use closed-ended questions that push people into the answers you want. Here is another finding:

- American college students overwhelmingly prefer Levis 501 to the jeans of any competitor.

Sound good? Before you rush out to buy this product, note what the researchers for Levis did: In asking a sample of students which clothes would be the most popular in the coming year, their list of choices included *no other jeans* but Levis 501!

4. *Discard undesirable results.* Researchers can simply keep silent about findings they find embarrassing, or they can even continue to survey samples until they find one that matches what they are looking for.

As stressed in this chapter, research must be objective before it can be considered scientific. Obviously, none of the preceding results qualifies. The underlying problem with the research cited here—and with so many similar surveys that are bandied about in the media—is that survey research has become big business. Simply put, the vast sums of money offered by corporations have corrupted some researchers.

The beginning of the corruption is subtle. Paul Light, associate dean of the Hubert Humphrey Institute at the University of Minnesota, put it like this: "A funder will never come to an academic and say, 'I want you to produce finding X, and here's a million dollars to do it.' Rather, the subtext is that if the researchers produce the right finding, more work—and funding—will come their way." He adds, "Once you're on that treadmill, it's hard to get off."

5. *Misunderstand the subjects' world.* This route can lead to errors every bit as great as those just cited. Even researchers who use an adequate sample, word their questions properly, and offer adequate choices can end up with skewed results. For example, surveys show that 80 percent of Americans are environmentalists. Most Americans, however, are probably embarrassed to tell a stranger otherwise. Today, that would be like going against the flag, motherhood, and apple pie.

6. *Analyze the data incorrectly.* Even when researchers strive for objectivity, the sample and wording are correct, and respondents answer the questions honestly, the results can still be skewed—the researchers may simply err in their calculations, such as entering incorrect data into computers.

The first four sources of bias constitute intentional, inexcusable fraud. The fifth and sixth sources of bias reflect sloppiness—which is also inexcusable in science.

Sources: Based on Reynolds 1982; Babbie 1985; Hunt 1986; Crossen 1991; and Goleman 1993.

seniors. If so, you could use a **stratified random sample.** You would first identify freshmen and seniors, and then use random numbers to select subsamples from each group.

Asking Neutral Questions   After you have decided on your population and sample, your next task is to make certain that your questions are neutral. Your questions must allow **respondents,** people who respond to a survey, to express their own ideas. Otherwise, you will end up with biased answers—and biased findings are worthless. (The Down-to-Earth Sociology box on page 125 gives examples of biased findings.) For example, if you were to ask, "Don't you agree that rapists deserve the death penalty?" you would be tilting the results toward agreement with the position being stated.

Questionnaires and Interviews   Sociologists not only strive to ask questions that reduce bias; they are also concerned about how **questionnaires,** the list of questions to be asked, are administered (carried out). There are two basic techniques for administering questionnaires. The first is for the respondents to fill them out. Although such **self-administered questionnaires** allow a larger number of people to be sampled at a relatively low cost, the researcher using this method loses control, because the conditions under which the questionnaires were filled out are unknown. For example, someone could have influenced the respondents' answers. In the second technique, called an **interview,** the researcher asks the questions directly, either face to face or by telephone. The advantage of this method is that the researcher can make certain that each question is asked in precisely the same way. This method also has disadvantages, however. Not only does it reduce the number of questionnaires that can be completed, while increasing the cost, but it also can result in **interviewer bias,** effects that interviewers themselves have on respondents that bias their answers. For example, respondents may be willing to write an anonymous answer but not to express the same opinion to another person directly. Respondents also sometimes try to make their answers match what they think an interviewer wants to hear.

In some cases, **structured interviews** work best. This type of interview uses **closed-ended questions,** questions followed by a list of possible answers. The advantages of structured interviews are that they are faster to administer and make it easier for the answers to be *coded* (categorized) so that they can be fed into a computer for analysis. The primary disadvantage is that respondents are limited to the answers listed on the questionnaire, which may or may not match their own opinions. For this reason, some researchers prefer **unstructured interviews.** Here the interviewer poses a series of **open-ended questions,** which people answer in their own words. Although unstructured interviews allow respondents to express the full range of their opinions they make it difficult to compare one set of answers with another. For example, how would you compare these answers to the question "What do you think causes rape?"

"They're sick."

"They haven't been raised right."

"I think they must have had problems with their mother."

"We ought to kill every one!"

"They're just *.*.* bastards!"

Establishing Rapport   Research on rape also brings up another significant issue. You may have been wondering if your survey of rape victims would be worth anything even if you rigorously followed scientific procedures. Would a rape victim really give honest answers? Would she even admit to a stranger that she had been raped?

If you were simply to walk up to female strangers on the street and ask if they had ever been raped, there understandably would be little basis for taking your findings seriously. It is therefore vital for researchers to establish **rapport** ("ruh-POUR"), a feeling of trust, with their respondents, especially when it comes to sensitive topics, areas about which they may feel embarrassment or other deep emotions.

---

stratified random sample: a sample of specific subgroups of the target population in which everyone in the subgroups has an equal chance of being included in the study

respondents: people who respond to a survey, either in interviews or in self-administered questionnaires

questionnaires: a list of questions to be asked

self-administered questionnaires: questionnaires filled out by respondents

interview: direct questioning of respondents

interviewer bias: effects that interviewers have on respondents that lead to biased answers

structured interviews: interviews that use closed-ended questions

closed-ended questions: questions followed by a list of possible answers to be selected by the respondent

unstructured interviews: interviews that use open-ended questions

open-ended questions: questions that respondents are able to answer in their own words

rapport: a feeling of trust between researchers and subjects

Sociologists who do surveys sometimes use interviews to collect data, conducted either by telephone or in person. One potential pitfall of the interview is interviewer bias. This occurs when respondents alter their responses to fit what they think the interviewer wants to hear or do not feel free to fully re-veal what they really think.

We know that once rapport is gained (for example, by first asking nonsensitive questions), victims will talk to researchers about rape. To go beyond police statistics, researchers conduct national crime surveys in which they interview a random sample of 100,000 Americans, asking them if they have been victims of burglary, robbery, and so on. After gaining rapport, the researchers then ask questions about rape. They find that rape victims do share their experiences with them, yielding results that parallel the official statistics (Shim and DeBerry 1988).

Participant Observation (Fieldwork)

In the second method, **participant observation,** the researcher *participates* in a research setting while *observing* what is happening in that setting. My research with the homeless, mentioned in Chapter 1, is an example of participant observation.

How is it possible to study rape by participant observation? Obviously, this method does not apply to being present during a rape. Rape, however, is a broad topic, and many questions about rape cannot be answered adequately by any other method.

Let's suppose that your interest is in how rape victims adjust to this traumatic event. You want to know what they think about themselves. You would like to learn how the rape has affected their behavior and their orientations to the world. For example, has their victimization affected their hopes and goals, their dating patterns, their ideas about men, and their ability to form intimate relationships? Participant observation can provide detailed answers to such questions.

Now let's go back to your campus again, assuming, for the sake of argument, that it has a rape crisis intervention center. Such a setting lends itself to participant observation, for here you can observe rape victims from the time they first report the attack to their later participation in counseling. With good rapport, you may even be able to spend time with victims outside this setting, observing other aspects of their lives. Their statements and other behaviors may be the keys that help you unlock answers about their attitudes and other orientations to life.

As you may have noticed, the researcher's personal characteristics are extremely important in fieldwork. For example, could a male researcher conduct such research? Technically, the answer is yes. But given the topic, which specifically centers on the emotions of females who have been brutally victimized by males, female sociologists may be better suited to conduct such research, and thus more likely to achieve results. Here again, however, our commonsense suppositions regarding how likely female rape victims are to disclose information to male versus female interviewers are just that—suppositions. Research

Because sociologists consider all human behavior to be valid research topics, they research both socially approved and disapproved behaviors. Rape, which reaches far back into antiquity, is among these topics. This painting by Peter Rubens (1577-1640), "Abduction of the Daughters of Leukippos," depicts an event that is supposed to have occurred in the fifth century B.C.

participant observation (or fieldwork): research in which the researcher *participates* in a research setting while *observing* what is happening in that setting

Because of the emotions surrounding it and the damage done to its victims, rape is a difficult topics for sociologists to research. Sociologists use different methods of research to answer different questions. Among the methods that could be used to study rape is to examine the documents kept by rape crisis centers, which log the number of calls and visits made by rape victims.

generalizability: the extent to which the findings from one group (or sample) can be generalized or applied to other groups (or populations)

secondary analysis: the analysis of data already collected by other researchers

documents: written sources

causation: if a change in one variable leads to a change in another variable, causation is said to exist

correlation: the simultaneous occurrence of two or more variables

spurious correlation: the correlation of two variables actually caused by a third variable; there is no cause–effect relationship

alone will verify or refute these assumptions. In conducting research, then, sociologists must be aware of how such variables as their sex, age, race, personality, and even height and weight can affect their findings (Henslin 1990a). Although these variables are important in all research methods, they are especially important in participant observation.

Participant observers face a problem with **generalizability,** the ability to apply their findings to larger populations. Most of their studies are exploratory in nature, documenting in detail what people in a particular setting are experiencing and how they are reacting to those experiences. Although such research suggests that other people who face similar situations react in similar ways, it is difficult to know just how far the findings apply beyond their original setting. The results of participant observation, however, can stimulate hypotheses and theories and be tested in other settings using other research techniques.

Secondary Analysis

In **secondary analysis,** a third research method, the researcher analyzes data that have already been collected by others. For example, if you were to examine the original data collected for studies reported later in this chapter (such as Rossi, page 134, or Scully and Marolla, pages 138–139), you would be doing secondary analysis. Ordinarily, researchers prefer to gather their own data, but lack of resources, especially money, may make that impossible. In addition, existing data may contain a wealth of information that was not pertinent to the goals of the original study, which can be analyzed for your specific purposes.

Like the other methods, this approach also poses its own problems. How can a researcher who did not directly carry out the research be sure that the data were systematically gathered, accurately recorded, and that biases were avoided? That may be an impossible task, especially if the original data were gathered by numerous researchers, not all of whom were equally qualified.

Documents

The use of **documents,** written sources, is a fourth research method employed by sociologists. To investigate social life, sociologists examine such diverse sources as books, newspapers, diaries, bank records, police reports, household accounts, immigration files, and records kept by various organizations.

To study rape, you might examine police reports. These might reveal what proportion of complaints result in arrest, what proportion of all arrests are for rape, how many of the men arrested for rape are brought to trial, what proportion are convicted, how many receive probation, how many are imprisoned, and so forth. If these were your questions, police statistics would be valuable.

But for other questions, those records would be useless. If you wanted to know about the social and emotional adjustment of rape victims, for example, they would tell you nothing. Other documents, however, might lend themselves to answering this question. A campus rape crisis center, for example, might have records that would provide key information. Diaries kept by rape victims would yield important insights into their reactions, especially how their attitudes and relationships with others change over time. If you couldn't locate such diaries, you might contact rape victims and ask them to keep diaries. Again, the rape crisis center might be the key in eliciting victims' cooperation. Their personnel might ask clients to keep such diaries. To my knowledge, no sociologist has yet studied rape in this way.

Of course, I am presenting an ideal situation in which the rape crisis center is opening its arms to you. In actual fact, the center might not cooperate at all, neither asking victims to keep diaries nor even letting you near its records. Access, then, is another problem researchers face constantly. Simply put, you can't study a topic unless you can gain access to it.

Table 5.3

Cause, Effect, and Spurious Correlations

In science, **causation** means that a change in one variable is due to another variable. Three conditions are necessary for causation: correlation, time order, and no spurious correlation. Let us apply each of these necessary conditions to rape and violent pornography.

1. The first necessary condition: **correlation**

If two variables exist together, they are said to be correlated. If rapists have viewed pornography that shows violence against women, rape and pornography are correlated.

Pornography ⟷ Rape

People sometimes assume that correlation is causation. In this instance, they conclude that pornography causes rape.

Pornography ⟶ Rape

But *correlation never proves causation*. In this instance, *either* variable could be the cause of the other. Perhaps raping arouses interest in pornography.

Rape ⟶ Pornography

2. The second necessary condition: *time order* (temporal priority)

For a variable to be a cause (the *independent* variable), it must precede that which is changed (the *dependent* variable). If the men had not seen pornography until after they had raped, pornography obviously could not be the cause of the rape. Although the necessity of time order is obvious, it is not always a simple matter to determine.

3. The third necessary condition: *no spurious correlation*

This is the necessary condition that really makes things difficult. Even if we identify correlation and can determine time order, we still don't know that pornography is the cause. It is possible that we have a **spurious correlation;** that is, the cause is not the variable we thought it was, but some underlying third variable that is not as easily visible. Some sociologists identify male culture as that underlying third variable.

Male Culture ⟶ Rape

Socialized into dominance, some males learn to view women as objects for their own pleasure and will not take no for an answer. In fact, this underlying third variable could be a cause of both rape and viewing pornography.

Male Culture ⟶ Rape
Male Culture ⟶ Pornography

But since only some men rape, while all males are exposed to male culture, other variables must also be involved. Perhaps specific subcultures that promote violence and denigrate women lead to both rape and the viewing of pornography.

Subculture ⟶ Rape
Subculture ⟶ Pornography

As indicated in the Scully–Marolla research reported on pages 138–139, we have a good indication that such subcultural socialization is an underlying variable.

If so, this does not mean that it is the only causal variable, for rape probably has many causes. Unlike the movement of amoebas or the action of heat on some object, human behavior is infinitely complicated. Human behavior involves people's definitions of the situation, including their views of right and wrong. To explain rape, then, we need to add such variables as men's definitions of the relative rights of women and men and their views of sex and violence. In fact, there is no reason to assume that some single variable such as pornography could ever account for rape. Indeed, rape is probably more prevalent among the Gusii, a preliterate group in western Kenya than any other human group,—and the Gusii don't have movies, videos, or porno magazines (Edgerton 1992). On the other hand, in societies that do have pornography, why should we assume that it is not a cause of at least some rape? It is precisely to help unravel such complicating factors in human behavior that we need the experimental method.

More on Correlations

Correlation simply means that two or more variables are present together. The more often they are found together, the greater the strength of their relationship. To indicate that strength, sociologists use a number called a *correlation coefficient*. If two variables are *always* related, they have what is called a *perfect positive correlation*. The number 1.0 represents this correlation coefficient. Nature has some 1.0's, such as the lack of water and the death of trees. 1.0's similarly apply to the human physical state, such as the absence of nutrients and the absence of life. But social life is much more complicated than physical conditions, and there are no 1.0's in human behavior.

In contrast, if two variables have a *perfect negative correlation*, it means that when one variable is present, the other is always absent. The number -1.0 expresses this correlation coefficient.

Weak positive correlations of 0.1, 0.2, 0.3, and 0.4 mean that one variable is associated with another only 1 time out of 10, 2 times out of 10, 3 times out of 10, and 4 times out of 10. In other words, in most instances the first variable is *not* associated with the second, indicating a weak relationship. The greater the correlation coefficient, the stronger the relationship. A strong relationship may indicate a causal relationship. Testing the relationship between variables is the goal of some sociological research.

Sociologists who put themselves directly in the research setting to discover their information are following a research method known as participant observation.

unobtrusive measures: various ways of observing people who do not know they are being studied

experiment: the use of control groups and experimental groups and dependent and independent variables to test causation

independent variable: a factor that causes a change in another variable, called the dependent variable

dependent variable: a factor that is changed by an independent variable

Unobtrusive Measures

The fifth method is **unobtrusive measures,** observing the behavior of people who do not know they are being studied. For example, social researchers have studied the level of whisky consumption in a town that was officially "dry" by counting empty bottles in trash cans and the degree of fear induced by ghost stories by measuring the shrinking diameter of a circle of seated children (Webb 1966). One of my graduate students studied gender differences by recording all the graffiti in every public rest room in two towns (Darnell 1971). Researchers have even gone high-tech in their unobtrusive measures. Some are outfitting shopping carts with infrared surveillance equipment. After tracing the customers' paths through a store and precisely measuring their stops, retailers use their findings to change the location of their items (McCarthy 1993).

How could we use unobtrusive measures to study rape? We could observe rapists in prison when they do not know that they are being watched. For example, we could arrange for the leader of a therapy group for rapists to be called out of the room. During his absence, social researchers could use a one-way mirror to observe the men's interactions and videotape them. This would probably tell us more about their real attitudes than most other techniques. Professional ethics, however, would likely prohibit this application of unobtrusive measures.

Experiments

The sixth method, the **experiment,** is especially useful to determine cause and effect. Causation has three necessary conditions, which are discussed in Table 5.3. You may want to devise an experiment to test the hypothesis that violent pornography creates attitudes that favor rape. Your **independent variable** (something that causes a change in another variable) would be violent pornography, your **dependent variable** (the variable that is changed) attitudes toward rape. Suppose that you have access to a laboratory on campus and to some male volunteers. You could randomly divide these subjects into two groups. The reason for doing this is that many of the characteristics of the men will differ—their experiences, attitudes, perhaps even their "suggestibility." If you randomly divide the subjects, making certain that each per-

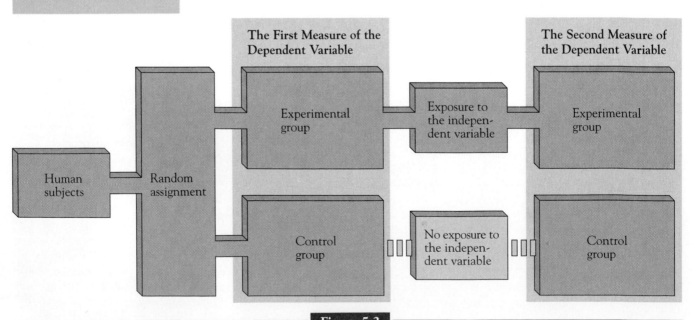

Figure 5.2

The Experiment

Down-To-Earth Sociology

The Hawthorne Experiments

THE PURPOSE OF SOCIOLOGICAL research is to determine how variables influence human behavior. One famous research attempt, now a classic in sociology, drives home how necessary it is to accurately identify independent and dependent variables.

In the mid-1920s, a series of studies was carried out at the Hawthorne plant of the Western Electric Company near Chicago. The management wanted to know how different levels of lighting affected productivity. Several groups of female employees participated in the Relay Room Experiments. In the control room, the level of lighting was held constant as the women worked, while in the test room the lighting was varied. To everyone's surprise, output increased in *both* locations. In the test room, productivity remained high even when the lights were dimmed to about the level of moonlight—so low that workers could barely see what they were doing!

To solve this mystery, management called in a team of researchers headed by Elton Mayo of the University of Chicago. This team tested thirteen different work conditions. When they changed the workers' pay from hourly wages to piecework, productivity increased. When they served refreshments, output again went up. When they added two 5-minute rest periods, productivity jumped. When they changed the rest periods to two 10-minute periods, again output increased. When they let the workers go home early, they found the same result. Confused, the researchers then restored the original conditions, offering none of the added benefits. The result? Even higher productivity.

The situation became even more confusing when male workers were observed in the Bank Wiring Room Study. Here, the researchers did not change the work conditions at all. They simply observed the men while they worked and interviewed them after work. But instead of there being no change in productivity, as might have been expected, productivity *decreased*.

None of this made sense. Finally, Mayo concluded that the results were due to the research itself. Aware that they were being studied and pleased at the attention paid to them, the female workers responded by increasing their efforts. The male workers, in contrast, reacted by becoming suspicious about why the researchers were observing them. They feared that an increase in productivity would increase the amount they were expected to produce each day, or that it might even cost some of them their jobs. Consequently, they deliberately decreased their output.

The Hawthorne research is important—not for its findings on worker productivity, but for what it revealed about the research process itself. Today, social researchers carefully monitor the *Hawthorne effect*, the change in subjects' behavior that occurs when they know they are being studied.

Sources: Based on Roethlisberger and Dickson 1939; Mayo 1966; Baron and Greenberg 1990.

---

son has an equal chance of becoming a member of either group, these unknown variables will be distributed between the groups.

As shown in Figure 5.2, you then measure the dependent variable, their attitudes toward rape. To one group, called the **experimental group**, you introduce the independent variable, showing them violent pornographic movies. The other men, the **control group,** are not exposed to the independent variable; that is, they are not shown these movies. You then measure the dependent variable again in both groups. In this way, the effects of unknown third variables are "washed out"; that is, you can assume that, whatever such variables may be, they have had the same effects on both groups. Any changes in the dependent variable in the experimental group can now be attributed to what only that group received, namely, the independent variable.

Because there is always some chance that the unknown third variables have not been evenly divided among the groups, you would need to replicate (retest) your results by doing the same experiment with other groups of men. You can be certain that other experimenters will test your findings. The Down-to-Earth Sociology box on this page describes a set of famous experiments undertaken in the 1920s that uncovered several surprising underlying third variables.

This classic method of the natural sciences is seldom used in sociology because sociologists are generally interested in broad features of society and social behavior, or in the actual workings of some group in a natural setting, neither of which lends itself

experimental group: the group of subjects exposed to the independent variable

control group: the group of subjects not exposed to the independent variable

well to an experiment. To study rape, however, we could devise experiments that might prove beneficial for society. For example, the independent variable could be therapy.

Convicted rapists could be randomly assigned to experimental and control groups to assure that individual characteristics (number of convictions, severity of crimes, length of prison sentence, education, rural and urban backgrounds, race, age, and so on) would be evenly distributed between the groups. The experimental group would receive some particular form of therapy, the control group no therapy. We would have to assume that, except for the therapy, the prison and postprison experiences had equal effects on the men. Differences in the re-arrest rates for rape could then be attributed to the independent variable, the therapy. Such results, if positive (that is, if they did not *increase* rape), would provide valuable guidelines for dealing with rapists.

Down-To-Earth Sociology

Applied Sociology: Marketing Research as a Blend of Quantitative and Qualitative Methods

TO SURVIVE IN THE highly competitive business world requires that companies figure out what consumers need and want and then supply it—or else convince people that they need or want what the company has to offer. Marketing researchers try to fill this niche. About eight years ago, Roger Straus was teaching sociology at a university when he answered an ad in the ASA (American Sociological Association) *Employment Bulletin*. He has been doing marketing research ever since.

A typical problem for marketing researchers is to help manufacturers "position" their products with the public in order to increase sales. The "position" of a product is marketing jargon for how customers think about a product. Marketing researchers determine the needs of customers, how they select and use products, and the images they hold of a product or service. They also assess how receptive the public will be to a new product or to a change in an established product. Some marketing researchers measure demand and track sales, while others help companies make their product stand out from its competitors.

To design, conduct, and analyze such studies, marketing researchers use a combination of qualitative and quantitative research techniques. Qualitative methods are used both as a prelude to survey research and as a "stand-alone" technique. An example is "focus groups," groups of about ten people who have been invited to discuss a product. A moderator leads a discussion before a one-way mirror, where other team members observe or videotape the session. To control for regional variations, other focus groups may be held at the same time in other cities. Straus points out that *Verstehen* and training in symbolic interactionism are especially valuable for interpreting the results.

Marketing researchers also use quantitative techniques. For example, they may conduct surveys to determine what the public thinks of a new product. They also gather sales data from the "bar codes" now found on almost all products. Marketing researchers use both basic and advanced statistics to analyze the data and to prepare tables and graphics that distill the findings for clients.

This summary would not be complete unless I point out a problem with the status of marketing research in sociology. As Straus says, most of the results of marketing research are proprietary (owned by the client) and are therefore confidential. This means that the researcher has little opportunity to generalize from findings in order to create social theory or even to publish results in sociology journals. In addition, clients are usually interested only in specific marketing problems and seldom commission research into important social issues. For such reasons, some sociologists do not consider marketing research a "legitimate" sociological activity. Some even say that sociologists who do marketing research are wasting their talents or even that they have "sold out," that they are using sociological methods to help companies exploit the public by convincing them to purchase unneeded goods and services.

Marketing researchers, of course, do not see things this way. They argue that marketing research is a neutral activity, and they help sell more than just diapers and soft drinks. Advocates point out that marketing research has been used to help communities assess public needs and colleges to attract students. They argue that the decision whether or not to do research for a particular product is a moral one based on the researcher's own values, that it is unreasonable for anyone to place a wholesale judgment on this activity. Straus and others also contend that sociologists can have an important impact on marketing research by bringing their research training and ethical values to this large and growing field.

Sources: Based on Straus 1991 and communication with Straus 1993.

Simply counting the number of homeless people who sleep in shelters or eat in soup kitchens will not yield an accurate total of homeless Americans. For Rossi and his associates, this was only the starting point for research that turned out to be controversial.

Other independent variables that we might want to consider are length of imprisonment, different forms of punishment, and degrees of isolation. Frankly, no one yet knows how to successfully change a rapist into a nonrapist, and such rigorous experiments are badly needed.

Deciding Which Method to Use

Four primary factors underlie a researcher's choice of method. First, resources are crucial, and researchers must always match methods to available resources. For example, although they may prefer to conduct a survey, they may find that finances will not permit it and instead turn to the study of documents. The second significant factor is access to subjects. If persons in a sample live in remote parts of the country, researchers may have to mail them questionnaires or conduct a telephone survey even if they would prefer face-to-face interviews. The third factor concerns the purpose of the research, the questions that the researcher wishes to answer. Each method is better for answering some questions than for others. Participant observation, for example, is a good method for uncovering people's real attitudes, while experiments work better for resolving questions of cause and effect. Fourth, the researcher's background or training comes into play. In graduate school, sociologists study many methods but are able to practice only some of them. Consequently, following graduate school they generally feel most comfortable using the methods in which they have had the most training and tend use these during their career. Thus, researchers who have been trained in **quantitative research methods,** which emphasize precise measurement, numbers, and statistics, are more likely to use surveys, while researchers who have been trained in **qualitative research methods,** which emphasize describing, observing, and interpreting people's behavior, lean toward participant observation. In the Down-to-Earth Sociology box on page 132, you can see how a combination of quantitative and qualitative methods are used in applied sociology. The following Thinking Critically section illustrates how significant the choice of research method is, and how sociologists can find themselves in the midst of controversy for applying rigorous research methods.

quantitative research methods: research in which the emphasis is placed on precise measurement, the use of statistics and numbers

qualitative research methods: research in which the emphasis is placed on observing, describing, and interpreting people's behavior

▼▲▼▲▼▲▼▲▼▲▼▲▼▲▼▲▼▲▼▲▼▲▼▲▼▲▼▲▼▲▼

Thinking Critically About Social Controversy

Doing Controversial Research—Counting the Homeless

▼ WHAT COULD BE SIMPLER, or more inoffensive, than counting the homeless? As sometimes happens, however, even basic research lands sociologists in the midst of controversy. This is what happened to sociologist Peter Rossi and his associates.

It happened this way. There was a dispute between advocates for the homeless and the federal government. The advocates said that there were three to seven million Americans homeless, while the government said there was about one-twelfth this number, only about a quarter of a million. Each side accused the other of gross distortion—the one to place undue pressure on Congress, the other to keep the public from knowing how bad the situation really was.

Only an accurate count could clear up the picture, for both sides were only guessing at the numbers. Peter Rossi and the National Opinion Research Center decided to carry out an accurate count. They had no vested interest in supporting one side or the other, only in answering this question honestly.

The challenge was immense. No federal, state, county, or city registers exist from which to add up names, and only some of the homeless stay at shelters. The *population* was evident, America's homeless. A *survey* would be appropriate, but how do you survey a *sample* of this population? And for *validity*, to make certain that they were counting only people who were really homeless, the researchers needed a good *operational definition* of homelessness. To include people who weren't really homeless would destroy the study's *reliability*. The researchers wanted results that would be consistent if others were to *replicate*, or repeat, the study.

As an operational definition, the researchers used the criterion of "literally homeless," persons "who do not have access to a conventional dwelling and who would be homeless by any conceivable definition of the term." Because a national count would cost about $6 million, far beyond their resources, the researchers decided to count just the homeless in Chicago. By using a stratified random sample, they were able to generalize to the entire country. The cost was still high, however—about $600,000.

To generalize about the homeless who sleep in shelters, the researchers used a stratified random sample of the city's shelters. For the homeless who sleep in the streets, vacant buildings, and so forth, they used a stratified random sample of the city's blocks. To make doubly certain that their count was accurate, the researchers conducted two surveys. At night, trained teams visited the shelters and searched the alleys, bridges, and vacant houses.

Many found the results startling. On an average night, Chicago has 2,722 homeless persons. Because people move in and out of homelessness, between 5,000 and 7,000 are homeless at some point during the year. On warm nights, only two out of five sleep in the shelters, and even in winter only three out of four do so. The median age is 40; 75 percent are men, and 60 percent are African Americans. One in four is a former mental patient, one in five a former prisoner. A homeless person's income from all sources is less than $6 a day. Projecting these findings to the entire nation results in a national figure of about 350,000 homeless people.

The reactions were predictable. While government officials rubbed their hands in glee, stunned homeless advocates began a sniping campaign, denying the findings.

Remember that Rossi and associates had no interest in proving which side in the debate was right, only in getting reliable figures. Using impeccable methods, this they did.

The researchers had no intention of minimizing the problem of homelessness. They stressed that several hundred thousand Americans are so poor that they slip through the welfare system, sleep in city streets, live in shelters, eat out of garbage cans, are undernourished, and suffer from severe health problems. In short, these people live hopeless, despairing lives.

It is good to *know* for certain how many such people there are. Even though the number is far less than the homeless advocates had estimated, this information can still serve their cause: Since there are fewer homeless people than many had thought, the problem is more manageable. It means that if we have the national resolve, we can put our resources to work with greater certainty of success.

Nevertheless, as in this instance, people whose positions are not supported by research are not pleased, and they tend to take potshots at the researchers. This, of course, is one of the risks of doing sociological research, for sociologists never know whose toes they will step on.

Sources: Based on Anderson 1986; Rossi et al. 1986; Rossi et al. 1987; Coughlin 1988; Rossi 1989; Rossi 1991; De Parle 1994. ▲

Ethics in Sociological Research

In addition to choosing an appropriate research method, sociologists must also bear in mind the matter of ethics. Sociologists cannot just do any type of research that they might desire. Their research must meet their profession's ethical criteria, which center on basic assumptions of science and morality (American Sociological Association 1989; Fichter and Kolb 1989). Research ethics require openness (sharing findings with the scientific community), honesty, and truth. Ethics clearly forbid the falsification of results or plagiarism—that is, stealing someone else's work. Another basic ethical guideline is that research subjects should not be harmed by the research. Ethics further require that researchers protect the anonymity of people who provide private, sometimes intimate, and often potentially embarrassing or otherwise harmful information. Finally, although not all sociologists are in agreement about this, it is generally considered unethical for researchers to misrepresent themselves.

Sociologists take these ethical criteria seriously. To illustrate the extent to which sociologists will go to protect their respondents, consider the research conducted by Mario Brajuha and Rik Scarce.

The Brajuha Research

Brajuha, a graduate student at the State University of New York at Stony Brook, was doing participant observation of restaurant work (Brajuha and Hallowell 1986). He lost his job as a waiter because the restaurant where he was working burned down. The fire turned out to be of "suspicious origin," and the police investigated it. During their investigation, detectives learned that Brajuha had taken extensive field notes, and they asked to see them. Brajuha refused. The district attorney then subpoenaed the notes. Brajuha still refused to hand them over. The district attorney then threatened to send Brajuha to jail. By this time, Brajuha's notes had become rather famous, and unsavory characters, perhaps those who had set the fire, also began to wonder what was in them. They, too, demanded to see them—accompanying their demands with threats of a different nature. Brajuha unexpectedly found himself in a very disturbing double bind.

For two years Brajuha steadfastly refused to hand over his notes, even though he had to appear at numerous court hearings and became filled with anxiety, until finally, the district attorney dropped the subpoena. Happily, when the two men under investigation for setting the fire died, so did the threats to Brajuha, his wife, and his children.

The Scarce Research

In 1993, a group calling itself the Animal Liberation Front broke into a research facility at Washington State University, released animals, and did extensive damage to computers and files. Rik Scarce, a doctoral student in sociology at the university and the author of *EcoWarriors: Understanding the Radical Environmental Movement* (listed as a suggested reading on page 615), was summoned before a federal grand jury investigating the break-in. Scarce was not a suspect, but law enforcement officers thought that during his research Scarce might have come across information that would help lead them to the guilty parties. Scarce answered scores of questions about himself and topics related to the raid, but he refused to answer questions that would violate his agreements of confidentiality with research subjects. He cited the American Sociological Association's Code of Ethics (1989): "Confidential information provided by research participants must be treated as such by sociologists, even when this information enjoys no legal protection or privilege and legal force is applied." A federal judge did not agree, and put Scarce in the Spokane County Jail for contempt of court. Although Scarce could have obtained his freedom at any time simply by testifying, he maintained his laudable ethical stance and continued to refuse, in his words, "to be bludgeoned into becoming an agent of the state." Scarce served 159 days in jail. The longest any scholar before this had been held in contempt was one week (Monaghan 1993; Scarce 1993a, 1993b, and communication with the author).

The Humphreys Research

Sociologists agree on the necessity to protect respondents, and they applaud the professional manner in which Brajuha and Scarce handled themselves. There is less than complete agreement, however, on the requirement that researchers not misrepresent themselves, and sociologists who violate this norm can become embroiled in ethical controversy as was Laud Humphreys, whose research forced sociologists to rethink and refine their ethical stance.

Laud Humphreys (1970, 1971, 1975), a classmate of mine at Washington University in St. Louis, was an Episcopal priest who decided to become a sociologist. For his Ph.D. dissertation Humphreys decided to study homosexuals. Specifically, he wanted to focus on social interaction in "tearooms," places where some male homosexuals go for quick, anonymous oral sex.

Humphreys found that some restrooms in Forest Park, just across from the campus, were tearooms. He first did a participant observation study, just hanging around these restrooms. He found that three people were always involved, the two having sex and a third person—called a "watchqueen"—who stayed on the lookout for police and other unwelcome strangers. Humphreys took the role of watchqueen, watching not only for strangers but also observing what the men did. He systematically recorded these encounters, and they became part of his dissertation.

Humphreys decided, however, that he also wanted to know more about the regular lives of these men. Impersonal sex in tearooms was a fleeting encounter, and the men must spend most of their time doing other things. What things? With whom? And what was the significance of the wedding rings that many of the men wore? Humphreys then hit on an ingenious technique. Many of the men parked their cars near the tearooms. After observing an encounter, he would leave the restroom and record the license number of the man's car. Through the help of a friend in the St. Louis police department, Humphreys then obtained each man's address. About a year later, Humphreys arranged for these men to be included in a medical survey conducted by some of the sociologists on our faculty. Disguising himself with a different hairstyle and clothing, and driving a different car, he visited some of these men at their homes. He then interviewed them, supposedly for the medical study.

Humphreys said that no one recognized him—and he did obtain the information he was looking for: family background, social class, health, religion, employment, and relationship with wife. He found that most of the men were in their mid-thirties and had at least some college education. Surprisingly, the majority were married, and a higher proportion than in the general population turned out to be Roman Catholic. Moreover, these men led very conventional lives. They voted, mowed their lawns, and took their kids to Little League games.

Humphreys also found that although most of the men were committed to their wives and families, their sex life was far from satisfactory. Many reported that their wives were not aroused sexually or were afraid of getting pregnant because their religion did not allow them to use birth control. Humphreys concluded that these were heterosexual men who were using the tearooms for an alternative form of sex that, unlike affairs, was quick (taking no time away from their families), inexpensive (zero cost), and nonthreatening (the encounter required no emotional involvement to compete with their wives). If a wife had discovered her husband's secret sex life, of course, it would have been devastating to their relationship. And today tearoom encounters present a much greater threat, for Humphreys conducted his research before the arrival of AIDS. Anyone participating in tearooms today risks death—both for himself and, by transmitting AIDS, also for his sexual partners, wife included.

This study stirred controversy among sociologists and nonsociologists alike (Goodwin et al. 1991). Humphreys was severely criticized by many sociologists, and a national columnist even wrote a scathing denunciation of "sociological snoopers" (Von Hoffman 1970). Concerned about protecting the identity of his respondents, Humphreys kept a master list in a safe deposit box. As the controversy grew more heated, however, and he feared that the names might be subpoenaed (a court case was being threatened), he gave me a list to take from Missouri to Illinois, where I had begun teaching. (It could have been some other list of respondents. I was told not to examine it, and I did not.) When he called and asked me to destroy it, I burned it in my backyard. Humphreys had a contract to remain at Washington University as an assistant professor, but he was fired before he could begin teaching. (Although other reasons were involved, his research was a central issue. There was even an attempt by one professor to have his doctorate revoked.)

Was the research ethical? That question is not easily decided. Although many sociologists sided with Humphreys and his book reporting the research won a highly acclaimed award, the criticisms mounted. At first Humphreys vigorously defended his position, but five years later, in a second edition of his book (1975), he stated that he should have identified himself as a researcher.

How Research and Theory Work Together

As discussed, sociological research is based on the sociologist's interests, the availability of subjects, appropriate methods, and ethical considerations. But the value of research is also related to sociological theory. On the one hand, as sociologist C. Wright Mills (1959) so forcefully argued, research without theory is of little value, simply a collection of meaningless "facts." On the other hand, if theory is unconnected to research it is abstract and empty, unlikely to represent the way life really is. Research and theory, then, are interdependent, and sociologists combine them in their work.

They do this in three major ways. First, as stressed in Chapters 1 and 2, sociologists use theory to interpret data. Functionalism, symbolic interactionism, and conflict theory are frameworks that sociologists use to interpret research findings. Second, theory helps to generate research. As sociologists develop hypotheses from theory, they identify areas that need to be explored further to test those hypotheses. Third, research helps to generate theory. When research findings do not fit a theory, they indicate that the theory needs to be modified.

Sociologists Diana Scully and Joseph Marolla, who interviewed rapists in prison, reported their findings in a book and in papers published in sociological journals. Who ends up in prison, and who escapes this punishment, is often the consequence of social class and the wealth, connections, and legal talent that can be purchased—or the lack thereof. Shown here is William Kennedy Smith, nephew of former President Jack Kennedy and Senator Ed Kennedy, smiling triumphantly after the jury in Palm Beach County found him not guilty of rape. To his left is Cathy Bennett, a specialist in how to select the members of a jury whom Smith was able to hire.

Research findings that contradict a theory can also indicate that the data are inaccurate, that more research needs to be done. If a study were to show little relationship between (1) poverty and (2) abduction and rape by strangers, it would fly in the face of several sociological theories that are based on existing studies. Consequently, if contradictory results came in, the research would be suspect and more research would need to be carried out. Theory and research, then, go hand in hand, each feeding the other.

The Real World: When the Ideal Meets the Real

Although one can list the ideals of research, real-life situations often force sociologists to settle for something that falls short of the ideal. Let's look at how two sociologists confronted the ideal and the real in the following Thinking Critically section.

▼▲▼▲▼▲▼▲▼▲▼▲▼▲▼▲▼▲▼▲▼▲▼▲▼▲▼▲▼▲▼

Thinking Critically About Social Controversy

Are Rapists Sick? A Closeup View of Research

▼ TWO SOCIOLOGISTS, DIANA SCULLY and Joseph Marolla, were not satisfied with the typical explanation that rapists are "sick," psychologically disturbed, or different from other men. They developed the hypothesis that rape, like most behavior, is learned socially through interaction with others. That is, some men learn to justify rape as appropriate behavior.

To test this hypothesis, Scully and Marolla would have liked to interview a random sample of rapists. But a random sample of this population is impossible, for there is no list that will allow all rapists the same chance of being included in a sample. Even prison populations won't permit a random sample, for many rapists have never been caught, some who were caught were found not guilty, and some who were found guilty were given probation. Consequently, Scully and Marolla confronted the classic dilemma of sociologists—to either not do the study or to do so under less than ideal conditions.

They chose to do the study. They knew that whatever they learned would be more than we already knew, and when they had the opportunity to interview convicted rapists in prison, they jumped at it. With no random sample possible, Scully and Marolla did systematic research that lends itself to replication. They sent out 3,500 letters to men serving time in seven prisons in Virginia, the state where they were teaching. About 25 percent of the prisoners agreed to be interviewed. From this pool of volunteers, they matched men on the basis of age, education, race, severity of offense, and previous criminal record. This resulted in a sample of 98 prisoners who were convicted for rape and a control sample of 75 nonrapists, men convicted for other offenses.

To prevent biases that might result from the sex of the interviewer, each interviewed half the sample. It took them 600 hours to go through sixty-two pages of questions with both samples and an additional thirty pages of open-ended questions with the rapists. Marolla and Scully gathered information on the prisoner's background, including their psychological, criminal, and sexual history. To guard against lies, they did what is called a "validity check"; in this case, they checked what the individuals said against their institutional record. They used twelve scales to measure the men's attitudes about women, rape, and themselves. They also presented nine vignettes of forced sexual encounters to measure the circumstances under which the men defined a situation as rape and viewed the victim as responsible.

Scully and Marolla discovered something that goes against common sense—that most rapists are not sick, that they are not overwhelmed by uncontrollable urges. They found that the psychological histories of the two samples were similar. Rapists, they concluded, are emotionally average men who have learned to view rape as appropriate in various situations. Rapists are men who find rape rewarding. The men feel good while they rape. Some even find pleasure in anticipating the rape. Some plan their rapes, sometimes with other like-minded individuals. Some even rape with friends on a regular basis, such as on weekends, using rape as a form of recreation. Others rape spontaneously. Some men even use rape to get even with someone (not necessarily the woman) ("revenge rape"). Others simply take an unexpected opportunity, such as a man Scully and Marolla interviewed. He said that while robbing a woman on a local supermarket parking lot,

> I wasn't thinking about sex. But when she said she would do anything not to get hurt, probably because she was pregnant, I thought, "Why not?"

Another man pinpointed how power was combined with sex in his rapes:

> Rape gave me the power to do what I wanted to do without feeling I had to please a partner or respond to a partner. I felt in control, dominant. Rape was the ability to have sex without caring about the woman's response. I was totally dominant.

To discover that most rapists engage in calculated behavior—that they are not "sick," and that the motivating force is power not passion, the criminal pursuit of pleasure not mental illness—is extremely significant and part of the thrill of the sociological quest.

Scully and Marolla also found something else very significant—that rapists are more likely than nonrapists to believe "rape myths." Comparing their samples of rapists and nonrapists, they discovered that the rapists were more likely to believe that most men accused of rape are innocent, that women cause their own rape by the way they act and the clothes they wear, and that a woman who charges rape has simply changed her mind after voluntary sex.

Such findings go far beyond simply adding to our storehouse of "facts." As indicated in Figure 5.1 on page 120, social research stimulates both the development of theory and the need for more research. As Scully and Marolla suggest, rape myths may act as neutralizers. They may allow "potential rapists to turn off social prohibitions against injuring others." This, in turn, pinpoints the need to determine how some males learn myths that justify rape. On the one hand, how do male subcultures transmit such myths? Do the mass media contribute to these myths? On the other hand, do family, religion, and education create respect for females and help keep males from learning such myths? If so, how?

At some point sociologists will build on this path-breaking research—done, as usual, under less than ideal conditions. The resulting theorizing and research may provide the basis for making changes that reduce rape in U.S. society.

Sources: Scully and Marolla 1984, 1985; Marolla and Scully 1986; Scully 1990.

This is how sociology develops, slowly adding one small unit of data and theory to another. And it is exactly what sociology needs more of—imaginative, and sometimes daring, research conducted in an imperfect world under less than ideal conditions. This is really what sociology is all about. Sociologists study what people do—whether those behaviors are pleasing to others, or whether they disgust them and arouse intense anger. In either case, the application of research methods takes us beyond common sense and allows us to penetrate surface realities so we can better understand human behavior—and, in the ideal case, to make changes in order to improve social life.

Summary and Review

What Is a Valid Sociological Topic?

Any human behavior is a valid sociological topic, even disreputable behavior. Rape is an example. Sociological research is based on the sociologist's interests, the availability of subjects, appropriate methods, and ethical considerations. P. 118.

Common Sense and the Need for Sociological Research

Why isn't common sense adequate?

Common sense is not a reliable tool in research. When subjected to scientific research methods, commonsense ideas often are found to be highly limited or false. Pp. 118–119.

A Research Model

What are the eight basic steps of scientific research?

1. Selecting a topic

2. Defining the problem

3. Reviewing the literature

4. Formulating a hypothesis

5. Choosing a research method

6. Collecting the data

7. Analyzing the results

8. Sharing the results

These steps are explained in detail on pp. 119–123.

Six Research Methods

How do sociologists gather data?

Sociologists use six research methods (or research designs) for gathering data: surveys, participant observation, secondary analysis, documents, unobtrusive measures, and experiments. Pp.123–133.

How do sociologists choose a particular research method?

Sociologists choose their research method on the basis of the research questions to be answered, their access to potential subjects, the resources available, their training, and ethical considerations. Pp. 133–134.

Ethics in Sociological Research

How important are questions of ethics in sociological research?

Ethics are of fundamental concern to sociologists, who are committed to openness, honesty, truth, and protecting their subjects from harm. Sociologists are not supposed to misrepresent themselves or their research. The Brajuha research on restaurants, the Scarce research on the environmental movement, and the Humphreys research on "tearooms" were cited to illustrate ethical issues of concern to sociologists. Pp. 135–137.

How Research and Theory Work Together

What is the relationship between theory and research?

Theory and research are interdependent. Sociologists use theory to interpret the data they gather. Theory also helps to generate research, while research, in turn, helps to generate theory. Theory without research is not likely to represent real life, while research without theory is merely a collection of empty facts. Pp. 137–138.

What happens when the ideal meets the real?

As illustrated by the Scully–Marolla research on rapists in prison, real-life situations often force sociologists to conduct research in less than ideal conditions. Although conducted in an imperfect world, social research stimulates sociological theorizing, more research, and the potential of improving human life. Pp. 138–139.

Where can I read more on this topic?

Suggested readings for this chapter are listed on page 639.

Beauford Delaney, Can Fire in the Park, 1946

Societies to Social Networks

J OHNNY SMILED AS HIS FINGER *tightened on the trigger. The explosion was pure pleasure to his ears. His eyes glistened as the bullet ripped into the dog. With an exaggerated swagger, Johnny walked away, surrounded by five buddies, all wearing Levis, Air Jordans, and jackets emblazoned with the logo of Satan's Servants.*

Johnny had never felt as if he belonged. His parents were never home much, and when they were, all they did was have one drunken quarrel after another. Many times he had huddled in a corner while the police separated his parents and handcuffed his father. One of Johnny's recurring memories was of his father being taken away in a police cruiser. School was a hassle, too, for he felt that the teachers were out to get him and that most of his classmates were jerks. It wasn't unusual for Johnny to spend most of his time in detention for disrupting classes and fighting during lunch period.

Johnny didn't want to be a loner, but that seemed to be what fate held in store. He once tried a church group, but that lasted just one meeting. He was lousy at skateboarding and had given that up after the guys laughed at him. It was the same with baseball and other sports.

But Satan's Servants—now that was different. For the first time in his life, Johnny felt welcome—even appreciated. All the guys got in trouble in school, and none of them got along with their parents. He especially liked the jackets, with the skull and crossbones and "Satan's Servants" emblazoned on the back. And finally, with the "Satan's Servettes," there were girls who looked up to him.

The shooting assured Johnny, now known as JB, of a firm place in the group. The old man wouldn't bother them anymore. He'd get the message when he found his dog.

When they returned to the abandoned building, which served as their headquarters, Johnny had never felt so good in his entire life. This was what life was all about. "There isn't anything I wouldn't do for these guys," he thought, as they gathered around him and took turns pointing the pistol.

Social Groups and Societies

Groups are the essence of life in society. Workers in a corporation form a group, as do neighbors on a block. The family is a group, as is the Los Angeles Lakers basketball team. The groups to which we belong help to determine our goals and values, how we feel about ourselves, and even how we feel about life itself. Groups can ignite a sense of purpose in life—or extinguish even the spark that makes life seem worthwhile. Just as Johnny found a sense of belonging in Satan's Servants, others find the same in the Scouts, in church and synagogue, in sports, in the family, at work.

LO1 Describe the relationship between a social group and a society.

Sociologists define **group** in many different ways. Albion Small (1905), mentioned in Chapter 1 as an early North American sociologist at the University of Chicago, used group in a very broad sense to mean people who have some sort of relationship so that they are thought of together. Sociologists Michael Olmsted and Paul Hare (1978) point out that the "essential feature of a group is that its members have something in common and that they believe what they have in common makes a difference." This is our general definition of group, and more specific types of groups are defined later as they are introduced.

Society, which consists of people who share a culture and a territory, is the largest and most complex group that sociologists study. The values, beliefs, and cultural characteristics of a society profoundly affect the smaller groups within it. In the former Soviet Union, for example, underground artists formed hundreds of groups, all of which shared opposition to the Soviet state. The members of one art movement, called "Apartment Art," visually depicted how stifling life was for the millions of Russians forced to live several families or more to one apartment. Because no one knew who was a government

group: defined differently by various sociologists, but in a general sense, people who have something in common and who believe that what they have in common is significant; also called a social group

society: people who share a culture and a territory

144

spy, an atmosphere of paranoia and unhappiness was often present—which the artists tried to depict in works such as that shown in the photograph on page 147.

Now that the communist government responsible for the spying has collapsed, the impetus for the formation of these artists' groups is gone. These groups will either disband or refocus their artistic perceptions on continuing problematic features of national life. Similarly, thousands of other groups in the former Soviet Union must also adapt to changing circumstances, for they, too, had defined themselves by the conditions of their society. As any society changes, then, so do the nature and types of its groups.

Later on, this chapter looks at the major types of groups in industrialized societies and the dynamics that occur within them. But first, let's trace the evolution of the largest social groups—societies—from those based on the simplest form of social organization to those based on increasingly complex social arrangements. Thus, before investigating the different types of groups and their dynamics, we need to examine how contemporary society came into being. How did the United States, for example, become an industrialized nation with literally millions of groups?

The Transformation of Societies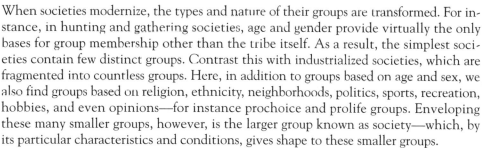

When societies modernize, the types and nature of their groups are transformed. For instance, in hunting and gathering societies, age and gender provide virtually the only bases for group membership other than the tribe itself. As a result, the simplest societies contain few distinct groups. Contrast this with industrialized societies, which are fragmented into countless groups. Here, in addition to groups based on age and sex, we also find groups based on religion, ethnicity, neighborhoods, politics, sports, recreation, hobbies, and even opinions—for instance prochoice and prolife groups. Enveloping these many smaller groups, however, is the larger group known as society—which, by its particular characteristics and conditions, gives shape to these smaller groups.

To better understand this envelope that surrounds us and sets the stage on which we grow up, let us trace the development of societies from their earliest beginnings. As we examine the evolution of societies portrayed in Figure 6.1, we will not only see how our own society emerged, but we will also see how each type of society is marked by fundamentally different characteristics. These patterns are significant because they determine our basic orientations to life.

Hunting and Gathering Societies

The simplest societies are called **hunting and gathering societies.** As the name implies, these groups depend on hunting and gathering for their survival. The men do the hunt-

Whether large or small, groups are the essence of life in society. As Durkheim pointed out, small groups such as these students performing an experiment in a high school chemistry class, serve as a buffer between us and the huge, impersonal, amorphous group called society. One of the chief functions of small groups is to provide meaning for our lives.

hunting and gathering society: a society dependent on hunting and gathering for survival

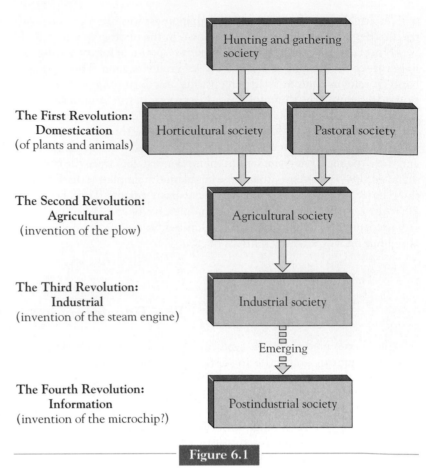

Figure 6.1

The Social Transformations of Society

ing (of animals), the females the gathering (of plants). Beyond this basic division of labor by sex, there are few social divisions. The groups usually have a **shaman,** or priest, but they, too, must help procure food. Although these groups give greater prestige to the male hunters, the women gatherers contribute much more food to the group, perhaps even four-fifths of their total food (Bernard 1992).

In addition to gender, the major unit of organization is the family. Most members are related by ancestry or marriage. Because the family is the only distinct social institution in these societies, it fulfills functions that are divided among many specialized institutions in modern societies. The family distributes food to its members, educates its children (especially in food skills), nurses the sick, and so on.

Because an area cannot support a large number of people who hunt animals and gather plants (they do not plant, only gather what is already there), hunting and gathering societies are small, usually consisting of only twenty-five to forty members. They are also nomadic, moving from one place to another as the food supply of an area gives out. These groups are usually peaceful and place high value on sharing food, which is essential to their survival. The high risk of destruction of the food supply, however—by disease, drought, famine, and pestilence—makes their death rate very high. Members of hunting and gathering groups have only about a fifty–fifty chance of surviving childhood (Lenski and Lenski 1987).

Of all societies, hunters and gatherers are the most egalitarian. Because what the people hunt and gather are perishable, they can't accumulate possessions. Consequently, no one becomes wealthier than anyone else. There are no rulers, and most decisions are arrived at through discussion. Because their needs are simple and they do not accumulate material possessions, hunters and gatherers also have the most leisure of all human groups (Lee 1979; Sahlins 1972).

shaman: a priest in a preliterate society

As a society—the largest and most complex type of group—changes, so too do the smaller groups that form the society. Until the collapse of communism in the former Soviet Union, many artists were forced to work underground. In this photograph, the artist Ilya Kabakov, a member of a now-defunct underground art movement called "Apartment Art," depicts his version of life in a typical Russian apartment under communism. Many people shared small flats and often one or more flat members were spies for the government. In "The Man Who Flew Into Space From His Apartment," Kabakov illustrates a fantasy of escape from the terrible tensions these crowded and suspicion-filled living conditions created.

All human groups were once hunters and gatherers, and until several hundred years ago such societies were still fairly common. Now, however, only a few remain, such as the pygmies of central Africa, the San of the Namibian desert, and the aborigines of Australia. Sociologists Gerhard and Jean Lenski (1987) pointed out that modern societies have increasingly taken over the areas on which such groups depend for their food. They suggested that the few remaining hunting and gathering societies will soon disappear from the human scene.

Pastoral and Horticultural Societies

About ten thousand to twelve thousand years ago, hunting and gathering societies branched in one of two directions. Very gradually, over thousands of years, some groups found that they could tame and breed some of the animals they hunted—primarily goats, sheep, cattle, and camels—others that they could cultivate plants.

The key to understanding the first branching is the word *pasture*; **pastoral societies** are based on the *pasturing of animals*. Pastoral societies developed in arid regions, where lack of rainfall made it impractical to build life around crops. Groups that took this turn remained nomadic, for they followed their animals to fresh pasture. The key to understanding the second branching is *horticulture*, or plant cultivation. **Horticultural societies** are based on the *cultivation of plants by the use of hand tools*. No longer having to abandon an area as the food supply gave out, these groups developed permanent settlements.

We can call the domestication of animals and plants the *first social revolution*. Although the **domestication revolution** was extremely gradual, it represented a fundamental break with the past and changed human history.

Horticulture apparently first began in the fertile areas of the Middle East. Primitive agricultural technology—hoes and digging sticks (to punch holes in the ground for

pastoral society: a society based on the pasturing of animals

horticultural society: a society based on cultivating plants by the use of hand tools

domestication revolution: the first social revolution, based on the domestication of plants and animals, which led to pastoral and horticultural societies

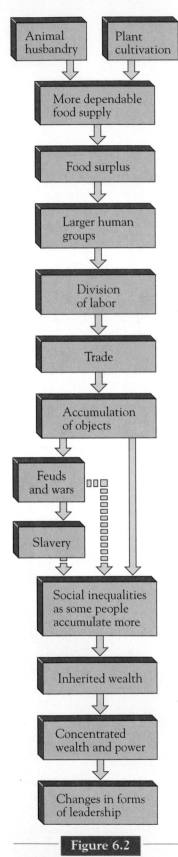

Figure 6.2

Fundamental Consequences of Animal Husbandry and Plant Cultivation

seeds)—gradually spread to Europe and China. Apparently these techniques were independently invented in Central and South America, although they may have arrived there through *cultural diffusion* (the spreading of items from one culture to another) due to contacts yet unknown to us.

These discoveries of animal husbandry and plant cultivation transformed human society. By creating a more dependable food supply, they ushered in a series of interrelated changes that altered almost every aspect of human life. Because a more dependable food supply could support more people, human groups became larger. There also was more food than was necessary for survival. This food surplus allowed groups to develop a specialized division of labor: not everyone had to produce food, and some became full-time priests, others the makers of jewelry, tools, weapons, and so on. This production of objects, in turn, stimulated trade. As groups that had lived largely in isolation traded with one another, people began to accumulate objects they considered valuable, such as gold, jewelry, utensils, and a greater variety of food.

These changes set the stage for social inequality, for now some families (or clans) accumulated more surplus goods or wealth than others. Feuds and wars then erupted, for groups now possessed animals, pastures, croplands, jewelry, and other material goods to fight about. War, in turn, let slavery enter the human picture, for people found it convenient to let captives from their battles do their drudge work. Social stratification remained limited, however, for the surplus itself was limited. As individuals passed on their possessions to their descendants, wealth grew more concentrated and power more centralized. Forms of leadership then changed as chiefs emerged. These changes are depicted in Figure 6.2.

Note that the primary pattern that runs through this fundamental transformation of group life is the change *from greater to lesser equality.* The essential significance of this change was that where people were located *within* a society came to be vital in determining what happened to them in life.

Agricultural Societies

About five to six thousand years ago came the *second social revolution,* much more sudden and dramatic than the first. The **agricultural revolution** was brought about by the invention of the plow, an invention with such far-reaching effects that it produced a new type of society. This new **agricultural society** was based on large-scale agriculture, which depended on plows drawn by animals. Compared with hoes and digging sticks, the use of animals to pull plows was immensely efficient. More nutrients were returned to the soil as the ground was turned up, and much more land could be farmed by a smaller number of people. The result was a huge agricultural surplus, which allowed more people to engage in activities other than farming—to develop the things popularly known as "culture," such as philosophy, art, literature, and architecture. The changes during this period in history were so profound that they are sometimes referred to as "the dawn of civilization." Not only the plow but also the wheel, writing, and numbers were invented. The developments just outlined, some of which were only tendencies during the earlier period, grew more pronounced.

One of the most significant changes was the growth of social inequality. When the agricultural surplus allowed the population to increase beyond anything previously known, cities developed. As groups began to be distinguished by their possessions, what earlier had been only a tendency now became a pronounced feature of social life. As conflict theorists point out, an elite gained control of the surplus resources and wielded them to reinforce their own power. This concentration of resources and power was the precursor of the state, or the political institution, for to protect their privileged positions, the elite surrounded themselves with armed men to maintain their position. After taking control, the elite levied taxes on groups who had now become their "subjects," a fundamental step in oppression.

The simplest form of societies are called hunting and gathering societies. They face particular hardships, but have adapted well to their environments. They have the most leisure of any type of society.

No one knows exactly how it happened, but sometime during this period females also became subjugated to males. Sociologist Elise Boulding (1976) theorized that this change occurred because men were in charge of plowing and the cows. She suggests that when metals were developed, men took on the new job of attaching the metal as tips to the wooden plows and doing the plowing. As a result,

> the shift of the status of the woman farmer may have happened quite rapidly, once there were two male specializations relating to agriculture: plowing and the care of cattle. This situation left women with all the subsidiary tasks, including weeding and carrying water to the fields. The new fields were larger, so women had to work just as many hours as they did before, but now they worked at more secondary tasks. . . . This would contribue further to the erosion of the status of women.

Although Boulding's theory hasn't been proven, it matches the available evidence. As new evidence comes to light, we must expect to modify the theory.

Industrial Societies

Just as the agricultural revolution was based on a single invention, so was the much later *third social revolution*. Just like the second revolution, it, too, turned society upside down. The **Industrial Revolution** began in Britain, where in 1765 the steam engine was first used to run machinery. Before this time some machines had harnessed nature (such as wind and water mills), but most had depended on human and animal power. This new source of energy led to the development of what is called **industrial society,** defined by sociologist Herbert Blumer (1990) as a society in which goods are produced by machines powered by fuels instead of by the brute force of humans or animals.

A group's technology is an essential part of its culture, and any change in technology requires that the group make some sort of adjustment. Sociologist William Ogburn (1922, 1961) concluded that a certain amount of time is required before people change their patterns of living in response to a change in technology. He called this time gap **cultural lag.** In other words, industrial societies are always playing catch-up: Nonmaterial culture (values, beliefs, folkways, and how we relate to one another) always trails the more rapidly changing material culture (technology). Critics of this view point out that the process is not always so one-sided and that changes in the nonmaterial culture, such as values, also stimulate change in the material culture (Barber 1959).

Let us look at some of the social changes that followed industrialization. This new form of production was far more efficient than anything the world had seen. Just as its surplus was greater, so were its effects on the human group. Highly significant was a growth in social inequality, especially during the first stage of industrialization. The individuals who first used the new technology accumulated great wealth, their riches in many instances outrunning the imagination of kings. Gaining an early position in the

agricultural revolution: the second social revolution, based on the invention of the plow, which led to agricultural societies

agricultural society: a society based on large-scale agriculture, dependent on plows drawn by animals

Industrial Revolution: the third social revolution, occurring when machines powered by fuels replaced most animal and human power

industrial society: a society based on the harnessing of machines powered by fuels

cultural lag: William Ogburn's term for the situation in which nonmaterial culture lags behind changes in material culture

A hallmark of postindustrial societies is the information revolution, which is based on the computer chip. Like other social revolutions before it, this one, too, will leave hardly any aspect of our lives untouched. Changes in social life ushered in by this invention are discussed in Chapter 22.

markets, they were able not only to control the means of production (factories, machinery, tools), but also to dictate the conditions under which people could work. A huge surplus of labor had already developed at this time, for feudal society was breaking up and masses of people were thrown off the lands that they and their ancestors had farmed as tenants for centuries. Moving to the cities, these landless peasants faced the choice of stealing, starving, or working for starvation wages (Chambliss 1964; Michalowski 1985).

At that time, workers had no legal rights to safe, or even humane, working conditions; nor had they the right to unionize to improve them. The law considered employment to be a private contract between the employer and the individual worker. If workers banded together to ask for higher wages or to improve some condition of their work, they were fired. If they returned to the factory, they were arrested for trespassing. In the United States—where striking was illegal—strikers were beaten or shot by private police, and even by the National Guard.

As workers gradually won their demands for better working conditions, however, wealth spread to ever larger segments of society. Eventually, home ownership became common, as did the ownership of automobiles and an incredible variety of consumer goods. Beyond the imagination of social reformers, in the later stages of industrial societies the typical worker enjoys a high standard of living in such terms as material conditions, health care, longevity, and access to libraries and education.

The progression of industrialization to some extent reversed the earlier pattern of growing inequality. Indicators of greater equality include better housing and a vast increase in consumer goods; the abolition of slavery; the shift from monarchies to more representative political systems; the right to be tried by a jury of one's peers and to cross examine witnesses; the right to vote; and greater rights for women and minorities.

It is difficult to overstate the sociological principle that the type of society we live in is the fundamental reason that we become who we are. To see how industrial society affects your life, note that you would not be taking this course if it were not for industrialization. Clearly you could not have a car, or your type of clothing or home, a telephone, stereo, television, computer, or even electric lights. On a deeper level, you would not feel the same about life or have your particular aspirations for the future. Actually, probably no aspect of your life would be the same, for you would be locked into an agricultural or horticultural way of life. The Perspectives box on page 151 reports on how the Hmong, a group from an agricultural society in Southeast Asia, are adapting to their sudden immersion in the postindustrial society of the United States.

▼▲▼▲▼▲▼▲▼▲▼▲▼▲▼▲▼▲▼▲▼▲▼▲▼▲▼▲▼▲▼▲▼▲▼▲▼

Perspectives

CULTURAL DIVERSITY IN U.S. SOCIETY

A Tribal Mountain People Meets Postindustrial Society

WHAT HAPPENS WHEN A proud, tribal people from an agricultural society is suddenly transplanted to a postindustrial society?

When U.S. forces withdrew from Vietnam and the North Vietnamese took over Laos in 1975, about 100,000 Hmong emigrated to the United States, mainly to California, Minnesota, and Wisconsin. The Hmong had fought loyally on the side of the United States against the North Vietnamese, sustaining a casualty rate five times that of U.S. forces. Part of a huge wave of immigration of some 850,000 postwar Southeast Asian refugees, this little-known people had distinctive needs that often went unmet by overwhelmed resettlement officials.

In Laos, the Hmong were tribal mountain dwellers whose agricultural life was light-years removed from the world they encountered in the United States. They had no knowledge of cars, telephones, televisions, not even plumbing or electricity. They did not even have a written language until American and French missionaries invented one in the mid-1950s.

Resettled to U.S. cities, the Hmong abruptly confronted a totally bewildering way of life for which their agricultural society had left them quite unprepared. Many did not understand what locks were for, or the purpose of light switches. They had never seen a stove, and refugee workers would find them huddled around open fires in their living rooms. Some tried to make inside gardens by bringing in soil from the outside and spreading it around the living room floor. The Hmong used the toilet to wash rice—a logical adaptation of "water bowl" from their culture—but were perplexed when the rice disappeared if the toilet were accidentally flushed.

Perhaps the most poignant story of all is told by Sgt. Marvin Reyes of the Fresno city police: One night he pulled over a driver who was jerking his way through an intersection. The driver would stop, suddenly dart a few feet, then stop again. Figuring that the man was drunk, the officer was astonished when the Hmong driver said that he had been told to stop at every red light. It was late; the stoplight was blinking.

The resettlement of the Hmong in cities across the United States proved a failure, for by isolating families, it undermined the clan and tribal bonds on which Hmong identity is based. The youth, knowing more English, began to take on greater authority, while Hmong women began to assert new, culturally unfamiliar independence.

As they make their perilous adjustment—holding on to what they can of their old way of life while changing what they must to survive in their new land—the Hmong are attempting to maintain their tribal closeness. So far, they have succeeded to an amazing degree; Hmong who travel to a strange town can look in the telephone book for a Hmong name and be welcomed into that home even if they do not know the family. "This keeps us alive as a people, as a clan," say the Hmong.

Yang Dao, the first Hmong to earn a Ph.D., says that the Hmong must shake off their refugee status. "We must start thinking like Hmong Americans," he says, "Take the best of Laos and the best of America and live like that."

Certainly the new identity destined to arise from this mixing of cultures will be sociologically interesting, another part of the cultural diversity that makes up the American folkscape.

Sources: Based on Meredith 1984; Jones and Strand 1986; Spencer 1988; Mitchell et al. 1989; Cerhan 1990; Snider 1990; Trueba et al. 1990; Lopez-Romano 1992.

Postindustrial Societies

Sociologists have identified the emergence of an entirely new type of society. The basic trend in advanced industrial societies is away from production and manufacturing to service industries. The United States was the first country to have more than 50 percent of its work force employed in service industries—health, education, research, the government, counseling, banking and investments, sales, law, and the mass media. Australia, New Zealand, western Europe, and Japan soon followed. The term **postindustrial society** refers to this emerging society—one *based on information, services, and high technology* rather than on raw materials and manufacturing (Bell 1973; Lipset 1979; Toffler 1980; Beck 1993).

The basic component of the postindustrial society is information. People who offer services either provide or apply information of one sort or another. Teachers pass on knowledge to students, repair technicians use knowledge to service technological gadgets, while lawyers, physicians, bankers, pilots, and interior decorators sell their specialized knowledge of law, the body, money, aerodynamics, and color schemes to clients. Unlike factory workers in an industrial society, they don't *produce* anything. Rather, they transmit or use knowledge to provide services that others are willing to pay for.

> **postindustrial society:** a society based on information, services, and high technology, rather than on raw materials and manufacturing

As reviewed, early technological developments brought wrenching changes to past cultures. What will happen to ours? It may be that social analysts in years to come will speak of the current changes as the *fourth revolution*. Often called the **information revolution,** it is based on technology that processes information. Specifically, the computer chip is the primary technological change that is transforming society and with it, our social relationships. This tiny device, with its miniaturized circuitry, allows some people to work at home, others to talk to people in distant cities and even other countries while they drive their automobiles. Because of it, we can peer farther into space than ever before. And because of it, millions of children spend countless hours struggling against video enemies, at home and in the arcades. The list of changes ushered in by this one technological advance is practically endless.

Although the full implications of the information explosion are still unknown, of this we can be certain: Just as the larger group called society has historically exerted a fundamental force on people's thinking and behavior, so it will in its new form. As society is transformed, then, shall be swept along with it. As history is our guide, the change will be so extensive that even our attitudes about the self and life will be transformed.

Groups Within Society

Sociologist Emile Durkheim (1933) viewed groups as a buffer between the individual and the larger society. He said that if it were not for small groups, we would feel oppressed by that huge, amorphous entity known as society. By establishing intimate relationships and offering a sense of meaning and purpose to life, small groups serve as a sort of lifeline that helps to prevent *anomie*. Sometimes, as with Johnny's group in our opening vignette, small groups stand in opposition to the larger society, but in most instances they reinforce society's major values.

Before we examine groups in more detail, we should distinguish between groups, aggregates, and categories. An **aggregate** consists of individuals who temporarily share the same physical space but who do not see themselves as belonging together, such as people walking on the same sidewalk or drivers parked at the same red light. A **category** consists of people who have similar characteristics, such as all college females who wear glasses or all males over 6 feet tall. Unlike groups, the individuals who make up a category neither interact with one another nor take one another into account.

Let us look at the types of groups that make up our society—primary, secondary, in-groups and out-groups, reference groups, and social networks.

Primary Groups

In the opening vignette, Johnny never felt as though he belonged anywhere until Satan's Servants welcomed him. It was with them that he found friendship, admiration, and the close, intimate, face-to-face relationships that he valued. That is what sociologist Charles H. Cooley calls a **primary group.** As Cooley (1909) put it,

> By primary groups I mean those characterized by intimate face-to-face association and cooperation. They are primary in several senses, but chiefly in that they are fundamental in forming the social nature and ideals of the individual.

Because primary groups, such as the family, friendship groups, and gangs mold our basic perceptions and ideals, Cooley calls them the "springs of life." As people internalize the views of their primary groups, those views become the lens through which they view life. Even as adults, no matter how far they may have come from their childhood roots, early primary groups remain "inside" people, where they continue to form part of the perspective from which they look out on the world.

information revolution: the fourth social revolution, based on technology that processes information

aggregate: individuals who temporarily share the same physical space but do not see themselves as belonging together

category: people who have similar characteristics

primary group: a group characterized by intimate, long-term, face-to-face association and cooperation

Primary groups are essential to an individual's emotional well-being. Humans have an intense need for ongoing, cooperative, face-to-face associations that provide feelings of self-esteem. By offering a sense of belonging, a feeling of being appreciated, and sometimes even love, primary groups are uniquely equipped to meet this basic need. The relationships provided by the primary group are so significant that the group becomes fused into the individual's identity. It is difficult, if not impossible, for the individual to separate his or her self from the primary group, for the self and the group merge into a "we."

Primary Groups That Fail Not all primary groups function positively, however. Some fail to provide the self-satisfactions that their members seek. Such groups, like Johnny's family, for example, are dysfunctional.

Three types of dysfunctions can be identified. First, the members of a primary group may quarrel and humiliate one another instead of providing reinforcement and support. (Note, however, that some members, such as those who dominate a family, may find personal rewards in such behavior.) Second, a primary group, such as the one Johnny joined, may purposely set itself against society. (Note, however, that as with Satan's Servants, the group may be dysfunctional for society but highly functional for its members.) The third dysfunction occurs when an essential primary group breaks down throughout society. An example would be if families in general were no longer to provide the essential benefits of a primary group. Some analysts think that this has already happened to the American family; others believe that the family is simply changing, but that it will continue to serve as an essential and beneficial primary group.

Primary groups such as the family, a key focus of sociological investigation, play a key role in the development of the self. As a small group, the family also serves as a buffer from the often-threatening larger group known as society. The family has been of primary significance in helping this couple from Nicaragua adjust to their new life in the United States.

Secondary Groups

Compared with primary groups, **secondary groups** are larger, relatively temporary, more anonymous, formal, and impersonal. Such groups are based on some interest or activity, and their members are likely to interact on the basis of specific roles, such as president, manager, worker, or student. Examples are a college classroom, the American Sociological Association, a factory, or the Democratic party.

As we have seen, in hunting and gathering and horticultural societies the entire society formed a primary group. In contrast, in industrial societies secondary groups have multiplied and become essential to our welfare. Over the course of our lives, we all join a variety of secondary groups. They are part of the way we get our education, make our living, and spend our money and leisure.

Although contemporary society could not function without secondary groups, such groups fail to satisfy deep human needs for intimate association. Consequently, *secondary*

secondary group: compared with a primary group, a larger, relatively temporary, more anonymous, formal, and impersonal group based on some interest or activity, whose members are likely to interact on the basis of specific roles

Relationships in secondary groups are more formal and temporary than those in primary groups. In order to satisfy basic emotional needs, members of secondary groups, such as workers in a large company, form smaller primary groups.

groups tend to break down into primary groups. For example, at school and work we tend to form friendship cliques, which provide such valued interaction that if it weren't for them we sometimes feel that school or work "would drive us crazy." Just as small groups serve as a buffer between us and the larger society, so the primary groups we form within secondary groups serve as a buffer between us and the demands that secondary groups place on us.

In-Groups and Out-Groups

Sometimes group membership is defined as much by what people are *not*, as by what they are; in other words, the antagonisms that some groups feel toward other groups become an integral part of their identity. Groups toward which individuals feel loyalty are called **in-groups;** those toward which they feel antagonisms, **out-groups.** For Johnny, Satan's Servants was an in-group, while the police, teachers, welfare workers, and all those associated with school represented out-groups.

This fundamental division of the world into in-groups and out-groups has far-reaching consequences for people's lives. To identify with a group generates not only a sense of belonging, but also loyalty and feelings of superiority. In-groups can therefore exert a high degree of control over their members. Johnny's shooting of the dog is such an example.

Not surprisingly, in-and out-group relations also lead to discrimination, for, with their strong identification and loyalties, people favor members of their in-groups. This aspect of in-and out-groups is, of course, the basis of many problems in contemporary society. Another consequence is the production of rivalries, which are usually mild, such as sports rivalries between nearby towns, where the most extreme act is likely to be the furtive invasion of the out-group's territory in order to steal a mascot, paint a rock, or uproot a goal post. In some cases, however, an out-group can come to symbolize such evil that it arouses hatred and motivates members of an in-group to extreme acts. In spite of the recent Israeli-Palestinian accord, for example, seething hatred remains, and extremists on both sides are still willing to sacrifice their lives to help bring about the destruction of the other.

As sociologist Robert Merton (1968) observed, in-and out-group relations also produce a very interesting double standard. The traits of one's in-group come to be viewed as virtues, while if those *same* traits characterize groups we don't like they are defined as vices (Schaller 1991). For example, men who see women as members of an out-group may define an aggressive male employee as assertive, but an aggressive female employee as pushy; a male who doesn't speak up as "knowing when to keep quiet," but his female counterpart as too timid to make it in the business world.

Negative feelings between out-groups can range from mild dislike to intense hatred, accompanied by the desire to destroy the other. Shaking hands after signing their historic peace accord are the heads of two of these latter types of out-groups, the Prime Minister of Israel, Yitzhak Rabin, and the Chairman of the Palestinian Liberation Organization, Yasir Arafat. Although no longer at war, the PLO and Israel remain bitter out-groups.

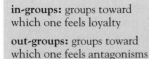

in-groups: groups toward which one feels loyalty

out-groups: groups toward which one feels antagonisms

Reference Groups

Suppose you have just received a good job offer. It pays double what you hope to make even after you graduate from college. Your prospective employer says that you have to make up your mind within three days. And you will have to drop out of college now if you accept the job. As you consider the matter, thoughts like this may go through your mind: "My friends will say I'm a fool if I don't take the job . . . but Dad and Mom will practically go crazy. They've made sacrifices for me, and they'd be so disappointed if I didn't finish college. They've always said I've got to get my education first, that good jobs will always be there. . . . But, then, I'd like to see the look on the faces of those neighbors who said I'd never amount to much!"

This is an example of how people use **reference groups,** the groups we use as standards to evaluate ourselves. Your reference groups may include family, the Scouts, the members of a church or synagogue, your neighbors, teachers, classmates, and co-workers. Your reference group need not be one you actually belong to; it may include a group to which you aspire. For example, if you are thinking about going to graduate school, graduate students or members of the profession you want to join may form your reference group as you evaluate your grades or writing skills.

Reference groups exert tremendous influence over people's behavior. For example, if you want to become the president of a corporation, you might have your hair cut fairly short, start dressing more formally, use more formal speech, read the *Wall Street Journal,* take business and law courses, try to obtain a "fast-track" job, and join the local chamber of commerce. In contrast, if you want to become a rock musician, you might let your hair grow long (or perhaps shave your head), wear three earrings in one ear, dress in ways your parents and many of your peers consider outlandish, read *Rolling Stone,* drop out of college, and hang around clubs and rock groups.

From these examples, you can see that the yardsticks provided by reference groups operate as a form of social control. When we see ourselves as measuring up to the yardstick, there is no conflict, but if our behavior, or even aspirations, do not match the

> **reference groups:** Herbert Hyman's term for the groups we use as standards to evaluate ourselves

All of us have reference groups—the groups we use as standards to evaluate ourselves. Although the groups by which we evaluate our own attitudes and behaviors certainly differ from the reference groups of these skinheads who are protesting the Martin Luther King holiday, both ours and theirs serve the same sociological functions.

The relationships we establish early in life may serve us well later in life, as in the case of these members of a social network of Harvard alumni.

standards held by a reference group, the mismatch can lead to internal turmoil. For example, to want to become a corporate officer would present no inner turmoil for most Americans, but it would if you had grown up in an Amish home, for the Amish strongly disapprove of such activities for their children. They ban high school and college education, three-piece suits, the *Wall Street Journal,* and corporate employment. Similarly, if you wanted to become a soldier and had been raised by dedicated pacifists, you would likely experience deep conflict, as such parents, disapproving of violence on principle, are likely to hold quite different aspirations for their children.

Given the highly mobile and pluralistic nature of contemporary society, many of us are exposed to contradictory ideas and standards from the various groups that become significant to us. The "internal recordings" that play contradictory messages from these reference groups, then, are simply one cost of social mobility in a postindustrial society.

Social Networks

If you are a member of a large group, there probably are a few people within that group with whom you regularly associate. In a sociology class I was teaching at a commuter campus, six women chose to work together on a project. They got along well, and they began to sit together. Eventually they planned a Christmas party at one of their homes. These clusters, or internal factions, are called **cliques.** The links between people—their cliques, as well as their family, friends, acquaintances, and even "friends of friends"—are called **social networks.** Think of a social network as ties that expand outward from yourself, gradually encompassing more and more people.

Although we live in an immense society, few of us experience social life as an ocean of nameless, strange faces. Instead, we interact within social networks that connect us to the larger society. The connections between people's social networks, in turn, are so extensive that they probably incorporate almost everyone in society. That is, if you list everyone you know, and each of those individuals lists everyone he or she knows, and you keep doing this, it seems that eventually almost everyone in the entire society will be included on those lists.

It would be too cumbersome to test this hypothesis by drawing up such lists, but psychologist Stanley Milgram (1967) hit on an ingenious way to find out just how interconnected our social networks are. In what has become a classic experiment, he selected names at random from across the United States. Some he designated as "senders," others as "receivers." Milgram addressed letters to the receivers and asked the senders to mail the letters to someone they knew on a first-name basis who they thought might know the receiver. This person, in turn, was asked to mail the letter to someone they knew who might know the receiver, and so on. The question was, Would the letters ever get to the receivers, and if so, how long would the chain be?

clique: a cluster of people within a larger group who choose to interact with one another; an internal faction

social network: the social ties radiating outward from the self that link people together

networking: the process of consciously using or cultivating networks for some gain

Think of yourself as part of this experiment. What would you do if you are a sender, but the receiver lives in a state in which you know no one? You would send the letter to someone you know who might know someone in that state. And this is just what happened. None of the senders knew the receivers, and Milgram kept a record of who sent the letters to whom. In the resulting chains, some links broke; that is, after receiving a letter, some people didn't send it on. Surprisingly, however, most letters did reach their intended receivers. Even more surprising, the average chain was made up of only *five* links.

Milgram's experiment shows just how small our world really is. Perhaps our social networks are so interrelated that most of us are connected to just about everyone else in society by just five links. At the very least, Milgram's experiment gives us insight into why strangers from different parts of the country sometimes find they have a mutual acquaintance.

The term **networking,** which has appeared in popular speech, refers to using or even developing social networks, usually for career advancement (Speizer 1983). Hoping to establish a circle of acquaintances who will prove valuable to them, people go to parties, join clubs, churches, synagogues, and political parties. Because many social networks are hard to break into, and some perpetuate social inequalities, people cultivate alternative networks. The "old boy network," for example, tends to keep good jobs moving in the direction of male friends and acquaintances (Hall 1987; Abramson 1992). To break this barrier—for most jobs are secured through social networks—many females do "gender networking," developing networks of working women to help advance their careers (Lin et al. 1981).

Group Dynamics

Now that we have surveyed the types of groups that make up society, let's look at what happens within groups, especially the ways in which individuals affect groups and the ways in which groups affect individuals. These reciprocal influences are known as **group dynamics.** We first discuss the differences that the size of the group makes and then examine the effects of the group on leadership, conformity, and decision making.

Before turning to small groups, let's first see what sociologists mean by this term. A **small group** is one that is small enough for everyone in it to interact directly with all the other members. Small groups can be either primary or secondary. Relatives at a family reunion and workers who take their breaks together represent primary small groups, while bidders at an auction and passengers on a flight from Boston to San Francisco are examples of secondary small groups.

Group Size

Writing at the turn of the century, sociologist Georg Simmel (1858–1918) noted the significance of group size. He used the term **dyad** for the smallest possible group, which consists of two persons. Dyads, he noted, which include marriages, love affairs, and close friendships, show two distinct qualities. First, they are the most intense or intimate of human groups. Because only two persons are involved, the interaction is focused exclusively between one and the other. Second, because dyads require the continuing active participation and commitment of both members, they are the most unstable of social groups. If one member loses interest, the dyad collapses. In larger groups, in contrast, even if one member withdraws the group can continue, for its existence does not depend on any single member (Simmel 1950).

A **triad** is a group of three persons, such as a married couple with their first child. As Simmel noted, the addition of a third person fundamentally changes the group. For example, with the birth of a child hardly any aspect of a couple's relationship goes untouched (Rubenstein 1992). In spite of difficulties that couples experience adjusting to their first child, however, their marriage is usually strengthened. Simmel's principle that groups larger than a dyad are inherently stronger helps explain this effect. Like dyads, triads are also intense, for interaction is shared by only three persons; but because interaction is shared with an additional person, the intensity lessens.

group dynamics: the ways in which individuals affect groups and the ways in which groups influence individuals

small group: a group small enough for everyone to interact directly with all the other members

dyad: the smallest possible group, consisting of two persons

triad: a group of three persons

Simmel also pointed out that triads, too, are inherently unstable. Because relationships among a group's members are seldom neatly balanced, they encourage the formation of a **coalition,** in which some group members align themselves against others. In a triad, it is not uncommon for two members to feel strong bonds with one another, leading them to act as a dyad and leaving the third feeling hurt and excluded. In addition, triads often produce an arbitrator or mediator, someone who tries to settle disagreements between the other two.

The general principle is that *as a small group grows larger its intensity, or intimacy, decreases and its stability increases.* To see why, look at Figure 6.3 on page 159. The addition of each person to a group greatly increases the connections among people. In a dyad, there is only 1 relationship; in a triad, 3; in a group of four, 6; in a group of five, 10. If we expand the group to six, we have 15 relationships; while a group of seven yields 21 relationships. If we continue adding members to the groups in this figure, we soon would be unable to follow the connections, for a group of eight has 28 possible relationships, a group of nine 36 relationships, a group of ten 45, and so on. It is not only the number of relationships that makes larger groups more stable. As groups grow, they tend to develop a more formal social structure to accomplish their goals. For example, leaders emerge and more specialized roles come into play, ultimately resulting in such formal offices as president, secretary, and treasurer.

Effects on Attitudes and Behaviors   Imagine that you are taking a class with social psychologists John Darley and Bibb Latané (1968) and that they have asked you to join a few students to discuss your adjustment to college life. When you arrive, they tell you that to make things totally anonymous, they would like you to sit unseen in a booth and participate in the discussion over an intercom. You are to speak when your microphone comes on. The professors say they will not listen in, and they leave.

You find the format somewhat strange, to say the least, but you participate. The other students, whom you have not seen, begin to freely exchange ideas, and you find yourself becoming wrapped up in the various problems they are sharing. One student even mentions how frightening he has found college because of his history of epileptic seizures. Soon after, this individual begins to breathe heavily into the microphone. Then he stammers and cries for help. A crashing noise follows; and you imagine him lying helpless on the floor. Then there is nothing but an eerie silence. What do you do?

coalition: the alignment of some members of a group against others

Group size has a significant influence on how people interact. When a group changes from a dyad (two people) to a triad, the relationships among each of the participants undergoes a shift.

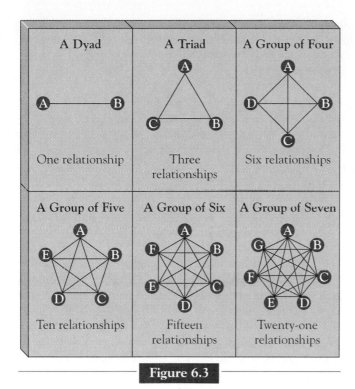

Figure 6.3

The Incremental Effects of Group Size on Relationships

It turns out the researchers staged the whole thing. No one had a seizure. In fact, no students were in other booths. Everything, except your comments, was on tape.

Some participants were told they would be discussing the topic with just one other student, others with two, others with three, and so on. Darley and Latané found that all students who thought they were part of a dyad rushed out to help. If they thought they were part of a triad, only 80 percent went to help—and they were slower in leaving the booth. In six-person groups, only 60 percent went to see what was wrong—and they were even slower in doing so.

Darley and Latané concluded that in the dyad, the students clearly knew it was up to them. The professor was gone, and if they didn't help there would be no help. In the triad, students felt less personal responsibility, while in the larger groups they felt a *diffusion of responsibility:* it was no more up to them than it was up to anyone else.

This experiment demonstrates one of the far-reaching consequences that group size has on our everyday lives—in this case, how it affects our willingness to help one another. In general, the smaller the group, the more willing we are to stick our necks out for strangers.

You probably have observed the second consequence of group size first hand. When a group is small, its members behave informally toward one another. As the group increases in size, however, its members grow more formal. A degree of intimacy is lost, for no longer can the members assume that the others are "insiders" in sympathy with what they say. Now they must take a "larger audience" into consideration, and instead of merely "talking," they now begin to "address" the group. As their language becomes more formal, their body language stiffens too.

The third aspect of group dynamics is also one that you probably have observed many times. In the very early stages of a party, when only a few people are present, almost everyone talks with everyone else. As others arrive, however, the guests soon break into smaller groups. This sometimes dismays hosts, who may want all their guests to mix together, and may even make a nuisance of themselves trying to achieve *their* ideas of what a group should be like. The division into small groups is inevitable, however, for it follows the basic sociological principles we have just reviewed. Because the addition of each person rapidly increases connections (in this case, "talk lines"), it makes conversation more difficult. The guests therefore break into smaller groups in which they can not only see one another, but also, unlike in the larger group, comfortably interact directly with each person.

Leadership

All groups, no matter what their size, have leaders, though they may not hold a formal position in a group. A **leader** is someone who influences the behaviors, opinions, or attitudes of others. Some people are leaders because of their personalities, but leadership involves much more than this, as we shall see.

Types of Leaders   Groups have two types of leaders (Bales 1950, 1953; Cartwright and Zander 1968). The first is easy to recognize as a leader. This person, called an **instrumental leader** (or task-oriented leader) tries to keep the group moving toward its goals. Such a leader tries to keep group members from getting sidetracked, reminding them of what they are trying to accomplish. The **expressive leader** (or socioemotional leader), in contrast, is not usually recognized as a leader, but he or she certainly is. This person is likely to crack jokes, to offer sympathy, or to do other things that help lift the group's morale. Both types of leadership are essential: the one to keep the group on track, the other to increase harmony and minimize conflicts.

It is difficult for one person to be both an instrumental and an expressive leader, for these roles contradict one another. Because instrumental leaders are task oriented, they sometimes create friction as they prod the group to get on with the job. Their actions often cost them popularity. Expressive leaders, in contrast, being peacemakers who stress personal bonds and the reduction of friction, are usually more popular (Olmsted and Hare 1978).

Leadership Styles   Let us suppose that the president of your college has asked you to head a task force to determine how the college can reduce sexual discrimination on your campus. The position requires you to be an instrumental leader. However, you can adopt a number of **leadership styles,** or ways of expressing yourself as a leader. The three basic styles are those of **authoritarian leader,** one who gives orders; **democratic leader,** one who tries to gain a consensus; and **laissez-faire leader,** one who is highly permissive. Which should you choose?

Social psychologists Ronald Lippitt and Ralph White (1958) carried out a classic study of these three leadership styles. Boys, matched for IQ, popularity, physical energy, and leadership, were assigned to "craft clubs" made up of five youngsters each. Adult males trained in the three leadership styles then rotated among the clubs, each playing all three styles to control possible effects of their individual personalities.

leader: someone who influences other people

instrumental leader: an individual who tries to keep the group moving toward its goals; also known as a task-oriented leader

expressive leader: an individual who increases harmony and minimizes conflict in a group; also known as a socioemotional leader

leadership styles: ways in which people express their leadership

authoritarian leader: a leader who leads by giving orders

democratic leader: a leader who leads by trying to reach a consensus

laissez-faire leader: an individual who leads by being highly permissive

Groups have both instrumental and expressive (affective) leaders. Even in such formal groups as those of the U.S. government, not all instrumental leaders serve in an official capacity, as is illustrated by Hillary Rodham Clinton's appearance at health care hearings held on Capitol Hill.

The authoritarian leaders assigned tasks to the children and set the working conditions. They also praised or condemned their work arbitrarily, giving no explanation for why it was good or bad. The democratic leaders held group discussions and outlined the steps necessary to reach the group's goals. They also suggested alternative approaches to these goals and let the children work at their own pace. When they evaluated the children's projects, they gave "facts" as the bases for their decisions. The laissez-faire leaders were very passive. They gave the group almost total freedom to do as they wished. They stood ready to offer help when asked but made few suggestions. They did not evaluate the children's projects, either positively or negatively. While all this action was taking place, researchers peered through peepholes, taking notes and making movies.

The results? Each leadership style produced different reactions. The boys who had authoritarian leaders became either aggressive or apathetic. Although both the aggressive and apathetic boys showed strong dependence on the leader, the aggressive ones also became hostile toward him. The boys also showed a high degree of internal solidarity. In contrast, the boys who had democratic leaders were more personal and friendly, more "group minded," and looked to one another for mutual approval. They did less scapegoating, and when the leader left the room they continued working at a steadier pace. The boys with laissez-faire leaders asked more questions, but they made fewer decisions. They were notable for their lack of achievement. The researchers concluded that the democratic style of leadership worked best. Those conclusions may have been colored by ideology, however, as the research was conducted by people who themselves favored a democratic style of leadership; and it was conducted during a highly charged political period (Olmsted and Hare 1978).

You may have noted that only males were involved in this experiment. It is interesting to speculate how the results might differ if the experiment were repeated with groups of girls who had male and female leaders, groups of boys with male and female leaders, and groups of both girls and boys with male and female leaders. Perhaps you will become the sociologist to do this.

Situations and Leadership Styles   It is important to note that different situations require different styles of leadership. Suppose, for example, that you are leading a dozen backpackers in California's Sierra Madre mountains, and it is time to make dinner. A laissez-faire style would be appropriate if everyone had brought their own food—or perhaps a democratic style if the meal were to be communally prepared. Authoritarian leadership—you telling everyone how to prepare their meals—would probably create resentment. This, in turn, would likely interfere with meeting the primary goals of the group, in this case, having a good time while enjoying nature.

Now assume the same group but a different situation: one of your party is lost and a blizzard is on its way. This situation calls for you to take charge and be authoritarian. To simply shrug your shoulders and say, "You figure it out," would invite disaster. It would also border on moral and legal negligence (Priest and Dixon 1991).

Who Becomes a Leader?   Are leaders people who are born with characteristics that propel them to the forefront of a group? No sociologist would agree with such a premise. In general, people who are seen as strongly representing the group's values or who are perceived as able to lead a group out of a crisis are likely to become leaders (Trice and Beyer 1991). Leaders also tend to be more talkative and to express determination and self-confidence. These findings may not be surprising, as such traits appear related to a leadership role. Researchers, however, have also discovered that traits seeming to have no bearing whatsoever on ability to lead are also significant. For example, taller people and those judged better looking are more likely to become leaders (Stodgill 1974; Crosbie 1975). (The taller and more attractive are also likely to earn more, but that is another story [Deck 1968; Feldman 1972; Katz 1995].)

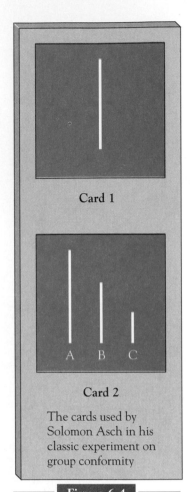

Card 1

Card 2

The cards used by Solomon Asch in his classic experiment on group conformity

---

Figure 6.4

Asch's Cards

(Source: Asch 1952: 452–453.)

Many other factors underlie people's choice of leaders, most of which are quite subtle. A simple experiment performed by social psychologists Lloyd Howells and Selwyn Becker (1962) uncovered one of these factors. They formed groups of five people each who did not know one another, seating them at a rectangular table, three on one side and two on the other. After each group had discussed a topic for a set period of time, they chose a leader. Their findings are startling: Although only 40 percent of the people sat on the two-person side, 70 percent of the leaders emerged from that side. The explanation is that we tend to direct more interactions to people facing us than to people to the side of us.

Conformity to Peer Pressure: The Asch Experiment

How influential are groups in people's lives? As we shall see, they wield a surprising amount of influence over our attitudes and behaviors. Let us look first at *conformity* in the sense of going along with your peers. They have no authority over you, only the influence that you allow.

Imagine that you are taking a course in social psychology with Dr. Solomon Asch and that you have agreed to participate in an experiment. As you enter his laboratory, you see seven chairs, five of them already filled by other students. You are given the sixth. Soon the seventh person arrives. Dr. Asch stands at the front of the room next to a covered easel. He explains that he will first show a large card with a vertical line on it, then another card with three vertical lines. All each of you has to do is tell him which of the three lines is identical to the line on the first card (see Figure 6.4).

Dr. Asch then uncovers the first card with a single line and the comparison card with the three lines. The correct answer is easy, for one of the lines is obviously too tall, another too short, and one exactly right. Each person, in order, states his or her answer aloud. You all answer correctly. The second trial is just as easy, and you begin to wonder what the point is of your being here. Then on the third trial something unexpected happens. Just as before, it is easy to tell which lines match. The first student, however, gives a wrong answer. The second gives the same incorrect answer. So do the third and the fourth. By now you are wondering what is wrong. How will the person next to you answer? You can hardly believe it when he, too, gives the same wrong answer. Then it is your turn, and you give what you know is the right answer. The seventh person also gives the same wrong answer. On the next trial, the same thing happens. You know the choice of the other six is wrong, yet they give what to you are obviously wrong answers. You don't know what to think. Why aren't you seeing things the same way they are? Sometimes they do, but in twelve trials they don't. Something is seriously wrong, and you are no longer sure what to do. . . .

When the eighteenth card is finished, you feel relief. The experiment is finally over, and you are ready to bolt for the door. Dr. Asch walks over to you with a big smile on his face, thanks you for participating in the experiment, and then explains that you were the only real subject in the experiment! The other six were all stooges! "I paid them to give those answers," he says. Now you feel real relief. Your eyes weren't playing tricks on you after all.

What were the results? Asch (1952) tested fifty people. About 33 percent gave in to the group about half the time and gave what they knew to be wrong answers. Another 40 percent also gave wrong answers, but not as often. And 25 percent stuck to their guns and always gave the right answer. I don't know how I would do on this test (if I knew nothing about it in advance), but I like to think that I would be part of the 25 percent. You probably feel the same way. But why should we feel that we wouldn't be like *most* people?

The results are disturbing. In our "land of individualism," the group is so powerful that most people are willing, at least to some extent, to say things that they know do not match objective reality. And this was simply a group of strangers! How much more can we expect the group to enforce conformity when it consists of friends, people we value highly and depend on for getting along in life? Again, perhaps you will become the sociologist to run that variation of Asch's experiment, and perhaps to use female subjects. Further implications of conformity are considered in the following Thinking Critically section.

▼▲▼▲▼▲▼▲▼▲▼▲▼▲▼▲▼▲▼▲▼▲▼▲▼▲▼▲▼▲

Thinking Critically About Social Controversy

If Hitler Asked You to Execute a Stranger, Would You? The Milgram Experiment

▼ IMAGINE THAT YOU ARE taking a course with Dr. Stanley Milgram (1963, 1965), a former student of Dr. Asch's. Assume that you did not take part in Dr. Asch's experiment and have no reason to be wary of these experimenters. You appear in the laboratory to participate in a study on punishment and learning. A second student arrives, and you draw lots for the roles of "teacher" and "learner." You are to be the teacher, he the learner. You are glad that you are the teacher when you see that the learner's chair has protruding electrodes and resembles an electric chair. Dr. Milgram shows you the machine you will run. You see that one side of the control panel is marked "Mild Shock, 15 volts," the center says "Intense Shock, 350 Volts," while the far right side reads, "DANGER: SEVERE SHOCK."

"As the teacher, you will read aloud a pair of words," explains Dr. Milgram. "Then you will repeat the first word, and the learner will reply with the second word. If the learner can't remember the word, you press this lever on the shock generator. The shock will serve as punishment, and we can then determine if punishment improves memory." You nod, now extremely relieved that you haven't been designated a learner.

"Every time the learner makes an error, increase the punishment by 15 volts," Dr. Milgram says. Then, seeing the look on your face, he adds, "The shocks can be extremely painful, but they won't cause any permanent tissue damage." He pauses, and then adds, "I want you to see." You then follow him to the "electric chair," and Dr. Milgram gives you a shock of 45 volts. "There. That wasn't too bad, was it?" "No," you mumble.

The experiment begins. You hope for the learner's sake that he is bright, but unfortunately he turns out to be rather dull. He gets some answers right, but you have to keep turning up the dial. Each turn of the dial makes you more and more uncomfortable. You find yourself hoping that the learner won't miss another answer. But he does. When he received the first shocks, he let out some moans and groans, but now he is screaming in agony. He even protests that he suffers from a heart condition. *How far do you continue turning that dial?*

By now, you have probably guessed that there was no electricity attached to the electrodes and that the "learner" was a stooge, only pretending to feel pain. The purpose of the experiment, of course, was to find out at what point people refuse to participate. Does anyone actually turn the lever all the way to DANGER: SEVERE SHOCK?

Milgram was motivated to do this research because the slaughter of so many Jews, Gypsies, and others designated by the Nazis as "inferior" required the cooperation of "good people" (Hughes 1993; Meyer 1993). The fact that millions of ordinary people did nothing to stop the deaths seemed bizarre, and Milgram wanted to see how ordinary, intelligent Americans might react to an analogous situation.

Milgram was upset by what he found. Many "teachers" broke into a sweat and protested to the experimenter that this was inhuman and should be stopped. But when the experimenter, who sat by calmly, supposedly recording how the "learner" was performing, replied that the experiment must go on, this assurance from the "authority" ("scientist, white coat, university laboratory") was enough for most "teachers" to continue, even though they were free to leave. Even some who were "reduced to twitching, stuttering wrecks" continued to follow orders.

Milgram did eighteen of these experiments (Miller 1986). He used both males and females and put some "teachers" and "learners" in the same room, where the "teacher" could clearly see the suffering. In some experiments, he had "learners" pound and kick on the wall during the first shocks and then go silent. No verbal feedback was involved. On other occasions he even added a second "teacher," this one a stooge who refused to go along with the experiment. The results varied from situation to situation. The highest proportion of "teachers" who pushed the lever all the way to 450 volts—65 percent—occurred when there was no verbal feedback from the "learner." Of those who could turn and look at the "learner," 40 percent turned the lever all the way. But only 5 percent carried out the severe shocking when the stooge-teacher refused to comply, a result that bears out some of Asch's results.

Milgram's experiments raised a ruckus in the scientific community. Not only were social researchers surprised, and disturbed, at the results, but they also were alarmed at Milgram's methods. Milgram's experiments became a stormy basis for rethinking the research ethics we reviewed in the previous chapter. Associations of social researchers adopted or revised their codes of ethics, and universities began to require that subjects be informed of the nature and purpose of social research. Not only did researchers agree that to reduce subjects to "twitching, stuttering wrecks" was unethical, but almost all deception was banned.

The results of the Asch and Milgram experiments leave us with the disturbing question: "How far would *I* go in following authority?" Truly the influence of the group extends beyond what most of us imagine.

Issues to Consider   In light of such significant findings, do you think that the scientific community overreacted to Milgram's experiment? Should we allow such research? In light of both the Asch and Milgram experiments, why do you think groups have such influence over us? How do you think we can reduce the power of authorities to motivate people to do evil? ▲

Groupthink and Decision Making

Among the disturbing implications of the Asch and Milgram experiments is the power of what is called **groupthink,** a narrowing of thought by a group of people. Sociologist Irving Janis (1972) coined this term to refer to situations in which a group of people think alike and any suggestion of alternatives becomes a sign of disloyalty, the group having decided that there is but one correct answer. Even moral judgments must be put aside, for the group is convinced that its welfare depends on a particular course of action. Groupthink often leads to overconfidence and a disregard for the risk that the group is taking (Hart 1991).

Groupthink, which leads to tunnel vision, is especially dangerous when it characterizes government officials. The options narrow, then finally disappear, and the officials are unable to see anything beyond what has already been decided on. They interpret all subsequent events from the framework of the "right" answer—that is, what the group has determined to be the only reasonable thing to do.

The Asch and Milgram experiments let us see how groupthink can develop. Suppose you are a member of the president's inner circle and the president has just called an emergency meeting in the middle of the night and announces a national crisis. At first, various options are presented. Eventually, these are narrowed to only a few choices, and at some point everyone seems to agree on what now seems "the only possible course of action." At that juncture, expressing doubts will bring you into direct conflict with *all* the other important people in the room, while actual criticism may mark you as not being a "team player." So you keep your mouth shut, with the result that each step commits you—and them—more and more to the "only" course of action.

U.S. history provides a fertile field of examples of groupthink: the refusal of President Roosevelt and his chiefs of staff to believe that the Japanese might attack Pearl Harbor and the subsequent decision to continue naval operations as usual; President Kennedy's invasion of Cuba; and the policies of Presidents Kennedy, Johnson, and Nixon in Vietnam. Watergate is especially noteworthy, for it plunged the United States into political crisis and for the first time in history forced the resignation of a U.S. president. In each of these cases, options closed as officials committed themselves to a single course of action, which became the equivalent of disloyalty to question. Those in power plunged ahead, no longer able to see different perspectives, no longer even try-

groupthink: Irving Janis's term for a narrowing of thought by a group of people, leading to the perception that there is only one correct answer, in which to even suggest alternatives becomes a sign of disloyalty

ing to objectively weigh evidence as it came in, interpreting everything as supporting their one correct decision. Like Milgram's subjects, they became mired deeper and deeper in actions that as individuals they would have considered unacceptable, and found themselves pursuing policies they may have found morally repugnant.

Groupthink is one of the dangers that faces any government, for leaders already tend to be isolated at the top and can easily become cut off from information that does not coincide with their own opinions. Leaders also foster groupthink by surrounding themselves with an inner circle that closely reflects their own views.

Preventing Groupthink

Perhaps the key to preventing the mental captivity and paralysis caused by groupthink is the widest possible circulation, especially among a nation's top government officials, of research that has been freely conducted by social scientists, and information that has been freely gathered by media reporters. In addition, it might be useful to pass a law requiring the president of the United States to consult regularly with at least two advisers known to disagree violently with his or her views.

If this conclusion comes across as an unabashed plug for sociological research and the free exchange of ideas, it is. Giving free rein to diverse opinions can effectively curb groupthink, which—if not prevented—can lead to the destruction of a society and, in today's world of sophisticated weapons, the mass destruction of the earth's inhabitants.

Summary and Review

Social Groups and Societies

What is a group?

Sociologists have many definitions of groups, but, in general, **groups** are people who have something in common and who believe that what they have in common is significant. **Societies** are the largest and most complex groups that sociologists study. Pp. 144–145.

The Transformation of Societies

What inventions are linked to the change from one type of society to another?

On their way to postindustrial society, humans passed through four types of societies, each due to a social revolution linked to an invention. The **domestication revolution,** pasturing animals and cultivating plants, transformed hunting and gathering societies into pastoral and horticultural societies. Then the **agricultural revolution,** brought about by the invention of the plow, ushered in the agricultural society, while the **Industrial Revolution,** caused by machines being powered by fuels, allowed the industrial society to develop. Today, the **information revolution,** based on the computer chip, is leading to the postindustrial society. Pp. 145–152.

How is social inequality linked to the transformation of societies?

Social equality was greatest in hunting and gathering societies, but as societies became more complex social inequality grew. The root of the transition to social inequality was the accumulation of a food surplus, made possible through the domestication revolution. This surplus stimulated the division of labor, trade, accumulation of material goods, the subordination of females by males, the development of the state, and the rule by a few over many. Pp. 145–152.

Groups Within Society

What is the significance of small groups?

Small groups, standing between the individual and the larger society, provide a sense of meaning to life. They help prevent *anomie,* Durkheim's term for a condition of normlessness. P. 152.

How do sociologists classify groups?

Sociologists divide groups into primary, secondary, in-groups, out-groups, reference groups, and networks. The cooperative, intimate, long-term, face-to-face relationships provided by **primary groups** are fundamental to our sense of self. **Secondary groups** are larger, relatively temporary, more anonymous, formal, and impersonal than primary groups. **In-groups** provide members with a strong sense of identification and belonging, while **out-groups** help create this identity by showing in-group members what they are *not*. **Reference groups** are groups we use as standards to evaluate ourselves. **Social networks** consist of social ties that link people together. Pp. 152–157.

Group Dynamics

How does a group's size affect its dynamics?

The term **group dynamics** refers to how individuals affect groups and how groups influence individuals. In a **small group,** everyone can interact directly with everyone else. As a group grows larger, its intensity decreases and its stability increases. A **dyad,** consisting of two persons, and the most unstable of human groups, provides the most intense or intimate relationships. The addition of a third person, forming a **triad,** fundamentally alters relationships. Triads are unstable, as they tend to form **coalitions,** the alignment of some members of a group against others. Pp. 157–160.

What characterizes a leader?

A **leader** is someone who influences others. **Instrumental leaders** try to keep a group moving toward its goals, even at the cost of causing friction. **Expressive leaders** focus on creating harmony and raising group morale. Both types are essential to the functioning of groups. P. 160.

What are the three main leadership styles?

Authoritarian leaders give orders, **democratic leaders** try to lead by consensus, and **laissez-faire leaders** are highly permissive. An authoritarian style appears to be more effective in emergency situations, a democratic style works best for most situations, and a laissez-faire style is usually ineffective. Pp. 160–162.

How do groups encourage conformity?

The Asch experiment was cited to illustrate the power of peer pressure, the Milgram experiment the influence of authority. Both experiments demonstrate how easily we can succumb to **groupthink,** a kind of collective tunnel vision. Preventing groupthink requires the free circulation of contrasting ideas. Pp. 162–165.

Where can I read more on this topic?

Suggested readings for this chapter are listed on page 639.

Unknown. Sign of the Watchmaker: Enseigne de l'Horloger. *Contemporary Folk Art*

CHAPTER 7

Bureaucracy and Formal Organizations

THIS WAS THE MOST EXCITING *day Joan could remember. Her first day at college. So much had happened so quickly. Her senior year had ended with such pleasant memories: the prom, the graduation—how proud she had felt at that moment. But best of all had been the SAT scores. Everyone, especially Joan, had been surprised at the results—she had outscored everyone in her class. "Yes, they're valid," her adviser had assured her. "You can be anything you want to be."*

Those words still echoed in Joan's mind. "Anything I want to be," she thought.

Then came the presidential scholarship! Full tuition for four years. Beyond anything Joan had ever dreamed possible. She could hardly believe it, but it was really hers.

"Next, Please!" Joan's reverie was interrupted as she reached the head of the line. "Your number 3 card, please."

Joan looked startled. "My what?" she asked.

"Your number 3 card," said the clerk, with more than a hint of exasperation.

"I don't know what that is," Joan replied, beginning to feel a little foolish.

The irritation in the clerk's voice was now quite noticeable: "You can't get your schedule approved without your number 3 card. Where is it?"

"I don't have one," said Joan, feeling her face redden at the sound of a snicker behind her.

"Then you'll have to go to Forsyth Hall and get one. Next!"

Joan felt thoroughly confused. She had waited in line for an hour. Somehow she had missed the instructions to get a number 3 card in Forsyth before going to Rendleman Building for course approval. Dejected, she crossed the quadrangle to Forsyth and joined a double line of students stretched from the building to the courtyard.

But nobody told Joan that this was the line for paying tuition. Number 3 cards were issued in the basement.

You can understand Joan's dismay. Things could have been clearer—a lot clearer. The problem is that many colleges must register thousands of students, most of whom are going to start classes on the same day. To do so, they have broken the registration process into tiny bits, with each piece making a small contribution to getting the job done. Of course, as Joan found out, things don't always go as planned.

This chapter looks at how society is organized to "get its job done." As you read, you may be able to trace the source of some of your frustrations to this social organization, as well as see how your welfare depends on it.

The Rationalization of Society

LO1 Explain what is meant by the "rationalization of society," and differentiate between the views of Max Weber and Karl Marx on this process.

rationality: the acceptance of rules, efficiency, and practical results as the right way to approach human affairs

traditional orientation: the idea, characteristic of tribal, peasant, and feudal societies, that the past is the best guide for the present

In the previous chapter, we discussed how, over the course of history, societies underwent transformations so extensive that whole new types of societies emerged. In addition to these transformations, a major development has been **rationality**—the acceptance of rules, efficiency, and practical results as the right way to approach human affairs. Let's examine how this approach to life—which we today take for granted—came about.

The Contribution of Max Weber

Max Weber (1864–1920), a sociologist whose studies incorporated an amazingly broad sweep of world history, concluded that until recently the world's groups and nations had been immersed in a **traditional orientation** to life—the idea that the past is the best guide for the present. In this view, what exists is good because it has passed the test of time. Customs—and relationships based on them—have served people well and should not be lightly abandoned. A central orientation of a traditional society is to protect the status quo. Change is viewed with suspicion, and comes but slowly, if at all.

Such a traditional orientation stands in the way of industrialization, which requires the willingness—even eagerness—to change. If a society is to industrialize, then, a deep-seated shift must occur in people's thinking—from wanting to hold onto things as they are to seeking the most efficient way to accomplish matters. Practical consequences must replace the status quo, while rule-of-thumb methods give way to explicit rules and procedures for measuring results. This change, called rationality, requires an entirely different way of looking at life. It flies in the face of human history, for it is opposed to the basic orientation of all human societies until the time of industrialization. How, then, did what Weber called the **rationalization of society**—a widespread acceptance of rationality and a social organization largely built around this idea—come about? How did people break through their profound resistance to change?

To Weber, this problem was like an unsolved murder is to a detective. Weber's primary clue was that capitalism thrived only in certain parts of Europe. If he could determine why this was so, he was convinced that he could discover the root of this fundamental change in human society. As Weber pursued the matter, he concluded that religion held the key, for it was in Protestant countries that capitalism flourished, while Roman Catholic countries held onto tradition and were relatively untouched by capitalism.

But why should Roman Catholics have continued to hold onto the past, while Protestants embraced change, welcoming the new emphasis on practical results? Weber's answer to this puzzle has been the source of controversy ever since he first proposed it in his highly influential book, *The Protestant Ethic and the Spirit of Capitalism* (1904–1905). He concluded that essential differences between the two religions held the answer. Roman Catholic doctrine emphasized the acceptance of present arrangements, not change: "God wants you where you are. You owe primary allegiance to the Church, to your family, to your community and country. Accept your lot in life and remain rooted." But Protestant theology was quite different, Weber argued, especially Calvinism, a religion he was intimately familiar with from his mother. Calvinists (followers of the teachings of John Calvin, 1509–1564) believed that before birth people are destined to go either to heaven or to hell—and they would not know their destiny until after they died. Weber believed that this doctrine filled Calvinists with an anxiety that pervaded their entire lives. Salvation became their chief concern in life—they wanted to know *now* where they were going after death.

To resolve their spiritual dilemma, Calvinists came up with an ingenious solution: God did not want his chosen ones to be ignorant of their destiny. Consequently, he would bestow signs of approval on those he had predestined for heaven. But what signs? The answer, they claimed, was found not in mystical, spiritual experiences, but in tangible achievements that people could see and measure. The sign of God's approval became success: those whom God had predestined for heaven, he would bless with visible success in this life.

This idea transformed Calvinists' lives, serving as an extraordinary motivation to work hard. Because Calvinists also believed that thrift is a virtue, their dedication to work led to an accumulation of money. Calvinists could not spend the excess on themselves, however, for to purchase items beyond the basic necessities was considered sinful. **Capitalism,** the investment of capital in the hope of producing profits, became an outlet for their excess money, while the success of those investments became a further sign of God's approval. Wordly success, then, became transformed into a spiritual virtue, and other branches of Protestantism, although less extreme, adopted the creed of thrift and hard work. Consequently, said Weber, Protestant countries embraced capitalism.

Until the 1500s the world's societies had a traditional orientation to life. The way things had "always" been was the guide to decision making. Change, which came very slowly, was viewed with suspicion, and one generation was very similar to the next. The rise of capitalism, however, changed this orientation, and for much of the West, rationality became the new guide to decision making. In this illustration from the fifteenth century, Tres Riches Heures of the Duke of Berry, you can see the slow pace of life.

rationalization of society: a widespread acceptance of rationality and a social organization largely built around this idea

capitalism: the investment of capital with the goal of producing profits

A central characteristic of formal organizations is the division of labor. Bureaucracies, for example, divide responsibilities into very small segments. Prior to capitalism and industrialization, however, there was little division of labor, and few formal organizations existed. In this woodcut of money coiners in Germany during the Middle Ages, you can see an early division of labor and perhaps the emergence of a formal organization.

Now, what has this to do with rationalization? Simply put, capitalism demands rationalization, the careful calculation of practical results. If profits are your goal, you must compute income and expenses. You must calculate inventories and wages, the cost of producing goods and how much they bring in. You must determine "the bottom line." In such an arrangement of human affairs, efficiency, not tradition, becomes the drum to which you march. Traditional ways of doing things, if inefficient, must be replaced, for what counts are the results.

Marx on Rationalization

Another sociologist, Karl Marx, looked at the same problem and came up with entirely the reverse interpretation of events. He, too, noted that tradition had given way to rationality. Unlike Weber, however, Marx attributed this fundamental change not to religion but to capitalism itself. It was not that people's changed ways of thinking brought about capitalism, Marx said, but, instead, that capitalism changed people's views about life. The new form of production, called capitalism, broke down traditional relationships, uprooting the old ways of doing things. Capitalism was much more efficient, and when people saw the greater abundance it brought, they altered their ideas. Rationality, argued Marx, was the result of economics, the material forces of production.

Who is correct? Weber, who concluded that Protestantism produced rationality, which then paved the way for capitalism? Or Marx, who concluded that capitalism produced rationality? No analyst has yet reconciled these two opposing answers to the satisfaction of sociologists: The two views still remain side by side.

Formal Organizations and Bureaucracy

Regardless of whether Marx or Weber was right about its cause, rationality was a totally different way of thinking that came to permeate society. This new orientation transformed the way in which society was organized. The resulting rationalization of society includes the widespread existence of formal organizations, predominantly in the form of bureaucracies.

Formal Organizations

Rationality brought the proliferation of **formal organizations,** secondary groups designed to achieve explicit objectives. Unlike primary groups, formal organizations have a defined structure, including a set of officers, whose task it is to keep the organization moving toward its objectives.

Prior to industrialization, only a few formal organizations existed. The guilds of western Europe during the twelfth century are an example. People who performed the same type of work organized to control their craft in a local area. They set prices and standards of workmanship (Bridgwater 1953). Much like modern unions, guilds also prevented craftsmen from other localities from encroaching on their area. Another example of an early formal organization is the army, with its structure of senior officers, junior officers, and ranks. Formal armies, of course, go back to early history.

With industrialization, secondary groups became common. Today we take their existence for granted and, beginning with grade school, all of us spend a good deal of time in them. Formal organizations tend to develop into bureaucracies, and in general, the larger the formal organization, the more likely it is to be bureaucratic.

formal organization: a secondary group designed to achieve explicit objectives

How powerful the traditional way of life was prior to the arrival of capitalism is still evident from the dominating position of the Lincoln Cathedral in Lincolnshire, England. Max Weber wrote that the rise of capitalism and the type of society it produced—one based on rationality versus tradition—emerged in response to the Protestant ethic, especially the Calvinist doctrine of predestination. Karl Marx saw things differently. He believed that capitalism itself was responsible for the breakdown of traditional society and the rise of rationality.

The Essential Characteristics of Bureaucracies

Although the army, the post office, a college, and General Motors may not seem to have much in common, they are all bureaucracies. As Weber (1947) analyzed them, the essential characteristics of a **bureaucracy** are as follows:

1 *A hierarchy with assignments flowing downward and accountability flowing upward.* The organization is divided into clear-cut levels. Each level assigns responsibilities to the level beneath it, while each lower level is responsible to the level above for fulfilling those assignments. The bureaucratic structure of a typical university is shown in Figure 7.1 on page 174.

2 *A division of labor.* Each member of a bureaucracy has a specific task to fulfill, and all of the tasks are then coordinated to accomplish the purpose of the organization. In a college, for example, a teacher does not run the heating system, the president does not teach, and a secretary does not evaluate textbooks. These tasks are accomplished by being distributed among people who have been trained to do them.

3 *Written rules.* In their attempt to become efficient, bureaucracies stress written procedures. In general, the longer a bureaucracy exists and the larger it grows, the more written rules it has. The rules of some bureaucracies cover just about every imaginable situation. In my university, for example, the rules are bound in handbooks: separate ones for faculty, students, administrators, civil service workers, and perhaps others that I do not even know exist. The guiding principle generally becomes, "If there isn't a written rule covering it, it is allowed."

4 *Written communications and records.* Records are kept of much of what transpires in a bureaucracy. ("Fill that out in triplicate.") Consequently, workers in bureaucracies spend a fair amount of time reading and writing memos to one another. They also produce written reports detailing their activities. My university, for example, requires that each faculty member fill out quarterly reports summarizing the number of hours per week spent on specified activities as well as an annual report listing what was accomplished in teaching, research, and service—all accompanied by copies of publications,

bureaucracy: a formal organization with a hierarchy of authority; a clear division of labor; emphasis on written rules, communications, and records; and impersonality of positions

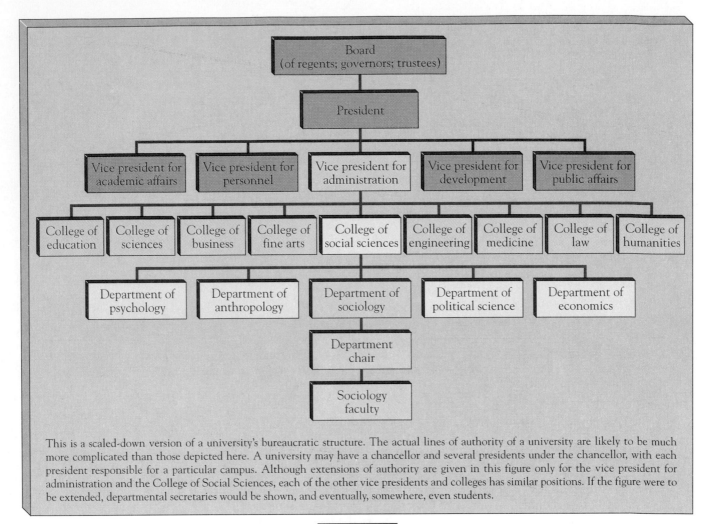

This is a scaled-down version of a university's bureaucratic structure. The actual lines of authority of a university are likely to be much more complicated than those depicted here. A university may have a chancellor and several presidents under the chancellor, with each president responsible for a particular campus. Although extensions of authority are given in this figure only for the vice president for administration and the College of Social Sciences, each of the other vice presidents and colleges has similar positions. If the figure were to be extended, departmental secretaries would be shown, and eventually, somewhere, even students.

Figure 7.1

The Typical Bureaucratic Structure of a Medium-Sized University

testimonies to service, and written teaching evaluations from each course. These materials go to committees whose task it is to evaluate the relative performance of each faculty member.

5 *Impersonality.* It is the office that is important, not the individual who holds the office. You work for the organization, not the replaceable person who heads some post in the organization. Consequently, members of a bureaucracy owe allegiance to the office, not to particular persons. If you work in a bureaucracy, you become a small cog in a large machine. Each worker is a replaceable unit, for many others are available to fulfill each particular function. For example, when a professor retires or dies, someone else is appointed to take his or her place.

These five characteristics not only help bureaucracies reach their goals but also allow them to grow and endure. One bureaucracy in the United States, the postal service, has become so large that one out of every 150 employed Americans now works for it (Frank 1990). If the head of a bureaucracy dies, retires, or resigns, the organization continues, ordinarily hardly skipping a beat, for unlike a "mom and pop" operation, the functioning of each unit and each person in those units does not depend on the individual who heads the organization. The expansion (some would say domination) of bureaucracies in contemporary society is illustrated by the Down-to-Earth Sociology box on the next page

Down-To-Earth Sociology

The McDonaldization of Society

SOCIOLOGIST GEORGE RITZER HAS coined the term, "the McDonaldization of society," to refer to the increasing rationalization and efficiency of routine tasks of life. The first systematic observations of bureaucracy were made by sociologist Max Weber at the turn of the century. He noted that new organizations had appeared, ones that did not leave people on their own to find solutions to problems, but, rather, set out a list of rules and regulations that guided them to solve tasks with maximum efficiency. This was a major development in the history of the world.

Ritzer notes that the characteristics of bureaucracy have expanded beyond factory and office and now pervade social life. He takes McDonald's as the supreme example. Ray Kroc, the founder, applied the principles developed by Henry Ford to the preparation and serving of food. A 1958 operations manual spelled out the exact procedure:

It told operators exactly how to draw milk shakes, grill hamburgers, and fry potatoes. It specified precise cooking times for all products and temperature settings for all equipment. It fixed standard portions on every food item, down to the quarter ounce of onions placed on each hamburger patty and the thirty-two slices per pound of cheese. It specified that french fries be cut at nine-thirty-seconds of an inch thick. . . . Grill men . . . were instructed to put hamburgers down on the grill moving from left to right, creating six rows of six patties each. And because the first two rows were farthest from the heating element, they were instructed (and still are) to flip the third row first, then the fourth, fifth, and sixth before flipping the first two.

Ritzer stresses that "McDonaldization" does not refer just to the robotlike assembly of food. Rather, this same process, occurring throughout contemporary society, is transforming our lives. Shopping malls are controlled environments of approved design, logo, colors, and opening and closing hours. Male employees of amusement parks are forbidden to wear beards, moustaches, long hair, or jewelry, while females cannot wear short skirts, use mascara, or have more than one ring per hand. Travel agencies transport middle-class Americans to ten European capitals in fourteen days, each visitor experiencing exactly the same hotels, restaurants, and other predictable settings. No one need fear meeting a "real" native. In rationalized campgrounds, one can enjoy the outdoors—without having to worry about such things as putting up with nature. *USA Today* produces the same bland, instant news—in short, unanalytic pieces that can be read between gulps of the McShake or the McBurger.

Is all this bad? Not necessarily. Efficiency brings reduced costs. But there is something very difficult to define that is lost, a quality of life no longer present. In my own travels, for example, had I taken packaged tours, I never would have had the enjoyable, eye-opening experiences that have added to my appreciation of human diversity. Of course, I would have had other experiences—and I wouldn't have known what I had missed in the first place.

In any event, the future has arrived. The trend is strongly toward the McDonaldization of human experience. For good or bad, we shall live within these new prepackaged settings. To resist will be futile, in most instances. At best we will be able to spark up our lives with some direct camping in the few remaining wilderness spots, to travel on our own from time to time, and to peel an occasional potato just to see what unprocessed food looks like.

Our children will no longer have to put up with the idiosyncrasies of real professors, those people who think that ideas must be endlessly discussed and who never come to decisive answers anyway. What we want are instant, preformed solutions to social issues, like those we find in mathematics and engineering. Fortunately, our children will be able to be instructed by standardized, computerized courses, in which everyone learns the same answer, the precise and proper way to think about social issues. That will be efficiency—and the iron cage of bureaucracy that Weber said would entrap us.

Source: Based on Ritzer 1993. The italics in the quotation were added by Ritzer.

"Ideal" Versus "Real" Bureaucracy

Just as people often act quite differently from the way the norms say they should, so it is with bureaucracies. The characteristics of bureaucracies identified by Weber are **ideal types;** that is, they are a composite of characteristics based on many specific examples. Think of a judge at a dog show. He or she has a mental image of what a particular breed of dog should look like, and judges each dog according to that mental image. No particular dog will have all the characteristics, but all dogs of that breed put together have them. Thus, a particular organization may be ranked high or low on some characteristic and still qualify as a bureaucracy. Instead of labeling a particular organization as a "bureaucracy" or "not a bureaucracy," it probably makes more sense to think in terms of the *extent* to which an organization is bureaucratized (Hall 1963; Udy 1959).

ideal type: a composite of characteristics based on many specific examples ("ideal" in this case means a description of the abstracted characteristics, not what one desires to exist)

Today's armies, no matter from what country, are bureaucracies. They have a strict hierarchy of rank, division of labor, impersonality (an emphasis on the office, not the person holding it), and they stress written records, rules, and communications—essential characteristics identified by Max Weber. This army in India, though its outward appearance may differ from Western standards, is no exception to this principle.

As with culture, the real nature of a bureaucracy often differs from its ideal image. The actual lines of authority ("going through channels"), for example, may be quite different from those portrayed on organizational charts, such as that shown in Figure 7.1. For example, suppose that before being promoted, the university president taught in the history department. As a result, friends from that department may have direct access to him or her. In giving their "input" (ranging from opinions about how to solve problems to personal grievances or even gossip), these individuals may skip their chairperson or even the dean of their college altogether.

Dysfunctions of Bureaucracies

Although no other form of social organization has been found to be more efficient in the long run, as Weber recognized, his model accounts for only part of the characteristics of bureaucracies. They also have a dark side. As Joan (in the opening vignette) discovered, bureaucracies do not always operate smoothly. They slip up, and individuals sometimes get hurt. Probably all of us have been frustrated by red tape—what bureaucrats call "correct procedures." Other dysfunctions, which we shall now examine, are alienation, trained incapacity, goal conflict, goal displacement, engorgement, and incompetence.

Bureaucratic Alienation As you may have sensed from reading about the characteristics of bureaucracies, they sometimes leave individual needs unfulfilled. Many workers find it disturbing to deal with others in terms of roles, rules, and functions rather than as individuals. Similarly, they may dislike writing memos instead of talking to people face to face.

The rules that bureaucrats come up with can be downright ridiculous. For example, county officials in Hackensack, New Jersey, wrote eighteen pages of contract specifications for shining shoes in the courthouse. Robert Taylor, who has been shining shoes there for twenty-seven years, says that he has been getting along just fine without such bureaucratic "guidelines" on how to perform his job. Nevertheless, Taylor must now meet the new specifications (Scism 1993).

It is not surprising that in large organizations workers often begin to feel more like objects than people, or, as Weber (1978) put it, "only a small cog in a ceaselessly moving mechanism which prescribes to [them] an endlessly fixed routine. . . ." Because workers must deal with one another in such formal ways, and because they constantly perform routine tasks, some come to feel that no one cares about them and that they are misfits in their surroundings.

Marx termed these reactions **alienation** and attributed them to the fact that workers are cut off from the finished product of their labor. Although assigning workers to repetitive tasks makes for efficient production, Marx argued that it also reduces their satisfaction by limiting their creativity and sense of contribution to the finished product. Underlying alienation is the workers' loss of control over their work because they no longer own their own tools. Before industrialization, individual workers used their own tools to produce an entire product, such as a chair or table. Now the capitalists own the machinery and tools and assign each worker only a single step or two in the entire production process. Relegated to repetitive tasks disassociated from the actual product, workers lose a sense of responsibility for what they produce. Ultimately they come to feel estranged not only from their products but from their whole work environment.

Resisting Alienation   Alienation, of course, is not a pleasant experience. Workers understandably want to feel useful, valued, and needed. They want to feel respected and worthwhile and to have a sense of control over their own work. To resist the alienation produced by bureaucracies, workers form primary groups. They band together in informal settings—at lunch, around desks, for a drink after work. There they give one another approval for jobs well done and express sympathy for the shared need to put up with cantankerous bosses, repetitive tasks, meaningless routines, and endless rules. Here they relate to one another not just as workers, but as people who value one another. They laugh and tell jokes, talk about their families, their problems, their goals, and, often, their sexual interests. Adding this multidimensionality to their work relationships restores their sense of being persons rather than mere cogs.

Sociologically, the tendency for workers to personalize their work areas with pictures and personal items is not simply an interesting trait. Rather, it is another way in which workers strive to overcome alienation—by claiming to be individuals, not just machines functioning at a particular job.

The Alienated Bureaucrat   Not all workers succeed in resisting alienation, however, and some become extremely alienated (see Robert Merton's typology in Chapter 8, pages 204–205). They remain in the organization because they see no viable alternative or because they have "only so many years until retirement." They hate every minute of it, however, and it shows—in their attitudes toward clients, toward fellow workers, and especially toward authority in the organization. The alienated bureaucrat does not take initiative, will not do anything for the organization beyond what he or she is absolutely required to do, and uses rules to justify doing as little as possible. If Joan had come across an alienated bureaucrat behind the registration window, she might have been told, "What's the matter with you—Can't you read? Everyone else manages to get their number 3 card, why can't you? I don't know what kind of students they are sending us nowadays." If the worker had been alienated even more, he or she might even have denied knowledge of where to get a number 3 card.

In spite of poor attitude and performance, alienated workers often retain their jobs, either because they may have seniority, or know the written rules backward and forward, or threaten expensive, time-consuming, and embarrassing legal action if anyone tries to fire them. Some alienated workers are shunted off into small bureaucratic corners, where they do trivial tasks and have little chance of coming in contact with the public. This treatment, of course, only alienates them further.

Goal Conflict   Sometimes a bureaucracy creates **goal conflict,** a situation in which the goals of one unit conflict with those of the organization as a whole. Unionized workers, for example, often care little about the company's "bottom line," demanding raises whether the year was profitable or not. This attitude is sometimes fed by managers, who have themselves replaced the goal of "the bottom line" with the sole aim of feathering

alienation: Marx's term for the experience of being cut off from the product of one's labor that results in a sense of powerlessness and normlessness

goal conflict: goals that conflict with one another; in this context, those of a unit in a formal organization and those of the organization as a whole

The March of Dimes was founded by President Franklin Roosevelt in the 1930s. When a vaccine for polio was discovered in the 1950s, the organization did not declare victory and disband. Instead, it kept the organization intact by creating new goals—fighting birth defects. Sociologists use the term goal displacement to refer to this process of adopting new goals. "Fighting birth defects" is now being replaced by an even vaguer goal, "campaigning for healthier babies." This last goal displacement may guarantee the organizations's existence forever, for it is a goal so elusive it can never be reached.

their own nests. Stockholders of public corporations, who see corporate managers continuing to vote themselves fat raises and bonuses in spite of decreased profits, frequently complain about such behavior. This point is discussed further in Chapter 14.

Goal Displacement   Bureaucracies sometimes take on a life of their own, adopting new goals in place of old ones. In this process, called **goal displacement,** even when the goal of the organization has been achieved and there is no longer any reason for it to continue, continue it does. A good example is the National Foundation for the March of Dimes, organized in the 1930s to fight polio, a crippling disease that strikes without warning (Sills 1957). The origin of polio was a mystery to the medical profession, and the public was alarmed and fearful. All sorts of rumors ran rampant about its cause. Everyone knew someone who had been crippled by this disease. Overnight, a healthy child would be stricken. Parents were fearful because no one knew whose child would be next. The March of Dimes began to publicize individual cases. An especially effective strategy was placing posters of a child on crutches near cash registers in almost every store in the United States. The American public took the goals of the organization to heart and contributed heavily.

The organization raised money beyond its wildest dreams. Then during the 1950s, when Dr. Jonas Salk developed a vaccine for polio this threat was wiped out almost overnight. The public breathed a collective sigh of relief. What then? Did the organization fold? After all, its purpose had been fulfilled. But, as you know, the March of Dimes is still around. Faced with the loss of their jobs, the professional staff that ran the organization quickly found a way to keep the bureaucracy intact by pursuing a new enemy—birth defects. Their choice of enemy is particularly striking, for it is doubtful that we will ever run out of birth defects—and thus unlikely that these people will ever run out of jobs.

goal displacement: a goal displaced by another; in this context, the adoption of new goals by an organization; also known as *goal replacement*

Peter principle: a bureaucratic "law" according to which the members of an organization are promoted for good work until they reach their level of incompetence, the level at which they can no longer do good work

Bureaucratic Incompetence   In a tongue-in-cheek analysis of bureaucracies, Laurence Peter proposed what has become known as the **Peter principle:** Each employee of a bureaucracy is promoted to his or her *level of incompetence* (Peter and Hull 1969). People who perform well in a bureaucracy come to the attention of those higher up the chain of command and are promoted. If they again perform well, they are again promoted. This process continues until finally they are promoted to

Under the totalitarian regime of Romania's Nicolae Ceausescu, which was overthrown in 1989, the government bureaucracy grew to incredible proportions. In his quest to house this bureaucracy, Ceausescu virtually bankrupted the country by pouring funds into bureaucratic monuments such as the House of the Republic in Bucharest, depicted here.

a level at which they can no longer handle the responsibilities well; this is their level of incompetence. There they hide behind the work of others, taking credit for what those under their direction accomplish. Although the Peter principle contains a grain of truth, if it were generally true, bureaucracies would be staffed entirely by incompetents, and none of these organizations could succeed. In reality, bureaucracies are remarkably successful.

Voluntary Associations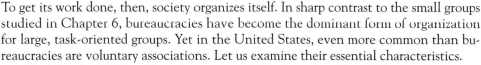

To get its work done, then, society organizes itself. In sharp contrast to the small groups studied in Chapter 6, bureaucracies have become the dominant form of organization for large, task-oriented groups. Yet in the United States, even more common than bureaucracies are voluntary associations. Let us examine their essential characteristics.

Back in the 1830s, a Frenchman traveled across the United States, observing the customs of this new nation. Alexis de Tocqueville wrote a book about his observations, *Democracy in America* (1835), which became widely read in Europe and in the United States and is still quoted for its insights into the American character. As an outsider, de Tocqueville was able to see patterns that people immersed in them could not. One of de Tocqueville's observations was that Americans joined a lot of **voluntary associations,** groups made up of volunteers who organize on the basis of some mutual interest.

Over the years, Americans have maintained this pattern and are extremely proud of it. A visitor entering any of the thousands of small towns that dot the landscape will be greeted with a highway sign proclaiming which volunteer associations that particular town has: Girl Scouts, Boy Scouts, Kiwanis, Lions, Elks, Eagles, Knights of Columbus, Chamber of Commerce, Junior Chamber of Commerce, Future Homemakers of America, Future Farmers of America, American Legion, Veterans of Foreign Wars, and perhaps a host of others. One form of voluntary association is so prevalent that a separate sign usually indicates which varieties are present in the town: Roman Catholic, Baptist, Lutheran, Methodist, Episcopalian, and so on. Not listed on these signs are many other voluntary associations, such as political parties, unions, professional associations, health clubs, the American Civil Liberties Union, the National Right to Life, the National Organization for Women, Alcoholics Anonymous,

voluntary association: a group made up of volunteers who have organized on the basis of some mutual interest

Voluntary organizations are extremely popular in the United States. In this photograph from World War II, members of the Women's Ambulance Association stand ready to offer their services, in this case picking crops in order to make up for the lack of male labor due to so many men being away at war.

Gamblers Anonymous, Association of Pinto Racers, and Citizens United For or Against This and That.

Americans love voluntary associations, using them to express a wide variety of interests, goals, opinions, and even dissatisfactions. Some groups are local, consisting of only a few volunteers; some are national, with a paid professional staff; and others are in between. Some are temporary, organized to accomplish a particular task such as arranging a town's next Fourth of July fireworks. Others, such as the Scouts and the Democratic and Republican political parties, are permanent, large, secondary organizations with clear lines of command; and they are also bureaucracies.

Functions of Voluntary Associations

Whatever their form, voluntary associations are so numerous because they meet people's basic needs. People do not *have* to belong to these organizations. They join because they obtain benefits from their participation. Functionalists have identified seven functions of voluntary associations.

1   Voluntary organizations advance the particular interests they represent. For example, adults who are concerned about children's welfare volunteer for the Scouts because they think that this group is superior to the corner pool hall. In short, voluntary associations get things done, whether ensuring that fireworks are purchased and shot off or that people become familiar with the latest legislation affecting their occupation.

2   Voluntary groups also offer people an identity, for some, even a sense of purpose in life. As in-groups, they provide their members with a feeling of togetherness, of belonging, and in many cases, of doing something worthwhile. This identity function becomes so important for some individuals that their participation in voluntary associations becomes the center of their lives.

3   Voluntary associations help govern the nation and maintain social order. Groups that help "get out the vote" or assist the Red Cross in coping with disasters are obvious examples.

Note that the first two functions apply to all voluntary associations. In a general sense, so does the third. Although few organizations are focused on politics and the social order, taken together, voluntary associations help to incorporate individuals into the general society, and by allowing the expression of desire and dissent, voluntary associations help to prevent anomie.

Sociologist David Sills (1968) identified four other functions, which apply only to some voluntary groups.

4   Some voluntary groups mediate between the government and the individual, for example by providing a way in which people can put pressure on lawmakers.

5   Some voluntary groups provide training in organizational skills, helping individuals climb the occupational ladder.

6   Some voluntary groups help bring people into the political mainstream. The National Association for the Advancement of Colored People (NAACP) is an example of such a group.

7   Finally, some voluntary groups pave the way to social change. Challenging society's definitions of "normal" and socially acceptable, these groups, usually labeled extremist and ranging from the Ku Klux Klan to Greenpeace, challenge society's established boundaries. They often indicate directions of social change.

Voluntary associations, then, represent no single interest or purpose. They can be reactionary, dragged screaming into the present as their nails claw the walls of the past, or they can lead the vanguard for social change, announcing their vision of a better world. In spite of their amazing diversity, however, a thread does run through all voluntary associations. That thread is mutual interest. Although the particular interest varies from group to group, shared interest in some view or activity is the tie that binds their members together.

Although a group's members are united by mutual interests, the specific motivations for joining a group differ from one individual to another. Some join because of their conviction concerning the stated purpose of the organization, but others become members for quite different reasons, such as the chance to make contacts that will help them politically or professionally—or even to be closer to some special person of the opposite sex.

With motivations for joining voluntary associations and commitment to their goals so varied, these organizations typically have a high turnover. Some people move in and out of groups almost as fast as they change clothes. Within each organization, however, is an inner core of individuals who stand firmly behind the group's goals, or at least are firmly committed to maintaining the organization itself. If this inner core loses commitment, the group is likely to fold.

The Problem of Oligarchy

Rather than losing its commitment, however, this inner core is likely to grow ever tighter, becoming convinced that most members can't be counted on and that it can trust only the smaller group to make the really important decisions. To see this principle at work, let us look at the Veterans of Foreign Wars (VFW).

Sociologists Elaine Fox and George Arquitt (1985) studied three local posts of the VFW, a national organization of former U.S. soldiers who have served in foreign wars. The constitution of the VFW is very democratic, giving every member of the organization the right to be elected to positions of leadership. Fox and Arquitt found three types of VFW members: the silent majority (members who rarely show up), the rank and file (members who show up, but mainly for drinking), and leaders (those have been elected to office or appointed to committees). Although the leaders of the posts are careful not to let their attitudes show, they look down on the rank and file, viewing them as a bunch of ignorant boozers.

Because the leaders can't stand the thought that such persons might represent them to the community and at national meetings, a curious situation arises. Although the VFW constitution makes rank-and-file members fully eligible for top leadership positions, they never become leaders. In fact, the leaders are so effective in keeping their own group in leadership that even before an election is held they can specify who is going to be their new post commander. "You need to meet Jim," the sociologists were told. "He's the next post commander after Sam does his time." At first the researchers found this puzzling. How could the elite be so sure? As they investigated further, however, they found that leadership is effectively decided behind the scenes. The elected leadership appoints their favored people to chair key committees. The members then become aware of their accomplishments, and these individuals are elected as leaders. The inner core, then, maintains control over the entire organization simply by appointing members of their inner circle to highly visible positions.

Like the VFW, most organizations are run by only a few of their members (Cnaan 1991). Building on the term *oligarchy,* a system in which many are ruled by a few, sociologist Robert Michels (1876–1936) coined the phrase **the iron law of oligarchy** to refer to how formal organizations inevitably come to be dominated by a small, self-perpetuating elite. The majority of the members become passive, and an elite inner group keeps itself in power by passing the leading positions from one clique member to another.

What many find depressing about the iron law of oligarchy is that it applies even to organizations strongly committed to democratic principles. Even U.S. political parties, for example, supposedly the backbone of the nation's representative government, have fallen prey to it. Run by an inner group that may or may not represent the community, they pass their leadership positions from one elite member to another. This principle is also demonstrated by the U.S. Senate. With their control of statewide political machinery and access to free mailing, about 97 percent of U.S. Senators who choose to run are re-elected (*Statistical Abstract* 1993: Table 442).

The iron law of oligarchy is not without its limitations, of course. Members of the inner group must remain attuned to the opinions of the other members, regardless of their personal feelings. If the oligarchy gets too far out of line, its members run the risk of a grassroots rebellion that would throw them out of office. It is this threat that often softens the iron law of oligarchy by making the leadership responsive to the membership.

Careers in Bureaucracies

Since you are likely to end up working in a bureaucracy, let's look at how its characteristics may affect your career.

The Corporate Culture: Consequences of Hidden Values

Who gets ahead in a large corporation? Although we might like to think that success is the consequence of intelligence and hard work, many factors other than merit underlie salary increases and promotions. As sociologist Rosabeth Moss Kanter (1977, 1983) stresses, the **corporate culture,** the orientations that characterize corporate work settings, is crucial in determining people's corporate fate. She explains how a corporation's "hidden values"—the values that are not officially part of the organization, but that nevertheless powerfully influence its members—operate as self-fulfilling stereotypes. The elite holds ideas about who are the best workers and colleagues, and those who fit this mold receive better access to information and networking, and are put in "fast-track" positions. Not surprisingly, these people perform better and become more committed to the organization, thus confirming the initial expectation. In contrast, those judged to be outsiders find opportunities closing up. They often work at a level beneath their capacity, come to think poorly of themselves, and become less committed to the organization.

The hidden values that created this self-fulfilling prophecy remain invisible to most. What is visible are the promotions of people with superior performances and greater

the iron law of oligarchy: Robert Michels's phrase for the tendency of formal organizations to be dominated by a small, self-perpetuating elite

corporate culture: the orientations that characterize corporate work settings

commitment to the company, not how a self-fulfilling prophecy has produced these attitudes and work performances.

The Down-to-Earth Sociology box below explores how ideas often are judged in corporations not by their merit, but according to *who* expresses them. You can see how such hidden values contribute to the iron law of oligarchy, for the corporate elite, the tight inner group that heads a corporation, sets in motion a self-fulfilling prophecy that tends to reproduce itself with people who "look" like themselves, generally white and male. Although women and minorities, who don't match the stereotype, are often "showcased"—placed in highly visible positions with little power in order to demonstrate to the public and affirmative action officials how progressive the company is (Benokraitis and Feagin 1991)—they often occupy "slow-track" positions, where accomplishments seldom come to the attention of top management.

Kanter found that the level people reach in the organization also shapes their behavior, and even their attitudes toward themselves and others. In general, the higher people go, the higher their morale. "This is a good company," they say to themselves. "They recognize my abilities." With their greater satisfaction, people in higher office also tend to be more helpful to subordinates and flexible in their style of leadership. In contrast, people who don't get very far in the organization are frustrated and tend to have lower morale. A less apparent result of their blocked opportunity, however, is that they are likely to be rigid supervisors and close defenders of whatever privileges they have.

There are two levels in a bureaucracy, then. Because the workers in a corporation tend to see only the level that is readily visible, they usually ascribe differences in behaviors and attitudes to people's individual personalities. Sociologists probe beneath this level, however, to examine how corporate culture shapes people's attitudes, and, by extension, the quality of their work.

Sociologist Rosabeth Moss Kanter has written extensively about life in corporations, including such titles as Men and Women of the Corporation, The Change Masters, *and* When Giants Learn to Dance.

▼▲▼▲▼▲▼▲▼▲▼▲▼▲▼▲▼▲▼▲▼▲▼▲▼▲▼▲▼▲▼▲▼▲

Down-To-Earth Sociology

Maneuvering the Hidden Culture—Women Surviving the Male-Dominated Business World

I WORK FOR A large insurance company. Of its twenty-five hundred employees, about 75 percent are women. Only 5 percent of the upper management positions, however, are held by women.

I am one of the more fortunate women, for I hold a position in middle management. I am also a member of the twelve-member junior board of directors, of whom nine are men and three are women.

Recently one of the female members of the board suggested that the company become involved in Horizons for Tomorrow, a program designed to provide internships for disadvantaged youth. Two other women and I spent many days developing a proposal for our participation.

The problem was how to sell the proposal to the company president. From past experiences, we knew that if he saw it as a "woman's project" it would be shelved into the second tier of "maybes." He hates what he calls "aggressive bitches."

We three decided, reluctantly, that the proposal had a chance only if it were presented by a man. We decided that Bill was the logical choice. We also knew that we had to "stroke" Bill if we were going to get his cooperation.

We first asked Bill if he would "show us how to present our proposal." (It is ridiculous to have to play the role of the "less capable female" in the 1990s, but, unfortunately the

corporate culture sometimes dictates this strategy.) To clinch matters, we puffed up Bill even more by saying, "You're the logical choice for the next chairmanship of the board."

Bill, of course, came to our next planning session, where *we* "prepped" *him* on what to say.

At our meeting with the president, we had Bill give the basic presentation. We then backed *him* up, providing the background and rationale for why the president should endorse the project. As we answered the president's questions, we carefully deferred to Bill.

The president's response? "An excellent proposal," he concluded, "an appropriate project for our company."

To be successful, we had to maneuver through the treacherous waters of the "hidden culture" (actually not so "hidden" to women who have been in the company for a while). The proposal was not sufficient on its merits, for the "who" behind a proposal is at least as significant as the proposal itself.

"We shouldn't' have to play these games," Laura said, summarizing our feelings.

But we all know that we have no choice. To become labeled "pushy" is to commit "corporate suicide"—and we're no fools.

Source: Written by an insurance executive in Henslin's introductory sociology class who, out of fear of retaliation at work, chooses to remain anonymous.

The following Thinking Critically section explores a recent trend designed to address the needs of those who have traditionally been powerless, or absent altogether, from the corporation.

▼▲▼▲▼▲▼▲▼▲▼▲▼▲▼▲▼▲▼▲▼▲▼▲▼▲▼▲▼▲

Thinking Critically About Social Controversy

Managing Diversity in the Workplace

▼ THE U.S. WORK FORCE is being transformed by diversity. Some of the signs: more than half of U.S. workers now are minorities, immigrants, and women. By the year 2000, only 57 percent of new workers will be native-born whites. In San Jose, California, families with the Vietnamese surname Nguyen outnumber the Joneses by nearly 50 percent. Diversity in the workplace is much more than skin color. Diversity also includes ethnicity, gender, age, religion, social class, and sexual orientation.

The huge successes of the women's movement and civil rights activism have encouraged pride in one's heritage and made many Americans comfortable with being different from the dominant group. Consequently, people are now less amenable to *assimilation*, the process by which minorities are absorbed into the dominant culture. Assimilation involves relinquishing distinctive cultural patterns of behavior in favor of those of the dominant culture. Two, three, four generations ago, immigrants to the United States routinely changed their names to help them enter the mainstream as soon and as completely as possible. No longer. As Roosevelt Thomas, president of the American Institute for Managing Diversity, says, "You don't have to aspire to be a white male or a member of the dominant group. People are willing to be part of a team, but they won't jump into the melting pot anymore."

Realizing that *assimilation* is probably not the way of the future, companies as diverse as IBM, Ford, and 3M have begun programs on managing diversity. The goals of these programs are threefold: (1) to uncover and root out biases and prejudices about people's differences, (2) to increase awareness and appreciation of those differences, and (3) to teach "people skills," especially communication and negotiation skills, for working with diverse groups. The bottom line of these programs is to develop leaders who can put a team of diverse people together so they can cooperatively and efficiently reach corporate goals.

Although many of these programs have been successful, some have produced a backlash of fear and anger. After the Washington State Ferry System spent $1 million to teach its 1,500 employees tolerance of diversity, a supervisor said, "We used to all be just ferry workers, but now everyone's divided up into little groups—blacks, women, gays, even white males." After the program, some supervisors even began to hesitate to give orders, and now the ferry system has to begin another program—this one to help supervisors who worry that they are going to be accused of harassment if they criticize someone's views.

Applying the Theoretical Perspectives From a *functionalist* perspective, programs in managing diversity are part of an ongoing adjustment in the economic system. If successful, these programs will help meet needs caused by a changing population and new international relations that require corporations to be more competitive.

From a *symbolic interactionist* perspective, these programs reflect changing symbols. They illustrate how being different from the dominant group means something different now from what it used to mean. The programs not only reflect this change, but they also bring about further change in the participants' understanding of diversity.

From a *conflict* perspective, the key term is not diversity, but *managing* diversity. No matter what their name, such programs are merely another way to exploit labor—to get workers to get along better in order to produce more profits for the elite owners of the corporations.

What do you think?

Sources: Based on Thomas 1990; Piturro and Mahoney 1991; Bradley 1993; Egan 1993; Sowell 1993. ▲

Humanizing the Corporate Culture

Bureaucracies, with all their faults, have transformed societies by harnessing people's energies to stated goals and monitoring progress to those goals. Weber (1946) predicted that because bureaucracies are so efficient and have the capacity to replace themselves indefinitely, they would come to dominate social life. More than any prediction in sociology, this one has withstood the test of time (Rothschild and Whitt 1986).

Bureaucracies appear likely to remain our dominant form of social organization, and most of us, like it or not, are destined to spend our working lives in bureaucracies. Many people have become concerned about the negative side of bureaucracies, however, and would like to make them more humane. **Humanizing a work setting** means organizing it in such a way that it develops rather than impedes human potential. Among the characteristics of more humane bureaucracies are (1) access to opportunities on the basis of ability and contributions rather than personal characteristics; (2) a more equal distribution of power; and (3) less rigid rules and more open decision making. In short, more people are involved in making decisions, their contributions are more readily recognized, and individuals feel freer to participate.

Can bureaucracies adapt to such a model? Contrary to some popular images, bureaucracies are not necessarily synonymous with unyielding, unwieldy monoliths. There is nothing in the nature of bureaucracies that makes them *inherently* insensitive to changing cultural needs or prevents them from humanizing corporate culture.

But how about the cost of such changes? The United States is in intense economic competition with other nations, especially Japan and western Europe, and it would be difficult to afford costly changes. To humanize corporate culture, however, does not require huge expense. Kanter (1983) compared forty-seven companies that were rigidly bureaucratic with competitors of the same size that were more flexible. It turned out that the more flexible companies were also the more profitable—probably because their greater flexibility encouraged greater company loyalty and productivity.

Quality Circles

In light of such findings, many corporations have taken steps to humanize their work settings, motivated not by any altruistic urge to make life better for their workers but by self-interest, the desire to make their organization more competitive. About two thousand U.S. companies—from the smallest to the largest—have begun to reform their work organizations. Some have developed "quality circles," which consist of perhaps a dozen workers and a manager or two who meet regularly to try to improve the quality of both the work setting and the company's products. To date, however, over half of these companies report that quality circles have yielded few benefits. Part of the reason may be that many companies set up quality circles for reasons of publicity, not intending to take employee suggestions seriously (Horn 1987; Saporito 1986). Disappointed with the results, companies such as Whirlpool and GE have abandoned quality circles. Each company continues to solicit ideas from its employees, however. GE now uses town hall–type meetings and rewards workers with cash and stock options (Naj 1993).

Employee Stock Ownership

Many companies provide an opportunity for their employees to purchase the firm's stock at a discount or as part of their salary, depending on the company's profitability. About eight thousand U.S. companies are now partially owned by their employees, but because each employee typically owns only a tiny amount of stock in the company, such "ownership" is practically meaningless. In about one thousand of these companies, however, the employees own the majority of the stock. Evidence has recently emerged

humanizing a work setting: organizing a workplace in such a way that it develops rather than impedes human potential

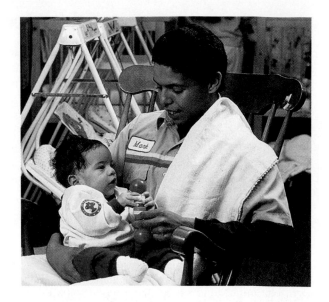

Some corporations have begun to humanize the work setting. Among the steps being taken to reach this goal is setting up onsite day care. In the unusual situation depicted here, a father is able to use his work break to take care of his 3-month-old baby.

that, on average, companies with at least 10 percent of their stock owned by employees are more profitable than other firms, probably because the workers are more committed and managers take a longer-term view (White 1992).

Even though the employees are the owners, this does not mean that working conditions and employee–management relations are automatically friction free. It seems, rather, that profitability is the key. Unprofitable firms pressure their employee–owners a great deal, creating resentment and tensions between workers and managers. Profitable companies show fewer tensions of this kind and resolve problems more quickly (Russell 1985; Horn 1987; Newman 1987).

Small Work Groups

Pioneered in the computer industry to increase productivity and cut down on absenteeism, small work groups, or self-managed teams, are now used by one in five employers in the United States, up from one in twenty just a decade ago. The results have been extraordinary, for employees who work in small groups not only feel a greater sense of loyalty to the company, work harder, and reduce their absenteeism, but small work groups also stimulate creative ideas and imaginative solutions to problems. Workers in these groups react more quickly to threats posed by technological change and competitors' advances. No less a behemoth than IBM has found that people work more effectively in a small group than in a distant, centralized command structure (Larson and Dolan 1983; Drucker 1992).

Materials discussed in the last chapter help to explain these results. The small work group establishes primary relationships among its members, and workers' identities become tied up with their group. This reduces alienation, for rather than being lost in a bureaucratic maze, here their individuality is appreciated, their contributions more readily recognized. The group's successes become the individual's successes—as do its failures—reflecting positively or negatively on the individual. As a consequence of their expanded personal ties, workers make more of an effort. The results have been so good that in what is known as "worker empowerment," some self-managed teams even replace bosses in controlling everything from schedules to hiring and firing (Lublin 1992).

Corporate Day Care

Another way to humanize the work setting is to set up day care facilities at work. This eases the strain on parents, especially on new mothers, who are able to go to work and still keep an eye on a baby or young child. Parents are also able to spend time with their children during breaks and lunch hours. Mothers can even nurse a child at these times.

Some have protested the cost of such facilities; others have questioned the involvement of corporations, whose goal is to produce a profit. An instructive example is the day care center set up by Union Bank in Monterey, California. Accountable to its stockholders and wanting to know the cost of the facility, the bank hired Sandra Burud, a social science researcher, to find out their net cost. Burud compared 87 employees who used the center with a control group of 105 employees who did not use it. She found that turnover in the control group was 9.5 percent, but among the center users it was only 2.2 percent. Users of the center were also absent an average of 1.7 days a year less than the control group, and their maternity leaves were 1.2 weeks shorter. The bottom line? After subtracting the $105,000 cost to open the center, as well as the costs of running it, the bank saved $232,000 (Solomon 1988).

Developing an Alternative: The Cooperative

In the 1970s, many Americans, especially those opposed to capitalism and what they considered to be the deadening effects of bureaucracy, began to seek an alternative organizational form. They began to establish cooperatives, organizations owned by members who collectively make decisions, determine goals, evaluate resources, set salaries, and assign work tasks. These tasks are all carried out without a hierarchy of authority, for all members can participate in the decisions of the organization. Since the 1970s, about five thousand cooperatives have been established.

As sociologists Joyce Rothschild and Allen Whitt (1986) pointed out, cooperatives are not new, but were introduced into the United States during the 1840s. Cooperatives attempt to achieve some specific social good (such as lowering food prices and improving food quality) and to provide a high level of personal satisfaction for their members as they accomplish that goal. Because all members can participate in decision making, cooperatives spend huge amounts of time in deciding even routine matters. The economic results of cooperatives are mixed. Many are less profitable than private organizations, others more so. A few have been so successful that they have been bought out by Wall Street corporations.

The Conflict Perspective

Conflict theorists point out that the basic relationship between workers and owners is confrontational regardless of how the work organization is structured (Edwards 1979; Derber and Schwartz 1988). Each walks a different path in life, the one exploiting workers to extract a greater profit, the other trying to resist that exploitation. Since their basic interests are fundamentally opposed, these critics argue, employers' attempts to humanize the work setting are mere window dressing, efforts to conceal their fundamental goal to exploit workers. If humanization of the work setting is not camouflage, then it is worse—an attempt to manipulate workers into active cooperation in their own exploitation. This analysis does not apply to cooperatives because they are owned by the workers.

The Japanese Corporate Model

The Japanese have developed a form of the corporate model that has stimulated great interest around the world. How were the Japanese able to arise from the defeat of World War II, including the nuclear destruction of two of their main cities, to become such a giant in today's global economy? Some analysts trace part of the answer to the way in which their major corporations are organized. Let's look at the conclusions of William Ouchi (1981), who pinpointed five major ways in which Japanese corporations differ from those in the United States.

Hiring and Promotion

In *Japan*, college graduates hired by a corporation are thought of as a team working toward the same goal, namely, the success of the organization. They are all paid about the same starting salary, and they are rotated through the organization to learn its various levels. Not only do they work together as a team, but they also are promoted as a team. Team members cooperate with one another, for the welfare of one represents the welfare of all. They also develop intense loyalty to one another and to their company. Only in later years are individuals singled out for recognition. When there is an opening in the firm, outsiders are not even considered.

In the *United States*, an employee is hired on the basis of what the firm thinks that individual can contribute. Employees try to outperform others, regarding salary and position as a sign of success. The individual's loyalty is to himself or herself, not to the company. When there is an opening in the firm, outsiders are considered.

Lifetime Security

In *Japan* lifetime security is taken for granted. Once hired, employees can expect to work for the same firm for the rest of their lives. Similarly, the firm expects them to be loyal to the company, to stick with it through good and bad times. On the one hand, employees will not be laid off or fired; on the other hand, they do not go job shopping, for their careers—and many aspects of their lives—are wrapped up in this one firm.

In the *United States*, lifetime security is unusual, being limited primarily to some college professors (who receive what is called *tenure*). A company is expected to lay off workers in slow times, and if it reorganizes it is not unusual for whole divisions to be fired. Given this context, workers are expected to "look out for number one," and that includes job shopping and job hopping, constantly seeking better pay and opportunities elsewhere.

Almost Total Involvement

In *Japan* work is like a marriage: The employee and the company are committed to each other. The employee supports the company with loyalty and long hours of dedicated work, while the company, in turn, supports its workers with lifetime security, health services, recreational activities, sports and social events, and perhaps a home mortgage or even a home. Involvement with the company does not stop when the workers leave the building. They are likely to associate with company employees both on and off the job, to spend evenings with co-workers in places of entertainment, and perhaps to be part of a company study or exercise group.

In the *United States*, the work relationship is assumed to be highly specific. An employee is hired to do a specific job, and employees who have done their jobs have thereby

The Japanese corporate model differs from the U.S. corporate model in several key ways, including its greater emphasis on employee and employer commitment, training, compensation, and collective decision making. Members of Japanese corporations work—and exercise—as a team.

fulfilled their obligation to the company. The rest of their hours are their own. They go home to their private lives, which are highly separated from the firm.

Broad Training

In *Japan*, employees move from one job to another within the corporation. Not only are they not stuck doing the same thing over and over for years on end, but they gain a broader picture of the corporation, of its goals and approaches, its particular problems, and the ways in which whatever job they are assigned fits into the bigger picture.

In the *United States*, employees are expected to perform one job, to do it well, and then to be promoted upward to a job with more responsibility. Their understanding of the company is largely tied to the particular corner they occupy, and it may be difficult for them to see how their job fits into the overall picture.

Decision Making by Consensus

In *Japan*, decision making is a lengthy process. The Japanese think it natural that after lengthy deliberations, to which each person to be affected by a decision contributes, everyone will agree on which suggestion is superior. This process broadens decision making, allowing workers to feel that they are an essential part of the organization, not simply cogs in a giant wheel.

In the *United States*, the individual who has responsibility for the unit in question does as much consulting with others as he or she thinks necessary and then makes the decision.

Limitations of the Model

This model of corporate life in Japan has always struck some sociologists as too idealized to accurately reflect reality. And, indeed, to peer beneath the surface gives a somewhat different view of this ideal image, as is illustrated in the following Perspectives box, with which we shall close this chapter.

▼▲▼

Perspectives

CULTURAL DIVERSITY AROUND THE WORLD

Cracks in the Corporate Façade

- *The Japanese are more productive than Americans.*
- *The living standard of Americans has fallen behind that of the Japanese.*
- *All Japanese workers enjoy lifetime job security.*
- *The Japanese work for cheaper wages than do Americans.*

WHAT IS WRONG WITH these statements? Nothing, except that they are untrue.

In recent years, the Japanese economic behemoth seemed unstoppable. Many nations felt threatened by it, and there was even talk that Japan had lost World War II, but was winning a new, undeclared economic war. Impressed with the Japanese success, many nations, including the United States, tried to emulate at least portions of their economic model. A closer look, however, reveals that not everything about the Japanese corporate system is good, and that not everything is as it appears on the surface.

One element, in fact, is so unfair from the American perspective that it is hard to imagine how the Japanese tolerate it. At age 60, workers are dismissed. Although early retirement may sound attractive, the problem is that retirement income does not begin until workers reach 65. Facing five years without income, these workers must depend on savings, part-time, low-paying jobs, and family and friends to get by until their retirement pay kicks in.

Nor is everything as it appears on the surface. During the current worldwide recession, Japan has been hit hard, and cracks in the seamless surface—the image that Japan so carefully cultivated—have become visible. It turns out that only employees of major corporations have lifetime job security, perhaps a third of Japanese workers. And Japan has found that paying the same wages to almost everyone in the same age group is costly and inefficient. Diligent but uninspired executives are compensated more by seniority than by output. Bottom–up decision making is also too slow to ad-

just to rapidly changing worldwide markets. Although still small by Western standards, unemployment has grown, while industrial output has fallen. Japanese labor costs have soared higher than those in the United States, while their much-vaunted productivity actually lags behind U.S. industry.

In a surprise move, Japan has turned to U.S. corporations to see why they are more efficient. The Japanese government has put through an American- or European-style tax cut to spur investment, and U.S. firms have now gone to Japan to teach seminars on business techniques. Flying in the face of their traditions, Japanese corporations have begun to lay off workers and to use merit pay. At Honda, for example, managers must now set annual goals, with their compensation depending on their success in meeting those goals. Although this is standard U.S. practice, it was unthinkable in Japan just a few years ago. Some firms have even begun to cut salaries and to demote managers who don't meet goals. And to meet the changing challenges of international markets, instead of waiting for "bottom-up" results, some managers now initiate decisions.

We will have to await the results, but we know that the Japanese were remarkably successful in their initial adapting of the West's manufacturing techniques to their culture. If they make the adjustment of this second phase as successfully, we can predict that an even stronger Japanese production machine will emerge from the recession.

The bottom line may be that both the West and Japan will feed off each other—the one learning greater cooperation in the production process, the other greater internal competitiveness.

Sources: Besser 1992; Nasar 1992; Naj 1993; Schlesinger and Sapsford 1993; Schlesinger et al. 1993; Shill 1993.

Summary and Review

The Rationalization of Society

How did the rationalization of society come about?

Weber used the phrase **rationalization of society** to refer to transformation in people's thinking and behaviors—the change from protecting time-honored ways to a concern with efficiency and practical results. Weber traced the rationalization of society to Protestant theology, which he said brought about capitalism, while Marx attributed the rationalization to capitalism itself. Pp. 170–172.

Formal Organizations and Bureaucracy

What are formal organizations?

Formal organizations are secondary groups designed to achieve explicit objectives. Their most common form is a **bureaucracy,** which Weber characterized as consisting of a hierarchy, a division of labor, written rules, written communications, and impersonality of positions—characteristics that allow bureaucracies to be efficient and enduring. Pp. 172–176.

What dysfunctions are associated with bureaucracies?

The dysfunctions of bureaucracies include **alienation, trained incapacity, goal conflict, goal displacement,** and incompetence (as seen in the **Peter principle**). In Weber's view, the impersonality of bureaucracies tends to produce alienation among workers—the feeling that no one cares about them and that they do not really fit in. Marx's view of alienation is somewhat different—workers are separated from the product of their labor because they participate in only a small part of the production process. The basic reason that workers have lost control over their work is that they no longer own their tools. Pp. 176–179.

Voluntary Associations

What social purposes do voluntary associations serve?

Voluntary associations are groups made up of volunteers who organize on the basis of common interests. These associations further mutual interests, provide a sense of identity and purpose, help to govern and maintain order, mediate between the government and the individual, give training in organizational skills, help provide access to political power, and pave the way for social change. Pp. 179–181.

What is the "iron law of oligarchy"?

Formal organizations, including voluntary associations, tend to resemble oligarchies, or systems in which the many are ruled by the few. Robert Michels called this tendency for formal organizations to eventually be dominated by a small, self-perpetuating group of leaders the **iron law of oligarchy.** Pp. 181–182.

Careers in Bureaucracies

How does the corporate culture affect workers?

The term **corporate culture** refers to an organization's traditions, values, and unwritten norms. Much of corporate culture is invisible, such as its hidden values. People who match a corporation's hidden values are put on tracks that enhance their chance of success, while those who do not match these values are set on a course that minimizes their performance. Pp. 182–184.

Humanizing the Corporate Culture

What does it mean to humanize the work setting?

Humanizing a work setting means organizing it in a way that develops rather than impedes human potential. Among the characteristics of more humane bureaucracies are expanded opportunities on the basis of ability and contributions rather than personal characteristics, a more even distribution of power, less rigid rules, and more open decision making. Attempts to modify bureaucracies include quality circles, small work groups, and self-management teams. Employee ownership plans give workers a greater stake in the outcomes of their work organizations. Cooperatives are an alternative to bureaucracies. Conflict theorists see attempts to humanize work as a way of manipulating workers. Pp. 185–187.

The Japanese Corporate Model

How do Japanese corporations differ from those in the United States?

The Japanese corporate model contrasts sharply with the U.S. model in its hiring and promotion practices, guarantee of lifetime security, worker involvement outside the work setting, broad training of workers, and collective decision making. Many critics however, believe that this model has been idealized and does not adequately reflect the reality of Japanese corporate life today. Pp. 187–190.

Where can I read more on this topic?

Suggested readings for this chapter are listed on page 639.

Ilona Anderson, Untitled, 1989

Deviance and Social Control

I N JUST A FEW MOMENTS *I was to meet my first Yanomamo, my first primitive man. What would it be like? . . . I looked up (from my canoe) and gasped when I saw a dozen burly, naked, filthy, hideous men staring at us down the shafts of their drawn arrows. Immense wads of green tobacco were stuck between their lower teeth and lips making them look even more hideous, and strands of dark-green slime dripped or hung from their noses. We arrived at the village while the men were blowing a hallucinogenic drug up their noses. One of the side effects of the drug is a runny nose. The mucus is always saturated with the green powder and the Indians usually let it run freely from their nostrils. . . . I just sat there holding my notebook, helpless and pathetic. . . .*

The whole situation was depressing, and I wondered why I ever decided to switch from civil engineering to anthropology in the first place. . . . (Soon) I was covered with red pigment, the result of a dozen or so complete examinations. . . . These examinations capped an otherwise grim day. The Indians would blow their noses into their hands, flick as much of the mucus off that would separate in a snap of the wrist, wipe the residue into their hair, and then carefully examine my face, arms, legs, hair, and the contents of my pockets. I said (in their language), "Your hands are dirty"; my comments were met by the Indians in the following way: they would "clean" their hands by spitting a quantity of slimy tobacco juice into them, rub them together, and then proceed with the examination.

Gaining a Sociological Perspective of Deviance

So went Napoleon Chagnon's eye-opening introduction to the Yanomamo tribe of the rain forests of Brazil. His ensuing months of fieldwork continued to bring surprise after surprise, and often Chagnon (1977) could hardly believe his eyes—or his nose.

Where would we start to list the deviant behaviors of these people? Appearing naked in public? Using hallucinogenic drugs? Letting mucus hang from one's nose? Rubbing hands filled with mucus, spittle, and tobacco juice over a frightened stranger who doesn't dare to protest? Perhaps. But it isn't this simple, for first we must deal with the question of what deviance is.

The Relativity of Deviance

Sociologists use the term **deviance** to refer to a violation of norms. This deceptively simple definition takes us to the heart of the sociological perspective of deviance, which sociologist Howard S. Becker (1966) identifies this way: *It is not the act itself, but the reactions to the act, that make something deviant.* In other words, people's behaviors must be viewed from the framework of the culture in which they take place. To Chagnon, the behaviors were frighteningly deviant, but to the Yanomamo they represented normal, everyday life. What was deviant to Chagnon was *conforming* to the Yanomamo. From their viewpoint of life, you *should* check out strangers as they did—and nakedness is good, as are hallucinogenic drugs and letting mucus be "natural."

Chagnon's abrupt introduction to the Yanomamo allows us to see the *relativity of deviance,* a major point made by symbolic interactionists such as Howard S. Becker (1966) and Malcolm Specter and John Kitsuse (1977, 1980). As the Perspectives box on the next page illustrates, because different groups have different norms, *what is deviant to some is not deviant to others.* This principle holds *within* a society as well as across cultures. Thus acts perfectly acceptable in one culture—or in one group within a society—may be considered deviant in another culture, or in another group within the same society.

What is similar about the following people: a college student cheating on an exam and a mugger lurking on a dark street; a child molester and a drunk; a jaywalker and a

deviance: the violation of rules or norms

194

▲▼▲▼▲▼▲▼▲▼▲▼▲▼▲▼▲▼▲▼▲▼▲▼▲▼▲▼▲▼▲▼▲▼

Perspectives

CULTURAL DIVERSITY AROUND THE WORLD

Deviance in Cross-Cultural Perspective

ANTHROPOLOGIST ROBERT EDGERTON (1976) reports how differently human groups react to similar behaviors. Of the many examples he provides, let's look at suicide and sexuality to illustrate how a group's *definitions* of a behavior, not the behavior itself, determine whether or not it will be considered deviant.

Suicide In some societies, suicide is seen not as deviance but as a positive act, at least under specified conditions. In traditional Japanese society, hara-kiri, a ritual disembowelment, was considered the proper course for disgraced noblemen or defeated military leaders. Similarly, kamikaze pilots in World War II who crashed their explosives-laden planes into U.S. warships were admired for their bravery and sacrifice. Traditional Eskimos approved the suicide of individuals no longer able to contribute their share to the group. Sometimes an aged father would hand his hunting knife to his son, asking him to drive it through his heart. For a son to refuse this request would be considered deviant.

Sexuality Norms of sexuality vary so widely around the world that many behaviors considered normal or desirable in one society are considered deviant in another. The Pokot people of northwestern Kenya, for example, place high emphasis on sexual pleasure and fully expect that both a husband and his wife will reach orgasm. If a husband does not satisfy his wife, he is in serious trouble. Pokot men often engage in adulterous affairs, and should a husband's failure to satisfy his wife be attributed to his adultery, when her husband is sleeping the wife will bring in female friends and tie him up. The women will then shout obscenities at him, beat him, and, as a final gesture of their utter contempt, slaughter and eat his favorite ox before releasing him. His hours of painful humiliation are assumed to make him henceforth more dutiful concerning his wife's conjugal rights.

Official Versus Covert Norms People can also become deviants for failing to understand that the group's official norms may not be its real norms. As with many groups, the Zapotec Indians of Mexico expect sexual activity to take place exclusively between husband and wife. Yet the *only* person in one Zapotec community who had had no extramarital affairs was considered deviant. Evidently these people have a covert, commonly understood norm that married couples will engage in discreet extramarital affairs, for when a wife learns that her husband is having an affair she does the same thing. One Zapotec wife, however, did not follow this informal pattern. Instead, she continually threw her virtue into her husband's face—and claimed headaches. Worse, she also informed all other husbands and wives in the village who their spouses' other partners were. As a result, this virtuous woman was condemned by everyone in the village. In other words, the official norms do not always represent the real norms—another illustration of the gap between ideal and real culture.

---

rapist; a killer and someone who breaks in line ahead of you? To a sociologist, these very different behaviors are all examples of deviance, for each is a violation of rules, or norms. Sociologists use the term **deviants** to refer to people who violate rules—whether the infraction is as minor as jaywalking or as serious as murder.

Unlike the general public, sociologists use the term *deviance* nonjudgmentally, to refer to acts to which people respond negatively. When sociologists use this term, it does not mean that they agree that an act is bad, just that others judge it negatively. To sociologists, then, all of us are deviants of one sort or another, for we all violate norms from time to time.

To be considered deviant, a person may not even have to *do* anything. Sociologist Erving Goffman (1963) used the term **stigma** to refer to attributes that discredit people. These attributes range from blindness, deafness, mental retardation, physical deformities, and obesity—characteristics that violate norms of appearance and ability—to involuntary membership in groups, such as relatives of criminals or victims of AIDS. The stigma becomes a person's master status, defining him or her as deviant. Recall from Chapter 4 that a person's master status cuts across all other statuses that a person occupies.

deviants: people who violate rules, as a result of which others react negatively to them

stigma: "blemishes" that discredit a person's claim to a "normal" identity

From a sociological perspective, deviance is relative. In U.S. culture, for instance, taking hallucinogenic drugs is considered deviant. Among the Yanomamo Indians, however, the normal route to initiation into manhood is accomplished through the administration of hallucinogens by a shaman, or holy man.

▼   **In Sum** In sociology, the term deviance refers to all violations of social rules, regardless of their seriousness. The term is not a judgment about the behavior. Deviance is relative, for what is conforming behavior in one group may be deviant in another. As symbolic interactionists stress, if we are to understand people, we must understand the meanings that they give to events. Consequently, we must consider deviance from *within* a group's own framework, for it is *their* meanings that underlie their behavior.

Who Defines Deviance?

If deviance does not lie in the act, but in definitions of the act, where do those definitions come from? To answer this question, let's look first at areas of agreement between functionalists and conflict theorists, then at how these views diverge.

Tribal Versus Industrial Societies Let's first consider preliterate groups without a written language. Each of these groups, such as the Yanomamo, has passed through a unique history. Each has faced and solved a set of problems that threatened their survival. These solutions, such as how to investigate strangers and protect themselves from enemies, have become part of their norms and now are an essential part of their way of life. Agreement on how life should be lived is relatively simple, for they are a small group, with strong social bonds.

Industrialized societies, in contrast, are made up of many competing groups. Each has its own history of problems, its own solutions, its own ideas about the way the world is and ought to be, and its own norms to uphold its ideas of right and wrong. Because they participate in the same general culture, these groups agree on many things. Yet due to their separate histories, they may differ sharply on many others—to the extent that what one group considers right, another may consider wrong.

Regardless of how they define deviance, to enforce their version of what is good all groups set up techniques of **social control.** Up to this point in the analysis, functionalists and conflict theorists are in basic agreement about social control. But now they diverge.

Functionalism and Social Control Functionalists stress how the various segments of the population in a pluralistic society coexist. Each enforces its own norms on its members, and the various groups attain a more or less balanced state. Although tensions between them may appear from time to time, the balancing of these tensions produces

social control: formal and informal means of enforcing norms

Michael Jackson is one of the most successful artists in the history of show business, with a personal fortune reputed to be in excess of $150 million. Whether innocent or guilty, Jackson will always carry the stigma brought by accusations of child abuse.

the whole that we call society. If some group threatens to upset the equilibrium, efforts are made to restore balance. For example, in a pluralistic society the central government often plays a mediating role between groups. In the United States, the executive, legislative, and judicial branches of the government mediate the demands of the various groups that make up society, preventing groups whose basic ideas deviate from those held by most members of society from taking political control (Riesman 1950). This view of mediation and balance among competing groups is broadly representative of what may be called the **pluralistic theory of social control.**

Conflict Theory and Social Control Conflict theorists, in contrast, stress that each society is dominated by a group of elite, powerful people, and that the basic purpose of social control is to maintain the current power arrangements. Consequently, society is made up not of groups in balance, but rather of competing groups uneasily held together. The group that holds power must always fend off groups that desire to replace it and take over the society themselves. If another group does gain power, it, too, immediately tries to neutralize competing groups. Some groups are much more ruthless than others; for example, before and during World War II the Nazis in Germany and the Communists in the Soviet Union systematically eliminated individuals and groups they deemed a threat to their vision of the ideal society. In more recent years, the Khmer Rouge did the same in Cambodia. Other dominant groups may be less ruthless, but they, too, are committed to maintaining power.

In U.S. society, for example, although political power is not as naked as it is in dictatorships, conflict theorists note that an elite group of wealthy, largely white males maintains power by working behind the scenes to control the three branches of government (Domhoff 1990, 1993). These men make certain that their interests are represented in the day-to-day decisions of Congress, by the nominees to the U.S. Supreme Court, and by the presidential candidates of the two major political parties. Thus, it is this group's views of capital and property, the basis of their power, that are represented in

pluralistic theory of social control: the view that society is made up of many competing groups, whose interests manage to become balanced

From a conflict perspective, the elite in power decide who is deviant based not on the act itself but, rather, on how it affects their own interests. Shown here is Pablo Escobar, who prior to his death at the hands of Colombian police used to direct the heroin operations in Colombia, the primary source of drugs imported to the United States. To answer why there was an intensive national hunt for Escobar, conflict theorists would point not to an anti-drug stance on the part of Colombian officials but to intense pressure from the U.S. government.

the laws of society. This means that **official deviance**—the statistics on victims, law-breakers, and the outcomes of criminal investigations and sentencing—centers on maintaining their interests.

Thus, conflict theorists stress, the state's machinery of social control represents the interests of the wealthy and powerful (Hall 1952). It is this group that determines the basic laws whose enforcement is essential to preserving its own power. Other norms, such as those that govern informal behavior (chewing with a closed mouth, appearing in public with combed hair, and so on), may come from other sources, but they simply do not count for much. Although they influence everyday behavior, they do not determine prison sentences.

How Norms Make Social Life Possible

Regardless of which of these views is correct regarding the origin of a group's norms, or whose interests they represent, *norms make social life possible by making behavior predictable*. Consequently, every group within a society, and even human society itself, depends on norms for its existence. Only because we can count on most people most of the time to meet the expectations of others can social life as we know it exist.

What would life be like if you could not predict what others would do? Imagine for a moment that you have gone to a store to purchase milk:

> Suppose that the clerk says: "I won't sell you any milk. We are overstocked with soda, and I'm not going to sell anyone milk until our soda inventory is reduced."
>
> You don't like it, but you decide to buy a case of soda. At the checkout, the clerk says, "I hope you don't mind, but there's a $5 service charge on each fifteenth customer." You, of course, are the fifteenth.
>
> Just as you start to leave, another clerk stops you and says, "We're not working anymore. We're having a party." Suddenly a stereo begins to blast, and everyone in the store is dancing. "Oh, good, you've brought the soda," says one clerk, who takes your package and passes sodas all around.

But life is not like this. You can depend on a grocery clerk selling you milk as long as it is in stock and that is what you want. You can also depend on paying the same price as everyone else. And you can depend on the clerks not to give a party in the store and force you to attend. Why can you depend on this? Because we are socialized to follow norms, to play the basic roles as society indicates we should.

Without norms we would have social chaos. Norms regulate our behavior; they dictate how we play our roles and how we interact with others. In short, norms allow **social order,** a group's usual and customary social arrangements, those on which we depend and on which we base our lives. This is precisely the reason that deviance is often seen as so threatening, for it undermines predictability, the foundation of social life. Consequently, human groups develop a system of *social control*, formal and informal means of enforcing norms.

Comparing Biological, Psychological, and Sociological Explanations

Since norms are essential for society, why do people violate them? To better understand the reasons, it is useful to know first how sociological explanations differ from biological and psychological ones, and then to examine how the three sociological perspectives explain deviance.

Psychologists and *sociobiologists* explain deviance by looking for answers *within* individuals. They assume that something in the makeup of people leads them to become deviant. By contrast, sociologists look for answers in factors *outside* the individual. They assume that something in the environment influences people to become deviant.

Biological explanations focus on **genetic predispositions** toward deviance such as juvenile delinquency and crime (Lombroso 1911; Sheldon 1949; Glueck and Glueck

official deviance: a society's statistics on lawbreaking; its measures of crimes, victims, lawbreakers, and the outcomes of criminal investigations and sentencing

social order: a group's usual and customary social arrangements, on which its members depend and on which they base their lives

genetic predispositions: inborn tendencies, in this context, to commit deviant acts

1956; Wilson and Hernstein 1985; Kamin 1975, 1986; Rose 1986). Biological explanations include (but are not restricted to) the following three theories: (1) intelligence—low intelligence leads to crime; (2) the "XYY" theory—an extra Y chromosome in males leads to crime; and (3) body type—people with "squarish, muscular" bodies are more likely to commit **street crime,** acts such as mugging, rape, and burglary.

How have these theories held up? Some criminals are very intelligent, and most people of low intelligence do not commit crimes. Most criminals have the normal "XY" chromosome combination, and most men with the "XYY" combination do not become criminals. In addition, no women have this combination of genes, so it wouldn't even deal with female criminals. Criminals also run the range of the body types exhibited by humanity, and most people with "squarish, muscular" bodies do not become street criminals. In short, these supposedly "causal" characteristics are also found among the general population of people who do not commit crimes.

Still, we cannot rule out the possibility that biological factors influence deviance. Advances in biology have renewed interest in this issue, and some of the findings are intriguing. Psychiatrist Dorothy Lewis (1981), for example, compared the medical histories of delinquents and nondelinquents. She found that delinquents had significantly more head injuries. Then she matched the delinquents by the seriousness of their crimes. When she compared their medical histories, she found that the more violent delinquents—those incarcerated for murder, assault, and rape—also had more head injuries than boys locked up for lesser violence such as fights and threats with weapons. Many of the injuries had occurred before the age of 2.

The answers, then, are not yet in, and we must await more research. Even if biological factors are involved in some forms of deviance, from a sociological perspective the causes of deviance cannot be answered by biology alone. Biological factors are always mediated through the social environment. That is, conditions of society channel different categories of people in different directions. For example, some of the expectations of the masculine role in U.S. society—to be braver, tougher, more independent, and less tolerant of insult—increase the likelihood that males will become involved in violence.

Psychological explanations of deviance focus on abnormalities in the individual personality, on what are called **personality disorders.** The supposition is that deviating individuals have deviating personalities (Kalichman 1988; Stone 1989; Heilbrun 1990), that various unconscious devices drive people to deviance. Neither specific negative childhood experiences nor particular personalities, however, are invariably linked with deviance. For example, children who had "bad toilet training," "suffocating mothers," or "emotionally aloof fathers" may become embezzling bookkeepers—or good accountants. Just as students, teachers, and bus drivers represent a variety of bad—and good—childhood experiences, so do deviants. In short, there is no inevitable outcome of particular childhood experiences.

Sociologists, in contrast, search for factors outside the individual. First, they stress that because deviance is relative there is no reason to expect that internal factors within individuals will account for deviance. For example, **crime** is the violation of norms that have been written into law. Since one society may pass a law against some behavior while another society passes no such law, why should we expect to find anything constant within people to account for a behavior that is conforming in one society and deviant in another?

Second, sociologists look for social influences that "recruit" some people rather than others to break norms. To account for why people commit crimes, for example, sociologists examine such external influences on them as socialization, subcultural membership, and social class. *Social class*, a concept discussed in depth in the next two chapters, refers to people's relative standing in terms of education, occupation, and especially income and wealth.

To see how sociologists study deviance, let's contrast the three sociological perspectives—symbolic interactionism, functionalism, and conflict theory—looking at how each theory accounts for criminal behavior.

street crime: crimes such as mugging, rape, and burglary

personality disorders: the view that a personality disturbance of some sort causes an individual to violate social norms

crime: the violation of norms that are written into law

The Symbolic Interactionist Perspective

As we examine symbolic interactionism, it will become more evident why sociologists are not satisfied with explanations rooted in biology and personality. A basic principle of symbolic interactionism is that each of us interprets social life through the symbols that we learn from the groups to which we belong. Let's consider the extent to which membership in a group influences people's behaviors and views of the world, also a focus of the Perspectives box on the next page.

Differential Association Theory

Contrary to theories of biology and personality, sociologist Edwin Sutherland stressed that people *learn* deviance. He coined the term **differential association** to indicate that learning to deviate or to conform to society's norms is influenced most by the people with whom we associate (Sutherland 1924, 1947; Sutherland and Cressey 1974; Sutherland et al. 1992). On the most obvious level, boys and girls who join Satan's Servants learn a way of looking at the world that is more likely to get them in trouble with the law than boys and girls who join the Scouts.

Sutherland's theory is actually more complicated than this, but he stressed that learning deviance is like learning anything else—which goes directly against the thinking that deviance is biological or due to deep personality needs. Sutherland said that the key to differential association is the learning of "definitions" (which you can translate as ideas or attitudes) favorable to following the law or favorable to breaking it. From the various people we associate with, each of us learns both, and the end result is an imbalance—an "excess of definitions" one way or the other. Consequently, we conform or deviate.

The extent to which some groups teach their members to violate the dominant norms of society has been documented by demographers Allen Beck, Susan Kline, and Lawrence Greenfeld (1988). After studying the family histories of a representative sample of the 25,000 delinquents confined in high-security state institutions nationwide, they found that significant numbers have a relative who has been in prison: 25 percent a father, 25 percent a brother or sister, 9 percent a mother, and 13 percent some other relative. Apparently families involved in crime tend to set their children on a law-breaking path.

The neighborhood is also likely to be influential, for sociologists have long observed that delinquents tend to come from neighborhoods in which their peers are involved in crime (Miller 1958; Wolfgang and Ferracuti 1967). Sociologist Ruth Horowitz (1983, 1987), who did participant observation of a Chicano neighborhood in Chicago, discovered how associating with people who have a certain concept of "honor" can propel young men to deviance. The formula is simple. An insult is defined as a threat to one's manliness. Honor requires a man to stand up to an insult. Not to stand up to someone is to be less than a real man. Suppose that you were a young man growing up in this neighborhood. You would likely do a fair amount of fighting, for you would see many statements and acts as infringing on your honor. You might make certain that you carried a knife or had access to a gun, for words and fists won't always do. Along with members of your group, you would define fighting, knifing, and shooting quite differently from the way most people do in American culture.

Studies of the Mafia also show a relationship between killing, manliness, and honor. *To kill is a primary measure of one's manhood.* Not all killings are accorded the same respect, however, for "the more awesome and potent the victim, the more worthy and meritorious the killer" (Arlacchi 1980). Some killings are very practical matters. A member of the Mafia who gives information to the police, for example, has violated the Mafia's *omerta* (the vow of secrecy its members take). Such an offense can never be tolerated, for it threatens the very existence of the group. This example further illustrates just how rel-

differential association: Edwin Sutherland's term to indicate that associating with some groups results in learning an "excess of definitions" of deviance, and, by extension, in a greater likelihood that one will become deviant

Perspectives

CULTURAL DIVERSITY IN U.S. SOCIETY

When Cultures Clash—Problems in Defining Deviance

HAVING DECIDED THAT IT was time to marry, a young Hmong refugee in Fresno, California, named Kong Moua, went to a local college campus along with a group of friends and forced the girl he had selected as his mate to his house. He then had sex with her.

In the Hmong culture, Kong Moua had performed *zij poj niam*, marriage by capture. While this method of obtaining a marriage partner is not the only, or even the most frequent, way of marrying among traditional Hmong, neither is it a rare occurrence. Universal to Hmong courtship is the idea that men appear strong, women resistant and virtuous.

The apparent sincerity of Kong Moua presented a dilemma to the judge who heard his case. Under the U.S. legal system, Kong Moua had committed two crimes: kidnap and rape. Given Moua's cultural background, however, the judge felt uncomfortable simply applying U.S. law. In an attempt to balance matters, he allowed Moua to plead to a lesser charge of false imprisonment, thus giving the court the leeway "to get into all these cultural issues and try to tailor

a sentence that will fulfill both our needs and the Hmong needs." Moua was ordered to pay $1,000 to the girl's family and serve a ninety-day jail term.

In Connecticut, with five friends assisting, Beinh Gia Pham doused himself with gasoline, flicked a lighter, and exploded into flames. He was protesting attempts by the Vietnamese government to suppress Buddhism. Pham's friends, who had videotaped his death, notified Connecticut police. The five were bewildered when they were charged with manslaughter for assisting a suicide. Taking into account that public suicide is a traditional Buddhist form of protest, the judge sentenced the men to probation.

For Your Consideration: What is the proper reaction when cultures clash? When the norms of the culture in which people were raised violate the norms of their host society, what should the proper reaction be? Should the full force of the law be applied in such cases? If not, how can we justify two types of application?

Sources: Based on Sherman 1988; La Cayo 1993.

ative deviance is. While the act of killing is deviant to the larger society, *not* to kill after certain rules are broken, such as "squealing" to the cops, is the deviant act for this group.

As symbolic interactionists stress, people are not merely pawns in the hands of others, destined by group membership to think and behave in the precise way their group wants. Rather, individuals *help to produce their own orientations to life*. Their choice of association, for example, helps to shape the self. For instance, one college student may join a feminist group that is trying to change the treatment of females in college; another may associate with a group of women who shoplift on weekends. Their choice of groups points them in two different directions. The one who associates with shoplifters may become even more oriented toward deviant activities, while the one who joins the feminist group may develop an even greater interest in producing social change.

Control Theory

Sociologist Walter Reckless (1973), who developed **control theory,** stresses that everyone is propelled toward deviance—by temptations, inner drives, hostility, resentment, pressure from peers, and so on. Two control systems work against these motivations to deviate. The *inner control* system is the individual's capacity to withstand these pressures. Inner controls include internalized morality—conscience, ideas of right and wrong, and reluctance to violate religious principles. Inner controls also include fears of punishment, feelings of integrity, and the desire to be a "good" person (Hirschi 1969; Rogers 1977). The *outer control* system involves groups—such as family, friends, and the police—that influence a person to stay away from crime. (Control theory is sometimes classified as a functional theory, because

control theory: the idea that two control systems—inner controls and outer controls—work against our tendencies to deviate

When O.J. Simpson was arrested and charged with the murder of his former wife and her male friend, because of his celebrity status the news instantly made headlines around the world. For several months it was even the primary news story in the United States, at times forcing international events into a secondary position. If guilty, control theory would be highly appropriate to explain the act. Whether innocent or guilty, however, the stigma of the accusation will remain with Simpson the rest of his life.

when outer controls operate well, the individual conforms to social norms and thereby does not threaten the status quo. Because symbols and meanings are central to this theory, however, it can also be classified as a symbolic interactionist theory.)

As sociologist Travis Hirschi (1969) noted, the more people feel bonds with society, the more effective are their inner controls. Bonds are based on *attachments* (in this case, having affection and respect for people who conform to society's norms), *commitments* (having a stake in society that you don't want to risk, such as a respected place in your family, a good standing at college, a good job), *involvements* (putting time and energy into approved activities), and *beliefs* (holding that certain actions are morally wrong).

The likelihood that someone will deviate from social norms, for example by committing a crime, depends on the strength of these two control systems relative to the strength of the pushes and pulls toward the deviance. If the control systems are weak, deviance results. If they are strong enough, however, the person does not commit the deviant act. This theory can be summarized as *self*-control, says Hirschi. The key to learning high self-control is socialization, especially in child rearing. Parents help their children develop self-control by supervising them and punishing their deviant acts (Gottfredson and Hirschi 1990).

Labeling Theory

labeling theory: the view, developed by symbolic interactionists, that the labels people are given affect their own and others' perceptions of them, thus channeling their behavior either into deviance or into conformity

Labeling theory, which focuses on the significance of the labels (names, reputations) given to people, also represents the symbolic interactionist perspective. According to labeling theory, acts are deviant only because people label them as such. Thus, the young

Hmong man, whose attempt to "capture" a wife is recounted in the Perspectives box on page 201, is not seen as deviant by traditional Hmong. Perhaps some of his own relatives had married in this manner. They would label his behavior as desirable and expected, and perhaps even applaud him for it. In U.S. society, however, different labels—those of kidnapper and rapist—are appropriate. Consequently, symbolic interactionists analyze the significance of labels in determining how people react to others.

In an ironic twist, symbolic interactionists have found that these labels, although intended to prevent or reduce deviance, sometimes make people even more deviant (Hewitt 1994). We shall examine such unintended consequences of labeling on pages 210–211, where we follow the careers of some high school youth who were labeled "Saints" and "Roughnecks."

▼ **In Sum** Symbolic interactionists examine how people's definitions of the situation underlie their deviation or conformance to social norms. Differential association theory focuses on the effects of group membership, control theory emphasizes how people balance pressures to conform and to deviate, and labeling theory examines the significance of the labels placed on people.

The Functionalist Perspective

When we think of deviance, its dysfunctions are likely to come to mind. Functionalists, in contrast, are as likely to stress the functions of deviance as its dysfunctions.

How Deviance Is Functional for Society

Most of us are upset by deviance, especially crime, and assume that society would be better off without it. The classic functionalist theorist Emile Durkheim (1933, 1964) came to a surprising conclusion, however. Deviance, including crime, he said, is functional for society, for it contributes to the social order. Its three main functions are:.

1 *Deviance clarifies moral boundaries and affirms norms*. A group's ideas about how people should act and think mark its *moral boundaries*. Deviant acts challenge those boundaries. To call a deviant member to account, saying in effect, "You broke a valuable rule, and we cannot tolerate that," affirms the group's norms and clarifies the distinction between conforming and deviating behavior. To deal with deviants is to assert what it means to be a member of the group.

2 *Deviance promotes social unity*. To affirm the group's moral boundaries by reacting to deviants develops a "we" feeling among the group's members. In saying, "You can't get by with that," the group collectively affirms the rightness of its own ways.

3 *Deviance promotes social change*. Groups do not always agree on what to do with people who push beyond their acceptable ways of doing things. Some group members may even approve the behavior. Boundary violations that gain enough support become new, acceptable behaviors. Thus, deviance may force a group to rethink and redefine its moral boundaries, helping groups, and whole societies, to change their customary ways.

Strain Theory: How Social Values Produce Crime

Functionalists argue that crime is a *natural* part of society, not an aberration or some alien element in our midst. Indeed, they say, some crime represents values that lie at the very core of society. This concept sounds strange at first. To understand how the acceptance of

On the left is Tonya Harding, shown as she admitted guilt in a failed plot to "kneecap" her chief figure skating rival, Nancy Kerrigan. On the right is Kerrigan as she receives a silver medal at the Olympics in Liljehamer, Norway. Harding's public admission of her guilt before a national audience was a type of degradation ceremony, a public removal of Harding as a legitimate competitor. Her status was so diminished by her deviance that she will never again be able to compete in figure skating.

strain theory: Robert Merton's term for the strain engendered when a society socializes large numbers of people to desire a cultural goal (such as success) but withholds from many the approved means to reach that goal; one adaptation to the strain is crime, the choice of an innovative means (one outside the approved system) to attain the cultural goal

cultural goals: the legitimate objectives held out to the members of a society

institutionalized means: approved ways of reaching cultural goals

cultural values can generate crime, consider what sociologists Richard Cloward and Lloyd Ohlin (1960) identified as the crucial problem of the industrialized world: the need to locate and train the most talented people of every generation—whether born in wealth or in poverty—so that they can take over the key technical jobs of modern society. When children are born, no one knows which ones will have the abilities to become dentists, nuclear physicists, or engineers. To get the most talented people to compete with one another, society tries to motivate *everyone* to strive for success. It does this by arousing discontent—making people feel dissatisfied with what they have so that they will try to "better" themselves.

Merton's Typology Sociologist Robert Merton (1956, 1968) developed **strain theory** to analyze what happens when people are socialized into desiring **cultural goals** (the legitimate objectives held out to everyone, such as owning material possessions) but are denied access to the institutionalized means of achieving those goals. By **institutionalized means,** Merton meant the socially acceptable ways to achieve goals, such as gaining an education or acquiring a good job. Large numbers of people who want to succeed, however, find their path to good jobs blocked because they grew up in poverty and received an inferior education. Due to racism or sexism, many others are denied access to the institutionalized means of achieving cultural goals. The result is anomie, a sense of normlessness as people find the conventional norms of society blocked.

Table 8.1 compares people's reactions to cultural goals and institutionalized means. The first reaction, which Merton said is the most common, is *conformity*, using socially

Table 8.1

Merton's Typology of Individual Adaptation to Anomie

Modes of Adaptation	Cultural Goals	Institutionalized Means
Conformity	+	+
Innovation	+	–
Ritualism	–	+
Retreatism	–	–
Rebellion	±	±

Note: + indicates acceptance, – rejection, and ± rejection of prevailing goals or means and substitution of new ones.

acceptable, legitimate means to strive to attain cultural goals. In industrialized societies most people try to get good jobs, a good education, and so on. If well-paid jobs are unavailable, they take less desirable jobs. If they are denied access to Harvard or Stanford, they go to a state university. Others take night classes and attend vocational schools. In short, most people take legally and socially acceptable actions to get ahead.

The remaining four types of responses are deviant. Let's look at each. Individuals turn to *innovation* when they accept the goals of society but use illegitimate means to achieve them. Drug dealers, for instance, accept the goal of achieving wealth but reject the legitimate avenues for doing so. Embezzlers, robbers, and con artists are other examples of what Merton called innovators.

The second deviant path is taken by people who find their way blocked, become discouraged and give up on achieving cultural goals, but nonetheless cling to conventional rules of conduct. Merton called this type of response *ritualism*. Although not seeking to excel or advance in position, ritualists nonetheless follow the rules of their job, sometimes with a vengeance. Teachers who suffer from "burnout" but continue to go through the motions of classroom performance after their idealism is shattered are examples of ritualists. Their response is considered deviant because they cling to the job although they have actually abandoned the goal, in this instance stimulating young minds and, possibly, making the world a better place.

People who choose the third deviant path, *retreatism*, reject both cultural goals and the institutionalized means of achieving them. Those who drop out of the pursuit of success by way of alcohol or drugs are retreatists. Such people do not even try to appear as though they share the goals of their society.

The final type of deviant response identified by Merton is *rebellion*. Convinced that the society in which they live is corrupt, rebels, like retreatists, reject both society's goals and its institutionalized means. Unlike retreatists, however, they seek to replace existing goals with new ones. Revolutionaries are the most committed type of rebels.

Merton's theory has held up under examination. Sociologists have found that anomie is higher among the lower social classes, and these classes do have less access to the institutionalized means to success (Bell 1957; Tumin and Collins 1959; Killian and Grigg 1962). Sociologists Chien Huang and James Anderson (1991) found that people in the lower classes perceive more obstacles to their goals and are more likely to give up on cultural values. In contrast, people in the upper classes, who perceive fewer obstacles to their success, are more committed to the dominant social values.

Strain theory underscores the main sociological point about deviance, namely, that deviants, including criminals, are not pathogenic individuals, but the product of society itself. Due to their social location, some people experience greater pressures to deviate from society's norms. Simply put, if a society emphasizes the goal of material success, groups deprived of access to this goal will be more involved in property crime. This is a good part of the reason that young males join the gangs discussed in the Down-to-Earth Sociology box on page 207.

Shown in this nineteenth-century lithograph are some of London's hungry unemployed as they lunge forward to receive a free meal ticket. Conflict theorists stress that the marginal working class provides the temporary workers who are hired during economic booms and then discharged to their misery during economic turndowns. Until these workers are needed, they are kept alive at substandard conditions. Whether in early or late capitalism, is it surprising that most street criminals come from the marginal working class?

Illegitimate Opportunity Theory: Explaining Social Class and Crime

That different social classes have unequal access to institutionalized means to success is also relevant to one of the more interesting sociological findings in the field of deviance: The social classes have distinct styles of crime. Let us look first at the poor.

Functionalists point out that industrialized societies have no trouble socializing the poor into desiring material success. Like others, they, too, are bombarded with messages urging them to purchase everything from designer jeans to new cars. Television portrays vivid images of the middle class enjoying luxurious lives, reinforcing the myth that all full-fledged Americans can afford the goods and services portrayed on programs and offered in commercials (Silberman 1978).

The school system, however, which constitutes the most common route to success, fails the poor. It is run by the middle class, and when the children of the poor enter it, already at an educational disadvantage, they confront a bewildering world for which their background ill prepares them. Their grammar and nonstandard language—liberally punctuated by what the middle class considers obscene and foul words and phrases—their ideas of punctuality and neatness, and their lack of preparation in paper-and-pencil skills are a mismatch with their new environment. Facing these barriers, the poor drop out of school in larger numbers than their more privileged counterparts. Educational failure, in turn, closes the door on many legitimate avenues to financial success.

Not infrequently, however, a different door opens to them, one that sociologists Richard Cloward and Lloyd Ohlin (1960) called **illegitimate opportunity structures.** Woven into the texture of life in urban slums, for example, are robbery, burglary, drug dealing, prostitution, pimping, gambling, and other remunerative crimes, commonly called "hustles" (Liebow 1967; Sullivan 1989; Anderson 1978, 1990). For many of the poor, the "hustler" is a role model—glamorous, in control, the image of "easy money," one of the few people in the area who approximates the cultural goal of success. For some, then, such illegal income-producing activities are functional—they provide income—and they attract disproportionate numbers of the poor.

White-Collar Crime   Other social classes are not crime-free, of course, but a different illegitimate opportunity structure beckons the more privileged classes. For them, *other forms of crime* are functional. Rather than mugging, pimping, and burglary, the more privileged encounter "opportunities" for income tax evasion, bribery of public officials,

illegitimate opportunity structures: opportunities for crimes that are woven into the texture of life

▼▲

Down-To-Earth Sociology

Islands in the Street: Urban Gangs in U.S. Society

THE UNITED STATES HAS always had gangs—from the out-laws of the West to Chicago's mobs during Prohibition. Today it is urban youth gangs. For over ten years, sociologist Martín Sánchez Jankowski (1991) did participant observation of thirty-seven Irish, African-American, Puerto Rican, Chicano, Dominican, Jamaican, and Central American gangs in Boston, Los Angeles, and New York City. Jankowski ate, slept, and sometimes fought with the gangs, but by mutual agreement did not participate in drugs or other illegal activities. He was seriously injured twice during the study.

Jankowski identified five character traits of gang members, almost all of whom were from low-income neighborhoods: competitiveness, a sense of mistrust, self-reliance, social isolation, and a survival instinct, by which he means that they fight for survival in a hostile world filled with predators seeking prey.

Surprisingly, Jankowski did not find that the motive for joining was to escape broken homes (there were as many members from intact as broken homes) or to seek a substitute family (as many members said they were close to their families as said they were not). Rather, the boys joined to gain access to steady money, recreation (including access to females and drugs), anonymity in criminal activities, protection, and to help the community. This last reason exists in areas where gangs transcend generations and help to protect community members from outsiders. In addition, the gang was seen as an alternative to the dead-end—and deadening—jobs held by the working parents.

The gangs earn the money by which they attract members through gambling, arson, mugging, armed robbery, making and wholesaling drugs to pushers, and selling moonshine, guns, stolen car parts, and protection. Some gangs are involved in legal economic activities such as running "mom and pop" stores and renovating and renting abandoned apartment buildings—but this is unusual.

Jankowski witnessed much gang violence. When the members of a gang quarrel over drugs or women, or fight to test one another, gang rules and other members usually keep such violence under control. In contrast, attacks against rival gangs often escalate into serious violence. Similarly, the gangs don't attack residents of their own community unless someone has insulted them or threatened to turn them in to the police, but individuals will attack people outside the community simply to test their strength or even because they don't like the way someone looks.

The residents of a gang's turf are ambivalent about gangs. On the one hand, they don't like the violence; on the other hand, they may complain that the police use unnecessary force against gangs. The reasons for the ambivalence are that many adults once belonged to gangs, gang members are the children of neighborhood residents, and the gangs often provide better protection than do the police.

Particular gangs will come and go, but gangs will likely always be part of the city, for from a functional standpoint gangs fulfill needs for poor youth who live on the margins of society.

---

securities violations, embezzlement, false advertising, and price fixing. Sociologist Edwin Sutherland (1949) coined the term **white-collar crime** to refer to crimes that people of respectable and high social status commit in the course of their occupations.

Although the general public seems to think that the lower classes are more crime-prone, numerous studies show that white-collar workers also commit many crimes (Weisburd et al. 1991; Zey 1993). The difference in public perception has much to do with visibility. While crimes committed by the poor are given much publicity, the crimes of the more privileged classes seldom make the evening news and go largely unnoticed. Yet white-collar crimes are very costly (Moore and Mills 1990). The cost of "crime in the suites" (as opposed to "crime in the streets") may total about $200 billion a year. This is about *eighteen* times the cost of all the street crimes committed in the United States (Gest and Scherschel 1985). These figures refer only to dollar costs. No one has yet figured out a way to compare, for example, the suffering of a rape victim with the pain experienced by an elderly couple who lose their life savings to white-collar fraud.

In terms of dollars, perhaps the most costly crime in U.S. history is the plundering of the savings and loan industry. Corporate officers, who had the trust of their depositors, systematically looted these banks of billions of dollars. The total cost may run as high as $500 billion—a staggering $2,000 for every man, woman, and child in the entire country (Kettl 1991; Newdorf 1991). Of the thousands involved, the most famous cul-

white-collar crime: Edwin Sutherland's term for crimes committed by people of respectable and high social status in the course of their occupations; for example, bribery of public officials, securities violations, embezzlement, false advertising, and price fixing

prit was Neil Bush, son of the president of the United States and an officer of Silverado, a Colorado savings and loan. Bush approved loans totaling $100 million to a company in which he secretly held interests, an act that helped bankrupt his firm (Tolchin 1991). Future generations will continue to suffer from the wholesale looting of this industry. The interest alone will be exorbitant (at 5 percent a year's interest on an increased national deficit of $500 billion would be $25 billion, at 10 percent $50 billion). Since the government does not pay its debt, but merely borrows more to keep up with the compounding interest, this extra $500 billion will double in just a few years. As the late Senator Everett Dirkson once said, "A billion here and a billion there, and pretty soon you're talking about real money."

Although white-collar crime is not as dramatic as a street killing or an abduction and rape—and therefore usually considered less newsworthy—it too can involve physical harm, and sometimes death (Reiman 1990). With the act clandestine and often a long lag between the act and the injury, the harm is difficult to measure. For example, although Dow Corning knew for twenty years that its silicone breast implants might leak, the company concealed that information. In the ensuing years, thousands of women suffered from ruptured implants, which apparently caused illnesses ranging from arthritis-type joint pain to severely swollen abdomens—and perhaps even increased their risk of cancer (Burton 1992; Burton and McMurray 1992; Ingersoll 1992; McMurray 1992; Woods and Arnold 1992). Similarly, unsafe working conditions, many the result of executive decisions to put profits ahead of workers' safety, claim about one hundred thousand American lives each year—about *five* times the number of people killed each year by street criminals (Simon and Eitzen 1993).

In Sum Functionalists conclude that much crime is the consequence of socializing people of all social classes into equating success with material possessions, while denying the lower classes the means to attain that success. People from different social classes encounter different opportunity structures to commit crimes.

The Conflict Perspective

Conflict theorists, agreeing that the social classes face different opportunity structures, place their primary focus on crimes of the powerful. They also analyze how the elite controls the criminal justice system.

Class, Crime, and the Criminal Justice System

Have you ever wondered what is going on when you read that top-level executives who defraud the public of millions through price fixing, insider trading, or stock manipulation receive only small fines and suspended sentences? In the same newspaper, furthermore, you may read that some young man who stole an automobile worth $5,000 was sentenced to several years in prison. An example is the Grumman Corporation, which, accused of fraud in federal contracts, agreed to pay a fine so no one would go to jail and the company could continue to bid on more federal contracts (Pasztor 1993). How can a legal system that is supposed to provide "justice for all" be so inconsistent? According to conflict theorists, this question is central to the analysis of crime and the **criminal justice system**—the police, courts, and prisons that deal with people who are accused of having committed crimes.

Conflict theorists look at power and social inequality as the primary characteristics of every society (Simon and Eitzen 1993). They see the most fundamental division in industrial society as that between the few who own the means of production and the many who do not, those who sell their labor and the privileged few who buy it. Those who

criminal justice system: the system of police, courts, and prisons set up to deal with people who are accused of having committed a crime

buy labor, and thereby control workers, make up the **capitalist class;** those who sell their labor form the **working class.** Toward the most depressed end of the working class is the **marginal working class,** people with few skills, who are subject to unexpected lay-offs, and whose jobs are low paying, part time, or seasonal. This class is marked by unemployment and poverty, and from its ranks come most of the prisoners in the United States. Desperate, these people commit street crimes, and because their crimes threaten the social order, they are severely punished.

According to conflict theorists, the idea that the law is a social institution that operates impartially and administers a code shared by all is simply a cultural myth promoted by the capitalist class. In contrast, they see the law as an instrument of repression, a tool designed to maintain the powerful in their privileged position (Spitzer 1975; Turk 1977; Ritzer 1992). Because the working class holds the potential of rebelling and overthrowing the current social order, when its members get out of line they are arrested, tried, and imprisoned.

For this reason, the criminal justice system does not focus on the owners of corporations and the harm they do to the masses with their unsafe products, wanton pollution, and price manipulations but instead directs its energies against violations by the working class (Gordon 1971; Platt 1978; Coleman 1989). The violations of the capitalist class cannot be totally ignored, however, for if they became too outrageous or oppressive, the working class might rise up in revolution. To prevent this, a flagrant violation by a member of the capitalist class is occasionally prosecuted. The publicity given to the case helps to stabilize the social system by providing visible evidence of the "fairness" of the criminal justice system.

Usually, however, the powerful bypass the courts altogether, appearing instead before some agency with no power to imprison (such as the Federal Trade Commission). Most cases of illegal sales of stocks and bonds, price fixing, restraint of trade, collusion, and so on are handled by "gentlemen overseeing gentlemen," for such agencies are directed by people from wealthy backgrounds who sympathize with the intricacies of the corporate world. It is not surprising, then, that the typical sanction is a token fine. In contrast, the property crimes of the masses are handled by courts that do have the power to imprison. The burglary, armed robbery, and theft by the poor not only threaten the sanctity of private property but, ultimately, the positions of the powerful.

From the perspective of conflict theory, then, the small penalties imposed for crimes committed by the powerful are typical of a legal system designed to mask injustice, to control workers, and, ultimately, to stabilize the social order. From this perspective, law enforcement is simply a cultural device through which the capitalist class carries out self-protective and repressive policies (Silver 1977).

Reactions to Deviants

Whether it be cheating on a sociology quiz or holding up a liquor store, any violation of norms invites reaction. Let's look first at reactions by others, and then at how people react to their own deviance.

Sanctions

As discussed in Chapter 2, people do not strictly enforce folkways, but they become very upset when mores are broken. Disapproval of deviance, called **negative sanctions,** ranges from frowns and gossip to imprisonment and capital punishment. **Positive sanctions,** in contrast—from smiles to formal awards—are used to reward people for conforming to norms. Getting a raise is a positive sanction, being fired a negative sanction. Getting an A in basic sociology is a positive sanction, getting an F a negative one.

capitalist class: the wealthy who own the means of production and buy the labor of the working class

working class: those who sell their labor to the capitalist class

marginal working class: the most desperate members of the working class, who have few skills, little job security, and are often unemployed

negative sanction: a punishment or negative reaction for disapproved behavior, for deviance

positive sanction: a reward or positive reaction for approved behavior, for conformity

As symbolic interactionists stress, humans categorize their experiences and then act on the basis of their classifications. The classifications, or stereotypes, developed by teachers, police, and others in authority can have far-reaching effects on people's lives, as illustrated by the Saints and the Roughnecks described in the text. How do you think high school teachers classify these students?

Most negative sanctions are informal. You will probably merely stare when someone dresses in what you consider inappropriate clothing, or just gossip if a married person you know spends the night with someone other than his or her spouse. Whether you consider the breaking of a norm simply an amusing matter that warrants no severe sanctions or a serious infraction that does, however, depends on your perspective. If a woman appears at your college graduation ceremonies in a swimsuit, you may stare and laugh, but if it is *your* mother you are likely to feel that different sanctions are appropriate. Similarly, if it is *your* father who spends the night with an 18-year-old college freshman, you are likely to do more than gossip.

Reacting to deviance is vital to the welfare of groups, for groups must maintain their boundaries if they are to continue to claim a unique identity. As we shall see in the next section, reactions to deviance can have far-reaching consequences for people's lives.

Labeling: The Saints and the Roughnecks

For two years, sociologist William Chambliss (1973) observed two groups of adolescent lawbreakers in Hanibal High School. He called one group the "Saints," the other the "Roughnecks." Both groups were "constantly occupied with truancy, drinking, wild parties, petty theft, and vandalism." As Chambliss catalogued their offenses, however, he noted that the Saints committed more criminal acts than the Roughnecks. Yet their teachers looked on the Saints as "headed for success" and the Roughnecks as "headed for serious trouble." Moreover, by the time they finished high school, not one Saint had been arrested, while the Roughnecks were in constant trouble with the police.

Why did the community see these boys so differently? Chambliss concluded that this double vision was due to their family background, especially to social class. As symbolic interactionists emphasize, social class is a powerful symbol that vitally affects people's perceptions and behavior. The Saints came from respectable, middle-class families, while the Roughnecks came from less respectable, working-class families. Because of their respective backgrounds, teachers and other authorities expected good, law-abiding behavior from the Saints but trouble from the Roughnecks. And like the rest of us, both teachers and police see what they expect to see.

Social class also had a practical effect in making one group more *visible* than the other. Because the Saints had automobiles, they were able to make their drinking and vandalism inconspicuous by spreading it around neighboring towns. Without cars, the Roughnecks could not even make it to the edge of town. Day after day, the Roughnecks hung around the same street corners, where their boisterous behavior made them conspicuous and confirmed the ideas that the community had of them.

Another significant factor was also at work. The boys' different social backgrounds had equipped them with distinct *styles of interaction*. When questioned by police or teachers, the Saints put on apologetic and penitent faces. Their deferential behavior elicited such positive reactions that they escaped serious legal problems. In contrast, the Roughnecks' attitude was "almost the polar opposite." They expressed open hostility to the authorities, and even when they pretended to show respect, the veneer was so thin that it fooled no one. Consequently, while the police simply let the Saints off with warnings, they came down hard on the Roughnecks, interrogating and arresting them when they had the chance.

This study provides an excellent illustration of the labeling theory described earlier in this chapter. As noted, the labels given to people affect how others perceive them and how they perceive themselves, thus helping to channel their behavior either into deviance or into conformity. In this case, all but one of the Saints went on to college, after which one earned a doctorate and one became a doctor, one a lawyer, and the others business managers. In contrast, only two of the Roughnecks went to college, both on athletic scholarships, after which they became coaches. The other Roughnecks did not fare so well. Two of them dropped out of high school, later became involved in separate killings, and received long prison sentences. One became a local bookie, and no one knows the whereabouts of the other.

While a lifetime career is not determined by a label alone, the Saints and the Roughnecks nevertheless did live up to the labels that the community gave them. You can easily see in this case how labels opened and closed the doors of opportunity. Being labeled a "deviant" (certainly far from a nonjudgmental term in everyday life!) can lock people out of conforming groups and force them into almost exclusive contact with people who have similar labels.

The Trouble with Official Statistics

Both the findings of symbolic interactionists concerning the authorities' reactions to such groups as the Saints and the Roughnecks and the conclusions of conflict theorists that the criminal justice system exists to serve the ruling elite demonstrate the need for caution in interpreting official crime statistics. Statistics are not tangible objects, like produce in a supermarket, waiting to be picked up. They are a human creation, produced within a specific social and intellectual context for some particular purpose.

According to official statistics, working-class boys clearly emerge as much more delinquent than middle-class boys. Yet, as we have just seen, *who actually gets arrested for what* is directly affected by social class, a point that has far-reaching implications. As symbolic interactionists point out, the police use a symbolic system as they enforce the law. Their ideas of "typical criminals" and "typical good citizens," for example, permeate their work. The more a suspect matches their ideas of the "criminal profile," the more likely that person is to be arrested. *Police discretion*, the decision whether or not to arrest someone or even to ignore a matter, is a routine part of police work. Consequently, official crime statistics always reflect these and many other biases.

Degradation Ceremonies

When someone wanders far from a group's standards, the reaction to the deviant is likely to be harsh. In some instances, groups attempt to mark an individual indelibly as a DE-VIANT for all the world to see. In Nathaniel Hawthorne's *The Scarlet Letter*, for example, Hester Prynne was forced to stand on a platform in public wearing a scarlet A sewn on her dress to mark her as an adulteress. Furthermore, she was expected by the community to wear this badge of shame every day for the rest of her life.

Sociologist Harold Garfinkel (1956) called such formal attempts to mark an individual with the status of an outsider **degradation ceremonies.** The individual is called to account before the group, witnesses denounce him or her, the offender is pronounced guilty, and, most important in sociological terms, steps are taken to *strip the individual of his or her identity as a group member.* Following a court martial, for example, officers found guilty stand at attention before their peers while the insignia of rank are ripped from their uniforms. A priest may be defrocked before a congregation, a citizen forced to wear a prison uniform. These procedures indicate that the individual is no longer a member of the group—no longer able to command soldiers, to preach or offer sacraments, to vote or to move about freely. Although Hester Prynne was not banished from the group physically, her degradation ceremony proclaimed her a *moral* outcast from the community, the scarlet A marking her as "not one" of them.

Imprisonment

Today, we don't make people wear scarlet letters, but we do remove them from society and make them wear prison uniforms. The prison experience follows a degradation ceremony involving a public trial and the public pronouncement that the person is "unfit to live among regular, law-abiding people" for some specified period of time.

Imprisonment is an increasingly popular reaction to crime. As Figure 8.1 shows, between 1970 and 1990 the number of Americans in prison more than tripled. About half of prison inmates are African Americans; about 95 percent are males (see Table 8.2).

——— **Figure 8.1** ———

Growth in the U.S. Prison Population

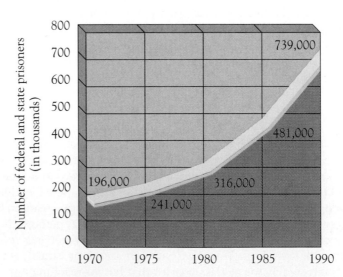

Note: To better understand the significance of this phenomenal growth, it is useful to compare it with the change in the general population during this same period. Between 1970 and 1990, the population of the United States grew 22 percent, while the prison population grew *seventeen* times as fast, increasing by 377 percent. If the number of prisoners had increased at the same rate as the general population, there would be 240,000 people in prison, only one-third of the actual number.

degradation ceremonies: rituals designed to strip an individual of his or her identity as a group member; for example, a court martial or the defrocking of a priest

As noted earlier in this chapter, because social class funnels some people into the criminal justice system and others away from it, official statistics on social class and crime are inherently biased.

Among the many problems with imprisonment is that prisons fail to teach their clients to stay away from crime. The **recidivism rate** (the proportion of people who are rearrested) runs as high as 85 to 90 percent (Blumstein and Cohen 1987). Within just six years of their release from prison 69 percent are re-arrested, most within just three years (Zawitz 1988). Those given probation—released into the community under the court's supervision—do no better, for within three years 62 percent are arrested for a felony or have a disciplinary hearing for violating their parole (Langan and Cunniff 1992).

Perhaps an underlying reason for this high recidivism rate is that Americans do not agree on *why* people should be put in prison. There appears to be widespread agreement that offenders should be imprisoned, but not on the reasons for doing so. Let's examine the four primary reasons for imprisoning people.

Retribution The purpose of **retribution** is to right a wrong by making offenders suffer, or to pay back what they have stolen. The offense is thought to have upset a moral balance; the punishment is an attempt to restore that balance (Cohen 1940). Attempts to make the punishment "fit the crime," such as sentencing someone who has stolen from a widow to work a dozen weekends in a geriatric center for the poor, are rooted in the idea of retribution.

Deterrence The purpose of **deterrence** is to create fear so that others won't break the law. The belief underlying deterrence is that if people know that they will be punished, they will refrain from committing the crime. Sociologist Ernest van den Haag (1975), a chief proponent of deterrence, believes, like many Americans, that the criminal justice system is too soft. He advocates that juveniles who commit adult crimes be tried as adults, that parole boards be abolished, and that prisoners be forced to work.

Does deterrence work? Evidence is mixed, but those who claim that it does not like to recall an example from the nineteenth century. When English law meted out the death penalty for pickpockets, other pickpockets looked forward to the hangings—for people whose attention was riveted on the gallows made easy victims (Hibbert 1963). At this point, no firm evidence resolves the issue.

Rehabilitation **Rehabilitation** switches the focus from punishing offenders to resocializing them so that they can become conforming citizens. One example of rehabilitation is teaching prisoners skills so they can support themselves after their release. Other examples include providing college courses in prison, encounter groups for prisoners, and **halfway houses**—community support facilities where ex-prisoners supervise many aspects of their own lives, such as household tasks, and still report to authorities.

Incapacitation **Incapacitation** means removing offenders from circulation. "Nothing works," some say, "but we can at least keep them off the streets." Criminologist James Wilson (1975, 1992) supports incapacitation, calling it the only policy that works. He

Table 8.2

Inmates in U.S. State Prisons

Characteristics of Prisoners	Percentage in Prison	Percentage in the U.S. Population
Age		
Under 18	0.5	25.9
18–24	26.7	10.2
25–34	45.7	16.6
35–44	19.4	15.7
45–54	5.2	10.8
55–64	1.6	8.2
65 and over	0.6	12.6
Race		
White	49.7	80.3
African American	46.9	12.1
Other races	3.4	7.6
Sex		
Male	95.6	48.8
Female	4.4	51.2

Note: The category "white" includes people of Latin descent.
Source: Statistical Abstract 1992: Table 330; 1993: Tables 14, 17, 18.

recidivism rate: the proportion of people who are rearrested

retribution: the punishment of offenders in order to restore the moral balance upset by the offense

deterrence: creating fear so people will refrain from breaking the law

rehabilitation: the resocialization of offenders so that they can become conforming citizens

halfway house: community support facilities where ex-prisoners supervise many aspects of their own lives, such as household tasks, but continue to report to authorities

incapacitation: to take away someone's capacity to commit crimes, in this instance, by putting the offender in prison

Overcrowding and the possibility of violence among inmates are just two of the problems created by the rising number of people imprisoned each year.

proposes what he calls "added incapacitation," increasing an offender's sentence each time he or she is convicted of a crime.

In the United States, the public is fearful of crime and despairing of solutions. Increasing dependence on prisons (see Table 8.2) may indicate that Americans are throwing up their hands as far as criminals are concerned and just trying to "keep them off the streets." It may also indicate attempts at retribution and deterrence. It certainly does not indicate efforts toward rehabilitation, for U.S. prisons are basically simply holding tanks, offering few, if any, programs of rehabilitation.

Reactions by Deviants

People not only react to the deviant behaviors of others; they also react to their own violations of norms. These self-reactions can set them on paths that help propel them into or divert them from deviance.

Primary, Secondary, and Tertiary Deviance

Sociologist Nanette Davis (1978), who interviewed young women to find out how they had become prostitutes, noted that they had experienced a gradual slide from sexual promiscuity to prostitution. Their first acts of selling sex were casual. A girl might have run away from home and "turned a few tricks" to survive—or she might have done so to purchase a prom dress. At this point, the girls were in a stage of deviance that sociologist Edwin Lemert (1972) calls **primary deviance**—fleeting acts that do not become part of the self-concept. The young women did not think of themselves as prostitutes. As one girl said, "I never thought about it one way or another."

Girls who prostitute themselves for a longer time, however, have to come to terms with their activities. They incorporate a deviant identity into their self-concept and come to think of themselves as prostitutes. When this occurs, they have entered **secondary deviance.**

primary deviance: Edwin Lemert's term for acts of deviance that have little effect on the self-concept

secondary deviance: Edwin Lemert's term for acts of deviance incorporated into the self-concept, around which an individual orients his or her behavior

The movement from primary to secondary deviance may be gradual. Through *self-labeling*, bit by bit the deviance becomes part of the self-concept. Often, however, the reactions of others facilitate this transition. For example, if a young woman is arrested for prostitution, it is difficult for her to define her activities as "normal," as she might in primary deviance. A face-to-face confrontation with a formal system that publicly labels her a sexual deviant challenges self-definitions. (Self-jarring labels can also be informal, as indicated by such terms as "nut," "queer," "pervert," and "whore.") Such powerful labels tend to lock people out of conforming groups and push them into contact with other deviants.

There is yet another stage, one that few deviants reach. In **tertiary deviance,** deviant behavior is normalized by *relabeling* it nondeviant (Kitsuse 1980; de Young 1989). Most people in this stage simply reject the judgment that the behavior is wrong, but some even turn matters on their head by relabeling it a virtue. Although none of the women in Davis's sample had reached this stage, other prostitutes have. They have formed an organization called COYOTE (Call Off Your Old Tired Ethics), which has chapters in several states (Weitzer 1991). This group takes the position that prostitution is a useful activity, a reasonable occupational choice, and that legislation should allow prostitutes to operate without interference from the government (Jenness 1990).

Neutralizing Deviance

Most people resist deviant labels and prefer to be known as conforming members of society, not outsiders. By neutralizing society's norms, some people involved in activities condemned by society still manage to consider themselves conformists (Jankowski 1991). When sociologists Gresham Sykes and David Matza (1988) studied a group of delinquents, they found that in spite of their vandalism, fighting, drinking, and attacks on people these boys successfully resisted the labels that others tried to pin on them. As Sykes and Matza probed further, they found that the boys used five **techniques of neutralization,** or rationalizations, in an attempt to deflect society's norms.

Denial of Responsibility   The youths frequently said, "I'm not responsible for what happened because . . ." and then were quite creative about the "becauses." The act may have been an "accident," or they may see themselves as "victims" of society, with no control over what happened—like billiard balls shot around the pool table of life.

Denial of Injury   Another favorite explanation of the boys was, "What I did wasn't wrong because no one got hurt." They would define vandalism as "mischief," gang fighting as a "private quarrel," and stealing cars as "borrowing." They might acknowledge the illegality of something they did but claim that it was "just having a little fun."

tertiary deviance: "normalizing" behavior considered deviant by mainstream society; relabeling behavior as nondeviant

techniques of neutralization: ways of thinking or rationalizing that help people deflect society's norms

All of us do deviant acts from time to time. To help us adjust to our own violations of rules, we use various techniques of neutralization. Few people, however, kill their own parents, as did the Menendez brothers of Beverly Hills. Their most visible neutralization device has been the denial of responsibility.

Denial of a Victim   Sometimes the boys thought of themselves as avengers. To vandalize a teacher's car is only to get revenge for an unfair grade; to steal is to even the score with "crooked" store owners; to attack someone is justified retaliation against someone who threatened them. In short, if the boys did accept responsibility and even admit that someone did get hurt, they rationalize this away by claiming that the people "deserved what they got."

Condemnation of the Condemners   Another technique the boys used was to deny the right of others to pass judgment on them. They might accuse people who pointed their fingers at them of being "a bunch of hypocrites": the police are "on the take," teachers have "pets," and parents cheat on their taxes. In short, they say, "Who are *they* to accuse *me* of something?"

Appeal to Higher Loyalties   A final technique the boys used to justify antisocial activities was to consider loyalty to the gang more important than following the norms of society. They might say, "I had to help my friends. That's why I got in the fight." Not incidentally, the boy may also have shot two members of the rival group as well as a bystander!

▼   **In Sum**   The identification of these five techniques of neutralization has implications far beyond the case of these boys, for it is not only delinquents who try to neutralize the views of the broader society. Look again at these five techniques: (1) "I couldn't help myself"; (2) "Who really got hurt?"; (3) "Don't you think she deserved that, after what *she* did?"; (4) "Who are *you* to talk?"; and (5) "I had to help my friends—wouldn't you have done the same thing under those circumstances?" Don't such statements have a familiar ring? All of us attempt to neutralize the moral demands of society, for such rationalizations help us sleep at night.

Embracing Deviance

Although most people resist being labeled deviant, there are those who revel in a deviant identity. Some teenagers, for example, make certain by their clothing, choice of music, and hairstyle that no one misses their purposeful status as outside adult norms. Their status among fellow members of a subculture, within which they are inveterate conformists, is vastly more important than any status outside it.

One of the best examples of a group that embraces deviance is motorcycle gangs. Sociologist Mark Watson (1988) did participant observation with outlaw bikers. He rebuilt Harleys with them, hung around their bars and homes, and went on "runs" (trips) with

Although most people don't want to be labeled deviant, members of some groups actively embrace deviance.

them. He concluded that outlaw bikers see the world as "hostile, weak, and effeminate," while they pride themselves on looking "dirty, mean, and generally undesirable," and take great pleasure in provoking shocked reactions to their appearance. Holding the conventional world in contempt, they also pride themselves on getting into trouble, laughing at death, and treating women as lesser people whose primary value is to provide them with services—especially sexual ones. Outlaw bikers also look at themselves as losers, a factor that becomes interwoven in their unusual embrace of deviance.

In Sum Reactions to deviants vary from such mild sanctions as frowns and stares to such severe responses as imprisonment and death. Some sanctions are formal—court hearings, for example—although most are informal, as when friends refuse to talk to each other. One sanction is to label someone a deviant, which can have powerful consequences for the person's life, especially if the label closes off conforming activities and opens deviant ones. The degradation ceremony, in which someone is publicly labeled "not one of us," is a powerful sanction.

People also react to their own deviant behaviors. As long as they commit deviant acts but still think of themselves as conformists, they are in primary deviance. When they incorporate deviance into the self-concept, they are in secondary deviance. And when they "normalize" acts considered deviant by their society, relabeling them nondeviant, they are in tertiary deviance. To try to neutralize negative reactions to their deviant behaviors, people use a variety of techniques, ranging from condemning the condemner to claiming that no one was hurt. Although most people resist the labels that others try to place on them, some people, like outlaw bikers, embrace deviance.

The Medicalization of Deviance: Mental Illness

Another way in which society deals with deviance is to "medicalize" it. Let us look at what this entails.

Neither Mental nor Illness?

To *medicalize* something is to make it a medical matter, to classify it as a form of illness that properly belongs in the care of physicians. For the past hundred years or so, especially since the time of Sigmund Freud (1856–1939), the Viennese physician who founded psychoanalysis, there has been a growing tendency toward the **medicalization of deviance.** In this view, deviance, including crime, is a sign of mental sickness. Rape, murder, stealing, cheating, and so on are external symptoms of internal disorders, consequences of a confused or tortured mind.

Thomas Szasz (1970, 1986, 1989, 1990), a renegade in his profession of psychiatry, argues that *mental illnesses are neither mental nor illnesses. They are simply problem behaviors.* Some forms of so-called mental illnesses have organic causes; that is, they are *physical* illnesses that result in unusual perceptions and behavior. Some depression, for example, is caused by a chemical imbalance in the brain, which can be treated by drugs. The depression, however, may show itself as crying, long-term sadness, and the inability to become interested in anything. When a person becomes deviant in ways that disturb others, and these others cannot find a satisfying explanation for why the person is "like that," they conclude that a "sickness in the head" causes the inappropriate, unacceptable behavior.

All of us have troubles. Some of us face a constant barrage of problems as we go through life. Most of us continue the struggle, encouraged by relatives and friends, motivated by job, family responsibilities, and life goals. Even when the odds seem hopeless, we carry on, not perfectly, but as best we can.

medicalization of deviance: to make deviance a medical matter, a symptom of some underlying illness that needs to be treated by physicians

Some people, however, fail to cope well with the challenges of daily life. Overwhelmed, they become depressed, uncooperative, or hostile. Some strike out at others, while some, in Merton's terms, become retreatists and withdraw into their apartments or homes and won't come out. These are *behaviors, not mental illnesses,* stresses Szasz. They may be inappropriate coping devices, but they are coping devices, nevertheless, not mental illnesses. Thus, Szasz concludes that "mental illness" is a myth foisted on a naive public by a medical profession that uses pseudoscientific jargon to expand its area of control and force nonconforming people to accept society's definitions of "normal."

Szasz's extreme claim forces us to look anew at the forms of deviance called mental illness. He points the analysis of behavior that people find bizarre away from causes hidden deep within the unconscious, placing the focus instead on how people learn behaviors that others find inappropriate. To ask, "What is the origin of inappropriate or bizarre behavior?" then becomes similar to asking, "Why do some women steal?" "Why do some men rape?" "Why do some teenagers cuss their parents and stalk out of the room slamming doors?" The answers depend on people's particular experiences in life, not an illness in their mind. In short, some sociologists find Szasz's renegade analysis refreshing because it indicates that social experiences, not some illness of the mind, underlies bizarre behaviors—as well as deviance in general.

The Homeless Mentally Ill

Regardless of whether or not Szasz is right, we do incarcerate people whose behaviors we deem bizarre in mental hospitals. Psychiatrists working in mental hospitals have noticed that most patients adjust fairly well to hospital routines, and that the longer patients are cut off from the outside community, the more difficult it is for them to readjust to it later. During the 1960s, the psychiatric profession, working with state budget planners who wanted to save money, came up with the idea of **deinstitutionalization.** Mental patients would be released into the community, where their needs would be met by a network of outpatient services. Ongoing counseling and medicine would then enable these former patients to make the adjustment to living in the community again.

With the approval of politicians who saw dollar signs flashing before their eyes, the doctors began to open the doors of the nation's mental hospitals (Warner 1989). There was just one problem—they did not set up the network of outpatient services. They simply released patients into the streets. In perhaps the most notorious case, patients from mental hospitals in Austin were placed in a van, driven to Houston, and dumped in front of the Greyhound bus station—located on Skid Row. In contrast, a paroled rapist or killer was given $200 and new clothing (Karlen and Burgower 1985).

Consider how you would survive if you were abruptly dumped onto Skid Row without warning and without money. You and I would have a hard time making it, but not nearly as hard a time as those whose coping skills are already extremely fragile.

The bizarre thinking of many of the homeless is often attributed to their being former mental patients. Consider Jamie, who sits on the low wall surrounding the landscaped open-air eating area of an exclusive restaurant.

> Jamie appeared unaware of the stares elicited by her many layers of mismatched clothing, her dirty face, and the ever-present shopping cart overflowing with her meager possessions.
>
> Every once in a while Jamie would pause, concentrate, and point to the street, slowly moving her finger horizontally. I asked her what she was doing.
>
> "I'm directing traffic," she replied. "I control where the cars go. Look, that one turned right there," she said, now withdrawing her finger.
>
> "Really?" I said.
>
> After a while she confided that her cart talked to her.
>
> "Really?" I said again.

deinstitutionalization: the release of mental patients from institutions into the community pending treatment by a network of outpatient services

"Yes," she replied. "You can hear it, too." At that, she pushed the shopping cart a bit.

"Did you hear that?" she asked.

When I shook my head, she demonstrated again. Then it hit me. She was referring to the squeaking wheels!

I nodded.

When I left Jamie, she was pointing to the sky, for, as she told me, she also controlled the flight of airplanes. To most of us, Jamie's behavior and thinking are bizarre. They simply do not match any reality we know.

In Jamie's case, there may be an underlying organic cause to her behavior, such as a chemical imbalance. Other homeless people, however, may have no psychiatric history, yet exhibit strange behaviors, for *just being on the streets can cause mental illness*—or whatever we want to label socially inappropriate behaviors that we find difficult to classify (McCarthy 1983; Belcher 1988; Nelson 1989).

Place yourself in the situation of the homeless. Suppose that you have no money, no place to sleep, no bathroom, do not know *if* you are going to eat, much less where, have no friends or anyone you can trust, and live in constant fear of rape and violence. Wouldn't that be enough to drive you "over the edge"? Maybe, maybe not. But it is certainly enough for some people.

All these conditions bring severe consequences, but consider just the problems involved in not having a place to bathe. (Shelters are often so dangerous that the homeless prefer to take their chances sleeping in public settings.) You will try at first to wash in the toilets of gas stations, bars, the bus station, or a shopping center. But you are dirty, and people stare when you enter, and they call the management when they see you wash your feet in the sink. You are thrown out, and told in no uncertain terms to never come back. So you get dirtier and dirtier. Eventually you come to think of being dirty as a fact of life. Soon, maybe, you don't even care. No longer do the stares bother you— at least not as much.

No one will talk to you, and you withdraw more and more into yourself. You begin to build a fantasy life. You talk openly to yourself. People stare, but so what? They stare anyway. Besides, they are no longer important to you. Perhaps, like a small child, you begin to imagine that you can control vehicles by pointing at them. Eventually you become convinced of it.

The point is that *homelessness and mental illness are reciprocal:* just as "mental illness" can cause homelessness, so the trials of being homeless, of living on cold, hostile streets, can lead to unusual and unacceptable thinking and behaviors.

The Need for a More Humane Approach

As Durkheim (1893/1958:68) pointed out, deviance is inevitable—even in a group of saints.

> Imagine a society of saints, a perfect cloister of exemplary individuals. Crimes, properly so called, will there be unknown; but faults which appear [invisible] to the layman will create there the same scandal that the ordinary offense does in ordinary [society].

With deviance inevitable, one measure of a society is how it treats its deviants. Deinstitutionalization certainly says little good about U.S. society. Nor do its prisons. Filled with the poor, they are warehouses of the unwanted, reflecting patterns of broad discrimination in the larger society. White-collar criminals continue to get by with a slap on the wrist while street criminals are severely punished. Some deviants, failing to meet current standards of admission to either prison or mental hospital, take refuge in shelters and cardboard boxes in city streets. Although no one has *the* answers, it does not take much reflection to see that there are more humane approaches than these.

With deviance inevitable, the larger issues are how to protect people from deviant behaviors that are harmful to themselves or others, to tolerate those that are not, and to develop systems of fairer treatment for deviants. In the absence of the fundamental changes that would bring about a truly equitable social system, most efforts are, unfortunately, Band-Aid work. What is needed is a more humane social system, one that would prevent the social inequalities that are the focus of the next five chapters.

Summary and Review

Gaining a Sociological Perspective of Deviance

How do sociologists view deviance?

From a sociological perspective, **deviance**—defined as the violation of norms—is relative. What people consider deviant varies from one culture to another and from group to group within the same society. Consequently, as symbolic interactionists stress, it is not the act itself, but the reactions to the act, that make something deviant. All groups develop systems of **social control** to punish those who violate its norms. Pp. 194–198.

How do biological, psychological, and sociological explanations of deviance differ?

To explain why people deviate, biologists and psychologists look for reasons *within* the individual, such as **genetic predispositions** or **personality disorders.** Sociologists, in contrast, look for explanations *outside* the individual, in social relations. Pp. 198–199.

The Symbolic Interactionist Perspective

How do symbolic interactionists explain deviance?

Symbolic interactionists have developed several theories to explain deviance such as **crime** (the violation of norms written into law). According to **differential association theory,** people learn to deviate from associating with others. According to **control theory,** each of us is propelled toward deviance, but most of us conform because of an effective system of inner and outer controls. People who have less effective controls deviate. From the perspective of **labeling theory,** acts are deviant only because people label them as such. Some labeling has a countereffect and increases deviance. Pp. 200–203.

The Functionalist Perspective

How do functionalists explain deviance?

Functionalists point out that deviance, including criminal acts, is functional for society. Functions include affirming norms and

promoting social unity and social change. According to **strain theory,** societies socialize their members into desiring **cultural goals,** but many people are unable to achieve these goals in a socially acceptable way—**by institutionalized means.** Deviants, then, are people who either give up on the goals or who use deviant means to attain them. Merton identified five types of responses to cultural goals and institutionalized means: conformity, innovation, ritualism, retreatism, and rebellion. **Illegitimate opportunity theory** stresses that some people have easier access to illegal means of achieving goals. Pp. 203–208.

The Conflict Perspective

How do conflict theorists explain deviance?

Conflict theorists take the position that the group in power (the **capitalist class**) imposes its definitions of deviance on other groups (the **working class** and the **marginal working class**). From the conflict perspective, the law is an instrument of oppression used to maintain the privilege of the few over the many. The marginal working class has little income, is desperate, and commits highly visible property crimes. The ruling class directs the criminal justice system, using it to punish the crimes of the poor while it diverts its own criminal activities away from this punitive system. Pp. 208–209.

Reactions to Deviants

How do societies react to deviance?

Deviance results in **negative sanctions,** acts of disapproval ranging from frowns to capital punishment. Labeling, as in the case of the Saints and the Roughnecks, is a common sanction. Some groups use **degradation ceremonies** to impress on their members that certain violations will not be tolerated. Imprisonment is motivated by the goals of **retribution, deterrence, rehabilitation,** and **incapacitation.** Pp. 209–214.

Are official statistics on crime reliable?

The conclusions of both symbolic interactionists (that the police operate with a large measure of discretion) and conflict theorists (that the legal system is controlled by the capitalist class) cast doubt on the accuracy of official crime statistics. P. 211.

Reactions by Deviants

How do people react to their own acts of deviance?

Reactions to one's own deviance depend on how extensively the self-concept is involved. In **primary deviance,** the acts are fleeting and have little effect on the self-concept. In **secondary deviance,** people incorporate their deviant acts into their self-concept. In **tertiary deviance,** acts commonly considered deviant are relabeled as normal. Pp. 214–215.

How do people neutralize the norms of society?

Many people commit deviant acts and still think of themselves as conformists. They apparently use five techniques of neutralization. Although most people resist being labeled deviants, some embrace deviance itself. Pp. 215–217.

The Medicalization of Deviance: Mental Illness

How does society medicalize deviance?

The medical profession has attempted to medicalize many forms of deviance, claiming that they represent mental illnesses. Thomas Szasz disagrees, claiming that they are just problem behaviors, not mental illnesses. Research on homeless people illustrates how problems in living can lead to bizarre behavior and thinking. Pp. 217–219.

The Need for a More Humane Approach

Deviance is inevitable, so the larger issues are how to protect people from deviance that harms themselves and others, to tolerate deviance that is not harmful, and to develop systems of fairer treatment for deviants. Pp. 219–220.

Where can I read more on this topic?

Suggested readings for this chapter are listed on page 640.

Pacita Abad, Haitians Waiting at Guantanamo Bay, 1994

Social Stratification in Global Perspective

JOHN F. KENNEDY WAS BORN in Brookline, Massachusetts, on May 29, 1917. The son of Joseph Patrick Kennedy and Rose Fitzgerald Kennedy, he was one of ten children. His paternal grandfather, Patrick J. Kennedy, who had immigrated from Ireland in 1847, had made a fortune in running saloons and had served in both houses of the Massachusetts State Legislature. His maternal grandfather, John F. ("Honey Fitz") Fitzgerald, had been mayor of Boston. Neither John (known as Jack) nor his three brothers and six sisters ever attended public schools. Jack went to Riverside Country Day School, an exclusive school for children of the wealthy in Brookline, Massachusetts. His high school years were spent at Choate School in Wallingford, Connecticut. He began college at Princeton University and graduated from Harvard University in 1940.

Joseph Patrick Kennedy, who contributed substantially to the presidential campaign of Franklin Delano Roosevelt, was appointed chairman of the Securities and Exchange Commission in 1933 and U.S. ambassador to Great Britain in 1937. He set up a trust fund so that at the age of 21 each of his children would receive $100,000 (about $1 million in today's money). He made plans for his eldest son, Joseph Patrick Kennedy, Jr., to become president of the United States. After Joe, Jr., was killed in World War II, his father decided to groom his next eldest son, Jack, for the presidency instead. Joseph Kennedy first had him run for the Senate. After winning the presidential election in 1960, Jack appointed his younger brother Bobby attorney general of the United States. Jack's youngest brother, Edward (Teddy), then took Jack's Senate seat.

When Mary Petrovitch signed into the hospital, she paid with a "green card," a state voucher given to welfare recipients that guarantees payment for each approved medical procedure. Her delivery was normal, and in three days she went home with her new daughter, Kim.

Kim attended Thomas Mann Elementary and Thomas Jefferson High. During her early years, Kim didn't even realize that she was poor, for everyone in the projects had about the same income, and all her neighbors bought groceries with food stamps. As time went on, however, Kim became more and more aware of differences between herself and others. During high school, where she attended classes with students from more privileged backgrounds, this distinction was always in her mind. She became determined to make her life different: She would go to college and make something of herself.

During the end of her junior year, Kim fell in love. She never made it back to high school. Instead, the earnings from her two part-time jobs went to rent and payments for their "almost new" car. On the day that she would have graduated, Kim checked into the hospital to have her first baby. She paid with a green card.

What Is Social Stratification?

The distance between Jack Kennedy and Kim Petrovitch illustrates the heart of social stratification, for to talk about social stratification is to refer to inequalities between people. Their inequalities are obvious: wealth versus poverty, private versus public schools, and power versus powerlessness. One was born to a life of privilege, the other to deprivation. In short, the son of a Kennedy and the daughter of a Petrovitch have far from equal chances in life—and that is what social stratification is all about.

It is important to emphasize at the outset that social stratification does not simply refer to individuals. It is a *way of ranking large groups of people into a hierarchy that shows their relative privileges*. **Social stratification** is a system in which people are divided into layers according to their relative power, property, and prestige.

social stratification: the division of people into layers according to their relative power, property, and prestige; applies to both a society and to nations

Social stratification exists in all societies. While some people live in poverty, others try to figure out what to do with their wealth. Deciding that her dog deserves the very best, the woman on the right has taken it to a specialist in gold pet jewelry. On the left are people "down the street."

Jack Kennedy, for example, was not only part of his family, but also part of a larger group of people who come from similarly privileged backgrounds. Their backgrounds are so similar, in fact, that members of this group share values, attitudes, and lifestyles. They even tend to think alike and to vote for the same candidates for political office. It is the same with Kim and her mother—and the millions of people who come from backgrounds like hers. Sharing similar life chances, they, too, tend to think alike. Finding life a struggle to survive, most of their attitudes contrast sharply with those of the Kennedys. And when it comes to politics, they aren't likely to run for office, or even to show up at the polls (Gilbert and Kahl 1982, 1993). In short, society is stratified into layers, and each layer has its own characteristics.

Just as it did for Kim Petrovitch and Jack Kennedy, the layer of society into which you were born has vitally affected your life. Membership in your layer, which sociologists call *social class,* even helps explain why you are in college and how many children you plan to have. Social class will continue to exert its powerful hold on you throughout your life, as you will see from this and the following chapter.

Let's look at how the various layers that make up society develop.

Systems of Social Stratification

Every society stratifies its members in some form. Some, like the agricultural societies studied in Chapter 6, draw firm lines that separate group from group, while others, like hunting and gathering societies, show much greater equality. Regardless of its forms, however, the existence of social stratification is universal. There are four major systems of social stratification: slavery, caste, clan, and class.

Slavery

Let's first look at the broad aspects of slavery—its major causes and conditions—and then at slavery in the New World. As we examine the characteristics of slavery, you will see how remarkably it has varied around the world.

Causes of Slavery **Slavery,** whose essential characteristic is *ownership of some people by others,* has been common in world history. The Romans had slaves, as did the ancient

slavery: a form of social stratification in which some people own other people

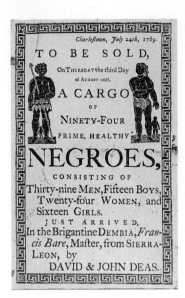

Slavery is an age-old system of social stratification. This 1769 broadside from Charleston, South Carolina, reminds us that this form of stratification was once the custom in the United States.

indentured service: a contractual system in which someone sells his or her body (services) for a specified period of time in an arrangement very close to slavery, except that it is voluntarily entered into

Africans. In classical Greece, slaves did the work while free citizens engaged in politics and the arts (Beck 1992). Slavery was least common among nomads, especially hunters and gatherers, and most common in agricultural societies (Landtman 1968).

Contrary to popular assumption, slavery was not usually based on racism, but on one of three other factors. The first was debt. In some cultures, an individual who could not pay a debt could be enslaved by the creditor. The second was a violation of the law. Instead of being killed, a murderer or thief might be enslaved by the family of the victim as compensation for the loss he or she had caused. The third was war and conquest. When one group of people conquered another, it was often convenient to enslave at least some of the vanquished (Starna and Watkins 1991). Historian Gerda Lerner (1986) notes that through this practice the first slaves were women. When premodern men raided a village or camp, they killed the men, raped the women, and then brought the women back as slaves. The women were valued for sexual purposes, for reproduction, and for extra labor.

Roughly twenty-five hundred years ago when Greece was but a collection of city-states, slavery was common. A city that became powerful and conquered another city would enslave some of the vanquished. Both slaves and slaveholders were Greek. Similarly, when Rome became the supreme power of the Mediterranean area about two thousand years ago, following the custom of the time the Romans enslaved some of the Greeks they had conquered. Some of these slaves, more educated than their conquerors, served as tutors in Roman homes. Slavery, then, was a sign of defeat in battle, of a criminal act, or of debt, not the sign of some supposedly inherently inferior status.

Conditions of Slavery   The conditions of slavery have varied widely around the world. *In some cases, slavery was temporary.* After serving a set number of years, a slave might be free to return to his or her home country. Slaves of the Israelites were set free in the year of jubilee, which occurred every fifty years. Roman slaves ordinarily had the right to buy themselves out of slavery. They knew what their purchase price was, and some were able to meet this price by striking a bargain with their owner and selling their services to others. Such was the case with some of the educated Greek slaves. In most instances, however, slavery was lifelong. Some criminals, for example, became slaves when they were given life sentences as oarsmen on Roman war ships. There they served until death, which under this exhausting service often did not take long.

Slavery was not necessarily inheritable. In most places, the children of slaves were automatically slaves themselves. But in some instances, the child of a slave who served a rich family might even be adopted by that family, becoming an heir who bore the family name along with the other sons or daughters of the household. In ancient Mexico, the children of slaves were always free (Landtman 1968:271).

Slaves were not necessarily powerless and poor. In almost all instances, slaves owned no property and had no power. Among some slaveholding groups, however, slaves could accumulate property and even rise to high positions in the community. Occasionally, a slave might even become wealthy, loan money to the master, and end up owning slaves himself or herself (Landtman 1968). Such instances, however, were not typical.

Slavery in the New World   **Indentured service** represents a fuzzy line between a contract and slavery (Main 1965; Elkins 1968). Many persons who desired to start a new life in the American colonies were unable to pay their passage. Ship captains would carry them on credit, depending on someone to "buy their paper" when they arrived. This arrangement provided passage for the penniless, payment for the ship's captain, and servants for wealthier colonists for a set number of years. During that specified period, the individuals had to serve their master—and could be captured and forcibly returned if they ran away. At the end of the period of indenture, the individuals became full citizens, able to live where they chose and free to sell their labor.

When the colonists found that there were not enough indentured servants to meet their growing need for labor, they tried to enslave Indians. This attempt failed miserably.

Among other reasons, when Indians escaped they knew how to survive in the wilderness and were able to make their way back to their tribe. The colonists then turned to Africans, who were being brought to North and South America by the Dutch, English, Portuguese, and Spanish.

Given this context, some analysts conclude that racism in the United States developed out of slavery. Finding it profitable to make people slaves for life, U.S. slave owners developed an **ideology,** a system of beliefs that justifies social arrangements. Essential to an ideology that would justify lifelong slavery was the view that the slaves were inferior to humans. Some even concluded that the slaves were not fully human. Others said that they were locked into a childlike, helpless state, which meant that they needed to be taken care of by superior people—white colonists, of course. With these views, the colonists developed elaborate justifications for slavery on the presumed superiority of one race and inferiority of another.

Later on, to make slavery even more profitable, slave states passed laws that made slavery *inheritable;* that is, the babies born to slaves became the property of the slave owners (Stampp 1956). Following the "rule of blood," these included children born to slaves who had been fathered by slave owners. These children could be sold, bartered, or traded. To strengthen their control, slave states passed laws making it illegal for slaves to marry, to be away from the master's premises without carrying a pass, to hold meetings, or to learn to read (Lerner 1972).

Patterns of legal discrimination did not end after the Civil War. For example, until 1954 the states operated two separate school systems. Even until the 1950s, to keep the races from "mixing," it was illegal in Mississippi for a white and an African American to sit together on the same seat of a car! The reason there was no outright ban on both races being in the same car was to allow for African-American chauffeurs.

Common Characteristics of Slavery   The practice of slavery, then, differed markedly from one region or time to another. However, whether slavery was the outcome of debt, punishment, conquests, or racism; whether it was permanent or temporary; whether it was inheritable or not, a slave was the property of another person, and a legal system dictated by slave owners enforced the slave's status. Slavery was a major divide between people, marking those who were free (and thus entitled to certain privileges by the law) and those who were slaves (and not so entitled).

> **ideology:** beliefs about the way things ought to be that justify social arrangements
>
> **caste system:** a form of social stratification in which one's status is determined by birth and is lifelong
>
> **endogamy:** marriage within one's own group

Caste: India and South Africa

The second system of social stratification is caste. In a **caste system** of social stratification, status is determined by birth and is lifelong. In sociological terms the basis of a caste system is ascribed status (discussed on page 94). Achieved status cannot change an individual's place in this system. People born into a low-status group will always have low status, no matter how much they personally may accomplish in life.

Societies with this form of stratification try to make certain that the boundaries between castes remain firm. They practice **endogamy,** marriage within their own group, and prohibit intermarriage. To prevent contact between castes, they even develop elaborate rules about *ritual pollution,* teaching that contact with inferior castes contaminates the superior caste.

India   India provides the best example of a caste system. Based not on race but on religion, it has existed for almost three thousand years (Chandra 1993a, b). India's four main castes, or *varnas,* are depicted in Table 9.1. The four main castes are subdivided into thousands of specialized subcastes, or *jati,* with each *jati* working in a

Table 9.1	
India's Caste System	
Caste	*Occupation*
Brahman	Priests or scholars
Kshatriya	Nobles and warriors
Vaishva	Merchants and skilled artisans
Shudra	Common laborers
Harijan	The outcastes; degrading labor

specific occupation. For example, knife sharpening is done only by members of a particular subcaste.

The lowest group listed on Table 9.1, the Harijan, is actually so low that it is beneath the caste system altogether. The Harijans, along with some of the Shudras, make up India's "untouchables." If someone of a higher caste is touched by one of them, that person becomes unclean. In some cases, even the shadow of an untouchable is contaminating. Early morning and late afternoons are especially risky, for the long shadows of these periods pose a danger to everyone higher up the caste system. Consequently, Harijans are not even allowed in some villages during these times. For those contaminated, their religion specifies **ablution,** or washing rituals, to restore purity (Lannoy 1975).

Although the Indian government declared the caste system abolished in 1949, the force of centuries-old practices cannot be so easily eliminated, and the caste system remains part of everyday life in India. What ceremonies one follows at births, marriages, and deaths, for example, are dictated by caste (Chandra 1993a). Due to industrialization and urbanization, however, this system is breaking down, for it is difficult to maintain caste divisions in crowded and anonymous cities (Robertson 1976).

South Africa   Until recently, South Africa provided another example of social stratification based on caste. Europeans of Dutch descent, a numerical minority called Afrikaaners, controlled the government, the police, and the military to enforce their ideas of proper social stratification in a system they called **apartheid** (ah-PAR-tate), the separation of the races. By law there were four different racial groups: Europeans (whites), Africans (blacks), Coloureds (mixed races), and Asians. To be classified in one of these groups—and everyone was—determined where one could live, work, and go to school. It also determined where one could swim or see movies—for by law whites and Africans were not allowed to mix socially.

After decades of trade sanctions, sports boycotts, and worldwide negative publicity, however, Afrikaaners reluctantly dismantled their caste system (Ford 1993; Melloan 1993). No longer must Africans carry special passes, public facilities are integrated, and all races have the right to vote and to hold office. In 1994, in the country's first postapartheid election, Nelson Mandela, an African who had been imprisoned for nineteen years for revolutionary activities, was elected president of South Africa. As one might expect, this caste system has left a bitter heritage—prejudice, hatred, and resentment that will remain for generations.

An American Racial Caste System   Before leaving the subject of caste, we should note that when slavery ended in the United States it was replaced by a *racial caste system,* in which birth marked a person for life (Berger 1993). In this system, *all* whites, no matter if they were poor and uneducated, considered themselves higher than *all* African Americans. Even into the earlier parts of this century, long after slavery had ended, this attitude persisted. When any white met any African American on a southern sidewalk, the latter had to move aside. And as in India and South Africa, the upper caste feared pollution from the lower, insisting on separate schools, hotels, restaurants, and even toilets and drinking fountains in public facilities.

Clan

The **clan system** used to be common in agricultural societies. In this system, each individual is linked to a large network of relatives called a **clan.** A clan is like a greatly extended family. Just as in a family, if the clan has a high status, so does the individual. Similarly, the clan's resources—whether few or many—are the individual's. And like a family, allegiance to the clan is a lifelong obligation.

Clans are also like castes in that membership is determined by birth and is lifelong. Unlike castes, however, marriages can cross clan lines. In fact, marriages may be used to forge alliances between clans, for the obligations that a marriage establishes between in-laws can bind clans together.

ablution: a washing ritual designed to restore ritual purity

apartheid: the separation of races as was practiced in South Africa

clan system: a form of social stratification in which individuals receive their social standing through belonging to an extended network of relatives

clan: an extended network of relatives

Just as industrialization and urbanization are eroding the lines that separate the castes of India, so they make clans more fluid, eventually replacing them by social classes. Like other systems of social stratification, clans can make a difference between life and death, as the following example illustrates:

> The Sultan clan consists of about 150 individuals, who occupy a dozen neighboring houses in Kuwait City. To survive the Iraqi occupation of Kuwait in 1989–90, members of this clan pooled their resources for the common good. Those in the appliance business bribed Iraqi officers with food processors, microwave ovens, and televisions; while those in the hotel business secreted away huge amounts of steak and shrimp from the hotel, which they shared with fellow clan members. Together they plotted—and obtained—the release of one of their members who had been imprisoned and were able to smuggle him into Saudi Arabia. (Horwitz 1991)

Class

As we have seen, stratification systems based on slavery, caste, and clan are rigid. The lines marking the divisions between people are so firm that, except for marriage between clans, there is no movement from one group to another. A **class system,** in contrast, is much more open, for it is based primarily on money or material possessions. It, too, begins at birth, when an individual is ascribed the status of his or her parents, but, unlike slavery, caste, and clan, one's social class may change due to what one achieves (or fails to achieve) in life. In addition, there are no laws that specify occupations on the basis of birth or that prohibit marriage between the classes.

class system: a form of social stratification based primarily on the possession of money or material possessions

In a caste system, status is determined at birth and is lifelong. Members of lower castes suffer deprivation in virtually all aspects of life. In the Indian caste system, even occupation is determined by birth. Just as this man's father fixed shoes, so will his son. Gender cuts across every form of social stratification. Birth gave the woman in the photo on the left membership in a lower caste, as well as a secondary status within that caste. So it will be for her daughter. The photo on the right illustrates gender stratification in the division of labor which has been found in all societies.

A major characteristic of this fourth system, then, is its relatively fluid boundaries. A class system allows **social mobility,** that is, movement up or down the class ladder. The potential for improving one's social circumstances, or class, is one of the major forces that drives people to go far in school and to work hard. As in the case of Kim Petrovitch, the family background that an individual inherits at birth may determine disprivileges that give the child little chance of climbing very far—or, as in the case of Jack Kennedy, it may provide privileges that make it almost impossible to fall down the class ladder.

A Note on Gender and Social Stratification

We shall examine the social class system in detail, but first let's note that in every society of the world gender is a basis for social stratification. In no society is gender the sole basis for stratifying people, but gender cuts across *all* systems of social stratification—whether slavery, caste, clan, or class (Huber 1990). On the basis of their gender, people in every society are sorted into categories and given different access to the good things offered by their society. Apparently these distinctions always favor males. Gender is so significant for human relations that we shall devote a separate chapter to this topic (Chapter 11).

What Determines Social Class?

In the early days of sociology, a disagreement arose concerning the meaning of social class in industrialized nations. Let us compare how Marx and Weber saw the matter.

Karl Marx: The Means of Production

As discussed in Chapter 1, Karl Marx (1818–1883) personally saw societies in upheaval. When the feudal system broke up, masses of peasants were displaced from their traditional lands and occupations. Fleeing to cities, they competed for the few available jobs. Offered only a pittance for their labor, they dressed in rags, went hungry, and slept under bridges and in hovels. In contrast, the factory owners built mansions, hired servants, and lived in the lap of luxury. Seeing this great disparity between owners and workers, Marx concluded that social class depends on a single factor—the **means of production**—the tools, factories, land, and investment capital used to produce wealth (Marx 1844/1964; Marx and Engels 1848/1967).

Marx argued that the distinctions people often make between themselves—such as clothing, speech, education, or relative salary—are superficial matters that camouflage the only real significant dividing line: People (the **bourgeoisie**) either own the means of production or they (the **proletariat**) work for those who do. This is the only distinction that counts, for these two classes make up modern society. In short, according to Marx, people's relationship to the means of production determines their social class.

Marx did recognize that other groups were part of industrial society: farmers and peasants; a *lumpenproletariat* (marginal people such as migrant workers, beggars, vagrants, and criminals); and a middle class (self-employed professionals). Marx did not consider these groups social classes, however, for they lacked **class consciousness**—a common identity based on their position in the means of production. They did not see themselves as exploited workers whose plight could be solved only by collective action. Consequently, Marx thought of these groups as insignificant in the coming workers' revolution that would overthrow capitalism.

As capital becomes more concentrated, Marx claimed that capitalists and workers will become increasingly hostile. The workers will perceive capitalists as the common source of their oppression and will unite and throw off the chains of their oppressors. They will take up arms, seize the means of production, and usher in a classless society, where no longer will the few grow rich at the expense of the many. What holds back the workers' unity and their revolution, however, is **false consciousness,** workers mis-

---

social mobility: movement up or down the social class ladder

means of production: the tools, factories, land, and investment capital used to produce wealth

bourgeoisie: Karl Marx's term for the people who own the means of production

proletariat: Karl Marx's term for the people who work for those who own the means of production

class consciousness: Karl Marx's term for awareness of a common identity based on one's position in the means of production

false consciousness: Karl Marx's term to refer to workers identifying with the interests of capitalists

takenly identifying with capitalists. Because they have a few dollars in the bank, for example, workers may forget that they are workers and instead see themselves as investors, or as capitalists who are about to launch a successful business.

The only distinction worth mentioning, then, is whether a person is an owner or a worker. That decides everything else, for property determines people's lifestyles, shapes their ideas, and establishes their relationships with one another.

Max Weber: Property, Prestige, and Power

Max Weber (1864–1920) became an outspoken critic of Marx. He said that seeing property as the whole picture is shortsighted. Social class, he said, is actually made up of three components—property, prestige, and power (Gerth and Mills 1958; Weber 1922/1968). Some call these the three P's of social class. (Although Weber used the terms *class, status,* and *power,* some sociologists find *property, prestige,* and *power* to be clearer terms. To make them even clearer, you may wish to substitute *wealth* for *property.*)

Property (or wealth), said Weber, is certainly significant in determining a person's standing in society. On that he agreed with Marx. But, added Weber, ownership is not the only significant aspect of property. For example, some powerful people, such as managers of corporations *control* the means of production although they do not *own* them. If managers can control property for their own benefit—awarding themselves huge bonuses and magnificent perks—it makes no practical difference that they do not own the property that they so generously use for their own benefit.

Prestige, the second element in Weber's analysis, is often derived from property, for people tend to look up to the wealthy. Prestige, however, may be based on other factors. Olympic gold medalists are an example. Even though such persons do not own property, they may have very high prestige. Some are even able to exchange their prestige for property—such as being paid a small fortune for saying that they start their day with "the breakfast of champions." In other words, property and prestige are not one-way streets: although property can bring prestige, prestige can also bring property.

Power, the third element of social class, is the ability to control others, even over their objections. Weber agreed with Marx that property is a major source of power, but he added that it is not the only source. Position, for instance, can also lead to power. A notable example is J. Edgar Hoover, who headed the FBI for forty-eight years, from 1924 to 1972. Hoover wielded such enormous power that during his later years even presidents Johnson and Kennedy were fearful of him. Hoover's power, however, did not come from ownership of property, for he lived simply and did not accumulate property. Rather, his power derived from his position as the head of this powerful government agency. Not only did he direct a well-trained secret police, but he also maintained files on presidents and members of Congress documenting their sexual indiscretions, files they knew he could leak to the public.

Max Weber identified three elements of social class—property, prestige, and power. J. Edgar Hoover, director of the FBI for forty-eight years, lacked great wealth but possessed enormous power. Hoover's deviance, revealed only several years after his death, has greatly diminished his reputation.

▼ **In Sum** For Marx, social class was based solely on a person's position in relationship to the means of production—as a member of either the bourgeoisie or the proletariat—while Weber argued that social class is a combination of property, prestige, and power.

Why Is Social Stratification Universal? ◣▼

What is it about social life that makes all societies stratified? At the very least, why aren't there some societies that are not stratified? We shall first consider the explanation proposed by functionalists, which has aroused much controversy in sociology, followed by criticisms of this position. We then explore explanations proposed by conflict theorists.

The Functionalist View of Davis and Moore: Motivating Qualified People

Functionalists take the position that a group's particular characteristics represent historical adaptations that have contributed to its survival. Since social inequality is universal, then, inequality must help societies survive. In applying this principle, sociologists Kingsley Davis and Wilbert Moore (1945, 1953) concluded that stratification is inevitable for the following reasons:

1   Society must make certain that its positions are filled.
2   Some positions are more important than others.
3   The more important positions must be filled by the more qualified people.
4   To motivate the more qualified people to fill these positions, society must offer them greater rewards.

Let us look at some examples to flesh out this functionalist argument. The positions of college president, chief executive officer of a corporation, and general of an army are deemed much more important for society than are those farther down the line of command in each institution—students, assembly-line workers, and privates. They are more important in the sense that their decisions affect many people. Any mistakes they make carry implications for a large number of students, workers, and privates—their careers, paychecks, and, in some cases, even life and death.

Positions with greater responsibility also require greater accountability. College presidents, CEOs, and army generals are accountable for how they perform—to boards of control, stockholders, and the leader of a country, respectively. How can society motivate highly qualified people to enter such high-pressure positions? What keeps people from avoiding them and seeking only less demanding jobs?

The answer, said Davis and Moore, is that society offers greater rewards for its more responsible, demanding, and accountable positions. If they didn't offer higher salaries, benefits, and greater prestige, why would anyone strive for them? Thus, a salary of $1 million, country club membership, a private jet, and a limousine may be necessary to get the most highly qualified people to compete with one another for a certain position, while a $30,000 salary without fringe benefits is enough to get hundreds of people to compete for some other, lower position. Similarly, higher rewards are necessary to recruit people to positions that require rigorous training.

The functionalist argument is simple and clear. Society works better if its most qualified people hold its most important positions. For example, to get highly talented people to become surgeons—to undergo many years of rigorous training and then cope with life-and-death situations on a daily basis, as well as withstand the Sword of Damocles known as malpractice suits—requires a high payoff.

Tumin: A Critical Response

Note that the Davis–Moore thesis is an attempt to explain *why* social stratification is universal, not an attempt to *justify* social inequality. Note also that their view nevertheless makes many sociologists uncomfortable, for they see it as coming close to justifying social inequality.

Melvin Tumin (1953) was the first sociologist to point out what he saw as major flaws in the functionalist position. Here are four of his arguments.

First, how do you measure the importance of a position? If importance is measured by the rewards a position carries, the argument is circular. There must be an independent measure of importance to test whether the more important positions actually carry higher rewards. For example, is a surgeon really more important to society than a garbage collector, since the garbage collector helps prevent contagious diseases?

Second, if stratification worked as Davis and Moore describe it, society would be a **meritocracy;** that is, all positions would be awarded on the basis of merit. Ability, then, should predict who goes to college. Instead, the best predictor of college entrance is family income—the more a family earns, the more likely those children are to go to college. Similarly, while some people do get ahead through ability and hard work, others simply inherit wealth and the opportunities that go with it. Moreover, a stratification system that places half the population above the other half solely on the basis of sex does not live up to the argument that talent and ability are the bases for holding important positions. In short, one look at people like Kim Petrovitch and John F. Kennedy shows that factors far beyond merit give people their relative positions in society.

Third, Davis and Moore place too much emphasis on money and fringe benefits. These aren't the only reasons people take jobs. An example is college teaching. If money were the main motivator, why would people spend four years in college, then average another six or seven years pursuing a Ph.D.—only to earn slightly more than someone who works in the post office? Obviously college teaching offers more than monetary rewards: high prestige (see Table 10.1, page 258), autonomy (college teachers have considerable discretion about how they do their job), rewarding social interaction (much of the job consists of talking to people), security (when given tenure, college teachers have a lifetime job), leisure and the opportunity to travel (professors work short days, enjoy several weeks of vacation during the school year, and have the entire summer off).

Fourth, if social stratification is so functional, it ought to benefit almost everyone. In actual fact, however, social stratification is *dysfunctional* to many. Think of the people who could have made invaluable contributions to society had they not been born in a slum and had to drop out of school, taking a menial job to help support the family; or the many who, born female, are assigned "women's work," ensuring that they do not maximize their mental abilities (Huber 1988).

Mosca: A Forerunner of the Conflict View

In 1896 Italian sociologist Gaetano Mosca wrote an influential book entitled *The Ruling Class.* He argued that every society will be stratified by power, for three main reasons:

1 A society cannot exist unless it is organized. This requires politics of some sort in order to coordinate people's actions and get society's work done.

2 Political organization always results in inequalities of power, for it requires that some people take leadership positions, while others follow.

3 It is human nature to be self-centered. Therefore, people in positions of power will use their positions to bring greater rewards for themselves.

There is no way around these facts of life, said Mosca. Social stratification is inevitable, and every society will stratify itself along lines of power. Because the ruling class is well organized and enjoys easy communication among its relatively few members, it is extremely difficult for the majority they govern to resist (Marger 1987). Mosca's argument is a forerunner of explanations developed by conflict theorists.

The Conflict View: Class Conflict and Competition for Scarce Resources

Conflict theorists such as William Domhoff (1990, 1993), C. Wright Mills (1956), and Irving Louis Horowitz (1966) sharply disagree with the functionalist position. They stress that conflict, not function, is the basis of social stratification. They point out that in every society groups struggle with one another to gain a larger share of

meritocracy: a form of social stratification in which all positions are awarded on the basis of merit

Apartheid was a form of social stratification practiced in South Africa. Nelson Mandela spent many years in prison as a result of his struggle against apartheid and the white government that developed it to keep blacks, who constitute a majority, powerless. Here, Mandela is being sworn in as the first black president of South Africa, the historic point in the transference of political power from whites to blacks.

their society's limited resources. Whenever some group gains power, it uses that power to extract what it can from the groups beneath it. It also uses the social institutions to keep other groups weak and itself in power. Class conflict, then, is the key to understanding social stratification, for society is far from being a harmonious system that benevolently distributes greater resources to society's supposedly more qualified members.

All ruling groups—whether slave masters or modern elites—develop an ideology to justify their position at the top. This ideology seduces the oppressed into believing that their welfare depends on keeping society stable. Consequently, the oppressed may support laws against their own interests and even sacrifice their children as soldiers in wars designed to enrich the bourgeoisie.

Marx predicted that the workers would revolt. The day will come, he claimed, when class consciousness will overcome ideology, and the workers, with their eyes finally opened, will throw off their oppressors. At first, this struggle for control of the means of production may be covert, showing itself only in such acts as industrial sabotage, but ultimately it will break out into open resistance. The struggle will be difficult, for the bourgeoisie control the police, the military, and even education (where they inculcate false consciousness in the workers' children).

Some conflict theorists have given a different focus to Marx's original emphasis. C. Wright Mills (1956), Ralf Dahrendorf (1959), and Randall Collins (1974, 1988), for example, stress that groups within the *same class* also compete for scarce resources—for power, wealth, education, housing, and even prestige—whatever benefits society has to offer. The result is conflict between the young and the old, labor unions and business owners, producers and consumers, women and men, and racial and ethnic groups. Unlike functionalists, then, conflict theorists hold that just beneath the surface of what may appear to be a tranquil society lies overt conflict—uneasily held in check.

Toward a Synthesis

In spite of vast differences between the functionalist and conflict views, some social analysts have tried to synthesize them. Sociologist Gerhard Lenski (1966), for example, used the development of surpluses as a basis for reconciling the two views. He said that the functionalists are right when it comes to societies that have only basic resources and do not accumulate wealth. In hunting and gathering societies, the limited resources are channeled to people as rewards for taking on important responsibilities. The conflict theorists are right, however, when it comes to societies with a surplus. Because humans pursue self-interest, they struggle to control those surpluses, and a small elite emerges. To protect its position, the elite builds social inequality into the society, which results in a full-blown system of social stratification.

How Do Elites Maintain Stratification?

Suppose that you are part of the ruling elite of your society. What can you do to maintain your privileged position? The key lies in controlling ideas and information, in social networks, and in the least effective of all, the use of force.

Ideology Versus Force

Medieval Europe provides a good example. At that time, land, which was owned by only a small group of people, was the primary source of wealth. With the exception of the clergy and some craftsmen, almost everyone was a peasant working for this small group of powerful landowners, called the aristocracy. The peasants farmed the land, took care of the cattle, and built the roads and bridges. Each year, they had to turn over a designated portion of their crops to their feudal lord. Year after year, for centuries, they did so.

Why didn't the peasants rebel and take over the land themselves? There were many reasons, not the least of which is that the army was controlled by the aristocracy. Coercion, however, only goes so far, for it breeds hostility and nourishes rebellion. How much more effective it is to get the people to *want* to do what the ruling elite desires. This is where ideology comes into play, and the aristocracy of that time used it to great effect. They stressed the **divine right of kings**—the idea that the king's authority comes directly from God—which can be traced back several thousand years to the Old Testament. The king could delegate authority to nobles, who as God's representatives also had to be obeyed. To disobey was a sin against God; to rebel meant physical punishment on earth and a sentence to suffer in eternal hell.

The control of ideas, then, can be remarkably more effective than brute force. Although this particular ideology no longer governs people's minds today, the elite in every society develops an ideology to justify its position at the top. For example, around the world schools teach that their country's form of government—*whatever form of government that may be*—is the best. Each nation's schools also stress the virtues of governments past and present, not their vices. Religion also teaches that we owe obedience to authority, that laws are to be obeyed. To the degree that their ideologies are accepted by the masses, political arrangements are stable.

To maintain their positions of power, elites also try to control information. In dictatorships this is accomplished through the threat of force, for dictators can—and do—imprison editors and reporters for printing critical reports, sometimes even for publishing information unflattering to them (Timerman 1981). The ruling elites of democracies, lacking such power, accomplish the same purpose by manipulating the media through the selective release of information, withholding what they desire "in the interest of national security." But just as coercion has its limits, so does the control of information—especially given its new forms (from satellite communications to modems and fax machines) that pay no respect to international borders (Kennedy 1993).

> **divine right of kings:** the idea that the king's authority comes directly from God

Depicted in this French miniature, painted about 1450, is the coronation of 15-year-old Philip Augustus (1165–1223) as king of France by the Archbishop of Reims in 1179 or 1180. During his reign serfdom practically disappeared, cities and the merchant class grew prosperous, and Philip began the building of great cathedrals. The church's stamp of approval was essential for the legitimacy of the monarchy, with the right to rule passed from one generation to the next.

Also critical in maintaining stratification are social networks—the social ties that link people together (Higley et al. 1991). As discussed in Chapter 6, social networks—contacts expanding outward from the individual that gradually encompass more and more people—supply valuable information and tend to perpetuate social inequality. Sociologist William Domhoff (1983, 1990) has documented that members of the elite move in a circle of power that multiplies their opportunities. As with the Kennedys in the opening vignette, these contacts with people of similar backgrounds, interests, and goals allow the elite to pass privileges from one generation to the next. In contrast, as with the Petrovitches, the social networks of the poor perpetuate disprivilege.

Underlying the maintenance of stratification is control of a society's institutions. The legal establishment enforces the laws passed under the influence of a society's elite. The elite also commands the police and military and can give orders to crush a rebellion—or even to run the post office if postal workers strike. As noted, however, force has its limits, and a nation's elite generally finds it preferable to maintain its stratification system by peaceful means, especially by influencing the thinking of its people.

Comparative Social Stratification

Now that we have examined different systems of social stratification and considered why stratification is universal, let us compare social stratification in Great Britain and in the former Soviet Union. For even more contrast, see the Perspectives box on the next page, where you can catch a glimpse of the social stratification that characterized Polish Jews prior to the Nazi inferno.

Social Stratification in Great Britain

Great Britain is often called England by Americans, but England is only one of the countries that make up the island of Great Britain. The others are Scotland and Wales. In addition, Northern Ireland is part of the United Kingdom of Great Britain and Northern Ireland.

Like other industrialized countries, Great Britain has a class system that can be divided into a lower, middle, and upper class. A little over half the population is in the lower or working class, while close to half the population is in the nation's very large middle class. A tiny upper class, perhaps 1 percent of the population, is powerful, highly educated, and extremely wealthy.

Compared with Americans (who, regardless of their social background, are likely to claim that they are middle class), the British are extremely class conscious. Like

The British remain far more class conscious than Americans, and they overwhelmingly wish to retain the monarchy. From it, they attain a sense of unity, and they revel in its strong ties with the past. The widely-publicized marital difficulties of Prince Charles and Princess Diana, however, have undermined the monarchy's credibility and posed a threat to its legitimacy. Symbolically, perhaps, this is a sign of a crumbling class system.

▼▲▼

Perspectives

CULTURAL DIVERSITY AROUND THE WORLD

Social Stratification Among Polish Jews

THE STRATIFICATION OF THE JEWS in Stoczek, Poland, between World Wars I and II provides a rich contrast with stratification in the United States. The four sources of social status for the Jews were occupation, wealth, learning, and lineage. In general, people were located at the same point on all four scales.

The first source of status, occupation was divided into men of labor (about 60 percent) and businessmen (about 39 percent). About 1 percent were learners, who did not work. Learners devoted themselves full time to studying the Torah, the Jewish law as written in the first five books of the Old Testament. Learners were supported by their wives or by their parents-in-law. High respect was given to a man who devoted his life to learning.

Wealth, the second base of prestige, had three acceptable uses. First, a person should eat well, dress well, and enjoy other pleasures, but anyone who spent money only on such things was considered a "pig." To be rich and command respect also required a second use of money—doing good deeds (*mitzvot*) for the needy. To give money to those who needed it, rather than to those who could repay, was a sign of having a true "Jewish heart." Doing a good deed for an orphan, for example, brought greater credit than doing a similar deed for a self-supporting person. In addition to gaining honor and respect, the doer of good deeds also stored up credit with God for the afterlife. The third use of money was to purchase status for one's children—to educate one's sons or to marry one's daughters into "better" family.

The third source of status, learning, referred to studying the Torah. Unlike education, learning was never completed. This lifelong endeavor was a goal in itself, not a means to obtain material benefits. Learning was the equivalent of "refinement," and was to be pursued with love and joy. To sit up late at night studying, after a long day's work, brought prestige in the community. The advice and opinions of a learned man were highly valued.

The fourth source of status, lineage, was the first thing to be established when strangers met or when people talked about a third person. People were accorded high prestige if they were descendants of learned, wealthy, and charitable ancestors. By itself, however, the connection was insufficient: individuals had to live up to their lineage by being learned and charitable themselves. Those who did not were seen as having squandered their inheritance.

These four sources of social status translated into three social classes. At the top of the social pyramid were people with much learning, wealth, and a reputation for giving to the needy. Next came the middle class, consisting of shopkeepers and traders who had some means and some learning. At the bottom were the plain Jews—workers and craftsmen who had little learning and little money.

In Stoczek, it was important for everyone to know their place and to act with proper respect toward those with higher status. To fail to do so was seen as insolence, and such persons were looked down on by the entire community. Social status was so significant that there were no friendships between adults of different classes, and status even determined where a man would sit in the synagogue. Reserved for men of highest status were the seats nearest to the eastern wall—those closest to Jerusalem.

Although anyone was supposed to be able to move up the class ladder through attaining wealth or learning, class membership was, for the most part, hereditary. Women who guided their children to love learning or to do good deeds were given higher status, as were those who were very religious and did good deeds themselves. A woman whose father was a rabbi or scholar was also accorded higher status, as was a woman who encouraged her husband to *mitzvot* or supported him so he could devote all his time to learning. Women were not allowed to worship alongside the men in the synagogue, but were permitted only in the balcony or some other separate place.

The world depicted by this stratification system was erased by Hitler in his systematic—and largely successful—campaign to destroy European Jewry.

Sources: Based on Heller 1953, 1991.

Americans the British recognize class distinctions on the basis of the type of car a person drives, or the stores that person patronizes. But the most striking characteristics of the British class system are language and education. Differences in speech have a powerful impact on British life. Accent almost always betrays class, and as soon as someone speaks, the listener is aware of that person's class—and treats him or her accordingly.

Education is the primary way by which the British perpetuate their class system from one generation to the next. Almost all children go to neighborhood schools, but the children of Great Britain's more privileged 5 percent—who own *half* the nation's wealth—attend exclusive private boarding schools (known as "public" schools), where they are trained in subjects considered "proper" for members of the ruling class. An astounding 50 percent of the students at Oxford and Cambridge, the country's most prestigious universities, come from this 5 percent of the population. To illustrate how powerfully this system of stratified education affects the national life of Great Britain, sociologist Ian Robertson (1987) says:

> [E]ighteen former pupils of the most exclusive of them, Eton, have become prime minister. Imagine the chances of a single American high school producing eighteen presidents!

Social Stratification in the Former Soviet Union

Vladimir Ilyich Lenin (1870–1924) and Leon Trotsky (1879–1940) heeded Karl Marx's call for a classless society. They led a revolution in Russia to bring this about. They, and the nations that followed their banner, never claimed to have achieved the ideal of communism, in which all contribute their labor to the common good and receive according to their needs. Instead, they used the term *socialism* to describe the intermediate step between capitalism and communism, in which social classes are abolished but some individual inequality remains.

Although the socialist nations often manipulated the world's mass media to tweak the nose of Uncle Sam because of the inequalities of the United States, they, too, were marked by huge disparities in privilege—much more than they ever acknowledged to the outside world. Their major basis of stratification—membership in the Communist party—often was the determining factor in deciding who would gain admission to the better schools or obtain the more desirable jobs. The equally qualified son or daughter of a nonmember would be turned down, for such privileges came with demonstrated loyalty to the Party.

Divided into three layers, even the Communist party was highly stratified. Most members occupied a low level, having such assignments as spying on other workers. For their services, they might be given easier jobs in the factory or occasional access to special stores to purchase hard-to-find goods. A smaller number were mid-level bureaucrats with better than average access to resources and privileges. The top level consisted of a small elite: party members who enjoyed not only power but also limousines, imported delicacies, vacation homes, and even servants and hunting lodges. As with other stratification systems around the world, women held lower positions in the Party, as was readily evident in each year's May Day photos of the top members of the Party reviewing the weapons paraded in Moscow's Red Square. The top officials were always male.

Rather than eliminating social classes, then, the Communist revolution merely ushered in a different set of classes. An elite continued to rule from the top. Before the revolution this elite was based on inherited wealth; afterward it consisted of top party officials. Below this elite was a middle class, much smaller than ours, consisting of white-collar and other skilled workers. At the bottom was a mass of peasants and unskilled workers, very similar to the lower class before the revolution.

Struggling with a bloated bureaucracy, the gross inefficiencies of central planning, workers who did not see a personal stake in their assignments, and the military taking 12 percent of the gross national product (*Statistical Abstract* 1993:1432), the leaders of the USSR became frustrated as they saw the West thrive. It added to their distress to see the prosperity of even the Japanese, the World War II adversary with whom they had arrogantly refused to make a peace treaty. Their ideology did not intend their citizens to be deprived, and in an attempt to turn things around, the Soviet leadership initiated reforms, allowing elections with more than one candidate for an office (unlike earlier elections) and even encouraging private investment and ownership. It is too soon to know the results of these reforms on their stratification system, but at this point we can see a class of the newly rich emerging—some who have had the political connections, others the foresight and initiative, to take advantage of the change to capitalism.

Global Stratification: The Three Worlds of Development

Just as the people within a nation are stratified into groups based on their relative power, prestige, and property, so are nations. The most common model divides nations into three groups according to how they rank in terms of wealth and industrialization. The richest and most industrialized nations generally rank highest in prestige and power. The differences between these groups of nations are so immense that it is as though their citizens live in different worlds. Consequently, nations can be categorized as belonging to the First World, Second World, and Third World. ("First" does not mean better, but richer, having higher prestige, and, above all, being more powerful.) Each of these Three Worlds' relative share of the world's land area and population is shown in Table 9.2.

The First World

The *First World* consists of the earth's most heavily industrialized nations: the United States and Canada in North America; Great Britain, France, Germany, Switzerland, and the other industrialized nations of western Europe; Japan in Asia; and Australia and New Zealand in the area of the world known as Oceania. Although there are variations in their economic systems, these nations are capitalistic. With 31 percent of the earth's land and only 16 percent of its people (Kurian 1990), these relatively few nations hold most of the world's wealth. Their wealth is so enormous that even the First World's poor live better and longer lives than do the Third World's average citizens. Figure 9.1 on pages 240–241 shows the tremendous disparities in income among nations.

The Second World

Until the breakup of the Soviet Union in 1989, the *Second World* referred to nations that were governed by socialism or communism. Now it is used to refer to nations that are in the process of industrializing, which includes most of the nations of the former Soviet Union and its former satellites in eastern Europe. These nations account for 20 percent of the earth's land and 16 percent of its people (Kurian 1991).

The dividing points between the three "worlds" are soft, making it difficult to know where to best place some nations. This is especially the case with the Second World. Exactly how much industrialization must a nation have to be a Second World nation? Although soft, these categories are useful, for they do pinpoint essential differences. Although most inhabitants of the Second World have much lower incomes and standards of living than people who live in the First World, most are better off than members of the Third World. For example, on such measures as access to electricity, indoor plumbing, automobiles, telephones, and even food, citizens of Second World nations rank lower than those in the First World, but higher than those in the Third World.

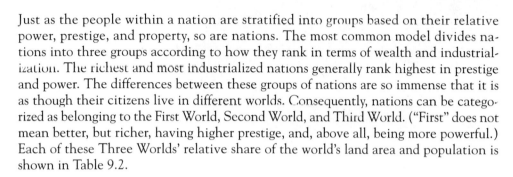

Table 9.2

The Three Worlds of Development

	Percentage of the World's:	
	Land	*Population*
First World	31%	16%
Second World	20	16
Third World	49	68

Source: Computed from Kurian 1990, 1991, 1992.

First World Nations

Nation	Income per Person
1 United States	US $22,470
2 Switzerland	$21,700
3 Austria	$20,895
4 Luxembourg	$20,200
5 Canada	$19,400
6 Japan	$19,100
7 France	$18,300
8 Australia	$18,054
9 Denmark	$17,700
10 Belgium	$17,300
11 Sweden	$17,200
12 Norway	$17,100
13 Italy	$16,700
14 Netherlands	$16,600
15 Iceland	$16,300
16 Finland	$16,200
17 Great Britain	$15,900
18 Germany	$14,600
19 New Zealand	$14,000
20 Israel	$12,500
21 Spain	$12,400
22 Ireland	$11,200

Second World Nations

Nation	Income per Person
23 Portugal	US $8,400
24 Greece	$7,730
25 Czech Republic	$7,700
26 South Korea	$6,300
27 Hungary	$5,700
28 Russia*	$5,448
29 Poland	$4,300
30 Mexico	$3,200
31 Romania	$3,100
32 Cuba	$2,644
33 South Africa	$2,600
34 Ukraine	$2,500
35 Thailand	$1,630
36 Indonesia	$630
37 Yugoslavia	$540

Oil-Rich Nations

Nation	Income per Person
80 Qatar	US $15,000
81 United Arab Emirates	$12,100
82 Bahrain	$7,300
83 Kuwait	$6,200
84 Saudi Arabia	$5,800
85 Iraq	$1,950
86 Iran	$1,500

Figure 9-1

The Three Worlds of Development

Variously listed as per capita domestic product and per capita income. The years vary, usually 1990 to 1992. Since there is such a variance in some of these figures from year to year, they must be taken as approximate.

*The mean of a figure computed from the table's source and the figure given for the Soviet Union in *Statistical Abstract*, 1992: Table 1371.

Source: *World Almanac and Book of Facts, 1994*

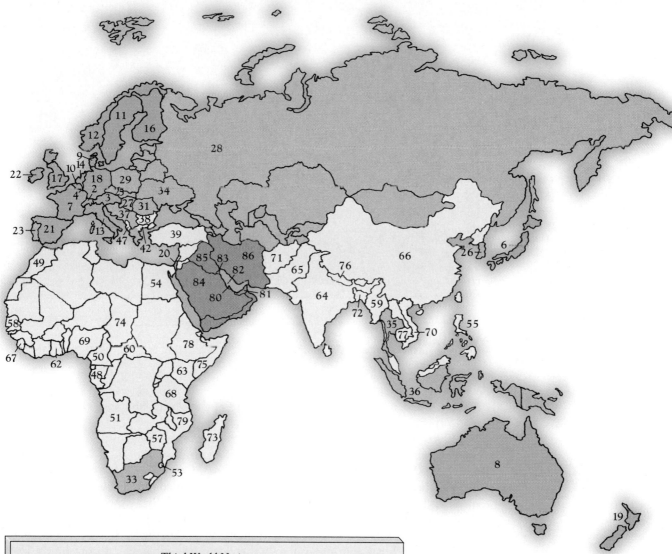

Third World Nations

Nation	Income per Person	Nation	Income per Person
38 Bulgaria	US $5,300	59 Myanmar (Burma)	US $530
39 Turkey	$3,400	60 Central African Republic	$440
40 Argentina	$3,100	61 Haiti	$440
41 Brazil	$2,540	62 Ghana	$400
42 Macedonia	$2,399	63 Kenya	$385
43 Chile	$2,200	64 India	$380
44 Costa Rica	$1,810	65 Pakistan	$380
45 Belize	$1,637	66 China	$360
46 Paraguay	$1,460	67 Sierra Leone	$330
47 Albania	$1,300	68 Tanzania	$260
48 Congo	$1,070	69 Nigeria	$230
49 Morocco	$1,060	70 Vietnam	$230
50 Cameroon	$1,010	71 Afghanistan	$220
51 Angola	$950	72 Bangladesh	$200
52 Peru	$920	73 Madagascar	$200
53 Swaziland	$752	74 Chad	$190
54 Egypt	$720	75 Somalia	$170
55 Philippines	$720	76 Nepal	$165
56 Bolivia	$690	77 Cambodia	$130
57 Zimbabwe	$660	78 Ethiopia	$130
58 Senegal	$615	79 Mozambique	$120

Haitians have endured corrupt leaders and persistent poverty for hundreds of years. Although Haitian slaves wrested power from their French colonial rulers in 1804, the country has been ruled by a ruthless, wealthy, elite ever since. This leadership has plundered the nation's coffers while oppressing those they govern. To survive, some Haitians have been reduced to picking over garbage.

The Third World

The rest of the world's nations make up the *Third World*, where there is little industrialization, most people are peasant farmers living on farms or in villages, and living standards are low. These nations account for 49 percent of the earth's land and 68 percent of the world's people (Kurian 1992).

It is difficult to imagine the poverty that characterizes the Third World. Although wealthy nations have their pockets of poverty, most people in the Third World live on less than $1,000 a year, in many cases considerably less. Most of them have no running water, indoor plumbing, central water supply, or access to trained physicians. Because modern medicine has cut infant mortality but not births, the population grows fastest in these nations, thus placing even greater burdens on their limited facilities, and causing them to fall farther behind each year (Sweezy and Magdoff 1992). The twin specters of poverty and death at an early age continuously stalk these countries. Some conditions in the Third World are gruesome, as discussed in the following Thinking Critically section.

▽▲▽▲▽▲▽▲▽▲▽▲▽▲▽▲▽▲▽▲▽▲▽▲▽▲▽▲▽▲▽

Thinking Critically About Social Controversy

Open Season: Children of the Third World

▼ WHAT IS CHILDHOOD LIKE in the Third World? The answer depends primarily on who your parents are. If you are the son or daughter of rich parents, childhood can be extremely pleasant. If you are born into poverty, but living in a rural area where there is plenty to eat, life can still be good—although there likely will be no books, television, and little education. If you live in a Third World slum, however, life can be horrible—worse even than in the slums of the First World. Let's take a glance at what is happening to children in the slums of Brazil.

Not having enough food, this you can take for granted—as well as broken homes, alcoholism, drug abuse, and a high crime rate. From your knowledge of First World ghettos, you would expect these things. What you may not expect, however, are the brutal conditions in which Brazilian slum (*favela*) children live.

Sociologist Martha Huggins, who has summarized life in these slums, reports that poverty is so deep that children and adults swarm over garbage dumps to try to find enough decaying food to keep them alive. And you might be surprised to discover that in Brazil the owners of these dumps hire armed guards to keep the poor out—so they can sell the garbage for pig food. And you might be shocked to learn that poor children are systematically killed. Each year, the Brazilian police and death squads murder about 2,000 children. Some associations of shop owners even put assassination teams on retainer and auction victims off to the lowest bidder! The going rate is half a month's salary—figured at the low Brazilian minimum wage.

One of the children killed by death squads operating in Brazil.

Life is cheap in the Third World—but death squads for children? To understand this situation, we must first note that Brazil has a long history of violence. Although it is one of the most industrialized of the developing countries, Brazil has an extremely high rate of poverty, only a tiny middle class, and is controlled by a small group of families who, under a veneer of democracy, make the country's major decisions. Hordes of homeless children, with no schools or jobs, roam the streets, washing windshields, shining shoes, begging, and stealing to survive. These children, part of the "dangerous classes," as they are known, threaten the status quo.

The "respectable" classes see these children as nothing but trouble. They hurt business, for customers feel intimidated when they see a group of adolescents clustered in front of stores. Some shoplift; others dare to sell items in competition with the stores. With no social institutions to care for these children, one solution is to kill them. As Huggins notes, murder sends a clear message—especially if it is accompanied by ritual torture—pulling out the eyes, ripping open the chest, cutting off the genitals, raping the girls, and burning the victim's body.

Not all life is bad in the Third World, but this is about as bad as it gets.

For Your Consideration

Do you think there is anything First World nations can do about this situation? Or is it any of their business? Is it, though unfortunate, just an "internal" affair that is up to the Brazilians to handle as they wish? ▲

Imperfections in the Model

This classification of nations into First, Second, and Third World is helpful in that it pinpoints gross differences among them, but it is also inadequate. I have mentioned the difficulty of classifying nations by their degree of industrialization. Another major problem is how to classify the oil-rich nations of the Middle East. These nations are not industrialized, but by providing the oil and gasoline that fuels the machinery of the industrialized nations, they have become wealthy. Consequently, to classify them as Third World nations glosses over significant material differences, such as their modern hospitals, extensive prenatal care, pure water systems, and high literacy. Kuwait, on whose formal behalf the United States and other industrialized powers fought Iraq in the Gulf War, is so wealthy that almost none of its citizens is employed. The government simply pays each a generous annual salary just for being citizens. Migrant workers from the Third World do most of the onerous chores that daily life requires, while highly skilled workers from the First World run the specialized systems that keep the nation's economy going and, on occasion, fight its wars for them as well. Granted this significant distinction, I suggest an alternative model of global stratification in Table 9.3.

Table 9.3
An Alternative Model of Global Stratification
The Four Worlds of Development
First World: Highly industrialized nations
Second World: Industrializing nations (such as Korea)
Third World: Nonindustrialized nations
Fourth World: Oil-rich, nonindustrialized nations

How the World's Nations Became Stratified

How did the globe become stratified into such distinct worlds of development? The obvious answer is that the poorer nations have fewer resources than the richer nations. As with so many other "obvious" answers, however, this one, too, falls short, for many of the Second and Third World nations are rich in natural resources, while one First World Nation, Japan, has few. Four competing theories explain how global stratification came about.

Imperialism and Colonialism

The first theory focuses on how European powers exploited weaker nations. The nations that industrialized earliest got the jump on the rest of the world. Beginning in Great Britain about 1750, industrialization spread throughout western Europe, reaching the United States about 1825. Its powerful new technology produced great wealth, resulting in surplus capital that needed to be invested. Economist John Hobson (1858–1940) proposed that the industrialized nations lacked enough consumers to make it profitable to invest all excess capital there. Consequently, business leaders persuaded their governments to embark on **imperialism,** to forcibly create an empire, so they could expand their markets and gain access to cheap raw materials.

Backed by the more powerful armaments developed by their new technology, the industrialized nations found others easy prey (Harrison 1993). The result was **colonization;** that is, these more powerful nations made colonies out of weaker nations. After invading and subduing them, they left a controlling force to exploit their labor and natural resources. At one point, there was even a free-for-all among the industrialized European nations as they frantically rushed to divide up an entire continent. As Africa was sliced into pieces, even tiny Belgium got into the act and acquired the Congo. While the more powerful European nations would plant their national flags in a colony and send their representatives to directly run the government and administer the territory's affairs, the United States usually chose to plant corporate flags in the colony and let these corporations dominate the territory's government. Central and South America are prime examples of such "economic imperialism" on the part of the United States. No matter what the form, and whether benevolent or harsh, the purpose was the same—to exploit the nation's people and resources for the benefit of the "mother" country.

Western imperialism and colonization, then, shaped the Third World. In some instances, the industrialized nations were so powerful that they were able to divide their booty among themselves by drawing lines across a map and forming new states without regard for tribal or cultural considerations (Kennedy 1993). Britain and France did just this in North Africa and parts of the Middle East, which is why the national boundaries of Libya, Saudi Arabia, Kuwait, and other nations are so straight. This legacy of European conquests still erupts into tribal violence because tribes with no history of national identity were arbitrarily included within the same political boundaries.

World System Theory

To explain how global stratification developed, Immanuel Wallerstein (1974, 1979, 1984, 1990), the major proponent of the second theory, argued that since the sixteenth century a **world system** has been developing; that is, the world's countries have been increasingly tied together by economic and political connections. Wallerstein identified four groups of interconnected nations. Capitalism first developed in what he calls the *core nations* (Britain, France, Holland, and later Germany). Capitalism made these nations rich and powerful. A second group, nations around the Mediterranean, called the *semiperiphery,* became highly dependent on trade with these core nations. Consequently, their own economies stagnated. The third group, the *periphery,* or fringe, consists of the eastern European countries. Primarily limited to selling cash crops to the core nations,

imperialism: a nation's attempt to create an empire; its pursuit of unlimited geographical expansion

colonization: the process by which one nation takes over another nation, usually for the purpose of exploiting its labor and natural resources

world system: economic and political connections that tie the world's countries together

Today's system of telecommunications that encircles the earth, connects small human groups around the world into a single, encompassing system. Here we see how this process, called globalization, is so extensive that this preliterate people, the Gaviao Indians in Brazil's remote Amazon, is being incorporated into this system.

their economies developed even less. The fourth group, which Wallerstein calls the *external area*, includes most of Africa and Asia. These nations were left out of the development of capitalism and had few if any economic connections with the core nations.

Capitalism's relentless expansion has given birth to a **capitalist world economy** dominated by the core nations (to which Canada, the United States, Japan, and a few other highly industrialized nations were added). This new world economy forged economic and political connections between the core nations and others. This economy has turned out to be so all-encompassing that today even the nations in the external area are being drawn into its commercial web.

Globalization   The extensive interdependence among the nations of the world ushered in by the expansion of capitalism is called **globalization** (Robertson 1992). Although globalization has been under way for the past several hundred years, today's new forms of communication and transportation have greatly speeded it up (Kennedy 1993). The interconnections are so extensive that no longer can a nation live in isolation. Events in remote parts of the world now affect us all—sometimes immediately, as when a revolution interrupts the flow of raw materials, or, perish the thought, if in Russia's unstable political climate terrorists managed to seize an arsenal of earth-destroying nuclear missiles—at other times in a slow ripple effect, as when a government's policy changes that country's ability to compete in world markets. All of today's societies, then, no matter where they are located, are part of a global social system.

Dependency Theory

The third theory is sometimes difficult to distinguish from world system theory. **Dependency theory** attributes the lack of economic development in the Third World to the dominance of the world economy by the industrialized nations (Cardoso 1972; Furtado 1984). According to this theory, the First World nations turned other nations into their plantations and mines, planting or extracting whatever they needed to meet their growing appetite for commodities and exotic foods. As a result, many Third World nations began to specialize in a single cash crop. Brazil became the primary source for coffee; Nicaragua and other Central American countries specialized in bananas (hence

capitalist world economy: the dominance of capitalism in the world along with the international interdependence that capitalism has created

globalization: the extensive interconnections among nations due to the expansion of capitalism

dependency theory: the belief that lack of industrial development in Third World nations is caused by the industrialized nations dominating the world economy

the term "banana" republic); Chile became the primary source of tin; and the Belgian Congo (Zaire) was turned into a gigantic rubber plantation. The Mideast nations became the First World's supplier of oil. By becoming dependent on the industrialized nations, the Third World countries did not develop independent economies of their own.

Culture of Poverty

An entirely different explanation of global stratification was proposed by economist John Kenneth Galbraith (1979), who claimed that it was the Third World's own culture that held them back. Building on the ideas of anthropologist Oscar Lewis (1966), Galbraith argued that some nations remained poor because they were crippled by a **culture of poverty,** a way of life that perpetuates poverty from one generation to the next. He explained it in this way: Most of the world's poor live in rural areas, where they barely eke out a living from the land. Their marginal life offers little room for error or risk, so they tend to stick closely to tried-and-true, traditional ways. Experimenting with new farming or manufacturing techniques is threatening, for if these fail they could lead to hunger or death. Their religion also reinforces traditionalism, for it teaches fatalism, the acceptance of their lot in life as God's will.

Evaluating the Theories

Most sociologists find imperialism, world systems, and dependency theory preferable to an explanation based on a culture of poverty, for this theory places blame on the victim, the poor nations themselves. It points to characteristics of the poor nations, rather than to international arrangements that benefit the First World at the expense of the Third. But even taken together, these theories yield only part of the picture, as becomes evident from the example of Japan. None of these theories would lead anyone to expect that after World War II, Japan—with a religion that stressed fatalism, two major cities destroyed by atomic bombs, and stripped of its colonies—would become an economic powerhouse able to turn the Western world on its head.

Each theory, then, yields but a partial explanation, and the grand theorist who will put the many pieces of this puzzle together has yet to appear.

Maintaining Global Stratification

Why are the same countries rich year after year, while the rest remain poor? Let us look at two explanations of how global stratification is maintained.

Neocolonialism

Sociologist Michael Harrington (1977) observed that although the First World nations no longer invade a country and make it a colony, they do control Third World nations through **neocolonialism.** This term means that the industrialized nations not only set the prices they charge for their manufactured goods but also control the international markets where they purchase the mineral and agricultural wealth of these Third World nations. Thus, the industrialized nations determine how much they will pay for tin from Bolivia, copper from Peru, coffee from Brazil, and so forth. Neocolonialism also means that First World nations move hazardous industries out of their own countries into Third World nations that, eager to get the employment, allow themselves to be used as dumping grounds for untreated factory waste (LaDou 1991).

The First World nations set up a cycle of indebtedness by selling weapons and other manufactured goods to the Third World. Making these nations eternal debtors keeps

culture of poverty: a culture that perpetuates poverty from one generation to the next

neocolonialism: the economic and political dominance of Third World nations by First World nations

Perspectives

CULTURAL DIVERSITY AROUND THE WORLD

The Patriotic Prostitute

Holidays with the most beautiful women of the world. An exclusive tour by Life Travel. . . . You fly to Bangkok and then go to Pattaya. . . . Slim, sunburnt and sweet, they . . . are masters in the art of making love by nature, an art we European people do not know. . . . In Pattaya costs of living and loving are low.
(from a Swiss pamphlet)

A NEW WRINKLE IN the history of prostitution is the "patriotic prostitute." These are young women who are encouraged by their governments to prostitute themselves to help the country's economy. Patriotic prostitution is one of the seediest aspects of global stratification. Some Third World nations encourage prostitution to help pay their national debts. A consequence is that perhaps 10 percent of all Thai women between the ages of 15 and 30 have become prostitutes. Bangkok alone reports 100,000 prostitutes—plus 200,000 "masseuses."

Government officials encourage prostitution as a service to their country. In South Korea, prostitutes are issued identification cards that serve as hotel passes. In orientation sessions, they are told, "Your carnal conversations [sic] with foreign tourists do not prostitute either yourself or the nation, but express your heroic patri-

otism." With such an official blessing, "sex tourism" has become big business. Travel agencies in Germany openly advertise "trips to Thailand with erotic pleasures included in the price." Japan Air Lines hands out brochures that advertise the "charming attractions" of Kisaeng girls, advising men to fly JAL for a "night spent with a consummate Kisaeng girl dressed in a gorgeous Korean blouse and skirt."

What the enticing advertising fails to mention is the misery underlying Third World prostitution. Many of the prostitutes are held in bondage. Some are only children, as in the accompanying photo. Some are forced into prostitution to pay family debts. Some are kept under lock and key to keep them from escaping. The advertisements also fail to mention the incidence of AIDS among Third World prostitutes. Somewhere between 25 percent and 50 percent of Nairobi's 10,000 prostitutes appear to be infected.

Women's groups protest this international sex trade, deploring in particular its exploitation of the world's most impoverished and underprivileged women.

Sources: Based on Gay 1985; Cohen 1986; Shaw 1987; O'Malley 1988; Srisang 1989.

---

them from developing their own industrial capacity. Because of the Third World's huge debts, the industrialized countries are able to dictate their trading terms (Tordoff 1992; Carrington 1993) and to extract more capital each year than they put in (Sweezy and Magdoff 1992). Thus, although the Third World nations have their own governments—whether elected or dictatorships—they remain almost as dependent on the industrialized nations as they were when those nations occupied them. For an example of neocolonialism today, see the Perspectives box above.

Multinational Corporations

A second way in which international stratification is maintained is through **multinational corporations,** companies that operate across many national boundaries. In some cases, multinational corporations exploit Third World nations directly. A prime example is the United Fruit Company, which for decades controlled national and local politics in the Central American nations, running them as a fiefdom for the company's own profit while the U.S. marines waited in the wings in case the company's interests needed to be backed up. Most commonly, however, multinational corporations help to maintain international stratification simply by doing business. A single multinational may do mining in several countries, manufacturing in many others, and run transportation and advertising networks around the globe. No matter where the particular profits are made, or where they are reinvested, the primary beneficiaries are First World nations, especially the one in which the multinational corporation has its central headquarters. As Michael Harrington (1977) stressed, the real profits are made in processing the products and in controlling their distribution—and these profits are withheld from the Third World. For more on multinational corporations, see Chapter 14.

According to sociologist Michael Lipton (1979), multinational corporations work closely with the Third World power elite. This elite, which lives a sophisticated upper-class life in the major cities of its home country, sends its children to Oxford, the Sorbonne, or Harvard to be educated. The multinational corporations funnel investments to this small circle of power, whose members favor projects such as building laboratories and computer centers in the capital city, projects that do not help the vast majority of their people living in poor, remote villages where they farm small plots of land.

This, however, is not the full story. Multinational corporations also play a role in changing international stratification. This is an unintentional by-product of their worldwide search for cheap resources and labor. By moving manufacturing from First World countries with high labor costs to Third World countries with low labor costs, they not only exploit cheap labor but in some cases also bring prosperity to those nations. Although in comparison with their counterparts in the First World these workers are paid a pittance, it is more than they can earn elsewhere. With new factories come opportunities to develop new skills and a capital base. This does not occur in all nations, but the Pacific Rim nations, nicknamed the "Asian tigers," have now developed such a strong capital base that they have begun to rival the older capitalist nations.

Summary and Review

What Is Social Stratification?

The term **social stratification** refers to a hierarchy of relative privilege based on power, property, and prestige. Every society stratifies its members. Pp. 224–225.

Systems of Social Stratification

What are the four major systems of social stratification?

The four major stratification systems are slavery, caste, clan, and class. The essential characteristic of **slavery** is that some people own other people. Initially, slavery was based not on race but on debt, punishment, or defeat in battle. Slavery could be temporary or permanent, and was not necessarily passed on to one's children. In North America slaves had no legal rights, and the system was gradually buttressed by a racist ideology. In a **caste system,** status is determined by birth and is lifelong. People marry within their own group and develop rules about ritual pollution. In a **clan system,** people's status depends on lineage that links them to an extended network of relatives. Class-based stratification is much more open than these other systems, for it is based primarily on money or material possessions. Industrialization encourages the formation of **class systems.** Gender discrimination cuts across all forms of social stratification. Pp. 225–230.

What Determines Social Class?

Karl Marx argued that a single factor determines social class: If you own the **means of production,** you belong to the bourgeoisie; if you do not, you are one of the proletariat. Max Weber theorized that three elements determine social class: *property, prestige,* and *power.* Pp. 230–231.

Why Is Social Stratification Universal?

To explain why stratification is universal, functionalists Kingsley Davis and Wilbert Moore argued that to attract the most capable people to fill its important positions, society must offer them higher rewards. Melvin Tumin criticized this view, arguing that if it were correct, U.S. society would be a **meritocracy,** with all positions awarded on the basis of merit. Gaetano Mosca argued that stratification is inevitable because every society must have leadership, and leadership always perpetuates inequality. Conflict theorists argue that stratification is inevitable because resources are always limited, and groups always struggle against one another for them. Gerhard Lenski suggested a synthesis between the functionalist and conflict perspectives. Pp. 231–234.

How do Elites Maintain Stratification?

How do nations maintain social stratification?

To maintain social stratification within a nation, the ruling class uses an ideology that justifies current arrangements. It also controls information, and, when all else fails, depends on brute force. The social networks of the rich and poor also perpetuate social inequality. Pp. 235–236.

Comparative Social Stratification

What are some key characteristics of stratification systems in other nations?

The most striking features of the British class system are differences in speech and in educational patterns. In Britain, accents nearly always betray class standing, and virtually all of the elite attend public schools (the equivalent of our private schools). In what is now the former Soviet Union, communism was supposed to abolish class distinctions. Instead, it merely ushered in a different set of classes. Pp. 236–239.

Global Stratification: The Three Worlds of Development

How are nations stratified?

The most common model divides nations into three groups— First, Second, and Third Worlds—according to how they rank in terms of wealth and amount of industrialization. The First World consists of the highly industrialized nations, the Second World of the industrializing nations, and the Third World of the nonindustrial nations. Pp. 239–243.

How the World's Nations Became Stratified

Why are some nations rich and others poor?

Four theories seek to account for global stratification: **imperialism** and **colonialism, world system theory, dependency theory,** and the **culture of poverty.** Pp. 244–246.

Maintaining Global Stratification

How is global stratification maintained?

There are two basic explanations for why nations remain stratified. **Neocolonialism** is the ongoing dominance of Third World nations by First World nations. The second explanation points to the influence of **multinational corporations,** which operate across national boundaries. Pp. 246–248.

Where can I read more on this topic?

Suggested readings for this chapter are listed on page 640.

Randy Stevens, Social Climbers, 1993

Social Class in Contemporary Society

*A*H, NEW ORLEANS, THAT FABLED CITY on the Gulf. *Images from its rich past floated through my head—pirates, wealth, intrigue. So did memories from a pleasant vacation—the exotic French Quarter with odors of Creole food and sounds of earthy jazz drifting through the air.*

The shelter for the homeless, however, forced me back to an unwelcome reality. The shelter was the same as those I had visited in the North—as well as the West and the East—only dirtier. The dirt, in fact, was the worst that I encountered during my research, and this was the only shelter to insist on payment to sleep in one of its filthy beds. The men looked the same—disheveled and haggard, wearing that unmistakable expression of despair—just like the homeless anywhere in the country. Except for the accent, you wouldn't know where you were. Poverty wears the same tired face, I realized. The accent may differ, but the look remains the same.

The next morning, just a block or so from the shelter, I felt indignation growing within me. I had grown used to the sights of abject poverty. I had come to expect what I saw in the shelters and on the streets. Those no longer held surprises. But this was startling.

Huge posters mounted on the glitzy transparent plastic shelter covering the bus stop, advertising wares available nearby, glared at me, obscenely out of joint with the reality of despair that I had just left. Almost life-sized pictures portrayed finely dressed men and women, proudly strutting elegant suits, dresses, jewelry, and furs. The prices were astounding—perhaps not to some, but certainly to the homeless I had just left.

A wave of disgust swept over me as I looked at the display. "Something is cockeyed in this society," I thought, my mind refusing to stop juxtaposing the images in the ads with those of the suffering I had witnessed in the shelter. I felt nauseated—and surprised at my urge to deface the sketches and photos of these people in their finery.

Occasionally the facts of social class in American life hit home with brute force. This was one of those moments. The disjunction that I felt in New Orleans was triggered by the ads, but it was not the first time that I had experienced this sensation. Whenever my research abruptly transported me from the world of the homeless to one of another social class, I felt unfamiliar feelings of disjointed unreality. Each social class has its own way of being, and because these fundamental orientations to the world contrast so sharply, the classes do not mix well.

What Is Social Class?

To gain an understanding of social class, the first question we need to examine is what social class is. The second question is how to measure social class.

Defining Social Class

"There are the poor and the rich—and then there are you and I, neither poor nor rich." That is just about as far as most Americans' consciousness of social class goes. Let's try to flesh this out.

Our task is made somewhat difficult because sociologists have no clear-cut, accepted definition of social class. As noted in Chapter 9, conflict sociologists (of the Marxist orientation) see only two social classes: those who own the means of production and those who do not. The problem with this view, say most sociologists, is that it lumps too many people together. Physicians and corporate executives with incomes of $250,000 a year are lumped together with hamburger flippers working at McDonald's for $10,000 a year.

Most sociologists agree with Weber that there are more components of social class than a person's relationship to the means of production. Consequently, most sociologists

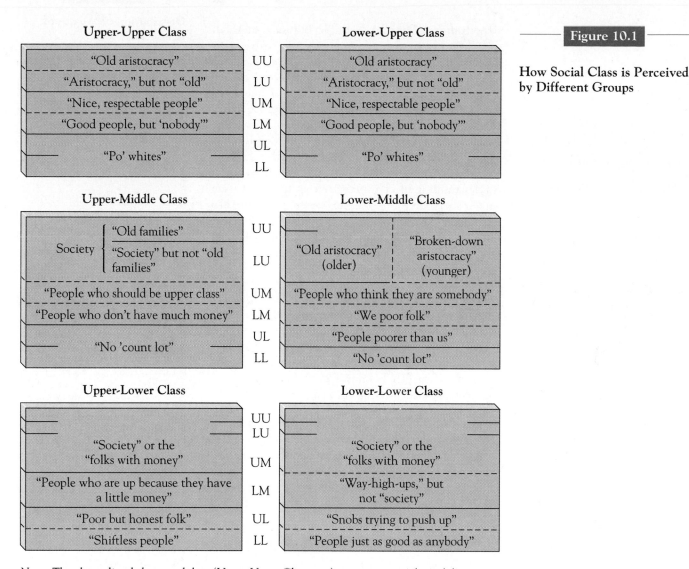

Figure 10.1

How Social Class is Perceived by Different Groups

Note: The classes listed above each box (Upper-Upper Class, etc.) represent a sociological division in common use at the time of this research, a six-fold division that is sometimes still used.

Source: Reprinted by permission from Davis, Gardner, and Gardner. Copyright 1941 by the University of Chicago.

use the components Weber identified and define a **social class** as a large group of people who rank closely to one another in wealth, power, and prestige. These three elements separate people into different lifestyles, give them different chances in life, and provide them with distinct ways of looking at the self and the world.

Measures of Social Class

We will examine wealth, power, and prestige in the next section, but first let's look at three different ways of measuring social class.

Subjective Method The **subjective method** is to ask people what their social class is. Although simple and direct, this approach is filled with problems. First, people may deny that they belong to any class, claiming, instead, that everyone is equal. Second, people may classify themselves according to their aspirations—where they would like to be—rather than where they actually are. Third, when asked to what class they belong, *nine out of ten Americans identify themselves as middle class* (Vanneman and Cannon 1987). This reply—more than likely prompted by the powerful U.S. ideology of equality—effectively removes the usefulness of the subjective method.

social class: according to Weber, a large group of people who rank closely to one another in wealth, power, and prestige; according to Marx, one of two groups: capitalists who own the means of production and workers who sell their labor

subjective method (of measuring social class): a system in which people are asked to define their own social class

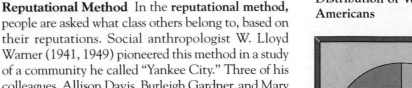

Figure 10.2

Reputational Method In the **reputational method,** people are asked what class others belong to, based on their reputations. Social anthropologist W. Lloyd Warner (1941, 1949) pioneered this method in a study of a community he called "Yankee City." Three of his colleagues, Allison Davis, Burleigh Gardner, and Mary Gardner (1941), used the reputational method to study Old City, a Southern town of 10,000 inhabitants. How the residents saw their town's social classes is depicted in Figure 10.1. This approach provides an understanding of how people in a community see major social divisions. Its use, however, is limited to small communities where people know one another. As you can see from Figure 10.1, this method produces several different snapshots of a class system, for people see life from the perspectives of their own class.

Objective Method In the **objective method,** researchers rank people according to objective criteria such as wealth, power, and prestige. Although there is always the possibility that researchers will err in their measurement, this method has the advantage of letting others know exactly what measurements were made, so that they can test them.

▽ **In Sum** Given the three choices of subjective, reputational, and objective methods to determine social class, sociologists use the objective method almost exclusively. The studies reported in this chapter are examples of the objective approach.

Distribution of Wealth of Americans

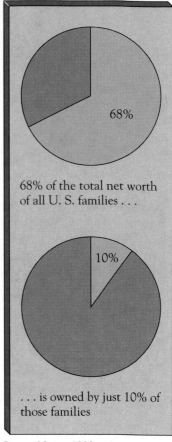

68% of the total net worth of all U. S. families . . .

. . . is owned by just 10% of those families

Source: Nassar 1992.

Most Americans identify themselves as middle class. How would you identify the individuals depicted by artist Duane Hanson in these lifesize polyvinyl figures? What status markers do you see?

▼▲ ## The Components of Social Class

Let us now turn to the three ways that most sociologists use to measure social class: wealth, power, and prestige.

Wealth

The primary dimension of social class is wealth. **Wealth** consists of property and income. *Property* comes in many forms, such as buildings, land, animals, machinery, cars, stocks, bonds, businesses, and bank accounts. *Income* is money received as wages, rents, interest, royalties, or the proceeds from a business.

reputational method (of measuring social class): a system in which people who are familiar with the reputations of others are asked to identify their social class

objective method (of measuring social class): a system in which people are ranked according to objective criteria such as wealth, power, and prestige

wealth: property and income

Distinction Between Wealth and Income Wealth and income are sometimes assumed to be the same, but they are not. Some people have much wealth and little income. For example, a farmer may own much land, but with the high cost of fertilizers and machinery, a little bad weather can cause the income to disappear. Others have much income and little wealth. For example, an executive with $150,000 annual income may actually be debt-ridden. Below the surface prosperity, he or she may be greatly overextended: unpaid bills for the children's exclusive private schools, the sports cars one payment away from being repossessed, and huge mortgage payments on the large home in the exclusive suburb. Typically, however, wealth and income go together.

Distribution of Wealth Who owns the wealth in the United States? One answer, of course, is "everyone." Although that statement has some merit, it overlooks how that wealth is divided among "everyone." How are the two forms of wealth—property and income—distributed among Americans?

Property Overall, Americans are worth a hefty sum, about $15 trillion (*Statistical Abstract* 1993: Table 754). Most of this wealth is in the form of real estate, corporate stocks, bonds, and business assets. As Figure 10.2 shows, this wealth is highly concentrated. The vast majority, 68 percent, is owned by only *10 percent* of the nation's families. How rich are they? This top 10 percent owns *50 percent* of the value of all real estate, *90 percent* of corporate stocks and business assets, and *95 percent* of bonds (Stafford et al. 1986). That leaves only 50 percent of the value of real estate, just 10 percent of stocks and businesses, and only 5 percent of all bonds for the other 90 percent of Americans.

And these figures are only part of the picture of how concentrated U.S. wealth is. The super-rich, *the wealthiest 0.5 percent of Americans, own 27 percent of the country's entire wealth*. In fact, about 325,000 families own 40 percent of all the corporate stock and business assets in the entire country (Stafford et al. 1986–1987; *Wall Street Journal*, July 28, 1986:38; *Statistical Abstract* 1990: Table 731).

Income How is income distributed in U.S. society? Economist Paul Samuelson (1989:644) put it this way: "If we made an income pyramid out of a child's blocks, with each layer portraying $500 of income, the peak would be far higher than Mount Everest, but most people would be within a few feet of the ground."

Actually, if each block were 1 1/2 inches tall, the typical American would be *less than 5 feet off the ground*, for the average per capita income in the United States is about $19,000 per year. See Figure 10.3. The typical family does better than this, for its average annual income, from all working members, runs about $36,000. Yet compared with the Mount Everest incomes of a few, these earnings of the typical U.S. family bring it to only 9 feet off the ground (*Statistical Abstract* 1993: Tables 705, 715).

The fact that some Americans reach past the top of Mount Everest while most live less than 5 feet up the slope presents a striking image of income inequality in the United States. Another picture emerges if we divide the U.S. population into five equal sections and rank them from the highest to lowest income. As Figure 10.4 shows, the top 20 percent of the population acquires 44 percent of all income in the United States, while the bottom 20 percent receives less than 5 percent of the nation's income.

The most striking feature of Figure 10.4 is the consistency of income inequality over the past 50 years. In spite of numerous antipoverty programs, *each fifth of the U.S. population receives the same proportion of the nation's income today as it did in 1945*. Some slight changes did occur over the years, such as a temporary decrease in the percentage going

Figure 10.3

Inequality of Income in the United States

Taller than   (Some Americans)
Mount Everest   29,028 feet

If a 1 1/2-inch child's block equals $500 of income, the average American is only about 4 feet off the ground, the average family just 9 feet, while the income of some families takes them past the top of Mount Everest.

(Average American)
4 feet   9 feet

In the United States, a mere 0.5 percent of the population owns over a quarter of the nation's wealth. Very few minorities are numbered among this 0.5 percent. Shown here is one who is, Bill Cosby, who through a successful career in entertainment has become the wealthiest African American in the United States.

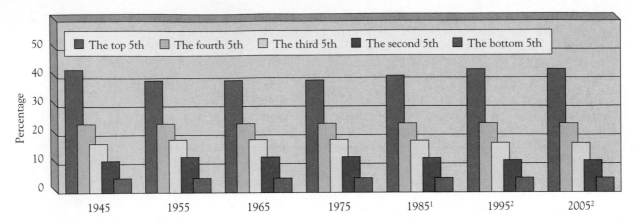

Note: The distribution of U.S. income—salaries, wages, and all other money received, except capital gains and government subsidies in the form of food stamps, health benefits, or subsidized housing. Because of rounding, totals for some years equal 101%.
[1]Because the 1985 data were not published, the average of the 1984 and 1986 figures are used.
[2]Author's estimate.

Sources: *Statistical Abstract* 1947, 1957, 1962, 1967, 1972, 1977, 1982, 1987, and 1992: Table 704.

Figure 10.4

The more things change the more they stay the same: the percentage of the nation's income received by each fifth of U.S. families since World War II.

Warren Buffett is the wealthiest man in the United States. His fortune of several billion dollars has been made through astute stock market investments.

to the top 20 percent of the population, but this division is now back to where it used to be. There also have been some slight variations not shown due to rounding. For example, in some years, the bottom fifth received as low as 4.5 percent, in other years as high as 5.4 percent. These changes were so slight, however, that during this entire period they did not change the poor's proportion by even 1 percent.

Apart from the very rich, whom we study later, the most affluent group in U.S. society consists of the chief executive officers (CEOs) of the nation's largest corporations. The *Wall Street Journal* ("The Boss's Pay," 1990) surveyed the 325 largest U.S. companies to determine what they paid their CEOs. The median annual compensation, including salaries and bonuses, came to $1 million a year. (Median means that half received more than this amount, and half less.) This figure does *not* include their stock options. Those who exercised options earned an *additional* $428,000. (Nor does this figure include their income from investments—interest, dividends, capital gains.)

Imagine how you could live with an income like this. And that is precisely the point. Beyond the numbers lies a reality that profoundly affects people's lives. The difference in wealth between those at the top and the bottom of the U.S. class structure means vast differences in lifestyles. For example, a colleague of mine who was teaching at an exclusive Eastern university piqued his students' curiosity when he lectured on poverty in Latin America. That weekend, one of his students borrowed his parents' corporate jet and pilot for the weekend, and in Monday's class he and his friends reported on their personal observations on the problem. Other Americans, in contrast, must choose whether to spend the little they have at the laundromat or on milk for their children. In short, divisions of wealth represent not "mere" numbers, but choices that make real differences in people's lives.

Power

Like many people, you may have said to yourself, "Sure, I can vote, but somehow the big decisions are always made in spite of what I might think. Certainly *I* don't make the decision to send soldiers to Vietnam, Grenada, Panama, Kuwait, Somalia, or Haiti. *I* don't decide to raise taxes. It isn't *I* who decide to change welfare benefits."

And then another part of you may say, "But *I* do it through my representatives in Congress." True enough—as far as it goes. The trouble is, it just doesn't go far enough. Such views of being a participant in the nation's "big" decisions are a playback of the ideology we learn at an early age—an ideology that Marx said is put forward by the elites to both legitimate and perpetuate their power (Marger 1987). Sociologists Daniel Hellinger and Dennis Judd (1991) call this the "democratic façade" that conceals where the real power in U.S. society lies.

Back in the 1950s, sociologist C. Wright Mills (1956) was criticized for insisting that **power**—the ability to carry out your will in spite of resistance—was concentrated in the hands of the few, for his analysis contradicted the dominant ideology of equality. As discussed in earlier chapters, Mills coined the term **power elite** to refer to those who make the big decisions in U.S. society. He and others have stressed how wealth and power coalesce in a group of like-minded individuals. They share ideologies and values, belong to the same private clubs, vacation at the same exclusive resorts, and even hire the same bands for their daughters' debutante balls. These shared backgrounds and vested interests all serve to reinforce their view of the world and of their special place in it (Domhoff 1974, 1978).

Those few wield extraordinary power in U.S. society. Although there are exceptions, *most* U.S. presidents have come from this group—millionaire white males from families with "old money" (Baltzell and Schneiderman 1988). As one social analyst pointed out, the 325,000 families that own 40 percent of all corporate stock and business assets in the entire country virtually control corporate America (Stafford et al. 1986–1987).

Sociologist William Domhoff (1990), continuing in the tradition of Mills, argues that the power of this group is so extensive that no major decision of the U.S. government is made without its approval. He has analyzed how this minority works behind the scenes with elected officials to set both the nation's foreign and domestic policy— from establishing Social Security rates to determining taxes and trade tariffs. Although Domhoff's conclusions are controversial—and alarming—they certainly follow logically from the principle that wealth brings power, and extreme wealth brings extreme power.

Prestige

Occupations and Prestige   Table 10.1 illustrates how people rank occupations according to **prestige** (respect or regard). From this table, you can see how your parents' occupations, those of your neighbors, and the one that you are striving for all stack up. Because we are moving toward a global society, this table also shows how the rankings given by Americans compare with those of the residents of sixty other countries.

Why do people give some jobs more prestige than others? If you look at Table 10.1, you will notice that the jobs at the top share four elements:

1 They pay more.
2 They require more education.
3 They entail more abstract thought.
4 They offer greater autonomy (freedom, or self-direction).

If we turn this around, we can see that people give *less* prestige to jobs that are low-paying, require less preparation or education, involve more physical labor, and are closely supervised. In short, the professions and white-collar jobs are ranked at the top of the list, blue-collar jobs at the bottom.

One of the more interesting aspects of these rankings is how consistent they are across countries and over time. For example, people in every country, rank college professors higher than nurses, nurses higher than social workers, and social workers higher

power: the ability to get your way in spite of the desires of other people

power elite: C. Wright Mills's term for the top people in U.S. corporations, military, and politics who make the nation's major decisions

prestige: respect or regard

Table 10.1

Occupational Prestige: How the United States Compares with 60 Countries

Occupation	United States	Average of 60 Countries	Occupation	United States	Average of 60 Countries
Supreme court judge	85	82	Professional athlete	51	48
College president	82	86	Undertaker	51	34
Physician	82	78	Social worker	50	56
Astronaut	80	80	Electrician	49	44
College professor	78	78	Secretary	46	53
Lawyer	75	73	Real estate agent	44	49
Dentist	74	70	Farmer	44	47
Architect	71	72	Carpenter	43	37
Psychologist	71	66	Plumber	41	34
Airline pilot	70	66	Mail carrier	40	33
Electrical engineer	69	65	Jazz musician	37	38
Civil engineer	68	70	Bricklayer	36	34
Biologist	68	69	Barber	36	30
Clergy	67	60	Truck driver	31	33
Sociologist	65	67	Factory worker	29	29
Accountant	65	55	Store sales clerk	27	34
Banker	63	67	Bartender	25	23
High school teacher	63	64	Lives on public aid	25	16
Author	63	62	Bill collector	24	27
Registered nurse	62	54	Cab driver	22	28
Pharmacist	61	64	Gas station attendant	22	25
Chiropractor	60	62	Janitor	22	21
Veterinarian	60	61	Waiter or waitress	20	23
Classical musician	59	56	Bellhop	15	14
Police officer	59	40	Garbage collector	13	13
Actor or actress	55	52	Street sweeper	11	13
Athletic coach	53	50	Shoe shiner	9	12
Journalist	52	55			

Sources: Treiman 1977, Appendices A and D; Nakao and Treas 1991.

---

than janitors. Similarly, the occupations that were ranked high back in the 1950s are still ranked high in the 1990s—and likely will be in future decades.

Table 10.1 also reveals a disadvantage of the objective method of studying social stratification; namely, how do you rank a two-career family? Should you use only the husband's occupation, only the wife's, or average their scores (which would really represent neither occupation)? In addition, how do part-time workers fit in? Note also that although occupations are the primary source of prestige for most people, they are not the only source. Some gain fame (prestige) through inventions, feats (mountain climbing, Olympic gold medals), or even doing good to others (Mother Teresa).

Displaying Prestige   For prestige to be of value, people must acknowledge it. In times past, some ruling elites even passed laws to emphasize their higher status. In ancient Rome, only the emperor and his family were allowed to wear purple, while in France only the nobility could wear lace. In England, no one could sit while the king was on his throne. Some kings and queens required that subjects depart by walking backward—so that they never "turned their back" on the "royal presence."

Although we have much greater equality today and no longer have consumption laws that specify who can and cannot wear particular clothing or colors, today's elite still manages to enforce its prestige. Western kings and queens expect curtsies and bows,

Successful novelists such as Toni Morrison are accorded a high level of occupational prestige. While many writers, even well-regarded ones, are not wealthy, the popularity of her books has made Morrison comparatively rich. Morrison, who now teaches at Princeton University, is shown as she receives the Nobel Prize in literature from Swedish King Carl Gustaf XVI. Not incidentally, this prize carries with it a cash award of $790,000.

while their Eastern counterparts expect their subjects to touch their faces to the ground. The U.S. president enters a room only after others are present (to show that *he* isn't the one waiting for *them*). If seated, the others rise when the president appears and remain standing until he is seated, or if he going to speak without sitting first, until he signals (gives permission) for them to sit. Military officers surround themselves with elaborate rules about who must salute whom, while uniformed officers in the courtroom make certain that everyone stands when judges enter.

Most people are highly conscious of prestige, a fact that advertisers know well and exploit relentlessly. Consequently, designers can charge more for a particular item of clothing not because it is of better quality but simply because it displays a particular label. Similarly, people buy cars not only for transportation, but also for their prestige. (How does a BMW compare with a Geo—not for power, but for prestige?) People gladly spend many thousands of dollars more for a home with a "good address," that is, one in a prestigious neighborhood. For many, prestige is a primary factor in deciding which college to attend. Everyone knows how the prestige of a generic sheepskin from Regional State College compares with a degree from Harvard, Princeton, Yale, or Stanford.

Interestingly, status symbols vary with social class. Clearly, only the wealthy can afford certain items, such as yachts. But beyond affordability lies a class-based preference in status symbols. For example, Yuppies (young upwardly mobile professionals) are quick to flaunt labels and other material symbols to show that they have "arrived," while the rich, more secure in their status, often downplay such images. The wealthy see designer labels of the more "common" classes as cheap and showy. They, of course, flaunt their own status symbols, such as $20,000 Rolex watches.

Status Inconsistency

Ordinarily a person ranks at the same point on all three dimensions of social class—wealth, power, and prestige. The homeless men in the vignette are an example—as were John F. Kennedy and Mary Petrovitch in the opening vignette of Chapter 9. Sometimes the match is not there, however, and someone has a mixture of high and low ranks, a condition called **status inconsistency.** This leads to some interesting situations.

status inconsistency: a condition in which a person ranks high on some dimensions of social class and low on others

People use a wide variety of ways to display their relative prestige and to set themselves off from other members of their society. How, then, are the debutante balls of the rich similar to wearing name-brand clothing?

Sociologist Gerhard Lenski (1954, 1966) pointed out that each of us tries to maximize our **status,** our social ranking. Thus individuals who rank high on one dimension of social class but lower on others will expect people to judge them on the basis of their highest status. Others, however, concerned about maximizing their own position, may respond to them according to their lowest status.

A classic study of status inconsistency was done by sociologist Ray Gold (1952). He found that after apartment-house janitors unionized, they made more money than some of the people whose garbage they carried out. Tenants became especially upset when they saw their janitors driving more expensive cars than they did. Some attempted to "put the janitor in his place" by making "snotty" remarks to him. Instead of addressing him by name, others would say, "Janitor." For their part, the janitors took secret pride in knowing "dirty" secrets about the tenants, gleaned from their garbage.

Individuals with status inconsistency, then, are likely to confront one frustrating situation after another. They claim the higher status, but are handed the lower. The sociological significance of this condition, said Lenski, is that such people are likely to be more politically radical. An example is college professors. Their prestige is very high, as we saw in Table 10.1, but their incomes are relatively low. Hardly anyone in society is more educated, and yet college professors don't even come close to the top of the income pyramid. In line with Lenski's prediction, the politics of most college professors are, indeed, left of center. This hypothesis may also hold true *among* academic departments; that is, the higher a department's pay, the less radical are its politics. Teachers in departments of business and medicine, for example, are among the most highly paid in the university—and they are also the most politically conservative. This hypothesis is also likely to hold true *within* departments, for in general, regardless of the department, higher-paid members tend to be more conservative, lower-paid members more liberal. Although age is a highly significant variable (age generally brings more conservative views of life, and older teachers generally earn more than younger ones), status inconsistency may be part of the explanation. Only testing, of course, can determine the validity of these observations.

status: social ranking

Sociological Models of Social Class

The question of how many social classes there are is a matter of debate. Sociologists have proposed various models, but no model has gained universal support. There are two main models: one that builds on Marx, the other on Weber.

Updating Marx: Wright's Model

As discussed in Chapters 1 and 9, Marx argued that there are just two classes—capitalists and workers—with membership based solely on a person's relationship to the means of production. Sociologist Erik Wright (1979, 1985) was dissatisfied with Marx's concept of social classes because he realized that not everyone falls neatly into these two categories. He concluded that Marx's category of "workers" is much too broad. Top executives, managers, and supervisors, for example, act like capitalists yet they are technically workers because they do not own the means of production.

Wright also concluded that Marx's category of "capitalist" is too broad. Take, for example, someone who owns a factory that employs one thousand workers. The owner's decisions, good or bad, directly affect one thousand families. Now consider a man I know in Godfrey, Illinois. Working on cars out of his own back yard, he gained a following, quit his regular job, and in a few years put up a building with five bays and an office. This mechanic is now a capitalist, for he employs five or six other mechanics and owns the tools and building (the "means of production"). But he has little in common with a factory owner who controls the lives of one thousand workers. Not only are his activities different, but so are his lifestyle and consciousness.

Wright resolved this problem by regarding some people as simultaneously members of more than one class, having what he called **contradictory class locations.** By this Wright meant that the person's position in the class structure generates contradictory interests. For example, the automobile mechanic–turned–businessowner may want his mechanics to have higher wages, since he has directly experienced their working conditions for most of his own working life. At the same time, his own interests—remaining profitable and competitive with other repair shops—cause him to resist pressures to raise wages.

Taking contradictory class locations into account, Wright then modified Marx's analysis. As summarized in Table 10.2, Wright identified four classes: (1) *capitalists* (or owners), who own businesses and employ many workers; (2) *petty bourgeoisie,* who own small businesses; (3) *managers,* who sell their own labor but also exercise authority over other employees; and (4) *workers,* who simply sell their labor to others. As you can see, this model allows finer divisions than the one Marx originally proposed, yet it maintains the primary distinction between employer and worker.

Updating Weber: Gilbert's and Kahl's Model

Sociologists Dennis Gilbert and Joseph Kahl (1993) developed a six-class model to portray the class structure of the United States and other capitalist countries. Think of their model, illustrated in Figure 10.5, as a ladder. Our discussion will start with the highest rung and move downward. In line with Weber, on each lower rung you find less wealth, less power, and less prestige. Note that in this model education is also a primary criterion of class.

The Capitalist Class   The super-rich who occupy the top rung of the class ladder consists of only about 1 percent of the population. This 1 percent is so wealthy that *its members are worth more than the entire bottom 90 percent of the nation* (Nasar 1992a). Their power is so great that their decisions open or close jobs for millions of people. Through their ownership of newspapers and magazines, radio stations and television companies, together with their generous contributions to political parties, this elite class even helps to shape the consciousness of the nation. Its members perpetuate themselves by passing on to their children their assets and influential social networks.

Table 10.2

Social Class and the Means of Production

Marx's Class Model (based on the means of production)

1. Capitalists (bourgeoisie)
2. Workers (proletariat)

Wright's Modification of Marx's Class Model (to account for contradictory class locations)

1. Capitalists
2. Petty bourgeoisie
3. Managers
4. Workers

---

contradictory class location: Erik Wright's term for a position in the class structure that generates contradictory interests

Social Class	Education	Occupation	Income	Percentage of Population
Capitalist	Prestige university	Investors and heirs, a few executives	$750,000+	1%
Upper-Middle	College or university, often with postgraduate study	Professionals and upper managers	$75,000+	14%
Lower-Middle	At least high school; perhaps some college or apprenticeship	Semiprofessionals and lower managers, craftspeople, foremen	About $40,000	30%
Working Class	High school	Factory workers, clerical workers, low-paid craftspeople, retail sales	About $25,000	30%
Working Poor	Some high school	Laborers, service workers, low-paid salespeople	Less than $20,000	22%
Underclass	Some high school	Unemployed and part-time, on welfare	Less than $13,000	3%

Source: Based on Gilbert and Kahl 1993.

Figure 10.5

The U.S. Social Class Ladder

Old Money The capitalist class can be divided into "old" and "new" money (Aldrich 1988). People whose wealth has been in the family longer have greater prestige. Many people entering the capitalist class have found it necessary to cut moral corners, at least here and there. This "taint" to the money disappears with time, however, and the later generations of Kennedys, Rockefellers, Vanderbilts, Mellons, DuPonts, Chryslers, Fords, Morgans, Nashes, and so on are considered to have "clean" money simply by virtue of the passage of time. Able to be philanthropic as well as rich, they establish foundations and support charitable causes. Subsequent generations attend prestigious prep schools and universities, and male heirs are likely to enter law. These old-money capitalists wield vast power as they use extensive political connections to protect their huge economic empires (Domhoff 1990, 1995; Persell et al. 1992).

New Money Those at the lower end of the capitalist class also possess vast sums of money and power, but it is new, and therefore suspect. Although these people may have made fortunes in business, the stock market, inventions, entertainment, or even sports, they have not gone to the right schools and lack the influential social networks that old money provides. Consequently, those with old money cannot depend on this newer group for adequate in-group loyalty. Their children, however, will ascend into the upper part of the capitalist class if they go to the right schools and marry old money.

The Upper Middle Class   Of all the classes, the upper middle is the one most shaped by education. Almost all members of this class have at least a bachelor's degree, and many have postgraduate degrees in business, management, law, or medicine. These people manage the corporations owned by the capitalist class or else operate their own business or profession. As Gilbert and Kahl (1982) say, these positions

> may not grant prestige equivalent to a title of nobility in the Germany of Max Weber, but they certainly represent the sign of having "made it" in contemporary America. . . . Their income is sufficient to purchase houses and cars and travel that become public symbols for all to see and for advertisers to portray with words and pictures that connote success, glamour, and high style.

Consequently, parents and teachers push children to prepare themselves for upper middle class jobs. About 14 percent of the population belong to this class.

The Lower Middle Class   About 30 percent of the population belong to the lower middle class. Members of this class follow orders on the job given by those who have upper-middle-class credentials. Their technical and lower-level management positions bring them a good living—albeit one constantly threatened by rising taxes and inflation—and they enjoy a generally comfortable, mainstream lifestyle. They usually feel secure in their positions and anticipate being able to move up the social class ladder.

The distinctions between the lower middle class and the working class on the next lower rung are more blurred than those between other classes. As a result, these two classes run into one another. The lower-middle class works at jobs that have slightly more prestige, however, and their incomes are generally higher.

The Working Class   This class consists of relatively unskilled blue-collar and white-collar workers who occupy highly routinized, closely supervised, manual and clerical jobs. Most of these workers have a high school education, their incomes are lower than those of the lower-middle class, and little prestige is attached to what they do. Their work is more insecure, and they are subject to layoffs during recessions. They feel vulnerable, but anticipate that layoffs will be temporary and that they will be able to support their families in a "simple but decent" manner. With only a high school diploma, the average member of the working class has little hope of climbing farther up the class ladder. Consequently, most concentrate on getting ahead by achieving seniority on the job rather than by changing their type of work. About 30 percent of the population belong to this class.

The Working Poor   Members of this class, about 22 percent of the population, work at unskilled, low-paying, temporary and seasonal jobs, such as share-cropping, migrant farm work, house cleaning, and day labor. Although many of the younger members of this class have high school diplomas, they are likely to have received them simply for putting in time and may be functionally illiterate, finding it difficult to read even the want ads. The working poor are not likely to vote (Gilbert and Kahl 1993), for they feel that no matter what party is elected to political office it simply means "business as usual."

With little education, low and undependable income, and low-prestige work, the working poor live from paycheck to paycheck—when there is a paycheck, that is. Constantly in debt, many depend on food stamps to supplement their meager incomes. In old age they rely entirely on Social Security, since their jobs do not provide retirement

Migrant workers, who perfrom seasonal work for low wages, are part of the group classified as the working poor. How would conflict theorists analyze migrant workers? How do you think people such as this avocado picker in California support themselves between crops?

The homeless are located at the lower end of the U.S. social class ladder. One might even say that their status is so low that the homeless are a step below its lowest rung. Why do you think the homeless exist in such a wealthy society?

underclass: a small group of people for whom poverty persists year after year and across generations

benefits. Because they cannot save money or depend on steady work, members of this class run the risk of falling onto the lowest rung. High stress is part of their daily lives, and one of their greatest fears is ending up "on the streets."

The Underclass   On the lowest rung, and with next to no chance of climbing anywhere, is the **underclass** (Myrdal 1962; Wilson 1987; Bagguley and Mann 1992). Concentrated in the inner city, this group has little or no connection with the job market. Those who are employed, and some are, do menial, low-paying, temporary work. Welfare is their main support, and most members of other classes consider these people the ne'er-do-wells of society. Although life is the toughest in this class, it is not hopeless, and research shows that their children's chances of getting out of poverty are fifty-fifty (Gilbert and Kahl 1982:353). About 3 percent of the population fall into this class.

Social Class in the Automobile Industry

The example of the automobile industry aptly illustrates this social class ladder. The Fords, for example, own and control a manufacturing and financial empire whose net worth is truly staggering. Their power matches their wealth, for through their multinational corporation their decisions affect plants, production, and employment in many countries. The family's vast accumulation of money, not unlike its accrued power, is now several generations old. Consequently, Ford children go to the "right" schools, know how to spend money in the "right" way, and can be trusted to make family and class interests paramount in life. They are without question at the top level of the *capitalist* class.

Next in line come top Ford executives. Although they may have an income of several hundred thousand dollars a year (and some, with stock options and bonuses, earn well over $1 million annually), most are new to wealth and power. Consequently, they would be classified at the lower end of the capitalist class.

A husband and wife who own a Ford agency are members of the *upper middle* class. Their income clearly sets them apart from the majority of Americans, and their reputation in the community is enviable. More than likely they also exert greater than average influence in their community, but their capacity to wield power is limited.

A Ford salesperson, as well as people who work in the dealership office, belongs to the *lower middle* class. Although there are some exceptional salespeople, perhaps a few of whom make a lot of money selling prestigious, expensive cars to the capitalist class, salespeople at a run-of-the-mill local Ford agency are lower middle class. Compared with the owners of the agency, their income is less, their education is also likely to be less, and their work brings them less prestige.

A mechanic who repairs customers' cars is a member of the *working* class, although one who has risen in rank and now supervises the repair shop is lower-middle class.

Janitors who are hired only during the busy season and then laid off, as well as those who "detail" used cars (making them appear newer by polishing the car, painting the tires, spraying "new car scent" into the interior, and so on) belong to the *working poor*. Their income and education are low, and the prestige accorded their work minimal.

Ordinarily, the *underclass* is not represented at all in the automobile industry. It is conceivable, however, that the agency might hire a member of the underclass, for the day or job only, to rake the grass or to clean up the used-car lot. In general, however, personnel at the agency do not trust members of the underclass and do not want to associate with them. They prefer to hire someone from the working poor for such jobs.

Below the Ladder: The Homeless

The homeless men described in the opening vignette of this chapter, and the women and children like them, are so far down the class structure that their position must be considered even lower than the underclass. Technically, the homeless are members of the underclass, but their poverty is so severe and their condition in life so despairing that we can think of them as occupying an unofficial rung below the underclass.

These are the people whom most Americans wish would just go away. Their presence on our city streets bothers passersby from the more privileged social classes—which includes just about everyone. "What are those obnoxious, foul-smelling people doing here, cluttering up my city?" appears to be a common response. Some people respond with sympathy and a desire to do something. But what? Almost all just shrug their shoulders and look the other way, despairing of a solution and somewhat intimidated by the presence of the homeless.

The homeless are the "fallout" of industrialization, especially the postindustrial developments reviewed in Chapter 6. In another era, society would offer them work. Most would dig ditches, shovel coal, and run the factory looms, while some would explore and settle the West. Others would follow the lure of gold to California, Alaska, and Australia. Today, however, since industrialized societies have no unsettled frontiers and little need of unskilled labor, these people are left to wander aimlessly about the city streets.

Consequences of Social Class

Each social class can be thought of as a broad subculture with distinct approaches to life. Social class has such profound influences on us that it even affects our chances of living and dying, our choice of mate, and how we rear our children. Let's examine some of the consequences of social class.

Life Chances

The primary significance of social class is that it determines **life chances,** the probabilities concerning the fate we can expect in life. Obviously not everyone has the same chances in life, and in industrialized societies the single most significant factor in determining life chances is money. The more money you have, the more control you have over your

> **life chances:** the probabilities concerning the fate an individual may expect in life

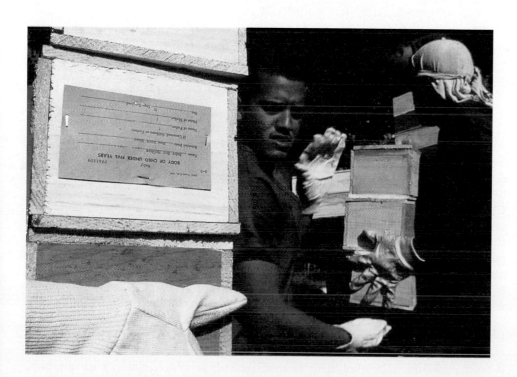

A crucial aspect of social class is that it directly affects our chances of living or dying. Children of the poor are much less likely to survive childbirth and childhood than are children of the middle classes. In a scene reminiscent of the Third World, or of some distant past, workers carry stacks of roughly-made pine coffins containing babies who will be buried in a mass grave in a Potter's Field in New York City.

life, and the more likely you are to find life pleasant. Beyond this obvious point, however, lies a connection between social class and life chances that is less evident—social class even affects our chances of living and dying. The principle is simple: the lower a person's class, the more likely that individual is to die before the expected age. This principle holds true at all ages. Infants born to the poor are more likely to die during their first year of life than are infants born into other classes. In old age—whether 70 or 90—the poor are more likely to die of illness and disease. During both childhood and adulthood, the poor are also more likely to be killed by accidents, fires, and homicide.

Physical and Mental Health

Part of the explanation for these different death rates lies in unequal access to medical care and nutrition. Medical care is expensive, and even with state-funded plans for the poor, the higher classes receive better medical treatment. Poorer people also suffer from inferior nutrition. They are considerably less educated concerning nutrition, and their meals tend to be heavy in fats and sugars, neither of which are healthy (Freedman 1990).

Social class also affects mental health. From the 1930s until now, sociologists have found that the mental health of the lower classes is worse than that of the higher classes (Faris and Dunham 1939; Srole et al. 1978; Brown and Gary 1988; Lundberg 1991). This difference reflects the greater stresses that those in the lower classes experience, such as unpaid bills, unemployment, dirty and dangerous work, the threat of eviction, unhappy marriages, and broken homes. People higher up the social class ladder also experience stress in daily life, of course, but their stress is generally less and their coping resources greater. Not only can they afford vacations, psychiatrists, and counselors, but *their class position gives them greater control over their lives, a key to good mental health.*

Family Life

Social class plays an especially significant role in family life. Of its many consequences in this vital area, let's look at choice of mate, divorce, and child rearing.

Choice of Mate   The capitalist class places very strong emphasis on family tradition and continuity. They stress the family's ancestors, history, and even a sense of purpose or destiny in life (Baltzell 1979; Aldrich 1989). Children of this class learn that their choice of husband or wife affects not just themselves but the whole family unit, that their mate will have an impact on the "family line." Consequently, their field of "eligibles" is much narrower than it is for the children of any other social class. In effect, parents in this class play a greater role in their children's mate selection.

Divorce   The more difficult life of the lower social classes, especially the many tensions and frustrations that come from inadequate incomes, leads to more marital friction and a greater likelihood of both spouse and alcohol abuse. Consequently, the marriages of the poor are more likely to fail and their children to grow up in broken homes.

Child Rearing   As discussed on page 443, sociologist Melvin Kohn (1977) found significant class differences in child rearing. Lower-class parents are more concerned that their children conform to conventional norms and obey authority figures. Middle-class parents, in contrast, encourage their children to be more creative and independent, and tolerate a wider range of behaviors (except in speech, where they are less tolerant of bad grammar and curse words).

Kohn concluded that lower and middle-class parents rear their children differently primarily because their occupations give them different visions of their children's futures. Lower-class parents are closely supervised in their jobs, and they anticipate that their children will work at similar jobs. Consequently, they try to teach their children to defer to authority. In contrast, parents from the more privileged classes work at jobs in which they enjoy greater creativity and self-expression. Anticipating similar work for their children, they encourage them to have greater freedom. Out of these contrasting orientations also arise different ways of enforcing discipline; lower-class parents are more likely to use the stick, while the middle classes rely more on verbal persuasion.

Politics

As has been stressed throughout this text, symbolic interactionists emphasize that people see events from their own corner in life. Political views are no exception to this principle. Americans tend to see the major political parties as promoting different class interests. Consequently, the working class, which feels much more strongly than the classes above it that government should intervene in the economy to make citizens financially secure, is more likely to vote Democrat, those in the higher classes Republican. Although the working class is more liberal on *economic* issues (those that favor government spending), this class is more conservative on *social* issues (such as opposing abortion and the Equal Rights Amendment). Finally, people toward the bottom of the class structure are less likely to become politically involved, to vote and to campaign for candidates (Erikson et al. 1980; Gilbert and Kahl 1993).

Religion

One area of social life that we might think would be unaffected by social class is religion. ("People are religious, or they are not. People are believers, or they are not.") This is not the case, however, for social class affects just about every aspect of religious orientation. First, members of the upper middle class are more likely to attend church than are the lower classes. In fact, this pattern holds for all types of voluntary organizations—the lower classes are always less likely to join. Second, as we shall discuss in Chapter 18, the classes tend to cluster in different denominations. Episcopalians, for example, are much more likely to recruit from the middle and upper classes, while Baptists draw heavily from the lower classes. Patterns of worship also follow class lines: those that attract the lower classes have more spontaneous worship services and louder music, while those that draw mostly from the middle and upper classes are more "subdued."

Education

As was shown in Figure 10.5, education increases as one goes up the social class ladder. It is not just the amount of education that changes, however, but also the type of education. As indicated by the account of John F. Kennedy in the opening vignette of the previous chapter, children of the capitalist class bypass public schools entirely in favor of exclusive private schools. Here their children are trained to take a commanding role in society. As their parents see matters, even preschools set children on a course in life, and parents in the more privileged classes make certain that their youngsters go to the "right" preschool. Aspiring members of the upper middle class, aware of the significance of the preschools for the elite, attempt to gain their children's entry by eliciting letters of recommendation for their 2-and 3-year-olds. Such differences in parental expectations and resources are major reasons that children from the more privileged classes do better in school and are more likely to enter and to graduate from college.

Crime and the Criminal Justice System

If justice is supposed to be blind, it certainly is not when it comes to one's chances of being arrested (Hurst 1992). In Chapter 8 (pages 206–208) we discussed how the upper and lower social classes have different styles of crime. There we also noted that the white-collar crimes of the more privileged classes are likely to be dealt with outside the criminal justice system, while the street crimes of the lower classes are dealt with by the police. One consequence of this double standard is that members of the lower classes are far more likely to be on probation, on parole, or in jail. In addition, since people tend to commit crimes in or near their own neighborhoods, the lower classes are more likely to be robbed, burglarized, or murdered.

Social Mobility

No aspect of life, then—from marriage to politics—goes untouched by social class. Because life is so much more satisfying in the more privileged classes, people strive for upward social mobility. What affects people's chances of climbing the class ladder? Keep this question in mind as we examine the three types of social mobility.

Intergenerational, Structural, and Exchange Mobility

There are three basic types of social mobility: intergenerational, structural, and exchange mobility. **Intergenerational mobility** is the change that family members make in their social class from one generation to the next. Children are initially assigned the social class of their parents, but they can pass their parents. For example, if the child of a salesperson who works for a new car dealer goes to college and eventually becomes the manager of the dealership, that person has experienced **upward social mobility.** Conversely, if a child of the dealer's owners becomes an alcoholic, fails to get through college, and takes a lower-status job, he or she experiences **downward social mobility.**

The second type is **structural mobility,** changes in society that affect the social class of huge numbers of people. In the preceding examples, the individual's change in social class was due to his or her own behavior—hard work, sacrifice, and ambition on the one hand, versus indolence and alcohol abuse on the other. Although some social mobility is due to such individual factors, sociologists consider structural mobility to be the crucial factor. To understand this term, think of how the invention of computers changed the positions available to people. New types of jobs opened up overnight. Corporations offered workshops and other on-site practical courses for their employees, and colleges offered crash night courses. As a result, huge numbers of people switched from blue-collar to white-collar work. Although in each case individual effort certainly was involved, the underlying cause was a change in the *structure* of society. Similarly, in a large-scale depression, millions of people are forced into downward mobility. In this instance, too, their changed status is due much less to individual behavior than to structural changes in the society.

The third type of mobility is **exchange mobility.** This term refers to large numbers of people moving up and down the social class ladder, where on balance, the relative proportions of the various classes remain about the same. Suppose that over a certain period of time a million or so working-class people are trained in computers, and their new jobs move them up the social class ladder. Suppose also that during this same period about a million skilled workers have to take lower-status jobs because of a vast surge in imports. In effect, there will be an exchange among large groups in the society. The net result more or less balances out, and the class system remains basically untouched.

Social Mobility in the United States

How much mobility is there on the U.S. social class ladder? Until recently, sociologists focused on men, because the large numbers of women now in the work force are a relatively new phenomenon. They found intergenerational mobility to be common. Com-

---

intergenerational mobility: the change that family members make in social class from one generation to the next

upward social mobility: movement up the social class ladder

downward social mobility: movement down the social class ladder

structural mobility: movement up or down the social class ladder that is attributable to changes in the structure of society, not to individual efforts

exchange mobility: about the same numbers of people moving up and down the social class ladder, such that, on balance, the social class system shows little change

pared with their fathers, about one-half of all men moved up, about one-third stayed at the same level, and only about one-sixth moved down (Blau and Duncan 1967; Featherman and Hauser 1978; Featherman 1979).

During the past generation, professional, managerial, and administrative positions increased from just 15 percent to 30 percent of the U.S. labor force. Eliminating millions of blue-collar jobs and opening even more white-collar positions, this extensive structural change paved the way for many women to move up the class ladder. Sociologists Elizabeth Higginbotham and Lynn Weber (1992) studied 200 women professionals, managers, and administrators in Memphis who came from working-class backgrounds. They found that the parents of these women played a significant role in their upward mobility. Almost without exception, their parents had encouraged them while they were still little girls to work toward a better life. The parents stressed that the way to get ahead was to postpone marriage and get an education. This study confirms findings of many sociologists, that the family is of utmost importance in the socialization process and that the primary entry to the upper middle class is a college education. At the same time, note that if there had not been a *structural* change in society that the millions of new positions to which these people moved would not have existed.

As discussed earlier, structural mobility can also work in the opposite direction—precisely what has struck fear in the hearts of many U.S. workers today. If the United States does not keep pace with global change and remain highly competitive by producing low-cost, quality goods, its economic position will decline. The result will be shrinking opportunities—with U.S. workers facing fewer good jobs and lower incomes. Such a decline would result in the next generation having slightly *less* status than their parents. Perhaps, indeed, this decline has already begun. The following Thinking Critically section illustrates some of the structural obstacles that U.S. workers face.

▼▲▼▲▼▲▼▲▼▲▼▲▼▲▼▲▼▲▼▲▼▲▼▲▼▲▼▲▼▲

Thinking Critically About Social Controversy

Upward Mobility for U.S. Workers—A Vanishing Dream?

▼ ROBERT MIDDLECOFF, A 35-YEAR-OLD Ohioan, spent most of the 1980s rebuilding furnaces at a metals foundry near Cleveland. When the plant closed, Middlecoff's $26,000-a-year job vanished with it. Today, while retraining for a career in computers, he and his wife live on her income of $15,400 and struggle to make their monthly mortgage payment of $611. Middlecoff worries about his chances of getting a new job in computers. He knows that even these jobs are scarce and that many employers look for college graduates to fill the positions.

Twenty-two years ago, Letitia Brown, daughter of a migrant worker, easily found work at an auto assembly plant in Flint, Michigan. Things are different for her son, Alphonse, who for the past ten years has moved from one low-paying job to the next. Now, at 28, he has given up hope of joining the assembly line. Says his mother, "In Buick City, there's nobody left with less than fourteen years' seniority. We're on our way back to being migrants."

Since 1979, out of twenty-one million manufacturing jobs, almost three million have disappeared—taking with them the dreams of upward mobility for millions of U.S. workers like the Middlecoffs and the Browns.

This large-scale job displacement presents daunting challenges to U.S. society. For generations, Americans considered a brighter future their birthright, and for most of U.S. history the nation's economy delivered. But with foreign competition nipping at the heels of U.S. industry, the richest rewards are reserved for the highly educated or for those who work at jobs sheltered from foreign competition. The result is that millions of workers in the lower half of the U.S. labor force are hitting a brick wall. They are doing worse than their parents did, and falling further behind.

How will this structural change in the economy affect you? You should note two points. First, as mentioned earlier, the key to social mobility is education, one of the major components of social class. The second point is highly related—the hardest hit during this economic transition are those who did not attend college. Figure 10.6 shows that a college degree translates directly into

Capitalists move their capital to areas where they anticipate the highest return, even though workers may be harmed in the process. The movement of capital from the United States to lower-wage Mexico is an example.

higher income. On average, college graduates obtain more secure jobs. They also average 47 percent more income than college dropouts and 78 percent more than high school graduates. What is also starkly apparent in Figure 10.6 is that education pays off much less for females than it does for males. In the next chapter, we shall take up this problem of gender discrimination, but for now let us note that—whether male or female—the more education you attain, the more you are likely to earn. Although life does not come with guarantees, education does provide excellent protection for surviving the structural change in which the United States is now immersed.

Sources: Based on Davis 1982; Olsen 1990; Dentzler 1991; Nussbaum et al. 1992; Thomas 1993.

Costs of Social Mobility

People who are socially mobile find unexpected costs. Sociologists Richard Sennett and Jonathan Cobb (1988) studied working-class men and women in Boston who had made financial sacrifices so that their children could get ahead. The men worked long hours, were

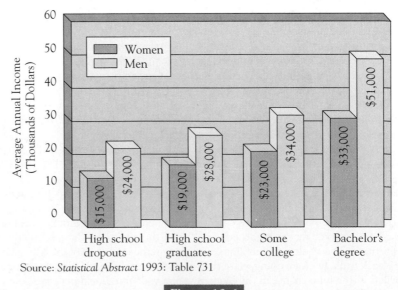

Source: *Statistical Abstract* 1993: Table 731

Figure 10-6

Education, Gender, and Income

seldom home, and, along with their wives, did without things to permit their children to finish high school and go on to college. The parents expected their children to appreciate what they were doing for them, but to their dismay they found estrangement, lack of communication, and even bitterness. Estrangement resulted because the father was seldom home and the children grew distant from him; lack of communication because the children's world of education was so remote from the parents' world that they no longer had much in common; and bitterness because, instead of receiving appreciation for their deep sacrifice, the parents felt betrayal by this estrangement and lack of communication.

In short, social class separates people into worlds so distinct that communication and mutual understanding become difficult. To change one's social class, then, is to risk losing one's roots.

Where Is Horatio Alger? The Social Functions of a Myth

Around the turn of the century, Horatio Alger was one of the most talked-about fictional heroes. The rags-to-riches exploits of this national character, and his startling successes in overcoming severe odds, motivated thousands of boys of that period. Although he has disappeared from U.S. literature, Horatio Alger remains alive and well in the psyche of Americans. From abundant, real-life examples of people from humble origins who climbed far up the social class ladder, Americans know that anyone can get ahead by *really* trying. In fact, they believe that most Americans, including minorities and the working poor, have an average or better than average chance of getting ahead—obviously a statistical impossibility (Kluegel and Smith 1986).

The accuracy of Horatio Alger is less important than the belief itself in *limitless possibilities for everyone*. Functionalists would stress that this belief is functional for society. On the one hand, it encourages people to compete for higher positions, or, as the song says, "to reach for the highest star." On the other hand, it places blame for failure squarely on the individual. If you don't make it—in the face of extensive opportunities to get ahead—the fault must be your own. The Horatio Alger belief helps to stabilize society, then, for since the fault is viewed as the individual's, not society's, current social arrangements are satisfactory. This reduces pressures to change the system.

Poverty ▼

A lot of Americans find the "limitless possibilities" of the American dream rather elusive. As illustrated in Figure 10.5, the working poor and underclass together form about 25 percent of the population of the United States. This percentage translates into a huge number, over sixty million people. Let's see who these people are.

Drawing the Line: What Is Poverty?

To define poverty, the U.S. government assumes that poor families spend one-third of their income on food and then multiplies a low-cost food budget by 3 (Banerjee 1994). Those whose incomes are lower than this amount are classified as below the **poverty line**. As sociologist Michael Katz observed (1989), this definition is unrealistic. It ignores changing standards of food consumption, does not allow for snacks, and assumes a careful shopper who cooks all meals at home and never has guests. Nevertheless, this is how the government draws the line that separates the poor from the nonpoor.

It is part of the magical sleight-of-hand of modern bureaucracy that a modification in this official measure of poverty instantly adds—or subtracts—millions of people from this category (Katz 1989; Ruggles 1990). Although the official definition of poverty does not make anyone poor, the way in which poverty is defined does have serious practical consequences.

poverty line: the official measure of poverty; calculated to include those whose incomes are less than three times a low-cost food budget

In recent years, poverty among the U.S. elderly has decreased, while the number of children living in poverty has risen dramatically. Is the one related to the other? Or is this a false alternative?

The government uses this definition to make choices about who will receive help and who will not. Based on this official definition of poverty, let us see who in the United States is poor.

Who Are the Poor?

Race/Ethnicity   Although two out of three poor people are white, in relationship to their numbers in the population most racial/ethnic minorities are more likely to be poor. As Figure 10.7 shows, only 11 percent of whites are poor, but 29 percent of Latinos and 33 percent of African Americans live in poverty.

Old Age   As Figure 10.7 also shows, old age has little effect on the likelihood that whites and African Americans will be poor, for their percentage of elderly poor is practically the same as their overall percentage. A few years ago this was not the case, but

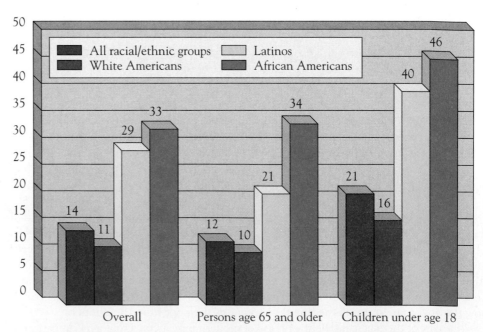

Figure 10-7

Poverty in the United States, by Age and Race/Ethnicity

Legend: All racial/ethnic groups — White Americans — Latinos — African Americans

Note: The poverty line on which these figures are based is $13,924 for a nonfarm family of four. See the source for figures for single individuals and families of different sizes.

Source: *Statistical Abstract* 1993: Tables 735, 736, 739

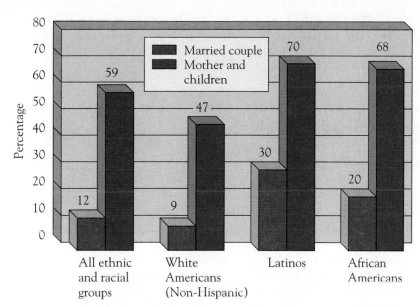

Source: *Statistical Abstract* 1993, Table 737

Figure 10-8

Poverty Rate of U.S. Children Age 6 Years and Younger, by Family Type

changes in government policies concerning Social Security and subsidized housing, food, and medicine have significantly cut the rate of poverty among the elderly. This is especially striking in the case of elderly Latinos, whose rate of poverty is considerably less than the overall Latino rate. The bottom line, however, is that the prevailing racial and ethnic patterns carry over into old age, and an elderly African American or Latino is two or three times more likely to be poor than is an elderly white person.

Sex The greatest predictor of whether a U.S. family is poor is not race, but the sex of the person who heads the family. *Most* poor families are headed by women (Gimenez 1990). If a single-parent family is headed by a male, the poverty rate is close to the national average; but if a female heads a family, that figure soars. As Figure 10.8 shows, a mother-headed family is *several* times more likely to be poor than is a family headed by a married couple. The three major causes of this phenomenon, called the **feminization of poverty,** are divorce, births to unwed mothers, and the lower wages paid to women.

The Rural Poor

Because almost all studies of poverty have focused on cities, sociologists have recently completed a national study of rural poverty. Of 56 million rural Americans, 9 million are poor. At 16 percent, this is higher than the national average shown on Figure 10.7. The rural poor reflect the racial and ethnic patterns of the nation; that is, poverty is least among whites, greatest among African Americans, while Latinos rank in between. The rural poor, however, do differ. They are less likely to be on welfare or to be single parents, and more likely to be married and to have jobs. Compared with urban Americans, the rural poor are less skilled and less educated, and the jobs available to them pay less than similar jobs in urban areas (Dudenhefer 1993).

Children of Poverty: A New Social Condition?

Children are more likely to live in poverty than are adults or the elderly. This holds true regardless of race, but as Figures 10.7 and 10.8 show, poverty is much greater among Latino and African-American children. That so many children are poor is shocking

feminization of poverty: a trend in U.S. poverty whereby most poor families are headed by women

when one considers the wealth of this country and the supposed concern for the well-being of children. This new, and tragic, aspect of poverty in the United States is the topic of the following Thinking Critically section.

▼△▼△▼△▼△▼△▼△▼△▼△▼△▼△▼△▼△▼△▼△▼△

Thinking Critically About Social Controversy

Children in Poverty

▼ DURING THE PAST DECADE or two, children have slipped into poverty faster than any other age group. As Figure 10.7 shows, one of six white U.S. children, two of every five Latino children, and almost one of every two African-American children are poor. These figures translate into incredible numbers—approximately *17 million* children live in poverty: 9 million white children, 3 1/2 million Latino children, and 5 million African-American children.

According to sociologist and U.S. Senator Daniel Moynihan, this high rate of child poverty is due primarily to a general breakdown of the U.S. family. He points his finger at the sharp increase in births outside marriage since 1960, when only 5 percent of all U.S. children were born to unmarried mothers. Since then, births to single mothers have jumped sixfold, and now account for 30 percent of all births in the United States. The relationship to social class is striking, for as Table 10.3 shows, births to unmarried mothers are not distributed evenly across the social classes. For women above the poverty line, only 6 percent of births are to single mothers, while for women below the poverty line this rate jumps to 44 percent. Only 4 percent of all single women who give birth are college educated, while 82 percent have only a high school education or less.

Regardless of causes—and there are many—the statement that millions of children live in poverty can be as cold and meaningless as saying that their shoes are brown. Easy to overlook is the significance of childhood poverty. Poor children are more likely to die in infancy, to go hungry and to be malnourished, to develop more slowly, and to have more health problems. They are more likely to drop out of school, to become involved in criminal activities, and to have children while still in their teens—thus perpetuating the cycle of poverty.

Many social analysts—liberals and conservatives alike—are alarmed at this increase in child poverty, believing that the current overall U.S. rate represents a new social condition. They emphasize that it is time to stop blaming the victim, and instead to focus on the structural factors that underlie child poverty. To relieve the problem, they say, we must take immediate steps to establish national programs of child nutrition and health care. Solutions will require at least these fundamental changes: (1) removing obstacles to employment; (2) improving education; and (3) strengthening the family. To achieve these changes, what specific programs would *you* recommend?

Sources: Based on Duncan and Rodgers 1991; Lawton 1991; Moynihan 1991; Grossfield 1993; Murray 1993; *Statistical Abstract* 1993: Tables 22, 23, 98, 101, 735–739. ▲

Table 10.3

U.S. Births to Single and Married Women

Births to Women Above the Poverty Line

Married	Single
94%	6%

Births to Women Below the Poverty Line

Married	Single
56%	44%

Education of Single Women Who Become Mothers

College	High School or Less
4%	82%

Note: Figures were available only for white women.

Source: Murray 1993.

Short-Term and Long-Term Poverty

In the 1960s Michael Harrington (1962) and Oscar Lewis (1966) suggested that some of the poor get trapped in a **culture of poverty.** They assumed that the values and behaviors of the poor "make them fundamentally different from other Americans, and that these factors are largely responsible for their continued long-term poverty" (Ruggles 1989:7).

Economist Patricia Ruggles (1989, 1990) wanted to see if this were true. Is there a self-perpetuating culture, transmitted across generations, which keeps its members in poverty? If so, it would confirm common stereotypes of the poor as lazy people who bring poverty on themselves. After studying national statistics, Ruggles found that about half the poor are *short-term poor;* that is, they move out of poverty in less than eight years, some within a few months. About half are *long-term poor,* their poverty lasting at least

culture of poverty: the assumption that the values and behaviors of the poor make them fundamentally different from other people, that these factors are largely responsible for their poverty, and that parents perpetuate poverty across generations by passing these characteristics to their children

While this may look like a scene from the Great Depression, it is not. This multigenerational family of the 1990s illustrates a type of poverty that is not easily visible—elderly women who, never having worked outside the home, qualify only for partial payment from their deceased husband's minimum Social Security; the middle-aged who are locked into patterns of temporary employment; and children who may or may not break the cycle of poverty.

eight years. She also found that most of the long-term poor eventually move out of poverty; that, contrary to popular belief, very few people pass poverty across generations. Many people might be surprised to learn that most children of the poor do *not* grow up to be poor. Only about 20 percent of people who are poor as children are still poor when they are adults (Corcoran et al. 1985; Sawhill 1988; Ruggles 1989).

Since the number of people in poverty remains fairly constant year after year, however, this means that in any given year about as many people move into poverty as move out of poverty. In addition, although most people who are poor today will not be poor in just a few years, about 1 percent of the U.S. population remains poor year in and year out. These two and a half million people were poor twenty years ago, and they are poor today. Ruggles found that this group has three primary characteristics: most are African American, unemployed, and live in female-headed households. About half are unmarried mothers with children.

Individual Versus Structural Explanations of Poverty

Where shall we place blame? On the poor, or on social conditions? On the one hand, we can believe the stereotypes that people are poor because of their own inadequacies, such as laziness or lack of intelligence. On the other hand, we can look at social structure as the source of poverty. Sociologists accept this second explanation—looking to such factors as inequalities in education and access to learning job skills, as well as other forms of discrimination and large-scale economic changes. For example, because U.S. society now needs relatively few unskilled workers, large numbers of unskilled people are unemployed or work only at marginal jobs that pay poverty incomes. Others are held back by racial, ethnic, age, and gender discrimination. The sociological approach, then, is to examine the structural features of society that create poverty.

Occasionally even well-intentioned scholars, however, blame the poor for their poverty. Edward Banfield (1974), for example, argued that people's orientation to time helps to explain their poverty. Banfield noticed that the poor are inclined toward immediate gratification, while the middle class opt for **deferred gratification,** that is, giving up something in the present for the sake of greater gains in the future. From this, he concluded that the "present orientation" of the one keeps them in poverty, while the "future orientation" of the other keeps them out of poverty.

deferred gratification: forgoing something in the present in the hope of achieving greater gains in the future

Let's take a closer look at life on the bottom and see how it is easy to mistake these behaviors as the cause rather than the consequence of people's social class. As we have seen, poverty is brutal. The poor face more illnesses, accidents, marital breakups, street crimes, and unemployment than do members of other social classes. They have less education and less control over what happens to them in life. Indeed, not knowing what is going to happen next is one of the hallmarks of poverty. The future is a series of question marks, punctuated by one emergency after another.

How can a person living in poverty plan far ahead when tomorrow may bring even more problems than today? From this perspective, the desire for immediate gratification can be seen as *a consequence, not a cause,* of the situations that the poor face on a daily basis. Sociologist Elliot Liebow (1967), who studied African-American street corner men in Washington, D.C., noted that these men, who live in abject poverty, are just as concerned about the future as anyone—only they perceive their future accurately, and it looks bleak. Consequently, lacking any grounds for the promise of something better, they conclude that they may as well enjoy what they have at the moment, for tomorrow is not likely to bring any improvement. In other words, their immediate gratification is not the cause of their poverty, but an accurate reflection of their life situation.

For the middle classes, deferred gratification reflects a different life situation. They have a surplus that they can deposit in a bank and retrieve at their leisure. As Liebow points out, the poor also save, but their savings come in a form invisible to the middle class: they buy material items such as musical instruments, watches, and video recorders from which they can get practical use, and yet pawn in an emergency.

Poor people would love the chance to practice deferred gratification, but they have little or nothing to defer. If the daily reality of the middle class were an old car that runs only half the time, threats from the utility company to shut off the electricity and gas, and a choice between buying medicine, diapers, and food or paying the rent, their orientations to life would surely undergo a radical change. Again, the behaviors of the poor are driven by their poverty more than they are a cause of it.

As Marx and Weber pointed out, social class penetrates our consciousness, shaping our ideas of life and our proper place in society. When the rich look around, they sense superiority and control over destiny. In contrast, the poor see defeat, and a buffeting by unpredictable forces. Each knows the dominant ideology, that their particular niche in life is due to their own efforts, that the reasons for success—or failure—lie solely with the self (Shepelak 1989; Gatewood 1990; Hurst 1992). Like the fish not seeing water, people tend not to see the effects of social class on their own lives.

Summary and Review

What Is Social Class?

What is social class, and how do sociologists measure it?

Most sociologists have adopted Weber's definition of **social class** as a large group of people who rank closely to one another in wealth, power, and prestige. There are three ways to measure social class. In the **subjective method,** people assign themselves their own social class. In the **reputational method,** people identify the social class of others based on knowledge of their circumstances. In the **objective method,** researchers assign subjects to a social class based on objective criteria such as wealth, power, and prestige. Pp. 252–254.

The Components of Social Class

What are the three criteria used to measure social class?

Wealth, power, and prestige are most commonly used to measure social class. **Wealth,** consisting of property and income, is concentrated in the upper classes. The distribution of wealth in the United States has changed little over the past couple of generations, and the poorest and richest quintiles now receive about the same share of the country's wealth as they did in 1945. **Power** is the ability to carry out one's will, even over the resistance of others. C. Wright Mills coined the term **power elite** to refer to the small group that holds the reins of power in business, government, and the military. **Prestige** is often linked to occupational status. People's rankings of occupational prestige have changed little over the decades and are similar from country to country. Cross culturally, occupations that pay more, require more education and abstract thought, and offer greater autonomy are given greater prestige. Pp. 254–259.

What is meant by the term status inconsistency?

Status is social ranking. Most people are status consistent; that is, they rank high or low on all three dimensions of social class. People who rank higher on some dimensions than on others are status inconsistent. The frustrations of **status inconsistency** tend to produce political radicalism. Pp. 259–260.

Sociological Models of Social Class

What models are used to portray the social classes?

Sociologists use two main models to portray the social class structure. Erik Wright developed a four-class model based on Marx: (1) capitalists or owners; (2) petty bourgeoisie or small business owners; (3) managers; and (4) workers. Gilbert and Kahl developed a six-class model. At the top is the capitalist class. In descending order are the upper middle class, the lower middle class, the working class, the working poor, and the underclass. Pp. 261–265.

Consequences of Social Class

How does social class affect people?

Social class leaves no aspect of life untouched. Its primary significance is the determination of **life chances**—an individual's chances of such things as dying early, receiving good health care, becoming mentally ill, and getting divorced. Class membership also affects child-rearing, political participation, religious affiliation, educational attainment, and contact with the criminal justice system. Pp. 265–268.

Social Mobility

What are the types of social mobility?

Intergenerational mobility concerns changes in social class from one generation to the next. **Exchange mobility** is the movement of large numbers of people from one class to another, with the net result that the relative proportions of the population in the classes remain about the same. **Structural mobility** refers to social changes that affect the social class membership of large numbers of people. Pp. 268–271.

How is the Horatio Alger myth functional for society?

The Horatio Alger myth—the belief that anyone can get ahead if only he or she tries hard enough—encourages people to strive to get ahead and deflects blame for failure from society to the individual. P. 271.

Poverty

Who are the poor?

Poverty is unequally distributed in the United States. Latinos, African Americans, Native Americans, children, female-headed households, and rural Americans are more likely than others to be poor. The poverty rate of the elderly is about the same as the general population. Pp. 271–275.

What are individual and structural explanations of poverty?

Some social analysts believe that characteristics of the poor, such as a desire for immediate gratification, cause poverty. Sociologists, in contrast, examine structural features of society, such as employment opportunities, to find the causes of poverty. Sociologists generally conclude that life orientations are a consequence, not the cause, of one's position in the social class structure. Pp. 275–276.

Where can I read more on this topic?

Suggested readings for this chapter are listed on page 640.

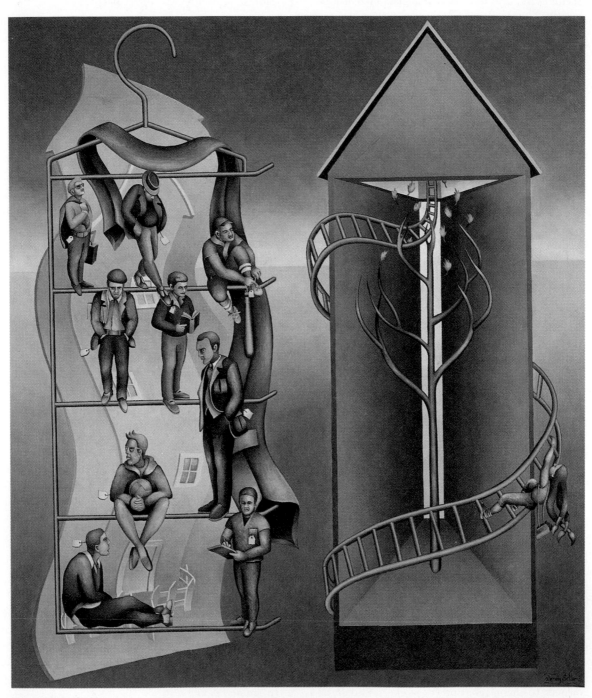

Wendy Seller, Dissension, 1993

CHAPTER

11

Inequalities of Gender

THE TEENAGE GIRLS CREPT CAUTIOUSLY *through the jungle. Blending into the silent streams of dawn, machine guns at their sides, the shadowy figures quickly stepped across the narrow opening. Masked by the thick veil of foliage, they waited for those carrying the T-81 Chinese assault rifles. The last to cross were the three with rocket launchers.*

"Ready?" whispered Kamir. Eyes glistening, the other young women nodded. Suddenly, the morning's silence was pierced by a lethal barrage. Panicked, the Sri Lankan troops tried to flee, only to be cut down by gunfire from all sides. Leaving the soldiers writhing in death agonies, the women slipped back into the jungle's cover, as silently as they had arrived.

The Tamils of Sri Lanka used to consider warfare to be "men's work." But all that changed when teenage girls joined Tamil separatists in their armed struggle for independence. Tamils traditionally believe that women should be demure, quietly blending into the background. But in the present circumstances, they have little time for such views. Maybe later.

And then, again, maybe not. The Tiger women, as they are called, operate check-points twenty-four hours a day. They drive heavy trucks captured from the Indian army and take part in active combat. And like the Tiger men, each young woman wears a cyanide capsule around her neck. If capture is imminent, rather than being questioned by the enemy—and almost certainly raped and tortured—they bite into that capsule (based on an Associated Press report of March 29, 1990).

Fierce revolution has ripped Tamil society apart. Of their traditional roles, relationships, and institutions nothing remains untouched. When the war ends, all will have to be reconstructed, a new culture astride the past and the present. What that new culture will be is not the subject here, although it would be fascinating to observe the transformation. What is significant for our purposes is the role that young Tamil women are playing in their revolution and the way in which the Tamil definition of "feminine" behavior has been transformed.

This chapter examines **gender stratification**—males' and females' unequal access to power, prestige, and property on the basis of sex. Gender stratification is especially significant because it cuts across all aspects of social life. No matter what our social class, age, race, or ethnic classification, we are labeled *male* or *female*. The images and expectations attached to these labels not only guide our behavior but they also serve as the basis of power relations (Rotundo 1993). In this chapter's fascinating journey, as we look at inequality between the sexes around the world and in U.S. society, we shall review such topics as whether it is biology or culture that makes us the way we are, how ideas of manhood vary from one culture to another, sexual harassment, unequal pay, and circumcision and other violence against women. This excursion will provide a good context for understanding the Tamil—and your own experience with gender.

Issues of Sex and Gender

gender stratification: males' and females' unequal access to power, prestige, and property on the basis of their sex

sex: biological characteristics that distinguish females and males, consisting of primary and secondary sex characteristics

When we consider how females and males differ, the first thing that usually comes to mind is **sex,** the *biological* characteristics that distinguish males and females. *Primary sex characteristics* consist of a vagina or a penis and other organs related to reproduction; *secondary sex characteristics* refer to the physical distinctions between males and females that are not directly connected with reproduction. Secondary sex characteristics become clearly evident at puberty when males develop more muscles, a lower voice, and more hair and height; while females form more fatty tissue, broader hips, and larger breasts.

What makes a man masculine and a woman femininity? The answer, stress most sociologists, is socialization into a culture's expectations concerning masculinity and femininity. The changes experienced by Tamil women, depicted here and featured in the opening vignette, vividly illustrate this point.

Gender, in contrast, is a *social*, not a biological characteristic. Gender, which varies from one society to another, is what a group considers proper for its males and females. Whereas *sex* refers to male or female, *gender* refers to masculinity or femininity. In short, you inherit your sex, but you learn your gender as you are socialized into specific behaviors and attitudes. The sociological significance of gender is that it serves as a primary sorting device by which society controls its members. Ultimately, gender determines the nature of people's access to their society's system of power, property, and even prestige. Like social class, gender is a structural feature of society.

Before examining inequalities of gender, let us consider why men and women differ socially. Are they, perhaps, just "born that way"?

Biology or Culture? The Continuing Controversy

Why do males and females act differently? For example, why are most males—unlike the Tamil—more aggressive than most females? Why do females tend to enter "nurturing" occupations such as nursing in far greater proportions than males? To answer such questions, many people respond with some variation of "They are just born that way."

Is this the correct answer? Certainly biology plays a significant role. Each of us begins as a fertilized egg. The egg, or ovum, is contributed by our mother, the sperm that fertilizes the egg by our father. At the very moment the egg is fertilized, our sex is determined. Each of us receives twenty-three pairs of chromosomes from the ovum and twenty-three from the sperm. The egg has an X chromosome. If the sperm that fertilizes the egg also has an X chromosome, we become female (XX). If the sperm has a Y chromosome, we become male (XY).

Does this difference in biology account for differences in male and female behaviors? Does it, for example, make females more comforting and more nurturing, and males more aggressive and domineering? Almost all sociologists take the side of "nurture" in this "nature versus nurture" controversy, but a few do not, as you can see from the Thinking Critically sections on pages 282 and 283.

The Dominant Position in Sociology

The dominant sociological position is represented by the symbolic interactionists. They stress that the visible differences of sex do not come with meanings built into them. Rather, each society interprets these physical differences, and on that basis assigns males and females to separate groups. Here they learn contrasting expectations of life and are given different access to their society's privileges.

Most sociologists find the argument compelling that if biology were the principle factor in human behavior, around the world we would find women to be one sort of person and men another. In fact, however, ideas of gender—and resulting male–female

gender: the social characteristics that a society considers proper for its males and females; masculinity or femininity

▼△▼△▼△▼△▼△▼△▼△▼△▼△▼△▼△▼△▼△▼△▼△▼△▼△▼△▼△

Thinking Critically About Social Controversy

Biology Versus Culture—Culture Is the Answer

▼ FOR SOCIOLOGIST CYNTHIA FUCHS EPSTEIN (1986, 1988, 1989), differences between males' and females' behavior are solely the result of social factors—specifically, socialization and social control. Her argument is as follows:

1. A re-examination of the anthropological record shows greater equality between the sexes in the past than we had thought. In earlier societies, women, as well as men, hunted small game, devised tools for hunting and gathering, and gathered food. Studies of today's hunting and gathering societies show that "both women's and men's roles have been broader and less rigid than those created by stereotypes. For example, the Agta and Mbuti are clearly egalitarian and thus prove that hunting and gathering societies exist in which women are not subordinate to men. Anthropologists who study them claim that there is a separate but equal status of women at this level of development."

2. The types of work that men and women perform in each society are determined not by biology but by rigidly enforced social arrangements. Few people, whether male or female, can escape these arrangements to perform work outside their allotted narrow range. This gender inequality of work, which serves the interests of males, is enforced by informal customs and formal systems of laws. Once these socially constructed barriers are removed, women can and do exhibit similar work habits as males.

3. The human behaviors that biology "causes" are limited to those involving reproduction or differences in body structure. These differences are relevant for only a few activities, such as playing basketball or "crawling through a small space."

4. Female crime rates, which are rising in many parts of the world, indicate that displays of aggressiveness, often considered a biologically dictated male behavior, are related instead to social rather than biological factors. When social conditions permit, such as in the practice of female attorneys, females also exhibit "adversarial, assertive, and dominant behavior." Not incidentally, this "dominant behavior" also appears in scholarly female challenges to the biased views about human nature that have been proposed by male scholars.

In short, rather than "women's incompetence or inability to read a legal brief, perform brain surgery, [or] to predict a bull market," social factors—socialization, gender discrimination, and other forms of social control—are responsible for gender differences in behavior. Arguments that assign "an evolutionary and genetic basis" to explain gender differences in sex status are simplistic. They "rest on a dubious structure of inappropriate, highly selective, and poor data, oversimplification in logic and in inappropriate inferences by use of analogy." ▲

---

behavior—vary greatly from one culture to another (see the Perspectives box on page 284). They also stress findings like that presented in the opening vignette, noting that the emergence of female warriors in Tamil society was obviously due to changes in their social conditions, not to changes in their biology.

Opening the Door to Biology

Without losing sight of the social experiences that mold femininity and masculinity, many sociologists acknowledge that biological factors may be involved. Alice Rossi (1977, 1984), a feminist sociologist and former president of the American Sociological Association, has suggested that women are better prepared biologically for "mothering" than are men, that women are more sensitive to such stimuli as the infant's soft skin or their nonverbal communications. Her basic point is that the issue is not biology *or* society; it is that nature provides biological predispositions, which are then overlaid with culture (see Renzetti and Curran 1992).

▼△▼△▼△▼△▼△▼△▼△▼△▼△▼△▼△▼△▼△▼△▼△▼△▼△

Thinking Critically About Social Controversy

Biology Versus Culture—Biology Is the Answer

▼ SOCIOLOGIST STEVEN GOLDBERG (1974, 1986, 1989) finds it astonishing that anyone should doubt "the presence of core-deep differences in males and females, differences of temperament and emotion we call masculinity and femininity." Goldberg's argument, that it is not environment but inborn differences that "give masculine and feminine direction to the emotions and behaviors of men and women" is summarized as follows:

1. The anthropological record shows that all societies for which evidence exists are (or were) **patriarchies** (societies in which men dominate women). Stories about past **matriarchies** (societies in which women dominate men) are myths.

2. In all societies, past and present, the highest statuses are associated with males. In every society, politics is ruled "by hierarchies overwhelmingly dominated by men."

3. The reason for this one-way dominance of societies is that males "have a lower threshold for the elicitation of dominance behavior . . . a greater tendency to exhibit whatever behavior is necessary in any environment to attain dominance in hierarchies and male–female encounters and relationships." Males are more willing "to sacrifice the rewards of other motivations—the desire for affection, health, family life, safety, relaxation, vacation and the like—in order to attain dominance and status."

4. Just as a 6-foot woman does not prove the social basis of height, so exceptional individuals, such as a highly achieving and dominant woman, do not refute "the physiological roots of behavior."

In short, only one interpretation of why every society from that of the Pygmy to that of the Swede associates dominance and attainment with males is valid. Male dominance of society is simply "an inevitable resolution of the psychophysiological reality." Socialization and social institutions merely *reflect*—and sometimes exaggerate—inborn tendencies. Any interpretation other than inborn differences is "wrongheaded, ignorant, tendentious, internally illogical, discordant with the evidence, and implausible in the extreme." The argument that males are more aggressive because they have been socialized that way is the equivalent of a claim that men can grow moustaches because boys have been socialized that way.

To acknowledge this reality is *not* to defend discrimination against women. Whether or not one approves what societies have done with these basic biological differences is not the point. The point is that biology leads males and females to different behaviors and attitudes—regardless of how we feel about this or wish it were different. ▲

This assumption is supported by a bizarre case, one that no ethical experimenter would dare to have attempted. The drama began in 1963, when 7-month-old identical twins were taken to a doctor for a routine circumcision (Money and Ehrhardt 1972). The inept physician, who was using electrocautery (a heated needle), turned the electric current too high and accidentally burned off the penis of one of the boys. You can imagine the parents' reaction of disbelief—followed by horror, as the truth sank in.

What can be done in a situation like this? The damage was irreversible. The parents were told that the child could never have sexual relations. After months of soul-wrenching agonies and tearful consultations with experts, the parents decided that their son should have a sex-change operation. When he was 17 months old, surgeons used the boy's own skin to construct a vagina. The parents then gave the child a girl's name, dressed him in frilly clothing, let his hair grow long, and began to treat him as a girl. Later, physicians gave the child female steroids to promote female pubertal growth.

At first the results were extremely promising. When the twins were 4 1/2 years old, the mother said (remember that the children are biologically identical):

patriarchy: a society in which men dominate women

matriarchy: a society in which women dominate men

▼▲▼

Perspectives

CULTURAL DIVERSITY AROUND THE WORLD

Manhood in the Making

THE BASIC PRESUPPOSITION of the sociological perspective on gender is that differences between the sexes are due entirely, or almost entirely, to socialization. Some analysts consider the possibility that biology may account for some differences in men's and women's behavior, possibly even for attitudinal differences, but if it does, they assume that its influence is minor. Without in any way intending to try to resolve this issue, the following materials illustrate how vastly different masculinity is conceived in diverse cultures.

Anthropologist David Gilmore wanted to find out if there were universal elements to the idea of masculinity. He surveyed anthropological data on cultures in southern Spain, the United States, Canada, Britain, Mexico, Sicily, Micronesia, Melanesia, equatorial Africa, aboriginal South America, South Asia, East Asia, the Middle East, New Guinea, and ancient Greece. He found four basic elements associated with masculinity: (1) not being like females (to be called feminine is an insult), (2) matching or outdoing other males (which takes such forms as fighting, drinking, and gaining wealth), (3) personal accomplishment (especially sexual prowess, but also being able to withstand adversity and pain), and (4) "bigness" (of sexual organ, body, wealth, or possessions). He also found a consistent theme running through these elements—that masculinity does not come naturally, but must be attained. Masculinity is validated by reputation.

If Gilmore's sample of cultures had ended with these groups, we might conclude that he had identified a cultural universal of masculinity. His sample, however, included two cultures where ideas of manliness differ sharply.

The first exception is Tahiti in the South Pacific, where both men and women are expected to be passive, yielding, and to ignore slights. Neither competitively strives for material possessions. Their blurred sex roles are manifested in the following ways: There is no expression of gender in their

language, not even pronouns; children's names are not sex specific; labor is not divided on the basis of gender.

The Semai of Central Malaysia are the second exception. The Semai, a racially mixed group of Malays, Chinese, and other people who have passed through their forest enclaves, also lack the differentiation between the sexes that most societies esteem. Their core value is not to make anyone feel bad, which means not denying or frustrating anyone. To do so could anger the spirits, which might take vengeance on the entire village. Consequently, the Semai have no contests or sporting competitions that might make a losing person feel bad. No one can give orders to another, for that might make the other feel bad. For the same reason, they can't resist someone's sexual advances. The Semai say that adultery, whether a man's or a woman's, is "just a loan." Nor are they to nag another person for sex, for that, too, would be aggressive. Not concerned about family lines, they love and treat all children well, regardless of paternity. Children may not be disciplined, for that might make them feel bad, and if a child says that he or she does not feel like doing something, that is the end of the matter. If the Semai, either men or women, encounter danger, they run away and hide without shame. Women become headmen, but less often than men, and men can become midwives, but rarely do. The one gender distinction that the Semai appear to make is that the men do the hunting.

Although Gilmore's survey of cultures failed to find a universal, he did confirm a significant sociological principle—that in each human group manhood (or in the exceptional cases of the Tahitians and the Semai, personhood) is a culturally imposed ideal to which men must conform whether or not they find it personally congenial. That we can also apply to cultural ideals of femininity.

Sources: Based primarily on Gilmore 1990, but also on Epstein 1988 and Rhode 1990.

One thing that really amazes me is that she is so feminine. I've never seen a little girl so neat and tidy. . . . She likes for me to wipe her face. She doesn't like to be dirty, and yet my son is quite different. I can't wash his face for anything. . . . She is very proud of herself, when she puts on a new dress, or I set her hair. . . . She seems to be daintier. (Money and Ehrhardt 1972)

About a year later, the mother described how their daughter imitated her while their son copied his father:

I found that my son, he chose very masculine things like a fireman or a policeman. . . . He wanted to do what daddy does, work where daddy does, and carry a lunch kit. . . .

And [my daughter] didn't want any of those things. She wants to be a doctor or a teacher. . . . But none of the things that she ever wanted to be were like a policeman or a fireman, and that sort of thing never appealed to her. (Money and Ehrhardt 1972)

If the matter were this clear-cut, we could use this case to conclude that gender is entirely up to nurture. Seldom are things in life so simple, however, and a twist occurs in this story. In spite of her parents' coaching and the initially encouraging results, the twin whose sex had been reassigned did not adapt well to femininity. Milton Diamond (1982), a medical researcher, reports that at age 13 she was unhappy and having a difficult time adjusting to being a female. She walked with a masculine gait, and was called "cavewoman" by her peers.

We certainly need more evidence about this individual's life experiences to understand what we can learn from this case. At this point, we do not know to what degree biology influences male and female behavior, but we do know that biological distinctions are not a legitimate reason for social inequality.

Gender Inequality in Global Perspective

As we have seen over and over in this text, to grasp a larger perspective helps us better understand our own situation in life. To help us understand gender relations, we can note that around the world gender is *the* primary division between people. Because each society sets up barriers to provide unequal access on the basis of sex, sociologists classify females as a *minority group.* Since women outnumber men, you may think it strange to consider women a minority group, but as sociologist Helen Hacker who proposed this idea in 1951 pointed out, since **minority group** means people who are discriminated against on the basis of physical or cultural characteristics, this concept applies perfectly to females. To better see why, in spite of their numbers, women are a minority group, let's survey occupations around the world, and then consider how gender discrimination may have originated.

Sex Typing of Work

Anthropologist George Murdock (1937), who surveyed 324 premodern societies around the world, found that in all of them activities are **sex typed;** in other words, every society associates activities with one sex or the other. He also found that activities considered "female" in one society may be considered "male" in another. In some groups, for example, taking care of cattle is women's work, while other groups assign this task to men.

Metalworking was the exception, being men's work in all the societies examined. Three other pursuits—making weapons, pursuing sea mammals, and hunting—were almost universally the domain of men. In a few societies, however, women participated in these activities. Although Murdock found no specific work that was universally assigned to women, he did find that making clothing, cooking, carrying water, and grinding grain were almost always female tasks. In a few societies, however, such activities were regarded as men's work.

From Murdock's cross-cultural survey, we can conclude that there is nothing about biology that requires men and women to be assigned different work. Anatomy does not have to equal destiny when it comes to occupations, for as we have seen, pursuits considered feminine in one society may be deemed masculine in another, and vice versa.

Prestige of Work

You might ask whether this division of labor really illustrates social inequality. Does it perhaps simply represent arbitrary forms of dividing up labor, not gender discrimination? That could be the case, except for this finding: *universally, greater prestige is given to male activities—regardless of what those activities are* (Linton 1936; Rosaldo 1974). If taking

minority group: a group that is discriminated against on the basis of its members' physical or cultural characteristics

sex typed: the association of behaviors with one sex or the other

When anthropologist George Murdock surveyed 324 premodern societies worldwide, he found that work activities in all of them were sex typed. In Somalia, women tend the livestock.

care of goats is men's work, then the care of goats is considered important and carries high prestige, but if it is women's work, it is considered less important and given less prestige. Or, to take an example closer to home, when delivering babies was "women's work" and done by midwives, it was given low prestige. But when men took over this task, its prestige increased sharply (Ehrenreich and English 1973). In short, it is not the work that provides the prestige, but the sex with which the work is associated.

The Genesis of Female Minority Status

Some analysts question whether *patriarchy*, male dominance, is universal, speculating that in some earlier societies women may have dominated, or at least been equal, to men. Apparently the horticultural and hunting and gathering societies reviewed on pages 145–148 had much less gender discrimination than do contemporary societies (Lerner 1986). Many analysts believe that in these societies women played a much more active role in all aspects of social life, that they even contributed about 60 percent of the group's total food. After reviewing the historical record, however, historian and feminist Gerda Lerner (1986) concluded that "there is not a single society known where women-as-a-group have decision-making power over men (as a group)."

How did it happen, then, that around the world women and their activities came to be held in less esteem than men and their activities and that in all societies women became systematically discriminated against in social life? Two interesting theories have emerged. Both assume that patriarchy is universal and, accordingly, look to universal conditions to explain its origins. Each focuses on universal biological factors coupled with universal social factors.

Childbirth and Social Experiences   The first theory points to the social consequences of the biology of human reproduction (Lerner 1986; Friedl 1990). In early human history, life was short and many children had to be born to reproduce the human group. Because only women get pregnant, carry a child nine months, give birth, and nurse, women were limited in activities for a considerable part of their lives. To survive, an infant needed a nursing mother. With a child at her breast or in her uterus, or one carried on her hip or on her back, women were physically encumbered. Conse-

One theory about the origin of patriarchy is that because of childbirth women assumed tasks associated with home and child care, while men hunted and performed other tasks requiring greater strength, speed, and absence from home.

quently, around the world women assumed tasks associated with the home and child care, while men took over the hunting of large animals and other tasks that required greater speed and absence from the base camp for longer periods of time (Huber 1990).

As a consequence, males became dominant. It was the men who left camp to hunt animals, who made contact with other tribes, who traded with these other groups, and who quarreled and waged war with them. It was also men who made and controlled the instruments of death, the weapons used for hunting and warfare. It was they who accumulated possessions in trade, who gained prestige by triumphantly returning with prisoners of war or with large animals to feed the tribe. In contrast, little prestige was given to the ordinary, routine, taken-for-granted activities of women—who were not seen as risking their lives for the group. Eventually, men took over society. Their weapons, items of trade, and knowledge gained from contact with other groups became sources of power. They used this power to make women second-class citizens, subject to male decisions.

Warfare and Physical Strength   The second theory was proposed by anthropologist Marvin Harris (1977), who attributed patriarchy to universal social conditions—threats to the existence of human groups and to universal biological conditions—differences in the physical strength of males and females.

Harris argued that in prehistoric times, each small human group was threatened with annihilation from other groups. To survive, each group had to recruit members to fight enemies in dangerous, hand-to-hand combat. As you can imagine, the threat of injury and death made this recruiting process difficult. People had to be coaxed into bravery through promises of rewards and coerced through threats of punishment. Females, on average 85 percent as large and only two-thirds as strong as men (Gallese 1980), found themselves at a huge disadvantage in hand-to-hand combat.

To encourage males to become the warriors, females became the reward. Males who did not live up to their group's expectations of bravery were banished from the tribe, while males who showed bravery were rewarded with sexual access to women. Some groups carried this idea to such an extent that only males who had proven their bravery by facing an enemy in combat were allowed to marry. Since some women were brawnier than some men, to exclude them from combat entirely might seem irrational. If women were to be the chief inducement for men to risk their lives, however, it was necessary to separate them from combat. To make the system work, men had to be trained from birth for combat, and women conditioned from birth to acquiesce in male demands.

According to this explanation, the reward for male bravery came at the direct expense of females. In almost all band and village societies, when men took control they assigned women the "drudge work": weeding, seed grinding, fetching water and firewood, carrying household possessions during moves, and routine cooking. Because men preferred to avoid these onerous tasks—and were able to do so if they had one or more wives—access to women proved an effective bait to induce men to fight.

Evaluating the Theories   Which theory is correct? Remember that the answer is buried in human history and there is no way of testing either explanation. Either theory may be correct, patriarchy could have arisen due to some combination of the two, or some third theory may be the right one. For example, Frederick Engels proposed that patriarchy developed with the origin of private property (Lerner 1986). He could not explain why private property should have produced patriarchy, however. Gerda Lerner (1986) suggests that patriarchy may even have had different origins in different places.

Whatever its origins, patriarchy became surrounded with cultural supports to justify gender inequality. A closed, circular system evolved. Men developed notions of their own inherent superiority—based on the evidence of their dominant position in society. They then consolidated their power, surrounded many of their activities with secrecy, and constructed elaborate rules and rituals to avoid "contamination" by the females whom they now openly deemed inferior.

As tribal societies developed into larger groups, men, enjoying their power and privileges, maintained their dominance long after hunting and hand-to-hand combat ceased to be routine, and even after large numbers of children were no longer needed to reproduce the human group. Male dominance in contemporary societies, then, is a continuation of a millennia-old pattern whose origin is lost in history.

Gender Inequality in the United States

Gender inequality, then, is worldwide. Rather than some accidental hit-or-miss affair, the institutions of each society work together to maintain the group's particular forms of inequality. Custom, grounded in history, both justifies and maintains arrangements of gender inequality. Although men have resisted sharing their privileged positions with women, change has come.

Fighting Back: The Rise of Feminism

To see how far we have come, it is useful to see where we used to be. In early U.S. society, the second-class status of females was taken for granted. Women could not serve on juries, nor could they vote, make legal contracts, or hold property in their own name. Women who worked for wages could not even collect their own paychecks—single women were often required to hand them over to their fathers; married women, to their husbands. These conditions were generally seen as part of the *proper* relations of the sexes. How could times have changed so much that such conditions sound like fiction?

A central lesson of conflict theory is that power yields tremendous privilege; that, like a magnet, it draws to the elite the best resources available. Because men held tenaciously onto their privileges and used social institutions to maintain their position, basic rights for women came only through a prolonged and bitter struggle (Offen 1990).

Feminism, the view that biology is not destiny, and, therefore, stratification by gender is wrong and should be resisted, met strong opposition—both by men who had privilege to lose and by many women who accepted their status as morally correct. In the United States, for example, women had to directly confront men, who first denied

feminism: the philosophy that men and women should be politically, economically, and socially equal, and organized activity on behalf of this principle

Against enormous opposition from men, women finally won the right to vote in the United States in 1919. They first voted in national elections in 1920.

them the right to speak and then ridiculed them when they persisted in speaking in public. Leaders of the feminist movement, then known as *suffragists*, chained themselves to posts and to the iron grillwork of public buildings—and then went on protesting while the police sawed them loose. When imprisoned, they continued to protest by going on hunger strikes. Threatened by such determination and confrontations, men spat on demonstrators for daring to question their place, slapped their faces, tripped them, pelted them with burning cigar stubs, and hurled obscenities at them (Cowley 1969).

In 1916, feminists founded the National Women's Party. In January 1917, they threw a picket line around the White House, which they picketed continuously for six months. On June 22, the pickets were arrested. Declaring their fines unjust, the women refused to pay them. Hundreds went to prison, including Lucy Burns and Alice Paul, two leaders of the National Women's Party. The extent to which these women had threatened male prerogatives is demonstrated by their treatment in prison.

> Two men brought in Dorothy Day, twisting her arms above her head. Suddenly they lifted her and brought her body down twice over the back of an iron bench. . . . They had been there a few minutes when Mrs. Lewis, all doubled over like a sack of flour, was thrown in. Her head struck the iron bed and she fell to the floor senseless. As for Lucy Burns, they handcuffed her wrists and fastened the handcuffs over head to the cell door. (Cowley 1969)

Although women enjoy fundamental rights today, gender inequality continues to exert a central influence on female welfare. In some instances, it can even be a life-and-death matter, as with the medical situations discussed in the Down-to-Earth Sociology box on page 290. Let's look at gender relations in education and everyday life, and then, in greater detail, at discrimination in the world of work.

Gender Inequality in Education

In education, too, a glimpse of the past sheds light on the present. About a century ago, leading educators claimed that a female's womb dominated her mind. Because females are equipped for childbirth, education was considered dangerous. Dr. Edward Clarke, of Harvard University's medical faculty, expressed the dominant sentiment this way:

▼▼▼▼▼▼▼▼▼▼▼▼▼▼▼▼▼▼▼▼

Down-To-Earth Sociology

Making the Invisible Visible—The Deadly Effects of Sexism

MEDICAL RESEARCHERS WERE PERPLEXED. Reports were coming in from all over the country indicating that women, who live much longer than men, were twice as likely to die after coronary bypass surgery. Researchers at Cedars-Sinai Medical Center in Los Angeles checked their own records. They found that of almost 2,300 coronary bypass patients, 4.6 percent of the women died as a result of the surgery, compared with only 2.6 percent of the men.

Initial explanations were based on biology. Coronary bypass surgery involves taking a blood vessel from one part of the body and stitching it to a coronary artery on the surface of the heart. This operation was supposedly more difficult to perform on women because of their smaller hearts and coronary arteries. The researchers tested this theory by measuring the amount of time that surgeons kept patients on the heart–lung machine while they operated. It turned out that women were kept on the machine for less time than men, indicating that the operation was not more difficult to perform on women.

As the researchers probed, a surprising answer slowly unfolded. It lay in neither biology nor lifestyle. Rather, the culprit was sexual discrimination by physicians. They simply had not taken the chest pains of the female patients as seriously as those of their male patients. Physicians, it turns out, are *ten* times more likely to give men exercise stress tests and radioactive heart scans. And they send male patients to surgery on the basis of abnormal stress tests but wait until a woman shows clear-cut symptoms of coronary heart disease before sending her to surgery. Being referred for surgery later in the course of the disease decreases the chances of survival.

Other researchers wondered if the sex of the physician matters when it comes to ordering Pap smears and mammography. They examined the records of 98,000 patients and found that it does make a difference—female physicians are much more likely to order these screening tests.

In short, gender bias is so pervasive in our society that it operates beneath our level of awareness and so severe that it can even be a matter of life or death. The doctors are unaware that they are discriminating. They have no intentions to do so. In what ways do you think gender bias affects your own perceptions and behavior?

Sources: Based on Bishop 1990; Lurie et al. 1993.

> A girl upon whom Nature, for a limited period and for a definite purpose, imposes so great a physiological task, will not have as much power left for the tasks of school, as the boy of whom Nature requires less at the corresponding epoch. (Andersen 1988)

Because females were so much weaker, Clarke urged them to study only one-third as much as young men—and not to study at all during menstruation.

This quotation, which allows us to glimpse the mind-set of earlier generations, reminds us how far we have come. In fact, some measures of education today make it look as though discrimination may be directed against males. For example, more females than males are enrolled in U.S. colleges and universities, and females earn 53 percent of all bachelor's degrees. As Figure 11.1 shows, with the exception of Latinos, female students also complete their bachelor's degrees faster than males (*Statistical Abstract* 1993: Tables 290, 291, 293).

To probe below the surface, however, reveals that degrees follow gender, thus reinforcing male–female distinctions. Two extremes at the bachelor's level highlight gender tracking. Females earn 90 percent of bachelor's degrees in home economics, while males earn 92 percent of bachelor's degrees in military "science." Similarly, men earn 86 percent of bachelor's degrees in the "masculine" field of engineering, while women are awarded 85 percent of bachelor's degrees in the "feminine" field of health sciences (*Statistical Abstract* 1993: Table 293). As reviewed on pages 71–74, gender socialization gives males and females different orientations to life. As a consequence, males and females enter college with sex-linked aspirations, and it is these—rather than any presumed innate characteristics—that channel males and females into different educational paths.

If we follow students into graduate school, we see that with each passing year the proportion of females decreases. Table 11.1 gives us a snapshot of doctoral programs in the sciences. Note how aspirations (enrollment) and accomplishments (doctorates conferred) are sex linked. In all but two scientific fields males outnumber females, and in *all* scientific fields women are less likely than men to complete work for the doctorate.

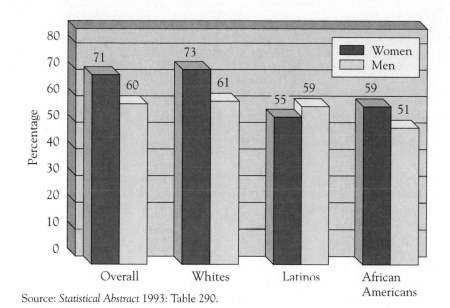

Figure 11.1

Five Years or Less to a Bachelor's Degree, by Sex and Race

Source: *Statistical Abstract* 1993: Table 290.

Note also that the highest female attrition is in engineering and mathematics, traditionally considered strongly masculine fields.

If we follow those who earn doctoral degrees back into colleges and universities, we find gender stratification in rank and pay. Throughout the United States, women are less likely be full professors, the highest rank. In addition, female full professors average less pay than male full professors. The higher the prestige of the university, the

Table 11.1

Doctorates in Science, by Sex and Field

Field	Students Enrolled in Doctoral Programs		Doctorates Conferred		Completion Ratio* (higher or lower than expected)	
	Female	Male	Female	Male	Female	Male
Engineering	14%	86%	9%	91%	-36%	+6%
Computer Sciences	23%	77%	15%	85%	-35%	+10%
Physical Sciences	24%	76%	18%	82%	-25%	+8%
Agriculture	31%	69%	20%	80%	-35%	+16%
Mathematics	31%	69%	19%	81%	-39%	+17%
Social Sciences	43%	57%	36%	64%	-16%	+12%
Biological Sciences	46%	54%	38%	62%	-17%	+15%
Psychology	66%	34%	61%	39%	-8%	+15%
Health Fields	76%	24%	57%	43%	-25%	+80%

*The difference between the proportion enrolled in a program and the proportion granted doctorates divided by the proportion enrolled in the program. Data are from 1991, except for doctorates granted in health fields, which are from 1988.

Source: *Statistical Abstract of the United States* 1993: Tables 992, 993.

greater the discrimination, and women are most likely to be full professors in community colleges (DePalma 1993).

Some very encouraging changes are taking place in higher education. Although we are still a long way from equality, as Figure 11.2 illustrates the proportion of professional degrees earned by females has increased markedly. The most startling change is dentistry, where in 1970 across the entire United States only 34 women earned this degree. Now that annual total is over 1,200 (*Statistical Abstract* 1993: Table 294).

Gender Inequality in Everyday Life

Of the many aspects of gender discrimination in everyday life that could be examined, we have space to look only at two: the general devaluation of femininity in U.S. society and male dominance of conversation.

General Devaluation of Things Feminine

Leaning against the water cooler, two men—both minor executives—are nursing their cups of coffee, discussing last Sunday's Giants game, postponing for as long as possible the moment when work must finally be faced.

A vice president walks by and hears them talking about sports. Does he stop and send them back to their desks? Does he frown? Probably not. Being a man, he is far more likely to pause and join in the conversation, anxious to prove that he, too, is "one of the boys," feigning an interest in football that he may very well not share at all. These men—all men in the office—are his troops, his comrades-in-arms.

Now, let's assume that two women are standing by the water cooler discussing whatever you please: women's liberation, clothes, work, any subject—except football, of course. The vice president walks by, sees them, and moves down the hall in a fury, cursing and wondering whether it is worth the trouble to complain—but to whom?—about all those bitches standing around gabbing when they should be working. "Don't they know," he will ask, in the words of a million men, "that this is an office?" (Korda 1973:20–21)

Figure 11.2

Gender Changes in Professional Degrees

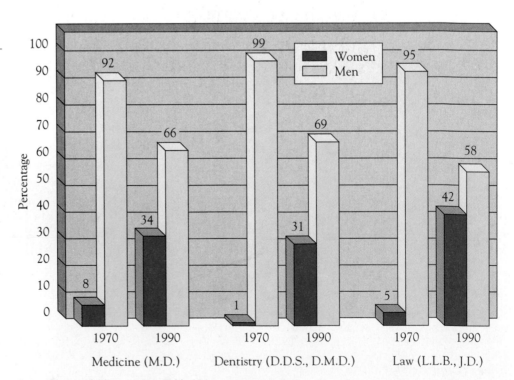

Source *Statistical Abstract* 1993: Table 294.

The expectations of others, whether teachers, parents, or even images presented in the media, help to produce sex-linked aspirations. This 1959 ad for a refrigerator assumes that women are the primary customers and that they will derive feelings of joy and self-worth from owning a fancy one.

As indicated in this scenario, women's capacities, interests, attitudes, and contributions are not taken as seriously as those of men. Masculinity is valued more highly, for it represents success and strength; while femininity is devalued, for it is perceived as failure and weakness (Schur 1984).

During World War II, sociologist Samuel Stouffer noted the general devaluation of things feminine. In his classic study of combat soldiers, *The American Soldier*, Stouffer reported that officers used feminine terms as insults to motivate soldiers (1949). To show less-than-expected courage or endurance was to risk the charge of not being a man. An officer might say, "Whatsa matter, bud—got lace on your drawers?" A generation later, to prepare soldiers to fight in Vietnam accusations of femininity were still used as motivating insults. Drill sergeants would mock their troops by saying, "Can't hack it, little girls?" (Eisenhart 1975). In the Marines, the worst insult to male recruits is to compare their performance to a woman's (Gilham 1989).

The same phenomenon occurs in male sports. Sociologist Douglas Foley (1993) notes that football coaches insult boys who don't play well by saying that they are "wearing skirts," and sociologists Jean Stockard and Miriam Johnson (1980), who observed boys playing basketball, heard boys who missed a basket called a "woman."

This name-calling is sociologically significant. As Stockard and Johnson (1980:12) point out, such insults embody the generalized devaluation of women in U.S. society. As they noted, "There is no comparable phenomenon among women, for young girls do not insult each other by calling each other 'man.'"

Gender Inequality in Conversation As you may have noticed, gender inequality also shows up in everyday talk. Because men are more likely to interrupt a conversation and to control changes in topics, sociologists have noted that talk between a man and a woman is often more like talk between an employer and an employee than between social equals (Hall 1984; West and Garcia 1988; Smith-Lovin and Brody 1989; Tannen 1990). Even in college, male students interrupt their instructors more often than do female students, especially if the instructor is female (Brooks 1982). In short, conversations between men and women mirror their relative positions of power in society.

Shown here is David Williams of the Houston Oilers holding his newborn child. Williams received national publicity when he missed a game in order to be present at the birth of his first child. Do you think he showed irresponsibility to his employer and to football fans by purposely missing the game?

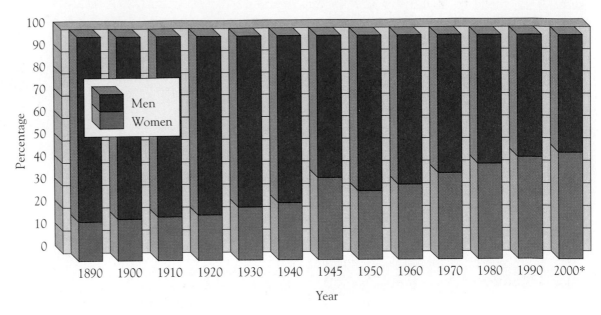

* Author's estimate.
Sources: 1969 Handbook on Women Workers, 1969: 10; Manpower Report to the President, 1971: 203, 205; Mills and Palumbo, 1980: 6, 45; Statistical Abstract 1993: Table 622 Note: Pre 1940 figures include women 14 and over: figures for 1940 and after are for women 16 and over.

Figure 11.3

Women's and Men's Proportion of the U.S. Labor Force.

Derogatory terms and conversation represent only the tip of the iceberg, however, for underlying these aspects of everyday life is a structural inequality based on gender that runs throughout society. Let's examine that structural feature in the workplace.

 ## Gender Relations in the Workplace

To examine the work setting is to make visible basic relations between males and females. Let us look at changes in the work force, then compare what males and females expect from their jobs, and, finally, examine discrimination at work.

Changes in the Work Force

Since 1890, the U.S. government has tracked the percentage of the work force that is male and female. From Figure 11.3, you can see that in 1890 about four of every five workers were male and that with each passing year women have made up a larger proportion of the U.S. labor force. The exception is the years immediately following World War II when millions of women left factories and offices to return home as full-time wives and mothers. Today, for every ten male workers, there are almost nine female workers.

Figure 11.4 shows the *labor force participation rate*; that is, the proportion of men and women age 16 and older who are in the labor force at least part time. A hundred years ago, less than one in five females was employed outside the home. By 1945, this total had doubled to about two of five. Following World War II, the percentage of females in the labor force declined for a few years and then resumed its upward march. Today it is about three of every five females. Note that while the rate has been increasing for females it has been dropping slowly for males, and at this point in U.S. history the gap between males and females is the smallest it has ever been.

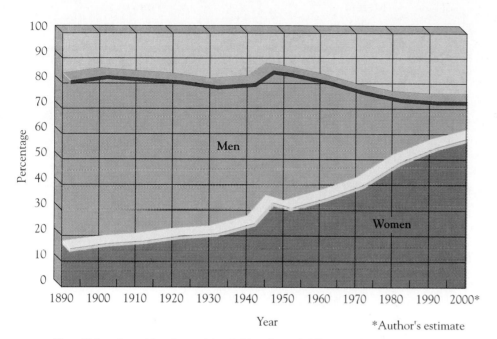

Figure 11.4

What Percentage of U.S. Men and Women Are in the Labor Force?

Note: U.S. males and females age 16 and older who work full time and part time.

Sources: Pre-1970, Blau and Winkler 1989; 1970–2000, *Statistical Abstract* 1993: Table 622

Differences in What Males and Females Expect from a Job

After you finish college, what will you expect from a job besides a paycheck? A good part of the answer may depend on your sex. Each year during the past couple of decades, sociologists have interviewed representative samples of high school seniors about their job attitudes. Just as these years have brought fundamental changes in male–female relationships, so they have brought interesting changes in job expectations. Both males and females continue to want their work to provide good income, status, and security, but it is now females who place greater value on jobs that give an opportunity to make decisions and to face challenges, while males place higher value on a slower pace and more leisure (Leverenz et al. 1993). Other differences are summarized in Figure 11.5 on page 296.

The Pay Gap

How would you like to earn an extra $700,000 on your job? If this sounds attractive, all you have to do is average an extra $17,000 or $18,000 a year between the ages of 25 and 65.

Is this hard to do? Not if you are a male—for, compared with female college graduates, this is precisely how much more the *average* male college graduate will earn. Hardly any single factor pinpoints gender discrimination better than this figure. Look at Table 11.2, and you will see that the gender gap in earnings

Table 11.2

Annual Earnings by Education

	High School		College	
	Dropout	*Graduate*	*Dropout*	*Bachelor's or Higher*
Male	$23,765	$28,230	$33,758	$50,747
Female	$15,352	$19,336	$22,833	$33,144
Gender Penalty	$8,413	$8,894	$10,925	$17,603

Note: For year-round, full-time workers 25 years old and over as of March 1992.

Source: *Statistical Abstract* 1993: Table 731.

Figure 11.5

What Do Young Men and Women Want from Their Jobs? Features of Work That Both Men and Women Rank High

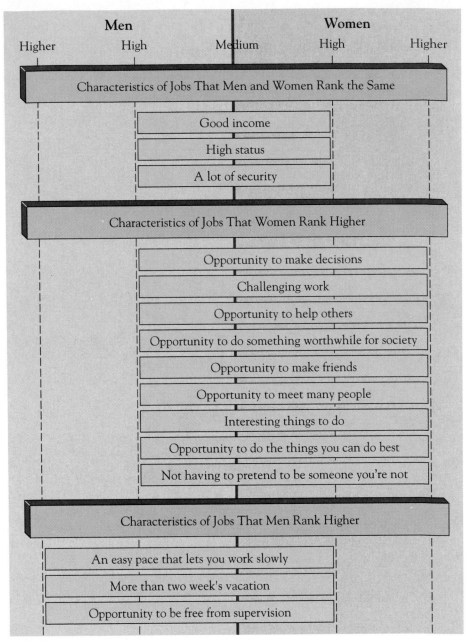

Source: Leverenz et al. 1993.

applies to all levels of education. In fact, if we consider all year-round, full-time workers in all fields in the United States, we find that women's wages average only 73 percent of men's. As Figure 11.6 shows, until 1985 women's earnings hovered between 58 and 61 percent of men's, so being paid just under three-fourths of what men make is actually an improvement. A gender gap in pay characterizes all industrialized nations, but only in Japan is the gap larger than in the United States (Blau and Kahn 1992).

There must be some logical explanation for the gender pay gap. Earlier we saw that college degrees are gender linked, so perhaps it is due to career choices. Maybe women tend to choose lower-paying jobs, such as grade-school teaching, whereas men are more likely to go into better-paying fields, such as business and engineering. Actually, this is true, and researchers have found that about *half* the pay gap is due to such factors. The balance, however, is due to gender discrimination (Kemp 1990).

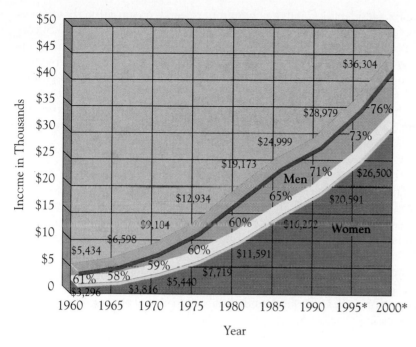

Figure 11.6

The Gender Pay Gap: The Annual Income of Full-Time Workers and the Percentage of the Men's Income Earned by Women

* Author's estimate.

Sources: Beeghley 1989: 239: *Statistical Abstract* 1993: Table 727.

Depending on your sex, then, you are likely to either benefit from gender discrimination—or to be its victim. Because this factor will be so important in your own work life, let's see how it actually takes place. A study by economists Rex Fuller and Richard Schoenberger (1991) is especially insightful. By focusing on gender inequality *within* the same occupation, they eliminated the variable of women choosing lesser-paying occupations. They examined the starting salaries of 230 business majors at the University of Wisconsin, of whom 47 percent were women, and found that females averaged 11 percent ($1,737) lower than males.

We might be able to think of valid reasons for this initial pay gap. For example, the female candidates might have been less qualified. Perhaps they didn't do as well in their courses and received lower grades. Or maybe they did fewer internships. If so, they would deserve lower salaries. To test this possibility, Fuller and Schoenberger reviewed the students' college records. To their surprise, it turned out that the female students had earned *higher* grades and done *more* internships than the men. In other words, if women were equally qualified, the women were offered lower salaries—and if the women were more highly qualified, they were offered lower salaries—a classic lose–lose situation.

What happened after these graduates were on the job? Did these starting salaries wash out, so that after a few years the males and females earned about the same? To find out, Fuller and Schoenberger checked on these graduates five years later. Instead of narrowing, however, the pay gap had grown even wider, and by this time the women earned 14 percent ($3,615) less than the men.

In short, work represents two separate worlds for men and women. In science, females are excluded from the "inner circle" that stimulates research and financing (Zuckerman et al. 1991). In the legal profession, women are only half as likely as men to receive a partnership in their legal firms—even women who graduated from quality law schools and received academic honors (Spurr 1990). The average female corporate lawyer makes $40,000 a year less than her male counterpart (Hagan 1990). A survey of the 325 largest U.S. corporations showed that the average chief executive officer receives an annual salary of $1 million and averages another $400,000 from stock options. *Not one of these 325 CEOs is a female* (*Wall Street Journal*, April 18, 1990).

Felice Schwartz, president of Catalyst, a nonprofit research organization that focuses on women's issues in the workplace, surveyed female executives in the largest U.S. corporations (Lopez 1992). She concluded that women are detoured away from core positions from which senior executives are tapped. Stereotyped as being better at providing "support," women are steered away from marketing, production, and sales and pushed into public relations and human resources—which do not provide the corporate experience needed for jobs in top management. This glass ceiling prevents women from advancing to top executive positions, while it lets men pass through. As a result, only 6 percent of the 12,000 directors of the largest one thousand corporations in the United States are women (Sharpe 1993).

In the upper ranks, an "old boys" network maintains the pay gap. That is, a network of acquaintances funnels men to job openings and encourages promotions of one another. Excluded from this network, female professionals find themselves at a disadvantage when it comes to career opportunities (Andersen 1988). In self-defense, some female professionals are cultivating their own networks (Cox 1986; Schwartz 1989), while others are suing for equal treatment (Pleck 1990; Holden 1993).

Most males and females, however, do not graduate from college, and most do not become professionals or work at jobs with high salaries and high prestige. To gain an idea of how people cope who work at the lower end of the occupational prestige scale, see the Down-to-Earth Sociology box below.

The "Mommy Track"

Wives are more likely than husbands to be the caretakers of the marriage, to nurture it through the hard times. Most wives also take greater responsibility for taking care of

Down-To-Earth Sociology

Maintaining Dignity in the Midst of Stigma

SUPPOSE FOR A MOMENT that you hadn't made it to college, but that, instead, you had ended up with a low-paying, low-status, dead-end job that consists of cleaning up other people's messes. How do you think you could maintain a sense of dignity?

Sociologist Mary Romero interviewed twenty-five Chicanas who were doing domestic work. All were poor; only nine had completed high school. They knew that people looked down on their work: vacuuming, washing and waxing floors, dusting, and cleaning bathrooms and kitchens. Some were angry or embarrassed, others defensive. They used three main symbolic interactionist strategies for dealing with the stigma.

The first was to define themselves as professionals and their employers as clients and customers. Rather than using the term "domestic," they referred to themselves as "professional housekeeper." Listen to the sharp distinction one worker makes between a maid and a housekeeper:

They (the employer's children) started to introduce me to their friends as their maid. "This is our maid, Angela." I would say, "I'm not your maid. I've come to clean your house, and a maid is someone who takes care of you and lives here or comes in every

day, and I come once a week and it is to take care of what you have messed up. I'm not your maid. I'm your housekeeper.

A second strategy is to emphasize the autonomy of their work, that they are able to work at their own pace and do the job in their own way. They stress how this benefit is not found in many jobs, such as hospital work, where an employer breathes down your neck.

The third strategy is to emphasize the flexibility of the work. All the women in Romero's sample had children of their own, and several stressed how their work helps them as mothers. One woman said,

I make my own hours so I can go to (school) programs when I'm needed. I go to conferences when I'm needed. When the kids are ill, I'm there. . . . It's one of the best jobs that I could find in my situation where I am home with my family before and after school. I'm always around.

Within a social structure that can be oppressive, then, these women symbolically define their work in such a way that they give a dignity to it—and to themselves—that is otherwise denied them by their society.

Source: Based on Romero 1988.

the children and spend considerably more time doing housework (see Chapter 16). Consequently, most employed wives face greater role conflict than do their husbands.

To help resolve this conflict, Felice Schwartz (1989) suggested that corporations offer women a choice of two parallel career paths. The "fast track" consists of the high-powered, demanding positions that may require sixty or seventy hours of work per week—regular responsibilities, emergencies, out-of-town meetings, and a briefcase jammed with work at night and on weekends. With such limited time outside of work, family life often suffers. Women can choose this "fast track" if they wish. Or instead they may choose the proposed "mommy track," which would stress both career and family. Less would be expected of a woman on the "mommy track," for her commitment to the firm would be lower and her commitment to her family higher.

That, of course, say critics, is exactly what is wrong with this proposal. A "mommy track" will encourage women to be satisfied with lower aspirations and fewer promotions and confirm male stereotypes of female executives. Because there is no "daddy track," it also assumes that child rearing is primarily women's work (Starrels 1992). To encourage women to slow up in the race to climb the corporate ladder would perpetuate, or even increase, the executive pay gap. The "mommy track," conclude critics, would keep men in executive power by relegating women to an inferior position in corporate life.

Critics suggest that a better way to confront the conflict between work and family is for husbands to take greater responsibilities at home and for firms to provide on-site day care, flexible work schedules, and parental leave without loss of benefits (Auerbach 1990; Galinsky and Stein 1990). Others maintain that the choice between family and career is artificial, that there are ample role models of family-oriented, highly successful women from Sandra Day O'Connor and Ruth Bader Ginsberg, Justices of the U.S. Supreme Court, to Ann Fisher, astronaut and physician (Ferguson and Dunphy 1991).

Sexual Harassment

In a third-floor hallway at a convention of Navy pilots at the Las Vegas Hilton, male officers lined up against the walls. When female pilots tried to walk by, the men pushed, touched, and rubbed the women. One female officer reported that a male officer grabbed her buttocks with both hands, then grabbed her breasts. Other women reported similar incidents (*U.S. News & World Report,* July 13, 1992).

When the women complained, male officers shrugged their shoulders and said with a wink that "boys will be boys." They felt that the women were being too sensitive. "What do you expect when you're around a bunch of drunk pilots, anyway?" A Navy investigation found no fault. When the female officers complained to the media, pressures mounted, and the Secretary of the Navy resigned.

Sexual harassment—unwanted sexual advances, whether touches, looks, pressures to have sex, or even jokes—was not recognized as a problem until the 1970s. Before this, women considered such things a personal matter. With the prodding of feminists, however, women began to see unwanted sexual advances at work as part of a structural problem. That is, they no longer saw them as a male here and there doing obnoxious things because he was attracted to a female, but, rather, as males in authority using their positions to force various forms of unwanted sex on females.

In 1976, feminists coined the term *sexual harassment* (MacKinnon 1979), and now even schoolchildren are familiar with it. Symbolic interactionists would say that a change in consciousness resulted from a "symbolic reinterpretation of experiences." In short, when females had a name to refer to their experiences, they saw them in a different light. To see how this same reinterpretation is occurring in another culture, see the Perspectives box on the next page.

When Felice Schwartz suggested in 1989 that corporations offer working women with children the option of selecting a separate—and slower-paced—career track than that of childless women, controversy flared. Some said that instead of offering women the option of lowering their work aspirations in favor of family, employers should encourage males to share equally in family tasks. These critics of the "mommy track" also called for family-oriented benefits such as onsite day care and parental leave for both parents.

sexual harassment: usually defined as the use of one's occupational position to force unwanted sexual demands on someone; the legal definition includes nonsexual behavior—an abusive or hostile work environment based on gender that impairs the ability to perform one's job (Fitzpatrick 1994)

Now that many women have moved into positions of power, sexual harassment is no longer an exclusively female problem (Lopez 1994). One study in 1981 and another in 1992 found that 15 percent of males had been sexually harassed (*Merit Systems Protection Board* 1981; Lawler 1994). Male victims are much less likely than female victims to receive a sympathetic ear, for people tend to find such situations humorous. These men, however, also report that they feel powerless and used. Social norms, I imagine, will eventually catch up to this changing reality.

Victims of sexual harassment have begun to fight back. They have demanded and received legal protection. The Equal Employment Opportunity Commission has broadened the definition of sexual harassment to include all unwelcome sexual attention that affects an employee's job conditions or creates a "hostile" working environment (Adler 1991). The legal concept has also become so fuzzy that in one case a female employee who was *not* asked for sexual favors while the others were was ruled a victim of sexual harassment (Hayes 1991).

When the congressional hearings for Judge Clarence Thomas's confirmation to the U.S. Supreme Court were viewed by a national television audience in 1991, *sexual harassment* became a household term overnight. Sexual harassment has become a top item in executive education programs, and many companies are trying to develop written policies specifying exactly which behaviors are intolerable (Adler 1991).

Perspectives

CULTURAL DIVERSITY AROUND THE WORLD

Sexual Harassment in Japan

THE PUBLIC RELATIONS DEPARTMENT had come up with an eye-catcher: Each month, the cover of the company's magazine would show a woman taking off one more piece of clothing. The men were pleased, looking forward to each new issue.

Six months later, with the cover girl poised to take off her tank top in the next edition, the objections of women employees had grown too loud to ignore. "We told them it was a lousy idea," said Junko Takashima, assistant director of the company's women's affairs division. The firm, dropped the striptease act.

The Japanese men didn't get the point. "What's all the fuss about?" they asked. "Beauty is beauty. We're just admiring the ladies. It's a wish, or maybe a hope. It's nothing serious. It just adds a little spice to boring days at the office."

"It's degrading to us, and it must stop," responded female workers, who, encouraged by the U.S. feminist movement, have broken their long tradition of passive silence.

The Japanese have no word of their own to describe this situation, so they have borrowed the English phrase "sexual harassment." They are now struggling to apply it to their own culture. In Japan a pat on the bottom has long been taken for granted as a boss's way of getting his secretary's attention.

Differing cultural expectations have led to problems when Japanese executives—always male—have been sent to overseas factories. A managing director of Honda learned this the hard way. During business meetings he repeatedly put his hand on the knee of an American employee. When she threatened to sue, he was transferred back to Japan.

The Japanese expectation that everyone will work together harmoniously does not make it easy complain. But some women are now speaking out, and discovering how to apply the Western concept "sexual harassment."

Source: Based on Graven 1990.

Gender and Violence

The high rate of violence in U.S. society shocks foreigners and frightens many Americans. Only a couple of generations ago many Americans left their homes and cars unlocked, in contrast with today when, fearful of carjackings, they even lock their cars while driving, and, fearful of rape and kidnappings, escort their children to school. Lurking behind these fears is the gender inequality of violence—that females are most likely to be victims of males, not the other way around. Let's briefly review this almost one-way street in gender violence.

Violence Against Women

Rape Because rape was the recurring theme of Chapter 5, where we reviewed research methods, here we shall simply review a couple of its primary features. Rape has become so common in U.S. society that each year 83 of every 100,000 females in the entire country are raped. Rapists are almost exclusively young males. Although males aged 14 to 25 make up about 18 percent of the U.S. male population, about 54 percent of those arrested for rape are in this age group (U.S. House of Representatives 1990; *FBI Uniform Crime Reports* 1992).

Date Rape What has shocked so many about date rape (also known as acquaintance rape) are studies showing that it is not an isolated event here and there. For example, about 21 percent of female students in the introductory psychology courses at Texas A&M University reported that they have been forced to have sexual intercourse. Date rape most commonly occurs not between relative strangers on first dates, but between couples who have known each other about a year (Muehlenhard and Linton 1987). Most date rapes go unreported. Those that are reported are difficult to prosecute, for juries tend to believe that if a woman knows the accused she wasn't "really" raped (Bourque 1989).

Murder Table 11.3 summarizes U.S. statistics on murder and gender. Note that although females make up about 51 percent of the U.S. population, they don't even come close to making up 51 percent of the nation's killers. Note also that when a female is the victim, nine times out of ten the killer is a male.

Table 11.3		
Killers and Their Victims		
	The Killers	
	Male	Female
The Victims		
Male	86%	14%
Female	91%	9%

Source: FBI Uniform Crime Reports 1991: 11.

Abuse against women has been studied extensively by sociologists. A major pattern in domestic abuse is relative power. Almost always, the victims are the family members with the lesser power. Many abused women remain in situations of abuse for years. Symbolic interactionists have identified lack of perceived alternatives as a basic reason that they endure such abuse. Conflict theorists point to women's lower status in society as the basic reason.

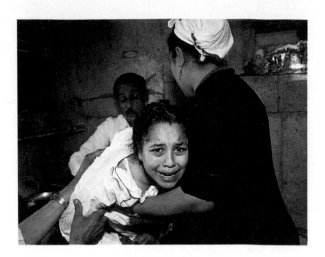

Shown here is a pre-adolescent girl as she is being circumcised without anethesia. Female circumcision, as well as the issue of cultural relativity versus ethnocentrism, are discussed in the Perspectives box on the facing page.

Violence in the Home   Spouse battering, marital rape, and incest are discussed in Chapter 16, pages 454–456. A particular form of violence against women, genital circumcision, is the focus of the Perspectives box on page 302.

A Feminist Understanding of Gender Patterns in Violence

Feminist sociologists have been especially effective in bringing violence against women to the public's attention. Some see symbolic interactionism as a key to understanding how U.S. culture promotes violence by males. An example is action video games in which barely clad females are hunted down and killed. In one of these games by Nintendo, zombies suck the blood of barely dressed sorority sisters (Pereira 1993). The result is not surprising, they point out, for to associate strength and virility with violence—as is done in so many areas of U.S. culture—is to produce violence. Feminist sociologists also use conflict theory. They argue that violence against females is an expression of male power, that males use violence to try to maintain a higher status (Adler 1992). They also point out that if males lose relative status as gender relations change, we can expect high rates of violence by males against females. For some assailants, they suggest, violence even offers a sense of power not available in other spheres of life.

Solutions

There is no magic bullet for this problem, but to be effective any solution must break the connection between violence and masculinity. This will require a wholesale educational program that must incorporate school, churches, homes, and the media. Given such aspects of U.S. history as gunslinging heroes of the West, and current messages in the mass media, it is difficult to see reasons for optimism that a change will come soon.

Our last topic, women in politics, gives us much more reason for optimism.

The Changing Face of Politics

What do these nations have in common?

- Canada in North America
- Argentina, Bolivia, and Nicaragua in Latin America
- Britain, France, Ireland, and Portugal in Western Europe

Perspectives

CULTURAL DIVERSITY AROUND THE WORLD

Female Circumcision

FEMALE CIRCUMCISION IS COMMON in parts of Muslim Africa and in some parts of Malaysia and Indonesia. This custom, often called *female genital mutilation* (FGM) by Westerners, is also known as *clitoral excision, clitoridectomy, infibulation,* and *labiadectomy,* depending largely on how much of the tissue is removed. Worldwide, between 100 million and 200 million females have been circumcised.

In some cultures only the girl's clitoris is cut off, in others the clitoris and both the labia majora and the labia minora. The Nubia in the Sudan cut away most of the girl's genitalia, then sew together the remaining outer edges with silk or catgut, so that when the wound is healed the vagina is fused together. They leave a very small opening—variously described as the size of a matchstick or a pinhole—for the passage of urine and menstrual fluids. In East Africa the vaginal opening is not sutured shut, but the clitoris and both sets of labia are cut off.

Among most groups, the surgery takes place between the ages of 4 and 8. In some cultures it occurs seven to ten days after birth, while in others it is not performed until girls reach adolescence. Often done without anesthesia, the pain is so excruciating that adults sometimes must hold the girl down. In urban areas, the operation is sometimes performed by physicians; in rural areas, it is usually performed by a neighborhood woman.

Some of the risks are shock, extensive bleeding, infection, infertility, and death. Ongoing complications include vaginal spasms, painful intercourse, and lack of orgasms. The tiny opening makes urination and menstruation difficult. Frequent urinary tract infections result from urine and menstrual flow building up behind the little opening.

When the woman marries, the opening is cut wider to permit sexual intercourse. In some groups, this is the husband's responsibility. Before a woman gives birth, the opening is enlarged further. After birth, the vagina is again sutured shut, a cycle of surgically closing and opening that begins anew with each birth.

One woman, circumcised at 12, described it this way:

"Lie down there," the excisor suddenly said to me, pointing to a mat stretched out on the ground. No sooner had I laid down than I felt my frail, thin legs tightly grasped by heavy hands and pulled wide apart. I lifted my head. Two women on each side of me pinned me to the ground. My arms were also immobilized. Suddenly I felt some strange substance being spread over my genital area. . . . It was supposed to facilitate the excision, it seems. . . . I would have given anything at that moment to be a thousand miles away; then a shooting pain brought me back to reality. . . . I underwent the ablation of the labia minor and then of the clitoris. The operation seemed to go on forever . . . I was in the throes of agony, torn apart both physically and psychologically. It was the rule that girls of my age did not weep in this situation. I broke the rule. I reacted immediately with tears and screams of pain . . . . Never

have I felt such excruciating pain!

[After the operation] they forced me, not only to walk back to join the other girls who had already been excised, but to dance with them . . . I was doing my best . . . then I fainted. . . . It was a month before I was completely healed. . . . When I was better, everyone mocked me, as I hadn't been brave, they said. (Walker and Parmar 1993:107–108)

What are the reasons for this custom? Some groups believe that it reduces female sexual desire, thus making it less likely that a wife will be unfaithful to her husband. Others believe that it enhances female fertility, prevents the clitoris from getting infected, and enhances vaginal cleanliness. A primary reason for the more extensive forms is that it guarantees that a woman will be a virgin when she marries.

Feminists, who call female circumcision a form of ritual torture to control female sexuality, point out that the societies that practice it are male dominated. Mothers cooperate with the circumcision because in these societies an unmarried woman has virtually no rights, and an uncircumcised woman is considered impure and is not allowed to marry. Grandmothers insist that the custom continue out of concern that their granddaughters marry well.

Some Muslims living in the United States take their daughters to Muslim countries for the operation. Although the surgery is legal in the United States, physicians refuse to perform it because they can be charged with child abuse. Pressure has been placed on the United Nations to campaign against female circumcision and to withhold development funds from countries that practice it.

Do you think that Western nations should try to make African nations stop this custom? Or would this be ethnocentric, the imposition of Western values on other cultures? As one Somali woman said, "The Somali woman doesn't need an alien woman telling her how to treat her private parts." What legitimate basis do you think there is for members of one culture to interfere with another? What if people from some culture did not like an American custom because it violated their values—such as surgery to enlarge or reduce breasts, remove fat, or change the shape of one's nose—would they have a proper basis for interfering with us? Or does female circumcision belong to some special category that justifies intervention? If so, what category?

Sources: Based on Mahran 1978, 1981; Ebomoyi 1987; Lightfoot-Klein 1989; Denney and Quadango 1992; Edgerton 1992; Hansen and Scroggins 1992; van der Kwaak 1992; Merwine 1993; Walker and Parmar 1993.

- Iceland and the Philippines in Asia
- Israel in the Mideast
- Poland in Eastern Europe
- India, Pakistan, and Sri Lanka on the subcontinent

The answer is that all have had a female president or prime minister. To this list we can add even such bastions of male chauvinism as Haiti, Turkey, Pakistan, and Bangladesh (Harwood and Brooks 1993).

Then why not the United States? Why don't women, who outnumber men, take political control of the nation? Nine million more women than men are of voting age, and about 53 percent of all voters in U.S. national elections are women. As Table 11.4 shows, however, women are greatly outnumbered by men in political office. Only a handful of women serve as governors and mayors of large cities. In spite of the political gains women have made in recent elections, since 1789 1,800 men have served in the U.S. Senate, but only 22 women, including the seven current senators. Not until 1992 was the first African-American woman (Carol Mosely-Braun) elected to the U.S. Senate (National Women's Political Caucus 1993; *Statistical Abstract* 1993: Table 454).

The reasons for women's underrepresentation? First, women are still underrepresented in law and business, the careers from which most politicians come. Further, most women do not perceive themselves as a class of people who need bloc political action in order to overcome domination. Most women also find the irregular hours needed to

---

Table 11.4

U.S. Women in Political Office, 1993

	Percentage and Number Held by Women	
	Percentage	Number
National Office		
U.S. Senate	7%	7
U.S. House of Representatives	11%	47
State Office		
Governors	6%	3
Attorneys general	16%	8
Secretaries of state	26%	13
Treasurers	38%	19
State auditors	10%	5
State legislature	20%	1,517
Local Office		
Mayors[a]	18%	175

Note: Does not include women elected to the judiciary, appointed to state cabinet-level positions, elected to executive posts by the legislature, or members of a university board of trustees.

[a]Of cities with a population over 30,000.

Source: National Women's Political Caucus 1993.

Although women still represent a minority of elected and appointed officials, in recent years they have become much more prominent in U.S. politics. Shown here is Ruth Bader Ginsburg, the second woman appointed to the U.S. Supreme Court, as she takes the oath to defend the Constitution of the United States. Administering the oath is Chief Justice William Rehnquist. Ginsburg's husband is holding the Bible, and President Clinton is looking on.

run for office incompatible with their role as mothers. Fathers, in contrast, whose ordinary roles are more likely to take them away from home, do not feel this same conflict. Women are also less likely to have a supportive spouse who is willing to play an unassuming background role while providing solace, encouragement, child care, and voter appeal. Finally, preferring to hold tightly onto their positions of power, males have been reluctant to incorporate women into centers of decision making or to present them as viable candidates.

These very factors are changing, and we can expect more women to seek and gain political office. As we saw in Figure 11.2, more women are going into law, where they are doing more traveling and making statewide and national contacts. The same is true for business. Increasingly, child care is seen as a mutual responsibility of both mother and father. And in some areas, such as my own political district, party heads are frantically searching for qualified candidates (read "people with voter appeal and without skeletons in their closets"), without regard to sex. The primary concern in at least some areas today is not gender, but whether a candidate can win. This generation, then, is likely to mark a fundamental change in women's political participation, and it appears only a matter of time until a woman occupies the Oval Office.

Glimpsing the Future—with Hope

As females come to play a fuller role in the decision-making processes of our social institutions, the stereotypes and role models, which lock males into exclusively male activities and push females into roles considered feminine, will be broken. As structural barriers fall and more activities become degenderized, both males and females will be free to pursue activities more compatible with their abilities and desires as *individuals*.

As sociologist Janet Giele (1978) pointed out, the ultimate possibility is a new conception of the human personality. At present structural obstacles, accompanied by supporting socialization and stereotypes, cast most males and females into fairly rigid molds along the lines that culture dictates. To overcome these obstacles and abandon traditional stereotypes is to give males and females new perceptions of themselves and one another. Both females and males will then be free to feel and to express needs and emotions that present social arrangements deny them. Females are likely to perceive themselves as more in control of their environment and to explore this aspect of the human personality. Males are likely to feel and to express more emotional sensitivity—to be warmer, more affectionate and tender, and to give greater expression to anxieties and stresses that their gender now forces them to suppress. In the future we may discover that such "greater wholeness" of males and females entails many other dimensions of the human personality.

As they develop a new consciousness of themselves and of their own potential, basic relationships between females and males will change. Certainly distinctions between the sexes will not disappear. There is no reason, however, for biological differences to be translated into social inequalities. The reasonable goal is appreciation of sexual differences coupled with equality of opportunity—which may well lead to a transformed society (Hubbard 1990; Offen 1990). If so, as sociologist Alison Jaggar (1990) observed, gender equality can become less a goal than a background condition for living in society.

Summary and Review

Issues of Sex and Gender

What is gender stratification?

The term **gender stratification** refers to unequal access to power, prestige, and property on the basis of sex. Each society establishes a structure that, on the basis of sex and gender, permits or limits access to the group's privileges. P. 280.

How do sex and gender differ?

Sex refers to biological distinctions between males and females. Sex consists of both primary and secondary sex characteristics. **Gender,** in contrast, is what a society considers proper behaviors and attitudes for its male and female members. Sex physically distinguishes males from females; gender defines what is "masculine" and "feminine." Pp. 280–281.

Is gender inequality due to biology or culture?

In the "nature versus nurture" debate—whether differences between male and female behaviors are caused by inherited (biological) or learned (cultural) characteristics—almost all sociologists take the side of nurture. Pp. 281–285.

Gender Inequality in Global Perspective

Is gender stratification universal?

George Murdock surveyed information on premodern societies and found not only that all of them have sex-linked activities, but also that, universally, greater prestige is given to male activities. **Patriarchy,** or male dominance, does appear to be universal. Pp. 285–286.

How did females become a minority group?

Two theories attempt to explain how females became a minority group in their own societies. One focuses on the physical limitations imposed by childbirth, the other on warfare and the need to encourage males to engage in combat. Pp. 286–288.

Gender Inequality in the United States

Is the feminist movement new?

Feminists made political demands for change in the early 1900s—and were met with much hostility, and even violence. Pp. 288–289.

What forms does gender stratification in education take?

Although more females than males now attend college, each tends to select "feminine" or "masculine" fields. In addition, males outnumber females in all but two scientific fields. Change is indicated by the growing numbers of females in such fields as law and medicine. Pp. 289–292.

Is there gender inequality in everyday life?

Two indications of gender inequality in everyday life are the general devaluation of femininity and the male dominance of conversation. Pp. 292–294.

Gender Relations in the Workplace

How is gender inequality manifested in the workplace?

Over the last century, females have made up an increasing proportion of the work force. Nonetheless, the gender gap in pay characterizes all occupations. For college graduates, the lifetime pay gap runs about $700,000 in favor of males. **Sexual harassment** also continues to be a reality of the workplace. Pp. 294–300.

Gender and Violence

What forms does violence against women take?

Females are overwhelmingly the victims of battering, rape, incest, and murder. Female circumcision is a special case of violence against women. Conflict theorists point out that males use violence to maintain their higher status. Pp. 301–303.

The Changing Face of Politics

What is the trend in gender inequality in politics?

A strict division of gender roles—females as child care providers and housekeepers, males as workers outside the home—has traditionally kept females out of politics. Although women continue to be underrepresented in U.S. politics, the trend toward greater political equality is firmly in place. Pp. 302–305.

Glimpsing the Future—with Hope

What progress has been made in reducing gender inequality?

In the United States, females are playing a fuller role in the decision-making processes of our social institutions. Males, too, are re-examining their traditional roles. The ultimate possibility of gender equality is a new conception of the human personality, one that allows both males and females to pursue their individual interests unfettered by gender. Pp. 305–306.

Where can I read more on this topic?

Suggested readings for this chapter are listed on page 641.

Pacita Abad, Korean Shopkeepers, 1993

Inequalities of Race and Ethnicity

T HE COLONEL WAS EXHAUSTED. HE *scowled as he looked at the long line facing him.*

"Sometimes I wonder if it's worth the effort," he thought. "But someone's got to do it. They're short of men, and we all have to make sacrifices in war."

The colonel looked at the young man and woman standing in front of his desk—disheveled, unkempt hair, the man unshaven for weeks, both reeking a strong odor. The body odor was one of the worst parts of his job. That was why he always kept a fan blowing across his desk. At least it helped a little.

"I'm glad I don't have to touch them," the colonel thought, as he scratched his shoulder. His shoulder was acting up again. He could hardly wait to get home to Hilda. She would rub it, as she always did after a hard day's work. "If it weren't for my wife and kids, I don't know how I could keep going," he mused.

The colonel glanced at the pair again. "He seems strong enough. There's still some work in him," he thought. "But she's too weak." He motioned the young man to the right, the young woman to the left.

There was no doubt about the next seven. Four were old, two were young children, and one hobbled as he walked. "They wouldn't last a day. Just a waste of time," the colonel said to himself. He motioned them to the left.

The line seemed to stretch to eternity. Indeed, the line did stretch to eternity. The colonel was a member of the Schutzstaffel, the infamous Nazi SS. As a physician, he had been assigned to Auschwitz, the concentration camp that served a double purpose: mass extermination and the employment of slave labor (Rubenstein 1987). His job was not to heal, but to sort people into two groups. Children, the elderly, and the weak were sent to one door—from which they were transported to the gas ovens. Those who looked strong entered the other door, from which they emerged as factory slaves. They labored until they dropped from overwork and lack of nutrition, ordinarily just a matter of a few weeks.

Although you and I are not likely to feel sympathy for the colonel—hurting shoulder or not—the fact is that quite ordinary people cooperated with the Nazi death machine (Browning 1993). Perhaps through this chapter you will come to better understand how that could be.

▼ Basic Concepts in Race and Ethnic Relations

Seldom do race and ethnic relations drop to such a brutal low as they did in Nazi Germany, but in our own society newspaper headlines and television evening news keep race relations constantly before us. Sociological findings on this topic, then, can contribute greatly to our better understanding of social life. To begin, let us consider to what extent race itself is a myth.

Race: Myth and Reality

With its almost six billion people, the world offers a fascinating variety of human shapes and colors. People see one another as black, white, red, yellow, and brown. Eyes come in various shades of blue, brown, and green. Thick and thin lips. Straight hair, curly hair, kinky hair, black, white, and red hair—and, of course, all hues of brown.

As humans spread throughout the world, their adaptations to diverse climate and other living conditions resulted in this fascinating variety of complexions, colors, and shapes. Genetic mutations added distinct characteristics to the peoples of the globe. In this sense the concept of **race,** a group with inherited physical characteristics that distinguish it from another group, is a reality. Humans do indeed come in a variety of colors and shapes.

race: inherited physical characteristics that distinguish one group from another

310

In two senses, however, race is a myth, a fabrication of the human mind. The *first* fabrication is the idea that any one race is superior to another. All races have their geniuses—and their idiots. As with language, no race is superior to another. Adolf Hitler's ideas were extreme. He believed that a superior race, the Aryan, was responsible for the cultural achievements of Europe. These tall, fair-skinned blonds—the "master race"— possessed the genetic stuff that made them inherently superior. (Never mind that Hitler was not a blond!) Consequently, the Aryans were destined to establish a higher culture and institute a new world order. This destiny required them to avoid the "racial contamination" that breeding with inferior races would engender and to isolate or destroy races that might endanger Aryan culture.

The colonel in our opening vignette, even though educated in one of the best medical schools of the time, bought that line. He gave up healing and began mass killing— all in the name of what was good for the "master race." Even many scientists of the time—not only in Germany but throughout Europe and the United States—espoused the idea of racial superiority. Not surprisingly, they considered themselves members of the supposedly superior race!

In addition to the myth of racial superiority, there is a *second* myth—that of the existence of a "pure" race. From the perspective of contemporary biology, humans show such a mixture of physical characteristics—in skin color, hair texture, nose shape, head shape, eye color, and so on—that "pure" races do not exist. Instead of falling into distinct types clearly separate from one another, human characteristics flow endlessly together. These minute gradations make arbitrary any attempt to draw definite lines.

Large groupings of people, however, can be classified by blood type and gene frequencies. Yet even these classifications do not uncover "race." Rather, they are so arbitrary that biologists and anthropologists can draw up listings showing any number of "races." Ashley Montagu (1964), a physical anthropologist, pointed out that some scientists have classified humans into only two "races" while others have found as many as two thousand. Montagu (1960) himself classified humans into forty "racial" groups.

This is not meant to imply that the *idea* of race is a myth. That idea is definitely very much alive. It is firmly embedded in our culture, a social reality that we confront daily (McLemore 1994). As noted in Chapter 4, sociologist W. I. Thomas observed that "if people define situations as real, they are real in their consequences." The fact that no race is superior or that we cannot even decide how people should be biologically classified into races is not what counts. What makes a difference for social life, rather, is that people *believe* these ideas, for *people act on beliefs, not facts*. As a result, we always have people like Hitler—and those like the colonel who agree with him. Most people, fortunately, do not believe in such extremes, yet most people also appear to be ethnocentric enough to believe, at least just a little, that their *own* race is superior to others.

Ethnic Groups

Whereas the term *race* refers to biological characteristics that distinguish one people from another, **ethnicity** and **ethnic** apply to cultural characteristics. Derived from the Greek *ethnos*, meaning "people" or "nation," these terms refer to people who identify with one another on the basis of common ancestry and cultural heritage. Their sense of belonging centers on country of origin, distinctive foods, dress, family names and relationships, language, music, religion, and other customs.

Although this distinction between race and ethnicity is clear—one is biological the other cultural—people often confuse the two. This confusion is due to the cultural differences people see *and* the way they define race. For example, many people consider the Jews a race—including many Jews. Jews, however, are more properly considered an ethnic group, for it is their cultural characteristics, especially religion, that bind them together. Wherever Jews have lived in the world, they have intermarried. Consequently, Jews in China may look mongoloid, while some Swedish Jews are blue-eyed blonds. This matter is even more strikingly illustrated in the case of the Ethiopian Jews, who look so

ethnic (and **ethnicity**): having distinctive cultural characteristics

Fanning hatred for Jews as a scapegoat for Germany's problems and preaching the superiority of the supposed racially pure Aryans, Adolf Hitler eventually put his ideas of race into practice. The result was the Holocaust, the wholesale and systematic slaughter of Jews and others deemed racially inferior. In the photo on the left, Hitler is addressing a group called "Hitler Youth," a sort of Boy Scouts dedicated to serving Hitler and his ideas. The photo on the right is of U.S. senators visiting the concentration camp at Buchenwald after Germany's defeat in World War II, where they view a small part of the consequences of Hitler's racial ideas.

different from European Jews that when they immigrated to Israel some felt that they could not *really* be Jews.

Minority Groups

Sociologist Louis Wirth (1945) defined a **minority group** as people who are singled out for unequal treatment and who regard themselves as objects of collective discrimination. Either physical (racial) or cultural (ethnic) differences can be the basis of the unequal treatment. Wirth added that discrimination excludes minorities from full participation in the life of their society.

Surprisingly, this term does not necessarily mean that a minority group is a numerical minority. For example, before India's independence in 1947, a handful of British colonial rulers collectively discriminated against millions of Indians, while under apartheid in South Africa a small group of whites discriminated against the black majority. And, as reviewed in the previous chapter, all over the world females are a minority group. Accordingly, sociologists refer to those who do the discriminating not as the majority but, rather, as the **dominant group,** for they have greater power, more privileges, and higher social status.

The dominant group almost always considers its privileged position to be due to its own innate superiority. Being in a position of political power (and unified by shared physical and cultural traits), the dominant group uses its position to discriminate against those with different—and supposedly inferior—traits.

Emergence of Minority Groups   A group becomes a minority in one of two ways. The *first* is through the expansion of political boundaries by another group. With the ex-

minority group: people who are singled out for unequal treatment, and who regard themselves as objects of collective discrimination

dominant group: the group with the most power, greatest privileges, and highest social status

ception of females, small tribal societies contain no minority groups. In tribal societies everyone is "related," speaks the same language, practices the same customs, and belongs to the same physical stock. When one group expands its political boundaries, however, it produces minority groups, as people with different customs, languages, values, and physical characteristics then become bound into the same political entity. For example, by defeating Mexico in war, the U.S. government annexed the Southwest. Consequently, the Mexicans living there, who had been the dominant group, were transformed into a minority group, a master status that has significantly influenced their lives ever since. A *second* way in which a group becomes a minority is by migration. This can be voluntary, as with the millions of people who have chosen to move from Mexico to the United States, or involuntary, as with the millions of Africans forcibly transported to the United States. (The way females became a minority group represents a third way, but as reviewed in the previous chapter, no one knows just how this occurred.)

Shared Characteristics   Anthroplogists Charles Wagley and Marvin Harris (1958) identified five characteristics shared by minorities worldwide.

1   Membership in a minority group is an ascribed status; that is, it is not voluntary, but comes through birth.
2   The physical or cultural traits that distinguish minorities are held in low esteem by the dominant group.
3   Minorities are unequally treated by the dominant group.
4   Minorities tend to marry within their own group.
5   Minorities tend to feel strong group solidarity (a sense of "we-ness").

These conditions—especially when combined with collective discrimination—tend to create a shared sense of identity among minorities, and, in many instances, even a sense of common destiny (Chandra 1993b).

Prejudice and Discrimination

Although virtually all Americans are familiar with prejudice and discrimination, the United States certainly has no monopoly on these negative features of social life. On the contrary, they appear to characterize every society, regardless of size. The Perspectives box on page 315 recounts the prejudice and discrimination now rampant in Europe. In Northern Ireland, Protestants discriminate against Roman Catholics; in Israel, Ashkenazi Jews, primarily of European descent, discriminate against Sephardi Jews from the Muslim world; and in Japan, the Japanese discriminate against just about anyone who isn't Japanese, especially the Koreans and the two million present-day descendants of the *Eta* caste. A stigma still attaches to the *Eta*, now renamed the Burakumin, who used to do the society's dirty work—working with dead animals (stripping the hides and tanning the leather) and serving as Japan's executioners and prison guards (Taylor 1983). In some places the elderly discriminate against the young, in others the young against the elderly. And, as discussed in Chapter 11, all around the world men discriminate against women.

As you can see from this list, **discrimination** is an *action*—unfair treatment directed against someone. When the basis of such discrimination is race, it is known as **racism,** but discrimination can be based on many characteristics other than race—including age, sex, height, weight, income, education, marital status, sexual orientation, disease, disability, religion, and politics. Discrimination is often the result of **prejudice**—a prejudging of some sort, usually in a negative way—which is an *attitude*. Positive prejudice exaggerates the virtues of a group, such as thinking that some group (usually one's own) is more capable than others. Most prejudice, however, is negative, a prejudgment that some groups are inferior.

discrimination: an *act* of unfair treatment directed against an individual or a group

racism: prejudice and discrimination on the basis of race

prejudice: an *attitude* or prejudging, usually in a negative way

Figure 12.1

The Relationship Between
Attitudes and Actions

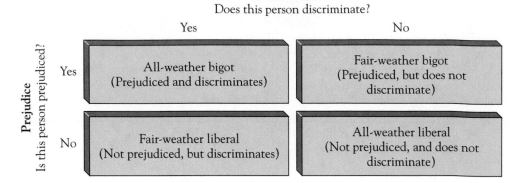

Discrimination
Does this person discriminate?

	Yes	No
Prejudice Is this person prejudiced? — Yes	All-weather bigot (Prejudiced and discriminates)	Fair-weather bigot (Prejudiced, but does not discriminate)
Prejudice Is this person prejudiced? — No	Fair-weather liberal (Not prejudiced, but discriminates)	All-weather liberal (Not prejudiced, and does not discriminate)

Source: Merton 1949, 1976.

When Prejudice and Discrimination Don't Match

Before you began reading this chapter, it is likely that you knew something "very obvious": prejudiced people discriminate—at least if they have the chance—and nonprejudiced people do not. As you have seen over and over in this text, however, sociologists have disproved many of the things people take for granted. So it is in this instance.

Back in 1934, when prejudice against Chinese Americans was widespread and there were no laws against discrimination, sociologist Richard LaPiere designed a simple study. He and a Chinese couple traveled around the United States, staying or eating at over 200 hotels and restaurants. Six months later, LaPiere wrote to these businesses asking if they were willing to serve "members of the Chinese race." Of the 128 replies, 92 percent said that they would not serve Chinese. Yet, on their entire trip, LaPiere and his friends *had been refused service only once.*

Sociologist Robert Merton (1949) found such inconsistencies fascinating. As he thought about the matter, Merton concluded that there were four possible connections between attitudes and actions. As shown in Figure 12.1, these are:

1   *The All-Weather Bigot.* The all-weather bigot meets our expectations, for attitudes match actions: he or she is both prejudiced *and* discriminates. This person is likely to say, "Of course I discriminate—they deserve it."

2   *The Fair-Weather Bigot.* The fair-weather bigot's attitudes and actions do not match. Although this person is prejudiced against the minority, he or she does not discriminate. With today's civil rights legislation, the most common reason for such failure to discriminate is to avoid legal penalties. If in business, this person is likely to say, "I don't like them, but I can't turn them away."

3   *The Fair-Weather Liberal.* The fair-weather liberal's attitudes and actions don't match either. Although the fair-weather liberal believes in equal treatment, he or she does discriminate. In the 1960s, when racial discrimination in hotels and restaurants was legal—as well as the norm—fair-weather liberals were common. The *social structure* kept them in line, for anyone who refused to discriminate would lose both customers and social standing. Although restaurants today cannot bar minorities, they can give them slower service (Farrell and Jones 1988; Feagin 1991), and servers who are not prejudiced may find themselves cooperating in this form of discrimination. They are likely to say, "What else can I do? I don't want to get fired."

4   *The All-Weather Liberal.* Like the all-weather bigot, this person's attitudes and behaviors are consistent. The all-weather liberal is neither prejudiced nor discriminates. He or she is likely to say, "Everyone should be treated equally. Anything less is un-American and immoral, and I would never be a part of it."

▲▼▲▼▲▼▲▼▲▼▲▼▲▼▲▼▲▼▲▼▲▼▲▼▲▼▲▼▲▼▲▼▲▼▲▼▲▼▲

Perspectives

CULTURAL DIVERSITY AROUND THE WORLD

Clashing Cultures

WESTERN EUROPEAN COUNTRIES THAT once sent their huddled masses to the United States are now fending off the tired and poor from the Third World. When the economy of western Europe boomed, accompanied by plummeting birthrates, a need was created for immigrant labor. Workers from the Third World answered that need. The result has been clashing cultures, accompanied by prejudice and discrimination—some of it mild, some violent, all of it ugly.

In France, immigrants from North Africa make up 8 percent of the population. A new party, the National Front, was first dismissed as a racist fringe group just a few years ago. Now the party's slogan, "Let's Make France for the French," has caught on. Jean-Marie Le Pen, the party's head, says, "If integration between Islamic immigrants and the French were possible, it would have happened already. We must send these people back home." Bruno Megret, the party's chief strategist, adds, "France must be made racially pure. There is a worldwide conspiracy that seeks to abolish national identity and infect the world with the AIDS virus."

But it is Germany that has people really worried. With its Nazi past still in living memory, racial disturbances in Germany send shivers down the back of Europe—and throughout the world.

It is the likes of Heiko Baumert of Berlin that frightens people. Sporting tattoos of swastikas and storm troopers on his arms, he says, "If you mix races in Germany, it never works." The young man next to him, with shaved head and black, steel-toed boots, adds, "We want to wake up Germans and pressure the state to kick the foreigners out."

Another of the young men, numbering about three hundred, who have battled Africans in an adjoining block, says, "It is demagoguery to ignore the achievements of the Nazis." The neo-Nazis have even gone so far as to burn down a home with immigrants inside. Although the authorities have cracked down on the neo-Nazis and citizens have turned out in large numbers to demonstrate against racism, one wonders if Germany and the rest of Europe have really learned how evil—and self-destructive—racism is.

For your Consideration:
How do you think this problem can be solved? What steps can be taken so these clashing cultures can peacefully coexist? What do you think will happen if Europe goes into a full-fledged economic depression?

Sources: Horwitz and Forman 1990; Aeppel 1992; Gumbel 1992; Shlaes 1992.

As we have seen, attitudes and behaviors do not always match. Although prejudiced people tend to discriminate and nonprejudiced people try to avoid discriminating, there is not always a one-for-one relationship; for the social environment, which *creates* prejudice in the first place, may encourage or discourage discrimination.

The Extent of Prejudice

You yourself may not be prejudiced, but sociologists have found that ethnocentrism is so common that each racial or ethnic group views other groups as inferior in at least some ways. In a random sample of adults in the Detroit area, sociologists Maria Krysan and Reynolds Farley (1993) found that whites and African Americans judge Latinos as less intelligent than themselves. Using a probability sample (from which we can generalize), sociologists Lawrence Bobo and James Kluegel (1991) found that younger and more educated whites are more willing to have close, sustained interaction with other groups than are older and less educated whites. Details of their findings are shown in Figure 12.2. We must await matching studies to test the prejudices of Latinos, Asian Americans, and Native Americans.

Figure 12.2

Social Distance

Percentage of white Americans who believe that different races should live in segregated housing, by education

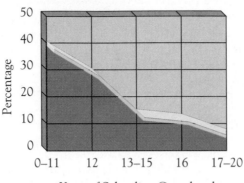

Percentage of white Americans who believe that racial intermarriage should be banned, by age

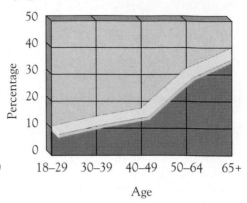

Source: Bobo and Kluegel 1991.

This finding does not mean, of course, that all younger people with the same education have the same amount of prejudice. At the University of Alabama, sociologist Donald Muir (1991) measured racial attitudes of white students who belonged to fraternities and sororities and compared them to nonmembers. He asked a variety of questions—from their ideas about dating African Americans to attending classes together. On all measures, the fraternity members were more prejudiced than the non-frats, a finding that has been confirmed on other campuses (Morris 1991).

Racism on college campuses—by no means limited to members of fraternities and sororitites, nor to any single racial or ethnic group—has become a major issue. We explore it in the following Thinking Critically section.

▼△▼△▼△▼△▼△▼△▼△▼△▼△▼△▼△▼△▼△▼△▼△▼△▼△▼△

Thinking Critically About Social Controversy

Racism on Campus

▼ AT A WHITE FRATERNITY party, the men did a vaudeville skit in which they painted their faces and hands black and sang "Mammy." "It's just good fun," the fraternity president said to his critics. The college administration ruled that blackface skits are within the students' right of free speech. Another fraternity and another campus. This time a slave auction to raise money for the poor. Females were "sold" to the highest bidder. The slaves had to walk their "masters" to class, carry their books, and stand in lunch line for them. Each had SLAVE written on her forehead. When African-American students complained, the response was, "Don't make a big deal out of nothing. This is our annual fund-raising event for the poor. You're too sensitive."

On still another campus, an economics professor said, "Not many blacks take my class. It's too tough for them." When he was accused of racism, he denied that he had a racist bone in his body. He pointed out that he had worked hard for thirty-two years to integrate students from different racial backgrounds. "What I said is the truth," he added.

At another university, a professor wrote in his weekly column in the student newspaper that Puerto Rican students "traveled in packs" and spoke English only when they wanted to. When criticized, he replied that he had written only the truth, that it was time for minorities to be integrated into student life instead of remaining aloof. When minority students went to the administration, one of the trustees replied, "You should settle down and concentrate on your studies. I think that's the main reason your group isn't doing as well as the whites."

In the 1920s, the Ku Klux Klan became a powerful political force in the
United States, especially in Indiana
where this photo was taken. Which
theories, sociological and psychological, would be most useful to explain
this upsurge in racism among ordinary
citizens?

What do you think: Are such incidents racist? If so, should they be banned and the participants disciplined? Or should they be tolerated to preserve free speech?

Now, consider this event. At Vassar, the Celtic Society and the Jewish Union asked to be assigned facilities in the college's Intercultural Center. They were refused. To make certain that
no white group would request its facilities again, the center was renamed the Intercultural Center: A Center for Asian, Black, and Latino Students. Is this racist?

At several universities, Louis Farrakhan has addressed students, delivering an anti-Semitic
message. So has rapper Sister Souljah. In each case, the consequence has been strained relationships between African-American and Jewish students. Should such speeches be banned as
racist, or protected as free speech?

What do you think? Is there a difference when racism is expressed by a minority group? Is it
worse when expressed by the dominant group? Should colleges have a speech code that bans all
racist speech—whether by appearance and gesture as with the fraternities, or by words as with
Farrakhan and Souljah? Do you think the Grand Dragon of the KKK should be allowed to address students on campus? Support your position by applying ideas from this chapter.

Sources: Farrell and Jones 1988; Brodie 1989; Fitzgerald 1989; Greene 1989; Belknap 1991; Boulard
1991; Ruffins 1991; Elfin 1993; Stains 1993.

Theories of Prejudice

Perhaps you have noticed that people who are prejudiced against one racial or ethnic
group are likely to be prejudiced against other groups. This principle was strikingly illustrated by the research of psychologist Eugene Hartley (1946), who asked people how
they felt about various racial and ethnic groups. Besides blacks, Jews, and so on, his list
included the Wallonians, Pireneans, and Danireans—names he had made up. Most people who expressed dislike for Jews and blacks also expressed dislike for these three ficti-
tious groups. The significance of Hartley's study is that prejudice does not depend on
negative experiences with others. People can be, and are, prejudiced against people
they have never met—and even against groups that do not exist!

Why are people prejudiced? Social scientists have developed several theories to explain the causes of prejudice. Let us look first at psychological theories, then at sociological explanations.

Psychological Perspectives

Frustration and Scapegoats   In 1939 psychologist John Dollard suggested that prejudice is the result of frustration. People who are unable to strike out at the real source of their frustration (such as low wages) find someone else to blame. They view this **scapegoat**—the group they unfairly blame for their troubles—as having few good traits. In this way a racial, ethnic, or religious minority, which is by no means the true cause of these people's frustration, becomes a convenient—and safe—target on which to vent it.

Even mild frustration can increase prejudice. In an ingenious experiment, psychologists Emory Cowen, Judah Landes, and Donald Schaet (1959) first measured the prejudice of a sample of students. They then gave the students two puzzles to solve, but made sure that they did not have enough time to solve them. After the students had worked furiously on the puzzles, the experimenters shook their heads in disgust and expressed disbelief that they had not finished. They then retested the students and found higher scores on prejudice. The students had directed their frustration outward, onto people who had nothing to do with their problem.

The Authoritarian Personality Have you ever wondered if personality is a cause of prejudice—if some people are more inclined to be prejudiced, and others more fair-minded? For psychologist Theodor Adorno, who had escaped from the Nazis, this was no idle speculation. With the horrors he had observed still fresh in his mind, Adorno wondered whether there was a certain type of individual who was more likely to fall for the racist utterances and policies of people like Hitler, Mussolini, and the Ku Klux Klan.

Adorno (1950) decided to test this idea. He and his associates developed three scales: a series of statements that measured ethnocentrism, anti-Semitism, and support for strong, authoritarian government. Testing about two thousand people, ranging from college professors to prison inmates, Adorno found that people who scored high on one scale also scored high on the other two. For example, people who agreed with anti-Semitic statements also agreed that it was good for a government to be highly authoritarian and that foreign ways of life posed a threat to the "American" way.

Adorno concluded that highly prejudiced people have an **authoritarian personality.** They are marked by excess conformity, intolerance, insecurity, respect for authority, and submissiveness to superiors. Such people see many threats to their world, believe that things are *either* right *or* wrong, and are disturbed by ambiguity, especially in matters of religion or sex. The authoritarian personality, Adorno said, is formed during childhood, the result of bigoted, cold, and aloof parents who discipline their children harshly. When such people confront norms and values that differ from their own, they become anxious. A scapegoat relieves their anxiety, for to define people who are different from themselves as inferior assures them that their own positions are right.

Adorno's research stirred the scientific community, and more than a thousand research studies followed. The general conclusion was that people who are older, less educated, less intelligent, and from a lower social class are more likely to be authoritarian. The research did not confirm the influence of family socialization during childhood. Critics say that these studies merely show that the less educated are more prejudiced than those with higher levels of education—which we already know (Yinger 1965; Ray 1991).

The surge of racism in Europe (discussed in the Perspectives box on page 315) has brought with it renewed interest in the authoritarian personality (Meloen 1991). The research currently underway will either end this controversy or stoke its fires even higher.

scapegoat: an individual or group unfairly blamed for someone else's troubles

authoritarian personality: Theodor Adorno's term for people who are prejudiced and rank high on scales of conformity, intolerance, insecurity, respect for authority, and submissiveness to superiors

Sociological Perspectives: Functionalism, Conflict, and Symbolic Interactionism

Sociologists find psychological explanations inadequate. They stress that the key to understanding prejudice is not the *internal* state of individuals, but factors *outside* the individual. Thus, sociological theories focus on how some environments foster prejudice, while others reduce it. These theories examine the problem from the functionalist, conflict, and symbolic interactionist perspectives.

Functionalism   In a telling scene from a television documentary, journalist Bill Moyers interviewed Fritz Hippler, a Nazi intellectual who at age 29 was put in charge of the entire German film industry. Hippler said that when Hitler came to power the Germans were not more anti-Semitic than the French, probably less so. He was told to create anti-Semitism, which he did by producing movies that contained vivid scenes comparing Jews to rats—their breeding threatening to infest the population.

Why was Hippler told to create hatred? Prejudice and discrimination were functional for the Nazis. The Jews provided (1) a scapegoat, a common enemy around which the Nazis were able to unite a Germany weakened by its defeat in World War I and bled by war reparations and rampant inflation; (2) businesses, bank accounts, and other property they could confiscate; and (3) key positions (university professors, reporters, judges, and so on whom they could replace with their own flunkies as they fired Jews). In short, making the Jews a target of hatred was functional for the Nazis because it helped unite the German people behind goals of nationalism and power. From the functionalists' point of view, in the end hatred also showed its dysfunctional side, as the Nazi officials who were sentenced to death at Nuremberg discovered.

To harness state machinery to hatred as the Nazis did—the schools, police, courts, mass media, and almost all aspects of the government—makes prejudice practically irresistible. Recall the identical twins featured in the Perspectives box on page 61. Oskar and Jack had been separated as babies. Jack was brought up as a Jew in Trinidad, while Oskar was raised as a Catholic in Czechoslovakia. Under the Nazi regime, Oskar learned to hate Jews, in spite of the fact that, unknown to himself, he was a Jew.

That prejudice is functional and shaped by the social environment was dramatically demonstrated by psychologists Muzafer and Carolyn Sherif (1953) in a simple but ingenious experiment. In a boys' summer camp, they first assigned friends to different cabins and then made the cabin the basic unit of competition. Each cabin competed against the others in sports and for status. In just a few days, strong in-groups had formed, and even former lifelong friends were calling one another "crybaby" and "sissy" and showing intense dislike for one another.

Sherif's study illustrates three major points. First, the social environment can be deliberately arranged to generate either positive or negative feelings about people. Second, prejudice, one of the products of pitting group against group in an "I-win-you-lose" situation, is functional in that it creates in-group solidarity and out-group antagonisms. Third, prejudice is dysfunctional in that it destroys social relationships.

Conflict Theory   Conflict theorists stress that the capitalist class systematically exploits the principle that pitting group against group in a win-or-lose situation creates prejudice. If white and minority workers are united, they will demand higher wages and better working conditions. In contrast, groups that fear, distrust, or even hate one another will actively work against one another. To reduce solidarity is to weaken bargaining power, drive down costs, and increase profits. Thus the capitalist class exploits racial and ethnic strife to produce a **split-labor market,** workers divided along racial, ethnic, and gender lines (Reich 1972; Wright 1979; James 1988).

Unemployment is a useful weapon to help maintain a split-labor market. If everyone were employed, the high demand for labor would put workers in a position to demand pay increases and better working conditions. Keeping some people unemployed, however,

split-labor market: a term used by conflict theorists for the practice of weakening the bargaining power of workers by splitting them along racial, ethnic, sex, age, or any other lines

provides a **reserve labor force** from which owners can draw when they need to expand production temporarily. When the economy contracts, these workers are easily released to rejoin the ranks of the unemployed. Minority workers are perfect for the reserve labor force, for their presence is a constant threat to white workers (Willhelm 1980).

The consequences are devastating, say conflict theorists. Just like the boys in the Sherif experiment, African Americans, Latinos, whites, and so on see themselves as able to make gains only at one another's expense. Their frustration, anger, and hostility are deflected away from the capitalists and directed toward the scapegoats whom they see as standing in their way. Pitted against one another, racial and ethnic groups learn to distrust one another instead of recognizing their common class interests and working for their mutual welfare (Blackwelder 1993).

Symbolic Interactionism   Where conflict theorists focus on the role of the capitalist class in exploiting racial and ethnic inequalities, symbolic interactionists examine how perception and labels produce prejudice.

How Labels Create Prejudice   "What's in a name?" asked Romeo. In answer he declared, "That which we call a rose / By any other name would smell as sweet." This may be true of roses, but it does not apply to human relations. Words are not simply meaningless labels. Rather, *the labels we learn color the way we see the world*.

Symbolic interactionists stress that labels are an essential ingredient of prejudice. Labels cause **selective perception;** that is, they lead people to see certain things and blind them to others. Through labels, people look at the members of a group as though they were all alike. As sociologists George Simpson and Milton Yinger (1972) put it, "New experiences are fitted into old categories by selecting only those cues that harmonize with the prejudgment or stereotype."

Racial and ethnic labels are especially powerful. They are shorthand for emotionally laden stereotypes. The term *nigger*, for example, is not, like Romeo's rose, simply a neutral name. Nor are *honky*, *spic*, *mick*, *kike*, *limey*, *kraut*, *dago*, or any of the other words people use to derogate ethnic groups. The nature of such words overpowers us with emotions, blocking out rational thought about the people they refer to (Allport 1954).

Symbolic interactionists stress that no one is born prejudiced. Rather, people learn their prejudices in interaction with others. At birth each of us joins some particular family and racial or ethnic group, where we learn beliefs and values. There, as part of our basic orientations to the world, we learn to like—or dislike—members of other groups and to perceive them positively or negatively. Similarly, if discrimination is the common practice, we learn to practice it routinely. Just as we learn any other attitudes and customs, then, so we learn prejudice and discrimination.

Stereotypes and Discrimination: The Self-Fulfilling Prophecy   The stereotypes that we learn not only justify prejudice and discrimination, but they also produce stereotypical behavior in those who are stereotyped. Let us consider Group X. Negative stereotypes, which characterize Group X as lazy, seem to justify withholding opportunities from this group ("because they are lazy and undependable") and placing its members in inferior positions. The result is a self-fulfilling prophecy. Denied jobs that require high dedication and energy, Group X members are confined to "dirty work," for it is seen as more fitting for "that kind" of people. Since much dirty work is irregular, members of Group X are also liable to be readily visible—standing around street corners. The sight of their idleness then reinforces the original stereotype of laziness, while the discrimination that created the "laziness" in the first place passes unnoticed.

reserve labor force: the term used by conflict theorists for the unemployed, who can be put to work during times of high production and then discarded when no longer needed

selective perception: seeing certain features of an object or situation, but remaining blind to others

Individual and Institutional Discrimination

Sociologists stress that we need to move beyond thinking in terms of **individual discrimination,** the negative treatment of one person by another. Although such behavior certainly creates problems, it is primarily a matter of one individual treating another badly. Focusing on human behavior at the group level, sociologists encourage us to think in broader terms, to examine **institutional discrimination,** that is, to see how discrimination is woven into the fabric of society. Let us look at two examples.

Home Mortgages

Mortgage lending provides an excellent illustration of institutional discrimination. As shown in Figure 12.3, race–ethnicity is a significant factor in getting a mortgage. When bankers looked at the statistics shown in this figure, however, they cried foul. They said that it might *look* like discrimination, but the truth was that whites had better credit histories. To see if this were true, researchers went over the data again, comparing the credit histories of applicants. Not only did they check for late payments, but they also compared the applicant's debts, loan size relative to income, and even characteristics of the property they wanted to buy. The lending gap did narrow a bit, but the bottom line was that even when two mortgage applicants were identical in all these areas, African Americans and Latinos were 60 percent more likely to be rejected than whites (Thomas 1992).

> **individual discrimination:** the negative treatment of one person by another on the basis of that person's perceived characteristics
>
> **institutional discrimination:** negative treatment of a minority group that is built into a society's institutions; also called *systematic discrimination*

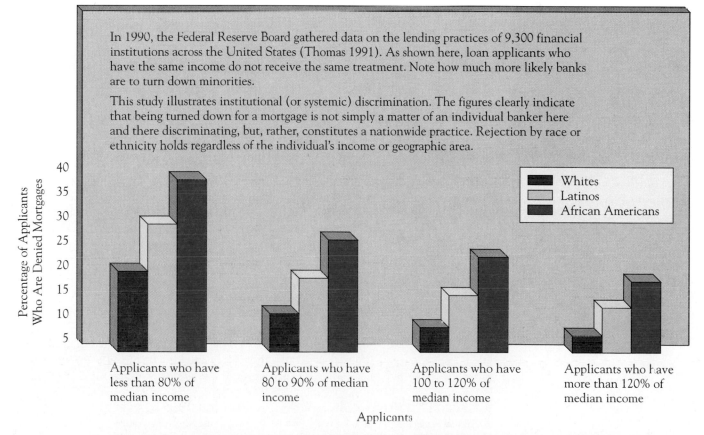

In 1990, the Federal Reserve Board gathered data on the lending practices of 9,300 financial institutions across the United States (Thomas 1991). As shown here, loan applicants who have the same income do not receive the same treatment. Note how much more likely banks are to turn down minorities.

This study illustrates institutional (or systemic) discrimination. The figures clearly indicate that being turned down for a mortgage is not simply a matter of an individual banker here and there discriminating, but, rather, constitutes a nationwide practice. Rejection by race or ethnicity holds regardless of the individual's income or geographic area.

Legend: Whites / Latinos / African Americans

y-axis: Percentage of Applicants Who Are Denied Mortgages

x-axis categories: Applicants who have less than 80% of median income | Applicants who have 80 to 90% of median income | Applicants who have 100 to 120% of median income | Applicants who have more than 120% of median income

x-axis label: Applicants

Note: The figures refer to applicants for conventional mortgages. Although applicants for government-backed mortgages had lower overall rates of rejection, the identical pattern showed up for all income groups. Median income is the income of each bank's local area.

Figure 12.3

Race–Ethnicity and Mortgages: An Example of Institutional discrimination

Because ideas of race and ethnicity are such a significant part of society, all of us are "properly" classified according to those ideas. This photo illustrates the difficulty such assumptions posed for Israel. The Ethiopians, although claiming to be Jews, looked so different from other Jews that it took several years for Israeli authorities to acknowledge this group's "true Jewishness."

Heart Surgery

Discrimination so pervades U.S. society that it can occur without either the person doing the discriminating or those being discriminated against being aware of it. An example is coronary bypass surgery. Mark Wenneker and Arnold Epstein (1989), two physicians, studied all patients admitted to Massachusetts hospitals for circulatory diseases or chest pain. Comparing patients by their age, sex, race, and income, they found that whites were 89 percent more likely to be given coronary bypass surgery. A national study of Medicare patients showed an even higher discrepancy—that whites were three times as likely as blacks to receive this surgery (Winslow 1992).

The particular interracial dynamics that cause medical decisions to be made on the basis of race are unknown at present. It is likely that physicians *do not intend* to discriminate, but that in ways we do not yet fully understand discrimination is somehow built into the medical delivery system. Race apparently works as gender does. Just as higher death rates for women following bypass surgery can be traced to attitudes that physicians have about their female patients (see page 290), so race seems to be an unconscious basis for giving or denying access to advanced medical procedures.

Table 12.1

Race and Health

	Infant mortality	Maternal deaths	Life expectancy Males	Life expectancy Females
White Americans	9.3	5.4	73.0	79.7
African Americans	19.2	22.4	65.6	74.3

Note: The national data base used for this table does not list these figures for other racial/ethnic groups. *White* refers to non-Hispanic whites. The rate for infant mortality is the number of deaths per year of infants under 1 year old per 1,000 live births; for maternal deaths, it is the number per 100,000.

Source: Statistical Abstract 1993: Tables 115, 121.

We can see, then, that institutional discrimination is much more than a matter of inconvenience, that it also translates into life and death. Another way of seeing the depth of institutional discrimination is shown in Table 12.1. You can see that an African-American baby has *twice* the chance of dying in infancy as does a white baby, that an African-American mother is *four* times as likely to die in childbirth as a white mother, and that African Americans live five to seven years less than whites. The underlying reason for these differences is income—the key factor in determining who has access to better nutrition, housing, and medical care.

Patterns of Intergroup Relations

In any society that contains minorities, basic patterns develop between the dominant group and the minorities. Let us look at each of the patterns shown in Figure 12.4.

Genocide

As has been observed repeatedly in this book, stereotypes (or labels) powerfully influence human behavior. Symbolic interactionists point out that labels are so powerful that they can even persuade people who have been taught from childhood that hurting others, much less killing them is wrong, to participate in mass murder.

This century's most notorious example is represented in the opening vignette, in which the Nazi colonel, educated in music, science, foreign languages, literature, and in sensitivities to the social graces and feelings of others, perceives his participation in **genocide**—the systematic slaughter of an entire people—as an act of patriotism and self-sacrifice. Hitler's attempt to destroy all Jews required the cooperation of ordinary citizens. Those who turned on their neighbors and fellow citizens were not some strange beasts brought forth from the bowels of the earth but, rather, ordinary men and women who were taught to think of Jews as *Untermenschen*, or subhuman. The result was the Holocaust, the slaughter of about six million Jews, half a million Gypsies, hundreds of thousands of Slavs, and unknown numbers of homosexuals and physically deformed or mentally ill persons—all defined as "subhumans." The slaughter occurred with the tacit and sometimes explicit complicity of ordinary German citizens (Huttenback 1991; Browning 1993; Hughes 1993).

genocide: the systematic annihilation or attempted annihilation of a race or ethnic group

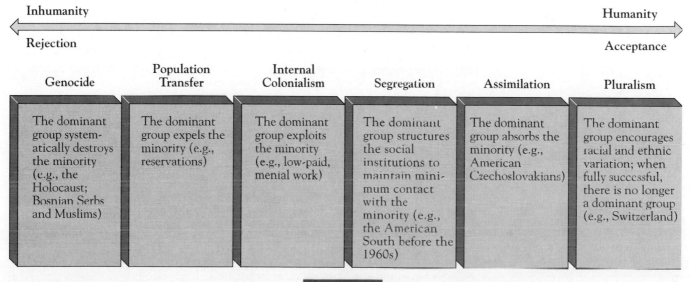

Figure 12.4

Patterns of Intergroup Relations: A Continuum

Amid hysterical fears that Japanese Americans were "enemies within" who would sabotage industrial and military installations on the West Coast, in the early days of World War II Japanese Americans were transferred to "relocation camps." Many returned home after the war to find that their property had been vandalized.

The Holocaust is, unfortunately, not the only example of the use of labels to justify genocide. The U.S. government and U.S. settlers did the same thing in referring to Native Americans as "savages." Labeling them as something less than human made it easier to justify killing them in order to take over their resources. Although most Native Americans actually died from diseases brought by the whites, against which they had no immunity (Dobyns 1983; Thornton 1987), the settlers ruthlessly destroyed the Native Americans' food base (buffalos, crops) and systematically killed those who resisted their advance toward the West. These policies resulted in the death of more than 90 *percent* of Native Americans (Garbarino 1976; Thornton 1987).

During the 1800s, when most of this slaughter occurred, the same thing was happening in other places. In South Africa, the Boers, or Dutch settlers, looked on the native Hottentots as jungle animals and totally wiped them out. In Tasmania, the British settlers ruthlessly stalked the local aboriginal population, hunting them for sport and sometimes even for dog food.

Labels, then, are powerful forces in human life. Labels that dehumanize others help people to **compartmentalize**—to separate their acts from feelings that would threaten their self-concept and make it difficult for them to participate in the act (Bernard et al. 1968). Thus, *genocide is facilitated by labeling the targeted group as less than fully human*.

Population Transfer

Population transfer is of two types, indirect and direct. *Indirect* population transfer is achieved by making life so unbearable for members of a minority that they leave "voluntarily." Under the bitter conditions of czarist Russia, for example, millions of Jews made this "choice." *Direct* transfer takes place when a minority is expelled. Examples include the relocation of Native Americans to reservations and the transfer of Americans of Japanese descent to relocation camps during World War II.

In the 1990s, a combination of genocide and population transfer occurred in Bosnia, a part of the former Yugoslavia. A hatred bred for centuries, so carefully nurtured that no slight was overlooked, had been kept under wraps during Tito's iron-fisted rule. After the breakup of communism, Yugoslavia split into warring factions and these suppressed,

compartmentalize: to separate acts from feelings or attitudes

population transfer: involuntary movement of a minority group

smoldering hatreds broke to the surface. During protracted armed conflict, the Serbs vented their hatred by what they termed **ethnic cleansing,** that is, slaughtering Muslims and some Croatians who lived in areas the Serbs captured and forcing survivors to flee through fear inspired by the slaughter, rape, and torture.

Internal Colonialism

In Chapter 9, the term *colonialism* was used to describe how the First World nations exploit the Third World. Conflict theorists use the term **internal colonialism** to refer to a country exploiting it's own minority groups, using social institutions to deny the minority access to the society's full benefits (Blauner 1972). Slavery, reviewed on pages 225–227, is an extreme example of internal colonialism. The more "routine" form is white dominance of minorities. Another example is the South African system of *apartheid*, described on page 228. Although the dominant Afrikaaners despised the minority, they found their presence necessary. As Simpson and Yinger (1972) put it, who else would do all the hard work?

Segregation

Segregation—the formal separation of racial or ethnic groups—accompanies internal colonialism. Segregation allows the dominant group to exploit the labor of the minority (butlers, chauffeurs, housekeepers, nannies, street cleaners) while maintaining social distance (Collins 1986). In the southern United States until the 1960s, by law African Americans and whites had to use separate public facilities such as hotels, schools, swimming pools, bathrooms, and even drinking fountains. In some states, laws also prohibited interracial marriage. In the North, too, a scattering of laws prohibited interracial marriage, while the legal structure upheld residential segregation.

Assimilation

Assimilation is the process by which a minority is absorbed into the mainstream culture. There are two types. In *forced assimilation* the dominant group refuses to allow the minority to practice its religion, speak its language, or follow its customs. Prior to the fall of the Soviet Union, for example, the dominant group, the Russians, required that Armenian schoolchildren be instructed in Russian and that Armenians honor Russian, not Armenian, holidays. *Permissible assimilation,* in contrast, permits the minority to adopt the dominant group's patterns in its own way and at its own speed. In Brazil, for example, an ideology favoring the eventual blending of diverse racial types into a "Brazilian stock" encourages its racial and ethnic groups to intermarry.

Pluralism

A policy of **pluralism** permits or even encourages racial and ethnic variation. For example, the United States has followed a "hands off" policy toward immigrant associations, foreign-language newspapers, and religion. Freedom of religion became such an important value in the United States that in 1972 sociologists Simpson and Yinger noted that "religious pluralism is now nearly fully the fact as well as the ideal." Today, as Muslim minarets adorn major U.S. cities, we see even greater religious pluralism. Switzerland provides perhaps the most outstanding example of pluralism. The Swiss are a nation made up of three separate ethnic groups—French, Italians, and Germans—who have kept their own languages, and live peacefully in political and economic unity. None of these groups can properly be called a minority.

ethnic cleansing: a policy of population elimination, including forcible expulsion and genocide. The term emerged in 1992 among the Serbians during their planned policy of expelling Croats and Muslims from territories claimed by them during the Yugoslav wars

internal colonialism: the systematic economic exploitation of a minority group

segregation: the policy of keeping racial or ethnic groups apart

assimilation: the process of being absorbed into the mainstream culture

pluralism: a philosophy that permits or encourages ethnic variation

Race and Ethnic Relations in the United States

Each of us belongs to a racial or ethnic group, and the consequences of that membership are felt in virtually all areas of social life. As shown in Figure 12.5, the major racial and ethnic groups in the United States are Americans of European descent, African Americans, Latinos, Asian Americans, and Native Americans. Let's explore some of the implications of racial and ethnic identity and group membership in the United States.

Figure 12.5

Racial and Ethnic Groups in the United States

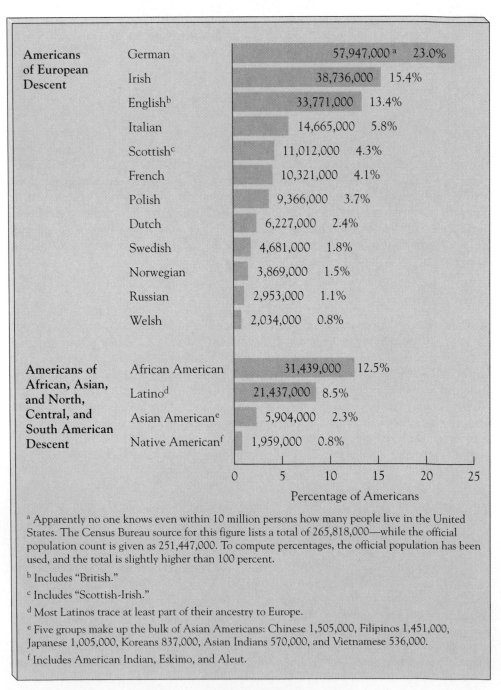

^a Apparently no one knows even within 10 million persons how many people live in the United States. The Census Bureau source for this figure lists a total of 265,818,000—while the official population count is given as 251,447,000. To compute percentages, the official population has been used, and the total is slightly higher than 100 percent.

^b Includes "British."

^c Includes "Scottish-Irish."

^d Most Latinos trace at least part of their ancestry to Europe.

^e Five groups make up the bulk of Asian Americans: Chinese 1,505,000, Filipinos 1,451,000, Japanese 1,005,000, Koreans 837,000, Asian Indians 570,000, and Vietnamese 536,000.

^f Includes American Indian, Eskimo, and Aleut.

Source: Statistical Abstract of the United States 1993: Tables 49, 51, 53, 56.

Constructing Ethnic Identity

Although every American is a member of an ethnic group, some people have a greater sense of ethnicity than others. For some, the boundaries between "us" and "them"—their group and the others in society—are firm. Others have assimilated so extensively into the mainstream culture that they are only vaguely aware of their ethnic origins. With extensive interethnic marrying, some do not even know the countries from which their families originated—nor do they care. If asked to identify themselves ethnically, they respond with something like "I'm German-Irish, with a little Italian and French thrown in—and I think someone said something about being 1/16th American Indian."

Why do some people feel an intense sense of ethnic identity, while others feel hardly any? Figure 12.6 portrays four factors identified by sociologist Ashley Doane (1993) that heighten or reduce a sense of ethnic identity. From this figure, you can see that the keys are relative size, power, appearance, and discrimination. If a group is relatively small, has little power, has a distinctive appearance, and is an object of discrimination, its members will have a heightened sense of ethnic identity. In contrast, members of the numerical majority who hold most of the power, look like most people in the society, and feel no discrimination are likely to experience a sense of "belonging," and wonder why ethnic identity is such a big deal.

We can use the term **ethnic work** to refer to how people construct their ethnicity. For people who already have a strong ethnic identity, this term refers to how they enhance and maintain their group's distinctions. For people with a lower sense of ethnicity, it refers to attempts to recover their ethnic heritage, such as trying to trace family lines. Millions of Americans are engaged in ethnic work, which has confounded the experts who thought that the United States would be a **melting pot,** its many groups quietly blending into a sort of ethnic stew. In recent years, however, as Americans have become fascinated with their "roots" and increasingly assertive and prideful of their ethnic background (Karnow and Yoshihara 1992; Wei 1993), some analysts think the term "tossed salad" more appropriate than "melting pot."

White Europeans

The term **WASP** stands for white Anglo-Saxon Protestant. In its narrow meaning, WASP refers to Protestant Americans whose ancestors came from England. These early

ethnic work: activities designed to discover, enhance, or maintain ethnic and racial identification

melting pot: the view that Americans of various backgrounds would blend into a sort of ethnic stew

WASP: a white Anglo-Saxon Protestant; narrowly, an American of English descent; broadly, an American of western European ancestry

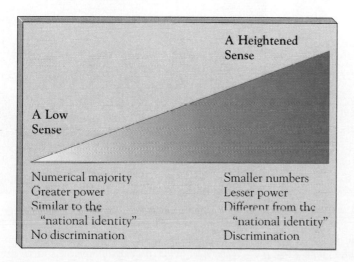

Figure 12.6

A Sense of Ethnicity

immigrants did not consider all WASPs to be equal, and class distinctions quickly developed. Lacking an official royalty, and somewhat envious of European royal courts, in 1890 some WASPs established the Society of Mayflower Descendants to certify which families possessed the right "blood lines." Membership was limited to those who could trace their ancestry to the immigrants who arrived on the Mayflower. Around this same time, the *Social Register* began to be published. To be listed in this book is to be deemed a member of the upper upper class, for only people with "old" money are included. Such organizations help isolate their members from the more "common" folk (Baltzell 1964).

The WASP colonists were highly ethnocentric, and they viewed white Europeans from countries other than England as inferior. They greeted **white ethnics**—immigrants from Europe whose language and other customs differed from theirs—with negative stereotypes. For example, they viewed the Irish as dirty, lazy drunkards. They painted Germans, Poles, Jews, Italians, and so on with similarly broad brush strokes.

The cultural and political dominance of the WASPs placed great pressure on immigrants to blend into the mainstream culture. The children of most immigrants embraced the new way of life and quickly came to think of themselves as Americans rather than as Germans, French, Hungarians, and so on. They dropped their distinctive customs, especially their language, often viewing them as symbols of shame. This second generation of immigrants was sandwiched between two worlds, that of their parents from "the old country" and their new home. With fewer inconsistencies and with fewer customs to discard, it was the children of the third generation who made the easier adjustment. As large numbers of immigrants from western Europe assimilated into this Anglo culture, the meaning of WASP expanded to include people of this descent.

white ethnics: white immigrants to the United States whose culture differs from that of WASPs

Because the English settled the Colonies, it was they who established the institutions to which later immigrants had to conform—from the dominant language to the dominant religion and family form. The customs of any group that differed from theirs were considered inferior and undesirable. In short, it was the European colonists who, taking power and determining the national agenda, controlled the destiny of the nation and dominated and exploited other ethnic groups. Throughout the years other ethnic groups have had to react to this institutional and cultural dominance of western Europeans, and it still sets the stage for current ethnic relations.

Shown on the left is Mrs. Rosa Parks being fingerprinted in Atlanta following her arrest in 1955 for refusing to give up her bus seat to a white. As detailed in the text, her arrest touched off a bus boycott that thrust Dr. Martin Luther King, Jr., to center stage in the civil rights movement—which eventually transformed U.S. society. On the right is Mrs. Parks in 1993, being honored on her 80th birthday.

African Americans

Discrimination was once so integral a part of U.S. life that it was not until 1944 that the U.S. Supreme Court decided that African Americans could vote in southern primaries, and not until 1954 that they had the legal right to attend the same public schools as whites (Carroll and Noble 1977; Polenberg 1980). Well into the 1950s, the South was still openly—and legally—practicing segregation.

King's Leadership and Civil Disobedience   It was 1955, in Montgomery, Alabama. As specified by law, whites took the front seats of the bus, while African Americans went to the back. As the bus filled up, the middle section was needed by whites.

In that section sat a 42-year-old African-American woman, Rosa Parks. Ordinarily she would have shrugged her shoulders and moved to the back when more whites got on—as she had so many time before. But today she was tired and didn't feel like moving. So she stubbornly sat there while the bus driver raged and whites felt insulted. Her arrest touched off mass demonstrations, led fifty thousand blacks to boycott the city's buses for a year, and thrust an otherwise unknown preacher into a historic role.

Rev. Martin Luther King, Jr., who had majored in sociology at Morehouse College in Atlanta, Georgia, took control. He organized car pools and preached nonviolence. Incensed at this radical organizer and at the stirrings in the normally compliant African-American community, segregationists also put their beliefs into practice—by bombing homes and dynamiting churches.

Under King's leadership, **civil disobedience,** the act of deliberately but peacefully disobeying laws considered unjust, became a tactic widely used by civil rights activists to break down institutional barriers. Inspired by Mohandas Ghandi, who had played a critical part in winning India's independence from Great Britain, King (1958) based his strategy on the following principles:

1   Pursuing active, nonviolent resistance to evil.

2   Not seeking to defeat or humiliate opponents, but to win their friendship and understanding.

3   Attacking the forces of evil rather than the people who are doing the evil.

4   Being willing to accept suffering without retaliating.

5   Refusing to hate the opponent.

6   Acting with the conviction that the universe is on the side of justice.

Rising Expectations and Civil Strife   The barriers came down slowly, but they did come down. Not until 1964 did Congress pass the Civil Rights Act, making it illegal to discriminate in hotels, theaters, and other public places. Then in 1965, Congress passed the Voting Rights Act, banning the literacy and other tests that had been used to keep eligible African Americans from voting.

Encouraged by such gains, African Americans then experienced what sociologists call **rising expectations;** that is, they believed better conditions would soon follow. The lives of the poor among them, however, changed little, if at all. Frustrations built, finally exploding in Watts in 1965, when people living in that African-American ghetto of central Los Angeles took to the streets in the first of what have been termed "the urban revolts." When King was assassinated by a white supremacist on April 4, 1968, ghettos across the nation again erupted in fiery violence. Under threat of the destruction of America's cities, Congress passed the sweeping Civil Rights Act of 1968.

civil disobedience: the act of deliberately but peacefully disobeying laws considered unjust

rising expectations: the sense that better conditions are soon to follow, which, if unfulfilled, creates mounting frustration

Continued Gains   Since then, African Americans have made remarkable political, educational, and economic gains. At 9 percent, African Americans have *quadrupled* their membership in the U.S. House of Representatives in just 15 years (Rich 1986, *Statistical*

Changes in African-American Family Income

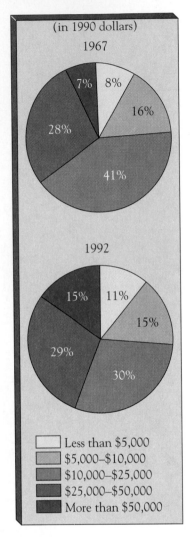

(in 1990 dollars)

1967

8%
16%
7%
28%
41%

1992

11%
15%
15%
29%
30%

☐ Less than $5,000
☐ $5,000–$10,000
☐ $10,000–$25,000
☐ $25,000–$50,000
☐ More than $50,000

Source: Barringer 1992; *Statistical Abstract* 1993: Table 49.

Abstract 1993: Table 443). As enrollment in colleges and in graduate schools increased, a new middle class emerged, one that holds three times the proportion of African Americans as it did in 1940. As shown in Figure 12.7, the proportion of African-American families making $50,000 or more has doubled since 1967, going from 1 out of 14 to 1 out of 7 today.

The extent of African-American political prominence was highlighted when Jesse Jackson (another sociology major) competed for the Democratic presidential nomination in 1984 and 1988. In 1989, this progress was further confirmed when L. Douglas Wilder of Virginia became the nation's first elected African-American governor (Perry 1990). The political prominence of African Americans came to the nation's attention again in 1991 at the televised Senate hearings held to confirm the appointment of Clarence Thomas to the Supreme Court. After grueling questioning concerning sexual harassment charges brought by Anita Hill, a former employee, Thomas was confirmed as the nation's second African-American Supreme Court Justice.

Current Reverses In spite of these gains, African Americans continue to lag behind in politics, economics, and education. Only one U.S. Senator is African American, when by ratio in the population we would expect 12 or 13. As Table 12.2 shows, African Americans average only 57 percent of white income, have much more unemployment and poverty, and are much less likely to own their home. As Table 12.3 shows, only 12 percent graduate from college, and the number earning doctorates has declined in recent years. The doubling of families with incomes over $50,000 mentioned earlier is also only part of the story, for as Figure 12.7 shows, African-American families making less than $5,000 have also increased, going from 8 percent to 11 percent.

This increase in the proportion of ultra-poor African Americans is significant. Here are concentrated those with the least hope, the highest despair, and the violence that so often dominates the evening news. African-American males are more than *seven* times as likely to be homicide victims as are white males, and African-American females are more than *four* times as likely as white females to die from homicide (*Statistical Abstract* 1993: Table 134). Homicide is now the leading cause of death for African-American males ages 15 to 24. Each year, more African-American males are killed by other African Americans than died in the entire nine years of the war in Vietnam.

Race or Social Class? A Sociological Debate Controversy has swirled around the conclusions of sociologist William Wilson (1978, 1987), who argues that social class is more important than race in determining the life chances of African Americans. Wilson notes that prior to civil rights legislation, the African-American experience was dominated by race. Throughout the United States, African Americans were systematically excluded from avenues of economic advancement—from good schools and good jobs. When civil rights legislation opened new opportunities, middle-class African Americans seized them. Following the path taken by other ethnic groups, as they advanced economically, they moved out of the inner city. Unfortunately, just as legal remedies began to open doors to African Americans, opportunities for unskilled labor declined: manufacturing jobs dried up and many other blue-collar jobs were transferred to the suburbs. As a result, while better-educated African Americans were able to obtain middle-class, white-collar jobs, a large group of African Americans—those with poor education and lack of skills—was left behind, trapped in poverty in the inner city.

The result, says Wilson, is two worlds of African-American experience. Those who are stuck in the inner city, live in poverty, confront violent crime daily, attend underfunded schools, face dead-end jobs or welfare, and are filled with hopelessness and despair, combined with apathy or hostility. In contrast, those who have moved up the social class ladder live in good housing in relatively crime-free neighborhoods, work at well-paid jobs that offer advancement, and send their children to good schools. Their middle-class experiences and lifestyle have changed their views on life. Their aspirations and values have so altered that they no longer have much in common with African

Americans who remain poor. According to Wilson, then, social class—not race—has become the most significant factor in the lives of African Americans today.

Many sociologists point out that this analysis omits the vital element—ongoing discrimination—that still underlies the relative impoverishment of African Americans. Sociologist Charles Willie (1991), for example, notes that even when they do the same work, whites average more income than do African Americans. This fact, he argues, points to ongoing discrimination on the basis of race rather than social class. He and other critics are concerned that Wilson's analysis can be used by people who want to turn back affirmative action. By "ongoing discrimination," Willie is referring to the many humiliations that African Americans continue to experience because of the color of their skin. Many middle-class and wealthy African Americans, for example, report being pulled over in traffic by police who assume their expensive cars must be stolen. Similarly, one *New York Times* reporter recounted that, while rushing to catch a plane, she was stopped by a white security officer who concluded that since she was black and in such a hurry, she must be carrying drugs (Cose 1993).

What is the answer to this debate? It is likely that *both* discrimination and social class are significant. It is also likely that African Americans who occupy an advantaged class position and enjoy greater opportunities face less discrimination—although what they do face is no less painful.

Latinos (Hispanic Americans)

Numbers, Origins, and Location   The second-largest ethnic group in the United States is the *Latinos* or Hispanic Americans, people of Spanish origin. In addition to the fourteen to twenty million **Chicanos** (those whose country of origin is Mexico), Latinos include about three million Puerto Ricans, a million Cuban Americans, and about three million people from Central or South America, primarily Venezuela and Colombia. Officially tallied at twenty-two million (see Figures 12.5 and 12.8), the actual number of Latinos is considerably higher, perhaps twenty-seven million. No one knows for certain because, although most Latinos are legal residents, large numbers have entered the country illegally. Not surprisingly, such individuals avoid contact with both public officials and census forms. Each year more than one million people are apprehended at the border or at points inland and deported to Mexico (*Statistical Abstract* 1993: Table 320), but perhaps another million or so manage to enter the United States. Most migrate for temporary work and then return to their homes and families. The Down-to-Earth Sociology box on page 335 explores this vast subterranean immigration.

Figure 12.8

Country of Origin of the Latino Population of the United States.

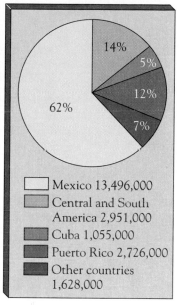

Mexico 13,496,000
Central and South America 2,951,000
Cuba 1,055,000
Puerto Rico 2,726,000
Other countries 1,628,000

Source: *Statistical Abstract* 1993: Tables 32, 53.

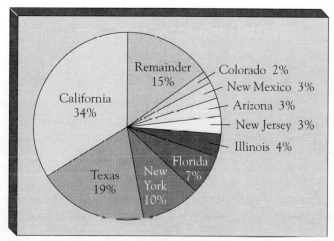

Source: *Statistical Abstract* 1993: Table 32.

Figure 12.9

Where Latinos live in the United States.

Chicanos: Latinos whose country of origin is Mexico

Table 12.2

Race and Ethnicity and Comparative Well-Being

	Median Family Income	Percentage of White Income	Percentage Unemployed	Percentage of White Unemployment
White Americans[a]	$37,783	—	6.5%	—
African Americans	21,548	57%	14.1	217%
Latinos	23,431	62	9.9	152
Country of origin				
Mexico	23,240	62	10.4	160
Puerto Rico	18,008	48	11.6	178
Cuba	31,439	83	8.1	125
Central and South America	23,445	62	NA[c]	NA
Asian Americans[b]	42,661	113	6.3	97
Country of origin				
China	43,381[d]	115	4.7	72
Japan	54,127	143	2.7	42
Korea	35,604	94	6.1	94
Philippines	49,027	130	4.7	72
Vietnam	32,077	85	8.9	137
Native Americans	NA[e]	NA	NA	NA

Note: The racial and ethnic groups are listed from largest to smallest.

[a]Non-Hispanic.

[b]Includes Pacific Islanders.

[c]For Asian Americans who have lived in the United States since before 1980, the poverty rate is only 6.1 percent.

To gain an understanding of these numbers, note that roughly as many Latinos live in the United States as there are Canadians in Canada. To midwesterners, such a comparison often comes as a surprise, for members of this minority are virtually absent from vast stretches of Middle America. As shown in Figure 12.9, 70 percent are concentrated in just four states: California, Texas, New York, and Florida. Most Puerto Ricans live in New York City, and Cuban Americans are concentrated in the Miami area. In California, Latinos are expected to soon *outnumber* Anglos (Engardio 1988). And by the year 2015 their population is expected to top forty million, making them the largest minority group in the United States (Corchado 1989). The Perspectives box on page 336 discusses other changes in the ethnic composition of the United States.

The Spanish Language   The Spanish language distinguishes Latinos from other ethnic minorities in the United States. With its large numbers of Latinos, the United States has become one of the largest Spanish-speaking nations in the world (Labov 1993). Because almost half of Latinos are unable to speak English, or can do so only with difficulty, many face a major obstacle to getting good jobs.

The growing use of Spanish has become a social issue. Perceiving the prevalence of Spanish in advertising and on radio and television as a threat, some Anglos have initi-

Race and Ethnic Relations in the United States

	Table 12.2		

Race and Ethnicity and Comparative Well-Being

Percentage Below Poverty Line	Percentage of White Poverty	Percentage Owning Their Homes	Percentage of White Home Ownership
11.3%	—	68%	—
32.7	289%	31	46%
28.1	249	39	57
28.1	249	44	65
40.6	359	23	34
16.9	150	47	69
25.4	225	22	32
13.8[c]	122	51	75
14.0	124	NA	NA
7.0	62	NA	NA
13.7	121	NA	NA
6.4	57	NA	NA
25.7	227	NA	NA
41.1	364	NA	NA

[d]Because incomes for these countries of origin were for 1989 while other income figures are for 1992, I have arbitrarily added a modest 5 percent.

[e]Not available.

Sources: Statistical Abstract 1993: Tables 49, 50, 53; Asian and Pacific Islanders in the United States August 1993: Tables 4, 5; Characteristics of American Indians by Tribes and Selected Areas 1980, September 1989: Table 15.

ated an "English Only" movement. They have succeeded in getting most states to consider a law to declare English their official language (Henry 1990; Auerbach 1992).

Politics and Disunity   For Latinos, country of origin is highly significant. Puerto Ricans, for example, feel little in common with Latinos from Mexico, Venezuela, or El Salvador—something akin to last century's immigrants from Germany, Sweden, and England who felt little in common with one another. A sign of these divisions among Latinos is the preference of many to use terms indicating their country of origin, such as Puerto Rican or Cuban American, rather than Latino or Hispanic (Otten 1994).

As with other ethnic groups, Latinos, too, find huge gulfs separating them on the basis of social class. The half-million Cubans who fled Castro's rise to power in 1959, for example, were mostly well-educated, well-to-do professionals or businesspeople. In contrast, the one hundred thousand "boat people" from Cuba who arrived in 1980 were mostly lower-class refugees, people with whom the earlier arrivals would not even have associated in Cuba. The earlier arrivals, firmly established in Florida and in control of many businesses and financial institutions, continue to feel a chasm between themselves and the more recent immigrants.

These divisions of national origin and social class are a major obstacle to Latino political unity (Skerry and Hartman 1991). One consequence is a severe underrepre-

With the recent arrival of large numbers of Latinos, the use of Spanish has become controversial. One issue is the use of Spanish in schools. Some feel that Spanish should be used in grade school to help assimilate the children of Latino immigrants, while others take the position that these children will assimilate better if instruction is given only in English.

sentation in politics. Although they make up about 9 percent of the U.S. population, Latinos hold only about 1 percent of elected offices nationwide (Schick and Schick 1991). In spite of these divisions, however, since 1900 six Latino governors have been elected in three states: New Mexico, Arizona, and Florida (Chavez 1990).

Fragmented among themselves, Latinos also find that a huge gulf separates them from African Americans (Skerry and Hartman 1991). With highly distinct cultures and differing ideas about life, these two minorities usually avoid each other. As Latinos have become more visible in U.S. society and more vocal in their demands for equality, they have come face to face with African Americans who fear that Latino gains in jobs and at the ballot box will come at their expense (Chavez 1990).

Comparative Conditions   Table 12.2 on pages 332–333 shows how Latinos compare with other groups. You can see that compared with non-Hispanic whites and with Asian Americans that Latinos are considerably worse off on all the indicators of well-being shown in this table. Compared with African Americans, however, most Latinos are better off on these indicators. This table also illustrates the significance of country of origin. You can see that Cuban Americans score much better on these indicators of well-being, while conditions for Puerto Rican Americans are the worst. Table 12.3 below shows that half of Latinos do not complete high school, and only 10 percent graduate from college. In a postindustrial society that increasingly stresses advanced skills, these figures indicate growing problems.

The Immigrant Backlash   The large numbers of illegal immigrants have led to growing resentment, especially in southern California and New York City, where they are concentrated (Mydans 1993; Reinhold 1993). Some are convinced that the immigrants are taking jobs away from citizens, others that they are an economic drag on taxpayers through their use of welfare and other social services. Many are disturbed that the United States has lost control over its borders. Whether the illegal immigrants pay more in taxes than they cost in benefits or the other way around has become a matter of heated debate, with experts differing in their interpretations of the same statistics (James 1993; Simon 1993).

Table 12.3

Education and Race or Ethnicity

	Less Than High School	*High School Graduates*	*1–3 Years Colleges*	*College Graduates*	*Number of Ph.D.s Awarded*	*Percent of Ph.D.s Awarded*	*Change in the Number of Ph.D.s Awarded in the Past 10 Years*
White Americans	19%	36%	23%	22%	23,077	89.6%	NA
African Americans	32	36	20	12	951	3.7	-9%
Latinos	49	29	12	10	755	2.9	+41
Asian Americans	16	27	18	39	828	3.2	+83
Native Americans	44	31	17	8	148	.6	+192

Note: NA = Not Available. Totals except for Ph.D.s refer to persons 25 years and over.

Source: Statistical Abstract 1993: Tables 49, 53; *Asian and Pacific Islanders in the United States* August 1993: Tables 4, 5; *Wall Street Journal*, January 18, 1994: A16; *Characteristics of American Indians by Tribes and Selected Areas*, September 1989: Table 5.

▼▲▼▲▼▲▼▲▼▲▼▲▼▲▼▲▼▲▼▲▼▲▼▲▼▲▼▲▼▲▼▲▼▲▼▲▼▲

Down-To-Earth Sociology

The Illegal Travel Guide

MANUEL WAS A DRINKING BUDDY of Jose's, a man I had met on an earlier trip to Mexico. At 45, Manuel can best be described as friendly, outgoing, and enterprising.

Manuel lived in the United States for seven years and speaks fluent English. Preferring his home town in Colima, Mexico, where he can pal around with his childhood friends, Manuel always seemed to have money and free time.

When Manuel invited me to go on a business trip with him, I quickly accepted. I never could figure out how Manuel made his living and how he was able to afford a car—a luxury that none of his friends had. As we traveled from one remote village to another, Manuel would gather a crowd and sell used clothing that he had heaped in the back of his older-model station wagon.

While chickens ran in and out of the dirt-floored, thatched-roof hut, Manuel spoke in whispers to a slender man of about 23. The sense of poverty was overwhelming. Juan, as his name turned out to be, had a partial grade-school education. He also had a wife, four hungry children under the age of 5—and two pigs, his main meat supply. Although eager to work, he had no job—and no prospects of getting one, for there was simply no work available.

As we were drinking a Coke, the national beverage of the poor of Mexico, Manuel explained to me that he was not only selling clothing—he was also lining up migrants

to the United States. For $200 he would take a man to the border and introduce him to a "wolf," who, for another $200 would make a night crossing into the promised land.

When I saw the hope in Juan's face, I knew nothing would stop him. He was borrowing every cent he could from every relative to get the $400 together. He would make the trip although he risked losing everything if apprehended—for wealth beckoned on the other side. He personally knew people who had been there and spoke in glowing terms of its opportunities.

Looking up from the children playing on the dirt floor with the chickens pecking about them, I saw a man who loved his family and was willing to suffer their enforced absence, as well as the uncertainties of a foreign culture whose language he did not know, in order to make the desperate bid for a better life.

Juan handed me something, and I looked at it curiously. I felt tears as I saw the tenderness with which he handled this piece of paper—his passport to opportunity—a Social Security card made out in his name, sent by a friend who had already made the trip and who was waiting for Juan.

It was then that I knew that the thousands of Manuels scurrying about the face of Mexico and the millions of Juans they were transporting could never be stopped—for the United States held their only dream of a better life.

Asian Americans

A Background of Discrimination It was December 7, 1941, a quiet Sunday morning destined to "live in infamy," as President Roosevelt described it. Wave after wave of Japanese bombers began their dawn attack on Pearl Harbor. Beyond their expectations, the pilots found the Pacific fleet anchored like sitting ducks.

This attack left behind not only destruction. It also changed the world political order by precipitating the United States into World War II. As the nation readied for war, no American was untouched. Many left home to battle overseas. Others left the farm to work in factories to support the war effort. All lived with the rationing of food, gasoline, coffee, sugar, meat, and other essentials.

Just as waves of planes had rolled over Pearl Harbor, so waves of suspicion and hostility now rolled over the Japanese Americans. Many feared that Japan would invade the United States and that the Japanese Americans would fight on Japan's side (Daniels 1975). They also feared that they would sabotage military installations on the West Coast. Although no Japanese American had been involved in even a single act of sabotage, on February 1, 1942, President Roosevelt signed Executive Order 9066, authorizing the removal of anyone considered a threat from specified military areas. All people on the West Coast who were *one-eighth Japanese or more* were imprisoned, sent to what were termed "relocation camps." They were charged with no crime. There were no indictments, no trials. Japanese ancestry was sufficient cause for being imprisoned.

This was not the first time that Asian Americans had met discrimination. Lured by gold strikes in the West and a vast need for unskilled workers, two hundred thousand

▼▲

Perspectives

CULTURAL DIVERSITY IN THE UNITED STATES

Implications of the Changing Racial/Ethnic Mix in the U.S.

STUDIES OF POPULATION TRENDS in the United States indicate a future that surprises many. Currently, almost one American in four defines himself or herself as Hispanic or non-white. If current trends in immigration and birth persist, by the year 2000 the population of Asian Americans will increase about 22 percent, that of Hispanic Americans about 21 percent, and that of African Americans about 12 percent. During this same period, whites are expected to increase by a puny 2 percent.

By the year 2020, the number of Hispanic Americans and nonwhites will double, to nearly 115 million, but the white population will show no increase at all (see Chapter 20). The year 2056, when someone born today will be in his or her sixties, is expected to be the watershed year, for then the "average" American will trace his or her descent to Africa, Asia, the Hispanic world, the Pacific Islands, Arabia—to almost anywhere but white Europe.

In California, the future has already arrived. In 1980, two-thirds of Californians were non-Latino whites. By 1990, this figure had fallen to 57 percent. By the year 2000, it is expected to drop below 50 percent, making California the first state in which ethnic and racial minorities together constitute the majority. Non-Latino white schoolchildren are already a *minority* in California, where the school population is 49 percent non-Latino whites, 31 percent Latinos, 11 percent Asian Americans, and 9 percent African Americans. Californians who request new telephone service from Pacific Bell can speak to customer representatives in English, Spanish, Korean, Vietnamese, Mandarin, or Cantonese.

A truly multicultural society will pose unique problems and opportunities. For example, in 2056, when "minorities" are expected to outnumber whites, there will be a large number of retirees but dwindling numbers of workers who pay taxes to pay for their Social Security benefits. For race and ethnic relations, the significance is that most of the retirees will be white, and most of the workers from today's minorities.

White Americans, who have enjoyed a privileged status in the United States, are unlikely to welcome this changed balance. Political backlashes of various sorts are likely. For example, the "English First" movement is a reaction to the growing influence of Spanish-speaking Americans. Similarly, African Americans, who feel that they have waited the longest and endured the most in the fight for equal opportunity, resist gains made by Latinos. They also feel that as affirmative action has been broadened to include even white women, it has become of less value for them.

Finally, this change will mean a rethinking of U.S. history as citizens debate the source of the nation's successes and just what its "unalterable" beliefs and other national symbols are. No longer, for example, will the meaning of the Alamo and the West be clear. Did the Alamo represent the heroic action of dedicated Americans against huge odds—or the well-deserved death of extremists bent on wrestling territory from Mexico? Was the West settled by individuals determined to find economic opportunity and freedom from oppression—or a savage conquest, just another brutal expression of white imperialism?

Although we cannot predict the particulars, of one thing we can be certain—that the future will be challenging as the United States undergoes this fundamental transformation in its population.

Sources: Whitman 1987; Henry 1990; Stevenson 1992.

Chinese had immigrated between 1850 and 1880. Feeling threatened by competing cheap labor, mobs and vigilantes intimidated the Chinese. Although 90 percent of the Central Pacific's labor force was Chinese, when the famous golden spike was driven at Promontory, Utah, in 1869 to mark the joining of the Union Pacific and the Central Pacific railroads, white workers prevented the Chinese from being present (Hsu 1971).

As fears of "alien genes and germs" grew, U.S. legislators passed anti-Chinese laws (Schrieke 1936). An 1850 California law, for example, required Chinese (and Latino) miners to pay a fee of $20 a month—at a time when wages were only $1 a day. The California Supreme Court even ruled that Chinese testimony against whites was inadmissible in court, a ruling that stood for almost twenty years (Carlson and Colburn 1972). In 1882 Congress passed the Chinese Exclusion Act, suspending all Chinese immigration for ten years. Four years later, the Statue of Liberty was dedicated. The tired, the poor, and the huddled masses it was to welcome were obviously not Chinese.

Spillover Bigotry   When immigrants from Japan began to arrive, they encountered "spillover bigotry," a stereotype that lumped Asians together, depicting them as sneaky, lazy, and untrustworthy. In 1913 California passed the Alien Land Act, prohibiting anyone ineligible for citizenship from owning land. Federal law, which had initially allowed only whites to be citizens, had been amended in the 1870s to extend that right to African Americans and some Native Americans—although most Native Americans were not granted citizenship in their own land until 1924 (Amott and Matthaie 1991). The Supreme Court ruled that since Asians had not been mentioned in these amendments, they could not become citizens (Schaefer 1979). In 1943, Chinese residents were finally allowed to become citizens, but those born in Japan were excluded from citizenship until 1952.

A World of Striking Contrasts   Today, Asian Americans are the fastest-growing minority in the United States, increasing at *fifteen* times the rate of non-Hispanic whites, and doubling in just the past ten years (Chun and Zalokar 1992). Most Asian Americans live in the West, as can be seen in Figure 12.10. The three largest groups of Asian Americans—of Chinese, Filipino, and Japanese descent—are concentrated in Los Angeles, San Francisco, Honolulu, and New York City.

Contrary to stereotypes, it is inaccurate to characterize Asian Americans as a single group. They are diverse peoples divided by separate cultures. Like Latinos, Asian Americans from different countries feel little in common with one another and are divided by social class. Table 12.2 on pages 332–333 illustrates some of this diversity. You can see that Japanese Americans score so highly that their income not only outstrips all other Asian Americans, but is almost half again as high as that of white Americans. Such figures have led to the stereotype that all Asian Americans are successful, a stereotype that masks huge ethnic differences. For example, with more than 30 percent of all households depending on welfare for survival, Southeast Asians have the highest rate of welfare dependency of any racial or ethnic group in the United States (Dunn 1994).

In spite of high poverty among some subgroups, on average Asian Americans have done very well. Their success can be traced to four major factors: family life, supportive community, educational achievement, and assimilation into mainstream culture.

Family life gives Asian Americans their basic strength, for they socialize their children into cultural values that stimulate cohesiveness and the motivation to succeed (Bell 1991). Most Asian-American children grow up in close-knit families that stress self-discipline, thrift, and industry (Suzuki 1985). The second factor, supportive community, means that the community supports the parents' efforts. For example, if a child is impolite, other adults will admonish the child and report the situation to the parents (McLemore 1994). This consistent socialization within a framework of encouragement and strict limits provides strong motivation for doing well in school. Their high rate of college graduation, shown in Table 12.3 on page 334, paves the way for high-paying professional and technical work, which, in turn, affords them better-than-average housing and health care.

Assimilation, the fourth element, is indicated by their high intermarriage rate. Figure 12.11 shows that almost one-fourth of all Asian Americans marry a non-Asian American. Japanese Americans, who rank highest on the economic and educational measures, also have the highest rate of interracial marriages (Lee and Yamanaka 1990).

Recent Immigrants   In 1975, after the United States was defeated in Vietnam, 130,000 Vietnamese, fearful for their lives because they had sided with the United States, were evacuated. Scattered to various locations across the United States, they were denied an avenue of adjustment used by previous immigrant groups, the ethnic community. On their own, however, most Vietnamese moved to California and Texas, where they established such communities.

Another group of Vietnamese arrived later, termed by the media and the public "the boat people." This group, too, barely escaped with their lives. Fleeing in leaky boats, they were attacked by pirates who robbed them and raped the women. Although no one knows the exact number, it is estimated that 200,000 drowned (McLemore 1994).

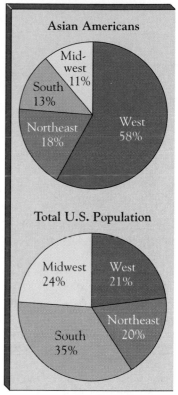

Figure 12.10

Residence of Asian Americans

Source: U.S. Bureau of the Census.

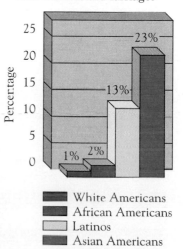

Figure 12.11

U.S. Interracial Marriages

White Americans
African Americans
Latinos
Asian Americans

Source: Lee and Yamanaka 1990.

To help them adjust to their host society, immigrants often band together for support, publish newspapers in their native language, establish churches, shop in stores that sell foods from their homeland, and live near one another. Recent immigrants to the United States are following this pattern, as depicted in this photo of Koreatown in Los Angeles, California.

In spite of their trauma and a huge language barrier, these immigrants adjusted well. Their children have done remarkably well in school, with three-fourths earning overall GPAs of A's and B's, and over 60 percent scoring in the top half on the standardized California Achievement Test (McLemore 1994). As Table 12.2 shows, their family income is approaching the average white income. Their high rate of interracial marriage is an indication of their assimilation: 35 percent of Vietnamese Americans born in the United States marry non-Asian Americans (Lee and Yamanaka 1990).

Native Americans

Diversity of Groups Thanks to countless grade-B Westerns, many Americans hold stereotypes of Native Americans on the frontier as wild, uncivilized savages, a single group of people subdivided into separate bands. The European immigrants of this period, however, encountered diverse groups of people with a variety of cultures, from nomadic hunters and gatherers to people living in wooden houses in settled agricultural communities. These groups had their own sets of norms and values—and the usual ethnocentric pride in their own cultures. Consider the following event:

> In 1744, the colonists of Virginia made what they considered a generous offer of college scholarships for "savage lads." They were somewhat taken aback, however, when the Iroquois replied, "Several of our young people were formerly brought up at the colleges of Northern Provinces. They were instructed in all your sciences. But when they came back to us, they were bad runners, ignorant of every means of living in the woods, unable to bear either cold or hunger, knew neither how to build a cabin, take a deer, or kill an enemy. . . . They were totally good for nothing." They then added, "If the English gentlemen would send a dozen or two of their children to Onondaga, the great Council would take care of their education, bring them up in really what was the best manner and make men of them" (Nash 1974 in McLemore 1994; Schweder 1994).

Perhaps numbering five million, the Native Americans had no immunity to the diseases the Europeans brought with them. With deaths due to disease and warfare—a much lesser cause—their number was reduced to about one-twentieth its size, reaching a low point of about a half million at the turn of the century. Native Americans, who now number about two million (see Figure 12.5 on page 326), still represent diverse groups. Like Latinos and

The massacre of Native Americans at Wounded Knee, South Dakota, in 1890 is discussed in the text. Shown here are some of the victims as they are buried in mass graves.

Asian Americans, Native Americans—who speak 150 different languages—do not think of themselves as a single people that justifies a single label (McLemore 1994).

From Treaties to Genocide and Population Transfer At first, relations between the European settlers and the Native Americans were by and large peaceful. The Native Americans accommodated the strangers, as there was plenty of land for both. As wave after wave of settlers continued to arrive, however, Pontiac, an Ottawa chief, saw the future—and didn't like it. He convinced several tribes to unite in an effort to push the Europeans into the sea. He almost succeeded, but failed when the English were reinforced by fresh troops (McLemore 1994).

To keep things peaceful, the U.S. government first made treaties. The general pattern was to buy some of a tribe's land, with the promise to honor forever the tribe's right to what it had not sold. European immigrants who continued to pour into the New World, however, disregarded these boundaries. The tribes would then resist, with death tolls on both sides, and Washington would intervene—not to enforce the treaty—but to force the tribe off its lands. In its relentless drive westward, the U.S. government embarked on a policy of genocide. The U.S. Cavalry was assigned the task of "pacification," which translates as slaughtering tens of thousands of Native Americans who "stood in the way" of this territorial expansion.

The acts of cruelty perpetrated by the Europeans against Native Americans appear endless, but two of the most grisly were the distribution of blankets contaminated with smallpox under the guise of a peace offering, and the Trail of Tears, a forced march of a thousand miles from the Carolinas and Georgia to Oklahoma. Scantily clad, four thousand Cherokees died on this midwinter march. The symbolic end to Native American resistance was the 1890 massacre at Wounded Knee, South Dakota, where of 350 Native Americans, the cavalry gunned down 300 men, women, and children (Kitano 1974; Thornton 1987). These acts took place after the U.S. government changed its policy from genocide to population transfer and began to confine Native Americans to specified areas called *reservations*.

The Invisible Minority and Self-Determination Native Americans can truly be called the invisible minority. Because about 50 percent live in rural areas and one-third in just three states—Oklahoma, California, and Arizona—most other Americans are hardly conscious of a Native American presence in U.S. society. The isolation of about one-quarter of all Native Americans on reservations further reduces their visibility (Thornton 1987; *Statistical Abstract* 1993: Table 51).

Poverty is more extensive among Native Americans than any other ethnic group in the U.S. Shown here is a Navajo woman and her three children. Note that you can see daylight through the walls of the shack in which she lives. To understand why this looks like a photo from the Third World, conflict theorists point to internal colonialism, discussed in the text.

The systematic attempts of European Americans to destroy the Native Americans' way of life and their resettlement onto reservations continue to have deleterious effects. Of all U.S. minorities, Native Americans are the worst off. As Table 12.2 on pages 332–333 shows, the poverty rate of Native Americans is the highest of any group. In addition, their life expectancy is lower than that of the nation as a whole, and their rates of suicide and alcoholism are higher (U.S. Department of Health and Human Services 1990). As Table 12.3 on page 334 shows, their education so lags behind the nation that only 8 percent graduate from college. Although the percentage of doctorates earned by Native Americans remains below their proportion of the population, an encouraging sign of positive change is that it has almost doubled in the past ten years.

These negative conditions are the consequence of Anglo domination. In the 1800s, U.S. courts determined that Native Americans did not own the land on which they had been settled and had no right to develop their resources. Native Americans were made wards of the state and treated like children by the Bureau of Indian Affairs (Mohawk 1991). Then, in the 1960s, Native Americans won a series of legal victories that restored their control over the land and their right to determine economic policy. As a result, several Native American tribes have opened businesses on their lands—ranging from industrial parks serving major metropolitan areas to fish canneries. Perhaps the development that has attracted the most attention is the opening of casinos, which may offer an exit from poverty for some tribes. More than two hundred tribes operate gambling businesses that generate about $2.5 billion a year (McLemore 1994).

A highly controversial issue is *separatism.* Because Native Americans were independent peoples when the Europeans arrived and they never willingly joined the United States, many tribes maintain the right to remain separate from the U.S. government and U.S. society. The chief of the Onondaga tribe in New York, a member of the Iroquois Federation, summarizes the issue this way:

> For the whole history of the Iroquois we have maintained that we are a separate nation. We have never lost a war. Our government still operates. We have refused the U.S. government's reorganization plans for us. We have kept our language and our traditions, and when we fly to Geneva to UN meetings, we carry Hau de no sau nee passports. We made some treaties that lost some land, but that also confirmed our separate-nation status. That the U.S. denies all this doesn't make it any less the case. (Mander 1991)

pan-Indianism: the emphasis of common elements in Native American culture in order to develop a mutual self-identity and to work toward the welfare of all Native Americans

One of the most significant changes is **pan-Indianism,** an emphasis on common elements that run through Native American cultures in the attempt to develop a self-identity that goes beyond any particular tribe. Whether Native Americans wish to work together as in pan-Indianism, or to stress separatism and to identify solely with their individual tribes, to assimilate into the dominant culture or to remain apart from it, to move to cities or to remain on reservations, to manufacture electronics or to engage only in traditional activities—"such decisions must be ours," say the Native Americans. "We are to be sovereign, not dictated to by the victors of the last centuries' wars."

Writing History: The Privilege of the Victor As symbolic interactionists stress, the events of life do not come with built-in meanings, but must be interpreted from some framework. Consequently, it is not surprising that the victors and the vanquished have quite contrasting ways of viewing the events that led to their relative conditions. After all, the past must be recounted from someone's perspective. This is the topic of the following Thinking Critically section.

▼▲▼▲▼▲▼▲▼▲▼▲▼▲▼▲▼▲▼▲▼▲▼▲▼▲▼▲▼▲

Thinking Critically About Social Controversy

Whose History?

▼ CONSIDER THE BATTLE OF Little Bighorn. U.S. history books usually recount the massacre of an outnumbered, brave band of cavalrymen, with Gen. George Custer going down to a sad but somehow glorious defeat. When Joe Marshall, a Lakota Sioux, heard this version as a fourth-grader, he mustered all the courage he could, raised his hand, and told the class the version he had heard as he was growing up among the descendants of survivors of the battle. This version refers to an armed group invading Native American lands. When the young boy finished, his teacher smiled indulgently and said, "That's nice, but we'll stick to the real story."

The U.S. history books say there were no survivors of this battle. Think about this for a moment, and the point about perspectives in history will become even more obvious. For the Native Americans, there were *many* survivors. Indeed, it is those survivors who used a technique called "oral tradition" to recount what took place during that battle. Their descendants have written a book that recounts those events, but the white officials who head the Little Bighorn Battlefield National Monument won't even let the book be sold there—only books that recount the event from the European-American perspective may be sold.

It is this issue of perspective that underlies the current controversy surrounding the teaching of history in U.S. schools. The question of *what* should be taught was always assumed, for the school boards, teachers, and textbook writers were united by a background of similar experiences. It was unquestioningly assumed, for example, that George Washington was the general-hero-founder of the nation. No question was raised about whether school curricula should mention that he owned slaves. In the first place, most white boards, teachers, and textbook writers were ignorant of such facts, and, secondly, on learning of them, thought them irrelevant.

But no longer. The issue now is one of balance—how to make certain that the accomplishments of both genders and our many racial and ethnic groups are included in teaching. This issue, called *multiculturalism,* is now central to school districts around the nation. Teachers, principals, school boards, and publishers are wrestling with a slew of difficult questions. How much space should be given to Harriet Tubman versus George Washington? Is there enough attention paid to discrimination against Asian Americans? To Latinos? Is the attempted genocide of Native Americans sufficiently acknowledged? What about the contributions to U.S. society of females and white ethnics—Poles, Russians, and so on?

No one yet knows the answers. What is certain at this point is that the imagery of U.S. society has changed—from a melting pot to a tossed salad. At the heart of the current issue is the fact that so many groups have retained separate identities, instead of fusing into one as was "supposed" to happen. The question being decided now is how much emphasis should be given to the salad as a whole, and how much to the cucumbers, tomatoes, lettuce, and so on.

The answers to such questions will give birth to new images of history, which, rather than consisting of established past events, as is commonly supposed, is a flowing, winding, and sometimes twisted perception that takes place in the present.

Sources: Glazer 1991; Charlier 1992). ▲

Principles for Improving Racial and Ethnic Relations

If a society can dedicate its energies to creating ethnic hatreds and pitting one group against another, as in Nazi Germany and in the former Yugoslavia, why can't a society organize to bring about racial and ethnic harmony?

No society can pass laws against prejudice, of course, for prejudice is an attitude. Laws banning discrimination, however, can significantly reduce prejudice. Following the civil rights movement of the 1950s and 1960s, when such laws were passed and enforced, national opinion polls indicated a decrease in prejudice (Harris 1978). The cause was the increased contact between racial groups, which reduced stereotypes that thrive on lack of personal, direct information about others.

Increased contact between groups, then, is the first step, but this is no guarantee that prejudice will decrease, for not all contact is positive. Recall the Sherif experiment with the boys at summer camp (page 319). Pitting group against group clearly increases prejudice and discrimination, and must therefore be avoided (Rouse and Hanson 1991). Social psychologist Gordon Allport (Pettigrew 1976) developed four guidelines that can promote the type of intergroup contact that decreases prejudice:

1   The groups should possess equal status in the situation (interethnic housing, for example, should involve occupants from the same social class background).

2   The groups should be seeking common goals (for example, parents from different ethnic backgrounds meeting to try to improve their children's school).

3   The groups should feel the need to pull together to obtain their goals (to improve an integrated school system, for example, voters from the various ethnic groups must vote for a bond proposal).

4   Authority, law, and custom should support interaction between the groups (if legal authorities strongly stand behind school integration, for example, more positive interaction is likely).

Summary and Review

Basic Concepts in Race and Ethnic Relations

How is race both a reality and a myth?

In the sense that different groups inherit distinctive physical characteristics, race is a reality. In the sense of one race being superior to another and of there being pure races, however, race is a myth. The *idea* of race is powerful, shaping basic relationships among people. Pp. 310–311.

How do race and ethnicity differ?

Race refers to inherited biological characteristics; **ethnicity,** to cultural ones. Ethnic groups identify with one another on the basis of common ancestry and cultural heritage. Pp. 310–312.

What are minority and dominant groups?

Minority groups are people singled out for unequal treatment by members of the **dominant group,** the group with more power, privilege, and social status. Minorities originate with the expansion of political boundaries or migration. Pp. 312–313.

Prejudice and Discrimination

Are prejudice and discrimination the same thing?

Prejudice refers to an attitude, **discrimination** to an act. Some people who are prejudiced do not discriminate, while others who are not prejudiced do. Pp. 313–317.

Theories of Prejudice

How do psychologists explain prejudice?

Psychological theories of prejudice stress frustration displaced toward **scapegoats** and **authoritarian personalities.** Pp. 317–318.

How do sociologists explain prejudice?

Sociological theories focus on how different social environments increase or decrease prejudice. Functionalists stress the benefits and costs that come from discrimination. Conflict theorists look at how the groups in power exploit racial and ethnic group divisions in order to hold down wages and otherwise maintain power. Symbolic interactionists stress how labels create **selective perception** and self-fulfilling prophecies. Pp. 319–320.

Individual and Institutional Discrimination

How do individual and institutional discrimination differ?

Individual discrimination is the negative treatment of one person by another, while **institutional discrimination** is discrimination built into a society's social institutions. Institutional discrimination often occurs without the awareness of either the perpetrator or the object of discrimination. Referral rates for coronary bypass surgery are but one example. Pp. 321–323.

Patterns of Intergroup Relations

What are the major patterns of minority and dominant group relations?

Dominant group practice to minority groups, beginning with the least humane, are **genocide, population transfer, internal colonialism, segregation, assimilation,** and **pluralism.** Pp. 323–325.

Race and Ethnic Relations in the United States

What are the major ethnic groups in the United States?

From largest to smallest, the major ethnic groups are European Americans, African Americans, Latinos, Asian Americans, and Native Americans. Pp. 326–341.

What heightens ethnic identity, and what is "ethnic work"?

A group's size, power, physical characteristics, and amount of discrimination heighten or reduce ethnic identity. **Ethnic work** is the process of constructing an ethnic identity. For people with strong ties to their culture of origin, ethnic work involves enhancing and maintaining group distinctions. For those without a firm ethnic identity, ethnic work is an attempt to recover one's ethnic heritage. P. 327.

What are some issues in race relations and characteristics of minority groups today?

African Americans are increasingly divided into middle and lower classes, with two sharply contrasting worlds of experience. Illegal immigration has led to a backlash against Latinos. The average income of Asian Americans is higher than that of white Americans. For Native Americans, the primary issues are poverty, nationhood, and settling treaty obligations. The overarching issue for all groups is overcoming discrimination. Pp. 329–341

Principles for Improving Racial and Ethnic Relations

How can intergroup relations be improved?

Intergroup relationships can be improved by following the principles of equal status, common goals, solidarity, and institutional support. To avoid pitting one group against another in a struggle for limited resources is essential. P. 342.

Where can I read more on this topic?

Suggested readings for this chapter are listed on page 641.

Diedre Scherer, Sisters, Too, 1992

Inequalities of Age

I N THE VILLAGE OF TAMISH in [the ex-Soviet region of] Abkhasia, I raised my glass of wine to toast a man who looked no more than 70. "May you live as long as Moses (120 years)," I said. He was not pleased. He was 119.

With these words, Sula Benet (1971) began a report on a people who commonly live to be 100, or even older. Even after spending months with the Abkhasians, Benet was unable to judge the age of older Abkhasians. He found that most work regularly—whether they are 70 or 107. They still have good eyesight, most still have their own teeth, they walk more than two miles a day, and are slim. The old women are dark-haired, slender, with fair complexions and shy smiles. A study of 123 people over 100 showed neither mental illness nor cancer.

The Abkhasians' perception of age is so different that they do not even have a word for "old people." The closest is a word designating persons over 100: "Long living people."

Do the Abkhasians really live this long? Some researchers doubt it, and have challenged the accuracy of Benet's report (Haslick 1974; Harris 1990). One problem is a lack of records—this people did not have a written language until after the Russian Revolution of 1917. Some investigators, however, have documented the Abkhasians' account through military records. They did find that a few Abkhasians were lying—some men claiming to be younger than they were. One man, who was going to marry, for example, said he was 95, but records indicated he really was 108.

Social Factors in Aging

As discussed in Chapters 1 and 3, the nature of childhood can vary tremendously depending on whether a society views children as miniature adults just about ready for adult roles, or as vulnerable, dependent beings in need of long years of protection. Sociologists stress that this same principle applies to growing old, that aging, too, is far from only a matter of biology. How, then, does society influence the aging process?

Aging Among Abkhasians

Abkhasia is a mountainous region within Georgia, a republic of the former Soviet Union. It is an agricultural society, with few inroads made by industrialization. Although we cannot determine with certainty why the Abkhasians live so long, a few clues indicate the *social* nature of their longevity. The Abkhasians themselves give three reasons: their customs regarding sex, work, and diet (Benet 1971). Let us consider each in turn, and then add a fourth factor.

1 *Sexual practices.* First, the Abkhasians feel that sexual energy should be conserved. Their traditional age for marriage is 30, and they believe that nothing sexual should occur before marriage. It is essential that a bride be a virgin. If not, she will be scornfully returned to her family. (The Abkhasians also have a special cultural problem—even a woman's armpit is considered an erogenous zone, and all women must carefully keep them covered.) In marriage, sex is considered a pleasure to be enjoyed, but for the sake of one's health it should not be overdone.

2 *Work.* Work is the second explanation they give for their longevity. Work begins in childhood. A 4-year-old might be responsible for feeding and watering the chickens, for example. As adults, the men work the land or herd goats, while the women work at home and care for farm animals. Only with advancing age do the Abkhasians gradually slow down: At about 80 a man may begin to stop plowing, while a woman may cut down on her housework and cooking. Still, after the age of 100, the average

Shown here is Khfaf Lasuria—who is between 133 and 145 years old—as she raises a glass of vodka to propose a toast. Although such longevity remains unusual even among the Georgians, about 39 of every 100 Georgians reach 100.

Abkhasian works about four hours a day. To them, retirement is unknown—and unthinkable. The Abkhasians have a saying, "Without rest, you cannot work; without work, rest gives you no benefit."

3 *Diet and eating customs.* Diet is the third reason the Abkhasians give for their longevity. They consider overeating dangerous, and when they see someone even a little overweight they inquire about the person's health. Abkhasians take in almost 25 percent fewer calories than do the industrial workers in their state, and they consume twice as much vitamin C. All food is freshly prepared, for they regard leftovers as unhealthy.

The Abkhasians eat meat only about once or twice a week. Always freshly slaughtered, their meat is broiled only until the blood stops running. Most of their diet consists of fresh fruits and vegetables, and includes large quantities of garlic. They also eat cornmeal and goat cheese daily. They do not drink tea or coffee, but do drink wine at lunch and dinner and consume about two glasses of buttermilk a day. They never eat sugar, but do use honey.

Meals are eaten leisurely. They eat their food with their fingers, taking only small bites and chewing them slowly. The presence of guests is a special occasion, with toasts made to the virtues of each person present. Such meals may last several hours.

4 *Social integration—A sense of community.* Researchers are impressed with the Abkhasians' approach to work and diet, but they doubt that their sexual practices contribute to their longevity. Perhaps a fourth factor is significant, which the Abkhasians take so much for granted that they are not aware of it: an integrated community that yields a strong sense of belonging and security.

From childhood, each individual is highly integrated into the group—and remains so throughout life. Because the elderly remain active, they don't feel that they are a burden to anyone. Continuing to do the same work (although less) and leisure activities as younger Abkhasians, they neither vegetate, nor do they have the need to "fill time" with such activities as bingo or shuffleboard. In short, they feel no sudden rupture between what they "were" and what they "are." (You never hear "I used to be a teacher [accountant, physician], but now I am retired.")

An example of their integration is their extraordinarily broad sense of kinship. Everyone who can be traced to the same ancestor is considered a brother or a sister, as are people who have the same last name. This means that each individual feels closely related to several hundred other people, and that he or she can count on them for help.

Because such reckoning of extended kinship was beyond anything Benet had known, he thought that the Abkhasians were exaggerating. One day, when a friend, Omar, took him to another village, however, Benet found that they meant what they said.

> Omar began to introduce Benet to his brothers and sisters. After about twenty such introductions, Benet asked how many brothers and sisters he had. When Omar explained that in this village he had thirty, Benet kept his disbelief to himself.
>
> In one of the homes they visited, the host played a recording of Abkhasian epic poetry. When Benet expressed admiration of the poetry, Omar took the record from the player and handed it to him as a gift. Benet declined, saying, "Omar, you know it isn't yours." "Oh, yes, it is," replied Omar. "This is the home of my brother." Perplexed, Benet looked at the "brother," who said, "Of course he can give it to you. He is my brother."

With this background, let us look at the process of aging in industrialized societies. As we do so, you may from time to time wish to make a mental note of the contrast with the Abkhasians.

Aging in Industrialized Nations

Along with other industrialized nations, the United States has experienced an increase in longevity. As Figure 13.1 shows, U.S. life expectancy has increased throughout this century. Public health measures, especially a safer water supply and developments in medicine—which have suppressed the killers of earlier years such as German measles, smallpox, and polio—have brought an uninterrupted march toward longer life.

To me, and perhaps to you, it is startling to realize that at the turn of this century the average American would not even see age 50. Since then, **life expectancy** has increased so greatly that Americans born today can expect to live until their 70s or 80s. (To apply this change to yourself, see the Down-to-Earth Sociology box on the next page.)

> **life expectancy:** The number of years that an average newborn can expect to live

Figure 13.1

Life Expectancy by Year of Birth

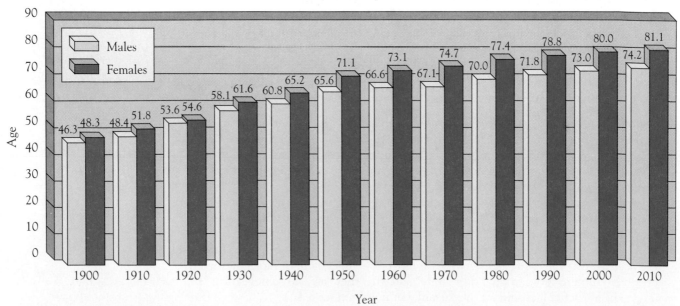

Sources: Statistical Abstract 1993; Table 115; Historical Statistics of the United States, Colonial Times to 1970, Bicentennial Edition, Part1, Series B, 107–115.

▼▲▼▲▼▲▼▲▼▲▼▲▼▲▼▲▼▲▼▲▼▲▼▲▼▲▼▲▼▲▼▲▼▲▼▲

Down-To-Earth Sociology

Applying Life Expectancy Figures

YOU CAN APPLY THE information in Figure 13.1 (on page 348) to your own family. If you are about 20, your grandparents could have expected to live to about 60. If they made it past that, they beat the odds. Your own life expectancy at birth, however, jumped to almost 70 if you are a male and to about 75 if you are a female. You can see the projections for your own children.

Your life expectancy now is actually higher than it was at birth, for life expectancy increases with each year you survive—at least it does on paper. Actually, your own life span is determined by biology (inherited disease and susceptibility to disease) and social factors (diet, medical care, and lifestyle). As death takes its toll on people in high-risk lifestyles, such as IV drug users, or on those who have less access to medical treatment because they are poor, for example, the life expectancy for survivors goes up because it leaves a larger proportion of people who have better access to good nutrition and medical care and who live less risky lives.

To gauge the current projections for your life expectancy, locate your age in the left column of Table 13.1. As these figures are only averages, they do not indicate how long any particular person will live, of course. Depending on your genetics, lifestyle (including those associated with social class), and a bit of luck (such as avoiding AIDS, car accidents, and homicide)—your own life expectancy may be higher (or lower) than these averages.

As illustrated in Figure 13.1 and Table 13.1, gender is a crucial factor in determining life expectancy. No matter in what year a person is born, the average female lives longer than the average male. Consequently, as more males die, with each year of advancing age females outnumber males by a larger margin. By age 65 and over, about three out of every five Americans are females.

Table 13.1 shows another major impact of the racial or ethnic inequalities reviewed in Chapter 12. At every age (except 85), the life expectancy of whites is greater than that of African Americans. Since the sources from which these data were drawn do not provide precise information for other ethnic groups, you may apply these general principles: the life expectancy for Latinos falls in between the figures for African Americans and whites, that of Asian Americans is closer to whites, and for Native Americans it is lower than for African Americans.

Table 13.1

Average Years You Can Expect To Live

If you are:	African American		White	
Age	Male	Female	Male	Female
0	65.2	73.6	72.2	78.9
5	61.7	70.0	68.1	74.7
10	56.8	65.1	63.1	69.7
15	51.9	60.2	58.2	64.8
16	51.0	59.2	57.3	63.8
17	50.1	58.2	56.4	62.8
18	49.1	57.2	55.4	61.9
19	48.2	56.3	54.5	60.9
20	47.3	55.3	53.6	59.9
21	46.4	54.4	52.6	59.0
22	45.5	53.4	51.7	58.0
23	44.7	52.4	50.8	57.0
24	43.8	51.5	49.9	56.1
25	42.9	50.5	49.0	55.1
26	42.0	49.6	48.0	54.1
27	41.2	48.6	47.1	53.1
28	40.3	47.7	46.2	52.2
29	39.4	46.8	45.3	51.2
30	38.6	45.8	44.3	50.2
35	34.4	41.2	39.7	45.4
40	30.4	36.7	35.1	40.6
45	26.6	32.3	30.6	35.9
50	22.9	28.1	26.2	31.3
55	19.5	24.1	22.1	26.9
60	16.2	20.4	18.3	22.7
65	13.5	17.1	14.9	18.8
70	10.9	13.9	11.8	15.1
75	8.7	11.1	9.1	11.8
80	6.8	8.6	6.9	8.8
85	5.6	6.8	5.2	6.4

Source: Vital Statistics of the United States, 1987, Life Tables, II, Section 6, February 1990: Table 6-3.

It is important to keep in mind, however, that the maximum length of life, the **life span,** has not increased. That is, people in industrialized societies are not living to age 120 or 150. Rather, because the diseases that kill people at younger ages are mostly under control, more people survive to later adulthood. Even the recent increase in deaths by homicides and AIDS, as alarming as they are, has not reversed this trend—but a warning flag is up: Between 1992 and 1993, life expectancy fell slightly (Otten 1994b). We must await data for future years to see if this is a trend or merely a blip in an onward march.

life span: The maximum length of life of a species

The Graying of America.

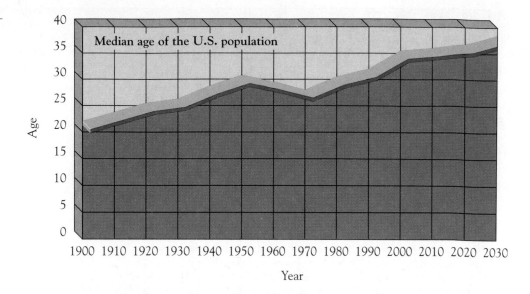

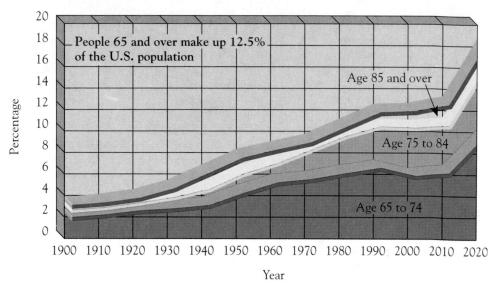

Source: Statistical Abstract, various editions.

The term **graying of America** refers to the proportion of older people in the U.S. population. Look at Figure 13.2 above. In 1900, only 4 percent of Americans were aged 65 or over. Since then, the proportion has tripled, and today it is almost 13 percent. U.S. society has become so "gray" that there now are four million *more* elderly Americans than teenagers (*Statistical Abstract* 1993: Table 22).

Race or Ethnicity and Aging   Due largely to social class, the U.S. racial-ethnic groups have different proportions of elderly. For example, compared with African Americans a larger proportion of non-Hispanic whites is over age 65. Of all racial-ethnic groups, Native Americans have the smallest proportion of elderly (Harper 1990).

As we noted in the previous chapter, the proportion of non-whites in the U.S. population is growing. As a result, although only about 10 percent of U.S. elderly are members of minority groups now, by 2025 it will be 15 percent and by 2050, 20 percent. The minority elderly, of course, are more numerous in states that attract larger numbers of minority groups. Consequently, in 25 years, about 40 percent of California's

graying of America: A term that refers to the rising proportion of older people as a percentage of the U.S. population

The elderly retain their ethnic cultures, as is illustrated by these Cuban Americans playing dominos in Little Havana's (Miami) Maximo Gomez Park.

elderly will belong to minority groups (Wray 1991). The implications of differences in cultural attitudes about aging, types of family relationships, work histories, and health practices will be important areas of sociological investigation in coming years.

Worldwide Trends   Because industrialization brings improved health, more people reach advanced age. This graying trend is occurring in all industrialized nations. Table 13.2, reflecting this change, shows that the proportion of people aged 65 and over is considerably greater in the industrialized nations than in the nonindustrialized nations.

Table 13.2

The Elderly in Cross-Cultural Perspective

Country	Total Population	Percentage over 65	Number over 65	Percentage of Payroll Taxes Paid to Support the Elderly
Sweden	9,000,000	18.0	1,6000,000	20.9
Germany	79,000,000	15.0	12,000,000	17.7
Italy	58,000,000	14.7	8,500,000	27.4
France	57,000,000	14.6	8,320,000	17.0
United States	255,000,000	12.6	32,000,000	12.4
Japan	124,000,000	11.9	14,800,000	14.5
Canada	27,000,000	11.5	3,100,000	4.6
China	1,134,000,000	5.8	65,800,000	N/A
Mexico	88,000,000	3.8	3,300,000	N/A
Egypt	54,000,000	3.4	1,800,000	N/A
Kenya	24,000,000	2.2	500,000	N/A

Sources: Kinsella and Taeuber 1993; Statistical Abstract 1993: Table 1400.

As a nation's elderly increase, so, too, does the bill paid by its younger citizens to provide for their needs. Table 13.2 also shows the proportion of their payrolls that several nations pay to fund benefits for the elderly. In spite of the common complaints of Americans that Social Security taxes are too high, this table shows that the U.S. rate is relatively low. In the nonindustrialized nations, there generally are no such taxes, and families are expected to care for the elderly.

The Symbolic Interactionist Perspective

To apply symbolic interactionism to aging, we will consider why people call themselves "old," what it means to be old, how negative stereotypes of the elderly developed, and, finally, how the mass media affect our perceptions of aging.

Self, Society, and Aging

You probably can remember when you thought a 12-year-old was "old"—and anyone older beyond reckoning, just "up there" someplace. You probably were 5 or 6 at the time. Similarly, to a 12-year-old someone of 21 seems "old." At 21, 30 may mark that line, and 40 may seem "quite old." And so it keeps on going, with "old" gradually receding from the self. To people who turn 40, 50 seems old; at 50, the late 60s look old (not the early 60s, for at that point in accelerating years they don't seem too far away).

At some point, of course, an individual must apply the label "old" to himself or herself. Often, cultural definitions of age force this label on people sooner than they are ready to accept it. In the typical case, the individual has become used to what he or she sees in the mirror. The changes have taken place very gradually, and each change, if not exactly taken in stride, has been accommodated. (Consequently, it comes as a shock, when meeting a friend one has not seen in years, to see how much that person has changed. At class reunions, *each* person can hardly believe how much older *the others* appear!)

If there is no single point at which people automatically cross a magical line and become "old," what, then, makes someone "old"? We can point to several factors that spur people to apply the label of old to themselves.

The first factor is biology. One person may experience "symptoms" of aging much earlier than another: wrinkles, balding, aches, inability to do certain things that he or she used to take for granted. Consequently, one person will feel "old" at an earlier or later age than others, and only at that time *adopt the role of an "old person,"* that is, begin to act in ways old people in that particular society are thought to act.

Stereotypes of the elderly as inactive people in ill health are inappropriate for the vast majority of Americans over 65. With higher life expectancy, most Americans can expect to live well past 65 and to enjoy years of active living—whether relaxing with grandchildren and great grandchildren, pursuing hobbies and volunteer work, continuing paid employment, or spending time at the beach.

Personal history or biography is a second factor that influences when people consider themselves old. An accident that limits mobility may make one person feel old sooner than others. Or a woman may have given birth at 16 to a daughter, who in turn has a child at 18. When this woman is 34, she is a biological grandmother. It is most unlikely that she will begin to play any stereotypical role—spending the day in a rocking chair, for example—but *knowing* that she is a grandmother has an impact on her self-concept. At a minimum, she must *deny* that she is old.

A third factor in determining when people label themselves old is **gender age,** the relative value that a culture places on men's and women's ages. For example, around the world, compared to most women most men are able to marry much younger spouses. Similarly, on men graying hair and even some wrinkles are likely to be seen as signs of "maturing," while on women those same features are likely to be interpreted as signs of "old." "Mature" and "old," of course, carry two quite different meanings in Western cultures—the first is desired, while the second is shunned. Two striking examples of gender age in U.S. society are found in the mass media. Older male news anchors are likely to be retained, while female anchors who turn the same age are more likely to be transferred to a less visible position. Similarly, in movies older men are much more likely to play romantic leads—and opposite much younger rising stars.

Although we see some change in these patterns, such differences in "gender aging" remain. Many individuals, of course, are exceptions to the pattern. Maria, for example, may marry Bill, who is fourteen years younger than she. But in most marriages in which there is a fourteen-year age gap between husband and wife, around the world the odds greatly favor the wife being the younger of the pair. Biology, of course, has nothing to do with this socially constructed reality.

The fourth factor is timetables, the signals societies use to inform their members that they are old. Since there is no automatic age at which people become "old," these timetables vary around the world. Native Americans, for example, often measure age by productive capacity and social roles. Birthdays were only introduced on U.S. reservations 100 years ago, and by itself, reaching the age of 60 is meaningless. Regardless of their age, however, adults who suffer from long-term ill health or those who become grandparents are likely to consider themselves old. In one survey, for instance, a woman with many disabilities described herself as elderly. She was only 37 (Kramer 1992).

The timetables adopted by a given culture are not fixed forever. Just as the management of a railroad or bus line adjusts the timetable when travelers shift their vacation habits, so groups sometimes adjust their expectations about the onset of old age. In Japan, for example, age 60 was so firmly marked as the beginning of old age that the Japanese had a special word for it. This term, *kanreki,* literally means "return of the calendar," a time at which people were expected to become dependent. At *kanreki,* it was acceptable to turn to one's children for support. Now that the Japanese have industrialized and established pension plans, however, they have advanced their idea of the onset of old age to 65 or 70—the time of eligibility for pensions (Maeda 1980; Palmore 1985).

The Relativity of Aging: Cross-Cultural Comparisons

To pinpoint the extent to which being old involves factors beyond biology, and how each society infuses old age with its own particular meanings, let us look at three cross-cultural examples.

Anthropologists who studied the Tiwi, a group who inhabit an island off the northern coast of Australia, discovered something different about what it means to be old (Hart and Pilling 1983):

> Bashti looked in envy at Masta. Masta strutted just a bit as he noticed Bashti glance his way. He knew what Bashti was thinking. Had he not thought the same just twenty years earlier? Then he had no wife; now he had three. Then he had no grand hut. Now he did, plus one for each wife. Then he had no respect, no power, no

In 1937, Mary Frances Grimes, an 11-year-old bride, and her 67-year-old husband, William H. Grimes, received national publicity. Married "in the woods" near Neelyville, Missouri, the bride said that she regretted the marriage and did not "love anyone but my doll." Is this an example of gender age, as symbolic interactionists might say? Or, as conflict theorists would say, of gender exploitation?

gender age: the relative values that cultures place on men's and women's ages

Aging depends on much more than biology, and classifying oneself as old depends on many factors, including cultural guidelines and biography. What biographical factors do you think were significant for this woman of the Great American Depression?

wealth. Now he was looked up to by everyone. "Ah, the marvels and beauty of gray hair," Masta thought.

Bashti hung his head as he slouched toward the fringe of the group. "But my turn will come. I, too, will grow old," he thought, finding some comfort in the situation.

Why did Bashti look forward to growing old, something that few people in the United States do? Traditional Tiwi society was a **gerontocracy,** a society run by the elderly. The old men were firmly entrenched in power and controlled everything. Their power was so inclusive that the old men married *all* the women—both young and old—leaving none for the young men. Only at about the age of 40 was a man able to marry. (In Tiwi society, females were the pawns, and aging was of no advantage to a woman.)

Traditional Eskimo society also provides a rich contrast to that of an industrialized society such as the United States.

Shantu and Wishta fondly kissed their children and grandchildren farewell. Then sadly, but with resignation at the sacrifice they knew they had to make for their family, they slowly climbed onto the ice floe. The goodbyes were painfully made as the large slab of ice inched into the ocean currents. Shantu and Wishta would now starve. But they were old, and their death was necessary, for it reduced the demand on the small group's scarce food supply.

As the younger relatives watched Shantu and Wishta recede into the distance, each knew that their turn to make this sacrifice would come. Each hoped that they would be able to face it as courageously.

To grow old in traditional Eskimo society meant a "voluntary" death, for no longer was one able to fulfill one's tasks. Survival was so precarious that all, except very young children, had to pull their own weight. The food supply was so limited that there was nothing left over to give to anyone who could not take an active part in the closely integrated tasks required for survival.

Finally, let's consider the meaning of age in traditional Chinese society.

Wong Fu bowed deeply as he met Ming Chau. When Ming Chau sat down, Wong Fu shyly took a seat at his side. Wong Fu had wanted to speak to Ming Chau for some time. Ming Chau was in his eighties, and his many years of experience had brought wisdom. Wong Fu was certain that Ming Chau would have the answer for his problem. He would remain silent until Ming Chau asked him about his family. Perhaps then he might be able to bring the matter up. If not, he would wait until the next time he was able to meet with Ming Chau.

Just as culture determines when old age begins, so it determines what that age category *means* for people. With the Tiwi, old age meant power (matched by envy on the part of the younger); with the traditional Eskimos, resignation to a deliberate death; and among the Chinese, reverence and respect from the younger. That does not, of course, exhaust the meanings of old age in these societies, but these are dominant emphases.

Symbolic interactionist stress that, by itself, old age has no particular meaning. There is nothing about adding years to one's life that automatically brings respect—or its opposite. Indeed, as noted earlier, there is nothing inherent in the aging process that requires a people even to have a word for "old" (the Abkhasians, remember, use "long living" instead). The symbolic interactionist perspective, then, helps us to see that what living a long life means comes not from the process of growing old, but from the ideas common in a culture. As a society changes, so might its meanings of aging. The modernization of China, for example, is resulting in less veneration of the elderly.

Let us look at how the meaning of aging has changed in U.S. society.

Ageism in U.S. Society

gerontocracy: a society (or some other group) run by the elderly

At first, the audience sat quietly as the developers explained their plans for a high-rise apartment building. After a while, people began to shift uncomfortably in their seats. Now they were showing open hostility.

"That's too much money to spend on those people," said one.

"You even want them to have a swimming pool?" asked another incredulously.

Finally, one young woman put it all in a nutshell when she asked, "Who wants all those old people around?"

When physician Robert Butler (1975, 1980) heard these responses to plans to construct an apartment building for senior citizens, he came to realize how deeply feelings against the elderly run in our society. He coined the term **ageism** to refer to prejudice, discrimination, and hostility directed against people because of their age.

Although old age means different things to different people, its general image is negative, and none of us wants the label "old" applied to us. We have "old and sick," "old and helpless," "old and crabby," "old and useless," and "old and dependent." Take your choice. None is pleasant.

As we have just seen, however, there is nothing inherent in old age to summon forth such images, and, apparently old age once had positive meanings in U.S. society (Cottin 1979; Kart 1990; Clair et al. 1993). Due to high death rates, not many people made it to old age. With growing old seen as a sort of accomplishment, the younger generation listened to the elderly's advice about how to live a long life. People also associated old age with virtue, and the younger looked to the elderly for guidance on how to live a good life. Because this was before Social Security and almost all the elderly continued to work, they also remained a source of knowledge about work skills.

Industrialization, however, eroded these bases of respect. With improved sanitation and medical care, more people reached old age, and being elderly lost its distinction. The new forms of mass production made young workers as productive as the elderly, and the new lifestyles and relationships ushered in by industrialization also created new ideas of morality—making many of the elderly's opinions outmoded. Finally, the growth of mass education stripped away the mystique that the elderly possessed superior knowledge (Cowgill 1974). As the social bases that had upheld respect for the elderly crumbled, a new set of images—from those of esteem to those of contempt—emerged. A sign of this shift in meanings is how people lie about their age—they used to claim they were older than they were, but now they say they are younger than they are (Clair et al. 1993).

It is a basic principle of symbolic interactionism that people perceive both themselves and others according to the symbols of their culture. Thus, as the meaning of old age was transformed—from usefulness to uselessness, from wisdom to foolishness, from an asset to a liability, and even to being associated with death—not only did younger people see the elderly differently, but the elderly, also internalizing cultural symbols, came to see themselves in a new light.

The Mass Media: Source of Powerful Symbols

Just as the mass media help to shape our ideas of gender and relationships between men and women (see pages 72–74), so they also influence our ideas of the elderly. Like females, the elderly are underrepresented on television, in advertisements, and in the most popular magazines. Their omission implies a lack of social value. The covert message is that the elderly are of little consequence and can be safely ignored. This message is not lost on television viewers, who also internalize the media's negative symbols and go to great lengths to deny that they are growing old. The mass media then exploit fears of losing youthful vitality to sell hair dyes, skin creams, and innumerable other products that supposedly conceal even the appearance of old age (Vernon et al. 1990).

The American Association of Retired Persons (AARP) contends that television advertising often depicts the elderly as feeble, foolish, or passing their time

ageism: prejudice, discrimination, and hostility directed against people because of their age; can be directed against any age group, including youth

endlessly in rocking chairs (Goldman 1993). The AARP complains that advertising firms are dominated by younger people who transmit their own negative images—picking up the "worst traits of the group, making everyone believe that old is something you don't want to be." Apparently the portrayal of the elderly is now improving (Vernon et al. 1990), and under pressure from the AARP this change is likely to continue.

The Functionalist Perspective

As explained in Chapter 1, functionalists examine how the various parts of society work together. We can consider an **age cohort,** people born at roughly the same time who pass through the life course together, as a component of society. This component affects other parts. For example, if the age cohort nearing retirement is large (a "baby boom" generation), many jobs will open at roughly the same time. If it is small (a "baby bust" generation), fewer jobs will open. A smooth transition at retirement requires a good adjustment between the parts.

Disengagement theory and activity theory focus on the mutual adjustments necessary between those who are retiring and society's other components.

Disengagement Theory

Elaine Cumming and William Henry (1961) developed **disengagement theory** to explain how society prevents disruption when the elderly vacate (or disengage from) their positions of responsibility. It would be very disruptive if the elderly left their positions only because of death or incompetence. Consequently, society encourages the elderly to hand over their positions to younger people. In industrialized societies the elderly are paid a pension in return for giving up these positions. Thus, disengagement is a mutual agreement between two parts of society that facilitates a smooth transition between the elderly and the younger.

Cumming (1976) also examined disengagement from the individual's perspective, pointing out that disengagement begins during middle age, long before retirement, when an individual senses that the end of life is closer than its start. The individual does not immediately disengage, however, but, realizing that time is limited, begins to assign priority to goals and tasks. Disengagement begins in earnest when children leave home, then with retirement, and eventually, widowhood.

age cohort: people born at roughly the same time who pass through the life course together

disengagement theory: the view that society prevents disruption by having the elderly vacate (or disengage from) their positions of responsibility so the younger generation can step into their shoes

Why is old age a source of satisfaction for some, but of despair for others? Researchers have found that people's level and type of activity are significant factors. Some of the elderly obtain immense satisfaction and a sense of purpose from volunteer activities that help the younger generation, as does this woman who is helping elementary school children with a class project.

Evaluation of the Theory   Disengagement theory has recently come under heavy criticism. Anthropologist Dorothy Jerrome (1992) points out that it contains an implicit bias against older people—assumptions that the elderly disengage from productive social roles, and then sort of sink into oblivion. Her own research shows that, instead of disengaging, the elderly actually exchange one set of roles for another. She found that the new roles, centering around friendship, are no less satisfying than were the earlier roles—although they are less visible to researchers who tend to have a youthful orientation, and who show their bias by assuming that productivity is the measure of self-worth.

Activity Theory

What happens to people when they disengage from their usual activities? For example, does retirement increase or decrease satisfaction with life? Are intimate activities more satisfying than formal ones? Such questions are the focus of **activity theory,** in which the general hypothesis is that the more activities that elderly people engage in, the more they find life satisfying. Although we could consider this theory under other perspectives, because its focus is how disengagement is functional or dysfunctional, it, too, can be considered from the functionalist perspective.

Evaluation of the Theory   The research results are mixed. In general, research has supported the central hypothesis that more active people are more satisfied. But not always. For example, a study of retired people in France found that some people are happier when they are very active, others when they are less involved (Keith 1992). Similarly, most people apparently find more informal, intimate activities, such as spending time with friends, to be more satisfying than formal activities. But not everyone. The 2,000 retired American men in one study reported formal activities to be as important as more intimate activities. Even solitary activities, such as doing home repairs, turned out to have about the same impact as intimate activities on these men's life satisfaction (Beck and Page 1988).

   With this mix, it is evident that researchers should search for key variables that underlie people's activities. I suggest three: finances, health, and individual orientations. The first may be related directly to social class, for older people with adequate finances are usually more satisfied with life (Atchley 1975: Krause 1993). The second is health, for healthier people are more active (Jerrome 1992; Johnson and Barer 1992). Third, the French and American studies just mentioned indicate the significance of individual orientations. Just as some people are happier doing less, others are satisfied only if they are highly involved. Similarly, some people prefer informal activities, while others derive greater satisfaction from more formal ones. To simply count people's activities, then, is far from adequate, and these variables, as well as others, may provide the key to understanding the relationship between disengagement, activities, and life satisfaction.

The Conflict Perspective

From the conflict perspective, the guiding principles of social life are competition, disequilibrium, and change. So it is with society's age groups. Whether the young and old recognize it or not, they are part of a basic struggle that threatens to throw society into turmoil. The passage of Social Security legislation is an example of this struggle.

Social Security Legislation

In the 1920s, before Social Security provided an income for the aged, two-thirds of all citizens over 65 had no savings and could not support themselves (Holtzman 1963; Hudson 1978). The

activity theory: the view that satisfaction during old age is related to a person's level and quality of activity

Great Depression made matters even worse, and in 1930 Francis Townsend, a social reformer, started a movement to rally older citizens. He soon had one-third of all Americans over 65 enrolled in his Townsend clubs, demanding that the federal government impose a national sales tax of 2 percent to provide $200 a month for every person over 65—the equivalent of about $2,000 a month today. In 1934, the Townsend Plan went before Congress. Because it called for such high payments and many were afraid that it would remove younger people's incentive to save for the future, Congress looked for a way to reject the plan without appearing to be opposed to old age pensions (Schottland 1963). When President Roosevelt announced his own, more modest Social Security plan in June 1934, Congress embraced it.

This legislation required that workers retire at 65. It did not matter how well people did their work, nor how much they needed an income. For decades, the elderly protested. Finally, in 1978 Congress raised the mandatory retirement age to 70, and eliminated it in 1986. Today, almost 90 percent of Americans retire by age 65, but they do so voluntarily. They can no longer be forced out of their jobs simply because of their age.

Conflict theorists point out that the retirement benefits Americans have today are not the result of generous hearts in Congress. They are, rather, the result of a struggle between competing interest groups. As conflict theorists stress, equilibrium is only a temporary balancing of social forces, one that is always ready to come apart. Perhaps, then, more direct conflict will emerge in the future. Let us consider that possibility.

The Question of Intergenerational Conflict

Will the future bring conflict between the elderly and the young? Although violence is not likely to result, the grumblings have begun—complaints about the elderly getting more than their share of society's dwindling resources in an era of high taxes, reduced services, and gigantic budget deficits. The huge costs of Social Security have become a national concern. As Figure 13.3 shows, Social Security taxes were only $784 million in 1950, but now they run 400 times higher. The nearby Down-to-Earth Sociology box examines stirrings of resentment that may become widespread.

Figure 13.3

Costs of Social Security

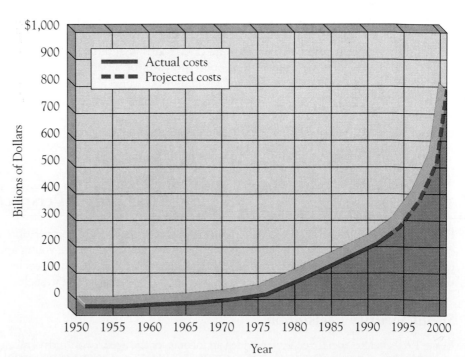

Sources: Statistical Abstract, various years. Recent years are from the 1991 edition, Table 592 and the 1993 edition, Table 511. Broken line indicates the author's estimates.

Down-To-Earth Sociology

Changing Sentiment About the Elderly

JUST A FEW YEARS back, there was widespread concern about extensive poverty among the elderly in the United States. As noted in the text, Congress took effective measures, and their rate of poverty dropped dramatically. At this point, is sentiment about the elderly changing?

There are indications that it is. Teresa Anderson (1985) recounts her resentment when she had to pay more than her parents for an identical room in the same motel. She says, "My parents work and own several pieces of property. Something is wrong when people are automatically entitled to a 'senior citizen discount,' regardless of need."

Robert Samuelson (1988) has gone further. He proposes eliminating tax breaks for the elderly, such as their extra standard deduction on federal income tax forms. He also suggests reducing the cost-of-living adjustments in Social Security.

A medical ethicist, Daniel Callahan (1987), even argues that because medical resources are limited we may have to ration medical care for the elderly. Considering costs, he asks if we should perform open-heart surgery on people in their 80s, which might prolong life only two or three years—or should we use those same resources for a kidney transplant to a child, which might prolong life by fifty years?

Samuelson accuses the elderly's powerful lobby, the American Association of Retired Persons (AARP), of using misleading stereotypes to take unfair advantage of the public and politicians. He says, "In the real world, the stereotypes of the elderly as sedentary, decrepit, and poor have long vanished, but in politics the cliché is promoted and perpetuated." He then accuses the AARP of outright hypocrisy: "They insist (rightfully) that age alone doesn't rob them of vitality and independence, while also arguing (wrongfully) that age alone entitles them to special treatment." They can't have it both ways, he says.

What do you think?

Some form of conflict seems inevitable. As the United States grays, the number of people who collect Social Security grows, but the proportion of working people—those who pay for these benefits out of their wages—shrinks. Some see this shift in the **dependency ratio,** the number of workers compared with the number of Social Security recipients, as especially troubling. Presently, five working-age Americans pay Social Security taxes to support each person who is over 65—but shortly this ratio will drop to less than three to one, and by the year 2035, to two to one. The following Thinking Critically section summarizes major problems with Social Security.

Thinking Critically About Social Controversy

Social Security—Fraud of the Century?

▼ EACH MONTH THE SOCIAL SECURITY Administration mails checks to about thirty-five million retired Americans. Across the country, in every occupation, U.S. workers dutifully pay into the Social Security system, looking to it to provide for their basic necessities—and, hopefully, a little more—in their old age.

How dependable is Social Security? The short answer is, "Don't bet your old age on it."

The first problem is well known. Social Security is not like a bank account into which individuals make deposits, and then, when they need the money, draw it out. Instead, the money that current workers pay into Social Security is paid to retired workers. When these current workers retire, they will be paid not from their own savings, but from the contributions of others who are still working.

This system is like a chain letter—it works well as long as enough new people join the chain. If you join early enough, you will collect much more than you paid in—but if you get in toward the end, you are simply out of luck. And, say some conflict theorists, we are nearing the end of the chain. When the number of workers supporting each retiree drops from five

dependency ratio: the number of workers required to support one person on Social Security

to just two, Social Security taxes may become so prohibitive that they will stifle the country's entire economy. To address this problem, Social Security taxes were raised in 1977 and again in 1983. These increased revenues were intended to build up a Social Security surplus in the trillions of dollars—a trust fund that would ease the burden on a future, smaller labor force.

The second problem with Social Security takes us to the root of the crisis, or, some say, fraud. In 1965 President Lyndon Johnson, bogged down in a horribly expensive war in Vietnam, wanted to conceal the war's true costs from the U.S. public. To produce a budget that would hide the red ink, politicians hit on an ingenious solution—they simply transferred what the workers pay into Social Security to the general fund (the general income of the U.S. government). The confiscation went unnoticed by the public, for it was accomplished simply by prohibiting the Social Security Administration from investing in anything but U.S. Treasury bonds—a form of government IOUs. Suppose that you buy a $1,000 U.S. Treasury bond (although they don't come that small). The government takes your $1,000 and gives you a document that says it owes you $1,000 plus interest. This is now what happens with the money that workers pay into Social Security. The Social Security Administration collects the money, pays the currently retired, and then hands the excess over to the U.S. government, which, in turn, gives out these gigantic IOUs.

Now, if the government were running a surplus, the shenanigans might be OK. But the fact that the public's pension money is being appropriated by an organization with an annual deficit of $250 billion or $350 billion does not exactly inspire confidence.

Social Security also helps conceal the true extent of the government's debt from the public, for the annual deficits announced by the government do *not* include these amounts confiscated from U.S. workers. The Gramm-Rudman provisions, designed to limit the amount of federal debt, do *not* count the funds "borrowed" from Social Security. It is as though this particular government spending does not exist.

It's a politician's ideal money machine. Workers, who have no choice about "contributing," are led to believe that they're building up a retirement nest egg for themselves when the money is actually being spent by the federal government.

Will Social Security still be there when you retire? Some conflict theorists say that you should not count on it, for every year the government wipes the Social Security trust fund clean. The federal government now owes the fund about $15 trillion, which means that the national debt is *several times* its official figures. If this process continues, it is estimated that to support future retirees, Social Security taxes will have to be raised so high that they will eat up 45 percent of the income of U.S. workers.

Will U.S. workers stand for such huge taxes? Will there one day be a taxpayers' revolt that will leave millions of retirees without their monthly payments? How can the federal government be prevented from spending revenues designated for Social Security? Are the current arrangements legitimate—or is the system a gigantic fraud?

Sources: Smith 1986; Smith 1987; Hardy 1991; Genetski 1993; and Gary North's newsletter, *Remnant Review.* Raw data in which Social Security receipts are listed as deficits can be found in *Monthly Treasury Statement of Receipts and Outlays,* the *Winter Treasury Bulletin,* and the *Statement of Liabilities and Other Financial Commitments of the United States Government*—all government publications. ▲

As shown in Figure 13.4, medical costs for the elderly have soared. Medicare and Medicaid now account for three-fourths of all federal money spent on health care (*Statistical Abstract* 1993: Tables 155, 159). Because of this, some fear that the health care of children is being shortchanged and Congress will be forced to "pick between old people and kids." Are the elderly and children, then, on a collision course? What especially alarms some are the data shown in Figure 13.5. As the condition of the elderly improved, that of children worsened. Although critics are glad that the elderly are better off than they were, they are bothered that this improvement has come at the cost of the nation's children.

But has it really? Conflict sociologists Meredith Minkler and Ann Robertson (1991) say that while the figures themselves are true, the comparison is misleading. The money that went to the elderly did *not* come from the children. Would anyone say that the money the government gives to flood or earthquake victims comes from the children? Of course not. The government makes choices about where to spend money, and it could

Figure 13.4

Health-Care Costs for the Elderly and Disabled.

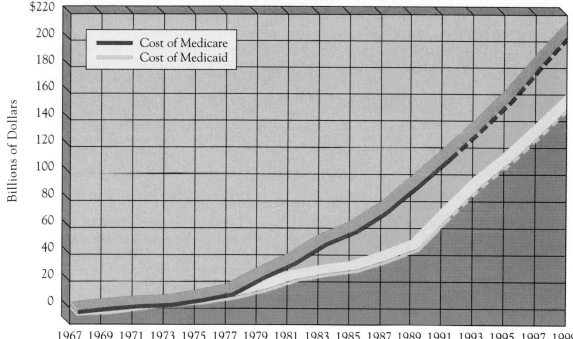

Note: Medicare is intended for the elderly and disabled, Medicaid for the poor. One–third of Medicaid payments ($25 billion) goes to the elderly (*Statistical Abstract* 1993: Table 162). Broken lines indicate the author's projections.
Sources: Statistical Abstract various years. Recent years are from the 1993 edition, Table 159.

very well have decided to increase spending on *both* the elderly and the children. It simply has not done so. To frame the issue as money going to one at the expense of the other is an attempt to divide the working class. If the working class can be made to think that they must make a choice between suffering children and suffering old folks, they will be divided and unable to work together to change U.S. society.

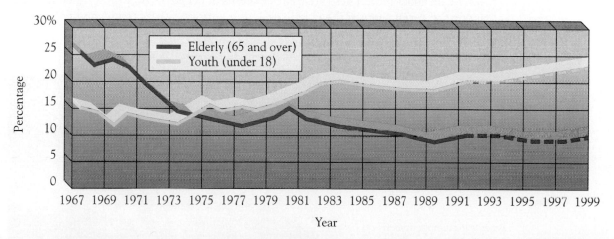

Note: For some years the government figures for youth refer to people under 18, for other years to people under 16 or under 15. Broken lines indicate the author's projections.
Sources: Congressional Research Service; Statistical Abstract 1991: Table 748.

Figure 13.5

Trends in Poverty.

Fighting Back

Some organizations work to protect the hard-won gains of the elderly. Let's consider two.

The Gray Panthers   The Gray Panthers are aware of the danger of dividing the working class along age lines. This organization, founded in the 1960s by Margaret Kuhn (1990), encourages people of all ages to work for the welfare of both the old and the young. On the micro level, the goal is to develop positive self-concepts. On the macro level, the goal is to build a power base that will challenge institutions that oppress the poor, whatever their age—and to fight attempts to pit people against one another along age lines. One indication of their effectiveness is that Gray Panthers frequently testify before congressional committees concerning pending legislation.

The American Association of Retired Persons   The AARP also combats negative images of the elderly. This thirty-three-million member organization is politically powerful (Clark 1994). It monitors proposed federal and state legislation and mobilizes its members to act on issues affecting their welfare. The organization can command tens of thousands of telephone calls, telegrams, and letters from irate elderly citizens. To protect their chances of re-election, politicians know better than to cross swords with the AARP. As you can expect, critics claim that the organization is too powerful, that it is able to muster forces to claim greater than its share of the nation's resources.

All this helps prove our point, say conflict theorists. Age groups are just one of society's many groups struggling for scarce resources, with conflict the inevitable result.

Before we close this chapter, let us look at problems of dependency and the sociology of death and dying.

Problems of Dependency

"Will I be able to take care of myself? Will I become frail and not able to get around? Will I end up poor and in some nursing home somewhere, in the hands of strangers who don't care about me?" These are some concerns of people as they grow older. Let's examine the dependency of the elderly: isolation, nursing homes, abuse, and poverty.

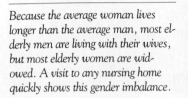

Because the average woman lives longer than the average man, most elderly men are living with their wives, but most elderly women are widowed. A visit to any nursing home quickly shows this gender imbalance.

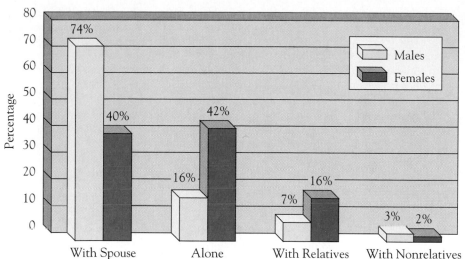

Figure 13.6

Where Do America's Elderly Live?

Source: Statistical Abstract 1993: Table 71.

Isolation and Gender

We need first to note that most U.S. elderly are not as isolated as stereotypes would have us believe. Half of all people over 65 live within a half hour of a child. Forty percent see or talk to one of their children daily, 80 percent at least weekly, and only 6 percent less than once a week (*Statistical Abstract* 1989: Tables 42, 43). Four-fifths of the elderly have a living brother or sister, and one-third see a sibling at least once a week.

Nevertheless, isolation is a problem for many people over 65, especially for women. Because of differences in mortality, most men over 65 are married, while most elderly women are not. As a result, most elderly men live with their wives, while most elderly women live alone or with relatives (see Figure 13.6). The intense feelings of isolation that widowhood brings (DiGiulio 1992), then, are more likely to be experienced by women. Note, however, that only a tiny proportion of U.S. elderly, either male or female, lives with people who are not relatives.

Nursing Homes

At any one time, about 5 percent of U.S. citizens over the age of 65 are in nursing homes (*Statistical Abstract* 1993: Tables 14, 191). With turnover—some residents return home after only a few weeks or a few months, others die after a short stay—perhaps 20 percent of elderly Americans spend at least some time in a nursing home. Nursing home residents are *not typical* of the elderly. They are likely to be widowed, or quite ill, or over 80, or never to have married and therefore without family to take care of them (Kinsella and Taeuber 1993). What is life like for them?

It is difficult to say good things about nursing homes, even those that are run well. First, nursing care is so expensive (averaging about $25,000 a year) that of people without family, 70 percent go broke within just three months (Ruffenbach 1988). The literature, both popular and scientific, is filled with horror stories—reports of patients neglected, beaten, and otherwise maltreated (Ellis 1991; Brink 1993). Of course, not all nursing homes are like that. On the contrary, most are probably at least halfway decent. Some even provide a pleasant decor and concerned help, but they still fall far short of being home (Butterworth 1990). Even the better ones have a tendency to strip away human dignity, as sociologist Sharon Curtin found (1976):

Nursing home residents, most of whom are either very old or very sick, are not typical of the elderly. Shown here is a Native American in an old age home at Pine Ridge Indian Reservation in South Dakota.

Miss Larson entered Montcliffe the last week of October. . . . Shortly after her admission, I arrived at 7 A.M. to find the night nurse indignant and angry. Miss Larson had climbed over the side rails during the night, and had been found in the bathroom. "She didn't ring or call out," said the nurse. . . . "Why, she might have been hurt, and she is so confused. I want the doctor to order me more sedation. We can't have her carrying on, and disturbing all the other patients."

I walked in the room and Miss Larson was in restraints. . . . "Get me out of these!" she ordered. "How dare they try to stop me from getting out of bed. I always have to relieve myself at night; and they never answer my bell. . . . So I crawl over the edge; I've been doing it ever since I came to this place. . . ."

Miss Larson was not confused; but in a place where all the patients are so sedated that they scarcely move a muscle during the night, she was counted a nuisance. I did not want them to increase her sedation; barbiturates frequently make old people confused and disoriented. Even if she was a pain in the neck, I like her better awake and making some sense. The problem was she had no rights. She was old, sick, feeble. Therefore she must shut up, lie still, take what little was offered and be grateful. And if she did that, she would be a "good girl."

The elderly bitterly resent being treated like children—in an institution or anywhere else. They resist, as did Miss Larson, but resistance is usually fruitless.

Not everything about nursing homes is bad, of course. They do provide care for those who have no families, or are so sick that their families can no longer care for them. Sometimes nursing homes even help family relationships. A study of a well-run, middle-class nursing home showed that 30 percent of the residents continued their pattern of alienation, but 70 percent either grew closer to one another or maintained an already close relationship. With professional care, the condition of some patients improved, and children whose affection had been strained by the parent's physical or mental traumas found themselves free to again provide emotional support to the parent (Smith and Bengston 1979).

As we have seen in many previous instances, one of the best ways to gain perspective on conditions in our own society is to take a cross-cultural view. Consequently, the Perspectives box on the next page on treatment of the elderly should prove enlightening.

What life is like for the elderly depends primarily on the same factors as for people of other ages, especially gender, social class, and historical period. On the left is an elderly farm couple of the 1930s, on the right a contemporary elderly urban couple.

▲▼▲

Perspectives

CULTURAL DIVERSITY AROUND THE WORLD

Trouble in Paradise: Death-Hastening Behaviors in "Idyllic" Societies

MYTHS ABOUND OF THE tender care lavished on the elderly in preliterate and agricultural societies. Like the Abkhasians, the elderly are perfectly integrated into a caring community. They gradually disengage from more demanding roles as they take on less rigorous, but highly appreciated tasks. As strength gradually diminishes, surrounded by caring, supportive kinfolk and lifelong friends, the individual departs from life, leaving misty-eyed relatives and friends filled with heartwarming memories of the departed.

Such perceptions bear little resemblance to the reality that many elderly people experience among their lifelong tribal friends. Consider this incident from the Tiwi:

The old lady had become too feeble to look after herself. She was now blind and constantly falling over logs or into fires. Her sons and the tribal elders agreed that the time had come for the "covering up" ceremony. They dug a hole in a lonely place, put the woman in, and heaped in earth until only her head was showing. Then they left. When they returned a couple of days later, they discovered—to their surprise—that the old woman was dead.

They all do express surprise, for she was alive when they last saw her. Things like this "just happen," they say—to feeble women, I would add, but not to the men in this culture.

Anthropologists have found numerous instances of what they call "death-hastening" behaviors, passive killing of the decrepit elderly.

Niue is a small island in Polynesia, a sort of tropical paradise. Here the elderly are held in high respect. Comfortably settled into a network of friends and responsibilities, the elders are stable and influential figures in the community. Competence, authority, and respect is how one would describe the role of elders in this culture—unless, that is, significant mental or physical decline sets in. Then the situation is turned on its head. If the elderly become incontinent, have wheezing chests, or if they drool or look vacantly about them—or even if they forget people's names and talk constantly about events in the remote past—they are left unattended or given only minimal care. Little effort is made to bathe them, they grow hungry and are clad in filthy rags, and their homes carry a strong stench of urine and other filth. One old man, too frail to summon a doctor and lying on the floor only half conscious, evoked smiles from visitors and kin, who commented that he was "going out the hard way." Then there was this event:

A woman of 85, partially blind, fell into a disused water tank. Lying there with a broken arm and dislocated shoulder, she feebly cried for help. Her pleas were met with curses for being such a nuisance. Other adults laughingly teased the woman about her helpless condition. After they helped her out, the old lady remained the butt of rude jokes about incompetence.

These examples are not meant to imply that all nonindustrial groups treat their frail elders in ways that appear so horrible by our standards. Most do not. In most cultures the elderly are treated well, although probably not quite as well as some of our mythical conceptions imply.

All human groups face the problem of how to care for their decrepit elderly. Because the numbers of such people in the industrialized nations are growing rapidly, this has become a pressing issue. Many are justifiably concerned about cost. Some propose that the elderly are the family's responsibility, not that of the general society. Yet we cannot turn back the clock—and, if we could, we aren't really certain what we would find. What was the past *really* like? As these examples from supposedly idyllic nonindustrial societies indicate, ideas often don't match reality. No one has the entire answer yet. Certainly no one would suggest that we choose the Tiwi or Niue as models.

What do you think?

Sources: Based on Barker 1990; Glascock 1990; Sokolovsky 1990.

Elder Abuse

Stories of elder abuse abound—and so does the abuse itself. In interviews with a random sample of nursing home staff, 40 percent admitted that during the preceding year they had abused patients psychologically, and 10 percent admitted to abusing them physically (Pillemer and Hudson 1993). Most abuse of the elderly, however, takes place at home, and most abusers are not paid staff, but family members, who hit, verbally and emotionally abuse, or financially exploit their aged relatives (Pillemer and Wolf 1987). Spouses are most likely to be the abusers (Nachman 1991; Pillemer and Suitor 1993).

Why do children, spouses, and other relatives abuse their own elderly? Sociologists Karl Pillemer and Jill Suitor (1993) interviewed over 200 people who were caring for family members who suffered from Alzheimer's disease. One husband told them,

Frustration reaches a point where patience gives out. I've never struck her, but sometimes I wonder if I can control myself. . . . This is . . . the part of her care that causes me the frustration and the loss of patience. What I tell her, she doesn't register. Like when I tell her, "You're my wife." "You're crazy," she says.

Apparently, the precipitating cause of this form of violence is stress from caring for a person who is highly dependent, demanding, and in some cases violent (Douglass 1983; Pillemer and Suitor 1993). Since most people who care for the elderly undergo stress, however, we still do not have the answer to why some caregivers become violent. For that, we must await future research.

Regaining Rights: Elderly Empowerment

For a nursing home resident to be restrained—tied into a chair or bed—used to be a common sight. After numerous complaints and years of neglect, the U.S. government finally took action. To change nursing homes from a warehouse of bodies to places of treatment and humane care, the U.S. Congress passed a bill of rights for nursing home residents. Now nursing home patients have the right to be informed about their treatment and to refuse it, the right to privacy, the right to complain without reprisal—and the right to be unfettered (Brink 1993). As with any other law, this one, too, will be only as good as its enforcement.

The Elderly Poor

Many elderly live in nagging fear of poverty. Since they do not know how long they will live, nor what the rate of inflation will be, they are uncertain whether their money will last as long as they will. How realistic is this fear? Although we cannot speak to any individual case, we can look at the elderly as a group.

Gender and Poverty As we reviewed in Chapter 11, during their working years most women have lower incomes than men. Table 13.3 shows that this pattern follows women

Table 13.3

The Elderly and Poverty

	Percentage Below the Poverty Line
Race or Ethnicity	
Whites	10.3%
Asian Americans	14.0
Latinos	20.8
African Americans	33.8
Head of Family Unit	
Male	6.1
Female	12.6
Living Arrangements	
Living in family	6.0
Living with unrelated persons	24.9

Sources: Statistical Abstract 1990: Table 746; 1993: Table 736; Wray 1991.

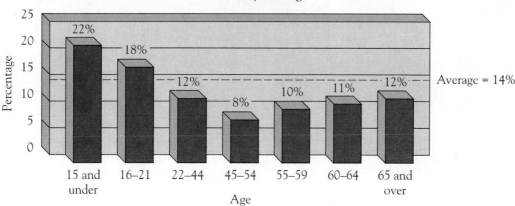

Figure 13.7

Poverty and Age

Source: Statistical Abstract 1993: Table 738.

and men into their old age. As you can see from this table, women are twice as likely to be poor as are men. This table also reflects one of the protective consequences of family life, for elderly people who live in families are only one-fourth as likely to be poor as those who live with unrelated individuals.

Race or Ethnicity and Poverty   Table 13.3 also shows how racial and ethnic patterns persist among the elderly. Latinos aged 65 and over are twice as likely as whites to be poor, while the poverty rate among elderly African Americans is over three times the white rate. Although the gap is not as large, a larger proportion of elderly Asian Americans is also likely to be poorer than whites. The poverty of elderly women also shows distinct patterns by race and ethnicity, with elderly Latinas and African-American women twice as likely as elderly white women to be poor (Wray 1991).

A Decline in Poverty   An image of poor, neglected grandparents was used in earlier decades to promote programs to benefit elderly Americans. This was an apt description during the 1960s and 1970s—for at that time the poverty rate of the elderly was greater than that of the general population—but today this is not the case. In spite of the gender and racial patterns shown in Table 13.3, federal programs for the elderly have been a remarkable success. In the 1950s, 33 percent of Americans aged 65 and over were living below the poverty line. By the 1970s, this rate had plunged to 15 percent (Hudson 1978; *Statistical Abstract* 1993: Table 739). As Figure 13.7 shows, the U.S. elderly are now *less* likely than the average American to be poor.

The Sociology of Death and Dying

In a fascinating subfield of sociology, death and dying, sociologists stress how death, like old age, is much more than a biological event. They examine how culture shapes the ways that people experience death. Let us look at some of their findings.

Effects of Industrialization

In preindustrial societies, the sick were taken care of at home, and they died at home. Because life was short, during childhood most people saw a sibling or parent die (Blauner 1966). As noted in Chapter 1, corpses were even prepared for burial at home.

Just as at other stages in the life course, having money adequate for one's needs and desires makes life more pleasant and satisfying. This elderly woman who must live out of her car is not likely to find this time of her life satisfying. Income, however, is hardly the sole determiner of satisfaction during old age. As indicated in the text, integration in a community in which one is respected is also a critical factor. Thus, these elderly men, although poor, are likely to find this time of life much more satisfying than the isolated homeless woman.

Industrialization radically altered the circumstances of dying. With modern medicine, dying was transformed into an event to be managed by professionals in hospitals. Consequently, most Americans have never seen anyone die. Fictional deaths on television are the closest most come to witnessing death. In effect, dying has become an event that takes place behind closed doors—isolated, disconnected, remote.

In consequence, the process of dying has become strange to us—and perhaps more fearful as well. To help put on a mask of immortality, we hide from the fact of death. We have even developed elaborate ways to refer to death without using the word itself, which uncomfortably reminds us of our human destiny. We carefully construct a language of avoidance, terms such as "gone," "passed on," "no longer with us," "gone beyond," "passed through the pearly gates," and "at peace now."

As people grow older, death becomes a less distant event. The elderly see many friends and relatives die, and often much of their talk centers on those persons. Often fears about dying focus more on the "how" of death than on death itself. The elderly are especially fearful of dying alone or in pain. One of their biggest fears is cancer, which seems to strike out of the blue.

Death as a Process

Through her interviews with people who had been informed that they had an incurable disease, psychologist Elisabeth Kübler-Ross (1969, 1981) found that coming face to face with one's own death sets in motion a five-stage process:

1 *Denial.* In this first stage, people cannot believe that they are really going to die. ("The doctor made a mistake. Those test results aren't right.") They avoid the topic of death and any situation that might remind them of it.

2 *Anger.* In this second stage, they acknowledge their coming death but see it as unjust. ("I didn't do anything to deserve this. So-and-so is much worse than I am, and he's in good health. It isn't right that I should die.")

3 *Negotiation.* Next, the individual tries to get around death by making a bargain with God, with fate, or even with the disease itself. ("I need one more Christmas with the family. I never appreciated them as much as I should have. Don't take me until after Christmas, and then I'll go willingly.")

4 *Depression*. In this stage, people are resigned to the fact that death is inevitable, but they are extremely unhappy about it. They grieve because their life is about to end, and they have no power to change the course of events.

5 *Acceptance*. In this final stage, people come to terms with the certainty of impending death. They are likely to get their affairs in order—to make wills, pay bills, give instructions to children on what kind of adults they should become and of how they should take care of Mommy (or Daddy), and express regret at not having done certain things when they had the chance. Devout Christians are likely to talk about the hope of salvation and their desire to be in heaven with Jesus.

Kübler-Ross noted that not everyone experiences all these stages, and that not everyone goes through them in this precise order. Some people never come to terms with their death and remain in the first or second stages throughout the process of dying. Others may move back and forth, vacillating, for example, between acceptance, depression, and negotiation. When my mother was informed that she had inoperable cancer, she immediately went into a vivid stage of denial. If she later went through anger or negotiation, she kept them to herself. After a short depression, she experienced a longer period of questioning why this was happening to her. She then moved quickly into stage 5, which occurred very much as Kübler-Ross described it. After her funeral, my two brothers and I went to her apartment, as she had instructed us. There, to our surprise, we found attached to each item in every room a piece of masking tape with one of our names on it—from the bed and television to the silverware and knickknacks. At first we found this strange, but as we sorted through things, reflecting on why she had given certain items to whom, we began to appreciate the "closure" she had given to this aspect of her material life. It was a strong indication of her acceptance of death.

Hospices

In earlier generations, when not many people made it to age 65 or beyond, death at an earlier age was taken for granted—much as people take it for granted today that most people *will* see 65. In fact, *most* deaths in the United States (about 75 percent) now occur after the age of 65. This has led to a concern about the *how* of dying. Few elderly people want to burden their children with their own death; they want to die with dignity and with the comforting presence of friends and relatives. Hospitals, to put the matter bluntly, are awkward places in which to die. There, patients are surrounded by strangers in formal garb, in an organization that puts its routines ahead of their needs. In addition to their coldness and formality, hospitals are also extremely expensive.

Hospices emerged as a solution to these problems. Originating in Great Britain, hospices attempt to reduce the emotional and physical burden on children and other relatives and to lower costs. Above all, hospices are intended to provide dignity in death and to make people comfortable in what Kübler-Ross (1989) called the living-dying interval, that period between discovering that death is imminent and death itself. The term **hospice** originally referred to a place, but increasingly it refers to services that are brought into a dying person's home. In the United States, the number of hospices has grown from one in 1974 to 1,800 today (Busby 1993).

Whereas hospitals are dedicated to prolonging life, hospices are dedicated to bringing comfort and dignity to a dying person's last days or months. In the hospital the patient is the unit, but in the hospice the unit changes to the dying person and his or her friends and family. In the hospital, the goal is to make the patient well; in the hospice, it is to relieve pain and suffering. In the hospital, the primary concern is the individual's physical welfare; in the hospice, although medical needs are met, the primary concern is the individual's social—and in some instances, spiritual—well-being.

hospice: a place, or services brought into someone's home, for the purpose of bringing comfort and dignity to a dying person

Suicide and the Elderly

In Chapter 1, we noted how Durkheim analyzed suicide as much more than an individual act. He stressed that each country has its own suicide rate, and that these rates remain quite stable year after year. This same stability can be seen in the age, sex, and race of people who kill themselves. Figure 13.8 shows striking patterns. One of the most notable is that at all ages males kill themselves at higher rates than do females. Similarly, at all ages the rates of white Americans are higher than those of African Americans (data are unavailable for other racial and ethnic groups).

Statistics often fly in the face of the impressions fostered by the mass media, and here you have such an example. Although self-inflicted deaths of youths are given high publicity, such deaths are relatively rare. Note that with the exceptions of African-American males age 55 to 64 and African-American females age 75 to 84, the suicide rate of adolescents is *lower* than all other ages. Because adolescents have such a low death rate, however, suicide does rank as their third leading cause of death—after accidents and homicide (*Statistical Abstract* 1993: Table 127).

What is also striking about this figure is the sharp rise in the suicide of white males when they reach their sixties. No one has a good explanation for this, but from a symbolic interactionist viewpoint it may indicate that white males experience aging differently from the other groups shown in this figure. Because white males generally enjoy greater power and status in U.S. society, it could be that aging for them represents a relatively greater loss of privilege. As noted, however, no one knows the explanation—nor, for that matter, has anyone been able to adequately explain why year after year the suicide rate of African Americans is lower than that of white Americans.

The primary sociological point of these findings on suicide is one that has been stressed throughout this text: recurring patterns of human behavior—whether education, marriage, work, or even suicide—represent underlying social forces. Consequently, if no basic changes take place in the social conditions under which the groups that make up U.S. society live, you can expect their suicide rates to be little changed five to ten years from now.

Figure 13-8

A Profile of Suicide

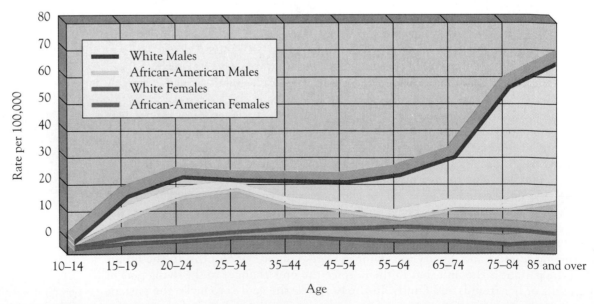

Note: Data are available only for whites and African Americans in the source, and for inconsistent years. Data are for 1990, except 1980 for African-American males 85 and over and African-American females 75 to 84, and 1970 for African-American females 85 and over.

Source: *Statistical Abstract* 1993: Tables 22, 137.

Summary and Review

Social Factors in Aging

How do social factors influence aging?

Cultural attitudes and beliefs about aging affect people's perceptions and behavior. The Abkhasians, for example, have a set of beliefs and practices regarding sex, work, diet, and community that apparently helps people live longer. The **graying of America** refers to the rising proportion of older people in the U.S. population. This trend, which due to industrialization is worldwide, brings about changes in attitudes toward the elderly. Pp. 346–352.

The Symbolic Interactionist Perspective

What factors influence perceptions of aging?

Symbolic interactionists stress that, by itself, reaching any particular age has no meaning. They identify four factors that influence when people label themselves as "old": biological changes, biographical events, gender age, and cultural timetables. Cross-cultural comparisons—for example, the traditional Tiwi, Eskimos, Chinese, and Native Americans—demonstrate the role of culture in determining how individuals experience aging. **Ageism,** negative reactions to the elderly, is based on stereotypes, which, in turn, are influenced by the mass media. Pp. 352–356.

The Functionalist Perspective

How is retirement functional for society?

Functionalists focus on how the withdrawal of the elderly from positions of responsibility benefits society. **Disengagement theory** examines retirement as a device for ensuring that a society's positions of responsibility will be passed smoothly from one generation to the next. **Activity theory** examines how people adjust when they disengage from productive roles. Pp. 356–357.

The Conflict Perspective

Is there conflict between different age groups?

Social Security legislation is an example of one generation making demands on another generation for limited resources. As the **dependency ratio,** the number of workers who support one retired person, decreases, workers may become resentful. The Social Security Trust Fund may be a gigantic fraud perpetrated by the power elite on the nation's elderly. The argument that benefits to the elderly come at the cost of benefits to children is fallacious. Organizations such as the Gray Panthers and the AARP recognize the potential for conflict between age groups. Pp. 357–362.

Problems of Dependency

What are some of the problems that today's elderly face?

Due to differences in mortality and work histories, women are more likely to live alone and to be poor. Perhaps 20 percent of Americans spend at least some time in nursing homes. Beyond the expense of this kind of care, nursing homes tend to foster dependency among the elderly. The U.S. Congress has passed laws to protect the rights of nursing home residents. Some elderly are victims of abuse, most often by their own family. Poverty in old age, greatly reduced through government programs, reflects the gender and racial or ethnic patterns of poverty in the general society. Pp. 362–367.

The Sociology of Death and Dying

How does culture affect the meaning—and experience—of death and dying?

Like old age, death is much more than a biological event. Industrialization, for example, brought modern medicine, and with it hospitals and the custom of dying in a formal setting surrounded by strangers. Kübler-Ross identified five stages in the dying process, which, though insightful, do not characterize all people. **Hospices** are a cultural device of recent origin designed to overcome the negative aspects of dying in hospitals. Suicide shows distinct patterns by sex and race. At all ages, whites are more likely to commit suicide than are African Americans, as are males than females. Pp. 367–370.

Where can I read more on this topic?

Suggested readings for this chapter are listed on page 642.

Thomas Hart Benton, City Building *from* America Today, *1930*

The Economy:
Money and Work

THE ALARM POUNDED IN KIM'S *ears. "Not Monday already," she groaned. "There must be a better way of starting the week." She pressed the snooze button on the clock (from Germany) to sneak another ten minutes' sleep. In what seemed just thirty seconds, the alarm shrilly insisted she get up and face the week.*

Still bleary-eyed after her shower, Kim peered into her closet and picked out a silk blouse (from China), a plaid wool skirt (from Scotland), and leather shoes (from India). She nodded, satisfied, as she added a pair of simulated pearls (from Taiwan). Running late, she hurriedly ran a brush (from Mexico) through her hair. As Kim wolfed down a bowl of cereal (from the United States), topped with milk (from the United States), bananas (from Costa Rica), and sugar (from the Dominican Republic), she turned on her kitchen television (from Korea) to listen to the weather forecast.

Gulping the last of her coffee (from Brazil), Kim grabbed her briefcase (from Wales), purse (from Spain), and jacket (from Malaysia), and quickly climbed into her car (from Japan). As she glanced at her watch (from Switzerland), she hoped the traffic would be in her favor. She muttered to herself as she glimpsed the gas gauge at a street light (from Great Britain). She muttered again when she paid for the gas (from Saudi Arabia), for the price had risen once more. "My check never keeps up with prices," she moaned to herself as she finished the drive to work.

The office was abuzz. Six months ago, New York headquarters had put the company up for sale, but there had been no takers. The big news this Monday was that both a Japanese and a Canadian corporation had put in bids over the weekend. No one got much work done that day, as the whole office speculated about how things might change.

As Kim walked to the parking lot after work, she saw a "Buy American" bumper sticker on the car next to hers. "That's right," she said to herself. "If people were more like me, this country would be in better shape."

While the vignette may be slightly exaggerated, it is not too far from the experience of most Americans. Many of us are like Kim—using a multitude of products from around the world, and yet somewhat concerned about the declining competitive position of our own country. In terms of trade and products, the world has certainly grown much smaller in recent years. We live in a global economy, and this chapter focuses on the consequences of this fact for the future of the United States.

The Transformation of Economic Systems

In Mexico, the market is a bustling scene—farmers selling fruits and vegetables, as well as poultry, goats, and caged songbirds—others selling homemade blankets, serapes, huaraches, pottery, belts. Women bend over open fires cooking tacos, which their waiting customers wolf down with soft drinks. The market is a combined business and social occasion, as people make their purchases and catch each other up on the latest gossip. Such scenes used to characterize the world, but now they are limited primarily to the Second and Third Worlds. The closest people come in the United States is a flea market, a farmer's market, or a bazaar.

Today, the term *market* means much more than such settings and activities. It has kept its original meaning of buying and selling, but it now refers to things much more impersonal. **Market,** the mechanism by which we establish values in order to exchange goods and services, today means the Dow Jones Industrial Average in New York City, and the Nikkei Average in Tokyo. Market also means the movement of vast amounts of goods across international borders, even across oceans and continents. Market means brokers taking orders for IBM, speculators trading international currencies, and futures

market: any process of buying and selling; on a more formal level, the mechanism that establishes values for the exchange of goods and services

Although the term market *now refers to the mechanisms by which people establish value so they can exchange goods and services, its original meaning referred to a direct exchange of goods, as shown in this photo of a market in Chiapas, Mexico. In peasant societies, where such markets are still a regular part of everyday life, people find the social interaction every bit as rewarding as the goods and money that they exchange.*

traders making huge bets on whether oil, wheat, and pork bellies will go up or down—and, of course, it also refers to making a purchase at the local food store.

People's lives have always been affected by the dynamics of the market, or as sociologists prefer to call it, the **economy.** Today, the economy, which many sociologists believe is the most important of our social institutions, differs radically from all but our most recent past. Economic systems have become impersonal and global. The products that Kim used in our opening vignette make it apparent that today's economy knows no national boundaries. The economy is essential to our welfare for it means inflation or deflation, high or low interest rates, high or low unemployment, economic recession or economic boom. The economy affects our chances of buying a new home, of having to work at a dead-end job or of being on a fast track in an up-and-coming company.

To better understand the U.S. economy and its relative standing in history, it is useful to review the historical stages that preceded it. These stages were discussed in some detail in Chapter 6 (pp. 145–152), in which the Lenskis (1987) described how societies were transformed from those based on relatively simple organization to those with more complex organization. Here we shall just briefly review them.

Hunting and Gathering Societies: Subsistence

The earliest human societies, *hunting and gathering societies*, had a simple **subsistence economy.** Groups of perhaps twenty-five to forty people lived off the land, simply gathering what they could find, moving from place to place as their food supply ran low. Hunting added to these people's knowledge and skills as they developed weapons and learned to prepare and store meat. Because there was little or no excess food or other items, there was little trade with other groups. With no excess to accumulate, there was a high degree of social equality in this earliest type of society.

Pastoral and Horticultural Societies: The Creation of Surplus

People then began to breed animals and cultivate plants. This development, called pastoral and horticultural societies, created a more dependable food supply. From this developed a *surplus,* which was one of the most significant events in human history, for it

economy: a system of distribution of goods and services

subsistence economy: a type of economy in which human groups live off the land with little or no surplus

Two hallmarks of postindustrial economies are information and a global village. Just a few decades ago, the value of goods in what used to be "far off" Japan had little or no relevance to the West. Today, in contrast, with Japan an integrated part of a global market, economic events there are significant for the stock exchanges in New York, London, Zurich, Bonn, Paris, Brussels, Madrid, and so on. Shown here are floor traders at the Tokyo Stock Exchange.

changed people's basic relationships. It allowed human groups to grow in size, to settle down in a single place, and to develop a specialized division of labor. For the first time in human history, some individuals were able to devote their energies to tasks other than food production. Some became leather workers, others weapon makers, and so on. This new division of labor had far-reaching effects on human life, for having an excess of items that were produced stimulated trade. The primary sociological significance of surplus and trade was that they fostered *social inequality*, for some members of the group were now able to accumulate more possessions than others. The effects of that change remain with us today.

Agricultural Societies: The Growth of Trade

The invention of the plow brought even greater surpluses to agricultural societies, magnifying the trends of the previous period. Even more people were freed from food production, more specialized divisions of labor followed, and trade expanded—a greater range of goods was exchanged over greater distances. As trading centers developed into cities, power passed from the heads of families and clans to a ruling elite. The result was even greater social, political, and economic inequality.

Industrial Societies: The Birth of the Machine

Industrial societies, which are based on machines powered by fuels, created a surplus unlike anything the world had seen. Following the invention of the steam engine in 1765, a minority of people could produce all the food a society needed, and the vast surplus of manufactured goods stimulated extensive trade between nations. The early part of the Industrial Revolution magnified social inequalities, as some individuals found themselves able to exploit the labor of many others and to manipulate the political machinery for their own purposes. Later on, bloody battles occurred as workers unionized to improve their working conditions.

As the surplus produced by industrialization increased, the emphasis changed from the production of goods to their consumption. Sociologist Thorstein Veblen (1912) used the term **conspicuous consumption** to describe this fundamental change in people's ori-

conspicuous consumption: Thorstein Veblen's term for a change from the Protestant ethic to an eagerness to show off wealth by the elaborate consumption of goods

The Industrial Revolution not only changed the way people worked, but also altered social relationships. Shown here is a scene from an early stage of the Industrial Revolution, power loom weaving in a textile mill about 1834. Two vital aspects of this fundamental change are immediately evident: the infinitely greater productive power of the machine as opposed to hand work, and the employment of women.

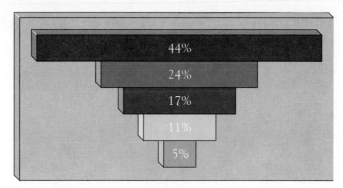

Figure 14.1

The Inverted Income Pyramid: The Proportion of Income Received by Each Fifth of the U.S. Population

Source: Statistical Abstract 1993: Table 722.
Note: Due to Rounding, the total is 101%

entations. By this term, Veblen meant that the Protestant ethic identified by Weber—an emphasis on hard work, savings, and a concern for salvation (discussed on pages 170–172)—had been replaced by an eagerness to show off wealth by the "elaborate consumption of goods."

Postindustrial Societies: The Information Age

In 1973, sociologist Daniel Bell noted the emergence of a *postindustrial society*. According to Bell, this new type of economy has six characteristics: (1) extensive trade among nations; (2) a large surplus of goods; (3) a service sector so large that it employs the majority of workers; (4) a wide variety and quantity of goods available to the average person; (5) an "information explosion"; and (6) a "global village," that is, technological advances that make possible instantaneous, worldwide communications.

Perhaps the two most striking characteristics are the information explosion and the emergence of a global village. Today, news of political and economic changes, instantaneously transmitted by satellite, not only affects prices on the New York Stock Exchange but reverberates on the Japanese Nikkei Stock Exchange as well. Because national boundaries now present less of a barricade than ever to the exchange of goods and information, the world has become far more accessible (Kennedy 1993).

Consequences are especially visible in Europe, where seventeen nations have formed an economic and political entity called the European Union (EU). Each nation remains sovereign and retains its own legislature, courts, and heads of state, but there is also a European Parliament, a European court, and, as proposed, a single military. Just as the currencies of the individual states continued to circulate for a time after the formation of the United States, so do those of EU members as it struggles to develop a unified currency. A goal is political unity, expected to be reached within a decade.

Continued Inequalities The postindustrial economy's cornucopia of material wealth allows the average citizen of the First World to live at a level only dreamed of just a few generations back. But, as you know from experience, the distribution of income is anything but equal. In the preceding five chapters, we examined these inequalities—from global stratification to inequalities of social class, gender, race, and age in the United States. There is little to add to that extensive presentation, but an overall snapshot of how the income of the United States is distributed may be useful.

The inverted pyramid shown in Figure 14.1 is that snapshot. The proportion of the nation's income going to the wealthiest fifth of the U.S. population is at the top, the proportion going to the poorest fifth at the bottom. Note that *44 percent* of the whole country's income goes to just one-fifth of Americans, while only *5 percent* goes to the poorest fifth. Rather than bringing equality, then, the postindustrial economy has perpetuated the income inequalities of the industrial economy.

The Transformation of the Medium of Exchange

As each type of economy evolved, so, too, did the **medium of exchange,** the means by which people value and exchange goods and services. As we review this transformation, you will see how the medium of exchange is vital to each society, both reflecting its state of development and contributing to it.

Earliest Mediums of Exchange

As noted, the lack of surplus in hunting and gathering and pastoral and horticultural societies meant that there was little to trade. Whatever trading did occur was by **barter,** the direct exchange of one item for another. The surplus that stimulated trade in later societies led to different ways of valuing goods and services for the purpose of exchange. Let us look at how the medium of exchange was transformed.

Medium of Exchange in Agricultural Societies

Although bartering continued in agricultural societies, people increasingly came to use **money,** a medium of exchange by which items are valued. In most places, money consisted of gold and silver coins, their weight and purity determining the amount of goods or services that they could purchase. In some places people made purchases with **deposit receipts,** receipts that transferred ownership to a specified number of ounces of gold, bushels of wheat, or amount of other goods that were on deposit in a warehouse or bank. Toward the end of the agricultural period, deposit receipts became formalized into **currency** (paper money), each piece of paper representing a specific amount of gold or silver that could be redeemed from a central warehouse. Thus currency (and deposit receipts) represented **stored value,** and no more currency could be issued than the amount of gold or silver that the currency represented. Gold and silver coins continued to circulate alongside the deposit receipts and currency.

Medium of Exchange in Industrial Societies

With but few exceptions, bartering became a thing of the past in industrial societies. Gold was replaced by paper currencies, which, in the United States, could be exchanged for a set amount of gold stored at Fort Knox. This policy was called the **gold standard,** and as long as each dollar represented a specified amount of gold the number of dollars that could be issued was limited. By the end of this period, U.S. paper money could no longer be exchanged for gold or silver, resulting in **fiat money,** currency issued by a government that is not backed by stored value.

One consequence of the move away from stored value was that coins made of precious metals disappeared from circulation. In comparison with fiat money, these coins were more valuable, and people became unwilling to part with them. Gold coins disappeared first, followed by the largest silver coin, the dollar. Then, as inferior metals (copper, zinc, and nickel) replaced the smaller silver coins, people began to hoard them, and silver coins also disappeared from circulation.

Even without a gold standard that restrains the issuing of currency to stored value, governments have a practical limit on the amount of paper money they can issue. In general, prices increase if a government issues currency at a rate higher than the growth of its **gross national product,** the total amount of a nation's goods and services. This condition, known as **inflation,** means that each unit of currency will purchase fewer goods and services. Governments try to control inflation, for it is a destabilizing influence.

As you can see from Figure 14.2, as long as the gold standard limited the amount of currency, the purchasing power of the dollar remained relatively stable. When the United States departed from the gold standard in 1937, the dollar no longer represented stored value, and it plunged in value. Today, the dollar is but a shadow of its former self, retaining only about 10 percent of its original purchasing power.

medium of exchange: the means by which people value goods and services in order to make an exchange, for example, currency, gold, and silver

barter: the direct exchange of one item for another

money: any item (from seashells to gold) that serves as a medium of exchange; today, currency is the most common form

deposit receipts: a receipt stating that a certain amount of goods is on deposit in a warehouse or bank; the receipt is used as a form of money

currency: paper money

stored value: the backing of a currency by goods that are stored and held in reserve

gold standard: paper money backed by gold

fiat money: currency issued by a government that is not backed by stored value

gross national product: the amount of goods and services produced by a nation

inflation: an increase in prices

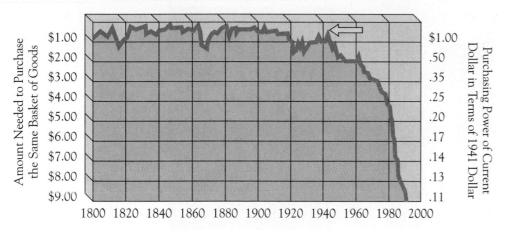

Source: "Alternative Investment Market Letter," November 1991

Figure 14-2

Declining Value of the Dollar.

In the industrial economy, checking accounts held in banks became common. A *check* is actually a type of deposit receipt, for it is a promise that the writer of the check has enough currency on deposit to cover the check. The latter part of this period saw the invention of the **credit card,** a device that allows its owner, who has been preapproved for a set amount of credit, to purchase goods without an immediate exchange of money—either metal or currency. The credit card owner is later billed for the purchases.

Medium of Exchange in Postindustrial Societies

During the first part of the postindustrial economy, paper money circulates freely. Paper money then becomes less common as it is gradually replaced by checks and credit cards. The **debit card,** a device by which a purchase is charged against its owner's bank account, comes into being. Increasingly, spending means not an exchange of physical money—whether paper or coins—but rather the electronic transfer of numbers residing in computer memory banks. In effect, the new medium of exchange is itself a part of the information explosion.

> **credit card:** a device that allows its owner to purchase goods but to be billed later
>
> **debit card:** a device that allows its owner to charge purchases against his or her bank account

World Economic Systems

Now that we have outlined the main economic changes in history, let us compare capitalism and socialism, the two main economic systems in force today.

Capitalism

People who live in a capitalist society are immersed in details that blur its essentials. It is difficult to see beyond the local shopping mall and fast-food chains. If we distill the businesses of the United States to their basic components, however, we see that **capitalism** has three essential features: (1) **private ownership of the means of production** (individuals own the land, machines, and factories, and decide what shall be produced); (2) the pursuit of **profit** (selling something for more than it costs); and (3) **market competition** (an exchange of items between willing buyers and sellers).

Welfare (or State) Capitalism Versus Laissez-Faire Capitalism Many people believe that the United States is an example of pure capitalism. Pure capitalism, however, known as **laissez-faire capitalism** (literally meaning "hands off"), exists only when market forces are able to operate without interference from the government. Such is not

> **capitalism:** an economic system characterized by the private ownership of the means of production, the pursuit of profit, and market competition
>
> **private ownership of the means of production:** the ownership of machines and factories by individuals, who decide what shall be produced
>
> **profit:** an amount in excess of an item's cost
>
> **market competition:** the exchange of items between willing buyers and sellers
>
> **laissez-faire capitalism:** unrestrained manufacture and trade (literally, "hands off" capitalism)

Essential to the exchange of goods and services is a medium of exchange. With extensive travel a characteristic of today's global market, currencies must be able to be exchanged instantaneously, a function served by this "camel bank" in Jaisalmer, India. As a global economy continues to develop, it is possible that one day there will be a single world currency.

the case in the United States, where many restraints to the laissez-faire model have been instituted. The current form of U.S. capitalism is **welfare** (or **state**) **capitalism,** in which private citizens own the means of production and pursue profits, but do so within a vast system of laws designed to protect the welfare of the population.

Suppose that you have discovered what you think is a miracle tonic: It will grow hair, erase wrinkles, and dissolve excess fat. If your product works, you will become an overnight sensation—not only a millionaire, but also the toast of television talk shows.

Before you count your money—and your fame—however, you must reckon with **market restraints,** the laws and regulations of welfare capitalism that limit your capacity to sell what you produce. First, you must comply with local and state rules. You must obtain a charter of incorporation, business license, and a state tax number that allows you to make untaxed purchases. Then come the federal regulations. You cannot simply take your item to local stores and ask them to sell it; you must first seek approval from federal agencies that monitor compliance with the Pure Food and Drug Act. This means that you must prove that your product will not cause harm to the public. In addition, you must be able to substantiate your claims—or else face being shut down by state and federal agencies that monitor the market for fraud. Your manufacturing process is also subject to government regulation: state and local laws concerning cleanliness and state and federal rules for the storage and disposal of hazardous wastes.

Suppose that you succeed in overcoming these obstacles, your business prospers, and the number of your employees grows. Other federal agencies will monitor your compliance with regulations concerning racial and sexual discrimination, the payment of minimum wages, and the remittance of Social Security taxes. State agencies will also ex-

welfare (state) capitalism: an economic system in which individuals own the means of production, but the state regulates many economic activities for the welfare of the population

market restraints: laws and regulations that limit the capacity to manufacture and sell products

An essential aspect of every society is economy, a system of exchanging goods and services. The boat vendors in Thailand provide an efficient means of getting fresh produce to consumers, where the goods are exchanged for cash. An exchange also occurs in postindustrial societies, but often the transaction is mediated through electronic numbers.

amine your records to see that you have paid unemployment compensation taxes on your employees and remitted sales taxes on items that you sell at retail. Finally, the Internal Revenue Service will constantly look over your shoulder. In short, the highly regulated U.S. economic system is far from an example of laissez-faire capitalism.

To see how welfare or state capitalism developed in the United States, let us go back to the 1800s when capitalism was considerably less restrained. At that time, you could have made your "magic" potion in your kitchen and sold it at any outlet willing to handle it. You could have openly advertised that it cured baldness, erased wrinkles, and dissolved fat, for no agency existed to monitor your product or your claims. In fact, that is precisely what thousands of individuals did at that time, producing numerous "elixirs" with whimsical names such as "Grandma's Miracle Medicine" and "Elixir of Health and Happiness." A single product could claim that it simultaneously restored sexual potency, purged the intestines, and made people more intelligent. People often felt better after drinking such tonics, for many elixirs were liberally braced with alcohol—and even cocaine (Ashley 1975). Indeed, until 1903 a main ingredient of Coca-Cola was cocaine. To protect the public's health, in 1906 the federal government passed the Pure Food and Drug Act and began to regulate products.

Government regulation of capitalism was also accelerated by John D. Rockefeller's remarkable success in unregulated markets. After a ruthless drive for domination—which included drastically reducing prices for oil and then doubling them after driving out the competition, and in some instances sabotaging competitors' pipelines and refineries—Rockefeller managed to corner the U.S. oil and gasoline market (Josephson 1949). With his competitors crippled or eliminated, his company, Standard Oil, was able to dictate prices to the entire nation. Rockefeller had achieved the capitalist's dream, a **monopoly,** the control of an entire industry by a single company.

Rockefeller had overplayed the capitalist game, however, for he had wiped out one of its essential components, competition. Consequently, to protect this cornerstone of capitalism, the federal government passed antimonopoly legislation and broke up Standard Oil. Today, the top firms of each industry—such as General Motors in automobiles and General Electric in household appliances—must obtain federal approval before acquiring another company in the same industry. If the government determines that one firm dominates a market, and thereby unfairly restricts competition, it can force that company to **divest** (sell off) some of its businesses.

Another characteristic of welfare capitalism is that although the government supports competition, it establishes its own monopoly over "common good" items—those presumed essential for the common good of the citizens, such as soldiers, war supplies, highways, and sewers.

▼   **In Sum**   As currently practiced, capitalism is far from the classical laissez-faire model. The economic system of the United States encourages the first two components of capitalism, the private ownership of the means of production and the pursuit of profit. But a vast system of government regulations both protects and restricts the third component, market competition. The government also controls "common good" items.

Socialism

Socialism also has three essential components: (1) the public ownership of the means of production; (2) central planning; and (3) distribution of goods without a profit motive.

In socialist economies, the government owns the means of production—not only the factories, but also the land, railroads, oil wells, and gold mines. Unlike capitalism, in which **market forces**—supply and demand—determine what shall be produced and the prices that will be charged, in socialism a central committee decides that the country needs X number of toothbrushes, Y toilets, and Z shoes. This group decides how many of each shall be produced, which factories will produce them, the prices that will be charged for the items, and where they will be distributed.

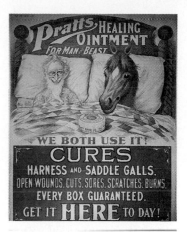

This advertisement from 1885 represents an earlier stage of capitalism when individuals were free to manufacture and market products with little or no interference from the government. Today, the production and marketing of goods take place under detailed, complicated government regulations.

monopoly: the control of an entire industry by a single company

divest: to sell off

socialism: an economic system characterized by the public ownership of the means of production, central planning, and the distribution of goods without a profit motive

market forces: the law of supply and demand

Socialism is designed to eliminate competition, for goods are sold at predetermined prices regardless of demand for an item or the cost to produce it. Profit is not the goal, nor is encouraging consumption of goods in low demand (by lowering the price), nor limiting the consumption of hard-to-get goods (by raising the price). Rather, the goal is to produce goods for the general welfare and to distribute them according to people's needs, not their ability to pay.

In a socialist economy *everyone* in the economic chain works for the government. The members of the central committee who determine production are government employees, as are the administrators who oversee production, the factory workers who do the producing, the truck drivers who move the merchandise, and the clerks who sell it. Although those who purchase the items work at entirely different jobs—in offices, on farms, in day care centers—even they are government employees.

Just as capitalism does not exist in a pure form, neither does socialism (Horowitz 1989). Although the ideology of socialism calls for resources to be distributed according to need and not position, in line with the functionalist argument of social stratification presented in Chapter 9 (page 232), socialist countries found it necessary to offer higher salaries for some jobs in order to entice people to take greater responsibilities. For example, factory managers always earn more than factory workers. By narrowing the huge pay gaps that characterize capitalist nations, however, socialist nations have been able to establish considerably greater equality of income.

Dissatisfied with the greed and exploitation of capitalism and the lack of freedom and individuality of socialism, some Western nations (most notably Sweden and Denmark) have adopted **democratic socialism,** or welfare socialism. In this form of socialism, both the state and individuals engage in production and distribution. Although the government owns and runs the steel, mining, forestry, and energy concerns, as well as the country's telephones, television stations, and airlines (*Wall Street Journal,* November 12, 1991), the retail stores, farms, manufacturing concerns, and most service industries remain in private hands.

Ideologies of Capitalism and Socialism

Capitalism and socialism not only have different approaches to the production and distribution of goods, but each also represents a distinct ideology.

Capitalists hold that market forces should determine both products and prices and that it is healthy for people to strive after profits. They believe that under such conditions people will seek to produce items that make a profit, and that the only items that will make a profit are those that are in demand. As the Down-to-Earth Sociology box on the facing page shows, the market also *creates* a demand for products. In short, market forces underlie the successful capitalist society. The potential for profit encourages people to develop and produce new products desired by the public, while workers are motivated to work hard so that they can make as much money as possible to purchase more goods.

In contrast, socialists believe that profit is immoral, that it represents *excess value* extracted from workers. Karl Marx made the point that because an item's value represents the work that goes into it, there can be no profit unless workers are paid less than the value of their labor. Profit, then, represents an amount withheld from workers. To protect workers from this exploitation, socialists believe that the government should own the means of production, using them not for profit, but to produce and distribute items according to people's needs rather than their ability to pay.

Criticisms of Capitalism and Socialism

The primary criticism leveled against capitalism is that it leads to social inequality. Capitalism, say its critics, produces a tiny top layer consisting of wealthy, powerful people, who exploit a vast bottom layer of unemployed and underemployed (**underemployment** is having to work at a job beneath one's training and abilities or being able to

democratic socialism: a hybrid economic system in which capitalism is mixed with state ownership

underemployment: the condition of having to work at a job beneath one's level of training and abilities, or of being able to find only part-time work

▼▲▼▲▼▲▼▲▼▲▼▲▼▲▼▲▼▲▼▲▼▲▼▲▼▲▼▲▼▲▼▲▼▲

Down-To-Earth Sociology

Selling the American Dream—The Creation of Constant Discontent

ADVERTISING IS SUCH AN integral part of contemporary life that it almost appears to be our natural state to be deluged with ads. We open a newspaper or magazine and expect to find that a good portion of its pages proclaim the virtues of products and firms. We turn on the television and on most stations are assailed with commercials for about ten minutes of every half hour. Some social analysts even claim that the purpose of television is to round up an audience to watch the commercials—making the programs a mere diversion from the medium's real objective of selling products!

A fascinating potential of advertising is its ability to increase our desire to consume products for which we previously felt no need whatsoever. American kitchens, filled with gadgets that slice and dice and machines that turn anything into a sandwich, attest to this power.

But advertising's power to make people gluttons for consumption goes beyond kitchen gadgets soon consigned to back drawers and later to garage sales. Many Americans today would not think of going out in public without first shampooing, rinsing, conditioning, and blow-drying their hair. Many also feel the need to apply an underarm deodorant so powerful that it overcomes the body's natural need to sweat. For many women, public appearance also demands the application of foundation, lipstick, eye shadow, mascara, rouge, powder, and perfume. For many men, after-shave lotion is essential. And only after covering the body with clothing bearing suitable designer labels do Americans feel that they are presentable to the public.

Advertising also penetrates our consciousness to such a degree that it determines not only what we put on our bodies, what we eat, and what we do for recreation, but to a large degree also how we feel about ourselves. Our ideas of whether we are too fat, too skinny, too hippy, too buxom, whether our hair is too oily or too dry, our body too hairy, or our skin too rough are largely a consequence of advertising. As we weigh our self-image against the idealized pictures that constantly bombard us in our daily fare of commercials, we conclude that we are lacking something. Advertising, of course, assures us that there is salvation—another new product that promises to deliver exactly what we lack.

The creation of constant discontent—continual dissatisfaction with ourselves compared to perfect images that are impossible to match in real life—is, of course, intentional. And it leaves most of us vulnerable to consuming more of the never-ending variety of products that the corporations have decided that we need—and that they are only too willing to sell.

---

find only part-time work). Another major criticism is that the few who own the means of production and reap huge profits are able to get legislation passed that goes against the public good merely to further their own wealth and power.

The primary criticism leveled against socialism is that it does not respect individual rights (Berger 1986). Others (in the form of some government body) control people's lives—making decisions about where they will live, where they will go to school, where they will work, how much they will be paid, and, in the case of China, even how many children they may have (Mosher 1983). Critics also argue that central planning is grossly inefficient (Kennedy 1993) and that socialism is not capable of producing much wealth. They say that its greater equality really amounts to giving almost everyone an equal chance to be poor.

The Systems in Conflict and Competition

These contrasting ideologies paint such different pictures—not only of the economy but also of the way the world "ought" to be—that proponents of each have come to see the other as inherently evil. Capitalists see socialists as violating basic human rights of freedom of decision and opportunity, while socialists see capitalists as violating basic human rights of freedom from poverty.

Although capitalism and communism were at each others' throats for three generations, apparently an uneasy accord has been reached. In line with convergence theory, capitalist countries have adopted some features of socialism, while communist nations have added features of capitalism. Advertising of products and their sale for profit, previously banned in China, are now becoming commonplace. This photo also illustrates the growing global economy.

As a result of these opposing views, *each sees the other as a system of exploitation*. With each side painting itself in moral colors while viewing the other as a threat to its very existence, this century witnessed the world split into two main blocs. The West armed itself to defend capitalism, the East to defend socialism. The remaining "nonaligned" nations were often able to receive vast sums of economic and military aid by playing the West and the East off against one another.

In recent years, fundamental changes have taken place. The former Soviet Union, which headed the Eastern bloc of nations, concluded that its system of central planning had failed. Suffering from shoddy goods and plagued by shortages, its standard of living severely lagged the West (Newman 1991). Consequently, the former Soviet Union began to reinstate market forces, including the private ownership of property and profits for those who produce and sell goods. Capitalism emerged victorious with the fall of the Berlin Wall in 1989, which precipitated the reunification of the two Germanys.

China watched in dismay as its one-time mentor abandoned basic premises of socialism (Szelenyi 1987). In 1989, at the cost of many lives and despite world opposition, Chinese authorities, in what is called the Tiananmen Square massacre, even put down an uprising by students and workers who were demanding greater freedom and economic reforms. In spite of these repressive measures, however, China began to encourage capitalism. Chinese leaders solicited Western investments, encouraged farmers to cultivate their own plots on the communal farms, allowed the use of credit cards, approved a stock market, and even permitted bits of that symbol of China itself, the "Great Wall," to be sold for profit as souvenirs (McGregor 1992). While still officially proclaiming Marxist-Leninist-Maoist principles, the Communist party—under the slogan "One China, Two Systems"—is trying to make Shanghai the financial center of East Asia (McGregor 1993; Schlesinger 1994). One consequence—besides the new Avon ladies and radio talk shows—is a rapidly rising standard of living (WuDunn 1993).

The democratic socialist nations of western Europe have not remained untouched by this rejection of socialism. Sweden is one of the best examples. In the 1930s, Sweden adopted socialist principles that eventually provided "from cradle-to-grave" security for all its citizens. Medical care, child care, higher education—all were free. Full pay was guaranteed even during unemployment or illness. But then the bill came due. As costs mounted, 70 percent of the nation's income went to the national welfare system

(Stevenson 1993). Taxes increased until more than 50 percent of the average paycheck went to the government (Meyerson 1992).

As taxes grew, profits declined, and private investment dropped. When Sweden's competitive position in the global market slipped, the Swedes embarked on **privatization,** the selling of state-run industries to private companies. They sold its steel mills, coal mines, national airline, and even some of its forests (*Wall Street Journal*, November 12, 1991). They also cut back on unemployment benefits, reduced payments to injured workers, and raised the age for retirement in order to try to get "a system we can pay for" (Stevenson 1993).

At least in this point in history, capitalism speaks with a much louder voice than does socialism. Capitalist economies, however, speak in a variety of accents, some more muted than others, with the versions in China, the former Soviet Union, Great Britain, Japan, Germany, Sweden, and the United States each differing from one another.

The Future: Convergence?

Clark Kerr (1960, 1983) suggested that as nations industrialize they grow similar to one another. They produce similar divisions of labor (such as professionals and skilled technicians), develop higher education, and urbanize extensively. Similar values also emerge, uniting its various groups. By themselves, these tendencies would make capitalist and socialist nations grow more alike, but some sociologists, such as William Form (1979), have identified another factor that brings these nations closer to one another: In spite of their incompatible ideologies, both capitalist and socialist systems have adopted features of the other. Known as **convergence theory,** this view points to a possible hybrid or mixed economy for the future.

Convergence theory is given support by the new emphasis on profit in socialist countries. But changes in U.S. capitalism also support this theory. Although the world sees the United States as the exemplar of capitalism, this nation has adopted many socialist practices. Each such feature, viewed with alarm when first proposed, eventually became a firm part of the economic system, blurring its socialist base. In each instance, some people are paying for benefits received by others—and the money to pay for the benefits is involuntarily extracted from them. Consider the following taken-for-granted aspects of the U.S. economic system: unemployment compensation (taxes paid by workers are distributed to those who no longer produce a profit); subsidized housing (shelter, paid for by the many, is distributed to the poor and elderly, with no motive of profit); welfare (taxes from the many are distributed to the needy); the minimum wage (the government, not the employer, determines the minimum that a worker shall be paid); and Social Security (as noted in the Thinking Critically section on pages 359–360, the retired do not receive what they paid into the system, but, rather, money collected from current workers). Such changes indicate that the United States has moved away from pure capitalism and, embracing some socialist principles, has produced its own version of a mixed type of economy.

Perhaps, then, the tremendous upheavals now occurring in the world's economic systems indicate that the hybrid is closer than ever. On the one hand, not even staunch capitalists want a system that does not provide at least minimum support during unemployment, extended illness, and old age. On the other hand, socialist leaders have reluctantly admitted that profit does motivate people to work harder. If the convergence does occur, it is likely to make the world a safer place, for there will be no need for any group to paint its economic system in stark moral colors and swear to defend it to the last drop of blood (Sakharov 1974; Wriston 1992). Other bases of conflict remain, of course—and convergence, if it occurs, will not mean the end of dictators and demagogues, regional ethnic conflicts, or inequalities and oppressions of all sorts.

privatization: the selling of a nation's state-run industries to the private sector

convergence theory: the view that as capitalist and socialist economic systems each adopt features of the other, a hybrid (or mixed) economic system will emerge

The Inner Circle of Capitalism

As we have seen, capitalism has undergone so many changes that its laissez-faire form is unrecognizable today. At this point, let us examine two further developments in capitalism: corporate capitalism and multinational corporations.

Corporate Capitalism

Corporations have altered the face of capitalism. The **corporation,** a legal entity treated in law as an individual, is the joint ownership of a business enterprise, whose liabilities and obligations are separate from those of its owners. For example, each shareholder of Xerox—whether the owner of one or 100,000 shares—owns a portion of the company. As a legal entity, Xerox can buy and sell, sue and be sued, make contracts, and incur debts. The corporation, however, not its individual owners, is responsible for the firm's liabilities—such as paying its debts and fulfilling its contracts.

Corporations have so changed capitalism that the term **corporate capitalism** has emerged to indicate that giant corporations dominate the economic system. Of the hundreds of thousands of businesses and tens of thousands of corporations in the United States, a mere five hundred dominate the economy. Called the "Fortune 500" (derived from *Fortune* magazine's annual profile of the largest five hundred companies), these firms are so large that their annual profits represent one-quarter of the United States' entire gross national product (*Statistical Abstract* 1990: Tables 690, 899).

One of the most significant aspects of corporations is the *separation of ownership and management.* Unlike most businesses, it is not the owners, those who own the company's stock, who run the day-to-day affairs of the company. Rather, a corporation is run by managers who are able to treat it *as though it were their own* (Cohen 1990). The result is the "ownership of wealth without appreciable control, and control of wealth without appreciable ownership" (Berle and Means 1932). Sociologist Michael Useem (1984) put it this way:

> When few owners held all or most of a corporation's stock, they readily dominated its board of directors, which in turn selected top management and ran the corporation. Now that a firm's stock [is] dispersed among many unrelated owners, each holding a tiny fraction of the total equity, the resulting power vacuum allow[s] management to select the board of directors; thus management [becomes] self-perpetuating and thereby acquire[s] de facto control over the corporation.
>
> Management determines its own salaries, sets goals and awards itself bonuses for meeting them, authorizes market surveys, hires advertising agencies, determines marketing strategies, and negotiates with unions. The management's primary responsibility to the owners is to produce profits. The greater the profit, the better their job performance (Useem 1984).

At the annual stockholders' meeting the owners consider broad company matters, including the selection of a board of directors and a firm to audit the company's books. As long as management reports a handsome profit, the stockholders rubber-stamp its recommendations. It is so unusual for this not to happen, that when it does not the outcome is called a **stockholders' revolt.** The irony of this term is generally lost, but remember that in such cases it is not the workers but the owners who are rebelling!

The world's largest corporations wield immense power. Forming **oligopolies**—several large companies that dominate a single industry, such as olive oil, breakfast cereal, or light bulbs—they dictate pricing, set the quality of their products, and protect their markets. Oligopolies also use their political connections to support legislation that gives them special tax breaks or protects their industry from imports. Oligopolies are tempted to abuse their power in more sinister ways as well. For example, in 1973 the International Telephone and Telegraph Company (ITT) joined the CIA in a plot to unseat Chile's elected government. After their attempt to bring about the economic collapse of Chile failed, they then plotted a coup d'état, which resulted in the assassination of the Chilean president, Salvador Allende (Coleman 1995).

corporation: the joint ownership of a business enterprise, whose liabilities and obligations are separate from those of its owners

corporate capitalism: the domination of the economic system by giant corporations

stockholders' revolt: the refusal of a corporation's stockholders to rubber-stamp decisions made by its managers

oligopoly: the control of an entire industry by several large companies

The largest corporations are headed by a group that sociologist Michael Useem (1984) calls the *inner circle*. Although these powerful leaders are competitors, their mutual interest in preserving capitalism pulls them together (Mizruchi and Koenig 1991). They support political candidates who stand firmly for the private ownership of property, promote legislation favorable to big business, consult with high-level politicians, and serve as trustees for foundations and universities.

Interlocking Directorates

One way in which the wealthy use corporations to wield power is by means of **interlocking directorates** (Mizruchi and Koenig 1991). The elite serve as directors of several companies. Their fellow members on those boards also sit on the boards of other companies, and so on. Like a spider's web that starts at the center and then fans out in all directions, eventually this interlocking includes all the top companies in the country (Mintz and Schwartz 1985). The chief executive officer of a firm in Great Britain, who also sits on the board of directors of half a dozen other companies, noted:

> If you serve on, say, six outside boards, each of which has, say, ten directors, and let's say out of the ten directors, five are experts in one or another subject, you have a built-in panel of thirty friends who are experts who you meet regularly, automatically each month, and you really have great access to ideas and information. You're joining a club, a very good club. (Useem 1984)

The resulting concentration of power minimizes competition, for a director is not going to approve a plan that will be harmful to another company in which he or she (mostly he) has a stake. The top executives of the top U.S. companies—part of the powerful capitalist class described on pages 261–263—also meet together in recreational settings, where they renew their sense of solidarity, purpose, and destiny (Domhoff 1991).

Multinational Corporations

Kim, in the opening vignette, illustrates the new distribution and consumption patterns of our global marketplace. Outgrowing national boundaries, the larger corporations have become more and more detached from the interests and values of their country of origin. They move investments and production from one part of the globe to another—with no concern for consequences other than profits. As the Cold War trading barriers have broken down and the global economy has become more integrated, these corporations play an increasingly significant role in global life (Kennedy 1993).

The domination of world trade shows an interesting pattern. After World War II, with Germany destroyed and France in shambles, the United States eclipsed Great Britain and became the major player in international business. Recently, the Japanese, also using the multinational corporate model, gained huge markets across the globe. Table 14.1 shows that of the world's largest twenty-five corporations, the United States and Japan tie with eleven each. Of the world's next twenty-five largest firms (not shown), the United States accounts for no less than twelve and Japan seven. Without doubt, these two countries are today's Goliaths of global trade.

The sociological significance of the giant multinational corporations is that they owe allegiance only to profits and market share, not to any nation, nor even to any particular culture. As a U.S. executive said, "The United States does not have an automatic call on our resources. There is no mind-set that puts the country first" (Kennedy 1993). This fundamental shift in orientation is so new that its implications are unknown at present. The millions of workers whose jobs have been pulled out from under them know the negative consequences. On the positive side, these corporations' global interconnections may be a force for peace, for removed from the tribal loyalties of national boundaries, the inner circle will expand to include the elite of the global giants. The downside, however, may be a New World Order dominated by a handful of corporate leaders.

interlocking directorate: the phenomenon of one person serving on the board of directors of several companies

Table 14.1

The Largest Twenty-Five Corporations in the World

Rank	Name	Country	Market Value[a]	Annual Sales	Annual Profit[b]
1	NT&T	Japan	$ 127,287	$ 61,565	$ 1,590
2	AT&T	U.S.	84,409	64,900	3,850
3	Exxon	U.S.	82,127	117,000	4,800
4	General Electric	U.S.	81,907	57,073	4,305
5	Royal Dutch/Shell	Neth./U.K.	81,606	83,031	4,623
6	Mitsubishi Bank	Japan	73,237	469,734	530
7	Sumitomo Bank	Japan	67,195	583,937	199
8	Industrial Bank of Japan	Japan	65,662	419,376	388
9	Dai-Ichi Kangyo Bank	Japan	64,688	561,957	445
10	Fuji Bank	Japan	64,134	572,919	549
11	Sanwa Bank	Japan	61,225	559,922	899
12	Wal-Mart Stores	U.S.	60,331	55,483	1,995
13	Coca-Cola	U.S.	56,191	13,074	1,905
14	Toyota Motor	Japan	53,546	96,200	2,253
15	Sakura Bank	Japan	51,130	508,495	546
16	Tokyo Electric Power	Japan	44,630	44,489	698
17	Philip Morris	U.S.	43,299	59,100	4,940
18	Merck	U.S.	40,637	9,663	2,447
19	British Telecom	U.K.	39,990	19,982	1,930
20	Nomura Securities	Japan	36,218	72,715	38
21	Procter & Gamble	U.S.	35,329	29,362	1,872
22	GTE	U.S.	33,921	19,984	1,787
23	Roche Holding	Switzerland	31,896	8,658	1,282
24	DuPont	U.S.	31,632	37,799	1,438
25	General Motors	U.S.	31,462	113,000	−2,620

[a]All money totals are in millions of U.S. dollars.
[b]As of December 31, 1992.
Source: Wall Street Journal, September 24, 1993: R26.

Work in U.S. Society

Let us now turn our focus on work in U.S. society. To understand the present situation, we must first review the large-scale changes in what are called economic sectors.

Three Economic Sectors

primary sector: that part of the economy that extracts raw materials from the environment

secondary sector: that part of the economy that turns raw materials into manufactured goods

Sociologists divide economic life into three sectors: primary, secondary, and tertiary. The primary sector is central to preindustrial societies. In the **primary sector,** workers extract natural resources from the environment. People who fish for a living or who mine copper work in the primary sector. So do hunters, cattle raisers, farmers, and lumberjacks. In the **secondary sector,** workers turn raw materials into manufactured goods. They package fish, process copper into electrical wire, and turn trees into lumber and paper. The secondary sector dominates industrial economies.

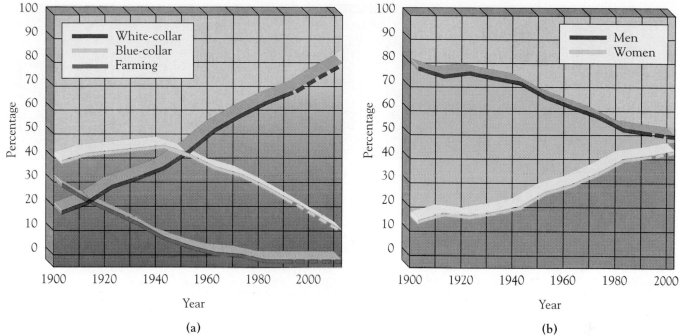

(a)   (b)

Note: From 1900 to 1940, "workers" refers to people age 14 and over, from 1970 on to people age 16 and over. Dotted lines are the author's projections.

Sources: Statistical Abstract Various years and 1993: Table 644.

Figure 14.3a & b

Percentage of U.S. Workers in Three Types of Work and Proportion of Workers by Sex.

The main focus of the **tertiary sector** is providing services. Some workers, such as computer technicians and automobile mechanics, install or service products. Others, such as private detectives and cab drivers, provide personal services. Although *most* of the labor force in postindustrial societies work in the tertiary sector, all three sectors exist side by side. Take the common lead pencil as an example. People who extract lead and cut timber work in the primary sector, those who turn the wood and lead into pencils are in the secondary sector, and those who advertise and sell the pencils work in the tertiary sector.

Farming provides a remarkable example of this transition, for which there is no parallel in history (Drucker 1987). Figure 14.3a shows the decline of employment in farming (the primary sector), where most of our ancestors once worked. As the number of farmers declined during the early and mid-1900s, manufacturing (the secondary sector) picked up the slack. During the 1800s, a typical farmer could produce only enough food for five people, while with today's powerful farming machinery and hybrid seeds he or she now feeds about eighty. In the 1800s over 50 percent of U.S. workers were engaged in farming, but this figure has dropped to only about 1 percent today (*Statistical Abstract* 1993: Tables 644, 1095).

Figure 14.3a also shows a major transition that occurred about 1955. Then, for the first time, most Americans worked in the tertiary sector, although a postindustrial economy requires few people to produce food or basic materials and few people to process them, the information explosion demands that large numbers of people work in the tertiary sector. Consequently, we have experienced a surge in "knowledge work"—managing information and designing and servicing products—and, as Figure 14.3a also shows, a severe decline in blue-collar jobs.

Women and Work

One of the chief characteristics of the U.S. workforce has been a steady increase in the numbers of women who work outside the home for wages. Figure 14.3b shows how

tertiary sector: that part of the economy that consists of service-oriented occupations

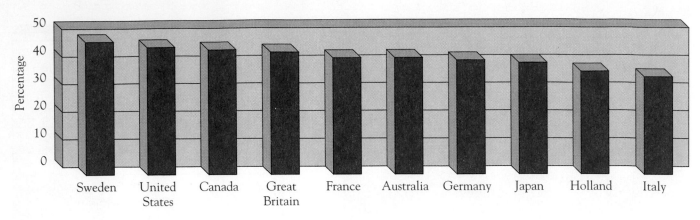

Source: Statistical Abstract 1993: Table 1402.

Figure 14.4

What Percentage of the Labor Force Is Female?

women have become an increasingly larger component of the U.S. workforce. At the turn of the century, one of five U.S. workers was a woman. By 1940, this ratio had grown to one of four, by 1960 it was one of three, and today it is almost one of two. As you can see from Figure 14.4, this ratio is one of the highest in the industrialized world.

How likely a woman is to work depends on several factors, especially her race or ethnicity, marital status, and if she has young children. Figure 14.5a shows that African-American and white women are slightly more likely to be in the labor force than Latinas. Note how the rates for African Americans and whites have dovetailed. From Figure 14.5b, you can see that single women are the most likely to work for wages; married women follow closely behind; and divorced, widowed, and separated women are the least likely to be in the workforce.

Researchers have found some major distinctions between women and men in the world of work. For one, women tend to be more concerned than men with maintaining a balance between their work and family lives (Statham et al. 1988). For another, men and women tend to follow different models for success: Men tend to emphasize individualism, power, and competition, while the female leadership model stresses collaboration, persuasion, and helping (Miller-Loessi 1992). A primary concern of many women is the extent to which they must adopt the male model of leadership in order to be successful in their careers. You should note that these findings represent tendencies. Although they characterize the average female or male, many people diverge from them.

The Quiet Revolution   Because its changes are so gradual but its implications so profound, sociologists use the term **"quiet revolution"** to refer to the continually increasing proportions of women who have joined the ranks of paid labor. This trend, shown in Figure 14.5a, b, and c, means a transformation of consumer patterns, relations at work, self-concepts, and relationships with boyfriends, husbands, and children. One of the most significant aspects of the quiet revolution is indicated by Figure 14.5c. Note that since 1960 the proportion of married women with preschool children who work for wages has tripled. It now equals the average of all U.S. women. We discuss implications of these changes in Chapter 16.

The Underground Economy

the quiet revolution: the fundamental changes in society that occur as a result of vast numbers of women entering the workforce

The underground economy. It has a sinister ring—suggestive of dope deals struck in alleys and wads of dollar bills hastily exchanged. The underground economy is this, but it is a lot more—and usually a lot more innocent. If you pay the plumber with a

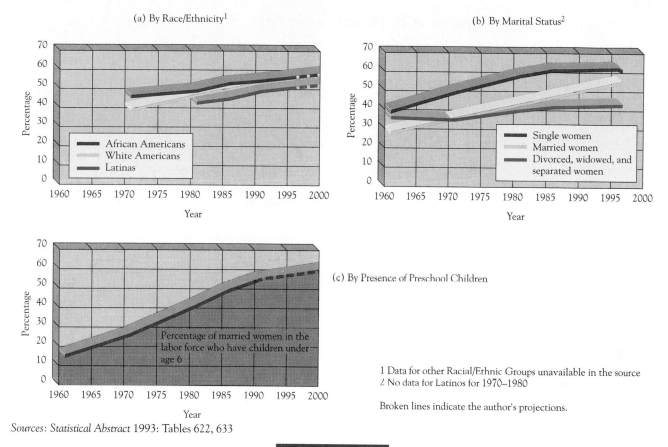

(a) By Race/Ethnicity[1]

(b) By Marital Status[2]

(c) By Presence of Preschool Children

Percentage of married women in the labor force who have children under age 6

1 Data for other Racial/Ethnic Groups unavailable in the source
2 No data for Latinos for 1970–1980

Broken lines indicate the author's projections.

Sources: Statistical Abstract 1993: Tables 622, 633

Figure 14.5a, b & c

Percentage of Women in the U.S. Labor Force by Race/Ethnicity, Marital Status, and Preschool Children.

check made out to "cash," if you purchase a pair of sunglasses from a street vendor or a kitchen gadget at a yard sale, if you so much as hand a neighbor's kid a $20 bill (or if you accept it) to mow the lawn or to baby sit, you are participating in the underground economy. (Pennar and Farrell 1993)

Also known as the informal economy and the off-the-books economy, the **underground economy** consists of economic activities—whether legal or illegal—that people don't report to the government. What interests most of us is not unreported baby-sitting money, but the illegal activities that people cannot report even if they wanted to. As a 20-year-old child care worker who also works as a prostitute two or three nights a week said, "Why do I do this? For the money! Where else can I make this kind of money in a few hours? And it's all tax free" (author's files). Drug dealing is perhaps the largest single source of illegal income, for billions of dollars flow from users to sellers and their networks of growers, importers, processors, transporters, dealers, and enforcers. These particular networks are so huge that each year three-quarters of a million Americans are arrested for illegal drug activities (*Statistical Abstract* 1993: Table 314).

Because of its subterranean nature, no one knows the exact size of the underground economy, but it probably runs 10 to 15 percent of the regular economy (Pennar and Farrell 1993). Since the official gross national product of the United States is about $6 trillion, the underground economy probably runs between $600 billion and $1 trillion. It is so huge that it distorts the official statistics of the country's gross national product, and the IRS loses over $100 billion a year in taxes.

underground economy: exchanges of goods and services that are not reported to the government and thereby escape taxation

Patterns of Work and Leisure

Suppose that it is 1860 and you work for a textile company in Lowell, Massachusetts. When you arrive at work one day, you find that the boss has posted a new work rule: All workers will have to come in at the same time and remain until quitting time. Like the other workers, you feel outrage. You join them as they shout, "This is slavery!" and march out on strike, indignant at such a preposterous rule (Zuboff 1991). Workers were used to coming and going when they wanted. To see why, let's consider how patterns of work and leisure are related to the transformation of economies.

Effects of Industrialization Hunting and gathering societies provided tremendous amounts of leisure. If people did not face some unusual event, such as drought or pestilence, it did not take long to gather what they needed for the day. In fact, *most of their time was leisure*, and the rhythms of nature were an essential part of their lives. Agricultural economies also allowed much leisure, for, at least in the western hemisphere, work peaked in the spring, let up in the summer, and then peaked again in the fall. During the winter work receded, for by this time the harvest was in, animals had been slaughtered, food had been canned and stored, and a wood supply had been laid up.

Industrialization, however, brought fundamental change. No longer was time harnessed to seasonal rhythms, as it had been for all of human history. Now rhythms were dictated by bosses and machines. At first, workers insisted on moving to their traditional rhythms. After working for several weeks, a worker would disappear, only to reappear when money ran out. For many, enjoying leisure was considerably more important than amassing money (Weber 1904–1905). Bosses, wanting to profit from regular, efficient production, began to insist that all workers start work at the same time. To workers, that seemed like slavery. Today, in contrast, those work patterns artificially imposed on us have become part of our culture and are taken for granted.

Trends in Leisure Leisure refers to time not taken up by work or required activities such as eating and sleeping. It is not the activity itself that makes something leisure, but the purpose for which it is done. Consider driving a car. If you do it for pleasure, it is leisure, but if you are an on-duty police officer or commuting to the office, it is work. If done for enjoyment, horseback riding and reading a book are leisure—but these activities are work for jockeys and students.

Patterns of leisure change with the life course, following the U-curve shown on Figure 14.6. Young children enjoy the most leisure, but teenagers still have considerably more leisure than their parents. Parents with small children have the least leisure, but after the children leave home, leisure picks up again. After the age of 65, the amount of leisure for adults peaks.

Most Leisure Time

Early childhood

Old age

Years after parenthood

Teen years

Years of parenthood

Least Leisure Time

Figure 14.6

Leisure and the Life Cycle: The "U" Curve of Leisure.

The underground economy, which escapes taxation, has become a significant part of the U.S. economy. Most of the underground economy consists of unreported earnings from legal activities, such as that shown here, but it also includes income from illegal activities.

Compared with early industrialization, workers today have far more leisure. A hundred years ago the workweek was half again as long as today's, for then workers had to be at their machines sixty hours a week. When workers unionized, they demanded a shorter workweek. Over the years, the workweek has gradually shrunk. In Germany the workweek is 35 hours, mainly with Friday afternoons taken off. In addition, German workers are guaranteed six weeks of paid vacation each year. Unlike western Europe, however, in the United States this trend to more leisure reversed course during the 1960s (Schor 1991). U.S. workers now average 1,948 hours of work a year, matched only by workers in Great Britain. They are soundly beaten, however, by Japanese workers, who average 2,120 hours a year (Ono and Schlesinger 1992; MacShane 1993).

The Global Marketplace and Downsizing A primary reason that the average workweek of U.S. workers has increased is the attempt of U.S. firms to remain competitive in the global marketplace. By paying overtime to their regular workers, companies add fewer full-time workers and thus avoid paying such additional benefits as unemployment, medical, and retirement. For the same reason, they are "downsizing" (reducing their workforces) and hiring temporary workers (whom they can release at will). Some analysts are concerned that these patterns may be permanent, foreshadowing an era of easily discharged workers who live with insecurity, low pay, and few benefits.

Applying Sociological Theories

Before we close this chapter, let's see what pictures emerge when we apply the three theoretical perspectives of sociology to our economic life.

The Functionalist Perspective

Work, of course, is functional for society. It is only because people work that we have electricity, roads, hospitals, schools, automobiles, and homes. Beyond this obvious point, however, lies a basic sociological principle: *work binds us together*. Let us review Durkheim's principles of mechanical and organic solidarity introduced in Chapter 4.

Mechanical Solidarity In preindustrial societies, people do similar work and directly share many aspects of life. Because of this, they look at the world in similar ways. Durkheim used the term **mechanical solidarity** to refer to this sense of unity—feeling as others feel and identifying with them—that comes from doing similar activities.

Organic Solidarity As societies industrialize, however, a division of labor develops, and people work at different occupations. Consequently, they feel less solidarity with one another. Grape growers in California, for example, may feel little in common with manufacturers of aircraft in Missouri. Yet, like an organism, each is part of the same economic system, and the welfare of each depends on the others. Durkheim called this economic interdependence **organic solidarity**.

Organic solidarity has expanded far beyond anything Durkheim envisioned. Today it engulfs the world. People who live in California or New York—or even Michigan— depend on workers in Tokyo to produce cars. Tokyo workers, in turn, depend on Saudi Arabian workers for oil, South American workers to operate ships, and workers in South Africa for palladium (for catalytic converters). Although we do not feel unity with one another—in fact, we sometimes even feel hostility—interdependence wraps us all in the same economic package. Like Kim in our opening vignette, our daily life depends on workers around the globe. Perhaps, then, the term *organic solidarity* is no longer adequate to depict this sweeping change, and we need a new term like "superorganic solidarity."

leisure: time not taken up by work or required activities such as eating, sleeping, commuting, child care, and housework

mechanical solidarity: Durkheim's term for the unity that comes from being involved in similar occupations or activities

organic solidarity: Durkheim's term for the interdependence that results from people needing others to fulfill their jobs

Functionalists stress the interdependence of nations, how the welfare of each depends on the work and products of many other nations. An example of the "superorganic solidarity" now developing is the reliance of Western nations on oil from North Yemen, depicted in this photo. Conflict theorists, in contrast, stress the exploitation of Third World nations by the First World, and of workers by the country's elite who own the oil and live off their investments—and the sweat of workers.

Economic Cycles Why is work sometimes easy to find, when just a few years later you can't pay someone to give you a job? Functionalists provide an interesting explanation for **economic cycles,** capitalism's cycle of "booms" and "busts." They say that booms occur when business owners are confident about the future. They then hire more workers and increase production. Money flows freely throughout the economy among workers, manufacturers, suppliers, salespeople, and planners. With easy credit and high consumption, expansion continues as though there were no tomorrow.

The "boom" ends in overexpansion. Some segments of the economy feel it first. When sales of new homes slow, for example, the market becomes glutted as houses already under construction are completed. Builders then lay off workers and reduce prices. Bankers, frightened that people won't be able to pay back their loans, tighten up credit. Fearful of layoffs, workers cut their purchases, and inventory in many industries builds up. Producers then cancel expansion plans and cut production. With more layoffs, fewer raises, and factories made idle, a full-blown recession follows.

Functionalists, however, spot something else within this gloomy picture. In their view, easy credit had lured many individuals and businesses into heavy debt; and too much money was circulating, causing inflation to heat up. The foreclosures and bankruptcies transfer property to more prudent hands. Inefficient factories close—and stay out of business—while efficient factories emerge from the recession leaner and even more competitive. For the particular businesses and workers who go bankrupt or barely make it, the cycle is dysfunctional—but not for the system itself.

As the recession continues, the Federal Reserve Board in Washington, which determines interest rates for the whole country, lowers interest rates to make borrowing easier and get more money circulating. This, in turn, stimulates demand, and as their excess inventory shrinks businesses increase production. Another boom period then follows, with high production and employment; and the cycle repeats itself.

Although socialist economies don't experience this cycle, neither are they as productive (Berger 1986). Thus workers in a socialist economy do not face the tortures of unemployment and bankruptcy, but neither do they enjoy as high a standard of living as their counterparts in capitalist societies.

economic cycle: periods of economic "booms" (expansion) followed by periods of "busts" (contraction)

The Conflict Perspective

As usual, each theoretical perspective paints only part of the picture. Let's see how conflict theorists view work and economic cycles.

Exploitation of Workers In contrast to the smoothly running and self-correcting machine that functionalists see, when conflict theorists view capitalism, they see oppression, exploitation, and anomie. They regard workers as exploited by those who own the means of production, mere tools to produce profits, whose exhausted bodies can be spewed out by the economic machine when it no longer needs them.

Economic Cycles How does the conflict view of economic cycles differ from that of functionalists? Following their basic orientation, conflict theorists are not concerned with how booms and busts tune the capitalist machinery. Rather, they see the economic cycle as powered by greed, power, and exploitation. Because profit, not people's welfare, is the goal, capitalists overexpand to wring every bit of profit they can. When profits decrease, they pull back, laying off workers until they need them again. That people get hurt in this process is of no concern to them—only profits count.

As noted in Chapter 12, conflict theorists also stress that capitalists maintain a **reserve labor force,** unemployed people whom they can hire for temporary work and then fire at will during the next economic downturn. People in dire need will work for low wages—happy to earn something—and they can be fired as soon as no longer needed. If workers knew the true extent of unemployment, however, it might feed discontent and destabilize society. Consequently, as the Perspectives box on page 397 shows, official statistics are manipulated to produce low unemployment figures.

Although economic recessions seem to hurt capitalists, and some do go under, the closing of less efficient businesses during recessions helps set the stage for the more powerful capitalists to make even more money in the economic boom that follows. They rid themselves of their least productive employees, reduce excess inventory, and buy out competitors cheaply. Workers forego raises, for they know that the unemployed are waiting to take their place. Owners also find recessions an excellent opportunity to replace strikers with nonunion employees. To capitalists, then, *full* employment, not unemployment, is the specter that haunts the economy. Workers could seize full employment as an opportunity to demand higher wages and better working conditions.

As conflict theorists stress, capitalist economies need a reserve labor force that can be put to work in boom times and laid off during economic downturns. A good example is silver mining in Idaho, depicted in this photo. When silver prices fall below the cost of producing silver, workers are laid off. This miner, and other members of the reserve labor force, will then survive on unemployment, and when that runs out, on low-paying, part-time work or welfare. When silver prices again rise, they will be called back to work, again putting in gruelling hours like this—until the next reduction in silver prices leads to a repetition of the process.

The Symbolic Interactionist Perspective

As we apply this perspective, let us explore two different aspects of work: The characteristics that make work a profession and the way in which work affects an individual's perception of self and life.

Profession or Job? Work as Status Symbol Just what distinguishes a job from a profession? We know that selling hamburgers from a drive-in window is not a profession, but why isn't selling shoes? Sociologists identify five characteristics of **professions** (Etzioni 1969; Goode 1960; Greenwood 1962; Parsons 1954).

1 *Rigorous education.* A high school education will not do. Nor will a six-week training course in cutting hair, or even a rigorous course in diesel repair. Today the professions require not only college but also graduate school. Ordinarily, those years are followed by an examination that determines whether or not you will be allowed into the profession. From personal experience, I would like to add that this examination is one of the most significant parts of the educational or-

reserve labor force: conflict theorists' term for the unemployed

profession: an occupation characterized by rigorous education, a theoretical perspective, self-regulation, authority over clients, and service to society (as opposed to a job)

deal. The gnawing threat of not knowing if your years of preparation will allow you to enter your chosen profession hangs over your head like the sword of Damocles.

2 *Theory*. The education is theoretical, not just "hands on." Instead of "Turn this nut, and it frees the main bolt that holds the carburetor," heavy stress is placed on causes and processes. In other words, concepts or objects that cannot be seen are used to explain what can be seen. For example, in medicine, microbes, viruses, and genetics are used to explain disease, while in sociology, social structure and social interaction are used to explain human behavior.

3 *Self-regulation*. Members of the profession claim that only they possess sufficient knowledge to determine the profession's standards and to certify those qualified to be admitted. As sociologist Ernest Greenwood (1962) put it, "Anyone can call himself a carpenter, locksmith, or metal-plater if he feels so qualified. But a person who assumes the title of physician or attorney without having earned it conventionally becomes an imposter." The group's members also determine who shall be decertified because of incompetence or moral problems.

4 *Authority over clients*. Members of a profession claim authority over clients on the basis of their specialized education and theoretical understanding. Unlike carpentry, in which any of us can see that the nail is bent, members of the profession claim that the matter is too complex for "laypeople" to understand. Thus it is the clients' obligation to follow the professional's instructions.

5 *Service to society, not self-interest*. The public good lies at the heart of a profession. Although some car salespeople may make preposterous claims about serving the public good, we all know that they sell cars to make money. In contrast, the professions claim that they exist "to provide service to whomever requests it, irrespective of the requesting client's age, income, kinship, politics, race, religion, sex and social status" (Greenwood 1962).

    Obviously, this fifth criterion is the weakest. Today, we expect the basic motivation of a physician to be not far different from that of an automobile mechanic. Although both physicians and automobile mechanics may want things to get better for their customers, most of us assume both do what they do for money.

Is it a profession or a job? In some ways, this is not an either–or matter. While we can identify the extremes—medicine is a profession and flipping burgers is not—we can also view any particular work as "more" or "less" professionalized. For example, we may wish to make the case that creating stained glass windows is a profession. We can measure it according to these five criteria and see that it ranks higher on some than on others. So it is with other work. Using these guidelines, we can see that practicing law is less professional than practicing medicine, for law is low on theory and, in the public's mind at least, even more questionable on its claim to be doing a service for society.

Work Satisfaction   Let us briefly examine a second aspect of work from the symbolic interactionist perspective—the question of what makes work satisfying. As is well known, pay is central to job satisfaction, for unless a person is independently wealthy, no matter how much he or she likes a job, if it does not pay enough to buy groceries or gasoline it will prove highly unsatisfying. Pay, however, provides only *the general context that makes work satisfying* (Jencks et al. 1988). The specific conditions that increase job satisfaction are good working relationships with others, autonomy (control over one's work), and a feeling of purpose and accomplishment (Mortimer and Lorence 1989; Kohn et al. 1990). When these characteristics are present, morale is high. When they are absent, work loses its luster in spite of good pay. For differences in work satisfaction, you may want to review Figure 11.5 on page 296.

CULTURAL DIVERSITY IN THE UNITED STATES

Who Is Unemployed?

IT IS HARD TO believe that Amy and Peter are not officially part of the unemployed. After all, they have no jobs. In fact, they have no home. They are among the 350,000 homeless and jobless Americans sleeping in alleys and shelters for the destitute (Rossi et al. 1987). That fact, however, is *not* enough to count them as unemployed.

To see how the calculation works, let us suppose that you lose your job. After six months' frustrating search for work you become so discouraged that you stay home and stare blankly at the television. Amazingly, you no longer are counted as unemployed. As far as official statistics are concerned, to be unemployed you must be *actively* seeking work. If not, the government leaves you out of its figures. People without jobs who are so discouraged that they have not looked for work during the previous four weeks are simply not included in the government's unemployment figures.

Now, suppose that you do keep on looking for work, and you remain part of the government's count. But if your neighbor pays you to clean out her garage and rake the leaves, and if you put in fifteen hours and report them, you won't be counted, for the government figures that you have a job. Now assume that you keep on looking for work, don't rake leaves for a few hours' pay, but can't pay your telephone bill. Again, you won't show up in the figures, for the Bureau of Labor Statistics counts only people it reaches in a random telephone survey. To get an accurate idea how many are unemployed, then, we need to add about 3 percent to the official unemployment rate (Myers 1992). If the Labor Department says it is 8 percent, the true rate is actually about 11 percent—a difference of about *eight million* people. This is a conservative figure, for some estimate that six million people who want to work have only part-time jobs or are so discouraged that they no longer look for work (Herbert 1993).

Granted these problems, certain patterns do show up year after year. As you can see from Table 14.2, unemployment varies by sex, race, education, and marital status. Whites are the least likely to be unemployed, African Americans the most likely, and Latinos between the two. You won't be surprised to see that the higher a person's education, the less the likelihood of unemployment, but you might be surprised to see that men are more likely to be unemployed than women—and that married people are the least likely to be unemployed, separated people the most likely, and that divorced workers fall in between. Although the particular percentages fluctuate with changing economic conditions, the patterns themselves hold from year to year.

Table 14.2

The Percentage of Americans Who Are Officially Unemployed

Category	Percentage	Category	Percentage	Category	Percentage
Sex		*Ethnic Background of Latinos*		*Education*	
Males	7.8%	Puerto Rican		1–3 years of high school	
Females	6.9	Males	15.6	Males	11.4
Race and Ethnicity		Females	12.3	Females	11.4
African Americans		Mexican		Graduated from high school	
Males	15.2	Males	11.7	Males	7.3
Females	13.0	Females	11.7	Females	6.2
Latinos		Cuban		1–3 years of college	
Males	11.5	Males	7.1	Males	5.9
Females	11.3	Females	8.9	Females	5.3
Whites		Other[b]		Graduated from college	
Males	6.9	Males	10.5	Males	3.3
Females	6.0	Females	10.5	Females	3.0
Asian Americans[a]				*Marital Status of Women[c]*	
Males	6.3			Married	4.9
Females	6.3			Single	9.1
				Divorced, widowed, and separated	7.6

[a]Source does not list employment of Asian Americans by sex, and this is the overall total listed for both males and females.

[b]Refers primarily to people from Central or South America.

[c]Source does not list totals for men.

Source: Statistical Abstract 1993: Tables 50, 625, 628, 629, 633, 635.

The Future of the U.S. Economy

To try to glimpse the future, it is helpful to first review what is happening to the U.S. economy as it makes a painful transition to a postindustrial society. Of the many wrenching changes, perhaps the one most keenly felt is a stagnating or even declining standard of living. Bennett Harrison and Barry Bluestone (1988) put it this way:

> The standard of living of American workers. . . is in serious trouble. For every affluent "yuppie" in an expensive big-city condominium, working as a white-collar professional for a high-flying, high-technology concern or a multibillion-dollar insurance company, there are many more people whose wages have been falling and whose families are finding it more and more difficult to make ends meet.

Look at Figure 14.7, which apparently indicates a handsome increase in U.S. wages. Since workers have more dollars in their paychecks each year, it seems that they are earning more. As this Figure makes clear, however, to translate these wages into constant dollars strips away the illusion. Factoring in inflation reveals that U.S. workers make *less* now than they did in 1970. Workers don't just *feel* that they are earning less—they really are. From the end of World War II to about 1973, their standard of living rose steadily. Inflation-adjusted pay, unemployment and health insurance, paid vacations—all improved. But more recent years show a net *decline* in wages and standard of living, what Harrison and Bluestone call *the great American U-turn.*

Why did the United States make this U-turn? One explanation is a surge in imports and a decline in exports. The United States used to sell (export) more than it purchased (imports). One result was a hefty annual profit that could be plowed back into building new factories and machinery—along with higher wages and an increasing standard of living. For about twenty years, however, the United States has imported more than it has exported—a troubling equation that results in spiraling debt and less money to invest in wages, education, factories, parks, or any other ways that increase a people's standard of living (*Statistical Abstract* 1993: Table 1344). In addition, Americans are saving less. In 1970, Americans saved 7 percent of their income. Today it is just 4 percent (*Statistical Abstract* 1993: Tables 700, 701). The result is the same—less money to invest in making the means of production more efficient. Like an individual, if a nation spends more each year than it takes in, economic problems are inevitable.

Perhaps the great American U-turn is best summarized by two statistics. First, in just a few short years the United States went from being the world's largest creditor to the world's largest debtor. Second, the national debt is so huge that the interest payments alone run more than all the money the U.S. government spends on health, science, space, agriculture, housing, protecting the environment, and the entire justice system (Kennedy 1993).

If these trends continue, the result could be a *"two-thirds society"* (Glotz 1986). An upper third would consist of well-educated and prosperous technocrats who would be in charge. In the middle third would be workers who, though insecure in their jobs, earn a more-or-less adequate income. At the bottom, however, would be another third of the entire population consisting of the unemployed and the underemployed—migrant workers, the physically and mentally handicapped, teenagers who cannot find their way into the job market, and older people who have been pushed out of the job market—with minorities a disproportionate share of this bottom third.

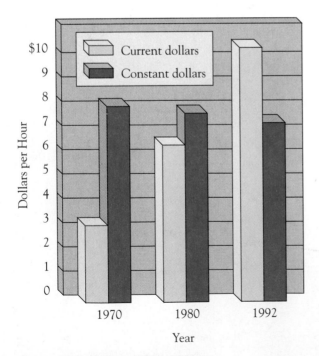

Source: Statistical Abstract 1993: Table 622.

Figure 14.7

Average Hourly Earnings of U.S. Workers in Current and Constant (1982) Dollars.

Will we be able to straighten out the great American U-turn? The economic fate of the United States is inextricably linked to many domestic events—economic planning, tax subsidies, savings rates, capital investments, even the quality of education. Beyond such domestic factors, however, lie worldwide events, especially the global demand for products and services and the relative competitiveness of other nations. While no one can say with certainty how such domestic and international forces will ultimately play out, we can be reasonably sure that the future will be wrenching. Industries will continue to be ripped out in some parts of the nation so that they can be transplanted onto foreign shores—whether across the ocean or to low-wage countries south of the U.S. border—workers will be retooled, and families will be forced to migrate from declining regions to others in the hope of finding work. Similar events occurred when the United States made the transition from an agricultural to an industrial economy, however, and earlier generations made the difficult adjustment. Based on the past, then, perhaps we should be cautiously optimistic as we approach the new economy.

Summary and Review

The Transformation of Economic Systems

How are economic systems linked to types of societies?

The earliest societies, hunting and gathering, were **subsistence economies:** small groups lived off the land and produced little or no surplus. Economic systems grew more complex as people discovered how to domesticate and cultivate (pastoral and horticultural societies), farm (agricultural societies), and manufacture (industrial societies). Each of these methods allowed people to produce a *surplus,* which fostered trade. Trade, in turn, brought social inequality as some people began to accumulate more than others. Pp. 374–377.

The Transformation of the Medium of Exchange

How has the medium of exchange evolved?

A **medium of exchange** is any means by which people exchange goods and services. In hunting and gathering and pastoral and horticultural societies, people **bartered** goods and services. In agricultural societies, **money** came into use, which evolved into **currency,** or paper representing a specific amount of gold or silver. Postindustrial societies rely increasingly on electronic transfer of funds in the form of **credit** and **debit cards.** Pp. 378–379.

World Economic Systems

How do the major economic systems differ?

The world's two major economic systems are capitalism and socialism. In **capitalism,** private citizens own the means of production and pursue **profits.** In **socialism,** the state owns the means of production and determines production with no goal of profit. Adherents of each have developed ideologies that defend their own systems and paint the other as harmful. Following **convergence theory,** in recent years each system has adopted features of the other. Pp. 379-385.

The Inner Circle of Capitalism

What is the role of the corporation in capitalism?

The term **corporate capitalism** indicates that giant corporations dominate capitalism today. At the top of the major corporations is an **inner circle,** whose mutual interests make certain that corporate capitalism is protected. The prominence of *multinational corporations* indicates that the interests of the inner circle lie beyond national boundaries. Pp. 386–388.

Work in U.S. Society

What are the three economic sectors of the labor force?

In the **primary sector** workers extract raw materials from the environment. In the **secondary sector** workers turn raw prod-

ucts into manufactured goods. In the **tertiary sector** workers produce services. Most Americans now work in the tertiary, or service sector. Pp. 388–389.

How has the ratio of women in the workforce changed?

In 1940, one in four women was a member of the labor force. Today, this figure is almost one in two, one of the highest ratios in the industrialized world. Pp. 389–390.

What is the underground economy?

The **underground economy** consists of any economic activity not reported to the government, from babysitting to prostitution. The size of the underground economy runs perhaps 10 to 15 percent of the regular economy. Pp. 390–391.

How have patterns of work and leisure changed?

In agricultural societies, work was dictated by the seasons. Industrialization initially brought a dramatic decrease in leisure, but workers have gained some back. Among the industrialized nations, currently only the Japanese work longer hours per week than do U.S. workers. Pp. 392–393.

Applying Sociological Theories

How do the three major perspectives apply to work?

From the *functionalist perspective,* work is a basis of social solidarity. Preindustrial societies foster **mechanical solidarity,** identifying with others who perform similar tasks. With industrialization comes **organic solidarity,** economic interdependence brought about by the division of labor. *Conflict theorists,* who are critical of capitalist economies, focus on worker exploitation and alienation. *Symbolic interactionists* analyze meanings and self-perceptions, asking why work is a job or a profession, what gives work status, and what makes work satisfying? Pp. 393–397.

The Future of the U.S. Economy

What does the future hold for U.S. workers?

A drop in real wages and a declining standard of living indicate serious economic problems on the way to postindustrial economy. Just as we adjusted to economic changes in the past, we are likely to do so now—but not without great difficulty. Pp. 398–399.

Where can I read more on this topic?

Suggested readings for this chapter are listed on page 642.

Pacita Abad, L.A. Liberty, 1993

CHAPTER

15

Politics:
Power and Authority

Micropolitics and Macropolitics

Power, Authority, and Coercion

Authority and Legitimate Violence
Traditional Authority
Rational-Legal Authority
Charismatic Authority
Authority as Ideal Type
The Transfer of Authority

Types of Government

Monarchies: The Rise of the State
Democracies: Citizenship as a Revolutionary Idea
Dictatorships and Oligarchies: The Seizure of Power

The U.S. Political System

Political Parties and Elections
Democratic Systems in Europe
Voting Patterns
Perspectives: Cultural Diversity in the United States:
   Immigrants—Ethnicity and Class as the Path to
   Political Participation

The Depression as a Transforming Event
Lobbyists and Special-Interest Groups
PACs in U.S. Politics

Who Rules the United States?

The Functionalist Perspective: Pluralism
The Conflict Perspective: Power Elite/Ruling Class
Which View Is Right?

War: A Means to Implement Political Objectives

Is War Universal?
How Common Is War?
Why Nations Go to War
Costs of War
Sowing the Seeds of Future Wars
War and Dehumanization

A New World Order?

Perspectives: Cultural Diversity Around the World:
   Nations Versus States—Implications for a
   New World Order

Summary and Review

I N THE **1930S**, GEORGE ORWELL WROTE *1984, a book about a future in which the government, known as "Big Brother," dominates society, dictating almost every aspect of everyone's life. To even love someone is considered a sinister activity, a betrayal of the first love and unquestioning allegiance that all citizens owe Big Brother.*

Two characters, Winston and Julia, fall in love. Because of Big Brother, they meet furtively, always with the threat of discovery and punishment hanging over their heads. When informers turn them in, expert interrogators separate Julia and Winston. They swiftly proceed to break their affection—to restore their loyalty to Big Brother.

Then follows a remarkable account of Winston and his tormentor, O'Brien. Winston is strapped so tightly into a chair that he can't even move his head. O'Brien explains that inflicting pain is not always enough, but that everyone has a breaking point, some worst thing that will push them over the edge.

O'Brien tells Winston that he has discovered his worst fear. Then he sets a cage with two giant, starving sewer rats on the table next to Winston, picks up a mask connected to the door of the cage and places it over Winston's head. In a quiet voice, O'Brien explains that when he presses the lever, the door of the cage will slide up, and the rats will shoot out like bullets and bore straight into Winston's face. Winston's eyes, the only part of his body that he can move, dart back and forth, revealing his terror. Still speaking so quietly that Winston has to strain to hear him, O'Brien adds that the rats sometimes attack the eyes first, but sometimes they burrow through the cheeks and devour the tongue. When O'Brien places his hand on the lever, Winston realizes that the only way out is for someone to take his place. But who? Then he hears his own voice screaming, "Do it to Julia! . . . Tear her face off, strip her to the bones. Not me! Julia! Not me!"

Orwell does not describe Julia's interrogation, but when they see each other later they realize that each has betrayed the other, and their love is gone. Big Brother has won.

Winston's crime was that he had given his loyalty to Julia, his lover, instead of to Big Brother, the overseeing, all-demanding, and all-controlling government. Winston's misplaced loyalty made him a political heretic, for it was the obligation of every citizen to place the state above all else in life. To preserve the state's dominance over the individual, Winston's allegiance had to be taken away from Julia. As you see it was.

Although seldom this dramatic, politics is always about power and authority, the focus of this chapter.

 ## Micropolitics and Macropolitics

Although the images that come to mind when we think of politics are those of government—kings, queens, coups, dictatorships, running for office, voting—politics, in the sense of power relations, is also an inevitable part of everyday life (Schwartz 1990). As Weber (1922/1968) said, **power** is the ability to carry out your will in spite of resistance, and in every group, large or small, some individuals have power over others. Symbolic interactionists use the term **micropolitics** to refer to the exercise of power in everyday life. Routine situations in which people jockey for power include employees' attempts to impress the new boss—who is going to decide which one of them will be promoted to manager—as well as efforts by parents to enforce their curfew on a reluctant daughter or son—and as has become a topic of comedians—who controls the remote to the TV. *Every group, then, is political, for in every group there is a power struggle of some sort.*

power: the ability to carry out one's will, even over the resistance of others

micropolitics: the exercise of power in everyday life, such as deciding who is going to do the housework

In contrast, **macropolitics**—the focus of this chapter—refers to the exercise of large-scale power over a broad group. Governments, whether the dictatorship faced by Winston or the elected forms in the United States and Canada, are examples of macropolitics. Let us turn, then, to macropolitics, considering first the matter of authority.

Power, Authority, and Coercion

For a society to exist, it must have a system of leadership. Some people will have to have power over others. As Max Weber (1913/1947) pointed out, however, people can perceive power as legitimate or illegitimate. Weber used the term **authority** to refer to legitimate power—that is, power that people accept as right. In contrast, illegitimate power—**coercion**—is power that people do not accept as just.

Let's imagine two situations. In the first, you are on your way to buy a CD player on sale for $250. As you approach the store, a man jumps out of the alley and shoves a gun in your back. He demands your money. Frightened for your life, you hand it over. In the second, you are on your way to a final examination, and you are running late. Afraid you might miss the test, you step on the gas. As the needle hits eighty-five just a mile from campus, you see flashing blue and red lights in your rear-view mirror. Your explanation about the final examination doesn't faze the officer—nor the judge who hears your case a few weeks later. She first lectures you on safety and then orders you to pay $50 court costs plus $10 for every mile an hour over sixty-five. You pay the $250.

What's the difference? The mugger, the police officer, and the judge—each has power and the end result is also the same. In each case you part with $250. The difference is that the mugger has no authority. His power is illegitimate—he has no *right* to do what he did. In contrast, you acknowledge that the officer has the right to stop you and that the judge has the right to fine you. Theirs is authority, or legitimate power.

macropolitics: the exercise of large-scale power, the government being the most common example

authority: power that people accept as rightly exercised over them; also called *legitimate power*

coercion: power that people do not accept as rightly exercised over them; also called *illegitimate power*

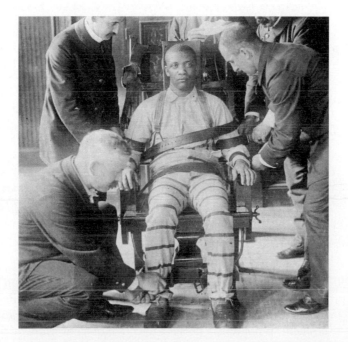

The ultimate foundation of any political order is violence. This is nowhere more starkly demonstrated than when a government takes human life. Shown in this 1910 photo from Sing Sing Prison is a man about to be executed.

The more that people see a government as legitimate, the more likely they are to cooperate with it, and the more stable it is. In 1989 in Beijing, China, students and workers protested the legitimacy of their government's power. The government then reasserted its authority through violence, massacring an unknown number of demonstrators. Shown here are demonstrators before the massacre.

Authority and Legitimate Violence

As sociologist Peter Berger observed, however, it makes little difference whether you pay the fine that the judge levies against you willingly or refuse to pay it. The court will get its money one way or another.

> There may be innumerable steps before its application [violence], in the way of warnings and reprimands. But if all the warnings are disregarded, even in so slight a matter as paying a traffic ticket, the last thing that will happen is that a couple of cops show up at the door with handcuffs and a Black Maria. Even the moderately courteous cop who hands out the initial traffic ticket is likely to wear a gun—just in case. (Berger 1963)

The **state,** then—a term synonymous with government—is the source of legitimate force or violence. This point, made by Max Weber (1946, 1922/1968)—that the state claims the exclusive right to use violence and the right to punish everyone else who does—is critical to our understanding of macropolitics. If someone owes you a debt, you cannot imprison that person or even forcibly take the money. The state can. The ultimate proof of the state's authority is that you cannot kill someone because he or she has done something that you consider absolutely horrible—but the state can. As Berger (1963) summarized this matter, *"Violence is the ultimate foundation of any political order."*

Before we explore the origins of the modern state, let us first look at a situation in which the state loses legitimacy.

The Collapse of Authority Sometimes the state oppresses its people, and they resist their government just as they do a mugger. The people cooperate reluctantly—but with a smile if that is what is required—while they eye the gun in the hand of the government's representatives. But, as they do with a mugger, if they are able they take up arms to free themselves. **Revolution,** armed resistance with the intention to overthrow a government, is not only a people's rejection of a government's claim to rule over them but also a rejection of its monopoly on violence. In a revolution, the people claim that

state: government; the source of legitimate violence in society

revolution: armed resistance designed to overthrow a government

right for themselves and if successful, they establish a new state in which they claim the right to monopolize violence.

What some see as coercion, however, others see as authority. Consequently, some people remain loyal to a government, willingly defend it, perhaps even die for it, although others are ready to take up arms against it. *The more that its power is seen as legitimate, then, the more stable a government is.*

But just why do people accept power as legitimate? Max Weber (1922/1968) identified three sources of authority: traditional, rational-legal, and charismatic. Let us examine each.

Traditional Authority

Throughout history, the most common form of authority has been traditional. **Traditional authority,** which is based on custom, is the hallmark of preliterate groups. In these societies, custom dictates basic relationships. For example, because of birth a particular individual becomes the chief, king, or queen. As far as members of that society are concerned, this is the right way to determine a ruler because "that is the way it has always been done."

Gender relations in most human groups are a good example of traditional authority, for they are based on custom. For example, in the villages of Spain and Portugal, widows are expected to wear only black until they remarry—which generally means that they wear black for the rest of their lives. By law, a widow is free to wear any color she wishes, but not by tradition. Tradition, decreeing black, is so strong that if a widow were to violate the dress code, she would be seen as having profaned the memory of her deceased husband and would be ostracized by the community.

When traditional society changes, traditional authority is undermined. As a society industrializes, for example, new perspectives on life open up, and no longer does traditional authority go unchallenged. Thus, in Spain and Portugal you can still see old women dressed in black from head to toe—and you immediately know their marital status. Younger widows, however, are likely to be indistinguishable from other women.

Even in postindustrial societies, traditional authority never totally dies out (Schwartz 1990). Parental authority provides an excellent example. Parents exercise authority over their children *because* they have always had such authority. From generations past, we inherit the idea that parents are not only responsible for providing their children with food and shelter, but also that they have the right to discipline them, to choose their doctors and schools, and to teach them religion and morality.

traditional authority: authority based on custom

For centuries, widows in the Mediterranean area were expected to dress in black. Their long dresses were matched by black stockings, black shoes, and black head covering. Widows conformed to this socially defined expression of ongoing sorrow for the deceased husband not because of law, but because of custom. Today, however, as industrialization erodes traditional authority, few widows follow this practice.

George Washington, shown here at the Constitutional Convention at Philadelphia in 1787, is an example of rational-legal authority. That is, he took office according to a system of rules that people had agreed on, in this case, the new Constitution of the United States.

Rational-Legal Authority

The second type of authority identified by Weber, **rational-legal authority,** is not based on custom but on written rules. "Rational" means reasonable, and "legal" means part of law. Thus "rational-legal" refers to matters agreed to by reasonable people and written into law (or regulations of some sort). The matters agreed to may be as broad as a constitution that specifies the rights of all members of a society or as narrow as a contract between two individuals. Because bureaucracies are based on written rules, rational-legal authority is also called *bureaucratic authority*.

In this system, authority comes from the position that an individual holds, not from the person who holds the position. In a democracy, for example, the president's authority comes from the office, as specified in a written constitution, not from custom or the individual's personal characteristics. In rational-legal authority everyone—no matter how high the office—is subject to the organization's written rules. In governments based on traditional authority the ruler's word may be law, but in those based on rational-legal authority the ruler's word is subject to the law.

Charismatic Authority

A few centuries back, in 1429, the English controlled large parts of France. When they prevented the coronation of a new French king, a farmer's daughter heard a voice telling her that God had a special assignment for her—that she should put on male clothing, recruit an army, and go to war against the English. Joan of Arc obeyed. She raised an army, conquered cities, and routed the English. Later that year, her visions were fulfilled as she stood next to Charles VII while he was crowned king of France (Bridgwater 1953).

Joan of Arc is an example of **charismatic authority,** the third type of authority Weber identified. (*Charisma* is a Greek word that means a gift freely and graciously given [Arndt and Gingrich 1957].) A charismatic individual is someone to whom people are drawn because they believe that person has been touched by God or has been endowed by nature with exceptional qualities (Lipset 1993). Note that the armies did not follow Joan of Arc because it was the custom to do so, as in traditional authority. Nor did they risk their lives alongside her because she held a position defined by written rules, as in

rational-legal authority: authority based on law or written rules and regulations; also called *bureaucratic authority*

charismatic authority: authority based on an individual's outstanding traits, which attract followers

rational-legal authority. Instead, people followed her because they were drawn to her outstanding traits. They saw her as a messenger of God, fighting on the side of justice, and accepted her leadership because of these attractive qualities.

The Threat Posed by Charismatic Leaders   Because the authority of charismatic leaders is based on their personal ability to attract followers, they pose a threat to the established political system. Whereas a king owes allegiance to tradition and a president to the system of law, to what does a charismatic leader owe allegiance? Working outside the political structure, he or she can direct followers according to personal preference—which can include the overthrow of traditional and rational-legal authorities.

Because charismatic leaders pose a threat to the established order, traditional and rational-legal authorities are often quick to oppose them. If they are not careful, however, they may create a martyr, arousing even higher sentiment in favor of the charismatic leader and in opposition to themselves. Occasionally, the Roman Catholic church faces such a threat when a priest claims miraculous powers, a claim perhaps accompanied by amazing healings. As people flock to this individual, they bypass parish priests and the formal ecclesiastical structure. To transfer allegiance from the organization to an individual is a threat to the church bureaucracy. Consequently, the church hierarchy may encourage the priest to withdraw from the public eye, perhaps to a monastery to rethink matters. Thus the threat is defused, rational-legal authority reasserted, and the stability of the organization maintained.

Charismatic authority—in which an individual is followed because others perceive that he or she possesses a special gift, perhaps even a touch from God—threatens both traditional and rational-legal authority. One of the best-known examples of charismatic authority is Joan of Arc, who raised a French army and defeated the English.

Authority as Ideal Type

Weber's classifications—traditional, rational-legal, and charismatic—represent ideal types of authority. As noted on page 175, ideal type does not refer to what is ideal or desirable, but to a composite of characteristics found in many real-life examples. A particular leader, then, may show a combination of characteristics.

An example is John F. Kennedy, who combined rational-legal and charismatic authority. As the elected head of the U.S. government, Kennedy represented rational-legal authority. Yet his mass appeal was so great that his public speeches aroused large numbers of people to action. When in his inaugural address Kennedy said, "Ask not what your country can do for you, but what you can do for your country," millions of Americans were touched. When Kennedy proposed a Peace Corps to help poorer countries, thousands of idealistic young people volunteered for challenging foreign service.

Charismatic and traditional authority can also overlap, as is illustrated by the Ayatollah Khomeini of Iran. Khomeini was a religious leader, holding the traditional position of ayatollah. His embodiment of the Iranian people's dreams, however, as well as his austere life and devotion to principles of the Koran, gave him such mass appeal that he was also a charismatic leader. Khomeini's followers were convinced that he had been chosen by God, and his speeches could arouse tens of thousands of followers to action.

In rare instances, then, traditional and rational-legal leaders possess charismatic traits. This is unusual, however, and most authority is clearly one type or another.

The Transfer of Authority

The orderly transfer of authority at the death, resignation, or incapacitation of a leader is critical for social stability. Under traditional authority, people know who is next in line. Under rational-legal authority, people may not know who the next leader will be, but they do know *how* that person will be selected. In both traditional and rational-legal systems of authority, the rules of succession are established.

Charismatic authority, however, poses a problem of succession, which makes it inherently less stable than either traditional or rational-legal authority. Because charismatic authority relies neither on custom nor law, but is built around a single individual, the death or incapacitation of a charismatic leader can mean a bitter struggle for succession. Consequently, some charismatic leaders make arrangements for an orderly transition of power by appointing a successor. This does not guarantee orderly succession, of course, for the followers may not perceive the designated heir in the same way as they did the charismatic leader. A second strategy is for the charismatic leader to construct an organization, which then perpetuates itself with a rational-legal leadership. Weber used the term the **routinization of charisma** to refer to the transfer of authority from a charismatic leader to either traditional or rational-legal authority.

Types of Government

How do the various types of government—monarchies, democracies, dictatorships, and oligarchies—differ? As we compare them, let's also look at how the institution of the state arose, and how the idea of citizenship was revolutionary.

Monarchies: The Rise of the State

Early societies were small and needed no extensive political system. They operated more like an extended family, with decisions being made as they became necessary. As surpluses developed and societies grew larger, cities evolved—perhaps about 3500 B.C. (Fischer 1976). **City-states** then came into being, with power radiating outward from a city like a spider's web. The city controlled the immediate area around it, but the areas between cities remained in dispute. Each city-state had its own **monarchy,** a king or queen whose right to rule was considered hereditary. If you drive through Spain, France, or Germany, you can still see evidence of former city-states. In the countryside you will see only scattered villages. Farther on, your eye will be drawn to the outline of a castle on a faraway hill. As you get closer, you will see that the castle is surrounded by a city. Several miles farther, you will see another city, also dominated by a castle. Each city, with its castle, was once a center of power.

As city-states warred with one another, the victorious ones would extend their rule. Eventually, one city-state would be able to wield power over an entire region. As the size of these regions grew, the people slowly developed an identity with the larger region (seeing distant inhabitants as a "we" instead of a "they"), and what we call the **state**—the political entity that claims a monopoly on the use of violence within a territory—came into being.

Democracies: Citizenship as a Revolutionary Idea

The United States had no city-states. Each colony, however, like a city-state, was small and independent. After the American Revolution, the colonies united. With the greater strength and resources that came from political unity, they conquered almost all of North America, bringing it under the power of a central government.

The government formed by this new country was called a **democracy.** (Derived from two Greek words—*kratos,* power and *demos,* common people—democracy literally means "power to the people.") Because of the bitter antagonisms associated with the revolution against the British king, the founders of the new country were distrustful of monarchies. They wanted to place political decision making into the hands of the people. This was not the first democracy the world had seen, but such a system had been tried before only with smaller groups. Athens, a city-state of Greece, practiced democracy two thousand years ago, with each male above a certain age having the right to be heard and to vote. Members of Native American tribes were also able to elect a chief, and in some, women were able to vote.

Because of their small size, tribes and cities were able to practice **direct democracy.** That is, they were small enough for the eligible voters to meet together, ex-

---

routinization of charisma: the transfer of authority from a charismatic figure to either a traditional or a rational-legal form of authority

city-state: an independent city whose power radiates outward, bringing the adjacent area under its rule

monarchy: a form of government headed by a king or queen

state: a political entity that claims a monopoly on the use of violence in some particular territory; commonly known as a country

democracy: a system of government in which authority derives from the people, derived from two Greek words that translate literally as "power to the people"

direct democracy: a form of democracy in which the eligible voters meet together to discuss issues and make their decisions

press their opinions, and then vote publicly—much like a town hall meeting today. As populous and spread out as the United States was, however, direct democracy was impossible, and **representative democracy** was invented. Certain citizens (at first only white landowners) voted for men to represent them in Washington. Later the vote was extended to nonowners of property, to African-American men, to women, and to others.

Today we take the idea of citizenship for granted. What is not evident to us is that the idea had to be conceived in the first place. There is nothing natural about citizenship—it is simply a way in which we choose to define ourselves. Throughout most of human history people were thought to belong to a clan, to a tribe, or even to a ruler. The idea of **citizenship**—that by virtue of birth and residence people have basic rights—is quite new to the human scene (Turner 1990).

Historically, people's rights usually depended on sex and family status. The rights of a resident of France in the 1600s, for example, depended on whether the individual was a male or female, a peasant or a member of the nobility. There were *no overarching rights* that people possessed simply because they were French. In essence, everyone belonged to the king, and the king had power of life and death over all his subjects.

The concept of representative democracy based on citizenship, perhaps the greatest gift the United States has given to the world, was revolutionary. Power was to be vested in the people themselves, and government was to flow from the people. The fact that at the time this concept was revolutionary is generally lost on us, but remember that its implementation meant the *reversal of traditional ideas, for the government was to be responsive to the people's wishes, not the people to the wishes of the government.* To keep the government responsive to the needs of its citizens, people not only had the right, but the obligation, to express dissent. Thomas Jefferson observed that

> a little rebellion now and then is a good thing. . . . It is a medicine necessary for the sound health of government. . . . God forbid that we should ever be twenty years without such a rebellion. . . . The tree of liberty must be refreshed from time to time with the blood of patriots and tyrants. It is its natural manure. (In Hellinger and Judd 1991)

The idea of **universal citizenship**—of *everyone* having the same basic rights by virtue of being born in a country (or by immigrating and becoming a naturalized citizen)—flowered very slowly, and came into practice only through fierce struggle. When the United States was founded, for example, that idea was still in its infancy. Today it seems inconceivable to us that any group should not have the right to vote, hold office, make a contract, or own property. For earlier generations of Americans, however, it seemed just as inconceivable that the poor, women, African Americans, Native Americans, and Asian Americans should have such rights. Over the years, then, rights have been extended, and in the United States citizenship and its privileges now apply to all. No longer does property, sex, or race determine the right to vote, to testify in court, and so on. These characteristics, however, do influence whether or not one votes, as we shall see in a later section on voting patterns.

Dictatorships and Oligarchies: The Seizure of Power

Democracies and monarchies are not the only systems of government. In some countries, an individual seizes power, sometimes by killing the king, queen, or president, and then dictates his will onto the people. A government run by a single person who has seized power is known as a **dictatorship.** If a small group seizes power, the government is called an **oligarchy.** The frequent coups in Central and South America, in which a few military leaders seize control of a country, are examples of oligarchies. Although one individual may be named president, it is often a group of high-ranking officers, working behind

The essence of a democracy is people being able to elect their leaders. Although the United States gave the world representative democracy, the vote was withheld from many on the basis of property, sex, and race. As reviewed in the text, minorities are still underrepresented. Shown here is Ben Nighthorse Campbell of Colorado. Campbell, a Northern Cheyenne, is the first Native American to serve in the U.S. Senate in 60 years.

representative democracy: a form of democracy in which voters elect representatives to govern and make decisions on their behalf

citizenship: the concept that birth (and residence) in a country impart basic rights

universal citizenship: the idea that everyone has the same basic rights by virtue of being born in a country (or by immigrating and becoming a naturalized citizen)

dictatorship: a form of government in which power is seized by an individual

oligarchy: a form of government in which power is held by a small group of individuals; the rule of the many by the few

Totalitarian leaders attempt to control every aspect of their subjects' lives that they find threatening— and, since threats abound, their inclination is to use iron-fisted control. Like many dictators, Saddam Hussein of Iraq operates prisons where political prisoners are tortured and killed. Unlike most such leaders, he also has personally executed army officers who displeased him.

the scenes, that makes the decisions. If their designated president becomes uncooperative, they remove him from office, and designate another.

Monarchies, dictatorships, and oligarchies can be benevolent, or they can be totalitarian. **Totalitarianism** refers to almost *total* control of a people by the government. As our opening vignette demonstrated, totalitarian regimes tolerate no opposing opinion. In Nazi Germany, for example, Hitler kept the populace in tight control through the Gestapo, a ruthless secret police force that looked for any sign of dissent. Control was so total that spies even watched moviegoers' reactions to newsreels, reporting those who did not respond "appropriately" (Hipler 1987).

In totalitarian regimes, the names of those who rule may change, but the techniques of control remain the same. Threats and terror force citizen compliance and allow the dictator to remain in power. Privacy is viewed as a threat to the regime, and the police keep a dossier on each citizen. A description of Nazi Germany could just as well be applied to the Soviet Union under Stalin or Iraq under Saddam Hussein. The police, courts, armed forces, and entire government bureaucracy are directly accountable to the dictator. Individual rights, if they existed prior to the dictator, simply disappear, while if individual citizens dissent, they disappear.

People around the world find the ideas of citizenship and of representative democracy appealing. Those who have no say in their government's decisions, or who face prison for expressing dissent, find in these ideas the hope for a brighter future. With today's efficient communications, people no longer remain ignorant of whether they are more or less privileged politically than others. This knowledge produces pressure for greater citizen participation in government. It looks as though the future will continue to step up this pressure.

 ## The U.S. Political System

At this point, let us turn to an overview of the U.S. political system. We shall consider the two major political parties, compare the U.S. political system with other democratic systems, examine voting patterns, analyze how the Great Depression of the 1930s transformed U.S. politics, and examine the role of lobbyists and PACs.

Political Parties and Elections

After the founding of the United States, numerous political parties emerged, but by the time of the Civil War, two parties dominated U.S. politics (Burnham 1983): the Democrats, who in the public mind are often associated with the working class and the Republicans, who are associated with wealthier people. Each party nominates candidates, and in pre-elections, called primaries, the voters decide which candidates will represent their party. Each candidate then campaigns, trying to appeal to the most voters. Table 15.1 shows how Americans align themselves with political parties.

Although the Democratic and Republican parties represent different philosophical principles, each appeals to such a broad membership that it is difficult to distinguish a conservative Democrat from a liberal Republican. The extremes, however, are easy to discern. Deeply committed Democrats support legislation that transfers income from one group to another or that controls wages, working conditions, and competition. Dyed-in-the-wool Republicans oppose such legislation.

Those elected to Congress may cross party lines. That is, some Democrats vote for legislation proposed by Republicans, and *vice versa*. This happens because officeholders support their party's philosophy but not necessarily all its specific proposals. For example, during elections Democrats espousing the principle that the poor should have more income may call Republicans callous representatives of the rich. The Republicans, in

totalitarianism: a form of government that exerts almost total control over the people

Table 15.1				
How Americans Identify with Political Parties				
	1960	*1970*	*1980*	*1990*
Democrats				
Strong Democrat	20%	20%	18%	20%
Weak Democrat	25	24	23	19
Independent Democrat	6	10	11	12
Total	51	54	52	51
Republicans				
Strong Republican	16	9	9	10
Weak Republican	14	15	14	15
Independent Republican	7	8	12	12
Total	37	32	35	37
Other				
Independent	10	13	13	11
Not political	3	1	2	2
Total	13	14	15	13

Note: Due to rounding, the totals do not always equal 100 percent.
Source: Statistical Abstract 1991: Table 452; 1993: Table 452.

turn, have their own choice words to arouse emotions—and votes—perhaps calling an opponent misguided, or even, if the contest really heats up, un-American. When it comes to a specific bill, however, such as raising the minimum wage, not all Democrats or Republicans see it the same way. Some conservative Democrats may view the measure as unfair to small employers, or too costly, and vote with the Republicans against the bill. At the same time, liberal Republicans—feeling that the proposal is just, or sensing a changing sentiment in voters back home—may side with its Democratic backers.

Regardless of their differences, however, the Democrats and Republicans represent *different slices of the center.* Although they may ridicule the opposing party and promote different legislation, each party firmly supports such fundamentals of U.S. political philosophy as free public education, a strong military, freedom of religion, speech, assembly, and, of course, capitalism—especially the private ownership of property.

Third parties also play a role in U.S. politics, but to have any influence they, too, must support these centrist ideas. To advocate their radical change is to doom a third party to a short life of little political consequence. Because most Americans consider a vote for a third party a waste, third parties do notoriously poorly at the polls. Two exceptions are Theodore Roosevelt's Bull Moose party, which won more votes in 1912 than Taft, the Republican presidential candidate, and the United We Stand party, headed by billionaire political hopeful Ross Perot, which won 19 percent of the vote in 1992 (Bridgwater 1953; *Statistical Abstract* 1993: Tables 427, 428).

Democratic Systems in Europe

We tend to take our political system for granted and assume that any other democracy looks like ours—even down to having two major parties. Such is not the case. To gain a comparative understanding, let us look at the European system.

Although both theirs and ours are democracies, there are fundamental distinctions between the two (Domhoff 1979, 1983; Lipset 1963). First, elections in most of Europe are not winner-take-all. In the United States, elections are determined by a simple

Although minorities are still underrepresented in U.S. politics, they have made remarkable gains in recent years. Shown here is Michael Woo as he voted in the Los Angeles mayoral race. Woo lost to millionaire Richard Riordan in a tight race for leadership of the nation's second largest city.

proportional representation: an electoral system in which seats in a legislature are divided according to the proportion of votes each political party receives

centrist party: a political party that represents the center of political opinion

noncentrist party: a political party that represents marginal ideas

coalition government: a government in which a country's largest party aligns itself with one or more smaller parties

majority. For example, if a Democrat wins 51 percent of the votes cast in an electoral district, he or she takes office. The Republican candidate, who may have won 49 percent, loses everything. In contrast, most European countries base their elections on a system of **proportional representation;** that is, the seats in the national legislature are divided according to the proportion of votes received by each political party. If one party wins 51 percent of the vote, for example, that party is awarded 51 percent of the seats; while a party with 49 percent of the votes receives 49 percent of the seats.

Second, proportional representation encourages minority parties, while the winner-take-all system discourages them. As we saw, the U.S. system pushes parties to the center as they strive to obtain the broadest possible support required to win elections. For this reason, the United States has **centrist parties.** The proportional representation followed in most European countries means that if a party gets 10 percent of the voters to support its candidate, it will get 10 percent of the seats. This system encourages the formation of **noncentrist parties,** those that propose less popular or even offbeat ideas. For example, a party may make its central platform a return to the gold standard, or the retirement of all nuclear weapons and the shutting down of all nuclear power reactors.

Three main results follow from being able to win even just a few seats in the national legislature. First, if a minority party has officeholders, it gains access to the media throughout the year, receiving publicity that helps keep its issues alive. Second, small parties gain power beyond their numbers. Because many parties compete in the elections, no single party is likely to gain a majority of the seats in the national legislature. To muster the required votes to make national decisions, the party with the most seats must align itself with one or more of the smaller parties and form a **coalition government.** A party with only 10 or 15 percent of the seats, then, may be able to trade its vote on some issues for the larger party's support on others. Third, because coalitions break down, the governments tend to be less stable. Italy, for example, has had 51 different governments since World War II, compared with ten presidents in the United States. To add greater stability, the Italians have voted that three-fourths of their Senate seats will be decided on the winner-take-all system (Melloan 1993b).

Voting Patterns

Year after year, Americans show consistent voting patterns. From Table 15.2, you can see how the percentage of people who vote increases with age. This table also shows the significance of race and ethnicity. Non-Hispanic whites are more likely to vote than are African Americans or Asian Americans, while Latinos are the least likely to vote. The difference is so great that whites are about twice as likely to vote as are Latinos. A crucial aspect of the socialization of newcomers to the United States has been learning the U.S. political system, which is the topic of the Perspectives box on page 416.

As with age, greater education also increases the likelihood of voting. People who finish college are more than twice as likely to vote as those who complete only grade school. Employment and income are also significant. People who make over $35,000 a year are twice as likely to vote as those who make less than $5,000. Finally, note that about the same proportion of males and females vote in presidential elections.

Social Integration How can we explain the voting patterns shown in Table 15.2? The people most likely to vote are older, more educated, affluent, employed whites, while those least likely to vote are poor, younger, ill-educated, unemployed Latinos. From these patterns, we can draw this principle: *the more that people feel they have a stake in the political system, the more likely they are to vote.* They have more to protect, and feel that voting can make a difference. In effect, people who have been rewarded by the political system feel more socially integrated. They vote because they perceive that elections directly affect their own lives and the type of society in which they and their children live.

Alienation In contrast, those who gain less from the system—in terms of education, income, and jobs—are more likely to be alienated. Such people feel that their vote will not affect their lives one way or another, that "next year will be more of the same, regardless of who is president," that "all politicians do is lie to us." Similarly, minorities who feel that the U.S. political system is a "white" system are less motivated to vote.

Voter Apathy Table 15.2 also indicates that a large proportion of people who do have jobs, high education, and good incomes also stay away from the polls. Many people do not vote because of **voter apathy,** or indifference. Like the alienated, they feel that their vote will not affect the outcome. A common attitude is "What difference does my one vote make when there are millions of votes?" Many of the apathetic see little difference between the two major political parties. The result is that two out of five eligible U.S. voters do not vote for president, and that less than half the nation's eligible voters (about 45 percent) vote for members of Congress (*Statistical Abstract* 1993: Table 454).

The Depression as a Transforming Event

Until Franklin Delano Roosevelt (FDR) became president in 1932, the country's ruling philosophy was that the government should play as small a part as possible in people's lives. The proper role of local government was to run schools, make the community safe, and operate a small maintenance department for garbage, sewers, and streets; that of the federal government was to build highways and bridges, deliver the mail, and maintain a small armed force. Government, at whatever level, was to collect as few taxes as possible. The poor were the responsibility of family, church, and local community.

During what became known as the Great Depression of the 1930s, which followed the stock market's collapse in 1929, employment around the country collapsed too. About one in every four workers had no job, and many of those who did worked for subsistence wages. Public opinion was transformed, and with it, the role of government in the economy. Previously, Americans had been convinced that only laziness kept people from work. Now they saw that millions desperately wanted to work, but no work was available. At this point,

---

Table 15.2

Percentage of Americans Who Vote for President

	1980	1984	1988	1992
Overall				
Americans Who Vote	59%	60%	57%	61%
Age				
18–20	36	37	33	39
21–24	43	44	38	46
25–34	55	55	48	53
35–44	64	64	61	64
45–64	69	70	68	70
65 and up	65	68	69	70
Sex				
Male	59	59	56	60
Female	59	61	58	62
Race or Ethnicity				
Whites (non-Hispanic)	61	61	59	64
African Americans	51	56	52	54
Latinos	30	33	29	29
Asian Americans and Pacific Islanders	NA	NA	NA	50
Education				
Grade school only	43	43	37	35
High school dropout	46	44	41	41
High school graduate	59	59	55	58
College dropout	67	68	65	69
College graduate	80	79	78	81
Labor Force				
Employed	62	62	58	64
Unemployed	41	44	39	46
Income				
Under $5,000	38	39	35	NA
$5,000 to $9,999	46	49	41	NA
$10,000 to $14,999	54	55	48	NA
$15,000 to $19,999	57	60	54	NA
$20,000 to $24,999	61	67	58	NA
$25,000 to $34,999	67	74	64	NA
$35,000 and over	74	74	70[a]	NA

[a]For 1988, the percentage is an average of $35,000 to $49,900 and over $50,000.

Sources: Statistical Abstract 1991: Table 450; 1993: Table 454; *Current Population Reports*, Series P-20, vol. 440; U.S. Bureau of the Census, "Voting and Registration in the Election of November 1992," no. 466, p. 20.

---

voter apathy: indifference and inaction on the part of individuals or groups with respect to the political process

▲▼▲▼▲▼▲▼▲▼▲▼▲▼▲▼▲▼▲▼▲▼▲▼▲▼▲▼▲▼▲▼▲▼

Perspectives

CULTURAL DIVERSITY IN THE UNITED STATES

Immigrants—Ethnicity and Class as the Path to Political Participation

THAT THE UNITED STATES is the land of immigrants is a truism; every schoolchild knows that since the English Pilgrims first landed on Plymouth Rock, successive groups—among them Germans, Scandinavians, Italians, Poles, and Greeks—crossed the Atlantic ocean to reach U.S. shores.

Some, such as the Irish immigrants in the late 1800s and early 1900s, left to escape brutal poverty and famine. Others, such as the Jews of czarist Russia, fled a government that singled them out for persecution. Some fled as refugees or asylum seekers from lands divided by war. Others, called *entrepreneurial immigrants*, sought economic opportunities absent in their native lands. Still others came as *sojourners*, planning to return home after a temporary stay.

Today the United States witnesses its second large wave of immigration of the twentieth century. The first, in the early 1900s, in which immigrants came to account for 13.2 percent of the population, consisted largely of Europeans. Today, the mix of immigrants—currently about 6.2 percent of the population—is far more diverse, with most coming from South and Central America and Asia. As in the past, there is widespread concern that "too many" immigrants will alter the character of the United States. "Throughout the history of American immigration," write sociologists Alejandro Portes and Ruben Rumbaut, "a consistent thread has been the fear that the 'alien element' would somehow undermine the institutions of the country and lead it down the path of disintegration and decay."

Thus, both immigration and the fear of its consequences are central to the history of the United States. A widespread fear held by native-born Americans in the early part of the century was that immigrants would subvert the democratic system in favor of socialism or communism. Today, some fear that the primacy of the English language is threatened. In ad-

dition, the age-old fear that immigrants will take jobs away from native-born Americans remains strong. Finally, minority groups that struggled for political representation fear that newer groups will gain political power at their expense.

What route to political participation do immigrants take? In general, they first organize as a group on the basis of *ethnicity* rather than *class*. In response to common problems, especially discrimination, they reaffirm their cultural identity. "This represents the first effective step in their social and political incorporation," note Portes and Rumbaut. "By mobilizing the collective vote and by electing their own to office, immigrant minorities have learned the rules of the democratic game and absorbed its values in the process."

This pattern of banding together on the basis of ethnicity can be seen in the case of Irish immigrants in Boston. They built a power base that put the Irish in political control of the city, and, ultimately, saw one of their own sworn in as president of the United States.

As Portes and Rumbaut observe, "Assimilation as the rapid transformation of immigrants into Americans 'as everyone else' has never happened." Instead, all immigrant groups began by fighting for their own interests as Irish, Italians, and so on. Only when they had attained enough political power to overcome discrimination did they become "like everyone else"—that is, like others who had power.

Thus, only when a certain level of political power is achieved, when groups gain political representation somewhat proportionate to their numbers, does the issue of class grow in significance. This, then, is the path that immigrants follow in their socialization into the U.S. political system.

Sources: Portes and Rumbaut 1990; Salholz 1990; Prud 'Homme 1991; James 1993.

Americans began to develop a sociological imagination, for they caught a glimpse of the economic system itself. They began to see that having a job or being unemployed was not simply the result of individual traits such as initiative or the lack of it, but the consequence of the social system itself. They demanded that the government do something about the economy.

In 1932 Herbert Hoover, the Republican incumbent, was defeated, and Roosevelt, a Democrat, took office with the promise to change things. That he did. He took the view that it was the government's responsibility to oversee the country's economy. Among other things, he instituted federal work programs such as the Works Progress Administration (WPA) to build parks and civic buildings, and the Rural Electrification Association (REA) to bring electricity to the country's farms. Because he put people back to work, FDR was re-elected in 1936, 1940, and 1944.

U.S. politics was never the same again. Although they disagree about the extent of government responsibility, both Republicans and Democrats support payments to unemployed workers, the elderly, and the poor. Parties and candidates may propose specific changes in these programs, but any party that suggested dismantling unemployment insurance, Social Security, and welfare would have no chance of being elected.

Lobbyists and Special-Interest Groups

Suppose that you are president of the United States, and you want to make dairy products more affordable for the public in general and the poor in particular. As you check into the matter, you find that prices for milk and cheese are high because the government is paying dairy farmers over $200 million a year in price supports (*Statistical Abstract* 1993: Table 1110). You therefore propose to eliminate these subsidies.

Immediately, large numbers of people leap into action. They send telegrams to your office, contact their senator and representatives, and call reporters for news conferences. The news media report that hardships will result from your proposed action and that across the land dairy farmers will be put out of business. The Associated Press distributes pictures of a farm family—their Holsteins grazing in the background—informing readers how this healthy, happy family of good Americans struggling to make a living will be destroyed by your proposal.

President or not, you don't have a chance of getting your legislation passed.

What happened? The dairy industry went to work to protect its special interests. A **special-interest group** consists of people who think alike on a particular issue and who can be mobilized for political action. The dairy industry is just one of thousands of such groups that employ **lobbyists,** people paid to influence legislation on behalf of their clients. Special-interest groups and lobbyists have become a major force in U.S. politics. Members of Congress who are interested in being re-elected must pay attention to them, for they represent blocs of voters who have a vital interest in the outcome of specific bills. Well financed and able to contribute huge sums, lobbyists can deliver votes to you—or to your opponent.

Because so much money was being passed under the table by special-interest groups to members of Congress, in the 1970s legislation limited the amount that any individual, corporation, or special-interest group could give a candidate, and required all contributions over $1,000 to be reported. Special-interest groups immediately did an end sweep around the new laws by forming **political action committees (PACs),** organizations that solicit contributions from many donors—each contribution within the allowable limits—and then use the large total to influence legislation.

PACs have become a powerful influence in Washington, for they bankroll lobbyists and legislators. More than four thousand PACs disburse over $350 million (*Statistical Abstract* 1993: Tables 460, 461). A few PACs represent broad social interests such as environmental protection, but most stand for narrow financial concerns, such as the dairy, oil, banking, and construction industries. Those PACs with the most clout in terms of money and votes gain the ear of Congress.

PACs in U.S. Politics

Suppose that you want to run for the Senate. To have a chance of winning, you must not only shake hands around the state, be photographed hugging babies, and eat a lot of chicken dinners at local civic organizations, but you must also send out hundreds of thousands of pieces of mail to solicit votes and financial support. During the home stretch, television ads may run $700,000 a week (Harwood 1994). If you are an *average* candidate for the Senate, you will spend almost $4 million on your campaign. To run for the House will cost a paltry $.5 million (*Statistical Abstract* 1993: Tables 442, 464).

Now suppose that it is only a few weeks from the election, the polls show you and your opponent neck and neck, and your war chest is empty. The representatives of a couple of PACs pay you a visit. One says that his organization will pay for a mailing, while

The Great Depression transformed Americans' attitudes toward government intervention in economic matters. Shown here is a 1939 poster that was displayed in post offices and other public buildings throughout the country.

special-interest group: a group of people who have a particular issue in common who can be mobilized for political action

lobbyists: people who influence legislation on behalf of their clients

political action committee (PAC): an organization formed by one or more special-interest groups to solicit and spend funds for the purpose of influencing legislation

Figure 15.1

Foreign Lobbyists:
The Top 10 Spenders

1. $60 million
   Japan

2. $23 million
   Canada

3. $13 million
   Germany

4. $12.8 million
   France

5. $11 million
   Mexico

6. $10.5 million
   Hong Kong

7. $9.5 million
   Kuwait

8. $8 million
   Taiwan

9. $8 million
   Australia

10. $7.8 million
    Ireland

Source: Engelberg and Tolchin, 1993.

the other offers to buy television and radio ads. You feel somewhat favorably toward their positions anyway, and you accept. Once elected, you owe them. When legislation that affects their interests comes up for vote, their representatives call you—at your unlisted number at home—and tell you how they want you to vote. It would be political folly to double-cross them.

It is said that the first duty of a politician is to get elected—and the second duty to get re-elected. If you are an average senator, to finance your re-election campaign you must raise $1,700 *every single day* of your six-year term. It is no wonder that money has been dubbed the "mother's milk of politics" (Abramson and Rogers 1991).

Criticism of Lobbyists and PACs   The major criticism leveled against lobbyists and PACs is that their money, in effect, buys votes. Rather than representing the people who elected them, legislators support the special interests of groups able to help them stay in power. The influence of foreign lobbyists has been a target of especially harsh criticism. As shown in Figure 15.1, the top ten foreign lobbyists spend $163 million annually to influence votes. Japan has hired over one hundred former U.S. government officials to support its interests, and spends $60 million a year to pressure members of Congress to reduce quotas and duties on imports of its products. During election years, Japan contributes to both presidential candidates. Critics argue that the playing field is not level, for Japan forbids foreigners to influence *its* legislation (Judis 1990; Duffy 1992).

Even if the United States were to outlaw PACs, special-interest groups would not disappear from the U.S. political process. Before PACs, lobbyists walked the corridors of the Senate, they always have had access to Senate staff, and since the time of Alexander Graham Bell they have carried the unlisted numbers of members of Congress. Lobbyists—for good or ill—play an essential role in the U.S. political system.

Who Rules the United States?

With special-interest groups and their lobbyists and PACs, just who do U.S. senators and representatives really represent? Do the people in general rule, or do special-interest groups? This question has led to a lively debate among sociologists. In previous chapters, we have discussed the contrasting views of sociologists on the control of U.S. society, and this is an opportune moment to review them.

The Functionalist Perspective: Pluralism

Functionalists view the state as having arisen out of the basic needs of the social group. To protect themselves from would-be oppressors, people formed a government and gave it the monopoly on violence. Their continuing need, however, is to prevent the state from turning that force against themselves. To return to the example used earlier, states have a tendency to become muggers. Thus, people must perform a balancing act between having no government—which would lead to **anarchy,** a state in which disorder and violence reign—and having a government that protects them from violence, but may itself turn against them. When functioning well, then, the state is a balanced system that protects its citizens—from themselves and from government.

What keeps the government of the United States from turning against its citizens? Functionalists say that **pluralism,** a diffusion of power among many interest groups, prevents any one group from gaining control of the government and using it to oppress

anarchy: a condition of lawlessness or political disorder caused by the absence or collapse of governmental authority

pluralism: the diffusion of power among many interest groups, preventing any single group from gaining control of the government

the people (Dahl 1961, 1982; Polsby 1959; Huber and Form 1973). The founders of the United States were determined that the government should not come under the control of any one group, or else they believed democracy would be doomed. To balance the interests of competing groups, the founders set up three branches of government—the executive (president), judiciary (courts), and legislative (the Senate and House of Representatives). Each is sworn to uphold the Constitution, which guarantees rights to citizens, and each is able to nullify the actions of the other two. This system, known as **checks and balances,** was designed to ensure that power remains distributed and that no one branch of government dominates.

From the functionalist perspective, ethnic groups, women, farmers, factory workers, religious groups, bankers, bosses, the unemployed, coal miners, the retired, as well as the broader categories of the rich, middle class, and poor, are all parts of our pluralist society. Each has political muscle to flex at the polls. To be re-elected, politicians promote legislation that benefits special-interest groups, or, at the very least, does not offend them. The competitive activities of our many interest groups balance the political system by preventing the dominance of any single group.

Thus, say functionalists, no one group rules the United States. Rather, power is widely dispersed among the many groups that make up U.S. society (Dahl 1982; Marger 1987). As each group pursues its own interests, it is balanced by many other groups pursuing theirs. As special-interest groups negotiate with one another and reach compromises, conflict is minimized, and the resulting policies gain wide support. Consequently, no one group rules, and the political system is responsive to the people.

The Conflict Perspective: Power Elite/Ruling Class

Conflict theorists come up with a different answer. If you focus on the lobbyists scurrying around Washington, they say, you get a blurred image of superficial activities, of laws being passed for specific purposes. What really counts is the big picture, not its fragments. The important question is who holds the power that determines the overarching policies of the United States. For example, who determines how many Americans will be out of work by raising or lowering interest rates? Who sets policies that transfer jobs from the United States to countries with low-cost labor? And the ultimate question of power: Who is behind decisions to go to war?

Power Elite/Ruling Class C. Wright Mills (1956) took the position that the most important matters are not decided by lobbyists, nor even by Congress. Rather, the decisions that have the greatest impact on the lives of Americans—and people across the face of the globe—are made by a coalition of individuals whose interests coincide and who have access to the center of political power in the United States. Mills called them the **power elite,** and said that it is this group that rules the United States. As depicted in Figure 15.2, the power elite consists of the top leaders of the largest corporations, the most powerful generals and admirals of the armed forces, and certain elite politicians—the president, his cabinet, and select senior members of Congress who chair the major committees. It is they who wield power, who make the decisions that direct the country—and shake the world (Hourani 1987; Hellinger and Judd 1991).

Are the three groups that make up the power elite—the top political, military, and corporate leaders—equal in power? Mills said they were not, but for his choice of dominance he did not point to the president and his staff or even to the generals and admirals, but rather to the corporate heads. Because all three segments of the power elite view capitalism as essential to the welfare of the country, business interests, he said, come foremost in setting national policy.

Sociologist William Domhoff (1967, 1990) uses the term *ruling class* to refer to the power elite. He focuses on the 1 percent of Americans who belong to the super rich, the powerful capitalist class studied in Chapter 10 (pages 261–263). Members of this

checks and balances: the separation of powers among the three branches of U.S. government—legislative, executive, and judicial—so that each is able to nullify the actions of the other two, thus preventing the domination of any single branch

power elite: C. Wright Mills's term for those who rule the United States: the top people in the leading corporations, the most powerful generals and admirals of the armed forces, and certain elite politicians

class control our top corporations and foundations, even the boards that oversee our major universities. It is no accident, says Domhoff, that from this group the president chooses most members of his cabinet and appoints the top ambassadors to the most powerful countries of the world.

Conflict theorists point out that we should not think of the ruling class as a group that meets together and agrees on specific matters. Rather, it consists of people whose backgrounds and orientations to life are so similar—they attend prestigious private schools, belong to exclusive private clubs, and are millionaires many times over—that they automatically share the same values and goals. Their behavior stems not from some grand conspiracy to control the country, but rather from a mutual interest in solving the problems that face large businesses (Useem 1984). Able to ensure that the social policies it deems desirable for the country are adopted, this powerful group sets the economic and political conditions under which the rest of the country operates (Domhoff 1990). We shall return to this line of inquiry later.

Which View Is Right?

The functionalist and conflict views of power in U.S. society cannot be reconciled. Either competing interests block the dominance of any single group, as functionalists assert, or a power elite oversees the major decisions of the United States, as conflict theorists maintain. Perhaps at the middle level of Mills's model, depicted in Figure 15.2, the competing interest groups do keep each other at bay, and none is able to dominate. If so, the functionalist view would apply to this middle level, as well as the lowest level of power. Perhaps functionalists have just not looked high enough, and activities at the peak remain invisible to them. If so, on that level lies the key to U.S. power, the dominance by an elite as it follows its mutual interests.

The answer, however, is not yet conclusive. For that, we must await more research.

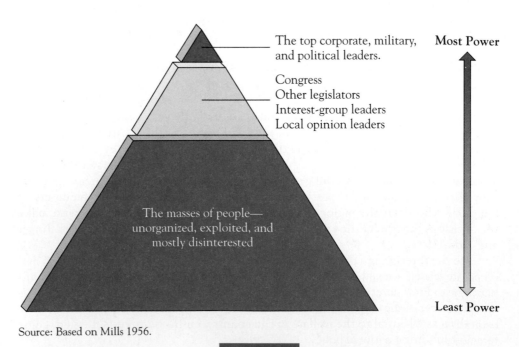

The top corporate, military, and political leaders.

Congress
Other legislators
Interest-group leaders
Local opinion leaders

The masses of people—
unorganized, exploited, and
mostly disinterested

Most Power

Least Power

Source: Based on Mills 1956.

Figure 15.2

Power in American Society: The Model Proposed by C. Wright Mills.

War: A Means to Implement Political Objectives

As we have noted, an essential characteristic of the state is that it claims a monopoly on violence. At times, a state may direct that violence against other nations. **War,** armed conflict between nations (or politically distinct groups), is often part of national policy. Let us look at this aspect of politics.

Is War Universal?

Although human aggression and individual killing characterize all human groups, war does not. War is simply *one option* that groups may choose for dealing with disagreements; but not all societies choose this option. The Mission Indians of North America, the Arunta of Australia, the Andaman Islanders of the South Pacific, and the Eskimos of the Arctic, for example, had procedures to handle aggression and quarrels, but they did not have organized battles that pitted one tribe against another. These groups do not even have a word for war (Lesser 1968).

How Common Is War?

One of the contradictions of humanity is that people long for peace while at the same time they glorify war. The glorification of war can be seen by noting how major battles hog the center of a country's retelling of its history and how monuments to its generals are scattered throughout the land. From May Day parades in Moscow's Red Square to the Fourth of July celebrations in the United States and the Cinco de Mayo victory marches in Mexico, war and revolutions are interwoven into the fabric of daily life.

To find out how often war occurred in European history, sociologist Pitirim Sorokin (1937) counted the wars from 500 B.C. to A.D. 1925. He documented 967 wars, an average of one war every two to three years. Counting years or parts of a year in which a country was at war, at 28 percent Germany had the lowest record of warfare, while Spain's 67 percent gave it the dubious distinction of being the most war-prone. Sorokin found that Russia, the land of his birth, had experienced only one peaceful quarter-century during the entire previous one thousand years. Since the time of William the Conqueror, who took power in 1066, England was at war an average of fifty-six out of each one hundred years. As noted, Spain fought even more often. It is worth noting

war: armed conflict between nations or politically distinct groups

Although war is a political act, the politicians who declare war somehow manage to keep themselves away from its carnage. In addition to the loss of human life, such as the victims at Sarajevo, other costs of war are the loss of property and a change in morality called dehumanization.

the history of the United States in this regard: Since 1850, it has intervened militarily around the world more than 150 times, an average of *more than once a year* (Kohn 1988).

Why Nations Go to War

Why do nations choose war to handle disputes? Sociologists answer this question by focusing not on factors *within* humans, such as aggressive impulses, but by looking for *social* causes—conditions in society that encourage or discourage combat between nations.

Sociologist Nicholas Timasheff (1965) identified three essential conditions of war. The first is a cultural tradition of war. Because their nations have fought wars in the past, the leaders of a group see war as an option for dealing with serious disagreements with other nations. The second is an antagonistic situation in which two or more states confront incompatible objectives. For example, each may want the same land or resources. The third is a "fuel" that heats the antagonistic situation to a boiling point, so that people cross the line from thinking about war to actually engaging in it. Timasheff identified seven such "fuels." He found that war is likely if a country's leaders see the antagonistic situation as an opportunity to achieve one of the following objectives:

1 Gain revenge or settle "old scores" from previous conflicts
2 Dictate their will to a weaker nation
3 Enhance their prestige, or save the nation's "honor"
4 Unite rival groups within their country
5 Protect or exalt their own position
6 Satisfy the national aspirations of ethnic groups, bringing under their rule "our people" who are living in another country
7 Forcibly convert others to religious and ideological beliefs

Table 15.3

What U.S. Wars Cost	
War of 1812	$615,000,000
Mexican War	$1,076,000,000
American Revolution	$1,918,000,000
Spanish-American War	$5,961,000,000
Civil War	$45,990,000,000
World War I	$369,580,000,000
Vietnam War	$553,088,000,000
Korean War	$262,062,000,000
World War II	$2,953,716,000,000
TOTAL	$4,194,006,000,000

Note: In the source, the costs are listed in 1967 dollars. To account for inflation, I increased these amounts by 350 percent, and added the costs of service-connected benefits. Where a range was listed, the mean was used.

The costs of the many "military interventions" such as in Grenada, Panama, and Somalia, and Haiti, are not listed in the source—nor is the more expensive "military intervention" on behalf of Kuwait. These costs do *not* include interest payments on war loans, nor are they reduced by the financial benefits to the United States, such as the acquisition of California and Texas in the Mexican War.

Source: Statistical Abstract 1993: Table 553.

Costs of War

One side effect of the industrialization stressed in this text is a growing capacity to inflict death. For example, during World War I bombs claimed fewer than 3 of every 100,000 people in England and Germany. With more powerful airplanes and bombs, accompanied by a diminished sense of it being wrong to kill noncombatants, by World War II this figure increased a hundredfold, to 300 of every 100,000 civilians. Further technological advances in human destruction have so increased our killing capacity that sociologist Hornell Hart (1957) estimated the death rate in a war fought with nuclear bombs at 100,000 per 100,000!

War is also extremely costly in terms of money. As shown in Table 15.3, the United States has spent $4 trillion on nine major wars. In spite of its massive cost in lives and property, warfare continues as a common technique of pursuing political objectives. For about seven years, the United States fought in Vietnam—at a cost of 59,000 American and about two million Vietnamese lives (Herring 1989; Hellinger and Judd 1991). For nine years, the Soviet Union waged war in Afghanistan—with a death toll of about one million Afghanistani and perhaps 20,000 Soviet soldiers (Armitage 1989). An eight-year war between Iran and Iraq cost about 400,000 lives. The total exacted by Cuban mercenaries in Africa and South America is unknown. Also unknown is the number of lives—almost exclusively Iraqi—lost in the brief war against Iraq by international forces led by the United States, although the figure of 100,000 losses on the Iraqi side has been suggested by media reports. Civil wars in Africa have killed hundreds of thousands. At a lower cost in lives, Israel and its Arab neighbors have engaged in a seemingly endless succession of "pre-emptive strikes" followed by "retaliatory measures."

Sowing the Seeds of Future Wars

While expressing concern about regional conflicts that can escalate into larger wars, some industrialized nations relentlessly pursue profits by selling powerful weapons to the developing nations. As Table 15.4 shows, Russia and the United States are the chief merchants of death to the Third World. When one country buys high-tech weapons, its neighbors get nervous, and an arms race is sparked among them (Cole and Lubman 1994; Ricks 1994). The seeds of future wars are also sown by nuclear proliferation, and developing nations such as India and China now have nuclear weapons. Always a threat to the world's safety, atomic weapons in the hands of a dictator can mean nuclear blackmail or nuclear attack to settle personal or nationalistic grudges.

On the positive side, most political analysts believe the cold war is now over. The United States and the former Soviet Union have announced that they no longer aim their nuclear missiles at the other's cities. Nonetheless, these two nations continue to eye each other suspiciously, neither of them wholly convinced that the other has truly peaceful intentions (Sherr 1993). The United States is especially concerned that the democratic reform movement in Russia may be undermined by reactionary politicians seeking to revert to military might, communism, and cold war foreign policies.

War and Dehumanization

War exacts many costs in addition to killing people and destroying property. One is its effect on morality. Exposure to brutality and killing often causes **dehumanization,** the process of reducing people to objects that do not deserve to be treated as humans.

As we review findings on dehumanization and see how it breeds callousness and cruelty, perhaps we can better understand how O'Brien in the opening vignette could have unleashed rats into someone's face, or how the colonel in the opening vignette of Chapter 12 could have unfeelingly sent people to their deaths. Physician-researchers Viola W. Bernard, Perry Ottenberg, and Fritz Redl (1971) identified four characteristics of dehumanization.

1 *Increased emotional distance from others.* People stop identifying with others, no longer seeing them as having basic human qualities similar to themselves. Instead of people, they become subhumans, "the enemy," or objects of some sort.

2 *An emphasis on following procedures.* Regulations become all-important. They are not questioned, for they are seen as a means to an end. People are likely to say, "I don't like this, but it is necessary to follow procedures," or "We all have to die some day. What difference does it make if these people die now?"

3 *Inability to resist pressures.* Fears of losing occupational security, losing the respect of one's peers, or having one's integrity and loyalty questioned take precedence over individual moral decisions.

4 *A diminished sense of personal responsibility.* People come to see themselves as only small cogs in a large machine. They are not responsible for what they do, for they are simply following orders. The higher-ups who give the orders are thought to have more complete or even secret information that justifies the act. They think, "The higher-ups are in a position to judge what is right and wrong, but in my humble place, who am I to question these acts?"

As the enemy comes to be thought of as an object, the conscience grows numb, and even acts of torture become dissociated from a person's "normal self." Brutality and

Table 15.4

The Business of Death

The Largest Arms Sellers	
Russia	$20 billion
United States	$11 billion
Great Britain	$3 billion
France	$3 billion
China	$2 billion
Germany	$1 billion

The Largest Customers	
Saudi Arabia	$4.2 billion
Afghanistan	$3.8 billion
India	$3.5 billion
Greece	$2.0 billion
Iraq	$1.9 billion
Iran	$1.3 billion
Vietnam	$1.3 billion
Cuba	$1.2 billion
Turkey	$1.1 billion
Syria	$1.0 billion

Note: Listed are nations whose sales or purchases total $1 billion or more. Purchases are limited to the developing nations. In the industrialized nations, Japan and the United States each import over $1 billion of weapons a year.

Source: Statistical Abstract 1993: Table 550.

dehumanization: the act or process of reducing people to objects that do not deserve the treatment accorded humans

killing become simply acts that must be done in order to accomplish a job. It is not the individual's responsibility to question whether or not the job should be done—one's responsibility as a soldier is limited to obedience. Torturing and killing are extremely unpleasant, but somehow they fit into the larger scheme of things—and someone has to do such "dirty work." Those who make the decisions are the ones who are responsible, not I, a simple soldier who is merely following orders.

As sociologist Tamotsu Shibutani (1970) stressed, dehumanization is helped along by the tendency for prolonged conflicts to be transformed into a struggle between good and evil. The enemy, of course, represents evil in the equation. To fight against absolute evil sometimes requires the suspension of moral standards—for one is dealing with an abnormal situation, an enemy that is less than human, and the precarious survival of good (Markhusen 1992). War, then, exalts treachery, bribery, and killing—and medals are given to glorify actions that would be condemned in every other context.

As soldiers participate in acts that they, too, would normally condemn, they neutralize their morality. This insulates them from acknowledging their behaviors as evil, which would threaten their self-concept and mental adjustment. Surgeons, highly sensitive to patients' needs in other medical situations, become capable of mentally removing an individual's humanity. By thinking of patients as mere "recipients of surgical techniques," surgeons are able to mutilate them just to study the results. Even torture can become so routine that a man can pause in the middle of torturing someone, take a call from his wife to plan dinner, and then calmly resume torturing his victim (Stockwell 1989).

Dehumanization does not always insulate the self from guilt, however, and its failure to do so can bring severe personal consequences. During the war, while soldiers are surrounded by army buddies who agree that the enemy is less than human and deserves inhuman treatment, such definitions ordinarily remain intact. After returning home, however, the dehumanizing definitions more easily break down. Many soldiers then find themselves seriously disturbed by what they did during the war. Although most eventually adjust, some cannot, for example, the soldier from California who wrote this note before putting a bullet in his head (Smith 1980):

> I can't sleep anymore. When I was in Vietnam, we came across a North Vietnamese soldier with a man, a woman, and a three-or four-year-old girl. We had to shoot them all. I can't get the little girl's face out of my mind. I hope that God will forgive me . . . I can't.

A New World Order?

The historical trend has been for states to grow larger and larger. Today, the embrace of capitalism and the worldwide flow of information, capital, and goods, has rendered national boundaries increasingly meaningless (Robertson 1992; Toffler and Toffler 1993). Not only have the United States, Canada, and Mexico formed a North American free-trade zone (NAFTA), but 117 nations have made an agreement to slash tariffs globally (Davis and Ingrassia 1993). Most European countries have formed an economic and political unit (the European Union) that supersedes their national boundaries. Similarly, the United Nations, transcending national borders and moderating disputes between countries, can authorize the use of international force against individual nations—as it has done against North Korea in 1950, Iraq in 1990, and on a smaller scale, Somalia in 1993 and Bosnia in 1994.

Will this process continue . . . until there is but one state or empire, the earth itself, under the control of one leader? That is a possibility, perhaps deriving not only from these historical trends but also from a push by a powerful group of capitalists who profit from global free trade (Domhoff 1990). Although the trend is in full tilt, even if it continues we are unlikely to see its conclusion during our lifetimes, for national boundaries and na-

▼▲▼

Perspectives

CULTURAL DIVERSITY AROUND THE WORLD

Nations Versus States—Implications for a New World Order

THE WORLD HAS ABOUT five thousand nations. What makes each a *nation* is that its people share a language, culture, territory, and political organization. A *state*, in contrast, claims a monopoly on violence over a territory. A state may contain many nations. The Kaiapo Indians are but one nation within the state called Brazil. The Chippewa and Sioux are two nations within the state called the United States. To nation peoples, group identity transcends political affiliation. The world's five thousand nations have existed for hundreds, some even for thousands of years. In contrast, most of the world's 171 states have been around only since World War II.

All modern states are empires, and they are increasingly seen as such by the nations that have been incorporated into them—usually by force. Some states have far better records than others, but overall, no ideology, left or right, religious or sectarian, has protected nations or promoted pluralism much better or worse than any other. In fact, the twentieth century has probably seen more genocides and ethnocides (the destruction of an ethnic group) than any other.

Clearly, the Palestinians who live within Israel's borders will not soon identify themselves as Israelis. But did you know that the Oromos in Ethiopia have more members than three-quarters of the states in the United Nations, and that they do not think of themselves as Ethiopians? The twenty million Kurds don't consider themselves first and foremost Turks, Iranians, Iraqis, or Syrians. There are about 130 nations in the former USSR, 180 in Brazil, 90 in Ethiopia, 450 in Nigeria, 350 in India. That so many nations are squeezed into so few states is, in fact, the nub of the problem.

In most states, power is in the hands of a few elites, who operate by a simple credo: Winner take all. They control foreign investment and aid, and use both to reinforce their power. They set local commodity prices, control exports, and levy taxes. They confiscate the resources of its nations, whether it be Indian land from North and South America or oil from the Kurds in Iraq. When nations resist, open conflict results.

Nearly all debt in Africa, and nearly half of all other Third World debt, comes from the purchase of weapons by states to fight their own citizens. Most of the world's twelve million refugees are the offspring of such conflicts, as are most of the hundred million internally displaced people who have been uprooted from their homelands. Conflict theorists view most of the colonization, resettlement, and villagization programs sponsored by states as an attempt, in the name of progress, to bring nation peoples to their knees.

A vicious cycle forms. The appropriation of a nation's resources leads to conflict, conflict leads to weapons purchases, weapons purchases lead to debt, and debt leads to the appropriation of more resources—and the cycle intensifies.

Now that the cold war is over, the United States and the former USSR are pulling back on aid to many rulers of Third World states. This is likely to unleash more struggle by nations that sense an opportunity to win greater control over their future. The number of shooting wars may increase just at the time when arms makers and NATO and Warsaw Pact countries are trying to dump obsolete weapons and find markets for new ones.

If nations and states are to peacefully coexist, a political system that is built from the bottom up—one that gives autonomy and power to nation peoples—will have to evolve. Beyond this guiding principle, there is no single model. Weak states with strong nations may break into new states. Newly independent nations, after trying to make a go of it for a while, may decide that it is to their advantage to be part of a larger political unit.

Of one thing we can be certain. The future is likely to be bloody if the world cannot find a better way to answer the demands of its now emboldened nations.

Sources: Clay 1990; Simons 1995.

tional patriotism will die only a hard death. And as borders shift, as occurred with the breakup of the Soviet Union, previously unincorporated nations such as Lithuania and Azerbaijan demand their independence and the right to full statehood. The Perspectives box above explores the rising tensions between nations and states worldwide.

If such global political and economic unity does come about, it is fascinating to speculate on what type of government will result. If Hitler had had his way, his conquests would have resulted in world domination—by a world dictator and a world totalitarian regime based on racial identification. Fortunately, the tendency now is toward greater rights of citizens and greater political participation. If this trend continues—and it is a big "if"—and if a world order does emerge, the potential for human welfare is tremendous. If, however, we end up with totalitarianism, and the world's resources and people come under the control of a dictatorship or an oligarchy, the future for humanity could be extremely bleak.

Summary and Review

Micropolitics and Macropolitics

What is the difference between micropolitics and macropolitics?

The essential nature of politics is **power,** and every group is political. The term **micropolitics** refers to the exercise of power in everyday life, **macropolitics** to large-scale power, such as governing a nation. Pp. 404–405.

Power, Authority, and Coercion

How are authority and coercion related to power?

Authority is power that people view as legitimately exercised over them, while **coercion** is power they consider unjust. The **state** is a political entity that claims a monopoly on violence over a particular territory. If enough people consider a state's power illegitimate, revolution is possible. Pp. 405–407.

Max Weber identified three types of authority. Power in **traditional authority** derives from custom—patterns set down in the past are the rules for the present. Power in **rational-legal authority** (also called *bureaucratic authority*) is based on law and written procedures. In **charismatic authority** power is based on loyalty to an individual to whom people are attracted and give allegiance. Charismatic authority, which undermines traditional and rational-legal authority, has built-in problems in transferring authority to a new leader. Pp. 407–410.

Types of Government

How are the types of government related to power?

In a **monarchy,** power is based on hereditary rule; in a **democracy,** power is given the ruler by citizens; and in a **dictatorship,** power is seized by an individual or small group. Pp. 410–412.

The U.S. Political System

What are the main characteristics of the U.S. political system?

The United States has a "winner take all" system, in which results are determined by a simple majority. Most European democracies, in contrast, have **proportional representation,** with legislative seats divided among political parties according to the percentage of votes each receives. With no single party in power, proportional representation creates the need of coalitions among many political parties, resulting in more frequent changes of government. In the 1992 U.S. presidential election, the strong showing of a third party indicated widespread dissatisfaction with the two dominant parties Pp. 412–414.

Voter turnout is higher among the more socially integrated, those who sense a greater stake in the outcome of elections, such as the more educated and well-to-do. The Great Depression of the 1930s marked a turning point in the U.S. political system. At that time, the government turned away from laissez-faire capitalism and accepted greater responsibility for economic conditions. Lobbyists and special-interest groups, such as **political action committees** (PACs), play a significant role in U.S. politics. Pp. 414–418.

Who Rules the United States?

Is the United States controlled by a ruling class?

Functionalists, in a view known as **pluralism,** say that no one group holds power, that the country's many competing interest groups balance one another. Conflict theorists, who focus on the top level of power, say that the United States is governed by a power elite, a ruling class made up of the top corporate, military, and political leaders. At this point, the matter is not decided. Pp. 418–420.

War: A Means to Implement Political Objectives

How is war related to politics—and what are its costs?

War, common in human history, is a means of attempting to reach political objectives. Because of technological advances in killing, the costs of war in terms of human lives have escalated. The Third World, which can least afford it, spends huge amounts on modern weapons. Another cost is **dehumanization,** whereby people no longer see others as worthy of human treatment. Pp. 421–424.

A New World Order?

Is humanity headed toward a one-world political order?

The global expansion of communications, transportation, and trade, and the trend toward larger political unions may indicate that a world political order is developing. If so, the possible consequences for human welfare range from excellent to calamitous. Pp. 424–425.

Where can I read more on this topic?

Suggested readings for this chapter are listed on page 642.

Carmen Lomas Garza, Sandia/Watermelon, 1986

The Family:
Initiation into Society

O N THIS WET AFTERNOON, A *dozen students, aged 10 to 12, are sitting in a circle at Kennedy Elementary School. They are all children of divorce. "It's called a support group," says the school counselor who meets with the children once a week. Despite the fact that divorce is now regarded as part of the American way of life, these children feel deep discomfort and alienation.*

Tony earnestly explains, "Sometimes you are too scared to tell your friends. You might be ashamed." Flora stares at the floor and adds, "Sometimes they say they are just going on a trip. They lied." Says Helen, "After all, the divorce is as much ours as our parents'."

Any adult who has tried to explain a divorce to a happily married friend will understand what the kids call "the brick wall." Happy people can't believe that the statement "They fight" can mean a father who says, "If I see your mother, I'll kill her"—and means it. And having to carry messages can mean being used as cannon fodder in support check battles.

Money is a big topic. "My father sends $350 a month, and I never get to see any of it," Billy says. "Last night he came over to pick up a lamp, and my mother said, 'Children, your father has just stolen a lamp.'"

The "divorced kids" find the parents' new relationships especially difficult. Julie says, "My mother had this man living in the house. I felt as if I was in the way. She would agree with him about things she would object to if it were just us. Mothers don't want to rock the boat with men." "My father wants to marry this woman," says Tony, "and he takes her kids out for doughnuts on Sunday mornings. It really upsets my sister; he never did that with us."

"Christmas is such a problem," says Janie. "You feel so guilty about the one you're not with." (Based on O'Reilly 1979)

Although husbands and wives often hurt one another during divorce, children are the real victims. They feel helpless and betrayed, caught between two people they love—but who can't stand each other. For them, the future is uncertain, the present unbearable.

Many feel that the real tragedy of divorce is children suffering from their parents' mistakes. Ruptured relationships between husbands and wives and between parents and their children—accompanied by feelings of betrayal, guilt, and anxiety—are symptoms of a major upheaval in the family today. The U.S. divorce rate, the highest in the industrialized world, is one aspect of marriage and family that we explore in this chapter.

Marriage and Family in Global Perspective

To better understand U.S. patterns of marriage and family, let's first sketch a cross-cultural portrait. The perspective it yields will give us a context for interpreting our own experience in this vital social institution.

Defining Family

"What is a family, anyway?" asked William Sayres (1992) at the beginning of an article on this topic. By this question, he meant that although the family is so significant to humans that it is universal—every human group in the world organizes its members in families—the world's cultures display so much variety that the term *family* is difficult to define. For example, although the Western world regards a family as consisting of a husband, wife, and children, other groups have family forms in which men have more than one wife (**polygyny**) or women more than one husband (**polyandry**). To define the family as the approved group into which children are born overlooks the Banaro of New Guinea. Among this group a young woman must give birth before she can marry, and she cannot marry the father of her child (Murdock 1949).

polygyny: a marriage in which a man has more than one wife

polyandry: a marriage in which a woman has more than one husband

430

And so it goes. For just about every element you might consider essential to marriage or family, some group has a different custom. Even the sex of the bride and groom may not be what you expect. Although in almost every instance the bride and groom are female and male, though rare, there are exceptions. In some Native American tribes, for example, a man or woman who wanted to be a member of the opposite sex went through a ceremony (*berdache*) and was *declared* a member of the opposite sex. From then on, not only did the "new" man or woman do the tasks associated with his or her new sex, but the individual also was allowed to marry. In this instance, the husband and wife were of the same biological sex. In the contemporary Western world, Denmark legalized homosexual marriages in 1992.

Even to say that the family is the unit in which children are disciplined and their parents are responsible for their material needs is not universally true. Among the Trobriand Islanders, the wife's eldest brother is responsible for making certain that his sister's children are fed and are properly disciplined when they get out of line (Malinowski 1927). Finally, even sexual relationships don't universally characterize a husband and wife. The Nayar of Malabar never *allow* a bride and groom to have sex. After a three-day celebration of the marriage, they send the groom packing—and never allow him to see his bride again (La Barre 1954). (In case you are wondering, the groom comes from another tribe, and Nayar women are allowed to have sex, but only with approved lovers—who can never be the husband. This system keeps family property intact—along matrilineal lines.)

Such remarkable variety means settling for a very broad definition. A **family** consists of two or more people who consider themselves related by blood, marriage, or adoption. A **household,** in contrast, consists of all people who occupy the same housing unit—a house, apartment, or other living quarters.

We can classify families as **nuclear** (husband, wife, and children) and **extended** (including people such as grandparents, aunts, uncles, and cousins in addition to the nuclear unit). There are also the **family of orientation** (the family in which an individual grows up) and the **family of procreation** (the family formed when a couple have their first child). Finally, regardless of its form, **marriage** can be viewed as a group's approved mating arrangements—usually marked out by a ritual of some sort (the wedding) to indicate the couple's new public status.

family: two or more people who consider themselves related by blood, marriage, or adoption

household: all people who occupy the same housing unit

nuclear family: a family consisting of a husband, wife, and child(ren)

extended family: a nuclear family plus other relatives, such as grandparents, uncles and aunts, who live together

family of orientation: the family in which a person grows up

family of procreation: the family formed when a couple's first child is born

marriage: a group's approved mating arrangements, usually marked by a ritual of some sort

Because who marries whom is important for society—not simply for the bride and groom—the human group sets up rules about who should marry whom, and then channels its members into its expectations. The norms that surround these newlyweds in Java may differ from those in the West, but they, too, function to channel mate selection, control sexuality, regulate child birth and inheritance, and so on.

Most Americans follow patterns of endogamy and marry someone whose race-ethnicity, religion, age, and social class are similar to their own. Marriages between African Americans and whites have increased in recent years.

Common Cultural Themes

In spite of this diversity, several common themes do run through marriage and family. All societies use marriage and family to establish patterns of mate selection, descent, inheritance, and authority. These patterns differ considerably between traditional and industrial societies, as illustrated on Table 16.1.

Patterns of Mate Selection   Each human group establishes norms to govern who marries whom. Norms of **endogamy** (such as those prohibiting interracial marriages) specify that people should marry within their own group, while norms of **exogamy** (such as the incest taboo) specify that they must marry outside their group. In some societies these norms are written into law, but in most cases they are informal. For example, in the United States most whites marry whites and most African Americans marry African Americans not because of any laws but because of informal norms. (For patterns of "outmarriage" in the United States, see Figure 12.11 on page 337.)

Patterns of Descent   How are you related to your father's father or to your mother's mother? The explanation is found in your society's **system of descent,** the pattern by which people trace kinship over generations. It certainly seems logical—and natural—to think of ourselves as related to people on both sides of the family, but this is only one of three logical ways to reckon descent. In the **bilateral** system, descent is traced on both the mother's and the father's side. In a **patrilineal** system, descent is traced only on the father's side, and children are not considered related to their mother's relatives. In a **matrilineal** system, descent is figured only on the mother's side, and children are not considered related to their father's relatives.

Patterns of Inheritance   A primary reason that all societies regulate mate selection and descent is the desire to provide an orderly way of passing property and other rights to the next generation. Marriage and family—in whatever form is customary in a society—are used to trace descent and to compute rights of inheritance. In the bilateral system, property is passed to both males and females, in the patrilineal system only to males, and in the matrilineal system (the rarest form) only to females. Each system matches a people's ideas of justice and logic.

Patterns of Authority   Historically, some form of **patriarchy,** a social system in which men dominate women, has formed a thread running through all societies. As noted in

endogamy: the practice of marrying within one's own group

exogamy: the practice of marrying outside one's group

system of descent: how kinship is traced over the generations

bilateral: (system of descent) a system of reckoning descent that counts both the mother's and the father's side

patrilineal: (system of descent) a system of reckoning descent that counts only the father's side

matrilineal (system of descent): a system of reckoning descent that counts only the mother's side

patriarchy: authority vested in males; male control of a society or group

Table 16.1

Marriage in Traditional and Industrial Societies

Characteristic	Traditional Societies	Industrial Societies
What is the structure of marriage?	Extended (marriage embeds spouses in a large kinship network of explicit obligations)	Nuclear (marriage brings fewer obligations toward spouse's kin)
What are the functions of marriage?	Encompassing (see the six functions listed on pp. 23–24)	More limited (many functions fulfilled by other social institutions)
Who holds authority?	Highly *patriarchal* (authority is held by males)	Although patriarchal features remain, authority is more evenly divided
How many spouses at one time?	Most have one spouse (*monogamy*), while some have several (*polygamy*)	One spouse
Who selects the spouse?	The spouse is selected by the parents, usually the father	Bride and groom choose their own spouse
Where does the couple live?	Couples most commonly reside with the groom's family (*patrilocal residence*), less commonly with the bride's family (*matrilocal residence*)	Couples establish a new home (*neolocal residence*)
How is descent figured?	Most commonly figured from male ancestors (*patrilineal kinship*); less commonly from female ancestors (*matrilineal kinship*)	Figured from male and female ancestors equally (*bilateral kinship*)
How is inheritance figured?	Rigid system of rules; either patrilineal or matrilineal	Highly individualistic; usually bilateral

Chapter 11, there are no historical records of a true **matriarchy,** a social system in which women dominate men. Our marriage and family customs, then, developed within a framework of patriarchy. Although family patterns in the United States are becoming more **egalitarian,** or equal, many customs practiced today still point to their patriarchal origin. Naming patterns, for example, reflect patriarchy. In spite of recent trends, the typical bride still takes the groom's last name; children, too, are usually given the father's last name. For information on a society that systematically promotes equality in marriage, see the Perspectives box on the next page.

Marriage and Family in Theoretical Perspective

The picture that emerges from a cross-cultural perspective, then, is that our own forms of marriage and family are just one of a wide variety of patterns that humans have chosen. Let's see what picture emerges when we apply the three sociological theories.

The Functionalist Perspective: Functions and Dysfunctions

As noted in Chapter 1, functionalists stress that to survive, a society must meet certain basic needs, or functions. When functionalists look at family, they examine how it is related to other parts of society, especially how it contributes to the well-being of society.

matriarchy: authority vested in females; female control of a society or group

egalitarian: authority more or less equally divided between people or groups, in this instance between husband and wife

Why the Family Is Universal As described on pages 23–24, the family serves six essential functions: (1) economic production; (2) socialization of children; (3) care of the sick and aged; (4) recreation; (5) sexual control; and (6) reproduction. Functionalists note that although the form of marriage and family may vary from one group to another, the fulfillment of these needs is so essential for society's well-being that *the family is universal*. That is, to make certain that these functions are performed, every human group has found it necessary to adopt some form of the family.

Functions of the Incest Taboo Functionalists have noted that the **incest taboo**—rules specifying which people are too closely related to have sex or to marry—helps families avoid role confusion. This, in turn, facilitates the socialization of children. If father–daughter incest were allowed, for example, consider how it would complicate family roles. For example, how should a wife treat her daughter—as a daughter, as a subservient second wife, or even as a rival? And should the daughter see her mother as a mother or as a rival wife? And would her father be a father or a lover? And would the wife be the husband's main wife, a secondary wife—or even "the mother of the other wife" (whatever role that might be)? Maternal incest would also lead to complications every bit as confusing as these (Henslin 1975).

> **incest taboo:** rules specifying the degrees of kinship that prohibit sex or marriage

---

Perspectives

CULTURAL DIVERSITY AROUND THE WORLD

Family Life in Sweden

SWEDISH LAWMAKERS HOLD A strong image of what good family life is. That image is of total equality in marriage and the welfare of children. They bolster this image with laws designed to put women and men on equal footing in marriage, to have mothers and fathers share responsibility for the home and children, and to protect the financially weaker party in the event of divorce or death.

At the center of family laws is the welfare of children. Health care for mothers and children, for example, is free of charge. This includes all obstetric care and all health care during pregnancy. Maternity centers offer free health checks and courses in preparation for childbirth. Fathers are also encouraged to attend the childbirth classes.

When a child is born, the parents are offered fifteen months' leave of absence with pay. The leave and compensation are available for either or both parents. Both cannot receive compensation at the same time, and the parents decide how they will split the leave between them. For the first twelve months the state pays 90 percent of gross income, and then a generous fixed rate for the remaining three months. The paid leave does not have to be taken all at once, but can be spread over eight years. The parents can stay at home full time, or they can work part time for a longer period. Parents who are not employed at the birth of a child receive a fixed amount for fifteen months.

The government also guarantees other benefits. All fathers are entitled to ten days leave of absence with full pay when a child is born. When a child is sick, either parent can care for the child and receive full pay for missed work—up to sixty days a year per child. Moreover, by law local governments must offer child care. And if a husband becomes violent or threatens his wife, the woman can have a security alarm installed in their home free of charge.

The divorce laws have also been drawn up with a view to what is best for the child. Local governments are required to provide free counseling to any parent who requests it. If both parties agree and if they have no children under the age of 16, a couple is automatically entitled to a divorce. Otherwise the law requires a six-month cooling-off period, so they can more calmly consider what is best for their children. Joint custody of children is automatic, unless one of the parents opposes it. The children may live only with one of the parents. The parent who does not live with the children is required to pay child support in proportion to his or her finances. If the parent fails to do so, the social security system makes the payments.

What do you think? How does the Swedish system compare with that of the United States? What "system" for watching out for the welfare of children does the United States have, anyway?

Source: Based on The Swedish Institute 1992.

Another function of the incest taboo is to force people to look outside the family for marriage partners (Degler 1991). Anthropologists theorize that exogamy was especially functional in primitive societies, for it forged alliances between tribes that otherwise might have killed each other off. Today, exogamy extends a bride's and groom's social networks beyond the nuclear family, building relationships with their spouse's family.

Shifting Foundations of the Family Functionalists also examine the family's dysfunctions. As noted in Chapter 1, by eroding some of the family's traditional functions, industrialization made the family more fragile. To weaken the family's functions is to weaken the "ties that bind" and to lessen the reasons for a family to struggle together against hardships. One consequence is higher divorce, and—as seen in our opening vignette—the pain experienced by the children of divorce. From the functionalist perspective, then, increased divorce does not represent "incompatible personalities" but a shifting foundation of the family itself.

Isolation and Emotional Overload Functionalists also analyze the dysfunctions that arise from the relative isolation of the nuclear family. Unlike members of extended families, who are enmeshed in kinship networks, members of nuclear families can count on fewer people for material and emotional support. This makes the members of a nuclear family vulnerable to "emotional overload." That is, because the stress that comes with crises such as the loss of a job or extended illness is spread around fewer people, greater strain is placed on each family member (Zakuta 1989; DiGiulio 1992). In addition, the relative isolation of the nuclear family makes it vulnerable to a "dark side"—incest and various other forms of abuse, matters that we examine later in this chapter.

The Conflict Perspective: Gender, Conflict, and Power

Conflict theorists focus on how the economic institution affects family life. Of the many aspects of family life that we could examine, let's look at how gender relations are being affected by families having two paychecks.

Power Struggles and Housework Among the consequences of married women working for pay is a reshuffling of power in the home. A husband who is the family's sole breadwinner tends to make most of the family's major decisions. When a wife goes to work for wages, however, along with her paycheck comes increased power in the family. Apparently a working wife no longer has to put up with her husband being so dominating, for her income gives her alternatives (Waite and Goldschneider 1992; Wright et al. 1992).

Sociologists Philip Blumstein and Pepper Schwartz (1985) point out that traditional roles used to provide clear answers about marital life—who should earn the living, do the home repairs, clean the house, bathe the children, do the cooking, and initiate the sex. Today, couples must work out these areas of married life for themselves. The absence of clear guidelines leads to an ongoing struggle between wives and husbands.

How to divide up housework is a special problem. The most common solution? Working wives do almost all the housework, as shown on Figure 16.1, based on a representative national sample of dual-earner marriages. As the researchers point out, even when wives do 81 percent of the cooking, 78 percent of the cleaning, and so on, the husbands are likely to see themselves as splitting the work fifty–fifty (Galinsky et al. 1993).

In her research, sociologist Arlie Hochschild (1989) found that in the *typical* case, after returning home from an eight-hour day of work for wages, the wife puts in a "second shift" doing cooking, cleaning, and child care. She calculated the difference in time spent on housework and found that wives in two-paycheck families average fifteen hours more work each week than their husbands. This means that wives work an *extra month of twenty-four-hour days a year.* Hochschild (1989) quoted the one-sided nature of the second shift as satirized by Garry Trudeau in the Doonesbury comic strip:

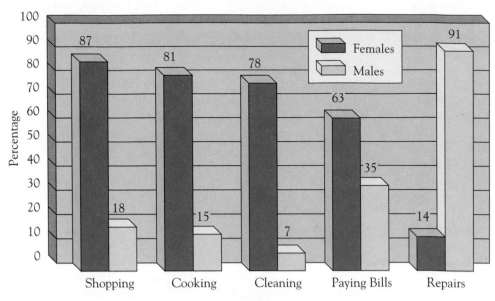

Source: Galinsky et al. 1993.

Figure 16.1

In Dual-Earner Families, Who says That They Have The Greater Responsibility for the Housework?

> A "liberated" father is sitting at his word processor writing a book about raising his child. He types: "Today I wake up with a heavy day of work ahead of me. As Joannie gets Jeffry ready for day care, I ask her if I can be relieved of my usual household responsibilities for the day. Joannie says, 'Sure, I'll make up the five minutes somewhere.'"

Not surprisingly, the burden of the second shift has created deep discontent among wives. These problems, as well as how wives and husbands cope with them, are discussed in the following Thinking Critically section.

▼△▼△▼△▼△▼△▼△▼△▼△▼△▼△▼△▼△▼△▼

Thinking Critically About Social Controversy

The Second Shift—Strains and Strategies

▼ To FIND OUT WHAT life is like in two-paycheck families, for nine years sociologist Arlie Hochschild (1989) and her research associates interviewed and reinterviewed fifty-odd families. Hochschild also did participant observation with a dozen of them. She "shopped with them, visited friends, watched television, ate with them, walked through parks, and came along when they dropped their children at day care."

Hochschild notes that women have no more time in a day than when they stayed home, but that now there is twice as much to get done. Most wives and husbands in her sample felt that the second shift—the household duties that follow the day's work for pay—is the wife's responsibility. But as they cook, vacuum, and take care of the children after their job in the office or factory, many wives feel overtired, emotionally drained, and resentful. Not uncommonly, these feelings show up in the bedroom, where the wives show a lack of interest in sex.

It isn't that men do nothing around the house. But since they see household responsibilities as the wife's duty, they "help out" when they feel like it—or when they get nagged into it. And since most of us prefer to tend to our children than clean house, men are more likely to "help out" on the second shift by taking children to do "fun" things—to see movies, or to go for outings in the park. In contrast, the woman's time with the children is more likely to be "maintenance"—feeding and bathing them, taking them to the doctor, and so on.

The strains from working the second shift affect not only the marital relationship, but also the self-concept. Here is how one woman tried to buoy her flagging self-esteem:

> After taking time off for her first baby, Carol Alston felt depressed, "fat," "just a housewife," and for a while became the supermarket shopper who wanted to call down the aisles, "I'm an MBA! I'm an MBA!"

Most wives feel strongly that the second shift should be shared, but many feel that it is hopeless to try to get their husbands to change. They work the second shift, but they resent it. Others have a "showdown" with their husbands, some even giving the ultimatum, "It's share the second shift, or it's divorce." Still others try to be the "supermom" who can do it all.

Some men cooperate and cut down on their commitment to a career. Others cut back on movies, seeing friends, doing hobbies. Most men, however, engage in what Hochschild describes as strategies of resistance. She identifies the following:

- *Playing dumb.* When they do housework, some men become incompetent. They can't cook rice without burning it; when they go to the store, they forget grocery lists; they can never remember where the broiler pan is. Hochschild did not claim that men do these things purposely, but rather that by withdrawing their mental attention from the task, they "get credit for trying and being a good sport"—but in such a way that they are not chosen next time.
- *Waiting it out.* Many men never volunteer, forcing their wives to ask them to do household chores. Since many wives dislike asking because it feels like "begging," this strategy often works. Some men make this strategy even more effective by showing irritation or becoming glum when they are asked, discouraging the wife from asking again.
- *Needs reduction.* An example of this strategy is a father of two who explained that he never shopped because he didn't "need anything." He didn't need to iron his clothes because he "[didn't] mind wearing a wrinkled shirt." He didn't need to cook because "cereal is fine." As Hochschild observed, "Through his reduction of needs, this man created a great void into which his wife stepped with her 'greater need' to see him wear an ironed shirt . . . take his shirts to the cleaners . . . and cook his dinner."
- *Substitute offerings.* Expressing appreciation to the wife for being so organized that she can handle both work for wages and the second shift at home can be a substitute for helping—and subtly encouraging the wife to keep on working the second shift.

Hochschild (1991) is confident that such problems can be solved. Use these materials to:

1. Identify the underlying social causes of the problem of the second shift.
2. Based on your answer to number 1, identify social solutions to this problem.
3. Determine how a working wife and husband might best reconcile this problem. ▲

The Symbolic Interactionist Perspective: Marital Communication

As noted in Chapter 1, symbolic interactionists focus on the meanings that people give their relationships. Let's look at the importance of talk in marriage, and how differently husbands and wives perceive their marriages.

The Importance of Talk Even if newlyweds have grown up in the same society, *she* has learned a world of feminine expectations, *he* a world of masculine ones. In marriage, the new couple must merge these two worlds, not an altogether easy task. As sociologists Peter Berger and Hansfried Kellner (1992) note, conversation is the primary means by which a couple unite their separate worlds. By talking about their experiences, a couple share their ideas and feelings. The more they talk to each other, the more their perceptions and ideas merge. Talking allows a couple to see things from closer perspectives, helping them to overcome the separateness that society creates by throwing males and females into different corners of life.

Talk is also an essential part of what sociologists call **emotional labor,** the building of intimacy by sharing deeply personal thoughts and feelings. Sociologists have found that women not only do most of the housework, but also most of the couples' emotional labor. When a husband's stress increases, wives typically increase their emotional

emotional labor: efforts to maintain intimacy, such as listening, being attentive to another's emotional needs, and sharing deep, personal thoughts, feelings, and aspirations

support, but when the wife's stress grows most husbands do not do the same (Tingey et al. 1993). As a consequence, men are more likely to depend on their wives for emotional support, while wives are more likely to depend on family and friends for theirs.

Two Marriages in One   Although talking may bring spouses closer to one another, huge gulfs often exist in their world. In a classic work, sociologist Jessie Bernard (1972) wrote that when researchers

> ask husbands and wives identical questions about the union they often get quite different replies. There is usually agreement on the number of children they have and a few other such verifiable items, although not, for example, on length of premarital acquaintance and of engagement, on age at marriage and interval between marriage and birth of first child. Indeed, with respect to even such basic components of the marriage as frequency of sexual relations, social interaction, household tasks, and decision making, they seem to be reporting on different marriages.

At first the researchers thought these differences were due to methodological flaws. They felt that if they could develop better ways to interview couples, the answers of husbands and wives would agree. Gradually, however, the researchers concluded that a husband and a wife hold down such different corners in a marriage that they perceive the marriage differently. As we just observed, for example, wives and husbands disagree about how much housework they do. In fact, their experiences contrast so sharply that *every marriage contains two separate marriages:* the wife's and the husband's.

With regard to sexual relations, for example, why—since the husband and wife are referring to the same instances of making love—wouldn't they agree on such a basic matter as how frequently they have sex? The answer lies in differing *perceptions* of lovemaking. It appears that in the typical marriage the wife desires greater emotional involvement from her husband, while the husband's desire is for more sex (Komter 1989; Barbeau 1992). When questioned about sex, then, the husband, feeling deprived, tends to underestimate it, while the wife, more reluctant to participate in sex because of unsatisfied intimacy needs, overestimates it (Bernard 1972).

The Family Life Cycle

Thus far we have seen that the forms of marriage and family vary widely and have examined marriage and family from the three sociological perspectives. We now discuss the family life cycle, diversity and trends in U.S. families, divorce, and remarriage. We shall also look at the "dark side" of families and, finally, examine what makes marriage work.

Love and Courtship

Until recently, social scientists thought that romantic love originated in western Europe during the medieval period (Mount 1992). Anthropologists William Jankowiak and Edward Fischer (1992), however, surveyed the data available on 166 societies around the world. They found that **romantic love**—people being sexually attracted to one another and idealizing the other—showed up in 88 percent (147) of these groups. The role of love, however, differs sharply from one society to another. As the Perspectives box on the next page details, for example, Indians don't expect love to occur until *after* marriage—if then.

Because love plays such a significant role in Western life—and is often thought to be the *only* proper basis for marriage—social scientists have probed this concept with the tools of the trade—laboratory experiments, questionnaires, interviews, and systematic observations. One of the more interesting experiments was conducted by

romantic love: feelings of erotic attraction accompanied by an idealization of the other

Perspectives

CULTURAL DIVERSITY AROUND THE WORLD

East Is East and West Is West . . . : Love and Arranged Marriage in India

AFTER ARUN BHARAT RAM returned home with a degree from the University of Michigan, his mother announced that she wanted to find him a wife. Arun would be a good "catch" anywhere: 27 years old, good education, well mannered, intelligent, handsome—and, not incidentally, heir to one of the largest fortunes in India. Nonetheless, Arun would not consider selecting a wife on his own.

Arun's mother already had someone in mind. Manju, who came from a solid, middle-class family, was also a college graduate. Arun and Manju met in a coffee shop in a luxury hotel—along with both sets of parents. He found her pretty and quiet. He liked that. She was impressed that he didn't boast about his background.

After four more meetings, one with the two alone, the parents asked their children if they were willing to marry. Neither had any major objections.

The Prime Minister of India and fifteen hundred other guests came to the wedding.

"I didn't love him," Manju says. "But when we talked, we had a lot of things in common." She then adds, "But now I couldn't live without him. I've never thought of another man since I met him."

Although India has undergone extensive social change, Indian sociologists estimate that about 95 percent of marriages are still arranged by the parents. Today, however, as with Arun and Manju, couples have veto power over their parents' selection. Another innovation is that the couple are allowed to talk to each other before the wedding—unheard of just a generation ago.

The fact that arranged marriages are the norm in India does not mean that this ancient land is without a tradition of passion and love. Far from it. The *Kamasutra* is worldrenowned for its explicit details about lovemaking, and the erotic sculptures at Khajuraho still startle Westerners today. Indian mythology extols the copulations of gods, and every Indian schoolchild knows the love story of the god Krishna

and Radha, the beautiful milkmaid he found irresistible.

Why, then, does India have arranged marriages, and why does this practice persist today, even among the educated and upper classes? We can also ask why the United States has such an individualistic approach to marriage.

To answer these questions takes us to a basic sociological principle—that a group's marriage practices match its values. Individual mate selection matches U.S. values of individuality and independence, while arranged marriages match Indian ideals of children deferring to parental authority. In addition, arranged marriages reaffirm caste lines by channeling marriage within the same caste.

To Indians, to practice unrestricted dating would be to trust important matters to inexperienced young people. It would encourage premarital sex, which, in turn, would break down family lines that virginity at marriage assures the upper castes. Consequently, Indian young people are socialized to think that parents have cooler heads and superior wisdom in these matters. In the United States, family lines are much less important, and caste is an alien concept.

Even ideas of love differ. For Indians, love is a peaceful emotion, based on long-term commitment and devotion to family. Indians also think of love as something that can be "created" between two people. To do so, one needs to arrange the right conditions—and marriage is one of those right conditions.

Thus, Indian and U.S. cultures have produced not just different, but opposite, approaches to love and marriage. For Indians, marriage produces love—while for Americans, love produces marriage. Americans see love as having a mysterious element, a passion that "grabs" the individual. Indians see love as a peaceful feeling that develops when a man and a woman are united in intimacy and share common interests and goals in life.

Sources: Based on Cooley 1962; Gupta 1979; Weintraub 1988; Bumiller 1992; Sprecher and Chandak 1992; Whyte 1992.

psychologists Donald Dutton and Arthur Aron who discovered that fear breeds love (Rubin 1985). Across a rocky gorge, about 230 feet above the Capilano River in North Vancouver, a rickety footbridge sways in the wind. Another footbridge, a solid structure, crosses only ten feet above a shallow stream. An attractive female approached men who were crossing these bridges, asking if they would take part in her study of "the effects of exposure to scenic attractions on creative expression." She showed them a picture, and they wrote down their associations. The researchers, who measured the sexual imagery in the men's stories, found that the men on the unsteady, frightening bridge were more sexually aroused than the men on the solid bridge. They were also more likely to call the young woman afterward—supposedly to get more information about the study.

Shown here is part of the largest wedding in history, the marriage of 25,000 couples from 120 countries in August 1992. Rev. Moon, head of the Reunification Church, used dossiers on these couples to make the matches. Most of the couples were married via satellite.

This research, of course, was really about sexual attraction, not love. The point, however, is that romantic love is usually initiated by sexual attraction. We find ourselves sexually attracted to someone and spend time with that person. If we discover mutual interests, we may eventually label our feelings "love." Apparently, then, romantic love has two components. The first is emotional, a feeling of sexual attraction. The second is cognitive, a label that we attach to our feelings. If we do attach this label, we describe ourselves as being "in love."

Marriage

In the typical case, marriage in the United States is preceded by "love," but contrary to folklore, whatever love is, it certainly is not blind. That is, love does not hit anyone willy-nilly, as if Cupid had shot darts blindly into a crowd. If it did, marital patterns would be practically unpredictable. An examination of who marries whom, however, reveals that love is socially channeled.

The Social Channels of Love and Marriage.   When we marry, we generally think that we have freely chosen our spouse. With very few exceptions, however, our choices follow highly predictable social channels, especially age, education, social class, race, and religion (Tucker and Mitchell-Kerman 1990; Kalmijn 1991). For example, a Latina with a college degree whose parents are both physicians is likely to fall in love and marry a Latino male slightly older than herself who has graduated from college. Similarly, a female high school dropout whose parents are on welfare is likely to fall in love with and marry a male who comes from a background similar to hers.

As with all social patterns, there are exceptions. Although 95 percent of all Americans marry someone of their same race, this means that 5 percent do not. Since there are 53 million married couples in the United States, those 5 percent add up, totaling two and a half million couples. As we saw in Figure 12.11 on page 337, Asian Americans are the most likely to marry someone of a different race, white Americans the least likely to do so. There is no doubt that interracial marriages have become more acceptable. For example, during the past twenty years or so the number of married couples increased only 20 percent, but the number of marriages between African Americans and whites almost quadrupled. This total is still relatively small, however, representing only 246,000 of the 53 million U.S. married

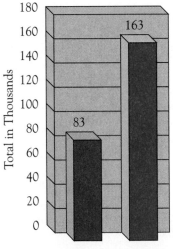

White husband, African–American wife

African–American husband, white wife

Source: Statistical Abstract 1993: Table 63.

Figure 16.2

The Racial Background of Husbands and Wives in Marriages Between Whites and African Americans

couples (*Statistical Abstract* 1993: Table 63). As shown on Figure 16.2, these marriages, in turn, have their own distinct pattern.

Sociologists use the term **homogamy** to refer to the tendency of people with similar characteristics to marry one another. Homogamy occurs largely as a result of *propinquity*, or spatial nearness. That is, we tend to "fall in love" and marry people who live near us or whom we meet at school, church, or work. The persons with whom we associate are far from a random sample of the population, for social filters produce neighborhoods, schools, and churches that follow racial and social class lines.

Childbirth

Sociologist Martin Whyte (1992), who interviewed wives in the greater Detroit area, found that marital satisfaction usually decreases with the birth of a child. To explain why, recall from Chapter 6 that a dyad (just two persons) provides greater intimacy than a triad (after adding a third person, interaction must be shared). To move from the theoretical to the practical, think about the implications of coping with a newborn—heavy expenses, less free time (feeding, soothing, and diaper changing), a lot less sleep, even a decrease in sexual relations (Rubenstein 1992).

Sociologist Lillian Rubin (1976, 1992b) compared fifty working-class couples with twenty-five middle-class couples. She found that social class is a key to how couples adjust to the arrival of children. For the average working-class couple, the first baby arrived just nine months after marriage. They hardly had time to adjust to being husband and wife before they were thrust into the demanding roles of mother and father. The result was financial problems, bickering, and interference from in-laws. The young husbands weren't ready to "settle down" and resented getting less attention from their wives. A working-class husband who became a father just five months after getting married made a telling statement to Rubin when he said, "There I was, just a kid myself, and I finally had someone *to take care of me*. Then suddenly, I had to take care of a kid, and she was too busy with him *to take care of me*" (italics added).

In contrast, the middle-class couples postponed the birth of the first child, which gave them more time to adjust to each other. On average, their first baby arrived three years after marriage. Their greater financial resources also worked in their favor, making life a lot easier and marriage more pleasant.

Child Rearing

Who's minding the kids while the parents are at work? A while back such a question would have been ridiculous, for the mother was at home taking care of the children. Now that three of five mothers work for wages, that assumption no longer holds. With so many mothers employed, who, then, is taking care of the children?

A national survey provides the answer. Figure 16.3 compares the child care arrangements of married couples and single mothers. As you can see, their overall child care arrangements are quite similar. For each, about one-third of preschoolers is cared for in the child's home. The main difference is the role of the child's father while the mother is at work. For married couples, almost one of four children is cared for by the father, while for single mothers such child care plummets to only one of fourteen. As you can see, grandparents step in to help fill the gap left by the absent father.

Sociologists have identified "gender styles" in parenting. As you might know, when it comes to talking to children about sex, fathers talk to the sons and mothers to the daughters. But researchers have found that fathers discuss with their sons only about a third of the topics that the mothers discuss with their daughters (Nolin and Petersen 1992). Play also shows gender styles. Fathers are much more likely to wrestle and roughhouse with the young children, while mothers tend to be more verbal and to play quieter games such as "peek-a-boo" (Easterbrooks and Goldberg 1984). Play is not a meaningless

homogamy: the tendency of people with similar characteristics to marry one another

Figure 16-3

Who Takes Care of Preschoolers While the Mother Is at Work?

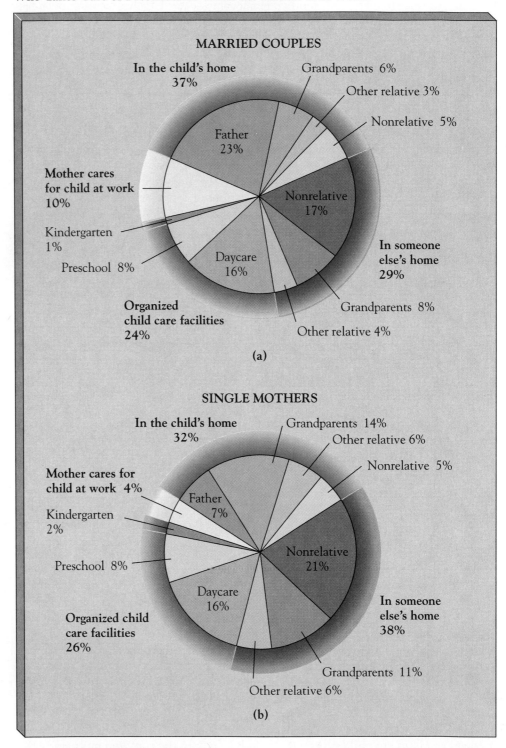

Source: O'Connell 1993.

activity, and distinct gender styles teach children to associate different kinds of behaviors with each sex and to adopt those themselves.

Birth order is also significant. Parents tend to discipline their firstborns more than their other children, and to give them more attention. When the second child arrives, the firstborn competes to maintain the attention. Researchers suggest that this instills in firstborns a greater drive for success, which is why they are more likely than their siblings to earn higher grades in school, to go to college, and to go further in college. Firstborns are even more likely to become astronauts, to appear on the cover of *Time* magazine, and to become president of the United States. Although subsequent children may not go as far, most are less anxious about being successful, and more relaxed in their relationships (Forer 1976; White et al. 1979; Snow et al. 1981; Goleman 1985).

Social class is also important in child rearing. As noted on pages 74–75 sociologist Melvin Kohn found that parents of each class socialize their children into the norms of their respective work worlds. Because members of the working class are more closely supervised and are expected to follow explicit rules laid down for them by others, their concern is less with their children's motivation and more with outward conformity. They are more apt to use physical punishment. In contrast, middle-class parents, who are expected to take more initiative on the job, are more concerned that their children develop curiosity, self-expression, and self-control. They are more likely to withdraw privileges or affection than to use physical punishment.

Some analysts are concerned that U.S. children are pressured into growing up too quickly. Psychologist David Elkind (1981) coined the term "hurried child" to describe the process in which social pressures from the family, school, and the mass media encourage children to take on roles beyond their age. As a consequence, many children no longer look like children; they wear clothing, hairstyles, makeup, and jewelry that make them look older. Many analysts are especially concerned that young children are exposed to highly violent and explicitly sexual television programs, videos, and music. The consequences of "hurrying" children in this way are yet to be seen.

The Family in Later Life

The later stages of family life bring their own pleasures to be savored and problems to be solved. Let's look at the empty nest, retirement, and widowhood.

The Empty Nest When the last child leaves home, the husband and wife are left, as at the beginning of their marriage, "alone together." This situation, sometimes called the **empty nest,** is thought to signal a difficult time of adjustment for women—especially those who have not worked outside the home—because they have devoted so much energy to a child-rearing role that is now gone. Sociologist Lillian Rubin (1992), who interviewed both career women and homemakers, found that this picture is largely a myth. Contrary to the stereotype, she found that women's satisfaction generally *increases* when the last child leaves home. A typical statement was made by a 45-year-old woman, who leaned forward in her chair as though to tell Rubin a secret.

> To tell you the truth, most of the time it's a big relief to be free of them, finally. I suppose that's awful to say. But you know what, most of the women I know feel the same way. It's just that they're uncomfortable saying it because there's all this talk about how sad mothers are supposed to be when the kids leave home.

Similar findings have come from other researchers, who report that most mothers feel relieved at finally being able to spend more time on themselves (Whyte 1992). Many couples also report a renewed sense of companionship at this time (Kalish 1982). This closeness appears to stem from four causes: (1) the couple is free of the many responsibilities of child rearing; (2) they have more leisure; (3) their income is at its highest; and (4) their financial obligations are reduced.

empty nest: a married couple's domestic situation after the last child has left home

The Not-So-Empty Nest   An interesting twist on leaving home has taken place in recent years. With prolonged education, an uncertain job market, and a growing cost of establishing households, U.S. children are leaving home later (Goldscheider and Goldscheider 1994). In addition, many who struck out on their own have found the cost or responsibility too great and are returning to the home nest. As a result, 54 percent of all U.S. 18-to 24-year-olds live with their parents, and one of eight 25-to 34-year-olds is still living at home (*Statistical Abstract* 1993: Table 72).

Widowhood   Women are more likely than men to face the problem of adjusting to widowhood, for not only does the average woman live longer than a man but she has also married a man older than herself. The death of a spouse is a wrenching away of identities that have merged through the years (DiGiulio 1992). Now that the one who had become an essential part of the self is gone, the survivor, as in adolescence, is forced once again to wrestle with the perplexing question, "Who am I?"

Sociologist Starr Hiltz (1989) documents how much more difficult adjustment is when the death is unexpected. Survivors who know that death is impending make preparations that smooth the transition—from arranging finances to psychologically preparing themselves for being alone. Saying goodbye and cultivating treasured last memories are important in adjusting to the death of an intimate companion.

Diversity in U.S. Families

It is important to note that there is no such thing as *the* American family. Rather, family life varies widely throughout the United States. The significance of social class, stressed above, will continue to be evident as we examine diversity in U.S. families.

African-American Families

Note that the heading is African-American *families*, not *the* African-American family. There is no such thing as *the* African-American family any more than there is *the* white

There is no such thing as the African-American family, anymore than there is the Native American, Asian-American, Latino, or Irish-American family. Rather, each racial-ethnic group has different types of families, with the primary determinant being social class.

family or *the* Latino family. The primary distinction is not between African Americans and other groups, but between social classes. Because African Americans who are members of the upper class follow the class interests reviewed in Chapter 10—preservation of privilege and family fortune—they are especially concerned about the family background of those whom their children marry (Gatewood 1990). To them, marriage is viewed as a merger of family lines. Children of this class marry later than children of other classes.

Middle-class African-American families focus on achievement and respectability. Both husband and wife are likely to work outside the home. Their concerns are that the family stay intact and that their children go to college, get good jobs, and marry well—that is, marry people like themselves, respectable and hardworking, who want to get ahead in school and pursue a successful career.

African-American families in poverty face all the problems that cluster around poverty. Because the men are likely to have few skills and to be unemployed, it is difficult for them to fulfill the cultural roles of husband and father. Consequently, these families are likely to be headed by a female and to have a high rate of unwed motherhood. Divorce and desertion are also more common than among other classes. Sharing scarce resources and stretching kinship are primary survival mechanisms. That is, people who have helped out in hard times are considered brothers, sisters, or cousins, to whom one owes obligations as though they were blood relatives (Stack 1974).

From Figure 16.4, you can see that African-American families are less likely to be headed by married couples and more likely to be headed by females. Because of a **marriage squeeze**—an imbalance in the sex ratio, in this instance fewer unmarried males per 100 unmarried females—African-American women are more likely than other racial groups to marry men who are less educated than themselves, who are unemployed, or who are divorced (South 1991).

Latino Families

As Figure 16.4 shows, the proportion of Latino families headed by married couples and females falls in between whites and African Americans. The effects of social class on families, sketched above, also apply to Latinos. In addition, families differ by country of origin. Families from Cuba, for example, are much more likely to be headed by a married couple than are families from Puerto Rico (*Statistical Abstract* 1993: Table 53).

> **marriage squeeze:** the difficulty a group of males or females have in finding marriage partners, due to an imbalanced sex ratio

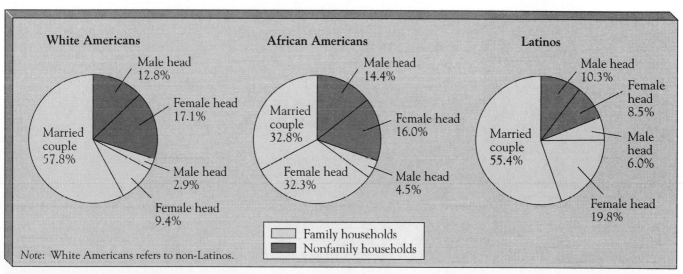

Note: White Americans refers to non-Latinos.

Source: Statistical Abstract 1993: Table 66.

Figure 16.4

Percentage of U.S. Households Headed by Males, Females, and Married Couples.

Regardless of race-ethnicity, the more resources a family has, the more it assumes the middle-class characteristics of a nuclear family, placing greater emphasis on educational achievement and deferred gratification.

What really distinguishes Latino families, however, is culture—especially the Spanish language, the Roman Catholic religion, and a strong family orientation with a disapproval of divorce. Although there is some debate among the experts, another characteristic seems to be **machismo**—an emphasis on male strength and dominance. In Chicano families (those originating from Mexico), the husband-father plays a stronger role than in either white or African-American families (Vega 1990). Machismo apparently decreases with each generation in the United States (Hurtado et al. 1992). In general, however, the wife-mother makes most of the day-to-day decisions for the family and does the routine disciplining of the children. She is usually more family centered than her husband, displaying more warmth and affection for her children.

Generalizations have limits, of course, and as with other ethnic groups individual Latino families vary considerably from one another.

Asian-American Families

Sociologist Bob Suzuki (1985) has analyzed cultural differences that distinguish Chinese-American and Japanese-American families from most others. Although they have adopted the nuclear family common in the United States, they have retained Confucian values that provide a distinct framework for family life: humanism, collectivity, self-discipline, hierarchy, respect for the elderly, moderation, and obligation. Obligation means that each individual owes respect to other family members and carries the responsibility never to bring shame on the family. Asian Americans tend to be more permissive than Anglos in child rearing and more likely to use shame and guilt rather than physical punishment to control their children's behavior.

▼ **In Sum** Social class and culture hold the keys to understanding family life. Race by itself signifies little, if anything. The more resources a family has, the more it assumes the middle-class characteristics of a nuclear family. Compared with the poor, middle-class families have fewer children and fewer unmarried mothers, and place greater emphasis on educational achievement and deferred gratification.

One-Parent Families

From TV talk shows to government officials, one-parent families have become a matter of general concern. The increase is no myth, and has occurred for two primary reasons. The first is the high divorce rate, which each year forces a million children from two-parent homes to one-parent homes (*Statistical Abstract* 1993: Table 144). The second is the sharp increase in unwed motherhood. Overall, 28 percent of U.S. children are born to women who are not married, a 50 percent increase in just ten years (*Statistical Abstract* 1993: Table 102).

The primary reason for the concern, however, may have less to do with children being raised by one parent than the fact that most of these families are poor. The poverty is primarily due to most one-parent families being headed by women. Although 90 percent of children of divorce live with their mothers, most divorced women earn less than their former husbands. In the case of unwed mothers, most have little education and few marketable skills, which condemns them to bouncing from one minimum-wage job to another, with welfare sandwiched in between.

To understand the typical one-parent family, then, we need to view it through the lens of poverty; for that is its primary source of strain. The results are serious, not just for these parents and their children, but for society as a whole. Children from single-parent families are more likely to drop out of school, to become delinquent, to have emotional problems, to get pregnant as teenagers, to bear children outside marriage, to be poor as adults, and to get divorced (Wallerstein and Blakeslee 1992; Whitehead 1993). The cycle of poverty should be apparent.

machismo: an emphasis on male strength and dominance

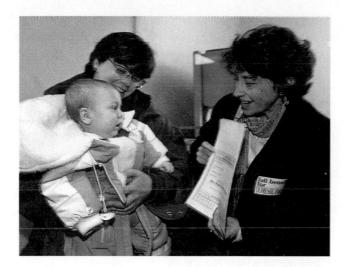

Although homosexual marriages are not legal in the United States, spousal benefits are available for city workers in several major U.S. cities. Shown here is a homosexual couple and their child in New York City, one of the cities offering such benefits.

Families Without Children

Why do some couples choose to not have children? Sociologist Kathleen Gerson (1985) found that some women see their marriage as unstable and either do not believe their relationship can withstand the strains that a child would bring or think that it may break up before the child is grown. Others feel a child would be too expensive. Finally, some career-oriented women consider that a child will bind them to the home, and that they will suffer from boredom, loneliness, and lost career opportunities. The trend toward greater childlessness is strong. Twenty-five percent of college-educated women between 35 and 45 do not have children (Lang 1991). The highest rate of voluntary childlessness is among Asian Americans and whites, the lowest among Latinos. More education, careers for women, effective contraception, abortion, the costs of rearing children, as well as changing attitudes toward children and goals in life—all contribute to this trend.

Blended Families

An increasingly significant type of family formation found in the United States is the **blended family,** one whose members were once part of other families. Two divorced persons who marry and each bring their children into a new family unit become a blended family. With divorce common, many children spend some of their childhood in blended families. One result is more complicated family relationships, exemplified by the following description written by one of my students:

> I live with my dad. I should say that I live with my dad, my brother (whose mother and father are also my mother and father), my half sister (whose father is my dad, but whose mother is my father's last wife), and two stepbrothers and stepsisters (children of my father's current wife). My father's wife (my current stepmother, not to be confused with his second wife who, I guess, is no longer my stepmother) is pregnant, and soon we all will have a new brother or sister. Or will it be a half brother or half sister?

> If you can't figure this out, I don't blame you. I have trouble myself. It gets very complicated around Christmas. Should we all stay together? Split up and go to several other homes? Who do we buy gifts for anyway?

Gay Families

When Denmark legalized marriage between people of the same sex in 1992, other nations did not follow suit. Although such marriages remain illegal in the United

blended family: a family whose members were once part of other families

States, same-sex couples in San Francisco can register as "domestic partners," publicly agreeing to be jointly responsible for their basic living expenses. The city offers health benefits to the domestic partners of its employees, and the employee can take paid bereavement leave if the partner dies. New York, Seattle, and a scattering of other cities have made similar arrangements for their employees (Hartinger 1992), as have more than 70 major corporations such as Ben & Jerry's, Lotus, and Apple (Jefferson 1994).

What are gay marriages like? As with everything else in life, same-sex couples who live in monogamous relationships cannot be painted with a single brush stroke. As with opposite-sex couples, social class is highly significant, and orientations to life differ according to education, occupation, and income. Sociologists Blumstein and Schwartz (1985) interviewed same-sex couples and found their main struggles to be housework, money, careers, problems with relatives, and sexual adjustment—the same as heterosexual couples. Same-sex couples are much more likely to break up, however, probably because of a combination of higher levels of sexual infidelity and a lack of legal and broad social support.

Trends in U.S. Families

As is apparent from this discussion, patterns of marriage and family life in the United States are undergoing a fundamental change. Other indicators of this change, which we shall now examine, include the postponement of marriage, cohabitation, child care for working parents, divorce, and remarriage.

Postponing Marriage

Figure 16.5 shows one of the most significant trends in U.S. marriages. After declining for about eighty years, the average age of first-time brides and grooms turned sharply

---

Figure 16.5

The Median Age at which Americans Marry for the First Time.

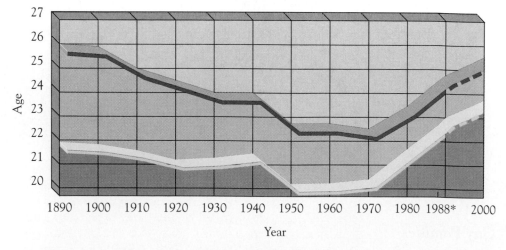

*Latest year available; data after this year are author's projections.

Source: Statistical Abstract 1993: Table 134, and earlier years.

Figure 16.6

Americans ages 20–24 who Have Never Married

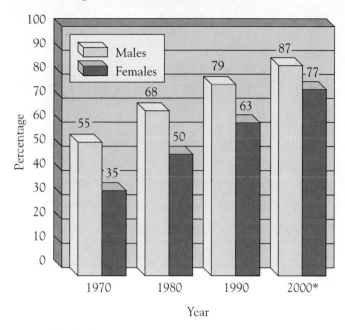

*Author's estimate.
Source: Statistical Abstract 1993: Table 60.

upward. In 1890 the typical first-time bride was 22, but by 1950 she had just left her teens. Today *the average first-time bride is older than at any time in U.S. history*. The age at first marriage for men is now about the same as it was in 1890. Figure 16.6 is another way of portraying this remarkable change. Note how the proportion of never-married younger Americans has climbed, with the percentage of unmarried females now almost *double* what it was in 1970.

Why did this change occur? The answer turns out to be very simple. Although young people have postponed the age at which they first marry, they have *not* postponed the age at which they first set up housekeeping together. In other words, the postponing of marriage has been offset by an increase in cohabitation. If cohabiting couples were counted as married, the rate of family formation and age at first marriage would show little change (Bumpass et al. 1991). Let's look at the trend in cohabitation.

Cohabitation

As Figure 16.7 shows, **cohabitation,** adults living together in a sexual relationship without being married, has increased about *seven times* in just over two decades. Cohabitation has become so common that about half of the couples who marry have cohabited (Gwartney-Gibbs 1986). The rate of cohabitation in the United States, however, is lower than in Canada and in most European countries (Sorrentino 1990). With this change in behavior have come changed attitudes. For example, when hiring executives, some corporations now pay for live-in partners to attend orientation sessions.

Commitment is the essential difference between cohabitation and marriage. While the assumption of marriage is permanence, cohabiting couples agree to remain together for "as long as it works out." Marriage requires public vows—and a judge to authorize its termination; cohabitation requires only that a couple move in together and move out when the relationship sours. Sociologists have found that couples who cohabit before

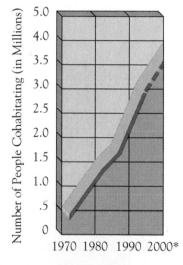

*Author's estimates.
Source: Statistical Abstract 1993: Table 62.

Figure 16.7

Cohabitation in the United States.

cohabitation: the condition of living together as an unmarried couple

With the U.S. divorce rate the highest of the industrialized nations, blended families have become increasingly common.

marriage are more likely to divorce than couples who do not first cohabit (Bennett et al. 1988; Whyte 1992). The reason, they conclude, is that cohabiting couples have a weaker commitment to marriage and to relationships.

Unmarried Mothers

Earlier we discussed the steady increase in births to unmarried U.S. mothers. To better understand this trend, we can place it in cross-cultural perspective. As Figure 16.8 shows, the United States is not alone in this increase. Of the ten industrial nations for which we have data, all except Japan have experienced sharp increases in births to unmarried mothers. Far from the highest, the U.S. rate falls in the middle third of these nations.

From this figure, it seems fair to conclude that industrialization sets in motion social forces that encourage out-of-wedlock births. The problem with this conclusion, however, is fourfold. First, why was the rate so low in 1960? Industrialization had been in process for many decades prior to that time. Second, why are the rates in the bottom four nations only a fraction of those in the top six nations? Third, why does Japan's rate remain so consistently low? Fourth, with but a couple of minor exceptions, the ranking of these nations in 1990 is the same as 1960. By itself, then, industrialization is too simple an answer. A fuller explanation will have to focus on customs and values embedded within the particular cultures. For that answer, we will have to await further research.

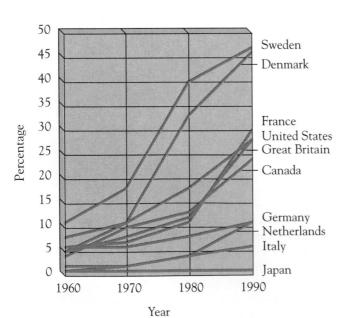

Source: Statistical Abstract 1993: Table 1380.

Figure 16.8

Births to Unmarried Women in Ten Industrial Nations, as a Percentage of All Births

Grandparenting

With longer life expectancy, more people are living to see their grandchildren and even their great-grandchildren. What does it mean to be a grandparent today? To find out, sociologists Andrew Cherlin and Frank Furstenberg interviewed a national sample of grandparents. They found three main styles of grandparenting. Fifty-five percent of grandparents are "recreational specialists." Their main contribution to their grandchildren is going on outings and other special activities. Twenty-nine percent are "ritualists." Often living a long way from their grandchildren, they carry on a symbolic relationship through letters and birthday and Christmas gifts. About 16 percent are "everyday actives." They participate in the routine care of their grandchildren, and often exercise a great deal of authority over them (Ahlburg and De Vita 1992). As we saw earlier, many grandparents step in to fill the void in childcare left by absent fathers.

The Sandwich Generation and Elder Care

The "sandwich generation" refers to people who find themselves sandwiched between two generations, responsible for the care of their children and for their own aging parents. Typically between the ages of 40 and 55, these people find themselves pulled in two equally compelling directions. Feeling responsible both for their children and their parents, they are plagued with guilt and anger because they can be in only one place at a time (Shellenbarger 1994a). Some corporations have begun to hold seminars, to offer referral services, and to experiment with flexible work schedules in order to help their employees meet their responsibilities without missing so much work (Shellenbarger 1994b).

Commuter Marriages

A commuter marriage used to refer to a husband who caught a 7:30 A.M. streetcar to work and returned to his wife and children on the 5:05. Today a commuter marriage can involve a husband who teaches in Akron and a wife who teaches in Chicago, who take turns meeting every other weekend in one city or the other. And with changes in our global marketplace and in gender roles, a commuter marriage can also refer to a wife who practices law in Paris and a husband who directs oil exploration in China. If fortunate, they are able to sneak a few days together every couple of months.

What are such marriages like? They certainly can be hectic and lonely. As one wife reported to me, when she and her husband get together, which is about monthly, they initially experience a period of high tension. Although happy to see each other, at first they feel uncomfortable. They bicker for a while, and only as the weekend goes on do they again feel relaxed in one another's presence. From a symbolic interactionist perspective, the basic reason for their initial discomfort is that while apart each has undergone different experiences. These experiences change each person slightly. Only as they spend time together and talk with one another does their shared world re-emerge.

The primary benefits for commuter couples are career development and the personal satisfactions and economic gains that this brings. Other benefits include independence, self-sufficiency, and an enhanced appreciation for spouse or family (Groves and Horm-Wingerd 1991). With continued changes in the marketplace and gender roles, we can expect commuter marriages to become more common (Lublin 1992). Although faxes, e-mail, and the telephone help reduce the problem of separate experiences pulling in different directions, we can also expect commuter marriages to be more fragile than those in which husband and wife live together. For long-distance couples with children, the complications can be almost unbearable (Shellenbarger 1993).

Divorce and Remarriage

The topic of family life would not be complete without considering divorce. Let us first try to determine how much divorce there really is.

Problems in Measuring Divorce

You probably have heard that the U.S. divorce rate is 50 percent, a figure popular with reporters. The statistic is true in the sense that each year about half as many divorces are granted as marriages are performed. In 1992, for example, 2,362,000 U.S. couples married and 1,215,000 couples divorced (*Monthly Vital Statistics Report* 1993).

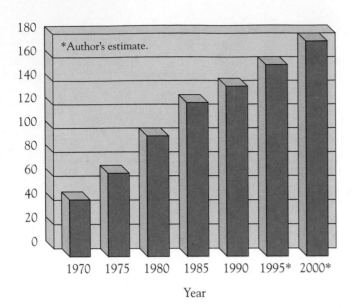

*Author's estimate.

Source: *Statistical Abstract* 1992: Table 50.

──────────── **Figure 16.9** ────────────

For Every Thousand Married Persons, How Many Divorced Persons Are There?

With these statistics, what is wrong with saying that the divorce rate is 50 percent? The real question is why these two figures should be compared in the first place. The couples who divorced do not—with rare exceptions—come from the group who married that year. The one set of figures has nothing to do with the other, so these statistics in no way establish the divorce rate.

What figures should we compare, then? Couples who divorce are drawn from the entire group of married people in the country. Since the United States has 56,350,000 married couples, and only 1,215,000 of them obtained divorces in 1992, the divorce rate is 2.1 percent, not 50 percent (*Statistical Abstract* 1993: Table 49). A couple's chances of still being married at the end of a year are 98 percent—not bad odds—and certainly much better than the mass media would have us believe.

Over time, of course, those annual 2.1 percentages add up. A third way of measuring divorce, then, is to ask, "For every thousand married people, how many divorced people are there?" As you can see from Figure 16.9, in just two decades this number *tripled*. Again, a cross-cultural comparison helps to place U.S. statistics in perspective—but the news is not good. As Table 16.2 illustrates, the United States has—by far—the highest divorce rate in the industrialized world (Sorrentino 1990). U.S. divorce is so high that sociologists Teresa Martin and Larry Bumpass (1989) estimate that as many as two-thirds of all couples getting married today may eventually divorce.

One hopeful note is that the U.S. divorce rate leveled off about 1981, and has even declined somewhat since then. Factors that make marriage successful are summarized at the end of this chapter.

Children of Divorce

As was apparent in the opening vignette, divorce profoundly threatens a child's world. Each year, the parents of over one million U.S. children divorce. Most divorcing parents become so wrapped up in their own problems that they are unable to prepare their children for the divorce—even if they knew how to do so in the first place. When the break comes, children become confused and insecure. For security, many cling to the unrealistic idea that their parents will be reunited (Wallerstein and Kelly 1992).

For ten years, researcher Judith Wallerstein tracked 131 children who had been functioning well until their parents divorced. She found that in the fifth year after divorce about a third of the children were depressed, could not concentrate in school, and had trouble making friends. In the tenth year, a "sleeper effect" turned up. Two-thirds of the young women were anxious about making the same mistake as their parents, expressing fears about marrying the wrong person (Wallerstein and Blakeslee 1992). What we need, of course, are comparative figures. How many young women (and men) of the same age from intact homes express these same fears?

The effects of divorce don't end with adolescence. A surprising finding, although still tentative, is that grown children of divorce feel more distant from their parents than do children from intact families—even from the parent they lived with. Why would this be so, considering all the sacrifices the custodial parent made for them? Some suggest that deep down the adult children of divorce believe that their parents reneged on an implicit contract to provide a stable two-parent family (Lye et al. 1993).

Table 16.2

Divorce Rates in Ten Industrial Nations per Thousand Married Women

	1960	1970	1980	1990
United States	9.9	15	23	21
Denmark	6	8	11	13
Canada	2	6	11	12
Great Britain	2	5	12	12
Sweden	5	7	11	12
Germany	4	5	6	8
France	3	3	6	8
Netherlands	2	3	8	8
Japan	4	4	5	5
Italy	NA	1	1	2

Note: For France, the last column is 1989; for Great Britain, it is 1988. Strangely, the source gives data only per 1,000 women.
Source: Statistical Abstract 1993: Table 1379.

Researchers have identified several factors that help children adjust to divorce. Adjustment is better if (1) both parents show understanding and affection; (2) the child lives with a parent who is making a good adjustment; (3) family routines are consistent; (4) the family has adequate money for its needs; and (at least according to preliminary studies) (5) the child lives with the parent of the same sex (Lamb 1977; Clingempeel and Reppucci 1982; Peterson and Zill 1986; Wallerstein and Kelly 1992). Sociologist Urie Bronfenbrenner (1992) reports that children adjust better if there is a second adult who can be counted on for support. This person makes the third leg of a stool, giving stability to the smaller family unit. Any adult can be the third leg, he says—a relative, friend, mother-in-law, or even co-worker—but the most powerful stabilizing third leg is the father, the ex-husband.

The Absent Father and Serial Fatherhood

With mothers given custody of about 90 percent of children of divorce, a new fathering pattern has emerged. In this pattern, known as **serial fatherhood,** divorced fathers tend to live with, support, and play an active fathering role with the children of the woman they are currently married to or living with (Ahlburg and De Vita 1992). Over time, contact with their children from a previous marriage diminishes. The usual pattern is for the father's contact to be fairly high during the first year or two after divorce, and then decline rapidly (Furstenberg and Harris 1992). The result is that only about one-sixth of children living apart from their fathers see their dad as often as every week, and in a typical month two-thirds of the children of divorce have no contact at all with their father.

The Ex-Spouses

Anger, depression, and anxiety are common feelings at divorce. But so is relief. Women are more likely than men to feel that the divorce is giving them a "new chance" in life. A few couples manage to remain friends through it all—but they are the exception. The spouse who initiates the divorce usually gets over it sooner (Stark 1989; Kelly 1992).

Divorce does not necessarily mean the end of a couple's relationship. Some divorced couples maintain contact because of their children, but for others the conti-

serial fatherhood: a pattern of parenting in which a father, after divorce, reduces contact with his own children, serves as a father to the children of the woman he marries or lives with, then ignores them after moving in with or marrying another woman; this pattern repeats

Figure 16.10

The Marital History of U.S. Brides and Grooms

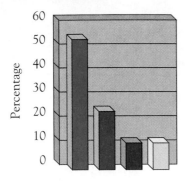

 First marriage of bride and groom

First marriage of bride and groom

Remarriage of bride and groom

First marriage of bride, remarriage of groom

First marriage of groom, remarriage of bride

Source: Statistical Abstract 1993: Table 141.

nuities represent a lingering attachment (Vaughan 1985; Masheter 1991). The former husband may help his former wife hang a picture and move furniture, for example, or she may invite him over for a meal. Some couples even continue to make love after their divorce.

After divorce, a couple's cost of living increases—two homes, two utility bills, and so forth. But the financial impact is very different for men and for women. Divorce often spells economic hardship for women, especially mothers of small children (Mauldin 1991). Sociologist Christine Grella (1990) found that in the first year following divorce the standard of living for women with dependent children drops 50 percent. Based on another sample, sociologist Lenore Weitzman (1985) found that the standard of living drops 73 percent for women, while for former husbands it increases 42 percent.

Remarriage

In spite of the number of people who emerge from the divorce court swearing, "Never again!" most do—and fairly soon at that. About four of every five divorced persons remarry, with an average lapse between divorce and remarriage of 2.3 years for men and 2.5 years for women (Ahlburg and De Vita 1992). As Figure 16.10 shows, most divorced people remarry other divorced people. You may be surprised that the women most likely to remarry are young mothers and those who have not graduated from high school (Glick and Lin 1986). Apparently the more educated and more independent (no children) women can afford to be more selective. Also there are fewer males of their status who are still unmarried. In all categories, men are more likely than women to remarry, perhaps because they have a larger pool of potential mates from which to select.

How do remarriages work out? The divorce rate of remarried people *without* children is the same as that of first marriages. Those who bring children into their new marriage, however, are more likely to divorce again (White and Booth 1985). Sociologist Andrew Cherlin (1989) suggests that remarriages with children are more difficult because we have not developed norms to govern these relationships. For example, we lack satisfactory names for stepmothers, stepfathers, stepbrothers, stepsisters, stepaunts, stepuncles, stepcousins, and stepgrandparents. At the very least, these are awkward terms to use, but they also represent ill-defined relationships.

▼ Two Sides of Family Life

Family life can be very rewarding or very brutal. Although most people find their experiences in marriage and family to be somewhere in between, the extremes inform us about the potential of family life as well as its dark side. Let's first look at situations in which marriage and family have gone seriously wrong and then try to answer the question of what makes marriage work.

Abuse: Battering, Marital Rape, and Incest

The dark side of family life involves situations and events that the people involved would rather keep in the dark. We shall look at battering, rape, and incest.

Battering   To determine the amount and types of violence in U.S. homes, sociologists Murray Straus, Susan Steinmetz, and Richard Gelles interviewed nationally representative samples of U.S. couples. They asked them about slapping, pushing, kicking, biting, beating, and so on—even about attacking with a knife or gun (Straus 1980; Straus, Gelles, and Steinmetz 1980; Straus and Gelles 1988; Straus 1992). They found that children are the most violent members of the family. During the year preceding the interview, two-thirds of them had physically attacked a brother or sister. Most acts of violence involved nothing more than shoving or throwing things, but one-third had kicked, bitten, or, in some instances, attacked with a knife or gun.

Although not all sociologists agree (Dobash et al. 1992, 1993; Pagelow 1992), Straus concludes that husbands and wives are about equally likely to attack one another. When it comes to the effects of violence, however, sexual equality vanishes (Gelles 1980; Straus 1980; Straus 1992). As Straus points out, even though *she* may throw the coffeepot first, it is generally *he* who lands the last and most damaging blow. Consequently, many more wives than husbands need medical attention because of marital violence. A good part of the reason, of course, is that most husbands are bigger and stronger than their wives, putting women at a disadvantage in this literal battle of the sexes.

Researchers have also found that violence between husbands and wives is not equally distributed among the social classes. Family violence, rather, follows certain "social channels," making some people much more likely to be abusers—or victims—than others. The highest rates of marital violence (Gelles 1980) are found among

- Families with low incomes
- Blue-collar workers
- People under 30
- Families in which the husband is unemployed
- Families with above-average numbers of children
- Families living in large urban areas
- Minority ethnic groups
- Individuals who have no religious affiliation
- People with low education

As Straus (1992) emphasizes, although no single route leads to marital violence, sexual inequality legitimizes force and coercion. That is, the sexist structure of society described in Chapter 11 makes some men think that they are superior and have a right to force their will on their wives.

Marital Rape How common is marital rape? Sociologist Diana Russell (1982), who used a sampling technique that allows generalization, found that 14 percent of married women report that their husbands have raped them. Similarly, 10 percent of a representative sample of Boston women interviewed by sociologists David Finkelhor and Kersti Yllo (1983, 1989) reported that their husbands had used physical force to compel them to have sex. Finkelhor's and Yllo's in-depth interviews with fifty of these victims showed that marital rape most commonly occurs during separation or during the breakup of a marriage. They found three types of marital rape.

- *Nonbattering rape* (40 percent). The husband forces his wife to have sex, with no intent to hurt her physically. These instances generally involve conflict over sex, such as the husband feeling insulted when his wife refuses to have sex.
- *Battering rape* (48 percent). In addition to sexually assaulting his wife, the husband intentionally inflicts physical pain to retaliate for some supposed wrongdoing on her part.
- *Perverted rape* (6 percent). These husbands, apparently sexually aroused by the violent elements of rape, force their wives to submit to unusual sexual acts. Anger and hostility can also motivate this type of rape. (The remaining 6 percent are mixed, containing elements of more than one type.)

Incest Sexual relations between relatives, such as brothers and sisters or parents and children, called **incest,** is most likely to occur in families that are socially isolated (Smith 1992). As with marital rape, sociological research has destroyed assumptions that incest is not common

incest: sexual relations between specified relatives, such as brothers and sisters or parents and children

Diana Russell (1986), who interviewed a probability sample (from which one can generalize) of 930 women in San Francisco, found that 16 percent were victims of incest before they turned 18. Russell used a very broad definition of incest, however, and included not only sexual intercourse but any unwanted sexual act—even an unwanted kiss. This information is not intended to minimize the problem of incest, which includes young victims and even forcible rape, but rather to point out the problem of operational definitions noted in Chapter 5. Russell (n.d.) also found that the incest victims who experience the most difficulty are those who have been victimized the most often, over longer periods of time, and whose incest was "more intrusive," for example, sexual intercourse as opposed to sexual touching.

Who are the offenders? Russell found that uncles are the most common offenders, followed by first cousins, then fathers (stepfathers especially), brothers, and, finally, relatives ranging from brothers-in-law to stepgrandfathers. Other researchers report that brother–sister incest is several times more common than father–child incest (Canavan et al. 1992). Incest between mothers and sons is rare.

Successful Marriages

After examining divorce and family abuse, one could easily conclude that marriages seldom work out. That would be far from the truth, however, for about two of every three married Americans report that they are "very happy" with their marriages (Cherlin and Furstenberg 1988; Whyte 1992). To find out what makes marriage successful, sociologists Jeanette and Robert Lauer (1992) interviewed 351 couples who had been married fifteen years or longer. They found that in 51 of these marriages one or both spouses was unhappy but stayed together for religious reasons, family tradition, or "for the sake of the children." The study revealed that the 300 happy couples all:

1   Think of their spouse as their best friend
2   Like their spouse as a person
3   Think of marriage as a long-term commitment
4   Believe that marriage is sacred
5   Agree with their spouse on aims and goals
6   Believe that their spouse has grown more interesting over the years
7   Strongly want the relationship to succeed
8   Laugh together

Sociologist Nicholas Stinnett (1992) used interviews and questionnaires to study 660 families from all regions of the country. He found that happy families all

1   Spend a lot of time together
2   Are quick to express appreciation
3   Are committed to promoting one another's welfare
4   Do a lot of talking and listening to one another
5   Are religious
6   Deal with crises in a positive manner

The Lauers also found that happy and unhappy couples approach problems differently. Happy couples are determined to confront and work through problems, while unhappy couples ignore, avoid, or endure them. Finally, these studies show that happily married couples do *not* agree that equality is the basis of marriage—not in the sense of believing that marriage is a fifty–fifty proposition. Rather, their attitude is that "you have to be willing to put in *more* than you take out."

The Future of Marriage and Family

What can we expect of marriage and family in the future? Will the high divorce rate, increasing cohabitation, and the postponement of marriage eventually make marriage a thing of the past for most people?

Quite the contrary, after completing a study of marriage, sociologist Martin Whyte (1992) concluded that we should side with the optimists regarding the state of marriage in the United States. In spite of severe problems—especially of family violence, incest, and mothers and children in poverty—marriage and family serve most people well. The vast proportion of Americans—between 90 and 95 percent—will continue to marry. So will most people who divorce, trying again for the satisfactions that eluded them the first time. If the percentage of Americans who marry does drop, it will not be a sign that Americans have forsaken marriage. Rather, it will only bring us back to the historical norm that was changed by the "marriage-happy" 1950s (Whyte 1992). We can safely assume that for the foreseeable future the vast majority of Americans will continue to reaffirm marriage as vital to their welfare.

Four trends are likely to continue: an increase in cohabitation, age at first marriage, births to unmarried mothers, and married women joining the work force. As more married women work for wages, it is likely that the marital balance of power will continue to shift in the direction of making husband–wife relationships more equal.

Additonal sociological research can help move us beyond the distorted images that haunt a culture: the rosy ones painted by cultural myths and the bleak ones portrayed by the mass media. Research can also bring our own family life into sharper focus, allowing us to see better how our own experiences fit into the patterns of our culture. Finally, sociological research can help to answer the big question of how to formulate social policy that will support and enhance family life.

Summary and Review

Marriage and Family in Global Perspective

What is a family—and what themes are universal?

Family is difficult to define. For just about every element one might consider essential, there are exceptions. Consequently, **family** is defined broadly—as two or more people who consider themselves related by blood, marriage, or adoption. Sociologists and anthropologists have documented extensive variation in family customs—from cultures in which babies are married to those in which husbands and wives refrain from sexual relations for years at a time. Universally, marriage and family are mechanisms for governing mate selection, reckoning descent, and establishing inheritance and authority. Pp. 430–433.

Marriage and Family in Theoretical Perspective

What is the functionalist perspective on marriage and family?

Functionalists examine the functions of families, analyzing such matters as the **incest taboo,** consequences of weakening family functions, and the dysfunctions of the family. Pp. 433–435.

What is the conflict perspective on marriage and family?

Conflict theorists examine how marriage and family help perpetuate inequalities, especially the subservience of women. Power struggles in marriage, such as those over housework, are an example. Pp. 435–437.

What is a symbolic interactionist perspective on marriage and family?

Symbolic interactionists examine how marriage produces contrasting experiences, and how these perspectives merge through communication. Pp. 437–438.

The Family Life Cycle

What are the major elements of the family life cycle?

The major elements are love and courtship, marriage, childbirth, child rearing, and the family in later life. Most marriages follow predictable patterns of age, social class, race, and religion. Childbirth and child-rearing patterns also vary by social class. Pp. 438–444.

Diversity in U.S. Families

How significant are race and ethnicity in family life?

While race and ethnicity are important, the primary distinction is social class. Families of the same social class are likely to be similar, regardless of their racial or ethnic makeup. Pp. 444–446.

What other diversity in U.S. families is there?

Also discussed were one-parent, childless, **blended,** and gay families. Although each has its own unique characteristics, social class is also significant in determining their primary characteristics. Poverty is especially significant for one-parent families, most of which are headed by women. Pp. 446–448.

Trends in U.S. Families

What major changes characterize U.S. families?

Two changes are postponement of first marriage and an increase in **cohabitation.** With more people living longer, grandparents are more common, and many middle-aged people find themselves sandwiched between caring for their own children and their own parents. Pp. 448–451.

Divorce and Remarriage

What is the current divorce rate?

Depending on what figures you choose to compare, you can produce almost any rate you wish, from 75 percent to just 2.1 percent. However you figure it, the U.S. divorce rate is higher than any other industrialized nation. Pp. 451–452.

How do children and their parents adjust to divorce?

Divorce is especially difficult for children, whose adjustment problems often continue into adulthood. Most divorced fathers do not pay child support and do not maintain ongoing relationships with their children. Financial problems are usually greater for the former wives. Most divorced people remarry in less than two and one-half years Pp. 452–454.

Two Sides of Family Life

What are the two sides of family life?

The dark side is family abuse—spouse battering, marital rape, and incest, activities that revolve around the misuse of family power. The bright side is families that provide intense satisfaction for spouses and their children. Pp. 454–456.

The Future of Marriage and Family

What is the likely future of marriage and family?

We can expect cohabitation, births to unmarried mothers, and postponement of marriage to increase. The growing numbers of women in the work force will likely continue to shift the marital balance of power. P. 457.

Where can I read more on this topic?

Suggested readings for this chapter are listed on page 643.

Honore Desmond Sharrer, Tribute to the American Working People, 1986

Education: Transferring Knowledge and Skills

WENDY STILL FEELS RESENTMENT WHEN *she recalls the memo that greeted her that Monday morning.*

With growing concern about international competition for our products, the management is upgrading several positions. The attached listing of jobs states the new qualifications that must be met.

Wendy quickly scanned the list. The rumors had been right, after all. The new position the company was opening up—the job she had been slated to get—was listed.

After regaining her composure somewhat, but still angry, Wendy marched to her supervisor's office. "I've been doing my job for three years," she said. "You always gave me good evaluations, and you said I'd get that new position."

"I know, Wendy. You'd be good at it. Believe me, I gave you a high recommendation. But what can I do? You know what the higher-ups are like. If they decide they want someone with a college degree, that's just what they'll get."

"But I can't go back to college now, not with all my responsibilities. It's been five years since I was in college, and I still have a year to go."

The supervisor was sympathetic, but she insisted that her hands were tied. Wendy would have to continue working at the lower job classification—and stay at the lower pay.

It was Wendy's responsibility to break in Melissa, the newcomer with the freshly minted college degree. Those were the toughest two weeks Wendy ever spent at work—especially since she knew that Melissa was already being paid more than she was.

Today's Credential Society

Sociologist Randall Collins (1979) observed that industrialized nations have become **credential societies,** that employers use diplomas and degrees to determine who is eligible for a job. In many cases the diploma or degree is irrelevant for the work that must be performed. The new job that Wendy wanted, for example, did not suddenly change into a task requiring a college degree. Her immediate supervisor knew Wendy's capabilities well and was sure she could handle the responsibility just fine—but the new company policy required a credential that Wendy didn't have. Similarly, is a high school diploma necessary to pump gas or to sell shoes? Yet employers routinely require such credentials.

In fact, it is often on the job, not at school, that employees learn the particular knowledge or skills that a job requires. A high school diploma teaches no one how to pump gas or to be polite to customers. Melissa had to be taught the ropes by Wendy. Why, then, do employers insist on diplomas and degrees? Why don't they simply use on-the-job training?

A major reason credentials are required is the larger size, urbanization, and consequent anonymity of industrial societies. Diplomas and degrees serve as automatic sorting devices. Because employers don't know potential workers personally or even by reputation, they depend on schools to weed out the capable from the incapable. By hiring a college graduate, the employer assumes that the individual is a responsible person; for evidently he or she has shown up on time for numerous classes, has turned in scores of assignments, and has demonstrated basic writing and thinking skills. The specific job skills that a position requires can then be grafted onto this base certified by the college.

In other cases, specific job skills must be mastered before an individual is allowed to do certain work. As a result of accelerated rates of change in technology and in knowl-

credential society: the use of diplomas and degrees to determine who is eligible for jobs, even though the diploma or degree may be irrelevant to the actual work

edge, simple on-the-job training will not do for physicians, engineers, and airline pilots. That is precisely why doctors so prominently display their credentials. Their framed degrees declare that they have been certified by an institution of higher learning, that they are qualified to work on our bodies.

Without the right credentials, you won't get hired. It does not matter that you can do the job better than someone else. You will never have the opportunity to prove what you can do, for you lack the credentials even to be considered for the job.

The Development of Modern Education

Credentialing is only one indicator of how central the educational institution is in our lives. Before exploring the role of education in contemporary society, let us first look at education in earlier societies, and then trace the development of universal education.

Education in Earlier Societies

In earlier societies there was no separate social institution called education. There were no special buildings called schools, and no people who earned their living as teachers. Rather, as an integral part of growing up children learned what was necessary to get along in life. If hunting or cooking were the essential skills, then people who already possessed those skills taught them. *Education was synonymous with* **acculturation,** the transmission of culture from one generation to the next—as it still is in today's preliterate groups.

In some societies, when a sufficient surplus developed—as in Arabia, China, North Africa, and classical Greece—a separate institution developed. Some people then devoted themselves to teaching, while those who had the leisure—the children of the wealthy—became their students. In ancient China, for example, Confucius taught a few select pupils, while in Greece Aristotle, Plato, and Socrates taught science and philosophy to upper-class males. **Education,** then, came to be something quite distinct from informal acculturation; education is a group's *formal* system of teaching knowledge, values, and skills. Such instruction stood in marked contrast to the learning of traditional skills such as farming or hunting, for it was clearly intended to develop the mind.

The flourishing of education during the period roughly marked by the birth of Christ, however, slowly died out. During the Dark Ages of Europe, the candle of enlightenment was kept burning by monks, who, except for a handful of the wealthy and nobility, were the only ones who could read and write. Although they delved into philosophy, the intellectual activities of the monks centered on learning Greek, Latin, and Hebrew so that they could read early texts of the Bible and writings of the church fathers. Similarly, Jews kept formal learning alive as they studied the Torah.

Formal education, however, remained limited to those who had the leisure to pursue it. (In fact *school* comes from the Greek word σχωλή [*scholē*] meaning "leisure.") Industrialization transformed this approach to learning, for the new machinery and new types of jobs brought a general need to be able to read, to write, and to work accurately with figures—the classic three R's of the nineteenth century (Reading, 'Riting, and 'Rithmetic.)

Democracy, Industrialization, and Universal Education

The development of universal education is linked to industrialization. Let us see how the United States pioneered free, universal education.

acculturation: the transmission of culture from one generation to the next

education: a formal system of teaching knowledge, values, and skills

In the years following the American Revolution, the founders of the new republic felt that formal education should be the principal mechanism for creating a uniform national culture out of its many nationalities and religions. Thomas Jefferson and Noah Webster proposed a universal system of schooling based on standardized texts that would instill patriotism and teach the principles of republican government (Hellinger and Judd 1991). They reasoned that if the American political experiment were to succeed, it needed educated voters who were capable of making sound decisions. Several decades later, however, in the early 1800s, the United States still had no comprehensive school system. The country remained politically fragmented, with many of its states still thinking of themselves as near-sovereign nations.

The system of education reflected the political situation. In effect, there was no *system*, just a hodgepodge of independent schools administered by separate localities, with no coordination among them. Most public schools were supported by tuition, with a few poor children being allowed to attend free. Parochial schools were run by Lutherans, Presbyterians, Congregationalists, and Roman Catholics (Hellinger and Judd 1991). Children of the rich attended private schools. Most children of the lower classes—and all slaves—received no formal education at all. Only the wealthy could afford to send their children to high school. College was beyond the reach of almost everyone.

Horace Mann, an educator from Massachusetts, found it deplorable that the average family could not afford to send its children even to grade school. In 1837 he proposed that "common schools," supported through taxes, be established throughout his state. Mann's idea spread throughout the country, as state after state directed more of its resources to public education. It is no coincidence that universal education and industrialization occurred simultaneously. Seeing that the economy was undergoing fundamental change, political and civic leaders recognized the need for an educated work force. They also feared the influx of foreign values and looked on public education as a way to Americanize immigrants (Hellinger and Judd 1991).

This 1893 photo of a school in Hecla, Montana, taught by Miss Blanche Lamont, provides a glimpse into the past, when free public education, itself pioneered in the United States, was still in its infancy. In these one-room rural schools, a single teacher had charge of grades 1 to 8. Children were assigned a grade not by age but by mastery of subject matter. Occasionally, adults who wished to learn to read, to write, or to do mathematics would join the class. Attendance was sporadic, for the needs of the family's economic survival came first.

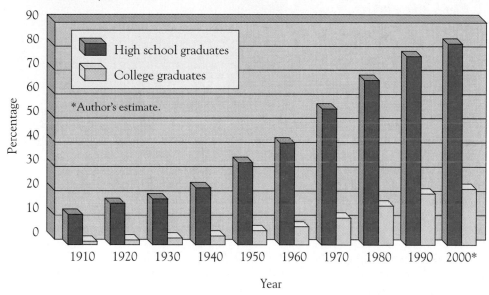

Figure 17.1

Educational Achievement in the United States.
Note: Americans 25 years and over

Source: National Center for Education Statistics, 1991: Table 8; *Statistical Abstract* 1993: Table 233.

Over time the amount of education considered necessary continued to expand. By 1918, all U.S. states had **mandatory education laws** requiring children to attend school, usually until they had completed the eighth grade or turned 16, whichever came first. In the early 1900s, graduation from the eighth grade was considered to be a full education for most people (Bettelheim 1982). "Dropouts" at that time were students who did not complete grade school, and high school was thought of as a form of "higher" education.

As industrialization progressed and as fewer people made their living from agriculture, formal education came to be thought of as essential to the well-being of society. Industrialized nations then developed some form of the credential society described earlier. As you can see from Figure 17.1, college graduation in the United States is now more common than high school graduation was in 1930. Just over 60 percent of all U.S. high school graduates now enter college, the highest rate of all industrialized nations (Rubinson 1986; *Statistical Abstract* 1993: Table 270).

Education in Global Perspective

To gain an idea of the variety of education around the world, and how education is directly related to a nation's economy, let's look at an example from each of the three worlds of development. Keep in mind that these are just examples, that no single nation represents the wide variety of educational approaches that characterizes each of these three worlds.

Education in the First World: Japan

A central sociological principle of education is that a nation's education reflects its culture. Since a core Japanese value is solidarity with the group, competition among individuals is downgraded. For example, in the work force people who are hired together work as a team. They are even promoted collectively (Ouchi 1991). Japanese education reflects this group-centered ethic. Children in grade school work as a group, all mastering the same skills and materials. Teachers stress cooperation and respect for elders and others in positions of authority. By law, Japanese schools even use the same textbooks.

> **mandatory education laws:** laws that require all children to attend school until a specified age or until they complete a minimum grade in school

Because examinations in Japan determine who can attend college—and thus seal one's occupational fate, and open and close privilege and status—after their regular school Japanese students attend intense cram schools such as this one, designed to prepare them for the national examinations.

College admission procedures in Japan and the U.S. also differ (Cooper 1991). Like the Scholastic Aptitude Test (SAT) required of U.S. college-bound high school seniors, Japanese seniors who want to attend college must take a national test. Only the top scorers in Japan, however—rich and poor alike—are admitted to college. In contrast, even a U.S. high school graduate who performs poorly on these tests can find some college to attend—as long as his or her parents can pay the tuition.

This Japanese practice poses a fascinating cultural contradiction. Although cooperation is a core Japanese value, students are admitted to college only on the basis of intense competition. Because this make-or-break process affects their entire lives, each day after high school children of affluent parents attend cram schools (*juku*) (Yee 1992). The annual college admission tests have become a national obsession. Families and friends nervously stand on college campuses at midnight awaiting the outcome that seals their fate. The results are posted on flood-lit bulletin boards. Families shout in joy—or hide their faces in shame and disappointment, while reporters photograph the results and rush back to their papers with the news. The next day, entire neighborhoods are abuzz about the results (Rohen 1983).

Just how highly do the Japanese value education? One way to tell how much a society values something is to see how much money it chooses to spend on it. By law, Japanese teachers are paid 10 percent more than the highest-paid civil service workers, putting teachers in the top 10 percent of the country's wage earners (Richburg 1985). In sharp contrast, as Figure 17.2 shows, the starting salaries of teachers in the United States are considerably less than those in other fields. Because the Japanese reward schoolteaching with both high pay and high prestige, each teaching opening is met by a barrage of eager, highly qualified applicants.

Education in the Second World: Post-Soviet Russia

After the Revolution of 1917, the Soviet Communist party attempted to upgrade the nation's educational system. At that time, as in most other countries, education was limited to the elite. The Revolution, meant to usher in social equality, was also intended to make education accessible to all. Just as the new central government directed the economy, so it directed the country's education. Following the sociological principle that education reflects culture, the government insisted that socialist values dominate education, for it saw education as a means to undergird the new political system. As a result, schoolchildren were taught that capitalism was evil and that communism was the salvation of the world.

With the country still largely agricultural, education remained spotty for the next two decades. The Nazi invasion of the Soviet Union during World War II dealt

Figure 17.2

**Starting Salaries of College Graduates:
Public School Teachers Compared with Private Industry.**

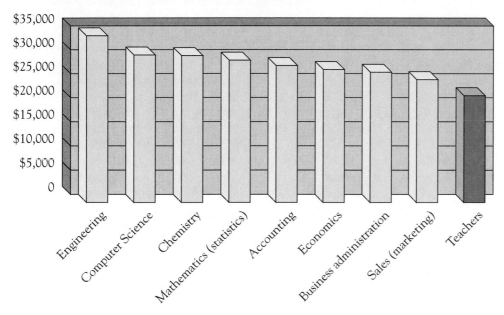

Source: *Statistical Abstract 1993: Table 246.*

a severe blow to the attempt to provide universal education, as military service disrupted the education of hundreds of thousands of young people. Even by 1950, only about half of Soviet young people were in school, and most of these came from the more privileged strata (children of the more educated and of party members) rather than from workers and peasants (Bell 1973; Grant 1979; Ballentine 1983; Matthews 1983; Tomiak 1983).

Eyeing the gains of the West, the Soviet leadership continued to struggle toward universal education, seeing education as a key to becoming a world power. Although the Soviet Union never succeeded in becoming a world industrial power—its power was based on military threat, not industrial might—its educational success did challenge the West. The launching of *Sputnik* in the 1950s caught Western leaders by surprise,

Since the breakup of the Soviet empire, education in the Second World has been in a state of rapid transition. Teachers and students are now free to explore ideas and to discuss social issues. Shown here is a classroom in Moscow, where the students are learning about acid rain.

forcing them to acknowledge how effective the Soviets had become in teaching mathematics, engineering, and the natural sciences.

The breakup of the Soviet empire in 1989 again caught Western experts by surprise, but this time they were surprised at the backwardness of Soviet education. Many schools lacked such basics as heat and indoor plumbing. To control ideas, education was totally centralized, with orders issued out of a remote educational bureaucracy in Moscow. The nation's schools followed the same state-prescribed curriculum, and throughout the country all students in the same grade used the same textbooks. Students memorized the materials, and were discouraged from discussing them (Bridgman 1994).

Today the post-Soviet Russians are in the midst of "reinventing" education. For the first time, private, religious, and even foreign-run schools are allowed, and teachers can encourage students to question and to think for themselves. The problems confronting the Russians are mind-boggling. Not only do they have to retrain tens of thousands of teachers set in their ways, used to teaching pat political answers, but school budgets are also shrinking while inflation is spiraling. Urban teachers are stampeding out of education into fields that, with the new capitalism, pay ten times the going rate for instructors (Bridgman 1994).

Because it is true of education everywhere, it is safe to conclude that beneath these changes Russia is developing an educational system designed to reflect its culture, that it will glorify its historical exploits and reinforce its values and worldviews. The primary difficulty at this point is that those values and worldviews are rapidly changing. For certain, however, if the adoption of a competitive market system goes forward, their basic ideas about profit and private property will be transformed—and their educational system will reflect those changed values.

Education in the Third World: Egypt

Education in the Third World stands in sharp contrast to the First and Second Worlds. Even if Third World nations have mandatory attendance laws, they are not enforced. Because most of their people work the land or take care of the household, they find little need for education. In addition, most of these nations simply cannot afford extensive formal education. As we saw on Figure 9.1 (on pages 240–241), the average income per person in some Third World nations is less than 5 percent of the average U.S. income. Consequently, in some nations most children do not go to school beyond the first couple of grades. As was once common around the globe, it is primarily the wealthy in the Third World who have either the means or the leisure for formal education—especially anything beyond the basics. As an example, let us look at education in Egypt.

Several centuries before the birth of Christ, Egypt's world-renowned centers of learning produced such acclaimed scientists as Archimedes and Eukleides. The primary areas of study during this classic period were physics, astronomy, geometry, geography, mathematics, philosophy, and medicine. The largest library in the world was at Alexandria. Fragments from the papyrus manuscripts of this library, which burned to the ground, have been invaluable in deciphering ancient manuscripts. After defeat in war, however, education declined, never again to rise to its former prominence.

Although the Egyptian constitution makes five years of grade school free and compulsory for all children, as in most Third World countries qualified teachers are few, classrooms are crowded, and education is highly limited. Many peasant children go completely uneducated, while others receive but rudimentary teaching of numbers and basic reading. Those who do receive a formal education attend grade school for five years, followed by three years in a preparatory school. High school lasts for three years. During the first two years, all students take the same required courses, and during the third year they specialize in arts, science, or mathematics. Examinations are held monthly, and a national exam is given at the end of the senior year. The Egyptian government specifies the manifest functions of higher education: to prepare graduates for the world of work, to develop scientific research, and to help solve the economic and social problems that confront Egypt's development (El-Meligi 1992). Although education is free at all levels, including college, children of the wealthy are several times as likely to get a college education.

Compared with farming skills, formal education is considered a luxury of little use in an agricultural society. Basic mathematics and reading are valued, however, because of the necessity to figure expenses and profits. Some agricultural countries are so poor that they can afford neither classrooms nor regular teachers, and few of their children attend school. Shown here is a math lesson in Nepal, taught by a traveling teacher who tries to acquaint children with addition and subtraction. For many children, such lessons will be the extent of their formal education.

The Functionalist Perspective: Providing Social Benefits

As stressed in previous chapters, a central position of functionalism is that when the parts of society are working properly, each contributes to the well-being or stability of that society. The intended consequences of people's actions are known as **manifest functions,** while those that are not intended are called **latent functions.** As we examine the functions of education, both its manifest and latent functions will become evident.

Teaching Knowledge and Skills

Education's most obvious manifest function is to teach knowledge and skills, whether those be the traditional three R's or their more contemporary version, such as computer literacy. Each society must train the next generation to fulfill its significant positions. From a functionalist perspective, this is the reason that schools are founded, parents support them, and taxes are raised to finance them.

Cultural Transmission of Values

At least as significant as teaching knowledge and skills is a function of education called **cultural transmission,** a process by which schools pass on a society's core values from one generation to the next. As discussed in Chapter 2, values lie at the center of every culture (see pages 45–48 for a summary of values that characterize U.S. culture). In addition to responding to the demands of industrialization, the need to produce an informed electorate, and the desire to Americanize immigrants, how else does the U.S. educational system reflect—and transmit—cultural values?

Schools are such an essential part of U.S. culture that it is difficult even to know where to begin. For example, the fact that instruction takes place almost exclusively in English, the dominant language of the society, reflects an intimate evolution from British institutions. Similarly, the architecture of school buildings themselves reflects Western culture, their often distinctive appearance identifying them as schools on sight, unlike, for example, the thatched-roof schools of some tropical societies.

Americans value "bigness," and this value is reflected in the U.S. educational system. With 47 million students attending grade and high schools, and another 14 million enrolled in college, U.S. education has become big business. Primary and secondary schools provide employment for 2.75 million teachers, while another 800,000 people

manifest functions: intended consequences of people's actions

latent functions: unintended consequences of people's actions

cultural transmission: in reference to education, the ways in which schools transmit a society's culture, especially its core values

teach in colleges and universities (*Statistical Abstract* 1993: Tables 239, 272, 274). Millions more work as support personnel—aides, administrators, bus drivers, janitors, and secretaries. Another several million earn their living in industries that service schools— from building schools to manufacturing pencils, paper, and desks.

To better understand the connection between education and values, let's look at how the educational system transmits individualism, competition, and patriotism.

Individualism Individualism forms a thread that is integrally woven into the U.S. educational system. Unlike their Japanese counterparts, U.S. teachers and students seldom focus on teamwork. Where Japanese schools stress that the individual is only one part of a larger, integrated whole, U.S. students learn that the individual is on his or her own. Pervasive but often subtle, such instruction begins in the early grades when teachers point out the success of a particular student. They might say, for example, "Everyone should be like José," or, "Why can't you be like María, who got all the answers right?" In such seemingly innocuous statements, the teacher thrusts one child ahead of the rest, holding the individual up for praise.

Competition Competitive games in the classroom and the schoolyard provide an apt illustration of how schools transmit this core value. In the classroom, a teacher may divide the class into competitive groups for a spelling bee, while on the playground children are encouraged to play hard-driving competitive games and sports. The school's formal sports program—baseball, football, basketball, soccer, hockey, volleyball, and so on— pits team against team in head-to-head confrontations, driving home the lesson that the competitive spirit is highly valued. Although organized sports stress teamwork, the individual is held up for praise. The custom of nominating an "outstanding player" (emphasizing which of these persons is *the* best) reinforces the related lesson of individualism.

Patriotism Finally, like schools around the world, U.S. schools feel a duty to teach patriotism. Consequently, U.S. students are taught that the United States is the best country in the world; Russians learn that no country is better than Russia; and French, German, British, Spanish, Japanese, Chinese, Afghani, and Egyptian students all learn the same about their respective countries. To instill patriotism, grade school teachers in every country extol the virtues of the society's founders, their struggle for freedom from oppression, and the goodness of the country's basic social institutions.

In the United States, grade school teachers wax eloquent when it comes to the exploits of George Washington—whether real or mythical (and each society tends to develop myths about its own early heroes). Throwing a silver dollar across the Potomac and chopping down the cherry tree are vivid memories many adults carry from their childhood classrooms—their hesitant suspicions about the waste of money or how such a

In addition to the manifest functions of education, a latent function is to produce social integration. Shown here is a classroom where students of contrasting backgrounds are not just learning the subject matter, but are being integrated.

good person could have chopped down a valued tree in the first place hushed by the teacher's stress on Washington's virtues: strength and accuracy in throwing the silver dollar, and honesty about the cherry tree.

Social Integration

Schools also perform the function of *social integration*, helping to mold students into a more or less cohesive unit. Indeed, as we just saw, forging a national identity by integrating immigrants into a common cultural heritage was one of the manifest functions of establishing a publicly funded system of education in the United States (Hellinger and Judd 1991). When children enter school, they come from many different backgrounds. Their particular family and social class may have taught them speech patterns, dress, and other behaviors or attitudes that differ from those generally recognized as desirable or acceptable. In the classroom and on the playground, those backgrounds take new shape. The end result is that schools help socialize students into the mainstream culture.

Peer culture is especially significant, for most students are eager to fit in. From their peers, they learn ideas and norms that go beyond their family and little corner of the world. Guided by today's powerful mass media, students in all parts of the country choose to look alike by wearing, for example, the same brands and styles of jeans, shirts, skirts, blouses, sneakers, and jackets. Parental influence rapidly declines as the peer culture molds not only the youths' appearance but even their ideas, speech patterns, and interaction with the opposite sex (Thorne and Luria 1993).

The classroom itself helps to produce social integration. As students salute the flag and sing the national anthem, for example, they become aware of the "greater government," and their sense of national identity grows. One of the best indicators of how education promotes political integration is the millions of immigrants who have attended U.S. schools, learned mainstream ideas, and given up their earlier national and cultural identities as they became Americans (Violas 1978).

How significant is this integrative function of education? It goes far beyond similarities of appearance or speech. To forge a national identity is to stabilize the political system itself. If people identify with a society's social institutions and *perceive them as the basis of their welfare* they have no reason to rebel. This function is especially significant when it comes to the lower social classes, the groups from which social revolutionaries would ordinarily be drawn. To get the lower classes to identify with the U.S. social system *as it is* goes a long way to preserving the system as it is.

Gatekeeping

Gatekeeping, or determining which people will enter what occupations, is another major function of education. Credentialing, the subject of the opening vignette, is an example of gatekeeping. Because Wendy did not have the credentials, but Melissa did, education closed the door to the one and opened it to the other.

Essential to the gatekeeping function is **tracking,** the sorting of students into different educational programs on the basis of real or perceived abilities. Tests are used to determine which students should be directed into "college prep" programs, while others are put onto a vocational track. The impact is lifelong, for, like Wendy and Melissa, throughout adulthood opportunities for jobs, raises, and promotions open or close on the basis of education.

Tracking begins in grade school, where on the basis of test results most students take regular courses, but some are placed in advanced sections of English and mathematics. In high school, tracking becomes more elaborate. In many schools, students are funneled into one of three tracks: general, college prep, or honors. All students who complete their sequence of courses receive a high school diploma and are eligible to go on to college. Those in the lowest track, however, are most likely to go to work after high school or at

gatekeeping: the process by which education opens and closes doors of opportunity; another term for the **social placement** function of education

tracking: the sorting of students into different educational programs on the basis of real or perceived abilities

best to attend a community college; those in the highest track usually enter the more prestigious colleges around the country; and those in between most often attend a local college or regional state university.

Gatekeeping sorts people on the basis of merit, say functionalists. Sociologists Talcott Parsons (1940), Kingsley Davis, and Wilbert Moore (1945), who pioneered this view, also known as **social placement,** argue that a major task of society is to fill its positions with capable people. Some positions, such as that of physician, require a high intellect and many years of arduous education. Consequently, to motivate capable people to postpone immediate gratification and submit to many years of rigorous education, society offers them high income and prestige. Other jobs require far fewer skills and can be performed by people of lesser intelligence. Thus, functionalists look on education as offering an opportunity for students with greater abilities and drive to get ahead. They see educational testing as a means of helping to determine people's abilities.

Promoting Personal Change

Personal change is achieved through critical thinking. Schools teach students to "think for themselves"—to critically evaluate ideas and social life. One consequence is that the further people go in school, the more open they tend to be to new ways of thinking and doing things. People with more education tend to hold more liberal ideas, while those with less education tend to be more conservative.

Promoting Social Change

The educational institution also contributes to social change by sponsoring research. Most university professors, for example, are given time off from teaching so that they can do research. Their findings become part of a body of accumulated knowledge that stimulates social change. Sociologists, for example, presented conclusions from sociological research before the U.S. Supreme Court that helped bring about the 1954 decision to desegregate U.S. schools. Some academic research has had an explosive impact on society—literally, in the case of the atomic and hydrogen weapons that were developed in part from university research. Nobody remains untouched by this function of education. For example, medical research conducted in universities across the world is partially responsible for the longer life span discussed in Chapter 13.

Mainstreaming

A new function of education is **mainstreaming,** incorporating people with disabilities into regular social activities. As a matter of routine policy, students with disabilities used to be placed in special schools. As the philosophy in the general society changed, educators also concluded that specialized schools did injustice to disabled students; in these settings they learned to adjust only to a world of the disabled and were left ill prepared to cope with the dominant world. The educational philosophy then changed to having disabled students attend regular schools.

Mainstreaming is easiest for students whose disabilities are minor, of course, for they fit more easily into regular schools. For people who cannot walk, wheelchair ramps are required; for those who cannot hear, "signers" (interpreters who use their hands) may attend classes with them. Most blind students still attend specialized schools, as do people with severe learning disabilities. Overall, two of five disabled school-age Americans attend school in regular classrooms, one of three splits the day between regular and specialized classrooms, and one of four spends most of the day in special classrooms (*Statistical Abstract* 1993: Table 256).

social placement: a function of education that funnels people into a society's various positions

mainstreaming: helping people to become part of the mainstream of society

Replacing Family Functions

U.S. education has become a rival for some family functions. Child care is an example. Grade schools do double duty as baby-sitters for parents who both work, or for single mothers in the work force. Child care has always been a latent function of formal education, for it was an unintended consequence of schooling. Now, however, since most families have two wage earners, child care has changed into a manifest function. Some schools even offer child care both before and after formal classes. Another example is providing sex education, which has stirred controversy, for some families resent this function being taken from them.

Other Functions

Education also fulfills many other functions. For example, because most students are unmarried, high schools and colleges effectively serve as *matchmaking* institutions. It is here that many young people find their future spouses. The sociological significance of this function of schools is that they funnel people into marriages with mates of similar social class background, interests, and educational level. Schools also establish *social networks*. Some older adults maintain friendship networks from high school and college, while others become part of business or professional networks that prove highly beneficial to their careers. Finally, schools also help to *stabilize employment*. Industrialized societies have little use for unskilled individuals. Schools keep part of the population out of the labor market, thereby reserving those positions for older workers.

The Conflict Perspective: Maintaining Social Inequality

Conflict theorists offer a sharply different view of education. Unlike functionalists, who see education as a social institution that performs functions for the benefit of society, conflict theorists see the educational system as a tool used by those in the controlling sector of society to maintain their dominance.

The Hidden Curriculum

From a conflict perspective, the real purpose of education is to teach a **hidden curriculum.** This term describes the unwritten rules of behavior and attitudes, such as obedience to authority and conformity to cultural norms, that are taught in the schools in addition to the formal curriculum (Gillborn 1992). The purpose of this hidden curriculum is to perpetuate existing social inequalities. For example, the values and work habits taught to help students "prepare for life" are merely devices to teach the middle and lower classes to support society's elite. Members of the elite need people to run their business empires, and they are more comfortable if their managers possess "refined" language and manners. Consequently, middle-class schools, whose teachers know where their pupils are headed, place high stress on "proper" English and "good" manners. Since few of the lower class will occupy managerial positions, teachers in inner-city schools allow ethnic and street language in the classroom. These children do not need "refined" speech and manners; they simply need to be taught to obey rules so they can take their place in the closely supervised, low-status positions for which they are destined (Bowles and Gintis 1976; Olneck and Bills 1980). From the conflict perspective, even kindergarten has a hidden curriculum, as the Down-to-Earth Sociology box on page 476 illustrates.

hidden curriculum: the unwritten goals of schools, such as obedience to authority and conformity to cultural norms

Table 17.1

What States Spend on Education, per Student

Rank	State	Expenditure	Rank	State	Expenditure	Rank	State	Expenditure
1.	New Jersey	10,219	18.	Virginia	5,487	35.	California	4,686
2.	Alaska	9,248	19.	Hawaii	5,453	36.	Nebraska	4,676
3.	New York	8,658	20.	Ohio	5,451	37.	Texas	4,651
4.	Connecticut	8,299	21.	Indiana	5,429	38.	Kentucky	4,616
5.	Vermont	6,992	22.	West Virginia	5,415	39.	South Carolina	4,537
6.	Pennsylvania	6,980	23.	Wyoming	5,333	40.	Missouri	4,534
7.	Rhode Island	6,834	24.	Washington	5,331	41.	Louisiana	4,378
8.	Massachusetts	6,323	25.	Colorado	5,259	42.	South Dakota	4,255
9.	Maryland	6,273	26.	Illinois	5,238	43.	North Dakota	4,119
10.	Delaware	6,080	27.	Kansas	5,131	44.	Oklahoma	3,939
11.	Oregon	5,972	28.	Montana	5,127	45.	Arkansas	3,770
12.	Wisconsin	5,972	29.	Iowa	4,949	46.	Tennessee	3,736
13.	Maine	5,969	30.	Nevada	4,910	47.	Alabama	3,675
14.	Florida	5,639	31.	North Carolina	4,857	48.	Idaho	3,528
15.	Michigan	5,630	32.	Arizona	4,750	49.	Mississippi	3,344
16.	Minnesota	5,510	33.	Georgia	4,720	50.	Utah	3,092
17.	New Hampshire	5,500	34.	New Mexico	4,692		AVERAGE	$5,486

Note: These are 1992 figures. They refer to the amount spent per student in grade school and high school.

Source: Statistical Abstract 1993: Table 251.

Stacking the Deck: Unequal Funding

Conflict theorists observe that funding for education is a scarce resource unequally distributed among rich and poor students, and even among different geographical regions. The geographical inequality becomes readily visible when we look at Table 17.1. You can see that for each of its students New Jersey spends more than three times what Utah spends for its students. If you divide the list in the middle, you can see that all eleven eastern states rank in the top half, while nine of the southern states fall in the bottom half. Although higher expenditure is generally associated with higher educational quality, high spending does not guarantee quality education. The students from Iowa, for example, which ranks only twenty-ninth in expenditure, score the highest on the SAT test. But this figure, too, is misleading, for compared with some other states not as many Iowan graduates take the test. Table 17.2 shows this same situation on an international level. Although Switzerland spends the most per student and gets the best test results, the United States is the third highest spender but gets the worst test results.

Conflict theorists go beyond this observation, however. They stress that how schools are funded stacks the deck against the poor of each state. Because public schools are largely supported by local property taxes, the more well-to-do communities (where property values are higher) have more to spend on their children, while the poorer communities end up with much less. Consequently, the richer communities are able to offer higher salaries (and take their pick of the most highly qualified and motivated teachers), afford the latest textbooks and microcomputers, as well as teach additional courses in foreign language, music, and so on. Because U.S. schools so closely reflect the U.S. social class system, then, the children of the privileged emerge from grade school best equipped for success in high school, and, in turn, come out of high school best equipped for success in college.

Table 17.2				
Educational Expenditures and Student Scores				
Rank by Student Performance	Country	Math Scores (percentage correct)	Science Scores (percentage correct)	Money Spent per Student
1.	Switzerland	71%	74%	$4,621
2.	Italy	64	70	3,082
3.	France	64	69	2,550
4.	Canada	62	69	4,268
5.	Ireland	61	63	1,769
6.	Spain	55	68	1,819
7.	United States	55	67	4,126

Note: These are the only countries in the source for which both expenditures and test scores are given. Based on testing of 13-year-olds. Expenditures are for 1988, test scores for 1991.

Source: Statistical Abstract 1992: Table 1369; 1993: Table 1384.

Discrimination by IQ: Tilting the Tests

How would you answer the following question?

A symphony is to a composer as a book is to a(n) _____.

___ paper ___ sculptor ___ musician ___ author ___ man

You probably had no difficulty coming up with "author" as your choice. Wouldn't any intelligent person have done so?

In point of fact, this question raises a central issue in intelligence testing. Not all intelligent people would know how to answer it, because it contains *cultural biases*. In other words, children from some backgrounds are more familiar with the concepts of symphonies, composers, sculptors, and musicians than are other children. Consequently, the test is tilted in their favor (Turner 1972; Ashe 1992).

Perhaps asking a different question will make the bias clearer. How would you answer this question?

If you throw dice and "7" is showing on the top, what is facing down?

___ seven ___ snake eyes ___ box cars ___ little Joes ___ eleven

This question, suggested by Adrian Dove (n.d.), a social worker in Watts, is slanted toward a lower-class experience. It surely is obvious that this *particular* cultural bias tilts the test so that children from some social backgrounds will perform better than others.

It is no different with IQ (intelligence quotient) tests that use words such as *composer* and *symphony*. A lower-class child may have heard about rap, rock, or jazz but not about symphonies. In other words, IQ tests measure not only intelligence but also culturally acquired knowledge. Whatever else we can say, the cultural bias built into the IQ tests used in schools is clearly *not* tilted in favor of the lower class.

A second inadequacy of IQ tests is that they focus on mathematical, spatial, symbolic, and linguistic abilities. Intelligence, however, consists of more than these components. The ability to compose music, to be empathetic to the feelings of others, or to be humorous or persuasive are also components of intelligence.

The significance of these factors, say conflict theorists, is that culturally biased IQ tests favor the middle classes and discriminate against students from lower-class backgrounds. These tests, used to track students, assign disproportionate numbers of minorities and the poor to noncollege tracks (Kershaw 1992). This outcome, as we have seen, destines them for lower-paying jobs in adult life. Thus, conflict theorists view IQ tests as another weapon in the arsenal designed to maintain the social class structure over the generations (Postman 1992).

Down-To-Earth Sociology

Kindergarten as Boot Camp

SOCIOLOGIST HARRY GRACEY (1991), who did participant observation in a kindergarten, concluded that kindergarten is a sort of boot camp for the entire educational system. Here, tender students are drilled in the behaviors and attitudes deemed appropriate for the "student role," which, he argued, is to follow classroom routines. The goal of kindergarten is to mold many individuals from diverse backgrounds into a compliant group that will, on command, unthinkingly follow classroom routines.

Kindergarten's famous "show and tell," for example, does not merely allow children to be expressive. It also teaches them to talk only when they are asked to speak. ("It's 'your turn,' Jarmay.") The format also teaches children to request permission to talk ("Who knows what Letitia has?") by raising a hand and being acknowledged. Finally, the whole ritual teaches children to acknowledge the teacher's ideas as superior. (She is the one who has the capacity to evaluate students' activities and ideas.)

Gracey found a similar hidden curriculum in the other activities he observed. Whether it was drawing pictures, listening to records, snack time, or rest time, the teachers would quiet talkative students, even scolding them at times, while giving approval for conforming behaviors. In short, the message is that the teacher—and, by inference, the entire school system—is the authority.

The purpose of kindergarten, Gracey concluded, is to teach children to "follow orders with unquestioning obedience." To accomplish this, kindergarten teachers "create and enforce a rigid social structure in the classroom through which they effectively control the behavior of most of the children for most of the school day." This produces three kinds of students: (1) "good" students who submit to school-imposed discipline and come to identify with it; (2) "adequate" students who submit to the school's discipline but do not identify with it; and (3) "bad" students who refuse to submit to school routines. This third type is also known as "problem children." To bring them into line, a tougher drill sergeant, the school psychologist, is called in.

Learning the student role prepares children for grade school, where they "will be asked to submit to systems and routines imposed by the teachers and the curriculum. The days will be much like those of kindergarten, except that academic subjects will be substituted . . ."

Gracey adds that these lessons extend well beyond the classroom, that they prepare students for the routines of the work world, whether those be of the assembly line or the office. Mastering the student role prepares them to follow unquestioningly the routines imposed by "the company."

The Correspondence Principle

Conflict sociologists Samuel Bowles and Herbert Gintis (1976) used the term **correspondence principle** to refer to the ways in which schools correspond to (or reflect) the social structure of society. This term means that the educational system reinforces the status quo and thus helps to perpetuate a society's social inequalities. The following list provides some examples.

correspondence principle: the sociological principle that schools correspond to (or reflect) the social structure of society

Society	Schools
Capitalism–free enterprise	Promote competition
Social inequality	Unequal funding of schools, track the poor to vocations
Racial–ethnic prejudice	Make minorities feel inferior, track minorities to vocations
Bureaucratic structure of the corporation	Authority structure of the classroom

Need for submissive workers	Make students submissive
Need for dependable workers	Promote punctuality
Need to maintain armed forces	Promote patriotism (to fight for capitalism)

Thus, conclude conflict theorists, the U.S. educational system is designed to produce dependable workers who will not question their bosses, as well as some individuals who will go on to be innovators in thought and action but can still be counted on to be loyal to the social system as it exists (Olneck and Bills 1980).

The Bottom Line: Reproducing the Social Class Structure

From unequal funding to IQ tests—what is the bottom line? For conflict theorists it is that education *reproduces the social class structure*; that is, education promotes the interests of a society's power elite and perpetuates a society's social class divisions. Regardless of their abilities, for example, children of the more well-to-do are likely to be placed in college-bound tracks, children of the poor into vocational tracks, and each to inherit matching life opportunities laid down before they were born.

If this is true, family background would be more important than test scores in predicting who attends college. Sociologist Samuel Bowles (1977) decided to find out. His results are shown in Figure 17.3. Of the *brightest* 25 percent of high school students, 90 percent of those from affluent homes went to college, while only half of those from low-income homes did so. Of the *weakest* students, 26 percent from affluent homes go to college, while only 6 percent from poorer homes do so. And today? This same general relationship still holds. If you rank families from the poorest to the richest, at each income level the likelihood that the children will attend college increases (Manski 1992–1993).

Chapters 10 and 12 reviewed how the U.S. class system is related to race and ethnicity. To see how the educational system reproduces this aspect of the social class structure, look at Figure 17.4 on page 478 which shows the *funneling effect* of education. You can see that whites are more likely to complete high school, to go to college, and to get a bachelor's degree. African Americans and Latinos, in contrast, are not only more likely to drop out of high school, but those who do complete high school are less likely to go to college, and those who do go to college are considerably less likely to graduate. In short, whites are more likely to be funneled in one direction, African Americans and Latinos in another. This is not due to the educational system alone, but mostly to the discrimination built into U.S. society, which we reviewed in earlier chapters.

The educational system, however, say conflict theorists, is an essential part of this process. Most children of the less privileged are funneled into community college vocational programs, while children of the middle classes attend state universities and small private colleges. The offspring of the elite, in contrast, attend exclusive boarding high schools, where their learning environment includes small classes and well-paid teachers (Persell et al. 1992). Here they inherit a cozy social network between the school's college advisers and the admissions officers of the nation's most elite colleges. Some of these networks are so efficient that half of these private school's graduating classes are admitted to Harvard, Yale, and Princeton (Persell and Cookson 1985).

▼ **In Sum** Conflict theorists stress that the best education is reserved for children of the elite, which prepares this group to continue its dominance of society. A middle

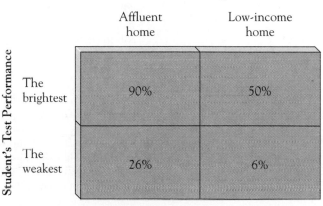

Student's Background

	Affluent home	Low-income home
The brightest	90%	50%
The weakest	26%	6%

Student's Test Performance

Note: A study by Sewell and Shah (1968) showed even greater effects of social class than did Bowles's (1977) study.

Source: Bowles 1977.

Figure 17.3

Who Goes to College? The Role of Social Class and Personal Ability in Determining College Attendance.

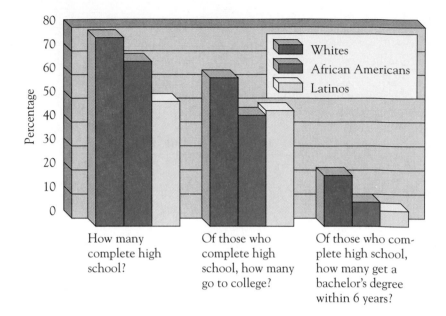

Figure 17.4

The Funneling Effects of Education: Race and Ethnicity.

Source: Statistical Abstract 1992: Table 283; 1993: Tables 263, 270.

level of education is reserved for children of the middle class, who are trained to serve the elite in managerial positions. Except for the very brightest and most industrious, children of the poor are blocked from higher education (Apple 1982; Hurn 1985; Useem 1992). The following Thinking Critically section explores how education helps some students accept a lesser status in life.

Thinking Critically About Social Controversy

The "Cooling-Out" Function of Higher Education

▼ SOCIOLOGIST BURTON CLARK found that most students who enter California's community colleges want to go on to study for a bachelor's degree. Although about two-thirds enroll in programs that permit them to transfer to a four-year college or university, only about one-third of those students actually do so.

Clark (1990) wanted to find out why one-third of the students change their minds. Why do they give up their original intention and accept a lower status? His research revealed that it was not so much that *they* change their minds as that the community college changes their minds for them. He referred to this process as "cooling out." Let's look at it.

First, pre-entrance testing funnels poorly qualified students into remedial classes, initiating a process of doubt about the reality of planning to go on for a higher degree. Significantly, the test results also become part of a folder that counselors use.

Second, a counselor meets with the students in order to "help students to accept their limitations" so they can "strive for success in worthwhile objectives that are within their grasp." The counselor begins to "gently" nudge the students toward a "terminal program" by getting them to enroll in "proper" courses.

Third, the students take a course entitled, "Orientation to College," in which the goal is "to assist students to evaluate their own abilities and vocational choices." As part of this course, the students must do a "self-appraisal of fitness" for occupations.

The "evidence" gradually accumulates: test scores, course grades, and recommendations from teachers and counselors. This procedure is designed to "heighten self-awareness in relation to choice." Counselors then begin to encourage students to move from a transfer major to a one- or two-year program of vocational, business, or semiprofessional training.

Fourth, the students face a different classroom reality from that of high school, for no longer are they automatically passed. When they receive low grades, they are referred back to a counselor who asks the student to do more "self-assessment."

Finally, students who continue to do poorly are put on probation. A primary effect of probation is the "slow killing off of lingering hopes" that students may still have of earning a bachelor's degree.

Why does Clark use the term "cooling out"? He argues that the process itself is kept hidden from the student and the community. The college advertises itself as a transfer college, yet most students never transfer to another college but instead are diverted to terminal programs. To "cool out" students—so that they feel good about themselves and the college—the school uses the following techniques.

- *Gradual disengagement.* The process just outlined is designed to let the student only gradually become aware that their original goals are inappropriate.
- *Objective denial.* The objective record (in the counselor's folder) is designed to "speak for itself." It is not the college or counselor who is dictating a new choice, but the record that shows another choice of career to be more appropriate.
- *Alternative achievement.* As students are diverted away from their original choice, an "alternative career" is made to appear not too different from the original goal. In this way, students do not "fail," but merely correct a "mistake."
- *Consolation.* Counselors try to be patient with the "overambitious." They gently teach them the value of alternative careers and console them about the lower status.

Clark found that dealing "softly" is essential to cooling out students. Counselors, for example, do not tell a student that he or she is not smart enough to become an engineer, an attorney, or a physician. Rather, counselors gradually steer them toward pursuits thought more appropriate to their abilities. If the cooling out is successful, the student will embrace the alternative career, find it a "more appropriate" choice than the original, while the underlying process of making that "right" choice will remain invisible to him or her.

For Your Consideration

1. Provide an alternative explanation for the points that Clark makes. (*Hint:* If you apply the functionalist perspective, the same points will look quite different.)
2. What do you think community colleges could do to increase the proportion of students who transfer to four-year colleges and do well there? ▲

The Symbolic Interactionist Perspective: Teacher Expectations and the Self-Fulfilling Prophecy

Whereas functionalists look at how education functions to benefit society and conflict theorists examine how education perpetuates social inequality, symbolic interactionists study face-to-face interactions inside the classroom. They have found that the expectations of teachers have profound consequences for their students.

The Rist Research

In 1970, sociologist Ray Rist did participant observation in an African-American grade school with an African-American faculty. Rist found that tracking begins with the teacher's perceptions. After only eight days in the classroom, the kindergarten teacher felt that she knew the children's abilities well enough to assign them to three separate worktables. To Table 1, Mrs. Caplow assigned those she considered to be "fast learners." They sat at the front of the room, closest to her. Those whom she saw as "slow learners," she assigned to Table 3, located at the back of the classroom. She placed "average" students at Table 2, in between the other tables.

This pattern seemed strange to Rist. He knew that the children had not been tested for ability, yet the teacher was certain that she could differentiate between bright and slow children. Investigating further, Rist found that social class was the underlying basis for assigning the children to the different tables. Middle-class students were separated out for Table 1, children from poorer homes to Tables 2 and 3. The teacher paid the most attention to the children at Table 1, who were closest to her, less to Table 2, and the least to Table 3. As the year went on, children from Table 1 perceived that they were treated better and that they were better students. They became the leaders in class activities and even ridiculed children at the other tables, calling them "dumb." Eventually, the children at Table 3 disengaged themselves from many classroom activities. Not surprisingly, at the end of the year only the children at Table 1 had completed the lessons that prepared them for reading.

This early tracking stuck. When these students entered the first grade, their new teacher looked at the work they had accomplished and placed students from Table 1 at her Table 1. She treated her tables much as the kindergarten teacher had, and the children at Table 1 again led the class.

The children's reputations continued to follow them. The second-grade teacher reviewed their scores and also divided her class into three groups. The first she named the "Tigers," and, befitting their name, gave them challenging readers. Not surprisingly, the Tigers came from the original Table 1 in kindergarten. The second group she called the "Cardinals." They came from the original Tables 2 and 3. Her third group consisted of children she had failed the previous year, whom she called the "Clowns." The Cardinals and Clowns were given less advanced readers.

Rist concluded that *the child's journey through school was preordained from the eighth day of kindergarten!* What had occurred was a **self-fulfilling prophecy,** a term coined by sociologist Robert Merton (1949) to refer to an originally false assumption of what is going to happen that comes true simply because it was predicted. For example, if people believe an unfounded rumor that a bank is in trouble and assume that they won't be able to get their money out, they all rush to the bank to demand their money. The prediction—although *originally false*—is now likely to be true.

In this case, of course, we are dealing with something more important than money the welfare of little children. As was the case with the Saints and the Roughnecks in Chapter 8, labels are powerful. They have a tendency to set people on courses of action that affect the rest of their lives. That, of course, is the significance of Rist's observations of these grade school children.

The Rosenthal-Jacobson Experiment

During the course of our education, most of us have seen teacher expectations at work. On one level, we know that if a teacher expects higher standards, then we must perform at a higher level to earn good grades. Teacher expectations, however, also work in ways that we don't perceive, as social psychologists Robert Rosenthal and Lenore Jacobson discovered. In what has become a classic experiment, Rosenthal and Jacobson (1968) tried out a new test in a San Francisco grade school. They tested the children's abilities and then told the teachers which students would probably "spurt" ahead during the year. They instructed the teachers to watch these students' progress, but not to let the students or their parents know about the test results. At the end of the year, they tested the students again and found that the IQs of the predicted "spurters" had jumped ten to fifteen points higher than those of the other children.

You might think that Rosenthal and Jacobson then became famous for developing a very useful scholastic aptitude test. Actually, however, this "test" was another of those covert experiments. Rosenthal and Jacobson had simply given routine IQ tests to the children and had then *randomly* chosen 20 percent of the students as "spurters." These students were *no different* from the others in the classroom. A self-fulfilling prophecy had taken place: The teachers expected more of those particular students, and the students responded. In short, expect dumb and you get dumb. Expect smart, and you get smart.

self-fulfilling prophecy:
Robert Merton's term for an originally false assertion that becomes true simply because it was predicted

As discussed in the text, high educational expenditures do not guarantee excellent results. More important are teacher expectations that motivate students to perform at a higher or lower level. Excellent facilities, however, certainly can help this process.

Although attempts to replicate this experiment have had mixed results (Pilling and Pringle 1978), a good deal of research confirms that students who are expected to do better generally do (Seaver 1973; Snyder 1991).

How Do Teacher Expectations Work?

How do teacher expectations actually work? Observations of classroom interaction give us some idea (Leacock 1969; Rist 1970; Buckley 1991; Farkas 1991). The teacher's own middle-class background comes into play, for teachers are pleased when middle-class students ask probing questions. They take these as a sign of intelligence. When lower-class students ask similar questions, however, teachers are more likely to interpret those questions as "smart aleck." In addition, lower-class children are more likely to reflect a subculture that "puts down" intellectual achievements, an attitude that causes teachers to react negatively.

Sociologist George Farkas (1990a, 1990b) led a team of researchers in probing how teacher expectations affect grades. Using a stratified sample of students in a large urban school district in the Southwest and a survey of their teachers, the researchers discovered that students who scored similarly on tests over the course materials did not necessarily receive the same grade for the course. They found that females and Asian Americans averaged higher course grades than males, African Americans, Latinos, and whites—even though they all had scored the same on the course work.

To explain this, the first conclusion most of us would jump to would be discrimination. In this case, however, such an explanation does not seem to work very well, for it is most unlikely that the teachers would be prejudiced against males and whites. Farkas used symbolic interactionism to interpret these unexpected results. He noted that some students "signal" to their teachers that they are "good students." The teachers pick up those "signals" and reward such persons with better grades. The "signals" that communicate "good student" are not surprising—greater docility (eagerness to cooperate and accept what the teacher says) combined with greater diligence (a show of effort and interest). In short, some students signal that they are interested in what the teacher is teaching and that they are "trying hard." Females and Asian Americans, the researchers concluded, are most likely to display these characteristics.

We do not yet have enough information on how teachers form their expectations, how they communicate them to students, or exactly how these expectations influence teacher–student interaction. Nor do we know very much about how students "signal" messages to teachers. Perhaps you will become the educational sociologist who will shed more light on this significant area of human behavior.

Problems in U.S. Education—and Their Solutions

To conclude this chapter, let us examine some of the major problems—and potential solutions—of U.S. education today.

Problems: SAT Scores, Grade Inflation, Social Promotion, Functional Illiteracy, Violence, and Teen Pregnancy

Failing Test Scores   Perhaps nothing so captures what is wrong with U.S. schools than this event reported by sociologist Thomas Sowell (1993):

> [A]n international study of 13-year-olds . . . found that Koreans ranked first in mathematics and Americans last. When asked if they thought they were "good at mathematics," only 23 percent of the Korean youngsters said "yes"—compared to 68 percent of American 13-year-olds. The American educational dogma that students should "feel good about themselves" was a success in its own terms—though not in any other terms.

In 1983, a blue-ribbon presidential panel gave a grim assessment of U.S. education, warning of a "rising tide of mediocrity that threatens our very future as a nation and as a people." Even the title of the report, *A Nation at Risk*, sounded an alarm. Among other problems, they were upset that national averages on the Scholastic Aptitude Test (SAT) had dropped. As Figure 17.5 shows, the math scores have recovered a good part of the lost ground. The verbal scores, however, are holding at their lows. Both are lower than they were twenty-five years ago.

The president of the American Federation of Teachers has come up with a unique defense of the decline in SAT scores—they are a sign that teachers are now doing a better job! The low test scores, he says, are the result of teachers being successful in getting more students to stay in high school and to go on to college. In the past, these students from poorer academic backgrounds would have dropped out and not have become part of the test results (Sowell 1993). Perhaps this is the reason. But if it is, it indicates not success, but a severe underlying problem— teachers are giving inferior education to disadvantaged students (Murray and Herrnstein 1992).

Others suggest that SAT scores have declined because children find television and video games more appealing than reading (Rigdon and Swasy 1990). Students who read little acquire a smaller vocabulary and less rigor in thought and verbal expression. Sociologists Donald Hayes and Loreen Wolfer (1993a, 1993b) are convinced that the culprit is the "dummied down" textbooks that pervade U.S. schools. Some point their fingers at other low standards: "frill" courses, less homework, fewer term papers, grade inflation, and burned-out teachers who are more interested in collecting paychecks than in educating their students. Some of the examples they offer are startling, such as the college freshman who couldn't understand why she was doing poorly in college since she had placed third in her Chicago high school graduating class. Testing showed that she ranked in the lowest 2 percent of the nation's high school graduates (Kotlowitz 1992).

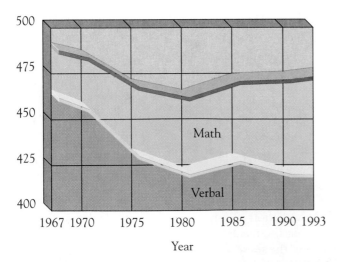

Sources: Powell and Steelman 1984; De Witt 1993; various editions of *Statistical Abstract.*

Figure 17.5

National Results of the Scholastic Aptitude Test (SAT)

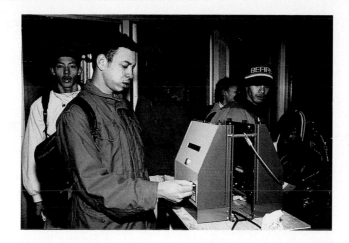

Violence in U.S. schools has become a major problem. As a consequence, New York City high school students are subject to random metal detector tests and, as shown here, they must pass a security check before being admitted to school. Do you think this is the future of most U.S. high schools?

The signs of a deteriorated educational system go on. Only 11 percent of California's eighth-graders can solve seventh-grade math problems (Sowell 1993). Overall, two-thirds of U.S. schoolchildren read below their grade level, and only one-third of high school seniors can competently understand their texts (Sharpe 1993).

Grade Inflation, Social Promotion, and Functional Illiteracy   At the same time that learning declined, grades went up. In the 1960s, high school teachers gave out about twice as many C's as A's, but now the A's exceed the C's. Another sign of **grade inflation** is that one-fifth of all entering college freshmen have an overall high school grade-point average of A– or higher (Sowell 1993).

Grade inflation in the face of declining standards has been accompanied by **social promotion,** the practice of passing students from one grade to the next even though they have not mastered basic materials. One unfortunate result is **functional illiteracy,** people who have difficulty with reading and writing even though they have graduated from high school. Some high school graduates cannot fill out job applications; other's can't figure out if they are given the right change at the grocery store.

Violence in Schools

James Murphy was teaching his government class at Dartmouth High, in a quiet university town 50 miles south of Boston, when two Dartmouth students and a third teenager suddenly burst through the door. One brandished a bat, another a billy club, and the third a hunting knife. When they asked for Shawn Pina, Jason Robinson made the fatal mistake of asking why they wanted him. When Murphy saw one go after Robinson with the bat, he wrestled the assailant to the floor. Another plunged his knife into Robinson's stomach, killing him. (Toch 1993)

Many U.S. schools have deteriorated to the point that basic safety is an issue, putting students' lives at peril, a condition that only a few years back would have been unimaginable. Consequently, in some schools uniformed guards have become a fixture, while in others students can gain entrance only after passing through metal detectors (Stecklow 1993). Some schools even supplement the traditional fire drills with "drive-by shooting drills" (Toch 1993).

Teenage Pregnancy   Students who lack a high school diploma face a severe handicap in life. At several points in this text, I have mentioned the highly negative consequences that often follow single motherhood, especially the cycle of poverty (see pages 274 and 446). Those consequences are especially stark for teenage mothers. Not only do these young women, some still girls, have the expense and responsibility of caring for a child, but they also are unlikely to complete high school, thus perpetuating a cycle of poverty and interrupted education.

grade inflation: higher grades given for the same work; a general rise in student grades without a corresponding increase in learning or test scores

social promotion: passing students to the next grade even though they have not mastered basic materials

functional illiterate: a high school graduate who has difficulty with basic reading and math

Solutions: Retention, Safety, Standards, and Other Reforms

It is one thing to identify problems, and quite another to find solutions for them. Let's begin by looking at a program designed to meet the problem of teen pregnancy, as described in the following Thinking Critically section, and then consider solutions to the other problems we have just reviewed.

▼▲▼▲▼▲▼▲▼▲▼▲▼▲▼▲▼▲▼▲▼▲▼▲▼▲▼▲▼▲▼

Thinking Critically About Social Controversy

High Schools and Teen Pregnancy: A Program That Works

▼ TO IMPROVE THE HIGH school graduation rates of teenage mothers, researchers in Ohio designed a program called LEAP—Learning, Earning, and Parenting. They made it tough for themselves by singling out teenage mothers on welfare, the group of teenage mothers that has the least chance of completing high school. The researchers randomly selected twelve of Ohio's eighty-eight counties, which included rural, suburban, and urban counties. All teens who were receiving Aid to Families with Dependent Children (AFDC), 7,000 individuals, became part of LEAP. They were required to stay in school or to return to school if they had dropped out—either to high school or to an Adult Basic Education program leading to a high school diploma (GED).

The teens were randomly assigned to either one of two groups. Those in the *experimental group* received a $62 bonus in their welfare check for providing evidence that they were enrolled in school and attending an assessment interview. Teens who did not comply had $62 deducted from their check. For each month they were absent no more than four times, the mothers received an additional $62 on their check, while those absent more than four times had $62 deducted from theirs. Sixty-two dollars may not sound like much, but since the monthly AFDC grant was $274, receiving a check with a bonus ($336) or a check with the penalty ($212) made a considerable difference. Mothers who enrolled in school were also eligible for assistance with child care and transportation to attend school. In contrast, teens assigned to the *control group* were treated as usual—no school attendance requirements, no child care or transportation, no bonuses, and no deductions.

The program design is simple and straightforward, and, as discussed in Chapter 5 (pages 130–132), random assignment to control and experimental groups allows us to separate cause and effect. What, then, were the results? These are shown in Figure 17.6.

As you can see, teen mothers are like the rest of us—we all desire incentives and try to avoid punishments. Because of the random assignment to the groups, we know that the higher rates of retention and returning to school are due to the experimental variable. Beyond its effectiveness, what is also good is the program's cost. There is little additional bureaucracy to feed, nor are there expensive educational programs to design and administer. There is little administrative work involved—simply identifying the teens and adjusting checks on the basis of attendance data. In addition, a good part of the cost is covered by an internal transfer of money: for every two teens who received bonuses, one teen received penalties.

If you were in charge of this program, how might you modify it to improve the results? Although the program had positive results, two of five teens in the experimental group still dropped out. If you were Ohio's administrator, would you recommend that the program be continued? Do you think this program should be applied nationally? Why or why not?

Source: Based on Bloom et al. 1993.

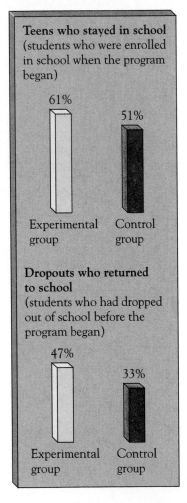

Figure 17.6

LEAP'S Impact on High School Retention and Dropouts

Teens who stayed in school
(students who were enrolled in school when the program began)

61% Experimental group
51% Control group

Dropouts who returned to school
(students who had dropped out of school before the program began)

47% Experimental group
33% Control group

A Secure Learning Environment The first criterion for a good education is security, to guarantee students' physical safety and freedom from fear. Granted the high rate of violence in U.S. society, some violence is bound to spill over into the schools, but basic steps can be taken to minimize that spillover. Fortunately, most U.S. schools are not yet violent, and those that are can be changed. School administrators and teachers can reclaim the schools by expelling all students who threaten the welfare of others and to refuse to tolerate threats, violence, drugs, and weapons (Toby 1992).

Higher Standards Within a secure learning environment, then, steps can be taken to improve the quality of education. The president's commission mentioned earlier concluded that U.S. schools need higher standards. The commission recommended that high school students take more courses in math, science, English, social studies, and computer science. The members also recommended that schools recruit more qualified teachers by paying higher salaries. To see why, review Figure 17.2 on page 467.

A study by sociologists James Coleman and Thomas Hoffer (1987) provides helpful guidelines for improving the quality of education. They wanted to see why students in Catholic schools average test scores 15 to 20 percent higher than students in public schools. Is it because they attract better students, while the public schools have to put up with everyone? To find out, Coleman and Hoffer measured the initial knowledge of 15,000 students in public and Catholic high schools. They then tracked those students for three years. Their findings? From their sophomore through their senior years, students at Catholic schools gain the equivalent of about a full grade in verbal and math skills. The superior test performance of students in Catholic schools, they concluded, is due not to better students, but to higher standards. Catholic schools have not watered down their curriculum as have public schools. The researchers also identified parental involvement as a significant factor, finding that parents and teachers in Catholic schools reinforced each other's commitment to the importance of learning.

Sociologist Michael Rutter (1979), who did a three-year study of twelve inner-city schools in London, drew similar conclusions—that the characteristics of the school are more important than the social class or abilities of their students. Learning was higher in schools where teachers stressed academic achievement and where they regularly assigned and checked homework. Not insignificantly, the teacher expectations that we studied earlier come into play, for the findings of Rutter, Coleman, and Hoffer support the basic principle that students do better in schools where they are expected to do well.

Other Reforms—From School Choice to Site-Based Management There is no lack of proposals for improving schools, but perhaps the one that has gained the most media attention—both because it is so controversial and because it holds such potential—is the use of tuition vouchers to bring about **school choice.** The main outline of this proposal is that the state would give the parents of each school-age child a voucher to be spent on the school of the parents' choice. As you can see from Table 17.1, the states have a great deal of money to work with, and the amount available per pupil would be rather large. Public and private schools—even those operated by individuals and business firms—would compete for the vouchers. With each school's test results published in the newspapers and otherwise readily available, parents would be able to shop around for the school they like best (Bolick 1994; Stecklow 1994).

Although many applaud this proposal, others fear that vouchers would mean the end of public schools as vouchers would drain away their resources. Proponents of the proposal reply that there is no reason why public schools can't compete in the marketplace, that vouchers would merely stimulate them to produce better results. Those that can't produce should fold.

Public school teachers and administrators are especially fearful of this proposal, for it threatens their jobs. In the face of persistent dissatisfaction with the performance of public schools and a growing demand for reform, administrators and teachers are developing proposals designed to keep public education out of private hands. At the center of these counterproposals is *site-based management,* a term that refers to schools designing their own reforms (Dunleavey 1994). We don't yet know the specifics of such reforms, but if they mean that students will be held accountable for meeting high academic standards and that teachers will be accountable for teaching at a high level, the potential is encouraging.

Reform in anything needs a guiding principle. I suggest that this serve as the guiding principle in reforming education: the problem is not the ability of the students, but rather the educational system itself. That this is true becomes apparent when we consider the results reported in the following Thinking Critically section, with which we close this chapter.

school choice: parents being able to choose the school their child will attend; often used in the context of expecting for-profit schools to compete for vouchers issued by the state

Breaking Through the Barriers: The Jaime Escalante Approach to Restructuring the Classroom

▼ CALLED "THE BEST TEACHER in America," Jaime Escalante taught in an East Los Angeles inner-city school plagued with poverty, crime, drugs, gangs, and the usual miserably low student scores. In this self-defeating environment, he taught calculus. His students scored so highly on national tests that test officials, suspecting cheating, asked his students to retake the test. They did. Again they passed—this time with even higher scores

Escalante's school ranks fourth in the nation in the number of students who have taken and passed the Advanced Placement SAT Calculus examination. In order for students to even take the test, they must complete Algebra I, Geometry, Algebra II, Trigonometry or Math Analysis, and Calculus for first-year college and/or Calculus for second-year college.

How did Escalante overcome such odds? His success is *not* due to a recruitment of the brightest students. Students' poor academic performance does not stand in the way of being admitted to the math program. The *only* requirement is an interest in math. What did Escalante do right, and what can we learn from his approach?

"Success starts with attitude" could be Escalante's motto. Few Latino students were taking math. Most were tracked into craft classes and made jewelry and birdhouses. "Our kids are just as talented as anyone else. They just need the opportunity to show it. And for that, they must be motivated," he said. "They just don't think about becoming scientists or engineers."

Here are the keys to what Escalante accomplished. First, teaching and learning can't take place unless there is discipline. For that the teachers, not gangs, must control the classroom. Second, the students must believe in themselves. The teacher must inspire students with the idea that they *can* learn (Remember teacher expectations). Third, the students must be motivated to perform, in this case to see learning as a way out of the barrio, the path to good jobs.

Escalante uses a team approach. He has his students think of themselves as a team, of him as the coach, and the national exams as a sort of Olympics for which they are preparing. To stimulate team identity, the students wear team jackets, caps, and T-shirts with logos that identify them as part of the team. Before class, his students do "warmups" (hand clapping and foot stomping to a rock song).

His team has practice schedules as rigorous as a championship football team. Students must sign a contract that binds them to participate in the summer program he has developed, to complete the daily homework, and to attend Saturday morning and after-school study sessions. To get in his class, even the student's parents have to sign the contract. To keep before his students the principle that self-discipline pays off, Escalante covers his room with posters of sports figures in action—Jerry West, Magic Johnson, Kareem Abdul-Jabbar, and Babe Ruth.

"How have I been successful with students from such backgrounds?" he asks. "Very simple. I use a time-honored tradition—hard work, lots of it, for teacher and student alike."

The following statement helps us understand how Escalante challenges his students to think of what is possible in life, instead of problems that destroy the possible:

> The first day when these kids walk into my room, I have a bunch of names of schools and colleges on the chalkboard. I ask each student to memorize one. The next day I pick one kid and ask, "What school did you pick?" He says USC or UCLA or Stanford, MIT, Colgate, and so on. So I say, "Okay, keep that in mind. I'm going to bring in somebody who'll be talking about the schools."

Escalante then has a college adviser talk to the class. But more than this, he has also arranged foundation money to help the students get to the colleges of their choice.

The sociological point is that the problem was *not* the ability of the students. Their failure to do well in school was not due to something *within* them. The problem was the *system*, the way classroom instruction is arranged. When Escalante changed the system of instruction, both attitudes and performance changed. Escalante makes this very point—that student performance does not depend on the charismatic personality of a single person, but on how we structure the learning setting.

What principles discussed in this or earlier chapters did Escalante apply? What changes do you think we can make in education to bring about similar results all over the country?

Sources: Based on Barry 1989; Meek 1989; Escalante and Dirmann 1990; Hilliard 1991.   ▲

Summary and Review

Today's Credential Society

What is a credential society, and how did it develop?

A **credential society** is one in which employers use diplomas and degrees to determine who is eligible for a job. One reason that credentialism developed is that large, anonymous societies lack the personal knowledge common to smaller groups; educational certification provides evidence of a person's ability. Pp. 462–463.

The Development of Modern Education

How did modern education develop?

In most of human history, education consisted of informal learning, equivalent to **acculturation.** In some earlier societies, centers of formal education did develop, such as among the Arabians, Chinese, Greeks, and Egyptians. Because modern education came about in response to industrialization, formal education is much less common in Third World nations. Pp. 463–465.

Education in Global Perspective

How does education compare in the First, Second, and Third Worlds?

In general, formal education reflects a nation's economy. Consequently, education is much more extensive in the First World, undergoing extensive change in the Second World, and very spotty in the Third World. Japan, post-Soviet Russia, and Egypt provide examples of education in the three worlds of development. Pp. 465–468.

The Functionalist Perspective: Providing Social Benefits

What is the functionalist perspective on education?

Among the functions of education are the teaching of knowledge and skills, **cultural transmission** of values, social integration, **gatekeeping,** promoting personal and social change, and **mainstreaming.** Functionalists also note that education has replaced some traditional family functions. Pp. 469-473.

The Conflict Perspective: Maintaining Social Inequality

What is the conflict perspective on education?

The basic view of conflict theorists is that education reproduces the social class structure; that is, through such mechanisms as unequal funding and operating different schools for the elite and for the masses, education reinforces a society's basic social inequalities. Pp. 473–479.

The Symbolic Interactionist Perspective: Teacher Expectations and the Self-Fulfilling Prophecy

What is the symbolic interactionist perspective on education?

Symbolic interactionists, who focus on face-to-face interaction, in this instance what occurs in the classroom, examine how teacher expectations cause a **self-fulfilling prophecy,** producing the very behavior the teacher is expecting. Basically, symbolic interactionists have found that student performance conforms to teacher expectations, whether they are high or low. Pp. 479–481.

Problems in U.S. Education—and Their Solutions

What are the chief problems that face U.S. education?

The major problems are low achievement as shown in low SAT scores, **grade inflation, social promotion, functional illiteracy,** violence, and teen pregnancy. Pp. 482–483.

What are the primary solutions to these problems?

The primary solution is to restore high educational standards, which can be done only after providing basic security for students. Specific problems, such as teen pregnancy, must have specific solutions, one of which is detailed in the text. Any solution for improving quality must be based on raising standards and expecting more of students and teachers alike. Pp. 484–486.

Where can I read more on this topic?

Suggested readings for this chapter are listed on page 643.

Orlando Agudelo-Botero, *Oración*, 1989

Religion: Establishing Meaning

*W*ITH HIS MOTHER'S CALL, *Tom's world had begun to crumble. Amidst sobs, she had told him that she had left his father. After twenty-two years, their marriage was over! Why? It just didn't make sense. Tom knew that his mother and father had problems, that they argued quite a bit. But they always had. And didn't every married couple? Where was he going to go for the summer? His parents had put the house up for sale, and each had moved to a small apartment. There was no home anymore.*

Life seemed a little brighter when Tom met Amy in English class. She was the only one he could talk to about his feelings—Amy's parents had divorced three years before, and she understood. When Amy was invited to a meeting of the Unification church, Tom agreed to go with her.

The meeting was a surprise. Everyone was friendly, and everything was low-key. And everyone seemed so sure. They all believed that Judgment Day was just around the corner.

Amy and Tom found the teachings rather strange, but, since the people had been so friendly, they came back. After Tom and Amy attended meetings for about a month, they became good friends with Marcia and Ryan. Later they moved into an apartment house where Marcia, Ryan, and other Moonies lived. After a while, they dropped out of college and immersed themselves in a new life as Moonies.

What Is Religion?

As we have seen in previous chapters, all human societies are organized by some form of the family, as well as by some kind of economic system and political order. These key social institutions touch on aspects of life that are essential to human welfare. This chapter examines religion, another universal social institution.

The goal of the sociological study of religion is to analyze the relationship between society and religion and to gain insight into the role that religion plays in people's lives. Sociologists do not seek to verify or disclaim individual faiths or to make value judgments about religious beliefs. As mentioned in Chapter 1, sociologists have no tools for deciding that one course of action is more moral than another, much less that one religion is "the" correct one or "more" correct than another. Religion is a matter of faith; sociologists deal with empirical matters, things they can observe or measure. Thus sociologists can measure the extent to which people are religious and can study the effects of religious beliefs and practices on social life. Sociologists can study how religion is organized and how systems of belief are related to culture, stratification systems, and other social institutions. Unlike theologians, however, they cannot evaluate the truth of a religion's teachings.

In 1912 Emile Durkheim published an influential book, *The Elementary Forms of the Religious Life,* in which he tried to identify the elements common to all religions. After surveying religions around the world, Durkheim discovered no specific belief or practice that they all shared. He did find, however, that all religions, regardless of their name or teaching, separate the sacred from the profane. By **sacred,** Durkheim referred to aspects of life having to do with the supernatural that inspire awe, reverence, deep respect, even fear. By **profane,** he meant aspects of life that are not concerned with religion or religious purposes but are instead part of the ordinary aspects of everyday life. Durkheim also found that all religions develop a community around their practices and beliefs. Durkheim (1912/1965) summarized his findings as follows:

sacred: Durkheim's term for things set apart or forbidden, that inspire fear, awe, reverence, or deep respect

profane: Durkheim's term for common elements of everyday life

A religion is a unified system of beliefs and practices relative to sacred things, that is to say, things set apart and forbidden—beliefs and practices which unite into one single moral community called a Church, all those who adhere to them.

Thus, he argued, a **religion** is defined by three elements:

1 *Beliefs* that some things are sacred (forbidden, set off from the profane)
2 *Practices* (rituals) concerning the things considered sacred
3 A *moral community* (a church) resulting from a group's beliefs and practices

Durkheim used the word **church** in an unusual sense, to refer to any "moral community" centered on beliefs and practices regarding the sacred. In Durkheim's sense, *church* means a moral community of Buddhists bowing before a shrine, Hindus dipping in the Ganges River, and Confucianists offering food to their ancestors. Similarly, the term *moral community* does not imply morality in the sense familiar to most of us. A moral community is simply people united by their religious practices—and that would include Aztec priests who each day gathered around an altar to pluck out the beating heart of a virgin.

To gain an understanding of the sociological approach to religion, let's see what picture emerges when we apply the three theoretical perspectives.

From his review of world religions, Durkheim concluded that all religions have beliefs, practices, and a moral community. Part of Hindu belief is that the Ganges is a holy river and bathing in it imparts spiritual benefits. Each year, millions of Hindus participate in this rite of ablution (purification).

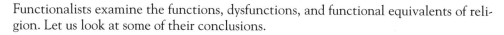

The Functionalist Perspective

Functionalists examine the functions, dysfunctions, and functional equivalents of religion. Let us look at some of their conclusions.

Functions of Religion

In Durkheim's sense of religion—dividing the world into the sacred and profane and establishing rituals around those beliefs—religion is universal (Alpert 1939; Galanter 1989; Caldwell et al. 1992; Nauta 1993). The reason for its universality, say functionalists, is that religion meets the following eight basic human needs.

Questions About Ultimate Meaning Around the world, religions provide answers to perplexing questions about ultimate meaning—such as the purpose of life, why people suffer, and the existence of an afterlife. Those answers give people a sense of purpose. Instead of seeing themselves buffeted by random events in an aimless existence, religious believers see their lives as fitting into a divine plan.

Emotional Comfort The answers that religion provides about ultimate meaning also comfort people by assuring them that there is a purpose to their suffering. Similarly, religious rituals that enshroud critical events as illness and death provide emotional comfort at such times of crisis. The individual knows that others care and can find consolation in following a familiar and prescribed pattern.

Social Solidarity Religious teachings and practices unite believers into a community that shares values and perspectives ("we Jews," "we Christians," "we Muslims"). The religious rituals that surround marriage, for example, link the bride and groom with a broader community that wishes them well. So do other religious rituals, such as those that celebrate birth and mourn death.

religion: according to Durkheim, beliefs and practices that separate the profane from the sacred and unite its adherents into a moral community

church: according to Durkheim, one of the three essential elements of religion—a moral community of believers; a second definition is the type of religious organization described on page 506, a large, highly organized group with little emphasis on personal conversion and formal, sedate worship services

Guidelines for Everyday Life The teachings of religion are not only abstract. They also apply to people's everyday lives. For example, four of the Ten Commandments delivered by Moses to the Israelites concern God, but the other six contain instructions on how to live everyday life, including how to get along with parents, employers, and neighbors.

Social Control Religion not only provides guidelines for everyday life, but it also controls people's behaviors. Most norms of a religious group apply only to its members, but some set limits on nonmembers also. An example is religious teachings that are incorporated into criminal law. In the United States, for example, blasphemy and adultery were once statutory crimes for which offenders could be arrested, tried, and sentenced. Laws that prohibit the sale of alcohol before noon on Sunday—or even Sunday sales of "nonessential items" in some places—are another example.

Adaptation Religion can help people adapt to new environments. For example, it is not easy for immigrants to adapt to the confusing customs of a new land. By maintaining the native language and familiar rituals and teachings, religion can provide continuity with an immigrant's cultural past.

The handful of German immigrants who settled in Perry County, Missouri, in the 1800s, for example, even brought their Lutheran minister with them. Their sermons and hymns continued to be in German, and their children also attended a school in which the minister conducted classes in German. Out of this small group grew the Lutheran Church–Missouri Synod, which, in spite of its name, is an international denomination that numbers almost three million people. Little by little, this group's descendants and converts entered mainstream U.S. culture. Today, except for Luther's basic teachings and some church practices, little remains of the past, for just as it helped the immigrants adapt to a new environment, so the religion itself underwent change.

Support for the Government Most religions provide support for the government. The U.S. flag so prominently displayed in many churches represents this support. Governments reciprocate by supporting God as witnessed in the inaugural speeches of U.S. presidents, which invariably ask God to bless the nation.

In some instances, the government sponsors a particular religion, bans all others, provides financial support for building churches and seminaries, and may even pay salaries to the clergy. The religions so sponsored are known as **state religions.** During the sixteenth and seventeenth centuries in Sweden, the government sponsored Lutheranism; in Switzerland, Calvinism; and in Italy, Roman Catholicism. In other instances, even though no particular religion is sponsored by the government, religious beliefs are so established in a nation's life that the country's history and social institutions are sanctified by being associated with God. For example, though U.S. officials may not belong to any particular religion, they take office by swearing that they will, in the name of God, fulfill their duty. Similarly, Congress is opened with prayer by its own chaplain, schoolchildren recite daily the pledge of allegiance (including the phrase "one nation under God"), and coins bear the inscription "In God We Trust." Sociologist Robert Bellah (1970) referred to this phenomenon as **civil religion.**

state religion: a government-sponsored religion

civil religion: Robert Bellah's term for religion that is such an established feature of a country's life that its history and social institutions become sanctified by being associated with God

Social Change Although religion is often so bound up with the prevailing social order that it resists social change, there are occasions when religion spearheads change. In the 1960s, for example, the civil rights movement, which fought to desegregate public facilities and reduce racial discrimination at southern polls, was led by religious leaders, especially leaders of African-American churches such as Martin Luther King, Jr. Churches also served as centers at which demonstrators were trained and rallies were organized (Jones 1992).

Religion can promote social change, as was evident with the civil rights movement in the United States in the 1950s and 1960s. The foremost leader of this movement was Dr. Martin Luther King, Jr., a Baptist minister, shown in this 1963 photo making a speech in Washington, D.C. King's repetition of the phrase, "I have a dream," helped to make this speech memorable. He was referring to his dream of the end of racial discrimination, when "all God's children" would live in harmony and peace. Although King was assassinated on April 4, 1968, his dream lives on in the hearts of many.

Functional Equivalents of Religion

The functions just described can also be fulfilled by other components of society. If another component answers questions about ultimate meaning, provides emotional comfort and guidelines for daily life, and so on, sociologists call it a **functional equivalent** of religion. Thus, for some people, Alcoholics Anonymous is a functional equivalent of religion (Chalfant 1992). For others, psychotherapy, humanism, transcendental meditation, or even a political party performs similar functions.

Some functional equivalents are difficult to distinguish from a religion (Brinton 1965; Luke 1985). For example, communism had its prophets (Marx and Lenin), sacred writings (everything written by Marx, Engels, and Lenin, but especially the *Communist Manifesto*), high priests (the heads of the Communist party), sacred buildings (the Kremlin), shrines (Lenin's body on display in Red Square), rituals (the annual May Day parade in Red Square), and even martyrs (Cuba's Che Guevara). Soviet communism, which was avowedly atheistic and tried to wipe out all traces of Christianity and Judaism from its midst, even tried to replace baptisms and circumcisions with state-sponsored rituals that dedicated the child to the state. The Communist party also produced rituals for weddings and funerals.

As sociologist Ian Robertson (1987) pointed out, however, there is a fundamental distinction between a religion and its functional equivalent. Although the substitute may perform similar functions, its activities are not directed toward God, gods, or the supernatural.

Dysfunctions of Religion

Functionalists also examine ways in which religion can be *dysfunctional*, that is, can bring harmful results. Two main dysfunctions are war and religious persecution.

War   History is filled with wars based on religion—comingled with politics. Between the eleventh and fourteenth centuries, for example, Christian monarchs conducted nine bloody Crusades in an attempt to wrest control of the Holy Land from the Muslims. Unfortunately, such wars are not just a relic of the past. Even in recent years we have seen Protestants and Catholics kill one another in Northern Ireland, while Jews and Muslims in Israel and Christians and Muslims in Bosnia have done the same thing.

functional equivalent: in this context, a substitute that serves the same functions (or meets the same needs) as religion, for example, psychotherapy

Religion as Justification for Persecution   Beginning in the 1200s and continuing into the 1800s, in what has become known as the Inquisition, Roman Catholic leaders burned convicted witches at the stake. In 1692, Protestant leaders in Salem, Massachusetts, did the same thing. (The last execution for witchcraft was in Scotland in 1722 [Bridgwater 1953].) Similarly, it seems fair to say that the Aztec religion had its dysfunctions—at least for the virgins offered to appease angry gods. In short, religion has been used to justify oppression and any number of brutal acts.

The Symbolic Interactionist Perspective

As discussed in previous chapters, symbolic interactionists focus on the role of meaning in people's lives, especially the ways in which people use symbols. Let's apply this perspective to religious symbols, rituals, and beliefs to see how they help to forge a community of like-minded people.

Religious Symbols

To see how significant religious symbols can be, suppose that it is about two thousand years ago and you have just joined a new religion. You have come to believe that a recently crucified Jew named Jesus is the Messiah, the Lamb of God offered for your sins. The Roman leaders are persecuting the followers of Jesus. They hate your religion because you and your fellow believers will not acknowledge Caesar as God.

Christians are few in number, and you are eager to have fellowship with other believers. But how can you tell who is a believer? Spies are all over. The government has sworn to destroy this new religion, and you do not relish the thought of being fed to lions in the Coliseum.

Woodcuts (engraved blocks of wood coated with ink to leave an impression on paper) were used to illustrate books shortly after the printing press was invented. This woodcut commemorates a dysfunction of religion, the burning of witches at the stake. This particular event occurred at Derenburg, Germany, in 1555.

You use a simple technique. While talking with a stranger, as though doodling absentmindedly in the sand or dust, you casually trace out the outline of a fish. Only fellow believers know the hidden symbolism—that, taken together, the first letter of the words in the Greek sentence, "Jesus (is) Christ the Son of God" spell the Greek word for *fish*. If the other person gives no response, you rub out the outline and continue the interaction as normal. If there is a response, you eagerly talk about your new faith.

All religions use symbols to provide identity and social solidarity for their members. For Muslims, the primary symbol is the crescent moon and star, for Jews the Star of David, for Christians the cross. For members, these are not ordinary symbols, but sacred symbols that evoke feelings of awe and reverence. In Durkheim's terms, religions use symbols to specify what is sacred and to separate the sacred from the profane.

A symbol is a condensed way of communicating. Worn by a fundamentalist Christian, for example, the cross says. "I am a follower of Jesus Christ. I believe that He is the Messiah, the promised Son of God, that He loves me, that He died to take away my sins, that He rose from the dead and is going to return to earth, and that through Him I will receive eternal life."

That is a lot to pack into one symbol—and it is only part of what the symbol means to a fundamentalist believer. To people in other traditions of Christianity, the cross conveys somewhat different meanings—but to all Christians, the cross is a shorthand way of expressing many meanings. So it is also with the Star of David, the crescent moon and star, the cow (expressing to Hindus the unity of all living things), and the various symbols of the world's many other religions.

Rituals

Rituals, ceremonies or repetitive practices, are also symbols that help unite people into a moral community. Some rituals, such as the bar mitzvah of Jewish boys and Holy Communion of Christians, are designed to create in the devout a feeling of closeness with God and unity with one another. Rituals include kneeling and praying at set times, bowing, crossing oneself, singing, lighting candles and incense, a liturgy, Scripture readings, processions, baptisms, weddings, funerals, and so on.

Beliefs

Symbols, including rituals, develop from beliefs. The belief may be vague ("God is") or highly specific ("God wants us to prostrate ourselves and face Mecca five times each day"). Religious beliefs not only include *values* (what is considered good and desirable in life—how we ought to live) but also a **cosmology,** a unified picture of the world. For example, the Jewish, Christian, and Muslim belief that there is only one God, the Creator of the universe, who is concerned about the actions of humans and who will hold us accountable for what we do, is a cosmology. It presents a unifying picture of the universe.

Religious Experience

The term **religious experience** refers to a sudden awareness of the supernatural or a feeling of coming in contact with God. Some people undergo a mild version, such as feeling closer to God when they look at a mountain or listen to a certain piece of music. Others report a life-transforming experience; for example, St. Francis of Assisi, who became aware of God's presence in every living thing.

Some Protestants use the term **born again** to describe people who have undergone such a life-transforming religious experience. These persons say that they came to the realization that they had sinned, that Jesus had died for their sins, and that God requires them to live a new life. Henceforth their worlds become transformed, they look forward to the Resurrection and a new life in heaven, and they see relationships with spouses, parents, children, and even bosses in a new light. They also report a need to

rituals: ceremonies or repetitive practices; in this context, religious observances or rites, often intended to evoke a sense of awe of the sacred

cosmology: teachings or ideas that provide a unified picture of the world

religious experience: a sudden awareness of the supernatural or a feeling of coming in contact with God

born again: a term describing Christians who have undergone a life-transforming religious experience so radical that they feel they have become new persons make changes in how they interact with others, so that their lives reflect their new, personal commitment to Jesus as their "Savior and Lord." They describe a feeling of beginning life again, hence the term "born again."

Community

Finally, the shared meanings that come through symbols, rituals, and beliefs (and for some, a religious experience) unite people into a moral community. People in a moral community feel a bond with one another, for their beliefs and rituals bind them together while at the same time separating them from those who do not share their unique symbolic world. Mormons, for example, feel a "kindred spirit" (as it is often known) with other Mormons. So do Baptists, Jews, Jehovah's Witnesses, and Muslims with members of their respective faiths.

As a symbol of their unity, members of some religious groups address one another as "brother" or "sister." "Sister Dougherty, we are going to meet at Brother and Sister Tedrick's on Wednesday" is a common way of expressing a message. The terms "brother" and "sister" are intended to symbolize a relationship so close that the individuals consider themselves members of the same family.

Community is powerful, not only because it provides the basis for mutual identity, but also because it establishes norms that govern the behavior of its members. Members either conform, or they lose their membership. In Christian churches, for example, an individual whose adultery becomes known, and who refuses to ask forgiveness, may be banned from the Church. He or she may be formally excommunicated, as in the case of Catholics, or more informally discharged, as is the usual Protestant practice.

The removal of community is a serious matter for people whose identity is bound up in the community. Sociologists John Hostetler (1980), William Kephart, and William Zellner (1994) describe the Amish practice *shunning*—ignoring an offender in all situations. Persons who are shunned are treated as though they do not exist (for if they do not repent by expressing sorrow for their act they have ceased to exist as members of the community). The shunning is so thorough that even family members, who themselves remain in good standing in the congregation, are not allowed to talk to the person being shunned.

Symbolic interactionists stress that a basic characteristic of humans is that they attach meaning to objects and events and then use representations of those objects or events to communicate with one another. Some religious symbols are used to communicate feelings of awe and reverence. For Roman Catholics, few such symbols are as effective as St. Peter's Basilica in the Vatican, depicted here.

The Conflict Perspective

The conflict perspective is quite different. Conflict theorists examine how religion supports the status quo, and helps to maintain social inequalities.

Opium of the People

In general, conflict theorists are highly critical of religion. Karl Marx, an avowed atheist who believed that the existence of God was an impossibility, set the tone for conflict theorists with his most famous statement on this subject: "Religion is the sigh of the oppressed creature, the sentiment of a heartless world. . . . It is the opium of the people" (Marx 1844/1964). By this statement, Marx meant that oppressed workers, sighing for release from their suffering, escape into religion. For them, religion is like a drug that helps them forget their misery. By diverting their eyes to future happiness in a coming world, religion takes their eyes off their suffering in this one, thereby greatly reducing the possibility that they will rebel against their oppressors.

A Reflection of Social Inequalities

Conflict theorists stress that religious teachings and practices are a mirror of a society's inequalities. Gender inequality illustrates this point. When males completely dominated U.S. society, U.S. churches and synagogues ordained only men, limiting women to such activities as teaching children in Sunday school or preparing meals for congregational get-togethers, which were considered appropriate "feminine" activities. As women's roles in the broader society changed, however, religion reflected those changes. First, many religious groups allowed women to vote. Then, as women attained prominent positions in the business world and professions, some Protestant and Jewish groups allowed women to be ordained. Similarly, just as women still face barriers in secular society, so some congregations still refuse to ordain women. In some congregations the barriers remain so high that women are still not allowed to vote.

A Legitimation of Social Inequalities

Not only does religion mirror the social inequalities of the larger society, conflict theorists say, but it also legitimates them. By this, they mean that religion, reflecting the interests of those in power, teaches that the existing social arrangements of a society represent what God desires. For example, during the Middle Ages Christian theologians decreed the "divine right of kings." This doctrine meant that God determined who would become king and set him on the throne. The king ruled in God's place, and it was the duty of a king's subjects to be loyal to him (and to pay their taxes). To disobey the king was to disobey God.

In what is perhaps the supreme technique of legitimating the social order, going even a step further than the "divine right of kings," the religion of ancient Egypt held that the Pharaoh was a god. The Emperor of Japan was similarly declared divine. If this was so, who could even question his decisions? How many of today's politicians would give their right arm for such a religious teaching!

Conflict theorists point to many other examples of how religion legitimates the social order. One of the more interesting took place in the decades before the American Civil War. Southern ministers used scripture to defend slavery, saying that it was God's will—while at the same time northern ministers legitimated *their* regional social structure and used scripture to denounce slavery as evil (Ernst 1988; Nauta 1993). In India, Hinduism supports the caste system by teaching that an individual who tries to change caste will come back in the next life as a member of a lower caste—or even as an animal.

Over the centuries, the office of clergy—whether priest, minister, or rabbi—has been reserved for men. Only in recent years has this office opened to some women in some groups. Shown here is the ordination of a woman in the Church of England.

 ## Religion and the Spirit of Capitalism

Max Weber disagreed intensely with the conflict perspective that religion merely reflects and legitimates the social order, and that religion impedes social change by encouraging people to focus on the afterlife. In contrast, Weber saw religion's focus on the afterlife as a source of profound social change.

Like Marx, Weber personally observed the European countries industrialize. Weber was intrigued with the question of why some societies embraced capitalism, while others had not broken out of their traditional ways. Tradition is strong and holds people in check, yet some societies had been transformed by capitalism, and others untouched. As he explored this problem, Weber concluded that religion held the key to **modernization**—the transformation of traditional societies to industrial societies.

Weber wrote *The Protestant Ethic and the Spirit of Capitalism* (1904–1905/1958) to explain his conclusions. Because Weber's argument was presented in Chapter 7 (pages 170–172), it is only summarized here.

1 Capitalism is not just a superficial change. Rather, capitalism represents a fundamentally different way of thinking about work and money. *Traditionally, people worked just enough to meet their basic needs, not so that they could have a surplus to invest.* To accumulate capital as an end in itself, not to spend it, was a radical departure from the past. People even came to consider it a duty to invest money in order to make profits, which, in turn, they reinvested to make more profits. Weber called this new approach to work and money the **spirit of capitalism.**

2 Why did the spirit of capitalism develop in Europe, and not, for example, in China or India, where the people had similar intelligence, material resources, education, and so on? According to Weber, *religion was the key.* The religions of China and India, and indeed Roman Catholicism in Europe, encouraged a traditional approach to life, not thrift and investment. Capitalism appeared when Protestantism came on the scene.

3 What was different about Protestantism, especially Calvinism? John Calvin taught that God had predestined some people to heaven, others to hell, and that in this life you couldn't know where you were headed. People could depend neither on church membership nor on feelings about their relationship with God to know they were saved.

modernization: the transformation of traditional societies into industrial societies

spirit of capitalism: Weber's term for the desire to accumulate capital as a duty—not to spend it, but as an end in itself—and to constantly reinvest it

4   This doctrine created intense anxiety among Calvin's followers: "Am I predestined to hell or to heaven?", people wondered. As Calvinists wrestled with this question, they concluded that each church member had a duty to prove that he or she was one of God's elect, and to live as though he or she were predestined to heaven—for good works were a demonstration of salvation.

5   This conclusion motivated Calvinists not only to lead highly moral lives, but also to work hard, to not waste time, and to be frugal—for idleness and needless spending were signs of worldliness. Weber called this self-denying approach to life the **Protestant ethic.**

6   The hard work, combined with spending money only on necessities (with luxuries narrowly defined), resulted in an accumulation of capital. This capital, in turn, since it couldn't be spent, was invested—which led to a surge in production.

7   Thus, a change in religion (from Catholicism to Protestantism, especially Calvinism) led to a fundamental change in thought and behavior (the Protestant ethic). The result was the "spirit of capitalism." Thus capitalism originated in Europe, and not in places where religion did not encourage capitalism's essential elements: the accumulation of capital through frugality and hard work, and its investment and reinvestment.

Although Weber's analysis has been highly influential, it has not lacked critics (Marshall 1982). Hundreds of scholars have attacked it, some for overlooking the lack of capitalism in Scotland (a Calvinist country), others for failing to explain why the Industrial Revolution was born in England (not a Calvinist country). Hundreds of other scholars have defended Weber's argument. There is currently no historical evidence that can definitively prove or disprove Weber's thesis.

Today the spirit of capitalism and the Protestant ethic are by no means limited to Protestants. U.S. Catholics, for example, have about the same approach to life as do U.S. Protestants. In addition, the Southeast Asian nations (Hong Kong, Japan, Malaysia, Singapore, South Korea, and Taiwan) have embraced capitalism—not exactly Protestant countries (Levy 1992).

At this point in history, the Protestant ethic and the spirit of capitalism are not confined to any specific religion or even part of the world. Rather, they have become cultural traits that have spread to societies around the world (Greeley 1964; Yinger 1970).

The World's Major Religions

Of the thousands of religions in the world, most people practice either Judaism, Christianity, Islam, Hinduism, Buddhism, or Confucianism. Let us briefly review each.

Judaism

The origin of Judaism is traced to Abraham, who lived about four thousand years ago in Mesopotamia. Jews believe that God (Jahweh) made a covenant with Abraham, setting aside his descendants as a chosen people and promising to make them "as numerous as the sands of the seashore" and give them a special land that would be theirs forever. The sign of this covenant was the circumcision of male children, to be performed when a newborn was eight days old. Descent is traced through Abraham and his wife, Sarah, their son Isaac, and their grandson Jacob (also called Israel).

Joseph, a son of Jacob, was sold by his brothers into slavery and taken to Egypt. Following a series of hair-raising adventures, Joseph became Pharaoh's right-hand man.

Protestant ethic: Weber's term to describe the ideal of a self-denying, highly moral life, accompanied by hard work and frugality

When a severe famine hit Canaan, where Jacob's family was living, Jacob and his eleven other sons fled to Egypt. Under Joseph's leadership, they were welcome. A subsequent Pharaoh, however, enslaved the Israelites. After about four hundred years, Moses, an Israelite who had been adopted by Pharaoh's daughter, confronted Pharaoh. He persuaded Pharaoh to release the slaves, numbering at that time about two million. Moses led them out of Egypt, but before they reached their Promised Land the Israelites spent forty years in desert wanderings. Sometime during those years, Moses delivered the Ten Commandments from Mount Sinai. Abraham, Isaac, Jacob, and Moses hold revered positions in Judaism. The events of their lives and the recounting of the early history of the Israelites are contained in the first five books of the Bible, called the Torah.

The founding of Judaism marked a fundamental change in religion, for it was the first religion based on **monotheism,** the belief that there is only one God. Prior to Judaism, religions were based on **polytheism,** the belief that there are many gods. In Greek religion, for example, Zeus was the god of heaven and earth, Poseidon the god of the sea, and Athena the goddess of wisdom. Other groups followed **animism,** believing that all objects in the world have spirits, some of which are dangerous and must be outwitted.

Contemporary Judaism in the United States comprises three main branches: Orthodox, Reform, and Conservative. Orthodox Jews adhere to the laws espoused by Moses. They eat only foods prepared in a designated manner (kosher), observe the Sabbath in a traditional way, and segregate males and females in their religious services. During the 1800s, a group that wanted to make their practices more compatible with the secular (nonreligious) culture broke from this tradition. This liberal group, known as Reform Judaism, mostly uses the vernacular (a country's language) in its religious ceremonies and has reduced much of the ritual. The third branch, Conservative Judaism, falls somewhere between the other two. No branch has continued polygyny (allowing a husband to have more than one wife), the original marriage custom of the Jews, which was outlawed by rabbinic decree about a thousand years ago.

The history of Judaism is marked by conflict and persecution. The Israelites were conquered by Babylon, and again made slaves. After returning to Israel and rebuilding the temple, they were later conquered by Rome, and after their rebellion at Masada in A.D. 70 failed, they were dispersed for almost two thousand years into other nations. During those centuries, they faced prejudice, discrimination, and persecution (called **anti-Semitism**) by many peoples and rulers. The most horrendous example is Hitler's attempt to eliminate the Jews as a people in the Nazi Holocaust of World War II. Under the Nazi occupation of Europe and North Africa, about six million Jews were slaughtered, perhaps half dying in gas ovens constructed specifically for this purpose.

Central to Jewish teaching is the requirement to love God and do good deeds. Good deeds begin in the family, where each member has an obligation toward the others. Sin is a conscious choice to do evil, and must be atoned for by prayers and good works. Jews consider Jerusalem their holiest city, where the Messiah will one day appear bringing redemption for them all.

Christianity

Christianity, which developed out of Judaism, is also monotheistic. Christians believe that Jesus Christ is the Messiah whom God promised the Jews.

Jesus was born in poverty, and traditional Christians believe, to a virgin. Within two years of his birth, Herod, named king of Palestine by Caesar, who had conquered Israel, was informed that people were saying that a new king had been born. When Herod sent soldiers to kill Jesus, his parents fled with him to Egypt. After Herod died, they returned, settling in the small town of Nazareth.

About the age of 30, Jesus began a preaching and healing ministry. His teachings challenged the contemporary religious establishment and as his popularity grew, the religious leaders plotted to have him killed by the Romans. Christians interpret the death of Jesus as a blood sacrifice for their sins. They believe that through his death they have peace with God and will inherit eternal life.

monotheism: the belief that there is only one God

polytheism: the belief that there are many gods

animism: the belief that all objects in the world have spirits, some of which are dangerous and must be outwitted

anti-Semitism: prejudice, discrimination, and persecution directed against Jews

The twelve main followers of Jesus, called *apostles,* believed that Jesus rose from the dead. They preached the need to be "born again," that is, to accept Jesus as Savior, give up selfish ways, and live a devout life. The new religion spread rapidly, and after initial hostility from imperial Rome—including the feeding of believers to the lions in the Coliseum—in A.D. 317 Christianity became the empire's official religion.

During the first thousand years of Christianity, there was only one church organization, directed from Rome. During the eleventh century, after disagreement over doctrine and politics, Greek Orthodoxy was established. It was headquartered in Constantinople (now Istanbul, Turkey). During the Middle Ages, the Roman Catholic church, aligned with the political establishment, grew corrupt. Some Church offices, such as that of bishop, were sold for a set price, and, in a situation that touched off the Reformation led by Martin Luther in the sixteenth century, the forgiveness of sins (including those not yet committed) could be purchased by buying an "indulgence."

Although Martin Luther's original goal was to reform the Church, not divide it, the Reformation began a splintering of Christianity. It coincided with the breakup of feudalism, and as the ancient political structure came apart, people clamored for independence not only in political but also in religious thought. Today, Christianity is the most popular religion in the world, with over one billion adherents. Christians are divided into hundreds of groups, some with doctrinal differences so slight that only members of the group can appreciate the extremely fine distinctions that, they feel, significantly separate them from others.

Islam

Islam, whose followers are known as Muslims, began in the same part of the world as Judaism and Christianity. Islam is the world's third monotheistic religion. It was founded by Muhammad, who was born in Mecca (now in Saudi Arabia) about A.D. 570. Muhammad married Khadija, a wealthy widow. About the age of 40, he reported that he had visions from God. These, and his teachings, were later written down in a book called the Koran. Few paid attention to Muhammad, although Ali, his son-in-law, believed him. When he found out that there was a plot to murder him, Muhammad fled to Medina, where he found a more receptive audience. There he established a *theocracy* (a government based on the principle that God is the ruler, his laws the statutes of the land, and priests his earthly administrators), and founded the Muslim empire. In A.D. 630 he returned to Mecca, this time as a conqueror (Bridgwater 1953).

After Muhammad's death, a struggle for control over the empire he had founded split Islam into two branches that remain today, the Sunni and the Shi'ite. The Shi'ite, who believe that the *imam* (the religious leader) is inspired as he interprets the Koran, are generally more conservative and inclined to **fundamentalism,** the belief that modernism threatens religion and that the faith as it was originally practiced should be restored. The Sunni, who do not share this belief, are generally more liberal.

fundamentalism: the belief that true religion is threatened by modernism and that the faith as it was originally practiced should be restored

Muslims kneeling or prostrating themselves in public are a common sight in Muslim countries, but still unusual in the United States. Shown here are Muslims praying on Madison Avenue in New York City during the Muslim Day Parade.

The pilgrimage to Mecca, the city of Muhammad's birth, is a sacred duty of Muslims. Each year millions make the pilgrimage. Shown here is the mosque complex at Mecca.

Like the Jews, Muslims trace their ancestry to Abraham. Abraham fathered a son, Ishmael, by Hagar, his wife Sarah's Egyptian maid (Genesis 25:12). Ishmael had twelve sons, from whom a good portion of today's Arab world are descended. For them also, Jerusalem is a holy city. The Muslims consider the Bibles of the Jews and the Christians to be sacred but take the Koran as the final word. They believe that the followers of Abraham and Moses (Jews) and Jesus (Christians) changed the original teachings and that Muhammad restored their purity. It is the duty of each Muslim to make a pilgrimage to Mecca during his or her lifetime.

Unlike the Jews, the Muslims continue to practice polygyny. They limit a man, however, to four wives.

Hinduism

Unlike the other religions described, Hinduism has no specific founder. Going back about four thousand years, Hinduism is the chief religion of India. The term *Hinduism*, however, is Western, and in India the closest term is *dharma* (law). Unlike Judaism, Christianity, and Islam, Hinduism has no canonical scripture, that is, no texts thought to be inspired by God. Instead, several books, including *Brahmanas*, *Bhagavad-Gita*, and *Upanishads*, expound on moral qualities that people should strive after. They also delineate the sacrifices people should make to the gods.

Hindus are *polytheists;* that is, they believe that there are many gods. They believe that one of these gods, Brahma, created the universe. Brahma, along with Shiva (the Destroyer) and Vishnu (the Preserver), form a triad at the center of modern Hinduism. A central belief is *karma*, spiritual progress. There is no final judgment, but **reincarnation,** a cycle of life, death, and rebirth. Death involves only the body, and each person's soul comes back in a form that matches the individual's moral progress in the previous life (which centers on proper conduct in following the rules of one's caste). If an individual reaches spiritual perfection, he or she has attained *nirvana*. This marks the end of the cycle of death and rebirth, when the soul is reunited with the universal soul. When this occurs, *maya*, the illusion of time and space, has been conquered.

reincarnation: in Hinduism and Buddhism, the return of the soul after death in a different form

As Durkheim pointed out, each religion has teachings about the sacred and profane and their relationship to one another. The goal of Buddhism is to escape reincarnation through denial of the self and compassion for others. Shown here are American Buddhists at the Buddhist temple in Los Angeles.

Some Hindu practices have been modified as a consequence of social protest—especially child marriage and *suttee*, the practice of cremating a surviving widow along with her deceased husband (Bridgwater 1953). Other ancient rituals remain unchanged, such as *kumbh mela*, a purifying washing in the Ganges River, which takes place every twelve years, and in which many millions participate.

Buddhism

About 600 B.C., Siddhartha Gautama founded Buddhism. (Buddha means the "enlightened one," a term Gautama was given by his disciples.) Gautama was the son of an upper-caste Hindu ruler in an area north of Benares, India. At the age of 29, he renounced his life of luxury and became an ascetic. Through meditation, he discovered the following "four noble truths," all of which emphasize self-denial and compassion.

1 Existence is suffering.
2 The origin of suffering is desire.
3 Suffering ceases when desire ceases.
4 The way to end desire is to follow the "noble eightfold path."

The noble eightfold path consists of

1 Right belief
2 Right resolve (to renounce carnal pleasure and to harm no living creature)
3 Right speech
4 Right conduct
5 Right occupation or living
6 Right effort
7 Right-mindedness (or contemplation)
8 Right ecstasy

Like Hinduism, the final goal of Buddhism is to escape from reincarnation into nonexistence or blissful peace (Bridgwater 1953).

Buddhism spread rapidly. In the third century B.C., the ruler of India adopted Buddhism and sent missionaries throughout Asia to spread the new teaching. By the fifth century A.D., Buddhism reached the height of its popularity in India, after which it died out. Buddhism, however, had been adopted in Ceylon, Burma, Tibet, Laos, Cambodia, Thailand, China, Korea, and Japan, where it flourishes today.

Confucianism

About the time that Gautama lived, K'ung–Fu-tsu (551–479 B.C.) was born in China. Confucius (his name strung together in English), a public official, was distressed by the corruption that he saw in government. Unlike Gautama, who urged withdrawal from social activities, Confucius urged social reform and developed a system of morality based on peace, justice, and universal order. His teachings were incorporated into writings called the *Analects*.

The basic moral principle of Confucianism is to maintain *jen,* sympathy or concern for other humans. The key to jen is to maintain right relationships—being loyal and placing morality above self-interest. In what is called the "Confucian Golden Rule," Confucius stated a basic principle for jen: to treat those who are subordinate to you as you would like to be treated by people superior to yourself. Confucius taught that right relationships within the family (loyalty, respect) should be the model for society. He also taught the "middle way," an avoidance of extremes.

Confucianism was originally atheistic, simply a set of moral teachings without reference to the supernatural. As the centuries passed, however, local gods were added to the teachings, and Confucius himself was declared a god. Confucius's teachings became the basis for the government of China. About A.D. 1000, the emphasis on meditation gave way to a stress on improvement through acquiring knowledge. This emphasis remained dominant until the twentieth century, by which time the government had become rigid, with approval of the existing order having replaced respectful relationships (Bridgwater 1953). Following the Communist revolution of 1949, political leaders attempted to weaken the people's ties with Confucianism.

Types of Religious Organizations

Just as different religions have distinct teachings and practices, so *within* a religion different groups contrast sharply with one another. Let's look at the types of religious organizations sociologists have identified: cult, sect, church, and ecclesia. The typology presented here is a modification of analyses by sociologists Ernst Troeltsch (1931), Liston Pope (1942), and Benton Johnson (1963). Figure 18.1 illustrates the relationship between each of these four types of religious organizations.

Cult

The word *cult* conjures up many bizarre images—shaven heads, weird music, brainwashing—even images of ritual murder may come to mind. In the opening vignette, Tom and Amy dropped out of college, and, to the dismay of their parents and friends, cut themselves off from their usual surroundings and activities.

Cults, however, are not necessarily weird, and few practice "brainwashing" or bizarre rituals. In fact, *all religions began as cults* (Stark 1989). A **cult** is simply a new or different religion, whose teaching and practices put it at odds with the dominant culture and religion. Cults often begin with the appearance of a **charismatic leader,** an individual who inspires people because he or she seems to have extraordinary qualities. **Charisma** refers to an outstanding gift or an exceptional quality. Finding something highly appealing about such an individual, people feel drawn to both the person and the message.

cult: a new religion with few followers, whose teachings and practices put it at odds with the dominant culture and religion

charismatic leader: literally, someone to whom God has given a gift; more commonly, someone who exerts extraordinary appeal to a group of followers

charisma: literally, an extraordinary gift from God; more commonly, an outstanding, "magnetic" personality

---

Figure 18.1

A Cult-Sect-Church-Ecclesia Continuum.

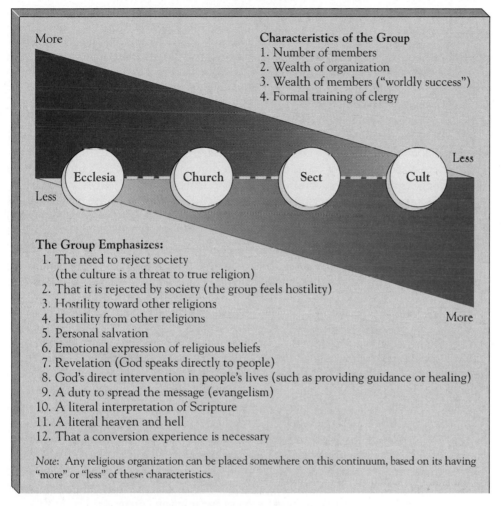

More

Characteristics of the Group
1. Number of members
2. Wealth of organization
3. Wealth of members ("worldly success")
4. Formal training of clergy

Less

Ecclesia — Church — Sect — Cult

Less

More

The Group Emphasizes:
1. The need to reject society
   (the culture is a threat to true religion)
2. That it is rejected by society (the group feels hostility)
3. Hostility toward other religions
4. Hostility from other religions
5. Personal salvation
6. Emotional expression of religious beliefs
7. Revelation (God speaks directly to people)
8. God's direct intervention in people's lives (such as providing guidance or healing)
9. A duty to spread the message (evangelism)
10. A literal interpretation of Scripture
11. A literal heaven and hell
12. That a conversion experience is necessary

Note: Any religious organization can be placed somewhere on this continuum, based on its having "more" or "less" of these characteristics.

Sources: Based on Troelsch (1931), Pope (1942), and Johnson (1963).

The most popular religion in the world today began as a cult. Its handful of followers believed that an unschooled carpenter who preached in remote villages in a backwater country was the Son of God, that he was killed and came back to life. Those beliefs made the early Christians a cult, setting them apart from the rest of their society. Persecuted by both religious and political authorities, these early believers clung to one another for support, many cutting off associations with their unbelieving families and friends. To others, the early Christians must have seemed deluded and brainwashed.

So it was with Islam. When Muhammad revealed his visions and said that God's name was really Allah, only a few people believed him. To others, he must have seemed crazy, deranged.

Each cult (or new religion) meets with rejection from society. Its message is considered bizarre, its approach to life strange. Its members antagonize the majority, who are convinced that they have a monopoly on the truth. The new message may claim revelation, visions, visits from God and angels, some form of enlightenment, or seeing the true way to God. The cult demands intense commitment, and its followers, confronting a hostile world, pull into a tight circle, separating themselves from nonbelievers.

Most cults fail. Not many people believe the new message, and the cult fades into obscurity. Some, however, succeed and make history. Over time, large numbers of people may come to accept the message, and become followers of the religion. If this happens, the new religion changes from a cult to a sect.

Sect

A **sect** is a group larger than a cult, whose members still feel a fair amount of tension with the prevailing beliefs and values of the broader society. The sect may even be hostile to the society in which it lives. At the very least, its members remain uncomfortable with many of the emphases of the dominant culture, while nonmembers, in turn, tend to be uncomfortable with members of the sect.

Ordinarily, sects are loosely organized and fairly small. They emphasize personal salvation and an emotional expression of one's relationship with God. Clapping, shouting, dancing, and extemporaneous prayers are hallmarks of sects. Like cults, sects also stress **evangelism,** the active recruitment of new members.

If a sect grows, its members gradually tend to make peace with the rest of society. They become more respectable in the eyes of the majority and feel much less hostility and little, if any, isolation. To appeal to the new, broader base, the sect shifts some of its doctrines, redefining matters to remove some of the rough edges that created tension between it and the rest of society. If a sect follows this course and becomes larger and more integrated into society, it has changed into a church.

Church

At this point, the religious group is highly bureaucratized—probably with national and international headquarters that give directions to the local congregations, enforce rules about who can be ordained, and control finances. The group's worship service is likely to have grown more sedate, with much less emphasis on personal salvation and emotional expression. Written prayers, for example, are now likely to be read before the congregation, sermons to be much more formal, and the relationship with God to be less intense. Rather than being recruited from the outside by fervent, personal evangelism, most new members now come from within, from children born to existing members. Rather than joining through conversion—seeing the new truth—children may be baptized, circumcised, or dedicated in some other way. When older, children may be asked to affirm the group's beliefs in a confirmation or bar mitzvah ceremony.

Ecclesia

Finally, some groups become so well integrated into a culture, and so strongly allied with their government, that it is difficult to tell where one leaves off and the other takes over. In these state religions, also called **ecclesia,** the government and religion work together to try to shape society. There is no recruitment of members, for citizenship makes everyone a member. The majority of the society, however, may belong to the religion in name only. The religion is part of a cultural identification, not an eye-opening experience. In Sweden, for example, where Lutheranism is the state religion, most Swedes come to church only for baptisms, marriages, and funerals. As shown in the Perspectives box on the next page, the culture and the religion interpenetrate one another.

Where cults and sects see God as personally involved and concerned with an individual's life, requiring an intense and direct response, an ecclesia's vision of God is more impersonal and remote. Church services reflect this view of the supernatural, for they tend to be highly formal, directed by ministers or priests who have undergone rigorous training in approved schools or seminaries, and follow set routines.

Examples of ecclesia include the Church of England (whose very name expresses alignment between church and state), the Lutheran church in Sweden and Denmark,

sect: a group larger than a cult that still feels substantial hostility from and toward society

evangelism: an attempt to win converts

ecclesia: a religious group so integrated into the dominant culture that it is difficult to tell where the one begins and the other leaves off; also called a *state religion*

▲▽▲▽▲▽▲▽▲▽▲▽▲▽▲▽▲▽▲▽▲▽▲▽▲▽▲▽▲▽▲▽▲▽▲▽▲▽

Perspectives

CULTURAL DIVERSITY AROUND THE WORLD

Religion and Culture in India

RELIGION AND CULTURE CAN be so interwoven that they totally blend into each other. As they interpenetrate, the religion reflects the culture and the culture reflects the religion. When religion is integral to a people's entire way of life, to change a cultural practice can threaten both the culture and the religion.

So it is in India, where Hinduism permeates the culture. A major teaching of Hinduism is that each person has a spiritual obligation to observe the limits set by the caste into which he or she was born. According to Hindu belief, an individual who does this well will be born into a higher caste in the next incarnation.

The cow also illustrates the interpenetration of religion and culture. The cow is worshiped as a sacred animal that represents the mother of life. To kill a cow is considered worse than to take a human life. The Indian constitution even includes a bill of rights for cows, and the government maintains "old-age homes" for cows (Harris 1974). To West-

ern thinking, it is irrational for 100 million cows to wander the countryside and cities while millions of people go to bed hungry and each day hundreds die of starvation. However, anthropologist Marvin Harris (1974), who analyzed the role of cattle in Indian life, pointed out that the taboo against killing cows produces a net benefit to the society. The cattle, which live off humanly inedible products, provide not only milk and energy for plowing but extremely valuable dung—used for fertilizer, cooking fuel, and even mortar and flooring. The taboo also prevents farmers from killing the animals during times of drought. Because farmers depend on oxen for plowing and for transportation (pulling their carts), they must overcome a short-term view. If they killed their cattle during droughts, when they and their families are starving, they would be left without energy for farming after the monsoon rains come. As Harris noted, Westerners do not realize that farmers would rather eat their cows than starve, but that they will surely starve later if they do eat them.

Islam in Iran and Iraq, and, during the time of the Holy Roman Empire, the Roman Catholic church, which was the official religion for what is today Europe.

Variations in Patterns

Obviously, not all religious groups go through all these stages—from cult to sect to church to ecclesia. Some die out because they fail to attract enough members. Others, such as the Amish, remain sects. And, as is evident from the few countries that have state religions, very few religions ever become ecclesias.

In addition, these classifications are not perfectly matched in the real world. For example, although the Amish are a sect, they place little or no emphasis on recruiting others. The early Quakers, another sect, shied away from emotional expressions of their beliefs. They would quietly meditate in church, with no one speaking, until God gave someone a message to share with others. Finally, some groups that become churches may retain a few characteristics of sects, such as an emphasis on evangelism or a personal relationship with God.

Although all religions began as cults, not all varieties of a particular religion have done so. For example, some **denominations**—"brand names" within a major religion, such as Methodism or Reform Judaism—may begin as splinter groups. A large group within a church may disagree with *some aspects* of the church's teachings (not its major message) and break away to form its own organization. An example mentioned earlier (page 497) is the Southern Baptist Convention, formed in 1845 to defend the right to own slaves (Ernst 1988; Nauta 1993).

Cults, Sects, and Culture Conflict

As we have seen, cults and sects represent a break with the past. Consequently, they challenge the social order. Three major patterns of adaptation occur when religion and the culture in which it is embedded find themselves in conflict.

denomination: a "brand name" within a major religion, for example, Methodist or Baptist

First, the members of a religion may reject the dominant culture and have as little as possible to do with nonmembers of their religion. Like the Amish, they may withdraw into closed communities. As noted in the Perspectives box on page 104, the Amish broke away from Swiss-German Mennonites in 1693. They try to preserve the culture of their ancestors, a simpler time when life was uncontaminated by television, movies, automobiles, or electricity. To do so, they emphasize family life, traditional male and female roles, and live on farms, which they work with horses. They continue to wear the same style of clothing as their ancestors did three hundred years ago, to light their homes with oil lamps, and to speak German at home and in church. They also continue to reject radio, television, motorized vehicles, and education beyond the eighth grade. They do mingle with non-Amish to the extent of shopping in town—where they are readily distinguishable by their form of transportation (horse-drawn carriages), clothing, and speech.

In the second pattern, a cult or sect rejects only specific elements of the prevailing culture. For example, religious teachings may dictate that immodest clothing—short skirts, swimsuits, low-cut dresses, and so on—is immoral, or that wearing makeup or going to the movies is wrong. Most elements of the main culture, however, are accepted. Although specific activities are forbidden, members of the religion are able to participate in most aspects of the broader society. They resolve this mild tension either by adhering to the religion or by "sneaking," doing the forbidden acts on the sly.

In the third pattern, the society rejects the religious group and may even try to destroy it. The early Christians are an example. The Roman emperor declared them enemies of Rome and ordered all Christians to be hunted down and destroyed. The Mormons provide another example. Their rejection of Roman Catholicism and Protestantism as corrupt, accompanied by their belief in polygyny, led to their persecution. In 1831, they left Palmyra, New York, and moved first to Kirtland, Ohio, and subsequently to Independence, Missouri. When the persecution continued, they moved to Nauvoo, Illinois. There a mob murdered the founder of the religion, Joseph Smith, and his brother Hyrum. The Mormons then decided to escape the dominant culture altogether by founding a community in the wilderness. Consequently, in 1847 they settled in the Great Salt Lake Valley of what is today the state of Utah (Bridgwater 1953). For a more current example, see the following Thinking Critically section.

▼▲▼▲▼▲▼▲▼▲▼▲▼▲▼▲▼▲▼▲▼▲▼▲▼▲▼▲▼▲▼▲▼

Thinking Critically About Social Controversy

How to Destroy a Cult:
A Conflict Interpretation of the Branch Davidians

▼ THE FIRST REPORT WAS STUNNING. About a hundred armed agents of the Bureau of Alcohol, Tobacco, and Firearms (ATF) attacked the compound of an obscure religious group in Waco, Texas. Four armed agents who assaulted the compound and six men who tried to defend it were shot to death. The result was a fifty-one-day standoff, televised to the U.S. public, with the ATF and FBI doing such strange things as bombarding the compound with loud music day and night. At 6 A.M. on the fifty-first day of the siege, following on-again, off-again negotiations with David Koresh, the charismatic 33-year-old leader of the Branch Davidians, a tank rammed the compound's main building and began pumping in gas consisting of chemicals that, by law, the U.S. military was unable to use against Iraqi soldiers. A second tank joined in, punching holes in the walls. In terror, the women and children fled to the second floor, while the men continued to shoot futilely at the armed vehicles. Suddenly an explosion rocked the compound, and the buildings burst into flames. Eighty-five men, women, and children were burned to death. Some of the charred bodies of the twenty-five children were found huddled next to their mothers.

The government claimed that the Branch Davidians set the fire. Survivors said the fire began when one of the tanks knocked over a lantern. After the fire, the government sealed off the area and bulldozed the charred remains of the buildings.

The following analysis of this controversial event does *not* take the government line. Rather, it is written from the conflict perspective, assuming a conspiracy of the elite to destroy a group that posed a threat to its power.

What crimes could have justified such a lethal assault against the Branch Davidians? At first, the government said that it took action because the group had violated firearms laws. Later, agents changed their story to make saving the children their primary goal. Was the death of those children—and their parents—just an ironic twist of events that marked the stunning end to a strange group? Or was it part of a conspiracy by U.S. government agencies to put an end to groups that dare to challenge their authority?

Koresh's teachings certainly were bizarre. He taught that he was Jesus Christ returned to earth. Many have made this same claim, but Koresh's twist was that he had returned in sinful form so he could better understand sinners. As a sinner, Koresh had a voracious sexual appetite. He demanded—and received—sex from the men's wives, while insisting that the men remain celibate. Some reports, perhaps sponsored by the government, indicate that he also had sex with their daughters, some as young as 12 and 13 years old. Koresh also taught that Armageddon was on its way, that the government, the enemy, would one day launch an armed attack against them. About this, at least, he was right.

Since the official version has been repeatedly published in the mass media, let's consider the case for the other side.

First, Koresh was no stranger to Waco. He regularly drove around the area, shopping in stores and eating in restaurants. If the government had wanted, it could have served warrants and arrested him in public, with no confrontation. Second, after the first assault, Koresh let anyone leave who wanted to go. Some parents and twenty-one children did leave. After studying the children, the worst the government could come up with was that the children had been spanked for disobedience. They also learned that the children had been taught Bible stories and had learned songs. Third, the accounts of some of the survivors certainly don't support government claims. Sheila Martin, whose husband, a Harvard-trained attorney, along with four of their children, died in the conflagration, says that people watching television saw only the outside of the building, not how nice it was to live there. "Those were the happiest days of my life," she said.

On the other hand, there may have been child abuse. But an armed attack by government agents for child abuse? No, the ATF's first accounts of the group stockpiling weapons is the key to explain the government's desire to annihilate the group. In the months before their destruction, the Branch Davidians had purchased many thousands of dollars of guns and ammunition. Although their purchases were legal, the government became concerned about reports of a strange group, heavily armed, holed up in its own compound. Who knows what they might do? The solution was to seek out and destroy. In this context, it is not without significance to note that the ATF is the trigger-happy group once headed by Elliot Ness of "The Untouchables" fame.

If this analysis is correct, what groups might be targeted next? One target could be militant Islamic groups, which government agents have already infiltrated. Other primary candidates are the survivalist groups that, believing the U.S. government is the Antichrist, reject the government's decrees as illegitimate, and, fearing an attack, have armed themselves. Like the Branch Davidians, some have retreated into their own compounds. One group calls itself Christian Identity. Its members believe that white "Aryans" are the direct descendants of the tribes of Israel and those who call themselves Jews are really the children of Satan. A specific candidate is the Prophet's Church Universal and Triumphant, which under the leadership of Elizabeth Clare, has built underground shelters near Yellowstone National Park—and is rumored to have stockpiled arms. Dozens of other groups have sprouted up, teaching that the world is soon coming to an end, that the Antichrist has been unleashed on the world. Like Koresh, they, too, have stockpiled weapons to defend themselves.

Will the future, then, bring more Wacos? Some say the answer is obvious. They ask if the power elite can afford to do nothing, while groups with paramilitary structures arm themselves and refuse to pay taxes to the Antichrist? Do you think the U.S. government, through specific agencies, will embark on a systematic plan to annihilate groups that spurn its authority?

What do you think lies behind the destruction of the Branch Davidians?

Sources: Barkun 1993; Chua-Eoan 1993; Corbin 1993; Dillin 1993; Lacayo 1993; Pressley 1993; Tye 1993; Paul 1994. ▲

During an attack by the Bureau of Alcohol, Tobacco, and Firearms the buildings in which the Branch Davidians lived went up in flames. Was the fire an accident? Set by the Branch Davidians themselves? The culmination of a conspiracy to destroy this group because it stockpiled arms and denied the authority of the U.S. government?

 Secularization

The term **secularization** refers to the process by which worldly affairs replace spiritual interests. (The term **secular** means "belonging to the world and its affairs.") As we shall see, both religions and cultures can become secularized.

The Secularization of Religion

The Splintering of Churches in the United States

> As the model, fashionably slender, paused before the head table of African-American community leaders, her gold necklace glimmering above the low-cut bodice of her emerald green dress, the hostess, a member of the Church of God in Christ, said, "It's now OK to wear more revealing clothes—as long as it is done in good taste." Then she added, "You couldn't do this when I was a girl, but now it's OK—and you can still worship God." (Author's files)

When I heard these words, I grabbed a piece of paper and quickly jotted them down, my sociological imagination stimulated at their deep implication. As strange as it may seem, this simple event pinpoints the essence of why the Christian churches in the United States have splintered. Let's see how that could possibly be.

The simplest answer to why Christians don't have just one church, or at most several, instead of the hundreds of sects and denominations that dot the U.S. landscape is disagreements about doctrine (church teaching). As theologian and sociologist Richard Niebuhr pointed out, however, there are many ways of settling doctrinal disputes beside splintering off and forming another religious organization. Niebuhr (1929) suggested that the answer lies more in *social* change than in *religious* conflict.

The explanation goes like this. As noted earlier, when a sect becomes more churchlike, tension between it and the main culture lessens. Quite likely, its founders and first members were poor, or at least not too successful in worldly pursuits. Feeling estranged from their general culture, they received a good part of their identity from their religion. Their services and customs stressed differences between their values and cosmology and those of the dominant culture. Typically, their religion also stressed the joys of the coming afterlife, when they would be able to escape from their present pain.

secularization: the process by which spiritual concerns are replaced by worldly concerns

secular: belonging to the world and its affairs

As time passes, the group's values—such as frugality and the avoidance of gambling, alcohol, and drugs—help later generations become successful. They attain more education, become more middle class, and grow more respectable in the eyes of society. They no longer experience the alienation felt by the founders of their group. Life's burdens don't seem as heavy, and the need for relief through an afterlife doesn't seem as pressing. Similarly, the pleasures of the world no longer appear as threatening to the "true" belief. Then, as in the preceding example of the fashion show, there follows an attempt to harmonize religious beliefs with their changing orientation to the culture.

In their early years, Protestant sects such as the Church of the Nazarene and the Church of God stressed that jewelry, makeup, and movies were worldly and that true believers had to separate themselves from such things. Over time, the groups became less vocal about movies, and then fell silent about them. Similarly, after initial protests, they gradually objected less and less to their younger members wearing makeup and jewelry. Finally came accommodation with the secular culture to such an extent that some ministers' wives dye their hair and wear makeup and jewelry. A sociological cycle has been completed: what was formerly called the "Jezebel" has become a role model for young women.

The particulars, of course, vary from one group to another, for not many groups choose avoidance of movies, makeup, and jewelry as central identifiers. But the process is the same. As the members of a sect become more middle class, the group's teachings change to match the members' new positions in life. Eventually, from groups that had prided themselves on their distinctive appearance, one hears, "Outward appearances aren't really important. It's what's in your heart that counts."

This process is called the **secularization of religion**—a group shifting its focus from spiritual matters to the affairs of this world. Such accommodation with the secular culture, however, displeases the group's members who have had less worldly success. They still feel estranged from the broader culture. For them, tension and hostility continue to be real. They see secularization as giving up the group's fundamental truths, a "selling out" to the secular world. After futile attempts to bring the group back to its senses, they break away, forming a sect that once again stresses its differences from the world, the need for more personal, emotional religious experiences, and salvation from the pain of living in this world. The cycle then repeats itself.

The secularization of religion also occurs on a much broader scale. As a result of modernization—the industrialization of society, urbanization, mass education, wide adoption of technology, and the transformation of *Gemeinschaft* to *Gesellschaft* societies—people depend much less on religious explanations for the problems of life (Berger 1967). Even a group's religious leaders turn to answers provided by sociology, philosophy, psychology, science, medicine, and so on. In some churches, sermons are based on novels and academic studies instead of the Bible, psychological encounter groups replace repentance and prayer, and "sin" is redefined as "bad choices." Abandoning its religious beliefs, the church nonetheless retains its rituals, which some now find devoid of the meaning they once held. This dissatisfaction with the accommodation to the general culture, in turn, provides fertile ground for the formation of splinter groups. (The Down-to-Earth Sociology box on the next page describes a group whose needs are not met by established religious organizations, but by a small, evangelizing, sectlike group.)

The Secularization of Culture

Just as a religion can be secularized, so can a culture. The term **secularization of culture** describes what happens when the influence of religion on a culture originally permeated by religion diminishes. The U.S. provides an example.

In spite of attempts to reinterpret history, the Pilgrims and most of the Founding Fathers of the United States were highly religious people. The Pilgrims were even convinced that God had guided them to found a new land, while many of the Founding Fathers felt that God had guided them to develop a new form of government.

secularization of religion: the replacement of a religion's "otherworldly" concerns with concerns about "this world"

secularization of culture: the process by which a culture becomes less influenced by religion

▼▼▼▼▼▼▼▼▼▼▼▼▼▼▼▼▼▼▼▼▼▼▼▼▼▼▼

Down-To-Earth Sociology

Bikers and Bibles

THE BIBLE BELT CHURCHGOERS in Eureka Springs, Arkansas, stare as Herbie Shreve, unshaven, his hair hanging over the collar of his denim vest, roars into town on his Harley Davidson. With hundreds of other bikers in town, it is going to be a wild weekend of drunks, nudity, and fights.

But not for Herbie. After pitching his tent, he sets up a table at which he offers other bikers free ice water and religious tracts. "No hard sell. They seek us out when it's the right time," says Herbie.

The ministry began when Herbie's father, a pastor, took up motorcycling to draw closer to his rebellious teenage son. As the pair rode around the heartland of America, they often were snubbed by fellow Christians when they tried to attend church. So Herbie's father hatched plans for a motorcycle ministry. "Jesus said, 'Go out to the highways and hedges,' and that always stuck with me," says the elder Shreve. "I felt churches ought to be wherever the people are."

Some Christian groups make evangelism, the conversion of others, a primary goal. One such group is the Christian Motorcyclists' Association, discussed in this box. Another is the Full Gospel Motorcycle Association, shown here joining hands in prayer before setting out to change tires, help stranded motorists, and preach the gospel. The bikers strike up conversations about their motorcycles, then change the topic to "how to reverse direction from the highway to hell to the highway to heaven."

They founded the Christian Motorcyclists Association (CMA), headquartered in Hatfield, Arkansas. It now has 33,000 members in more than 300 chapters in the United States and Canada. Members of the CMA call themselves "weekend warriors."

"Riding for the Son" is emblazoned on their T-shirts and jackets, which in the midst of the nudity and drunkenness, makes them stand out.

No MCA member has ever been harmed by a biker. But they have come close. In the early days, bikers at a rally surrounded Herbie's tent and threatened to burn it down. "Some of those same people are friends of mine today," says the elder Shreve.

Stepping over a biker who has passed out in front of his tent, Herbie goes through the campground urging last night's carousers to join them by a lake for a Sunday service. Four years ago no one took him up on it. Today twenty bikers straggle down to the dock.

Herbie's brief sermon is plain-spoken. He touches on the biker's alienation—the unpaid bills, the oppressive bosses, the righteous church ladies "who are always mad and always right." He tells them that Jesus loves them, and that they can call him anytime. "I'll help fix your life," he says.

They have several conversions this weekend. They give away more tracts—and a couple of the group come up to thank Herbie.

"You just stay at it. You don't know when their hearts are touched. Look at these guys," Herbie says, pointing to fellow CMA members. "They were all bikers headed for hell, too. Now they follow the Son."

Herbie gets on his Harley. In town, the churchgoers stare as he roars past, his long hair sweeping behind him.

Sources: Based on Graham 1990; Shreve 1991.

The clause in the Constitution that guarantees the separation of church and state was not an attempt to keep religion out of government, but a (successful) device to avoid the establishment of a state religion like that in England. Here, people were to have the freedom to worship as they wished. The assumption of the founders was even more specific—that Protestantism represented the true religion.

The phrase in the Declaration of Independence, "All men are created equal," refers to a central belief in God as the creator of humanity. A member of the clergy opened Congress with prayer. Many colonial laws were based on principles derived explicitly from the Old and the New Testaments. In some colonies, blasphemy was listed as a crime, as was failing to observe the Sabbath. Similarly, adultery was a crime that carried the death penalty. Even public kissing between husband and wife was considered an offense, punishable by being placed in the public stocks (Frumkin 1967). In other words, religion permeated U.S. culture. It was part and parcel of the way early Americans saw life. Their lives, laws, and other aspects of the culture all reflected their religious beliefs.

Today, however, U.S. culture has been secularized; that is, the influence of religion on public affairs has greatly lessened. Laws are no longer passed on the basis of religious principles. In general, ideas of what is "generally good" have replaced religion as an organizing principle for the culture.

The causes of this secularization are many. One is science, which, as it advanced, developed explanations for many aspects of life that people previously had attributed to God. Similarly, industrialization, urbanization, and mass education represented not just external changes but brought with them a more secular view of the world. One consequence is that such conditions as wealth and poverty, high and low intelligence, the election of one candidate and defeat of another, are attributed to natural processes, not to God's intervention or will.

Although the secularization of culture means that religion is less important in public life, personal religious involvement among Americans has not diminished. Ninety-four percent believe that there is a God, 77 percent believe there is a heaven, and 57 percent claim membership in a church or synagogue. On any given weekend, 42 percent of all Americans attend a church or synagogue (Woodward 1989; Gallup 1990; *Statistical Abstract* 1993: Tables 86, 89).

To underscore the paradox of how religious participation has increased while the culture has secularized (see Table 18.1). The proportion of Americans who belong to a church or synagogue is now *four* times as high as it was when the country was founded. Church membership is, of course, only a rough indicator of how significant religion is in people's lives, for some church members are not particularly religious, while many intensely religious people—Abraham Lincoln, for one—never join a church.

Table 18.1

Growth in Religious Membership: The Percentage of Americans who Belong to a Church or Synagogue

	Percentage who claim membership
1776	17%
1860	37%
1890	45%
1926	58%
1975	71%
1991	68%

Sources: Finke 1992; *Statistical Abstract* 1993: Table 86.

Characteristics of Religion in the United States

With its hundreds of denominations and sects, how can we generalize about religion in the United States? What do these many religious groups have in common? It certainly isn't doctrine, but doctrine is not the focus of sociology. As stated at the beginning of this chapter, sociologists are interested in the relationship between society and religion, and the role that religion plays in people's lives. Sociologically, then, we can identify the following major characteristics of religion in U.S. society.

Diversity

The United States has neither a state church nor a single denomination that dominates the country. As Table 18.2 shows, the largest group is the Roman Catholic church. Although more than twice as many Americans claim to be Protestants, they are divided among hundreds of different religious organizations.

Pluralism and Freedom

It is the U.S. government's policy not to interfere with religions. The government's position is that its obligation is to ensure an atmosphere in which people can worship as they see fit. At times, however, the government grossly violates this policy, as was discussed in the Thinking Critically section on pages 508–509.

Table 18.2	
U.S. Churches with at least 100,000 Members	
Roman Catholics	58,267,000
Baptists	34,600,000
Pentecostals	30,693,000
Methodists	14,627,000
Lutherans	8,398,000
Moslems	6,000,000
Church of God in Christ	5,000,000
Mormons	4,489,000
Jews	4,300,000
Presbyterians	4,252,000
Episcopal Church	2,472,000
Reformed Churches	2,169,000
Eastern Orthodox	2,116,000
Churches of Christ	1,742,000
Christian Churches	1,071,000
Disciples of Christ	1,023,000
Jehovah's Witnesses	914,000
Adventists	767,000
Church of the Nazarene	574,000
Salvation Army	446,000
Churches of God	265,000
Mennonites	259,000
Evangelical Free Church	188,000
Unitarian Universalists	141,000
Christian Congregation	111,000
Baha'i Faith	110,000

Source: World Almanac and Book of Facts 1994: 726–727.

Competition and Recruitment

The many religions of the United States compete for clients. Various congregations advertise in the Yellow Pages of the telephone directory and insert appealing advertising—under the guise of news—in the religious section of the Saturday or Sunday edition of the local newspapers.

Commitment

Americans are a deeply religious people, as demonstrated by the high proportion who believe in God and attend a church or synagogue. This religious commitment is underscored by generous support for religion and its charities. Each year Americans donate about $50 billion to religious causes (*Statistical Abstract* 1991: Table 79). To appreciate the significance of this huge figure, keep in mind that, unlike a country in which there is an ecclesia, those billions of dollars are not taxes but voluntary contributions that are the result of religious commitment.

Toleration

The general religious toleration can be illustrated by three prevailing attitudes (1) "All religions have a right to exist—as long as they don't try to brainwash anyone or bother me." (2) "With all the religions to choose from, how can anyone tell which one—if any—is true?" (3) "Each of us may be convinced about the truth of our religion—and that is good—but to try to convert others is a violation of the individual's dignity."

Fundamentalist Revival

The fundamentalist churches are undergoing a revival. Fundamentalist churches teach that the Bible is literally true and that salvation comes only through a personal relationship with Jesus Christ. They also decry what they see as the permissiveness of U.S. culture: sex on television and in movies, abortion, corruption in public office, premarital pregnancy, cohabitation, and drugs. Their answer to these problems is firm, simple, and direct: people whose hearts are changed through religious conversion will change their lives. The approach of the mainstream churches, which offer a remote God and a corresponding lack of emotional involvement, fails to meet the basic religious needs of large numbers of Americans. Consequently, as Figure 18.2 shows, during the past twenty-five years the mainstream churches have lost membership. The exception is the Roman Catholics, whose gain is primarily due to heavy immigration from Catholic countries.

The Electronic Church

What began as a ministry to shut-ins and those who do not belong to a church has blossomed into its own type of church. Its preachers, called "televangelists," reach millions of viewers and raise millions of dollars. Some of its most famous ministries are those of Robert Schuler (the "Crystal Cathedral") and Pat Robertson (the 700 Club). Its most infamous preachers are Jim Bakker and Jimmy Swaggert. Jim Bakker was sentenced to federal prison for misappropriation of funds, while Jimmy Swaggert lost his national television ministry (which brought in over $50 million a year) when revelations of his involvements with prostitutes became public.

Many local ministers view the electronic church as a competitor. They complain that it competes for the attention and dollars of their members. The electronic church

Figure 18.2

U.S. Churches: Gains and Losses in Twenty-Five Years

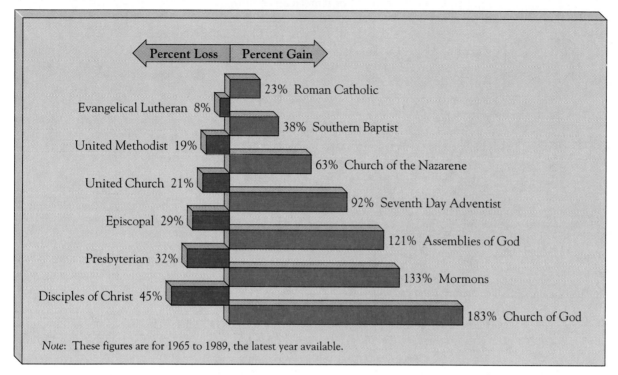

Note: These figures are for 1965 to 1989, the latest year available.

Source: Yearbook of American and Canadian Churches, various editions.

replies that its money goes to good causes and that through its conversions it feeds members into the local churches, strengthening, not weakening them.

An interesting combination of local congregations and the electronic church has emerged. Some independent fundamentalist groups now subscribe to the electronic church. They pay a fee in return for having "name" ministers piped "live" into their local congregation. They build services around these electronic messages, supplementing them with songs and adding other "local touches."

Characteristics of Members

About 68 percent of Americans belong to a church or synagogue. Let us look at the characteristics of people who hold formal membership in a religion.

Region Membership is not evenly distributed around the country. As shown on Table 18.3, membership is highest in the South, followed by the East and the Midwest. Membership in the West is lower than the other regions, perhaps because the West is both the newest region in the nation and has the highest net migration. If so, when its residents have put down firmer roots, the West's proportion of religious membership will increase.

Social Class Religion in the United States is stratified by social class. As can be seen from Figure 18.3, each religious group draws members from all social classes, but some are "top-heavy" and others "bottom-heavy." The most top-heavy are the Episcopalians and Jews, the most bottom-heavy the Baptists and Evangelicals. This figure is further confirmation

Table 18.3

Church and Synagogue Membership, Percentage of Population by Region	
South	76%
East	69%
Midwest	66%
West	54%

Source: Statistical Abstract 1993: Table 86.

that churchlike groups tend to appeal more to the successful, the more sectlike to the less successful.

Americans have a tendency to change their religion. About 40 percent of Americans belong to a denomination different from the one in which they were raised (Sherkat and Wilson 1991). People who change their social class are also likely to change their denomination. An upwardly mobile person is likely to seek a religion that draws more people from his or her new social class. An upwardly mobile Baptist, for example, may become a Methodist or a Presbyterian. For Roman Catholics, the situation is somewhat different. Since each parish is a geographical unit, an upwardly mobile individual who moves into a more affluent neighborhood is likely to automatically transfer into a congregation that has a larger proportion of affluent members.

Table 18.4

Age and Church or Synagogue Membership

Age	Membership
18–29	60%
30–49	67%
50+	76%

Source: Statistical Abstract 1993: Table 86.

Age   As shown on Table 18.4, the chances that an American will belong to a church or synagogue increase with age. Possibly this is because people become more concerned about an afterlife as they age. Another explanation is that membership is seen as part of the adult role, and as people marry, become parents, or become more established, they are more likely to join.

Race and Ethnicity   It is common for religions around the world to be associated with race and ethnicity: Islam with Arabs, Judaism with Jews, Hinduism with Indians, and Confucianism with Chinese. Sometimes, as with Hinduism and Confucianism, a religion and a particular country are almost synonymous. Christianity is not associated with any one country, although it is associated primarily with Western culture.

In the United States, all major religious groups draw from the nation's various racial and ethnic groups. Like social class, however, there is a clustering that connects religion with race and ethnicity. Persons of Latino or Irish descent are likely to be Roman Catholics, those of Greek origin to belong to the Greek Orthodox church. African Americans are likely to be Protestants, more specifically Baptists, or to belong to fundamentalist sects.

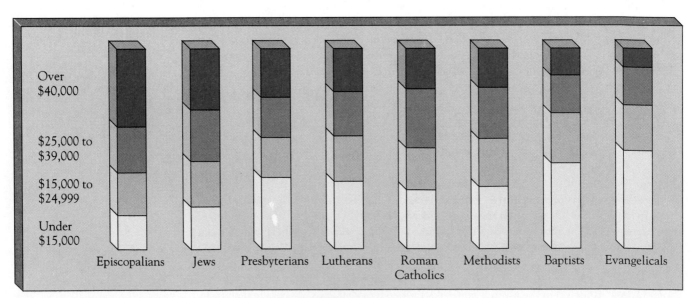

Source: Compiled from data in *Gallup Opinion Index,* 1987: 20–27, 29.

Figure 18.3

Average Income and Religious Affiliation.

Although many churches are integrated, it is not without cause that Sunday morning between ten and eleven has been called "the most segregated hour in the United States." African Americans tend to belong to exclusively or largely African-American churches, while most whites see only whites in theirs. The segregation of churches is based not on law, but on custom.

The Future of Religion

Marx was convinced that religion would crumble when the workers threw off their chains of oppression. When the workers usher in a new society based on justice, he argued, there will no longer be a need for religion, for religion is the refuge of the miserable, and people will no longer be miserable. Religion will wither away, for people will see that thoughts about an afterlife are misdirected, and that they must put their energies into developing a workers' paradise here on earth (De George 1968).

After communist countries were established, however, people continued to be religious. At first, the leaders thought they were simply a remnant that would eventually dwindle to nothing. Old people might cling to the past, but the young would give it up, and with the coming generation religion would cease to exist.

The new Marxist states, avowing atheism, were not content to let this withering occur on its own, however; they began a concerted effort to eradicate religion from their midst. (Keep in mind that Marx said that he was not a Marxist. He did not advocate the persecution of religion, for he felt that religion would crumble on its own.) The Communist government in the Soviet Union declared that church buildings were state property and turned them into museums or office buildings. The school curriculum was designed to ridicule religion, and, as noted, a civil marriage ceremony was substituted for the religious ceremony (complete with an altar and a bust of Lenin), while a ceremony dedicating newborns to the state was even substituted for baptism. Ministers and priests were jailed as enemies of the state, and parents who dared to teach religion to their children were imprisoned or fired from their jobs, their children taken from them to be raised by the state where they would learn the "truth." In spite of such persecution, religion remained strong, even among many of the youth.

Another group of thinkers, who placed their faith not in socialism or communism but in science, foresaw a similar end to religion. As science advanced, it would explain everything. Science would transform human thought and replace religion, which was merely mistaken prescientific thinking. For example, in 1966 Anthony Wallace, one of the world's best-known anthropologists, made the following observation:

> The evolutionary future of religion is extinction. Belief in supernatural beings . . .
> will become only an interesting historical memory. . . . doomed to die out, all over
> the world, as a result of the increasing adequacy and diffusion of scientific knowledge.

Marx, Wallace, and the many other social analysts who took this position were wrong. Religion thrives in the most advanced scientific nations, in capitalist and socialist countries. It is evident that these analysts did not understand the fundamental significance that religion plays in people's lives.

Humans are inquiring creatures. They are aware that they have a past, a present, and a future. They reflect on their experiences to try to make sense out of them. One of the questions that people develop as they reflect on life is the purpose of it all. Why are we born? Is there an afterlife? If so, where are we going, and what will it be like when we get there? Out of these concerns arises this question: If there is a God, what does God want of us in this life? Does God have a preference about how we should live?

A recent innovation in U.S. religion is the electronic church, consisting of millions of television viewers of religious programs. Some viewers belong to local congregations, but many do not. Pictured here is one of the more successful television preachers (also called televangelists), Robert Schuler, who has constructed a unique church he calls the "Crystal Cathedral" in Orange, California.

Science cannot answer such questions. By its very nature, science cannot tell us about four main concerns that many people have: (1) the existence of God; (2) the purpose of life; (3) morality; and (4) the existence of an afterlife. About the first, science has nothing to say (no test tube has either isolated God or refuted God's existence); for the second, while science can provide a definition of life and describe the characteristics of living organisms, it has nothing to say about ultimate purpose; for the third, science can demonstrate the consequences of behavior but not the moral superiority of one action compared with another; for the fourth, again science can offer no information, for it has no tests that it can use to prove or disprove a "hereafter."

Science simply cannot replace religion. Nor can political systems, as demonstrated by the experience of socialist and communist countries. Science cannot even prove that loving your family and neighbor is superior to hurting and killing them. It can describe death and compute consequences, but it cannot dictate the *moral* superiority of any action, even in such an extreme example.

There is no doubt that religion will last as long as humanity lasts—or until humans develop adequate functional alternatives. And even though such alternatives had different names, wouldn't they, too, be a form of religion?

Summary and Review

What Is Religion?

Durkheim identified three essential characteristics of religion: beliefs that set the sacred apart from the profane, rituals, and a moral community (a church). Pp. 490–491.

The Functionalist Perspective

What are the functions and dysfunctions of religion?

Among the functions of religion are answering questions about ultimate meaning, providing emotional comfort, social solidarity, guidelines for everyday life, social control, adaptation, support for the government, and fostering social change. Groups or activities that provide these same functions are called **functional equivalents** of religion. Among the dysfunctions of religion are war and religious persecution. Pp. 491–494.

The Symbolic Interactionist Perspective

What aspects of religion do symbolic interactionists study?

Symbolic interactionists focus on the meanings of religion for its followers. They examine religious symbols, rituals, beliefs, experiences, and the sense of community provided by religion. Pp. 494–496.

The Conflict Perspective

What aspects of religion do conflict theorists study?

Conflict theorists examine the relationship of religion to social inequalities, especially how religion is a conservative force that reinforces a society's social class system. P. 497.

Religion and the Spirit of Capitalism

What does the spirit of capitalism have to do with religion?

Max Weber disagreed with Marx's conclusion that religion impedes social change. In contrast, Weber saw religion as a primary source of social change. He analyzed how Protestantism gave rise to **the Protestant ethic,** which stimulated what he called **the spirit of capitalism.** The result was capitalism, which transformed society. Pp. 498–499.

The World's Major Religions

What are the world's major religions?

Judaism, Christianity, and Islam, all **monotheistic** religions, can be traced to the same Old Testament roots. Hinduism, the chief religion of India, has no specific founder, as do Judaism (Abraham), Christianity (Jesus), Islam (Muhammad), Buddhism (Gautama), and Confucianism (K'ung Fu-tsu). Specific teachings and history of these six religions are given in the text. Pp. 499–504.

Types of Religious Organizations

What types of religious organizations are there?

Sociologists divide religious organizations into cults, sects, churches, and ecclesias. All religions began as **cults.** Those that survive tend to develop into **sects** and eventually into **churches.** Sects, often led by charismatic leaders, are unstable. Some are perceived as a threat and are persecuted by the state. **Ecclesias,** or state religions, are rare. Pp. 504–509.

Secularization

What is the connection between secularization of religion and the splintering of churches?

Secularization, a change in a religion's focus from spiritual matters to concerns of "this world," is a key to understanding why churches divide. Basically, a cult or sect changes to accommodate its members' upward social class mobility, forming a church. Left dissatisfied, members who are not upwardly mobile tend to splinter off and form new cults or sects, and the cycle repeats itself. Cultures permeated by religion also secularize. This, too, leaves many dissatisfied and promotes social change. Pp. 510–513.

Characteristics of Religion in the United States

What are the main characteristics of religion in the United States?

The major characteristics are diversity, pluralism and freedom, competition, commitment, toleration, a fundamentalist revival, and the electronic church. Religious membership varies by region, social class, age, and race or ethnicity. Pp. 513–517.

The Future of Religion

Although industrialization led to the secularization of culture, this did not spell the end of religion, as many social analysts assumed it would. Because science and education cannot answer questions of ultimate meaning, the existence of God or an afterlife, or provide guidelines for morality, the need for religion will remain. In any foreseeable future, religion—or its functional equivalents—will prosper. Pp. 517–518.

Where can I read more on this topic?

Suggested readings for this chapter are listed on page 643.

Diego Rivera, Drs. Neftali Rodriguez and Antonio Diaz Lombardo, *detail from mural* The History of Medicine in Mexico: The People's Demand for Better Health, *1953*

Medicine: Health and Illness

The Sociological Perspective on Health and Illness

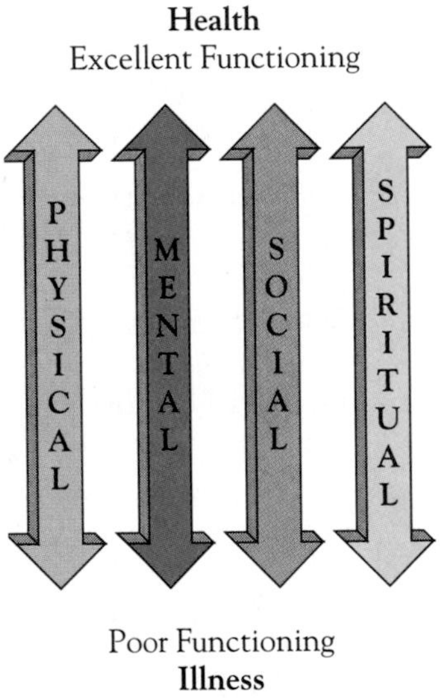

As the case of Terry Takewell illustrates, health is much more than a biological matter. In this chapter, we will look at how health is intimately related to society—to such matters as cultural beliefs, a country's stage of development, lifestyle, and social class. We will also examine developments in medicine that affect your health.

Defining Health and Illness

The definition of health seems so obvious that the question does not merit being asked. We all know what health is—or do we?

Trying to define health is like reaching for a bar of soap in a bathtub—just as you think you have it in your hand, it manages to slip away. A commonsense definition of health is the absence of disease or injury, but that is like defining marriage by saying that it is the absence of being single. It only says what it is *not*, not what it is.

When international health experts wrestled with this question back in the 1940s, they identified three components of **health:** physical, mental, and social (World Health Organization 1946). In consideration of the material covered in the previous chapter on religion, the spiritual dimension qualifies as a fourth component.

Figure 19.1 portrays this definition of health, which has several implications. First, rather than thinking of people as either healthy or unhealthy, it is useful to think of them as healthier in some areas and less healthy in others. A "certified" mentally ill person, for example, may be in fine physical shape, while a person who is physically ill may enjoy excellent mental health. Second, very few people are entirely healthy; that is, not many people are at peak performance in all four areas.

Effects of Cultural Beliefs on How People View Health and Illness

Health, therefore, is a relative matter, as is most apparent in its mental and spiritual components. For example, in Western culture officials might lock up a person who hears voices and sees visions, while in a tribal society such an individual might be honored and made a **shaman** ("witch doctor") for being in close contact with the gods. The social component is similarly relative. For example, does a person who fails to get along with others and causes problems at work necessarily demonstrate bad "social" health? Consider someone whose morals set her at odds with co-workers. She refuses to go along with padding a

---

Health
Excellent Functioning

PHYSICAL MENTAL SOCIAL SPIRITUAL

Poor Functioning
Illness

Figure 19.1

A Continuum of Health and Illness

health: a human condition measured by four components: physical, mental, social, and spiritual

shaman: the healing specialist of a preliterate tribe who attempts to control the spirits thought to cause a disease or injury; commonly called a witch doctor

government payroll and threatens to blow the whistle. If some see her as a hero and others as a villain, what is her "social" health?

Even the physical component is relative. Suppose one morning you look in the mirror and see strange blotches covering your face and chest. Hoping against hope that it is not serious, you rush to a doctor. If the doctor said that you had "dyschromic spirochetosis," your fears would be confirmed. Now, wouldn't everyone around the world draw the conclusion that the spots are a disease? No, not everybody. In one South American tribe this skin condition is so common that the few individuals who *aren't* spotted are seen as the unhealthy ones—and they are excluded from activities (Zola 1983).

The effects of cultural beliefs on health can also be illustrated by anorexia nervosa, a condition in which individuals—primarily young females—try to make themselves excessively thin by eating little and secretly vomiting much of what they do eat. Such a condition depends on the belief that thin is beautiful, a belief not shared in many parts of the world. For example, Arab men associate female beauty with greater weight than do Americans.

Over time, a group's definitions of what makes people healthy or sick may change. For example, Americans used to think that it was unhealthy for women to go to college because, as noted on page 290, experts presumed that a woman's uterus and her brain fought over a limited supply of energy (Fisher 1986). Similarly, U.S. health experts used to teach that masturbation caused mental illness.

Effects of Social Location on People's Health

Besides examining how people define health and illness, sociologists also study how social location affects people's chances of remaining healthy or getting sick. Let's look at how international stratification does this, then at lifestyle, social class, and social roles.

International Stratification and Health Care The intimate connection between social location and health is readily apparent when we view health and medical care on a global scale.

Suppose, for example, that you had been born in a poor country located in the tropics. Instead of facing cancer or a heart attack in old age, during your much shorter life you would constantly face illness and death from four major sources: malaria (from mosquitos), internal parasites (from contaminated water), diarrhea (from food and soil contaminated with human feces), and malnutrition. Heart disease and cancer, in contrast, are "luxury" diseases; that is, they characterize people in the rich First World where people live long enough to get them. As the Third World develops economically their people will live longer, and its population will likely trade their four primary killers in and begin to worry about cancer and heart attacks instead.

International stratification in medical care is a fact of global life. Just like the poor in the United States, Third World countries have little money to spend on health care. They can afford neither the facilities to train many medical personnel nor expensive medicines and equipment. Consequently, they lag far behind the industrialized nations in terms of medical care. One consequence is huge disparities in infant mortality rates and life spans. As Figure 19.2 shows, less than 10 of every 1,000 babies born in the industrialized nations die before they are a year old. In contrast, in some Third World countries such as Afghanistan, Angola, and Ethiopia, the death rate of infants is more than ten times higher. Similarly, whereas people in the First World can expect to live to about 75, in many Third World countries—Afghanistan, Angola, Cambodia, and Somalia—life expectancy is less than fifty years (*Statistical Abstract* 1993: Table 1376).

Many diseases that ravage the populations of these poorer countries could be brought under control if their meager funds were spent on public health. Cheap drugs can prevent malaria, while safer water supplies and increased food production would go a long way toward eliminating the other major killers. Instead, these countries train a

How Many Babies Die Before Their First Birthday?

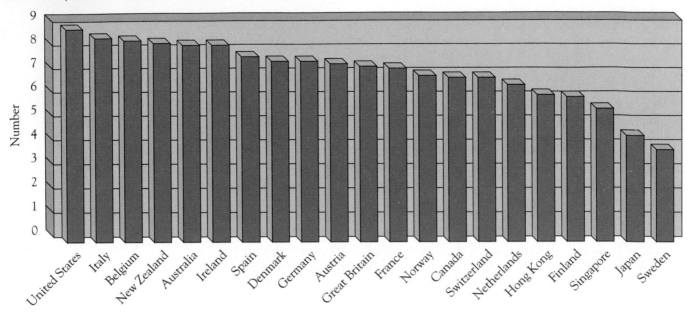

Note: Infant deaths (babies who die before 1 year of age) per thousand live births in twenty-one industrialized countries.

Source: Demographic Yearbook, 1992 (United Nations).

Figure 19.2

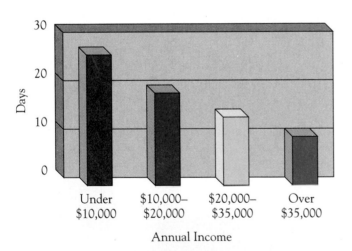

Source: Statistical Abstract 1993: Table 199.

Figure 19.3

Number of Days That People Were So Sick They Had to Cut Down on Their Usual Activities

few doctors in the West, who then primarily serve the country's elite. The elite receive Western-style medical treatment—including high technology, from X rays to life support systems—while the poor go without even basic medical services, and continue to die at an early age due to lack of preventive health measures.

Effects of Social Class   From this last example, you can see how significantly social class affects health. Figure 19.3 also illustrates this connection. As you can see, on average the more money Americans have, the less often they get sick. And, as the case of Terry Takewell illustrates, poor people have a more difficult time gaining access to medical treatment—which further undermines their health.

Subcultural Patterns and Lifestyle   Subcultural patterns and lifestyle also directly affect health and illness. Utah and Nevada provide a remarkable illustration. Although they are adjacent states with similar levels of income, education, medical care, urbanization, crime, and even climate (Fuchs 1981), Nevada's overall death rate is 45 percent higher than Utah's (*Statistical Abstract* 1993: Table 130). Nevadans are half again as likely to commit suicide and more than twice as likely to die from lung and liver diseases. Lifestyle accounts for most of the difference—Utah is inhabited mostly by Mormons, who encourage conservative living and disapprove of tobacco and alcohol. Similarly, due to their lifestyle (see pages 104 and 508), the Amish have lower rates of high blood pressure than do non-Amish people (Fuchs et al. 1990).

Work and Marriage   People's health is also deeply related to their social roles. For example, employed and married people don't get sick as often as do the unemployed and unmarried. But which is the cause, and which the effect? Is it that marriage and work help keep people healthy, or, rather, that healthy people are more likely to work and also more likely to marry? To find out, sociologists Beth Rushing, Christian Ritter, and Russell Burton (1992) studied a national sample of U.S. citizens who were interviewed eleven times over a period of 18 years. In order not to confuse cause and effect, they eliminated from their sample people who could not work. It turns out that marriage and work do keep people healthier. The researchers suggest that these social roles help give purpose and meaning to life, which, in turn, affects people's mental and physical well-being.

The Sick Role

Do you remember when your throat began to hurt and when your mom or dad took your temperature the thermometer registered 102°F? Your parents took you to the doctor, and despite your protests that tomorrow was (your birthday or the first day of vacation), you had to spend the next three days in bed taking medicines. You were forced to play what sociologists call the sick role. What do they mean by this term?

Elements of the Sick Role   Sociologist Talcott Parsons (1948, 1951 1975) identified four elements to the **sick role**—that you are not held responsible for being sick, that you are exempt from normal responsibilities, that you don't like the role, and that will get competent help so you can return to your routines. Parsons, a functionalist, pointed out that because society needs people to perform their regular roles of student, worker, parent, and so on, it is stingy with this role. Except for minor illnesses, which it grants on a very temporary basis, anyone who takes this role is obligated to seek competent help and to follow the prescribed remedy. People who don't are considered responsible for being sick. They are denied the right to claim sympathy from others and to be legitimately excused from their normal routines. The one is given sympathy and encouragement, the other a cold shoulder for wrongfully claiming the sick role.

Ambiguity in the Sick Role   Instead of a fever of 102°F, suppose that you feel "somewhat" ill and the thermometer registers 99.3 degrees. Do you then "become" sick or not? That is, do you decide to claim the sick role? Because clear-cut events such as heart attacks and limb fractures are rare, decisions to claim the sick role often are based more on social considerations than physical health. Let's also suppose that you are facing a midterm for which you are drastically underprepared, and you are allowed to make it up. The more you think about the test, the worse you are likely to feel—legitimating to yourself the need to claim the sick role. Now assume that you have no test, but your friends are coming over to take you out to celebrate your 21st birthday. You are much less likely to play the sick role. Note that in both cases your physical condition is the same.

Gatekeepers to the Sick Role   Parents and physicians are the primary gatekeepers to the sick role. That is, they mediate between our feelings of illness and our claim to being sick. Before parents call the school to excuse a child's absence, they decide whether the child is faking or has genuine symptoms serious enough to allow him or her to remain home from school. For adults, physicians are the main gatekeepers of the sick role. A "doctor's excuse"—actually permission to play the sick role—removes the need for employers and teachers to pass judgment on the individual's claim.

sick role: a social role that excuses people from normal obligations because they are sick or injured, while at the same time expecting them to seek competent help and cooperate in getting well

 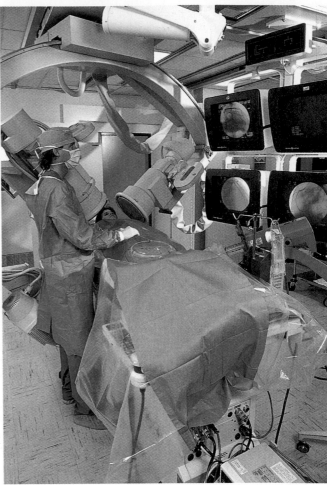

International stratification in health care is starkly contrasted in these two photographs. The one on the left shows medical treatment in Papua, New Guinea. The items on the table represent the extent of medical technology available to most residents of the Third World. The photo on the right, a catheterization laboratory in Austin, Texas, illustrates the medical technology available in the First World. Not all citizens of the First World, however, have equal access to such technology.

Gender Differences in the Sick Role   Although on average, females are healthier than males and live longer lives, they also go to doctors more frequently and are sick more often. How can we reconcile these seemingly incompatible findings? Testing college students from working-class backgrounds, researchers Elizabeth Klonoff and Hope Landrine (1992) found that women are more willing to claim the sick role when they feel poorly. They identified two primary reasons for this. Because fewer women were employed, they found less role conflict in claiming the sick role. The researchers also gave the men and women tests of "masculinity" and "femininity," and found that the women had been socialized for greater dependency and self-disclosure.

    This research helps to pinpoint some of the social factors that underlie the sick role. As we reviewed in Chapter 11, gender roles—ideas of what is properly feminine or masculine—vary from one culture to another. An ideal that men should be strong, keep their hurts to themselves, and "tough it through," while women should share their feelings and seek help from others, then, underlies this riddle of why women can be healthier than men and yet be sick and go to doctors more often.

Figure 19.4

The Top Ten Causes of Death in the United States, 1900 and 1990

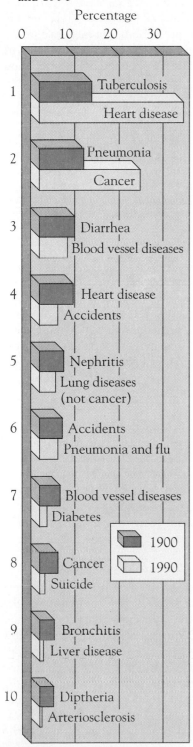

Percentage

Sources: National Center for Health Statistics; Statistical Abstract 1993: Table 130.

Historical Patterns of Health ▼

How have patterns of health and illness in the United States changed? The answer to this question takes us into the field of **epidemiology,** the study of how medical disorders are distributed throughout a population.

Physical Health

Leading Causes of Death One way to see how the physical health of Americans has changed is to compare the leading causes of death in two time periods. To get an idea of how extensively health problems have changed, look at Figure 19.4. Note that only half of the leading causes of death in 1900 are the same today. Heart disease and cancer, which placed fourth and eighth in 1900, have now jumped to the top of the list, while tuberculosis and diarrhea, which were the number 1 and 3 killers in 1900 don't even show up in today's top 10. This indicates extensive change in the society, somewhat like the change, mentioned earlier, that we expect will occur in the Third World.

Were Americans Healthier in the Past? A second way to see how the physical health of Americans has changed is to ask if they are healthier—or sicker—than they used to be. This question brings us face to face with the definitional problem discussed at the beginning of the chapter. "Healthy" by whose standards? An additional problem is that many of today's diseases went unrecognized in the past. Mortality rates, however, help us to answer this question. Because most people today live longer than their ancestors, we can conclude that contemporary Americans are healthier.

Some may see this conclusion as flying in the face of polluted air and water and today's high rates of heart disease and cancer, shown in Figure 19.4. And it does. Sometimes older people say, "When I was a kid, cancer wasn't even around. I never knew anyone who died from cancer, and now it seems everyone does." What they overlook is that in the past most cancer went unrecognized. People were simply said to have died of "old age" or "heart failure." In addition, most cancers strike older people, and the younger that most people die, the less chance that cancer is the cause of death.

epidemiology: the study of disease and disability patterns in a population

Mental Health

When it comes to mental health, we have no rational basis at all for making comparisons. The elderly may paint a picture of a past with lower suicide rates, less mental illness, and so on, but we need measures of mental illness or mental health, not anecdotes. The idyllic past—where everyone grew up in a happy home, married for life, and was at one with the universe—never existed. All groups have had their share of mental problems—and commonsense beliefs that mental illness is worse today represent perceptions, not measured reality. Such perceptions may be true, of course, but the opposite could also be true. Since we don't even know how extensive mental illness is today (Miller 1993), we certainly can't judge how much there was in the past.

The Professionalization of Medicine

Let's look at how medicine grew into the *largest* business in the United States. To do so, we first need to understand how medicine became professionalized.

Setting Standards

Imagine that you are living in the American colonies in the 1700s and that you want to become a physician. There are no course prerequisites, no entrance exams—in fact, there are no medical schools. You don't have to have *any* education at all. You simply ask a physician to train you and assist with menial tasks in return for the opportunity to learn. When *you* think that you have learned enough, you hang out a shingle and thereby proclaim yourself a physician. The process was similar to how someone becomes an automobile mechanic today. And like mechanics today, you could even skip the apprenticeship if you wished, and simply hang out the shingle. If you could convince people that you were good, you made a living. If not, you turned to something else.

During the 1800s, a few medical schools opened, and there was some licensing. Medical schools then, however, were like religious sects today; they competed for clients and represented different claims on truth. That is, medical schools had competing philosophies about both the causes of illnesses and the most effective treatments. Training was short, often not even a high school diploma was required, there was no clinical training, and lectures went unchanged from year to year. Even Harvard University's medical school took only two school years to complete—and the school year in those days lasted only four months (Starr 1982; Rosenberg 1987; Riessman 1994).

In 1906 the American Medical Association (AMA) examined the 160 medical schools in the United States and found only 82 acceptable (Starr 1982). The Carnegie Foundation asked Abraham Flexner, a renowned educator of the time, to investigate the matter. Flexner visited every medical school. Even the most inadequate opened their doors to him, for they thought that gifts from the Carnegie Foundation would follow (Rodash 1982). Flexner found glaring problems. The laboratories of some schools consisted only of "a few vagrant test tubes squirreled away in a cigar box." Other schools had libraries with no books. Flexner (1910) recommended that admissions and teaching standards be raised and that philanthropies fund the most promising schools. As a result, those schools that were funded were able to upgrade their facilities and attract more capable faculty and students. Left with inadequate funds and few students, most of the other schools had to close their doors.

The Flexner report led to the **professionalization of medicine.** Physicians began to (1) undergo a rigorous education; (2) claim a theoretical understanding of illness; (3) regulate themselves; (4) claim that they were performing a service for society (rather

professionalization of medicine: the development of medicine into a field in which education becomes rigorous, and in which physicians claim a theoretical understanding of illness, regulate themselves, claim to be doing a service to society (rather than just following self-interest), and take authority over clients

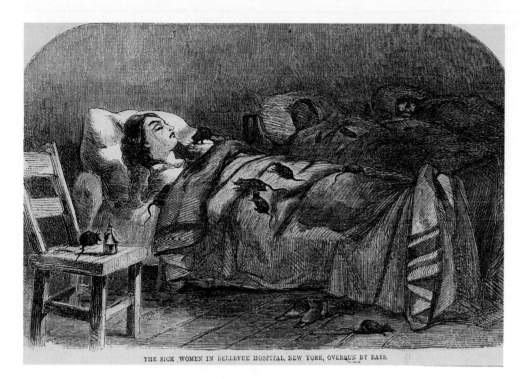

THE SICK WOMEN IN BELLEVUE HOSPITAL, NEW YORK, OVERRUN BY RATS.

In the 1860s, medical care in the United States was a hit-or-miss affair run by untrained and poorly trained medical personnel who were unaware of germs. Conditions in hospitals were miserable, as illustrated by this lithograph showing a patient in Bellevue Hospital in New York City in 1860.

than just following self-interest); and (5) take authority over clients (Goode 1960). (For differences between professions and jobs, see pages 395–396.)

The Monopoly of Medicine

When medicine professionalized, it also became a monopoly. The group that gained control over U.S. medicine set itself up as *the* medical establishment. This group was able to get laws passed to restrict medical licenses to graduates of approved schools, and make it so only graduates of those schools could become the faculty members who trained the next generation of physicians. In short, by controlling the education and licensing of physicians, they silenced most competing philosophies of medicine. The WASP males who took control also either refused to admit women and minorities to medical schools or placed severe enrollment limits on them.

The legal elimination of competitors paved the way for medicine to become big business. Only this select group of men—a sort of priesthood of medicine—was allowed to diagnose and treat medical problems. Only they knew what was right for people's health. Only they could scribble the secret language (Latin) on special pieces of parchment (prescription forms) for translators (pharmacists) to decipher (Miner 1995). This select group was able to shape itself into the most lucrative profession in the country— for they set their own fees and had little competition. This group of males became so powerful that it was even able to take over childbirth—the focus of the Down-to-Earth Sociology box on the next page.

Usually this **fee-for-service** (the patient paying a physician to diagnose and treat) approach to medicine went unquestioned. As the monopoly drove up the price of medical care, however, there was a public outcry that the poor and many of the elderly were priced out of health care. The AMA fought every proposal for the government to fund medical treatment as furiously as someone fending off a mad dog. Physicians were convinced that government funding would "socialize" medicine, remove the fee for service, and turn them into government employees—not unlike the 1990s' skirmishes between the AMA and proponents of national health care.

fee for service: payment by a patient to a physician to diagnose and treat the patient's medical problems

▼▲

Down-To-Earth Sociology

To Establish a Monopoly, Eliminate Your Competition: How Physicians Dealt with Midwives

MIDWIFERY HELPS US UNDERSTAND the professionalization of medicine and provides insight into the founding of the U.S. medical establishment. It had been the custom in the United States, as in Europe and elsewhere, for midwives to deliver babies. Pregnancy and childbirth were considered natural events, for which women were best equipped to help women. It was also considered indecent for a man to know much about pregnancy, much less to see a woman deliver a baby. Some midwives were trained; others were simply neighborhood women who had experience in childbirth. In many European countries, midwives were licensed by the state—as they still are. In the United States, physicians came to see midwives as business competitors.

Their desire for expansion ran up against a major problem, however: few physicians knew anything about delivering babies. To learn, they first sneaked into the bedrooms where midwives were assisting births. To say "sneaked" is no exaggeration, for some physicians crawled on their hands and knees so that the mother-to-be would not know a man was present. Since many midwives refused to cooperate, the training of most physicians was limited to lessons with mannequins. Physicians gradually gained admission to childbirth, but the issue of indecency persisted. At first the physician was limited to fumbling blindly under a sheet in a dark room, his head decorously turned aside.

As physicians grew more powerful politically, they launched a bitter campaign against midwives, attacking them as "dirty, ignorant, and incompetent," even calling them a "menace to the health of the community." Using the new political clout of the AMA, physicians succeeded in persuading many states to pass laws that made it illegal for anyone but a physician to deliver babies. Some states, however, continued to allow nurse-midwives to practice. The struggle is not yet over, and nurse-midwives and physicians still clash over who has the right to deliver babies.

Conflict theorists emphasize that this struggle was an attempt by males to gain control over what had been women's work. They stress that political power was central to the physicians' success in expanding their domain. Without denying the political aspect, symbolic interactionists stress that the key was the redefinition of pregnancy and childbirth from a natural event to a medical condition. To eliminate midwives, physicians launched a campaign of images, stressing that pregnancy and childbirth were not normal conditions. Their new definitions, which flew in the face of the millennia-old tradition of women helping women to have babies, transformed pregnancy and childbirth from a natural process to a "medical condition" that required the assistance of an able man. When this redefinition made childbirth "man's work," not only did the prestige of the work go up—so did the price.

Sources: English 1973; Wertz and Wertz 1981; Rodash 1982; Danzi 1989; Rothman 1994.

After *Medicaid* (government-paid medical care for the poor) and *Medicare* (government-sponsored medical insurance for the elderly) were instituted in the 1960s, however, U.S. physicians found that these programs did not lead to socialization. Instead, they provided millions of additional customers, for persons who previously could not afford medical services now had their medical bills guaranteed by the government. As Figure 13.4 on page 361 illustrates, these programs have become extremely expensive—and they put much wealth into physicians' pockets.

From its humble origins, medicine has grown into the largest business in the United States. Today it consists not only of physicians, but also of nurses, paraphysicians, hospital personnel, druggists, the manufacturers and sales force of medical technology, and especially pharmaceutical companies and the corporations that own hospitals. Medicine has become much more than hearing people's health complaints and prescribing medications. The medical monopoly not only wages national advertising campaigns to drum up customers but also lobbies all the state legislatures and the U.S. Congress. Some hospitals even pay million-dollar sign-up bonuses to lure big-name surgeons (McCartney 1993). To see how hospitals have contributed to the professionalization of medicine—as well as to the high cost of medical care—see the following Thinking Critically section.

▼▲▼▲▼▲▼▲▼▲▼▲▼▲▼▲▼▲▼▲▼▲▼▲▼▲▼▲▼▲

Thinking Critically About Social Controversy

In the Care of Strangers—The Hospital in U.S. Society

▼ IT TOOK A STRONG STOMACH to enter a hospital in 1810. Because the sick were the responsibility of families, neighbors, and towns, the few hospitals that existed then were places of last resort—places where the destitute, the mentally ill, the syphilitics, and old and diseased prostitutes went to die.

Ezra Ely, a visitor to a hospital for the poor in 1810, reports that there were not enough beds to go around. On one pallet he found two abandoned girls, aged 13 and 15. A victim of typhus fever in another room had lain dead for a full day among his fellow patients before being removed. The smell was unbearable, barely disguised by the use of vinegar and the burning of linen.

Despite efforts at classification, most wards were a hodgepodge of ages and sexes, of disabilities and ailments. Children wandered aimlessly through the hospital. The many young, diseased prostitutes engaged in "all intercourse with wicked men."

According to medical thinking of the time, moral depravity was a cause of physical illness. Syphilis, then practically incurable, was an example. So were the ravages of alcoholism. People suffering from such diseases were considered undeserving. They were left in the streets, locked in jails, or sent to almshouse hospitals.

But where were the deserving sick to go? Hardworking men who were too ill to work? Aged widows of "irreproachable character who had spent a lifetime in piety and hard work" whose families couldn't care for them? To build hospitals to serve "good people who had become ill through no fault of their own," fundraisers told contributors that they would discriminate between the deserving and the undeserving. Consequently, admission to these hospitals required "a written testimonial from a 'respectable' person attesting to the moral worth of the applicant."

For nurses, hospitals meant hard work, long hours, and low pay. A nurse's shift ran from 5 A.M. to 9 P.M. During those sixteen hours (six days a week), nurses not only dispensed medicines but also "scrubbed the floors, washed the sheets, and fetched dinner." Healthier patients had to pitch in, too, for one nurse might be assigned seventy-five patients. At night, nurses were not on duty, and the less sick had to help the worse off. Physicians seldom appeared.

Due to lack of hygiene, hospitals were sources of disease and death. It was not yet known in the early 1800s that germs caused disease, and deaths from fevers and infections in hospitals were so common that people referred to them as "hospitalism." As the theory of germs came to be more widely accepted, surgeons began to wash before surgery, and the death rate from postoperative infections declined. Medical schools saw the advantage of being affiliated with hospitals and began to require clinical training of their students. As technology developed, hospitals became more dependent on expensive x-ray machines and the like.

By 1910, the hospital had become a national institution, not just a refuge for the urban poor. Most towns of any size had their own hospital. Nurses became better trained, more disciplined, and more focused on patient care. Physicians came to look at hospitals as places where they could practice careers in surgery or other specialties. Following a national pattern of transferring social functions from family and neighborhood to institutions, hospitals came to be seen as places that offered better care than that available at home.

Already by the 1920s, more technology and higher wages of hospital workers made the high cost of hospital care a public concern. In the forefront of the controversy were questions that have still not been resolved: Should the hospital be the provider of medical care on the basis of need, or a profit-making enterprise like a department store? Does the hospital belong to the community, or is it simply part of the "marketplace of discrete and impersonal cash transactions"? Just what is the public's right to health care?

Source: Rosenberg 1987. ▲

Issues in Health Care

With this background, let's look at issues in health care in the United States.

Medical Care as a Costly Commodity

Why was Terry Takewell denied medical treatment and his life cut short? The fundamental reason is that in the United States health care is not the right of citizens, but a commodity to be sold at the highest price (Kaufmann 1994). Like potatoes, those with more money can buy the better quality, while, like Terry Takewell, the poor and uninsured can go without—or wait on handouts.

As Figure 19.5 shows, in 1960 the average American spent just $150 a year on health care. Today that average cost has skyrocketed to almost $3,000. The price of televisions can help put this increase in perspective. If their price had risen at the same rate as health care since 1960, a 17-inch black-and-white television would now cost over $3,000 (*Consumer Reports* 1960). Several factors have fueled medical costs, including a larger segment of the population that is elderly, and advanced—and expensive—technology undreamed of just a few years back. With health care considered a commodity, the result is a *two-tier system of medical care*—superior care for those who can afford the cost, and inferior care for those who cannot.

Social Inequality

> Standing among the police, I watched as the elderly, nude man, looking confused, struggled to put on his clothing. The man had ripped the wires out of the homeless shelter's main electrical box, and then led the police a merry chase as he had run from room to room.
>
> I asked the officers where they were going to take the man, and they replied, "To Malcolm Bliss" (the state hospital). When I said, "I guess he'll be in there for quite a while," they replied, "Probably for just a day or two. We picked him up last week—he was crawling under cars at a traffic light—and they let him out in two days."

The police then explained that one must be a danger to others or to oneself to be admitted as a long-term patient. Visualizing this old man crawling under cars in traffic and the possibility of electrocution in ripping out electrical wires with bare hands, I marveled at the definitions of "danger" that the psychiatrists must be using. The two-tier system was readily visible, stripped of its coverings. Certainly a middle-class or rich person would receive different treatment, and would not, of course, be in this shelter in the first place.

Since 1939, sociologists have found an inverse correlation between mental problems and social class. In other words, the lower the social class, the higher the proportion of serious mental problems. This finding has been confirmed in numerous studies (Faris and Dunham 1939; Hudson 1988; Ortega and Corzine 1990; Miller 1994). Sociologists have little difficulty understanding why people in the lower social classes have greater mental problems. These problems are part of a stress package that comes with poverty. Compared with middle- and upper-class Americans, the poor have less job security, lower wages, more unpaid bills and insistent bill collectors, and more divorce, greater vulnerability to crime, more alcoholism, more violence, and more physical illness. Such conditions certainly deal severe blows to people's emotional well-being.

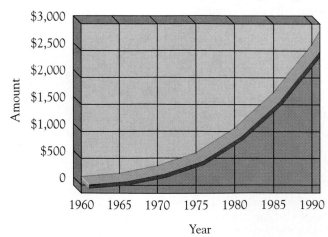

Source: Statistical Abstract 1993: Table 148.

Figure 19.5

The Soaring Cost of Medical Care: The Amount the Average American Pays Each Year.

Stories about a mythic, idyllic past are sometimes told by older people. The past was far from idyllic, as shown by this photo of a mental hospital in the 1950s. Is mental health better or worse today? We cannot tell, as we have no firm baselines to compare.

As noted on pages 218–219, the policy of deinstitutionalization carried out in the 1960s, intended to cut costs and integrate mental patients into the community, backfired. One consequence is that the poor—such as the nude man in the homeless shelter—find it difficult to get into mental hospitals. If they are admitted, they are sent to the dreaded state hospitals. In contrast, private hospitals serve the wealthy and those who have good insurance. The rich are also likely to be treated with "talk" therapy (various forms of psychotherapy), the poor with "medicinal straightjackets."

When it comes to physical illnesses, we find similar inequalities by social class. Unlike the middle and upper classes, few poor people have a personal physician, and they are likely to spend hours waiting in crowded public health clinics. After waiting most of a day, some don't even get to see a doctor, but are told to come back the next day (Fialka 1993). Finally, when hospitalized, the poor are likely to find themselves in understaffed and underfunded public hospitals, where they are treated by rotating interns who do not know them and cannot follow up on their progress.

Malpractice Suits and Defensive Medicine

Some analysts have observed that prior to this century physicians may have killed more patients than they ever cured. Granted that physicians didn't know about germs and didn't wash before surgery or child birth, this may be true. Back then, doctors thought that sickness was caused by "bad fluids," and they had four techniques for getting rid of these fluids: (1) bleeding (cutting a vein and draining out bad blood); (2) blistering (applying packs so hot they burned the skin and made the bad pus come to the surface); (3) vomiting (feeding patients liquids that made them vomit up the bad fluids); and (4) purging (feeding patients substances that caused diarrhea).

Comparing today's vastly superior technology and treatment, one might think that malpractice suits would have been a problem in the past but not today. The opposite, however, is true. Back then, the law didn't allow patients to recover damages. "People make mistakes," was the thinking, and that included doctors. Today, in contrast, physicians are held to much higher standards—some say to impossible ones. Awards are high, and doctors are anxious. One physician told me, "I'm looking for something else to do, because medicine is no longer fun. Every time I treat a patient, I wonder if this is the one who is going to turn around and sue me."

To protect themselves, physicians practice **defensive medicine.** They consult with colleagues and order lab tests not because the patient needs them but to leave a paper trail

defensive medicine: medical practices done not for the patient's benefit but in order to protect a physician from malpractice suits

Unequal access to medical care is one of the primary problems with the U.S. health care system. Shown here are patients waiting to see a physician. Many of them will wait for hours. To what social class do you think they belong?

that can be used in case they are sued. These consultations and tests—done for the doctor's benefit, not the patient's—boost the cost spiral even further. To reduce the costs of defensive medicine, the state of Maine has given checklists to physicians. If they follow them, malpractice suits are dismissed (Felsenthal 1993). Although physicians complain about a "paint-by-numbers" or cookbook approach to medicine, they apparently prefer this to the threat of lawsuits.

Depersonalization: The Cash Machine

One of the main criticisms leveled against the medical profession is **depersonalization,** the practice of dealing with people as though they were cases and diseases, not individuals. Many patients get the impression that they have been trapped by a cash machine—a physician who, while talking to you, is impatiently counting minutes and tabulating dollars so that he or she can move on to the next customer, and more dollars. After all, extra time spent with a patient is money down the drain.

Sociologist Sue Fisher (1986), who was examined for an ovarian mass, gives this account:

> As a new person in the community, I was without a doctor. The nurse-practitioner referred me to a gynecologist. My years of research (on the medical profession) did not prepare me for what followed. On my initial visit a nurse called me into an examination room, asked me to undress, gave me a paper gown to put on and told me the doctor would be with me soon. I was stunned. Was I not even to see the doctor before undressing? . . . How could I present myself as a competent, knowledgeable person sitting undressed on the examining table? But I had a potentially cancerous growth, so I did as I had been told.
>
> In a few minutes the nurse returned and said, "Lie down. The doctor is coming." Again I complied. The doctor entered the examining room, nodded in my direction while reading my chart, and proceeded to examine me without ever having spoken to me.

depersonalization: dealing with people as though they were objects; in the case of medical care, as though patients were merely cases and diseases, not persons

Participant observation of medical students at McMaster University in Canada by sociologists Jack Haas and William Shaffir (1991) provides insight into how physicians learn to depersonalize patients. Haas and Shaffir found that students begin medical school wanting to "treat the whole person." As vast amounts of material are thrown at them, their feelings for patients are overpowered by the need to be efficient. This student's statement picks up the change:

> Somebody will say, "Listen to Mrs. Jones's heart. It's just a little thing flubbing on the table." And *you forget about the rest of her* . . . and it helps in learning in the sense that you can go in to a patient, put your stethoscope on the heart, listen to it, and walk out. . . . The advantage is that *you can go in a short time and see a patient, get the important things out of the patient, and leave* (italics added).

Another student's statement illustrates the extent to which patients become objects.

> You don't know the people that are under anesthesia—just practice putting the tube in, and the person wakes up with a sore throat, and well, it's just sort of a part of the procedure. . . . Someone comes in who has croaked (and you say), "Well, come on. Here is a chance to practice your intubation" (inserting a tube in the throat).

Sexism in Medicine

As the box below illustrates, sexism in medicine often involves communication. Although usually quite subtle, often even below people's awareness, sexism in medicine can

---

Down-To-Earth Sociology

The Doctor–Nurse Game

LEONARD STEIN (1988), a physician who observed nurses and doctors for many years, analyzed their interactions in terms of a game. Because physicians have higher status, nurses must try to give the impression that the doctor is always "in control." Although nurses spend more time with patients and, therefore, are often more familiar with their needs, nurses can never be perceived as giving recommendations to a doctor. Consequently, nurses disguise their recommendations. Consider the following dialogue between a nurse and a resident physician whom the nurse has called at 1 A.M. The rotating resident does not know the patient.

"This is Dr. Jones." (*An open and direct communication*)

"Dr. Jones, this is Nurse Smith on 2W. Mrs. Brown learned today that her father died, and she is unable to fall asleep." (*This apparently direct, open communication of factual information—that the patient is unable to sleep and has learned of a death in the family—contains a hidden recommendation. The nurse has diagnosed the cause of the sleeplessness and is suggesting that a sedative be prescribed.*)

The conversation continues: "What sleeping medication has been helpful to Mrs. Brown in the past?" (*This communication, supposedly a mere request for facts, is actually a request for a recommendation of what to prescribe.*)

"Pentobarbital, 100 milligrams, was quite effective the night before last." (*This is actually a specific recommendation from the nurse to the physician, but it comes disguised in the form of factual information.*)

"Pentobarbital, 100 milligrams before bedtime, as needed for sleep. Got it?" (*This communication is spoken with audible authority—a little louder, a little firmer.*)

"Yes, I have, and thank you very much, doctor."

The two have successfully played the doctor–nurse game. The lower-status person has made a recommendation to the higher-status person in a covert manner that requires neither of them to acknowledge what really occurred and does not threaten their relative statuses.

When I interviewed Stein, he said that the doctor–nurse game is breaking down because of the larger number of males in nursing, the feminist movement challenging male authority, and the larger number of female physicians. As a consequence, nurses are less subservient, and physicians are less able to exert unquestioned authority.

Some version of the game will continue to be played, however, as long as status differences remain. The rules will simply be modified to meet changing circumstances.

carry very serious consequences. As we saw in the Down-to-Earth Sociology box on page 290, physicians don't take women's health complaints as seriously as they do men's. As a result, women are operated on at a later stage in heart disease, making it more likely that they will die from their surgery.

Sociologists who have done participant observation of physicians report a bias *against* the female reproductive organs. Sue Fisher (1986), whose encounter with de-personalized medicine was cited earlier, was surprised to hear surgeons recommend total hysterectomy (removal of both the uterus and the ovaries) when no cancer was present. As she probed the matter, she found that male doctors regarded the uterus and ovaries as "potentially disease-producing" and unnecessary after the childbear-ing years. Since surgeons don't make money if a woman does not have this surgery, they "sell" the operation. Here is how one resident explained it to sociologist Diana Scully (1994):

> You have to look for your surgical procedures; you have to go after patients. Because no one is crazy enough to come and say, "Hey, here I am. I want you to operate on me." You have to sometimes convince the patient that she is really sick—if she is, of course [laughs], and that she is better off with a surgical procedure.

The way the doctor "convinces" the woman is to say that, unfortunately, the examination has turned up fibroids in her uterus—and they *might* turn into cancer. This statement is often sufficient, for it frightens women, who can picture themselves ready to be buried. What the surgeon does *not* say is that the fibroids probably will not turn into cancer and there is a variety of nonsurgical alternatives.

Underlying this sexism is male dominance of medicine in the United States. This is not a worldwide phenomenon. For example, while only 20 percent of U.S. physicians are women, in the former Soviet Union three out of four physicians are women (Knaus 1981; *Statistical Abstract* 1993: Table 644). Following the changes in gender relations discussed in Chapter 11, the percent of U.S. medical degrees earned by women rose rapidly, going from only 6 percent in 1960 to 36 percent today. Women also now comprise 42 percent of applicants to medical schools (Alt-man 1993). This changing sex ratio should considerably reduce sexism in medical practice.

Medicalization of Society

As we have seen, childbirth and the female organs have become defined as medical matters. Sociologists use the term **medicalization** to refer to the process of turning something that was not previously considered medical into a medical matter. Exam-ples include balding, weight, wrinkles, acne, anxiety, depression, a sagging chin or buttocks, small breasts, and even the inability to achieve orgasm. As Susan Sontag (1994) says, even many criminal behaviors have become matters to be understood and treated.

There is nothing inherently medical in such human conditions, yet we have be-come so used to medicalization that we tend to consider them somehow naturally med-ical concerns. Symbolic interactionists would stress that medicalization is based on a view of life that is bound to a specific historical period. Functionalists would stress how such medicalization helps the medical establishment, and patients who have some-one to listen to their problems and are sometimes helped. Conflict sociologists would argue that this process is another indication of the growing power of the medical es-tablishment—the more physicians can medicalize human affairs, the greater their power and profits.

medicalization: the transforma-tion of something into a matter to be treated by physicians

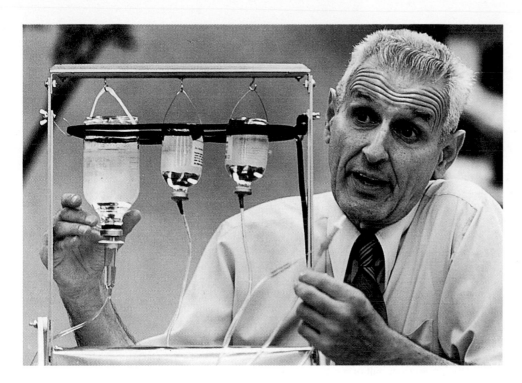

Unacknowledged, but covertly practiced, euthanasia has been a part of the practice of medicine for centuries. Retired physician Jack Kevorkian, shown here with his suicide machine, has brought euthanasia into the open and made it a matter of public debate. Using this machine, an individual self-administers poison at will. Proponents of euthanasia insist that people have the right to die, while opponents insist that it is morally wrong and also opens the door to abuse.

Medically Assisted Suicide

> I started the intravenous dripper, which released a salt solution through a needle into her vein, and I kept her arm tied down so she wouldn't jerk it. This was difficult as her veins were fragile. And then once she decided she was ready to go, she just hit the switch and the device cut off the saline drip and through the same needle released a solution of thiopental that put her to sleep in ten to fifteen seconds. A minute later, through the same needle flowed a lethal solution of potassium chloride.

This is how Jack Kevorkian described his death machine (Denzin 1992). Kevorkian, a retired pathologist who introduced his machine to the American public on the *Donahue* show, is known by some as Dr. Death. One side defends Kevorkian as a courageous trail blazer, while another side decries his acts as perverted. Some even call him "Jeffrey Dahmer in a lab coat" (Morganthau 1993). The topic fascinates the American public. A how-to book on suicide, *Final Exit*, sold over a half million copies. The Hemlock Society, a group advocating voluntary **euthanasia** (mercy killing) for terminally ill people, has grown to seventy chapters.

With new technology that can keep the body alive even after the heart, lung, and other vital organs no longer function on their own, a burning question, yet undecided, is "Who has the right to pull the plug?" Should someone's body be kept alive for years while the person's mind can no longer work? To resolve this issue, some people sign a **living will**—a declaration they make while in good health of what they want medical personnel to do in case they become dependent on artificial life support systems.

Our technology and the acts of Kevorkian have brought us face to face with matters of death that are both disturbing and unresolved. Should "medically assisted suicide" be legal? In some instances, perhaps even encouraged? Few find this medical-ethical issue easy to resolve. The following Thinking Critically section explores these issues.

euthanasia: mercy killing

living will: a statement people in good health sign that clearly expresses their feelings about being kept alive on artificial life support systems

▼△▼△▼△▼△▼△▼△▼△▼△▼△▼△▼△▼△▼△▼△▼△▼△▼

Thinking Critically About Social Controversy

Euthanasia in Holland

▼ PROPONENTS OF EUTHANASIA base their claim on "people's right to die." "If someone wants to be disconnected from feeding tubes," they say, "he or she should be able to die in peace. And if someone wants to commit suicide, that person should have the right to do so. What right does the rest of society have to interfere?"

Framed in this way, many Americans would agree that euthanasia should be permitted. "The problem," say its opponents, "is that most euthanasia involves other types of dying."

The best example, critics point out, is Holland, which has allowed euthanasia for over twenty years. According to Dutch law, a physician can assist a patient in dying if the patient makes "a free, informed, and persistent request." Euthanasia must be a "last resort," and physicians are accountable to the courts for following the letter of the law.

A Dutch government committee, however, has found that the practice is very different from what the law specifies. Although only about 150 cases of euthanasia are reported annually to government officials, this doesn't come even close to the actual number. The committee found 2,300 cases of "voluntary" euthanasia and 400 assisted suicides. They also found 8,750 deaths due to the physicians withholding or withdrawing treatment—*in not one of these cases did the patients consent to their deaths*. Doctors killed another 8,100 people by giving them pain-killing drugs—and more than half of these patients had *not* consented to their deaths.

Leading Dutch physicians who practice euthanasia oppose its legalization in the United States. Said one, "If euthanasia were allowed in the United States, I would not want to be a patient there. In view of the financial costs that the care of patients can impose on relatives and society under the United States health-care system, the legalization of euthanasia in America would be an open door to get rid of patients."

What do you think?

Sources: Gomez 1991; Keown 1991; Markson 1992.   ▲

Curbing Costs: Issues in Private and National Health Insurance

Although the soaring price of medical care in the United States has led to a clamor to reduce costs, attempts to do so have failed. Instead, medical costs have risen at about twice the rate of inflation. We have seen some of the basic reasons: advanced—and expensive—technology for diagnosis and treatment, a growing elderly population, tests performed for defensive rather than medical reasons, and health care as a commodity to be sold to the highest bidder. As long as these conditions are in effect, the price of medical care will continue to soar. Let's look at some attempts to reduce costs.

Health Maintenance Organizations   In a **health maintenance organization (HMO),** a company pays a set fee to a group of physicians to take care of the medical needs of its employees. The employer knows its annual medical bill in advance, and since the physicians are paid a set fee for the year, to make a profit they must be efficient and avoid unnecessary procedures. Because hospitalization costs are included in the annual fee, physicians use surgery and hospitalization as a last resort. HMOs lower expenses, but patients complain about their lack of choice of physicians and hospitals.

There are worse criticisms. In their rush to reduce costs, some HMO physicians discharge patients from hospitals before they are well. A woman I know was discharged even though she was still bleeding and running a fever. Even high social class is no guarantee that the physician's need to trim costs will not harm the patient. Les

health maintenance organization (HMO): a health care organization that provides medical treatment to its members for a fixed annual cost

Aspin, a former secretary of defense under President Clinton, was given a vaccination for his foreign travels that landed him in intensive care. The doctor didn't ask him if he wanted to pay the $1.55 extra for the vaccination that carried less risk (Matthews 1993).

Diagnosis-Related Groups   To interrupt the cost spiral, the federal government has classified all illnesses into 468 DRGs and specified the amount it will pay for the treatment of each. Hospitals make a profit only if they move patients through the system quickly. If patients are discharged before the hospital has spent the allotted amount, the hospital makes money. One consequence is that some patients are discharged before they are fully ready to go home. Others are refused admittance because they appear to have a "worse than average" case of a particular illness, which would cost the hospital money instead of making them a profit (Easterbrook 1987; Feinglass 1987).

Cost-Saving Measures by Insurance Companies   To try to control costs, insurance companies have increased deductibles (the initial amount patients pay before the insurance goes into effect); instituted coinsurance (patients pay a fixed percentage of medical costs); begun utilization reviews (payments are made only if medical personnel determine that a treatment is warranted); and introduced capping (setting a maximum amount to be paid for each procedure—one price to remove an appendix, another for a blood test, and so on).

National Health Insurance

> A young woman who was five months pregnant was taken to a hospital complaining of stomach pains. The hospital refused to admit her because she had no money or credit. As they were about to transfer her to a hospital for the poor, she gave birth. The baby was stillborn. The hospital went ahead and transferred the woman—dead baby, umbilical cord, and all. (Ansberry 1988)

One consequence of the desire to turn a profit on patient care is **dumping,** sending unprofitable patients to public hospitals. Most cases are less dramatic than this woman and her stillborn baby, but the same principle applies. With about 34 million Americans uninsured, primarily the poor (*Statistical Abstract* 1993: Table 167), pressure has grown for national health insurance. Advocates point out that it will reduce costs through centralized, large-scale purchases. They also cite the social inequalities of medicine and the inadequacy of care for the poor. Such horror stories as the one just told make their point. Those against national health insurance stress the immense red tape such plans would require. They ask if federal agencies—such as those that monitored the savings and loan associations—inspire so much confidence that they should be entrusted with administering something so vital as the nation's health care. This debate is not new, and even if some form of national health insurance is adopted the argument is likely to continue.

Threats to Health

Let's look at four threats to health: disease; drugs; disabling environments; and misguided, foolish, and callous experiments.

Disease

Perhaps the most pressing issue in American—and global—health today is AIDS (acquired immune deficiency syndrome). Although the first case of this virus that attacks

dumping: the practice of sending unprofitable patients to public hospitals

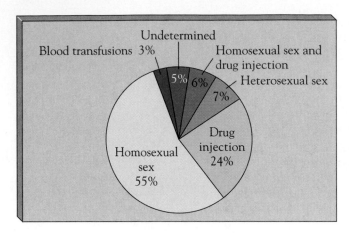

Source: Centers for Disease Control 1993: Table 3.

Figure 19.6

How People Get AIDS

the human immune system was not documented until 1981, AIDS has become the eleventh leading cause of death in the United States. AIDS has become so widespread that the United States has four national magazines for people with the virus (Cox 1994).

Origin   The origin of AIDS is unknown. The most prevalent theory is that the virus was first present in monkeys and chimpanzees in Africa and then transmitted to humans. If so, just how the transmission to humans took place remains a matter of conjecture. It may have occurred during the 1920s and 1950s when, in a peculiar test of malaria, people were experimentally inoculated with blood from monkeys and chimpanzees. The blood may unknowingly have been infected with viral ancestors of HIV (Rathus and Nevid 1993). Another possibility is that humans were bitten by infected monkeys. Finally, since monkeys are considered food in several parts of Africa, the ingestion of animal tissues that were not adequately cooked may have been responsible (Dwyer 1988:119). Although at this point scientists do not know the origin of AIDS, genetic sleuths may eventually unravel the mystery.

The Transmission of AIDS   In the United States, AIDS first appeared in the male homosexual population. Male bisexuals provided the bridge that passed AIDS on to the heterosexual population. As a result of having sex with bisexuals and sharing needles for intravenous drugs, prostitutes quickly become a second bridge to the heterosexual population. Others were infected with AIDS through blood transfusions. Figure 19.6 summarizes how people have become infected.

A person cannot become infected with AIDS unless bodily fluids pass from one person to another. AIDS is known to be transmitted by the exchange of blood and semen, as well as, in

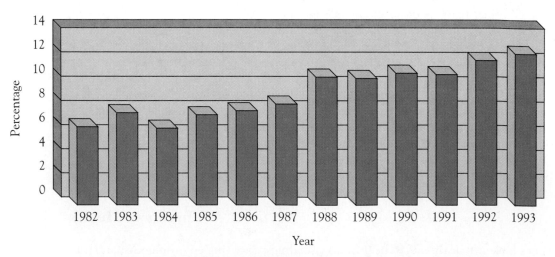

Note: When AIDS was first identified, the diagnosis was extremely unreliable, and for the purpose of computing a trend, the percentages for the early years should be discounted.

Source: Centers for Disease Control.

Figure 19.7

Percentage of People Diagnosed with AIDS Who Are Women.

rare cases, by mother's milk to newborns. Since the AIDS virus is present in all bodily fluids (including sweat, tears, spittle, and urine), some people think that AIDS can also be transmitted in these forms. The U.S. Centers for Disease Control, however, say that AIDS cannot be transmitted by casual contact in which traces of these fluids would be exchanged (Edgar 1994).

Women and Aids   Although in North America AIDS first appeared among males, in parts of Africa males and females are equally likely to have the disease. Figure 19.7 shows that women now make up *twice* the proportion of AIDS victims that they did in 1982. AIDS is now the fourth leading cause of death of U.S. women 25–44 (it is *the* leading cause of death for men of this age). Keep in mind that AIDS has a lengthy incubation period, and that most women diagnosed with AIDS this year were infected several years ago. The Centers for Disease Control predict that, worldwide, in a few years as many women as men will have AIDS (Pearl 1990). This does not mean that the proportions will be equal in every country.

The Threat AIDS Poses to Public Health   As portrayed on Figure 19.8, AIDS has claimed almost a quarter of a million American lives. These figures represent only the tip of the iceberg, for about one million Americans are infected with the AIDS virus. Most of these persons show no symptoms and are even unaware that they carry the deadly disease. Many thousands of them, however, have AIDS-related complex (ARC)—which means that they test positive for the virus and show mild symptoms of the disease, mild enough to allow them to continue their normal lives. An unknown percentage of people with ARC will develop full-blown cases of AIDS.

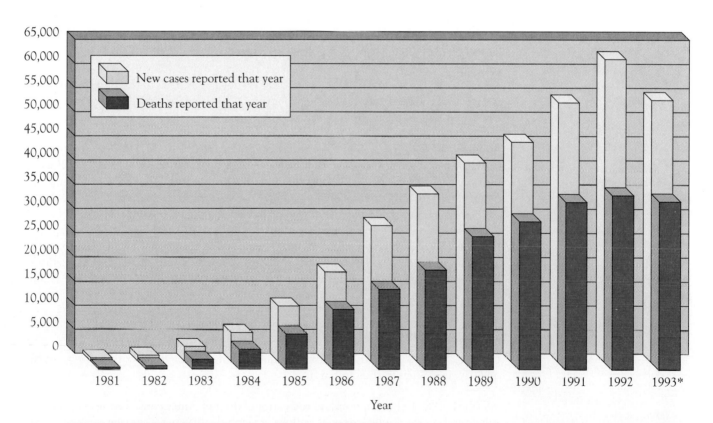

*The Centers for Disease Control changed its definition of AIDS in 1993, and these are provisional totals. The actual totals may run higher.

Source: Centers for Disease Control 1993.

Figure 19.8

The Inroads of AIDS in the United States.

As the first plague of modern times, AIDS is spreading rapidly around the globe. The number of people with the AIDS virus now numbers many millions. Currently, there is no cure. Prevention, however, is effective.

Table 19.1

The Drugs College Students Most Frequently Used in the Last Year

Drug	Males	Females
Alcohol	85%	85%
Tobacco	46	36
Marijuana	30	24
Cocaine	7	4
Hallucinogens	8	3
Amphetamines	6	4

Source: Presley et al. 1993.

Some experts estimate this proportion to be 50 to 75 percent, others as high as 100 percent. In either case, we are talking about vast numbers of people.

AIDS is far from just a U.S. problem; it is a global disease. The former director of the World Health Organization's AIDS project reports that AIDS "is gyrating out of control." In no country has the disease peaked, he says, and as many as 120 million people worldwide will have AIDS by the year 2000 (Stout 1992). Due to the huge sex industry in Asia (see the Perspectives box, "The Patriotic Prostitute," p. 247), the majority of new cases are likely to be in Asia (Bohrer 1992).

Is There a Cure for AIDS?   Several drugs, such as AZT and DDI, slow the progress of AIDS, but no cure has yet been found for the disease. Because AIDS is a rapidly mutating virus, finding a cure is especially difficult. Just developing tests that identify the new strains of the disease is a challenge. It is encouraging, however, that new medicines are being developed to block the action of an enzyme crucial to HIV replication (Chase and Waldholz 1993). Initial testing of a vaccine has also shown positive results, for healthy volunteers who were immunized against one strain of the virus have created antibodies in their blood that also react against different strains of AIDS (Chase 1993). Although promising, such medications and vaccines are still in the testing stage and no cure or effective vaccine yet exists.

Drugs: Alcohol and Nicotine

Let us examine some of the health consequences of alcohol and nicotine, the most frequently used drugs in the United States.

Alcohol   Alcohol is the standard recreational drug of Americans. The *average* American consumes the equivalent of 38 gallons of alcoholic beverages per year—about 33 gallons of beer, 3 gallons of wine, and 2 gallons of whiskey or other distilled spirits. Alcohol is so popular that most Americans drink more beer than milk or coffee (*Statistical Abstract* 1993: Table 220).

College students are no exception to this pattern. As Table 19.1 shows, 85 percent of both male and female college students have drunk at least some alcohol

Although such an ad strikes us as strange, in the 1950s newspapers and magazines were filled with testimonials about how cigarettes were good for people's health. They were even said to "soothe the throat." The health hazards of smoking were not unknown at this time. Today's cigarette advertising may be more subtle, but it has the same effects—to seduce the young into smoking, and to assure current smokers that it is all right to continue.

during the past year. Male students, however, drink considerably more than females, and are more likely to suffer negative consequences—from poorer grades to being arrested (Presley et al. 1993). (As Table 19.1 also makes evident, male college students tend to consume more of whatever drug is available.) As Table 19.2 shows, the more students drink the less well they do in college. Gender differences are highly evident on this table also.

Alcohol is far more harmful to health than its broad social acceptability would imply. Drunken drivers are responsible for about half the 41,000 lives lost in motor vehicle accidents each year (*Statistical Abstract* 1993: Table 1029). Pregnant women who drink are more likely than abstainers to give birth to children with birth defects. Drinkers are more likely to die violent deaths—to be murdered, to die in accidents, or to commit suicide. They also run a higher risk than nondrinkers of developing cancer of the tongue, mouth, esophagus, larynx, stomach, liver, lung, colon, and rectum.

Nicotine   Of all drugs, nicotine is the most harmful to health. Sociologist Erich Goode (1989) points out that compared with nonsmokers smokers are three times as likely to die before reaching the age of 65. Smoking doubles a person's risk of heart attack and causes progressive emphysema and several types of cancer. These cancers kill about 390,000 Americans each year, making nicotine the most lethal of all drugs. Overall, one of six Americans dies from cigarette smoking (Brecher et al. 1972; Gartner 1988).

Table 19.2

Grade-Point Average (GPA) and Average Number of Drinks per Week

GPA	Number of Drinks per Week	
	Males	Females
A	5	2
B	7	3
C	9	4
D or F	15	5

Source: Presley et al. 1993.

Table 19.3			
Percentage of Americans Who Smoke Cigarettes			
Sex	*1965*	*1985*	*1991*
Male	52%	33%	28%
Female	34%	28%	24%

Source: *Statistical Abstract* 1993: Table 210.

Stressing the health hazards of smoking and of secondhand smoke, an antitobacco campaign has ended smoking in airlines and brought about smoking and nonsmoking areas in restaurants and offices. As Table 19.3 shows, this message has really hit home with males, although females are still less likely to smoke.

Why do people smoke when it is so destructive? There are two major reasons, addiction and advertising. Some conclude that nicotine is as addictive as heroin (Tolchin 1988). While this may sound far-fetched, consider Buerger's disease:

> In this disease, the blood vessels, especially those supplying the legs, become so constricted that circulation is impaired whenever nicotine enters the bloodstream. If a patient continues to smoke, gangrene may eventually set in. First a toe may have to be amputated, then the foot at the ankle, then the leg at the knee, and ultimately at the hip. . . . Patients are informed that if they will only stop smoking, it is virtually certain that the otherwise inexorable march of gangrene up the legs will be curbed. Yet surgeons report that some patients with Buerger's disease vigorously puff away in their hospital beds following a second or third amputation (Brecher et al. 1972).

The second reason is advertising. Even though cigarette ads were banned from television in the 1980s, cigarettes continue to be heavily advertised on billboards and in print. The tobacco industry has a huge advertising budget, spending $2 billion a year to encourage people to smoke (Public Information Bureau 1994). Most of this money is spent on seducing youth into smoking by associating cigarette smoking with success, high fashion, and independence (Warner 1986). With the tobacco industry's clout in Washington and with 49,000 Americans depending on it for their livelihood, further attempts to stop cigarette advertising have thus far failed (*Statistical Abstract* 1993: Table 648).

Disabling Environments

A **disabling environment** is one that is harmful to health. The health risk of some occupations is evident: lumberjacking, riding rodeo bulls, and taming lions are obvious examples. In many occupations, however, people become aware of the risk only years after they worked at jobs they thought were safe. For example, several million people worked with asbestos during and after World War II. Now the federal government estimates that one-quarter of them will die of cancer from having breathed asbestos dust. It is likely that many other substances that we have not yet identified also cause slowly developing cancers—including, ironically, some asbestos substitutes (Meier 1987).

Although industrialization has increased the world's standard of living, it also now threatens to disable the basic environment of the human race, posing what may be the greatest health hazard of all time. The burning of vast amounts of carbon fuels is leading to the *greenhouse effect*, a warming of the earth that may change the globe's climate, melt its polar ice caps, and flood the earth's coastal shores. Use of fluorocarbon gases in such items as aerosol cans, refrigerators, and air conditioners is threatening the *ozone shield*, the protective layer of the earth's upper stratosphere that screens out a high proportion of the sun's ultraviolet rays. High-intensity ultraviolet radiation is harmful to most forms of life. In humans, it causes skin cancer. The pollution of land, air, and water, especially through nuclear waste, pesticides, herbicides, and other chemicals, poses additional risks to life on our planet.

To identify environmental threats to world health is only the first step. The second is to introduce short- and long-term policies to reduce such problems. The sociology of the environment is discussed on pages 629–634.

Misguided, Foolish, and Callous Experiments

disabling environment: an environment that is harmful to health

At times, physicians and government officials become so arrogant with power that they callously disregard the health of the people they are sworn to protect. Let's look at two notorious instances.

The Tuskegee Syphilis Experiment   Imagine that you are living in Macon County, Alabama, during the Depression years. You are dirt poor. You live in a little country shack with a dirt floor and no electricity or running water. You never finished grade school, and you make a living, such as it is, by doing odd jobs. You can't afford a doctor, but you haven't been feeling quite right lately.

Then you rub your eyes in disbelief. It is just like winning the lottery. You are offered free physical examinations at Tuskegee University, free rides to and from the clinic, hot meals on examination days, and free treatment for minor ailments. Your survivors are even guaranteed a burial payment. You eagerly accept.

You have just become part of what is surely slated to go down in history as one of the most callous experiments with human life, outside the infamous Nazi experiments. The U.S. Public Health Service told 399 African-American men that they had joined a social club and burial society called "Miss Rivers' Lodge." They also told them that they had "bad blood," and if they went to a private doctor they would lose their benefits.

What the men were *not* told was that they had syphilis. For forty years, the "Public Health Service" let their disease go untreated just "to observe what happened." There was even a control group of 201 men free of the disease (Jones 1993).

By the way, there was one further benefit for the men—free autopsies to determine the ravages of syphilis on the body.

The Cold War Radiation Experiments   Now assume that you are a soldier stationed in Nevada, and the U.S. Army orders your platoon to march through an area just after an atomic bomb is detonated. Because you are a soldier, you obey. Nobody knows much about radiation, and you don't know that the army wants you as a guinea pig, just to see if you'll be able to withstand the fallout—without any radiation equipment. Or suppose that you are a patient at the University of Rochester in 1946, and your doctor, whom you trust implicitly, says that he is going to give you something "to help you." You are pleased. But the injection, it turns out, is uranium (Noah 1994).

Like the Tuskegee experiment, such radiation experiments were conducted with uninformed subjects simply because officials of some agency of the U.S. government decided that they wanted information.

Playing God   To most of us, it is incredible that government officials and medical personnel would so callously disregard human life, but it obviously happens. Those in official positions can come to the point that they think they can play God and determine who shall live and who shall die. And obviously the most expendable citizens are the poor and powerless. It is inconceivable that an experiment such as the syphilis study would be forced on the wealthy and powerful. The elite are protected from such callous disregard of human rights and life. The only protection the rest of us have against such gross abuse of professional positions is to publicize each known instance and to insist on vigorous prosecution of those who direct and carry out such experiments.

The Search for Alternatives

What alternatives to the U.S. health care system are there? The suggestion we shall explore here is that we shift the emphasis away from the treatment of disease to prevention. We shall close with a look at health care systems of other countries—which might contain ideas to follow, or to avoid.

Treatment or Prevention?

Programs of "Wellness"   Most people prefer not to hear that they are largely responsible for their own health. Few people like responsibility, and that is a large one.

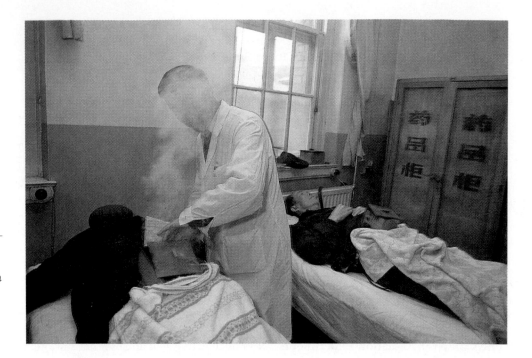

Much of Chinese medicine is based on different assumptions about the causes of disease and their proper cure. Shown here is a patient at the Beijing Institute for Traditional Medicine. The physician is treating the patient for internal disorders by burning herbs.

Individuals, of course, bear no responsibility for some health problems, such as congenital defects or, as discussed, those that result from the medical establishment failing to deliver good medical care to the poor. And no one can help being exposed to germs and viruses, for work and school require being among people who carry them.

As you have seen in this chapter, however, many of the current threats to health are preventable. Prevention implies both an individual and a group responsibility. On the individual level, doing exercises regularly, eating nutritious food, maintaining sexual monogamy, and avoiding smoking and alcohol abuse go a long way to preventing disease. Following these guidelines can add years to our lives—and make those years healthier and more enjoyable.

On the group level, one alternative is preventive medicine. Instead of the treatment of disease, U.S. medicine could have "wellness" as its goal. What would it require to implement a national policy of "prevention, not intervention"? First, the medical establishment must change its basic philosophy, not an easy task to accomplish. Essentially, physicians, nurses, and hospitals would have to be convinced that prevention is profitable. One possibility is that a group of doctors and a hospital would be paid an annual fee for keeping people well (Cooper 1993). Second, the public's attitude would also have to be turned around so they, too, can see the benefit of "wellness." This would require a program of education in the schools and the media showing how some practices of nutrition, exercise, sex, and drug use pay off with healthier and more satisfying lives. Such a change in attitude does not come easily, but the growing number of health clubs indicates that it is occurring among some segments of the population.

On yet a broader scale is comprehensive prevention—eliminating disabling environments and the use of harmful drugs. Some businesses continue to spew industrial wastes into the air and to use rivers and oceans as industrial sewers. This simply cannot be tolerated, and pollution control laws must be firm and enforced. The advertising of harmful drugs and the seduction of youths to use them are unconscionable. Since we now live in a global village, the creation and maintence of a health-producing environment requires international controls and cooperation.

Health Care in Other Nations

The search for alternatives also leads us to examine health care in other nations. Consequently, we shall close this chapter with a comparison of health care in the three worlds of development. As with education in the First, Second, and Third Worlds (see pages 465–468), no one nation can adequately illustrate the varieties of medicine that are practiced in nations in a particular stage of development. Nevertheless, the following nations do illustrate contrastive themes that characterize health care around the world. Because they are so different—one socialized, the other modified capitalist—we shall consider two First World nations. The following materials, then, help us place both positive and negative aspects of the U.S. system in cultural perspective.

Perspectives

CULTURAL DIVERSITY AROUND THE WORLD

Health Care in the Three Worlds of Development: Sweden, Canada, Post-Soviet Russia, and China

Health Care in the First World: Sweden

SWEDEN HAS THE MOST comprehensive health care system in the world. All Swedish citizens and alien residents are covered by national health insurance financed by contributions from the state and employers. Most physicians are paid a salary by the government to treat patients, but 5 percent work full time in private practice (Swedish Institute 1990). Except for a small consultation fee, medical and dental treatment by these government-paid doctors is free, and most of the charges of private physicians are also paid by the government. The government also reimburses travel expenses for patients, as well as for the parents of a hospitalized child. Only minimal fees are charged for prescriptions and hospitalization.

Medical treatment is just one component of Sweden's broad system of social welfare. For example, people who are sick or must stay home with sick children receive 90 percent of their salaries. Swedes are given parental leave at the birth of a child, and all Swedes are guaranteed a pension. This comprehensive system does not come cheap, running about 35 percent of each employee's salary (Cockerham 1989).

Sweden's socialized medicine is not only very expensive, but also very inefficient. Swedes have not solved the twin problems of getting rid of waiting lines and getting physicians to work. With salaries of medical personnel guaranteed, regardless how many patients they see, the system is marked by lack of productivity. When reporters of a Stockholm newspaper visited Sweden's largest hospital on a weekday morning, a peak period when 80 of 120 surgeons were on duty, they found 19 of 24 operating rooms not in use. Their photos of dark and empty operating rooms—at a time when there was a one- to two-year waiting period for hip replacements and cataract operations—provoked a public outcry (Bergström 1992).

Health Care in the First World: Canada

In 1971, the Canadian government instituted a national health insurance program. Medical costs are shared equally between the federal and provincial governments. Unlike most doctors in Sweden, Canadian physicians work in private practice and charge a fee for service. Patients can choose any doctor they wish. The government acts as the patient's insurer and pays the physician's bill. Physicians face no restrictions in choosing a medical specialty or deciding where they will practice. If they wish, physicians can practice private medical care instead of participating in the government program, but only a handful do (Coburn et al. 1981; Grant 1984; Vayda and Deber 1984).

Canada's bill for medical care runs 10 percent of its gross national product, compared with 13 percent in the United States (*Statistical Abstract* 1993: Table 1383). Costs are held down in three main ways. (1) A fixed fee is established annually by the government for each medical service after negotiations with professional medical associations; (2) physicians' incomes are capped—once a general practitioner hits $39,474 in quarterly fees, the government pays only 25 percent of each bill submitted over that amount until the next quarter starts; and (3) overhead costs are low because hospitals run at full capacity, compared with 65 percent capacity in the United States. Fixed costs are thus spread over the greatest possible number of patients. Nor do hospitals need large accounting departments to deal with a myriad of insurance companies, for only the provincial government is billed (Goad 1991). The savings in overhead account for half the difference between the cost of health care in Canada and the United States (Walker 1991).

Although the health of Canadians is among the best in the world, access to major medical procedures is much more limited than in the United States. Canada, with 10 percent of the population of the United States, has only 12 magnetic resonance imagers, the United States 1,375. In all of Canada only 11 facilities do open-heart surgery, compared with 793 in the United States (Barnes 1990). There are waiting lines for coronary bypass surgery and even for ultrasound treatment of kidney stones (Blinick 1992). Seeing greener pastures, about 10,000 Canadian physicians have moved to the United States to practice medicine (Goodman 1993). To discourage patients with minor complaints from clogging up the system, the province of Ontario has put up billboards that say, "A cold lasts a week, but if you see a doctor it lasts seven days" (Greenberg 1994).

Health Care in the Second World: Post-Soviet Russia

The government owns all health care facilities, all medical equipment, and determines how many students will attend the medical schools that it also owns and operates. The physicians, most of whom are women, are government employees, earning about the same salary as factory workers and high school teachers. Physicians are not trained well, and the health of the population has declined in the past two decades. At this point, as shown on Table 19.4, the health of Post-Soviet Russians is closer to that of China than to First World nations. The only hospitals comparable with those of the United States are the hospitals reserved for the elite (Light 1992). In the rest, basic supplies and equipment are in such short supply that surgical scalpels are resharpened until they break. Sometimes even razor blades are used for surgery (Donelson 1992). Although health care is free, patients have no choice about which doctor they see or where they will be treated. Some hospitals do not even have a doctor on staff. The length of the average hospital stay is three times longer than it is in the United States. Medical care is so inefficient that the *majority* of X rays are uninterpretable because of poor quality. Some of the radical changes now being introduced in the former Soviet Union include employer-based health insurance (Light 1992).

Health Care in the Third World: China

Because this nation of 1.1 billion people has a vast shortage of trained physicians, hospitals, and medicine, most Chinese see "barefoot doctors," people who have only a rudimentary knowledge of medicine, are paid low wages, and travel from village to village. Physicians are employees of the government, and as in post-Soviet Russia, the government owns all the country's medical facilities. With its emphases on medicinal herbs and acupuncture, Chinese medicine differs from that of the West. Although Westerners have scoffed at the Chinese approach, some have changed their minds, and at least on a limited basis, medicinal herbs and acupuncture have been imported into the United States.

Recent changes include payment for medical treatment. A hospital stay can now cost several hundred yuan, when the average monthly wage is 200 yuan. A system of private medical clinics is also developing. Some physicians take extra jobs because they cannot survive on their salaries, and bribery of medical personnel who are supposed to give free treatment has become routine. In some cases bribery is demanded, as with the surgeons who, arms scrubbed and held high in the air, refused to enter the operating room until the patient's relatives had stuffed their pockets with cash (Sampson 1992).

For Your Consideration

It is important to note that no nation has discovered the perfect medical system, and that today each country faces a medical crisis of "too much demand at too great a cost" (Moore and Winslow 1993). The preceding examples illustrate a variety of medical systems that can be compared to that of the United States. In what ways would you say that the U.S. medical system is superior—and inferior—to each of these four systems? If you had a choice, is there one that you would pick over the U.S. system? Why or why not? Short of socializing medicine, which goes against the value system of Americans, what modifications do you think can realistically be made in the U.S. medical system to overcome the deficiencies reviewed in this chapter—and to maintain its strengths?

			Table 19.4		

Indicators of Health

	Sweden	*Canada*	*United States*	*Post-Soviet Russia*	*China*
Life expectancy at birth	78.1 years	78.0 years	75.8 years	68.7 years	67.7 years
Infant mortality[a]	5.8	7.0	8.4	27.6	52.1
Suicide[b]					
Males	26.4	20.4	20.0	NA	NA
Females	11.5	5.3	4.8	NA	NA

[a]Per 1,000 live births.
[b]Per 100,000 population.
Source: Statistical Abstract 1993: Tables 1376, 1382.

Summary and Review

The Sociological Perspective on Health and Illness

What is the sociological perspective on health and illness?

Health is not only a biological matter, but is intimately related to society. Illness is also far from an objective matter, for illness is always viewed from the framework of culture, and such definitions vary from one group to another. Social location—from location in the international stratification system to social class, lifestyle, and marital and work status—directly affects people's health. Pp. 522–525.

What is the sick role?

The **sick role** is society's permission to not perform one's usual activities. In return for this permission, the individual assumes responsibility to seek competent help and to cooperate in getting well so he or she can quickly resume normal activities. Although healthier, women are more likely than men to claim the sick role. P. 525.

Historical Patterns of Health

How have health patterns changed over time?

Patterns of disease in the United States have changed so extensively that of today's top ten killers five did not even show up on the 1900 top ten list. Because most Americans live longer than their ancestors, we can conclude that contemporary Americans are healthier. For mental illness, we have no idea how today compares with the past, for we have no baselines from which to make comparisons. Pp. 527–528.

The Professionalization of Medicine

How did medicine become a profession?

In the American colonies, no training or licensing was necessary to call oneself a doctor. Even until the early 1900s medical training was a hit-or-miss affair. In 1910, the education of physicians came under the control of a group of men who eliminated most of their competition and turned medicine into the largest business in the United States. The development of hospitals parallels—and reinforces—the professionalization of medicine. Pp. 528–531.

Issues in Health Care

How does treating health care as a commodity lead to social inequalities?

Because medical care is a commodity to be sold to the highest bidder, the United States has a two-tier system of medical care in which the poor receive inferior health care for both their mental and physical illnesses. Pp. 532–533.

What is defensive medicine?

Defensive medicine refers to medical practices done in order to protect physicians from lawsuits. Done for the physician's benefit, not the patient's, these tests and consultations add huge amounts to the nation's medical bill. Pp. 533–534.

How does sexism in medicine hurt patients?

Sexism leads to tests on females being done too late and to much unnecessary surgery. Pp. 535–536.

Why is medically assisted suicide an issue now?

Due to advanced technology, people can be kept technically alive even when they have no brain waves. Physicians who openly assist in suicides have come under severe criticism. Research findings on **euthanasia** in Holland have fueled this controversy. Pp. 537–538.

What attempts have been made to cut medical costs?

Health maintenance organizations, diagnosis-related groups, and various procedures instituted by private insurance companies are among the measures taken to reduce medical costs. National health insurance, which has run into immense opposition, has been proposed as another solution. Pp. 538–539.

Threats to Health

What are some threats to the health of Americans?

Discussed here are AIDS, which is rapidly increasing; alcohol and nicotine, the most lethal drugs used by Americans; **disabling environments,** environments that are harmful to health, such as work-related diseases or pollution of air and water; and unethical experiments, with the Tuskegee syphilis and the radiation experiments cited as examples. Pp. 539–545.

The Search for Alternatives

Are there alternatives to our current health care system?

The primary alternative discussed here is a change from treatment to the prevention of disease. Other alternatives may be found by examining health care systems in other countries. Both positive and negative characteristics of health care in Sweden, Canada, Russia, and China were reviewed. Pp. 545–548.

Where can I read more on this topic?

Suggested readings for this chapter are listed on page 644.

Red Grooms, Subway (detail) from Ruckus Manhattan, 1976

CHAPTER

20

Population and Urbanization

T HE IMAGE STILL HAUNTS ME. *There stood Celia, age 30, her distended stomach obvious proof that her thirteenth child was on its way. Her oldest was only 14 years old! A mere boy by our standards, he had already gone as far in school as he ever would. Each morning, he joined the men to work in the fields. Each evening around twilight, we saw him return home, exhausted from hard labor in the sun.*

My wife and I, who were living in Colima, Mexico, had eaten dinner in Celia's and Angel's home, which clearly proclaimed the family's poverty. A thatched hut consisting of only a single room served as home for all fourteen members of the family. At night, the parents and younger children crowded into a double bed, while the eldest boy slept in a hammock. As in many other homes in the village, the others slept on mats spread on the dirt floor.

The home was meagerly furnished. It had only a gas stove, a cabinet where Celia stored her cooking utensils and dishes, and a table. There being no closets, clothes were hung on pegs in the wall. There were no chairs, not even one. This really startled us. The family was so poor that they could not afford even a single chair.

Celia beamed as she told us how much she looked forward to the birth of her next child. Could she really mean it? It was hard to imagine that any woman would want to be in her situation.

Yet Celia meant every word. She was as full of delightful anticipation as she had been with her first child—and with all the others in between.

How could Celia have wanted so many children—especially when she lived in such poverty? That question bothered me. I couldn't let it go until I had the solution.

This chapter helps provide an answer.

The Specter of Overpopulation

Celia's story takes us into the heart of **demography,** the study of the size, composition, growth, and distribution of human populations. It brings us face to face with the question of whether we are doomed to live in a world so filled with people that there will be practically no space for anybody. Will our planet be able to support its growing population? Or is chronic famine and mass starvation the sorry fate of most earthlings? Let's look at how this concern first began, and then at what today's demographers say about it.

Thomas Malthus: Sounding the Alarm

Sometimes the cultural diffusion of a simple item can have far-reaching consequences on nations. An example is the potato, which the Spanish Conquistadors found among the natives of the Andes. When the Spanish brought this food back to Europe, Europeans first viewed it suspiciously, but they gradually came to accept it. Eventually, the potato became the principal food of the lower classes. With more abundant food, fertility increased, and the death rate dropped. As a result, Europe's population almost doubled during the 1700s (Griffith 1926; McKeown 1977).

This rapid growth alarmed Thomas Malthus (1766–1834), an English economist. He saw it as a sign of coming doom. In 1798, he wrote a book that became world famous, *An Essay on the Principle of Population.* In it, Malthus proposed what became known as the **Malthus theorem.** He argued that while population grows geometrically (from 2 to 4 to 8 to 16 and so forth), the food supply increases only arithmetically (from 1 to 2 to 3 to 4 and so on). This meant, he claimed, that if births go unchecked, the population of a country, or even of the world, will outstrip its food supply.

demography: the study of the size, composition, growth, and distribution of human populations

Malthus theorem: an observation by Thomas Malthus that although the food supply increases only arithmetically (from 1 to 2 to 3 to 4 and so on), population grows geometrically (from 2 to 4 to 8 to 16 and so forth)

The New Malthusians doubt that families in the Third World will reduce their birth rate without strong government intervention, such as that being done in China. The Zambian husband, his two wives, and their nine children are of special concern to the New Malthusians, who predict that the world will soon run out of food and other resources. The Anti-Malthusians, in contrast, say that there is nothing to be concerned about, that as nations industrialize they will follow the same demographic transition that occurred in Europe.

The New Malthusians

Was Malthus right? This question has become a matter of heated debate among demographers. One group, which can be called the "New Malthusians," is convinced that today's situation is at least as grim, if not grimmer, than Malthus ever imagined. Figure 20.1 shows how fast the world's population is growing. *In just the time it takes you to read this chapter, another fifteen thousand to twenty thousand people will be born!* By this time tomorrow, the earth will have an additional quarter of a million people to support (Weeks 1994). This increase goes on hour after hour, day after day, without letup.

The New Malthusians point out that the world's population is following an **exponential growth curve.** In other words, if growth doubles during approximately equal intervals of time, it suddenly accelerates. To illustrate the far-reaching implications of exponential growth, sociologist William Faunce (1981) told a parable about a man who saved a rich man's life. The rich man was grateful and said that he wanted to reward the man for his heroic deed.

The man replied he would like his reward to be spread out over a four-week period, with each day's amount being twice what he received on the preceding day. He also said he would be happy to receive only one penny on the first day. The rich man immediately handed over the penny and congratulated himself on how cheaply he had gotten by. At the end of the first week, the rich man checked to see how much he owed and was pleased to find that the total was only $1.27. By the end of the second week he owned only $163.83. On the twenty-first day, however, the rich man was surprised to find that the total had grown to $20,971.51. When the twenty-eighth day arrived the rich man was shocked to discover that he owned $1,342,177.28 for that day alone and that the total reward had jumped to $2,684,354.56!

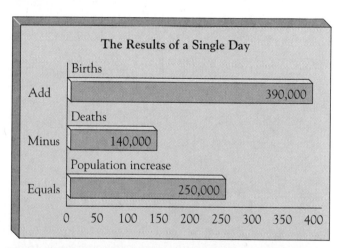
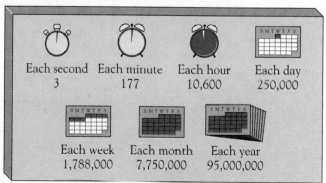

Source: Weeks 1994: 33.

Figure 20.1

How Fast is World Population Growing?

exponential growth curve: a pattern of growth in which numbers double during approximately equal intervals, thus accelerating in the latter stages

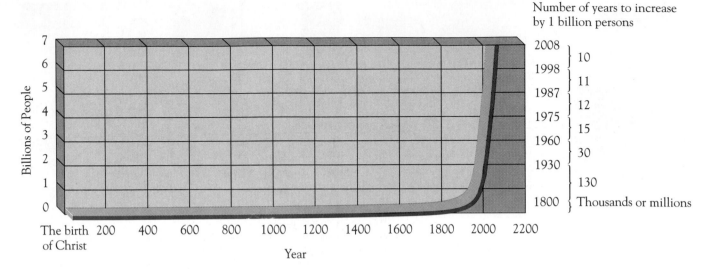

Source: Modified from Piotrow 1973: 4.

Figure 20.2

World Population Growth over 2,000 Years

This is precisely what alarms the New Malthusians. They claim that humanity has just entered the "fourth week" of an exponential growth curve. Figure 20.2 shows why they think the day of reckoning is just around the corner. They point out that it took all of human history for the world's population to reach its first billion around 1800. It then took about one hundred thirty years (1930) to add the second billion. Just thirty years later (1960), the world population hit three billion. The time needed to reach the fourth billion was cut in half, to only fifteen years (1975). It then took just twelve more years (1987) for the total to hit five billion. Right now, the world population is almost six billion (Haub and Yinger 1994).

To illustrate this increase, the new Malthusians have come up with some mind-boggling statistics. They point out that prior to Christ's birth it took 1,500 years for the world's population to double, but now it takes only about 35 years. They add that between 8000 B.C. and A.D. 1750 the world added an average of only 67,000 people a year—but now that many people are being added *every six to seven hours* (Weeks 1994).

It is obvious, claim the New Malthusians, that there is going to be less and less for more and more.

The Anti-Malthusians

It does seem obvious, and no one wants to live in a shoulder-to-shoulder world and face the constant threat of famine. How, then, can anyone argue with the Malthusians?

A much more optimistic group of demographers, whom we can call the "Anti-Malthusians," claim that such an image of the future is ridiculous. "Ever since Malthus reached his faulty conclusions," they argue, "people have been claiming that the sky is falling—that it is only a matter of time until the world is overpopulated and we all starve to death." The New Malthusians erroneously think that people breed like germs in a bucket, as illustrated by the following example.

> Assume there are two germs in the bottom of a bucket, and they double in number every hour. . . . If it takes one hundred hours for the bucket to be full of germs, at what point is the bucket one-half full of germs? A moment's thought will show that after ninety-nine hours the bucket is only half full. The title of this volume [*The 99th Hour*] is not intended to imply that the United States is half full of people but to emphasize

that it is possible to have "plenty of space left" and still be precariously near the upper limit. (Price 1967)

Anti-Malthusians, such as economist Julian Simon (1981, 1992), regard this image as dead wrong. In their view, people simply do not blindly reproduce until there is no room left. It is ridiculous to project the world's current population growth into the indefinite future; for such a calculation fails to take into account people's intelligence and rational planning when it comes to having children. To understand human reproduction, we need to look at the historical record more closely.

The Anti-Malthusians believe that Europe's **demographic transition** provides a more accurate picture of the future. This transition is diagrammed in Figure 20.3. During most of its history, Europe was in Stage I. High birthrates offset by high death rates led to a fairly stable population. Then came Stage II, the "population explosion" that so upset Malthus. Europe's population surged because birthrates remained high, while death rates went down. Finally, Europe made the transition to Stage III—the population stabilized as people brought their birthrates into line with their lower death rates.

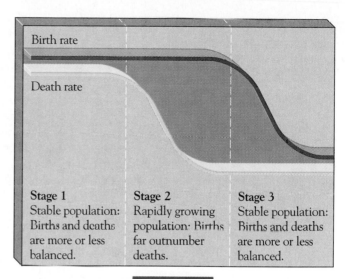

Stage 1 Stable population: Births and deaths are more or less balanced.

Stage 2 Rapidly growing population: Births far outnumber deaths.

Stage 3 Stable population: Births and deaths are more or less balanced.

Figure 20.3

The Demographic Transition

This, continue the Anti-Malthusians, is precisely what will happen in the poorer countries of the world. Their current surge in growth simply indicates that they have reached the second stage of the demographic transition. Hybrid seed and modern medicine imported from industrialized nations have cut their death rate, but their birthrate remains high. When they move into the third stage, as surely they will, we will wonder what all the fuss was about.

The Anti-Malthusians point out that Europe's demographic transition has been so successful that governments there are concerned about their citizens *not having enough babies.* They worry about **population shrinkage,** the result of not producing enough children to replace people who die (Bacon 1986). Already, workers from the Third World have migrated to Europe to fill this gap, which, as discussed in the Perspectives box on page 315, has created a volatile mixture of ethnic groups in Germany, France, and Italy. Japan is another highly developed nation that is not reproducing itself.

Who Is Correct?

As you can see, both the New Malthusians and the Anti-Malthusians have projected trends into the future. The New Malthusians project world growth trends and are alarmed. The Anti-Malthusians project the demographic transition onto the nonindustrialized countries and are reassured.

Only the future will prove the accuracy of either of these projections. There is no question that the Third World is in Stage II of the demographic transition. The question is, will these nations ever enter Stage III? After World War II, Western medicine, techniques of public hygiene, hybrid seeds, herbicides, and farm machinery were exported around the globe. Death rates plummeted as the food supply increased and health improved. At first, almost everyone was ecstatic. As the birthrate of Third World nations stayed high, however, and their populations mushroomed, misgivings set in. Demographers such as Paul and Anne Ehrlich (1972, 1978) predicted worldwide catastrophe if something were not done immediately to halt the population explosion.

We can use the conflict perspective to understand what happened when this message reached the leaders of the industrialized world. They saw the mushrooming populations of the Third World as a force that could upset the balance of power they had so carefully worked out. Fearing that the poorer countries, with swollen populations, might demand a larger share of the earth's resources, they used the United Nations to spearhead global efforts to reduce world population growth. At first, those efforts looked as though they were doomed to fail

demographic transition: a three-stage historical process of population growth: first, high birthrates and high death rates; second, high birthrates and low death rates; and, third low birthrates and low death rates

population shrinkage: the process by which a country's population becomes smaller because its birthrate and immigration are too low to replace those who die and emigrate

as populations in the Third World continued to surge. Then, gradually, the birthrates in countries such as China, India, South Korea, and Sri Lanka began to fall. Their populations did not decrease, but the rate at which they were growing slowed down, dropping from an average 2.1 percent a year in the late 1960s to 1.7 percent today (Haub and Yinger 1994).

The Malthusians and Anti-Malthusians greeted this news with significantly different interpretations. The New Malthusians stressed, as they still do, that this was but a dent in the increase. The populations of the Third World are still increasing, only not as fast as they were. A slower growth rate still spells catastrophe, they insist—it just takes a little longer for it to hit. For the Anti-Malthusians, however, this decrease in the rate of growth is the signal that Stage III of the demographic transition is arriving. First the death rate in the Third World fell—now, just as expected, the birthrate is falling.

Who is right? It simply is too early to tell. Like the proverbial pessimists who call the glass of water half empty, the New Malthusians interpret world population growth negatively. And like the optimists, the Anti-Malthusians view the figures positively and call the same glass half full. Sometime during our lifetimes we should know the answer.

Why Is There Starvation?

Pictures of starving children haunt us. They gnaw at our conscience; we live in such abundance, while these children and their parents starve before our very eyes. Why don't these children have enough food? Is it because there are too many of them, as the New Malthusians claim, or simply that the abundant food produced around the world does not reach them, as the Anti-Malthusians argue?

The basic question is this: does the world produce enough food to feed everyone? Here, the Anti-Malthusians make a point that seems irrefutable. As Figure 20.4 shows,

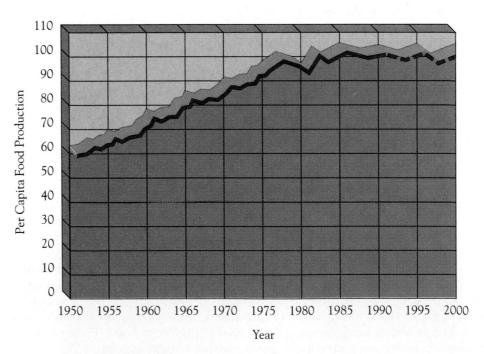

Note: 1979–1981 = 100

Years 1975 to 1991 are U.N. figures; years prior to 1975 have been recomputed from Simon to 1979-81 base; years beyond 1991 are the author's projections.

Sources: Simon 1981: 58; *United Nations Statistical Yearbook:* 1985–1986: Table 7; and 1990–1991: Table 4.

Figure 20.4

How Much Food Does the World Produce per Person?

Do people starve because the world does not produce enough food—or because there is abundant food, but it is maldistributed? This issue is at the heart of the New and Anti-Malthusian debate.

the amount of food produced for each person in the world is now much more than it was in 1950. Although the world's population has more than doubled during this time, improved seeds, fertilization, and harvesting techniques have made more food available for each person on earth (Avery 1991).

Then why do people die of hunger? From Figure 20.4, we can conclude that starvation does not occur because the earth produces too little food, but because particular places lack food. Some countries produce more food than their people can consume, others less than they need for survival. In short, the cause of starvation is an imbalance between supply and demand. One of the most notable examples is that at the same time as widespread famine is ravishing West Africa, the U.S. government is paying farmers to *reduce* their crops. *The United States'* problem is too much food, *theirs* too little.

The New Malthusians counter with the argument that the world's population is continuing to grow and that we do not know how long the earth will continue to produce sufficient food. They remind us of the penny doubling each day, as well as the germs multiplying in a bucket. It is only a matter of time, they say, until it no longer does—not "if," but "when."

The way in which governments view this matter is crucial for deciding social policy. If the problem is too many people it may call for one course of action, whereas an imbalance of resources would indicate another solution entirely. The New Malthusians would attempt to reduce the number of people in the world, while the Anti-Malthusians would instead try to distribute food more equitably.

Both the New Malthusians and the Anti-Malthusians have contributed significant ideas, but theories will not eliminate the problem of famines. Starving children are going to continue to peer out at us from our televisions and magazines, their tiny, shriveled bodies calling for us to do something. It is important to understand the underlying cause of such human misery, some of which could certainly be alleviated by transferring food from nations that have a surplus.

Perhaps this point can be driven home by noting that Africa, where recent famines have been concentrated, represents 22 percent of the earth's land surface, but only 10.5 percent of the earth's population (Nsamenang 1992). The reason for famines in Africa, then, certainly is *not* too many people living on too little land. Rather, these famines are due to two primary causes: outmoded farming techniques and ongoing political instability—revolutions and other warfare—that disrupts harvests and food distribution.

Population Growth

Even if famines are due to a maldistribution of food rather than world overpopulation, the fact remains that the Third World is growing at *three times* the rate of the First World (1.7 percent a year compared with 0.6 percent). Why do those who can least afford it have so many children?

Why the Poor Nations Have So Many Children

To understand why the population is increasing so much more rapidly in the Third World, let's figure out why Celia is so happy about having her thirteenth child. To do so, we need to apply the symbolic interactionist perspective, taking the role of the other, so that we can understand the world of Celia and Angel as *they* see it. As ours does for us, their culture provides a perspective on life that guides their choices. In this case, Celia's and Angel's culture tells them that twelve children are *not* enough, that they ought to have a thirteenth—as well as a fourteenth and fifteenth. How can that be? Let us consider three reasons that bearing many children plays a central role in their lives—and in the lives of millions of poor people around the world.

First is the status of parenthood. In the Third World, motherhood, the most highly exalted status a woman can achieve, provides personal and social fulfillment. The more children a woman bears, the more she is thought to have achieved the purpose for which she was born. Similarly, a man proves his manhood by fathering children. The more children he fathers, especially sons, the better—for through them his name lives on.

Second, the community supports this view. Celia and those like her live in *Gemeinschaft* communities, where people share values and closely identify with one another. This community awards or withholds status. And everyone agrees that children are a sign of God's blessing and that a couple should have many children. As people produce children, then, they achieve status in one of the primary ways held out by their community. The barren woman, not the woman with a dozen children, is to be pitied.

While the first two factors provide strong motivations for bearing many children, there is yet a third incentive. Poor people in nonindustrialized countries consider children economic assets. They have no Social Security or medical and unemployment insurance. As a result, they are motivated to bear *more* children, not fewer, for when parents become sick or too old to work—or when no work is to be found—they rely on their families to take care of them. The more children they have, the broader their base of support. Moreover, like the eldest son of Celia and Angel, children begin contributing to the family income at a young age. See Figure 20.5.

To those of us who live in the First World, it seems irrational to have many children. And *for us it would be*. Within the framework of the Third World, however—the essence of the symbolic interactionist position—it makes perfect sense to have many children. For example, consider the following incident, reported by an Indian government worker:

> Thaman Singh (a very poor man, a water carrier). . . . welcomed me inside his home, gave me a cup of tea (with milk and "market" sugar, as he proudly pointed out later), and said: "You were trying to convince me in 1960 that I shouldn't have any more sons. Now, you see, I have six sons and two daughters and I sit at home in leisure. They are grown up and they bring me money. One even works outside the village as a laborer. *You told me I was a poor man and couldn't support a large family. Now, you see, because of my large family I am a rich man.*" (Mamdani 1973, italics added)

Is this the whole story? In contrast to this symbolic interactionist view, the conflict perspective stresses the domination of females by males in all spheres of life, including that of reproduction. Conflict theorists would argue that Celia has internalized values

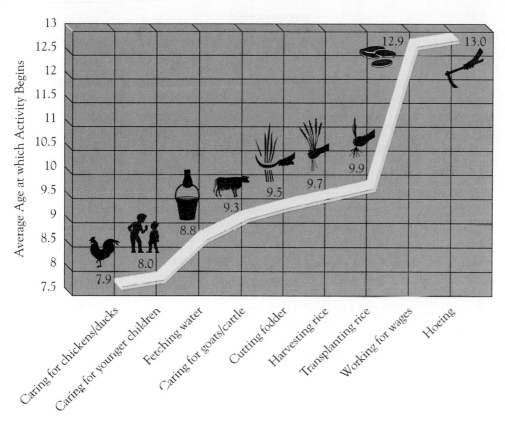

Figure 20.5

Why the Poor Need Children.

Source: U.N. Fund for Population Activities.

Surviving children are an economic asset in the developing nations. Based on a survey in Indonesia, this figure shows that boys and girls can be net income earners for their families by the age of 9 or 10.

that support male dominance. For example, in Latin America machismo is common. This emphasis on male strength and dominance includes fathering many children as a means of achieving status in the community. From a conflict perspective, then, the reason poor people have so many children is that males continue to control reproductive choices.

Implications of Different Rates of Growth

The result of Celia's and Angel's desire for many children—and of the millions of Celias and Angels like them—is that Mexico's current population will double in only thirty years. In sharp contrast, Sweden's population is growing at only 0.1 percent a year, making it one of the world's slowest-growing populations. In the thirty years in which Mexico's population will double, Sweden's population will increase by a mere 3 percent. To illustrate a country's population dynamics, demographers use **population pyramids,** depicting a population by age and sex. Figure 20.6 contrasts Mexico, in Stage II of the demographic transition, with the United States, in advanced Stage III.

The implications of a doubled population are mind-boggling. *Just to stay even,* within those thirty years Mexico must double its jobs and all other factors thought to constitute "decent" living standards. Consider food production and factories; hospitals and schools; transportation, communication, water, gas, sewer, and electrical systems; housing, churches, civic buildings, theaters, stores, and parks. If Mexico fails to double these facilities, its already very low standard of living will drop even further.

A declining standard of living poses the threat of political instability, followed by severe repression by the government to eliminate it. As conflict theorists point out, this

population pyramid: a graphic representation of a population, divided into age and sex

---
Figure 20.6

Population Pyramids of Mexico and the United States.

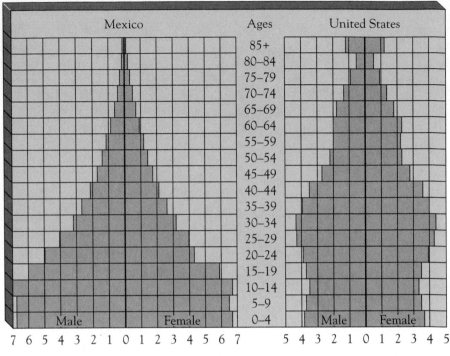

possibility is one reason that the First World is so insistent on United Nations support for worldwide birth control. Political instability in one country can spill over into others, threatening an entire region's balance of power. Consequently, to help preserve political stability, with one hand the First World gives agricultural aid, IUDs, and condoms to the masses in Third World countries—while with the other it sells arms and munitions to their elites. Both actions serve the same purpose, say conflict theorists.

Think of the worldwide attempt to achieve a higher standard of living as a contest. The Third World appears destined to fall still farther behind, for not only do its countries start with less, but their swelling numbers drain the limited financial resources that might otherwise be used for industrial development. In contrast, nations such as Sweden and the United States, already becoming post-industrialized nations, are far ahead and have *fewer people on whom to spend much more*.

Estimating Population Growth: The Three Demographic Variables

demographic variables: the three factors that influence population growth: fertility, mortality, and net migration

fertility rate: the number of children that the average woman bears

fecundity: the number of children that women are theoretically *capable* of bearing

To accurately project the future of human populations is obviously highly significant in today's world. Educators want to know how many schools to build. Manufacturers want to anticipate changes in demand for their products. The government needs to know how many doctors, engineers, and executives to train, as well as how many people will be paying taxes and how many young people will be available to fight a war.

To project population trends, demographers use three basic **demographic variables:** fertility, mortality, and migration. Let us look at each.

Fertility   The **fertility rate** refers to the number of children that the average woman bears. A term sometimes confused with fertility is **fecundity,** the number of children

Awareness of death, the second demographic variable, is incorporated into all cultures. Shown here is the Day of the Dead celebrated in Mexico each November 1 and 2. Cemeteries become places for singing, dancing, and picnicking, and children are given candy in the shape of skulls or coffins.

that women are *capable* of bearing. The fecundity of women around the world is around twenty children each. Their fertility rate, however (the actual number of children they bear), is much lower. The world's overall fertility rate is 3.6, which means that the average woman in the world can expect to bear 3.6 children during her lifetime. At 2.0, the fertility rate of U.S. women is considerably less (*Statistical Abstract* 1993: Table 95). The record for the world's lowest rate is held jointly by Germany, Austria, and Italy, where the average woman bears only 1.4 children. The world's highest rate is 8.5, a record shared by North Yemen and Rwanda in East Africa. This means that the average woman in North Yemen and Rwanda gives birth to *six* times as many children as the average Italian woman (Population Reference Bureau, 1988).

To compute the fertility rate of a country, demographers usually depend on a government's records of births. From these, they figure the country's **crude birthrate,** that is, the annual number of live births per 1,000 population. There may be considerable slippage here, of course, since birth records in the Third World may be haphazard. From Figure 20.6, you can see how a country's age structure affects its birthrate. If by some miracle Mexico were transformed overnight into a nation as industrialized as Sweden, its birthrate would continue to rapidly outpace Sweden's—simply because a much higher percentage of Mexican women are in their childbearing years.

Mortality   The second demographic variable, **crude death rate,** refers to the number of deaths per 1,000 population. It, too, varies around the world. Look again at Figure 20.6. Because the United States has a much higher proportion of old people than Mexico, we would expect the United States also to have a much higher crude death rate. Because of inadequate diets, poor public health, and inferior medical treatment, however, Mexico's death rate is higher.

Migration   The third major demographic variable is the **net migration rate,** the difference between the number of *immigrants* (people moving in) and *emigrants* (people moving out) per 1,000 population. Unlike fertility and mortality rates, this rate does not affect the global population, for people are simply shifting their residence from one country to another.

As is apparent, immigrants are seeking a better life. To find it, they are willing to give up the security of their family and friends and to move to a country with a strange language and unfamiliar customs. What motivates people to embark on such a venture? To understand migration, we need to look at both *push* and *pull* factors. The push factors are those things that people want to escape—poverty, the lack of religious and political freedoms, even political persecution. The pull factors are the magnets that draw people to a new land, such as a chance for higher wages and better jobs. Around the

crude birthrate: the annual number of births per 1,000 population

crude death rate: the annual number of deaths per 1,000 population

net migration rate: the difference between the number of immigrants and emigrants per 1,000 population

world, the flow of migration is from the less developed nations to the more industrialized countries (Kalish 1994). After "migrant paths" are established, immigration often accelerates as networks of kin and friends become further magnets that attract more people from the same nation—and even from the same villages.

With the United States the world's number-one choice of immigrants, this country admits more legal immigrants each year than all the other nations of the world combined. Table 20.1 shows the countries of origin of U.S. immigrants. In an attempt to escape the poverty experienced by Celia and Angel, a large number of people, primarily from Mexico and Central and South America, also enter the United States illegally. Although their total is unknown, it is so large that each year about a million people are apprehended at the Rio Grande or at points inland and deported. The Perspectives box on page 336 examines changes in the racial-ethnic mix of the United States that are resulting from immigration.

As mentioned, experts cannot agree whether immigrants are a net contributor to or a drain on the U.S. economy. Economist Julian Simon (1986, 1993) claims that the net results benefit the country. After subtracting what immigrants collect in welfare and adding what they produce in jobs and taxes, he concludes that immigrants make an overall positive contribution to the U.S. economy. Other economists such as Donald Huddle (1993) dispute this conclusion, producing figures showing that immigrants are a huge drain on taxpayers. At this point, not enough evidence is in to allow us to come to a rational conclusion.

The Demographic Equation and Problems in Forecasting Population Growth

The total of the three demographic variables—fertility, mortality, and net migration—gives us a country's **growth rate,** the net change after people have been added to and subtracted from a population. What demographers call the **basic demographic equation** is quite simple:

GROWTH RATE = BIRTHS − DEATHS + NET MIGRATION.

With such a simple equation, it might seem that it also would be a simple matter to project a country's future population. To forecast population growth, however, is to invite yourself to be wrong. Consider the following instance.

During the depression of the late 1920s and early 1930s, birthrates plunged as unemployment reached unprecedented heights. Demographers issued warnings about the dangers of depopulation almost as alarmist as some of today's forecasts of overpopulation. Because each year fewer and fewer females would enter the childbearing years, they felt that the population of countries such as Great Britain would shrink. (Waddington 1978)

Table 20.1

Country of Birth of Immigrants to the United States

Place of Birth	Total	Place of Birth	Total
North America	1,100,000	**Central and South America**	191,000
Mexico	946,000	El Salvador	47,000
Haiti	48,000	Guatemala	26,000
Domin. Rep.	41,000	Colombia	20,000
Jamaica	24,000	Nicaragua	18,000
Canada	14,000	Peru	16,000
Cuba	10,000	Guyana	12,000
Asia	359,000	Honduras	12,000
Philippines	64,000	Ecuador	10,000
Vietnam	55,000	**Europe**	135,000
India	45,000	Soviet Union (former)	57,000
China	44,000	Poland	19,000
Korea	27,000	Great Britain	14,000
Iran	20,000	**Africa**	36,000
Bangladesh	11,000		
Laos	10,000	**Total**	**1,821,000**
Hong Kong	10,000		

Note: The countries listed for each continent are only those from which at least 10,000 immigrants came in 1991. The total for each continent, then, is larger than listed here.

Source: Statistical Abstract 1993: Table 8.

growth rate: the net change in a population after adding births, subtracting deaths, and either adding or subtracting net migration

basic demographic equation: growth rate = births - deaths + net migration

▼▲▼

Perspectives

CULTURAL DIVERSITY IN THE UNITED STATES

Where the U.S. Population Is Headed—The Shifting Racial-Ethnic Mix

DURING THE NEXT FIFTY years, the population of the United States is expected to grow by about 44 percent. To see what the population will look like in fifty years, can we simply multiply the current racial-ethnic mix by 44 percent?

The answer is a resounding no. During the next fifty years some groups will increase much more than others. The result will be a different-looking United States. Let's try to catch a glimpse of the future.

You can see momentous changes (as illustrated in the table below). First, with low birthrates, almost all the population growth will come from immigration. Second, with 80 percent of immigration to the United States now coming from Latin America and Asia, the number of Asian Americans and Latinos is expected to quintuple and triple respectively. Third, although in fifty years there will still be more non-Hispanic whites than all other groups combined,

their majority will be slight (dropping from about 76 percent of the population to about 59 percent). Fourth, Latinos are expected to outnumber African Americans sometime during the first decade of the twenty-first century, when they will become the largest minority in the United States. Fifth, immigration is so vast that in fifty years about 50 million Americans will have been born outside the United States.

This population shift is one of the most significant events occurring in the United States. (You may wish to compare the materials in the Perspectives box on page 336.) Who do you think will be threatened by this shift in racial-ethnic mix? What measures to you think U.S. institutions should take to prepare for the future? Do you think, as some do, that "America should be for Americans" and that we should cut off immigration now? Why or why not?

Projecting the Future

Racial-Ethnic Group	Current Size	Expected Size in 50 Years	Growth Rate	Foreign Born Now	Foreign Born in 50 Years
Asian Americans	7,000,000	35,000,000	500%	67%	50%
Latinos	21,000,000	64,000,000	300	41	33
African Americans	30,000,000	44,000,000	47	5	9
White Americans (non-Hispanics)	187,000,000	211,000,000	13	3	4
Native Americans	2,000,000	2,000,000	0	0	0
Total	247,000,000	356,000,000	44	8.6	14.2

Source: Crispell 1992.

What actually happened? With the end of the Great Depression and the outbreak of war, the birthrate took a sharp turn downward. Then during the postwar years, it increased again. The result was a "baby boom" from 1946 to 1950 in both the United States and Great Britain.

If population increase depended only on biology, the demographer's job would be relatively simple. But economic booms and busts, wars, plagues, and famines can become unanticipated "push" factors for hundreds of thousands of a country's citizens. Even infanticide affects a country's birthrate, as shown in the Perspectives box on the next page. Government programs also make accurate projections difficult. Sometimes governments want their people to bear more children, sometimes less. Hitler, for example, decided that Germany needed more "Aryans," and the German government outlawed abortions and offered cash bonuses for women who gave birth. The population increased.

▲▼

Perspectives

CULTURAL DIVERSITY AROUND THE WORLD

"Killing Little Girls: An Ancient and Thriving Practice"

"THE MYSTERIOUS CASE OF the Missing Girls" could have been the title of this box. Around the globe, the norm for the girl–boy ratio is 100 girls to 105 boys. In China, however, for every 100 girls, 111 boys are born. This imbalance in the girl–boy ratio indicates that about 400,000 baby girls are missing each year. What is happening to them?

The answer is rooted in deep sexism. Around the world boy babies are generally preferred. To ensure the birth of boys, for millennia people have experimented with a variety of folk techniques, none of which has worked. Only in recent years, with the development of technology that separates semen, has a technique become available that is 80-percent effective. China, however, is not technologically advanced. Have the Chinese, then, stumbled on some effective folk technique?

The answer points in a different direction—to the ancient practice of *female infanticide*, the killing of girl babies. When a Chinese woman goes into labor, village midwives sometimes grab a bucket of water. If the newborn is a girl, she is plunged into the water before she can draw her first breath.

At the root of China's infanticide is economics. The people are extremely poor, and they have no pensions. When parents can no longer work, sons support them. In contrast, a daughter must be married off, at great expense, and at that point her obligations transfer to her husband and his family.

In just the past few years, China's girl–boy ratio has increased. Again, economics is the reason. As China has opened the door to capitalism, making profits no longer an official curse word, the men find themselves better able to travel, to work and trade, and to bring profits home to the family—one more push toward preferring male children.

By no means is female infanticide limited to China. Although this practice was banned in India by the British in 1870, it continues. Western technology has even been put to work. Many Indian women use amniocentesis to learn the sex of their child, and then decide whether or not to abort. In 99.9 percent of these abortions, the fetus is female.

This use of amniocentesis for sex selection led to a public outcry in India. The indignation was not due to outrage against this extreme form of sexism, however, nor was it due to some antiabortion movement. Rather, the public became indignant when a physician mistakenly gave the parents wrong information and aborted a *male* baby!

It is likely that the preference for boys, and the consequent female infanticide, will not disappear until the social structures that perpetuate sexism are dismantled. That will not take place until women hold as much power as men, a time, should it ever occur, that apparently lies far in the future.

Source: Giarelli 1988; Lagaipa 1990; McGowan 1991; Polumbaum 1992; Renteln 1992.

In contrast, when Chinese authorities decided that their population should not grow any larger, they not only launched a "One couple, one child" advertising campaign, but they fined couples who had a second child. They also instituted a severe abortion policy. Steven Mosher (1983, 1993), an anthropologist who did fieldwork in China, reports,

> Each population unit, such as a rural collective, is limited to a certain number of births per year, which it allots to couples who have yet to have children. Women who have had their allotted quota of one who get pregnant are forced to attend round-the-clock study courses until they submit to an abortion. In some cases abortions are physically forced on resisting women, some of whom are nine months pregnant. (Erik 1982)

Letting such policies pass without comment, we can see that a government's efforts to change a country's growth rate greatly complicate the demographer's task of projecting future populations.

The primary unknown factor that influences a country's growth rate, however, is its rate of industrialization. *In every country that industrializes, the growth rate declines.* Not only do people have new economic opportunities, but children become more expensive and, with more education expected, remain dependent longer. Significantly, the group's system of conferring status also changes—from having children to attaining education and displaying material wealth. People like Celia and Angel then begin to see life differently, and their motivation to have many children drops sharply. Not knowing how rapidly industrialization will progress, or how quickly changes in values and reproductive behavior will follow, adds to the difficulty of making accurate projections.

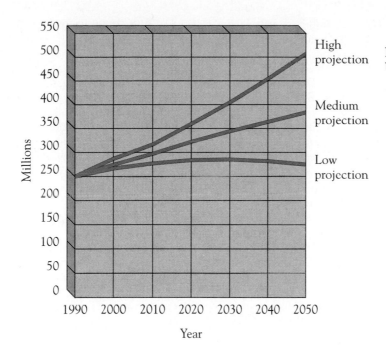

Figure 20.7

Population Projections of the United States

Source: Statistical Abstract 1993: Table 17.

Because of such complications, demographers play it safe by making *several* projections of future populations. For example, what will the population of the United States be in the year 2010? Perhaps we will be at **zero population growth,** with every 1,000 women giving birth to 2,100 children (the extra 100 children make up for those who do not survive). The college education of females is likely to increase, but by how much? (The more education women have, the fewer children they bear.) How will immigration trends change during the coming years? Will AIDS come under control? Will some other horrible disease appear? What will happen to the economy? With such huge variables, it is easy to see why demographers make the three projections of the U.S. population shown on Figure 20.7.

The Challenge of the Twenty-First Century

With the Third World's deep poverty and even starvation, one crisis follows another. Before concluding these materials on population, then, let's take a final glance at the challenge that confronts the world's nations as we enter the twenty-first century.

▼▲▼▲▼▲▼▲▼▲▼▲▼▲▼▲▼▲▼▲▼▲▼▲▼▲▼▲▼▲

Thinking Critically About Social Controversy

On the Doorstep of the Twenty-First Century

▼ THERE IS NO DOUBT that Malthus's pessimistic predictions were wrong—for his time, that is. Malthus could not foresee the new technology of the Industrial Revolution, which created new wealth and caused the national product to skyrocket.

But what about today, as we stand on the doorstep of the twenty-first century? Economist Paul Kennedy (1993) says that our greatest challenge is how to use modern technology to free the Third World from "the growing Malthusian trap of malnutrition, starvation, resource depletion, unrest, enforced migration, and armed conflict—developments that will also endanger the richer nations, if less directly."

zero population growth: a demographic condition in which women bear only enough children to reproduce the population

The past, unfortunately, may not provide guidelines for the future. During the last century, both the population and technology exploded in the same place, the British Isles. Today, however, technology is exploding in one part of the world, population in another. In the First World, which has the technology explosion, population is slow-growing and in some places even declining. The areas with the population explosion, however, find themselves with "limited technological resources, very few scientists and skilled workers, inadequate investment in research and development . . . and cultural and ideological prejudices are much more tilted against change than they were in the England of the Industrial Revolution" (Kennedy 1993). To complicate matters even more, adds Kennedy, overgrazing and erosion are also concentrated in these countries, reducing their agricultural resources just as their populations are mushrooming.

For Your Consideration

On the threshold of the twenty-first century, then, we face a severe challenge—with the fate of millions, if not billions, of people hanging in the balance. Considering the materials so far in this chapter, do you think that we should open our borders to anyone and everyone who wants to immigrate? Or would closing them entirely and concentrating on taking care of our own problems be a better approach? Do you think that the population problem is so severe that the First World should subsidize world condom distribution? Or pay people to be sterilized? Should the First World support such policies as the enforced abortions in China? Finally, how do you think that the First World can harness its vast technologies to benefit today's global community?   ▲

Let's look at a different aspect of population, where people live. Since the world is rapidly becoming urban, we shall concentrate on urban trends and urban life.

The City in History

*T*HE TRANSFORMATION OF THE SAN FRANCISCO *streets was as intriguing as it was unexpected. My interviewing of the homeless had gone on somewhat longer than I had planned, and dusk had begun to settle in. Heading back to the fleabag hotel, I had spotted a 20-year-old male carrying a backpack. Trying for one more interview, I sat on the sidewalk, with my back against a building. In this self-protective stance, I felt comfortable until the man stopped mid-sentence, stared at me intently, and in a voice so low I had to concentrate to hear what he was saying, slowly said, "I know why you are here."*

Somewhat taken back, I said, "What?"

He replied, "I know why you are here."

In measured tones, I said that I had already explained that to him, that I was doing sociological interviews.

"No," he said, not taking his eyes off me. "I know why you are here." He paused, then said, "You are here to help me. I can tell because of the way you move your hands."

I felt a strange sensation as the man nodded at me, looking as though he possessed some secret knowledge. He then began to mutter something about the FBI being after him.

Not taking my eyes off him, I looked past him to seek out an escape route—just in case.

The man fell into silence. He continued to stare intensely at me. Then, as I uttered a prayer, he picked up his knapsack, stood up, and walked briskly away into the falling darkness.

Ordinarily I would have felt badly at losing an interview. But not this time.

I had begun to take too much for granted in my homeless research, and this experience put me on guard once again, forcing on my consciousness a keener awareness of the city. As I looked for my hotel with dusk gently falling about the city streets, I saw the area change.

The men and women in business dress carrying briefcases, who had been scurrying around these streets as though time pursued them, and the fashionably dressed shoppers going in and out of the shops, were now replaced by people with hair adorned in bright hues.

A woman with a tattoo on her left breast, mostly exposed by her half-zipped leather jacket and absence of bra or blouse, leaned against a building. A man on roller skates, wearing a white jump suit with the zipper opened to his navel, rhythmically moved his feet back and forth to a beat only he heard, never leaving the tiny space he had claimed. Women in short, tight skirts, keenly watching passing cars, strolled slowly on the outside of the sidewalk.

And there was the couple whose image is forever emblazoned on my memory. The man, in his forties, shirtless and riding a Harley hog, wore an open denim vest. Other than his flowing beard and unkempt, long hair, his most pronounced characteristic was the huge beer gut that kept his vest from closing. On the back of his motorcycle, her arms tightly clutched about the man, but not quite able to reach around his stomach, sat a skinny blonde who couldn't have been more than 16.

This transformation took place in San Francisco in the mid-1980s. But if I had been in New Orleans or Atlanta in the South, New York or Boston in the East, Houston or Dallas in the Southwest, Miami in the Southeast, or Chicago in the Midwest, the scene would have been similar. This is a distinctly *urban* phenomenon. That is, there are specific characteristics of cities that give them their unique "flavor." Their "urbanness" comes not only from their size, but especially from the anonymity they provide, which allows people to both blend in with others and to stand out at the same time.

Such behaviors as I have just described whet the sociological imagination. Earlier (pages 101–103), we reviewed Emile Durkheim's conclusions about organic and mechanical solidarity and Ferdinand Tönnies contrasts of rural and urban life (*Gemeinschaft* and *Gesellschaft*). In the 1920s, Chicago was a vivid mosaic of newly arrived immigrants, gangsters, prostitutes, the homeless, the rich and the poor—much as it is today. Sociologists at the University of Chicago began to study these contrasting ways of life. From what became known as the Chicago School of Sociology emerged numerous studies of city life—from hobos (Anderson 1923) and gangs (Thrasher 1927) to a contrast of the lives of the poor and the rich (Zorbaugh 1929). Today, sociologists still enjoy studying why and how some people find the city a place of refuge, while others find it a threatening, foreboding sort of place.

To better understand urban life, let's first find out how the city itself came about.

Early cities were small economic centers surrounded by walls to keep out enemies. These cities had to be fortresses, for they were constantly threatened by armed, roving tribesmen and by local leaders who raised armies to enlarge their domain and enrich their coffers by sacking neighboring cities.

The Development of Cities

Cities are not new to the world scene. Perhaps as early as seven to ten thousand years ago people built small cities with massive defensive walls, such as Catal Hüyük (Schwendinger and Schwendinger 1983) and biblically famous Jericho (Homblin 1973). Cities on a larger scale originated about 3500 B.C., about the same time as the invention of writing (Chandler and Fox 1974; Hawley 1981). At that time, cities appeared in several parts of the world—first in Mesopotamia (Iran) and later in the Nile, Indus, and Yellow River valleys, around the Mediterranean, in West Africa, Central America, and the Andes (Fischer 1976; Flanagan 1990).

The key to the origin of cities is the development of more efficient agriculture (Lenski and Lenski 1987). Only when farming produces a surplus can some people stop being food producers and gather in cities to spend time in other pursuits. A **city,** in fact, can be defined as a place in which a large number of people are permanently based and do not produce their own food. The invention of the plow between five and six thousand years ago created widespread agricultural surpluses, stimulating the development of towns and cities (Curwin and Hart 1961). (For a review of the sweeping historical changes that laid the organizational groundwork for the rise and expansion of cities, see pages 145–150.)

The Industrial Revolution and the Size of Cities

Most early cities were tiny by comparison with those of today, merely a collection of a few thousand people in agricultural centers or on major trade routes. The most notable exceptions are two cities that reached one million for a brief period of time before they declined—Changan in China about A.D. 800 and Baghdad in Persia about A.D. 900 (Chandler and Fox 1974). Even Athens at the peak of its power in the fifth century B.C. had less than 200,000 inhabitants. Rome, at its peak, may have had a million or more (Flanagan 1990).

city: a place in which a large number of people are permanently based and do not produce their own food

Vast immigration into U.S. cities is nothing new, as shown by this 1905 photo of the intersection of Orchard and Hester Streets in New York City's Lower East Side. From this photo, can you identify any of the "pulls" that have drawn these people to the city?

Even 200 years ago, the only city in the world that had a population of more than a million was Peking, China (Chandler and Fox 1974). Then in just 100 years, by 1900, the number of such cities jumped to sixteen. The reason is the Industrial Revolution, which drew people to cities by providing work. It also stimulated the invention of mechanical means of transportation and communication, and allowed people, resources, and products to be moved efficiently—all essential factors (called "infrastructure") on which large cities depend. Today there are about 200 cities with a million or more people, and by the year 2000 there will be about 300 (Frisbie and Kasarda 1988).

Urbanization, Metropolises, and Megalopolises

Although cities are not new to the world scene, urbanization is. **Urbanization** refers to masses of people moving to cities and a growing urban influence on society. This process is worldwide. Just 200 years ago, in 1800, only 3 percent of the world's population lived in cities (Hauser and Schnore 1965). Now about 50 percent do. Each year the world's urban population grows by about 0.5 percent, and by the year 2020 about three of every five people on earth will live in cities (Palen 1987).

Without the Industrial Revolution this remarkable growth could not have taken place, for an extensive infrastructure is needed to support hundreds of thousands and even millions of people in a relatively small area. To understand the city's attraction, however, we cannot discount the "pull" of urban life. Due to its exquisite division of labor, the city offers incredible variety—music ranging from rock and country to classic and opera, diets for vegetarians and diabetics as well as imported delicacies from around the world for the rest of us. Nor can we discount the anonymity that cities offer, which so many find highly refreshing in light of the much tighter controls of village and small-town life. And, of course, the city offers work.

Some cities have grown so large and influential over a region that the term *city* is no longer adequate to describe them. The term **metropolis** is used instead. This term refers to a central city surrounded by smaller cities and their suburbs. They are connected economically, sometimes politically through county boards and regional governing bodies, and socially by ties of transportation and communication.

urbanization: the process by which an increasing proportion of a population lives in cities

metropolis: a central city surrounded by smaller cities and their suburbs

With its arch proclaiming its status as "The Gateway to the West," St. Louis's skyline has become famous the world over. Beneath the facade of imposing structures—stadium, convention center, high-rise hotels and restaurants—lies a less welcome reality, that of the poor and powerless who have been displaced in the name of "progress."

St. Louis is an example. Although this name, St. Louis, properly refers to a city of less than 400,000 people in Missouri, it also refers to another two million people living in over a hundred separate towns in both Missouri and Illinois, vaguely known as the "St. Louis or Bi-State Area." Although these towns are independent politically, they form a larger unit united economically (many people in the smaller towns work in St. Louis, or are served by industries from St. Louis), by communications (the same area newspaper and radio and television stations), and by transportation (the same three interstates, "Bi-State Bus" system, and international airport). As symbolic interactionists would note, a common identity also arises from the area's shared symbols (the Arch, the Mississippi River, Busch Brewery, the Cardinals, the Blues—both the hockey team and the music). Most of the towns run into one another, and if you were to drive through this metropolis you would not know that you were leaving one town and entering another—unless you had lived here some time and were aware of the fierce small-town identifications and rivalries that exist side by side with this larger identification.

Some metropolises have grown so large and influential that the term **megalopolis** is used to describe them. This term refers to an overlapping area consisting of at least two metropolises and their many suburbs. This urban area is also connected economically, socially, and sometimes even politically. Of the twenty or so megalopolises in the United States, the three largest are the Eastern seaboard running from Maine to Virginia, the area between Miami, Orlando, and Tampa in Florida, and California's coastal area between San Francisco and San Diego.

This process of urban areas turning into a metropolis and metropolises developing into a megalopolis is also worldwide. Table 20.2 lists the sixteen largest cities in the world. Note that most of them are located in the Third World.

megalopolis: an urban area consisting of at least two metropolises and their many suburbs

---

Table 20.2

The World's Sixteen Largest Cities

City	Country	Rank	Population (in millions)
Tokyo-Yokohama	Japan	1	28
Mexico City	Mexico	2	24
São Paulo	Brazil	3	22
Seoul	South Korea	4	19
New York	United States	5	15
Osaka-Kobe-Kyoto	Japan	6	14
Bombay	India	7	14
Calcutta	India	8	13
Rio de Janeiro	Brazil	9	13
Buenos Aires	Argentina	10	12
Tehran	Iran	11	12
Manilla	Philippines	12	11
Cairo	Egypt	13	11
Jakarta	Indonesia	14	11
Moscow	Russia	15	11
Los Angeles	United States	16	10

Source: Statistical Abstract 1993: Table 1377.

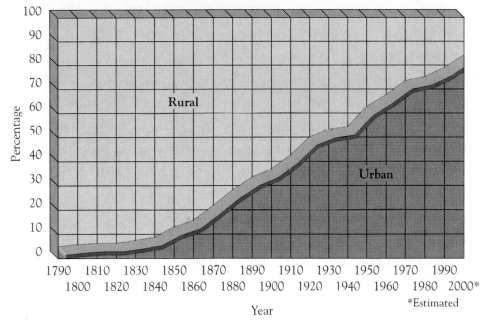

Figure 20.8

Urban Makeup of the U.S. Population, 1790–2000

Sources: *Statistical Abstract 1988:* Table 33 and *Patterns of Urban and Rural Population Growth* 1980: 159–162.

Urbanization in the United States

When the United States was founded, it was almost exclusively rural. Figure 20.8 illustrates the country's changing rural to urban ratio. In 1790, only about 5 percent of Americans lived in cities. By 1920, this figure had jumped to 50 percent. Urbanization has continued without letup, and today about 80 percent of Americans live in cities.

The U.S. Census Bureau has divided the country into 283 **metropolitan statistical areas (MSAs).** Each MSA consists of a central city and the urbanized county areas linked to it. As Table 20.3 shows, over half of the entire U.S. population lives in just 44 MSAs (Haub and Lang 1993).

metropolitan statistical area (MSA): a central city and the urbanized counties adjacent to it

Table 20.3

Metropolitan Statistical Areas over 1 Million			
Census Year	Number of MSAs	Population (millions)	Percentage of U.S. Population
1950	14	45	30%
1960	22	64	36
1970	31	84	41
1980	35	104	46
1990	39	125	50
1995[a]	44	150	57
2000[a]	50	170	63

[a]Author's estimate. *Source:* Census Bureau 1991: 2.

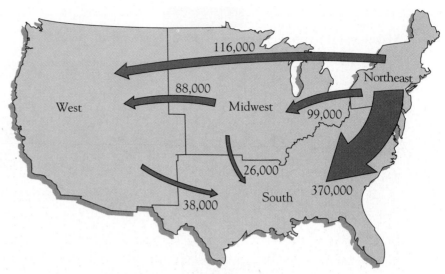

Source: U.S. Bureau of the Census 1992.

Figure 20.9

Net Migration Flows Between Regions, 1990–1991

As Americans migrate in search of work and better lifestyles, distinct patterns appear. As Figure 20.9 shows, the general movement is from the North and the East to the West and the South, or, as it is known, from the "snow belt" to the **sun belt.** A comparison of the ten fastest-and slowest-growing cities in the United States makes this pattern especially evident. As Table 20.4 shows, all the fastest-growing cities are in the West and the South, while all but two of the slowest-growing cities are in the Northeast.

As Americans migrate and businesses move, to serve them **edge cities** have developed. This term refers to a clustering of shopping malls, hotels, office parks, and residential areas near the intersection of major highways (Gans 1991; Garreau 1992; Rybczynski 1991; Walker 1991). Although this clustering of services may overlap the boundaries of several cities or towns, it provides a sense of place to those who live there.

sun belt: the southern and western states to which most U.S. migrants move

edge city: a large clustering of service facilities and residential areas near highway intersections that provides a sense of place to people who live, shop, and work there

Table 20.4

The Fastest- and Slowest-Growing U.S. Cities

The Fastest-Growing Cities		The Slowest-Growing Cities	
1. Las Vegas, NV	8.5	1. Shreveport LA	−0.5
2. Bremerton, WA	6.0	2. Boston, MA	−0.5
3. Olympia, WA	5.2	3. Springfield, MA	−0.3
4. Riverside, CA	5.1	4. New London, CT	−0.1
5. Boise City, ID	4.7	5. New Haven, CT	−0.1
6. Modesto, CA	4.4	6. Nashua, NH	−0.1
7. Bakersfield, CA	4.3	7. Bridgeport, CT	−0.1
8. McAllen, TX	4.1	8. Providence, RI	0.1
9. Brazoria, TX	3.9	9. Hartford, CT	0.1
10. Melbourne, FL	3.8	10. Flint, MI	0.2

Note: Population change from 1990–1991. A minus sign indicates a loss of population. Santa Cruz, California, actually ranks as fourth slowest in the source, but when I called the city's planning director, he said Santa Cruz had grown during this period and quoted statistics to illustrate its growth. Consequently, Santa Cruz has been dropped from the list.

Source: Statistical Abstract 1993: Table 42.

Edge cities are one of the newest developments of urban life. This aerial photo of an edge city near Corte Madera, California, shows San Francisco in the background.

Another major U.S. urban pattern is **gentrification,** the movement of middle-class people into rundown areas of a city. They are attracted by the low prices for quality housing that, though deteriorated, can be restored. One consequence is an improvement in the appearance of urban neighborhoods—freshly painted buildings, well-groomed lawns, and the absence of boarded-up windows. Another consequence is that the poor residents are displaced as the more well-to-do newcomers move in. There often is tension between these groups (Anderson 1990).

Models of Urban Growth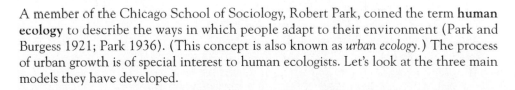

A member of the Chicago School of Sociology, Robert Park, coined the term **human ecology** to describe the ways in which people adapt to their environment (Park and Burgess 1921; Park 1936). (This concept is also known as *urban ecology.*) The process of urban growth is of special interest to human ecologists. Let's look at the three main models they have developed.

The Concentric-Zone Model

To explain how cities expand, sociologist Ernest Burgess (1925) proposed a *concentric-zone model.* As shown in segment A of Figure 20.10, Burgess noted that a city expands outward from its center. Zone I is the central business district. Encircling this downtown area is a zone in transition (Zone II). It contains deteriorating housing and rooming houses, which, as Burgess noted, breed poverty, disease, and vice. Zone III is the area to which thrifty workers have moved to escape the zone in transition and yet maintain easy access to their work. Zone IV contains more expensive apartments, residential hotels, single-family dwellings, and exclusive areas where the wealthy live. Still

gentrification: the displacement of the poor by the relatively affluent, who renovate the former's homes

human ecology: Robert Park's term for the relationship between people and their environment (natural resources such as land)

farther out, beyond the city limits, is Zone V, a commuter zone consisting of suburban areas or satellite cities that have developed around rapid transit routes.

Burgess intended this model to represent "the tendencies of any town or city to expand radially from its central business district." He noted, however, that no "city fits perfectly this ideal scheme." Some cities have physical obstacles, such as a lake, river, or railroad, which cause their expansion to depart from the model. While Burgess also noted in 1925 that businesses were deviating from the model by locating in outlying zones, he was unable to anticipate the extent of this trend—the suburban shopping malls that replaced downtown stores and now account for more than half the country's retail sales (Palen 1987).

The Sector Model

Sociologist Homer Hoyt (1939, 1971) noted that a city's concentric zones do not form a complete circle, and he modified Burgess's model of urban growth. As shown in segment B of Figure 20.10, a concentric zone might contain several sectors—one of working-class housing, another of expensive housing, a third of businesses, and so on, all competing for the same land.

What sociologists call an **invasion–succession cycle** is an example of this dynamic competition of urban life. When poor immigrants or rural migrants enter a city, they settle in the lowest-rent area they can. As their members swell, they spill over into adjacent areas. Upset at their presence, the middle class moves out, thus expanding the sector of low-cost housing. The invasion–succession cycle is never complete, for later another group of immigrants will replace this earlier one, or gentrification may occur.

The Multiple-Nuclei Model

Geographers Chauncey Harris and Edward Ullman noted that some cities have several centers or nuclei (Harris and Ullman 1945; Ullman and Harris 1970). As shown in segment C of Figure 20.10, each nucleus is the focus of some specialized activity. A familiar example is the clustering of fast-food restaurants in one area and automobile dealerships in another. Sometimes similar activities are grouped together because they profit from cohesion; retail districts, for example, draw more customers if there are more stores. Other clustering occurs because some activities, such as factories and expensive homes, are incompatible

invasion–succession cycle: the process of one group of people displacing a group whose racial-ethnic or social class characteristics differ from their own

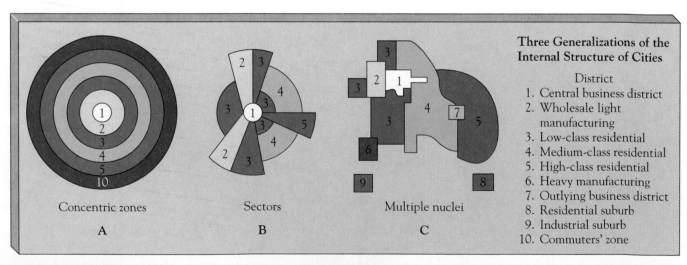

Three Generalizations of the Internal Structure of Cities

District
1. Central business district
2. Wholesale light manufacturing
3. Low-class residential
4. Medium-class residential
5. High-class residential
6. Heavy manufacturing
7. Outlying business district
8. Residential suburb
9. Industrial suburb
10. Commuters' zone

Concentric zones — A

Sectors — B

Multiple nuclei — C

Source: Cousins and Nagpaul, *Urban Man and Society,* 1970 McGraw-Hill, Inc.

Figure 20.10

Models of Urban Growth

with one another. Thus, push–pull factors separate areas by activities, and services are not evenly spread throughout an urban area.

Critique of the Models

Cities are complex, and no single model does justice to their complexity. Medieval cities looked quite different from modern cities, and cities in the Second and Third Worlds do not necessarily follow these North American models. For example, a common pattern in Latin America, striking to the North American visitor, is for the wealthy to stake a claim to the inner city, where fine restaurants and other services are readily accessible. Luxurious homes and gardens are tucked behind walls, protecting the rich from public scrutiny. For their part, the poor, especially rural migrants, settle unclaimed, fringe areas outside the city, as discussed in the Perspectives box below. Neither do the models make allowance for the extent to which elites influence the development of cities. Some individuals and groups, much more powerful than others, operate singly and in coalitions to promote policies that push a city's growth in a direction that suits them (Molotch 1976; Orum 1988; Feagin and Parker 1990).

▼▲

Perspectives

CULTURAL DIVERSITY AROUND THE WORLD

Urbanization in the Third World

IMAGES OF THE THIRD WORLD that portray quiet pastoral scenes distort today's reality. In the nonindustrialized nations, poor rural people have flocked to the cities in such numbers that, as we saw in Table 20.2, the Third World now contains most of the world's largest cities. Unlike the First World where industrialization generally preceded urbanization, the Third World's vast urbanization is *preceding* industrialization. Their limited technology makes it difficult to support these mushrooming urban populations.

When rural migrants and immigrants move to U.S. cities, they usually settle in the low-rent districts, mostly deteriorating housing located near the city's center. The wealthy reside in exclusive suburbs and in luxurious city enclaves. In contrast, Third World migrants settle in illegal squatter settlements outside the city. There, they build shacks from scrap boards, cardboard, and bits of corrugated metal. Even flattened tin cans are considered valuable building material. These squatters enjoy no city facilities—roads, transportation lines, water, sewers, or garbage pickup. After thousands of squatters settle in an area, bus lines are added, and the city acknowledges their de facto right to live there and eventually runs a water line to the area. Several hundred people then enjoy the use of one spigot. About four *million* of Mexico City's inhabitants live in such conditions.

Reflecting on conditions in its cities, India's leading news magazine published the following report.

[The city is] heading for a total breakdown. The endless stream of migrants pour in, turning metropolises into giant slums. A third of

the urban population lives in ramshackle huts with gunny sacks as doors and pavements for toilets. Another half of the populace is squeezed into one-room tenements or lives in monotonous rows of multi-storeyed flats. (Singh 1988)

Why is this vast rush to Third World cities occurring? At its core, it represents a breakdown of the rural way of life. These countries are caught in the second leg of the demographic transition—low death rates and high birthrates—and the rural populations are multiplying. Consequently, there is no longer enough land to divide up among descendants. Recall the poor Mexican peasant preparing to migrate illegally to the United States as recounted in the Down-to-Earth Sociology box on page 335. No longer does rural life hold the key to people's well-being. In addition, as discussed in this chapter, there are the pull factors—from jobs, education, and better housing to a more stimulating life.

Will Third World cities satisfy the people's longing for a better life? As miserable as life for the poor is in these cities, for many it is apparently an improvement over what they left behind. If not, they would flee the city to return to pastoral pleasures. If the Anti-Malthusians are right, this second stage of the demographic transition will come to an end, the populations of the Third World will stabilize—and so will both rural and urban life. In the meantime, however, the Third World cannot catch up with its population explosion—or its urban growth.

Sources: Based on Palen 1987; Singh 1988; Huth 1990; Kasarda and Crenshaw 1991.

Experiencing the City

Cities are intended to be solutions to problems. They are human endeavors to improve life collectively, to develop a way of life that transcends the limitations of farm and village. Cities hold out the hope of gaining employment, education, and other advantages. The perception of such opportunities underlies mass migration to cities throughout the world (Brueckner 1990; Huth 1990; Kasarda and Crenshaw 1991).

Just as cities provide opportunities, however, they also create problems. Humans not only have physical needs—food, shelter, and safety—but also a need for **community,** a feeling of belonging—the sense that others care what happens to you, and that you can depend on the people around you. Some people find this sense of community in the city; others find only its opposite, *alienation*, a sense of not belonging, and a feeling that no one cares what happens to you. Still others live in isolation and fear.

Alienation

> Twenty-eight-year-old Catherine Genovese, who was called Kitty by almost everyone in the Queens neighborhood, was returning home from work. After she had parked her car, a man grabbed her. She screamed, "Oh my God, he stabbed me! Please help me! Please help me!"
>
> For more than half an hour, thirty-eight respectable, law-abiding citizens looked out their windows and watched as the killer stalked and stabbed Kitty in three separate attacks. Twice the sudden glow from their bedroom lights interrupted him and frightened him off. Each time he returned, sought her out, and stabbed her again. Not one person telephoned the police during the assault. (*New York Times*, March 26, 1964)

When the police interviewed them, some witnesses said, "I didn't want to get involved." Others said, "We thought it was a lovers' quarrel." Some simply said, "I don't know." People throughout the country were shocked. It was as though Americans awoke one morning to find out that the country had changed overnight. They took this event as a sign that people could no longer trust one another, that the city was a cold, forbidding place.

Why should the city be alienating? In a classic essay, "Urbanism as a Way of Life," sociologist Louis Wirth (1938) argued that the city undermines kinship and neighborhood, which are the traditional bases of social control and social solidarity. Urban dwellers live in anonymity, he pointed out, their lives marked by segmented and superficial encounters. This causes them to grow aloof from one another and indifferent to other people's problems—as did the neighbors of Kitty Genovese. In short, the very sense of personal freedom that the city provides comes at the cost of alienation.

Wirth built on some of the ideas discussed on pages 102–103. *Gemeinschaft*, the sense of community that comes from everyone knowing everyone else, is ripped apart as a country industrializes. A new society emerges, characterized by *Gesellschaft*, secondary, impersonal relationships. The end result can be alienation so deep that people can sit by while someone else is being murdered. People lack identification with one another and develop the attitude, "It's simply none of *my* business."

Community

Such attitudes, however, do not do justice to the city. The city is more than a mosaic of strangers who feel disconnected and distrustful of one another. It is also made up of a series of smaller worlds, within which many people develop a sense of community or belonging (Bell and Boat 1970; Keans 1991). Some sociologists use the term *urban village* to refer to an area of the city that people know well and in which they live, work, shop, and play (Leinberger and Lockwood 1986). Even the run-down areas of a city, commonly called "slums," can provide a sense of belonging. In a classic study, sociologist Herbert Gans (1962) made the following observations.

community: a place people identify with, where they sense that they belong and that others care what happens to them

After a few weeks of living in the West End (of Boston), my observations—and my perceptions of the area—changed drastically. The search for an apartment quickly indicated that the individual units were usually in much better condition than the outside or the hallways of the buildings. Subsequently, in wandering through the West End, and in using it as a resident, I developed a kind of selective perception, in which my eye focused only on those parts of the area that were actually being used by people. Vacant buildings and boarded-up stores were no longer so visible, and the totally deserted alleys or streets were outside the set of paths normally traversed, either by myself or by the West Enders. . . .

Since much of the area's life took place on the street, faces became familiar very quickly. I met my neighbors on the stairs and in front of my building. And, once a shopping pattern developed, I saw the same storekeepers frequently, as well as the area's "characters" who wandered through the streets every day on a fairly regular route and schedule. In short, the exotic quality of the stores and the residents also wore off as I became used to seeing them.

Living in the West End, Gans gained an insider's perspective. He found that in spite of its narrow streets, substandard buildings, and even piled-up garbage, most West Enders had chosen to live there, for to them *the West End was a low-rent district, not a slum*. Gans had located a community in the West End, discovering that its residents visited back and forth with relatives and were involved in extensive networks of friendships and acquaintances. Gans therefore titled his book *The Urban Villagers* (1962). These residents were extremely upset when well-intentioned urban planners embarked on an urban renewal scheme to get rid of the "slum." And their distrust proved well founded, for the result of the gleaming new buildings was that people with more money took over the area. Its former residents were dispossessed, and their intimate patterns destroyed.

The city dwellers whom Gans identified as ethnic villagers find community in the city. Living in tightly-knit neighborhoods, they know many other residents. Some first-generation immigrants have even come from the same village in the "old country."

Types of Urban Dwellers

Whether you find alienation or community in the city largely depends on who you are, for the city offers both. People from different backgrounds experience the city differently. In what has become a classic analysis, Gans (1962, 1968, 1970) identified five different types of people who live in the city. The first three types live in the city by choice, for they find a sense of community.

The Cosmopolites The cosmopolites are the city's students, intellectuals, professionals, artists, and entertainers. They have been drawn to the city because of its conveniences and cultural benefits.

The Singles Young, unmarried people come to the city seeking jobs and entertainment. Businesses and services such as singles bars, singles apartment complexes, and computer dating have sprung up to cater to their needs. Their stay in the city reflects a particular stage in their life course. Few put down community roots, and most will move to the suburbs after they marry.

The Ethnic Villagers These people live in tightly knit neighborhoods that resemble villages and small towns. United by race–ethnicity and social class, their neighborhoods are far from depersonalized or disorganized. Family- and peer-oriented, the ethnic villagers try to isolate themselves from what they view as the harmful effects of city life.

Although an occasional individual from these first three groups is alienated, most of the city's alienated come from the next two types. Outcasts of industrial society, with little choice about where they live, they are always skirting the edge of disaster.

The Deprived City inhabitants in this category live in neighborhoods more like urban jungles than urban villages. Consisting of the very poor, the emotionally disturbed, and the handicapped, this group represents the bottom of society in terms of income, education, social status, and work skills. Some of them stalk their jungle in search of prey, their victims usually deprived persons like themselves. Their future holds little chance for anything better in life, either for themselves or their children.

The Trapped   The trapped can find no escape either. They consist of four subtypes: (1) those who could not afford to move when their neighborhood was "invaded" by another ethnic group; (2) "downwardly mobile" people who have fallen from a higher social class; (3) elderly people who have drifted into the slums because they are not wanted elsewhere and are powerless to prevent their downward slide; and (4) alcoholics and other drug addicts. Like the deprived, the trapped also suffer high rates of assault, mugging, robbery, and rape.

Gans's typology illustrates that not all urban dwellers experience the city in the same way. Recall the observations I reported on San Francisco. Some find the streets a stimulating source of cultural contrasts. For others, however, the same events pose a constant threat as they try to survive in what for them amounts to an urban jungle.

Urban Sentiment: Finding a Familiar World

Sociologists note that *the city is divided into little worlds* that people come to know down to their smallest details. Gregory Stone (1954) and Herbert Gans (1970) observed how city people create a sense of intimacy for themselves by *personalizing* their shopping. By frequenting the same stores, they become recognized as "regulars," and after a period of time customers and clerks greet each other by name. Particular taverns, restaurants, laundromats, and shops are more than just buildings in which to purchase items and services. They are meeting places where neighborhood residents build social relationships with one another and share informal news about the community.

Spectator sports also help urban dwellers find a familiar world in the city (Hudson 1991). When the Cardinals won the World Series, for example, the entire St. Louis metropolitan area celebrated the victory of "our" team—even though less than one in seven of the area's 2.5 million people live in the city. Sociologists David Karp and William Yoels (1990) note that such identification is so intense that long after moving to other parts of the country many people maintain an emotional allegiance to the sports teams of the city in which they grew up.

As sociologists Richard Wohl and Anselm Strauss (1958) pointed out, city dwellers also develop strong feelings for particular objects and locations in the city, such as trees, buildings, rivers, lakes, parks, and even street corners. In some cases objects become a type of logo that represents the city:

> We need only show persons New York's skyline, or San Francisco's Golden Gate Bridge, or New Orleans's French Quarter, and the city will be quickly identified by most. For those who live in these respective cities, such objects and places do not merely identify the city; they are also sources for personal identification *with* the city. (Karp et al. 1991, italics added)

Urban Networks

Think of the city as a series of overlapping circles. Each circle consists of one person and everyone in the city that that person knows. As you draw those circles, eventually everyone in the entire city is included in several overlapping circles, with the exception of a few loners and persons who have just moved into the city. These linkages unite people into social relationships, where, ultimately, community is found in the city—not in buildings and space, but in relationships. Regardless of where they live in the city, then, people who are not integrated into social networks are likely to find alienation, while those who are integrated are likely to find community.

Urban Overload

Whether male or female, urban dwellers are careful to protect themselves from unwanted intrusions from strangers. They follow a *norm of noninvolvement* as they traverse everyday life in the city, trying to avoid encounters with people they do not know.

> To do this, we sometimes use props such as newspapers to shield ourselves from others and to indicate our inaccessibility for interaction. In effect, we learn to "tune others out." In this regard, we might see the Walkman as the quintessential urban prop in that it allows us to be tuned in and tuned out at the same time. It is a device that allows us to enter our own private world and thereby effectively to close off encounters with others. The use of such devices to protect our "personal space," along with our body demeanor and facial expression (the passive "mask" or even scowl that persons adopt on subways) ensures that others will not bother us. One of the chief claims or rights that urban persons maintain in public places is the right to be left alone. In most instances people respect that right and behave mutually in a fashion to sustain it. (Karp et al. 1991)

Similarly, urban dwellers use a variety of filters to reduce overload. To prevent unwanted stimuli from reaching them, they use unlisted telephone numbers, telephone answering machines (to screen calls), apartment house doormen, post office boxes (to avoid revealing home addresses), as well as a series of locks—on cars, gates, houses, and mailboxes. Mace and burglar alarms can also be classified as filters. Giving and preventing access also differs sharply by gender, as discussed in the Down-to-Earth Sociology box below.

▼▲▼▲▼▲▼▲▼▲▼▲▼▲▼▲▼▲▼▲▼▲▼▲▼▲▼▲▼▲▼▲▼▲▼▲

Down-To-Earth Sociology

Giving and Concealing Access Information—
The Contrasting Perspectives of Females and Males

JUST AS URBANITES TRY to prevent anonymity, so they also try to preserve it. Males and females are especially different in this regard. Sociologist Carol Gardner (1988) spent eighteen months in Santa Fe, New Mexico, observing men and women interacting in public places. She found that single women who meet attractive male strangers face a dilemma: They may wish to give *access information,* information that will allow them to meet in the future, yet they fear that this might lead to harassment, obscene telephone calls, or even rape. They assess the risk and give information accordingly. Interestingly, the *place* is important, for Gardner reports that women see less risk in giving access information in stores and restaurants than in bars and bar-cafes. Giving a telephone number is also seen as less dangerous than giving a name and address. But even here, women perceive the risk of harassing or obscene phone calls.

Common tactics women employ to keep men at arm's length are to give only their first name, to use a false name (sometimes an outrageous one), to give a wrong telephone number (perhaps the number for "Dial-a-Prayer" or the local rape crisis center), or to say that they are married, even though they are not. If a man in whom a woman has no interest asks her name, she may reply, "*Mrs.* Westbrook," with the emphasis on the "Mrs." As some men have found to their dismay, a woman may even give another woman's name and the telephone number of *her* boyfriend.

Men, in contrast, see no danger in meeting female strangers. Unlike women, who are "not supposed to" strike up acquaintances with strangers, men are given society's blessing to initiate such encounters (Gardner 1988). The man's approach is to "size up" the situation—to determine that a woman is available—and then to try to get access information from her. Apparently unable to take her perspective, men see a woman's reluctance to give access information as a sign of coyness or false modesty.

Because their perceptions of danger differ so sharply, men and women live city life very differently. In short, although they use the same urban facilities, men experience much more freedom in the city.

Diffusion of Responsibility

The norm of noninvolvement helps to explain what happened to Kitty Genovese, whose story was recounted on page 576. That troubling case disturbed social psychologists John Darley and Bibb Latané (1970), who ran the series of experiments featured in Chapter 6, pages 158–159. As you may recall, they found that the *more* bystanders there are, the *less* likely people are to help. People's sense of responsibility becomes diffused, with each person assuming that *another* will do the responsible thing, "With these other people here, it is not *my* responsibility," they reason.

The norm of noninvolvement and the diffusion of responsibility help explain the response to Kitty Genovese's murder. The bystanders at her death were *not* uncaring, alienated people. They *did* care that a woman was being attacked. They were simply abiding by an urban norm—one helpful in getting them through everyday city life, but, unfortunately, dysfunctional in some critical situations.

The Decline of the City

The poverty, decay, and general decline of U.S. cities are among the primary problems of urban life today. Let's examine underlying reasons for these conditions and consider how to develop social policy to solve urban problems and improve our quality of life.

Suburbanization

On Suburbs and Ghettos   Suburbanization, which refers to people moving from cities to **suburbs,** the communities located just outside a city, is not new. The dream of a place of one's own with green grass, a few trees, and kids playing in the yard was not discovered by this generation (Riesman 1970). For the past hundred years or so, as transportation became more efficient, especially with the development of automobiles, people have moved to towns next to the cities in which they worked. Minorities joined this movement about 1970. The extent to which people have left the city in search of their dreams is remarkable. In 1957, only 37 million Americans lived in the suburbs (Karp et al. 1991), but today about as many Americans live in the suburbs as in the cities.

The city has been the loser in this transition. As people moved out of the city, businesses and jobs followed, shrinking the city's tax base. The resulting budget squeeze not only affected parks, zoos, libraries, and museums, but even the city's basic services— its schools, streets, sewer and water systems, and police and fire departments.

suburbanization: the movement from the city to the suburbs

suburb: the communities adjacent to the political boundaries of a city

Can you identify the city in which this photo was taken? Conditions in U.S. cities have deteriorated so badly that, unfortunately, this photo could have been taken in almost any large U.S. city.

As this shift in population and resources occurred, left behind were the people who had no choice but to stay in the city. The net result, says sociologist William Wilson, who has written extensively on cities, racism, and poverty, was the transformation of the inner city into a ghetto. Left behind were the highly disadvantaged

> families that have experienced long-term spells of poverty and/or welfare dependency, individuals who lack training and skills and have either experienced periods of persistent unemployment or have dropped out of the labor force altogether, and individuals who are frequently involved in street criminal activity. The term ghetto . . . suggests that a fundamental social transformation has taken place . . . that groups represented by this term are collectively different from and much more socially isolated from those that lived in these communities in earlier years. (quoted in Karp et al. 1991)

Barriers to Mutual Identification: City Versus Suburb   Having made the move out of the city, suburbanites prefer the city to keep its problems to itself. They fight movements to share suburbia's revenues with the city and oppose measures that would allow urban and suburban governments joint control over what has become a contiguous mass of people and businesses. Suburban leaders generally see it as in their best interests to remain politically, economically, and socially separate from their nearby city. They do not mind coming into the city to work, or venturing there on weekends for the diversions it offers, but they do not want to help shoulder the city's burdens.

It is likely that the mounting bill will ultimately come due, however, and that suburbanites will eventually have to pay for their uncaring attitude toward the urban disadvantaged. Karp et al. (1991) put it this way.

> It may be that suburbs can insulate themselves from the problems of central cities, at least for the time being. In the long run, though, there will be a steep price to pay for the failure of those better off to care compassionately for those at the bottom of society.

It may be that the L.A. riots were part of that bill—perhaps just the down payment.

Disinvestment

Already by the 1940s, the movement out of cities to suburbs had begun to undermine the cities' tax base, a problem only accelerated as poor rural migrants, mostly African American, moved in huge numbers to northern cities (Lemann 1994). As the tax base eroded, services declined—from garbage pickup to quality education. Buildings deteriorated, and banks began **redlining:** Afraid of loans going bad, banks drew a line on a map around a problem area and refused to make loans for housing or businesses there. The **disinvestment,** withdrawal of investment, pushed these areas into further decline. Not unconnected, youth gangs, murders, and robberies are high in these areas, while education, employment, and income are low.

Deindustrialization and Globalization

The development of a global market has also left a heavy imprint on U.S. cities. As sociologist Victor Rodríguez (1994) points out, to compete in the global market many U.S. industries have abandoned local communities and located their manufacturing processes in places where costs of production are lower. Although this makes U.S. industries more competitive, it also has eliminated hundreds of thousands of manufacturing jobs, locking many poor people out of the postindustrial economy that is engulfing the United States. Left behind in the inner cities, many live in despair as a distant economy charges into the uncharted waters of a brave new world without them.

Social Policy: Failure and Potential

The Failure   Social policy usually takes one of two forms. The first is to tear down and rebuild in the fancifully named effort called **urban renewal.** The result is the renewal of an area—but not for its inhabitants. Stadiums, high-rise condos, luxury hotels, and

redlining: the officers of a financial institution deciding not to make loans in a particular area

disinvestment: the withdrawal of investments by financial institutions, which seals the fate of an urban area

urban renewal: the rehabilitation of a rundown area, which usually results in the displacement of the poor who are living in that area

expensive shops are built. Outpriced, the area's inhabitants, are displaced. They flow into adjacent areas, adding to their problems. The second is some sort of **enterprise zone,** economic incentives such as reduced taxes to encourage businesses to move into the area. Although the intention is good, failure is the result. Most businesses refuse to locate in high-crime areas. Those that do may find that the costs of additional security run higher than the tax savings. If workers are hired from the problem area, and the jobs pay a decent wage, which most do not, the workers move to better neighborhoods, frustrating the purpose of establishing an enterprise zone (Lemann 1994). After all, who chooses to live with the fear of violence?

The Potential: An Urban Manhattan Project   In spite of the problems facing U.S. cities—problems so severe that they are discussed not only around dinner tables in New York and Los Angeles, but also in Tokyo and London—government policies remain uncoordinated and ineffective (Flanagan 1990; Lemann 1994).

A "nothing works" mentality will solve nothing. U.S. cities can be revitalized and made into safe and decent places to live. There is nothing in their nature that turns cities into dangerous, deteriorating slums. Most cities of Europe, for example, are both safe and pleasant. If U.S. cities are to change, they must become top agenda items of the U.S. government, with adequate resources in terms of money and human talents focused on overcoming urban woes.

Granted the deplorable condition of many U.S. cities, and the flight of the middle classes—both whites and minorities—to greener pastures, an urban Manhattan Project seems in order. During World War II the United States and the Allies faced a triumphant Hitler in Europe and Tojo in Asia. The United States gathered its top scientific minds, gave them all the resources they needed, and produced the atomic bomb. Today, a similar gathering of top social scientists and similar resources may be required to triumph over urban ills.

Guiding Principles   Sociologist William Flanagan (1990) suggests three guiding principles for working out specific solutions to our pressing problems:

- *Scale.* Regional and national planning is necessary. Currently, the many local jurisdictions, with their many rivalries, competing goals, and limited resources, lead to a hodgepodge of mostly unworkable solutions.

- *Livability.* Growth needs to be channeled in such a way that cities are appealing and meet human needs, especially the need of community discussed earlier. This will attract the middle classes into the city and increase the tax base. In turn, this will help finance the services that make the city more livable.

- *Social justice.* In the final analysis, social policy must be evaluated by its effects on people. "Urban renewal," for example, that displaces the poor for the benefit of the middle class and wealthy does not pass this standard. The same would apply to solutions that create "livability" but do not make the poor and the homeless beneficiaries of urban policy.

Unless the *root* causes of urban problems are addressed—housing, education, and jobs—solutions, at best, will be only Band-Aids that cover up problems, or, at worst, window dressing for politicians who want to *appear* as though they are doing something about the problems that affect our quality of life.

enterprise zone: the use of economic incentives in a designated area with the intention of encouraging investment there

Summary and Review

The Specter of Overpopulation

What debate did Thomas Malthus initiate?

In 1798, Thomas Malthus analysed the surge in Europe's population. His conclusion, called the **Malthus theorem,** was that because the population grows geometrically but food only arithmetically, the world will outstrip its food supply. The debate between today's New Malthusians and those who disagree, the Anti-Malthusians, continues. Pp. 552–556.

Why is there starvation?

Starvation is not due to a lack of food in the world, for there now is more food for each person in the entire world than there was fifty years ago, but to a maldistribution of food. Pp. 556–557.

Population Growth

Why do the poor nations have so many children?

The role of children is different. In the Third World, children are generally viewed as gifts from God, cost little to rear, and represent the parents' social security. Pp. 558–559.

What are the three demographic variables?

To compute population growth, demographers use **fertility, mortality,** and **migration.** The **basic demographic equation** is births – deaths + net migration = growth rate. Pp. 560–562.

Why is forecasting population difficult?

A nation's growth rate is affected by unanticipated variables—from economic conditions, wars, plagues, and famines to government policies and industrialization. Pp. 562–565.

What population challenges do we face today?

The population explosion is occurring in those nations that have the least wealth and technology. The challenge is how to use the First World's technology to help the Third World avoid starvation and resource depletion. Pp. 565–566.

The City in History

What is the relationship of cities to farming?

Cities can develop only if there is a large agricultural surplus, which frees people from food production. The primary impetus to the development of cities was the invention of the plow about five or six thousand years ago. Pp. 566–568.

How did the Industrial Revolution affect the size of cities?

Almost without exception, throughout history cities have been small. After the Industrial Revolution stimulated mechanical transportation and communication, the infrastructure on which modern cities depend, cities grew quickly and much larger. Pp. 568–569.

What are metropolises and megalopolises?

Urbanization is so extensive that some cities have become **metropolises,** dominating the area adjacent to them, and the area of influence of some metropolises has merged, forming a **megalopolis.** Pp. 569–570.

What are some major trends in U.S. urbanization?

Two trends are **gentrification,** and migration from the North and East to the South and the West. Pp. 571–573.

Models of Urban Growth

What models of urban growth have been proposed?

The primary models are concentric-zone model, a sector model, and a multiple–nuclei model. Pp. 573–575.

Experiencing the City

Is the city inherently alienating?

Some people do experience alienation in the city, but others find community in it. What people find depends largely on their background and urban networks. Herbert Gans identified five major types of people who live in cities: cosmopolites, singles, ethnic villagers, the deprived, and the trapped, indicating the great variety of people who make up city life. Pp. 576–580.

The Decline of the City

Why have U.S. cities declined?

Three primary reasons for their decline are **suburbanization,** (as people moved to the suburbs, the tax base of cities eroded, and services deteriorated), **disinvestment** (financial institutions withdrawing their financing), and **deindustrialization** (which has caused a loss of jobs). Pp. 580–581.

What social policy can salvage U.S. cities?

Although the particulars of that policy are unknown, a Manhattan Project on Urban Problems could likely produce workable solutions. Three guiding principles for developing social policy are scale, livability, and social justice. Pp. 581–582.

Where can I read more on this topic?

Suggested readings for this chapter are listed on page 644.

Diego Rivera, Parade in Moscow, 1956

Collective Behavior
and Social Movements

*T*HE NEWS SPREAD LIKE WILDFIRE. *A police officer had been killed. In just twenty minutes, the white population was armed and heading for the cabin. Men and mere boys, some not more than 12 years old, carried rifles, shotguns, and pistols.*

The mob, now about four hundred, surrounded the log cabin. Tying a rope around the man's neck, they dragged him to the center of town. While the men argued about the best way to kill him, the women and children looked on. Some yelled to hang him, others to burn him alive.

Someone pulled a large wooden box out of a store and placed it in the center of the street. Others filled it with straw. Then they lifted the man, the rope still around his neck, and shoved him head first into the box. One of the men poured oil over him. Another lit a match.

As the flames shot upward, the man managed to lift himself out of the box, his body a mass of flames. Trying to shield his face and eyes from the fire, he ran the length of the rope, about twenty feet, when someone yelled, "Shoot!" In an instant, dozens of shots rang out. Men and boys walked to the lifeless body and emptied their guns into it.

They dragged the man's body back to the burning box, then piled on more boxes from the stores, and poured oil over them. Each time someone threw more oil onto the flames, the crowd broke into shouts.

Standing about seventy-five feet away, I could smell the poor man's burning flesh. No one tried to hide their identity. I could clearly see town officials help in the burning. The inquest, dutifully held by the coroner, concluded that the man met death "at the hands of an enraged mob unknown to the jury." What else could he conclude? Any jury from this town would include men who had participated in the man's death.

They dug a little hole at the edge of the street, and dumped in it the man's ashes and what was left of his body.

The man's name was Sam Pettie, known by everybody to be quiet and unoffensive. I can't mention my name. If I did, I would be committing suicide.

(Based on a May 1914 letter to *The Crisis*)

Collective Behavior

Why did the people in this little town "go mad"? These men—and the women who watched in agreement—were ordinary, law-abiding citizens. Even some of the "pillars of the community" joined in the vicious killing of Sam Pettie, who may have been innocent.

Lynching is a form of **collective behavior,** a group of people bypassing the usual norms that guide their behavior and doing something unusual (Turner and Killian 1987; Lofland 1993). Collective behavior is a very broad term, for it includes not only such violent acts as lynchings and riots, but also panics, rumors, fads, and fashions. Before examining its specific forms, let us look at theories that seek to explain collective behavior.

Early Explanations: The Transformation of the Individual

collective behavior: extraordinary activities carried out by groups of people; includes lynchings, rumors, panics, urban legends, and fads and fashions

When people can't figure something out, they often resort to some form of "madness" as an explanation. People are apt to say, "She went 'off her rocker'; that's why she drove her car off the bridge." "He must have 'gone nuts,' or he wouldn't have shot into the crowd." Early explanations of mobs were not far from such assumptions. The behavior seemed so bizarre that it could be accounted for only by something bizarre within people. Let's look at how these ideas developed.

Contemporary sociologists analyze collective behavior as rational behavior; that is, the group is seen as utilizing accessible means to reach a goal, even though that goal may be barbaric, as in this photo of a lynching in Rayston, Georgia, on April 28, 1936. Earlier in the day, the 40-year-old victim, Lint Shaw, accused of attacking a white girl, had been rescued from a mob by National Guardsmen. After the National Guard left, the mob forced their way into the jail.

Charles Mackay, Gustave LeBon, and Robert Park: How the Crowd Transforms the Individual

The field of collective behavior began when Charles Mackay (1814–1889), a British journalist, noticed that "country folks," who ordinarily are reasonable sorts of people, sometimes "went mad" and did "disgraceful and violent things" when they got in a crowd. The best explanation Mackay (1841) could come up with was that people had a "herd mentality"—they were like a herd of cows that suddenly stampede.

About fifty years later, Gustave LeBon (1841–1931), a French psychologist, built on this initial idea. In an 1895 book, LeBon stressed how crowds make people feel anonymous, as though they are not accountable for what they do. In a crowd, people even develop feelings of invincibility, and come to think that they can do almost anything. A **collective mind** develops, he said, and people are swept up with almost any suggestion. Then contagion, something like mass hypnosis, takes over, releasing the destructive instincts that society has so carefully repressed.

Robert Park (1864–1944), an American sociologist who studied in Germany and wrote a 1904 dissertation on the crowd, was greatly influenced by LeBon (McPhail 1991). After Park joined the faculty at the University of Chicago, he added the ideas of social unrest and circular reaction. He said,

> Social unrest . . . is transmitted from one individual to another . . . so that the manifestations of discontent in A (are) communicated to B, and from B reflected back to A. (Park and Burgess 1921)

Park used the term **circular reaction** to refer to this back-and-forth communication. Circular reaction, he said, creates a "collective impulse" that comes to "dominate all members of the crowd." If "collective impulse" sounds just like LeBon's "collective mind," that's because it really is. As noted, Park was heavily influenced by LeBon, and his slightly different term did not change the basic idea at all.

collective mind: Gustave LeBon's term for the tendency of people in a crowd to feel, think, and act in extraordinary ways

circular reaction: Robert Park's term for a back-and-forth communication between the members of a crowd whereby a "collective impulse" is transmitted

Figure 21.1

Blumer's Model of How an Acting Crowd Develops

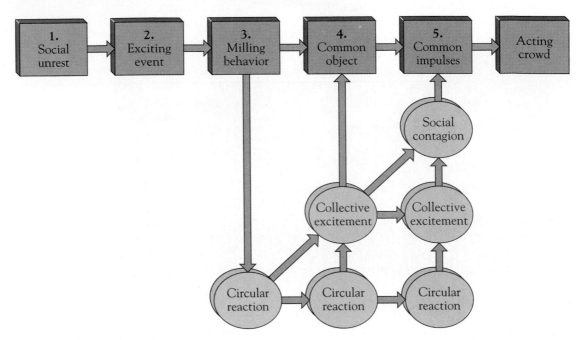

Source: Based on McPhail 1991: 11.

Herbert Blumer: The Acting Crowd

Herbert Blumer (1900–1987), who studied under Park, synthesized LeBon's and Park's ideas. As you can see from Figure 21.1, Blumer (1939) identified five stages that preceded what he called an **acting crowd,** an excited group that moves toward a goal. As we examine his model, which still dominates today's police manuals on crowd behavior (McPhail 1989), let's apply it to the lynching of Sam Pettie.

1 *Social unrest.* At the root of collective behavior is a background condition of social unrest. Disturbed about some condition of society, people are restless, apprehensive, and vulnerable to rumors and suggestions. When Sam Pettie was lynched, it was during the early 1900s when traditional southern life was undergoing upheaval. Due to industrialization, millions of Americans were moving to where the jobs were, from farm to city and from South to North. Left behind were many poor, rural southerners, white and black, who faced a bleak future. In addition, African Americans were questioning the legitimacy of their low status and deprivation.

2 *Exciting event.* An exciting event occurs, one so startling that people become preoccupied with it. In this instance, that event was the killing of a police officer.

3 *Milling.* Next comes **milling,** people standing or walking around, talking about the exciting event. A circular reaction then sets in. That is, as people pick up cues to the "right" way of thinking and feeling, they reinforce them in one another. During the short period in which Sam Pettie's lynch mob milled, the inhabitants of this small town became increasingly agitated as they discussed the officer's death.

4 *A common object of attention.* In this stage, people's attention becomes riveted on some aspect of the event. They get caught up in the collective excitement. In this case, people's attention turned to Sam Pettie. Someone may have said that he had been talking to the officer or that they had been arguing.

acting crowd: Herbert Blumer's term for an excited group that collectively moves toward a goal

milling: a crowd standing or walking around as they talk excitedly about some event

5 *Common impulses.* A sense of collective agreement about what should be done emerges. What stimulates these common impulses is *social contagion,* the collective excitement that is passed from one person to another. In this instance, people concluded that the killer had to be punished, and that only an immediate, public death would be adequate vengeance—as well as a powerful warning for other African Americans who might even think about getting "out of line."

The objective of acting crowds can be positive, such as an attempt to free a political prisoner, or as negative as the event just recounted. Acting crowds include not only lynch mobs but also people engaged in riots, food fights, mutinies, picketing, and sit-ins.

The Contemporary View: The Rationality of the Crowd

If we were to witness a lynching—or a screaming mob or a prison riot—most of us probably would agree with LeBon that some sort of "madness" had swept over the crowd. Sociologists today, however, point out that crowds are actually quite rational. By this, they mean that crowds take deliberate steps to reach some desired goal. As sociologist Clark McPhail (1991) points out, even a lynch mob is cooperative—someone gets the rope while others hold the victim, some tie the knot, and others hoist the body.

Richard Berk: The Minimax Strategy

A general principle of human behavior is that we try to minimize our costs and maximize our rewards. Sociologist Richard Berk (1974) calls this a **minimax strategy.** The fewer costs and the more rewards that we anticipate from some act, the more likely we are to do it. For example, if we believe that others will approve an act, a high reward, the likelihood that we will do that act increases. Whether it is yelling for the referee's blood at a bad call in football, or shouting for real blood as a member of a lynch mob, this principle applies. In short, whether people are in small groups or in crowds, the principles of human behavior remain the same.

Ralph Turner and Lewis Killian: Emergent Norm Theory

Since collective behavior always involves something unusual, however, it seems that something besides the usual norms of behavior are involved. Sociologists Ralph Turner and Lewis Killian get at the heart of this matter. They point out that life usually goes much as we expect, and our usual norms are adequate. When an extraordinary event disrupts our usual ways of doing things, however, our ordinary norms may not cover the new situation. People then develop *new* norms to deal with the problem. Sometimes they even produce new definitions of right and wrong that *under the new circumstances* justify actions that they themselves would otherwise consider immoral. Turner and Killian (1987) use the term **emergent norms** to describe this change.

To understand how new norms emerge, we first should note that not all members of a crowd share the same emotions and attitudes (Snow et al. 1993; Rodríguez 1994). Turner and Killian (1987) identify five kinds of crowd participants.

1 The *ego-involved* feel a high personal stake in the extraordinary event.

2 The *concerned* have a personal interest in the event, but less so than the ego-involved.

3 The *insecure* care little about the issue. They join the crowd because it gives them a sense of power and security.

4 The *curious spectators* also care little about the issue, but they are inquisitive about what is going on.

5 The *exploiters,* who also do not care about the event personally, use it for their own purposes, such as hawking food or T-shirts.

minimax strategy: Richard Berk's term for the effort people make to minimize their costs and maximize their rewards

emergent norms: Ralph Turner's and Lewis Killian's term for the development of new norms to cope with a new situation, especially among crowds

These five types of participants play different roles in the emergence of norms. The most significant role goes to the "ego-involved," who make suggestions about what should be done. If they act on these suggestions, the "concerned" help to set the crowd on a particular course of action. The "insecure" join in, and even the "curious spectators" may take part. The "exploiters," unlikely to interfere because they are concerned with other matters, lend the crowd passive support. If a common mood develops, new norms are likely to emerge. The particular activity—whether "mooning" the cops or cursing the college dean—is now "OK." As more and more people participate in the crowd's activities, the rest find it increasingly difficult to cling to their old norms.

The significance of Turner's and Killian's theory of emergent norms is that it points to a *rational* process as the essential component of collective behavior. Turner and Killian note, for example, that the crowd does not consider all suggestions made by the ego-involved to be equal: to be acceptable, a suggestion must match predispositions that the crowd already has. This analysis is a far cry from earlier interpretations that people were so transformed by a crowd that they went out of their minds.

Forms of Collective Behavior

Sociologists, then, treat collective behavior the same as other forms of behavior (Turner and Killian 1987; Lofland 1993; Turner 1993). They view it as ordinary people responding to extraordinary situations (Rodríguez 1994). They ask their usual questions about interaction such as: How do people influence one another? What is the significance of the members' age, gender, and social class? What role do pre-existing attitudes play? Just how do people's perceptions get translated into action?

In addition to lynchings, collective behavior includes riots, panics, moral panics, rumors, fads, fashions, and urban legends. Let's look at each.

Riots

The nation watched in horror. White Los Angeles police officers had been caught on videotape beating an African-American traffic violator with their nightsticks. The videotape clearly showed the officers savagely bringing their nightsticks down on a man prostrate at their feet. Television stations around the United States—and the world—broadcast the pictures to stunned audiences.

When the officers went on trial fourteen months later for the beating of the man identified as Rodney King, no one who had seen that videotape had any doubt that the men would be found guilty. With evidence so vivid and irrefutable, how could the verdict be anything but guilty? Yet in May 1992, a jury consisting of eleven whites and one Asian American found the officers innocent of using excessive force. The trial had been moved to Ventura County, California, because the defense attorneys claimed the accused could not get a fair trial in Los Angeles.

The result was a **riot**—violent crowd behavior aimed against people and property. Within minutes of the verdict, angry crowds began to gather in Los Angeles. That night, mobs set fire to businesses in South–Central Los Angeles, and looting and arson began in earnest. The rioting spread to other cities, including Atlanta, Georgia, Tampa, Florida, and even Madison, Wisconsin, and Las Vegas, Nevada. Whites and Koreans were favorite targets of violence.

Again Americans sat transfixed before their television sets as they saw parts of Los Angeles go up in flames and looters carrying television sets and lugging sofas in full view of the Los Angeles Police Department, which took no steps to stop them. Memorably seared into the American public's collective consciousness was the sight of Reginald Denny, a 36-year-old white truck driver who was pulled from his truck in the riot area. As he sat dazed in the street, one man hit him over the head with a hammer; then another man, laughing, knocked him senseless with a brick.

riot: violent crowd behavior aimed against people and property

The Los Angeles riot of 1992 was different only in the extent of its violence. This riot followed a familiar pattern, being set off by a precipitating event against a background of mounting frustrations. It was also a media event, as shown by these rioters posing for cameras in front of the Los Angeles Police Department.

On the third night, after four thousand fires had been set and more than thirty lives had been lost, President George Bush announced on national television that the U.S. Justice Department had appointed special prosecutors to investigate possible federal charges against the police officers for violating the civil rights of Rodney King. He then stated that he had ordered the Seventh Infantry, SWAT teams, and the FBI into Los Angeles. The president also federalized the California National Guard and placed it under the command of General Colin Powell, the African-

American chairman of the Joint Chiefs of Staff. Even Rodney King went on television and tearfully pleaded for peace.

The Los Angeles riot was the bloodiest in U.S. history. Before it was over, sixty people lost their lives, 2,300 people were injured, thousands of small businesses were burned, and about $750 million of property was destroyed. Two officers were later sentenced to 2 1/2 years in prison on federal charges, and King was awarded several million dollars in damages. (Associated Press April 30, 1992; May 1, 1992; May 2, 1992; Rose 1992; Stevens and Lubman 1992; Holden and Rose 1993)

Urban riots are usually caused by frustration and anger at deprivation. Frustrated at being kept out of mainstream society—limited to a meager education, denied jobs and justice, and kept out of good neighborhoods—frustration builds to such a boiling point that it takes only a precipitating event to erupt in collective violence. In the Los Angeles riot all these conditions existed, and the jury's verdict was the precipitating event.

Sociologists have found that it is not only the deprived, however, who participate in riots. After the assassination of Dr. Martin Luther King, Jr., in 1968, many U.S. cities erupted in riots, and even people with good jobs participated (McPhail 1991). In the L.A. riots, the first outbursts didn't come from the poorest neighborhoods but the most stable neighborhoods. Why would middle-class people participate in riots? The answer, says sociologist Victor Rodríguez (1994), is a sense of frustration that many minorities feel with being treated as second-class citizens even when they are gainfully employed and living stable lives.

In fact, the event that precipitates a riot is much less important than the riot's general context. The precipitating event is only the match that lights the fuel. The fuel is the area's background of unrest—a perceived sense of injustice that is being ignored or even condoned and encouraged by officials. It is this seething rage just underneath the surface that erupts following incidents such as the Rodney King verdict. Because this rage is felt by the poor and the unemployed and by those who are materially better off, both groups participate. In addition, there are opportunists—individuals who participate not out of rage, or even because they are particularly concerned about the precipitating event, but because the riot provides an opportunity for looting.

Panics

In 1938, on the night before Halloween, a radio program of dance music was interrupted with a report that explosions had been observed on the surface of Mars. The announcer breathlessly added that a cylinder of unknown origin had been discovered embedded in the ground on a farm in New Jersey. The radio station then switched to the farm, where an alarmed reporter gave details of horrible-looking Martians coming out of the cylinder. Their death-ray weapons had destructive powers unknown to humans. An interview with an astronomer confirmed that Martians had invaded the Earth.

Perhaps six million Americans heard this broadcast. About one million were frightened, and thousands panicked. Unknown numbers simply burst into tears, while thousands more grabbed weapons and hid in their basements or ran into the streets. Hundreds of others bundled up their families and jumped into their cars, jamming the roads as they headed to who knows where.

Of course, there was no invasion. This was simply a dramatization of H. G. Wells's *War of the Worlds*, starring Orson Welles. There had been an announcement at the beginning of the program and somewhere in the middle that the account was fictional, but apparently many people missed it. Although the panic reactions to this radio play may appear humorous to us, to anyone who is in a panic the situation is far from humorous. **Panic** is a behavior that results when people become so fearful that they cannot function normally, and may even flee.

Why did people panic? Psychologist Hadley Cantril (1941) attributed the result to widespread anxiety about world conditions. The Nazis were marching in Europe, and millions of Americans (correctly, as it turned out) were afraid that the United States would get involved. War jitters, he said, created fertile ground for the broadcast to touch off a panic.

Contemporary analysts, however, question whether there even was a panic. Sociologist William Bainbridge (1989) acknowledges that some people did become frightened, and that a few actually did get in their cars and drive like maniacs. But he says that most of this famous panic was an invention of the news media. Reporters found a good story and milked it, exaggerating as they went along.

Bainbridge points to a 1973 event in Sweden. To dramatize the dangers of atomic power, Swedish Radio broadcast a play about an accident at a nuclear power plant. Knowing about the 1938 broadcast in the United States, Swedish sociologists were waiting to see what would happen. Might some people fail to realize that it was a dramatization and panic at the threat of ruptured reactors spewing out radioactivity? The sociologists found no panic. A few people did become frightened. Some telephoned family members and the police; others shut windows to keep out the radioactivity—reasonable responses, considering what they thought had occurred.

The Swedish media, however, reported a panic! Apparently, a reporter had telephoned two police departments and learned that each had received calls from concerned citizens. With a deadline hanging over his head, the reporter decided to gamble. He reported that police and fire stations were jammed with citizens, that people were flocking to the shelters, and that others were fleeing south (Bainbridge 1989).

Panics do occur, of course—which is why nobody has the right to shout "Fire!" in a public building when no such danger exists—for if people fear immediate death, they will lunge toward the nearest exit in a frantic effort to escape. Such a panic occurred on Memorial Day weekend in 1977 at the Beverly Hills Supper Club, in Southgate, Kentucky. About half the 2,500 patrons were crowded into the Cabaret Room, awaiting the appearance of singer John Davidson. The fire, which began in a small banquet room near the front of the building, burned undetected until it was beyond control. When employees discovered the fire, they warned patrons. People began to exit in orderly fashion, but when flames rushed in the result was sheer panic. Patrons trampled one another in a furious attempt to reach the exits, which were immediately blocked by masses of screaming people simultaneously trying to push their way through. The writhing bodies at the exits created further panic among the remainder, who pushed even harder to force their way through the bottlenecks. One hundred sixty-five people died, all but two within thirty feet of two exits of the Cabaret Room.

Sociologists who studied this panic found what other researchers have discovered in analyzing other disasters. *Not everyone panics.* Many people continue to act responsibly within their primary group bonds, such as parents helping their children. Gender roles also persist, and more men help women than women help men (Johnson 1993). Even work roles continue to guide some behavior. Sociologists Drue Johnston and Norris Johnson (1989) found that only 29 percent of the employees of the Beverly Hills Supper Club left when they learned of the fire. As noted on Table 21.1, 41 percent helped customers, 17 percent reported or fought the fire, 7 percent simply went about their routines, and 5 percent did such things as search for friends and relatives.

Sociologists use the term **role extension** to describe the actions of most of the employees. In other words, the employees incorporated other activities into their occupational roles. For example, servers extended their role to include helping people to safety. How do we know that giving help was an extension of the occupational role, not simply helping in general? Johnston and Johnson found that servers who were away from their assigned stations returned to them in order to help *their* customers.

Table 21.1

Employees' First Action After Learning of the Fire

Action	Percentage
Left	29%
Helped others to leave	41%
Fought or reported the fire	17%
Continued routine activities	7%
Other (e.g., looked for a friend or relative)	5%

Note: These figures are based on interviews with 95 of the 160 employees present at the time of the fire: 48 males and 47 females, ranging in age from 15 to 59.

Source: Based on Johnston and Johnson 1989.

---

panic: the condition of being so fearful that one cannot function normally, and may even flee

role extension: the incorporation of additional activities into a role

This kindly looking grandmother stood accused of horrible sex crimes against little children who had been entrusted to her care. Was she guilty or innocent? Perhaps the victim of a moral panic? Why is the public no longer panicked about day care workers?

Moral Panics

Moral panics occur when large numbers of people become so fearful about some supposed deteriorating condition in society that it is difficult for them to carry on normal life. A moral panic does not come on as suddenly as the panics we have just discussed. Involving larger numbers of people and fostered by the mass media, they take a while to build up. An example is the fear of sexual abuse of children in day care centers that spread across the United States during the 1980s (Cockburn 1990). At one point, almost every day care worker became suspect in someone's eyes, and only with fear and trepidation did parents leave their children in day care centers. Although sexual abuse at day care centers has occurred, the highly publicized stories of children subjected to bizarre rituals with devil worshippers and naked priests and weird sex have not been substantiated. The hysteria has since died down.

Like other panics, moral panics center around a sense of danger. The supposed thousands of U.S. children who are snatched by strangers from playgrounds, city streets, and their own back yards are part of a moral panic that has made parents fearful and others perplexed at how U.S. society could so suddenly go to hell in a hand basket. This moral panic is destined to meet the same fate as others. The fear and hysteria will gradually subside, and people will feel less fear as they do the activity around which the moral panic occurred, such as dropping children off at school or letting children play in parks.

Moral panics are fed by **rumor**, information for which there is no discernible source and which is usually unfounded. For example, a rumor, still continuing, is that these children are being sold to Satanists who abuse them sexually and then ritually murder them. This rumor is intensely believed by some, and has been supported by testimony from people who claim to have been involved in such sacrifices. Investigations by the police, however, have uncovered no evidence to substantiate it. In addition, the actual number of stranger kidnappings per year is between 200 and 300 (Bromely 1991).

Moral panics thrive on uncertainty and anxiety. Satanic activities of the 1980s and early 1990s created anxiety among many Americans and helped to propel kidnapped children to national prominence. So did the uncertainties surrounding the changing family. Concerns over children receiving proper care as large numbers of mothers left home for paid work became linked with dangers to children from sinister sources lurking almost everywhere.

Rumors

rumor: unfounded information spread among people

"Did you hear about . . . ?" can be the introduction to a joke or to a rumor. Rumors are part of everyday life. Every work setting has them—especially when times are uncertain. The function of rumors is to fill in missing information (Shibutani 1966). People want to know about conditions that will have an impact on them, so when hard information is lacking, the void provides fertile ground for rumors, as people jump at cues and read into them what they are searching for.

The key to understanding rumors is *uncertainty,* some ambiguous situation that the rumor solves. During a period of economic downturn, for example, large work settings are filled with rumors concerning impending layoffs, mass firings, and what is now called "downsizing." Smaller work settings apparently do not provide the same fertile ground for rumors, because individuals there have more direct access to the sources of information. In smaller settings, however, **gossip** serves the same purpose, as information of a more personal nature is passed from one person to another to fill in missing gaps about people's lives. The information is usually distorted or blatantly untrue, but some is not. Some bosses do sleep with their secretaries, get divorced, steal from the company, and so on.

Most rumors are short-lived. They arise in a situation of ambiguity, only to dissipate when they are replaced by factual information—or by another rumor. Occasionally, however, a rumor has a long life. In the eighteenth and nineteenth centuries, for no known reason, healthy people would gradually grow weak, and slowly waste away. No one understood the cause and people said they had *consumption* (now known as tuberculosis). People were terrified as they saw their loved ones wither into shells of their former selves. With no one knowing when the disease would strike, or who its next victim would be, the rumor began that some of the dead weren't really dead. What had happened, people said, was that they had turned into vampire-like beings, and at night they were coming back from the grave and draining the life out of the living. The evidence was irrefutable—loved ones wasting away before their very eyes. To kill these ghoulish "undead," on dark nights people began to sneak into graveyards. They would dig up a grave, remove the leg bones and place them over the skeleton's chest, then lay the skull at the feet, forming a skull and crossbones. Having thus killed the "undead," they would rebury the remains. These rumors and resulting mutilations of the dead continued off and on in New England until the 1890s (Associated Press, November 30, 1993).

Everyone is interested in a juicy bit of gossip, or so it seems. Or is this a rumor? Differences between gossip and rumor are discussed in the text.

Procter & Gamble, the maker of numerous household products such as Tide, Crest, Pampers, Folger's, and Ivory soap, has been the victim of a persistent rumor. According to the rumor, the company logo—the man in the moon and thirteen stars—represents witchcraft (Turner 1993). (See Figure 21.2.) The rumor also reported that the president of the company gave a percentage of his earnings to satanic causes (Brunvand 1984). At the height of the rumor, when the company was receiving fifteen thousand calls a month, Procter & Gamble employed fifteen people simply to deny the rumor.

Why do people believe rumors? Three main factors have been identified. First, rumors deal with a subject that is important to an individual. Second, they replace ambiguity with some form of certainty. Third, they are attributed to a creditable source. An office rumor may be preceded by "Jane has it on good authority that . . . ," or "Bill overheard the boss say that . . ."

Ambiguity or uncertainty is especially important in giving life to rumors. That is why the New Englanders speculated about the cause of people slowly dying, their rather bizarre conclusions giving them

Persons predisposed to believe in conspiracies report that if the company's logo is viewed in a mirror the beard's curlicues read 666, the number of Satan and that another 666 shows up if the stars are connected by curving lines. Due to this rumor, Procter & Gamble changed its logo.

Procter & Gamble's Logo

Figure 21.2

gossip: information of a more personal nature than a rumor, often false, distorted, or blatantly untrue

certainty in the face of threatening, bewildering events. The uncertainty that sparked the Procter & Gamble rumor was satanic activity: self-proclaimed witches and warlocks granting media interviews, satanic graffiti in public places, and satanic churches such as the one led by Anton LaVey in San Francisco.

Fads and Fashions

A **fad** is a novel form of behavior that briefly catches people's attention. The new behavior appears suddenly and spreads by suggestion, imitation, and identification with people already involved in the fad. Publicity by the mass media also helps to spread the fad. After a short life, the fad fades into oblivion, although it may reappear from time to time (Aguirre et al. 1993).

Sociologist John Lofland (1985) identified four types of fads. First are object fads, such as the Hula Hoop of the 1950s, pet rocks of the 1970s, the Rubik's Cube and Cabbage Patch dolls of the 1980s, and baseball cards of the 1990s. Second are activity fads, such as eating goldfish in the 1920s and bungee jumping in the 1990s. Third are idea fads, such as astrology. Fourth are personality fads, such as Elvis Presley, Vanna White, and Michael Jordan. Some fads are extremely short-lived, such as "streaking" (running naked in a public place), which lasted only a couple of months in 1974. Some fads involve millions of people, but die just as quickly as they appeared. For example, in the 1950s the Hula Hoop sold so quickly that stores couldn't keep them in stock. Children cried and pleaded for these brightly colored plastic hoops. Across the nation, children, and some adults, gyrated with this object encircling their waists. Hula Hoop contests were held to see who could keep the hoops up the longest or who could rotate the most hoops at one time. Then, in a matter of months it was over, and parents wondered what to do with the abandoned items, now useless for any other purpose.

When a fad lasts, it is called a **fashion.** Some fashions, as with clothing, are the result of a coordinated international marketing system that includes designers, manufacturers, advertisers, and retailers. Billions of dollars worth of clothing are sold by manipulating the tastes of the public. Fashion, however, also refers to hairstyles, home decorating, even the design and colors of buildings. Sociologist John Lofland (1985) pointed out that fashion even applies to language, as demonstrated by these roughly comparable terms: "Neat!" in the 1950s, "Right on!" in the 1960s, "Really!" in the 1970s, "Awesome!" in the 1980s, and "Bad!" in the early 1990s.

Urban Legends

Did you hear about Nancy and Bill? They were parked at Echo Bay. They were listening to the car radio, and the music was interrupted by an announcement that a rapist-killer had escaped from prison. Instead of a right hand, he had a hook. Nancy said they should leave, but Bill laughed and said there wasn't any reason to go. When they heard a strange noise, Bill agreed to take her home. When Nancy opened the door, she heard something clink. It was a hook hanging on the door handle!

For the past generation, some version of "The Hook" story has circulated among Americans. It has appeared as a "genuine" letter in "Dear Abby," and some of my students heard it as preteens. **Urban legends** are stories with an ironic twist that sound realistic but are false. Although untrue, they usually are told by people who believe that they happened.

Another urban legend that has made the rounds is the "Kentucky Fried Rat."

One night, a woman didn't have anything ready for supper, so she and her husband went to the drive-through at Kentucky Fried Chicken. While they were eating in their car, the wife said, "My chicken tastes funny."

Her husband said, "You're always complaining about something." When she insisted that the chicken didn't taste right, he put on the light. She was holding fried rat— crispy style. The woman went into shock and was rushed to the hospital.

What do you want to do on your honeymoon? Immediately after their wedding, this couple in Atlantic City, New Jersey, bungee jumped 170 feet over the Atlantic Ocean while tightly clutching each other. Is bungee jumping a fad or a fashion?

fad: a temporary pattern of behavior that catches people's attention

fashion: a pattern of behavior that catches people's attention, which lasts longer than a fad

urban legend: a story with an ironic twist that sounds realistic but is false

A lawyer from the company offered them $100,000 if they will sign a release and not tell anyone. This is the second case they have had.

Folklorist Jan Brunvand (1981, 1984, 1986) reported that urban legends are passed on by people who think that the event happened just one or two people down the line of transmission, often to a "friend of a friend." The story has strong appeal and gains credibility from naming specific people or local places. Brunvand views urban legends as "modern morality stories," with each teaching a moral lesson about life.

If we apply Brunvand's analysis to these two urban legends, three major points emerge. First, their moral serves as a warning. "The Hook" warns young people that they should be careful about where they go, with whom they go, and what they do. The world is an unsafe place, and "messing around" is risky. "The Kentucky Fried Rat" contains a different moral: Do you *really* know what you are eating when you buy food from a fast-food outlet? Maybe you should eat at home, where you know what you are getting.

Second, each story is related to social change: "The Hook" to changing sexual morality; the "Kentucky Fried Rat" to changing male–female relationships, especially to changing sex roles at home. Third, each is calculated to instill guilt and fear: guilt—the wife failed in her traditional role of cooking supper, and she gets punished—and fear, the dangerous unknown, whether the dark countryside or fast food. The ultimate moral of these stories is that we should not abandon traditional roles or the safety of the home.

These principles can be applied to an urban legend that made the rounds in the late 1980s. I heard several versions of this one, each narrator swearing that it had just happened to a friend of a friend.

> Jerry (or whoever) went to a night club last weekend. He met a good-looking woman, and they hit it off. They spent the night in a motel, and when he awoke the next morning, the woman was gone. When he went into the bathroom, he saw a message scrawled on the mirror in lipstick: "Welcome to the wonderful world of AIDS."

Social Movements

When the Nazis, a small group of malcontents in Bavaria, first appeared on the scene in the 1920s, their ideas appeared laughable to the world. They believed that the Germans were a race of supermen (Übermenschen) who would launch a Third Reich (rule or nation) that would control the world for a thousand years. Their race destined them for greatness, lesser races to their service and exploitation.

From a little band of comic characters who looked as though they had stepped out of a grade-B movie, the Nazis gained such power that they threatened the existence of Western civilization. How could a little man with a grotesque moustache, surrounded by a few sycophants in brown shirts, ever come to threaten the world? Such things don't happen in real life—only in novels or movies, the deranged nightmare of some imaginative author. Only this was real life, the Nazi appearance on the human scene causing the deaths of millions of people and changing the course of world history.

How could this have happened? Social movements, the second major topic of this chapter, hold the answer. **Social movements** consist of large numbers of people who organize to promote or resist social change. Examples of such deliberate and sustained efforts include the temperance movement, civil rights movement, the white supremacist movement, the women's movement, the peace movement (anti-Vietnam War), the animal rights crusade, the nuclear freeze movement, the movement against drunken driving, and the environmental movement.

At the heart of social movements lie grievances and dissatisfactions. For some people, a current condition of society is intolerable, and their goal is to *promote* social change. Theirs is called a **proactive social movement.** In contrast, others perceive a threat because some condition of society is changing, and they organize to *resist* that change. Theirs is a **reactive social movement.**

To further their goals, people often develop **social movement organizations.** Those whose goal is to promote social change develop such organizations as the National Organization for Women (NOW) and the National Association for the Advancement of Colored People (NAACP). In contrast, for those who are trying to resist these changes, the Stop-ERA and the Ku Klux Klan serve the same purpose. To recruit followers and sympathizers, leaders of social movements use various attention-getting devices, from marches and protest rallies to sit-ins and boycotts. They also try to manipulate the mass media to get their point across, some doing so very effectively.

Social movements are like a rolling sea (Zald 1992). During one period of time, few social movements appear, but shortly afterward a wave of them rolls in, each competing for the public's attention. Sociologist Mayer Zald (1992) suggests that a *cultural crisis* can give birth to a wave of social movements. By this, he means that there are times when a society's institutions fail to keep up with social changes, many people's needs go unfulfilled, massive unrest follows, and social movements come into being to bridge this gap.

Types and Tactics of Social Movements

Let's see what types of social movements there are and then examine their tactics.

Types of Social Movements

Since social change is always their goal, we can classify social movements according to their *target* and the *amount of change* they seek. Figure 21.3 summarizes the classification developed by sociologist David Aberle (1966). If you read across, you will see that the target of the first two types of social movements is *individuals*. **Alterative social movements** seek only to *alter* some particular behavior of people. An example is a powerful social movement of the early 1900s, the Women's Christian Temperance Union (WCTU), whose goal was to get people to stop drinking alcohol. Its members were convinced that if they could close the saloons such problems as poverty and spouse abuse would go away. **Redemptive social movements** also target individuals, but here the aim is for total change. An example is a religious social movement that stresses conversion. In fundamentalist Christianity, for example, when someone converts to Christ, the entire person is supposed to change, not just some specific behavior. Self-centered behaviors are to be replaced by loving behaviors toward others as the convert becomes, in their terms, a "new creation."

Social movements involve large numbers of people who, upset about some condition in society, organize to do something about it. Shown here is Carrie Nation, a temperance leader who in 1900 began to break up saloons with a hatchet. Her social movement eventually became popular enough to result in Prohibition.

proactive social movement: a social movement that promotes some social change

reactive social movement: a social movement that resists some social change

social movement organization: an organization developed to further the goals of a social movement

alterative social movement: a social movement that seeks to alter only particular aspects of people

redemptive social movement: a social movement that seeks to change people totally

Amount of Change

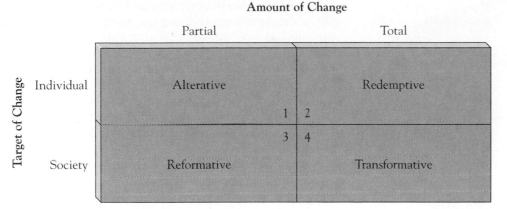

Source: Aberle 1966.

Figure 21.3

Types of Social Movements

The target of the next two types of social movements is *society*. **Reformative social movements** seek to *reform* some specific aspect of society. The environmental movement, for example, seeks to reform the ways society treats the environment, from its disposal of garbage and nuclear wastes to its use of forests and water. **Transformative social movements,** in contrast, seek to *transform* the social order itself and to replace it with a new version of the good society. Revolutions, such as those in the American colonies, France, Russia, and Cuba, are examples. So was the Nazi takeover of Germany in the 1930s, and its horrible consequences discussed in the Down-to-Earth Sociology box on 601.

One of the more interesting examples of transformative social movements is **millenarian movements,** which are based on prophecies of social upheaval. Of particular interest is a type of millenarian movement called a **cargo cult** (Worsley 1957). About one hundred years ago, Europeans colonized the Melanesian Islands of the South Pacific. From the home countries of the colonizers arrived ship after ship, each loaded with items the Melanesians had never seen. As the Melanesians watched the cargo being unloaded, they expected some of it to go to them. They noted, however, that it all went to the Europeans. Melanesian prophets then revealed the secret of this exotic merchandise. Their own ancestors were manufacturing and sending the cargos to them, but the colonists were intercepting the merchandise. Since the colonists were too strong to fight, and too selfish to share the cargo, there was little the Melanesians could do.

Then further prophecies came, which revealed the solution. If they would destroy their crops and food and build harbors, their ancestors would see their sincerity and send the cargo directly to them. The Melanesians did so. Surprisingly, the prophecies came true, but in a rather strange way. When the colonial administrators of the island saw that the natives had destroyed their crops and were just sitting in the hills waiting for the cargo ships to arrive, they informed the home government. The prospect of thousands of islanders patiently starving to death was too horrifying to allow, and the British government sent ships to the islands with cargo earmarked for the Melanesians.

Tactics of Social Movements

The leaders of a social movement can choose from a variety of tactics. Should they peacefully boycott, march, or hold an all-night candle-lit vigil? Or should they bomb a building, blow up an airplane, or assassinate a key figure? To understand why the leaders of social movements choose their tactics, we need to examine a group's levels of membership, the publics it addresses, and its relationship to authorities.

reformative social movement: a social movement that seeks to change only particular aspects of society

transformative social movement: a social movement that seeks to change society totally

millenarian movement: a social movement based on the prophecy of coming social upheaval

cargo cult: a social movement in which South Pacific islanders destroyed their possessions in the anticipation that their ancestors would send items by ship

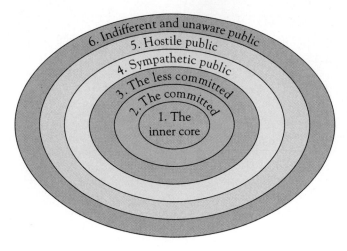

6. Indifferent and unaware public
5. Hostile public
4. Sympathetic public
3. The less committed
2. The committed
1. The inner core

The Membership and Publics of Social Movements

Figure 21.4

Levels of Membership   Figure 21.4 shows the composition of social movements. Beginning at the center and moving outward, you can see that there are three levels of membership. At the inner core are those people most committed to the movement. This inner core sets the group's goals, timetables, strategies, and inspires the other members. Those at the second level are also committed to the movement, but somewhat less so than the inner core. People at this level, however, can be counted on to show up for demonstrations and to do the grunt work—to run copy machines, to make telephone calls, and to pass out leaflets. At the third level is a wider circle of people who are less committed and less dependable. Their participation is primarily a matter of convenience. If an activity does not interfere with something else they want to do, they participate.

The predispositions and backgrounds of the inner core are essential in the choice of tactics. Because of their background, the inner core of some groups is predisposed to use peaceful means, others confrontational, while still others prefer violence. Tactics also depend on the number of committed members. Different tactics are called for if the inner core can count on seven hundred—or only seven—committed members to show up.

The Publics   Lying outside the membership is the **public,** a dispersed group of people who usually have an interest in the issue. Just outside the third circle of members, and blending into it, is the sympathetic public. Although their sympathies lie with the movement, these people have no commitment to it. Sympathy with the movement's goals, however, makes this public fertile ground for recruiting new members. The second public is hostile. It is keenly aware of the group's goals and dislikes them. This public wants to stop the social movement, for the movement's values go against its own. The third public consists of disinterested people. They are either unaware of the social movement, or if aware, indifferent to it.

In selecting tactics, the leadership pays attention to these publics. The sympathetic public is especially significant as it is the source of new members and support at the ballot box. Tactics that appear likely to alienate the sympathetic public will be avoided, while tactics will be chosen if they look as though they will elicit greater sympathy from this group. The leadership may even force a confrontation with the hostile public, trying to make itself appear a victim, a group whose rights are being trampled on. Tactics directed toward the unaware or indifferent public are designed to neutralize their indifference and increase their awareness.

Relationship to Authorities   The movement's relationship to authorities is also significant in determining tactics—especially in choosing peaceful or violent tactics. If a social movement is *institutionalized,* accepted by authorities, violence will not be directed against the authorities, for they are on the same side. This, however, does not rule out violence directed against the opposition. If authorities are hostile to a social movement, aggressive or even violent tactics are more likely. For example, since the goal of a transformative (revolutionary) social movement is to replace the government, the movement and the government are clearly on a collision course.

Social Movements and the Mass Media

In selecting tactics, the leaders of social movements are keenly aware of their effects on the mass media (Zald 1992). Their goal is to influence **public opinion,** how people think

public: a dispersed group of people who usually have an interest in the issue on which a social movement focuses; the sympathetic and hostile publics have such an interest, but a third public is either unaware of the issue or indifferent to it

public opion: how people think about some issue

▼▲▼▲▼▲▼▲▼▲▼▲▼▲▼▲▼▲▼▲▼▲▼▲▼▲▼▲▼▲▼▲▼

Down-To-Earth Sociology

On Social Movements and Morality: Looking into the Face of Evil

HITLER'S RISE TO POWER in the 1930s came during a period of general unrest: the shame of Germany's defeat in World War I, high unemployment, the devastation of hyperinflation. Hitler promised the restoration of national pride, jobs, and a stable currency. In the midst of this turmoil, a highly organized social movement masterminded by Hitler thrust him to power. One of the consequences was the mass slaughter of Jews, gypsies, the handicapped, and homosexuals—in order to "cleanse" the "Aryan" race. Behind the Nazi slaughter was the skillful manipulation of public opinion.

Dr. Paul Joseph Goebbels (1897–1945) headed the Nazi propaganda machine. Hitler considered his work as important as the manufacture of tanks and ammunition, for then, as now, the manufacture of opinion was essential to waging war. Goebbels's philosophy of propaganda was simple: "It is just as easy to tell a big lie as a small one. If you repeat it often enough, most people will believe it." Two basic principles underlay Goebbels's campaign to unify the German people for the war effort and to destroy "inferior" racial stock. The first was to simplify, to break a complex issue into simple parts. The second, Goebbels said, was to repeat, to continue to recite the simplified version of reality over and over again. The way that Goebbels (Moyers 1989) put the matter drives home the point. "Simplify! Simplify! Simplify! Then, Repeat! Repeat! Repeat!"

In order for the mass killing to take place, the public had to either support it or at least not interfere. Goebbels's success was not due only to propaganda, however, for terror also played its part. If the Nazis couldn't convince someone to buy their ideas, they could convince them to remain silent—or the Gestapo would make a midnight call.

People who carried out the slaughter faced more than propaganda. They confronted humans face to face. They shot men and women lined up at the edge of trenches ready to receive their lifeless bodies. They gassed children. How could they do such barbaric acts? Most were extremely troubled by what they saw and did (Browning 1993; Katz 1993). Some managed to get transfers. Others committed suicide. Still others took the killing as part of a job that had to be done. They didn't like it, but someone had to do it. Those were the orders, after all.

The concept of dehumanization discussed on pages 423–424 helps to explain how ordinary people can do such

things. *Dehumanization* is the process of reducing people to objects not deserving the treatment accorded humans. Dehumanization involves four main characteristics: increased emotional distance from others, an emphasis on following orders, inability to resist pressures, and a diminished sense of responsibility (Bernard 1971).

Symbolic interactionists stress that at the essence of dehumanization is a label that classifies people as less than human. The Nazis' use of labels was extremely effective, transforming killing from an unusual act to a normal part of work. This process is chillingly illustrated by letters written home by camp guards who were far more disturbed by delayed vacations or by shortages of butter than by the executions they carried out. As the guards became more efficient in their killing, they found more time to gather informally, where they played musical instruments, drank and laughed together—all after a hard day's "work" (Klee et al. 1991).

Some guards even came to enjoy the killing and to pride themselves in how evil they had become (Katz 1993). A witness at a Nazi war trial reported,

One particular day in November, 1944 . . . Jewish children were brought to Auschwitz. A truck came and stopped for a moment. . . . A little boy jumped off. He held an apple in his hand. [SS men] Boger and Drasner were standing in the doorway. I was standing at the window. The child was standing next to the car with the apple and was enjoying himself. Suddenly Boger went over to the boy, grabbed his legs, and smashed his head against the wall. Then he calmly picked up the apple. And Drasner told me to wipe "that" off the wall. About an hour later I was called to Boger to interpret in an interrogation and saw him eating the child's apple. (Naumann 1966)

As difficult as it is for us to grasp, these were "normal" people, not monsters. Their morality had been so neutralized through dehumanization that they could participate in acts that they, too, would otherwise condemn. This process is alive today. War continues to exalt treachery and killing, and we award medals to soldiers glorifying actions for which they would in all other contexts be imprisoned.

From the Nazis, we can conclude that social movements are not intrinsically moral or immoral, good or evil. These powerful forces of social change follow principles of human behavior that can be abstracted and analyzed by sociologists, principles that can be put to use to enhance life or to destroy it.

about some issue. The right kind of publicity enables them to arouse the sympathetic public and to lay the groundwork for recruiting a wider membership. Pictures of bloodied, dead baby seals, for example, go a long way to getting the group's message across.

A key to understanding social movements, then, is **propaganda.** Although this word often evokes negative images, it actually is neutral. Propaganda is simply the presentation of information in the attempt to influence people. Its original meaning was positive,

propaganda: in its broad sense, the presentation of information in the attempt to influence people; in its narrow sense, one-sided information used to try to influence people

The use of propaganda is popular among those committed to the goals of a social movement. They can see only one side to the social issue about which they are so upset. Do you think there is another side to this social issue?

for *propaganda* referred to a committee of cardinals of the Roman Catholic church whose assignment was the care of foreign missions. (They were to *propagate* the faith.) The term has traveled a long way since then, however, and today it usually refers to a one-sided presentation of information that distorts reality.

Propaganda, then, in the sense of organized attempts to manipulate public opinion, is a regular part of modern life. Advertisements, for example, are a form of propaganda, for they present a one-sided version of reality. Underlying effective propaganda are seven basic techniques, discussed in the Down-to-Earth Sociology box on the next page. Perhaps by understanding these techniques, you will be able to resist one-sided appeals—whether they come from social movements or from hawkers of some new product.

Sociology can be a liberating discipline (Berger 1963, 1993). It sensitizes us to the existence of *multiple realities*; that is, for any single point of view on some topic, there likely are competing points of view, which some find equally as compelling. Each represents reality as the individual sees it, but different experiences lead to different perceptions. Consequently, although the committed members of a social movement are sincere, and perhaps even sacrificing for "the cause," theirs is but one view of the way the world is. If other sides were presented, the issue would look quite different.

The mass media, then, play a crucial role in social movements. They have become, in effect, the gatekeepers to social movements. If those who control and work in the mass media—from owners to reporters—are sympathetic to some particular "cause," you can be sure that it receives sympathetic treatment. If the social movement goes against their own biases, it will either be ignored or receive unfavorable treatment. If you ever get the impression that the U.S. media are trying to manipulate your opinions and attitudes on some particular social movement—or some social issue—you probably are right. Far from doing unbiased reporting, the media are under the control and influence of people who have an agenda to get across. To the materials in the Down-to-Earth Sociology box on propaganda, then, we need to add the biases of the media establishment, the issues to which they choose to give publicity, those that they ignore, and their favorable and unfavorable treatment of issues and movements.

Down-To-Earth Sociology

"Tricks of the Trade"—The Fine Art of Propaganda

SOCIOLOGISTS ALFRED AND ELIZABETH LEE (1939) found that propaganda relies on seven basic techniques, which they termed "tricks of the trade." To be effective, the techniques should be subtle, with the audience remaining unaware of just which part of their mind or emotions is being manipulated. If propaganda is effective, people will not know *why* they support something, only that they do—as they fervently defend it.

1. *Name calling.* This technique aims to arouse opposition to the competing product, candidate, or policy by associating it with a negative image. By comparison, one's own product, candidate, or policy appears attractive. Political candidates who call an opponent "soft on crime" are using this technique.

2. *Glittering generality.* Essentially the opposite of the first, this technique surrounds the product, candidate, or policy with "virtue words," phrases that arouse positive feelings. "She's a *real* Democrat" has little meaning, but it makes the audience feel that something has been said. "He stands for individualism" is so general that it is meaningless, yet the audience thinks that it has heard a specific message about the candidate.

3. *Transfer.* In its positive form, this technique associates the product, candidate, or policy with something that the public respects or approves; in its negative form, with something of which it disapproves. Let's look at the positive form: You might not be able to get by with saying, "Busch beer is patriotic," but surround a beer with the American flag, and beer drinkers will somehow get the idea that it is more patriotic to drink this brand of beer than another.

4. *Testimonials.* Famous and admired individuals are used to endorse a product, candidate, or policy. Movie stars hawk skin cream, or perhaps extol the relief offered by a hemorrhoid ointment. Candidates for political office may solicit the endorsement of movie stars—who may know next to nothing about the candidate, or even about politics itself. In the negative form of this technique, a despised person is associated with the competing product. If propagandists could manage it, they would show Saddam Hussein drinking a competing beer or announcing support for an opposing candidate.

5. *Plain folks.* Sometimes it pays to take a contrasting approach and associate the product, candidate, or policy with "just plain folks." "If Mary or John Q. Public like it, you will, too." A political candidate who kisses babies, dons a hard hat, and has lunch at McDonald's while photographers "catch him or her in the act"—is using the "plain folks" strategy. "I'm just a regular person," is the message of the presidential candidate posing for photographers in jeans and work shirt—while making certain that the Mercedes and chauffeur do not show up in the background.

6. *Card stacking.* The aim of this technique is to present only positive information about what you support, only negative information about what you oppose. Make it sound as though there is only one conclusion that a rational person can draw. Use falsehoods, distortions, and illogical statements if you must.

7. *Bandwagon.* "Everyone is doing it" is the idea behind this technique. After all, "20 million Frenchmen can't be wrong," can they? Emphasizing how many others buy the product or support the candidate or policy conveys the message that anyone who doesn't join in is on the wrong track.

The Lees (1939) added, "Once we know that a speaker or writer is using one of these propaganda devices in an attempt to convince us of an idea, we can separate the device from the idea and see what the idea amounts to on its own merits."

Why People Join Social Movements

As we have seen, social movements arise from widespread, deeply-felt discontent, from the conviction that some condition of society is no longer tolerable. Not everyone, however, who feels strongly dissatisfied about an issue joins a social movement. Let's look at three explanations that explain why some people join social movements.

Mass Society Theory

To explain why people are attracted to social movements, sociologist William Kornhauser (1959) proposed **mass society theory.** Kornhauser argued that **mass society**—an industrialized, highly bureaucratized, impersonal society—makes many people feel

mass society theory: an explanation for participation in social movements based on the assumption that such movements offer a sense of belonging to people who have weak social ties

mass society: industrialized, highly bureaucratized, impersonal society

isolated. Social movements fill a void by offering people a sense of belonging. In geographical areas where social ties are supposedly weaker, such as the western United States, one would then expect to find more social movements than in areas where traditional ties are supposedly stronger, such as in the Midwest and South.

This theory seems to match commonsense observations. Certainly, social movements seem to proliferate on the West Coast. But sociologist Doug McAdam (1988), who interviewed people who had risked their lives in the civil rights movement, found that these people were firmly rooted in families and communities. It was their strong desire to right wrongs and to overcome injustices, not their isolation, that motivated their participation. Even the Nazis attracted many people firmly rooted in their communities (Oberschall 1973). Finally, those most isolated of all, the homeless, generally do not join anything—except food lines.

Deprivation Theory

A second explanation to account for why people join social movements is *deprivation theory*. According to this theory, people who are deprived of things deemed valuable in society—whether money, justice, status, or privilege—join social movements with the hope of redressing their grievances. This theory may seem so obvious as to need no evidence. Aren't the thousands of African Americans who participated in the civil rights movement of the 1950s and the World War I soldiers who marched on Washington after Congress refused to pay their promised bonuses ample evidence that the theory is true?

Deprivation theory does provide a beginning point. But there is more to the matter than this. We must also pay attention to what Alexis de Tocqueville (1856/1955) noted almost 150 years ago. The peasants of Germany were worse off than the peasants of France, and from deprivation theory we would expect the Germans to have rebelled and to have overthrown their king. Revolution, however, occurred in France, not Germany. The reason, said de Tocqueville, is *relative* deprivation. French peasants had experienced improving living conditions, and could imagine even better conditions, while German peasants, having never experienced anything but depressed conditions, had no comparative basis for feeling deprived.

According to **relative deprivation theory,** then, it is not people's actual negative conditions (their *absolute* deprivation) that matters. Rather, the key to participation is *relative* deprivation—that is, what people *think* they should have relative to what others have, or even compared with their own past or perceived future. This theory, which has provided excellent insight into revolutions, also holds a surprise. Because improving conditions fuel human desires for even better conditions, in some instances *improving* conditions can spark revolutions.

What about the civil rights movement of the 1950s and 1960s? At the center of the sit-ins in the South were relatively well-off African Americans. It was college students, Boy Scouts, and leaders of the churches who went to restaurants and lunch counters reserved for whites, who when refused service sat peacefully while abuse—and even food—were heaped on them (Morris 1993). What is significant for this theory, however, is the people with whom one compares oneself. The sit-ins were a form of rebellion against the white establishment, and compared with whites these demonstrators felt quite deprived.

Another example from this same social movement, however, offers greater challenge to this theory, for many of the later demonstrators who risked their lives in marches and other protests were white, middle-class college students from the North (McAdam 1988; Fendrich and Lovoy 1993). This is an example of people whose own personal welfare is not at stake who become active in social movements for *moral* reasons, a motivation to which we shall now turn.

Moral Issues and Ideological Commitment

As sociologists James Jasper and Dorothy Nelkin (1992) point out, we would miss the basic reason for many people's involvement in social movements if we overlooked the

relative deprivation theory: in this context, the belief that people join social movements based on their evaluations of what they think they should have compared with what others have

Activists in social movements become committed to "the cause." The social movement around abortion, currently one of the most dynamic in the United States, has split Americans, is highly visible, and has articulate spokespeople on both sides.

moral issue. Some people see the concerns of a particular social movement in stark moral terms. For them, great issues hang in the balance, and they feel that they must choose sides and do what they can to make a difference. As sociologists put it, they join because of *ideological commitment* to the movement. Many members on both sides of the abortion issue see their involvement in such terms. Similarly, most activists in the animal rights movement are convinced that there can be no justification for animals to suffer in order to make safer products for humans. Some see nuclear weapons and power in similar moral terms, and they risk arrest and ridicule for their participation in demonstrations. For others, matters of the environment are moral issues, and to not act would be an inexcusable betrayal of future generations. The *moral* component of a social movement, then, is a primary reason for some people's involvement.

A Special Case: The Agent Provocateur

A unique type of social movement participant is the **agent provocateur,** an agent of the government or even of a rival social movement, whose job is to spy on the leadership and perhaps to sabotage their activities. Some are recruited from the membership itself, traitors to the organization for a few Judas dollars, while others are members of the police or a rival group who go underground and join the movement.

On occasion an agent is converted to the social movement on which he or she is spying. Sociologist Gary Marx (1993) explains that to be credible, the agent must share at least some of the class, age, gender, ethnic, racial, or religious characteristics of the group. This makes the agent more likely to sympathize with the movement's goals and to become disenchanted with trying to harm the group. Also, to be effective, the agent must work his or her way into the center of the group. This requires frequent interaction with the group's committed members, which tends to produce liking. In addition, while the agent is building trust he or she is cut off from people who oppose the group, and concerns about betraying and deceiving people who have placed their trust in the agent may creep in.

Since the social change that some social movements represent is radical, threatening the power elite, the use of agent provocateurs is not surprising. What may be surprising, however, is how far these agents go. During the 1960s, when a wave of militant

agent provocateur: someone who joins a group in order to spy on it and to sabotage it by *provoking* its members to commit illegal acts

social movements rolled across the United States, the FBI and other police were busy recruiting agents. To sabotage groups, these agents provoked activities that otherwise would not have occurred, setting the leadership up for arrest, and in some instances, even death. Three examples will let us see how agent provocateurs operate (Marx 1993). A student at Northeastern Illinois University who proposed schemes for sabotaging public facilities and was suspended for two semesters for throwing the school's president off the stage turned out to be a police agent. One of the four men involved in a plot to blow up the Statue of Liberty by a small New York group called the Black Liberation Front was an undercover agent. It was he who drew up the plans and even provided police funds to pay for the dynamite and rent the car. Finally, the FBI reportedly paid $36,500 to two members of the White Knights of the Ku Klux Klan to arrange for two other Klansmen to bomb a Jewish businessman's home. A trap was set in which one Klansman was killed and another arrested in the unsuccessful attempt.

 In Sum   Recruitment generally follows channels of social networks. Perhaps most commonly, people join a social movement because they have friends and acquaintances already in the movement (McCarthy and Wolfson 1992; Snow et al. 1993). Some join purely out of self-interest, to further their own careers, because it is fun, or because they achieve recognition or find a valued identity.

Certainly not everyone who participates in a social movement does so from the same motives and convictions. Some people even participate in a social movement even though they *don't want to*. The Cuban government, for example, compels people to turn out for mass demonstrations in support of the communist regime (Aguirre 1993), and, as we just saw, police officials may join social movements in order to spy on them and sabotage their activities. In no social movement, then, is there a single cause for people joining. As in all other activities in life, people remain a complex bundle of motivations—which provides a challenge to sociologists to unravel.

On the Success and Failure of Social Movements

Large industrial societies produce the fertile ground of discontent that spawns social movements, but most social movements are not successful. Let's look at the reasons for their success or failure.

The Life Course of Social Movements

Social movements have a life course; that is, they go through different stages as they grow and mature. Sociologists have identified five stages of social movements (Lang and Lang 1961; Maus 1975; Spector and Kitsuse 1977; Tilly 1978; Jasper 1991).

1 *Initial unrest and agitation.* During this first stage, people are upset about some condition in society and want to change it. Leaders emerge who verbalize people's feelings and crystallize issues. Most social movements fail at this stage. Unable to gain enough support, after a brief flurry of activity they quietly die.

2 *Resource mobilization.* The crucial factor that enables social movements to make it past the first stage is **resource mobilization.** By this term, sociologists mean the mobilization of resources such as time, money, people's skills, technologies such as direct mailing and fax machines, attention by the mass media, and even legitimacy among the public and authorities (Benford 1992; Oliver and Marwell 1992). In some cases, an indigenous leadership arises to mobilize available resources. Other groups, having no capable leadership of their own, turn to outsiders, "specialists for hire," to mobilize resources for the group. As sociologists John McCarthy and Mayer Zald

resource mobilization: a theory that social movements succeed or fail based on their ability to mobilize resources such as time, money, and people's skills

(1977; Zald and McCarthy 1987) point out, even though large numbers of people may be upset over some condition of society, without resource mobilization they are only upset people, perhaps even agitators, but not a social movement.

3 *Organization*. A division of labor is set up. The leadership makes policy decisions, and the rank and file carry out the daily tasks necessary to keep the movement going. There is still much collective excitement about the issue, the movement's focal point of concern.

4 *Institutionalization*. At this stage, the movement has developed a bureaucracy, the type of formal hierarchy described in Chapter 7. The collective excitement is gone, and control lies in the hands of career officials, who may care more about their own position in the organization than the movement for which the organization's initial leaders made sacrifices.

5 *Organizational decline and possible resurgence*. As managing the day-to-day affairs of the organization comes to dominate the leadership, their attention is diverted away from the issues around which the movement originated. No longer a collection of committed people who share a common cause, the movement may decline at this point.

Decline is not certain, however. Emerging groups committed to the same goal led by more idealistic and committed leaders may step to the forefront and reinvigorate the movement with new strength. Or, as in the case of abortion, social movements in conflict with each other may fight on opposite sides of the issue, each continuously invigorating the other and preventing its decline. The following Thinking Critically section contrasts the two opposing groups in regard to abortion.

▼▲▼▲▼▲▼▲▼▲▼▲▼▲▼▲▼▲▼▲▼▲▼▲▼▲▼▲▼▲▼

Thinking Critically About Social Controversy

Which Side of the Barricades? Abortion as a Social Movement

▼ NO ISSUE SO DIVIDES Americans as abortion does. Polls show that in regard to abortion in the first trimester (the first three months) of pregnancy, opinion is evenly divided. While 45 percent favor a woman's right to obtain an abortion during this time, 45 percent oppose it. This polarization constantly invigorates life in the movement.

When the U.S. Supreme Court determined in its 1973 decision, *Roe v. Wade*, that states could not restrict abortion, the prochoice side relaxed. Victory was theirs, and they thought their opponents would quietly disappear. Instead, large numbers of Americans were disturbed by what they saw as gross immorality. For them, the legal right to abortion amounted to the right to murder unborn children.

The two sides see matters in totally incompatible ways. On the one hand, those in favor of choice view the 1.5 million abortions performed annually in the United States as examples of women exercising their basic reproductive rights. On the other, antiabortionists see them as legalized murder. To the prochoice side, those who oppose abortion stand in the way of women's rights, setting basic gender relations on their head by forcing women to continue pregnancies they desire to terminate. To the prolife forces, those who favor abortion are seen as condoning the murder of children, of putting their own desires for school, career, or convenience ahead of the lives of the unborn.

There is no way to reconcile such opposing views. Each sees the other as unreasonable and extremist. And each uses propaganda by focusing on worst-case scenarios: prochoice images of young women, raped at gunpoint, forced to bear the children of rapists; or prolife images of women who are eight months pregnant killing their children instead of nurturing them.

These views are in permanent conflict. And as each side fights for what it considers basic rights, it reinvigorates the other. When in 1989 the U.S. Supreme Court decided in *Webster* v. *Reproductive Services* that states could restrict abortion, one side hailed it as a defeat, the other as a victory. Seeing the political battle going against them, the prochoice side regrouped for a determined struggle. The prolife side, sensing judicial victory within its grasp, gathered forces for a push to complete the overthrow of *Roe* v. *Wade*.

This goal of the prolife side came close to becoming reality in *Casey* v. *Planned Parenthood*. On June 30, 1992, in a 6-to-3 decision the Supreme Court upheld a Pennsylvania law that requires a woman to wait 24 hours between the confirmation of pregnancy and abortion, girls under 18 to obtain the consent of one parent to have an abortion, and women to be informed about options to abortion and to be given materials that describe the fetus. In the same case, by a 5-to-4 decision, the Court ruled that a wife does not have to inform her husband if she intends to have an abortion.

Because the two sides see reality in entirely contrasting ways, this social movement cannot end unless the vast majority of Americans commit to one side or the other. Otherwise, all legislative and judicial outcomes—whether the overthrow of *Roe* v. *Wade* or such extremes as a constitutional amendment declaring abortion either murder or a woman's right—are victories to one and defeats to the other. Nothing, then, is ever complete, but each action is only a way station in a moral struggle.

Typically, the last stage of a social movement is decline. Why does this last stage not apply to this social movement? What is different about it? Do you see this ongoing back-and-forth struggle as temporary? Under what conditions other than those listed above will this social movement decline?

As just stated, the abortion issue has produced the most polarizing of all social movements. Americans are less than evenly divided, however, when it comes to abortions after the first trimester of pregnancy. The longer the pregnancy, the smaller the proportion of Americans who approve abortion. What is your opinion about abortion? Does it change depending on the length of pregnancy? For example, how do you feel about abortion during the second month versus the eighth month? What do you think about abortion in cases of rape and incest? Finally, can you identify some of the *social* reasons that underlie your opinions?

Sources: Luker 1984; Henslin 1990; Jasper 1991; Neikirk and Elsasser 1992; Rosenblatt 1992; Rothenberg 1992. ▲

The Difficult Road to Success

In spite of their significance in contemporary society, social movements seldom solve social problems. Resource mobilization helps to explain why. In order to mobilize resources, a movement must appeal to a broad constituency. This means that the group must focus on large-scale issues, which are deeply embedded in society. For example, the fact that workers at one particular plant are upset about their low wages is not adequate to recruit the broad support necessary for a social movement. At best, it will result in local agitation. The low wages and unsafe working conditions of millions of workers, however, have a chance of becoming the focal point of a social movement.

By their nature, such broad problems are entrenched in society and not easy to solve. They require more than merely tinkering with some small part. Just as the problem touches many interrelated components of society, so the solutions require changes in those many parts. With no short-term solutions available, the social movement must stay around. But longevity brings its own danger of failure, for as we just noted, as time passes social movements tend to become bureaucratized, to turn inward and to focus their energies on running the organization.

Many social movements, however, do vitally affect society. Some become powerful forces for social change. They highlight problem areas and turn the society on a path that solves the problem. Others become powerful forces in resisting the social change that its members—and the public it is able to mobilize—consider undesirable. In either case, social movements are highly significant for contemporary society, and we can anticipate that new ones will be a regular feature of our social landscape.

Summary and Review

Early Explanations of Collective Behavior:

How did early theorists explain the effects of crowds on individuals?

Early theorists argued that individuals are transformed by crowds. Charles Mackay used the term *herd mentality* to explain why people did wild things when they were in crowds. Gustave LeBon said that a **collective mind** develops, and people are swept away by suggestions. Robert Park said that collective unrest develops which, fed by a **circular reaction**, leads to collective impulses. Pp. 586–587.

What stages of crowd behavior are there?

Herbert Blumer identified five stages that crowds go through before they become an **acting crowd:** social unrest, an exciting event, **milling,** a common object of attention, and common impulses. Pp. 588–589.

The Contemporary View of Collective Behavior

What is the current view of crowd behavior?

Current theorists view crowds as rational. Richard Berk stresses a **minimax strategy;** that is, people try to minimize their costs and maximize their rewards, whether or not they are in crowds. Ralph Turner and Lewis Killian analyze how new norms develop that allow people to do things in crowds that they otherwise would not do. Pp. 589–590.

Forms of Collective Behavior

What forms of collective behavior are there?

Some of the major forms of collective behavior are **lynchings, riots, panics, moral panics, rumors, fads, fashions,** and **urban legends.** Conditions of discontent or uncertainty provide fertile ground for collective behavior, and each form provides a way of dealing with these conditions. Pp. 590–597.

Types and Tactics of Social Movements

What types of social movements are there?

Depending on their target (individuals or society) and the amount of social change desired (partial or complete), social movements can be classified as **alterative, redemptive, reformative,** and **transformative.** Pp. 597–599.

How do social movements select their tactics?

Tactics are chosen on the basis of a group's levels of membership, its publics, and its relationship to authorities. The three levels of membership are *the inner core, the committed,* and *the less committed.* The predispositions of the inner core are crucial in choosing tactics, but so is the public they wish to address. If relationships with authorities are bad, the chances of aggressive or violent tactics increase. Pp. 599–600.

How are the mass media related to social movements?

Because the mass media are gatekeepers for social movements, their favorable or unfavorable coverage greatly affecting a social movement, tactics are chosen with the media in mind. Social movements also make use of **propaganda** to further their cause. Pp. 600–603.

Why People Join Social Movements

Why do people join social movements?

There is no single, overriding reason why people join social movements. According to **mass society theory,** social movements relieve feelings of isolation created by an impersonal, bureaucratized society. According to **relative deprivation theory,** people join movements in order to address their grievances. Morality, values, and ideological commitment also motivate people to join social movements. The **agent provocateur** illustrates that even people who hate a cause can end up participating in it. Pp. 603–606.

On the Success and Failure of Social Movements

Why do social movements succeed or fail?

Social movements go through distinct stages—initial unrest and agitation, mobilization, organization, institutionalization, and, finally, organizational decline and possible resurgence. Groups that appeal to few people are likely to fail. But to appeal to a broad level in order to accomplish **resource mobilization,** the movement must focus on very broad concerns, problems deeply embedded in society, which also makes success extremely difficult. Pp. 606–608.

Where can I read more on this topic?

Suggested readings for this chapter appear on page 645.

Lisa Houck, Between Flights, 1993

Social Change, Technology, and the Environment

THE MORNING OF JANUARY 28, 1986, *dawned clear but near freezing, strange weather for subtropical Florida. At the Kennedy Space Center, launch pad 39B was lined with three inches of ice. Icicles 6 to 12 inches long hung like stalactites from the pad's service structure.*

Shortly after 8 A.M., the crew took the elevator to the white room, where they entered the crew module. By 8:36 A.M., the seven members of the crew were strapped in their seats. They were understandably disappointed when liftoff, scheduled for 9:38 A.M., was delayed because of the ice.

After a strong public relations campaign, public interest in the flight ran high. Attention focused on Christa McAuliffe, a 37-year-old high school teacher from Concord, New Hampshire, the first private citizen to fly aboard a space shuttle. Across the nation, schoolchildren watched with great anticipation, for Mrs. McAuliffe, selected from thousands of applicants, was to give two televised lessons during the flight. The first was to describe life aboard a spacecraft in orbit, the second to discuss the prospects of using space's microgravity to manufacture new products.

At the viewing site, thousands of spectators had joined the families and friends of the crew eagerly awaiting the launch. They were delighted to see Challenger's two solid-fuel boosters ignite and broke into cheers as the Challenger, amid billows of white smoke, lifted into the air. This product of technical innovation thundered majestically into space.

The time was 11:38 A.M. Seventy-three seconds later, the Challenger, racing skyward at 2,900 feet per second, had reached an altitude of 50,000 feet and was 7 miles from the launch site. Suddenly, a brilliant glow appeared on one side of the external tank. In seconds, the glow blossomed into a gigantic fireball. Screams of horror arose from the crowd as the Challenger, now 19 miles away, exploded, and bits of debris began to fall from the sky.

In classrooms across the country, children burst into tears. Adult Americans stared at their televisions in stunned disbelief.

Sources: Based on Broad 1986; Magnuson 1986; Lewis 1988; Malone 1988; Nelson 1988; Sanders 1988.

If any characteristic describes social life today, it is rapid social change. As we shall see in this chapter, technology, such as that which made the *Challenger* first a reality and then a disaster, is a driving force in this change. To understand the forces of social change is to better understand the forces that affect our lives, both positively and negatively.

Social Change: An Overview

Social change, a shift in the characteristics of culture and society, is such a vital part of social life that it has been a theme throughout this book. To make this theme more explicit, let's review the main points about social change made in the preceding chapters.

The Four Social Revolutions

The rapid, far-reaching social change that the world is currently experiencing did not "just happen." Rather, it is the result of fundamental forces set in motion thousands of years ago, beginning with the gradual domestication of plants and animals. This first social revolution allowed hunting and gathering societies to develop into horticultural and pastoral societies (see pages 145–148). The plow brought about the second social revolution, from which agricultural societies emerged. Then the invention of the steam en-

social change: the alteration of culture and societies over time

612

From the internal combustion engine to the telephone and the computer, technology lies at the center of our lives. The Challenger represents both the success and failure of technology: the general success of space exploration, but the stunning failure of this particular endeavor.

gine ushered in the Industrial Revolution, and now we are witnessing the fourth social revolution, stimulated by the invention of the microchip.

From Gemeinschaft to Gesellschaft

Although most of the consequences of this fourth revolution are yet to be seen, we can assume that they will be so fundamental that little of our way of life will be left untouched. This is how it was with the first three social revolutions. For example, the Industrial Revolution so remade society that early sociologists were disturbed by what they saw. The change from agricultural to industrial society meant not only that people moved from villages to cities but also that intimate, lifelong relationships were replaced by impersonal, short-term relationships. Paid work, contracts, and especially money, rather than the reciprocal obligations required by kinship, social position, and friendship, came to dominate social life. As reviewed on pages 102–103, sociologists use the terms *Gemeinschaft* and *Gesellschaft* to indicate this fundamental shift in society.

Capitalism and Industrialization

Just why did societies change from *Gemeinschaft* to *Gesellschaft*? Karl Marx pointed to a social invention called *capitalism*. He analyzed how the breakup of feudal society threw people off the land, creating a surplus of labor. Moving to cities, these masses were exploited by the owners of the means of production (factories, machinery, tools), setting in motion antagonistic relationships between capitalists and workers that remain today.

Max Weber agreed that capitalism was changing the world but he traced capitalism to the Protestant Reformation (see pages 170–172). He noted that the Reformation removed from Protestants the assurance that church membership saved them. As they agonized over heaven and hell, they concluded that God did not intend to leave his elect in uncertainty, that God would provide visible evidence of people's predestination to heaven. That sign, they decided, was prosperity. The unexpected consequence of the Reformation, then, was to make Protestants work hard and to be thrifty. The result was an economic surplus, the stimulation of capitalism, and, eventually, the Industrial Revolution that transformed the world.

Table 22.1

A Typology of Traditional and Modern Societies

Characteristics	Traditional Societies	Modern Societies
General Characteristics		
Social change	Slow	Rapid
Size of group	Small	Large
Religious orientation	More	Less
Formal education	No	Yes
Place of residence	Rural	Urban
Demographic transition	First stage	Third stage
Family size	Larger	Smaller
Infant mortality	High	Low
Life expectancy	Low	High
Health care	Home	Hospital
Temporal orientation	Past	Future
Material Relations		
Industrialized	No	Yes
Technology	Simple	Complex
Division of labor	Simple	Complex
Economic sector	Primary	Tertiary
Income	Low	High
Material possessions	Few	Many
Social Relationships		
Basic organization	*Gemeinschaft*	*Gesellschaft*
Families	Extended	Nuclear
Respect for elders	More	Less
Social stratification	Rigid	More open
Statuses	More ascribed	More achieved
Gender equality	Less	More
Norms		
View of reality, life, and morals	Absolute	Relativistic
Social control	Informal	Formal
Tolerance of differences	Less	More

Modernization

The term given to the sweeping changes ushered in by the Industrial Revolution is **modernization.** Table 22.1 reviews these changes. This table is an ideal type in Weber's sense of the term, for no society comprises to the maximum degree all the traits listed here. For example, although most Americans now work in the tertiary sector of the economy, many millions still work in the primary and secondary sectors. Thus all characteristics shown in Table 22.1 should be interpreted as "more" or "less" rather than "either/or."

Traditional, or *Gemeinschaft*, societies are small and rural, slow changing, with little stress on formal education. Most illnesses are treated at home. People live in extended families, look to the past for guidelines to the present, usually show high respect for elders, and have rigid social stratification and much inequality between the sexes. Life and morals tend to be seen in absolute terms, and few differences are tolerated. Modern societies, in contrast, are large, more urbanized, and fast changing. They stress formal education, are future oriented, and are less religiously oriented. In the third stage of the demographic transition, their members have smaller families, lower rates of infant mortality, longer lives, higher incomes, and more material possessions.

As capitalism and industrialization stimulated city life and ushered in short-term contractual relationships, people's views of the world changed. Their fundamental beliefs about what life should be like, their attitudes toward one another—nothing was to remain untouched. Just one example will help to make this point. In *Gemeinschaft* societies, people's rhythms of life were regulated by the seasons. For many, agriculture meant short periods of intense work, followed by long periods of a slower pace at routine tasks. Work was always available, and people worked as family units, with all but the youngest children contributing to the family's economic survival. Industrialization brought fundamental change, separating workers from family life for twelve to fourteen hours, six days a week. Work was no longer seasonal, but year round, except for unemployment, which now hung over people's heads, threatening their survival.

As technology from the industrialized world is introduced into the traditional societies of the Third World, we are able to witness how far-reaching the changes are. Take just modern medicine as an example. Its introduction into Third World nations helped to usher in the second stage of the demographic transition. As death rates dropped and birthrates remained high, the population exploded, bringing hunger and starvation, mass migration to cities, and mass migration from the Third World to the First World. This rush to Third World cities that have little industrialization, new to the world scene, is creating a host of problems yet to be solved. (See the Perspectives box on page 575.)

modernization: the process by which a *Gemeinschaft* society is transformed into a *Gesellschaft* society

A group known as G7, the world's most powerful nations, holds an annual economic summit, such as this one in Tokyo. At these meetings this tiny group makes decisions that affect the global map and the welfare of the world.

Globalization, Dependency, and Shifts in the Global Map

Already during the sixteenth century, today's Third World had begun to emerge. Trade alliances, forged by those nations with the most advanced technology of the time (the swiftest ships and the heaviest armaments), created a division into rich and poor nations. Then, according to *dependency theory*, as capitalism emerged the nations that industrialized exploited the resources of those that did not. As these nations, called the Third World, grew dependent on the First World, they were unable to develop their own resources (see pages 244–246). Today's information revolution will have similar consequences on global stratification. Those nations that take the fast lane on the information superhighway, primarily the First World, will dominate in the coming generation.

Since World War II, a realignment of national–regional powers has resulted in a triadic division of the world: a Japan-centered East, a Germany-centered Europe, and a United States-centered Western hemisphere (Robertson 1992). These three global powers, along with four lesser ones—Canada, France, Great Britain, and Italy—constitute the nations that today control the globe. These industrial giants—collectively known as G7 (meaning something like "*the* seven governments" or the "Global 7")—hold annual meetings at which they decide how to divide up the world's markets and regulate global economic policy, such as interest rates, tariffs, and currency exchanges. Their goal is to perpetuate their global dominance, which includes keeping prices down on raw materials from the Second and Third Worlds. Cheap oil is especially significant to this goal, making the domination of the Mideast essential, whether that be accomplished through peaceful means or a joint war effort by the United Nations.

Because of Russia's nuclear arsenal, the G7 have carefully courted Russia—giving Russia observer status at its annual summits and providing loans, encouragement, and some expertise to help Russia's transition to capitalism. The breakup of the Soviet Union has been a central consideration in G7's plans for a new world order, and events there will help determine the shape of future international alliances.

The Resurgence of Ethnic Conflicts

Threatening the global map so carefully divided by the G7 is the resurgence of ethnic conflicts across the globe. The breakup of the Soviet empire lifted the cover that had held in check the centuries' old hatreds and frustrated nationalistic ambitions of many ethnic groups. With the Soviet military and the KGB in disarray, these groups have turned violence on one another. In Africa, similar seething hatreds have brought warfare to groups only formally united by artificial political boundaries. In Europe, the former

The resurgence of ethnic conflicts around the world has come as a surprise to most social analysts. Fed by a history of discrimination and other injustices, the seething hatreds behind these conflicts can erupt into brutal violence, such as this haunting scene from Rwanda.

Yugoslavia divided, with parts self-destructing as pentup fury was unleashed. Ethnic conflicts threaten to erupt in Germany, France, Italy, the United States, and Mexico. At what point these resentments and hatreds will play themselves out, if ever, is unknown.

For the most part, the industrial nations care little if the entire continent of Africa self-destructs in ethnic slaughter, but the interethnic warfare of Bosnia cannot be tolerated. If it spreads, the resulting inferno could engulf Europe. For global control, the G7 must be able to depend on political and economic stability in its own neighborhood and in those countries that provide the essential raw materials for its industrial machine.

Social Movements

As we saw in the preceding chapter, social movements can be powerful forces for social change. From wide discontent emerge movements organized to address social issues—either to promote or to resist social change. If we want to examine the cutting edge of social change in an industrialized society, for the most part we need to look no further than its social movements. Indicating the issues of greatest concern to its citizens, social movements point to the areas that contain the greatest pressures for change. To see the future, we also need to examine the second part of the cutting edge of social change—a nation's new technology.

 ## Social Change and Technology

A simple and useful definition of **technology** is *tools*, items used to accomplish tasks. In this sense, technology refers both to clubs used to kill animals and to telephones and spacecraft. The explosion of the *Challenger*, described in the opening vignette, is a stunning example both of the failure of technology and of how far technology has advanced. A design flaw, troublesome in previous flights, proved fatal in this one. A simple gasket, an O-ring found in household appliances, did not fit properly. During the thirty-seven days that the *Challenger* stood on the launch pad, seven inches of rain had fallen. Some bypassed the ill-fitting O-ring, lodged in a joint, and froze during the inclement weather. Inadequate sealing allowed the combustion gases to leak—and ignite.

technology: often defined as the applications of science, but can be conceptualized as tools, items used to accomplish tasks

At the root of the design failure lay human error, complicated by political pressure. NASA needed a striking success to show Congress what it was getting for the huge sums of money pumped into the nation's space program. A highly publicized success by *Challenger* would pave the way for approval of the billions of dollars it would take to build a base on the moon and to send astronauts to Mars. Facing this pressure, NASA officials made the fateful decision to overlook certain flaws.

In spite of occasional glaring failures like the *Challenger*, modern technology is so advanced that experts are able to build space platforms and send people to the moon. We can pick up a telephone at home and call any city in the world. In just seconds, we can fax copies of documents overseas. Although the devices that allow such feats are fascinating, technology is more than the apparatus. Technology changes society. Without automobiles, telephones, televisions, computers, and so on, our entire way of life would be strikingly different. Let's look at how technology spreads, then at how technology affects the way people live, and, finally, at its impact on the natural environment.

Ogburn's Theory of Social Change

Sociologist William Ogburn (1922, 1938, 1961, 1964) identified three processes of social change. Technology, he said, can lead to social change through invention, discovery, and diffusion.

Invention   Ogburn defined **invention** as the combination of existing elements and materials to form new ones. While we think of inventions as being only material, such as computers, there are also social inventions, such as capitalism and the corporation. As we have seen, inventions, whether material or social, can have far-reaching consequences for a society. Later on, we will explore ways in which the automobile and the computer have transformed society, affecting not just some small part of social life but having ramifications for almost everything we do.

Discovery   Ogburn's second process of change is **discovery**, a new way of seeing reality. The reality is already present, but people now see it for the first time. For example, in 1992 the Cosmic Background Explorer (COBE), a satellite located 560 miles above the earth, provided data for the discovery of "ripples" in space. These ripples, 50 billion trillion miles across, are supposedly left over from density fluctuations in the afterglow of radiation from the birth of the cosmos. They are, presumably, the seeds that gave rise to the stars and planets three hundred thousand years after the "Big Bang" (Begley and Glick 1992; Wilford 1992).

Some discoveries, such as this one, may have little or no impact on a society. Other discoveries, in contrast, such as Columbus's "discovery" of North America, can produce such large-scale effects that they even alter the course of history. This example also illustrates another principle: a discovery brings extensive change only when it comes at the right time. Other groups, such as the Vikings, had already "discovered" America in the sense of learning that a new land existed (the land, of course, was no discovery to the Native Americans already living in it). Viking settlements disappeared into history, however, and Norse culture was untouched by the discovery.

Diffusion   **Diffusion,** said Ogburn, is the spread of an invention or discovery from one area to another. The usual reasons for diffusion are travel, trade, and conquest. As people migrate or visit an area, trade with one another, or one group conquers another, change occurs not only in material objects but also in human thought. Each can extensively affect social life.

On the material level, steel implements may replace stone items, and an economy may be transformed. Today, telecommunications are being diffused throughout the world, with similar far-reaching effects. On the intellectual level, citizenship illustrates

invention: the combination of existing elements and materials to form new ones; identified by William Ogburn as the first of three processes of social change

discovery: new way of seeing reality; identified by William Ogburn as the second of three processes of social change

diffusion: the spread of invention or discovery from one area to another; identified by William Ogburn as the final of three processes of social change

how ideas change social relationships. For example, this idea changed the political structure, for no longer was the monarch an unquestioned source of authority. Today, the concept of gender equality is circling the globe, with the basic idea that it is wrong to withhold rights on the basis of someone's sex. This idea, though now taken for granted in a few parts of the world, is revolutionary, and it is destined to transform basic human relationships and even social orders.

Cultural Lag Ogburn coined the term **cultural lag** to describe the situation in which some elements of a culture adapt to an invention or discovery more rapidly than others. Technology, he suggested, usually changes first, followed by culture. The nine-month school year is an example. In the nineteenth century, the school year matched the technology of the time, which required that children work with their parents at the critical times of planting and harvesting. Current technology has eliminated the need for the school year to be so short, but the cultural form has lagged severely behind technology.

Types of Technology

There are three types of technology. The first is **primitive technology,** natural items that people have adapted for their use such as spears, clubs, and animal skins. Both hunting and gathering societies and pastoral and horticultural societies are based on primitive technology. Most technology of agricultural societies is also primitive, for it centers on harnessing animals to do work. The second type, **industrial technology,** corresponds roughly to industrial society. It uses machines powered by fuels instead of natural forces such as winds and rivers. The third type, **postindustrial technology,** centers on information, transportation, and communication. At the core of postindustrial technology is the microchip.

A fourth type, which we might call the **new technology,** has yet to make its appearance on the human scene. If it does, it will be such a leap forward that we will not want to classify it as part of postindustrial technology. For example, should the transporters of *Star Trek* ever become reality, they would be part of the "new technology."

How Technology Transforms Society

When a technology is introduced into a society, it forces other parts of society to give way. In fact, *a new technology can reshape an entire society.* Let's look at five ways that technology changes society.

cultural lag: Ogburn's term for human behavior lagging behind technological innovations

primitive technology: the adaptation of natural items for human use

industrial technology: technology centered on machines powered by fuels instead of natural forces such as wind and rivers

postindustrial technology: technology centering on information, transportation, and communication

new technology: technology, if it is ever developed, that will be such a leap forward that it cannot be classified as simply an extension of current technology

Transformation of Existing Technologies The first impact is felt by the technology that is being displaced. Currently, for example, the rotary dial telephone is a living dinosaur. Some of us still use these machines, but they are clearly doomed to extinction in the wake of newer, more efficient touchtone telephones, and eventually, devices into which we will simply speak the number we desire. Similarly, IBM electric typewriters, "state of the art" equipment just a few years ago, have been rendered practically useless by the desktop computer.

Changes in Social Organization Technology also changes social organization. As discussed in Chapter 6, for example, machine technology gave birth to the factory. Prior to machine technology, most workers labored at home, but the advent of power-driven machinery made it more efficient for people to gather in one place to do their work. Then it was discovered that workers could produce more items if they did specialized tasks. Instead of each worker making an entire item, as had been the practice, each individual worked on only part of an item. One worker would do so much hammering on a single part, or turn so many bolts, and then someone else would take the item and do some other repetitive task before a third person took over, and so on. Henry Ford then built on this innovation by developing the assembly line: Instead of workers moving to the parts, a machine moved the parts to the workers. In addition, the parts were made interchangeable and easy to attach (Womack et al. 1990).

Changes in Ideology   Technology also spurs ideology. Karl Marx saw the change to the factory system as a source of **alienation.** He noted that workers who were assigned repetitive tasks on just a small part of a product no longer felt connected to the finished product and could therefore no longer take pride in it. They became alienated from the product of their labor, Marx said, which bred dissatisfaction and unrest.

Marx also noted that the new mode of production, factories, gave power to owners to exploit workers. Before factories came on the scene, workers owned their tools and were essentially independent. If they did not like their work situation, they could pack up their hammers and saws and leave. Others would hire them to build a wagon or make a harness. In the factory, however, the capitalists owned the tools and machinery, and they used the power that came with ownership to extract every ounce of sweat and blood they could. The workers had to submit, for if they left the tools stayed, and other workers took their place. Only a workers' revolution will change this exploitation, said Marx. When the workers realize the common basis of their exploitation, they will take over the means of production and establish a workers' state.

Note how the new technology that led to the factory stimulated new ideologies. First, defenders of capitalism developed an ideology to support the principle of maximizing profits. Then followers of Marx built theories of socialism to attack capitalism. As we shall see shortly, just as changes in technology stimulated the development of communism, changes in technology have been crucial in bringing about its end.

Transformation of Values   Just as ideology follows technology, so do values. If technology is limited to clubbing animals, then strength and cunning are valued. So are animal skins. No doubt some primitive man and woman walked with heads held high as they wore the skins of some especially unusual or dangerous animal—while their neighbors looked on in envy as they trudged along wearing only the same old sheepskins. In contrast, today's technology produces an abundance of synthetic fabrics for clothing. Unlike this primitive couple, Americans brag about cars, hot tubs, and jacuzzis—and make certain that their jeans have the right labels prominently displayed. In short, while jealousy, envy, and pride may be basic to human nature, the particular emphasis on materialism depends on the state of technology.

Transformation of Social Relationships   Technology also changes social relationships. As men were drawn out of their homes to work in factories, family relationships changed. No longer present in the home on a daily basis, the husband-father became isolated from many of the day-to-day affairs of the family. One consequence of husbands becoming strangers to their wives and children was a higher divorce rate. As current technology draws more and more women from the home to offices and factories, the consequences are similar—greater isolation from husbands and children, and one more impetus toward a higher divorce rate.

An Extended Example: Effects of the Automobile

If we try to pick the single item that has had the greatest impact on social life in this century, among the many candidates the automobile and the microchip stand out, though it is still too early to judge the full effects of the latter technology. Let us first look at some of the ways in which the automobile changed U.S. society.

Displacement of Existing Technology   The automobile gradually pushed aside the old technology, a replacement that began in earnest when Henry Ford began to mass-produce the Model T in 1908. People immediately found automobiles attractive (Flink 1990). They considered them cleaner, safer, more reliable, and more economical than

alienation: Marx's term for workers' lack of connection to the product of their labor; caused by their being assigned repetitive tasks on a small part of a product

This 1879 engraving of Third Avenue in New York City shows the city prior to the automobile. Other than walking and the steam engine, shown here powering an elevated train, horses were the primary means of transportation. Note that horses were even used to pull streetcars. The automobile transformed not only transportation, but, as analyzed in the text, even the shape of cities and basic social relationships.

horses. Cars also offered the appealing prospect of lower taxes, for no longer would the public have to pay to clean up the tons of horse manure that accumulated on the city streets each day. Humorous as it sounds now, it was even thought that automobiles would eliminate the cities' parking problems, for an automobile took up only half as much space as a horse and buggy.

The automobile also replaced a second technology. The United States had developed a vast system of urban transit, with electric streetcar lines radiating outward from the center of our cities. As the automobile became affordable and more dependable, Americans demonstrated a clear preference for the greater convenience of private transportation. Instead of walking to a streetcar and then having to wait in the cold and rain, people were able to travel directly from home on their own schedule.

Effects on Cities The decline in the use of streetcars actually changed the shape of U.S. cities. Before the automobile, U.S. cities were web-shaped, for residences and businesses were located along the streetcar lines. Freed from having to live so close to the tracks, people filled in the areas between the "webs."

The automobile also stimulated mass suburbanization. Already in the 1920s, U.S. residents had begun to leave the city, for they found that they could commute to work in the city from outlying areas where they benefitted from more room and fewer taxes (Preston 1979). Their departure significantly reduced the cities' tax base, thus contributing, as discussed in Chapter 20, to many of the problems that U.S. cities experience today.

Effects on Farm Life and Villages The automobile had a profound impact on farm life and villages. Prior to the 1920s, most farmers were isolated from the city. Because using horses for a trip to town was slow and cumbersome, they made such trips infrequently. By the 1920s, however, the popularity and low price of the Model T made the "Saturday trip to town" a standard event. There, farmers would market products, shop, and visit with friends. As a consequence, farm life was altered; for example, mail order catalogs stopped being the primary source of shopping, and access to better medical care and education improved (Flink 1990). Farmers were also able to travel to bigger towns, where they found a greater variety of goods. As farmers began to use the nearby villages only for immediate needs, these flourishing centers of social and commercial life dried up.

Changes in Architecture The automobile's effects on commercial architecture are clear—from the huge parking lots that decorate malls like necklaces to the drive-up windows of banks and restaurants. But the automobile also fundamentally altered the architecture of U.S. homes (Flink 1990). Before the car, each home had a stable in the back where the family kept its buggy and horses. The stable was the logical place to shelter the family's first car, and it required no change in architecture. The change occurred in three steps. First, new homes were built with a detached garage located like the stable, at the back of the home. Second, as the automobile became a more essential part of the U.S. family, the garage was incorporated into the home by moving it from the back to the front of the house, and connecting it by a breezeway. In the final step the breezeway was removed, and the garage integrated into the home so that Americans could enter their automobiles without even going outside.

Changed Courtship Customs and Sexual Norms By the 1920s, the automobile was used extensively for dating, thereby removing children from the watchful eye of parents and undermining parental authority. The police began to receive complaints about "night riders" who parked their cars along country lanes, "doused their lights, and indulged in orgies" (Brilliant 1964). Automobiles became so popular for courtship that by the 1960s about 40 percent of marriage proposals took place in them (Flink 1990).

In 1925 Jewett introduced cars with a foldout bed, as did Nash in 1937. The Nash version became known as "the young man's model" (Flink 1990). Since the 1970s, mobile lovemaking has declined, partly because urban sprawl (itself due to the automobile) left fewer safe trysting spots, and partly because changed sexual norms made beds more accessible.

Effects on Women's Roles The automobile may also lie at the heart of the changed role of women in U.S. society. To see how, we first need to see what a woman's life was like before the automobile. Historian James Flink (1990) described it this way:

> Until the automobile revolution, in upper-middle-class households groceries were either ordered by phone and delivered to the door or picked up by domestic servants or the husband on his way home from work. Iceboxes provided only very limited space for the storage of perishable foods, so shopping at markets within walking distance of the home was a daily chore. The garden provided vegetables and fruits in

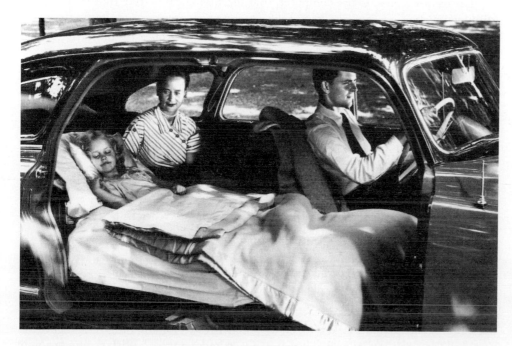

The automobile transformed society, from gender roles and architecture to courtship and sexual norms. Cars with fold-out beds were part of this transformation. Shown here is the 1949 Nash, with a feature in high demand by some dating couples.

season, which were home-canned for winter consumption. Bread, cakes, cookies, and pies were home-baked. Wardrobes contained many home-sewn garments.

Mother supervised the household help and worked alongside them preparing meals, washing and ironing, and house cleaning. In her spare time she mended clothes, did decorative needlework, puttered in her flower garden, and pampered a brood of children. Generally, she made few family decisions and few forays alone outside the yard. She had little knowledge of family finances and the family budget. The role of the lower-middle-class housewife differed primarily in that far less of the household work was done by hired help, so that she was less a manager of other people's work, more herself a maid-of-all-work around the house.

Because automobiles required skill rather than strength, women were able to drive as well as men. This new mobility freed women physically from the narrow confines of the home. As Flink (1990) observed, the automobile changed women "from producers of food and clothing into consumers of national-brand canned goods, prepared foods, and ready-made clothes. The automobile permitted shopping at self-serve supermarkets outside the neighborhood and in combination with the electric refrigerator made buying food a weekly rather than a daily activity." When women began to do the shopping, they gained greater control over the family budget, and as their horizons extended beyond the confines of the home, they also gained different views of life.

In short, the automobile changed women's roles at home, including their relationship with their husbands, altered their attitudes, transformed their opportunities, and stimulated them to participate in areas of social life not connected with the home.

▼   **In Sum** With changes this extensive, it would not be inaccurate to say that the automobile also shifted basic values and changed the way we look at life. No longer isolated, women, teenagers, and farmers began to see the world differently. So did husbands and wives, whose marital relationship had also been altered. The automobile even transformed views of courtship, sexuality, and gender relations.

No one attributes such fundamental changes solely to the automobile, of course, for many other technological changes, as well as historical events, occurred during this same period, each making its own contribution to social change. Even this brief overview of the social effects of the automobile, however, illustrates that technology is not merely an isolated tool but exerts a profound influence on social life.

Let us now consider the computer, that technological marvel that is also transforming society.

An Extended Example: Effects of the Computer

The ominous wail seemed too close for comfort. Sally looked in her rearview mirror and realized that the flashing red lights and the screaming siren might be for her. She felt confused. "I'm just on my way to Soc class," she thought. "I'm not speeding or anything." After she pulled over, an angry voice over a loudspeaker ordered her out of the car.

As she got out, someone barked the command, "Back up with your hands in the air!" Bewildered, Sally stood frozen for a moment. "Put 'em up now! Right now!" She did as she was told.

The officer crouched behind his open door, his gun drawn. When Sally reached the car—still backing up—the officer grabbed her, threw her to the ground, and handcuffed her hands behind her back. She heard words she would never forget, "You are under arrest for murder. You have the right to remain silent. Anything you say can and will be used against you in a court of law. You have the right to an attorney. If you cannot afford one, one will be provided for you."

Traces of alarm still flicker across Sally's face when she recalls her arrest. She had never even been issued a traffic ticket, much less been arrested for anything. The nightmare that Sally experienced happened because of a "computer error." With the inversion of

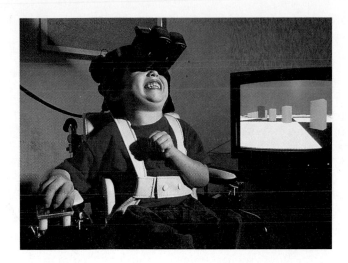

A developing aspect of computer technology is virtual reality, in which the viewer "enters" a computerized world. In this invention, based on the microchip, the world inside the mask seems as real as the ordinary world outside it. The viewer's angle of vision changes in response to head movements. Shown here is an application of this technology to help disabled children.

two numbers, her car's license number had been entered instead of that of a woman wanted for a brutal killing earlier that day.

The police later apologized. "These things happen," they said, "but not very often. We're sorry, but I'm sure you understand."

None of us is untouched by the computer, but it is unlikely that many of us have felt its power as directly and dramatically as Sally did. For most of us, the computer's control lies quietly behind the scenes. Although the computer has intruded into our daily lives, most of us never think about it. Our grades are computerized, and probably our paycheck as well. When we buy groceries, a computer scans our purchases and presents a printout of the name, price, and quantity of each item. Essentially the computer's novelty has given way to everyday routine; it is simply another tool.

Many people rejoice over the computer's capacity to improve their quality of life. They are pleased with the quality control of manufactured goods and the ease with which they can keep detailed records. Computers have also reduced the drudgery of many jobs. A typist can now type just one letter and let the computer print and address it to ten individuals—or ten thousand. Architects use software programs that show buildings in three dimensions.

Some individuals, however, worry about errors that can creep into computerized records, aware that something like Sally's misfortune may happen to them. Others fear that confidentiality of computer data will be abused, in the way that Orwell's Big Brother used information to achieve total control. Let us first look at how the computer is changing medicine, the military, education, and the workplace, then consider the concerns it has raised about the invasion of privacy.

Medicine   Computers have transformed medicine. They allow medical personnel to peer within the body's hidden recesses to determine how its parts are functioning or to see if surgery is necessary. They allow surgeons to operate on unborn babies and on previously inaccessible parts of the brain. Computers produce complicated test results in minutes instead of days. Physicians can feed vital information into a computer—sex, age, race, family medical history, symptoms, and test results—and find out what the chances are that a patient has cancer or some other disease.

Will the computer lead to "doctorless" medical offices? Will we perhaps one day feed vital information about ourselves into a computer and receive a printout of what is wrong with us—and, of course, a prescription? (Somehow, "Take two aspirins and key me in the morning" doesn't sound comforting.) Such an office is likely to remain only a concept in some futurist's fanciful imagination, for physicians would repel such an onslaught on their expertise, even if computers do outperform them in diagnostics (Waldholz 1991). Many patients are also likely to resist, for they would miss interacting with their doctors, especially the assurances and other psychological support that good physicians provide. It is likely that the computer will remain a diagnostic tool for physicians, not a replacement for them.

The Military and War The military has also been profoundly affected by the computer. This point was dramatically driven home to the U.S. public—and the world—during the Persian Gulf War by televised footage of "smart" weapons honing in on targets. Most impressive were pictures videotaped from the nose of a ballistic missile as it hit a designated air shaft in Iraq's military headquarters in the heart of Baghdad.

The computer apparently allowed pinpoint accuracy, and television brought the war into the world's living rooms. But on another level these machines also made the war less real. The only pictures that were shown were of exploding buildings, looking for all the world like computerized targets on a video game. The literal blood and guts were strangely absent. No suffering was visible, no screams of agony were heard. Indeed they were there, but not on the screen.

During the months in which the West's soldiers trained in the desert before the attack against Saddam Hussein's army, a sociology student, like thousands of other civilians, wrote a letter "to any soldier in Desert Shield." Her military pen pal sent her unauthorized photos of the slaughter of Iraqi troops as they fled Kuwait City. They showed the charred remains of teenaged soldiers, bodies clutched in agony. When the soldier's commander discovered that he had disclosed his "photo album of the war," the student had to return it immediately, or her pen pal's military career would have been over (author's files).

Education Almost every grade school in the United States introduces its students to the computer. Children learn how to type on it, as well as how to use mathematics software. Successful educational programs use a gamelike, challenging format that makes students forget that they are "studying." The question of social inequality becomes significant in this context. Those schools most able to afford the latest in computer technology are able to better prepare their students for the future. That advantage, of course, is given students of private schools and the richest public school districts, thus helping to perpetuate social inequalities that arise from the chance of birth.

The computer will transform the college of the future. Each office and dormitory room and off-campus residence will be equipped with fiber-optic cable, and a professor will be able to transmit a 250-page book directly from his or her office to a student's bedroom, or back the other way, in *less* time than it took to read this sentence ("Harvard Wired," 1994). To help students and professors write papers or prepare reports, computers will search millions of pages of text. Digital textbooks will replace printed versions such as this one. You will be able to key in the terms *social interaction* and *gender*, and select your preference of historical period and geographical area—and the computer will give you maps, moving images, and sounds. It will be the same for riots and Los Angeles, lynching and the South. If you wish, the computer will give you a test—at your chosen level of difficulty—so you can immediately check your mastery of the material.

The Workplace The computer is transforming the workplace. On the simplest level is how we do work. For example, I am composing this book on a computer, which will immediately print what I write. A series of archaic, precomputer processes follows, however, in which the printed copy is sent via the postal service to an editor, who physically handles the manuscript and sends it to others who do the same. The manuscript is eventually returned to me via the postal service for final corrections—a rather primitive process, much as would have occurred during Benjamin Franklin's day. Eventually I will be able to zap my manuscript electronically from my computer to my editor's computer—when practice catches up with potential.

On another level, the computer is changing things much more fundamentally, for it alters social relationships. For example, no longer do I bring my manuscript to a university secretary, wait, and then retrieve it several days later. The secretary is bypassed entirely, for with corrections made at the computer the secretary is no longer necessary. In this instance, the computer enhances social relationships, for the department secretary has much less work, and this new process eliminates the necessity of excuses when a manuscript is not ready on time—and the tensions in the relationship that this brings.

On the negative side, however, are increased surveillance of workers and depersonalization. Social psychologist Shoshana Zuboff (1991) reports how managers are able to increase surveillance without face-to-face supervision. Computers can report the number of strokes a word processor makes each minute or hour, or inform supervisors how long each telephone operator takes per call. Operators who are "underperforming" can then be singled out for discipline. It does not matter that the slower operators may be more polite or more helpful, only that the computer reports slower performance.

The computer's effect may be so radical that it reverses the work location ushered in by industrialization. As discussed earlier, industrialization caused work to shift from home to factory and office. Since workers now can be linked via computers, this fundamental change may be reversed as workers remain at home and perform their work on computers.

Telecommuters, people who work at home and communicate with the office by computer, illustrate these positive and negative consequences of computers. They don't miss losing the frustration and wasted time of commuting, and they like the flexibility of schedules. If they want to take a break or work at night instead of the day, they can. Telecommuting gives *them* control, which reduces the alienation of workers that Marx observed. Some, however, miss the office interaction, especially the give and take of joking, sharing the latest gossip, and giving and receiving sympathy, approval, and encouragement. A message on their computer doesn't provide the same satisfaction. To avoid depersonalization, some telecommuters go into the office a day a week, where they can "read the look" on the boss's face—missing from their computer terminal—and to keep their own face in the boss's mind when it comes to raises and promotions.

In some instances, the computer is reducing corporate hierarchies. Because hundreds of workers can share information simultaneously, in offices that have networks connecting their computers low-status workers have access to information that just a short time ago was available only to their bosses (Wilke 1993). These networks also allow low-level employees to join on-line discussions with senior executives. In these interactions, people are judged more by what they say than by their rank on the corporate ladder. In addition, visual cues that influence interaction—gender, race, age, weight, height, clothing, beauty, and physical ability—disappear. The content of the message becomes paramount. A remarkable example is the network software used at Wright-Patterson Air Force base in Ohio, where enlisted men can share ideas with a colonel, bypassing the sergeant—unheard of in the armed forces.

One effect of computers is called **job multiskilling,** which means that skills are added to those a worker already possesses. Secretaries, for example, had to learn to use a keyboard, monitor, printer, fax, and e-mail. Computers cut both ways, however, and they also cause **job deskilling;** that is, computers can reduce the skills necessary to do a job by telling workers what to do. For example, in a certain biscuit factory a master baker used to be in charge of mixing the dough, but now a computer has taken over. No longer is there a master baker, just an unskilled employee who presses a button to start the mixing process (Hodson and Parker 1988).

Power, Secrecy, and National Boundaries

A surprising effect of telecommunications is the weakening of national boundaries. Much to the dismay of dictators who want to keep their people ignorant so they can control them more easily, information can no longer be contained. Even during the Tiananmen Square massacre in Beijing, Chinese students faxed reports to Americans (Cleveland 1990). Telecommunications also contributed to the

job multiskilling: adding skills to those a worker already possesses

job deskilling: reducing the amount of skills that a job requires

collapse of the Soviet empire, for no matter what the ruling elite told the people, they were acutely aware through telecommunications (from television to fax) that the citizens of the capitalist countries enjoyed a much higher standard of living.

Secrecy, limiting access to information, is desired by people in power. To keep their plans secret, governments, businesses, and individuals sometimes use encryption; that is, they put their messages into code. With many affairs now dependent on worldwide communications that can be intercepted by enemies, competitors, or even the idly curious, encryption has become more significant than ever.

Up to now, secrecy was uncertain, for all encrypting devices were able to be broken—until 1993, that is, when Philip Zimmerman, an American anti–nuclear war activist, became a folk hero. Zimmerman decided that encryption should belong to the people and give them privacy from snooping governments. He took a six-month leave of absence from his job and worked twelve-hour days. He gave away the results of his work, the PGP—Pretty Good Privacy—a program that cannot be broken because it requires two different keys (Burkeley 1994). The sender needs only one to send a message, while the receiver decodes the message with a different key—which never needs to leave his or her computer.

The implications of this invention span the globe. Government leaders are upset because their spying on other governments is more difficult, and criminal investigators are concerned because organized crime can operate more easily. But when Russia's freedom hung in the balance after Russia's premier, Boris Yeltsin, dismissed the Russian parliament, Zimmerman received a message from Latvia: "If dictatorship takes over Russia, your PGP is widespread from Baltic to Far East now and will help democratic people if necessary. Thanks."

The Shrinking World and Cultural Leveling

Computers are causing the world to shrink in both space and time. Homes and businesses in the First World are being united by the satellite relays paving an information superhighway. In the jungles of Brazil, the Kayapo Indians used to spend their evenings gathered around the dancing flames of a camp fire, the children listening attentively as the elders told stories. These stories were not mere entertainment, but a primary means of imparting the tribe's history and culture. They integrated the people by creating shared beliefs, values, and life goals.

And now? Television has come to the Amazon. After selling mahogany trees and gold, the Kayapo bought a satellite dish. Now at night the children sit transfixed before the dancing images of cultures utterly foreign to them. The elders lament their loss of audience, wondering if they should destroy what they call the "Big Ghost" before it destroys their culture. This topic is explored further in the Perspectives box on the next page.

The Information Superhighway and Social Inequalities

The term *information superhighway* carries the idea of information traveling at a high rate of speed among homes and businesses. Just as a highway allows physical travel from one place to another, so homes and businesses will be connected by the rapid flow of information. Already 20 million people around the world are able to communicate by Internet, while other services such as Prodigy, America Online, and CompuServe allow electronic access to libraries of information. Some programs sift, sort, and transmit scanned images, sound, even video among participants (Wilke 1993). Using electronic mail (e-mail), people are able to zap messages without regard to national boundaries. This is the future, a world linked by almost instantaneous communications, with information readily accessible around the globe, and few places to be called remote.

Much as the telephone does now, interactive television will connect most U.S. households. Ten thousand movies will be available on demand on robot-accessed tape (Press 1993). You may be able to key in a list of groceries and see the total prices those items are selling for in several food stores in your area—or to "walk" through your local mall, "visit" individual shops, even "pick up" merchandise, and order what you want.

The implications of the information superhighway for national and global stratification are severe. On the national level, we can end up with information have-nots among inner-city and rural residents, thus perpetuating present inequalities (Carey and Lewyn 1994). On the global level, the question is who will control the information superhighway. The answer, of course, is obvious, for it is the First World that is developing the communications system, seemingly destining the Third World to a perpetual pauper status.

Since knowledge is power, these are no idle issues.

Perspectives

CULTURAL DIVERSITY AROUND THE WORLD

Lost Tribes, Lost Knowledge

SINCE 1900, 90 OF Brazil's 270 Indian tribes have disappeared. As settlers have taken over their lands, other tribes have settled in villages. With village life comes a loss of tribal knowledge.

Tribal groups are not just "wild" people barely surviving in spite of their ignorance. On the contrary, they possess intricate forms of social organization and knowledge accumulated over thousands of years. The 2,500 Kayapo Indians, for example, belong to one of the Amazon's endangered tribes. The Kayapo make use of 250 types of wild fruit and hundreds of nut and tuber species. They cultivate thirteen distinct bananas, eleven kinds of manioc (cassava), sixteen sweet potato strains, and seventeen different yams. Many of these varieties are unknown to non-Indians. The Kayapo also use thousands of medicinal plants, one of which contains a drug effective against intestinal parasites.

Until recently, Western scientists dismissed tribal knowledge as superstitious and worthless. Now, however, the West is coming to realize that to lose tribes is to lose knowledge. In the Central African Republic, a man whose chest was being eaten away by a subcutaneous amoeboid infection lay dying because he did not respond to drugs. Out of desperation, the Catholic nuns who were treating him sought the advice of a native doctor, who applied crushed soldier termites to the open wounds. The "dying" man made a remarkable recovery.

Along with the disappearance of a language goes a tribe's collective knowledge—and about half of the world's six thousand languages are doomed because no children speak them. And the disappearance of the forests destroys many species yet unknown that may hold healing properties. Of the earth's 265,000 species of plants, only 1,100 have been thoroughly studied by Western scientists. Yet 40,000 may possess medicinal or undiscovered nutritional value for humans. For example, scientists have recently discovered that the leaves of *Taxus baccata*, a Himalayan tree found in mountainous parts of India, contain taxol, a drug effective against ovarian cancer.

On average, one tribe of Amazonian Indians has been lost each year of this century—due to violence against them, greed by non-Indians for their native lands, and exposure to infectious diseases against which they have little resistance. Ethnocentrism underlies much of this assault. Perhaps the extreme is represented by the cattle ranchers in Colombia who killed eighteen Cueva Indians. The cattle ranchers were perplexed when they were put on trial for murder. They asked why they should be charged with a crime, since everyone knew that the Cuevas were animals, not people. They pointed out that there was even a verb in Colombian Spanish, *cuevar*, which means "to hunt Cueva Indians." So what was their crime, they asked? The jury found them innocent because of "cultural ignorance."

Sources: Simons 1989; Durning 1990; Gorman 1991; Linden 1991; Stipp 1992.

Other Theories of Social Change

Before turning to the environment, let's look at other explanations of why societies change. Let's first consider two major types of theories—evolutionary and cyclical—and then look at conflict theory.

Evolutionary Theories

Evolutionary theories can be classified into three basic types: unilinear, multilinear, and cyclical. Let's consider each.

The dominating assumption during the 1800s and in the earlier part of this century was that European and European-derived cultures represented the pinnacle of human evolution. Consequently, other groups represented a lesser stage of development. When they evolved, they, too, would become like the Europeans. Such an assumption underlies this 1828 portrait of Hoowaunneka, a Native American of the Winnebago tribe, as the painter, C.B. King (inadvertently) gave Hoowaunneka European features.

Unilinear Evolution   *Unilinear* evolutionary theories assume that all societies follow the same path, evolving from the simple to the complex through uniform sequences (Barnes 1935). Lewis Henry Morgan (1877), for example, proposed that societies go through three stages: savagery, barbarism, and civilization. In his eyes English society served as the epitome of civilization, which all others were destined to follow. Sociologists Herbert Spencer (1884) and Robert MacIver (1937) also held evolutionary views of social change. Since the basic assumption of this theory, that all preliterate groups have the same form of social organization, has been found to be untrue, views of unilinear evolution have been discredited. In addition, seeing one's own society as the top of the evolutionary ladder is now considered unacceptably ethnocentric.

Multilinear Evolution   *Multilinear* views of evolution have replaced unilinear theories. The assumption remains that societies evolve from smaller to larger, more complex forms as they adapt to their environments, but instead of assuming that all societies follow the same path, multilinear theories presuppose that different routes can lead to a similar stage of development. Thus, to become industrialized, societies need not pass through the same sequence of stages (Sahlins and Service 1960; Lenski and Lenski 1987).

Evaluating Evolutionary Theories   Central to evolutionary theories, whether unilinear or multilinear, is the idea of *progress*, that societies evolve toward a higher state. Growing appreciation of the rich diversity of traditional cultures, however, has brought this idea under attack. Now that Western culture is in crisis (poverty, racism, discrimination, war, alienation, violent sexual assaults, unsafe streets, rampant fear) and no longer regarded as holding the answers to human happiness, the assumption of progress has been cast aside and evolutionary theories have been rejected (Eder 1990; Smart 1990).

Cyclical Theories

Cyclical theories attempt to account for the rise of entire civilizations, not a particular society. Why, for example, did Egyptian, Greek, and Roman civilizations rise to a peak of power and then disappear? Cyclical theories assume that civilizations are like organisms: they are born, see an exuberant youth, come to maturity, decline as they reach old age, and finally die (Hughes 1962).

Historian Arnold Toynbee (1946) proposed that all civilizations follow a typical life course. He said that each time a society successfully meets a challenge, oppositional forces are set up that must later be overcome. At its peak, when a civilization has become an empire, the ruling elite loses its capacity to keep the masses in line "by charm rather than by force." The fabric of society is then ripped apart. Although force may hold the empire together for hundreds of years, the civilization is doomed.

In a book that provoked widespread controversy, *The Decline of the West* (1926–1928), Oswald Spengler, a German teacher and social critic, proposed that Western civilization was on the wane. Although the West succeeded in overcoming the crises provoked by Hitler and Mussolini that so disturbed Spengler, as Toynbee noted, civilizations do not necessarily end in a sudden and total collapse. Since the decline can last hundreds of years, some analysts think that the crisis in Western civilization mentioned earlier (poverty, assault, and so on) may indicate that Spengler was right.

Conflict Theory

Prior to Toynbee, Marx identified a recurring process in human history. He viewed social change as a **dialectical process,** in which a *thesis* (the status quo) contains within it its own *antithesis*, or opposition. The resulting struggle between the thesis and its antithesis leads to a new state, or *synthesis*. This new social order, in turn, becomes a thesis that will be challenged by its own antithesis, and so on.

In short, Marx saw the history of a society as a series of confrontations in which each ruling group sows the seeds of its own destruction. Capitalism, for example, sets workers and capitalists on a collision course. Capitalism is the thesis, the misery of workers the antithesis, and a classless state the synthesis. The dialectical process will not stop until workers establish this classless state.

The analysis of G7 given earlier follows conflict theory. Consider the current division of world resources and global markets a thesis. This arrangement contains contradictions, or an antithesis, such as the dissatisfactions that some G7 nation may have with its status in the arrangement. Another antithesis is resentments on the part of have-not nations. Still another is change that may occur in a nation's relative status. If one of the G7 nations loses or gains relative wealth, or substantially changes the size of its military, the arrangement threatens to come unglued. A new arrangement, or synthesis, will have to be worked out. Similarly, nations of the Second or Third World that gain in relative wealth or military power will also press for synthesis, a redistribution of power and resources. A population explosion in some area of the globe can place similar pressures on the arrangement, as can the ethnic conflicts we reviewed earlier. Any resulting new arrangement, or synthesis, will also contain its own contradictions, or antithesis, that will present problems that must later be resolved.

Social Change and the Natural Environment

Of all the changes in which societies today are immersed, perhaps those affecting the natural environment hold the most serious implications for human life. Industrialization and technology have brought such changes to the earth's air, water, soil, and atmosphere that some experts believe human existence itself is threatened. As we shall see, all three worlds of development face severe environmental problems.

Environmental Problems in the First World

Although even primitive technology produced pollution, the frontal assault on the natural environment did not begin in earnest until nations industrialized. The more extensive the industrialization, the better it was considered for a nation's welfare, and the slogan for the First World has been, "Growth at any cost."

Industrial growth came, but at a high cost to the natural environment. Today, for example, formerly pristine streams are polluted sewers, the water supply of many cities is unfit to drink, and Los Angeles announces "smog days" on radio and television, keeping children inside during recess and warning everyone to stay indoors. Of all the consequences of pollution in the First World that we could discuss—such as the depletion of the ozone layer in order to have the convenience of spray bottles and air conditioners, which may yet prove to be a folly that harms all of humanity—we shall consider just the implications of fossil fuels.

Fossil Fuels and Environmental Degradation The burning of fossil fuels for factories, motorized vehicles, and power plants has been especially harmful. Fish can no longer survive in some lakes in Canada and the northeastern United States because of **acid rain**—the burning fossil fuels release sulfur dioxide and nitrogen oxide, which react with moisture

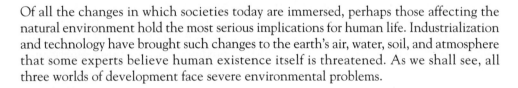

dialectical process: each arrangement, or thesis, contains contradictions, or antitheses, which must be resolved; the new arrangement, or synthesis, contains its own contradictions, and so on

acid rain: rain containing sulfuric and nitric acids (produced by the reaction of sulfur dioxide and nitrogen oxide with moisture when released into the air with the burning of fossil fuels) in the air to become sulfuric and nitric acids (Luoma 1989). An invisible but infinitely more serious consequence is the **greenhouse effect.** Like the glass of a greenhouse, the gases emitted from burning fossil fuels allow sunlight to enter the earth's atmosphere freely, but inhibit the release of heat. It is as though the gases have closed the atmospheric window through which our planet breathes. Some scientists say that the resulting **global warming** may melt the polar ice caps and inundate the world's shorelines, cause the climate boundaries to move about four hundred miles north, and may make many animal and plant species extinct (Smith and Tirpak 1988; Thomas 1988; Weisskopf 1992). Not all scientists agree with this scenario, however; some even doubt that a greenhouse effect exists (Balling 1992; Davis 1992).

The Energy Shortage, Internal Combustion Engines, and Multinational Corporations   If you ever read about an energy shortage, you can be sure that it is false. There is no energy shortage, nor can there ever be. The earth holds the potential of producing unlimited low-cost power, which can help to raise the living standards of humans across the globe. The sun, for example, produces more energy than humanity could ever need. Boundless energy is also available from the tides and the winds. In some cases, we need better technology to harness these sources of energy, while in others we need only to apply technology that we already have.

Since burning fossil fuels in internal combustion engines is the main source of pollution in the First World, and vast sources of alternative energy are available, why doesn't the First World use its scientific expertise to develop the technology to utilize these alternative sources of energy? From a conflict perspective, such abundant sources of energy present a threat to the energy monopoly ruled by the multinationals, and, to maintain their profits, they make certain that internal combustion engines remain dominant. We cannot expect the practical development and widespread use of alternative sources of power until the multinationals have cornered the market on the technology that will harness them—and conclude that the alternative sources of energy will yield as huge profits as those they now reap.

Environmental Racism and Social Class   Pollution in the United States has a racial and social class bias (Cushman 1993; Noah 1994). Racial minorities and the poor are disproportionately exposed to air pollution, hazardous wastes, pesticides, and the like. The basic reasons are that the land where the poor live sells cheaply, and the rich would not stand for factories to spew pollution near their homes. For the same reasons, hazardous waste landfills are likely to be located in predominantly African-American or Latino communities. To deal with this issue, a new specialty, environmental poverty law, is developing (Hayes 1992).

Environmental Problems in the Second World

Environmental degradation is not only a First World problem, and such severe consequences of industrialization as ozone depletion, the greenhouse effect, and global warming cannot be laid solely at the feet of the First World. With the dissolution of the Soviet Union came revelations of extensive pollution throughout its territory (Feshbach 1992). Until then, pollution had been treated as a state secret. Scientists and journalists could not mention pollution in public, and even a peaceful demonstration to call attention to pollution could net its participants a two-year prison sentence. With protest stifled, no environmental protection laws, and production quotas to be met, environmental pollution was rampant.

The extent of pollution in Russia and its former colonies, however, is difficult to grasp (Holman 1992, 1994). Russia is so polluted that its life expectancy has declined (Rich 1992), half of its arable land is unsuitable for farming, and half of its tap water is unfit to drink. Almost all of Russia's rivers are severely polluted. More than a third of Russians live in cities where air pollution is at least ten times greater than permitted lev-

greenhouse effect: the buildup of carbon dioxide in the earth's atmosphere that allows light to enter but inhibits the release of heat; believed to cause global warming

global warming: an increase in the earth's temperature due to the greenhouse effect

Under the leadership of the Communist party, environmental degradation was extensive. The Second World continues to suffer its effects, as it will for many decades. Shown here is the Aral Sea, an inland body of water that used to be more than 24,000 square miles and teeming with fish.

els. Most of Russia's former colonies face a similar situation. The level of pollution in Budapest, for example, makes a one-hour walk there as damaging to the lungs as smoking a pack of cigarettes (Diehl 1992; Okie 1992).

The dissolution of the Soviet Union brought new freedoms, including the right to environmental protest. For the most part, however, the protests have fallen on deaf ears. Considering the Second World's rush to compete industrially with the West, the desire to improve a low standard of living, and the lack of funds to purchase expensive pollution controls, it seems doubtful that the curtain will be pulled back on pollution for many years. Instead, it is likely that pollution will increase.

Environmental Problems in the Third World

With its greater poverty and swelling population, the Third World has an even greater incentive to industrialize at any cost. Most of the world population increase of a quarter of a million people every day occurs in the Third World. The combined pressures of population growth and almost nonexistent environmental regulations destine the Third World to become the earth's major source of pollution. The Third World's lack of environmental protection laws has not gone unnoticed by opportunists in the First World, who have begun to use those countries as a garbage dump for hazardous wastes and for producing chemicals that their own will no longer tolerate (La Dou 1991). The relentless cutting of the rain forests not only threatens plant and animal species but also causes huge amounts of soil erosion (Noah 1993). Alarmed at the implications of increasing environmental destruction, the World Bank, a monetary arm of First World nations, has placed pressure on Third World nations to reduce pollution and soil erosion (Lachica 1992). Understandably, the basic concern of the people of the Third World is to produce food and housing first, and to worry about environmental matters later.

Extinction Holding unknown consequences for the future of humanity is the extinction of numerous plant and animal species as tropical rain forests are relentlessly cleared for lumber, farms, and pastures. Although the rain forests cover just 7 percent of the planet's land area, they are home to half of all its plant species. With these rain forests disappearing at a rate of nearly *2,500 acres every hour* (McCuen 1993), it is estimated that ten thousand species are becoming extinct each year—about one per hour (Durning 1990).

The Environmental Movement

Concern about the world's severe environmental problems has produced a worldwide social movement. This quest for a healthy environment has produced an unexpected consequence: the political radicalization of many of its participants (Krauss 1989, 1991). In one instance, a dump leaking chemicals into local wells and making families sick caused working-class people, who placed high trust in their government, to assume, naively, that officials would be happy to solve the problem when they learned of it. Instead, they were told that it wasn't the government's business, or that it was the cost they had to pay for a "better" life! Frustrated, they pursued the matter on their own, but were shocked and disillusioned to find that in the courts deep pockets make a difference in justice. The small groups of protesters could not afford lawyers to deal with the endless barrage of legal motions filed by the polluters. Many underwent a political awakening as a result, having lost their trust in government, and gaining a disturbing insight into the relationship between wealth and political power.

In some countries, the environment has become such an issue that Green parties campaign in local and national elections. Germany's Green party has won seats in the national legislature (Kiefer 1991). Green parties have also arisen in Great Britain (Rootes 1990), Switzerland (Hug 1990), and even Mexico (Golden 1991) and Russia (Gordon 1993). In the United States, a Green party tried to field a candidate in the 1992 presidential election and managed to get on the ballot in only two or three states.

The environmental movement, which often transcends social class, gender, and race (Bullard 1990; Krauss 1991), generally sees solutions in education, legislation, and political activism. Some activists, however, seeing that pollution continues, that the rain forests are still being cleared, and that species are swiftly becoming extinct, have become convinced that the planet is doomed if immediate steps are not taken. They have chosen a more radical course. Using extreme tactics, they try to arouse indignation among the public and thus force the government to act. Convinced that they stand for true morality, many are willing to break the law and go to jail for their actions. These activists are featured in the following Thinking Critically section.

▼▲▼▲▼▲▼▲▼▲▼▲▼▲▼▲▼▲▼▲▼▲▼▲▼▲▼▲▼▲▼

Thinking Critically About Social Controversy

Ecosabotage

▼ BLOCKING A LOGGING ROAD by standing in front of a truck; climbing atop a giant Douglas fir slated for cutting; pouring sand down the gas tank of a bulldozer; tearing down power lines and ripping up survey stakes; driving spikes into redwood trees and sinking whaling vessels—are these the acts of dangerous punks, intent on vandalism and with little understanding of the needs of modern society, or of brave men and women willing to put their freedom, and even their lives, on the line on behalf of the earth itself?

To get some idea of why ecosabotage is taking place, consider the Medicine Tree, a three-thousand-year-old redwood in the Sally Bell Grove near the northern California coast. Georgia Pacific, a lumber company, was determined to cut down the Medicine Tree, the oldest and largest of the region's redwoods, which rests on an ancient sacred site of the Sinkyone Indians. Members of Earth First! chained themselves to the tree. After they were arrested, the sawing

With environmental degradation having implications for all of humanity, the environmental movement is worldwide. Shown here is an anti-nuclear rally on the anniversary of the Chernobyl disaster.

began. Other protesters jumped over the police-lined barricade and planted themselves in front of the axes and chain saws. A logger swung an axe and missed a demonstrator. At that moment, the sheriff radioed a restraining order, and the cutting stopped.

How many three-thousand-year-old trees remain on this planet? Do picnic tables and fences for backyard barbecues justify cutting them down? It is questions like these, as well as the slaughter of seals, the destruction of the rain forests, and the drowning of dolphins in mile-long drift nets that have spawned Earth First! and other organizations, such as Greenpeace and Sea Shepherds, which are devoted to preserving the environment at any cost.

"We feel like there are insane people who are consciously destroying our environment, and we are compelled to fight back," explains a member of one of the militant groups. "No compromise in defense of Mother Earth!" says another. "With famine and death approaching, we're in the early stages of World War III," adds another.

The dedication of some of these activists has brought them close to martyrdom. When Paul Watson, founder of the Sea Shepherds, sprayed seals with green dye, which destroys the value of their pelts but doesn't hurt the animals, hunters hogtied him, dragged him across the ice, and threatened to toss him into the sea. "It's no big deal," says Watson, "when you consider that one hundred million people in this century have died in wars over real estate."

Radical environmentalists represent a broad range of activities and purposes. They are united neither on tactics nor goals. Some want to stop a specific action, such as the killing of whales, or to destroy all nuclear weapons and dismantle nuclear power plants. Others want everyone to become vegetarians. Still others want the earth's population to be reduced to one billion, roughly what it was in 1800. Some even want humans to return to hunting and gathering bands. Most espouse a simpler lifestyle that will consume less energy and place less pressure on the earth's resources. These groups are so splintered that the founder of Earth First!, Dave Foreman, quit his own organization when it became too confrontational for his tastes.

Among their successes, the radical groups count a halt to the killing of dolphins off Japan's Iki Island, a ban on whaling, trash recycling in many communities, hundreds of thousands of acres of uncut trees, and, of course, the Medicine Tree.

For Your Consideration

Who, then, are these people? Should we applaud them or jail them? As symbolic interactionists stress, it all depends on your definition. And as conflict theorists emphasize, your definition likely depends on your location in the economic structure. That is, if you are the owner of a lumber company you will see ecosaboteurs differently than if you are a camping enthusiast. What is your own view of ecosaboteurs, and how does your view depend on your life situation?

Radical groups often call attention to social issues. If a movement gains public acceptance and becomes mainstream, as environmentalism has, do you think radical acts do more harm than good? Do they alienate people who support the movement, rather than unite them? What effective alternatives to ecosabotage are there for people who are convinced that modernization is destroying the very life support system of the planet itself?

Sources: Rhyne 1987; Russell 1987; Borrelli 1988; Guha 1989; Carpenter 1990; Eder 1990; Foote 1990; Martin 1990; Parfit 1990; Reed and Benet 1990; Keyser 1991. ▲

Environmental Sociology

Environmental sociology, which examines the relationship between human societies and the environment, emerged as a subdiscipline of sociology about 1970 (Dunlap and Catton 1979, 1983; Albrecht and Murdoch 1986; Buttel 1987; Freudenburg and Gramling 1989; Laska 1993). Its main assumptions are listed here:

> **environmental sociology:** a subdiscipline of sociology that examines how human activities affect the physical environment and how the physical environment affects human activities

1 The physical environment is a significant variable in sociological investigation.

2 Human beings are but one species among many that are dependent on the natural environment.

3 Because of intricate feedbacks to nature, human actions have many unintended consequences.

4   The world is finite, so there are potential physical limits to economic growth.

5   Economic expansion requires increased extraction of resources from the environment.

6   Increased extraction of resources leads to ecological problems.

7   These ecological problems place restrictions on economic expansion.

8   Governments create environmental problems by trying to create conditions for the profitable accumulation of capital.

As you can see, the goal of environmental sociology is not to stop pollution or nuclear power, but rather to study the ways in which human cultures, values, and behavior affect the physical environment and the ways in which the physical environment affects human activities. Environmental sociologists, however, are generally also environmental activists, and the Section on Environment and Technology of the American Sociological Association tries to influence governmental policies (American Sociological Association, n.d.).

The Goal of Harmony Between Technology and the Environment

It is inevitable that humans will continue to develop new technologies. But the extensive abuse of those technologies is not inevitable. Neither is the destruction of the planet. That is simply an unwise choice.

If we are to have a world that is worth passing on to coming generations, we must seek harmony between technology and the natural environment (Stead and Stead 1991). This will not be easy. At one extreme are people who claim that to protect the environment we must eliminate industrialization and go back to some sort of preindustrialized way of life. At the other extreme are people unable to see the harm that industrialization does to the natural environment, who want the entire world to continue industrializing at full speed. Somewhere, there must be a middle ground, one that recognizes that industrialization is here to stay but that we *can* control it, for it is our creation. Industrialization, controlled, can enhance our quality of life, not destroy us.

As a parallel to the development of technologies, then, we must develop a greater awareness of their harmful effects on the planet, systems to reduce or eliminate technologies' harm to the environment, and mechanisms to enforce rules for the production, use, and disposal of technology. The question, of course, is whether we have the resolve to do these things.

Will we use technology for exploitation, to make short-term gains regardless of long-term consequences? Or will we apply technology not just to enhance our quality of life but also to preserve the environment for future generations? These are issues that this generation must decide. The stakes—no less than the welfare of the entire planet—are surely high enough to motivate us to make the correct choices.

Summary and Review

Social Change: An Overview

What are the major trends in social change over the course of human history?

The primary changes in human history can be identified as the four social revolutions: the change from *Gemeinschaft* to *Gesellschaft* types of societies, capitalism and industrialization, modernization, and globalization, and the division of the globe into three worlds of development. Ethnic conflicts and social movements indicate cutting edges of social change. Pp. 612–616.

Social Change and Technology

What is Ogburn's theory of social change?

Ogburn identified technology as the basic cause of social change, which comes through three processes: invention, discovery, and diffusion. Pp. 617–618.

What types of technology are there, and what effects does a changed technology have on society?

Technology can be classified as primitive, industrial, postindustrial, and a new technology yet to emerge. Because technology is an organizing force of social life, when technology changes its effects can be profound. The automobile and the computer were used as extended examples. The automobile changed the development of cities, buying patterns, architecture, and even courtship and women's roles. The computer is changing the way we practice medicine, wage war, learn, and work. It bypasses national borders and stimulates cultural leveling. The information superhighway is affecting national and international stratification. Pp. 618–627.

Other Theories of Social Change

Besides technology, capitalism, modernization, and so on, what other theories of social change are there?

Evolutionary theories presuppose that societies are moving from the same starting point to some similar ending point. Unilinear theories, which assumed the same path for everyone, have been replaced with multilinear theories, which assume that different paths can lead to the same stage of development. Cyclical theories, in contrast, view civilizations as going through a process of birth, youth, maturity, decline, and death. Conflict theorists views social change as inevitable, for each thesis (basically a development of a status quo) contains an antithesis (contradictions). A new synthesis develops to resolve these contradictions, but it, too, contains contradictions that will have to be resolved, and so on. This is called a **dialectical process**. Pp. 628–629.

Social Change and the Natural Environment

What are the environmental problems of the First World?

The First World's environmental problems are severe, ranging from city smog and **acid rain** to the **greenhouse effect.** Scientists debate whether the greenhouse effect is real; if it is, it may cause **global warming** that will fundamentally affect social life. The burning of fossil fuels in internal combustion engines lies at the root of many environmental problems, but alternative sources of energy are unlikely to be developed until the multinational corporations can turn them into a profit. Environmental problems have a greater impact on minorities and the poor than on whites and the rich or the middle classes (sometimes called environmental racism). This is due to locating polluting factories and hazardous waste sites near minorities and the poor. Pp. 629–630.

What are the environmental problems of the Second and Third Worlds?

The worst environmental problems are found in the Second World, a legacy of the unrestrained exploitation of resources by the Communist party. Environmental problems in the Third World are primarily related to the process of industrialization. As industrialization in both the Second and Third Worlds increases, so will their environmental problems. Pp. 629–632.

What is the environmental movement?

The environmental movement is an attempt to restore a healthy environment for the world's people. This global movement takes many forms, from peacefully influencing the political process to *ecosabotage*, sabotaging the efforts of people thought to be legally harming the environment. Pp. 632–633.

What is environmental sociology?

Environmental sociology is not an attempt to change the environment, but a study of the relationship between humans and the environment. Environmental sociologists are generally also environmental activists. Pp. 633–634

Where can I read more on this topic?

Suggested readings for this chapter are listed on page 645.

Chapter 1

Berger, Peter L. *Invitation to Sociology: A Humanistic Perspective.* New York: Doubleday, 1963. This delightful analysis of how sociology applies to everyday life is highly recommended.

Charon, Joel M. *Symbolic Interactionism: An Introduction, an Interpretation, an Integration.* Englewood Cliffs, N.J.: Prentice Hall, 1985. As it lays out the main points of symbolic interactionism, this book provides an understanding of why symbolic interactionism is important in sociology.

Henslin, James M., ed. *Down to Earth Sociology: Introductory Readings,* 8th ed. New York: Free Press. 1995. This collection of readings about everyday life is designed to broaden the reader's understanding of society, and of the individual's place within it.

Homans, George Caspar. *Coming to My Senses: The Autobiography of a Sociologist.* New Brunswick, N.J.: Transaction, 1984. Homans emphasizes how being born into one of Boston's most privileged families shaped his orientations.

Merton, Robert K. *Social Theory and Social Structure.* New York: Free Press, 1968. This classic work on functionalism covers the theory's main points, but is perhaps best read by advanced students.

Mills, C. Wright. *The Sociological Imagination.* New York: Oxford University Press, 1959. This classic work provides an overview of sociology from the framework of conflict theory.

Straus, Roger, ed. *Using Sociology.* Bayside, N.Y.: General Hall, 1985. The author examines how applied and clinical sociology are used in the practical world.

Turner, Stephen Park, and Jonathan H. Turner. *The Impossible Science: An Institutional Analysis of American Sociology.* Newbury Park, Calif.: Sage, 1990. After tracing the history of American sociology from the Civil War, the authors reflect on its future.

Journals

Clinical Sociology Review, Journal of Applied Sociology, and *Sociological Practice Review* are three journals that report the experiences of sociologists who work in a variety of applied settings, from peer group counseling and suicide prevention to recommending changes to school boards.

Humanity & Society, the official journal of the Association for Humanist Sociology, publishes articles that "serve to advance the quality of life of the world's people."

About a Career in Sociology

The following pamphlets or brochures are available free of charge from the American Sociological Association: 1722 N Street, N.W., Washington, DC 20036   Tel. (202) 833-3410.

Careers in Sociology. American Sociological Association. What can you do with sociology? You like the subject and would like to major in it, but. . . . This pamphlet provides information about jobs available for sociology majors.

Majoring in Sociology: A Guide for Students. American Sociological Association. This brochure provides an overview of the programs offered in sociology departments, possible areas of specialization, and how to find information on jobs.

Huber, Bettina J. *Embarking Upon a Career in Sociology with an Undergraduate Sociology Major.* American Sociological Association. Designed for undergraduate sociology majors who are seeking employment, this brochure discusses how to identify interests and skills, pinpoint suitable jobs, prepare a résumé, and handle an employment interview.

Ferris, Abbott L. *How to Join the Federal Workforce and Advance Your Sociological Career.* American Sociological Association. This pamphlet gives tips on how to find employment in the federal government, including information on how to prepare a job application.

Miller, Delbert C. *The Sociology Major as Preparation for Careers in Business.* American Sociological Association. What careers can a sociology major pursue in business or industry? This brochure includes sections on job prospects, graduate education, and how to practice sociology in business careers.

Chapter 2

Chagnon, Napoleon A. *Yanomamo: The Fierce People,* 3rd ed. New York: Holt, Rinehart & Winston, 1983. This fascinating account of a preliterate people whose customs are extraordinarily different from ours will help you to see the arbitrariness of choices that underlie human culture.

Edgerton, Robert B. *Sick Societies: Challenging the Myth of Primitive Harmony.* New York: Free Press, 1992. The author's thesis is that cultural relativism is misinformed, that we have the obligation to judge cultures that harm its members as inferior to those that do not.

Goodall, Jane. *In the Shadow of Man*. Boston: Houghton Mifflin, 1988. First published in 1971. Goodall presents a fascinating first-person account of her research with wild chimpanzees.

Harris, Marvin. *Good to Eat: Riddles of Food and Culture*. New York: Simon & Schuster, 1986.

Harris, Marvin. *Cannibals and Kings: The Origins of Cultures*. New York: Random House, 1977. To read Harris's books is to read about cultural relativism. Using a functional perspective, this anthropologist analyzes cultural practices that often seem bizarre to outsiders. He interprets those practices within the framework of the culture being examined.

Shames, Laurence. *The Hunger for More: Searching for Values in an Age of Greed*. New York: Vintage Books, 1991. A critical account of changing U.S. values.

Spindler, George, Louise Spindler, Henry T. Trueba, and Melvin D. Williams. *The American Cultural Dialogue and Its Transmission*. Bristol, Penn.: Falmer Press, 1990. The authors analyze values central to American culture: individuality, freedom, community, equality, and success.

Tucker, David M. *The Decline of Thrift in America: Our Cultural Shift from Saving to Spending*. New York: Praeger, 1991. Tucker traces the change in American values from thrift to spending and consumption, indicating how this change has affected the competitiveness of the United States in world markets.

Yinger, Milton J. *Countercultures: The Promise and Peril of a World Turned Upside Down*. New York: Free Press, 1982. The author examines the rise and maintenance of countercultures, showing them as important elements—whether creative or destructive—in the process of social change. The countercultures presented include goodness, beauty, the disadvantaged, politics, economics, religion, education, families, and sex norms.

Journal

Urban Life, a sociological journal that focuses on social interaction, contains many detailed studies of the culture of small, off-beat groups.

Chapter 3

Ariès, Philippe. *Centuries of Childhood: A Social History of Family Life*. New York: Vintage Books, 1965. This pathbreaking study of childhood in Europe during the Middle Ages provides a sharp contrast to child-rearing patterns in modern society.

Curtiss, Susan. *Genie: A Psycholinguistic Study of a Modern Day "Wild Child."* New York: Academic Press, 1977. The psycholinguist who worked with Genie for several years tells the story of a girl who was locked in a small room for twelve years.

Elkin, Frederick, and Gerald Handel. *The Child and Society*, 4th ed. New York: Random House, 1984. This classic overview of the socialization of children emphasizes social class, race, sex, and place of residence as significant factors in socialization.

Gilmore, David D. *Manhood in the Making: Cultural Concepts of Masculinity*. New Haven, Conn.: Yale University Press, 1990. A survey of societies around the world aimed at determining if masculinity is constant; contains fascinating anthropological data.

Lieberman, Alicia F. *The Emotional Life of the Toddler*. New York: Free Press, 1993. The author analyzes challenges in socializing young children and presents many interesting case materials on problems that toddlers confront.

Mead, George Herbert. *Mind, Self and Society from the Standpoint of a Social Behaviorist*, Charles W. Morris, ed. Chicago: University of Chicago Press, 1962. First published in 1934. Put together from notes taken by Mead's students, this book presents Mead's analysis of how mind and self are products of society.

Piaget, Jean, and Barbel Inhelder. *The Psychology of the Child*. New York: Basic Books, 1969. The authors provide an overview of Piaget's experiments and conclusions about the thought processes of children.

Rymer, Russ. *Genie: An Abused Child's Flight from Silence*. New York: HarperCollins, 1993. This moving account of Genie includes the battles among linguists, psychologists, and social workers, who all claimed to have Genie's best interests at heart.

White, Merry. *The Material Child: Coming of Age in Japan and America*. New York: Free Press, 1993. Comparing adolescence in the United States and Japan, the author examines sexuality, friendship, plans for the future, and relationships with peers, family, and school.

Chapter 4

Couch, Carl J. *Social Processes and Relationships: A Formal Approach*. Dix Hills, N.Y.: General Hall, 1989. This analysis covers a wide range of processes and relationships, including bargaining, negotiating, solidarity, accountability, authority, romance, and tyranny.

Ebaugh, Helen Rose Fuchs. *Becoming an EX: The Process of Role Exit*. Chicago: University of Chicago Press, 1988. To become a former "something" especially when that "something" was important to you, can be an excruciating experience that wrenches the self-concept. The author analyzes this process by looking at ex-nuns, divorce, losing custody of one's children, and so on.

Fields, Mamie Garvin, and Karen Fields. *Lemon Swamp and Other Places*. New York: Free Press, 1985. The second author is a sociologist who has recorded her grandmother's oral history. By providing rich details of an African-American woman's life, this book fills a valuable niche in our understanding of life in U.S. society.

Goffman, Erving. *The Presentation of Self in Everyday Life*. New York: Doubleday, 1990. First published in 1959. This is the classic statement of dramaturgical analysis; it provides a different way of looking at everyday life.

Gouldner, Helen, and Mary Symons Strong. *Speaking of Friendship: Middle-Class Women and Their Friends*. New York: Greenwood Press, 1987. Drawing on extensive interviews, the author explores the significance of friendship for middle-class women in U.S. society.

Hatfield, Elaine, and Susan Sprecher. *Mirror, Mirror . . . : The Importance of Looks in Everyday Life*. Albany, N.Y.: SUNY Press, 1986. All of us consider appearance to be very important in everyday life. You may be surprised, however, at just how significant good looks are for determining what happens to us.

Helmreich, William B. *The Things They Say Behind Your Back: Stereotypes and the Myths Behind Them*. New Brunswick, N.J.: Transaction, 1984. Spiced with anecdotes and jokes, yet sensitively written, the book explores the historical roots of stereotypes. The author also illustrates how stereotypes help produce behaviors that reinforce them.

Karp, David A., and William C. Yoels. *Sociology and Everyday Life*. Itasca, Ill.: Peacock, 1986. The authors examine how social order is constructed and how it provides the framework for our interactions.

Schellenberg, James A. *Exploring Social Behavior: Investigations in Social Psychology*. Boston: Allyn and Bacon, 1993. The author takes the reader on an intellectual journey, exploring such "mysteries" as identity, conscience, intelligence, attraction, and aggression.

Tönnies, Ferdinand. *Community and Society (Gemeinschaft und Gesellschaft)*. New Brunswick, N.J.: Transaction, 1988. Originally published in 1887, this classic work, focusing on social change, provides insight into how society influences personality. Rather challenging reading.

Journals
The following three journals feature articles on symbolic interactionism and analyses of everyday life: *Qualitative Sociology*, *Symbolic Interaction*, *Urban Life*.

Chapter 5
Baker, Therese L. *Doing Social Research*, 2nd ed., New York: McGraw-Hill, 1994. This "how-to" book of sociological research describes the major ways in which sociologists gather data and the logic that underlies each method.

Burgess, Robert, ed. *Studies in Qualitative Sociology: Reflections on Field Experience*. London: JAI Press, 1990. First-person accounts by sociologists provide an understanding of the problems and rewards of fieldwork.

Holmstrom, Lynda Lyttle. *The Victims of Rape: Institutional Reactions*. New Brunswick, N.J.: Transaction, 1983. The writer follows rape victims as they come in contact with the police, hospitals, and courts, illustrating how these contacts are often devastating to the victim.

Jorgensen, D. L. *Participant Observation: A Methodology for Human Studies*. Newbury Park, Calif.: Sage, 1989. The book explains the value of participant observation and summarizes interesting studies. From it, you may understand why *you* are uniquely qualified for doing participant observation.

Merton, Robert K., Marjorie Fiske, and Patricia L. Kendall. *The Focused Interview: A Manual of Problems and Procedures*, 2nd ed. New York: Free Press, 1990. Interviewing techniques are outlined; of value primarily to more advanced students.

Reynolds, Paul D. *Ethics and Social Science Research*. Englewood Cliffs, N.J.: Prentice Hall, 1982. The author explores ethical dilemmas confronted by social researchers.

Scully, Diana. *Understanding Sexual Violence: A Study of Convicted Rapists*. Boston: Unwin Hyman, 1990. The author's examination of the rationalizations of rapists helps us understand why some men rape and what they gain from it.

Smith, Carolyn D., and William Kornblum. *In the Field: Readings on the Field Research Experience*. New York: Praeger, 1989. These sociologists' first-person accounts of their experiences of fieldwork help bring the research process to life.

Webb, Eugene J., Donald T. Campbell, Richard D. Schwartz, Lee Sechrest, and Janet Below Grove. *Unobtrusive Measures: Nonreactive Research in the Social Sciences*. Chicago: Houghton Mifflin, 1981. The clear overview of unobtrusive measures also contains concise summaries of a great deal of research.

Whyte, William Foote, and Kathleen King Whyte. *Learning from the Field: A Guide from Experience*. Beverly Hills, Calif.: Sage, 1984. Focusing on the extensive field experience of the senior author, this book provides insight into the critical involvement of the self in this research method.

Writing Papers for Sociology
The Sociology Writing Group. *A Guide to Writing Sociology Papers*, 3rd ed. New York: St. Martin's Press, 1994. The guide walks students through the steps in writing a sociology paper, from choosing the initial assignment to doing the research and turning in a finished paper. Also explains how to manage your time and correctly cite sources.

Cuba, Lee J. *A Short Guide to Writing About Social Science*. Glenview, Ill.: Scott, Foresman, 1988. The author summarizes the various types of social science literature, presents guidelines on how to organize and write a research paper, and explains how to prepare an oral presentation.

Journal
Visual Sociology Review. A specialized journal in qualitative sociology that focuses on the analysis of social life through visual means such as photos, movies, and videos.

Chapter 6
Bernstein, Carl, and Bob Woodward. *All the President's Men*. New York: Simon & Schuster, 1974. A fascinating account of groupthink, written by the reporters who broke the story of Watergate.

Homans, George. *The Human Group*. New York: Harcourt, Brace, 1950. Homans develops the idea that all human groups share common activities, interactions, and sentiments and examines various types of social groups from this point of view.

Janis, Irving. *Victims of Groupthink*. Boston, Mass.: Houghton Mifflin, 1972. Janis analyzes how groups can become cut off from alternatives, interpret evidence in light of their preconceptions, and embark on courses of action that they should have seen as obviously incorrect.

Kephart, William M., and William W. Zellner. *Extraordinary Groups: An Examination of Unconventional Lifestyles*, 4th ed. New York: St. Martin's Press, 1991. This sketch of the history and characteristics of eight groups—the Old Order Amish, Oneida Community, Gypsies, Shakers, Hasidim, Father Divine Movement, Mormons, and Jehovah's Witnesses—illustrates the effects of groups on their members.

Mills, Theodore M. *The Sociology of Small Groups*. Englewood Cliffs, N.J.: Prentice Hall, 1984. Mills provides an overview of research on small groups, focusing on the interaction that occurs within them (group dynamics).

Whyte, William H. *The Organization Man*. New York: Simon & Schuster, 1956. Although this book was written at midcentury, its analysis of how bureaucracies reward conformity and stifle creativity is still insightful.

Chapter 7
Ferguson, Kathy E. *The Feminine Case Against Bureaucracy*. Philadelphia: Temple University Press, 1984. Documenting how bureaucracies are male bastions of power and prestige, Ferguson illustrates the relative disadvantage they provide females.

Fucini, Joseph J., and Suzy Fucini. *Working for the Japanese: Inside Mazda's American Auto Plant*. New York: Free Press, 1990. The authors report on how U.S. workers at the wholly-owned Japanese auto plant in Flat Rock, Michigan, have found that the team system requires them to sacrifice individual interests to the welfare of the group.

Kaminer, Wendy. *Women Volunteering: The Pleasure, Pain, and Politics of Unpaid Work from 1830 to the Present*. Garden City, N.Y.: Anchor, 1984. The book summarizes 150 years of female participation in volunteer associations.

Kanter, Rosabeth Moss. *The Change Masters: Innovations for Productivity in the American Corporation*. New York: Simon & Schuster, 1983. By examining the basis of their capacity for innovation, the author explains why some corporations are more successful than others, illustrates how sociology is useful in solving practical problems, and explains how Americans can become more competitive.

Matyko, Alexander J. *The Self-Defeating Organization: A Critique of Bureaucracy*. New York: Praeger, 1986. The author explains that bureaucracies face a crisis because their hierarchical structure is too authoritarian to meet the demands of contemporary life.

Ouchi, William. *Theory Z: How American Business Can Meet the Japanese Challenge*. Reading, Mass.: Addison-Wesley, 1981. Contrasting the U.S. and Japanese corporate models, the author shows how features of the Japanese model can be adapted to meet changing needs in the United States.

Parkinson, C. Northcote. *Parkinson's Law*. Boston: Houghton Mifflin, 1957. While this exposé of the inner workings of bureaucracies is delightfully satirical, if what Parkinson analyzes were generally true, bureaucracies would always fail.

Rothschild, Joyce, and J. Allen Whitt. *The Cooperative Workplace: Potentials and Dilemmas of Organizational Democracy and Participation*. New York: Cambridge University Press, 1986. Exploring the movement toward a more cooperative workplace, the authors discuss the advantages and pitfalls of such reforms.

Chapter 8

DiUlio, John J., Jr. *Governing Prisons: A Comparative Study of Correctional Management*. New York: Free Press, 1990. In a proposal called "constitutional management," the author argues that U.S. prisons can be made safe and humane through a new governing system that "employs prison managers who are strong enough to control the inmates yet obliged to control themselves."

Jackson, Bruce, *Outside the Law: A Thief's Primer*. New Brunswick, N.J.: Transaction, 1972. An insider's perspective explains what it is like to make a living by cracking safes and passing bad checks.

Jankowski, Martín Sánchez. *Islands in the Street: Gangs and American Urban Society*. Berkeley: University of California Press, 1991. The author presents an overview of urban gangs in the United States; findings from this book are featured in the box on page 207.

Matza, David. *Delinquency and Drift*. New Brunswick, N.J.: Transaction, 1990. This analysis of how the delinquent subculture reflects the standards of conventional society explains how the drift toward delinquency is sometimes unwittingly aided by the enforcers of the social order.

Prus, Robert, and Styllianoss Irini. *Hookers, Rounders, and Desk Clerks*. Salem, Wis.: Sheffield, 1988. A look at the underground life of a hotel—how the social worlds of prostitutes, pimps, thieves, strippers, and hotel personnel intersect.

Rafter, Nicole Hahn. *Partial Justice: Women, Prisons, and Social Control*, 2nd ed. New Brunswick, N.J.: Transaction, 1990. The author documents the development of separate prisons for women, the goal of reform in women's prisons, and current concerns to produce more than "partial justice."

Schur, Edwin M. *Labeling Women Deviant: Gender, Stigma, and Social Control*. New York: Random House, 1984. Using the perspective of labeling theory, the author examines the process by which females are devalued and "female deviance" produced.

Szasz, Thomas S. *The Myth of Mental Illness*, rev. ed. New York: Harper & Row, 1986. Szasz takes the controversial position that mental illness is a myth, a mere label used by the medical establishment to broaden its control.

Weisburd, David, Stanton Wheeler, and Elin Waring. *Crimes of the Middle Classes: White-Collar Offenders in the Federal Courts*. New Haven, Conn.: Yale University Press, 1991. In examining the diversity of crime that comes under the term "white collar," the author explores the relationship between harm and blame and the sentences handed out by judges.

Zey, Mary. *Banking on Fraud: Drexel, Junk Bonds, and Buyouts*. Hawthorne, N. Y.: Aldine de Gruyter, 1993. An account of the networks of power that facilitated the fraudulent leveraged buyouts carried out by Michael Milken and his securities firm, Drexel Burnham Lambert.

Chapter 9

Carter, Bob. *Capitalism, Class Conflict and the New Middle Class*. London: Routledge & Kegan Paul, 1985. Carter explains why capitalism was not overthrown by the workers' revolution as Marx predicted.

Freedman, Robert. *The Mind of Karl Marx: Economic, Political, and Social Perspectives*. Chatham, N.J.: Chatham House, 1986. A conflict theorist provides an overview of social stratification from his perspective.

Harrison, Paul. *Inside the Third World: The Anatomy of Poverty*, 3rd ed. London: Penguin Books, 1993. The book's vivid examples make conditions in the Third World come alive.

International Monetary Fund. *World Economic Outlook: A Survey*. Washington, D.C.: International Monetary Fund, 1992. Comparative data on the world's economies provide insight into the interrelationships of the three worlds of development.

Kennedy, Paul. *Preparing for the Twenty-First Century*. New York: Random House, 1993. A thorough analysis of the relationship between the three worlds of development.

Lane, David, ed. *Russia in Flux: The Political and Social Consequences of Reform*. Brookfield, Vt.: Ashfield, 1992. The author analyzes the political and economic changes in Russia, the consequences of which are being felt throughout the world.

Miles, Rosalind. *The Woman's History of the World*. New York: HarperCollins, 1990. The author examines the importance of gender in human history.

Said, Edward W. *Culture and Imperialism*. New York: Knopf, 1993. The author analyzes the relationship of national power to cultural dominance, especially that of the First World to the Third World.

United Nations. *World Economic Survey 1990: Current Trends and Policies in the World Economy*. New York: United Nations, 1990. This survey of the economic characteristics of the world's nations provides a detailed contrast between the rich and poor nations.

Wills, David K. *Klass: How Russians Really Live*. New York: Avon, 1987. An American sociologist provides an overview of social stratification in the former Soviet Union.

Chapter 10

Domhoff, G. William. *The Power Elite and the State: How Policy Is Made in America*. New York: Aldine de Gruyter, 1990. The author analyzes the network of power that underlies the major policy decisions of the United States—and the plans of the power elite for a world economic order.

Ehrenreich, Barbara. *Fear of Falling: The Inner Life of the Middle Class*. New York: HarperCollins, 1990. Ehrenreich dissects the middle class by examining a wide variety of sources, including films, child-rearing manuals, and even the "class cues" built into clothing, furniture, and shopping habits. She also explains why from the 1960s to the 1980s the professional middle class "retreated from liberalism" to a "meaner, more selfish outlook, hostile to the aspirations of those less fortunate."

Funiciello, Theresa. *Tyranny of Kindness*. New York: Atlantic Monthly Press, 1993. The author, a former welfare recipient, suggests that the welfare industry, which funds an army of bureaucrats, be shut down and the money given directly to the poor.

Gatewood, Willard B. *Aristocrats of Color: The Black Elite, 1880–1920*. Bloomington: Indiana University Press, 1990. Analyzing the rise and decline of the African-American upper class that developed after the Civil War, Gatewood focuses on marriage, occupations, education, religion, clubs, and relationships with whites and with African Americans of lower classes.

Gilbert, Dennis, and Joseph A. Kahl. *The American Class Structure: A New Synthesis*, 4th ed. Belmont, Calif.: Wadsworth, 1993. Two sociologists provide an overview of social stratification in the United States.

Himmelfarb, Gertrude. *Poverty and Compassion: The Moral Imagination of the Late Victorians*. New York: Knopf, 1991. This account of poverty and the system of charity in Victorian England shows that the question of structural and individual causes of poverty is not new.

Hurst, Charles E. *Social Inequality: Forms, Causes, and Consequences*. Boston: Allyn and Bacon, 1992. Hurst analyzes social stratification in the United States.

Katz, Michael B. *The Undeserving Poor: From the War on Poverty to the War on Welfare*. New York: Pantheon, 1989. Katz looks at major changes in social policy regarding poverty and examines why Americans define poverty in terms of family, race, and culture rather than in terms of inequality, power, and exploitation.

Rural Sociological Society Task Force on Persistent Rural Poverty. *Persistent Poverty in Rural America*. Boulder, Colo.: Westview Press, 1993. This analysis of rural poverty, sponsored by the Rural Sociological Society, includes sections on racial and ethnic minorities, the elderly, women, and children.

Snow, David A., and Leon Anderson. *Down on Their Luck: A Study of Homeless Street People*. Berkeley: University of California Press, 1993. The authors use data from participant observation and interviews to explain how people end up on the streets and how they survive this brutal life.

Wilson, William Julius. *The Truly Disadvantaged: The Inner City, the Underclass, and Public Policy*. Chicago: University of Chicago Press, 1987. The author looks at how the conditions of the ghetto poor have deteriorated and suggests what can be done to improve matters.

Chapter 11

Bem, Sandra L. *The Lenses of Gender: Transforming the Debate on Sexual Inequality*. New Haven, Conn.: Yale University Press, 1993. Based primarily on psychological studies, the author examines "gender polarization," arguing the need of a social revolution that results in fused gender identities.

Campbell, Anne. *Men, Women, and Aggression*. New York: Basic Books, 1993. This comparison of male–female differences in aggression includes fights, robbery, marital violence, and street gangs.

Driscoll, Dawn-Marie, and Carol R. Goldberg. *Members of the Club: The Coming of Age of Executive Women*. New York: Free Press, 1993. Based on interviews with senior women executives, the authors suggest strategies for reaching the top of the corporate ladder.

Faludi, Susan. *Backlash: The Undeclared War Against American Women*. New York: Crown Publishers, 1991. This book is an argument against those who take the position that feminism has robbed women of their happiness.

Moore, Robert. *The Warrior Within: The Warrior in the Male Psyche*. New York: Morrow, 1992. One of a new genre of books written in reaction to changing gender relations and based on the fear that males are being feminized, this book presents techniques for getting in contact with the "real" man within.

Rotundo, E. Anthony. *American Manhood: Transformations in Masculinity from the Revolution to the Modern Era*. New York: Basic Books, 1993. Based on historical materials (letters, diaries, autobiographies, and printed advice to men), the author traces changes in

the social anchors of manhood among white, middle-class, Yankee Northerners.

Tannen, Deborah. *You Just Don't Understand: Women and Men in Conversation*. New York: Morrow, 1990. A psycholinguist documents the extent to which speech patterns of men and women are related to basic differences in their social worlds.

Witt, Linda, Karen M. Paget, and Glenna Matthews. *Running as a Woman: Gender and Power in American Politics*. New York: Macmillan, 1994. This history of women in politics includes successful strategies for running for political office as a woman.

Zuckerman, Harriet, Jonathan R. Cole, and John T. Bruer. *The Outer Circle: Women in the Scientific Community*. New York: Norton, 1991. The authors explore the degree to which the exclusion of women from the "inner circle" of male-dominated science results in an alienation that has profound effects on their work.

Journals

The following four journals focus on the role of gender in social life: *Feminist Studies*, *Sex Roles*, *Signs: Journal of Women in Culture and Society*, and *Gender & Society*, the official journal of Sociologists for Women in Society.

Chapter 12

Alba, Richard D. *Ethnic Identity: The Transformation of White America*. New Haven, Conn.: Yale University Press, 1990. The author analyzes the assimilation of white ethnics and the development of what he calls "unhyphenated Americans."

Allen, Irving Lewis. *Unkind Words: Ethnic Labeling from Redskin to WASP*. Westport, Conn.: Bergin & Garvey, 1990. Allen explores ethnic labeling in popular speech, showing how ethnic slurs reflect social change and the diversity and complexity of U.S. society.

Blee, Kathleen M. *Women of the Klan: Racism and Gender in the 1920s*. Berkeley: University of California Press, 1991. An overview of female activism motivated by fear, bigotry, and hatred directed against Catholics, Jews, and African Americans.

Browning, Christopher R. *Ordinary Men: Reserve Police Battalion 101 and the Final Solution in Poland*. New York: HarperPerennial, 1993. A startling account of how a government turned ordinary men into mass murderers.

Cose, Ellis. *The Rage of the Privileged Class*. New York: HarperCollins, 1993. The author details the humiliations faced by affluent middle-class African Americans when whites don't differentiate them from the black underclass.

Duneier, Mitchell. *Slim's Table: Race, Respectability, Masculinity*. Chicago: University of Chicago Press, 1992. Based on participant observation, the author analyzes the relationships of a group of working-class African-American men in Chicago, with an emphasis on how they maintain their sense of moral worth.

Hagan, William Thomas. *American Indians*. Chicago: University of Chicago Press, 1993. This analysis of Native Americans has a focus on relationships between Native Americans and the U.S. government.

Mander, Jerry. *In the Absence of the Sacred: The Failure of Technology and the Survival of the Indian Nations*. San Francisco, Calif.: Sierra Club Books, 1992. With a focus on the impact of technology, the author analyzes past and present relations of Native Americans and the U.S. government.

Moore, Joan, and Raquel Pinderhughes, eds. *In the Barrios: Latinos and the Underclass Debate*. New York: Sage, 1993. With an emphasis on immigration, discrimination, and gangs, the authors of the nine essays in this volume examine the overall social and economic conditions of poor Latinos.

Rodriguez, Clara. *Puerto Ricans: Born in the U.S.A.* Boston: Unwin Hyman, 1989. The author presents an overview of Puerto Rican Americans.

Trueba, Henry T., Lilly Cheng, and Kenji Ima. *Myth or Reality: Adaptive Strategies of Asian Americans in California.* Washington, D.C.: Falmer Press, 1993. With an emphasis on family, school, community, and work, the authors examine conflicts and adaptations of Asian-American immigrants.

Wei, William. *The Asian American Movement.* Philadelphia: Temple University Press, 1993. The author analyzes the "invisible" social movement, the efforts of Asian Americans to articulate their position in U.S. society.

Chapter 13

Chambre, Susan Maizel. *Good Deeds in Old Age: Volunteering by the New Leisure Class.* Lexington, Mass.: Lexington Books, 1987. With larger numbers of Americans retiring each year and a high level of activity considered essential to good health, volunteer activities have become increasingly important.

DiGiulio, Robert C. *Beyond Widowhood.* New York: Free Press, 1989. Based on personal experience as well as research, the author presents a sensitive and moving analysis of the grieving process.

Pillemer, Karl A., and Rosalie S. Wolf, eds. *Elder Abuse: Conflict in the Family.* Dover, Mass.: Auburn House, 1987. This collection of readings presents an overview of this disturbing topic.

Clair, Jeffrey Michael, David A. Karp, and William C. Yoels. *Experiencing the Life Cycle: A Social Psychology of Aging,* 2nd ed. Springfield, Ill.: Thomas, 1993. The authors examine social factors that underlie the ajustments that the elderly make to life changes.

Cockerham, William C. *This Aging Society.* Englewood Cliffs, N.J.: Prentice Hall, 1991. The social consequences of the growing numbers of elderly in society are the focus of this book.

Cox, Harold G. *Late Life: The Realities of Aging,* 3rd ed. Englewood Cliffs, N.J.: Prentice Hall, 1993. Using a symbolic interactionist framework, the author presents an overview of issues in aging.

Jerrome, Dorothy. *Good Company: An Anthropological Study of Old People in Groups.* Edinburgh, England: Edinburgh University Press, 1992. The day-to-day interactions that provide the primary bases for satisfying adjustment in old age are the primary focus of this book.

National Center for Health Statistics. *Common Beliefs About the Rural Elderly: What Do National Data Tell Us?* Washington, D.C.: U.S. Government Printing Office, 1993. This book provides a broad overview of a neglected topic, U.S. elderly in rural areas.

Journals

The Gerontologist, Journal of Aging and Social Policy, Journal of Aging Studies, Journal of Cross-Cultural Gerontology, Journal of Elder Abuse and Neglect, Journal of Gerontology, and *Journal of Women and Aging* focus on issues of aging, while *Youth and Society* examines adolescent culture.

Chapter 14

Bensman, David, and Roberta Lynch. *Rusted Dreams: Hard Times in a Steel Community.* New York: McGraw-Hill, 1987. The authors analyze plant closings in Chicago and illustrate some of the wrenching adjustments required by the change to a postindustrial economy.

Berger, Peter L. *The Capitalist Revolution: Fifty Propositions About Prosperity, Equality, and Liberty.* New York: Basic Books, 1991. Berger's explanation of why capitalism is highly productive and why it enhances personal liberty is especially useful in light of changes in the Second World.

Cohen, Stephen S., and John Zysman. *Manufacturing Matters: The Myth of the Post-Industrial Economy.* New York: Basic Books, 1987. The authors argue that manufacturing remains essential to the U.S. economy.

Harrison, Bennett, and Barry Bluestone. *The Great U-Turn: Corporate Restructuring and the Polarizing of America.* New York: Basic Books, 1990. The authors investigate major changes taking place in the U.S. economy, focusing on the declining standard of living of the average American.

Marx, Karl. *Selected Writings in Sociology and Social Philosophy,* Thomas B. Bottomore and Maximilian Rubel, eds. New York: McGraw-Hill, 1964. If you are unfamiliar with Marx's ideas, you will benefit from this useful introduction, especially Marx's analysis of social class and alienation.

Porter, Michael E. *The Competitive Advantage of Nations.* New York: Free Press, 1990. Based on research in ten countries, the author first examines how productivity is the key to a nation's competitive market position and then provides an explanation for the economic success of Japan and the decline of Great Britain.

Ritzer, George, and David Walczak. *Working: Conflict and Change,* 3rd ed. Englewood Cliffs, N.J.: Prentice Hall, 1986. This analysis of work in U.S. society emphasizes the transition to a postindustrial economy.

Rothschild, Joyce, and J. Allen Whitt. *The Cooperative Workplace: Potentials and Dilemmas of Organizational Democracy and Participation.* Cambridge, Mass.: Cambridge University Press, 1989. Focusing on the basic values that unite people in worker-owned and worker-run enterprises, the authors identify ten conditions that support democracy in organizations.

Statham, Anne, Eleanor M. Miller, and Hans O. Mauksch, eds. *The Worth of Women's Work.* Albany: State University of New York Press, 1988. The authors examine women's work, both unpaid housework and paid work in the labor force.

Womack, James P., Daniel T. Jones, and Daniel Roos. *The Machine That Changed the World.* New York: HarperPerennial, 1991. This analysis of the international automobile industry stresses how the lean production techniques developed by Toyota revolutionized mass production.

Journals

Two journals that focus on issues presented in this chapter are *Insurgent Sociologist* and *Work and Occupations.*

Chapter 15

Allen, Oliver E. *The Tiger.* New York: Addison-Wesley, 1993. An entertaining account of Tammany Hall, the corrupt political group that controlled New York City from the 1800s to past the middle of this century.

Amnesty International. *Amnesty International Report.* London: Amnesty International Publications, published annually. The reports summarize human rights violations around the world, listing specific instances country by country.

Chirot, Daniel. *Modern Tyrants: The Power and Prevalence of Evil in Our Age.* New York: Free Press, 1994. From Hitler and Stalin to Trujillo, Mao, and Pol Pot, the author analyzes the political expediency that underlies tyranny.

Domhoff, G. William. *The Power Elite and the State: How Policy Is Made in America.* New York: Aldine de Gruyter, 1990. Domhoff develops the thesis that coalitions within the power elite shape the major policies of the United States.

Keegan, John. *A History of Warfare*. New York: Knopf, 1993. With panoramic historical sweep, the author examines human aggression from the Stone Age to the present.

Mills, C. Wright. *The Power Elite*. New York: Oxford University Press, 1956. This classic analysis elaborates the conflict thesis summarized in this chapter that U.S. society is ruled by the nation's top corporate leaders, together with an elite from the military and political institutions.

Porter, Bruce D. *War and the Rise of the State: The Military Foundations of Modern Politics*. New York: Free Press, 1994. The author presents an intriguing analysis of how war and the military underlie the creation of the state and of changed relations within it.

Randall, Vicky. *Contemporary Feminist Politics: Women and Power in Britain*. New York: Oxford University Press, 1993. The author analyzes changes in the role and participation of women in British politics.

Said, Edward W. *Culture and Imperialism*. New York: Knopf, 1993. Drawing on a wide breadth of historical information, the author examines how attitudes and values, determined by culture, underlie people's justifications of political acts, especially the building of empires and the suppression of indigenous peoples.

Skerry, Peter. *Mexican Americans: The Ambivalent Minority*. New York: Free Press, 1993. An understanding of how the immigrant experience affects political attitudes and participation can be gained from this focus on Mexican Americans.

Journals

Most sociology journals publish articles on politics. Three that focus on this area of social life are *American Political Science Review*, *Journal of Political and Military Sociology*, and *Social Policy*.

Chapter 16

Biller, Henry B. *Fathers and Families: Paternal Factors in Child Development*. Westport, Conn.: Auburn House, 1993. This book provides an overview of research findings on the "special contribution of the father in the context of his sharing of parenting responsibilities with the mother."

Clausen, John A. *American Lives: Looking Back at the Children of the Great Depression*. New York: Free Press, 1993. Based on a sample of children born in the 1920s, this analysis makes visible the direct effects of social conditions on the dynamics and diversity of the life course.

Conger, Rand D., and Glen H. Elder, Jr., eds. *Families in Troubled Times: Adapting to Change in Rural America*. Hawthorne, N.Y.: Aldine de Gruyter, 1994. An examination of how farm families adjust during precipitous economic decline.

Coontz, Stephanie. *The Way We Never Were: American Families and the Nostalgia Trap*. New York: Basic Books, 1992. This provocative analysis of family history shows that current concerns about marriage and families are not new.

Dobasch, R. E., and R. P. Dobasch. *Women, Violence, and Social Change*. London: Routledge, 1992. This analysis of the battered-women's movement focuses on its goals of providing safety, shelter, and autonomy for abused women and eliminating violence against women.

Hochschild, Arlie. *The Second Shift: Working Parents and the Revolution at Home*. New York: Viking Penguin, 1989. Based on interviews and participant observation, the author provides an in-depth report on family life in homes where both husband and wife are employed full time.

Mount, Ferdinand. *The Subversive Family: An Alternative History of Love and Marriage*. New York: Free Press, 1992. Is almost everything that academics have concluded about families in the past incorrect? This author thinks so.

Ross, Jacob Joshua. *The Virtues of the Family*. New York: Free Press, 1994. The author, a philosopher, argues that the family is not a rigid, static institution with inflexible rules, but rather a dynamic social structure from which human morality and human nature emerge.

Journals

Family Relations, International Journal of Sociology of the Family, Journal of Comparative Family Studies, Journal of Divorce, Journal of Family and Economic Issues, Journal of Family Issues, Journal of Family Violence, Journal of Marriage and the Family, and *Marriage and Family Review* publish articles on almost every aspect of marriage and family life.

Chapter 17

Howe, Quincy, Jr. *Under Running Laughter: Notes from a Renegade Classroom*. New York: Free Press, 1990. A tenured professor of classics recounts his experiences and describes the unorthodox techniques he used to teach "throwaway" adolescents in the inner city.

Hurn, Christopher J. *The Limits and Possibilities of Schooling: An Introduction to the Sociology of Education*, 3rd ed. Boston: Allyn and Bacon, 1993. This overview of the sociology of education reviews in greater depth many of the topics discussed in this chapter.

Kozol, Jonathan. *Savage Inequalities*. New York: Crown Publishers: 1991. Kozol presents a journalistic account of educational inequalities that arise from social class.

Postman, Neil. *Technopoly: The Surrender of Culture to Technology*. New York: Knopf, 1992. An analysis of how technology is destroying vital aspects of social life and how education can lead the resistance against technological tyranny.

Schoolland, Ken. *Shogun's Ghost: The Dark Side of Japanese Education*. Westport, Conn.: Bergin & Garvey, 1990. The author, a college teacher in Japan for five years, shatters the myth of excellence in Japanese education in his account of unruly classrooms, general lack of discipline and study habits, truancy, and rampant cheating on exams.

Sowell, Thomas. *Inside American Education: The Decline, The Deception, the Dogmas*. New York: Free Press, 1993. The author, a thoroughgoing conservative, scathingly denounces most trends in U.S. education.

Trueba, Henry T., Lila Jacobs, and Elizabeth Kirton. *Cultural Conflict and Adaptation: The Case of Hmong Children in American Society*. Bristol, Penn.: Falmer Press, 1990. In examining problems of Hmong children living in California, the author probes the multi-ethnic challenges facing U.S. schools.

Journals

The following journals contain articles that examine almost every aspect of eduction: *Education and Urban Society, Harvard Educational Review, Sociology of Education*.

Chapter 18

Berger, Peter L. *A Far Glory: The Quest for Faith in an Age of Credulity*. New York: Free Press, 1992. A sociologist explains how faith is possible in an age of pluralistic relativism.

Berger, Peter L. *The Sacred Canopy: Elements of a Sociological Theory of Religion*. New York: Doubleday Anchor, 1969. Applying the functionalist, symbolic interactionist, and conflict perspectives to the analysis of religion, the author synthesizes the writings of Emile Durkheim, Max Weber, and Karl Marx.

Haddad, Yvonne Yazbeck, and Adair T. Lummis. *Islamic Values in the United States: A Comparative Study*. New York: Oxford University Press, 1987. Like the millions of immigrants before them, the large numbers of Muslims who have recently immigrated to the United States have brought their religion with them. The authors examine the adaptation of Islam to its new environment.

Hunter, James Davidson. *Evangelicalism: The Coming Generation.* Chicago: University of Chicago Press, 1987. What will the evangelical churches be like in coming years? Since they will be shaped by people now being trained, the author focuses on people studying for the ministry.

Lippy, Charles H., and Peter W. Williams, eds. *Encyclopedia of the American Religious Experience: Studies of Traditions and Movements.* New York: Scribners, 1988. This overview of religions in the United States focuses on their histories, as opposed to their teachings.

Marty, Martin E., and R. Scott Appleby. *The Glory and the Power: The Fundamentalist Challenge to the Modern World.* Boston: Beacon Press, 1992. Examining fundamentalism in the United States, Israel, Egypt, and elsewhere, the authors explain why fundamentalism is enjoying a revival.

Schoenherr, Richard A., and Lawrence A. Young. *Full Pews and Empty Altars: Demographics of the Priest Shortage.* Madison: University of Wisconsin Press, 1993. The authors analyze the implications of why, in spite of growing numbers of Roman Catholics, the number of priests is shrinking.

Smart, Ninian. *The World's Religions.* Englewood Cliffs, N.J.: Prentice Hall, 1989. The author presents a summary of the teachings and characteristics of religions around the world.

Journals

The following three journals publish articles that focus on the sociology of religion: *Journal for the Scientific Study of Religion, Review of Religious Research,* and *Sociological Analysis: A Journal in the Sociology of Religion.*

Chapter 19

Albrecht, Gary L. *The Disability Business: Rehabilitation in America.* Newbury Park, Calif.: Sage, 1992. This examination of how the megabillion-dollar rehabilitation industry functions focuses on how the desire for profit combines with marketing techniques to influence the quality of patient care.

Cockerham, William C. *The Sociology of Mental Disorder.* Englewood Cliffs, N.J.: Prentice Hall, 1992. How is sociology a tool for understanding mental illness? This book presents the answers.

Davis, Fred. *Passage Through Crisis: Polio Victims and Their Families.* New Brunswick, N.J.: Transaction, 1990. The book focuses on communications between doctors and their patients and the meaning of physical disability in U.S. society.

Fox, Renée C., and Judith P. Swazey. *Spare Parts: Organ Replacement in American Society.* New York: Oxford University Press, 1992. The authors explore moral and ethical aspects of organ replacement, a social issue destined to grow in importance as medical technology continues to advance.

Grob, Gerald N. *The Mad Among Us: A History of the Care of America's Mentally Ill.* New York: Free Press, 1994. From colonial to contemporary times, a detailed history of attitudes and approaches toward the mentally ill, some enlightened, most repressive.

Isaac, Rael Jean, and Virginia C. Armat. *Madness in the Streets: How Psychiatry and the Law Abandoned the Mentally Ill.* New York: Free Press, 1990. Why have so many sidewalks and parks become open-air mental wards? The authors analyze the social and political delusions that created a cultural base for justifying the abandonment of thousands of mentally ill people to the streets.

Konner, Melvin. *Medicine at the Crossroads: The Crisis in Health Care.* New York: Pantheon Books, 1993. This volume explores major social and professional issues facing U.S. medicine.

Payer, Lynn. *Disease Mongers: How Doctors, Drug Companies, and Insurers Are Making You Feel Sick.* New York: Wiley, 1992. Since profits underlie the U.S. medical system, could it be that the U.S. medical establishment has a vested interest in keeping people ill? The author of this radical analysis thinks so.

Rosenberg, Charles E. *The Care of Strangers: The Rise of America's Hospital System.* New York: Basic Books, 1987. The author examines how the development of hospitals in the United States is related to social class, ideology, philanthropy, education, and economics.

Smith, Barbara Ellen. *Digging Our Own Graves: Coal Miners and the Struggle over Black Lung Disease.* Philadelphia: Temple University Press, 1987. Smith relates the coal miners' struggle to get black lung disease recognized by the medical community.

Journals

Journal of Health and Social Behavior, Research in the Sociology of Health Care, Social Science and Medicine, and *Sociological Practice: Health Sociology* publish research articles and essays in the field of medical sociology.

Chapter 20

Anderson, Elijah. *StreetWise: Race, Class, and Change in an Urban Community.* Chicago: University of Chicago Press, 1992. A participant observation study that explores the relationships between those who are gentrifying an inner-city area and those who are being displaced.

Burgess, Ernest W., ed. *Urban Community.* New York: AMS Press, 1993. This reprint of a classic 1926 book allows you a glimpse of earlier life in the United States.

Department of Agriculture. *Yearbook of Agriculture.* Washington, D.C.: Department of Agriculture, published annually. The yearbook focuses on specific aspects of U.S. agribusiness, especially international economies and trade.

Flora, Cornelia Butler, Jan L. Flora, Jacqueline D. Spears, and Louis E. Swanson. *Rural Communities: Legacy and Change.* Boulder, Colo.: Westview Press, 1992. The authors examine profound changes that are transforming rural life.

Gans, Herbert J. *The Urban Villagers: Group and Class in the Life of Italian-Americans.* New York: Free Press, 1982. This participant observation study of the West End of Boston provides insight into and understanding of white lower-class urban life.

Garreau, Joel. *Edge City: Life on the New Frontier.* New York: Doubleday Anchor, 1992. Garreau gives the first overview of "edge cities," discussed in this chapter.

Karp, David A., Gregory P. Stone, and William C. Yoels. *Being Urban: A Sociology of City Life,* 2nd ed. New York: Praeger, 1991. This overview of urban life stresses the everyday lives of city dwellers—what people *do* in cities, how they adjust and get along.

Liebow, Elliot. *Tally's Corner: A Study of Negro Streetcorner Men.* Boston: Little, Brown, 1967. This participant observation study of black street corner men and their families in Washington, D.C., has become a classic in sociology.

Savitch, H. V. *PostIndustrial Cities.* Princeton, N.J.: Princeton University Press, 1993. The author examines how fundamental social and economic changes are affecting cities.

Simon, Julian L. *The Ultimate Resource.* Princeton, N.J.: Princeton University Press, 1981. This controversial, path-breaking book presents the anti-Malthusian position and defends population growth, indicating that the problem is political arrangements, not too many people or too few resources.

Weeks, John R. *Population: An Introduction to Concepts and Issues*. 5th ed. Belmont, Calif.: Wadsworth, 1992. Focusing on both the United States and the world, the author analyzes the major issues in population.

Whyte, William Foote. *Street Corner Society: The Social Structure of an Italian Slum*. Chicago: University of Chicago Press, 1993. First published in 1943. Still quoted and reprinted, this classic participant observation study provides insight into the social organization of an area of a U.S. city that, from an outsider's perspective, appeared socially disorganized.

Chapter 21

Brunvand, Jan Harold. *The Vanishing Hitchhiker: American Urban Legends and Their Meanings*. New York: Norton, 1981. This humorous analysis of urban legends helps us better understand how people adapt to social change. If you enjoy this book, you might try its 1984 sequel by the same author and publisher: *The Choking Doberman and Other "New" Urban Legends*.

Curtis, Russell L., Jr., and Benigno E. Aguirre, eds. *Collective Behavior and Social Movements*. Boston: Allyn and Bacon, 1993. The thirty-five readings in this collection, some at an advanced level, provide an overview of the major topics of this chapter.

Gitlin, Todd. *The Sixties: Years of Hope, Days of Rage*. New York: Bantam, 1987. The author, now a sociologist, was a leader in the peace movement that arose during the social unrest of the 1960s. He combines personal experience with a sociological perspective.

Jasper, James M., and Dorothy Nelkin. *The Animal Rights Crusade: The Growth of a Moral Protest*. New York: Free Press, 1992. With an emphasis on their philosophy, motivation, and tactics, the authors provide a kaleidoscopic overview of the animal rights movement, from its beginnings to its international participation.

Klee, Ernst, Willi Dressen, and Volker Riess. *"The Good Old Days": The Holocaust as Seen by Its Perpetrators and Bystanders*, Deborah Burnstone, trans. New York: Free Press, 1991. This chilling account of massacres by the SS is based on the photographs they took of their "work," their letters home, and their scrapbooks.

McPhail, Clark. *The Myth of the Madding Crowd*. New York: Aldine de Gruyter, 1991. McPhail provides an overview of the history of research and theorizing about collective behavior.

Turner, Patricia. *I Heard It Through the Grapevine*. Berkeley: University of California Press, 1993. The author analyzes rumors among African Americans, including their effects on specific businesses.

Turner, Ralph H., and Lewis M. Killian. *Collective Behavior*, 3rd ed. Englewood Cliffs, N.J.: Prentice Hall, 1987. This overview of collective behavior and social movements contains fascinating materials from real-life cases.

Yuan, Gao. *Born Red: A Chronicle of the Cultural Revolution*. Stanford, Calif.: Stanford University Press, 1987. This first-person account chronicles the cultural revolution in China during the late 1960s.

Chapter 22

Brown, Lester R., ed. *State of the World*. New York: Norton, published annually. Experts on environmental issues analyze environmental problems throughout the world.

Council on Environmental Quality. *Environmental Quality*. Washington, D.C.: U.S. Government Printing Office, published annually. Each report evaluates the condition of some aspect of the environment.

Feshbach, Murray, and Alfred Friendly. *Ecocide in the USSR*. New York: Basic Books, 1992. The authors analyze the political repression of environmentalists and the government's willing sacrifice of the environment for the sake of "building a brighter, industrial future."

Flink, James J. *The Automobile Age*. Cambridge, Mass.: MIT Press, 1990. This wide-ranging overview of the U.S. automobile industry also discusses the automobile's effects on society.

Hafner, Katie, and John Markoff. *Cyberpunk: Outlaws and Hackers on the Computer Frontier*. New York: Simon & Schuster, 1991. The stories of three of the most famous computer hackers—their crimes and their downfall—are revealed.

McCuen, Gary E., ed. *Ecocide and Genocide in the Vanishing Forest: The Rainforests and Native People*. Hudson, Wis.: GEM Publications, 1993. Eighteen brief readings examine why the rainforests are vanishing and explore possible solutions to this problem.

Mokyr, Joel. *The Lever of Riches: Technological Creativity and Economic Progress*. New York: Oxford University Press, 1992. Using a broad historical and cross-cultural sweep to analyze how advances in technology raise productivity, spur economic growth, and increase wealth, the author probes why some societies are more technologically creative than others.

Scarce, Rik. *Eco-Warriors: Understanding the Radical Environmental Movement*. Chicago: Noble Press, 1990. Written by a sociologist featured in Chapter 5 who was jailed for refusing to reveal his research sources, this book provides an overview of the origins, philosophy, and strategies of radical environmental activists.

Stead, W. Edward, and Jean Garner Stead. *Management for a Small Planet*. Newbury Park, Calif.: Sage, 1992. The authors examine how we can reconcile our need for economic production with our need to protect the earth's ecosystem.

Journals

Earth First! Journal and *Sierra*. These magazines, published by Earth First! and the Sierra Club respectively, are excellent sources for keeping informed of major developments in the environmental movement.

Aberle, David. *The Peyote Religion Among the Navaho*. Chicago: Aldine, 1966.

Aberle, David F., A. K. Cohen, A. K. David, M. J. Leng, Jr., and F. N. Sutton. "The Functional Prerequisites of a Society." *Ethics*, 60, January 1950:100–111.

Abramson, Jill. "How Outsider Clinton Built a Potent Network of Insider Contacts." *Wall Street Journal*, March 12, 1992:A1, A4.

Abramson, Jill, and David Rogers. "The Keating 535." *Wall Street Journal*, January 10, 1991:A1, A8.

Achenbaum, W. Andrew. *Old Age in the New Land: The American Experience Since 1870*. Baltimore: Johns Hopkins University Press, 1978.

Acker, Joan. "Class, Gender, and the Relations of Distribution." *Signs: Journal of Women in Culture and Society*, 13, 3, 1988:473–497.

Addams, Jane. *Twenty Years at Hull House*. New York: Signet, 1981. First published in 1910.

Adler, Patricia A., Steven J. Kless, and Peter Adler. "Socialization to Gender Roles: Popularity Among Elementary School Boys and Girls." *Sociology of Education*, 65, July 1992:169–187.

Adler, Stephen J. "Lawyers Advise Concerns to Provide Precise Written Policy to Employees." *Wall Street Journal*, October 9, 1991:B1, B4.

Adorno, Theodor W., Else Frenkel-Brunwick, D. J. Levinson, and R. N. Sanford. *The Authoritarian Personality*. New York: Harper & Row, 1950.

Aeppel, Timothy. "Germany Looks Less Like a Solid Citizen." *Wall Street Journal*, September 22, 1992:A12.

Aguirre, Benigno E. "The Conventionalization of Collective Behavior in Cuba." In *Collective Behavior and Social Movements*, Russell L. Curtis, Jr., and Benigno E. Aguirre, eds. Boston: Allyn and Bacon, 1993:413–428.

Aguirre, B. E., E. L. Quarantelli, and Jorge L. Mendoza. "The Collective Behavior of Fads: The Characteristics, Effects, and Career of Streaking." In *Collective Behavior and Social Movements*, Russell L. Curtis, Jr., and Benigno E. Aguirre, eds. Boston: Allyn and Bacon, 1993:168–182.

Ahlburg, Dennis A., and Carol J. De Vita. "New Realities of the American Family." *Population Bulletin*, 47, 2, August 1992:1–44.

Alba, Richard D. *Ethnic Identity: The Transformation of White America*. New Haven, Conn.: Yale University Press, 1990.

Albert, Ethel M. "Women of Burundi: A Study of Social Values." In *Women of Tropical Africa*, Denise Paulme, ed. Berkeley: University of California Press, 1963:179–215.

Albrecht, Donald E., and Steven H. Murdoch. "Natural Resource Availability and Social Change." *Sociological Inquiry*, 56, 3, Summer 1986:381–400.

Aldrich, Nelson W., Jr. *Old Money: The Mythology of America's Upper Class*. New York: Vintage Books, 1989.

Allport, Floyd. *Social Psychology*. Boston: Houghton Mifflin, 1954.

Alpert, Harry. *Emile Durkheim and His Sociology*. New York: Columbia University Press, 1939.

Altman, Lawrence K. "Medical Schools Discover an Unexpected Popularity." *New York Times*, May 18, 1993:A1, A19.

American Sociological Association. "Code of Ethics." Washington, D.C.: American Sociological Association, August 14, 1989.

American Sociological Association, "Section on Environment and Technology." Pamphlet, no date.

Amott, Teresa, and Julie Matthaei. *Race, Gender, and Work: A Multicultural Economic History of Women in the United States*. Boston: South End Press, 1991.

Andersen, Margaret L. *Thinking About Women: Sociological Perspectives on Sex and Gender*. New York: Macmillan, 1988.

Anderson, Chris. "NORC Study Describes Homeless," *Chronicle*, 1986:5, 9.

Anderson, Elijah. *A Place on the Corner*. Chicago: University of Chicago Press, 1978.

Anderson, Elijah. *Streetwise*. Chicago: University of Chicago Press, 1990.

Anderson, Nels. *The Hobo*. Chicago: University of Chicago Press, 1923.

Anderson, Nels. *Desert Saints: The Mormon Frontier in Utah*. Chicago: University of Chicago Press, 1966. First published in 1942.

Anderson, Teresa A. "The Best Years of Their Lives," *Newsweek*, January 7, 1985:6.

Angell, Robert C. "The Sociology of Human Conflict." In *The Nature of Human Conflict*, Elton B. McNeil, ed. Englewood Cliffs, N.J.: Prentice Hall, 1965.

Ansberry, Clare. "Despite Federal Law, Hospitals Still Reject Sick Who Can't Pay." *Wall Street Journal*, November 29, 1988:A1, A4.

Apple, Michael W. *Education and Power: Reproduction and Contradiction in Education*. London: Routledge & Kegan Paul, 1982.

Ariés, Philippe. *Centuries of Childhood: A Social History of Family Life*. Robert Baldick, trans. New York: Vintage, 1962.

Ariés, Philippe. *Centuries of Childhood*. R. Baldick, trans. New York Vintage Books, 1965.

Arlacchi, P. *Peasants and Great Estates: Society in Traditional Calabria*. Cambridge, England: Cambridge University Press, 1980.

Armitage, Richard L. "Red Army Retreat Doesn't Signal End of U.S. Obligation." *Wall Street Journal*, February 7, 1989:A20.

Arndt, William F., and F. Wilbur Gingrich. *A Greek-English Lexicon of the New Testament and Other Early Christian Literature*. Chicago: University of Chicago Press, 1957.

Asch, Solomon. "Effects of Group Pressure Upon the Modification and Distortion of Judgments." In *Readings in Social Psychology*, Guy Swanson, Theodore M. Newcomb, and Eugene L. Hartley, eds. New York: Holt, Rinehart and Winston, 1952.

Ash, Arthur. "A Zero-Sum Game That Hurts Blacks." *Wall Street Journal*, February 27, 1992:A10.

Ashley, Richard. *Cocaine: Its History, Uses, and Effects*. New York: St. Martin's, 1975.

Associated Press. "Death Rates for Minority Infants Were Underestimated, Study Says." January 7, 1992.

Atchley, Robert C. "Dimensions of Widowhood in Later Life," *Gerontologist*, 15, April 1975:176–178.

Auerbach, Elsa. "The Challenge of the English Only Movement." *College English*, 54, 7, November 1992:843–851.

Auerbach, Judith D. "Employer-Supported Child Care as a Women-Responsive Policy." *Journal of Family Issues*, 11, 4, December 1990:384–400.

Ausubel, Jesse H. "Rat-Race Dynamics and Crazy Companies: The Diffusion of Technologies and Social Behavior." *Technological Forecasting and Social Change*, 39, 1991:11–22.

Avery, Dennis T. "Mother Earth Can Feed Billions More." *Wall Street Journal*, September 19, 1991:A14.

Bacon, Kenneth H. "The 'Birth Dearth' and Immigration." *Wall Street Journal*, October 13, 1986:1.

Bagguley, Paul, and Kirk Mann. "Idle Thieving Bastards? Scholarly Representations of the 'Underclass.'" *Work, Employment, and Society*, 6, 1, March 1992:113–126.

Bagne, Paul. "High-Tech Breeding." In *Marriage and Family in a Changing Society*, 4th ed., James M. Henslin, ed. New York: Free Press, 1989:226–234.

Bahr, Howard M. *Skid Row: An Introduction to Disaffiliation*. New York: Oxford University Press, 1973.

Bahr, Stephen. "Effects of Power and Division of Labor in the Family." In *Working Mothers*, Lois W. Hoffman and F. Ivan Nye, eds. San Francisco: Jossey-Bass, 1974:167–185.

Bailey, Michael J., Richard C. Pillard, Michael C. Neale, and Yvonne Agyei. "Heritable Factors Influence Sexual Orientation in Women." *Archives of General Psychiatry*, 50, 3, March 1993:217–223.

Bainbridge, William Sims. "Collective Behavior and Social Movements." In *Sociology*, Rodney Stark. Belmont, Calif.: Wadsworth, 1989:608–640.

Bales, Robert F. *Interaction Process Analysis*. Reading, Mass.: Addison-Wesley, 1950.

Bales, Robert F. "The Equilibrium Problem in Small Groups." In *Working Papers in the Theory of Action*, Talcott Parsons et al., eds. New York: Free Press, 1953:111–115.

Ballentine, Jeanne H. *The Sociology of Education: A Systematic Analysis*. Englewood Cliffs, N.J.: Prentice Hall, 1983.

Balling, Robert C. "A Climate of Doubt About Global Warming." *Wall Street Journal*, April 22, 1992:A18.

Baltzell, E. Digby. *The Protestant Establishment: Aristocracy and Caste in America*. New York: Vintage, 1964.

Baltzell, E. Digby. *Puritan Boston and Quaker Philadelphia*. New York: Free Press, 1979.

Banerjee, Nela. "Debate over Measuring the Poverty Line Will Come to a Head in Senate Hearings." *Wall Street Journal*, May 12, 1994:A2.

Banfield, Edward C. *The Unheavenly City Revisited*. Boston: Little, Brown, 1974.

Barbeau, Clayton, "The Man–Woman Crisis." In *Marriage and Family in a Changing Society*, 4th ed. James M. Henslin, ed. New York: Free Press, 1992:193–199.

Barber, Bernard. "The Sociology of Science." In *Sociology Today: Problems and Prospects*, Robert K. Merton, Leonard Broom, and Leonard S. Cottrell, Jr., eds. New York: Basic Books, 1959: 215–228.

Barker, Judith C. "Between Humans and Ghosts: The Decrepit Elderly in a Polynesian Society." In *The Cultural Context of Aging: Worldwide Perspectives*, Jay Sokolovsky, ed. New York: Bergin & Garvey, 1990:295–313.

Barkun, Michael. "Reflections After Waco: Millenialists and the State." *Christian Century*, June 2–9, 1993:596–600.

Barnes, Harry Elmer. *The History of Western Civilization*, Vol. 1. New York: Harcourt, Brace, 1935.

Barnes, John A. "Canadians Cross Border to Save Their Lives." *Wall Street Journal*, December 12, 1990:A14.

Baron, Robert, and Gerald Greenberg. *Behavior in Organizations*. Boston: Allyn and Bacon, 1990.

Barringer, Felicity. "Rich–Poor Gulf Widens Among Blacks." *New York Times*, September 25, 1992:A12.

Barry, Paul. "Strong Medicine: A Talk with former Principal Henry Gradillas." *College Board Review*, Fall 1989: 2–13.

Baum, Steven K. "Adult Development in Women." Paper presented at the annual meetings of the American Psychological Association, Atlanta, 1988. (In *Psychology*, 2nd ed., Carole Wade and Carol Tavris, eds. New York: Harper & Row, 1990.)

Beals, Ralph L., and Harry Hoijer. *An Introduction to Anthropology*, 3rd ed. New York: Macmillan, 1965.

Beardsley, Tim. "Getting Warmer?" *Scientific American*, July 1988:32.

Beck, Allen J., Susan A. Kline, and Lawrence A. Greenfeld. "Survey of Youth in Custody, 1987." Washington, D.C.: U.S. Department of Justice, September 1988.

Beck, E. M., and Stewart E. Tolnay. "The Killing Fields of the Deep South: The Market for Cotton and the Lynching of Blacks 1882–1930." *American Sociological Review*, 55, August 1990:526–539.

Beck, Scott H., and Joe W. Page. "Involvement in Activities and the Psychological Well-Being of Retired Men." *Activities, Adaptation, & Aging*, 11, 1, 1988:31–47.

Beck, Ulrich. *Risk Society: Towards a New Modernity*, Mark Ritter, trans. London: Sage, 1992. First published as *Risikogesellschaft* in 1986.

Becker, Howard S. *Outsiders: Studies in the Sociology of Deviance*. New York: Free Press, 1966.

Beeghley, Leonard. *The Structure of Social Stratification in the United States*. Boston: Allyn and Bacon, 1989.

Begley, Sharon. "Twins: Nazi and Jew." *Newsweek, 94*, December 3, 1979:139.

Begley, Sharon, and Daniel Glick. "The Handwriting of God." *Newsweek*, May 4, 1992:76.

Belcher, John R. "Are Jails Replacing the Mental Health System for the Homeless Mentally Ill?" *Community Mental Health Journal, 24*, 3, Fall 1988:185–195.

Belknap, Joanne. "Racism on Campus: Prejudice Plus Power." *Vital Speeches, 57*, 10, March 1, 1991:308–312.

Bell, Daniel. *The Coming of Post-Industrial Society: A Venture in Social Forecasting*. New York: Basic Books, 1973.

Bell, Daniel. "The Third Technological Revolution and Its Possible Socioeconomic Consequences." *Dissent*, Spring 1989:164–176.

Bell, David A. "An American Success Story: The Triumph of Asian-Americans." In *Sociological Footprints: Introductory Readings in Sociology*, 5th ed., Leonard Cargan and Jeanne H. Ballantine, eds. Belmont, Calif.: Wadsworth, 1991:308–316.

Bell, Wendell. "Anomie, Social Isolation, and the Class Structure." *Sociometry, 20*, 1957:105–116.

Bell, Wendell, and Marion D. Boat. "Urban Neighborhoods and Informal Social Relations." In *Urban Man and Society: A Reader in Urban Ecology*, Albert N. Cousins and Hans Nagpaul, eds. New York: Knopf, 1970:211–220.

Bellah, Robert N. *Beyond Belief*. New York: Harper & Row, 1970.

Bellah, Robert N., Richard Madsen, William M. Sullivan, Ann Swidler, and Steven M. Tipton. *Habits of the Heart: Individualism and Commitment in American Life*. Berkeley: University of California Press, 1985.

Benales, Carlos. "70 Days Battling Starvation and Freezing in the Andes: A Chronicle of Man's Unwillingness to Die." *New York Times*, January 1, 1973:3.

Bender, Sue, "Everyday Sacred: A Journey to the Amish." *Utne Reader*, September–October 1990:91–97.

Benet, Sula. "Why They Live to Be 100, or Even Older, in Abkhasia." *New York Times Magazine, 26*, December 1971.

Benford, Robert D. "Dramaturgy and Social Movements: The Social Construction and Communication of Power." *Sociological Inquiry, 62*, 1, February 1992:36–55.

Benokraitis, Nijole V., and Joe R. Feagin. *Modern Sexism*. Englewood Cliffs, N.J.: Prentice Hall, 1986.

Berger, Arthur S., and Joyce Berger, eds. *To Die or Not to Die: Cross-Disciplinary, Cultural, and Legal Perspectives on the Right to Choose Death*. Westport, Conn.: Praeger, 1990.

Berger, Peter L. *Invitation to Sociology: A Humanistic Perspective*. New York: Doubleday, 1963:3–7.

Berger, Peter L. *The Sacred Canopy: Elements of a Sociological Theory of Religion*. Garden City, N.Y.: Doubleday, 1967.

Berger, Peter L. "Invitation to Sociology." In *Down to Earth Sociology: Introductory Readings*, 7th ed. James M. Henslin, ed. New York: Free Press, 1993.

Berger, Peter L., and Hansfried Kellner. "Marriage and the Construction of Reality." In *Marriage and Family in a Changing Society*, 4th ed., James M. Henslin, ed. New York: Free Press, 1992:165–174.

Berger, Peter L., and Thomas Luckmann. *The Social Construction of Reality: A Treatise in the Sociology of Knowledge*. Garden City, N.Y.: Anchor Books, 1967.

Bergström, Hans. "Pressures Behind the Swedish Health Reforms." *Viewpoint Sweden, 12*, July 1992:1–5.

Berk, Richard A. *Collective Behavior*. Dubuque, Iowa: Brown, 1974.

Berle, Adolf, Jr., and Gardiner C. Means. *The Modern Corporation and Private Property*. New York: Harcourt, Brace and World, 1932. As cited in Useem 1980:44.

Bernard, Jessie. *The Future of Marriage*. New York: Bantam, 1972.

Bernard, Jessie. "The Good-Provider Role." In *Marriage and Family in a Changing Society*, 4th ed., James M. Henslin, ed. New York: Free Press, 1992:275–285.

Bernard, Viola W., Perry Ottenberg, and Fritz Redl. "Dehumanization: A Composite Psychological Defense in Relation to Modern War." In *The Triple Revolution Emerging: Social Problems in Depth*, Robert Perucci and Marc Pilisuk, eds. Boston: Little, Brown, 1971:17–34.

Bessen, Jim. "No Need for More Unemployed." *New York Times*, August 4, 1993.

Besser, Terry L. "A Critical Approach to the Study of Japanese Management." *Humanity and Society, 16*, 2, May 1992:176–195.

Bettelheim, Bruno. "Difficulties Between Parents and Children: Their Causes and How to Prevent Them." In *Family Strengths 4: Positive Support Systems*, Nick Stinnett, John DeFrain, Kay King, Herbert Lingren, George Row, Sally Van Zandt, and Roseanne Williams, eds. Lincoln: University of Nebraska Press, 1982:5–14.

Billingsley, Andrew. *Black Families in White America*. Englewood Cliffs, N.J.: Prentice Hall, 1968.

Bishop, Jerry E. "Study Finds Doctors Tend to Postpone Heart Surgery for Women, Raising Risk." *Wall Street Journal*, April 16, 1990:B4.

Blackwelder, Stephen P. "Duality of Structure in the Reproduction of Race, Class, and Gender Inequality." Paper presented at the 1993 meetings of the American Sociological Association.

Blau, Francine D., and Lawrence M. Kahn. "The Gender Earnings Gap: Some International Evidence." Working Paper No. 4224, National Bureau of Economic Research, December 1992.

Blau, Francine D., and Anne E. Winkler. "Women in the Labor Force: An Overview." In *Women: A Feminist Perspective*, 4th ed., Jo Freeman, ed. Palo Alto, Calif.: Mayfield, 1989:265–286.

Blau, Peter M. *Exchange and Power in Social Life*. New York: Wiley, 1964.

Blauner, Robert. "Death and Social Structure." *Psychiatry, 29*, 1966:378–394.

Blauner, Robert. *Racial Oppression in America*. New York: Harper & Row, 1972.

Blinick, Abraham. "Socialized Medicine Is No Cure-All." *Wall Street Journal*, January 17, 1992:A11.

Blood, Robert O., Jr., and Donald M. Wolfe. *Husbands and Wives*. New York: Free Press, 1960.

Bloom, Dan, Veronica Fellerath, David Long, and Robert G. Wood. *LEAP: Interim Findings on a Welfare Initiative to Improve School Attendance Among Teenage Parents*. New York: Manpower Demonstration Research Corporation, May 1993.

Blumer, Herbert George. "Collective Behavior." In *Principles of Sociology*, Robert E. Park, ed. New York: Barnes and Noble, 1939:219–288.

Blumer, Herbert. "Sociological Implications of the Thought of George Herbert Mead." *American Journal of Sociology, 71,* 1966:535–544.

Blumer, Herbert. *Industrialization as an Agent of Social Change: A Critical Analysis,* David R. Maines and Thomas J. Morrione, eds. New York: Aldine de Gruyter, 1990.

Blumstein, Alfred, and Jacqueline Cohen. "Characterizing Criminal Careers." *Science, 237,* August 1987:985–991.

Blumstein, Philip, and Pepper Schwartz. *American Couples: Money, Work, Sex.* New York: Pocket Books, 1985.

Bobo, Lawrence, and James R. Kluegel. "Modern American Prejudice: Stereotypes, Social Distance, and Perceptions of Discrimination Toward Blacks, Hispanics, and Asians." Paper presented at the 1991 annual meeting of the American Sociological Association.

Boden, Deirdre, Anthony Giddens, and Harvey L. Molotch. "Sociology's Role in Addressing Society's Problems Is Undervalued and Misunderstood in Academe." *Chronicle of Higher Education,* February 21, 1990:B1, B3.

Bogardus, Emory S. *A History of Social Thought,* 2nd ed. Los Angeles: Jesse Ray Miller, 1929.

Bogdanich, Walt. "The People-Pushers." In *Dominant Issues in Medical Sociology,* 3rd ed., Howard D. Schwartz, ed. New York: McGraw-Hill, 1994:331–338.

Bogue, Donald J. *Skid Row in American Cities.* Chicago: University of Chicago Press, 1963.

Bohrer, Linda. "AIDS Impact Grows in Asia." *Wall Street Journal,* April 13, 1992:A11.

Bolick, Clint. "Puerto Rico: Leading the Way in School Choice." *Wall Street Journal,* January 14, 1994:A11.

Borrelli, Peter. "The Ecophilosophers." *Amicus Journal,* Spring 1988:30–39.

"The Boss's Pay." *Wall Street Journal,* April 18, 1990:R13–R20.

Boudon, Raymond. "What Middle-Range Theories Are." *Contemporary Sociology, 20,* 4, July 1991: 519–522.

Boulard, Gerry. "Student Staffers May Lose Control of Campus Paper." *Editor and Publisher, 124,* 41, October 12, 1991:20, 40.

Boulding, Elise. *The Underside of History.* Boulder, Colo.: Westview Press, 1976.

Bourque, L. B. *Defining Rape.* Durham, N.C.: Duke University Press, 1989.

Bowen, Crosswell. "Donora, Pennsylvania." In *Society and Environment: The Coming Collision,* Rex R. Campbell and Jerry L. Wade, eds. Boston: Allyn and Bacon, 1972:163–168.

Bowles, Samuel. "Unequal Education and the Reproduction of the Social Division of Labor." In *Power and Ideology in Education,* J. Karabel and A. H. Halsey, eds. New York: Oxford University Press, 1977.

Bowles, Samuel, and Herbert Gintis. *Schooling in Capitalist America.* New York: Basic Books, 1976.

Brajuha, Mario, and Lyle Hallowell. "Legal Intrusion and the Politics of Fieldwork: The Impact of the Brajuha Case." *Urban Life, 14,* 4, January 1986:454–478.

Brandt, Norman. U.S. National Center for Education Statistics. Telephone interview, March 8, 1994.

Brauchli, Marcus W. "China Cranks Up Propaganda Machine and Releases Dissident in Olympics Bid." *Wall Street Journal,* September 15, 1993a:A11.

Brauchli, Marcus W. "A Satellite TV System Is Quickly Moving Asia into the Global Village." *Wall Street Journal,* May 10, 1993b:A1, A8.

Brecher, Edward M., and the Editors of Consumer Reports. *Licit and Illicit Drugs.* Boston: Little, Brown, 1972.

Bridgwater, William, ed. *The Columbia Viking Desk Encyclopedia.* New York: Viking Press, 1953.

Brilliant, Ashleigh E. *Social Effects of the Automobile in Southern California During the 1920s.* Unpublished doctoral dissertation, University of California at Berkeley, 1964.

Brink, Susan. "Elderly Empowerment." *U.S. News & World Report,* April 26, 1993:65–70.

Brinton, Crane. *The Anatomy of Revolution.* New York: Vintage Books, 1965.

Broad, William J. "The Shuttle Explodes." *New York Times,* January 29, 1986, A1, A5.

Brodie, H. Keith H. "We Must Engage Intolerance and Inhumanity Openly and Publicly, as a Community, at Every Opportunity." *Chronicle of Higher Education, 36,* 4, September 27, 1989:B3.

Bromley, David G. "The Satanic Cult Scare." *Culture and Society,* May–June 1991:55–56.

Bronfenbrenner, Urie, as quoted in Diane Fassel. "Divorce May Not Harm Children." In *Family in America: Opposing Viewpoints,* Viqi Wagner, ed. San Diego, Calif.: Greenhaven Press, 1992a:115–119.

Bronfenbrenner, Urie. "Principles for the Healthy Growth and Development of Children." In *Marriage and Family in a Changing Society,* 4th ed., James M. Henslin, ed. New York: Free Press, 1992b:243–249.

Bronner, Ethan. "Unveiled." *The New Republic,* June 8, 1992:17–18, 20.

Brooks, Geraldine. "Saudi Duty Brings Novel Challenges." *Wall Street Journal,* August 16, 1990:A8.

Brooks, Virginia R. "Sex Differences in Student Dominance Behavior in Female and Male Professors' Classrooms." *Sex Roles, 8,* 7, 1982:683–690.

Brown, Diane Robinson, and Lawrence E. Gary. "Unemployment and Psychological Distress Among Black American Women." *Sociological Focus, 21,* 1988:209–221.

Brown, G. T., and T. Harris. *Social Origins of Repression: A Study of Psychiatric Disorder in Women.* London: Tavistock, 1978.

Brown, Lester R. *State of the World 1991.* New York: Norton, 1991.

Browning, Christopher R. *Ordinary Men: Reserve Police Battalion 101 and the Final Solution in Poland.* New York: HarperPerennial, 1993.

Brueckner, Jan K. "Analyzing Third World Urbanization: A Model with Empirical Evidence." *Economic Development and Cultural Change, 38,* 3, April 1990:587–610.

Brunvand, Jan Harold. *The Vanishing Hitchhiker: American Urban Legends and Their Meanings.* New York: Norton, 1981.

Brunvand, Jan Harold. *The Choking Doberman and Other "New" Urban Legends.* New York: Norton, 1984.

Brunvand, Jan Harold. *The Study of American Folklore.* New York: Norton, 1986.

Bryant, Clifton D. "Cockfighting: America's Invisible Sport." In *Down to Earth Sociology: Introductory Readings,* 7th ed., James M. Henslin, ed. New York: Free Press, 1993.

Buckley, Stephen. "Shrugging Off the Burden of a Brainy Image." *The Washington Post,* June 17, 1991:D1.

Bulkeley, William F. "Popularity Overseas of Encryption Code Has the U.S. Worried." *Wall Street Journal*, April 28, 1994:A1, A7.

Bullard, Robert D. *Dumping in Dixie: Race, Class, and Environmental Quality*. Boulder, Colo.: Westview Press, 1990.

Bullard, Robert, and Beverly Hendrix Wright. "Environmentalism and the Politics of Equity: Emergent Trends in the Black Community." *Mid-American Review of Sociology*, 12, 2, 1987:21–38.

Bullard, Robert, and Beverly Hendrix Wright. "The Quest for Environmental Equality: Mobilizing the African-American Community for Social Change." *Society and Natural Resources*, 3, 1990:301–311.

Bumiller, Elisabeth. "First Comes Marriage—Then, Maybe, Love." In *Marriage and Family in a Changing Society*, 4th ed., James M. Henslin, ed. New York: Free Press, 1992:120–125.

Bumpass, Larry. "What's Happening to the Family? Interactions Between Demographic and Institutional Change." *Demography*, 27, 4, 1990:483–498.

Bumpass, Larry L., James A. Sweet, and Andrew Cherlin. "The Role of Cohabitation in Declining Rates of Marriage." *Journal of Marriage and the Family*, 53, November 1991:913–927.

Bureau of the Census. Statistical Abstract of the United States. Washington, D.C.: U.S. Government Printing Office, published annually.

Burgess, Ernest W. "The Growth of the City: An Introduction to a Research Project." In *The City*, Robert E. Park, Ernest W. Burgess, and Roderick D. McKenzie, eds. Chicago: University of Chicago Press, 1925:47–62.

Burgess, Ernest W., and Harvey J. Locke. *The Family: From Institution to Companionship*. New York: American Book, 1945.

Burnham, Walter Dean. *Democracy in the Making: American Government and Politics*. Englewood Cliffs, N.J.: Prentice Hall, 1983.

Burr, Chandler. "Homosexuality and Biology." *Atlantic Monthly*, March 1993:47–65.

Burton, Thomas M. "How Industrial Foam Came to Be Employed in Breast Implants." *Wall Street Journal*, March 25, 1992:A1, A4.

Burton, Thomas M., and Scott McMurray. "Dow Corning Still Keeps Implant Data from Public, Despite Vow of Openness." *Wall Street Journal*, February 18, 1992:B8.

Busby, Jim. "Hospices: Help for the Dying." *Current Health*, January 1993:30–31.

Butler, Robert N. *Why Survive? Being Old in America*. New York: Harper & Row, 1975.

Butler, Robert N. "Ageism: Another Form of Bigotry." *Gerontologist*, 9, Winter 1980:243–246.

Buttel, Frederick H. "Sociology and the Environment: The Winding Road Toward Human Ecology." *International Social Science Journal*, 38, 1986:337–356.

Buttel, Frederick H. "New Directions in Environmental Sociology." *Annual Review of Sociology*, 13, W. Richard Scott and James F. Short, Jr., eds. Palo Alto, Calif.: Annual Reviews, 1987:465–488.

Butterworth, Katharine M. "The Story of a Nursing Home Refugee." In *Social Problems 92/93*, LeRoy W. Barnes, ed. Guilford, Conn.: Dushkin, 1992:90–93.

Caldwell, Cleopatra Howard, Angela Dungee Greene, and Andrew Billingsley. "The Black Church as a Family Support System: Instrumental and Expressive Functions." *National Journal of Sociology*, 6, 1, Summer 1992:21–40.

Callahan, Daniel. *Setting Limits: Medical Goals in an Aging Society*. New York: Simon & Schuster, 1987.

Canavan, Margaret M., Walter J. Meyer, III, and Deborah C. Higgs. "The Female Experience of Sibling Incest." *Journal of Marital and Family Therapy*, 18, 2, 1992:129–142.

Cantril, Hadley. *The Psychology of Social Movements*. New York: Wiley, 1941.

Caplow, Theodore. "The American Way of Celebrating Christmas." In *Down to Earth Sociology: Introductory Readings*, 6th ed., James M. Henslin, ed. New York: Free Press, 1991:88–97.

Cardoso, Fernando Henrique. "Dependent Capitalist Development in Latin America." *New Left Review*, 74, July–August 1972:83–95.

Carey, John, and Mark Lewyn. "Yield Signs on the Info Interstate." *Business Week*, January 24, 1994:88–90.

Carlson, Lewis H., and George A. Colburn. *In Their Place: White America Defines Her Minorities, 1850–1950*. New York: Wiley, 1972.

Carpenter, Betsy. "Redwood Radicals." *U.S. News & World Report*, 109, 11, September 17, 1990:50–51.

Carr, Donald E. "The Disasters." In *Society and Environment: The Coming Collision*, Rex R. Campbell and Jerry L. Wade, eds. Boston: Allyn and Bacon, 1972:129–134.

Carrington, Tim. "Developed Nations Want Poor Countries to Succeed on Trade, But Not Too Much." *Wall Street Journal*, September 20, 1993:A10.

Carroll, Peter N., and David W. Noble. *The Free and the Unfree: A New History of the United States*. New York: Penguin, 1977.

Cartwright, Dorwin, and Alvin Zander, eds. *Group Dynamics*, 3rd ed. Evanston, Ill.: Peterson, 1968.

Celis, William, III. "10 Years After a Scathing Report, Schools Show Little Progress." *New York Times*, April 28, 1993:A19.

Centers for Disease Control. *HIV/AIDS Surveillance Report*, September 1993.

Cerhan, Jane Ugland. "The Hmong in the United States: An Overview for Mental Health Professionals." *Journal of Counseling and Development*, 69, 1, September–October 1990:88–92.

Chafetz, Janet Saltzman. *Sex and Advantage: A Comparative Macro-Structural Theory of Sex Stratification*. Totowa, N.J.: Rowman and Allenheld, 1984.

Chagnon, Napoleon A. *Yanomamo: The Fierce People*, 2nd ed. New York: Holt, Rinehart and Winston, 1977.

Chalfant, H. Paul. "Stepping to Redemption: Twelve-Step Groups as Implicit Religion." *Free Inquiry in Creative Sociology*, 20, 2, November 1992:115–120.

Chalfant, H. Paul, Robert E. Beckley, and C. Eddie Palmer. *Religion in Contemporary Society*, 2nd ed. Palo Alto, Calif.: Mayfield, 1987.

Chamberlain, John. "Should We Auction Immigration Visas?" *St. Louis Post-Dispatch*, September 11, 1986:3E.

Chambliss, William J. "A Sociological Analysis of the Law of Vagrancy." *Social Problems*, 12, Summer 1964:67–77.

Chambliss, William J. "The Saints and the Roughnecks." *Society*, 11, November–December 1973:24–31.

Chambliss, William J. "The Saints and the Roughnecks." In *Down to Earth Sociology: Introductory Readings*, 7th ed., James M. Henslin, ed. New York: Free Press, 1993.

Chandler, Tertius, and Gerald Fox. *3000 Years of Urban Growth*. New York: Academic Press, 1974.

Chandra, Vibha P. "Fragmented Identities: The Social Construction of Ethnicity, 1885–1947." Unpublished paper, 1993a.

Chandra, Vibha P. "The Present Moment of the Past: The Metamorphosis." Unpublished paper, 1993b.

Chase, Marilyn. "Genentech, Chiron Report Advances in Research Toward an AIDS Vaccine." *Wall Street Journal*, June 19, 1993:B6.

Chase, Marilyn, and Michael Waldholz. "Progress Is Shown in Race for HIV Drug." *Wall Street Journal*, June 9, 1993:B6.

Chavez, Linda. "Rainbow Collision." *New Republic*, November 19, 1990:14–16.

Chen, Edwin. "Twins Reared Apart: A Living Lab." *New York Times Magazine*. December 9, 1979:112.

Cherlin, Andrew. "Remarriage as an Incomplete Institution." In *Marriage and Family in a Changing Society*, 3rd ed., James M. Henslin, ed. New York: Free Press, 1989:492–501.

Cherlin, Andrew, and Frank F. Furstenberg, Jr. "The American Family in the Year 2000." In *Down to Earth Sociology*, 5th ed., James M. Henslin, ed. New York: Free Press, 1988:325–331.

Chodorow, Nancy J. "What Is the Relation Between Psychoanalytic Feminism and the Psychoanalytic Psychology of Women?" In *Theoretical Perspectives on Sexual Difference*, Deborah L. Rhode, ed. New Haven, Conn.: Yale University Press, 1990:114–130.

Chua-Eoan, Howard. "Tripped Up by Lies." *Time*, October 11, 1993:39–40.

Chun, Ki-Taek, and Jadja Zalokar. *Civil Rights Issues Facing Asian Americans in the 1990s*. Washington, D.C.: U.S. Commission on Civil Rights, February 1992.

Clair, Jeffrey Michael., David A. Karp, and William C. Yoels. *Experiencing the Life Cycle: A Social Psychology of Aging*, 2nd ed. Springfield, Ill.: Thomas, 1993.

Clark, Burton R. "The 'Cooling-Out' Function in Higher Education." In *Social Problems Today: Coping with the Challenges of a Changing Society*, James M. Henslin, ed. Englewood Cliffs, N.J.: Prentice Hall, 1990:309–316.

Clark, Candace. "Sympathy in Everyday Life." In *Down to Earth Sociology: Introductory Readings*, 6th ed., James M. Henslin, ed. New York: Free Press, 1991:193–203.

Clark, Lindley H., Jr. "How the Biggest Lobby Grew." *Wall Street Journal*, January 27, 1994:A14.

Clay, Jason W. "What's a Nation?" *Mother Jones*, November–December 1990:28, 30.

Cleveland, Harlan. "The Age of Spreading Knowledge." *The Futurist*, 24, 2, March–April 1990:35–39.

Clingempeel, W. Glenn, and N. Dickon Repucci. "Joint Custody After Divorce: Major Issues and Goals for Research." *Psychological Bulletin*, 9, 1982:102–127.

Cloward, Richard A., and Lloyd E. Ohlin. *Delinquency and Opportunity: A Theory of Delinquent Gangs*. New York: Free Press, 1960.

Cnaan, Ram A. "Neighborhood-representing Organizations: How Democratic Are They?" *Social Science Review*, December 1991:614–634.

Coburn, David, Carl D'Arcy, Peter New, and George Torrance. *Health and Canadian Society*. Toronto: Fitzhenry and Whiteside, 1981.

Cockburn, Alexander. "Abused Imaginings." *New Statesman & Society*, January 26, 1990:19–20.

Cockerham, William. *Medical Sociology*, 4th ed. Englewood Cliffs, N.J.: Prentice Hall, 1989.

Cohen, Erik. "Lovelorn Farangs: The Correspondence Between Foreign Men and Thai Girls." *Anthropological Quarterly*, 59, 3, July 1986:115–127.

Cohen, Laurie P., William Power, and Michael Siconolfi. "Financial Firms Act to Curb Office Sexism, with Mixed Results." *Wall Street Journal*, November 5, 1991:A1, A6.

Cohen, Morris R. "Moral Aspects of the Criminal Law." *Yale Law Journal*, 49, April 1940:1009–1026.

Cohen, Ronald. "Brittle Marriage as a Stable System: The Kanuri Case." In *Divorce and After: An Analysis of the Emotional and Social Problems of Divorce*. Paul Bohannan, ed. New York: Doubleday, 1971:205–239.

Cole, Jeff, and Sarah Lubman. "Weapons Merchants Are Going Great Guns in Post-Cold War Era." *Wall Street Journal*, January 28, 1994:A1, A4.

Coleman, James S. *Public and Private High Schools: The Impact of Communities*. New York: Basic Books, 1987.

Coleman, James, and Thomas Hoffer. *Public and Private Schools: The Impact of Communities*. New York: Basic Books, 1987.

Coleman, James S., Thomas Hoffer, and Sally Kilgore. *High School Achievement: Public, Catholic, and Private Schools Compared*. New York: Basic Books, 1982.

Coleman, James William. *The Criminal Elite: The Sociology of White Collar Crime*. New York: St. Martin's Press, 1989.

Coleman, James William. "Politics and the Abuse of Power." In *Down to Earth Sociology: Introductory Readings*, 8th ed., James M. Henslin, ed. New York: Free Press, 1995: 442–450.

Collins, Patricia Hill. "Learning from the Outsider Within: The Sociological Significance of Black Feminist Thought." *Social Problems*, 33, 6, December 1986:514–532.

Collins, Randall. *Conflict Sociology: Toward an Explanatory Science*. New York: Academic Press, 1974.

Collins, Randall. *The Credential Society: An Historical Sociology of Education*. New York: Academic Press, 1979.

Collins, Randall. *Theoretical Sociology*. San Diego, Calif.: Harcourt Brace Jovanovich, 1988.

Comstock, George, and Victor C. Strasburger. "Deceptive Appearances: Television Violence and Aggressive Behavior." *Journal of Adolescent Health Care*, 11, 1, January 1990:31–44.

Cooley, Charles Horton. *Human Nature and the Social Order*. New York: Scribner's, 1902.

Cooley, Charles Horton. *Social Organization*. New York: Scribner's, 1909.

Cooley, Charles Horton. *Social Organization*. New York: Schocken, 1962.

Cooper, Helene. "Offering Aerobics, Karate, Aquatics, Hospitals Stress Business of 'Wellness.'" *Wall Street Journal*, August 9, 1993:B1, B3.

Cooper, Kenneth J. "New Focus Sought in National High School Exams: NEH Backs Approach Used in Europe and Japan to Assess Knowledge Rather Than Aptitude." *Washington Post*, May 20, 1991:A7.

Corbett, Thomas. "Child Poverty and Welfare Reform: Progress or Paralysis?" *Focus*, 15, 1, Spring 1993:1–17.

Corbin, Robert K. "The President's Column." *American Rifleman*, December 1993:56.

Corchado, Alfredo. "Hispanic Supermarkets Are Blossoming." *Wall Street Journal*, January 23, 1989:B1.

Corcoran, Mary, Greg J. Duncan, Gerald Gurin, and Patricia Gurin. "Myth and Reality: The Causes and Persistence of Poverty." *Journal of Policy Analysis and Management*, 4, 4, 1985:516–536.

Cose, Ellis. *The Rage of the Privileged Class*. New York: Harper-Collins, 1993.

Coser, Lewis A. *Masters of Sociological Thought: Ideas in Historical and Social Context*, 2nd ed. New York: Harcourt Brace Jovanovich, 1977.

Cottin, Lou. *Elders in Rebellion: A Guide to Senior Activism*. Garden City, N.Y.: Anchor Doubleday, 1979.

Couch, Carl J. *Social Processes and Relationships: A Formal Approach*. Dix Hills, N.Y.: General Hall, 1989.

Coughlin, Ellen K. "Studying Homelessness: The Difficulty of Tracking a Transient Population." *Chronicle of Higher Education*, October 19, 1988:A6–A12.

Cowen, Emory L., Judah Landes, and Donald E. Schact. "The Effects of Mild Frustration on the Expression of Prejudiced Attitudes." *Journal of Abnormal and Social Psychology*. January 1959:33–38.

Cowgill, Donald. "The Aging of Populations and Societies." *Annals of the American Academy of Political and Social Science, 415*, 1974:1–18.

Cowley, Joyce. *Pioneers of Women's Liberation*. New York: Merit, 1969.

Cox, Meg. "Clearer Connections." *Wall Street Journal*, March 24, 1986:200.

Cox, Meg. "New Magazines Cater to People with HIV." *Wall Street Journal*, March 1, 1994:B1.

Crispell, Diane, "People Patterns." *Wall Street Journal*, March 16, 1992:B1.

Crosbie, Paul V., ed. *Interaction in Small Groups*. New York: Macmillan, 1975.

Crossen, Cynthia. *Wall Street Journal*, November 14, 1991:A1, A7.

Cumming, Elaine. "Further Thoughts on the Theory of Disengagement." In *Aging in America: Readings in Social Gerontology*, Cary S. Kart and Barbara B. Manard, eds. Sherman Oaks, Calif.: Alfred Publishing, 1976:19–41.

Cumming, Elaine, and William E. Henry. *Growing Old: The Process of Disengagement*. New York: Basic Books, 1961.

Curtin, Sharon. "Nobody Ever Died of Old Age: In Praise of Old People." In *Growing Old in America*. Beth Hess, ed. New Brunswick, N.J.: Transaction, 1976:273–284.

Curwin, E. Cecil, and Gudmond Hart. *Plough and Pasture*. New York: Collier Books, 1961.

Cushman, John H. "U.S. to Weigh Blacks' Complaints About Pollution." *New York Times*, November 19, 1993:A16.

Cuzzort, R. P. *Using Social Thought: The Nuclear Issue and Other Concerns*. Mountain View, Calif.: Mayfield, 1989.

Cuzzort, Ray P., and Edith W. King. *20th Century Thought*, 3rd ed. New York: Holt, Rinehart and Winston, 1980.

Dahl, Robert A. *Who Governs?* New Haven, Conn.: Yale University Press, 1961.

Dahl, Robert A. *Dilemmas of Pluralist Democracy: Autonomy vs. Control*. New Haven, Conn.: Yale University Press, 1982.

Dahrendorf, Ralf. *Class and Class Conflict in Industrial Society*. Palo Alto, Calif.: Stanford University Press, 1959.

Daniels, Roger. *The Decision to Relocate the Japanese Americans*. Philadelphia: Lippincott, 1975.

Dannefer, Dale. "Adult Development and Social Theory: A Reappraisal." *American Sociological Review, 49*, 1, February 1984:100–116.

Danzi, Angela D. "Savaria, The Midwife: Childbirth and Change in the Immigrant Community." In *Contemporary Readings in Sociology*. Judith N. DeSena, ed. Dubuque, Iowa: Kendall/Hunt, 1989:47–56.

Darley, John M., and Bibb Latané. "Bystander Intervention in Emergencies: Diffusion of Responsibility." *Journal of Personality and Social Psychology, 8*, 4, 1968:377–383.

Darnell, Victor. "Qualitative-Quantitative Content Analysis of Graffiti in the Public Restrooms of St. Louis, Missouri, and Edwardsville, Illinois." Master's thesis, Southern Illinois University, Edwardsville, May 1971.

Darwin, Charles. *The Origin of Species*. Chicago: Conley, 1859.

Davies, James C. "Toward a Theory of Revolution." *American Sociological Review, 27*, 1, February 1962:5–19.

Davis, Allison, Burleigh B. Gardner, and Mary R. Gardner. *Deep South: A Social-Anthropological Study of Caste and Class*. Chicago: University of Chicago Press, 1941.

Davis, Bob. "In Rio, They're Eyeing Greenhouse Two-Step." *Wall Street Journal*, April 21, 1992:A1.

Davis, Bob, and Lawrence Ingrassia. "Trade Pact Is Set by 117 Nations, Slashing Tariffs, Subsidies Globally." *Wall Street Journal*, December 16, 1993:A3, A13.

Davis, Fred. "The Cabdriver and His Fare: Facets of a Fleeting Relationship." *American Journal of Sociology, 65*, September 1959:158–165.

Davis, James. "Up and Down Opportunity's Ladder." *Public Opinion, 5*, June–July 1982:11–15, 48–51.

Davis, Kingsley. "Extreme Isolation." In *Down to Earth Sociology: Introductory Readings*, 7th ed., James M. Henslin, ed. New York: Free Press, 1993.

Davis, Kingsley, and Wilbert E. Moore. "Some Principles of Stratification." *American Sociological Review, 10*, 1945:242–249.

Davis, Kingsley, and Wilbert E. Moore. "Reply to Tumin." *American Sociological Review, 18*, 1953:394–396.

Davis, Nanette J. "The Prostitute: Developing a Deviant Identity." In *Studies in the Sociology of Sex*, James M. Henslin, ed. New York: Appleton Century Crofts, 1971:297–322.

Davis, Nanette J. "Prostitution: Identity, Career, and Legal-Economic Enterprise." In *The Sociology of Sex: An Introductory Reader*, rev. ed., James M. Henslin and Edward Sagarin, eds. New York: Schocken Books, 1978:195–222.

de Beauvoir, Simone. *The Second Sex*. New York: Knopf, 1953.

Deck, Leland P. "Buying Brains by the Inch." *Journal of the College and University Personnel Association, 19*, 1968:33–37.

de Cordoba, Jose. "One Newspaper Finds Way to Lure Readers: Publish in Spanish." *Wall Street Journal*, April 23, 1992:A1, A8.

De George, Richard T. *The New Marxism: Society and East European Marxism Since 1956*. New York: Pegasus 1968.

Degler, Carl N. *In Search of Human Nature: The Decline and Revival of Darwinism in American Social Thought*. New York: Oxford University Press, 1991.

DeMartini, Joseph R. "Basic and Applied Sociological Work: Divergence, Convergence, or Peaceful Co-existence?" *The Journal of Applied Behavioral Science, 18*, 2, 1982:203–215.

DeMause, Lloyd. "Our Forebears Made Childhood a Nightmare." *Psychology Today 8*, 11, April 1975:85–88.

Denney, Nancy W., and David Quadagno. *Human Sexuality*, 2nd ed. St. Louis: Mosby Year Book, 1992.

Dentzler, Susan. "The Vanishing Dream." *U.S. News and World Report*, April 22, 1991:39–43.

Denzin, Norman K. "The Suicide Machine." *Society*, July–August, 1992:7–10.

DePalma, Anthony. "Rare in Ivy League: Women Who Work as Full Professors." *New York Times*, January 24, 1993:1, 23.

DeParle, Jason. "Report to Clinton Sees Vast Extent of Homelessness." *New York Times*, February 17, 1994:A1, A10.

Derber, Charles, and William Schwartz. "Toward a Theory of Worker Participation." In *The Transformation of Industrial Organization: Management, Labor, and Society in the United States*. Frank Hearn, ed. Belmont, Calif.: Wadsworth, 1988:217–229.

De Witt, Karen. "S.A.T. Scores Improve for 2d Consecutive Year." *New York Times*, August 19, 1993:A16.

deYoung, Mary. "The World According to NAMBLA: Accounting for Deviance." *Journal of Sociology and Social Welfare*, *16*, 1, March 1989:111–126.

Diamond, Milton. "Sexual Identity: Monozygotic Twins Reared in Discordant Sex Roles and a BBC Follow-Up." *Archives of Sexual Behavior*, *11*, 2, 1982:181–186.

Dickson, Tony, and Hugh V. McLachlan. "In Search of 'The Spirit of Capitalism': Weber's Misinterpretation of Franklin." *Sociology*, *23*, 1, 1989:81–89.

Diehl, Jackson. "New Breeze in Eastern Europe Is Fouled by Pollution: Large Areas May Become Uninhabitable." In *Ourselves and Others: The Washington Post Sociology Companion*, Washington Post Writers Group, eds. Boston: Allyn and Bacon, 1992:290–296.

DiGiulio, Robert C. "Beyond Widowhood." In *Marriage and Family in a Changing Society*, 4th ed., James M. Henslin, ed. New York: Free Press, 1992:457–469.

Di Leonardo, Micaela. "The Female World of Cards and Holidays: Women, Families, and the Work of Kinship." *Signs*, *12*, Spring 1987:40–53.

Dillin, John. "Congress Begins Search for Answers in Waco Tragedy." *Christian Science Monitor*, April 22, 1993:1, 4.

Doane, Ashley W., Jr. "Bringing the Majority Back In: Towards a Sociology of Dominant Group Ethnicity." Paper presented at the annual meetings of the Society for the Study of Social Problems, 1993.

Dobash, Russell P., and R. Emerson Dobash. "Community Response to Violence Against Wives: Charivari, Abstract Justice and Patriarchy." *Social Problems*, *28*, June 1981:563–581.

Dobash, Russell P., R. Emerson Dobash, Margo Wilson, and Martin Daly. "The Myth of Sexual Symmetry in Marital Violence." *Social Problems*, *39*, 1, February 1992:71–91.

Dobash, Russell P., R. Emerson Dobash, Margo Wilson, and Martin Daly. "Marital Violence Is Not Symmetrical: A Response to Campbell." *SSSP Newsletter*, *24*, 3, Fall 1993:26–30.

Dobriner, William M. "The Football Team as Social Structure and Social System." In *Social Structures and Systems: A Sociological Overview*. Pacific Palisades, Calif.: Goodyear, 1969:116–120.

Dobriner, William M. *Social Structures and Systems*. Pacific Palisades, California: Goodyear, 1969.

Dobson, Richard B. "Mobility and Stratification in the Soviet Union." *Annual Review of Sociology*. Palo Alto, Calif.: Annual Reviews, 1977.

Dollard, John, et al. *Frustration and Aggression*. New Haven, Conn.: Yale University Press, 1939.

Domhoff, G. William. *Who Rules America?* Englewood Cliffs, N.J.: Prentice Hall, 1967.

Domhoff, G. William. *The Higher Circles: The Governing Class in America*. New York: Random House, 1970.

Domhoff, G. William. *Who Really Rules? New Haven and Community Power Reexamined*. New Brunswick, N.J.: Transaction, 1978.

Domhoff, G. William. *The Powers That Be*. New York: Random House, 1979.

Domhoff, G. William. *The Power Elite and the State: How Policy Is Made in America*. New York: Aldine de Gruyter, 1990.

Domhoff, G. William. "The Bohemian Grove and Other Retreats." In *Down to Earth Sociology: Introductory Readings*, 8th ed., James M. Henslin, ed. New York: Free Press, 1995:334–346.

Doughtery, Wilma Holden, and Rosalind E. Engel. "An 80s Look for Sex Equality in Caldecott Winners and Honor Books." *Reading Teacher*, *40*, 4, January 1987:394–398.

Douglass, Richard L. "Domestic Neglect and Abuse of the Elderly: Implications for Research and Service." *Family Relations*, *32*, July 1983:395–402.

Dove, Adrian. "Soul Folk 'Chitling' Test or the Dove Counterbalance Intelligence Test." no date. (Mimeo)

Doyal, Lesley, and Imogen Pennell. *The Political Economy of Health*. London: Pluto Press, 1981.

Draper, R. "The History of Advertising in America." *New York Review of Books 33*, June 26, 1986:14–18.

Drucker, Peter F. "The Rise and Fall of the Blue-Collar Worker." *Wall Street Journal*, April 22, 1987:36.

Drucker, Peter F. "There's More Than One Kind of Team." *Wall Street Journal*, February 11, 1992:A16.

Dudenhefer, Paul. "Poverty in the Rural United States." *Focus*, *15*, 1, Spring 1993:37–46.

Duffy, Michael. "When Lobbyists Become Insiders." *Time*, November 9, 1992:40.

Duncan, Greg J., and Willard Rodgers. "Has Children's Poverty Become More Persistent?" *American Sociological Review*, *56*, August 1991:538–550.

Dunlap, Riley E., and William R. Catton, Jr. "Environmental Sociology." *Annual Review of Sociology*, *5*, 1979:243–273.

Dunlap, Riley E., and William R. Catton, Jr. "What Environmental Sociologists Have in Common Whether Concerned with 'Built' or 'Natural' Environments." *Sociological Inquiry*, *53*, 2/3, 1983:113–135.

Dunleavey, M. P. "Reforming the 3 R's: Blueprints for the Schools of Tomorrow." *Publisher's Weekly*, February 21, 1994:33–35.

Dunn, Ashley. "Southeast Asians Highly Dependent on Welfare in U.S." *New York Times*, May 19, 1994:A1, A23.

Durkheim, Emile. *The Division of Labor in Society*. George Simpson, trans. New York: Free Press, 1933. First published in 1893.

Durkheim, Emile. *The Elementary Forms of the Religious Life*. New York: Free Press, 1965. First published in 1912.

Durkheim, Emile. *The Rules of Sociological Method*. Sarah A. Solovay and John H. Mueller, trans. Glencoe, Ill.: Free Press, 1958.

Durkheim, Emile. *The Rules of Sociological Method*. New York: Free Press, 1964. First published in 1893.

Durkheim, Emile. *Suicide: A Study in Sociology*. John A. Spaulding and George Simpson, trans. New York: Free Press, 1966. First published in 1897.

Durning, Alan. "Cradles of Life." In *Social Problems 90/91*, LeRoy W. Barnes, ed. Guilford, Conn.: Dushkin, 1990:231–241.

Dutton, Diana B. "Social Class, Health, and Illness." In *Dominant Issues in Medical Sociology*, 3rd ed., Howard D. Schwartz, ed. New York: McGraw-Hill, 1994:470–482.

Dwyer, John M. *The Body at War: The Miracle of the Immune System*. New York: New American Library, 1989:119.

Easterbrooks, M. Ann, and Wendy A. Goldberg. "Toddler Development in the Family: Impact of Father Involvement and Parenting Characteristics." *Child Development*, 55, 1984:740–752.

Ebaugh, Helen Rose Fuchs. *Becoming an EX: The Process of Role Exit*. Chicago: The University of Chicago Press, 1988.

Ebomoyi, Ehigie. "The Prevalence of Female Circumcision in Two Nigerian Communities." *Sex Roles*, 17, 3/4, 1987:139–151.

Eder, Klaus. "The Rise of Counter-culture Movements Against Modernity: Nature as a New Field of Class Struggle." *Theory, Culture & Society*, 7, 1990:21–47.

Edgar, Gary. Author's interview with Gary Edgar of the Surveillance Branch of the CDC, March 28, 1994.

Edgerton, Robert B. *Deviance: A Cross-Cultural Perspective*. Menlo Park, Calif.: Benjamin/Cummings, 1976.

Edgerton, Robert B. *Sick Societies: Challenging the Myth of Primitive Harmony*. New York: Free Press, 1992.

Edwards, Richard. *Contested Terrain: The Transformation of the Workplace in the Twentieth Century*. New York: Basic Books, 1979.

Egan, Timothy. "Teaching Tolerance in Workplaces: A Seattle Program Illustrates Limits." *New York Times*, October 8, 1993:A18.

Ehrenreich, Barbara, and Deidre English. *Witches, Midwives, and Nurses: A History of Women Healers*. Old Westbury, N.Y.: Feminist Press, 1973.

Ehrensaft, Diane. *Parenting Together: Men and Women Sharing the Care of Their Children*. New York: Free Press, 1987.

Ehrensaft, Diane. "Shared Parenting." In *Marriage and Family in a Changing Society*, 3rd ed., James M. Henslin, ed. New York: Free Press, 1989:242–247.

Ehrlich, Paul R., and Anne H. Ehrlich. *Population, Resources, and Environment: Issues in Human Ecology*, 2nd ed. San Francisco: Freeman, 1972.

Ehrlich, Paul R., and Anne H. Ehrlich. "Humanity at the Crossroads." *Stanford Magazine*, Spring–Summer 1978:20–23.

Eibl-Eibesfeldt, Irrenäus. *Ethology: The Biology of Behavior*. New York: Holt, Rinehart, and Winston, 1970.

Eisenhart, R. Wayne. "You Can't Hack It, Little Girl: A Discussion of the Covert Psychological Agenda of Modern Combat Training." *Journal of Social Issues*, 31, Fall 1975:13–23.

Ekman, Paul, Wallace V. Friesen, and John Bear. "The International Language of Gestures." *Psychology Today*, May 1984:64.

Elder, Glen H., Jr. "Age Differentiation and Life Course." *Annual Review of Sociology*, 1, 1975:165–190.

Elkind, David. *The Hurried Child: Growing Up Too Fast Too Soon*. Reading, Mass.: Addison-Wesley, 1981.

Elkins, Stanley M. *Slavery: A Problem in American Institutional and Intellectual Life*, 2nd ed. Chicago: University of Chicago Press, 1968.

El-Meligi, M. Helmy. "Egypt." In *Handbook of World Education: A Comparative Guide to Higher Education and Educational Systems of the World*, Walter Wickremasinghe, ed. Houston, Texas: American Collegiate Service, 1992:219–228.

Elfin, Mel. "Race on Campus." *U.S. News & World Report*, April 19, 1993:52–56.

Ellis, Caroline. "Punish and Be Damned." *New Statesman and Society*, 17, 1991:17.

Engardio, Pete. "Fast Times on *Avenida Madison*." *Business Week*, June 6, 1988:62–64, 67.

Engelberg, Stephen, and Martin Tolchin. "Foreigners Find New Ally in U.S. Industry." *New York Times*, November 2, 1993:A1, B8.

Engels, Friedrich. *The Origin of the Family, Private Property, and the State*. New York: International Publishing, 1942. First published in 1884.

Epstein, Cynthia Fuchs. "Inevitabilities of Prejudice." *Society*, September–October 1986:7–15.

Epstein, Cynthia Fuchs. *Deceptive Distinctions: Sex, Gender, and the Social Order*. New Haven, Conn.: Yale University Press, 1988.

Epstein, Cynthia Fuchs. Letter to the author, January 26, 1989.

Erik, John. "China's Policy on Births." *New York Times*, January 3, 1982: IV, 19.

Erikson, Robert S., Norman R. Luttberg, and Kent L. Tedin. *American Public Opinion: Its Origins, Content, and Impact*, 2nd ed. New York: Wiley, 1980.

Ernst, Eldon G. "The Baptists." In *Encyclopedia of the American Religious Experience: Studies of Traditions and Movements*, Vol. 1, Charles H. Lippy and Peter W. Williams, eds. New York: Scribners, 1988:555–577.

Eron, Leonard D. "Parent–Child Interaction, Television Violence, and Aggression of Children. "*American Psychologist*, 37, 2, February 1982:197–211.

Etzioni, Amitai, ed. *The Semi-Professions and Their Organization*. New York: Free Press, 1969.

Escalante, Jaime, and Jack Dirmann. "The Jaime Escalante Math Program." Journal of Negro Education, 59, 3, Summer 1990: 407–423.

Etzioni, Amitai. *An Immodest Agenda: Rebuilding America Before the Twenty-First Century*. New York: McGraw-Hill, 1982.

"Europe's Economies Are Dragging Along Despite Hopes for 1992." *Wall Street Journal*, November 26, 1991:A1, A11.

Evanier, David. "Invisible Man." *New Republic*, October 14, 1991:21–25.

Farber, Susan I. *Identical Twins Raised Apart*. New York: Basic Books, 1981.

Faris, Robert E. L., and Warren Dunham. *Mental Disorders in Urban Areas*. Chicago: University of Chicago Press, 1939.

Farkas, George, Daniel Sheehan, and Robert P. Grobe. "Coursework Mastery and School Success: Gender, Ethnicity, and Poverty Groups Within an Urban School District." *American Educational Research Journal*, 27, 4, Winter 1990b:807–827.

Farkas, George, Robert P. Grobe, Daniel Sheehan, and Yuan Shuan. "Cultural Resources and School Success: Gender, Ethnicity, and Poverty Groups Within an Urban School District." *American Sociological Review*, 55, February 1990a:127–142.

Farley, John E. *Sociology*. Englewood Cliffs, N.J.: Prentice Hall, 1990.

Farrell, Walter C., Jr., and Cloyzelle K. Jones. "Recent Racial Incidents in Higher Education: A Preliminary Survey." *Urban Review*, 20, 3, 1988:211–226.

Faunce, William A. *Problems of an Industrial Society*, 2nd ed. New York: McGraw-Hill, 1981.

FBI Uniform Crime Reports. Washington, D.C.: U.S. Government Printing Office, 1990.

Feagin, Joe R. "The Continuing Significance of Race: Antiblack Discrimination in Public Places." *American Sociological Review*, 56, February 1991:101–116.

Feagin, Joe R., and Robert Parker. *Building American Cities: The Urban Real Estate Game,* 2nd ed. Englewood Cliffs, N.J.: Prentice Hall, 1990.

Featherman, David L. "Opportunities Are Expanding." *Society, 13,* 1979:4–11.

Featherman, David L., and Robert M. Hauser. *Opportunity and Change.* New York: Academic Press, 1978.

Feiler, Bruce S. "Cliff Notes." *New Republic,* March 23, 1992:8–10.

Feldman, Saul D. "The Presentation of Shortness in Everyday Life—Height and Heightism in American Society: Toward a Sociology of Stature." Paper presented at the 1972 meetings of the American Sociological Association.

Felsenthal, Edward. "Maine Limits Liability for Doctors Who Meet Treatment Guidelines." *Wall Street Journal,* May 3, 1993:A1, A9.

Fendrich, James Max, and Kenneth L. Lovoy. "Back to the Future: Adult Political Behavior of Former Student Activists." In *Collective Behavior and Social Movements,* Russell L. Curtis, Jr., and Benigno E. Aguirre, eds. Boston: Allyn and Bacon, 1993:429–434.

Ferguson, Trudi, and Joan S. Dunphy. *Answers to the Mommy Track: How Wives and Mothers in Business Reach the Top and Balance Their Lives.* New York: New Horizon Press, 1991.

Feshbach, Murray. "Soviet Health Problems." *Society,* March–April, 1984:79–89.

Feshbach, Murray. "Russia's Farms, Too Poisoned for the Plow." *Wall Street Journal,* May 14, 1992:A14.

Feshbach, Murray, and Alfred Friendly, Jr. *Ecocide in the USSR: Health and Nature Under Siege.* New York: Basic Books, 1992.

Fialka, John J. "Demands on New Orleans's 'Big Charity' Hospital Are Symptomatic of U.S. Health-Care Problem." *Wall Street Journal,* June 22, 1993:A18.

Fichter, Joseph H., and William L. Kolb. "Ethical Limitations on Sociological Reporting." *Sociological Practice, 7,* 1989:148–157.

Finke, Roger. *The Churching of America, 1776–1990: Winners and Losers in Our Religious Economy.* New Brunswick, N.J.: Rutgers University Press, 1992.

Finkelhor, David. *Sexually Victimized Children.* New York: Free Press, 1979.

Finkelhor, David. "Long-Term Effects of Childhood Sexual Victimization in a Non-Clinical Sample." Unpublished paper, Family Research Laboratory, Durham, New Hampshire, October 2, 1980.

Finkelhor, David. "Common Features of Family Abuse." In *Marriage and Family in a Changing Society,* 3rd ed., James M. Henslin, ed. New York: Free Press, 1989:403–410.

Finkelhor, David, and Kersti Yllo. "Marital Rape: The Myth Versus the Reality." In *Marriage and Family in a Changing Society,* 3rd ed., James M. Henslin, ed. New York: Free Press, 1989:382–391.

Finsterbusch, Kurt, and H. C. Greisman. "The Unprofitability of Warfare in the Twentieth Century." *Social Problems, 22,* February 1975:450–563.

Fischer, Claude S. *The Urban Experience.* New York: Harcourt, 1976.

Fisher, Sue. *In the Patient's Best Interest: Women and the Politics of Medical Decisions.* New Brunswick, N.J.: Rutgers University Press, 1986.

Fitzgerald, Mark. "Other Michigan College Papers Embroiled in Controversies." *Editor and Publisher, 122,* 16, April 22, 1989:55.

Fitzpatrick, Kellyanne. "What to Expect from Plaintiff Jones and Defendant Clinton." *Wall Street Journal,* May 11, 1994:A21.

Flanagan, William G. *Urban Sociology: Images and Structure.* Boston: Allyn and Bacon, 1990.

Flavell, J. H., et al. *The Development of Role-Taking and Communication Skills in Children.* New York: Wiley, 1968.

Fleming, Joyce Dudney. "The State of the Apes." *Psychology Today, 7,* 1974:31–38.

Flexner, Abraham. *Medical Education in the United States and Canada: A Report to the Carnegie Foundation for the Advancement of Teaching.* Bulletin No. 4. Boston: Merrymount Press, 1910.

Flink, James J. *The Automobile Age.* Cambridge, Mass.: MIT Press, 1988.

Foley, Douglas E. "The Great American Football Ritual." In *Down to Earth Sociology: Introductory Readings,* 7th ed., James M. Henslin, ed. New York: Free Press, 1993:418–431.

Foote, Jennifer. "Trying to Take Back the Planet." *Newsweek, 115,* 6, February 5, 1990:24–25.

Ford, Constance Mitchell. "South Africa Is Drawing Enthusiasm from Wall Street." *Wall Street Journal,* December 23, 1993:C1, C21.

Forer, Lucille K. *The Birth Order Factor: How Your Personality Is Influenced by Your Place in the Family.* New York: McKay, 1976.

Form, William. "Comparative Industrial Sociology and the Convergence Hypothesis." In *Annual Review of Sociology, 5,* 1, 1979, Alex Inkeles, James Coleman, and Ralph H. Turner, eds.

Fox, Elaine, and George E. Arquitt. "The VFW and the 'Iron Law of Oligarchy.'" In *Down to Earth Sociology,* 4th ed., James M. Henslin, ed. New York: Free Press, 1985:147–155.

Frank, Anthony. "Through the Open Door: What Is It Like to Be an Immigrant in America?" *Wall Street Journal,* July 3, 1990:A8.

Freudenburg, William R., and Robert Gramling. "The Emergence of Environmental Sociology: Contributions of Riley E. Dunlap and William R. Catton, Jr." *Sociological Inquiry, 59,* 4, November 1989:439–452.

Friedl, Ernestine. "Society and Sex Roles." In *Conformity and Conflict: Readings in Cultural Anthropology.* James P. Spradley and David W. McCurdy, eds. Glenview, Ill.: Scott, Foresman, 1990:229–238.

Fritz, Jan M. "The History of Clinical Sociology." *Sociological Practice, 7,* 1989:72–95.

Frumkin, Robert M. "Early English and American Sex Customs." In *Encyclopedia of Sexual Behavior,* Vol. 1. New York: Hawthorne Books, 1967.

Fuchs, Janet A., Richard M. Levinson, Ronald R. Stoddard, Maurice E. Mullet, and Diana H. Jones. "Health Risk Factors Among the Amish: Results of a Survey." *Health Education Quarterly, 17,* 2, Summer 1990:197–211.

Fuchs, Victor R. "A Tale of Two States." In *The Sociology of Health and Illness: Critical Perspectives,* Peter Conrad and Rochelle Kern, eds. New York: St. Martin's Press, 1981:67–70.

Fuchsberg, Gilbert. "Well, at Least 'Terminated with Extreme Prejudice' Wasn't Cited." *Wall Street Journal,* December 7, 1990:B1.

Fuller, Rex, and Richard Schoenberger. "The Gender Salary Gap: Do Academic Achievement, Internship Experience, and College Major Make a Difference?" *Social Science Quarterly, 72,* 4, December 1991:715–726.

Furstenberg, Frank F., Jr., and Kathleen Mullan Harris. "The Disappearing American Father? Divorce and the Waning Significance of Biological Fatherhood." In *The Changing American Family: Sociological and Demographic Perspectives,* Scott J. South and Stewart E. Tolnay, eds. Boulder, Colo.: Westview Press, 1992:197–223.

Galanter, Marc. *Cults: Faith, Healing, and Coercion.* New York: Oxford University Press, 1989.

Galbraith, John Kenneth. *The Nature of Mass Poverty.* Cambridge Mass.: Harvard University Press, 1979.

Galinsky, Ellen, James T. Bond, and Dana E. Friedman. *The Changing Workforce: Highlights of the National Study.* New York: Families and Work Institute, 1993.

Galinsky, Ellen, and Peter J. Stein. "The Impact of Human Resource Policies on Employees: Balancing Work/Family Life." *Journal of Family Issues, 11*, 4 December 1990:368–383.

Gallese, Liz Roman. "Blue-Collar Women." *Wall Street Journal,* July 28, 1980.

Galliher, John F. *Deviant Behavior and Human Rights.* Englewood Cliffs, N.J.: Prentice Hall, 1991.

Gallup, George, Jr. *The Gallup Poll: Public Opinion 1989.* Wilmington, Dela.: Scholarly Resources, 1990.

Gallup Opinion Index. *Religion in America, 1987.* Report 259, April 1987.

Gans, Herbert J. *The Urban Villagers.* New York: Free Press, 1962.

Gans, Herbert J. *People and Plans: Essays on Urban Problems and Solutions.* New York: Basic, 1968.

Gans, Herbert J. "Urbanism and Suburbanism." In *Urban Man and Society: A Reader in Urban Ecology,* Albert N. Cousins and Hans Nagpaul, eds. New York: Knopf, 1970:157–164.

Gans, Herbert J. "The Way We'll Live Soon." *Washington Post,* September 1, 1991:BW3.

Garbarino, Merwin S. *American Indian Heritage.* Boston: Little, Brown, 1976.

Gardner, Carol Brooks. "Access Information: Public Lies and Private Peril." *Social Problems, 35,* 4, October 1988:384–397.

Gardner, R. Allen, and Beatrice T. Gardner. "Teaching Sign Language to a Chimpanzee." *Science, 165,* 1969:664–672.

Garfinkel, Harold. "Conditions of Successful Degradation Ceremonies." *American Journal of Sociology, 61,* 2, March 1956: 420–424.

Garfinkel, Harold. *Studies in Ethnomethodology.* Englewood Cliffs, N.J.: Prentice Hall, 1967.

Garreau, Joel. *Edge City: Life on the New Frontier.* New York: Doubleday, 1992.

Gartner, Michael. "Legal 'Killer' Under Attack with the Wrong Weapons." *Wall Street Journal,* January 12, 1988:A11.

Gatewood, Willard B. *Aristocrats of Color: The Black Elite, 1880–1920.* Bloomington, Ind.: Indiana University Press, 1990.

Gay, Jill. "The Patriotic Prostitute." *Progressive,* February 1985:34–36.

Gelles, Richard J. "The Myth of Battered Husbands and New Facts about Family Violence." In *Social Problems 80–81,* Robert L. David, ed. Guilford, Conn.: Dushkin, 1980.

Genetski, Robert. "Privatize Social Security." *Wall Street Journal,* May 21, 1993.

Gerson, Kathleen. *Hard Choices: How Women Decide about Work, Career, and Motherhood.* Berkeley: University of California Press, 1985.

Gerson, Kathleen. "Hard Choices." In *Marriage and Family in a Changing Society,* 4th ed., James M. Henslin, ed. New York: Free Press, 1992:286–296.

Gerth, H. H., and C. Wright Mills. *From Max Weber: Essays in Sociology.* New York: Galaxy, 1958.

Gest, Ted, and Patricia M. Scherschel. "Stealing $200 Billion 'The Respectable Way.'" *U.S. News & World Report,* May 20, 1985:83–85.

Giarelli, Andrew. "Regional Report: Asia/Pacific." *World Press Review,* April 1988:44.

Giele, Janet Zollinger. *Women and the Future: Changing Sex Roles in Modern America.* New York: Free Press, 1978.

Gilbert, Dennis, and Joseph A. Kahl. *The American Class Structure: A New Synthesis.* Homewood, Ill.: Dorsey Press, 1982.

Gilbert, Dennis, and Joseph A. Kahl. *The American Class Structure: A New Synthesis.* 4th ed. Homewood, Ill.: Dorsey Press, 1993.

Gilham, Steven A. "The Marines Build Men: Resocialization in Recruit Training." In *The Sociological Outlook: A Text with Readings,* 2nd ed., Reid Luhman, ed. San Diego, Calif.: Collegiate Press, 1989:232–244.

Gill, Derek. "A National Health Service: Principles and Practice." In *The Sociology of Health and Illness,* 2nd ed., Peter Conrad and Rochelle Kern, eds. New York: St. Martin's Press, 1986:454–467.

Gillborn, David. "Citizenship, 'Race' and the Hidden Curriculum." *International Studies in the Sociology of Education, 2,* 1, 1992:57–73.

Gilmore, David D. *Manhood in the Making: Cultural Concepts of Masculinity.* New Haven, Conn.: Yale University Press, 1990.

Gimenez, Martha E. "The Feminization of Poverty: Myth or Reality?" *Social Justice, 17,* 3, 1990:43–69.

Githens, Marianne, and Jewel L. Prestage. *A Portrait of Marginality: The Political Behavior of the American Woman.* New York: McKay, 1977.

Glascock, Anthony P. "By Any Other Name, It Is Still Killing: A Comparison of the Treatment of the Elderly in America and Other Societies." In *The Cultural Context of Aging: Worldwide Perspectives,* Jay Sokolovsky, ed. New York: Bergin & Garvey, 1990:43–56.

Glazer, Nathan. "In Defense of Multiculturalism." *New Republic,* September 2, 1991:18–22.

Glick, Paul C., and S. Lin. "More Young Adults Are Living with Their Parents: Who Are They?" *Journal of Marriage and Family,* 48, 1986:107–112.

Glotz, Peter. "Forward to Europe." *Dissent, 33,* 3, Summer 1986:327–339. (As quoted in Harrison and Bluestone 1988)

Glueck, Sheldon, and Eleanor Glueck. *Physique and Delinquency.* New York: Harper & Row, 1956.

Goad, G. Pierre. "Canada Seems Satisfied with a Medical System That Covers Everyone." *Wall Street Journal,* December 3, 1991:A1, A10.

Goffman, Erving. *The Presentation of Self in Everyday Life.* New York: Doubleday, 1959.

Goffman, Erving. *Asylums: Essays on the Social Situation of Mental Patients and Other Inmates.* Chicago: Aldine, 1961.

Gold, Ray. "Janitors Versus Tenants: A Status–Income Dilemma." *American Journal of Sociology,* 58, 1952:486–493.

Goldberg, Steven. *The Inevitability of Patriarchy,* rev. ed. New York: Morrow, 1974.

Goldberg, Steven. "Reaffirming the Obvious." *Society,* September–October 1986:4–7.

Goldberg, Steven. Letter to the author, January 18, 1989.

Goldberg, Susan, and Michael Lewis. "Play Behavior in the Year-Old Infant: Early Sex Differences." *Child Development,* 40, March 1969:21–31.

Golden, Tim. "For Mexico's Green Party, It's a Very Grey World." *New York Times,* August 14, 1991:A3.

Goldman, Kevin. "Seniors Get Little Respect on Madison Avenue." *Wall Street Journal*, September 20, 1993:B6.

Goldscheider, Frances, and Calvin Goldscheider. "Leaving and Returning Home in 20th Century America." *Population Bulletin*, 48, 4, March 1994:2–33.

Goleman, Daniel. "Spacing of Siblings Strongly Linked to Success in Life." *New York Times*, May 28, 1985:C1, C4.

Goleman, Daniel. "Girls and Math: Is Biology Really Destiny?" *New York Times*, August 2, 1987:42–44, 46.

Goleman, Daniel. "Pollsters Enlist Psychologists in Quest for Unbiased Results." *New York Times*, September 7, 1993:C1, C11.

Gomez. Carlos F. *Regulating Death: Euthanasia and the Case of the Netherlands*. New York: Free Press, 1991.

Goode, William J. "Encroachment, Charlatanism, and the Emerging Profession: Psychology, Sociology, and Medicine." *American Sociological Review*, 25, 6, December 1960:902–914.

Goodman, William E. "Why Canada's Doctors Flee South." *Wall Street Journal*, September 16, 1993:A25.

Goodwin, Glenn A., Irving Louis Horowitz, and Peter M. Nardi. *Sociological Inquiry*, 61, 2, May 1991:139–147.

Gordon, David M. "Class and the Economics of Crime." *The Review of Radical Political Economics*, 3, Summer 1971:51–57.

Gordon, Michael R. "Moscow Is Making Little Progress in Disposal of Chemical Weapons." *New York Times*, December 1, 1993:A1, A16.

Gordon, Milton M. "The Concept of Sub-Culture and Its Application." *Social Forces*, 26, 1947:40–42.

Gordon, Robert J. *Macroeconomics*, 4th ed. Boston: Little, Brown, 1987.

Gorman, Peter. "A People at Risk: Vanishing Tribes of South America." *The World & I*. December 1991:678–689.

Gottfredson, Michael R., and Travis Hirschi. *A General Theory of Crime*. Stanford, Calif.: Stanford University Press, 1990.

Gracey, Harry L. "Kindergarten as Boot Camp." In *Down to Earth Sociology*, 7th ed., James M. Henslin, ed. New York: Free Press, 1993.

Graham, Ellen. "Christian Bikers Are Holy Rollers of a Different Kind." *Wall Street Journal*, September 19, 1990:A1, A6,

Grant, Karen R. "The Inverse Care Law in the Context of Universal Free Health Insurance in Canada: Toward Meeting Health Needs Through Social Policy." *Sociological Focus*, 17, 2, April 1984:137–155.

Grant, Nigel. *Soviet Education*. New York: Pelican Books, 1979.

Graven, Kathryn. "Sex Harassment at the Office Stirs Up Japan." *Wall Street Journal*, March 21, 1990:B1, B7.

Greeley, Andrew M. "The Protestant Ethic: Time for a Moratorium." *Sociological Analysis*, 25, Spring 1964:20–33.

Greenberg, Larry M. "Take Two Tablespoons of Mustard and Call If You Don't Feel Better." *Wall Street Journal*, February 22, 1994:B1.

Greene, Elizabeth. "Minority-Affairs Officials, Picked to Help Campuses Improve Racial Climate, Report Some Progress." *Chronicle of Higher Education*, 35, 28, March 22, 1989:A32–A34.

Greenwood, Ernest. "Attributes of a Profession." In *Man, Work, and Society: A Reader in the Sociology of Occupations*, Sigmund Nosow and William H. Form, eds. New York: Basic Books, 1962:206–218.

Grella, Christine E. "Irreconcilable Differences: Women Defining Class after Divorce and Downward Mobility." *Gender and Society*, 4, 1, March 1990:41–55.

Grossfield, Stan. "Wasting Away: America's Losing Battle Against Hunger." *Boston Globe*, July 28, 1993:1, 36.

Groves, Melissa M., and Diane M. Horm-Wingerd. "Commuter Marriages: Personal, Family, and Career Issues." *Sociology and Social Research*, 75, 4, July 1991:212–217.

Guha, Ramachandra. "Radical American Environmentalism and Wilderness Preservation: A Third World Critique." *Environmental Ethics*, 11, 1, Spring 1989:71–83.

Gumbel, Peter. "France First! Election Gives Voice to Far-Right Party." *Wall Street Journal*, March 23, 1992:A1, A6.

Gupta, Giri Raj. "Love, Arranged Marriage, and the Indian Social Structure." In *Cross-Cultural Perspectives of Mate Selection and Marriage*, George Kurian, ed. Westport, Conn.: Greenwood Press, 1979.

Gwartney-Gibbs, Patricia A. "The Institutionalization of Premarital Cohabitation: Estimates for Marriage License Applications, 1970 and 1980." *Journal of Marriage and Family*, 48, 2, May 1986:423–434.

Haas, Jack. "Binging: Educational Control Among High-Steel Iron Workers." *American Behavioral Scientist*, 16, 1972:27–34.

Hacker, Helen Mayer. "Women as a Minority Group." *Social Forces*, 30, October 1951:60–69.

Hagan, John. "The Gender Stratification of Income Inequality Among Lawyers." *Social Forces*, 68, 3, March 1990:835–855.

Hagerty, Bob. "The Squeamish Had Better Close Their Eyes and Not Take a Gander." *Wall Street Journal*, April 11, 1990:B1.

Hall, Edward T. *The Silent Language*. New York: Doubleday, 1959.

Hall, Edward T. *The Hidden Dimension*. Garden City, N.Y.: Anchor Books, 1969.

Hall, G. Stanley. *Adolescence: Its Psychology and Its Relations to Physiology, Anthropology, Sociology, Sex, Crime, Religion, and Education*. New York: Appleton, 1904.

Hall, J. A. *Nonverbal Sex Differences: Communication Accuracy and Expressive Style*. Baltimore: Johns Hopkins University Press, 1984.

Hall, Jerome. *Theft, Law, and Society*, 2nd ed. Indianapolis: Bobbs-Merrill, 1952.

Hall, Peter M. "Interactionism and the Study of Social Organization." *Sociological Quarterly*, 28, November 1987:1–22.

Hall, Richard H. "The Concept of Bureaucracy: An Empirical Assessment." *American Journal of Sociology*, 69, July 1963:32–40.

Hamilton, Richard F. "Work and Leisure: On the Reporting of Poll Results." *Public Opinion Quarterly*, 55, 1991:347–356.

Hammes, Sara, and Richard S. Teitelbaum. "The Global 500: How They Performed." *Fortune*, July 29, 1991:238–273.

Hansen, Jane, and Deborah Scroggins. "Female Circumcision: U.S., Georgia Forced to Face Medical, Legal Issues." *Atlanta Journal*, November 15, 1992:A1, A10, A11.

Hardy, Dorcas. *Social Insecurity: The Crisis in America's Social Security and How to Plan Now for Your Own Financial Survival*. New York: Villard Books, 1991.

Hardy, Quentin. "Death at the Club Is Par for the Course in Golf-Crazed Japan." *Wall Street Journal*, June 16, 1993a:A1, A8.

Hardy, Quentin. "Fortunately, Many Japanese Have Training in the Art of Self-Defense." *Wall Street Journal*, June 29, 1993b:B1.

Harlow, Harry F., and Margaret Kuenne Harlow. "Social Deprivation in Monkeys." *Scientific American*, 207, 1962:137–147.

Harlow, Harry F., and Margaret K. Harlow. "The Affectional Systems." In *Behavior of Nonhuman Primates: Modern Research Trends*,

Vol. 2, Allan M. Schrier, Harry F. Harlow, and Fred Stollnitz, eds. New York: Academic Press, 1965:287–334.

Harper, Mary S., ed. *Minority Aging: Essential Curricula Content for Selected Health and Allied Health Professions*. Washington, D.C.: U.S. Government Printing Office, 1990.

Harrington, Michael. *The Other America: Poverty in the United States*. New York: Macmillan, 1962.

Harrington, Michael. *The Vast Majority: A Journey to the World's Poor*. New York: Simon & Schuster, 1977.

Harris, Chauncey, and Edward Ullman. "The Nature of Cities." *Annals of the American Academy of Political and Social Science*, 242, 1945:7–17.

Harris, Diana K. *The Sociology of Aging*. New York: Harper, 1990.

Harris, Louis, and Associates. *A Study of Attitudes Toward Racial and Religious Minorities and Toward Women*. New York: National Conference of Christians and Jews, November 1978.

Harris, Marvin. *Cows, Pigs, Wars, and Witches: The Riddles of Culture*. New York: Vintage Books, 1974.

Harris, Marvin. "Why Men Dominate Women." *New York Times Magazine*, November 13, 1977:46, 115, 117–123.

Harrison, Bennett, and Barry Bluestone. *The Great U-Turn: Corporate Restructuring and the Polarizing of America*. New York: Basic Books: 1988.

Harrison, Paul. *Inside the Third World: The Anatomy of Poverty*, 3rd ed. London: Penguin Books, 1993.

Hart, Charles W. M., and Arnold R. Pilling. *The Tiwi of North Australia*. New York: Holt, Rinehart, and Winston, 1960.

Hart, Hornell. "Acceleration in Social Change." In *Technology and Social Change*, Francis R. Allen, Hornell Hart, Delbert C. Miller, William F. Ogburn, and Meyer F. Nimkoff. New York: Appleton, 1957:27–55.

Hart, Paul. "Groupthink, Risk-Taking and Recklessness: Quality of Process and Outcome in Policy Decision Making." *Politics and the Individual*, 1, 1, 1991:67–90.

Hartinger, Brent. "Homosexual Partners Are Changing the Family." In *Family in America: Opposing Viewpoints*, Viqi Wagner, ed. San Diego, Calif.: Greenhaven Press, 1992:55–62.

Hartley, Eugene. *Problems in Prejudice*. New York: King's Crown Press, 1946.

"Harvard Wired." *Economist*, February 5, 1994, p. 87.

Harwood, John. "For California Senator, Fund Raising Becomes Overwhelming Burden." *Wall Street Journal*, March 2, 1994:A1, A13.

Harwood, John, and Geraldine Brooks. "Other Nations Elect Women to Lead Them, So Why Doesn't U.S.?" *Wall Street Journal*, December 14, 1993:A1, A9.

Haslick, Leonard. *Gerontologist*, 14, 1974:37–45.

Haub, Carl, and Anne Lang. "U.S. Metro Data Sheet," 2nd ed. Washington, D.C.: Population Reference Bureau, 1993.

Haub, Carl, and Nancy Yinger. "The U.N. Long-Range Population Projections: What They Tell Us." Washington, D.C.: Population Reference Bureau, 1994.

Hauser, Philip, and Leo Schnore, eds. *The Study of Urbanization*. New York: Wiley, 1965.

Hayes, Arthur S. "How the Courts Define Harassment." *Wall Street Journal*, October 11, 1991:B1, B3.

Hayes, Arthur S. "Environmental Poverty Specialty Helps the Poor Fight Pollution." *Wall Street Journal*, October 9, 1992:B5.

Hayes, Donald P., and Loreen T. Wolfer. "Have Curriculum Changes Caused SAT Scores to Decline?" Paper presented at the annual meetings of the American Sociological Association, 1993a.

Hayes, Donald P., and Loreen T. Wolfer. "Was the Decline in SAT-Verbal Scores Caused by Simplified Schoolbooks?" Technical Report Series 93-8. Ithaca, N.Y.: Cornell University Press, 1993b.

Hearn, Frank, ed. *The Transformation of Industrial Organization: Management, Labor, and Society in the United States*. Belmont, Calif.: Wadsworth, 1988.

Heilbrun, Alfred B. "Differentiation of Death-Row Murderers and Life-Sentence Murderers by Antisociality and Intelligence Measures." *Journal of Personality Assessment*, 64, 1990:617–627.

Heintz, Katherine E. "An Examination of Sex and Occupational-Role Presentations of Female Characters in Children's Picture Books." *Women's Studies in Communication*, 10, 2, Fall 1987:76–78.

Heller, Celia Stopnicka. "Social Stratification of the Jewish Community in a Small Polish Town." *American Journal of Sociology*, 59, 1, July 1953:1–10.

Heller, Celia Stopnicka. Letter to the author. May 7, 1991.

Hellinger, Daniel, and Dennis R. Judd. *The Democratic Facade*. Pacific Grove, Calif.: Brooks/Cole, 1991.

Helson, Ravenna, Valory Mitchell, Geraldine Moane. "Personality and Patterns: The Adherence and Nonadherence to the Social Clock." *Journal of Personality and Social Psychology*, 46, 1984:1079–1097.

Henley, Nancy, Mykol Hamilton, and Barrie Thorne. "Womanspeak and Manspeak." In *Beyond Sex Roles*. Alice G. Sargent, ed. St. Paul, Minn.: West, 1985.

Henry, William A., III. "Beyond the Melting Pot." *Time*, April 9, 1990:28–31.

Henslin, James M. *Introducing Sociology: Toward Understanding Life in Society*. New York: Free Press, 1975.

Henslin, James M. "Cohabitation: Its Context and Meaning." In *Marriage and Family in a Changing Society*, 3rd ed., James M. Henslin, ed. New York: Free Press, 1980:101–115.

Henslin, James M. *Social Problems*, 2nd ed. Englewood Cliffs, N.J.: Prentice Hall, 1990b.

Henslin, James M. "When Life Seems Hopeless: Suicide in American Society." In *Social Problems Today: Coping with the Challenges of a Changing Society*. Englewood Cliffs, N.J.: Prentice Hall, 1990c:99–107.

Henslin, James M. "Centuries of Childhood." In *Marriage and Family in a Changing Society*, 4th ed., James M. Henslin, ed. New York: Free Press, 1992a:214–225.

Henslin, James M., ed. *Marriage and Family in a Changing Society*, 4th ed. New York: Free Press, 1992b.

Henslin, James M. "Why So Much Divorce?" In *Marriage and Family in a Changing Society*, 4th ed., James M. Henslin, ed. New York: Free Press, 1992c:389–396.

Henslin, James M. "Trust and Cabbies." In *Down to Earth Sociology: Introductory Readings*, 7th ed., James M. Henslin, ed. New York: Free Press, 1993.

Henslin, James M. "On Becoming Male: Reflections of a Sociologist on Childhood and Early Socialization." In *Down to Earth Sociology*, 8th ed., James M. Henslin, ed. New York: Free Press, 1995a.

Henslin, James M. "Sociology and the Social Sciences." In *Down to Earth Sociology: Introductory Readings*, 8th ed., James M. Henslin, ed. New York: Free Press, 1995b:9–18.

Henslin, James M., and Mac A. Biggs. "The Sociology of the Vaginal Examination." In *Down to Earth Sociology: Introductory Read-*

ings, 7th ed., James M. Henslin, ed. New York: Free Press, 1993:235–247.

Herbert, Bob. "The Real Jobless Rate." *New York Times*, August 4, 1993:A19.

Herring, George C. "Vietnam War." *World Book Encyclopedia, 20*. Chicago: World Book, 1989:389–393.

Hertzler, Joyce O. *A Sociology of Language*. New York: Random House, 1965.

Hevesi, Dennis. "Rooted in Slavery, Pogrom and Stereotypes, Crown Heights Is No Blend." *New York Times*, August 21, 1991:B1, B3.

Hibbert, Christopher. *The Roots of Evil: A Social History of Crime and Punishment*. New York: Minerva, 1963.

Higginbotham, Elizabeth, and Lynn Weber. "Moving with Kin and Community: Upward Social Mobility for Black and White Women." *Gender and Society, 6, 3*, September 1992:416–440.

Higley, John, Ursula Hoffmann-Lange, Charles Kadushin, and Gwen Moore. "Elite Integration in Stable Democracies: A Reconsideration." *European Sociological Review, 7, 1*, May 1991:35–53.

Hilliard, Asa, III. "Do We Have the *Will* to Educate All Children?" *Educational Leadership, 49*, September 1991:31–36.

Hilts, Philip J. "Forecast of AIDS Cases Is Cut by 10%." *New York Times*, January 4, 1990:Y11.

Hiltz, Starr Roxanne. "Widowhood." In *Marriage and Family in a Changing Society*, 3rd ed., James M. Henslin, ed. New York: Free Press, 1989:521–531.

Hipler, Fritz. Interview in a television documentary with Bill Moyers in *Propaganda*, in the series "Walk Through the 20th Century," 1987.

Hirschi, Travis. *Causes of Delinquency*. Berkeley: University of California Press, 1969.

Hobson, John A. Imperialism: A Study, rev. ed. London: Allen, 1939. First published in 1902.

Hochschild, Arlie Russell. "The Sociology of Feeling and Emotion: Selected Possibilities." In *Another Voice: Feminist Perspectives on Social Life and Social Science*, Marcia Millman and Rosabeth Moss Kanter, eds. Garden City, N.Y.: Anchor Books, 1975.

Hochschild, Arlie. *The Second Shift: Working Parents and the Revolution at Home*. New York: Viking, 1989.

Hochschild, Arlie. "Note to the Author." 1991.

Hodson, Randy, and Robert E. Parker. "Work in High-Technology Settings: A Review of the Empirical Literature." *Research in the Sociology of Work, 4*, 1988:1–29.

Holden, Benjamin A. "American Stores to Settle Sex-Bias Suit by Paying as Much as $107.3 Million." *Wall Street Journal*, December 17, 1993:A2.

Holden, Benjamin A., and Frederick Rose. "Two Policemen Get 2 1/2-Year Jail Terms on U.S. Charges in Rodney King Case." *Wall Street Journal*, August 5, 1993:B2.

Holden, Constance. "Twins Reunited." *Science, 80*, 1980:1, 55–59.

Holman, Richard L. "World Wire." *Wall Street Journal*, October 8, 1992:A7.

Holman, Richard L. "World Wire." *Wall Street Journal*, January 3, 1994:8.

Holtzman, Abraham. *The Townsend Movement: A Political Study*. New York: Bookman, 1963.

Homans, George Caspar. "Social Behavior as Exchange." *American Journal of Sociology, 62*, May 1958:597–605.

Homans, George Caspar. *Social Behavior: Its Elementary Forms*. New York: Harcourt, Brace & World, 1961.

Homblin, Dora Jane. *The First Cities*. Boston: Little, Brown, Time-Life Books, 1973.

Honig, Alice Sterling. "The Gifts of Families: Caring, Courage, and Competence." In *Family Strengths 4: Positive Support Systems*, Nick Stinnett, John DeFrain, Kay King, Herbert Lingren, George Rowe, Sally Van Zandt, and Roseanne Williams, eds. Lincoln: University of Nebraska Press, 1982:331–349.

Horowitz, Irving Louis. *Three Worlds of Development: The Theory and Practice of International Stratification*. New York: Oxford University Press, 1966.

Horowitz, Irving Louis. "Socialist Utopias and Scientific Socialists: Primary Fanaticisms and Secondary Contradictions." *Sociological Forum, 4*, 1989:107–113.

Horowitz, Ruth. *Honor and the American Dream: Culture and Identity in a Chicano Community*. New Brunswick, N.J.: Rutgers University Press, 1983.

Horowitz, Ruth. "Community Tolerance of Gang Violence." *Social Problems, 34, 5*, December 1987:437–450.

Horwitz, Tony. "Toughing It Out in Kuwait Tested the 'Sultan' Family." *Wall Street Journal*, March 4, 1991:A1, A6.

Horwitz, Tony, and Craig Forman. "Immigrants to Europe from the Third World Face Racial Animosity." *Wall Street Journal*, August 14, 1990:A1, A9.

Hostetler, John A. *Amish Society*, 3rd ed. Baltimore: Johns Hopkins University Press, 1980.

Hourani, Benjamin T. "Toward the 21st Century: The Organization of Power in Post-Industrial Society." *Science and Public Policy, 14, 4*, August 1987:217–229.

House, Karen Elliott. "Iraqi President Hussein Sees New Mideast War Unless America Acts." *Wall Street Journal*, June 28, 1990:A1, A11.

Howe, Henry, John Lyne, Alan Gross, Harro VanLente, Aire Rip, Richard Lewontin, Daniel McShea, Greg Myers, Ullica Segerstrale, Herbert W. Simons, and V. B. Smocovitis. "Gene Talk in Sociobiology." *Social Epistemology, 6, 2*, April–June 1992:109–163.

Howells, Lloyd T., and Selwyn W. Becker. "Seating Arrangement and Leadership Emergence." *Journal of Abnormal and Social Psychology, 64*, February 1962:148–150.

Hoyt, Homer. *The Structure and Growth of Residential Neighborhoods in American Cities*. Washington, D.C.: Federal Housing Administration, 1939.

Hoyt, Homer. "Recent Distortions of the Classical Models of Urban Structure." In *Internal Structure of the City: Readings on Space and Environment*, Larry S. Bourne, ed. New York: Oxford University Press, 1971:84–96.

Hsu, Francis L. K. *The Challenge of the American Dream: The Chinese in the United States*. Belmont, Calif.: Wadsworth, 1971.

Huang, Chien Ju, and James G. Anderson. "Anomie and Deviancy: Reassessing Racial and Social Status Differences." Paper presented at the annual meetings of the American Sociological Association, 1991.

Huber, Joan. "Trends in Gender Stratification, 1970–1985." *Sociological Forum, 1*, 1986:476–495.

Huber, Joan. "From Sugar and Spice to Professor." In *Down to Earth Sociology*, 5th ed., James M. Henslin, ed. New York: Free Press, 1988:92–101.

Huber, Joan. "Micro-Macro Links in Gender Stratification." *American Sociological Review*, 55, February 1990:1–10.

Huber, Joan, and William H. Form. *Income and Ideology*. New York: Free Press, 1973.

Huddle, Donald. "The Net National Cost of Immigration." Washington, D.C.: Carrying Capacity Network, 1993.

Hudson, Christopher G. "The Social Class and Mental Illness Correlation: Implications of the Research for Policy and Practice." *Journal of Sociology and Social Welfare*, 15, 1, March 1988:27–54.

Hudson, James R. "Professional Sports Franchise Locations and City, Metropolitan and Regional Identities." Paper presented at the annual meetings of the American Sociological Association, 1991.

Hudson, Robert B. "The 'Graying' of the Federal Budget and Its Consequences for Old-Age Policy." *Gerontologist*, 18, October 1978:428–440.

Huesmann, L. R., and L. D. Eron, eds. *Television and the Aggressive Child*. Hillsdale, N.J.: Erlbaum, 1986.

Huesmann, L. R., L. D. Eron, M. M. Lefkowitz, et al. "Stability of Aggression over Time and Generations." *Developmental Psychology*, 20, 1984:1120–1134.

Hug, Simon. "The Emergence of the Swiss Ecological Party: A Dynamic Model." *European Journal of Political Research*, 18, 6, November 1990:645–670.

Huggins, Martha K. "Lost Childhoods: Assassinations of Youth in Democratizing Brazil." Paper presented at the annual meetings of the American Sociological Association, 1993.

Huggins, Martha K. Personal communication, January 25, 1994.

Hughes, Everett C. "Good People and Dirty Work." In *Down to Earth Sociology*, 7th ed., James M. Henslin, ed. New York: Free Press, 1993.

Hughes, H. Stuart. *Oswald Spengler: A Critical Estimate*, rev. ed. New York: Scribner's, 1962.

Hughes, Kathleen A. "Even Tiki Torches Don't Guarantee a Perfect Wedding." *Wall Street Journal*, February 20, 1990:A1, A16.

Humphreys, Laud. *Tearoom Trade: Impersonal Sex in Public Places*. Chicago: Aldine, 1970.

Humphreys, Laud. "Impersonal Sex and Perceived Satisfaction." In *Studies in the Sociology of Sex*, James M. Henslin, ed. New York: Appleton-Century-Crofts, 1971:351–374.

Humphreys, Laud. *Tearoom Trade: Impersonal Sex in Public Places*, enlarged ed. Chicago: Aldine, 1975.

Hurn, Christopher J. *The Limits and Possibilities of Schooling*, 2nd ed. Boston: Allyn and Bacon, 1985.

Hurst, Charles E. *Social Inequality: Forms, Causes, and Consequences*. Boston: Allyn and Bacon, 1992.

Hurtado, Aída, David E. Hayes-Bautista, R. Burciaga Valdez, and Anthony C. R. Hernández. *Redefining California: Latino Social Engagement in a Multicultural Society*. Los Angeles: UCLA Chicano Studies Research Center, 1992.

Huth, Mary Jo. "China's Urbanization under Communist Rule, 1949–1982." *International Journal of Sociology and Social Policy*, 10, 7, 1990:17–57.

Huttenbach, Henry R. "The Roman *Porajmos*: The Nazi Genocide of Europe's Gypsies." *Nationalities Papers*, 19, 3, Winter 1991:373–394.

Ingersoll, Bruce. "Dow Corning Corp. Agrees to the Release of More Data on Breast-Implant Safety." *Wall Street Journal*, February 10, 1992:A8.

Inkeles, James Coleman, and Ralph H. Turner, eds. Palo Alto, Calif.: Annual Reviews, 1979.

Institute for Social Research. "Televised Violence and Kids: A Public Health Problem?" *ISR Newsletter*, 18, 1, February 1994:5–7.

Iori, Ron. "The Good, the Bad and the Useless." *Wall Street Journal*, June 10, 1988:18R.

Itard, Jean Marc Gospard. *The Wild Boy of Aveyron*. Translated by George and Muriel Humphrey. New York: Appleton-Century-Crofts, 1962.

Jackall, Robert. "Moral Mazes: Bureaucracy and Managerial Work." *Harvard Business Review*, 61, 5, September–October, 1983:118–130.

Jackson, Kenneth. *Crabgrass Frontier: The Suburbanization of the United States*. New York: Oxford University Press, 1985. (In Karp, Stone, and Yoels, 1991.)

Jackson, Phillip W. *Life in Classrooms*. New York: Holt, Rinehart, and Winston, 1968.

Jacobson, Louis. "Animal-Rights Battle Spills into Schools as Both Sides Target Next Generation." *Wall Street Journal*, September 2, 1992:B1, B3.

Jacquet, Constant H., Jr., ed. *Yearbook of American and Canadian Churches 1993*. Nashville, Tenn.: Abingdon Press, 1993.

Jaggar, Alison M. "Sexual Difference and Sexual Equality." In *Theoretical Perspectives on Sexual Difference*, Deborah L. Rhode, ed. New Haven, Conn.: Yale University Press, 1990:239–254.

James, Daniel. "To Cut Spending, Freeze Immigration." *Wall Street Journal*, June 24, 1993:A13.

James, David R. "The Transformation of the Southern Racial State: Class and Race Determinants of Local-State Structures." *American Sociological Review*, 53, 1988:191–208.

Janis, Irving. *Victims of Groupthink*. Boston, Mass.: Houghton Mifflin, 1972.

Jankowiak, William R., and Edward F. Fischer. "A Cross-Cultural Perspective on Romantic Love." *Journal of Ethnology*, 31, 2, April 1992:149–155.

Jankowski, Martín Sánchez. *Islands in the Street: Gangs and American Urban Society*. Berkeley: University of California Press, 1991.

Jaspar, James M. "Moral Dimensions of Social Movements." Paper presented at the annual meetings of the American Sociological Association, 1991.

Jasper, James M., and Dorothy Nelkin. *The Animal Rights Crusade: The Growth of a Moral Protest*. New York: Free Press, 1992.

Jaspar, James M., and Dorothy Nelkin. *Animal Crusades*. New York: Free Press, 1993.

Jefferson, David J. "Gay Employees Win Benefits for Partners at More Corporations." *Wall Street Journal*, March 18, 1994:A1, A2.

Jencks, Christopher, Lauri Perman, and Lee Rainwater. "What Is a Good Job? A New Measure of Labor-Market Success." *American Journal of Sociology*, 93, 1988:1322–1357.

Jenness, Valerie. "From Sex as Sin to Sex as Work: COYOTE and the Reorganization of Prostitution as a Social Problem." *Social Problems*, 37, 3, August 1990:103–120.

Jerrome, Dorothy. *Good Company: An Anthropological Study of Old People in Groups*. Edinburgh, England: Edinburgh University Press, 1992.

Johnson, Benton. "On Church and Sect." *American Sociological Review*, 28, 1963:539–549.

Johnson, Cathryn. "The Emergence of the Emotional Self: A Developmental Theory." *Symbolic Interaction*, 15, 2, Summer 1992:183–202.

Johnson, Colleen L., and Barbara M. Barer. "Patterns of Engagement and Disengagement Among the Oldest Old." *Journal of Aging Studies*, 6, 4, Winter 1992:351–364.

Johnson, Dirk. "Murder Charges Are Met by Cries of Compassion." *New York Times*, August 8, 1988:A14.

Johnson, Norris R. "Panic at 'The Who Concert Stampede': An Empirical Assessment." In *Collective Behavior and Social Movements*, Russell L. Curtis, Jr., and Benigno E. Aguirre, eds. Boston: Allyn and Bacon, 1993:113–122.

Johnston, Drue M., and Norris R. Johnson. "Role Extension in Disaster: Employee Behavior at the Beverly Hills Supper Club Fire." *Sociological Focus*, 22, 1, February 1989:39–51.

Johnston, William B., and Arnold E. Packer. *Workforce 2000: Work and Workers for the Twenty-First Century*. Indianapolis, Ind.: Hudson Institute, 1987.

Jones, Lawrence N. "The New Black Church." *Ebony*, November 1992:192, 194–195.

Jones, James H. *Bad Blood: The Tuskegee Syphilis Experiment*, 2nd ed. New York: Free Press, 1993.

Jones, Timothy K. "American Anabaptists: Where They Are Going." *Christianity Today*, October 22, 1990:34–36.

Jones, Woodrow, Jr., and Paul Strand. "Adaptation and Adjustment Problems Among Indochinese Refugees." *Sociology and Social Research*, 71, 1, October 1986:42–46.

Josephson, Matthew. "The Robber Barons." In *John D. Rockefeller: Robber Baron or Industrial Statesman?* Earl Latham, ed. Boston: Heath, 1949:34–48.

Josephy, Alvin M., Jr. "Indians in History." *Atlantic Monthly*, 225, June 1970:67–72.

Judis, John B. "The Japanese Megaphone." *New Republic*, 202, 4, January 22, 1990:20–25.

Kagan, Jerome. "The Idea of Emotions in Human Development." In *Emotions, Cognition, and Behavior*, Carroll E. Izard, Jerome Kagan, and Robert B. Zajonc, eds. New York: Cambridge University Press, 1984:38–72.

Kahn, Joan R., and Kathryn A. London. "Premarital Sex and the Risk of Divorce." *Journal of Marriage and the Family*, 53, November 1991:845–855.

Kain, Edward L. *The Myth of Family Decline*. New York: Lexington Books, 1990.

Kalichman, Seth C. "MMPI Profiles of Women and Men Convicted of Domestic Homicide." *Journal of Clinical Psychology*, 44, 6, November 1988:847–853.

Kalish, Richard A. *Late Adulthood: Perspectives on Human Development*, 2nd ed. Monterey, Calif.: Brooks/Cole, 1982.

Kalish, Susan. "International Migration: New Findings on Magnitude, Importance." *Population Today*, 22, 3, March 1994:1–2.

Kalmijn, Matthijs. "Shifting Boundaries: Trends in Religious and Educational Homogamy." *American Sociological Review*, 56, December 1991:786–800.

Kamin, Leon J. *The Science and Politics of I.Q.* Hillsdale, N.J.: Erlbaum, 1975.

Kamin, Leon J. "Is Crime in the Genes? The Answer May Depend on Who Chooses What Evidence." *Scientific American*, February 1986:22–27.

Kanter, Rosabeth Moss. *Men and Women of the Corporation*. New York: Basic Books, 1977.

Kanter, Rosabeth Moss. *The Change Masters: Innovation and Entrepreneurship in the American Corporation*. New York: Simon & Schuster, 1983.

Kantrowitz, Barbara. "Sociology's Lonely Crowd." *Newsweek*, February 3, 1992:55.

Kapferer, Jean-Noël. "How Rumors Are Born." *Society*, 29, 5, July–August 1992:53–60.

Kaplan, H. Roy. "Lottery Winners and Work Commitment." *Journal of the Institute for Socioeconomic Studies*, 10, 2, 1985:82–94.

Karlen, Neal, and Barbara Burgower. "Dumping the Mentally Ill." *Newsweek*, 105, January 7, 1985:17.

Karnow, Stanley, and Nancy Yoshihara. *Asian Americans in Transition*. New York: Asia Society, 1992.

Karp, David A., Gregory P. Stone, and William C. Yoels. *Being Urban: A Sociology of City Life*, 2nd ed. New York: Praeger, 1991.

Karp, David A., and William C. Yoels. "Sport and Urban Life." *Journal of Sport and Social Issues*, 14, 2, 1990:77–102.

Kart, Cary S. *The Realities of Aging: An Introduction to Gerontology*, 3rd ed. Boston: Allyn and Bacon, 1990.

Kasarda, John D., and Edward M. Crenshaw. "Third World Urbanization: Dimensions, Theories, and Determinants." *Annual Review of Sociology*, 17, 1991:467–501.

Katz, Fred E. *Ordinary People and Extraordinary Evil: A Report on the Beguilings of Evil*. Albany: State University of New York Press, 1993.

Katz, Michael B. *The Undeserving Poor: From the War on Poverty to the War on Welfare*. New York: Pantheon, 1989.

Katz, Sidney. "The Importance of Being Beautiful." In *Down to Earth Sociology: Introductory Readings*, 8th ed., James M. Henslin, ed. New York: Free Press, 1995:301–307.

Kaufmann, Caroline. "Rights and the Provision of Health Care: A Comparison of Canada, Great Britain, and the United States." In *Dominant Issues in Medical Sociology*, 3rd ed., Howard D. Schwartz, ed. New York: McGraw-Hill, 1994:376–396.

Keans, Carl. "Socioenvironmental Determinants of Community Formation." *Environment and Behavior*, 23, 1, January 1991:27–46.

Keith, Jennie. *Old People, New Lives: Community Creation in a Retirement Residence*, 2nd ed. Chicago: University of Chicago Press, 1982.

Kellogg, W. N., and L. A. Kellogg. *The Ape and the Child: A Study of Environmental Influence upon Early Behavior*. New York: Whittlesey House, 1933.

Kelly, Joan B. "How Adults React to Divorce." In *Marriage and Family in a Changing Society*, 4th ed., James M. Henslin, ed. New York: Free Press, 1992:410–423.

Kemp, Alice Abel. "Estimating Sex Discrimination in Professional Occupations with the *Dictionary of Occupational Titles*." *Sociological Spectrum*, 10, 3, 1990:387–411.

Keniston, Kenneth. *Youth and Dissent: The Rise of a New Opposition*. New York: Harcourt, Brace, Jovanovich, 1971.

Kennedy, Paul. *Preparing for the Twenty-First Century*. New York: Random House, 1993.

Kephart, William M., and William W. Zellner, *Extraordinary Groups: An Examination of Unconventional Life-Styles*, 5th ed. New York: St. Martin's Press, 1994.

Kerr, Clark. *The Future of Industrialized Societies*. Cambridge, Mass.: Harvard University Press, 1983.

Kerr, Clark, et al. *Industrialism and Industrial Man: The Problems of Labor and Management in Economic Growth.* Cambridge, Mass.: Harvard University Press, 1960.

Kershaw, Terry. "The Effects of Educational Tracking on the Social Mobility of African Americans." *Journal of Black Studies, 23,* 1, September 1992:152–169.

Kettl, Donald F. "The Savings-and-Loan Bailout: The Mismatch Between the Headlines and the Issues." *PS, 24,* 3, September 1991:441–447.

Keyser, Christine. "Compromise in Defense of Earth First!" *Sierra, 76,* 6, November 1991:45–47.

Kiefer, Francine S. "Radical Left Exits German Green Party After Sharp Dispute." *Christian Science Monitor,* April 29, 1991:4.

Killian, Lewis M., and Charles M. Grigg. "Urbanism, Race, and Anomie." *American Journal of Sociology, 67,* 1962.661–665.

King, Martin Luther, Jr. *Stride Toward Freedom: The Montgomery Story.* New York: Harper & Brothers, 1958.

Kinsella, Kevin, and Cynthia M. Taeuber. *An Aging World.* Washington, D.C.: U.S. Bureau of the Census, 1993.

Kitsuse, John I. "Coming Out All Over: Deviants and the Politics of Social Problems." *Social Problems, 28,* 1, October 1980:1–13.

Klandermans, Bert. "Mobilization and Participation: Social- Psychological Expansions of Resource Mobilization Theory." *American Sociological Review, 49,* October 1984:583–600.

Klandermans, Bert. "New Social Movements and Resource Mobilization: The European and the American Approach." *Journal of Mass Emergencies and Disasters, 4,* 1986:13–37.

Klee, Ernst, Willi Dressen, and Volker Riess. *"The Good Old Days": The Holocaust as Seen by Its Perpetrators and Bystanders,* Deborah Burnstone, trans. New York: Free Press, 1991.

Klein, Alan M. "Managing Deviance: Hustling, Homophobia, and the Bodybuilding Subculture." In *Constructions of Deviance: Social Power, Context, and Interaction.* Belmont, Calif.: Wadsworth, 1994:529–544.

Klonoff, Elizabeth A., and Hope Landrine. "Sex Roles, Occupational Roles, and Symptom-Reporting: A Test of Competing Hypotheses on Sex Differences." *Journal of Behavioral Medicine, 15,* 4, August 1992:355–364.

Kluegel, James R., and Eliot R. Smith. *Beliefs About Inequality: America's Views of What Is and What Ought to Be.* Hawthorne, N.Y.: Aldine de Gruyter, 1986.

Koenig, Frederick. *Rumor in the Market Place: The Social Psychology of Commercial Hearsay.* Dover, Mass.: Auburn House, 1985.

Kohfeld, Carol W., and Leslie A. Leip. "Bans on Concurrent Sale of Beer and Gas: A California Case Study." *Sociological Practice Review, 2,* 2, April 1991:104–115.

Kohlberg, Lawrence, and Carol Gilligan. "The Adolescent as a Philosopher: The Discovery of the Self in a Postconventional World." *Daedalus, 100,* 1971:1051–1086.

Kohn, Alfie. "Make Love, Not War." *Psychology Today,* June 1988:35–38.

Kohn, Melvin L. "Social Class and Parental Values." *American Journal of Sociology, 64,* 1959:337–351.

Kohn, Melvin L. "Social Class and Parent–Child Relationships: An Interpretation." *American Journal of Sociology, 68,* 1963:471–480.

Kohn, Melvin L. "Occupational Structure and Alienation." *American Journal of Sociology, 82,* 1976:111–130.

Kohn, Melvin L. *Class and Conformity: A Study in Values,* 2nd ed. Homewood, Ill.: Dorsey Press, 1977.

Kohn, Melvin L., Atsushi Naoi, Carrie Schoenbach, Carmi Schooler, and Kazimierz M. Slomczynski. "Position in the Class Structure and Psychological Functioning in the United States, Japan, and Poland." *American Journal of Sociology, 95,* 1990:964–1008.

Kohn, Melvin L., and Carmi Schooler. "Class, Occupation, and Orientation." *American Sociological Review, 34,* 1969:659–678.

Kohn, Melvin L., and Carmi Schooler. *Work and Personality: An Inquiry into the Impact of Social Stratification.* New York: Ablex Press, 1983.

Kohn, Melvin L., Kazimierz M. Slomczynski, and Carrie Schoenbach. "Social Stratification and the Transmission of Values in the Family: A Cross-National Assessment." *Sociological Forum, 1,* 1, 1986:73–102.

Komarovsky, Mirra, and S. S. Sargent. "Research into Subcultural Influences Upon Personality." In *Culture and Personalities,* S. S. Sargent and M. W. Smith, eds. New York: Viking Fund, 1949:143–159.

Komisar, Lucy. "The Image of Woman in Advertising." In *Woman in Sexist Society: Studies in Power and Powerlessness,* Vivian Gornick and Barbara K. Moran, eds. New York: Basic Books, 1971:207–217.

Komter, Aafke, "Hidden Power in Marriage." *Gender and Society, 3,* 2, June 1989:187–216.

Korda, Michael. *Male Chauvinism: How It Works.* New York: Random House, 1973.

Kornhauser, William. *The Politics of Mass Society.* New York: Free Press, 1959.

Kotlowitz, Alex. "A Businessman Turns His Skills to Aiding Inner-City Schools." *Wall Street Journal,* February 25, 1992:A1, A6.

Kramer, Josea B. "Serving American Indian Elderly in Cities: An Invisible Minority." *Aging Magazine,* Winter–Spring 1992:48–51.

Krause, Neal. "Race Differences in Life Satisfaction Among Aged Men and Women." *Journal of Gerontology, 48,* 5, 1993:235–244.

Krauss, Celene. "Community Struggle and the Shaping of Democratic Consciousness." *Sociological Forum, 4,* 2, 1989:227–239.

Krauss, Celene. "Blue-Collar Women and Toxic Waste Protests: The Process of Politicization." Proceedings of the Second Annual Conference of the Institute for Women's Policy Research, 1991.

Kraybill, Donald B. *The Riddle of Amish Culture.* Baltimore: Johns Hopkins University Press, 1989.

Krich, John. "Here Come the Brides: The Blossoming Business of Imported Love." In *Men's Lives,* Michael S. Kimmel and Michael A. Messner, eds. New York: Macmillan, 1989:382–392.

Kristof, Nicholas D. "China Sees 'Market-Leninism' as Way to Future." *New York Times,* September 6, 1993:5.

Kübler-Ross, Elisabeth. *On Death and Dying.* New York: Macmillan, 1969.

Kübler-Ross, Elisabeth. *Living with Death and Dying.* New York: Macmillan, 1981.

Kübler-Ross, Elisabeth. *Death: The Final Stage of Growth.* Englewood Cliffs, N.J.: Prentice Hall, 1989.

Kuhn, Margaret E. "The Gray Panthers." In *Social Problems,* James M. Henslin ed. Englewood Cliffs, N.J.: 1990:56–57.

Kurian, George Thomas. *Encyclopedia of the First World,* Vols. 1, 2. New York: Facts on File, 1990.

Kurian, George Thomas. *Encyclopedia of the Second World,* New York: Facts on File, 1991.

Kurian, George Thomas. *Encyclopedia of the Third World*, Vols. 1, 2, 3. New York: Facts on File, 1992.

La Barre, Weston. *The Human Animal*. Chicago: University of Chicago Press, 1954.

Labov, Teresa G. "Spanish-English Bilingualism and Gender." Paper presented at the annual meetings of the American Sociological Association, 1993.

Lacayo, Richard. "The 'Cultural' Defense." *Time*, Fall 1993a:61.

Lacayo, Richard. "In the Grip of a Psychopath." *Time*, May 3, 1993b:34–36, 39–43.

Lachica, Eduardo. "Third World Told to Spend More on Environment." *Wall Street Journal*, May 18, 1992:A2.

Ladner, Joyce A. "Teenage Pregnancy: The Implications for Black Americans." In *The State of Black America*, James D. Williams, ed. New York: National Urban League, 1986:65–84.

LaDou, Joseph. "Deadly Migration: Hazardous Industries' Flight to the Third World." *Technology Review*, 94, 5, July 1991:46–53.

Lagaipa, Susan J. "Suffer the Little Children: The Ancient Practice of Infanticide as a Modern Moral Dilemma." *Issues in Comprehensive Pediatric Nursing*, 13, 1990:241–251.

Lamb, Michael E. "The Effect of Divorce on Children's Personality Development." *Journal of Divorce*, 1, Winter 1977:163–174.

Landtman, Gunnar. *The Origin of the Inequality of the Social Classes*. New York: Greenwood Press, 1968. First published in 1938.

Lang, Kurt, and Gladys E. Lang. *Collective Dynamics*. New York: Crowell, 1961.

Lang, Susan S. *Women Without Children: The Reasons, the Rewards, the Regrets*. New York: Pharos Books, 1991.

Langan, Patrick A., and Mark A. Cunniff. "Recidivism of Felons on Probation, 1986–89." Washington, D.C.: U.S. Department of Justice, February 1992.

Lannoy, Richard. *The Speaking Tree: A Study of Indian Culture and Society*. New York: Oxford University Press, 1975.

LaPiere, Richard T. "Attitudes Versus Action." *Social Forces*, 13, December 1934:230–237.

Larson, Jeffry H. "The Marriage Quiz: College Students' Beliefs in Selected Myths About Marriage." *Family Relations*, January 1988:3–11.

Lasch, Christopher. *Haven in a Heartless World: The Family Besieged*. New York: Basic, 1977.

Laska, Shirley Bradway. "Environmental Sociology and the State of the Discipline." *Social Forces*, 72, 1, September 1993:1–17.

Laslett, Peter. *The World We Have Lost: England Before the Industrial Age*, 3rd ed. New York: Scribner's, 1984.

Lauer, Jeanette, and Robert Lauer. "Marriages Made to Last." In *Marriage and Family in a Changing Society*, 4th ed., James M. Henslin, ed. New York: Free Press, 1992:481–486.

Lawlor, Julia. "Women Gain Power, Means to Abuse It." *USA Today*, January 12, 1994:1A, 2A.

Lawton, Millicent. "Poverty Rate Seen Rising Fastest for Latino Children." *Education Week*, September 11, 1991:10.

Lazarsfeld, Paul F., and Jeffrey G. Reitz. "History of Applied Sociology." *Sociological Practice*, 7, 1989:43–52.

Leacock, Eleanor. *Teaching and Learning in City Schools*. New York: Basic Books, 1969.

LeBon, Gustave. *Psychologie des Foules (The Psychology of the Crowd)*. Paris: Alcan, 1895. Various editions in English.

Lee, Alfred McClung, and Elizabeth Briant Lee. *The Fine Art of Propaganda: A Study of Father Coughlin's Speeches*. New York: Harcourt Brace, 1939.

Lee, Felicia R., and Ari L. Goldman. "The Bitterness Flows in 2 Directions." *New York Times*, August 21, 1991:B1, B3.Lee, Marcia M. "Toward Understanding Why Few Women Hold Public Office: Factors Affecting the Participation of Women in Local Politics." In *A Portrait of Marginality: The Political Behavior of the American Woman*, Marianne Githens and Jewel L. Prestage, eds. New York: McKay, 1977:118–138.

Lee, Richard B. *The !Kung San: Men, Women, and Work in a Foraging Society*. New York: Cambridge University Press, 1979.

Lee, Sharon M., and Keiko Yamanaka. "Patterns of Asian American Intermarriage and Marital Assimilation." *Journal of Comparative Family Studies*, 21, 2, Summer 1990:287–305.

Leinberger, Christopher B., and Charles Lockwood. "How Business is Reshaping America." *Atlantic Monthly*, 10, October 1986:43–52.

Lemert, Edwin M. *Human Deviance, Social Problems, and Social Control*, 2nd ed., Englewood Cliffs, N.J.: Prentice Hall, 1972.

Lenski, Gerhard. "Status Crystallization: A Nonvertical Dimension of Social Status." *American Sociological Review*, 19, 1954:405–413.

Lenski, Gerhard. *Power and Privilege: A Theory of Social Stratification*. New York: McGraw-Hill, 1966.

Lenski, Gerhard, and Jean Lenski. *Human Societies: An Introduction to Macrosociology*, 5th ed. New York: McGraw-Hill, 1987.

Lerner, Gerda. *The Creation of Patriarchy*. New York: Oxford, 1986.

Lesser, Alexander. "War and the State." In *War: The Anthropology of Armed Conflict and Aggression*, Morton Fried, Marvin Harris, and Robert Murphy, eds. Garden City, N.Y.: Natural History, 1968:92–96.

Leverenz, Erica Finley, Pi-Ling Fan, Margaret Mooney Marini, and Ann Beutel. "Gender and Job Values." Paper presented at the annual meetings of the American Sociological Association, 1993.

Levinson, D. J. *The Seasons of a Man's Life*. New York: Knopf, 1978.

Levy, Marion J., Jr. "Confucianism and Modernization." *Society*, 24, 4, May–June 1992:15–18.

Lewin, Tamar. "Hospitals Pitch Harder for Patients." *New York Times*, May 10, 1987:F1, F27–28.

Lewis, Bernard. "The Roots of Muslim Rage." *Atlantic*, September 1990:47–54, 56, 59–60.

Lewis, Charlie, Deidre Scully, and Susan Condor. "Sex Stereotyping of Infants: A Re-Examination." *Journal of Reproductive and Infant Psychology*, 10, 1992:53–63.

Lewis, David L. "Sex and the Automobile: From Rumble Seats to Rockin' Vans." In *The Automobile and American Culture*, David L. Lewis and Lawrence Goldstein, eds. Ann Arbor: University of Michigan Press, 1983.

Lewis, Dorothy Otnow, ed. *Vulnerabilities to Delinquency*. New York: Spectrum Medical and Scientific Books, 1981.

Lewis, Oscar. "The Culture of Poverty." *Scientific American*, 115, October 1966a:19–25.

Lewis, Oscar. *La Vida*. New York: Random House, 1966b.

Lewis, Richard S. *Challenger: The Final Voyage*. New York: Columbia University Press, 1988.

Liebow, Elliot. *Tally's Corner: A Study of Negro Streetcorner Men*. Boston: Little, Brown, 1967.

Light, Donald W. "Perestroika for Russian Health Care?" *Footnotes*, 20, 3, March 1992:7, 9.

Lightfoot-Klein, A. "Rites of Purification and Their Effects: Some Psychological Aspects of Female Genital Circumcision and Infibulation (Pharaonic Circumcision) in an Afro-Arab Society (Sudan)." *Journal of Psychological Human Sexuality*, 2, 1989:61–78.

Lin, Nan, Walter M. Ensel, and John C. Vaughn. "Social Resources and Strength of Ties: Structural Factors in Occupational Status Attainment." *American Sociological Review*, 46, 4, August 1981:393–405.

Linden, Eugene. "Lost Tribes, Lost Knowledge." *Time*, September 23, 1991:46, 48, 50, 52, 54, 56.

Linton, Ralph. *The Study of Man*. New York: Appleton-Century-Crofts, 1936.

Lippitt, Ronald, and Ralph K. White. "An Experimental Study of Leadership and Group Life." In *Readings in Social Psychology*, 3rd ed., Eleanor E. Maccoby, Theodore M. Newcomb, and Eugene L. Hartley, eds. New York: Holt, Rinehart and Winston, 1958:340–365. (As summarized in Olmsted and Hare 1978:28–31.)

Lipset, Seymour Martin. *The First New Nation*. New York: Basic Books, 1963.

Lipset, Seymour Martin, ed. *The Third Century: America as a Post-Industrial Society*. Stanford Calif.: Hoover Institution Press, 1979.

Lipset, Seymour Martin. "The Social Requisites of Democracy Revisited." Presidential address to the American Sociological Association, Boston, Massachusetts, 1993.

Lipton, Michael. *Why Poor People Stay Poor: Urban Bias in World Development*. Cambridge, Mass.: Harvard University Press, 1979.

Lofland, John. "Collective Behavior: The Elementary Forms." In *Collective Behavior and Social Movements*, Russell L. Curtis, Jr., and Benigno E. Aguirre, eds. Boston: Allyn and Bacon, 1993:70–75.

Logan, John R., and Harvey L. Molotch. *Urban Fortunes: The Political Economy of Place*. Berkeley: University of California Press, 1987.

Lombroso, Cesare. *Crime: Its Causes and Remedies*, H. P. Horton, trans. Boston: Little, Brown, 1911.

Lopez, Julie Amparano. "Study Says Women Face Glass Walls as Well as Ceilings." *Wall Street Journal*, March 3, 1992:B1, B8.

Lopez, Julie Amparano. "Managing Your Career." *Wall Street Journal*, January 12, 1994.

Lopez-Romano, Sylvia Silva. "Integration of Community and Learning Among Southeast Asian Newcomer Hmong Parents and Children." Unpublished doctoral dissertation, University of San Francisco, 1992.

Lublin, Joann S. "Trying to Increase Worker Productivity, More Employers Alter Management Style." *Wall Street Journal*, February 13, 1991:B1, B7.

Lublin, Joann S. "Spouses Find Themselves Worlds Apart as Global Commuter Marriages Increase." *Wall Street Journal*, August 19, 1992:B1, B5.

Luebke, Barbara F. "Out of Focus: Images of Women and Men in Newspaper Photographs." *Sex Roles*, 20 (3/4), 1989:121–133.

Luke, Timothy W. *Ideology and Soviet Industrialism*. Westport, Conn.: Greenwood Press, 1985.

Luker, Kristin. *Abortion and the Politics of Motherhood*. Berkeley: University of California Press, 1984.

Lundberg, Olle. "Causal Explanations for Class Inequality in Health—An Empirical Analysis." *Social Science and Medicine*, 32, 4, 1991:385–393.

Luoma, Jon R. "Acid Murder No Longer a Mystery." In *Taking Sides: Clashing Views on Controversial Environmental Issues*, 3rd ed.,

Theodore D. Goldfarb, ed. Guilford, Conn.: Dushkin, 1989:186–192.

Lurie, Nicole, Jonathan Slater, Paul McGovern, Jacqueline Ekstrum, Lois Quam, and Karen Margolis. "Preventive Care for Women: Does the Sex of the Physician Matter?" *New England Journal of Medicine*, 329, August 12, 1993:478–482.

Lye, Diane N., Daniel H. Klepinger, Patricia Davis Hyle, and Anjanette Nelson. "Childhood Living Arrangements and Adult Children's Relations with Their Parents." 1993 revisions of a paper presented at the annual meetings of the Population Association of America, 1992.

Lynd, Robert S., and Helen Merell Lynd. *Middletown: A Study in American Culture*. New York: Harcourt, Brace, 1929.

Lynd, Robert S., and Helen Merell Lynd. *Middletown in Transition: A Study in Cultural Conflicts*. New York: Harcourt, Brace, 1937.

Lynn, Naomi, and Cornelia Butler Flora. "Societal Punishment and Aspects of Female Political Participation: 1972 National Convention Delegates." In *A Portrait of Marginality: The Political Behavior of the American Woman*, Marianne Githens and Jewel L. Prestage, eds. New York: McKay, 1977:139–149.

Maccoby, Eleanor E. "Current Changes in the Family and Their Impact upon the Socialization of Children." In *Major Social Issues*, J. M. Yinger and S. J. Cutler, eds. New York: Free Press, 1978.

MacIver, Robert M. *Society*. New York: Holt, Rinehart and Winston, 1937.

Mack, Raymond W., and Calvin P. Bradford. *Transforming America: Patterns of Social Change*, 2nd ed. New York: Random House, 1979.

Mackay, Charles. *Memories of Extraordinary Popular Delusions and the Madness of Crowds*. London: Office of the National Illustrated Library, 1852.

MacKinnon, Catharine A. *Sexual Harassment of Working Women: A Case of Sex Discrimination*. New Haven, Conn.: Yale University Press, 1979.

MacShane, Denis. "Lessons for Bosses and the Bossed." *New York Times*, July 19, 1993:A15.

Maeda, Daisaku. "Japan." In *International Handbook on Aging: Contemporary Developments and Research*. Westport, Conn.: Greenwood Press, 1980:253–270.

Magnuson, E. "A Cold Soak, a Plume, a Fireball." *Time*, February 17, 1986:25.

Mahran, M. *Proceedings of the Third International Congress of Medical Sexology*. Littleton, Mass.: PSG Publishing, 1978.

Mahran, M. "Medical Dangers of Female Circumcision." *International Planned Parenthood Federation Medical Bulletin*, 2, 1981:1–2.

Main, Jackson Turner. *The Social Structure of Revolutionary America*. Princeton, N.J.: Princeton University Press, 1965.

Mainardi, Pat. "The Politics of Housework." In *Social Problems in American Society*, 3rd ed., James M. Henslin and Larry T. Reynolds, eds. Boston: Holbrook Press, 1979:174–177.

Malinowski, Bronislaw. *Sex and Repression in Savage Society*. Cleveland, Ohio: World, 1927.

Malinowski, Bronislaw. *The Dynamics of Culture Change*. New Haven, Conn.: Yale University Press, 1945.

Malson, Lucien. *Wolf Children and the Problem of Human Nature*. New York: Monthly Review Press, 1972.

Mamdani, Mahmood. "The Myth of Population Control: Family, Caste, and Class in an Urban Village." New York: Monthly Review Press, 1973.

Mander, Jerry. *In the Absence of the Sacred: The Failure of Technology and the Survival of the Indian Nations.* San Francisco, Calif.: Sierra Club Books, 1992.

Mann, Arthur. "When Tammy was Supreme." In *Plunkitt of Tammany Hall,* William L. Riordan. New York: Dutton, 1963:vii–xxii.

Manski, Charles F. "Income and Higher Education." *Focus, 14,* 3, Winter 1992–1993:14–19.

Marger, Martin N. *Elites and Masses: An Introduction to Political Sociology,* 2nd ed. Belmont, Calif.: Wadsworth, 1987.

Markson, Elizabeth W. "Moral Dilemmas." *Society,* July–August, 1992:4–6.

Markusen, Eric. "Comprehending the Cambodian Genocide: An Application of Robert Jay Lifton's Model of Genocidal Killing." *Psychohistory Review, 20,* 2, Winter 1992:145–169.

Marolla, Joseph, and Diana Scully. "Attitudes Toward Women, Violence, and Rape: A Comparison of Convicted Rapists and Other Felons." *Deviant Behavior, 7,* 4, 1986:337–355.

Marshall, Gordon. *In Search of the Spirit of Capitalism: An Essay on Max Weber's Protestant Ethic Thesis.* New York: Columbia University Press, 1982.

Martin, Michael. "Ecosabotage and Civil Disobedience." *Environmental Ethics, 12,* 4, Winter 1990:291–310.

Martin, Teresa Castro, and Larry Bumpass. "Recent Trends in Marital Disruption." *Demography, 26,* 1989:37–51.

Martineau, Harriet. *Society in America.* Garden City, N.Y.: Doubleday 1962. First published in 1837.

Marx, Gary T. "Thoughts on a Neglected Category of Social Movement Participant: The Agent Provocateur and the Informant." In *Collective Behavior and Social Movements,* Russell L. Curtis, Jr., and Benigno E. Aguirre, eds. Boston: Allyn and Bacon, 1993:242–258.

Marx, Karl. "Contribution to the Critique of Hegel's Philosophy of Right." In *Karl Marx: Early Writings,* T. B. Bottomore, ed. New York: McGraw-Hill, 1964:45. First published in 1844.

Marx, Karl, and Friedrich Engels. *Communist Manifesto.* New York: Pantheon, 1967. First published in 1848.

Masheter, Carol. "Postdivorce Relationships Between Ex-spouses: The Role of Attachment and Interpersonal Conflict." *Journal of Marriage and the Family, 53,* February 1991:103–110.

Matthews, Marvyn. "Long Term Trends in Soviet Education." In *Soviet Education in the 1980s,* J. J. Tomiak, ed. London: Croom Helm, 1983:1–23.

Matthews, Merrill, Jr. "Medisave Accounts: The Ethical Health Reform." *Wall Street Journal,* September 16, 1993:A24.

Mauldin, Teresa A. "Economic Consequences of Divorce or Separation Among Women in Poverty." *Journal of Divorce and Remarriage, 14,* 3–4, 1991:163–177.

Mauss, Armand. *Social Problems as Social Movements.* Philadelphia, Penn.: Lippincott, 1975.

Mayo, Elton. *Human Problems of an Industrial Civilization.* New York: Viking, 1966.

McAdam, Doug. *Freedom Summer.* New York: Oxford University Press, 1988.

McAdam, Doug, John D. McCarthy, and Mayer N. Zald. "Social Movements." In *Handbook of Sociology,* Neil J. Smelser, ed. Newbury Park, Calif.: Sage, 1988:695–737.

McAlexander, James H., and John W. Schouten. "Hair Style Changes as Transition Markers." *Sociology and Social Research, 74,* 91, October 1989:58–62.

McCabe, J. Terrence, and James E. Ellis. "Pastoralism: Beating the Odds in Arid Africa." In *Conformity and Conflict: Readings in Cultural Anthropology,* James P. Spradley and David W. McCurdy, eds. Glenview, Ill.: Scott, Foresman, 1990:150–156.

McCall, Michal. "Who and Where Are the Artists?" In *Fieldwork Experience: Qualitative Approaches to Social Research,* William B. Shaffir, Robert A. Stebbins, and Allan Turowetz, eds. New York: St. Martin's, 1980:145–158.

McCarthy, Colman. "America's Homeless: Three Days Down and Out in Chicago." *Nation, 236,* 9, March 5, 1983:1, 271.

McCarthy, John D., and Mark Wolfson. "Consensus Movements, Conflict Movements, and the Cooperation of Civic and State Infrastructures." In *Frontiers in Social Movement Theory,* Aldon D. Morris and Carol McClurg Mueller, eds. New Haven, Conn.: Yale University Press, 1992:273–297.

McCarthy, John D., and Mayer N. Zald. "Resource Mobilization and Social Movements: A Partial Theory." *American Journal of Sociology, 82,* 6, 1977:1212–1241.

McCarthy, Michael J. "James Bond Hits the Supermarket: Stores Snoop on Shoppers' Habits to Boost Sales." *Wall Street Journal,* August 25, 1993:B1, B8.

McCartney, Scott. "People Most Needing Transplantable Livers Now Often Miss Out." *Wall Street Journal,* April 1, 1993:A1, A7.

McCoy, Elin. "Childhood Through the Ages." In *Marriage and Family in a Changing Society,* 2nd ed., James M. Henslin, ed. New York: Free Press, 1985:386–394.

McCuen, Gary E., ed. *Ecocide and Genocide in the Vanishing Forest: The Rainforests and Native People.* Hudson, Wis.: GEM Publications, 1993.

McGowan, Jo. "Little Girls Dying: An Ancient & Thriving Practice." *Commonweal,* August 9, 1991:481–482.

McGregor, James. "China's Aging Leader Seems Set to Carve Reformist Idea in Stone." *Wall Street Journal,* March 20, 1992:A9.

McGregor, James. "Running Bulls." *Wall Street Journal,* September 24, 1993:R16.

McKeown, Thomas. *The Modern Rise of Population.* New York: Academic Press, 1977.

McLemore, S. Dale. *Racial and Ethnic Relations in America.* Boston: Allyn and Bacon, 1994.

McMurray, Scott. "Studies of Women with Breast Implants Show Risk of Human Immune Diseases." *Wall Street Journal,* February 19, 1992:A3.

McPhail, Clark. "Blumer's Theory of Collective Behavior: The Development of a Non-Symbolic Interaction Explanation." *Sociological Quarterly, 30,* 3, 1989:401–423.

McPhail, Clark. *The Myth of the Madding Crowd.* New York: Aldine de Gruyter, 1991.

Mead, George Herbert. *Mind, Self and Society.* Chicago: University of Chicago Press, 1934.

Mead, Margaret. *Sex and Temperament in Three Primitive Societies.* New York: William and Morrow, 1935.

Mead, Margaret. *Sex and Temperament in Three Primitive Societies.* New York: New American Library, 1950.

Meek, Anne. "On Creating 'Ganas': A conversation with Jaime Escalante." *Educational Leadership, 46,* 5, February 1989: 46–47.

Meier, Barry. "Health Studies Suggest Asbestos Substitutes Also Pose Cancer Risk." *Wall Street Journal,* May 12, 1987:1, 21.

Melbin, Murray. "Night as Frontier." In *Down to Earth Sociology: Introductory Readings*, 5th ed., James M. Henslin, ed. New York: Free Press, 1988:397–403.

Melloan, George. "Breaking the Cycle of Failure." In *Social Problems Today: Coping with the Challenges of a Changing Society*. James M. Henslin, ed. Englewood Cliffs, N.J.: Prentice Hall, 1990:302–304.

Melloan, George. "Apartheid Is Dead—Now Comes the Hard Part." *Wall Street Journal*, November 22, 1993a:A15.

Melloan, George. "Italy 'Steps into the Tunnel' Toward Change." *Wall Street Journal*, April 26, 1993b:A15.

Meloen, Joseph D. "The Fortieth Anniversary of 'The *Authoritarian Personality*.'" *Politics and the Individual*, 1, 1, 1991:119–127.

Meltzer, Bernard N., John W. Petras, and Larry T. Reynolds. *Symbolic Interactionism: Genesis, Varieties, and Criticism*. London: Routledge & Kegan Paul, 1975.

Melucci, Alberto. "The New Social Movements: A Theoretical Approach." *Social Science Information*, 19, 1980:199–226.

Meredith, William H. "Level and Correlates of Perceived Quality of Life for Lao Hmong Refugees in Nebraska." *Social Indicators Research*, 14, January 1984:83–97.

Merit Systems Protection Board. *Sexual Harassment in the Federal Workplace: Is It a Problem?* Washington, D.C.: Office of Merit Systems Review and Studies, 1981.

Merton, Robert K. "Discrimination and the American Creed." In *Discrimination and National Welfare*, R. M. MacIver, ed. New York: Harper & Brothers, 1948:99–126.

Merton, Robert K. "Discrimination and the American Creed." In *Sociological Ambivalence and Other Essays*. New York: Free Press, 1976:189–216.

Merton, Robert K. "The Social-Cultural Environment and Anomie." In *New Perspectives for Research on Juvenile Delinquency*, Helen L. Witmer and Ruth Kotinsky, eds. Washington, D.C.: U.S. Department of Health, Education, and Welfare, 1956:24–50.

Merton, Robert K. *Social Theory and Social Structure*. Glencoe, Ill.: Free Press, 1949.

Merton, Robert K. *Social Theory and Social Structure*, enlarged ed. New York: Free Press, 1968.

Merwine, Maynard H. "How Africa Understands Female Circumcision." *New York Times*, November 24, 1993.

Messner, Michael. "Boyhood, Organized Sports, and the Construction of Masculinities." *Journal of Contemporary Ethnography*, 18, 4, January 1990:416–444.

Messner, Steven F. "Television Violence and Violent Crime: An Aggregate Analysis." *Social Problems*, 33, 3, February 1986:218–234.

Meyer, Philip. "If Hitler Asked You to Electrocute a Stranger, Would You? Probably." In *Down to Earth Sociology: Introductory Readings*, 7th ed., James M. Henslin, ed. New York: Free Press, 1993:165–171.

Meyerson, Per-Martin. "Where Is Sweden Heading?" New York: Swedish Information Service, January 1992.

Meyrowitz, Joshua. "The Adultlike Child and the Childlike Adult: Socialization in an Electronic Age." *Daedalus*, 113, 1984:19–48.

Michalowski, Raymond J. *Order, Law, and Crime: An Introduction to Criminology*. New York: Random House, 1985.

Michels, Robert. *Political Parties*. Glencoe, Ill.: Free Press, 1949. First published in 1911.

Miles, Rufus E., Jr. "The Population Challenge of the 70's: Achieving a Stationery Population." In *The Crisis of Survival*, editors of *The Progressive*, eds. Glenview, Ill.: Scott Foresman, 1970:122–140.

Milgram, Stanley. "Behavioral Study of Obedience." *Journal of Abnormal and Social Psychology*, 67, 4, 1963:371–378.

Milgram, Stanley. "Some Conditions of Obedience and Disobedience to Authority." *Human Relations*, 18, February 1965:57–76.

Milgram, Stanley. "The Small World Problem." *Psychology Today*, 1, 1967:61–67.

Milgram, Stanley. "The Experience of Living in Cities." *Science*, 67, March 1970:1461–1468.

Miller, Dan E. "Milgram Redux: Obedience and Disobedience in Authority Relations." In *Studies in Symbolic Interaction*, Norman K. Denzin, ed. Greenwich, Conn.: JAI Press, 1986:77–106.

Miller, Michael W. "Dark Days: The Staggering Cost of Depression." *Wall Street Journal*, December 2, 1993:B1, B6.

Miller, Michael W. "Survey Sketches New Portrait of the Mentally Ill." *Wall Street Journal*, January 14, 1994:B1, B10.

Miller, Walter B. "Lower Class Culture as a Generating Milieu of Gang Delinquency." *Journal of Social Issues*, 14, 3, 1958:5–19.

Miller-Loessi, Karen. "Toward Gender Integration in the Workplace: Issues at Multiple Levels." *Sociological Perspectives*, 35, 1, 1992:1–15.

Mills, C. Wright. *The Power Elite*. New York: Oxford University Press, 1956.

Mills, C. Wright. *The Sociological Imagination*. New York: Oxford University Press, 1959.

Mills, Karen M., and Thomas J. Palumbo. A *Statistical Portrait of Women in the United States: 1978*. U.S. Bureau of the Census, *Current Population Reports*, Series P-23, no. 100, 1980.

Miner, Horace. "Body Ritual among the Nacirema." In *Down to Earth Sociology: Introductory Readings*, 8th ed., James M. Henslin, ed. New York: Free Press, 1995:73–77.

Minkler, Meredith, and Ann Robertson. "The Ideology of 'Age/Race Wars': Deconstructing a Social Problem." *Ageing and Society*, 11, 1, March 1991:1–22.

Mintz, Beth A., and Michael Schwartz. *The Power Structure of American Business*. Chicago: University of Chicago Press, 1985.

Mitchell, G., Stephanie Obradovich, Fred Harring, Chris Tromborg, and Alyson L. Burns. "Reproducing Gender in Public Places: Adults' Attention to Toddlers in Three Public Locales." *Sex Roles*, 26, 7/8, 1992:323–330.

Mitchell, Rogert, Touly Xiong, Charles Vue, Moua Xiong, and Leanne Martin. "The Eau Claire Hmong Community: A Cooperative Study." *Wisconsin Sociologist*, 26, 1, Winter 1989:33–37.

Mizruchi, Mark S., and Thomas Koenig. "Size, Concentration, and Corporate Networks: Determinants of Business Collective Action." *Social Science Quarterly*, 72, 2, June 1991:299–313.

Modell, John, and Tamara K. Hareven. "Urbanization and the Malleable Household: An Examination of Boarding and Lodging in American Families." In *Family and Kin in Urban Communities, 1700–1930*. New York: New Viewpoints, 1977:167–186.

Mohawk, John C. "Indian Economic Development: An Evolving Concept of Sovereignty." *Buffalo Law Review*, 39, 2, Spring 1991:495–503.

Molotch, Harvey L. "The City as a Growth Machine." *American Journal of Sociology*, 82, 2, September 1976:309–333.

Monaghan, Peter. "Facing Jail, a Sociologist Raises Questions About a Scholar's Right to Protect Sources." *Chronicle of Higher Education*, April 7, 1992:A10.

Money, John, and Anke A. Ehrhardt. *Man and Woman, Boy and Girl*. Baltimore: Johns Hopkins University Press, 1972.

Montagu, M. F. Ashley. *The Concept of Race*. New York: Free Press, 1964.

Montagu, M. F. Ashley. *Introduction to Physical Anthropology*, 3rd ed. Springfield, Ill.: Thomas, 1960.

Montero, Darrel M. *Japanese Americans: Changing Patterns of Ethnic Affiliation over Three Generations*. Boulder, Colo.: Westview, 1980.

Montero, Darrel M. "Japanese Americans: Changing Patterns of Assimilation over Three Generations." *American Sociological Review*, 46, December 1981:829–839.

Moore, Elizabeth, and Michael Mills. "The Neglected Victims and Unexamined Costs of White-Collar Crime." *Crime and Delinquency*, 36, 3, July 1990:408–418.

Moore, Stephen D., and Ron Winslow. "Health-Care Systems in 12 Countries Near Crisis, Drug Maker Study Says." *Wall Street Journal*, September 15, 1993:B6.

Moore, Wilbert E. "Occupational Socialization." In *Handbook on Socialization: Theory and Research*, David A. Goslin, ed. Chicago: Rand McNally, 1968:861–883.

Morgan, Lewis Henry. *Ancient Society*. 1877.

Morgan, M. "Television and Adolescents' Sex-Role Stereotypes: A Longitudinal Study." *Journal of Personality and Social Psychology*, 43, 1982:947–955.

Morgan, M. "Television, Sex-Role Attitudes, and Sex-Role Behavior." *Journal of Early Adolescence*, 7, 3, 1987:269–282.

Morganthau, Tom. "Dr. Kevorkian's Death Wish." *Newsweek*, March 8, 1993:46–48.

Morris, Aldon. "Black Southern Student Sit-In Movement: An Analysis of Internal Organization." In *Collective Behavior and Social Movements*, Russell L. Curtis, Jr., and Benigno E. Aguirre, eds. Boston: Allyn and Bacon, 1993:361–380.

Morris, J. R. "Racial Attitudes of Undergraduates in Greek Housing." *College Student Journal*, 25, 1, March 1991:501–505.

Mortimer, Jeylan T., and Jon Lorence. "Satisfaction and Involvement: Disentangling a Deceptively Simple Relationship." *Social Psychology Quarterly*, 52, 1989:249–265.

Mosca, Gaetano. *The Ruling Class*. New York: McGraw-Hill, 1939. First published in 1896.

Mosher, Steven W. "Why Are Baby Girls Being Killed in China?" *Wall Street Journal*, July 25, 1983:9.

Mosher, Steven W. *A Mother's Ordeal: One Woman's Fight Against China's One-Child Policy*. New York: Harcourt, Brace, 1993.

Mount, Ferdinand. *The Subversive Family: An Alternative History of Love and Marriage*. New York: Free Press, 1992.

Moyers, Bill. "Propaganda." In the series "A Walk Through the 20th Century." 1989. (video)

Moynihan, Daniel Patrick. *The Negro Family: The Case for National Action*. Washington, D.C.: U.S. Department of Labor, U.S. Government Printing Office, 1965.

Moynihan, Daniel Patrick. "Social Justice in the Next Century." *America*, September 14, 1991:132–137.

Muir, Donal E. "'White' Fraternity and Sorority Attitudes Toward 'Blacks' on a Deep-South Campus." *Sociological Spectrum*, 11, 1, January–March, 1991:93–103.

Murdock, George Peter. "Comparative Data on the Division of Labor by Sex." *Social Forces*, 15, 4, May 1937:551–553.

Murdock, George Peter. "The Common Denominator of Cultures." In *The Science of Man and the World Crisis*, Ralph Linton, ed. New York: Columbia University Press, 1945.

Murdock, George Peter. *Social Structure*. New York: Macmillan, 1949.

Murray, Charles. "The Coming White Underclass." *Wall Street Journal*, October 29, 1993:A16.

Murray, Charles, and R. J. Hernstein. "What's Really Behind the SAT-score Decline?" *Public Interest*, 106, Winter 1992:32–56.

Murray, G. W. *Sons of Ishmael*. London: Routledge, 1935.

Mydans, Seth. "Poll Finds Tide of Immigration Brings Hostility." *New York Times*, June 27, 1993:A1, A16.

Myerts, Henry F. "Look for Jobless Rate to Stay High in '90s." *Wall Street Journal*, March 2, 1992:1.

Myrdal, Gunnar. *Challenge to Affluence*. New York: Pantheon Books, 1962.

Nachman, Sharon. "Elder Abuse and Neglect Substantiations: What They Tell Us About the Problem." *Journal of Elder Abuse and Neglect*, 3, 3, 1991:19–43.

Naj Amal Kumar. "Some Manufacturers Drop Efforts to Adopt Japanese Techniques." *Wall Street Journal*, May 7, 1993:A1, A12.

Nakao, Keiko, and Judith Treas. "Occupational Prestige in the United States Revisited: Twenty-Five Years of Stability and Change." Paper presented at the annual meetings of the American Sociological Association, 1990. (As referenced in Kerbo, Harold R. *Social Stratification and Inequality: Class Conflict in Historical and Comparative Perspective*. 2nd ed. New York: McGraw-Hill, 1991:181.)

Nasar, Sylvia. "Fed Gives New Evidence of 80's Gains by Richest." *New York Times*, April 21, 1992a.

Nasar, Sylvia. "Why International Statistical Comparisons Don't Work." *New York Times*, March 8, 1992b.

Nash, Gary B. *Red, White, and Black*. Englewood Cliffs, N.J.: Prentice Hall, 1974.

Nash, Nathaniel C. "Bolivia's Rain Forest Falls to Relentless Exploiters." *New York Times*, June 21, 1993:A1, A8.

National Center for Education Statistics. *Digest of Education Statistics*. Washington, D.C.: U.S. Government Printing Office, 1989.

National Center for Education Statistics. *Digest of Education Statistics*. Washington, D.C.: U.S. Government Printing Office, 1991.

National Safety Council. *Accident Facts*. Itasca, Ill.: 1993.

Naumann, Bernd. *Auschwitz: A Report on the Proceedings Against Robert Karl, Ludwig Mulka and Others Before the Court at Frankfurt*. New York: Praeger, 1966. As cited in Katz 1993:88.

Nauta, André. "That They All May Be One: Can Denominationalism Die?" Paper presented at the annual meetings of the American Sociological Association, 1993.

Neikirk, William, and Glen Elsasser. "Ruling Weakens Abortion Right." *Chicago Tribune*, June 30, 1992:1, 8.

Nelson, Ruth K. "Letter to the Editor." *Wall Street Journal*, November 2, 1989:A23.

Neugarten, Bernice L. "Grow Old with Me. The Best Is Yet to Be." *Psychology Today*, 5, December 1971:45–48, 79, 81.

Neugarten, Bernice. "Age Groups in American Society and the Rise of the Young-Old." *Annals of the American Academy of Political and Social Science*, September 1974:736–745.

Neugarten, Bernice L. "Middle Age and Aging." In *Growing Old in America*, Beth B. Hess, ed. New Brunswick, N.J.: Transaction, 1976:180–197.

Neugarten, Bernice L. "Personality and Aging." In *Handbook of the Psychology of Aging*, James E. Birren and K. Warren Schaie, eds. New York: Van Nostrand Reinhold. 1977:626–649.

"The New Alchemy: How Science Is Molding Molecules into Miracle Materials." *Business Weekly*, July 29, 1991:48–55.

Newdorf, David. "Bailout Agencies Like to Do It in Secret." *Washington Journalism Review*, 13, 4, May 1991:15–16.

"New Government in Sweden Unveils Plans for Sale of State-Run Industries." *Wall Street Journal*, November 12, 1991:A13.

Newman, Barry. "Amid Soviet Disarray, Some Farmers Refuse to Ship Food to Cities." *Wall Street Journal*, November 12, 1991:A1, A10.

Niebuhr, H. Richard. *The Social Sources of Denominationalism*. New York: Holt, 1929.

Niebuhr, R. Gustav. "Catholic Church Faces Crisis as Priests Quit and Recruiting Fails." *Wall Street Journal*, November 13, 1990:A1, A13.

Noah, Timothy. "Sierra Club Takes an Edifying Tour of Black America." *Wall Street Journal*, June 24, 1993:A1, A6.

Noah, Timothy. "White House Forms Panel to Investigate Cold War Radiation Tests on Humans." *Wall Street Journal*, January 4, 1994:A12.

Nolin, Mary Jo, and Karen Kay Petersen. "Gender Differences in Parent–Child Communication About Sexuality: An Exploratory Study." *Journal of Adolescent Research*, 7, 1, January 1992:59–79.

Nussbaum, Bruce, Ann Therese Palmer, Alice Z. Cuneo, and Barbara Carlson. "Downward Mobility." *Business Week*, March 23, 1992:56–60, 62–63.

Oberschall, Anthony. *Social Conflict and Social Movements*. Englewood Cliffs, N.J.: Prentice Hall, 1973.

O'Connel, Martin. "Where's Papa? Father's Role in Child Care." Population Trends and Public Policy no. 20. Washington, D.C.: Reference Bureau, September 1993.

"Of Channel Jockeys and Tyrants." *Wall Street Journal*, August 3, 1993:A14.

Offen, Karen. "Feminism and Sexual Difference in Historical Perspective." In *Theoretical Perspectives on Sexual Difference*, Deborah L. Rhode, ed. New Haven, Conn.: Yale University Press, 1990:13–20.

Ogburn, William F. *On Culture and Social Change: Selected Papers*, Otis Dudley Duncan, ed. Chicago: University of Chicago Press, 1964.

Ogburn, William F. "The Family and Its Functions." In *Recent Social Trends in the United States, Report of the President's Research Committee on Social Trends*. New York: McGraw-Hill, 1933:661–708.

Ogburn, William F. *Social Change, with Respect to Culture and Original Nature*. New York: Viking Press, 1938. First published in 1922.

Ogburn, William F. "The Hypothesis of Cultural Lag." In *Theories of Society: Foundations of Modern Sociological Theory*, Vol. 2, Talcott Parsons, Edward Shils, Kaspar D. Naegele, and Jesse R. Pitts, eds. New York: Free Press, 1961:1270–1273.

O'Hare, William P., and Judy C. Felt. "Asian Americans: America's Fastest Growing Minority Group." Washington, D.C.: Population Reference Bureau, February 1991.

Okie, Susan. "Developing World's Role in Global Warming Grows: Population Rise, Technology Spread Cited." In *Ourselves and Others: The Washington Post Sociology Companion*, Washington Post Writers Group, eds. Boston: Allyn and Bacon, 1992:288–289.

Oliver, Pamela E., and Gerald Marwell. "Mobilizing Technologies for Collective Action." In *Frontiers in Social Movement Theory*, Aldon D. Morris and Carol McClurg Mueller, eds. New Haven, Conn.: Yale University Press, 1992:251–272.

Olmsted, Michael S., and A. Paul Hare. *The Small Group*, 2nd ed. New York: Random House, 1978.

Olneck, Michael R., and David B. Bills. "What Makes Sammy Run? An Empirical Assessment of the Bowles-Gintis Correspondence Theory." *American Journal of Education*, 89, 1980:27–61.

Olsen, Marvin E. "The Affluent Prosper While Everyone Else Struggles." *Sociological Focus*, 23, 2, May 1990:73–87.

Olson, Mancur. *The Logic of Collective Action*. Cambridge, Mass.: Harvard University Press, 1965.

O'Malley, Jeff. "Sex Tourism and Women's Status in Thailand." *Society and Leisure*, 11, 1, Spring 1988:99–114.

Ono, Yumiko. "By Dint of Promotion Japanese Entrepreneur Ignites a Soccer Frenzy." *Wall Street Journal*, September 17, 1993:A1, A6.

Ono, Yumiko, and Jacob M. Schlesinger. "With Careful Planning, Japan Sets Out to Be 'Life Style Superpower.'" *Wall Street Journal*, October 10, 1992:A1, A11.

O'Reilly, Jane. "In Massachusetts: 'Divorced Kids'" *Time*, June 11, 1979, pp. 6–7.

Ortega, Suzanne T., and Jay Corzine. "Socioeconomic Status and Mental Disorders." *Research in Community and Mental Health*, 6, 1990:149–182.

Orum, Anthony M. "Political Sociology." In *Handbook of Sociology*, Neil J. Smelser, ed. Newbury Park, Calif.: Sage, 1988:393–423.

Orwell, George. *1984*. New York: Harcourt Brace, 1949.

Otten, Alan L. "People Patterns." *Wall Street Journal*, January 18, 1994:B1.

Otten, Alan L. "People Patterns." *Wall Street Journal*, September 23, 1994:B1.

Ouchi, William. *Theory Z: How American Business Can Meet the Japanese Challenge*. Reading, Mass.: Addison-Wesley, 1981.

Ouchi, William. "Decision-Making in Japanese Organizations." In *Down to Earth Sociology*, 7th ed., James M. Henslin, ed. New York: Free Press, 1993:503–507.

Pagelow, Mildred Daley. "Adult Victims of Domestic Violence: Battered Women." *Journal of Interpersonal Violence*, 7, 1, March 1992:87–120.

Palen, John J. *The Urban World*, 3rd ed., New York: McGraw-Hill, 1987.

Palmore, Erdman. "What the USA Can Learn from Japan About Aging." *Gerontologist*, 15, February 1975:64–67.

Palmore, Erdman. *The Honorable Elders Revisited*. Durham, N.C.: Duke University Press, 1985.

Parfit, Michael, "Earth First!ers Wield a Mean Monkey Wrench." *Smithsonian*, 21, 1, April 1990:184–204.

Park, Robert Ezra. "Human Ecology." *American Journal of Sociology*, 42, 1, July 1936:1–15.

Park, Robert E., and Ernest W. Burgess. *Human Ecology*. Chicago: University of Chicago Press, 1921a.

Park, Robert E., and Ernest W. Burgess. *Introduction to the Science of Sociology*. Chicago: University of Chicago Press, 1921b. (As quoted in McPhail 1991:6)

Parkinson, C. Northcote. *Parkinson's Law and Other Studies in Administration*. New York: Ballantine Books, 1957.

Parsons, Talcott. "An Analytic Approach to the Theory of Social Stratification." *American Journal of Sociology*, 45, 1940:841–862.

Parsons, Talcott. "The Sick Role and the Role of the Physician Reconsidered." *Milbank Memorial Fund Quarterly/Health and Society*, 53, 3, Summer 1975:257–278.

Parsons, Talcott. "Illness and the Role of the Physician: A Sociological Perspective." In *Personality in Nature, Society, and Culture*, 2nd ed., Clyde Kluckhohn and Henry A. Murray, eds. New York: Knopf, 1953:609–617.

Parsons, Talcott. "The Professions and Social Structure." In *Essays in Sociological Theory*, rev. ed., Talcott Parsons, ed. New York: Free Press, 1954:34–49.

Parsons, Talcott. *The Social System*. New York: Free Press, 1951.

Pasztor, Andy. "U.S., Grumman Reach Accord in Pentagon Case." *Wall Street Journal*, November 23, 1993:A3.

Patterson, Gregory A. "Black Middle Class Debates Merits of Cities and Suburbs." *Wall Street Journal*, August 6, 1991:B1, B8.

Paul, Ron. "Congressman Ron Paul." Newsletter issued April 1994.

Pearl, Daniel. "AIDS Spreads More Rapidly Among Women." *Wall Street Journal*, November 30, 1990:B1, B2.

Pearlin, L. I., and Melvin L. Kohn. "Social Class, Occupation, and Parental Values: A Cross-National Study." *American Sociological Review*, 31, 1966:466–479.

Pebley, Anne R., and David E. Bloom. "Childless Americans." *American Demographics*, 4, January 1982:18–21.

Pennar, Karen, and Christopher Farrell. "Notes from the Underground Economy." *Business Week*, February 15, 1993:98–101.

Pepinsky, Harold E. "A Sociologist on Police Patrol." In *Fieldwork Experience: Qualitative Approaches to Social Research*, William B. Shaffir, Robert A. Stebbins, and Allan Turowetz, eds. New York: St. Martin's, 1980:223–234.

Pereira, Joseph. "Toys 'R' Us Decides to Pull Night Trap from Store Shelves." *Wall Street Journal*, December 17, 1993:A9A.

Perry, James M. "Virginia's Wilder to Base Run for White House on Blend of Fiscal Conservatism and Compassion." *Wall Street Journal*, December 19, 1990:A18.

Persell, Caroline Hodges, and Peter W. Cookson, Jr. "Where the Power Starts." *Signature*, August 1986:51–57.

Persell, Caroline Hodges, Sophia Catsambis, and Peter W. Cookson, Jr. "Family Background, School Type, and College Attendance: A Conjoint System of Cultural Capital Transmission." *Journal of Research on Adolescence*, 2, 1, 1992:1–23.

Peter, Laurence J., and Raymond Hull. *The Peter Principle: Why Things Always Go Wrong*. New York: Morrow, 1969.

Peters, Gary L., and Robert P. Larkin. *Population Geography: Problems, Concepts, and Prospects*. Dubuque, Iowa: Kendall/Hunt, 1989.

Peterson, James L., and Nicholas Zill. "Marital Disruption, Parent–Child Relationships, and Behavior Problems in Children." *Journal of Marriage and the Family*, 48, 1986:295–307.

Pettigrew, Thomas. "How the People Really Feel." *The Center Magazine*, 9, January–February 1976:35.

Phillips, John L., Jr. *The Origins of Intellect: Piaget's Theory*. San Francisco: Freeman, 1969.

Piaget, Jean. *The Construction of Reality in the Child*. New York: Basic Books, 1954.

Piaget, Jean. *The Psychology of Intelligence*. London: Routledge & Kegan Paul, 1950.

Pillard, R. C., and J. D. Weinrich. "Evidence of Familial Nature of Male Homosexuality." *Archives of Sexual Behavior*, 43, 1986:808–812.

Pillemer, Karl. "Dangers of Dependency: New Findings on Domestic Violence Against the Elderly." *Social Problems*, 33, December 1985:146–158.

Pillemer, Karl, and Beth Hudson. "A Model Abuse Prevention Program for Nursing Assistants." *Gerontologist*, 33, 1, 1993:128–131.

Pillemer, Karl, and J. Jill Suitor. "Violence and Violent Feelings: What Causes Them Among Family Caregivers?" *Journal of Gerontology*, 47, 4, 1992:165–172.

Pillemer, Karl, and Rosalie S. Wolf. *Elder Abuse: Conflict in the Family*. Dover, Mass.: Auburn House, 1987.

Pilling, D., and M. Kellmer Pringle. *Controversial Issues in Child Development*. London: Paul Elek, 1978.

Pines, Maya. "The Civilizing of Genie." *Psychology Today*, 15, September 1981:28–34.

Piotrow, Phylis Tilson. *World Population Crisis: The United States' Response*. New York: Praeger, 1973.

Piturro, Marlene. "Managing Diversity." *Executive Female*, May–June 1991:45–46, 48.

Piven, Frances Fox, and Richard A. Cloward. *Why Americans Don't Vote*. New York: Pantheon Books, 1988.

Platt, Tony. "'Street' Crime—A View from the Left." *Crime and Social Justice: Issues in Criminology*, 9, 1978:26–34.

Pleck, Elizabeth. "The Unfulfilled Promise: Women and Academe." *Sociological Forum*, 5, 3, September 1990:517–524.

Ploski, Harry A., and Warren Marr, II, eds. *The Afro Americans*. New York: Bellwether, 1976.

Polenberg, Richard. *One Nation Divisible: Class, Race, and Ethnicity in the United States Since 1938*. New York: Penguin, 1980.

Pollak, Lauren Harte, and Peggy A. Thoits. "Processes in Emotional Socialization." *Social Psychological Quarterly*, 52, 1, 1989:22–34.

Polsby, Nelson W. "Three Problems in the Analysis of Community Power." *American Sociological Review*, 24, 6, December 1959:796–803.

Polsky, Ned. *Hustlers, Beats, and Others*. Chicago: Aldine, 1967.

Polumbaum, Judy. "China: Confucian Tradition Meets the Market Economy." *Ms.*, September–October 1992:12–13.

Pope, Liston. *Millhands and Preachers: A Study of Gastonia*. New Haven, Conn.: Yale University Press, 1942.

Population Reference Bureau. *1988 World Population Data Sheet*. Washington, D.C.: Population Reference Bureau, 1988.

Portes, Alejandro, and Ruben G. Rumbaut. *Immigrant America*. Berkeley: University of California Press, 1990.

Powell, Brian, and Lala Carr Steelman. "Variations in State SAT Performance: Meaningful or Misleading?" *Harvard Educational Review*, 54, 4, November 1984:389–412.

Presley, Cheryl A., Philip W. Meilman, and Rob Lyerla. *Alcohol and Drugs on American College Campuses*. Carbondale, Ill.: Southern Illinois University, 1993.

Press, Lary. "The Internet and Interactive Television." *Personal Computing*, 36, 12, December 1993:19–23, 140.

Pressley, Sue Anne. "The Curious Continue Waco Siege." *Washington Post*, August 28, 1993:A1, A12.

Preston, Howard L. *Automobile Age Atlanta: The Making of a Southern Metropolis, 1900–1935*. Athens: University of Georgia Press, 1979.

Price, Daniel O., ed. *The 99th Hour*. Chapel Hill: University of North Carolina Press, 1967.

Priest, Simon, and Timothy Dixon. "Research Note: Towards a New Theory of Outdoor Leadership Style." *Leisure Studies*, 10, 2, May 1991:163–170.

Prud'Homme, Alex. "Getting a Grip on Power." *Time*, July 29, 1991:15–16.

Prus, Robert. "Sociologist as Hustler: The Dynamics of Acquiring Information." In *Fieldwork Experience: Qualitative Approaches to Social Research*, William B. Shaffir, Robert A. Stebbins, and Allan Turowetz, eds. New York: St. Martin's, 1980:132–145.

Public Information Bureau. "Information given by telephone." New York, March 24, 1994.

Rathus, Spencer, and Jeffrey Nevid. *Human Sexuality in a World of Diversity*. Boston: Allyn and Bacon, 1993.

Ray, J. J. "Authoritarianism Is a Dodo: Comment on Scheepers, Felling and Peters." *European Sociological Review*, 7, 1, May 1991:73–75.

Raymond, Chris. "New Studies by Anthropologists Indicate Amish Communities Are Much More Dynamic and Diverse Than Many Believed." *Chronicle of Higher Education*, December 19, 1990:A1, A9.

Read, Piers Paul. *Alive. The Story of the Andes Survivors*. Philadelphia: Lippincott, 1974.

Reckless, Walter C. *The Crime Problem*, 5th ed. New York: Appleton, 1973.

Reed, Susan, and Lorenzo Benet. "Ecowarrior Dave Foreman Will Do Whatever It Takes in His Fight to Save Mother Earth." *People Weekly*, 33, 15, April 16, 1990:113–116.

Reich, Michael. "The Economics of Racism." In *The Capitalist System*, Richard C. Edwards, Michael Reich, and Thomas E. Weiskopf, eds. Englewood Cliffs, N.J.: Prentice Hall, 1972:313–321.

Reiman, Jeffrey H. "A Crime by Any Other Name." In *Taking Sides: Clashing Views on Controversial Social Issues*, 7th ed., Kurt Finsterbusch and George McKenna, eds. Guilford, Conn.: Dushkin, 1992:288–295.

Reinhold, Robert. "A Welcome for Immigrants Is Turning into Resentment." *New York Times*, August 25, 1993:A1, A12.

Renteln, Alison Dundes. "Sex Selection and Reproductive Freedom." *Women's Studies International Forum*, 15, 3, 1992:405–426.

Renzetti, Claire M., and Daniel J. Curran. *Women, Men, and Society*, 2nd ed. Boston: Allyn and Bacon, 1992.

Resnick, Melvyn C. "Beyond the Ethnic Community: Spanish Language Roles and Maintenance in Miami." *International Journal of the Sociology of Language*, 69, 1988:89–104.

Rhode, Deborah L., ed. *Theoretical Perspectives on Sexual Difference*. New Haven, Conn.: Yale University Press, 1990.

Rhyne, Edwin H. "Making Environmental Sociology Sociological." *Sociological Spectrum*, 7, 4, 1987:335–346.

Rich, Spencer. "Number of Elected Hispanic Officials Doubled in a Decade, Study Shows." *Washington Post*, September 19, 1986:A6.

Rich, Vera. "Russia: Pollution Takes Its Toll." *Lancet*, 339, February 1, 1992:295–296.

Richardson, Lewis F. *Statistics of Deadly Quarrels*. Chicago: Quadrangle, 1960.

Ricks, Thomas E. "Pentagon Considers Selling Overseas a Large Part of High-Tech Weaponry." *Wall Street Journal*, February 14, 1994:A16.

Rieder, Jonathan. "Crown of Thorns." *New Republic*, October 14, 1991:26–31.

Riesman, David. *The Lonely Crowd*. New Haven, Conn.: Yale University Press, 1950.

Riesman, David. "The Suburban Dislocation." In *Urban Man and Society: A Reader in Urban Ecology*, Albert N. Cousins and Hans Nagpaul, eds. New York: Knopf, 1970:172–184.

Riessman, Catherine Kohler. "Women and Medicalization: A New Perspective." In *Dominant Issues in Medical Sociology*, 3rd ed., Howard D. Schwartz, ed. New York: McGraw-Hill, 1994:190–211.

Rigdon, Joan E., and Alecia Swasy. "Distractions of Modern Life at Key Ages Are Cited for Drop in Student Literacy." *Wall Street Journal*, October 1, 1990:B1, B3.

Riger, Stephanie, Margaret T. Gordon, and Robert LeBailly. "Women's Fear of Crime." *Victimology*, 3, 1978:274–284.

Rist, Ray C. "Student Social Class and Teacher Expectations: The Self-Fulfilling Prophecy in Ghetto Education." *Harvard Educational Review*, 40, 3, August 1970:411–451.

Ritzer, George. *Sociological Theory*, 3rd ed. New York: McGraw-Hill, 1992.

Ritzer, George. *The McDonaldization of Society: An Investigation into the Changing Character of Contemporary Life*. Thousand Oaks, Calif.: Pine Forge Press, 1993.

Robert Wood Johnson Foundation. *Special Report: Updated Report on Access to Health Care for the American People*. Princeton, N.J.: Robert Wood Johnson Foundation, 1983.

Robertson, Ian. "Social Stratification." In *The Study of Anthropology*, David E. Hunter and Phillip Whitten, eds. New York: Harper & Row, 1976.

Robertson, Ian. *Sociology*, 3rd ed. New York: Worth, 1987.

Robertson, Roland. *Globalization: Social Theory and Global Culture*. London: Sage, 1992.

Robinson, John P. "I Love My TV." *American Demographics*, 12, 9, September 1990:24–27.

Rodash, Mary Flannery. "The College of Midwifery: A Sociological Study of the Decline of a Profession." Unpublished doctoral dissertation, Southern Illinois University at Carbondale, 1982.

Rodriguez, Richard. "The Education of Richard Rodriquez." *Saturday Review*, February 8, 1975:147–149.

Rodriguez, Richard. *Hunger of Memory: The Education of Richard Rodriguez*. Boston: Godine, 1982.

Rodriguez, Richard. *Mexico's American Children*. Harper's Magazine, 273, July 1986:12–14.

Rodriguez, Richard. "The Fear of Losing a Culture." *Time*, 132, July 11, 1988:84.

Rodriguez, Richard. "The Late Victorians: San Francisco, AIDS, and the Homosexual Stereotype." *Harper's Magazine*, October 1990:57–66.

Rodriguez, Richard. "Mixed Blood." *Harper's Magazine*, 283, November 1991:47–56.

Rodríguez, Victor M. "Los Angeles, U.S.A. 1992: 'A House Divided Against Itself . . .'" *SSSP Newsletter*, Spring 1994:5–12.

Roethlisberger, Fritz J., and William J. Dickson. *Management and the Worker*. Cambridge, Mass.: Harvard University Press, 1939.

Rogers, Joseph W. *Why Are You Not a Criminal?* Englewood Cliffs, N.J.: Prentice Hall, 1977.

Rohen, Thomas P. *Japan's High Schools*. Berkeley: University of California Press, 1983.

Rohner, Sharon W. "Fetal Alcohol Effects Linked to Moderate Drinking Levels." In *Formation and Feature Service of the National*

Clearinghouse for Alcohol Information of the National Institute of Alcohol Abuse and Alcoholism, 72, June 1980:4.

Romero, Mary. "Day Work in the Suburbs: The Experience of Chicana Private Housekeepers." In *The Worth of Women's Work: A Qualitative Synthesis,* Anne Statham, Eleanor M. Miller, and Hans O. Mauksch, eds. Albany, N.Y.: State University of New York Press, 1988.

Rootes, Chris A. "The Future of the 'New Politics': A European Perspective." *Social Alternatives,* 8, 4, January 1990:7–12.

Rosaldo, Michelle Zimbalist. "Women, Culture and Society: A Theoretical Overview." In *Women, Culture, and Society,* Michelle Zimbalist Rosaldo and Louise Lamphere, eds. Stanford: Stanford University Press, 1974.

Rose, Frederick. "Los Angeles Tallies Losses; Curfew Is Lifted." *Wall Street Journal,* May 5, 1992:A3, A18.

Rose, Steven. "Stalking the Criminal Chromosome." *Nation 242* (20), 1986:732–736.

Rosenberg, Charles E. *The Care of Strangers: The Rise of America's Hospital System.* New York: Basic Books, 1987.

Rosenblatt, Roger. *Life Itself: Abortion in the American Mind.* New York: Random House, 1992.

Rosenthal, Robert, and Lenore Jacobson. *Pygmalion in the Classroom: Teacher Expectation and Pupils' Intellectual Development.* New York: Holt, Rinehart, and Winston, 1968.

Ross, Catherine E. "The Division of Labor at Home" *Social Forces,* 65, 1987:816–833.

Rossi, Alice S. *The Feminist Papers: From Adams to de Beauvoir.* New York: Bantam, 1974.

Rossi, Alice S. "A Biosocial Perspective on Parenting." *Daedalus,* 106, 1977:1–31.

Rossi, Alice S. "Gender and Parenthood." *American Sociological Review,* 49, 1984:1–18.

Rossi, Peter H. *Down and Out in America: The Origins of Homelessness.* Chicago: University of Chicago Press, 1989.

Rossi, Peter H. "Going Along or Getting It Right?" *Journal of Applied Sociology,* 8, 1991:77–81.

Rossi, Peter H., Gene A. Fisher, and Georgianna Willis. *The Condition of the Homeless of Chicago.* Amherst: University of Massachusetts, September 1986.

Rossi, Peter H., James D. Wright, Gene A. Fisher, and Georgianna Willis. "The Urban Homeless: Estimating Composition and Size." *Science,* 235, March 13, 1987:1136–1140.

Rothenberg, Stuart. "Abortion's New Battlefield Is Congress." *Wall Street Journal,* April 27, 1992:A16.

Rothman, Barbara Katz. "Midwives in Transition: The Structure of a Clinical Revolution." In *Dominant Issues in Medical Sociology,* 3rd ed. Howard D. Schwartz, ed. New York: McGraw-Hill, 1994:104–112.

Rothschild, Joyce, and J. Allen Whitt. *The Cooperative Workplace: Potentials and Dilemmas of Organizational Democracy and Participation.* Cambridge, England: Cambridge University Press, 1986.

Rouse, Linda P., and Jeffery R. Hanson. "American Indian Stereotyping, Resource Competition, and Status-based Prejudice." *American Indian Cultural and Research Journal,* 15, 3, 1991:1–17.

Rubenstein, Carin. "Is There Sex After Baby?" In *Marriage and Family in a Changing Society,* 4th ed., James M. Henslin, ed. New York: Free Press, 1992:235–242.

Rubenstein, Richard L. "The Modernization of Slavery." In *Structured Social Inequality: A Reader in Comparative Social Stratification,* Celia S. Heller, ed. New York: Macmillan, 1987:74–81.

Rubin, Lillian Breslow. *Worlds of Pain: Life in the Working-Class Family.* New York: Basic Books, 1976.

Rubin, Lillian Breslow. "The Empty Nest." In *Marriage and Family in a Changing Society,* 4th ed., James M. Henslin, ed. New York: Free Press, 1992a:261–270.

Rubin, Lillian Breslow. "Worlds of Pain." In *Marriage and Family in a Changing Society,* 4th ed., James M. Henslin, ed. New York: Free Press, 1992b:44–50.

Rubinson, Richard. "Class Formation, Politics, and Institutions: Schooling in the United States." *American Journal of Sociology,* 92, 3, November 1986:519–548.

Ruesch, Hans. *Top of the World.* New York: Permabooks, 1959.

Ruffenbach, Glenn. "Nursing-Home Care as a Work Benefit." *Wall Street Journal,* June 30, 1988:23.

Ruffins, Paul. "How to Survive Campus Bigotry." *Washington Post,* June 16, 1991:B2.

Ruggles, Patricia. "Short and Long Term Poverty in the United States: Measuring the American 'Underclass.'" Washington, D.C.: Urban Institute, June 1989.

Ruggles, Patricia. *Drawing the Line: Alternative Poverty Measures and Their Implication for Public Policy.* Washington, D.C.: Urban Institute, 1990.

Rummel, R. J. *Lethal Politics: Soviet Genocide and Mass Murder Since 1917.* New Brunswick, N.J.: Transaction, 1990.

Rushing, Beth, Christian Ritter, and Russell P. D. Burton. "Race Differences in the Effects of Multiple Roles on Health: Longitudinal Evidence from a National Sample of Older Men." *Journal of Health and Social Behavior,* 33, June 1992:126–139.

Russell, Diana E. H. "Preliminary Report on Some Findings Relating to the Trauma and Long-Term Effects of Intrafamily Childhood Sexual Abuse." Unpublished paper, no date.

Russell, Diana E. H. *The Politics of Rape: The Victim's Perspective.* New York: Scarborough, 1979.

Russell, Diana E. H. *Rape in Marriage* New York: Macmillan, 1982.

Russell, Diana E. H. *Sexual Exploitation: Rape, Child Sexual Abuse, and Workplace Harassment.* Beverly Hills, Calif.: Sage, 1984.

Russell, Diana E. H. *The Secret Trauma: Incest in the Lives of Girls and Women.* New York: Basic Books, 1986.

Russell, Dick. "The Monkeywrenchers." *Amicus Journal,* Fall 1987:28–42.

Ruth, John L. "American Anabaptists: Who They Are." *Christianity Today,* October 22, 1990:25–29.

Rutter, Michael, Barbara Maughan, Peter Mortimore, Janet Ouston, and Alan Smith. *Fifteen Thousand Hours.* Cambridge, Mass.: Harvard University Press, 1979.

Rybczynski, Withold. "'Edge Cities': The People's Answer to Planners." *New York Times,* November 17, 1991:36.

Sahlins, Marshall D. *Stone Age Economics.* Chicago: Aldine, 1972.

Sahlins, Marshall D., and Elman R. Service. *Evolution and Culture.* Ann Arbor: University of Michigan Press, 1960.

Sakharov, Andrei D. *Sakharov Speaks,* Harrison E. Salisbury, ed. New York: Vintage, 1974.

Salholz, Eloise. "The Push for Power." *Newsweek,* April 9, 1990:19–20.

Samuelson, Paul A., and William D. Nordhaus. *Economics*, 13th ed. New York: McGraw-Hill, 1989.

Samuelson, Robert J. "The Elderly Aren't Needy." *Newsweek*, March 21, 1988:68.

Sampson, Catherine. "Corrupt Care." *World Press Review, 39*, 5, May 1992:46.

Sarnoff, Irving, and Suzanne Sarnoff. "Love-Centered Marriage." In *Marriage and Family in a Changing Society*, 4th ed., James M. Henslin, ed. New York: Free Press, 1992:158–164.

Sawhill, Isabel V. "Poverty in the U.S.: Why Is It So Persistent?" *Journal of Economic Literature, 26*, 3, September 1988:1073–1119.

Sawin, Douglas B. "Aggressive Behavior Among Children in Small Playground Settings with Violent Television." *Advances in Learning and Behavioral Disabilities, 6*, 1990:157–177.

Sayres, William. "What Is a Family Anyway?" In *Marriage and Family in a Changing Society*, 4th ed., James M. Henslin, ed. New York: Free Press, 1992:23–30.

Scanzoni, John. *Opportunity and the Family*. New York: Free Press, 1970.

Scarce, Rik. *Eco-Warriors: Understanding the Radical Environmental Movement*. Chicago: Noble Press, 1990.

Scarce, Rik. "Rik Scarce Responds: A Clear-cut Case of Academic Freedom at Risk." *Daily News* (Moscow-Pullman), June 12–13, 1993a:1B.

Scarce, Rik. "Turnabout: Jailed for No Crime at All." *Morning Tribune* (Lewiston), June 15, 1993b.

Schachter, Stanley, and Jerome Singer. "Cognitive, Social, and Physiological Determinants of Emotional State." *Psychological Review, 69*, 1962:379–399.

Schaeffer, Richard T. *Sociology*, 3rd ed. New York: McGraw-Hill, 1989.

Schaller, Mark. "Social Categorization and the Formation of Group Stereotypes: Further Evidence for Biased Information Processing in the Perception of Group-Behavior Correlations." *European Journal of Social Psychology, 21*, 1, January–February 1991:25–35.

Schick, Frank L., and Renee Schick. *Statistical Handbook on U.S. Hispanics*. New York: Oryx Press, 1991.

Schlesinger, Jacob M. "For What Ails Japan, Some Think the Cure Is a Good Hot Slogan." *Wall Street Journal*, January 31, 1994:A1, A7.

Schlesinger, Jacob M., and Jathon Sapsford. "Japan, Shaken by Plunging Stocks, Mulls Further Economic Measures." *Wall Street Journal*, December 1, 1993:A14.

Schlesinger, Jacob M., Michael Williams, and Craig Forman. "Japan Inc., Wracked by Recession, Takes Stock of Its Methods." *Wall Street Journal*, September 29, 1993:A1, A4.

Schlossberg, Nancy. *Overwhelmed: Coping with Life's Ups and Downs*. Boston: Lexington Books, 1990.

Schor, Juliet B. "Americans Work Too Hard." *New York Times*, July 25, 1991:A21.

Schottland, Charles I. *The Social Security Plan in the U.S.* New York: Appleton, 1963.

Schrieke, Bertram J. *Alien Americans*. New York: Viking, 1936.

Schur, Edwin M. *Labeling Women Deviant: Gender, Stigma, and Social Control*. New York: Random House, 1984.

Schwartz, Felice N. "Management Women and the New Facts of Life." *Harvard Business Review, 89*, 1, January–February 1989:65–76.

Schwartz, Howard D., ed. *Dominant Issues in Medical Sociology*, 3rd ed. New York: McGraw-Hill, 1994:373–375.

Schwartz, Mildred A. *A Sociological Perspective on Politics*. Englewood Cliffs, N.J.: Prentice Hall, 1990.

Schwendinger, Julia R., and Herman Schwendinger. *Rape and Inequality*. Beverly Hills, Calif.: Sage, 1983.

Scism, Leslie. "Rule No. 99b: Vendor Must Buff Every Shoe from Left to Right." *Wall Street Journal*, September 17, 1993:B1.

Scully, Diana. *Understanding Sexual Violence: A Study of Convicted Rapists*. Boston: Unwin Hyman, 1990.

Scully, Diana. "Negotiating to Do Surgery." In *Dominant Issues in Medical Sociology*, 3rd ed., Howard D. Schwartz, ed. New York: McGraw-Hill, 1994:146–152.

Scully, Diana, and Joseph Marolla. "Convicted Rapists' Vocabulary of Motive: Excuses and Justifications." *Social Problems, 31*, 5, June 1984:530–544.

Scully, Diana, and Joseph Marolla. "'Riding the Bull at Gilley's': Convicted Rapists Describe the Rewards of Rape." *Social Problems, 32*, 3, February 1985:251–263.

Seaver, W. J. "Effects of Naturally Induced Teacher Expectancies." *Journal of Personality and Social Psychology, 28*, 1973:333–342.

Seidman, Steven A. "An Investigation of Sex-Role Stereotyping in Music Videos." *Journal of Broadcasting and Electronic Media*, Spring 1992:210–216.

Sennett, Richard, and Jonathan Cobb. "Some Hidden Injuries of Class." In *Down to Earth Sociology*, 5th ed., James M. Henslin, ed. New York: Free Press, 1988:278–288.

Seubert, Virginia R. "Sociology and Value Neutrality: Limiting Sociology to the Empirical Level." *American Sociologist*, Fall–Winter 1991:210–220.

Sewell, William H., and Vimal P. Shah. "Parents' Education and Children's Educational Aspirations and Achievements." *American Sociological Review, 33*, 2, April 1968:191–209.

Shanas, Ethel. "The Family as a Social Support System in Old Age." *Gerontologist, 19*, April 1979:169–174.

Sharp, Deborah. "Miami's Language Gap Widens." *USA Today*, April 3, 1992:A3.

Sharpe, Rochelle. "Number of Women on Firms' Boards Rose 1% in Year." *Wall Street Journal*, November 10, 1993a:B5.

Sharpe, Rochelle. "Two-Thirds of Children in U.S. Read Below Their Grade Level, Study Finds." *Wall Street Journal*, September 16, 1993b:A4.

Shaw, Sue. "Wretched of the Earth." *New Statesman, 20*, March 1987:19–20.

Sheldon, William. *Varieties of Delinquent Youth: An Introduction to Constitutional Psychiatry*. New York: Harper, 1949.

Shellenbarger, Sue. "Longer Commutes Force Parents to Make Tough Choices on Where to Leave the Kids." *Wall Street Journal*, August, 18, 1993:B1, B6.

Shellenbarger, Sue. "The Aging of America Is Making 'Elder Care' a Big Workplace Issue." *Wall Street Journal*, February 16, 1994a:A1, A8.

Shellenbarger, Sue. "How Some Companies Help with Elder Care." *Wall Street Journal*, February 16, 1994b:A8.

Shepelak, Norma J. "Ideological Stratification: American Beliefs about Economic Justice." *Social Justice Research, 3*, 1, September 1989:217–231.

Sherif, Muzafer, and Carolyn Sherif. *Groups in Harmony and Tension*. New York: Harper & Row, 1953.

Sherkat, Darren E., and John Wilson. "Status, Denomination, and Socialization: Effects on Religious Switching and Apostasy." Presented at the annual meetings of the American Sociological Association, 1991.

Sherr, James. "Russia's New Threat to Neighbors." *Wall Street Journal*, December 17, 1993:A14.

Shibutani, Tamotsu. *Improvised News: A Sociological Study of Rumor*. Indianapolis, Ind.: Bobbs-Merrill, 1966.

Shibutani, Tamotsu. "On the Personification of Adversaries." In *Human Nature and Collective Behavior*, Tamotsu Shibutani, ed. Englewood Cliffs, N.J.: Prentice Hall, 1970.

Shill, Walt. "Lessons of the Japanese Mavericks." *Wall Street Journal*, November 1, 1993:A18.

Shim, Kelly H., and Marshall DeBerry. *Criminal Victimization in the United States, 1986*. Washington, D.C.: U.S. Department of Justice, Bureau of Justice Statistics, August 1988.

Shingles, Richard D. "Class, Status, and Support for Government Aid to Disadvantaged Groups." *Journal of Politics, 51*, 4, November 1989:933–962.

Shipler, David K. *Russia: Broken Idols, Solemn Dreams*. New York: Times Books, 1982.

Shirer, William L. *The Rise and Fall of the Third Reich*. Greenwich, Conn.: Fawcett, 1960.

Shively, JoEllen. "Cowboys and Indians: Perceptions of Western Films Among American Indians and Anglos." *American Sociological Review, 57*, December 1992:725–734.

Shlaes, Amity. "Germany 'Manages' Away an Asset." *Wall Street Journal*, January 23, 1992:A18.

Shreve, Herbie. Personal communication, 1991.

Shweder, Richard A. "What Do Men Want? A Reading List for the Male Identity Crisis." *New York Times Book Review*, January 9, 1994:3, 24.

Sibbison, Jim. "Death at Work." *The New Physician*, May 1979:18–21.

Signorielli, Nancy, "The Demography of the Television World." In *Proceedings from the Tenth Annual Telecommunications Policy Research Conference*, O. H. Gandy, P. Espinosa, and J. A. Ordover, eds. Norwood, N.J.: Ablex, 1983.

Signorielli, Nancy. "Television and Conceptions About Sex Roles: Maintaining Conventionality and the Status Quo." *Sex Roles, 21*, 5/6, 1989:341–360.

Signorielli, Nancy. "Children, Television, and Gender Roles: Messages and Impact." *Journal of Adolescent Heath Care, 11*, 1990:50–58.

Silberman, Charles E. *Criminal Violence, Criminal Justice*. New York: Random House, 1978.

Sills, David L. *The Volunteers*. Glencoe, Ill.: Free Press, 1957.

Sills, David L. "Voluntary Associations: Sociological Aspects." In *International Encyclopedia of the Social Sciences, 16*, David L. Sills, ed. New York: Macmillan, 1968:362–379.

Silver, Isidore. "Crime and Conventional Wisdom." *Society, 14*, March–April, 1977:9, 15–19.

Silverman, Deidre. "Sexual Harassment: The Working Women's Dilemma." *Building Feminist Theory: Essays from Quest*. New York: Longman, 1981.

Simmel, Georg, *The Sociology of Georg Simmel*, Kurt H. Wolff, ed. and trans. Glencoe, Ill.: Free Press, 1950. First published between 1902 and 1917.

Simon, David R., and D. Stanley Eitzen. *Elite Deviance*, 2nd ed. Boston: Mass.: Allyn and Bacon, 1986.

Simon, David R., and D. Stanley Eitzen. *Elite Deviance*, 4th ed. Boston: Allyn and Bacon, 1993.

Simon, Julian L. *The Ultimate Resource*. Princeton, N.J.: Princeton University Press, 1981.

Simon, Julian L. *Theory of Population and Economic Growth*. New York: Blackwell, 1986.

Simon, Julian L. "Population Growth Is Not Bad for Humanity." In *Taking Sides: Clashing Views on Controversial Social Issues*, Kurt Finsterbusch and George McKenna, eds. Guilford, Conn.: Dushkin, 1992:347–352.

Simon, Julian L. "The Nativists Are Wrong." *Wall Street Journal*, August 4, 1993:A10.

Simons, Marlise. "The Amazon's Savvy Indians." In *Down to Earth Sociology: Introductory Readings*, 8th ed. James M. Henslin, ed. New York: Free Press, 1995:463–470.

Simpson, George Eaton, and J. Milton Yinger. *Racial and Cultural Minorities: An Analysis of Prejudice and Discrimination*, 4th ed. New York: Harper & Row, 1972.

Singer, Dorothy G. "A Time to Reexamine the Role of Television in Our Lives." *American Psychologist, 38*, 7, July 1983:815–816.

Singer, Jerome L., and Dorothy G. Singer. "Psychologists Look at Television: Cognitive, Developmental, Personality, and Social Policy Implications." *American Psychologist, 38*, 1, July 1983:826–834.

Singh, Ajit. "Urbanism, Poverty, and Employment: The Large Metropolis in the Third World." Unpublished monograph, Cambridge University, 1988. As quoted in Giddens, Anthony. *Introduction to Sociology*. New York: W. W. Norton, 1991:690.

Skeels, H. M. *Adult Status of Children with Contrasting Early Life Experiences: A Follow-up Study*. Monograph of the Society for Research in Child Development, *31*, 3, 1966.

Skeels, H. M., and H. B. Dye. "A Study of the Effects of Differential Stimulation on Mentally Retarded Children." *Proceedings and Addresses of the American Association on Mental Deficiency, 44*, 1939:114–136.

Skerry, Peter, and Michael Hartman. "Latin Mass." *New Republic*, June 10, 1991:18–20.

Sklair, Leslie. *Sociology of the Global System*. Baltimore: Johns Hopkins University Press, 1991.

Small, Albion W. *General Sociology*. Chicago: University of Chicago Press, 1905. As cited in Olmsted and Hare 1978:10.

Smart, Barry. "On the Disorder of Things: Sociology, Postmodernity and the 'End of the Social.'" *Sociology, 24*, 3, August 1990:397–416.

Smith, Beverly A. "An Incest Case in an Early 20th-Century Rural Community." *Deviant Behavior, 13*, 1992:127–153.

Smith, Clark. "Oral History as 'Therapy': Combatants' Account of Vietnam War." In *Strangers at Home: Vietnam Veterans Since the War*, Charles R. Figley and Seymore Leventman, eds. New York: Praeger, 1980:9–34.

Smith, Daniel Scott, and Michael Hindus. "Premarital Pregnancy in America, 1640–1971: An Overview and Interpretation." *Journal of Interdisciplinary History, 4*, Spring 1975:537–570.

Smith, Harold. "A Colossal Cover-Up." *Christianity Today*, December 12, 1986:16–17.

Smith, Joel B., and Dennis A. Tirpak. *The Potential Effects of Global Climate Change in the United States*. Washington, D.C.: United States Environmental Protection Agency, October 1988.

Smith, Kristen F., and Vern L. Bengston. "Positive Consequences of Institutionalization: Solidarity Between Elderly Parents and

Their Middle-Aged Children." *Gerontologist, 19,* October 1979:438–447.

Smith, Lee. "The War Between the Generations." *Fortune,* July 20, 1987:78–82.

Smith-Lovin, Lynn, and Charles Brody. "Interruptions in Group Discussions: The Effects of Gender and Group Composition." *American Sociological Review, 54,* 1989:424–435.

Snider, William. "Fresno Schools, Hmong Refugees Seek Common Ground." *Education Week, 10,* 14, December 5, 1990:1, 12–13.

Snow, David A., Louis A. Zurcher, Jr., and Sheldon Ekland-Olson. "Social Networks and Social Movements: A Microstructural Approach to Differential Recruitment." In *Collective Behavior and Social Movements,* Russell L. Curtis, Jr., and Benigno E. Aguirre, eds. Boston: Allyn and Bacon, 1993:323–334.

Snow, David A., Louis A. Zurcher, and Robert Peters. "Victory Celebrations as Theater: A Dramaturgical Approach to Crowd Behavior." In *Collective Behavior and Social Movements,* Russell L. Curtis, Jr., and Benigno E. Aguirre, eds. Boston: Allyn and Bacon, 1993:194–208.

Snow, Margaret E., Carol Nagy Jacklin, and Eleanor E. Maccoby. "Birth-Order Differences in Peer Sociability at Thirty-Three Months." *Child Development, 52,* 1981:589–595.

Snyder, Mark. "Self-Fulfilling Stereotypes." In *Down to Earth Sociology,* 7th ed., James M. Henslin, ed. New York: Free Press, 1993:153–160.

Sokolovsky, Jay. "Introduction." In *The Cultural Context of Aging: Worldwide Perspectives,* Jay Sokolovsky, ed. New York: Bergin & Garvey, 1990.

Solis, Dianne. "'Coyotes' Along the Rio Grande Scoff at U.S. Plans for Immigration Controls." *Wall Street Journal,* August 9, 1993:A8.

Solomon, Jolie. "Companies Try Measuring Cost Savings from New Types of Corporate Benefits." *Wall Street Journal,* December 29, 1988:B1.

Sontag, Susan. As quoted in Catherine Kohler Riessman, "Women and Medicalization: A New Perspective." In *Dominant Issues in Medical Sociology,* 3rd ed., Howard D. Schwartz, ed. New York: McGraw-Hill, 1994:190–211.

Sorokin, Pitirim A. *Social and Cultural Dynamics.* 4 vols. New York: American Book Company, 1937–1941.

Sorokin, Pitirim A. *The Crisis of Our Age.* New York: Dutton, 1941.

South, Scott J. "Sociodemographic Differentials in Mate Selection Preferences." *Journal of Marriage and the Family, 53,* November 1991:928–940.

Sowell, Thomas. "Effrontery and Gall, Inc." *Forbes,* September 27, 1993a:52.

Sowell, Thomas. *Inside American Education: The Decline, the Deception, the Dogmas.* New York: Free Press, 1993b.

Special Report: On Family. Knoxville, Tenn.: Whittle Communications, 1989.

Spector, Malcolm, and John Kitsuse. *Constructing Social Problems.* Menlo Park, Calif.: Cummings, 1977.

Speizer, Jeanne J. "Education." In *The Women's Annual, 1982–1983,* Barbara Haber, ed. Boston: Hall, 1983:29–54.

Spencer, Herbert. *Principles of Sociology.* 3 vols. New York: Appleton, 1884.

Spengler, Oswald. *The Decline of the West,* 2 vols. Charles F. Atkinson, trans. New York: Knopf, 1926–1928. First published in 1919–1922.

Sperber, Irwin. "The Marketplace Personality: On Capitalism, Male Chauvinism, and Romantic Love." In *Social Problems in American Society,* James M. Henslin and Larry T. Reynolds, eds. Boston: Holbrook Press, 1973:131–139.

Spitz, Renée. "Hospitalism." *Psychoanalytic Study of the Child, 1,* 1945:53–72.

Spitzer, Steven. "Toward a Marxian Theory of Deviance." *Social Problems, 22,* June 1975:608–619.

Sprecher, Susan and Rachita Chandak. "Attitudes About Arranged Marriages and Dating Among Men and Women from India." *Free Inquiry in Creative Sociology, 20,* 1, May 1992:59–69.

Spurr, Stephen J. "Sex Discrimination in the Legal Profession: A Study of Promotion." *Industrial and Labor Relations Review, 43,* 4, April 1990:406–417.

Srisang, Koson. "The Ecumenical Coalition on Third World Tourism." *Annals of Tourism Research, 16,* 1, 1989:119–121.

Srole, Leo, et al. *Mental Health in the Metropolis: The Midtown Manhattan Study.* New York: New York University Press, 1978.

Stack, Carol B. *All Our Kin: Strategies for Survival in a Black Community.* New York: Harper, 1974.

Stafford, Linda, Sonya R. Kennedy, Joanne E. Lehman, and Gail Arnold. "Wealth in America." *ISR Newsletter,* Winter 1986–1987.

Stains, Laurence R. "Speech Impediment." *Rolling Stone,* August 5, 1993:45–52.

Stampp, Kenneth M. *The Peculiar Institution: Slavery in the Ante-Bellum South.* New York: Vintage Books, 1956.

Stark, Elizabeth. "Friends Through It All." In *Marriage and Family in a Changing Society,* 3rd ed., James M. Henslin, ed. New York: Free Press, 1989:441–449.

Stark, Rodney. *Sociology,* 3rd ed. Belmont, Calif.: Wadsworth, 1989.

Starna, William A., and Ralph Watkins. "Northern Iroquoian Slavery." *Ethnohistory, 38,* 1, Winter 1991:34–57.

Starr, Paul. *The Social Transformation of American Medicine.* New York: Basic Books, 1982.

Starrels, Marjorie. "The Evolution of Workplace Family Policy Research." *Journal of Family Issues, 13,* 3, September 1992:259–278.

Statistical Abstract. See U.S. Bureau of the Census.

Stecklow, Steve. "Metal Detectors Find a Growing Market, But Not Many Guns." *Wall Street Journal,* September 7, 1993:A1, A8.

Stecklow, Steve. "Private Groups Compete for the Chance to Create New Schools with Public Funds." *Wall Street Journal,* January 24, 1994:B1, B4.

Stein, Leonard I. "The Doctor–Nurse Game." In *Down to Earth Sociology: Introductory Readings,* 5th ed., James M. Henslin, ed. New York: Free Press, 1988:102–109.

Stevens, Amy, and Sarah Lubman. "Deciding Moment of the Trial May Have Been Five Months Ago." *Wall Street Journal,* May 1, 1992:A6.

Stevenson, Richard W. "Catering to Consumers' Ethnic Needs." *New York Times,* January 23, 1992.

Stevenson, Richard W. "Swedes Facing Rigors of Welfare Cuts." *New York Times,* March 14, 1993:18.

Stinnett, Nicholas. "Strong Families." In *Marriage and Family in a Changing Society,* 4th ed., James M. Henslin, ed. New York: Free Press, 1992:496–507.

Stipp, David. "Einstein Bird Has Scientists Atwitter over Mental Feats." *Wall Street Journal,* May 9, 1990:A1, A4.

Stipp, David. "Himalayan Tree Could Serve as Source of Anticancer Drug Taxol, Team Says." *Wall Street Journal*, April 20, 1992:B4.

Stockard, Jean, and Miriam M. Johnson. *Sex Roles: Sex Inequality and Sex Role Development*. Englewood Cliffs, N.J.: Prentice Hall, 1980.

Stockwell, John. "The Dark Side of U.S. Foreign Policy." *Zeta Magazine*, February 1989:36–48.

Stodgill, Ralph M. *Handbook of Leadership: A Survey of Theory and Research*. New York: Free Press, 1974.

Stone, Gregory P. "City Shoppers and Urban Identification: Observations on the Social Psychology of City Life." *American Journal of Sociology*, 60, November 1954:276–284.

Stone, Gregory P. "Sport as a Community Representation." In *Handbook of Social Science and Sport*, Gunther Luschen and George H. Sage, eds. Champaign, Ill.: Stipes, 1981:214–245.

Stone, Michael H. "Murder." *Psychiatric Clinics of North America*, 12, 3, September 1989:643–651.

Stouffer, Samuel A., Arthur A. Lumsdaine, Marion Harper Lumsdaine, Robin M. Williams, Jr., M. Brewster Smith, Irving L. Janis, Shirley A. Star, and Leonard S. Cottrell, Jr. *The American Soldier: Combat and Its Aftermath*, Vol. 2. New York: Wiley, 1949.

Stout, Hillary. "Harvard Team Says That AIDS Is Accelerating." *Wall Street Journal*, June 4, 1992:B10.

Straus, Murray A. "Victims and Aggressors in Marital Violence." *American Behavioral Scientist*, 23, May–June 1980:681–704.

Straus, Murray A. "Explaining Family Violence." In *Marriage and Family in a Changing Society*, 4th ed., James M. Henslin, ed. New York: Free Press, 1992:344–356.

Straus, Murray A., and Richard J. Gelles. "Violence in American Families: How Much Is There and Why Does It Occur?" In *Troubled Relationships*, Elam W. Nunnally, Catherine S. Chilman, and Fred M. Cox, eds. Newbury Park, Calif.: Sage, 1988:141–162.

Straus, Murray A., Richard J. Gelles, and Suzanne K. Steinmetz. *Behind Closed Doors: Violence in the American Family*. New York: Anchor/Doubleday, 1980.

Straus, Roger A. "The Sociologist as a Marketing Research Consultant." *Journal of Applied Sociology*, 8, 1991:65–75.

Stryker, Sheldon. "Symbolic Interactionism: Themes and Variations." In *Social Psychology: Sociological Perspectives*, Morris Rosenberg and Ralph H. Turner, eds. New Brunswick, N.J.: Transaction, 1990.

Sullivan, Mercer L. *"Getting Paid:" Youth Crime and Work in the Inner City*. Ithaca, N.Y.: Cornell University Press, 1989.

Sumner, William Graham. *Folkways: A Study in the Sociological Importance of Usages, Manners, Customs, Mores, and Morals*. New York: Ginn, 1906.

Sutherland, Edwin H. *Criminology*. Philadelphia: Lippincott, 1924.

Sutherland, Edwin H. *The Professional Thief*. Chicago: University of Chicago Press, 1937.

Sutherland, Edwin H. *Principles of Criminology*, 4th ed. Philadelphia: Lippincott, 1947.

Sutherland, Edwin H. *White Collar Crime*. New York: Dryden Press, 1949.

Sutherland, Edwin H., and Donald Cressey. *Criminology*, 9th ed. Philadelphia: Lippincott, 1974.

Sutherland, Edwin H., Donald R. Cressey, and David F. Luckenbill. *Principles of Criminology*, 11th ed. Dix Hills, N.Y.: General Hall, 1992.

Suzuki, Bob H. "Asian-American Families." In *Marriage and Family in a Changing Society*, 2nd ed., James M. Henslin, ed. New York: Free Press, 1985:104–119.

Swafford, Michael. *Perceptions of Social Status in the USSR*. Champaign, Ill.: Soviet Interview Project, 1986.

Swedish Institute, The. "Health and Medical Care in Sweden." July 1990:1–4.

Swedish Institute, The. "Fact Sheets on Sweden." February 1992.

Sweet, Stuart J. "A Looming Federal Surplus." *Wall Street Journal*, March 28, 1984:28.

Sweezy, Paul M., and Harry Magdoff. "Globalization—to What End? Part II." *Monthly Review*, 43, 10, March 1992:1–19.

Sykes, Gresham M., and David Matza. "Techniques of Neutralization." In *Down to Earth Sociology*, 5th ed., James M. Henslin, ed. New York: Free Press, 1988:225–231.

Szasz, Thomas S. *The Manufacture of Madness: A Comparative Study of the Inquisition and the Mental Health Movement*. New York: Harper & Row, 1970.

Szasz, Thomas. *Ceremonial Chemistry: The Ritual Persecution of Drugs, Addicts, and Pushers*. Garden City, N.Y.: Anchor/Doubleday, 1975.

Szasz, Thomas S. *The Myth of Mental Illness*, rev. ed. New York: Harper & Row, 1986.

Szasz, Thomas S. "Psychiatric Injustice." *British Journal of Psychiatry*, 154, June 1989:864–869.

Szasz, Thomas S. "Law and Psychiatry: The Problems That Will Not Go Away." *Journal of Mind and Behavior*, 11, 3–4, 1990:557–563.

Szelenyi, Szonja. "Social Inequality and Party Membership: Patterns of Recruitment in the Hungarian Socialist Workers' Party." *American Sociological Review*, 52, 1987:559–573.

Szymanski, Albert. "Racial Discrimination and White Gain." *American Sociological Review*, 41, June 1976:403–414.

Taeuber, Cynthia M., and Arnold A. Goldstein. "Profiles of America's Elderly: Growth of America's Oldest-Old Population." Washington, D.C.: U.S. Bureau of the Census and the National Institute on Aging, July 1992.

Tannen, Deborah. *You Just Don't Understand: Women and Men in Conversation*. New York: Morrow, 1990.

"Terror and Death at Home Are Caught in F.B.I. Tape." *New York Times*, October 28, 1991:A14.

Thayer, Stephen. "Encounters." *Psychology Today*, March 1988:31–36.

Thomas, Paulette. "EPA Predicts Global Impact from Warming." *Wall Street Journal*, October 21, 1988:B5.

Thomas, Paulette. "U.S. Examiners Will Scrutinize Banks with Poor Minority-Lending Histories." *Wall Street Journal*, October 22, 1991:A2.

Thomas, Paulette. "Boston Fed Finds Racial Discrimination in Mortgage Lending Is Still Widespread." *Wall Street Journal*, October 9, 1992:A3.

Thomas, Paulette. "Poverty Spread in 1992 to Total of 36.9 Million." *Wall Street Journal*, October 5, 1993:A2, A8.

Thomas, R. Roosevelt, Jr. "From Affirmative Action to Affirming Diversity." *Harvard Business Review*, 90, 2, March–April, 1990:107–117.

Thomas, William I., and Florian Znaniecki. *The Polish Peasant in Europe and America*. Chicago: University of Chicago Press, 1918.

Thompson, William E. "Hanging Tongues: A Sociological Encounter with the Assembly Line." In *Down to Earth Sociology: Introductory Readings*, 7th ed., James M. Henslin, ed. New York: Free Press, 1993:225–234.

Thorne, Barrie. "Children and Gender: Constructions of Difference." In *Theoretical Perspectives on Sexual Difference*, Deborah L. Rhode, ed. New Haven, Conn.: Yale University Press, 1990:100–113.

Thorne, Barrie, and Zella Luria. "Sexuality and Gender in Children's Daily Worlds." In *Down to Earth Sociology*, 7th ed., James M. Henslin, ed. New York: Free Press, 1993:133–144.

Thornton, Russell. *American Indian Holocaust and Survival: A Population History Since 1492*. Norman: University of Oklahoma Press, 1987.

Thornton, Arland. "The Influence of the Parental Family on the Attitudes and Behavior of Children." In *The Changing American Family: Sociological and Demographic Perspectives*, Scott J. South and Stewart E. Tolnay, eds. Boulder, Colo.: Westview Press, 1992:247–265.

Thrasher, Frederic M. *The Gang*. Chicago: University of Chicago Press, 1927.

Tilly, Charles. *From Mobilization to Revolution*. Reading, Mass.: Addison-Wesley, 1978.

Timasheff, Nicholas S. *War and Revolution*. Joseph F. Scheuer, ed. New York: Sheed & Ward, 1965.

Timerman, Jacobo. *Prisoner Without a Name, Cell Without a Number*. New York: Knopf, 1981.

Tingey, Holly, Gary Kiger, and Pamela Riley. "Emotional Labor in Dual-Earner Households." Unpublished paper, Department of Economics, Utah State University, 1993.

Tiryakian, Edward A., ed. *The Phenomenon of Sociology: A Reader in the Sociology of Sociology*. New York: Appleton-Century-Crofts, 1971.

Toby, Jackson. "To Get Rid of Guns in Schools, Get Rid of Some Students." *Wall Street Journal*, March 23, 1992:A12.

Toch, Thomas. "Violence in Schools." *U.S. News & World Report*, 115, 18, November 8, 1993:31–36.

Tocqueville, Alexis de. *Democracy in America*, J. P. Mayer and Max Lerner, eds. New York: Harper & Row, 1966. First published in 1835.

Tocqueville, Alexis de. *The Old Regime and the French Revolution*. Stuart Gilbert, trans. Garden City, N.Y.: Doubleday Anchor, 1955. First published in 1856.

Tönnies, Ferdinand. *Community and Society (Gemeinschaft und Gesellschaft)*, with a new introduction by John Samples. New Brunswick, N.J.: Transaction, 1988. First published in 1887.

Toffler, Alvin. *The Third Wave*. New York: Morrow, 1980.

Toffler, Alvin, and Heidi Toffler. "Societies at Hyper-Speed." *New York Times*, October 31, 1993:E17.

Tolchin, Martin. "Surgeon General Asserts Smoking Is an Addiction." *New York Times*, May 17, 1988:A1, C4.

Tolchin, Martin. "Mildest Possible Penalty Is Imposed on Neil Bush." *New York Times*, April 19, 1991:D2.

Tordoff, William. "The Impact of Ideology on Development in the Third World." *Journal of International Development*, 4, 1, 1992:41–53.

Toynbee, Arnold. *A Study of History*, D. C. Somervell, abridger and ed. New York: Oxford University Press, 1946.

Treiman, Donald J. *Occupational Prestige in Comparative Perspective*. New York: Academic Press, 1977.

Trice, Harrison M., and Janice M. Beyer. "Cultural Leadership in Organization." *Organization Science*, 2, 2, May 1991:149–169.

Troeltsch, Ernst. *The Social Teachings of the Christian Churches*. New York: Macmillan, 1931.

Trueba, Henry T., Lila Jacobs, and Elizabeth Kirton. *Cultural Conflict and Adaptation: The Case of Hmong Children in American Society*. Bristol, Penn.: Falmer Press, 1990.

Tucker, Belinda M., and Claudia Mitchell-Kernan. "New Trends in Black American Interracial Marriage: The Social Structural Context." *Journal of Marriage and the Family*, 52, 1990:209–218.

Tumin, Melvin M., and Roy C. Collins. "Status Mobility and Anomie: A Study in Readiness for Desegregation." *British Journal of Sociology*, 10, 1959.253–267.

Turk, Austin T. "Class, Conflict, and Criminalization." *Sociological Focus*, 10, 1977:209–220.

Turner, Bryan S. "Outline of a Theory of Citizenship." *Sociology*, 24, 2, May 1990:189–217.

Turner, Jonathan H. *American Society: Problems of Structure*. New York: Harper & Row, 1972.

Turner, Jonathan H. *The Structure of Sociological Theory*. Homewood, Ill.: Dorsey, 1978.

Turner, Ralph. "Race Riots Past and Present: A Cultural-Collective Behavior Approach." Paper presented at the annual meetings of the American Sociological Association, 1993.

Turner, Ralph H., and Lewis M. Killian. *Collective Behavior*, 2nd ed. Englewood Cliffs, N.J.: Prentice Hall, 1972.

Tye, Larry. "After Waco, the Focus Shifts to Other Cults." *The Boston Globe*, April 30, 1993:1, 22.

Udy, Stanley H., Jr. "Bureaucracy and Rationality in Weber's Organizational Theory: An Empirical Study." *American Sociological Review*, 24, December 1959:791–795.

Ullman, Edward, and Chauncey Harris. "The Nature of Cities." In *Urban Man and Society: A Reader in Urban Ecology*, Albert N. Cousins and Hans Nagpaul, eds. New York: Knopf, 1970:91–100.

"U.S. Arrests Boy, 5 Others in Computer Hacker Case." *Wall Street Journal*, August 17, 1990:B2.

U.S. Bureau of the Census. *World Population Profile: 1985*. Washington, D.C.: U.S. Government Printing Office, October 1986.

U.S. Bureau of the Census. "Census and You: April 1991." Washington, D.C.: U.S. Government Printing Office, 1991.

U.S. Bureau of the Census. *Statistical Abstract of the United States: The National Data Book*. Washington, D.C.: U.S. Government Printing Office. Published annually.

U.S. Department of Health and Human Services, Public Health Service. *Healthy People 2000*. Washington, D.C.: U.S. Government Printing Office, 1990.

U.S. House of Representatives. "Victims of Rape." Fact Sheet. June 28, 1990.

Usdansky, Margaret L., "English a Problem for Half of Miami." *USA Today*.

Useem, Elizabeth L. "Middle Schools and Math Groups: Parents' Involvement in Children's Placement." *Sociology of Education*, 65, October 1992:263–279.

Useem, Michael. "Corporations and the Corporate Elite." In *Annual Review of Sociology*, 6, Alex Inkeles, Neil J. Smelser, and Ralph H. Turner, eds. Palo Alto, Calif.: Annual Reviews, 1980:41–77.

Useem, Michael. *The Inner Circle: Large Corporations and the Rise of Business Political Activity in the U.S. and U.K.* New York: Oxford University Press, 1984.

Vande Berg, Leah R., and Diane Streckfuss. "Prime-Time Television's Portrayal of Women and the World of Work: A Demographic Profile." *Journal of Broadcasting and Electronic Media,* Spring 1992:195–208.

van den Haag, Ernest. *Punishing Criminals: Concerning a Very Old and Painful Question.* New York: Basic Books, 1975.

van der Kwaak, Anke. "Female Circumcision and Gender Identity: A Questionable Alliance." *Social Science and Medicine,* 35, 6, September 1992:777–787.

Van Lawick-Goodall, Jane. *In the Shadow of Man.* Boston: Houghton Mifflin, 1971.

Vanneman, Reeve, and Lynn Weber Cannon. *The American Perception of Class.* Philadelphia: Temple University Press, 1987.

Vaughan, Diane. "Uncoupling: The Social Construction of Divorce." In *Marriage and Family in a Changing Society,* 2nd ed., James M. Henslin, ed. New York: Free Press, 1985:429–439.

Vayda, Eugene, and Ralsa B. Deber. "The Canadian Health Care System: An Overview." *Social Science and Medicine,* 18, 1984:191–197.

Veblen, Thorstein. *The Theory of the Leisure Class.* New York: Macmillan, 1912.

Veevers, Jean E. "Voluntarily Childless Wives." *Sociology and Social Research,* 57, April 1973:356–366.

Veevers, Jean E. *Childless by Choice.* Toronto: Butterworths, 1980.

Vega, William A. "Hispanic Families in the 1980s: A Decade of Research." *Journal of Marriage and the Family,* 52, November 1990:1015–1024.

Vernon, JoEtta A., J. Allen Williams, Jr., Terri Phillips, and Janet Wilson. "Media Stereotyping: A Comparison of the Way Elderly Women and Men Are Portrayed on Prime-Time Television." *Journal of Women and Aging,* 2, 4, 1990:55–58.

Vincent, Richard C., Dennis K. Davis, and Lilly Ann Boruszkowski. "Sexism on MTV: The Portrayal of Women in Rock Videos." *Journalism Quarterly* 64, 4, Winter 1987:750–755, 941–942.

Vinokur, Aaron, and Gur Ofer. *Inequality of Earnings, Household Income and Wealth in the Soviet Union in the 70s.* Champaign, Ill.: Soviet Interview Project, 1986.

Violas, P. C. *The Training of the Urban Working Class: A History of Twentieth Century American Education.* Chicago: Rand McNally, 1978.

Von Hoffman, Nicholas. "Sociological Snoopers." *Transaction 7,* May 1970:4, 6.

Voslensky, Michael. *Nomenklatura: The Soviet Ruling Class.* New York: Doubleday, 1984.

Waddington, Conrad H. *The Man-Made Future.* New York: St. Martin's, 1978.

Wagley, Charles, and Marvin Harris. *Minorities in the New World.* New York: Columbia University Press, 1958.

Waldholz, Michael. "Computer Brain' Outperforms Doctors in Diagnosing Heart Attack Patients." *Wall Street Journal,* December 2, 1991:7B.

Waite, Linda, and Frances K. Goldscheider. "Work in the Home: The Productive Context of Family Relationships." In *The Changing American Family: Sociological and Demographic Perspectives,* Scott J. South and Stewart E. Tolnay, eds. Boulder, Colo.: Westview Press, 1992:267–299.

Walker, Alice, and Pratibha Pamar. *Warrior Marks: Female Genital Mutilation and the Sexual Blinding of Women.* New York: Harcourt Brace, 1993.

Walker, Michael. "Canadian Health Care Is a Model for Disaster." *Wall Street Journal,* October 18, 1991:A15.

Walker, Tom. "'Edge Cities' Represent a Quiet Social Revolution." *Atlanta Journal,* September 29, 1991:C1.

Wallace, Anthony F. C. *Religion: An Anthropological View.* New York: Random House, 1966.

Wallerstein, Immanuel. *The Modern World System: Capitalist Agriculture and the Origins of the European World-Economy in the Sixteenth Century.* New York: Academic Press, 1974.

Wallerstein, Immanuel. *The Capitalist World-Economy.* New York: Cambridge University Press, 1979.

Wallerstein, Immanuel. *The Politics of the World-Economy: The States, the Movements, and the Civilizations.* Cambridge, England: Cambridge University Press, 1984.

Wallerstein, Immanuel. "Culture as the Ideological Battleground of the Modern World-system." In *Global Culture: Nationalism, Globalization, and Modernity,* Mike Featherstone, ed. London: Sage, 1990:31–55.

Wallerstein, Judith S., and Sandra Blakeslee. "Divorce Harms Children." In *Family in America: Opposing Viewpoints,* Viqi Wagner, ed. San Diego, Calif.: Greenhaven Press, 1992:108–114.

Wallerstein, Judith S., and Joan B. Kelly. "How Children React to Parental Divorce." In *Marriage and Family in a Changing Society,* 4th ed., James M. Henslin, ed. New York: Free Press, 1992:397–409.

Walters, Jonathan. "Chimps in the Mist." *USA Weekend,* May 18–20, 1990:24.

Warner, Kenneth E. *Selling Smoke: Cigarette Advertising and Public Health.* Washington, D.C.: American Public Health Association, 1986.

Warner, Richard. "Deinstitutionalization: How Did We Get Where We Are?" *Journal of Social Issues,* 45, 3, Fall 1989:17–30.

Warner, W. Lloyd, and Paul S. Hunt. *The Social Life of a Modern Community.* New Haven, Conn.: Yale University Press, 1941.

Warner, W. Lloyd, Paul S. Hunt, Marchia Meeker, and Kenneth Eels. *Social Class in America.* New York: Harper, 1949.

Watson, J. Mark. "Outlaw Motorcyclists." In *Down to Earth Sociology: Introductory Readings,* 5th ed., James M. Henslin, ed. New York: Free Press, 1988:203–213.

Webb, Eugene J., Donald T. Campbell, Richard D. Schwartz, and Lee Sechrest. *Unobtrusive Measures: Nonreactive Research in the Social Sciences.* Chicago: Rand McNally, 1966.

Weber, Max. *From Max Weber: Essays in Sociology.* Hans Gerth and C. Wright Mills, trans. and ed. New York: Oxford University Press, 1946a.

Weber, Max. "Politics as a Vocation." In *From Max Weber: Essays in Sociology,* Hans Gerth and C. Wright Mills, eds. New York: Oxford University Press, 1946b:77–128.

Weber, Max. *The Theory of Social and Economic Organization,* A. M. Henderson and Talcott Parsons, trans., Talcott Parsons, ed. Glencoe, Ill.: Free Press, 1947. First published in 1913.

Weber, Max. *The Protestant Ethic and the Spirit of Capitalism.* New York: Scribner's, 1958. First published 1904–1905.

Weber, Max. *Economy and Society.* Ephraim Fischoff, trans. New York: Bedminster Press, 1968. First published in 1922.

Weber, Max. *Economy and Society,* G. Roth and C. Wittich, eds. Berkeley: University of California Press, 1978.

Weeks, John R. *Population: An Introduction to Concepts and Issues*, 5th ed. Belmont, Calif.: Wadsworth, 1994.

Wei, William. *The Asian American Movement*. Philadelphia: Temple University Press, 1993.

Weinstein, Deena. *Heavy Metal: A Cultural Sociology*. New York: Lexington Books, 1991.

Weintraub, Richard M. "A Bride in India." *Washington Post*, February 28, 1988.

Weisburd, David, Stanton Wheeler, and Elin Waring. *Crimes of the Middle Classes: White-Collar Offenders in the Federal Courts*. New Haven, Conn.: Yale University Press, 1991.

Weisskopf, Michael. "Scientist Says Greenhouse Effect Is Setting In." In *Ourselves and Others: The Washington Post Sociology Companion*, Washington Post Writers Group, eds. Boston: Allyn and Bacon, 1992:297–298.

Weitz, Rose. "From Accommodation to Rebellion: Tertiary Deviance and the Radical Redefinition of Lesbianism." In *Studies in the Sociology of Social Problems*, Joseph W. Schneider and John I. Kitsuse, eds. Norwood, N.J.: Ablex, 1984:140–161.

Weitzer, Ronald. "Prostitutes' Rights in the United States: The Failure of a Movement." *Sociological Quarterly*, 32, 1, Spring 1991:23–41.

Weitzman, Lenore J. *The Divorce Revolution*. New York: Free Press, 1985.

Weitzman, Lenore J., Deborah Eifler, Elizabeth Hokada, and Catherine Ross. "Sex Role Socialization in Picture Books for Pre-School Children." *American Journal of Sociology*, 77, May 1972:1125–1150.

Wellman, Barry. "Domestic Work, Paid Work, and Net Work." In *Understanding Personal Relationships*, Steve Duck and Daniel Perlman, eds. London: Sage, 1985.

Wenneker, Mark B., and Arnold M. Epstein. "Racial Inequalities in the Use of Procedures for Patients with Ischemic Heart Disease in Massachusetts." *Journal of the American Medical Association*, 261, 2, January 13, 1989:253–257.

Werner, Dennis. "Gerontocracy Among the Mekranoti of Central Brazil." *Anthropological Quarterly*, 54, 1, January 1981:15–27.

Wertz, Richard W., and Dorothy C. Wertz. "Notes on the Decline of Midwives and the Rise of Medical Obstetricians." In *The Sociology of Health and Illness: Critical Perspectives*, Peter Conrad and Rochelle Kern, eds. New York: St. Martin's Press, 1981:165–183.

West, Candace, and Angela Garcia. "Conversational Shift Work: A Study of Topical Transitions Between Women and Men." *Social Problems*, 35, 1988:551–575.

Westergaard, John, and Henrietta Resler. *Class in a Capitalist Society: A Study of Contemporary Britain*. New York: Basic Books, 1975.

"What's Wrong with the Navy?" *U.S. News and World Report*, July 13, 1992:22–28.

White, Burton L., Barbara T. Kaban, and Jane S. Attanucci. *The Origins of Human Competence*. Lexington, Mass.: Heath, 1979.

White, James A. "When Employees Own Big Stake, It's a Buy Signal for Investors." *Wall Street Journal*, February 13, 1991:C1, C19.

White, Joseph B., and Melinda Grenier Guiles. "GM's Plan for Saturn, to Beat Small Imports, Trails Original Goals." *Wall Street Journal*, July 9, 1990:A1, A4.

White, Lynn K., and Alan Booth. "The Quality and Stability of Remarriages: The Role of Stepchildren." *American Sociological Review*, 50, 1985:689–698.

Whitehead, Barbara Dafoe. "Dan Quayle Was Right." *Atlantic Monthly*, April 1993:47–84.

Whyte, Martin King. *Dating, Mating, and Marriage*. New York: Aldine de Gruyter, 1990.

Whyte, Martin King. "Choosing Mates—The American Way." *Society*, March–April 1992:71–77.

Whyte, Merry. *The Japanese Educational Challenge: A Commitment to Children*. New York: Free Press, 1987.

Whyte, William H. *The City: Rediscovering the Center*. New York: Doubleday, 1989.

Whyte, William H. "Street People." In *Down to Earth Sociology: Introductory Readings*, 6th ed., James M. Henslin, ed. New York: Free Press, 1991:165–178.

Wilford, John Noble. "In the Glow of Discovery: Scientist Ponders Fame." *New York Times*, May 5, 1992:B5.

Wilke, John R. "Computer Links Erode Hierarchical Nature of Workplace Culture." *Wall Street Journal*, December 9, 1993:A1, A7.

Willhelm, Sidney M. "Can Marxism Explain America's Racism?" *Social Problems*, 28, December 1980:98–112.

Williams, J. Allen, JoEtta A. Vernon, Martha C. Williams, and Karen Malecha. "Sex Role Socialization in Picture Books: An Update." *Social Science Quarterly*, 68, 1, March 1987:148–156.

Williams, Robin M., Jr. *American Society: A Sociological Interpretation*, 2nd ed. New York: Knopf, 1965.

Williams, T. B. *The Impact of Television: A Natural Experiment in Three Communities*. New York: Academic Press, 1986.

Willie, Charles V. "Caste, Class, and Family Life Experiences." *Research in Race and Ethnic Relations*, 6, 1991:65–84.

Wilson, Edward O. *Sociobiology: The New Synthesis*. Cambridge, Mass.: Harvard University Press, 1975.

Wilson, James Q. "Lock 'Em Up and Other Thoughts on Crime." *New York Times Magazine*, March 9, 1975:11, 44–48.

Wilson, James Q. "Is Incapacitation the Answer to the Crime Problem?" In *Taking Sides: Clashing Views on Controversial Social Issues*, 7th ed., Kurt Finsterbusch and George McKenna, eds. Guilford, Conn.: Duchkin, 1992:318–324.

Wilson, James Q., and Richard J. Hernstein. *Crime and Human Nature*. New York: Simon & Schuster, 1985.

Wilson, William Julius. *The Declining Significance of Race: Blacks and Changing American Institutions*. Chicago: University of Chicago Press, 1978.

Wilson, William Julius. "Race, Class, and Public Policy." *American Sociologist*, 16, 1981:125–134.

Wilson, William Julius. "The Black Underclass." *Wilson Quarterly*, 8, Spring 1984:88–99.

Wilson, William Julius. *The Truly Disadvantaged: The Inner City, the Underclass, and Public Policy*. Chicago: University of Chicago Press, 1987.

Winslow, Ron. "Study Finds Blacks Get Fewer Bypasses." *Wall Street Journal*, March 18, 1992:B1.

Wirth, Louis. "Urbanism as a Way of Life." *American Journal of Sociology*, 44, July 1938:1–24.

Wirth, Louis. "The Problem of Minority Groups." In *The Science of Man in the World Crisis*, Ralph Linton, ed. New York: Columbia University Press, 1945.

Wohl, R. Richard, and Anselm Strauss. "Symbolic Representation and the Urban Milieu." *American Journal of Sociology*, 63, March 1958:523–532.

Wolff, Michael, et al. *Where We Stand: Can America Make It in the Global Race for Wealth and Happiness?* New York: Bantam Books, 1992.

Wolfgang, Marvin E., and Franco Ferracuti. *The Subculture of Violence: Toward an Integrated Theory in Criminology.* London: Tavistock, 1967.

Woods, John E., and Phillip G. Arnold. "Fiction Obscures the Facts of Breast Implants." *Wall Street Journal*, April 7, 1992:A16.

Woodward, Kenneth L. "Heaven." *Newsweek, 113,* 13, March 27, 1989:52–55.

Woon, Yuen-Fong. "Growing Old in a Modernizing China." *Journal of Comparative Family Studies, 12,* 2, Spring 1981:245–257.

World Population Profile: 1985. Washington, D.C.: U.S. Bureau of the Census, U.S. Department of Commerce, 1986.

World Population Profile: 1986. Washington, D.C.: U.S. Bureau of the Census, U.S. Department of Commerce, 1987.

World Health Organization. *Constitution of the World Health Organization.* New York: World Health Organization Interim Commission, 1946.

"The World's Wars." *Economist*, March 12, 1988:19–22.

Worsley, Peter. *The Trumpet Shall Sound.* London: MacGibbon and Kee, 1957.

Wouters, Cas. "On Status Competition and Emotion Management: The Study of Emotions as a New Field." *Theory, Culture & Society,* 9, 1992:229–252.

Wray, Linda A. "Public Policy Implications of an Ethnically Diverse Elderly Population." *Journal of Cross-Cultural Gerontology, 6,* 1991:243–257.

Wright, Erik Olin. *Class, Crisis, and the State.* London: Verso, 1979a.

Wright, Erik Olin. *Class, Structure and Income Determination.* New York: Academic Press, 1979b.

Wright, Erik Olin. *Class.* London: Verso, 1985.

Wright, Erik Olin, Karen Shire, Shu-Ling Hwang, Maureen Dolan, and Janeen Baxter. "The Non-Effects of Class on the Gender Division of Labor in the Home: A Comparative Study of Sweden and the United States." *Gender & Society,* 6, 2, June 1992:252–282.

Wriston, Walter B. *The Twilight of Sovereignty.* New York: Scribner's, 1992.

Wrong, Dennis H. "The Over-Socialized Conception of Man in Modern Sociology." *American Sociological Review, 26,* April 1961:185–193.

WuDunn, Sheryl. "As China Leaps Ahead, the Poor Slip Behind." *New York Times,* May 23, 1993:3.

Yaukey, David. *Demography: The Study of Human Population.* New York: St. Martin's, 1985.

Yee, Albert H. "Asians as Stereotypes and Students: Misperceptions That Persist." *Educational Psychology Review,* 4, 1, March 1992:95–132.

Yinger, J. Milton. *Toward a Field Theory of Behavior: Personality and Social Structure.* New York: McGraw-Hill, 1965.

Yinger, J. Milton. *The Scientific Study of Religion.* New York: Macmillan, 1970.

Yuan, D. Y. "Voluntary Segregation: A Study of New York Chinatown." *Phylon,* 24, Fall 1963:255–265.

Zald, Mayer N., and John D. McCarthy, eds. *Social Movements in an Organizational Society.* New Brunswick, N.J.: Transaction, 1987.

Zald, Mayer N. "Looking Backward to Look Forward: Reflections on the Past and the Future of the Resource Mobilization Research Program." In *Frontiers in Social Movement Theory,* Aldon D. Morris and Carol McClurg Mueller, eds. New Haven, Conn.: Yale University Press, 1992:326–348.

Zawitz, Marianne W. *Report to the Nation on Crime and Justice,* 2nd ed. Washington, D.C.: U.S. Department of Justice, Bureau of Justice Statistics, July 1988.

Zerubavel, Eviatar. *The Fine Line: Making Distinctions in Everyday Life.* New York: Free Press, 1991.

Zey, Mary. *Banking on Fraud: Drexel, Junk Bonds, and Buyouts.* Hawthorne, N.Y.: Aldine de Gruyter, 1993.

Ziegenhals, Gretchen E. "Confessions of an Amish Watcher." *Christian Century,* August 21–28, 1991:764–765.

Zinn, Mazine Baca, and D. Stanley Eitzen. *Diversity in Families,* 2nd ed. New York: HarperCollins, 1990.

Zola, Irving K. *Socio-Medical Inquiries.* Philadelphia: Temple University Press, 1983.

Zorbaugh, Harvey W. *The Gold Coast and the Slum.* Chicago: University of Chicago Press, 1929.

Zuboff, Shoshana. *In the Age of the Smart Machine: The Future of Work and Power.* New York: Basic Books, 1984.

Zuckerman, Harriet, Jonathan R. Cole, and John T. Bruer. *The Outer Circle: Women in the Scientific Community.* New York: Norton, 1991.

ablution: a washing ritual designed to restore ritual purity

acculturation: the transmission of culture from one generation to the next

achieved statuses: positions that are earned, accomplished, or involve at least some effort or activity on the individual's part

acid rain: rain containing sulfuric and nitric acid

acting crowd: Herbert Blumer's term for an excited group that collectively moves toward a goal

activity theory: the view that satisfaction during old age is related to a person's level and quality of activity

age cohort: people born at roughly the same time who pass through the life course together

ageism: prejudice, discrimination, and hostility directed against people because of their age; can be directed against any age group, including youth

agent provocateur: someone who joins a group in order to spy on it and to sabotage it by *provoking* its members to commit illegal acts

agents of socialization: people or groups that affect our self-concept, attitudes, or other orientations toward life

aggregate: individuals who temporarily share the same physical space but do not see themselves as belonging together

agricultural revolution: the second social revolution, based on the invention of the plow, which led to agricultural societies

agricultural society: a society based on large-scale agriculture, dependent on plows drawn by animals

alienation: Marx's term for workers being cut off from the product of their labor, caused by their being assigned repetitive tasks on a small part of a product; results in a sense of powerlessness and normlessness

alterative social movement: a social movement that seeks to alter only particular aspects of people

anarchy: a condition of lawlessness or political disorder caused by the absence or collapse of governmental authority

Anglo-conformity: the expectation that immigrants to the United States would adopt the English language and other Anglo-Saxon ways of life

animal culture: learned, shared behavior among animals

animism: the belief that all objects in the world have spirits, some of which are dangerous and must be outwitted

anomie: Emile Durkheim's term for a condition of society in which people become detached, cut loose from the norms that usually guide their behavior; this lack of social integration results in a feeling of being out of place, of not belonging, of having lost a sense of direction or purpose in life, of being detached or uprooted

anticipatory socialization: learning parts of a future role because one anticipates entering that role

anti-Semitism: prejudice, discrimination, and persecution directed against Jews

apartheid: the separation of races as was practiced in South Africa

appearance: how an individual looks when playing a role

applied sociology: the use of sociology to solve problems—from the micro level of family relationships to the macro level of war and pollution

ascribed statuses: positions an individual either inherits at birth or receives involuntarily later in life

assimilation: the process of being absorbed into the mainstream culture

authoritarian leader: a leader who leads by giving orders

authoritarian personality: Theodor Adorno's term for people who are prejudiced and rank high on scales of conformity, intolerance, insecurity, respect for authority, and submissiveness to superiors

authority: power that people accept as rightly exercised over them; also called *legitimate power*

back stage: where people rest from their performances (interactions), discuss their presentations, and plan future performances

background assumptions: deeply embedded common understandings, or basic rules, concerning our view of the world and of how people ought to act

barter: the direct exchange of one item for another

basic demographic equation: growth rate = births − deaths + net migration

bilateral: (system of descent) a system of reckoning descent that counts both the mother's and the father's side

blended family: a family whose members were once part of other families

born again: a term describing Christians who have undergone a life-transforming religious experience so radical that they feel they have become new persons

bourgeoisie: Karl Marx's term for capitalists, those who own the means of production

bureaucracy: a formal organization with a hierarchy of authority; a clear division of labor; emphasis on written rules, communications, and records; and impersonality of positions

bureaucratic engorgement: the tendency for bureaucracies to keep on growing

capitalism: an economic system characterized by the private ownership of the means of production, the pursuit of profit, and market competition

capitalist class: the wealthy who own the means of production and buy the labor of the working class

capitalist world economy: the dominance of capitalism in the world along with the international interdependence that capitalism has created

cargo cult: a social movement in which South Pacific islanders destroyed their possessions in the anticipation that their ancestors would send items by ship

caste system: a form of social stratification in which one's status is determined by birth and is lifelong

category: people who have similar characteristics

causation: if a change in one variable leads to a change in another variable, causation is said to exist

centrist party: a political party that represents the center of political opinion

charisma: literally, an extraordinary gift from God; more commonly, an outstanding, "magnetic" personality

charismatic authority: authority based on an individual's outstanding traits, which attract followers

charismatic leader: literally, someone to whom God has given a gift; more commonly, someone who exerts extraordinary appeal to a group of followers

checks and balances: the separation of powers among the three branches of U.S. government—legislative, executive, and judicial—so that each is able to nullify the actions of the other two, thus preventing the domination of any single branch

Chicanos: Latinos whose country of origin is Mexico

Church: according to Durkheim, one of the three essential elements of religion—a moral community of believers; a second definition is a large, highly organized religious group with formal, sedate worship services and little emphasis on personal conversion

circular reaction: Robert Park's term for a back-and-forth communication between the members of a crowd whereby a "collective impulse" is transmitted

citizenship: the concept that birth (and residence) in a country impart basic rights

city: a place in which a large number of people are permanently based and do not produce their own food

city-state: an independent city whose power radiates outward, bringing the adjacent area under its rule

civil disobedience: the act of deliberately but peacefully disobeying laws considered unjust

civil religion: Robert Bellah's term for religion that is such an established feature of a country's life that the country's history and social institutions become sanctified by being associated with God

clan: an extended network of relatives

clan system: a form of social stratification in which individuals receive their social standing through belonging to an extended network of relatives

class conflict: Karl Marx's term for the struggle between the proletariat and the bourgeoisie

class consciousness: Karl Marx's term for awareness of a common identity based on one's position in the means of production

class system: a form of social stratification based primarily on the possession of money or material possessions

clinical sociology: the direct involvement of sociologists in bringing about social change

clique: a cluster of people within a larger group who choose to interact with one another; an internal faction

closed-ended questions: questions followed by a list of possible answers to be selected by the respondent

coalition: the alignment of some members of a group against others

coalition government: a government in which a country's largest party aligns itself with one or more smaller parties

coding: categorizing data

coercion: power that people do not accept as rightly exercised over them; also called *illegitimate power*

cohabitation: the condition of living together as an unmarried couple

collective behavior: extraordinary activities carried out by groups of people; includes lynchings, rumors, panics, urban legends, fads, and fashions

collective mind: Gustave LeBon's term for the tendency of people in a crowd to feel, think, and act in extraordinary ways

colonization: the process by which one nation takes over another nation, usually for the purpose of exploiting its labor and natural resources

common sense: those things that "everyone knows" are true

community: a place people identify with, where they sense that they belong and that others care what happens to them

compartmentalize: to separate acts from feelings or attitudes

compensatory education: educational programs designed to fill a gap in the background of students, usually lower-class children

conflict theory: a theoretical framework in which society is viewed as composed of groups competing for scarce resources

conspicuous consumption: Thorstein Veblen's term for a change from the Protestant ethic to an eagerness to show off wealth by the elaborate consumption of goods

content analysis: the examination of a source, such as a magazine article, a television program, or even a diary, to identify its themes

contradictory class location: Erik Wright's term for a position in the class structure that generates contradictory interests

control group: the group of subjects in an experiment not exposed to the independent variable

control theory: the idea that two control systems—inner controls and outer controls—work against our tendencies to deviate

convergence theory: the view that as both capitalist and socialist economic systems adopt features of the other, a hybrid (or mixed) economic system will emerge

corporate capitalism: the domination of the economic system by giant corporations

corporate culture: the orientations that characterize corporate work settings

corporation: the joint ownership of a business enterprise, whose liabilities and obligations are separate from those of its owners

correlation: the simultaneous occurrence of two or more variables

correspondence principle: the sociological principle that schools correspond to (or reflect) the social structure of society

cosmology: teachings or ideas that provide a unified picture of the world

counterculture: a group whose values place its members in opposition to the values of the broader culture

credential society: the use of diplomas and degrees to determine who is eligible for jobs, even though the diploma or degree may be irrelevant to the actual work

credit card: a device that allows its owner to purchase goods but to be billed later

crime: the violation of norms that are written into law

criminal justice system: the system of police, courts, and prisons set up to deal with people who are accused of having committed a crime

crude birthrate: the annual number of births per 1,000 population

crude death rate: the annual number of deaths per 1,000 population

cult: a new religion with few followers, whose teachings and practices put it at odds with the dominant culture and religion

cultural diffusion: the spread of cultural characteristics from one group to another

cultural goals: the legitimate objectives held out to the members of a society

cultural lag: William Ogburn's term for human behavior lagging behind technological innovations

cultural leveling: the author's term for the process by which cultures become similar to one another, and especially by which Western industrial culture is imported and diffused into developing nations

cultural relativism: understanding a people from the framework of its own culture

cultural transmission: in reference to education, the ways by which schools transmit a society's culture, especially its core values

cultural universal: a value, norm, or other cultural trait that is found in every group

culture: the language, beliefs, values, norms, behaviors, and even material objects that are passed from one generation to the next

culture contact: contact with a different culture

culture of poverty: the values and behaviors of the poor that are assumed to make them fundamentally different from other people; these factors are assumed to be largely responsible for their poverty, and parents are assumed to perpetuate poverty across generations by passing these characteristics on to their children

culture shock: the disorientation that people experience when they come in contact with a fundamentally different culture and can no longer depend on their taken-for-granted assumptions about life

currency: paper money

debit card: a device that allows its owner to charge purchases against his or her bank account

defensive medicine: medical practices done not for the patient's benefit but in order to protect a physician from malpractice suits

deferred gratification: forgoing something in the present in the hope of achieving greater gains in the future

degradation ceremony: a term coined by Harold Garfinkel to describe rituals designed to strip an individual of his or her identity as a group member; for

example, a court martial or the defrocking of a priest

dehumanization: the act or process of reducing people to objects that do not deserve the treatment accorded humans

deinstitutionalization: the release of mental patients from institutions into the community pending treatment by a network of outpatient services

democracy: a system of government in which authority derives from the people; the term's origin is two Greek words that translate literally as "power to the people"

democratic leader: a leader who leads by trying to reach a consensus

democratic socialism: a hybrid economic system in which capitalism is mixed with state ownership

demographic transition: a three-stage historical process of population growth: first, high birthrates and high death rates; second, high birthrates and low death rates; and, third low birthrates and low death rates

demographic variables: the three factors that influence population growth: fertility, mortality, and net migration

demography: the study of the size, composition, growth, and distribution of human populations

denomination: a "brand name" within a major religion, for example, Methodist or Baptist

dependency ratio: the number of workers required to support one person on Social Security

dependency theory: the belief that lack of industrial development in Third World nations is caused by the industrialized nations dominating the world economy

dependent variable: a factor that is changed by an independent variable

depersonalization: the practice of dealing with people as though they were objects; in the case of medical care, as though patients were merely cases and diseases, not persons

deposit receipts: a receipt stating that a certain amount of goods is on deposit in a warehouse or bank; the receipt is used as a form of money

deterrence: creating fear so people will refrain from an act

deviance: the violation of rules or norms

deviants: people who violate rules, as a result of which others react negatively to them

dialectical process: each arrangement, or thesis, contains contradictions, or antitheses, which must be resolved; the new arrangement, or synthesis, contains its own contradictions, and so on

dictatorship: a form of government in which power is seized by an individual

differential association: Edwin Sutherland's term to indicate that associating with some groups results in learning an "excess of definitions" of deviance, and, by extension, in a greater likelihood that their members will become deviant

diffusion: the spread of invention or discovery from one area to another; identified by William Ogburn as a major process of social change

direct democracy: a form of democracy in which voters meet together to discuss issues and make their decisions

disabling environment: an environment that is harmful to health

discovery: a new way of seeing reality; identified by William Ogburn as a major process of social change

discrimination: an act of unfair treatment directed against an individual or a group

disengagement theory: the view that society prevents disruption by having the elderly vacate (or disengage from) their positions of responsibility so the younger generation can step into their shoes

disinvestment: the withdrawal of investments by financial institutions, which seals the fate of an urban area

divest: to sell off

divine right of kings: the idea that the king's authority comes directly from God

division of labor: Emile Durkheim's term for the allocation of people into occupational specialties

documents: written sources

domestication revolution: the first social revolution, based on the domestication of plants and animals, which led to pastoral and horticultural societies

dominant group: the group with the most power, greatest privileges, and highest social status

downward social mobility: movement down the social class ladder

dramaturgy: an approach, pioneered by Erving Goffman, analyzing social life in terms of drama or the stage; also called *dramaturgical analysis*

dumping: private hospitals sending unprofitable patients to public hospitals

dyad: the smallest possible group, consisting of two persons

ecclesia: a religious group so integrated into the dominant culture that it is difficult to tell where the one begins and the other leaves off; also called a *state religion*

economic cycle: periods of economic "booms" (expansion) followed by periods of "busts" (contraction)

economy: a system of distribution of goods and services

edge city: a large clustering of service facilities and residences near a highway intersection that provides a sense of place to people who live, shop, and work there

education: a formal system of teaching knowledge, values, and skills

ego: Freud's term for a balancing force between the id and the demands of society

emergent norms: Ralph Turner's and Lewis Killian's term for the development of new norms to cope with a new situation, especially among crowds

emotional labor: efforts to maintain intimacy, such as listening, being attentive to another's emotional needs, and sharing deep, personal thoughts, feelings, and aspirations

empty nest: a married couple's domestic situation after the last child has left home

endogamy: the practice of marrying within one's own group

enterprise zone: the use of economic incentives in a designated area with the intention of encouraging investment there

environmental sociology: a subdiscipline of sociology that examines how human activities affect the physical environment and how the physical environment affects human activities

epidemiology: the study of disease and disability patterns in a population

ethnic (and **ethnicity**): having distinctive cultural characteristics

ethnic cleansing: a policy of population elimination, including forcible expulsion and genocide; the term emerged in 1992 among the Serbians during their planned policy of expelling Croats and Muslims from territories claimed by them during the Yugoslav wars

ethnic work: activities designed to discover, enhance, or maintain ethnic and racial identification

ethnocentrism: the use of one's own culture as a yardstick for judging the ways of other individuals or societies, generally leading to a negative evaluation of their values, norms, and behaviors

ethnomethodology: the study of how people use background assumptions to make sense of life

euthanasia: mercy killing

evangelism: an attempt to win converts

exchange mobility: about the same numbers of people moving up and down the social class ladder, such that, on balance, the social class system shows little change

exchange theory: a theory of behavior that assumes human actions are motivated by a desire to maximize rewards and minimize costs

exogamy: the practice of marrying outside one's group

experiment: the use of control groups and experimental groups and dependent and independent variables to test causation

experimental group: the group of subjects exposed to the independent variable

exponential growth curve: a pattern of growth in which numbers double during approximately equal intervals, thus accelerating in the latter stages

expressive leader: an individual who increases harmony and minimizes conflict in a group; also known as a socioemotional leader

extended family: a nuclear family plus other relatives, such as grandparents, uncles and aunts, who live together

face-saving behavior: techniques used to salvage a performance that is going sour

fad: a temporary pattern of behavior that catches people's attention

false consciousness: Karl Marx's term to refer to workers identifying with the interests of capitalists

family: two or more people who consider themselves related by blood, marriage, or adoption

family of orientation: the family in which a person grows up

family of procreation: the family formed when a couple's first child is born

fashion: a pattern of behavior that catches people's attention, which lasts longer than a fad

fecundity: the number of children that women are theoretically capable of bearing

fee for service: payment by a patient to a physician to diagnose and treat the patient's medical problems

feminism: the philosophy that men and women should be politically, economically, and socially equal, and organized activity on behalf of this principle

feminization of poverty: a trend in U.S. poverty whereby most poor families are headed by women

feral children: children assumed to have been raised by animals, in the wilderness isolated from other humans

fertility rate: the number of children that the average woman bears

fiat money: currency issued by a government that is not backed by stored value

folkways: norms that are not strictly enforced

formal organization: a secondary group designed to achieve explicit objectives

front stage: where performances are given

functional analysis: a theoretical framework in which society is viewed as composed of various parts, each with a function that, when fulfilled, contributes to society's equilibrium; also known as functionalism and structural functionalism

functional equivalent: one item or activity that serves the same functions (or meets the same needs) as another; for example, religion and psychotherapy

functional illiterate: a high school graduate who has difficulty with basic reading and math

functional requisites: the major tasks that a society must fulfill if it is to survive

fundamentalism: the belief that true religion is threatened by modernism and that the faith as it was originally practiced should be restored

gatekeeping: the process by which education opens and closes doors of opportunity; another term for the social placement function of education

Gemeinschaft: a type of society in which life is intimate; a community in which everyone knows everyone else and people share a sense of togetherness

gender: the social characteristics that a society considers proper for its males and females; masculinity or femininity

gender age: the relative values that cultures place on men's and women's ages

gender role: the behaviors and attitudes considered appropriate because one is a female or a male

gender socialization: the ways in which society sets children onto different courses in life *because* they are male or female

gender stratification: males' and females' unequal access to power, prestige, and property on the basis of their sex

generalizability: the extent to which the findings from one group (or sample) can be generalized or applied to other groups (or populations)

generalization: a statement that goes beyond the individual case and is applied to a broader group or situation

generalized other: taking the role of a large number of people

genetic predispositions: inborn tendencies

genocide: the systematic annihilation or attempted annihilation of a race or ethnic group

gentrification: the displacement of the poor in a section of a city by the relatively affluent, who renovate the former's homes

gerontocracy: a society (or some other group) run by the elderly

Gesellschaft: a type of society dominated by impersonal relationships, individual accomplishments, and self-interest

gestures: the ways in which people use their bodies to communicate with one another

globalization: the extensive interconnections among nations due to the expansion of capitalism

global warming: an increase in the earth's temperature due to the greenhouse effect

goal conflict: goals that conflict with one another, such as those of a unit in a formal organization and those of the organization as a whole

goal displacement: a goal displaced by another, such as the adoption of new goals by an organization; also known as *goal replacement*

gold standard: paper money backed by gold

gossip: information of a more personal nature than a rumor; often false, distorted, or blatantly untrue

grade inflation: higher grades given for the same work; a general rise in student grades without a corresponding increase in learning or test scores

graying of America: the process by which older people make up an increasing proportion of the U.S. population

greenhouse effect: the buildup of carbon dioxide in the earth's atmosphere that allows light to enter but inhibits the release of heat; believed to cause global warming

gross national product: the amount of goods and services produced by a nation

group: defined differently by various sociologists, but people who regularly and consciously interact with one another; in a general sense, people who have something in common and who believe that what they have in common is significant; also called a social group

group dynamics: the ways in which individuals affect groups and the ways in which groups influence individuals

groupthink: Irving Janis's term for a narrowing of thought by a group of people, leading to the perception that there is only one correct answer, in which the suggestion of alternatives becomes a sign of disloyalty

growth rate: the net change in a population after adding births, subtracting deaths, and either adding or subtracting net migration

halfway house: community support facilities where ex-prisoners supervise many aspects of their own lives, such as household tasks, but continue to report to authorities

health: a human condition measured by four components: physical, mental, social, and spiritual

health maintenance organization (HMO): a health care organization that provides medical treatment to its members for a fixed annual cost

hidden curriculum: the unwritten goals of schools, such as obedience to authority and conformity to cultural norms

holistic medicine: an approach to medical care centering on the idea that a person's body, feelings, attitudes, and actions are all intertwined and cannot be segregated into discrete organ systems

homogamy: the tendency of people with similar characteristics to marry one another

horticultural society: a society based on cultivating plants by the use of hand tools

hospice: a place, or services brought into someone's home, for the purpose of bringing comfort and dignity to a dying person

household: all people who occupy the same housing unit

human ecology: Robert Park's term for the relationship between people and their environment (natural resources such as land)

humanizing a work setting: organizing a workplace in such a way that it develops rather than impedes human potential

hunting and gathering society: a society dependent on hunting and gathering for survival

hypothesis: a statement of the expected relationship between variables according to predictions from a theory

id: Freud's term for the individual's inborn basic drives

ideal culture: the ideal values and norms of a people, the goals held out for them

ideal type: a composite of characteristics based on many specific examples; "ideal" in this case means a description of the abstracted characteristics, not what one desires to exist

ideology: beliefs about the way things ought to be that justify social arrangements

illegitimate opportunity structures: opportunities for crimes that are woven into the texture of life

imperialism: a nation's pursuit of unlimited geographical expansion

impression management: the term used by Erving Goffman to describe people's efforts to control the impressions that others receive of them

incapacitation: the removal of offenders from "normal" society; taking them "off the streets," thereby removing their capacity to commit crimes against the public

incest: sexual relations between specified relatives, such as brothers and sisters or parents and children

incest taboo: rules specifying the degrees of kinship that prohibit sex or marriage

indentured service: a contractual system in which someone sells his or her body (services) for a specified period of time in an arrangement very close to slavery, except that it is voluntarily entered into

independent variable: a factor that causes a change in another variable, called the *dependent variable*

individual discrimination: the negative treatment of one person by another on the basis of that person's perceived characteristics

Industrial Revolution: the third social revolution, occurring when machines powered by fuels replaced most animal and human power

industrial society: a society based on the harnessing of machines powered by fuels

industrial technology: technology centered on machines powered by fuels instead of natural forces such as wind and rivers

inflation: an increase in prices

information revolution: the fourth social revolution, based on technology that processes information

in-groups: groups toward which one feels loyalty

institutional discrimination: negative treatment of a minority group that is built into a society's institutions; also called *systemic discrimination*

institutionalized means: approved ways of reaching cultural goals

instrumental leader: an individual who tries to keep the group moving toward its goals; also known as a *task-oriented leader*

intergenerational mobility: the change that family members make in social class from one generation to the next

interlocking directorates: the phenomenon of one person serving on the board of directors of several companies

internal colonialism: the systematic economic exploitation of a minority group

interview: direct questioning of respondents

interviewer bias: effects that interviewers have on respondents that lead to biased answers

invasion–succession cycle: the process of one group of people displacing a group whose racial-ethnic or social class characteristics differ from their own

invention: the combination of existing elements and materials to form new ones; identified by William Ogburn as a major process of social change

involuntary memberships: (or involuntary associations) groups in which people are assigned membership rather than choosing to join

the iron law of oligarchy: Robert Michels's phrase for the tendency of formal organizations to be dominated by a small, self-perpetuating elite

job deskilling: reducing the amount of skills that a job requires

job multiskilling: adding skills to those a worker already possesses

labeling theory: the view, developed by symbolic interactionists, that the labels people are given affect their own and others' perceptions of them, thus channeling their behavior either into deviance or into conformity

labor force participation rate: the proportion of the population or of some group 16 years and older in the work force

laissez-faire capitalism: unrestrained manufacture and trade (literally, "hands off" capitalism)

laissez-faire leader: an individual who leads by being highly permissive

language: a system of symbols that can be combined in an infinite number of ways and can represent not only objects but also abstract thought

latent functions: the unintended consequences of people's actions that help to keep a social system in equilibrium

leader: someone who influences other people

leadership styles: ways in which people express their leadership

leisure: time not taken up by work or required activities such as eating, sleeping, commuting, child care, and housework

life chances: the probabilities concerning the fate an individual may expect in life

life course: the sequence of events that we experience on our journey from birth to death

life expectancy: The number of years that an average newborn can expect to live

life span: The maximum length of life of a species

living will: a statement people in good health sign that clearly expresses their feelings about being kept alive on artificial life support systems

lobbyists: people who try to influence legislation on behalf of their clients or interest groups

looking-glass self: a term coined by Charles Horton Cooley to refer to the process by which our self develops through internalizing others' reactions to us

machismo: an emphasis on male strength and dominance

macro-level analysis: an examination of large-scale patterns of society

macropolitics: the exercise of large-scale power, the government being the most common example

macrosociology: analysis of social life focusing on broad features of social structure, such as social class and the relationships of groups to one another; an approach usually used by functionalist and conflict theorists

mainstreaming: helping people to become part of the mainstream of society

Malthus theorem: an observation by Thomas Malthus that although the food supply increases only arithmetically (from 1 to 2 to 3 to 4 and so on), population grows geometrically (from 2 to 4 to 8 to 16 and so forth)

mandatory education laws: laws that require all children to attend school until a specified age or until they complete a minimum grade in school

manifest function: the intended consequences of people's actions designed to help some part of a social system

manner: the attitudes that people show as they play their roles

marginality: the condition of belonging to two groups whose values are incompatible with each other and not feeling fully accepted and comfortable in either

marginal working class: the most desperate members of the working class, who have few skills, little job security, and are often unemployed

market: any process of buying and selling; on a more formal level, the mechanism that establishes values for the exchange of goods and services

market competition: the exchange of items between willing buyers and sellers

market forces: the law of supply and demand

market restraints: laws and regulations that limit the capacity to manufacture and sell products

marriage: a group's approved mating arrangements, usually marked by a ritual of some sort

marriage squeeze: the difficulty a group of males or females have in finding marriage partners, due to an imbalanced sex ratio

mass media: forms of communication directed to huge audiences

mass society: industrialized, highly bureaucratized, impersonal society

mass society theory: an explanation for participation in social movements based on the assumption that such movements offer a sense of belonging to people who have weak social ties

master status: a status that cuts across the other statuses that an individual occupies

material culture the material objects that distinguish a group of people, such as their art, buildings, weapons, utensils, machines, hairstyles, clothing, and jewelry

matriarchy: a society in which authority is vested in females; female control of a society or group

matrilineal (system of descent): a system of reckoning descent that counts only the mother's side

means of production: the tools, factories, land, and investment capital used to produce wealth

mechanical solidarity: Durkheim's term for the unity or shared consciousness that comes from being involved in similar occupations or activities

medicalization: the transformation of something into a matter to be treated by physicians

medicalization of deviance: to make some deviance a medical matter, a symptom of some underlying illness that needs to be treated by physicians

medium of exchange: the means by which people measure the value of goods and services in order to make an exchange; currency, gold, and silver are examples

megalopolis: an urban area consisting of at least two metropolises and their many suburbs

melting pot: the idea that Americans of various backgrounds would melt into a sort of ethnic stew

meritocracy: a form of social stratification in which all positions are awarded on the basis of merit

metropolis: a central city surrounded by smaller cities and their suburbs

metropolitan statistical area (MSA): a central city and the urbanized counties adjacent to it

micro-level analysis: an examination of small-scale patterns of society

micropolitics: the exercise of power in everyday life, such as deciding who is going to do the housework

microsociology: analysis of social life focusing on social interaction; an approach usually used by symbolic interactionists

middle-range theories: explanations of human behavior that go beyond a particular observation or research but avoid sweeping generalizations that attempt to account for everything

millenarian movement: a social movement based on the prophecy of coming social upheaval

milling: a crowd standing or walking around as they talk excitedly about some event

minimax strategy: Richard Berk's term for people's attempts to minimize their costs and maximize their rewards

minimum competency tests: national tests on which students must attain some minimum score

minority group: people who are singled out for unequal treatment on the basis of their physical and cultural characteristics, and who regard themselves as objects of collective discrimination

modernization: the transformation of traditional societies into industrial societies

monarchy: a form of government headed by a king or queen

money: a general term for a medium of exchange, currency being the most common form in industrialized societies

monopoly: the control of an entire industry by a single company

monotheism: the belief that there is only one God

mores (MORE-rays)**:** norms that are strictly enforced because they are thought essential to core values

multinational corporations: companies that operate across many national boundaries; also called *transnational corporations*

natural sciences: the intellectual and academic disciplines designed to comprehend, explain, and predict events in our natural environment

negative sanction: an expression of disapproval for breaking a norm; ranging from a mild, informal reaction such as a frown to a formal prison sentence

neocolonialism: the economic and political dominance of Third World nations by First World nations

net migration rate: the difference between the number of immigrants and emigrants per 1,000 population

networking: the process of consciously using or cultivating networks for some gain

new technology: a technology, if it is ever developed, that will be such a leap forward that it cannot be classified as simply an extension of current technology

noncentrist party: a political party that represents marginal ideas

nonmaterial culture: a group's ways of thinking (including its beliefs, values, and other assumptions about the world) and doing (its common patterns of behavior, including language and other forms of interaction)

nonverbal interaction: communication without words through gestures, space, silence, and so on

normative order: the socially approved ways of doing things that make up our everyday lives

norms: the expectations, or rules of behavior, that develop out of values

nuclear family: a family consisting of a husband, wife, and child(ren)

objective method (of measuring social class)**:** a system in which people are ranked according to objective criteria such as wealth, power, and prestige

objectivity: total neutrality

object permanence: Piaget's term for children's ability to realize that objects continue to exist even when they are not visible

official deviance: a society's statistics on lawbreaking; its measures of crimes, victims, lawbreakers, and the outcomes of criminal investigations and sentencing

oligarchy: a form of government in which power is held by a small group of individuals; the rule of the many by the few

oligopoly: the control of an entire industry by several large companies

open-ended question: questions that respondents are able to answer in their own words

operational: Piaget's term for abstract reasoning skills

operational definition: the way in which a variable in a hypothesis is measured

organic solidarity: Durkheim's term for the interdependence that results from people needing others to fulfil their jobs; solidarity based on the division of labor

out-groups: groups toward which one feels antagonisms

panic: the condition of being so fearful that one cannot function normally, and may even flee

pan-Indianism: the emphasis of common elements in Native American culture in order to develop a mutual self-identify and to work toward the welfare of all Native Americans

participant observation research in which the researcher *participates* in a research setting while *observing* what is happening in that setting; also called fieldwork

pastoral society: a society based on the pasturing of animals

patriarchy: a society in which authority is vested in males; male control of a society or group

patrilineal (system of descent)**:** a system of reckoning descent that counts only the father's side

patterns: recurring characteristics or events

peer group: a group of individuals roughly the same age linked by common interests

personal identity kit: items people use to decorate their bodies

personality disorders: the view that a personality disturbance of some sort causes an individual to violate social norms

Peter principle: a bureaucratic "law" according to which the members of an organization are promoted for good work until they reach their level of incompetence, the level at which they can no longer do good work

pluralism: there are two basic meanings: a) a philosophy that permits or encourages ethnic variation, and b) the diffusion of power among many interest groups, preventing any single group from gaining control of the government

pluralistic society: a society made up of many different groups

pluralistic theory of social control: the view that society is made up of many competing groups, whose interests manage to become balanced

political action committee (PAC): an organization formed by one or more special-interest groups to solicit and spend funds for the purpose of influencing legislation

polyandry: a marriage in which a woman has more than one husband

polygyny: a marriage in which a man has more than one wife

polytheism: the belief that there are many gods

population: the target group to be studied

population pyramid: a graphic representation of a population, divided into age and sex

population shrinkage: the process by which a country's population becomes smaller because its birthrate and immigration are too low to replace those who die and emigrate

population transfer: involuntary movement of a minority group

positive sanction: a reward or positive reaction for following norms, ranging from a smile to a prize

positivism: the application of the scientific approach to the social world

postindustrial society: a society based on information, services, and high technology, rather than on raw materials and manufacturing

postindustrial technology: technology centering on information, transportation, and communication

poverty line: the official measure of poverty calculated to include those whose incomes are less than three times a low-cost food budget

power: the ability to get your way, even over the resistance of others

power elite: C. Wright Mills's term for the top leaders of U.S. corporations, military, and politics who make the nation's major decisions

prejudice: an *attitude* or prejudging, usually in a negative way

prestige: respect or regard

primary deviance: Edwin Lemert's term for acts of deviance that have little effect on the self-concept

primary group: a group characterized by intimate, long-term, face-to-face association and cooperation

primary sector: that part of the economy that extracts raw materials from the environment

primitive technology: the adaptation of natural items for human use

private ownership of the means of production: the ownership of machines and factories by individuals, who decide what shall be produced

privatization: the selling of a nation's state-run industries to the private sector

proactive social movement: a social movement that promotes some social change

profane: Durkheim's term for common elements of everyday life

profession: an occupation characterized by rigorous education, a theoretical perspective, self-regulation, authority over clients, and service to society (as opposed to a job)

professionalization of medicine: the development of medicine into a field in which education becomes rigorous, and in which physicians claim a theoretical understanding of illness, regulate themselves, claim to be doing a service to society (rather than just following self-interest), and take authority over clients

profit: the amount gained from selling something for more than it cost

proletariat Karl Marx's term for the people who work for those who own the means of production

propaganda: in its broad sense, the presentation of information in the attempt to influence people; in its narrow sense, one-sided information used to try to influence people

proportional representation: an electoral system in which seats in a legislature are divided according to the proportion of votes each political party receives

Protestant ethic: Max Weber's term to describe the ideal of a self denying highly moral life, accompanied by hard work and frugality

public: a dispersed group of people who usually have an interest in the issues on which a social movement focuses

public opinion: how people think about some issue

pure or basic sociology: sociological research whose only purpose is to make discoveries about life in human groups, not to make changes in those groups

qualitative research methods: research in which the emphasis is placed on observing, describing, and interpreting people's behavior

quantitative research methods: research in which the emphasis is placed on precise measurement, the use of statistics and numbers

questionnaires: a list of questions to be asked

quiet revolution (the): the fundamental changes in society that follow when vast numbers of women enter the work force

race: inherited physical characteristics that distinguish one group from another

racism: prejudice and discrimination on the basis of race

random sample: a sample in which everyone in the target population has the same chance of being included in the study

rapport: a feeling of trust

rational-legal authority: authority based on law or written rules and regulations; also called *bureaucratic authority*

rationality: the acceptance of rules, efficiency, and practical results as the right way to approach human affairs

rationalization of society: a widespread acceptance of rationality and a social organization largely built around this idea

reactive social movement: a social movement that resists some social change

real culture: the norms and values that people actually follow

recidivism rate: the proportion of people who are rearrested

redemptive social movement: a social movement that seeks to change people totally

reference group: Herbert Hyman's term for the groups we use as standards to evaluate ourselves

rehabilitation: the resocialization of offenders so that they can become conforming citizens

reformative social movement: a social movement that seeks to change only particular aspects of society

reincarnation: in Hinduism and Buddhism, the return of the soul after death in a different form

relative deprivation: people's evaluations of their own condition or behavior based on their comparisons with what others have

relative deprivation theory: an explanation for participation in social movements based on the assumption that people see themselves deprived relative to others and see the social movement as able to help solve the imbalance

reliability: the extent to which data produce consistent results

religion: according to Durkheim, beliefs and practices that separate the profane from the sacred and unite its adherents into a moral community

religious experience: a sudden awareness of the supernatural or a feeling of coming in contact with God

replication: the repetition of a study in order to test its findings

representative democracy: a form of democracy in which voters elect representatives to govern and make decisions on their behalf

reputational method (of measuring social class): a system in which people who are familiar with the reputations of others are asked to identify their social class

research method: one of six procedures sociologists use to collect data: surveys, participant observation, secondary analysis, documents, unobtrusive measures, and experiments; also called research design

reserve labor force: the term used by conflict theorists for the unemployed, who can be put to work during times of high production and then discarded when no longer needed

resocialization: the process of learning new norms, values, attitudes, and behaviors

resource mobilization: a theory that social movements succeed or fail based on their ability to mobilize resources such as time, money, and people's skills

respondents: people who respond to a survey, either in interviews or by self-administered questionnaires

retribution: the punishment of offenders in order to restore the moral balance upset by the offense

revolution: armed resistance designed to overthrow a government

riot: violent crowd behavior aimed against people and property

rising expectations: the sense that better conditions are soon to follow, which, if unfulfilled, creates mounting frustration

rituals: ceremonies or repetitive practices; in this context, religious observances or rites, often intended to evoke a sense of awe of the sacred

role: the behaviors, obligations, and privileges attached to a status

role conflict: conflicts that someone feels *between* roles because the expectations attached to one role are incompatible with the expectations of another role.

role extension: the incorporation of additional activities into a role

role performance: how people play a role; their "style" or "personality"

role strain: conflicts that someone feels *within* a role

romantic love: feelings of erotic attraction accompanied by an idealization of the other

routinization of charisma: the transfer of authority from a charismatic figure to either a traditional or a rational-legal form of authority

rumors: unfounded information spread among people

sacred: Durkheim's term for things set apart or forbidden, that inspire fear, awe, reverence, or deep respect

sample: the individuals intended to represent the population to be studied

sanction: an expression of approval or disapproval given to people for upholding or violating norms

Sapir-Whorf hypothesis: Edward Sapir's and Benjamin Whorf's hypothesis that language itself creates a particular way of thinking and perceiving

scapegoat: an individual or group unfairly blamed for someone else's troubles

school choice: parents being able to choose the school their child will attend; often used in the context of expecting for-profit schools to compete for vouchers issued by the state

science: the application of systematic methods to obtain knowledge and the knowledge obtained by those methods

scientific method: The use of objective, systematic observations to test hypotheses and theories

secondary analysis: the analysis of data already collected by other researchers

secondary deviance: Edwin Lemert's term for acts of deviance incorporated into the self-concept, around which an individual orients his or her behavior

secondary group: compared with a primary group, a larger, relatively temporary, more anonymous, formal, and impersonal group based on some interest or activity, whose members are likely to interact on the basis of specific roles

secondary sector: that part of the economy which turns raw materials into manufactured goods

sect: a group larger than a cult that still feels substantial hostility from and toward society

secular: belonging to the world and its affairs

secularization: the process by which spiritual concerns are replaced by worldly concerns

secularization of culture: the process by which a culture becomes less influenced by religion

secularization of religion: the replacement of a religion's "otherworldly" concerns with concerns about "this world"

segregation: the policy of keeping racial or ethnic groups apart

selective perception: seeing certain features of an object or situation, but remaining blind to others

self: the concept, unique to humans, of being able to see ourselves "from the outside"; to gain a picture of how others see us

self-administered questionnaires: questionnaires filled out by respondents

self-fulfilling prophecy: Robert Merton's term for an originally false assertion that becomes true simply because it was predicted

serial fatherhood: a pattern of parenting in which a father, after divorce, reduces contact with his own children, serves as a father to the children of the woman he marries or lives with, then ignores them after moving in with or marrying another woman; this pattern repeats

sex: biological characteristics that distinguish females and males, consisting of primary and secondary sex characteristics

sex typing: the associating behaviors with one sex or the other

sexual harassment: usually defined as the use of one's occupational position to force unwanted sexual demands on someone; the legal definition includes nonsexual behavior—an abusive or hostile environment based on gender that impairs the ability to perform one's job (Fitzpatrick 1994)

shaman: the healing specialist of a preliterate tribe who attempts to control the spirits thought to cause a disease or injury; commonly called a *witch doctor*

sick role: a social role that excuses people from normal obligations because they are sick or injured, while at the same time expecting them to seek competent help and cooperate in getting well

significant other: an individual who significantly influences someone else's life

sign-vehicles: Goffman's term to refer to the social setting, appearance, and manner which people use to communicate information about the self

slavery: a form of social stratification in which some people own other people

small group: a group small enough so everyone can interact directly with all the other members

social change: the alteration of culture and societies over time

social class: a large number of people with similar amounts of income and education who work at jobs that are roughly comparable in prestige; according to Weber, a large group of people who rank close to one another in wealth, power, and prestige; according to Marx, one of two groups: capitalists who own the means of production and workers who sell their labor

social cohesion: the degree to which members of a group or a society feel united by shared values and other social bonds

the social construction of reality: what people define as real because of their background assumptions and life experiences

social control: formal and informal means of enforcing norms

social devaluation: a reduction in the value or social worth placed on something or someone

social environment: the entire human environment, including direct contact with others

social facts: Durkheim's term for the patterns of behavior that characterize a social group

social inequality: a state in which privileges and obligations are given to some but denied to others

social institutions: the organized, usual, or standard ways by which society meets its basic needs

social integration: the degree to which people feel a part of social groups

social interaction: what people do when they are in one another's presence

social location: one's location in history and society; roughly equivalent to one's group memberships

social mobility: movement up or down the social class ladder

social movement: unusual behavior that, compared with other forms of collective behavior, usually involves more people, is more prolonged, is more organized, and focuses on social change

social movement organization: an organization developed to further the goals of a social movement

social network: the social ties radiating outward from the self, that link people together

social order: a group's usual and customary social arrangements

social placement: a function of education that funnels people into a society's various positions

social promotion: passing students to the next grade even though they have not mastered basic materials

social sciences: the intellectual and academic disciplines designed to understand the social world objectively by means of controlled and repeated observations

social setting: the place where the action of everyday life unfolds

social stratification: the division of people into layers according to their relative power, property, and prestige; applies to both a society and a nation

social structure: the relationship of people and groups to one another

socialism: an economic system characterized by the public ownership of the means of production, central planning, and the distribution of goods without a profit motive

socialization: the process by which people learn the characteristics of their group—the attitudes, values, and actions thought appropriate for them

society: a term used by sociologists to refer to a group of people who share a culture and a territory

sociobiology: a framework of thought that views human behavior as the result of natural selection and considers biological characteristics to be the fundamental cause of human behavior

sociological perspective: an approach to understanding human behavior by placing it within its broader social context

sociology: the scientific study of society and human behavior

special-interest group: a group of people who have a particular issue in common and can be mobilized for political action

spirit of capitalism (the): Weber's term for the desire to accumulate capital as a duty—not to spend it, but as an end in itself—and to constantly reinvest it

split-labor market: a term used by conflict theorists for the practice of weakening the bargaining power of workers by splitting them along racial, ethnic, sex, age, or any other lines

spurious correlation: the correlation of two variables actually caused by a third variable; there is no cause–effect relationship

state: government; the source of legitimate violence in society

state religion: a government-sponsored religion; also known as an *ecclesia*

status: the position that someone occupies in society or a social group; one's social ranking

status inconsistency: a contradiction or mismatch between statuses; a condition in which a person ranks high on some dimensions of social class and low on others

status set: all the statuses or positions that an individual occupies

status symbols: items used to identify a status

stereotype: assumptions of what people are like, based on previous associations with them or with people who have similar characteristics—or based on information, whether true or false

stigma: "blemishes" that discredit a person's claim to a "normal" identity

stockholders' revolt: the refusal of a corporation's stockholders to rubberstamp decisions made by its managers

stored value: the backing of a currency by goods that are stored

strain theory: Robert Merton's term for the strain engendered when a society socializes large numbers of people to desire a cultural goal (such as success) but withholds from many the approved means to reach that goal; one adaptation to the strain is crime, the choice of an innovative means (one outside the approved system) to attain the cultural goal

stratified random sample: a sample of a specific subgroup of the target population in which everyone in the subgroups has an equal chance of being included in the study

street crime: crimes such as mugging, rape, and burglary

structural mobility: movement up or down the social class ladder that is attributable to changes in the structure of society, not to individual efforts

structured interviews: interviews that use closed-ended questions

subculture: the values and related behaviors of a group that distinguish its members from the larger culture; a world within a world

subjective meanings: the meanings that people give their own behavior

subjective method (of measuring social class): a system in which people are asked to define their own social class

subsistence economy: a type of economy in which human groups live off the land with little or no surplus

suburb: the communities adjacent to the political boundaries of a city

suburbanization: the movement from the city to the suburbs

superego: Freud's term for the conscience, which consists of the internalized norms and values of our social groups

survey: the collection of data by having people answer a series of questions

symbol: something to which people attach meanings and then use to communicate with others

symbolic culture: another term for nonmaterial culture

symbolic interactionism: a theoretical perspective in which society is viewed as composed of symbols that people use to establish meaning, develop their views of the world, and communicate with one another

system of descent: how kinship is traced over the generations

taboo: a norm so strong that it brings revulsion if violated

taking the role of the other: putting oneself in someone else's shoes; understanding how someone else feels and thinks and thus anticipating how that person will act

teamwork: the collaboration of two or more persons who, interested in the success of a performance, manage impressions jointly

techniques of neutralization: ways of thinking or rationalizing that help people deflect society's norms

technology: often defined as the applications of science, but can be conceptualized as tools, items used to accomplish tasks

tertiary deviance: "normalizing" of behavior considered deviant by mainstream society; relabeling the behavior as nondeviant

tertiary sector: that part of the economy that consists of service-oriented occupations

theory: a general statement about how some parts of the world fit together and how they work; an explanation of how two or more facts are related to one another

Thomas theorem: basically, that people live in socially constructed worlds; that is, people jointly build their own realities; summarized in William I. Thomas's statement: "If people define situations as real, they are real in their consequences."

tool: an object that is modified for a specific purpose

total institution: a place in which people are cut off from the rest of society and are almost totally controlled by the officials who run the place

totalitarianism: a form of government that exerts almost total control over the people

tracking: the sorting of students into different educational programs on the basis of real or perceived abilities

traditional authority: authority based on custom

traditional orientation: the idea, characteristic of tribal, peasant, and feudal societies, that the past is the best guide for the present

trained incapacity: a bureaucrat's inability to see the goals of the organization and to function as a cooperative, integrated part of the whole; caused by the highly specific nature of the tasks he or she performs

transformative social movement: a social movement that seeks to change

society totally

triad: a group of three persons

underclass: a small group of people for whom poverty persists year after year and across generations

underemployment: the condition of having to work at a job beneath one's level of training and abilities, or of being able to find only part-time work

underground economy: exchanges of goods and services that are not reported to the government and thereby escape taxation

universal citizenship: the idea that everyone has the same basic rights by virtue of being born in a country (or by immigrating and becoming a naturalized citizen)

unobtrusive measures: techniques of observing people who do not know they are being studied

unstructured interviews: interviews that use open-ended questions

upward social mobility: movement up the social class ladder

urban legend: a story with an ironic twist that sounds realistic but is false

urban networks: the social networks of city dwellers

urbanization: the process by which an increasing proportion of a population lives in cities

urban renewal: the rehabilitation of a rundown area of a city, which usually results in the displacement of the poor who are living in that area

validity: the extent to which an operational definition measures what it was intended to measure

value contradictions: values that contradict one another; to follow the one means to come into conflict with the other

value clusters: a series of interrelated values that together form a larger whole

value free: the view that a sociologist's personal values or biases should not influence social research

values: the standards by which people define what is desirable or undesirable, good or bad, beautiful or ugly

variable: a factor or concept thought to be significant for human behavior, which varies from one case to another

Verstehen: a German word used by Max Weber that is perhaps best understood as "to have insight into someone's situation"

voluntary association: a group made up of volunteers who have organized on the basis of some mutual interest

voluntary memberships (or voluntary associations): groups that people choose to join

voter apathy: indifference and inaction on the part of individuals or groups with respect to the political process

war: armed conflict between nations or politically distinct groups

WASP: a white Anglo-Saxon Protestant; narrowly, an American of English descent; broadly, an American of western European ancestry

wealth: property and income

welfare (state) capitalism: an economic system in which individuals own the means of production but the state regulates many economic activities for the welfare of the population

white-collar crime: Edwin Sutherland's term for crimes committed by people of respectable and high social status in the course of their occupations; for example, bribery of public officials, securities violations, embezzlement, false advertising, and price fixing

white ethnics: white immigrants to the United States whose culture differs from that of WASPs

working class: those who sell their labor to the capitalist class

world system: economic and political connections that ties the world's countries together

zero population growth: a demographic condition in which women bear only enough children to reproduce the population

Subject Index

Political power, 405
    authority and coercion, 405–10. *See Also* Authority.
    conflict perspective, 419–20
    elections and, 412–13, 414–15
    functionalist perspective, 418–19
    lobbyists, 417–18
    new world order, 424–25
    political parties, 412–13
    special–interest groups, 417–18
    types of governments and, 410–12
    violence and, 406
    war as, 421–24
    women's, 303–5
Political science, 6
Politics, 6
    African Americans in, 329–30
    social class and, 260, 267
    as social institution, 97
    status inconsistency and, 260
    women in, 303–5
Pollution, 630–31
Polyandry, 430
Polygyny, 430, 502
Polytheism, 500
Poor, 272–73
    defining, 271–72
    rural, 273
    working, 263–64
Population, 555
    in surveys, 124
Population growth, 558–65
    estimating, 560–62
    in Europe, 555
    forecasting, 562–65
    industrialization and, 564–65
    rates of, and implications, 558–60
    in Third World, 242, 558–59
    in U. S., 559, 561
    zero, 565
Population shrinkage, 55
Population transfer, 324–25, 339
    indirect and direct, 324–25
Pornography, 129
Positive sanctions, 42, 209–10
Positivism, 10
Postindustrial economies, 377, 379
    medium of exchange in, 379
Postindustrial societies, 146, 151–52, 377
Postindustrial technology, 152
Poverty
    children in, 273–74
    culture of, 246, 274
    defining, 271–72
    among the elderly, 272–73, 359, 366–67
    feminization of, 273
    health care and, 532–33
    individual vs. structural explanations of, 275–76
    mental illness and, 532–33
    short–term and long–term, 274–75
    race/ethnicity and, 272, 273
    in Third World, 242–43, 246
    in U. S., 271–76
Poverty line, 271, 272

Power, 404, 405
    concentration of, 257
    exercise of, 404, 405
    legitimate and illegitimate, 405–10
    social class and, 231, 233
    telecommunications and, 625–26
    wealth and, 256–57
Power elite, 149, 234, 235–36, 248, 257, 419–20
Prediction, as goal, 7
Prejudice
    behavior vs., 314–15
    discrimination and, 313–17
    extent of, 315–16
    labels that create, 320
    Merton's categories of, 314
    psychological explanations of, 318
    sociological perspectives, 319–20
    theories of, 317–20
Preliterate societies, 83
Preoperational stages (Piaget's theory), 67–68
Prestige. *See Also* Status.
    displaying, 258–59
    occupations and, 257–58
    social class and, 231
    of work, 285–86
Preventive medicine, 545
Primary deviance, 214–15
Primary groups, 152–53
    family as, 152
    failure of, 152
Primary sector, 388
Prisons, 81–82, 212–14
Private ownership of the means of production, 379
Privatization, 385
Privilege. See Social stratification.
Proactive social movement, 598
Problem behaviors, 217–18
Pro–choice, 607–8
Productivity, 131
Profane, 490
Profession, job vs., 395–96
Professionalization of medicine, 528–31
Profit, 379
    socialist, 381, 382
Progress
    idea of, 628
    value of, 45
Proletariat, 12, 25, 230
Pro–life, 607–8
Promotion, in Japan, 188
Propaganda, 602–3
    Nazi, 601
    seven basic techniques of, 603
Property
    crimes of, 209
    income and wealth vs., 254
    social class and, 231
    U. S. statistics on, 255–56
Propinquity, 441
Proportional representation, 414
Prostitution, 206, 214–15, 247
    Third World, 247
Protestant ethic, 171, 377, 499

Protestant Ethic and the Spirit of Capitalism, The, (Weber), 171, 498
Protestantism,
    capitalism and, 171, 498–99
    social change and, 14
    suicide and, 13
Psychology, 6, 7
    on deviance, 199
    on prejudice, 318
Psychotherapy, 81, 493
Public distance, 107
Public health, 539–45
Public opinion, 600
Public ownership, 381
Puerto Ricans, 316, 331, 332, 333, 334, 445
Punishment
    corporal, 82
    crime and, 208–9, 212–14
    Milgram experiment, 163–64
    parenting and, 443
Pure Food and Drug Act, 381
Pure sociology, 28
Pygmies, 147, 283
Provocateur, agent, 605–6

Qualitative techniques, 132, 133
Quality circles, 185
Quantitative techniques, 132, 133
Questionnaires, 126
    self–administered, 126
Questions
    biased, 125
    types of, 126
Quiet revolution, 390

Race
    aging and, 350–51
    education and, 291, 334
    health and, 323
    heart surgery and, 322
    home mortgages and, 321
    imprisonment rates and, 213
    longevity and, 330, 349
    as master status, 95
    myth and reality, 310–11
    poverty and, 272, 273, 367
    rate of women working and, 390
    religion and, 516–17
    social class vs., 330–31
    U. S. population trends and, 563
Race relations
    basic concepts in, 310–13
    principles for improving, 342
    in U. S., 314, 326–42
Racial caste system, 229
Racism, 17, 313. See Prejudice.
    on college campuses, 316–17
    core values and, 45
    education level and, 315, 316, 318
    environmental, 630
    in Europe, 315
    social class and, 318
Radiation experiment, 544–45
Rape, 303

Name Index